European Union Politics

European Union Politics

SEVENTH EDITION

Michelle Cini

Nieves Pérez-Solórzano Borragán

OXFORD

UNIVERSITY PRESS

OXFORD
UNIVERSITY PRESS

Great Clarendon Street, Oxford, OX2 6DP,
United Kingdom

Oxford University Press is a department of the University of Oxford.
It furthers the University's objective of excellence in research, scholarship,
and education by publishing worldwide. Oxford is a registered trade mark of
Oxford University Press in the UK and in certain other countries

© Oxford University Press 2022

Fourth edition 2013
Fifth edition 2016
Sixth edition 2019

Impression: 1

Published in the United States of America by Oxford University Press
198 Madison Avenue, New York, NY 10016, United States of America

British Library Cataloguing in Publication Data
Data available

Library of Congress Control Number: 2021945728

ISBN 978–0–19–886223–9

Printed in Great Britain by
Bell & Bain Ltd., Glasgow

Preface

This seventh edition of *European Union Politics* builds on the success of the previous six editions by retaining and updating the chapters published in the previous version of the book. Innovations in this edition include new chapters on the Migration and Refugee Crisis and on the COVID-19 pandemic.

The book remains true to its earlier ambition, which was to offer students of EU politics an introductory text that would be both accessible and challenging, written by authors who are experts in their field. It was designed with undergraduates in mind, particularly those coming to the topic of the EU for the first time; but we know that it has also proven a useful basic text for more advanced students. As in previous editions, we aim to make the study of the European Union an appealing prospect for students. All students should, however, be reading beyond this book, and we provide some guidance on reading at the end of each chapter with that recommendation in mind.

The large number of chapters in this volume should not be taken to imply that the book is comprehensive; rather, it aims to provide a solid overview of a range of topics falling loosely under the rubric of EU politics. Other textbooks focus more specifically on history, theories, institutions, or policies. This book aims to give a taste of all these areas of EU study. We thank our contributors, without whom this book really would not have been possible. We also owe a debt of gratitude to the editorial and production team at Oxford University Press, and in particular to Anna Galasinska for her flexibility and sensitivity in supporting us through the challenges we faced in putting together this edition, and for her extremely efficient handling of this project.

Michelle Cini
Nieves Pérez-Solórzano Borragán
June 2021

New to this edition

- Extensive empirical updating of content taking account of recent developments in the European Union.
- New chapter on COVID-19 and the European Union.
- New chapter on the Migration and Refugee Crisis.

Contents

Detailed contents

PART 2   Theories and Conceptual Approaches   51

4 Neo-functionalism   53
Carsten Strøby Jensen

5 Intergovernmentalism   67
Michelle Cini

6 Theorizing the European Union after Integration Theory   81
Ben Rosamond

List of figures

List of boxes

List of tables

List of contributors

David Benson is a Senior Lecturer in Politics in the Department of Politics, University of Exeter, UK.

Edward Best is Senior Expert at the European Institute of Public Administration (EIPA) and Senior Fellow of Maastricht University, Netherlands.

Tanja A. Börzel is Professor of Political Science, holds the chair for European integration and is Director of the Center for European Integration, Freie Universität Berlin, Germany.

Eleanor Brooks is a lecturer in health policy at the Global Health Policy Unit (GHPU), School of Social and Political Science, University of Edinburgh, UK.

Charlotte Burns is Professor of Politics in the Department of Politics and International Relations, University of Sheffield, UK.

Paul James Cardwell is Professor of Law and Vice Dean (Education) at the Dickson Poon School of Law, King's College London, UK.

Thomas Christiansen is Professor of Political Science and European Integration in the Political Science department at Luiss University Guido Carli, Rome, Italy.

Clive H. Church is Emeritus Professor in the Department of Politics and International Relations, University of Kent, UK.

Michelle Cini is Professor of European Politics in the School of Sociology, Politics, and International Studies (SPAIS) at the University of Bristol, UK.

Michelle Egan is Professor and Jean Monnet Chair ad personam in the School of International Service at the American University, Washington DC, USA.

Morten Egeberg is Emeritus Professor of Public Policy and Administration in the Department of Political Science and at ARENA, University of Oslo, Norway.

Rainer Eising is Professor of Political Science in the Faculty of Social Science, Ruhr University, Bochum, Germany.

Ève Fouilleux is a Director of Research in Public Policy Analysis at the National Centre for Scientific Research (CNRS) and Gustave Eiffel University, and associated researcher at the French agricultural research and cooperation organization (CIRAD), in Montpellier, France.

Anna Maria Friis is an independent researcher.

Andrew Geddes is Professor of Migration Studies and Director of the Migration Policy Centre at the European University Institute, Florence, Italy.

Viviane Gravey is a Lecturer in European Politics in the School of History, Anthropology, Philosophy and Politics at Queen's University Belfast, Northern Ireland, UK.

Scott L. Greer is Professor of Health Management and Policy, Global Public Health and Political Science at the University of Michigan, USA.

Simona Guerra is Senior Lecturer in Comparative Politics in the Department of Politics at the University of Surrey, Guildford, UK.

Dermot Hodson is Professor of Political Economy in the Department of Politics, Birkbeck College, University of London, UK.

Andrew Jordan is Professor of Environmental Sciences in the School of Environmental Sciences, University of East Anglia, Norwich, UK.

Ana E. Juncos is a Professor of European Politics in the School of Sociology, Politics, and International Studies (SPAIS) at the University of Bristol, UK.

Brigid Laffan is a Director and Professor at the Robert Schuman Centre for Advanced Studies and Director of the Global Governance Programme at the European University Institute, Fiesole, Italy.

Jeffrey Lewis is Professor in the Department of Political Science at Cleveland State University, USA.

Diana Panke is Professor of Political Science at the Albert-Ludwigs University, Freiburg, Germany.

Nieves Pérez-Solórzano Borragán is a Senior Lecturer in European Politics at the School of Sociology, Politics, and International Studies (SPAIS) at the University of Bristol, UK.

David Phinnemore is Professor of European Politics and Jean Monnet Chair in the School of Politics, International Studies, and Philosophy, Queen's University Belfast, Northern Ireland, and Visiting Professor at the College of Europe, Bruges, Belgium.

Uwe Puetter is Professor of Empirical European Research at the Institute of Social Sciences and Theology at Europa-Universität Flensburg, Germany.

Ben Rosamond is EURECO Professor and Deputy Director of the Centre for European Politics, Department of Political Science, University of Copenhagen, Denmark.

Sarah Rozenblum is a PhD candidate in Health Management and Policy at the University of Michigan, USA.

Anniek de Ruijter is Associate Professor of European Law and Director of Amsterdam Law Practice at the University of Amsterdam, Netherlands.

Stijn Smismans is Professor in Law, Jean Monnet Chair in European Law and Governance, and Director of the Jean Monnet Centre of Excellence at the Cardiff Law School, Cardiff University, UK.

Michael Smith is Emeritus Professor of European Politics at the Department of Politics, History, and International Relations, Loughborough University, UK, and Professor in European Politics at the University of Warwick, UK.

Julia Sollik is Research Assistant in Sustainability Science at Bochum University of Applied Sciences, Germany.

Carsten Strøby Jensen is Associate Professor of Sociology at the University of Copenhagen, Denmark.

Hans-Jörg Trenz is Professor of Sociology of Culture and Communication at the Scuola Normale Superiore, Pisa/Florence, Italy.

Emek M. Uçarer is Professor of International Relations in the Department of International Relations at Bucknell University, Pennsylvania, USA.

Amy Verdun is Professor of Political Science at the University of Victoria, Canada, and visiting professor at the Institute of Political Science, Leiden University.

List of abbreviations

ACP	African, Caribbean, and Pacific
ACTA	Anti-Counterfeiting and Trade Agreement
AER	Assembly of European Regions
AFCO	Constitutional Affairs Committee, European Parliament
AfD	Alternative für Deutschland
AFET	Committee on Foreign Affairs
AFSJ	Area of Freedom, Security, and Justice
AG	Advocate-General
AGFISH	Council for Agriculture and Fisheries
AGS	Annual Growth Survey
ALDE	Alliance of Liberals and Democrats for Europe
AmCham	American Chamber of Commerce
AMM	Aceh Monitoring Mission
AoA	Agreement on Agriculture
APA	advance purchase agreement
APEC	Asia Pacific Economic Co-operation
ARNE	Antiracist Network for Equality in Europe
ASEAN	Association of Southeast Asian Nations
BDI	Federation of German Industries
BEPGs	Broad Economic Policy Guidelines
BEUC	*Bureau Européen des Unions des Consommateurs* [European Consumer Union Bureau]
BLEU	Belgium Luxembourg Economic Union
BNP	Banque Nationale de Paris
BRIC	Brazil, Russia, India, China
BSE	bovine spongiform encephalopathy ('mad cow disease')
BTO	Brussels Treaty Organization
BUAV	British Union for the Abolition of Vivisection
BUSINESSEUROPE	Confederation of European Business
CALRE	Conference of European Regional Legislative Parliaments
CAP	Common Agricultural Policy
CAR	Central African Republic

CARDS	Community Assistance for Reconstruction, Development and Stabilization
CCP	Common Commercial Policy
CdT	Translation Centre for the Bodies of the European Union
CDU	Christian Democratic Union (Germany)
CEAS	Common European Asylum System
CEB	Council of Europe Development Bank
CEC	European Confederation of Executives and Managers Staff
CEDEC	European Federation of Local Public Energy Distribution Companies
CEDEFOP	European Centre for the Development of Vocational Training
CEE	Central and Eastern Europe
CEEP	*Centre Européen des Entreprises Publics* [European Association for Public Sector Firms]
CEFIC	European Chemical Industry Council
CEMR	Council for European Municipalities and Regions
CEN	European Committee for Standardization
CENELEC	European Committee for Electro-technical Standardization
CEO	Corporate European Observatory
CEPOL	European Police College
CETA	Comprehensive Economic and Trade Agreement
CFC	chlorofluorocarbon
CFCA	Common Fisheries Control Agency
CFI	Court of First Instance
CFP	Common Fisheries Policy
CFR	Charter of Fundamental Rights
CFSP	Common Foreign and Security Policy
CGS	Council General Secretariat
CIREA	Centre for Information, Discussion and Exchange on Asylum
CIREFI	Centre for Information, Discussion and Exchange on the Crossing of Frontiers and Immigration

CIVAM	Network of French Alternative Farmers	DG NEAR	European Neighbourhood Policy and Enlargement Negotiations Directorate-General
CivCom	Committee for Civilian Crisis Management		
CJEU	Court of Justice of the European Union	DG SANTE	Directorate-General for Health and Food Safety
CLA	Country Landowners Association	DI	differentiated integration
CLRA	Congress of Local and Regional Authorities	DIT	Department for International Trade (UK)
CMO	common market organization	DQL	Directorate for Quality of Legislation
CNG	Compressed Natural Gas	DRC	Democratic Republic of Congo
CNJA	*Centre National des Jeunes Agriculteurs* [French Young Farmers' Association]	DUP	Democratic Unionist Party
		E&T	education and training
CO₂	carbon dioxide	EACEA	Education, Audiovisual and Culture Executive Agency
CoA	Court of Auditors		
CoE	Council of Europe	EACI	Executive Agency for Competitiveness and Innovation
CoFE	Conference on the Future of Europe		
COGECA	General Committee for Agricultural Cooperation in the European Union	EAEC	European Atomic Energy Community
		EAGGF	European Agricultural Guidance and Guarantee Fund
COMPET	Competitiveness (including Internal Market, Industry, and Research) (EU Council)	EAHC	Executive Agency for Health and Consumers
CONECCS	Consultation, the European Commission and Civil Society database	EAM	European Agenda on Migration
		EAP	Environmental Action Programme
		EASA	European Aviation Safety Agency
COPA	Committee of Professional Agricultural Organizations	EAW	European Arrest Warrant
		EBA	European Banking Authority
COPS	*See* PSC	EBRD	European Bank for Reconstruction and Development
CoR	Committee of the Regions		
Coreper	Committee of Permanent Representatives	EC	European Community; European Communities
CPMR	Conference of Peripheral Maritime Regions	ECA	European Court of Auditors
		ECB	European Central Bank
CPVO	Community Plant Variety Office	ECDC	European Centre for Disease Prevention and Control
CSDP	Common Security and Defence Policy		
CSG	Council Secretariat General	ECHA	European Chemicals Agency
CSO	civil society organization	ECHO	European Community Humanitarian Office
CSR	country-specific recommendation		
CSU	Christian Social Union (Germany)	ECHR	European Convention on Human Rights
CT	Constitutional Treaty		
CWP	Commission Work Programme	ECJ	European Court of Justice
DAC	Development Assistance Committee	ECOFIN	Council of Economics and Finance Ministers
DCFTA	deep and comprehensive free trade area		
		Ecosoc	*See* EESC
DExEU	Department for Exiting the European Union	ECR	European Conservative Reform Group
DG	Directorate-General	ECSC	European Coal and Steel Community
DG DEVCO	Directorate-General for Development and Cooperation	ECTC	European Counter Terrorism Center
		ecu	European currency unit
DG ECHO	Directorate-General for Civil Protection and Humanitarian Operations	EDA	European Defence Agency
		EDC	European Defence Community
DG MOVE	Directorate-General for Transport and Mobility	EdF	Électricité de France
		EDFs	European Development Funds

EDIS	European Deposit Insurance Scheme
EDP	excessive deficit procedure
EDU	European Drug Unit
EEA	European Economic Area; European Environment Agency
EEAS	European External Action Service
EEB	European Environmental Bureau
EEC	European Economic Community
EES	European Employment Strategy
EESC	European Economic and Social Committee
EFA	European Free Alliance
EFC	Economic and Financial Committee (of ECOFIN)
EFD	Europe of Freedom and Democracy
EFDD	Europe of Freedom and Direct Democracy
EFSA	European Food Safety Authority
EFSF	European Financial Stability Facility
EFSM	European Financial Stabilization Mechanism
EFTA	European Free Trade Association
EGC	European General Court
EGD	European Green Deal
EGF	European Globalization Adjustment Fund
EIA	environmental impact assessment
EIB	European Investment Bank
EIoP	*European Integration Online Papers*
EJA	European Judicial Area
ELO	European Landowners Organization
EMA	European Medicines Agency
EMCDDA	European Monitoring Centre for Drugs and Drug Addiction
EMEA	European Medicines Agency
EMS	European Monetary System
EMSA	European Maritime Safety Authority
EMU	economic and monetary union
ENDS	Environmental Data Services Ltd
ENF	Europe of Nations and Freedom
ENISA	European Network and Information Security Agency
ENP	European Neighbourhood Policy
ENPI	European Neighbourhood Partnership Instruments
ENV	Environment (EU Council)
EONIA	European Overnight Index Average
EP	European Parliament
EPA	economic partnership agreement
EPC	European Political Community; European political cooperation
EPERN	European Parties Elections and Referendums Network
EPFSF	European Parliamentary Financial Services Forum
EPI	environmental policy integration; European policy integration
EPP	European People's Party
EPPO	European Public Prosecutor's Office
EPSCO	Council for Employment, Social Policy, Health and Consumer Affairs
ERA	European Railway Agency
ERC	European Research Council Executive Agency
ERDF	European Regional Development Fund
ERICs	European Research Infrastructure Consortiums
ERM	Exchange Rate Mechanism
ERPA	European Research Papers Archive
ERRF	European Rapid Reaction Force
ERT	European Round Table of Industrialists
ESC	Economic and Social Committee
ESCB	European System of Central Banks
ESDP	European Security and Defence Policy
ESF	European Social Fund
ESM	European Stability Mechanism
ESMA	European Securities Markets Authority
ESS	European Security Strategy
ETCG	Education and Training 2010 Coordination Group
ETF	European Training Foundation
ETI	European Transparency Initiative
ETS	Emissions Trading Scheme
ETSI	European Telecommunications Standards Institute
ETSO	European Association of Transmission Systems Operators
ETUC	European Trade Union Congress/ Confederation
EU	European Union
EUAM	European Union Advisory Mission
EUBAM	European Union Border Assistance Mission
EUBG	EU battlegroups
EUCAP	European Union Capacity Building Mission
EUDO	European Union Democracy Observatory, European University Institute
EUFOR	European Union Force
EUGS	EU Global Strategy
EUJUST	European Union integrated rule of law mission

EUL	European United Left
EULEX	European Union Rule of Law Mission
EU MAM	European Union Military Advisory Mission
EU MAM-RCA/RAC	European Union Military Advisory Mission—Central African Republic
EUMC	European Union Military Committee
EUMM	European Union Monitoring Mission
EUMS	European Union Military Staff
EUNAVFOR	European Naval Force (Somalia)
EU-OSHA	European Agency for Safety and Health at Work
EUPAT	EU Political Advisory Team
EUPM	European Union Police Mission
EUPOL	European Union Police Office
EUPOL COPPS	European Union Coordinating Office for Palestinian Police Support
Euratom	*See* EAEC
EURELECTRIC	Union of the Electricity Industry
EUROCADRES	Council of European Professional and Managerial Staff
EUROCHAMBRES	Federation of the Chambers of Commerce in the European Union
EURO-COOP	European Consumer Co-operatives Association
EURODAC	European dactyloscopy (fingerprint database)
EUROFOUND	European Foundation for the Improvement of Living and Working Conditions
Eurojust	European Union's Judicial Cooperation Unit
Europol	European Police Office
Eurostat	European Statistical Office
EUSA	European Union Studies Association
EUSC	European Union Satellite Centre
EUSEC	European Union Security Sector Reform Mission
EUTM	European Union Training Mission
EWG	Eurogroup Working Group
EWL	European Women's Lobby
EYCS	Education, Youth, Culture, and Sport (EU Council)
FAC	Foreign Affairs Council (EU Council)
FAO	Food and Agriculture Organization
FDI	foreign direct investment
FDP	Free Democratic Party (Germany)
FEU	full economic union
FIFG	Financial Instrument for Fisheries Guidance
FN	Front National

FNSEA	*Fédération Nationale des Syndicats d'Exploitants Agricoles* [French National Federation of Farmers' Unions]
FoodSovCAP	European Movement for Food Sovereignty and another Common Agricultural Policy
FPU	full political union
FTE	full-time equivalent
FRA	European Fundamental Rights Agency
Frontex	European Agency for the Management of Operational Cooperation at the External Borders of the Member States of the European Union
FTA	Free Trade Agreement; free trade area
FYR	former Yugoslav Republic
FYROM	Former Yugoslav Republic of Macedonia
GAC	General Affairs Council
GAERC	General Affairs and External Relations Council
GAMM	Global Approach to Migration and Mobility
GATT	General Agreement on Tariffs and Trade
GDP	gross domestic product
GDR	German Democratic Republic
GEMU	Genuine Economic and Monetary Union
GEODE	*Groupement Européen de Sociétés et Organismes de Distribution d'Énergie* [European Group of Societies for the Distribution of Energy]
GMO	genetically modified organism
GNI	gross national income
GNP	gross national product
GNSS	Global Navigation Satellite System
GSA	European GNSS Supervisory Authority
GSC	General Secretariat of the Council
HERA	Health Emergency preparedness and Response Authority
HLWG	High-Level Working Group on Asylum and Immigration
HoA	Horn of Africa
HOSG	heads of state and government
HR	High Representative of the Union for Foreign Affairs and Security Policy
HSC	Health Security Committee
HSG	harder soft governance
IIA	inter-institutional agreement
IIABL	Interinstitutional Agreement on Better Law-Making
ICJ	International Court of Justice

ICT	Information and Communications Technology	MC	Monetary Committee
ICTY	International Criminal Tribunal of former Yugoslavia	MDG	Millennium Development Goals (UN)
ID	Identity and Democracy	MDR	Medical Devices Regulation
IEEP	Institute for European Environmental Policy	MENA	Middle-East and North African
		MEP	member of the European Parliament
IFIEC	International Federation of Industrial Energy Consumers	MEQR	measures having equivalent effect
		Mercosur	*Mercado Común del Sur* [Southern Common Market]
IFOAM	International Federation of Organic Agricultural Movements	MFA	Minister of Foreign Affairs; Multi-Fibre Arrangement
IGC	intergovernmental conference	MFF	Multi-Annual Financial Framework
IHRs	International Health Regulations	MGQ	maximum guaranteed quantity
ILO	International Labour Organization	MINEX	System for the Promotion of Mineral Production and Exports
IMF	International Monetary Fund		
IMP	Integrated Mediterranean Programmes	MIP	Macroeconomic Imbalance Procedure
IMPEL	Network for Implementation and Enforcement of Environmental Law	MLG	multilevel governance
		MP	member of Parliament
IPA	Instrument for Pre-Accession Assistance	MTR	mid-term review (CAP)
		NAFTA	North Atlantic Free Trade Agreement
IPE	international political economy	NAP	national action plan
IR	international relations	NATO	North Atlantic Treaty Organization
ISAF	International Security Assistance Force	NBs	notified bodies
ISPA	Instrument for Structural Policies for Pre-accession	NECP	National Energy and Climate Plan
		NEPI	new environmental policy instrument
ISR	intelligence, surveillance, and reconnaissance	NFU	National Farmers' Union (UK)
		NGEU	Next Generation EU
ISS	European Union Institute for Security Studies	NGL	Nordic Green Left
		NGO	non-governmental organization
IT	Information Technology	NHS	National Health Service
ITER	International Thermonuclear Experimental Reactor	NI	Northern Ireland
		NI	*non-inscrit*
ITRE	Committee on Industry, Research and Energy	NLG	Nordic Green Left
		NMGs	new modes of governance
JAC	*Jeunesse Agricole Chrétienne* [Young Christian Farmers]	NPE	Normative Power Europe
		NPF	national policy framework
JASPERS	Joint Assistance in Supporting Projects in European Regions	NUTS	Nomenclature of Units for Territorial Statistics
JEREMIE	Joint European Resources for Micro and Medium Enterprises	OCA	optimum currency area
		ODA	overseas development assistance
JESSICA	Joint European Support for Sustainable Investment in City Areas	OECD	Organisation for Economic Co-operation and Development
JHA	Justice and Home Affairs	OEEC	Organization for European Economic Cooperation
JNA	Joint National Army (of Serbia)		
JPCCM	judicial and police cooperation in criminal matters	OHIM	Office for the Harmonization of the Single Market (Trade Marks and Designs)
JTR	Joint Transparency Register		
LI	liberal intergovernmentalism	OJ	Official Journal (of the European Union)
LMU	Latin monetary union		
LPF	Level playing field	OLP	ordinary legislative procedure
LT	Lisbon Treaty	OMC	open method of coordination
MBS	mortgage-backed security		

OMT	Outright Monetary Transactions		RSPB	Royal Society for the Protection of Birds
OSCE	Organization for Security and Cooperation in Europe		S&D	Social and Democratic Alliance
			SAA	stabilization and association agreement
PCTF	European Police Chiefs Task Force		SAP	Stabilization and Association Process
PD	Political Declaration		SAPARD	Special Accession Programme for Agriculture and Rural Development
PDB	preliminary draft Budget			
PDCA	Political Dialogue and Cooperation Agreement		SARS	severe acute respiratory syndrome
			SCA	Special Committee on Agriculture (of AGFISH)
PEPP	pandemic emergency purchase programme			
			SDGs	Sustainable Development Goals
PES	Party of European Socialists		SDR	special drawing right
PESCO	Permanent structured cooperation		SEA	Single European Act
PHARE	Poland and Hungary Aid for Economic Reconstruction		SEM	Single European Market
			SFP	Single Farm Payment
PHEIC	Public Health Emergency of International Concern		SGP	Stability and Growth Pact
			SIS	Schengen Information System
PIIGS	Portugal, Ireland, Italy, Greece, and Spain		SitCen	Situation Centre (GSC)
			SLIM	Simpler Legislation for the Internal Market
PIREDEU	Providing an Infrastructure for Research on Electoral Democracy in the European Union			
			SMEs	small and medium-sized enterprises
			SMET	Single Market Enforcement Task Force
PiS	Law and Justice Party (Poland)		SMP	Securities Markets Programme
PJCCM	Policy and Judicial Cooperation in Criminal Matters		SRM	Single Resolution Mechanism
			SSC	Scientific Steering Committee
plc	public limited company		SSM	Single Supervisory Mechanism
PLO	Palestine Liberation Organization		SSR	security sector reform
PM	Prime Minister		STABEX	System for the Stabilisation of ACP and OCT Export Earnings
PNR	passenger name record			
PNV	*El Partido Nacionalist Vasco* [Basque Nationalist Party]		STF	Sustainable Transport Forum
			TA	Treaty of Amsterdam
PP	Permanent President of the European Council		TACIS	Programme for Technical Assistance to the Independent States of the Former Soviet Union and Mongolia
PPE	personal protective equipment			
PPP	purchasing power parity		TCA	Trade and Cooperation Agreement
PR	proportional representation; public relations		TCN	third-country national
			TEC	Treaty on the European Community
PSC	Political and Security Committee (also COPS)		TEN-TEA	Trans-European Transport Network Executive Agency
PTCF	(European) Police Chiefs Task Force		TESM	Treaty Establishing the European Stability Mechanism
QMV	qualified majority voting			
R&D	research and development		TEU	Treaty on European Union
R&T	research and technology		TFE	Task Force Europe
RABIT	rapid border intervention teams (Frontex)		TFEU	Treaty on the Functioning of the European Union
RAC	Central African Republic		TRAN	Committee on Transport and Tourism
REA	Research Executive Agency		TSCG	Treaty of Stability, Coordination and Governance in the Economic and Monetary Union
REGLEG	Conference of European Regions with Legislative Powers			
RIA	regulatory impact assessment		TTIP	Transatlantic Trade and Investment Partnership
RQMV	Reverse Qualified Majority Voting			
RRF	Recovery and Resilience Facility		UCPM	Union Civil Protection Mechanism
RRP	Recovery and Resilience Plan			

UEAPME	European Association of Craft, Small and Medium Sized Enterprises	UNSC	UN Security Council
UK	United Kingdom	US	United States
UKIP	United Kingdom Independence Party	VAT	value added tax
UKTF	Task Force for Relations with the United Kingdom	VCI	*Verband Chemischer Industrie* [(German) Chemical Industry Association]
UN	United Nations	VIS	Visa Information System
UNFCCC	UN Framework Convention on Climate Change	VOC	volatile organic compound
UNHCR	Office of the United Nations High Commissioner for Refugees	WA	Withdrawal Agreement
		WEU	Western European Union
UNICE	*See* BUSINESSEUROPE	WFP	World Food Programme
UNIPEDE	International Union of Producers and Distributors of Electrical Energy	WPEG	White Paper on European Governance
		WTO	World Trade Organization
		WWF	World Wide Fund for Nature
UNMIK	UN Mission in Kosovo	YES	Young Workers' Exchange Scheme

How to use this book

This textbook is enriched with a range of learning features to help you navigate the text and reinforce your understanding of the European Union. This guided tour shows you how to get the most out of your textbook package.

Reader's Guides

Reader's guides at the beginning of each chapter set the scene for the themes and issues to be discussed, and indicate the scope of the chapter's coverage.

12

The European Parliament

Charlotte Burns

Chapter Contents

Reader's Guide

This chapter focuses upon the European Parliament (EP) matically increase in recent times. The EP has been tr institution into one that is able to have a genuine say in Union's executive bodies (the Commission and Counc count in a range of policy areas. However, increases been matched by an increase in popular legitimacy: tu elections up to 2014, and whilst turnout increased in 20 populist Eurosceptic parties. Thus, while the EP's legisl many national parliaments, it has struggled to connect chambers now has to find ways to accommodate populist Eurosceptic MEPs. The chapter explores these issues in detail. In the first section, the EP's evolution from talking shop to co-legislator is reviewed; its powers and influence are explained in the next section; the EP's internal structure and organization are then outlined with a focus upon the role and behaviour of the political groups, and finally, the European Parliament's representative function as the EU's only directly elected institution is discussed.

Reader's Guide

This chapter focuses upon the European Parliament (EP), an institution that has seen its power dramatically increase in recent times. The EP has been transformed from being a relatively powerless institution into one that is able to have a genuine say in the legislative process and hold the European Union's executive bodies (the Commission and Council, introduced in Chapters 10 and 11) to account in a range of policy areas. However, increases in the Parliament's formal powers have not been matched by an increase in popular legitimacy: turnout in European elections fell in successive

Boxes

Throughout the book, boxes provide you with additional information and relevant examples to complement and further your understanding of the main chapter text.

 BOX 12.5   KEY DEBATES: ACCOMMODATING EUROSCEPTIC MEPS

In both the eighth (2014–19) and ninth (2019–24) Parliamentary elections, Eurosceptic parties performed well, raising the prospect that MEPs from these groups would seek to undermine parliamentary business. The larger mainstream political groups sought to prevent this eventuality by putting in place a cordon sanitaire, which has limited the access of Eurosceptic parties to positions of responsibility in the

1992 Programme The Commission's programme and timetable for implementation of the internal market. In its 1985 White Paper, the Commission listed some 300 legislative measures to be taken to implement the single market programme. These included the elimination of physical, technical, and tax frontiers. *See* single market (programme); Single European Act.

à la carte A non-uniform method of integration that would allow member states to select policies as if

Glossary Terms

Key terms appear in bold throughout the text, and are defined in a glossary at the end of the book to help you broaden your vocabulary and aid exam revision.

KEY POINTS

- The European Parliament started life as an unelected Common Assembly to the ECSC.

- Its powers were limited to dismissing the High Authority and being consulted on legislative proposals, but the Council could ignore its suggestions.

- Until 1979, MEPs were national parliamentarians, hence the EP was a part-time institution, which, with its limited powers,

Key Points

Each section ends with a set of key points which summarize the most important ideas and arguments discussed.

? QUESTIONS

1. Why was the European Parliament created?
2. How and why have the EP's power increased?
3. Do MEPs vote according to nationality or ideology? To what ex
4. What impact has the empowerment of the European Parlia
5. How is it possible to account for the turnout in European elec
6. What impact does the emergence of a larger bloc of Eur Parliament? What, if any, impact has Brexit had in this regard?

Questions

A set of carefully devised questions at the end of each chapter help you to check your understanding and critically reflect on core themes and issues. These may also be used as the basis of seminar discussion or coursework.

GUIDE TO FURTHER READING

Corbett, R., Jacobs, F., and Neville, D. (2016) *The European Parliament*, 9th edn (Lond comprehensive guide to the history and day-to-day operation of the European Parlia

Hix, S., Noury, A. G., and Roland, G. (2007) *Democratic Politics in the European P* University Press). A study of the internal politics of the European Parliament that c voting behaviour in the Plenary.

Ripoll Servent, A. (2018) *The European Parliament* (Basingstoke: Palgrave Macmillan). / organization and powers of the Parliament.

Ripoll Servent, A. and Roederer-Rynning, C. (2018) 'The European Parliament: A (Different Kind" in *Oxford Research Encyclopaedias, Politics* (New York: Oxford Univers

Further Reading

Each chapter includes a further reading list to guide you towards the key academic literature in the field, and to help you find out more about the issues raised within the chapter.

How to use the online resources

The **online resources** that accompany this textbook provide both students and instructors with helpful and ready-to-use teaching and learning materials to help you broaden your knowledge of EU politics.

© Oxford University Press, 2018   Privacy Policy | Cookie Policy | Terms of Use | Contact Us   OXFORD
UNIVERSITY PRESS

FOR STUDENTS:

Interactive timeline

An interactive timeline provides summaries of key events in the history of European Union politics as you click on each date.

Multiple-choice questions

A bank of self-marking multiple-choice questions accompanies each chapter, enabling you to test your knowledge and receive instant feedback to reinforce your understanding of the text.

Flashcard glossary

A series of interactive flashcards containing key terms and concepts has been provided to test your understanding of key terminology of the European Union, and to aid exam revision.

Answer guidance

A list of key points to consider in answering end-of-chapter questions will help keep your revision on track.

Web links

A series of annotated web links points you in the direction of helpful and relevant sources of information, enabling you to take your learning further.

Updates to the book

Biannual updates to content in the book will help you stay up-to-date on all of the key developments in EU politics.

FOR INSTRUCTORS:

PowerPoint presentations

Fully customizable PowerPoint slides complement each chapter of the book, providing a useful resource to instructors preparing lectures and in-class handouts.

Essay, seminar, and quiz questions

Essay and seminar questions designed to reinforce key themes are provided for each chapter.

Boxes and figures from the text

All boxes and figures from the text have been provided in high resolution format for downloading into presentation software, or for use in assignments and exam material.

I

Introduction

Michelle Cini and Nieves Pérez-Solórzano Borragán

Reader's Guide

This chapter comprises a very brief introduction to European Union (EU) politics. It aims to help those students who are completely new to the EU by drawing attention to some general background information and context, which should help to make sense of the chapters that follow. To that end, this introductory chapter begins by explaining what the EU is, why it was originally set up, and what the EU does. The chapter ends by explaining how the book is organized.

1.1 Introduction

The European integration process has moved in fits and starts. Periods of heightened activity and enthusiastic reform have been followed by years of stagnation, pessimism, and crisis. Indeed, some scholars claim that a crucial explanatory factor driving the evolution of first the European Community (EC), and later—after 1993—the European Union (EU), has been the crises that the EC/EU and its member states have had to address over the past six decades or so. That may be so; but even if crises have (re-)invigorated European integration in the past, this does not mean that they will continue to do so in the future. Relying on crises as a driver of European integration is a risky strategy.

Especially since the onset of the financial crisis in 2007–08, the European Union has been experiencing multiple and overlapping crises, including an economic crisis, which also provoked a social crisis for the citizens it affected; a refugee, migration, or borders crisis, which has contributed to thousands of deaths and which has exacerbated tensions between member states; a 'rule of law' crisis, which threatens the independence of judicial systems in some member states; 'Brexit', the first time a member state—and a large one at that—has left the Union; and finally a public health crisis in the form of the COVID-19 pandemic. The cumulative effect of these crises and talk of an 'existential crisis' has led some commentators to argue that the very existence of the EU is in jeopardy; rather than focusing on European integration, these scholars have directed their attention to the theme of Europe's (potential) 'disintegration'. However, amid the gloom, the EU has proven itself to be remarkably resilient amid calls for reform and the circulation of new or rediscovered ideas about what the future of European integration might look like. To paraphrase the American author, Mark Twain, reports of the death of the EU have—so far—been exaggerated, but that is not to say that its survival is inevitable (on this point see Gillingham, 2016).

1.2 Why a European Union?

Understanding the EU from an historical perspective means stepping back to the post-1945 era. The European integration process was initiated in the 1950s largely because of the negative experiences of the six founding member states during and in the immediate aftermath of the Second World War. This period was also marked by the 'end of Empire', with the European integration project constructed as a way of offering Europe new purpose in a new world order, whether to rescue the European nation state from decline or to address geopolitical challenges resulting from the onset of the Cold War.

Maintaining peace was a primary objective at the time. So too was economic recovery. And even though the idea of a formalized system of European cooperation was not entirely new, the shape that the post-1945 Communities (and later Union) would take was—while drawing on familiar models of government—innovative (see Chapter 2).

From the standpoint of the twenty-first century, it is perhaps easy to forget how important the anti-war rationale for European integration was in the 1940s and 1950s. But this ambition to prevent a repeat of the two world wars also went hand-in-hand with a general awareness that (Western) Europe had to get back on its feet economically after the devastation of the war years. Inter-state cooperation was considered a step towards a new post-war order. Fundamental to this objective was the reconstruction and rehabilitation of Germany as the engine of the West European economy. One can only imagine how controversial such an idea was at the time. Surely, encouraging the re-emergence of a strong Germany would pose a serious threat to the security of Western Europe? Was this not a case of short-term economic objectives trumping long-term geopolitical ones? Ultimately, however, these two ostensibly contradictory objectives of 'peace' and 'economic reconstruction' began to be viewed as mutually reinforcing. European integration—or rather the prospect of it—was the instrument that allowed this change of perspective to become credible.

The EU has altered dramatically since the early days of the Community (see Figure 1.1), and some argue that the original objectives of the 1950s are no longer relevant. Certainly, despite an absence of solidarity among EU member states, and different preferences on the nature and direction of European integration, the prospect of war between them seems extremely slim now, demonstrating, one might argue, the success of the integration project. However, European integration has been criticized and challenged on several fronts, and not least for substituting technocratic governance for democracy, for failing to deliver on promised economic growth and global competitiveness, at times for its insularity and conservatism, and for failing to be responsive to its citizens. Moreover, the EU has only very recently begun to address seriously the challenges posed by the new digital economy and society, and by climate change.

For the time being, however, it seems that the European Union will continue to exist in one form or another, even if its future shape and trajectory is unpredictable. Any explanation of why this is the case must rest on an understanding of the importance of the external or 'security' dimension of the EU's role. It is almost a truism now to state that since the early 1990s the discourse around 'old' definitions of security which implies *military* security—closely related to the notion of *defence*—has been subsumed within a more wide-ranging (comprehensive) notion of security. Even if the actions of governments do not always live up to the ambitions of this discourse, security issues can now be said to encompass environmental hazards and energy supply issues, migration flows, financial crisis, public health, and demographic change—as well as military threats. Two contextual 'events' have been crucial in accounting

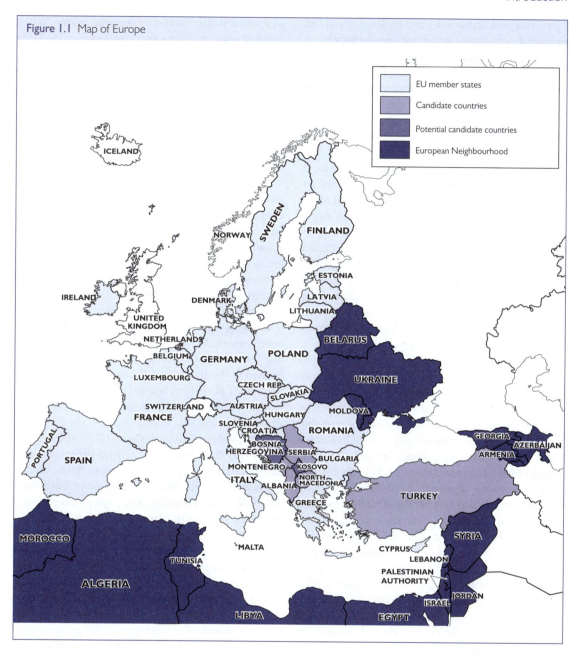

Figure 1.1 Map of Europe

Legend:
- EU member states
- Candidate countries
- Potential candidate countries
- European Neighbourhood

for the broadening out of the concept: the end of the Cold War in 1989; and the terrorist attacks on the World Trade Center in New York and the Pentagon in Washington DC on 11 September 2001 (often referred to as '9/11'). While the former ended the **bipolarity** of the post-1945 period, the latter redefined security threats as internal as well as external, as more multi-dimensional and fluid, and as less predictable. Add to this a growing awareness of the threats posed to future generations from climate change, and to current populations from environmental pollution, extreme instability in financial markets, the rise of non-Western economies, such as Brazil, India, and China, and the economic crisis and more recent COVID-19 crises, challenges to the dominant neo-liberal, capitalist paradigm, and it seems that the period after 1989 marked a transition to a newly emerging world order. However, this new world order is not static as the changing and challenging relations with Russia, the problematic aftermath of the Arab Spring, the instability derived from Western intervention in

Libya, Iraq, and Afghanistan, and the lengthy and continuing fallout from the Syrian war have demonstrated.

The EU is as much a product of this new world order as it is an actor seeking to manage change, or an arena in which other actors attempt to perform a similar function. Thus, there is no claim here that the EU alone can address these issues. It is but one response, one that is highly institutionalized, that facilitates agreement through procedural mechanisms such as qualified majority voting and norms of consensus, all overseen by a goal-orientated, politically involved bureaucracy, a directly elected co-legislature, and (arguably) an activist judicial system. Even though recent events often present the European Union as a 'problem' to be solved, this book demonstrates in many different ways that it also has the potential to provide solutions to the challenges facing Europe in the third decade of the twenty-first century, while acknowledging the EU's flaws, and the tensions and paradoxes that plague the Union, both at the level of integration, broadly cast, and within specific policy domains.

The EU is not just an agent of security, however, no matter how broadly we define the concept. It also concerns itself with welfare-related issues, albeit within certain constraints. From a normative perspective, which accepts that the state ought to take responsibility for the well-being and social condition of its citizens (rather than leaving them to fend for themselves), the notion of the EU as a neo-liberal entity with a strong focus on economic governance and financial stability accounts for only part of what the EU is or does. In its original form, the welfare state was a European construct, so it should come as no surprise to find that the EU has had ambitions in this direction. But it is important not to overstate the EU's capacity in this respect. Although redistribution and EU-level intervention finds expression in many European policies, when this is compared to the functions performed by its member states, the EU performs a very limited welfare role. While some argue that this is right and proper, others would like to see the EU developing its activities further in this direction, perhaps in the form of a revival of the idea of a 'Social Europe'. These ideas have gained more purchase as a consequence of the political fall-out from the COVID-19 public health crisis.

1.3 What is the European Union?

But what is the European Union? One way of answering this question is to view the EU as a family of 27 **liberal-democratic** states, acting collectively through an institutionalized system of decision-making. When joining the EU, members sign up not only to the body of EU treaties, legislation, and norms (the so-called *acquis communautaire*), but also to a set of shared common values, based on democracy, human rights, and principles of social justice. This does not prevent member states challenging these 'agreed' norms and values. Members, and indeed agents of the European institutions, are keen to stress the diversity of the Union—most obviously in cultural and linguistic terms.

Since its establishment in the 1950s, commentators have argued over the kind of body the European Community (now Union) is. Whilst there is a growing consensus that the EU sits somewhere between a traditional international organization and a state, the question of whether it resembles one of these 'models' more than the other is contested. Although it might seem fair to claim that the European Union is unique, or a hybrid body, even this point can be contentious because it could prevent researchers from comparing the EU to national systems of government and international organizations. Such issues are addressed in the theories of European integration and theories of EU politics covered in this book.

The common institutions of the EU, the Commission, Parliament, EU Council, Court, the European Council, and the European Central Bank (ECB) along with many other bodies, are perhaps the most visible manifestations of the European Union. These institutions, discussed at length in the chapters that follow, are highly interdependent; and together they form a nexus for joint decision-making in a now extremely wide range of policy areas. While many argue that the EU Council (comprising the EU's governments and support staff) still predominates as the primary legislator, the importance of the European Parliament has grown substantially since the 1980s, so that it is now generally considered as a co-legislature. Ultimately, however, the member states remain in a privileged position within the EU, as it is they (or rather their governments) who can change the general institutional framework of the Union through treaty reform; or even withdraw from the Union.

1.4 What does the European Union do?

One answer to the question 'what is the European Union?' might be to say that the EU *is* what it *does*. This leads us to focus on the wide range of activities in which the EU is involved, the highest profile and important of which are the making and management of European-level policies, and the representation of the EU and its member states externally, beyond Europe's borders. European policies, once agreed, must (or should) be implemented across all EU member states. But as implementation is usually the responsibility of national or sub-national governments, the EU-level actors tend to devote most of their attention to developing policy ideas and turning those ideas into legislation or actions which have concrete effects. Many of those policy initiatives respond to problems that have arisen in Europe because of increasing transnational (or cross-border) movements. There are exceptions to this; but the EU is most competent to act where the Single Market is concerned. Examples of this have included the EU's involvement in the reduction of Europe-wide 'roaming' charges for mobile phone calls, a more transparent pricing of airline tickets on the Internet, the legal obligation to clearly label the presence of any genetically modified organism (GMO) in food, or protecting the four freedoms (free movement of goods, capital, services, and people) in the aftermath of Brexit.

How, then, is European policy made? It is not easy to summarize the European policy process in just a few paragraphs. One reason for this is that there is no *one* way of making European policy. Some policies, such as foreign policy and policy on certain aspects of justice and home affairs, are very intergovernmental, and use a decision-making process that is based largely on government-to-government cooperation. By contrast, there is much more of a supranational (EU-level) quality to policies, such as agricultural policy and policy on, say, European-wide mergers. Focusing on policy types, Wallace and Reh have grouped similar types of policies together, identifying five 'modes' of European decision-making: the classical Community method; the EU regulatory mode; the EU distributional mode; the policy coordination mode; and intensive transgovernmentalism (Wallace and Reh, 2015; see also Chapter 16). These five modes give some indication of the extent of variation across the EU's policy process.

In some of the earliest textbooks on the EC, the adage that 'the Commission proposes, the Council disposes' was often repeated. As a general statement of how EU policy-making operates today, this is now far from an accurate depiction. It is certainly true that in the more supranational policy areas, the Commission proposes legislation; however, this does not provide a good summary of the Commission's role across the board.

It is fair to say that policy now emerges from the interaction of several actors and institutions. First among these is what is sometimes referred to as the 'institutional triangle' of the European Commission, European Parliament, and the Council of the European Union (the EU Council). However, many other European, national, and sub-national bodies, including interest groups, also play an important role (see Chapter 14). The functions, responsibilities, and obligations of these actors and institutions depend on the rules that apply to the policy under consideration. While there are rather different rules that apply to budgetary decisions and to the agreement of international agreements, and indeed for economic and monetary union, much of the work of the European Union involves regulatory activities.

Although different procedures still govern the way that policy is made, this variation is arguably not as extreme as it once was. Most legislation is now made using the ordinary legislative procedure (OLP). This procedure used to be called 'co-decision'; older books and articles will refer to it as such, and sometimes the concept of 'co-decision' is still used to reflect the sharing of legislative power across the EU Council and Parliament. This is because the OLP allows both the Parliament and the Council, as co-legislators, two successive readings of legislative proposals drafted by the Commission. In broad terms it means that the EU Council, comprising national ministers or their representatives, and the European Parliament, made up of elected representatives, together 'co-decide' EU laws. Together, then, they make up the EU's legislature. The Commission, by contrast, is often labelled the EU's executive body (note however that the Council also performs some executive functions). The Commission is not a government as such but has some government-type functions in that it proposes new laws; and has responsibility for managing policies once they have been agreed (see Chapter 10).

For the EU's member states who sit in the EU Council, policy is determined through either unanimity, where all countries have a potential veto, or a weighted voting system called 'qualified majority voting' (or QMV). Most EU policies are now decided upon using a qualified majority (see Chapter 11). However, increasingly, other 'modes' of policy-making are being used beyond the formal kinds of decisions that require a vote from the Council and the Parliament. This includes a process called the 'open method of coordination' (OMC), which provides a framework for member states to work towards policy convergence in areas of national competence such as employment, social protection, social inclusion, education, and youth and training, through sharing common objectives, policy instruments, best practice, and peer pressure to achieve policy convergence. The Commission, the Parliament, and the Court of Justice of the EU have a limited or no role in the process, which makes this form of policy largely intergovernmental in character.

Focusing solely on the legislative process, then, tells only part of the story of what the EU does. It does not tell us anything about the role the EU plays in distributing money, through its Structural Funds, or by providing research grants to university researchers, or for creating temporary recovery plans to address the effects of the economic and COVID-19 crises; nor does it say anything about the substance of EU activities, such as the foreign policy actions which take place under the European flag, EU efforts to forge consensus on economic governance, or the environmental initiatives that shape the EU's position in international negotiations on climate change. Neither does it tell us about what the EU means for democracy in Europe, the extent to which the EU is a union for European citizens, or how the EU has been affected by or contributed to various crises, such as the financial crisis, the migration and refugee crisis, Brexit, or the COVID-19 pandemic. All of these issues are addressed in the chapters that follow.

1.5 The organization of the book

The book is organized into five parts. Part One covers the historical evolution of the European Community from 1945. Chapter 2 focuses on the origins and early years of the European integration process, taking the story of the European integration up to the Nice Treaty and Chapter 3 then covers the period from the Constitutional Treaty to the Lisbon Treaty, the financial crisis, Brexit, and the COVID-19 pandemic.

Part Two deals with theoretical and conceptual approaches that have tried to explain European integration and EU politics. Chapter 4 reviews the fortunes of

neo-functionalism; while Chapter 5 summarizes the key elements of the intergovernmental approaches to European integration. Chapter 6 has a wide remit, focusing on how European integration and EU politics have been theorized since the 1990s. Chapter 7 focuses on governance approaches; Chapter 8 on Europeanization; and Chapter 9 on democracy and legitimacy in the EU.

Part Three introduces the European institutions: the European Commission (Chapter 10); the European Council and the EU Council (Chapter 11); the European Parliament (Chapter 12); and the Court of Justice of the EU (Chapter 13). It also includes chapters on interest intermediation (Chapter 14) and the EU's citizens and public opinion (Chapter 15).

Part Four covers a sample of European policies, which, though not aiming to be in any way comprehensive, demonstrates the various ways in which such policies have evolved, and—though to a lesser extent—how they operate. It starts in Chapter 16 with an overview of the EU policy process. Thereafter, Chapter 17 tackles trade and development policies; Chapter 18 focuses on enlargement; Chapter 19, foreign, security, and defence policies; and Chapter 20, the Single Market. Chapter 21 discusses the policies on freedom, security, and justice. Chapters 22 and 23 deal, respectively, with economic and monetary union (EMU) and the Common Agricultural Policy (CAP). Finally, Chapter 24 examines the EU's environmental policy.

The final part of the book, Part Five, comprises four chapters, each of which deals with specific issues related to the politics of the European Union and the future of European integration and a chapter focusing on the future of the EU. The first, Chapter 25, covers the post-2007 financial and economic crisis, Chapter 26 performs a similar function for the migration and refugee crisis; Chapter 27 addresses Brexit; and Chapter 28 reviews the EU's handling of the COVID-19 pandemic from early 2020 to mid-2021. Chapter 29 concludes the book by considering the prospects for the European Union, focusing on four possible scenarios for the EU's future development.

 This book is accompanied by online resources designed to take your learning and understanding further. Visit the website to access materials including extra multiple-choice questions with instant feedback, web links, answer guidance to end-of-chapter questions, and updates on new developments in EU politics.

www.oup.com/he/cini-borragan7e

PART I
The Historical Context

2

The European Union: Establishment and Development

David Phinnemore

Reader's Guide

The focus of this chapter is the emergence of the European Communities in the 1950s, their evolution in the three decades thereafter, and the establishment and early development of the European Union (EU) in the 1990s. The chapter explores key developments in the first five decades of European integration and some of the tensions that have shaped them. It considers the ambitions of the architects and supporters of the European Communities and how their hopes and aspirations played out as integration became a reality in the 1950s and 1960s. It looks at how their ambitions grew and how the process then lost momentum in the 1970s before the idea of 'European union' was rekindled in the 1980s with the Single European Act (1986) and the Single Market project. These acted as catalysts for a new era of dynamic European integration with the now expanded Communities at its core. The chapter then explores how, through the adoption and implementation of the Treaty on European Union (1992), the European Union was established. The chapter assesses the unique and incomplete form of the new 'union' and examines the impact on it of reforms introduced by the Treaty of Amsterdam (1997) and the Treaty of Nice (2000) as the EU sought to prepare itself for further enlargement and the challenges of the initial years of the twenty-first century.

2.1 Introduction

The European Union (EU) today is firmly established as the pre-eminent organization in the multi-faceted and dynamic process of European integration. It was not ever thus. The EU was formally established only on 1 November 1993, more than four decades after early efforts at promoting institutionalized cooperation between European states bore initial fruit with the establishment of the **Council of Europe** in 1949. The EU's emergence in the early 1990s should not therefore be seen as a radical and wholly new initiative of post-Cold War European politics even if its creation certainly gained some inspiration from the momentous events of 1989 in Central and Eastern Europe and the desire, according to the authors of its founding treaty, to establish 'firm bases for the construction of the future Europe'. The establishment of the EU in 1993 also needs to be viewed as a further stage in a process of ever closer integration between an increasing number of states. The roots of the process can be clearly traced back to the early years of European cooperation in the 1940s and in particular to the efforts of '**the Six**'—Belgium, France, (West) Germany, Italy, Luxembourg, and the Netherlands—in the 1950s to establish new forms of **supranational integration** in a concerted effort to promote peaceful reconciliation and coexistence, economic growth and security, and social development.

This chapter explores two important and related developments. The first is the emergence of the European Communities created by 'the Six' in the 1950s and their evolution during subsequent decades. Here, the chapter notes the progress 'the Six' made in establishing supranational institutions, moving towards common policies and raising their ambitions for further economic and political integration. The chapter draws attention, however, to the fact that there was far from universal support for the activities of 'the Six'. States were divided over what forms and in what areas cooperation and integration should take place. Tensions existed over how far integration should go and who should be involved. And new divisions and tensions were created with the establishment of the Communities; rather than uniting 'Europe', integration was—initially at least—focused on a limited number of continental Western European states, with Western Europe split between an 'inner six' and an 'outer seven'. Over time, the core would expand as other states, the United Kingdom among them, joined 'the Six'; a process that would actually increase tensions within the

Communities and contributed, against a backdrop of industrial decline and economic recession in the 1970s, to a slowdown in integration. By the early 1980s, albeit with the Communities established, enlarged to ten members with two more soon to follow, and its institutions functioning, European integration had seemingly lost its dynamism. It appeared unlikely that the more ambitious hopes and aspirations of the architects and supporters of the Communities would be realized; any prospect of moving to a European 'union' appeared to have faded. In fact, the complete opposite occurred.

This leads to the second important development covered by the chapter: the establishment and early development of the EU in the 1990s. The chapter explores how the idea of 'European union' was rekindled in the 1980s with the **Single European Act** (1986) and the Single Market project acting as catalysts for a new era of dynamic Communities-based integration. It considers how, through 'Maastricht' and the adoption and implementation of the Treaty on European Union (1992), the European Union was established and assesses the unique and incomplete form of the new 'union'. The chapter outlines the original structure of the EU and how this was affected by certain key developments during its first decade and later. The chapter therefore examines not only the origins of the EU, but also the background to and content of the Treaty of Amsterdam (1997) and the Treaty of Nice (2000) as well as the launch of the economic and monetary union (EMU) in 1999. The chapter concludes with an assessment of what sort of union the EU had become by the turn of the twenty-first century, what hopes and aspirations its supporters had for it as EU leaders in 2000 launched a 'Future of Europe' debate, and as ideas of adopting a European constitution came to the fore.

2.2 Integration and cooperation in Europe: ambitions, tensions, and divisions

The EU owes its existence to the process of European integration that has been a defining feature of post-Second World War Europe. Ideas for European 'unity' did not simply emerge in the post-1945 period, however. Throughout the 1920s and 1930s and also during the war years, various proposals had been drafted for federal or pan-European union. Among these was **Altiero Spinelli**'s 1941 **Ventotene Manifesto** 'For A

Free and United Europe', a blueprint for a federation of European states. A number of political leaders and governments-in-exile were also considering ideas and plans for post-war integration. Consequently, when hostilities in Europe did end in May 1945 the new governments of Belgium, Luxembourg, and the Netherlands moved quickly to establish a 'Benelux' customs union, and opportunities opened up for advocates of new forms of supranational political organization to advance their case. Fears of German military revival also led France and the United Kingdom in 1947 to sign the **Treaty of Dunkirk** on establishing a defensive alliance and mutual assistance pact; a year later they were joined through the **Treaty of Brussels** by the Benelux countries, and the following year, on 4 April 1949, military and defence cooperation was extended even further with the establishment of the North Atlantic Treaty Organization (NATO) and the incorporation, in a new 'Atlantic Alliance', of the Treaty of Brussels signatories, the United States, Canada, Portugal, Italy, Norway, Denmark, and Iceland (see Box 2.1).

BOX 2.1   BACKGROUND: KEY DATES IN EUROPEAN INTEGRATION: EARLY EFFORTS

1947	March	United States announces Truman Doctrine
	March	Treaty of Dunkirk signed
	June	United States announces Marshall Plan
1948	January	Benelux Customs Union established
	March	Treaty of Brussels signed
	April	Organisation for European Economic Cooperation (OEEC) established
	May	Congress of Europe in The Hague
1949	April	Washington Treaty establishing the North Atlantic Treaty Organization (NATO) signed
	May	Statute of the Council of Europe signed
1950	May	**Schuman Plan** circulated
	October	Pleven Plan for a European Defence Community (EDC) circulated
1951	April	Treaty of Paris—establishing the European Coal and Steel Community (ECSC)—signed
1952	May	Treaty constituting a European Defence Community signed
	July	ECSC established
1953	March	Draft Treaty embodying the Statute of the European Political Community adopted
1954	August	*Assemblée Nationale* rejects EDC
	October	West European Union (WEU) established
1955	June	Messina Declaration on further European integration
1957	March	Treaties of Rome—establishing the European Economic Community (EEC) and the European Atomic Energy Community (EAEC)—signed
1958	January	EEC and EAEC (Euratom) established
1959	November	OEEC negotiations on a European free trade area collapse
1960	May	European Free Trade Association (EFTA) established

Not all governments warmed to the idea of integration even if past, present, and future political leaders (e.g., Winston Churchill, Paul-Henri Spaak, **Konrad Adenauer**, Francois Mitterrand) who attended The Hague Congress of 1948 did resolve to pursue the creation of a European 'Union' or 'Federation'. They may have agreed to establish a 'European Assembly', draft a 'Charter of Human Rights', and include Germany in their endeavours, but the appetite to pursue the ambitious goal of a 'United Europe' was far from universal. Governments in the Benelux countries and in France and Italy were broadly enthusiastic and willing to consider supranational integration, but those in the United Kingdom, Switzerland, and the Scandinavian countries were at best lukewarm, maintaining a preference for much looser forms of intergovernmental cooperation. Germany under Adenauer's leadership was interested, seeing engagement as a means for rehabilitation. For the countries of Central and Eastern Europe, however, the emerging realities of Europe's division between a capitalist and democratic West and the Soviet Union-dominated East, and the onset of the Cold War, ruled out involvement. Moreover, post-war economic recovery was a far more pressing concern than the pursuit of political integration.

Nevertheless, on 5 May 1949, Belgium, Denmark, France, Ireland, Italy, Luxembourg, the Netherlands, Norway, Sweden, and the United Kingdom did establish the Council of Europe. Soon Greece and Turkey joined, and in 1950 the accession of Iceland and (West) Germany brought the membership to 14. The essentially intergovernmental nature of the Council of Europe's activities and ambitions disappointed federalists and other supporters of integration such as Spaak, but an important first step had been taken in establishing institutionalized political cooperation in Europe. Initial steps in promoting economic integration had also been taken in April 1948 with the establishment of the **Organisation for European Economic Cooperation (OEEC)**. Created at the insistence of the US government to administer US financial assistance from the Marshall Plan, the OEEC was also committed to promoting trade liberalization among the 17 participating 'West' European states. For integrationists, the OEEC, like the Council of Europe, lacked ambition. Incorporating as many states as possible promoted inclusivity, but it tended to mean that the goals to be achieved were limited to the pragmatically possible. The two organizations were also unwieldy, relying on unanimity for taking decisions,

their intergovernmental nature conferring on each member state a veto.

Advocates of more supranational integration involving the creation of new institutions and the pooling of sovereignty did not abandon all hope of realizing some form of 'United Europe'. In May 1950, the French Foreign Minister, **Robert Schuman**, proposed the pooling under a supranational authority of French and German coal and steel resources. The brainchild of the French diplomat and internationalist, Jean Monnet, this would not only facilitate the modernization of production and increase the supply of coal and steel and so contribute to further economic development, it would also make war between France and Germany 'materially impossible'. Other states, notably the United Kingdom, were encouraged to join. Yet Schuman was clear that this new initiative of narrowly focused **sectoral integration** was but a first step in a process of establishing closer supranational economic and political integration; it was intended to be 'the first concrete foundation of a European federation indispensable to the preservation of peace' (see Box 2.2).

The governments of the Benelux countries, Germany, and Italy responded positively, and negotiations commenced in Paris in June 1950. Other European states watched on, leaving 'the Six' to draft the treaty that would lead to the establishment of the **European Coal and Steel Community (ECSC)** in 1952 and the creation of Europe's first supranational institutions: the High Authority, the Common Assembly, the Special Council of Ministers, and the Court of Justice. The successful negotiation of the Treaty of Paris encouraged ideas of pursuing sectoral integration in other areas. A pressing priority with the onset of war on the Korean Peninsula in 1950 was the defence of Western Europe. With the USA committing resources to contain Soviet expansionism in the Far East, Western Europe appeared vulnerable. German rearmament was deemed necessary. But how could German rearmament take place so soon after the end of the Second World War? The solution, proposed by Monnet and the French Prime Minister, René Pleven, lay in incorporating German military forces in a supranational **European Defence Community (EDC)** modelled on the ECSC. In 1954, a treaty establishing the EDC was drawn up.

Once again, this new, elite-driven, supranational initiative would be limited to 'the Six', the United Kingdom having refused to participate in the creation of a

↘ BOX 2.2   CASE STUDY: THE SCHUMAN DECLARATION

The contribution which an organized and living Europe can bring to civilization is indispensable to the maintenance of peaceful relations. In taking upon herself for more than 20 years the role of champion of a united Europe, France has always had as her essential aim the service of peace. A united Europe was not achieved, and we had war.

Europe will not be made all at once, or according to a single plan. It will be built through concrete achievements which first create a de facto solidarity. The coming together of the nations of Europe requires the elimination of the age-old opposition of France and Germany. Any action taken must in the first place concern these two countries . . .

The pooling of coal and steel production should immediately provide for the setting up of common foundations for economic development as a first step in the federation of Europe, and will change the destinies of those regions which have long been devoted to the manufacture of munitions of war, of which they have been the most constant victims.

The solidarity in production thus established will make it plain that any war between France and Germany becomes not merely unthinkable, but materially impossible. The setting up of this powerful productive unit, open to all countries willing to take part and bound ultimately to provide all the member countries with the basic elements of industrial production on the same terms, will lay a true foundation for their economic unification . . .

By pooling basic production and by instituting a new High Authority, whose decisions will bind France, Germany and other member countries, this proposal will lead to the realization of the first concrete foundation of a European federation indispensable to the preservation of peace . . .

Source: Schuman Declaration, 9 May 1950 (http://europa.eu/about-eu/basic-information/symbols/europe-day/schuman-declaration/index_en.htm, accessed 6 April 2021).

---

de facto European army. So too would the **European Political Community (EPC)** that was being planned by Spaak and others to complement the EDC. Neither the EDC nor the EPC, though, came into being. In August 1954, the French parliament, the *Assemblée Nationale* failed to ratify the treaty establishing the EDC; with it fell plans for the EPC. Integrationists' immediate hopes for a new community to complement the ECSC were dashed. One new organization did, however, emerge, and this time involved more than just 'the Six'. On 23 October 1954, the Brussels Treaty (1948) was modified to include West Germany, and the **Western European Union (WEU)** involving 'the Six' and the United Kingdom was established. It would be through the WEU that Germany would rearm and on 9 May 1955 join NATO.

The failure of the EDC was a blow for advocates of integration. Yet almost immediately, new proposals were being made for extending economic integration. In June 1955, Foreign Ministers of 'the Six' gathered in Messina and agreed on *'une rélance européenne'*, a re-launch of the integration process, through a **customs union** as well as integration in specific economic sectors. Discussions chaired by Spaak, which initially involved the United Kingdom, ensued before negotiations to establish two new supranational communities—the **European Economic Community (EEC)**, and the **European Atomic Energy Community (EAEC)**—were launched in 1956 and concluded in 1957 with the signing on 25 March of the Treaties of Rome. Drawing on the model of the ECSC, 'the Six' committed themselves not only to the establishment of a **customs union** but also to the adoption of common commercial, agricultural, and transport polices and the establishment of a common market with common rules governing competition. The EEC would also involve the free movement of workers and capital, certain social policy activities and an investment bank. The purpose of the EAEC was, through supranational integration, 'the speedy establishment and growth of nuclear industries'.

These were ambitious goals, and, as the ratification process revealed, not ones universally shared by domestic political elites and political parties. Each of 'the Six' completed ratification, however, and on 1 January 1958, the EEC and EAEC were established. With new institutions—a Commission, an Assembly (which immediately referred to itself as the European Parliament), a Court of Justice, and a Council—a new era of integration was launched, albeit one that in addition to promising deeper integration also heralded an era of deeper divisions with Western Europe. With efforts within the OEEC to complement the establishment of the EEC's customs union with the establishment of a

European free trade area covering 18 countries collapsing in November 1958, Western Europe was effectively split in trading terms between an 'inner Six' and the rest. With the establishment by Austria, Denmark, Norway, Portugal, Sweden, Switzerland, and the United Kingdom of the looser, intergovernmental **European Free Trade Association (EFTA)** in 1960, an 'outer seven' was created and the division of Western Europe into two trade blocs was formalized.

> ### KEY POINTS
>
> - Early efforts at integration after the Second World War revealed major differences between states over the extent to which they were willing to pursue supranational integration rather than intergovernmental cooperation.
>
> - The early years of integration saw a variety of organizations with different memberships and purposes established.
>
> - In the 1950s 'the Six'—Belgium, France, (West) Germany, Italy, Luxembourg, and the Netherlands—emerged as the core of European integration.
>
> - The Treaties of Rome established the basis of the European Union's institutional architecture.

2.3 The Communities and a Europe of 'the Six'

The establishment of the EEC and EAEC in 1958 heralded a new era of supranational integration among 'the Six'. Yet considerable energies had to be invested in realizing the goals set out in the Treaties of Rome. For the EEC, a challenging timetable of tariff cuts and quota removals had to be implemented if the customs union was to be achieved by the target date of 31 December 1969. Common policies for agriculture, external trade, and for transport had to be drawn up and agreed. New institutions, notably the Commission, had to be created and their operations coordinated with those of the ECSC. Common rules governing the **common market** had to be adopted, and relations, particularly regarding trade, regulated with non-members and overseas territories. The tasks ahead were challenging, and only if aims and objectives were met would the new Communities be contributing to the broader political ambition of many of the treaties' drafters: 'to lay the foundations of an

ever closer union among the peoples of Europe'. The predominantly economic focus of activities could not hide the fact that the Communities were part of a political process and far from being the limit of integrationists' ambitions (see Box 2.3).

It was this reality that in many respects accounted for the fact that 'the Six' were not joined by others. Greece and Turkey were interested, but had yet to reach a level of economic development such that they could compete in the common market; they were soon granted 'associate' status with the prospect of possible membership at some future point. Other, often fiercely independent, states were very wary about the perceived and actual 'loss' of sovereignty that membership of a supranational entity entailed. This was true of most of the EFTA states. The Scandinavian members were in any case already pursuing their own regional forms of 'Nordic cooperation'. Neutrality precluded Austria from participating, just as it would have Switzerland and Sweden had they shown any interest in membership, which they did not. As for the United Kingdom, although committed to trade liberalization in Europe, successive governments had long been wary of political integration. Moreover, why should a post-imperial power with a history of playing a role on the global stage become embroiled in a regional project between continental European states which, given historical tensions and war, had little prospect, so London thought, of success? Portugal and Spain, meanwhile, effectively ruled themselves out, as dictatorships, from participating.

The early years of the EEC and EAEC demonstrated that integration was possible, at least between 'the Six'. The new institutions were established, thus adding to the 'neo-functionalist' pressures for closer integration (see Chapter 4); tariff reductions were introduced; and some envisaged common policies were drafted. Soon the United Kingdom was reassessing its decision to stand aside and in August 1961, a few days after Ireland, applied for membership. Denmark soon followed, with Norway eventually applying too. The UK application, broadly welcomed by most of 'the Six', did lead to accession negotiations. In January 1963, however, the French President, **Charles de Gaulle**, announced his opposition to the United Kingdom joining and vetoed the application, seeing in the United Kingdom a Trojan horse for US influence. Others suspected de Gaulle of fearing a rival for leadership of the Communities. Not that de Gaulle was an enthusiast for supranational integration. His clear preference

BOX 2.3   BACKGROUND: KEY DATES IN EUROPEAN INTEGRATION: THE ESTABLISHMENT AND GROWTH OF THE COMMUNITIES

1958	January	EEC and EAEC established
1959	January	First tariff cuts made by the EEC
1961	July	The Fouchet Plan for a 'union of states' proposed
1962	January	The EEC develops basic regulations for a Common Agricultural Policy
1963	January	de Gaulle vetoes UK membership
	January	Elysée Treaty on Franco-German Friendship and Reconciliation signed
1965	April	Merger Treaty establishing a single institutional structure for the ECSC, EEC, and EAEC signed
	June	'Empty-Chair' Crisis begins
1966	January	Luxembourg Compromise ends 'Empty-Chair' Crisis
1967	July	Merger Treaty enters into force
	November	de Gaulle vetoes UK membership
1968	July	EEC customs union established
1969	December	Hague Summit supports enlargement, greater policy cooperation, and economic and monetary union (EMU)
1970	October	Werner Report on EMU published
		Davignon Report on foreign policy cooperation leads to the establishment of European political cooperation
1972	March	Currency **'snake'** established
1973	January	Denmark, Ireland, and the United Kingdom join the Communities
1974	December	Paris Summit agrees to establish a **European Council** and accepts the principle of direct elections to the European Parliament (EP)
1976	January	Tindemans Report on 'European Union' published
1979	March	European Monetary System (EMS) established
	June	First direct elections to the EP
1981	January	Greece joins the Communities

was for intergovernmentalism (see Chapter 5), as reflected in his 1961 proposal, in the **Fouchet Plan**, for a 'Union of the European peoples'. His preference was most in evidence four years later when he sparked a major crisis in the EEC by opposing a scheduled move to **qualified majority voting** and French ministers refused to participate in Council meetings.

The seven-month 'empty chair' crisis threatened to paralyse decision-making and was only resolved with the adoption of the '**Luxembourg Compromise**' (see Box 2.4).

De Gaulle's hostility towards anything that might undermine French sovereignty did not, however, prevent integration among 'the Six'. During the 1960s,

> **BOX 2.4   CASE STUDY: THE LUXEMBOURG COMPROMISE**
>
> The Luxembourg Compromise is the political declaration agreed in January 1966 by the European Communities' then six member states to resolve the 'empty chair' crisis of 1965–66. The declaration states that 'Where, in the case of decisions which may be taken by majority vote on a proposal of the Commission, very important interests of one or more partners are at stake, the Members of the Council will endeavour, within a reasonable time, to reach solutions which can be adopted by all the Members of the Council while respecting their mutual interests and those of the Community'. Although not legally binding, the Luxembourg Compromise has in effect provided member states with a de facto veto over Council decisions that formally only require a qualified—now double—majority to be adopted. Although only very rarely invoked, the Luxembourg Compromise is still available to be used.

a Common Agricultural Policy was drawn up, tariff reductions accelerated so that the customs union was established ahead of schedule in 1968, and the institutions of the ECSC, EEC, and EAEC merged. The European Court of Justice also issued important rulings on the primacy and **direct effect** of EEC law (see Chapter 13). However, the launch of any new initiatives to take the EEC beyond its original objectives had to wait until after de Gaulle had left office in April 1969. Advocates of integration were eager to proceed. No sooner had de Gaulle resigned the French Presidency and been replaced by Georges Pompidou than the heads of state and government of 'the Six' gathered in The Hague to discuss not just enlargement to include the United Kingdom, Denmark, Ireland, and Norway—all of which had applied again in 1967—but also further integration. Accession negotiations were soon opened; a plan for EMU agreed; talks on establishing 'own resources' financing of the Communities launched; and a proposal for **European political cooperation (EPC)**, the forerunner of the Common Foreign and Security Policy, drawn up.

The early years of the 1970s appeared to bode well for integration. In 1970 the **Werner Report** on EMU was published, initial attempts were launched to limit currency fluctuations, and agreement was reached on an 'own resources' funding mechanism (see Chapter 22). Three years later, on 1 January 1973, the Communities enlarged to include Denmark, Ireland, and

the United Kingdom. The 'Six' had become 'Nine'. In addition, there were now industrial free trade agreements in place with the remaining EFTA states—including Iceland. First tentative steps at foreign policy coordination were taken, and later in the decade two Structural Funds—**the European Regional Development Fund (ERDF)** and the **European Social Fund (ESF)**—were established. In December 1975 agreement was reached on holding direct elections for the European Parliament (EP) (see Chapter 12). Six months earlier, Greece had applied for membership; two years later Spain and Portugal would submit their applications. Further enlargement was on the agenda.

Such developments could not mask the fact that the 1970s was a challenging decade for the Communities and for integration. International currency instability, the 1973 oil crises, and inflation brought an end to the sustained economic growth of the post-war period. Governments in Europe generally reacted to the economic crisis by pursuing national as opposed to coordinated European responses. The appetite for new projects appeared to be drying up. Moreover, the Communities were adjusting to new members. Neither the United Kingdom—which soon set about renegotiating the terms of its membership and held a referendum in 1975 on staying in the 'common market'—nor Denmark was particularly minded to support further integration. With governments' attention firmly on trying to mitigate the effects of economic recession and high unemployment, Europe entered a period of '**Eurosclerosis**' with integration apparently stagnating.

Efforts nevertheless continued to be made to sustain and deepen integration. A boost of sorts came with the regularization of meetings of heads of state and government as the 'European Council' from 1975 onwards and so the beginnings of greater institutionalized intergovernmentalism. This undermined the supranational nature of the Communities and the executive role of the Commission. It did, however, provide opportunities for more high-profile political leadership with successive leaders of France (e.g., Valéry Giscard d'Estaing, Mitterrand, Jacques Chirac) and Germany (e.g., Helmut Schmidt, Helmut Kohl) in particular pushing for further integration (see Chapters 10 and 11). In 1975, at the request of his fellow members of the European Council, **Leo Tindemans**, the Belgian Prime Minister, produced a report on 'European Union', setting out proposals for, inter alia, institutional reform, EMU, and a common foreign policy. The European Council responded to the second of these and a **European Monetary System (EMS)** was established in 1979. The same year, the first direct elections to the EP were held; turnout was 63 per cent. Agreement was also reached on admitting Greece in 1981. By now negotiations on the accession of Portugal and Spain had also begun.

With its expanding membership, the Communities reinforced their status as the main vehicle for increasingly pan-West European integration. Enlargement had its costs, however. The membership had become more diverse with more interests having to be accommodated; countries that were economically less developed than the original Six stretched the Communities' finances, and so, for integrationists, widening threatened to undermine the prospects for deepening integration and furthering the avowed goal of 'ever closer union'. Indeed, supporters of widening were suspected of championing enlargement precisely in order to prevent deeper integration (see Chapter 18). With the Communities in the early 1980s getting bogged down in battles over budgetary contributions and reform of the CAP, and with the United Kingdom under Margaret Thatcher proving particularly combative and insisting on a rebate from the budget, integrationists' fears appeared borne out. As the 25th anniversary of the signing of the Treaties of Rome approached, the mood was far from upbeat. The front cover of *The Economist* of 20 March 1982 depicted a headstone declaring the EEC 'moribund' with the epitaph *Capax imperii nisi imperasset*—'it seemed capable of power until it tried to wield it'.

2.4 Establishing the European Union

Ultimately, developments in the 1980s proved to be a turning point in the history of the Communities, much to the delight of champions of integration, such as the new French President, Mitterrand, the new German Chancellor, Kohl, and Jacques Delors, Commission President from 1985 to 1995. Whereas in the 1970s the intention, expressed by heads of state and government of 'the Six' in 1972, to convert 'their entire relationship into a European Union before the end of the decade' came to nothing, by the end of the 1980s the prospects appeared increasingly real. The commitment to 'European Union' had not fallen victim to the Eurosclerosis and Europessimism of the 1970s. This was evident in June 1983 when the Stuttgart European Council proclaimed a 'Solemn Declaration on European Union' and agreed to a 'general review' within five years of the Communities' activities with the possibility of a new 'Treaty on European Union'. Members of the European Parliament (MEPs)—now directly elected and predominantly enthusiastic supporters of integration—were soon proffering ambitious ideas in a Draft Treaty establishing the European Union (1984). These tended to be ignored in those member states, notably the United Kingdom, where governments were both generally opposed to ideas for closer integration and somewhat dismissive of the prospects for realizing the flowery rhetoric of 'solemn' declarations. The preference was for more pragmatic action. And here the Thatcher government's advocacy of deregulation and more liberal markets soon found common cause with the Commission and its proposals—encouraged by European multinationals—to remove remaining non-tariff **barriers to trade** within the EEC and establish a genuine 'single'—or 'internal'—market. The logics of intergovernmentalism and neo-functionalism both appeared to be driving closer integration (see Chapters 4 and 5).

The Single Market project, conceived in 1984–85, was a major stage in the process of European integration. It not only provided the Communities with a new sense of purpose, it would also ultimately act as a significant catalyst for integration in other areas. Thus, and following the logic of neo-functionalism, pressures for integration spilled over from the efforts to establish the free movement of goods, services, capital, and people. If the project were to be implemented, however, decision-making needed to be

---

KEY POINTS

- Supranational integration was initially limited to 'the Six' and was established through three 'Communities': the ECSC, the EEC, and the EAEC.

- The 1960s witnessed both progress in developing the EEC but also a failure to enlarge and the 'empty chair' crisis.

- Plans for economic and monetary union and further integration foundered in the 1970s as the now enlarged Communities entered recession.

- The enlarged Communities were faced with the challenges of a more diverse membership.

relieved of member state vetoes. A timeframe was also needed. With Germany effectively agreeing to finance an expansion of the Structural Funds to assist economically less-developed existing and soon-to-be member states to compete in the brave new world of the Single Market, Greece, Ireland, Portugal, and Spain signed up. The United Kingdom was also on board. Necessary treaty changes were soon negotiated in an **intergovernmental conference (IGC)** (see Box 2.5) with more integrationist-minded member states pushing, with MEPs and the Commission, for other policy and supranational political ambitions to be incorporated in the revisions, including more powers for the EP. The result was the **Single European Act (SEA)** of 1986 (see Box 2.6).

2.4.1 **The Single European Act**

In adopting the SEA, the member states agreed some significant amendments to the Treaty of Rome. They also signalled that the SEA was not simply about Single Market-orientated reforms, but an attempt, genuine as far as most member states were concerned, to realize their desire to 'transform' their relations into 'a European Union', to 'implement' this new entity, and to invest it 'with the necessary means of action'. So, the unanimously agreed SEA introduced a range of new **competences** (environment, research and development, and economic and social **cohesion**); established 31 December 1992 as

the deadline for the completion of the internal market; facilitated the adoption of **harmonized** legislation to achieve this; committed the member states to cooperate on the convergence of economic and monetary policy (see Chapter 22); and expanded social policy competences to include health and safety in the workplace and dialogue between management and labour. As regards the institutions, it expanded the decision-making role of the EP through the introduction of a **cooperation procedure** to cover mainly internal market issues, and the **assent procedure** governing **association agreements** and **accession**. The SEA also extended the use of **qualified majority voting (QMV)** in the Council, allowed the Council to confer implementation **powers** on the Commission, and established a Court of First Instance (CFI) to assist the European Court of Justice in its work. In addition, it gave formal recognition to the European Council and EPC. The fact that neither was technically part of the Communities reflected member states' differences on how much **supranational integration** they were willing to pursue. For some, there was a clear preference for intergovernmental cooperation, and any commitment to 'European union' was at best rhetorical.

Agreement on establishing a European Union was not, however, far off. As indicated, the SEA, and the goal of completing the internal market by the end of 1992, ushered in a period of renewed dynamism for the Communities. This was accompanied by calls for further steps towards European Union being made by senior European leaders such as Mitterrand and Kohl, as well as by Delors. Others—most notably, Thatcher—resisted, often vehemently. Momentum towards new plans for EMU became particularly strong, inspired in part by a spillover logic from the Single Market project, in part by a French desire to gain some influence over the Deutschmark and German monetary policy. Agreement was soon reached on launching a new IGC in 1991. Before long a second IGC—on political union—was being proposed. The motivation was less the spillover from the renewed internal dynamism of the Communities, but more the momentous geopolitical changes that were taking place in Central and Eastern Europe (CEE). Communist **regimes** had been collapsing since 1989, the Cold War had ended, and there was now the prospect of German unification. Out of these emerged the Treaty on European Union (TEU).

BOX 2.5   CASE STUDY: FROM INTERGOVERNMENTAL CONFERENCE (IGC) TO TREATY

The European Union and the European Communities were all established by constitutive treaties concluded between their founding member states. If the member states wish to reform the EU, they need to amend the constitutive treaties. This has historically been done via an intergovernmental conference (IGC), in which the member states negotiate amendments. Agreed amendments are then brought together in an **amending treaty** that all member states must sign and ratify. **Ratification** normally involves each member state's parliament approving the treaty by vote. In some member states, for either procedural or political reasons, treaties are also put to a referendum.

BOX 2.6   BACKGROUND: KEY DATES IN EUROPEAN INTEGRATION: FROM SINGLE EUROPEAN ACT TO EASTERN ENLARGEMENT, 1983–2003

1983	June	Solemn Declaration on European Union is proclaimed by heads of state and government
1984	February	EP adopts a Draft Treaty establishing the European Union
	June	Fontainebleau European Council agrees to take action on a number of outstanding issues hindering progress on integration
1985	March	The European Council agrees to the establishment of a **Single Market** by the end of 1992
1986	January	Portugal and Spain join the Communities
	February	Single European Act (SEA) signed
1987	July	SEA enters into force
1991	December	Maastricht **European Council** agrees Treaty on European Union (TEU)
1992	February	TEU signed
1993	November	European Union established
1995	January	Austria, Finland, and Sweden join the EU
1996	March	1996 **Intergovernmental Conference (IGC)** launched
1997	June	Amsterdam European Council agrees Treaty of Amsterdam
	July	**Agenda 2000** published
	October	Treaty of Amsterdam signed
1999	January	Stage III of **economic and monetary union (EMU)** launched
	May	Treaty of Amsterdam enters into force
2000	February	2000 IGC launched
	December	Nice European Council agrees Treaty of Nice
2001	February	Treaty of Nice signed
2002	January	Introduction of the euro
2003	February	Treaty of Nice enters into force

2.4.2 **The Treaty on European Union**

Agreed by the member states at Maastricht in December 1991, the TEU—often referred to as the '**Maastricht Treaty**'—was designed to expand the scope of European integration, to reform the EC's institutions and decision-making procedures, and to bring about EMU (see Box 2.7). It also furthered the goal of 'ever closer union' by bringing together the EEC—now renamed the European Community—the ECSC, and the EAEC as part of an entirely new entity, the 'European Union'. This was to be more than simply the existing supranational Communities. Established on 1 November 1993, it comprised not only their supranational activities, but also intergovernmental cooperation on common foreign and security policy matters (CFSP) and justice and home affairs (JHA) (see Chapters 19 and 21).

BOX 2.7   CASE STUDY: THE TREATY ON EUROPEAN UNION

The impact of the TEU on the process of achieving 'ever-closer union' was considerable. Most significantly, through it the member states formally established the EU. In turn, the TEU promoted European integration in a whole variety of ways, whether through the promotion of cooperation in the two new intergovernmental CFSP and JHA pillars or through the expansion of EEC—now EC—activities. Indeed, thanks to the TEU, the EC was given new competences in the fields of education, culture, public health, consumer protection, trans-European networks, industry, and development cooperation. Citizenship of the EU was also established and, of course, the TEU set out the timetable for EMU by 1999. As for existing competences, some were expanded—notably in the areas of social policy, the environment, and economic and social cohesion—although, in an attempt to assuage concerns about the over-centralization of power, the principle of **subsidiarity** was introduced. Moreover, the TEU saw the establishment of new institutions and bodies, including the **European Central Bank**, the **Committee of the Regions**, and the **Ombudsman**. As for existing institutions, the powers of the EP were increased (not least through the introduction of the new **co-decision** procedure), greater use of QMV in the Council was agreed, the Court of Auditors was upgraded to an institution, and the European Court of Justice gained the power to fine member states.

This mix of supranational integration and intergovernmental cooperation meant that the new EU fell short of what might normally be considered a union: a political and legal entity with a coherent and uniform structure. Indeed, an early assessment of the EU, referred to its constitutional structure as a 'Europe of bits and pieces' (Curtin, 1993). Depending, for example, on the policy area, the decision-making roles of the relevant institutions differed. Prior to the EU, there was essentially one approach, the so-called '**Community method**'—that is, the use of **supranational institutions** and decision-making procedures to develop, adopt, and police policy (see Chapter 16). This would no longer be the case.

That the EU lacked uniformity in terms of its structures and policy-making procedures was evident from the terminology widely used to describe the new construct. For many, whether practitioners, academics, or others, the EU was structurally akin to a Greek temple consisting of three pillars. It would remain thus until the Treaty of Lisbon. The first pillar comprised the three Communities (losing the ECSC in mid-2002—see Box 2.8) whereas the second and third consisted of essentially intergovernmental cooperation in the areas of CFSP and, originally, JHA (see Figure 2.1). Changes in the relationship between the pillars after 1993 meant that the boundaries between them became blurred. Indeed, with the entry into force of the Treaty of Lisbon on 1 December 2009, the pillars disappeared (see Chapter 3).

 BOX 2.8   BACKGROUND: THE EUROPEAN COMMUNITIES: FROM THREE TO TWO TO ONE

The TEU introduced reforms to the three Communities. It also renamed the EEC the 'European Community', although that name had often been used informally as shorthand for the EEC before that date. The ECSC was later disbanded in July 2002, its founding treaty having expired, as envisaged, after 50 years. Since then, through the Treaty of Lisbon, the EC has been merged into the EU, leaving only the EAEC as a discrete 'Community'.

To supporters of supranational integration, the establishment of the pillar-based EU in 1993 represented a clear setback. This was because the intergovernmental pillars threatened to undermine the supremacy of the Community method. For others, adopting a mix of supranational and intergovernmental pillars merely formalized existing practices and preferences. Even prior to the TEU, the member states were pursuing intergovernmental cooperation outside the framework of the EC. The most obvious examples were EPC and Schengen activities relating to the removal of border controls (see Chapter 21). These had been taking place since the early 1970s and mid-1980s respectively. All the same, the mix of **supranationalism** and **intergovernmentalism**—particularly given that the Community institutions, with the exception of the Council, were at best marginal players in Pillars II and III—meant that the EU, when established, was less of a union than many had either hoped or feared. The idea of the new EU as a union was also undermined by other features

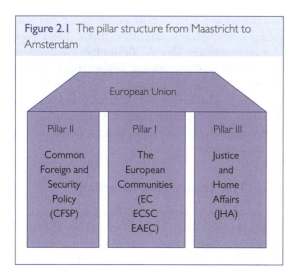

Figure 2.1 The pillar structure from Maastricht to Amsterdam

European Union

Pillar II	Pillar I	Pillar III
Common Foreign and Security Policy (CFSP)	The European Communities (EC ECSC EAEC)	Justice and Home Affairs (JHA)

integration. Such fears were initially assuaged when, at the time of the 1995 enlargement, the EU refused to consider any permanent exemptions or opt-outs from the existing *acquis communautaire* for the new member states. Austria, Finland, and Sweden had to accept all of the obligations of membership, including those concerning social policy, EMU, and the CFSP, the latter being significant because each of the three countries was still notionally neutral.

of the TEU. First, plans for EMU—the most important new area of EC activity—were set to create a three-tier EU, with member states divided between those that would become full participants, those that would fail, initially at least, to meet the **convergence criteria** and so be excluded from the single currency, and those—the UK and Denmark—that either had availed or could avail themselves of opt-outs (see Chapter 22). Semi-permanent **differentiation** between member states in a major policy area would characterize the new EU. Second, it was agreed that closer integration in the area of social policy would be pursued only by 11 of the then 12 member states. Resolute opposition to increased EU competences meant that new legislation resulting from the so-called '**Social Chapter**' would not apply to the UK. Third, Denmark was later granted a de facto opt-out from involvement in the elaboration and implementation of foreign policy decisions and actions having defence implications. All of this created the image of a new but partially fragmented EU.

That the TEU's provisions did not all apply to the same extent to all member states was significant, because such differentiated integration had never before been enshrined in the EU's treaties. Differentiation between member states had existed, but it had always been temporary, notably when new member states had been given strict time limits for fulfilling their membership obligations. Hence there were fears that the Maastricht opt-outs would set a precedent leading, at worst, to an **à la carte** EU, with member states picking and choosing the areas in which they were willing to pursue closer

2.5 Reviewing the Union: the 1996 Intergovernmental Conference and the Treaty of Amsterdam

That the European Union, when it was created, was less than its title implied was recognized not only by those studying the EU, but also those working in its institutions and representing its member states. Those who drafted the TEU acknowledged that what they were creating was not the final product, but part of an ongoing process. In the TEU's very first Article, the member states proclaimed that the establishment of the EU 'marks *a new stage* in the process of creating an ever closer union among the peoples of Europe' (emphasis added). They then proceeded to facilitate the process by scheduling an IGC for 1996 at which the TEU would be revised in line with its objectives.

Views on the purpose of the 1996 IGC differed. For the less integrationist member states, notably the UK, it would provide an opportunity to review and fine-tune the functioning of the EU and its structures. It was too soon to consider anything radical. Other member states did not want to rule out a more substantial overhaul. The IGC would provide an opportunity to push ahead with the goal of creating 'ever closer union', something that the European Parliament was particularly keen to see, as its draft Constitution of February 1994 demonstrated. Ever closer union, it was argued, was necessary if the EU wished to rectify the shortcomings of the structures created at Maastricht and prepare itself, having enlarged in 1995 to 15 member states, to admit the large number of mainly Central and Eastern European (CEE) applicants (see Chapter 18). Enlargement was now on the agenda: at Copenhagen in June 1993, the European Council had committed the EU to admit CEE countries once they met the accession criteria. Moreover, several member states were growing increasingly impatient with the reluctance of less integrationist member states, particularly the UK and Denmark, to countenance closer integration and there was also a need to bring the EU closer to its citizens. Popular reaction to the TEU had shown that elites—the drivers and designers of the Communities and now the EU—needed to do more to convince people of the value of union. Not only had the Danish people initially rejected the TEU in June 1992, but also the French people had only narrowly approved it three months later. Securing parliamentary ratification in the UK had also proven to be a tortuous affair.

The shortcomings of the EU's structures were highlighted in reports produced by the Council, Commission, and EP in 1995. They all agreed that the pillar structure was not functioning well and that the intergovernmental nature of decision-making in Pillar III was a significant constraint on the development of JHA cooperation. As for Pillar II, also intergovernmental, its inherent weaknesses had been highlighted by the EU's ineffective foreign policy response to the disintegration of **Yugoslavia**. Such shortcomings, it was argued, needed to be addressed, particularly given the commitment to enlargement. Preparations would have to be made, notably where the size and composition of the institutions were concerned. In addition, QMV would have to be extended to avoid decision-making paralysis. Also needed within an enlarged EU, at least in the eyes of supporters of closer and more dynamic integration, were mechanisms that would allow those member states keen on closer integration to proceed without the need for the unanimous agreement of the others. There was consequently much discussion of ideas concerning a '**core Europe**', **variable geometry**, and a **multi-speed** EU.

Preparations for reforming the EU began in earnest in 1995 with the formation of a '**Reflection Group**'. Its report suggested three key aims for the 1996 IGC: bringing the EU closer to its citizens; improving its

functioning in preparation for enlargement; and providing it with greater external capacity. The report also promoted the idea of '**flexibility**' mechanisms that would facilitate '**closer cooperation**' among groups of willing member states. The IGC was then launched in March 1996 and eventually concluded in June 1997, after the more integration-friendly Labour Party under Tony Blair had come to power in the United Kingdom.

2.5.1 The Treaty of Amsterdam

Signed on 2 October 1997, the Treaty of Amsterdam attracted far less popular attention than the TEU had. This does not mean that it was an insignificant treaty. In terms of substantive changes, it added the establishment of an 'area of freedom, security and justice' (AFSJ) to the EU's objectives and shifted much of JHA activity from Pillar III into Pillar I—in what is referred to as **communitarization**. In doing so, the thrust of cooperation in Pillar III was refocused on police and judicial cooperation in criminal matters (PJCCM), and the pillar renamed accordingly (see Figure 2.2). At the same time, provision was made for Schengen cooperation to be incorporated into the EU. These reforms gave greater coherence to EU activity. Yet the changes were also accompanied by increased differentiation. The UK, Ireland, and Denmark gained various opt-outs from both the new AFSJ and Schengen cooperation (see Chapter 21).

There was also the potential for further differentiation, with the introduction of mechanisms for 'closer cooperation'. Under these, member states that wished to do so could use the EC framework to pursue **enhanced cooperation** among themselves. This was possible provided that the mechanisms were only used as a last resort, that a majority of member states would be participating, and that the cooperation would be open to all other member states. Moreover, closer cooperation could not detract from either the principles of the EU and the *acquis* or from the rights of member states, nor could it be pursued for CFSP matters. Such restrictions, as well as the de facto veto that each member state had over closer cooperation, meant that the provisions would be difficult to use. In fact, the first formal request to use them was not made until 2008, when nine member states proposed closer cooperation to pursue common rules on cross-border divorce. All the same, the possibility of increasing differentiation within the EU was being established.

Figure 2.2 The pillar structure from Amsterdam to Lisbon

European Union

Pillar II	Pillar I	Pillar III
Common Foreign and Security Policy (CFSP)	The European Communities (EC ECSC/EAEC)	Police and Judicial Co-operation in Criminal Matters (PJCCM)

Where the Treaty of Amsterdam lessened differentiation within the EU was in its repeal, at the behest of the Blair government, of the UK opt-out from social policy. There was a bolstering of the EC's social policy competences too. Moreover, an employment policy chapter was introduced, in part as an attempt to assuage popular concerns that the EU did not have its citizens' interests at heart. Similar concerns were behind other new emphases, notably the enhanced EC competences concerning consumer and environmental protection, greater efforts to promote **transparency** and subsidiarity, and a reassertion that **EU citizenship** does not undermine national citizenship (see Chapter 9).

In terms of addressing the shortcomings of Pillar II, member states in the IGC resisted calls for a communitarization of the CFSP, preferring to maintain existing intergovernmental arrangements. Reforms were, however, introduced in an attempt to improve the consistency of EU action by involving the European Council more, by creating the post of **High Representative**, by establishing a policy planning and early warning unit, by seeking to develop long-term strategies, by clarifying the nature of the different instruments available, by defining more precisely the EU's concept of security (the so-called '**Petersberg tasks**' of humanitarian and rescue tasks, peacekeeping, and crisis management, including peacemaking), and by allowing for '**constructive abstention**' so that member states abstaining would not block CFSP initiatives (see Chapter 19). The commitment to deeper integration was evident in renewed references to a common defence policy and a common defence.

Finally, the Treaty of Amsterdam was supposed to prepare the EU institutionally for enlargement. In this regard, it failed, deferring to a later date the resolution of key questions, such as the size of the Commission, the redistribution of votes in the Council, and the nature of majority voting. Unanimity was replaced by QMV in some 19 instances, but even here, thanks to German insistence, progress was far less than anticipated or desired by many member states. This was underlined in a declaration issued by Belgium, France, and Italy to the effect that further treaty reform should be a precondition for the signing of the first **accession treaties** with applicant countries (see Chapter 18). The Treaty of Amsterdam did not fail totally, however, regarding institutional reform. The size of the European Parliament was capped at 700 members, and use of the assent and co-decision procedures was extended, thus enhancing the EP's legislative role. The EP's hand in the appointment of the Commission was also increased, as was its right to set its own rules for its elected members (see Chapter 12).

> **KEY POINTS**
>
> - Early experiences of the EU raised concerns about the functioning of the pillar structure.
>
> - The desire not to be held back by less integration-minded member states led to mechanisms for closer cooperation between interested and willing member states.
>
> - The Treaty of Amsterdam incorporated Schengen cooperation into the EU.
>
> - Despite the acknowledged need to introduce institutional reforms in preparation for enlargement, the Treaty of Amsterdam failed to prepare the EU sufficiently to admit more than a handful of new members.

2.6 Preparing for enlargement and the twenty-first century: the 2000 Intergovernmental Conference, the Treaty of Nice, and the 'Future of Europe' debate

With momentum in the late 1990s building towards enlargement to include the ten Central and Eastern European countries as well as Cyprus and potentially Malta, the need to introduce institutional reform remained on the EU's agenda. Without such reform it was feared that policy-making could grind to a halt. Moreover, there were concerns that enlargement could challenge the whole idea of union. Admitting ten CEE countries, most of which had been undergoing processes of wholesale transformation from command economies to fully functioning market economies, and some of which had only recently (re-)established themselves as independent states, was something that the EU had never done before. How to accommodate and integrate the new members became a major question. At the same time, integrationists, particularly within the EU institutions, were determined to ensure that the EU's *acquis* and the notion of union would be neither impaired nor undermined by enlargement, and that its institutions could continue to function as decision-making and decision-shaping bodies. Moreover, confronted with the prospect of what amounted to almost a doubling of the EU's membership, integrationists were faced with the challenge of ensuring that the commitment towards 'ever closer union' would be maintained. Opponents of 'ever closer union', notably the United Kingdom, often welcomed enlargement precisely because it complicated integration efforts.

2.6.1 Enlargement moves centre-stage

Preparing the EU institutionally for enlargement had been a key objective of the 1996 IGC. Yet the Treaty of Amsterdam, as noted, failed to deliver. Instead, reform was postponed. However, a Protocol did envisage that, at the time of the next enlargement, the Commission would consist of one national representative per member state provided, by then, the weighting of votes within the Council had been modified either via a re-weighting or through the adoption of a **dual majority** system of voting (see Chapter 11). The idea behind the re-weighting was to compensate the larger member states for giving up 'their' second Commissioner. The Protocol also provided for an IGC to carry out a 'comprehensive review of . . . the composition and functioning of the institutions' at least one year before the membership of the EU exceeds 20 member states.

In reality, the provisions of the Protocol were mainly ignored. Even before the Treaty of Amsterdam entered into force on 1 May 1999, the European Council in 1998 had identified institutional reform as

an issue of primary concern. Then, in June 1999, it agreed to hold an IGC the following year to address the key institutional questions. The issues—the size and composition of the Commission, the weighting of votes in the Council, and the possible extension of qualified majority voting (QMV) in the Council—became known as the 'Amsterdam leftovers'.

What pushed the European Council into calling an IGC for 2000 were changes in the EU's handling of the enlargement process. In July 1997, a matter of weeks after the Amsterdam European Council, the Commission had published *Agenda 2000*, its blueprint for enlargement. Following its recommendations, the Luxembourg European Council, in December 1997, agreed to launch an inclusive accession process with all applicant states (except Turkey), but to open actual accession negotiations with only six of the applicants (Cyprus, the Czech Republic, Estonia, Hungary, Poland, and Slovenia). It was felt at the time that six new members could be squeezed into the EU without necessarily holding an IGC. Within 18 months, however, attitudes towards enlargement had changed and, in the aftermath of the 1998–99 Kosovo conflict, a new Commission under the leadership of integrationist Italian former Prime Minister, Romano Prodi, was proposing to open accession negotiations with six more applicants—Bulgaria, Latvia, Lithuania, Malta, Romania, and Slovakia—and to recognize all applicants, including Turkey, as '**candidate countries**' (see Chapter 18). Opening up the possibility of large-scale enlargement made the need to address the Amsterdam leftovers more urgent. Hence an IGC was called.

2.6.2 The 2000 IGC

The 2000 IGC opened in February 2000 with a limited agenda. Most member states preferred to focus on the Amsterdam leftovers. Others, as well as the Prodi Commission and most MEPs, favoured a broader agenda. Strong support was voiced for a reorganization of the treaties and the integration of the WEU into the EU as a step towards a common defence policy. A Commission report also reminded the member states that it was incumbent on them to ensure that the IGC reformed the EU in such a way that it would remain flexible enough 'to allow continued progress towards our goal of European integration. What the Conference decides will set the framework for the political Europe of tomorrow'. The EU, it warned, 'will be profoundly changed by enlargement, but must not be weakened by it'. The EP came out strongly in favour of a wider agenda, dismissing the 'excessively narrow agenda' adopted by the Helsinki European Council in December 1999 as one that 'might well jeopardize the process of integration'.

Such calls were initially overlooked by the IGC, although 'closer cooperation' was added to its agenda by the Feira European Council in June 2000. By this time, however, certain member states were beginning to think more openly about the future of the EU. Hence negotiations were soon taking place against a backdrop of speeches from German Foreign Minister Joschka Fischer, advocating in a personal capacity 'a European **federation**', and French President Chirac, championing proposals for a European constitution. Other proposals on the future shape of the EU from, among others, Blair and his Spanish counterpart, José María Aznar, soon followed.

Many of the proposals were too ambitious for the IGC, in which progress was already proving to be slow, not least due to major differences on how best to deal with the Amsterdam leftovers. The situation was not helped by the heavy-handed manner in which France, holding the Council presidency, was managing the IGC, purportedly abusing its position to promote essentially a French agenda rather than seeking to broker compromises between the member states. At no point were the accusations louder than at the Nice European Council, which, after more than four days, eventually agreed a treaty. Once tidied up, the Treaty of Nice was signed on 26 February 2001.

2.6.3 The Treaty of Nice

What the member states agreed at Nice attracted much criticism. Although it was rightly heralded as paving the way for enlargement, for many it produced suboptimal solutions to the institutional challenges increased membership raised. On the former, QMV was extended to nearly 40 more treaty provisions, albeit in many instances ones concerned with the nomination of officials rather than policy-making, although some ten policy areas did see increased use of QMV. Reaching a decision using QMV did not, though, become any easier. Despite a reweighting of votes—each member state saw its number of votes increase, with the larger member states enjoying roughly a trebling and the smaller member states

roughly a doubling—the proportion of votes required to obtain a qualified majority remained at almost the same level as before and was actually set to increase. Moreover, a new criterion was introduced: any decision could, at the behest of any member state, be required to have the support of member states representing 62 per cent of the EU's total population.

Provision was also made for a staged reduction in the size of the Commission. From 2005, each member state would have one Commissioner. Then, once the EU admitted its 27th member, the next Commission would comprise a number of members less than the total number of member states, provided an equitable rotation system had been agreed. Staying with the institutions, the cap on the size of the EP was revised upward to 732 and maximum sizes were agreed for the **Committee of the Regions** and the **European Economic and Social Committee**. Reforms were also introduced to the competences and organization of the European Court of Justice and the Court of First Instance (renamed the General Court in 2009).

The imminence of enlargement to relatively young democracies in CEE, coupled with an awareness of existing institutional difficulties, also accounted for an enhanced stress on democracy and rights. Hence a '**yellow card**' procedure was introduced for member states deemed to be at risk of breaching the principles on which the EU is founded, the Treaty of Amsterdam having already provided for the suspension of voting and other rights. The Treaty of Nice also made closer cooperation—now referred to as 'enhanced cooperation'—easier to pursue, reducing the number of member states needed to start a project as well as the opportunities to block such a project. Enhanced cooperation could also now be used for non-military aspects of the CFSP.

All of this opened up the possibility of the EU becoming a less uniform entity. However, the Treaty of Nice also gave the EU a greater sense of coherence. In the area of CFSP and following the development of the European **Rapid Reaction Force**, it made the EU rather than the WEU responsible for implementing the defence-related aspects of policy (see Chapter 19). It also increased the focus on Brussels as the de facto capital of the EU. With enlargement, all European Council meetings would be held in the Belgian capital.

Yet although the Treaty of Nice paved the way for a more 'European' EU by introducing the institutional reforms necessary for enlargement, it did little in terms of furthering the avowed goal of 'ever closer union'. Integration-minded MEPs were quick to express their concerns, voicing particular criticism of a perceived drift towards intergovernmentalism and the consequent weakening of the Community method. The member states did, with the new Treaty, however, set in motion a process that drew on the speeches made by Fischer et al. to promote a debate on the future of the EU (see Chapter 3). To some, the Commission especially, this would provide an opportunity to create a stronger, more integrated EU with a less fragmented structure. Others, however, envisaged greater flexibility, a clear delimitation of competences, and a weakening of commitments to 'ever closer union'. As with all previous rounds of treaty reform the Treaty of Nice was not being seen as determining the *finalité politique* of the EU. It was but the latest stage in a larger process.

KEY POINTS

- Changes in the approach that the EU was adopting towards enlargement in 1999 gave greater urgency to the need to address the 'Amsterdam leftovers' and to agree institutional reform.

- *Agenda 2000* provided the European Commission's blueprint for enlargement.

- The Treaty of Nice may have paved the way for enlargement, but to many it provided suboptimal solutions to the institutional challenges posed by a significantly larger EU.

- While criticized for potentially weakening the EU, the Treaty of Nice initiated a process designed to respond to calls for a European Federation and a European Constitution.

2.7 Conclusion

The history of European integration is a history of competing preferences and ambitions, primarily of states and their leaders but also of institutions and other elite actors. The early years of integration, with its multiplicity of organizations and efforts to establish more reflected the tensions that existed between supporters of bold new supranational forms of political organization and those limiting their perspectives to looser, less ambitious forms of intergovernmental cooperation. Out of these tensions emerged the European Communities, initially based around 'the Six', but soon attracting interest from others and eventually enlarging its membership. From the outset, the Communities were conceived not as an end in themselves, but as staging posts to a more integrated Europe, with some form of 'European union' ultimately being established. During the 1950s, the 1960s, and the 1970s, few ambitions beyond the establishment of the Communities and their supranational institutions, and progress towards some original policy goals, were realized. Initially, there was as much division within Western Europe as there was unity, not least because of differing attitudes towards supranational integration as a model for political cooperation between states. Divisions were gradually overcome as the Communities enlarged, but differences on what forms

integration should take, what areas it should cover, and in which directions it should go persisted, and still do today.

From the mid-1980s, however, treaty reform and intergovernmental conferences (IGCs) became almost permanent items on the agenda of the EU. As a result, the EU was established and evolved in a variety of ways: the member states agreed to expand the range of policies in which the EU has a competence to act; they adjusted the decision-making powers of the institutions; and they embarked on some major integration projects—notably EMU and the adoption of the euro in 2002, and enlargement that subsequently brought the membership to 28 before returning to 27 with the UK's withdrawal in 2020. Driving these was a complex mix of state interests and institutional preferences generally advanced by political elites, albeit often with the support of business interests.

Consequently the EU assumed, during its first decade, many of the characteristics of a union. For some, especially eurosceptics, it soon resembled, or was deemed to be becoming, a **superstate**. Yet for many, particularly supporters of integration and political union, it has always been a much looser and more fluid organization than its name suggests. Its initial pillar structure—which would eventually disappear with the Treaty of Lisbon—embodied a complex mix of intergovernmental cooperation and supranational integration that brought together, in various combinations, a range of supranational institutions and the member states to further a variety of policy agendas. Adding to the complexity, and reflective of the tensions which persisted between member states over integration, were the various opt-outs that Denmark, Ireland, and the UK introduced, notably regarding certain JHA matters and in particular Schengen, as well as the differentiated integration created by EMU and the emergence of the **eurozone**. Moreover, successive rounds of treaty reform sought to facilitate a more multi-speed EU through the introduction and refinement of mechanisms for enhanced cooperation. All of this raised questions about how uniform the EU was and would be in the future.

What the various rounds of treaty reform also reveal, however, is that the EU and its member states were aware of the challenges raised by its complex structure and procedures, particularly in the light of enlargement. This is not to say that its member states ever really warmed to the challenges, introduced appropriate reforms, streamlined the EU, or decided what its *finalité politique* should be. There was, and there remains, considerable difference of opinion. This was evident in the subsequent 'future of Europe' debate and the negotiation of the **Constitutional Treaty** (2004), its rejection, the adoption of the replacement Treaty of Lisbon (2007), and more recently, **Brexit**. As Chapter 3 shows, several reforms in the 2000s and the 2010s have made the EU more like the union that its name implies. However, since its establishment in 1993, it has been, and remains, a complex—indeed messy—evolving mix of supranationalism, intergovernmentalism, and differentiated forms of integration.

QUESTIONS

1. Why was supranational integration limited to 'the Six' in the 1950s and 1960s?

2. What is meant by 'ever closer union'?

3. Have opt-outs and mechanisms for enhanced cooperation undermined the EU as a union?

4. What impact did the Treaty of Amsterdam have on the pillar structure of the EU?

5. Why did the 1996 Intergovernmental Conference fail to adopt the institutional reforms necessary to prepare the EU for enlargement?

6. Did the Treaty of Nice prepare the EU adequately for enlargement?

7. To what extent has the EU been characterized structurally by a complex mix of supranationalism, intergovernmentalism, and differentiated forms of integration?

8. To what extent has European integration been an entirely elite-led process?

GUIDE TO FURTHER READING

Dedman, M. (2009) *The Origins and Development of the European Union: A History of European Integration* (London: Routledge). A useful and concise introduction to the history of European integration.

Dinan, D. (2014) *Origins and Evolution of the European Union*, 2nd Edition (Oxford: Oxford University Press). An authoritative account of the history of the European Communities and the European Union.

Gilbert, M. (2020) *European Integration: A Political History*, 2nd Edition (Lanham: Rowman & Littlefield). An introduction to the political development of European integration since 1945

Laursen, F. (ed.) (2006) *The Treaty of Nice: Actor Preferences, Bargaining and Institutional Choice* (Leiden: Martinus Nijhoff). An analysis of the making of the Treaty of Nice, paying particular attention to member states and key issues on the agenda of the IGC.

Lynch, P., Neuwahl, N., and Rees, W. (eds) (2000) *Reforming the European Union from Maastricht to Amsterdam* (London: Longman). A volume assessing developments in the EU during the 1990s, paying particular attention to the reforms introduced by the Treaty of Amsterdam.

 Access the online resources to take your learning and understanding further, including extra multiple-choice questions with instant feedback, web links, answer guidance to end-of-chapter questions, and updates on new developments in EU politics.

www.oup.com/he/cini-borragan7e

3

Carrying the EU Forward: The Era of Lisbon

Clive Church and David Phinnemore

Chapter Contents

Reader's Guide

This chapter explores how the EU ended a long period of constitutional change by agreeing the Treaty of Lisbon and then used it to face new challenges of a financial crisis, Brexit, and COVID-19. All of these contributed to thinking that further treaty change might be needed. The process started in the Convention on the Future of Europe in 2002–03, which led to the Constitutional Treaty of 2004. Despite its rejection, the EU persisted with treaty change, and produced not a constitution, but, in October 2007, an orthodox amending treaty—the Treaty of Lisbon—carrying forward much of the Constitutional Treaty into two consolidated treaties. Although ratification was held up by an initial referendum rejection in Ireland in June 2008, reflecting both doubts about some elements of the Treaty and a deeper unease about the EU, this was overcome, and the Treaty entered into force on 1 December 2009. Its implementation proceeded relatively smoothly but was complicated by the eurozone crisis, which in turn pushed the EU to pursue further treaty reform, this time resulting, because of UK objections, in an extra EU compact as well as a treaty amendment. Thereafter, increasing Euroscepticism, populism, and persistent question marks over the popular legitimacy of the EU caused the official appetite for treaty reform to all but evaporate for much of the 2010s, even if integrationists believed further reform was needed. Then, after the UK's June 2016 vote to quit the EU, many thought that further changes were possible, with France's President Macron calling for a 're-founding' of the Union. However, Brexit was negotiated within the terms of the Treaty of European Union. Equally, despite limits to the EU's treaty responsibility for health, measures to deal with the COVID-19 pandemic were agreed. Calls for treaty revision, including from populist leaders, have continued but, despite EU member states committing in 2020 to a Conference on the Future of Europe (CoFE), active steps to re-negotiate the consolidated treaties have not yet begun.

3.1 Introduction

Given the political tensions in the EU that accompanied the process of treaty reform in the 1990s (see Chapter 2), it is perhaps surprising that the EU continued to pursue its own reform so doggedly during the first decade of the 2000s, initially with a Future of Europe debate and a European Convention, then with a Constitutional Treaty (CT) in 2004, and later with the Treaty of Lisbon in 2007. Moreover, the pursuit of reform in the second half of the decade occurred against the backdrop of the CT's decisive rejection in referendums in France and the Netherlands in 2005, its rapid abandonment in a number of other member states, and increasing evidence of rising Euroscepticism and concerns about the popular legitimacy of the EU. Eurosceptics and opponents put this seemingly unrelenting commitment to more integration down to an unholy and ideological lust for power on the part of a basically anti-democratic European elite seeking to replace national and popular sovereignty by a centralized, and probably neo-liberal, superstate (see Chapter 15).

The truth is less dramatic. Many European decision-makers and commentators believed that enlarging EU—which would increase in size during 2004–07 from 15 to 27 member states—needed substantial institutional reform if it was to develop effectively. This had to take precedence over the opposition of those who queried integration and the EU project. Moreover, the opposition overlooked the fact that the reforms contained in the much-maligned CT were far less radical than many assumed and had been more democratically devised and directed than in previous treaty reforms. In other words, treaty reform was not a Manichean war between good and evil, but a normal political conflict over the governance and direction of the EU.

So, although many observers assumed that with the blows inflicted by the French and Dutch electorates in 2005 the CT was dead, during the so-called 'period of reflection' that followed, other states continued to ratify it. Little serious reflection actually took place. Eventually, however, the German Council presidency during the first half of 2007 led a push for a new deal, securing agreement among the member states on a detailed mandate for a new intergovernmental conference (IGC) that would preserve many of the innovations of the CT but within an orthodox treaty that would have nothing of the 'constitutional' about it. A rapid and technical IGC followed, and the new Treaty was signed in Lisbon in December 2007. The thought behind this strategy was that it was the constitutional element that had alarmed people; removing this would therefore permit easy parliamentary ratification.

To begin with, this was indeed the case. However, on 12 June 2008, the Irish electorate rejected the Treaty of Lisbon, just as they had initially rejected the Treaty of Nice. The reasons for this were partly related to the text itself, but also to specific Irish issues and, especially, to an underlying popular angst. The rejection nevertheless threw the EU into a new crisis. This time, there was no reflection period, the ball being quickly and firmly left in the Irish court. By the end of the year, with all except three other member states having completed ratification, the Irish government, having secured various clarifications and concessions, committed itself to holding a second referendum. This it won, and ratification of the new Treaty was soon completed, despite the obstructionism of Czech President Vaclav Klaus. The Treaty of Lisbon entered into force on 1 December 2009.

Although many expected—and hoped—that this would usher in a period in which the EU might cease tinkering with its **treaty base**, treaty reform was soon back on the agenda. This was essentially driven by the eurozone crisis and in particular the decision to create a **European Stability Mechanism (ESM)** to help address the sovereign debt crisis and to establish more effective mechanisms for coordinated economic governance and improved **fiscal discipline**, particularly within the eurozone. In the face of UK opposition to a treaty amendment, extra-EU means had to be found to establish a **Fiscal Compact** (see Chapter 25). As the sense of crisis surrounding the eurozone began to abate from mid-2012, calls for treaty reform to provide for banking union, **fiscal union**, and economic union dissipated.

This scuppered UK government plans to use eurozone reform as an opportunity to leverage a renegotiation of its membership status in advance of an 'in–out' referendum. Instead, it had to settle for a deal that postponed associated treaty amendments (e.g., to remove the applicability of 'ever closer union' to the UK) to an unspecified later date (see Chapter 27). While integrationists continued to murmur about the need for further treaty reform, and with the prospect of Brexit failing to induce a sense of existential crisis for the EU, it was not until the election of Emmanuel Macron in France in 2017 and his call for the *'refondation d'une Europe souveraine, unie et démocratique'* that there was any sense of a real political impetus for reform emerging (see Chapter 29). This was followed by plans in 2020 for a new Conference on the Future of Europe (CoFE).

This chapter explores the background to the CT and the emergence and adoption of the Treaty of Lisbon. It explains and assesses the Treaty's main points, before reviewing its ratification and assessing the significance for the EU of the Treaty and the experience of securing its ratification. The chapter then explores how the EU and its institutions have adapted to the reforms introduced by the Treaty and have also eschewed further major treaty reform in response to the eurozone and subsequent crises (see Chapter 26). It concludes with a discussion of the prospects for further treaty reform in the light of the UK's withdrawal from the EU and the various new calls for reform, noting the continuing resistance to treaty change.

3.2 From the 'Future of Europe' debate to the Constitutional Treaty

The origins of the Treaty of Lisbon owe much to the 'Future of Europe' debate started by the Nice **European Council** in 2000 and the Constitutional Treaty which grew out of it. Awareness of the Treaty of Nice's own weaknesses together with pressures from outside for clarification and **constitutionalization** were key drivers. The initial terms of reference for the 'Future of Europe' debate were outlined by the 2000–01 IGC that drew up the Treaty of Nice. It was to focus on: how to establish and monitor a more precise delimitation of powers between the EU and its member states; the status of the **Charter of Fundamental Rights** (CFR), proclaimed at the Nice European Council; a simplification of the treaties, with a view to making them clearer and better understood; and the role of national parliaments in the EU's institutional architecture. In addition, ways of bringing the EU closer to its citizens would be sought. However, by the time the debate was formally launched with the European Council's **Laeken Declaration** in December 2001, a whole raft of new and often wide-ranging questions had been tabled for discussion.

Although the 'debate' attracted little popular input, this time the question of how to reform the EU would not be left simply to an IGC (see Box 3.1). Instead, drawing on the approach for the CFR in 1999–2000, a **'Convention on the Future of Europe'** was established to debate options and to make proposals. This **'European Convention'** comprised representatives of national governments, and members of the EP (MEPs) and of national parliaments, as well as representatives from the Commission and the 13 **candidate countries**, including Turkey, along with observers from other EU institutions and bodies. It met from February 2002 until July 2003 and was chaired by a **Praesidium**, led by former French President and MEP Valéry Giscard d'Estaing.

Although there were doubts about the potential of the Convention, it proved itself an active and, up to a point, open forum. It followed Giscard's advice that it was best to produce a single text rather than a set of possibilities. Through a mixture of plenary sessions, working groups, study circles, and Praesidium meetings, it began to move towards a European constitution and not just a new treaty. In a spirit of openness and **transparency**, all its papers were posted on the

> **BOX 3.1 BACKGROUND: KEY DATES IN EUROPEAN INTEGRATION: FROM THE TREATY OF NICE TO THE CONSTITUTIONAL TREATY**

2001	26 February	Treaty of Nice signed
	7 March	'Future of Europe' debate launched
	15 December	Laeken Declaration
2002	1 January	Introduction of the euro as single currency in 11 member states
	28 February	Inaugural plenary session of the European Convention
2003	20 June	Parts I and II of the Draft Treaty establishing a Constitution for Europe presented to the Thessaloniki European Council
	18 July	Complete Draft Treaty presented to the President of the European Council
	29 September	IGC opens
2004	1 May	Cyprus, the Czech Republic, Estonia, Hungary, Latvia, Lithuania, Malta, Poland, Slovakia, and Slovenia join the EU
	10–13 June	European Parliament election
	18 June	European Council agrees a Treaty establishing a Constitution for Europe
	29 October	Treaty establishing a Constitution for Europe signed
2005	29 May	French electorate reject the Constitutional Treaty (CT) in a referendum
	1 June	Dutch electorate reject the CT in a referendum
	16–17 June	European Council announces a 'pause' in ratification

Internet and its plenary sessions were opened to the public. Yet the Convention failed to attract media or popular attention, leaving things to an essentially self-selecting EU elite, skilfully steered by Giscard.

KEY POINTS

- The Treaty of Nice's weaknesses explain the agreement on the need for further EU reform.
- The Laeken Declaration provided the parameters for the next stage of treaty reform.
- The European Convention attempted to be both more open and more innovative than a typical intergovernmental conference.
- The Convention failed to attract popular attention and was perceived as an elite-driven process.

3.3 The 2003–04 Intergovernmental Conference and the Constitutional Treaty

The Convention was only just able to meet its deadline and present its draft to the European Council in June 2003. Although a minority of Eurosceptics sketched an alternative vision, the vast majority of *convention-nels* accepted it, which made it hard to ignore. The Thessaloniki European Council duly declared that the draft was a 'good basis' for further negotiations and the IGC began soon afterwards, in September 2003. However, no member state was willing to adopt the draft without amendment. In particular, Spain and Poland objected to a proposed new **double majority** voting system in the Council. Others had doubts about provisions on the Commission, the proposed Union

Minister for Foreign Affairs, the reformed European Council presidency, the respective powers of the EP and the Council, the extension of **qualified majority voting (QMV)**, and the new treaty revision processes. Given this, it proved impossible to get agreement until the European Council in Brussels in June 2004. The Treaty establishing a Constitution for Europe—90 per cent of which had come from the Convention draft, despite the IGC's 80 amendments—was subsequently signed on 29 October 2004 at a ceremony in Rome, in the same building where representatives of the **original six** member states had signed the 1957 **Treaty of Rome**.

The document that they signed was a lengthy one: 482 pages in length, complex and sometimes impenetrable, and doing little to promote transparency and **accountability**. It was designed to replace all the existing treaties and become the single constitutional document of the EU. It began with a Preamble, setting out the purpose of the EU. This was followed by a core Part I outlining the fundamentals of the EU. This included everything one needed to know about the EU's institutions, competences, and procedures, making it the most innovative and constitutional of the four parts. Part II contained the Charter of Fundamental Rights. The longest element was Part III, which contained detailed rules expanding on the provisions of Part I by bringing much of the existing Treaty on European Union (TEU) and Treaty establishing the European Community (TEC) into line with them. Part IV and the Final Act contained legal provisions common in international treaties, such as revision and ratification procedures. The protocols and declarations provided more detailed specifications and interpretations of what was found in the four parts.

In terms of content, not much was new. The vast bulk of the CT came from the existing treaties, albeit slightly altered. Innovations were mainly structural. Policy and powers changed rather less. The nature of the EU, its style of operation, its institutions, and the revision process were all altered. The CT abolished the three-pillared Union with a more singular EU. This inherited the legal personality of the Community, along with its symbols and the primacy of its law. However, the EU committed itself to respecting its member states, which were recognized as conferring powers on it, and, significantly, were given the right to leave.

The CT changed the way the EU made rules through the **ordinary legislative procedure (OLP)**. **Directives** and **regulations** were renamed 'laws'.

There was also a new focus on values and rights, along with democratic improvements, including new powers for both the EP and national parliaments. The CT also envisaged **citizens' initiatives** (see Chapter 9). Accompanying all of this was an extended use of QMV, although **unanimity** was still required for a range of sensitive and constitutional issues, such as measures relating to tax **harmonization**, the **accession** of new members, and treaty revisions. A change to what constitutes a qualified majority was also planned, with a double majority consisting of 55 per cent of member states representing 65 per cent of the EU's population becoming the norm.

The CT also upgraded the European Council and gave it a permanent president, limited the size of the EP and the Commission, formalized the use of team presidencies in the Council, and established a new post of Union Minister for Foreign Affairs. The holder was to be at the same time a member of the Commission and Chair of the Foreign Affairs Council, while heading a **European External Action Service** (EEAS; see Chapters 10, 11, and 19). The constitutional nature of the CT was intensified by the addition of the Charter of Fundamental Rights. This was made binding on the member states, but only when they were applying EU law. Guarantees were given to the UK that the CFR did not increase EU powers. Part IV also introduced simplified revision procedures, to avoid the EU being forced to call an IGC for all alterations to its treaties.

As to what the EU could do, the CT clarified its policy **competences**, dividing them into **exclusive competences—customs union**, competition, monetary policy for the **euro area**, and common commercial policy—and those in which competence is 'shared' with the member states, including the internal market, social policy, the environment, and the area of freedom, security, and justice (AFSJ). In other areas, the EU's role was restricted to supporting and coordinating complementary actions. Few new competences were conferred. A number of areas—tourism, civil protection, administrative **cooperation**, and energy— were specifically mentioned for the first time in any detail, but each of these was an area in which the EU had already been active.

Generally speaking, the CT simplified the EU, and attempted to make it more comprehensible, democratic, and efficient. Unfortunately, people rarely recognized this, and Eurosceptics in particular were quick to seize on the CT's more constitutional features as proof of a relentless drive towards the establishment of a European superstate. Moreover, the Convention and the IGC failed to involve the people and to increase the EU's legitimacy in the desired way.

With little popular and, in many cases, political understanding or appreciation of the CT, ratification by all 25 member states was always going to be a challenge. At first, it proceeded relatively smoothly even if not in a uniform or coordinated manner, since some member states, as was their right, chose to hold referendums. Most stuck with parliamentary ratification. Spain was the first to hold a referendum in February 2005. The outcome was, as expected, positive, although low turnout and scant knowledge of the CT meant that the vote was essentially an expression of support for EU membership. The second member state to hold a referendum was France. On 29 May, 53.3 per cent of voters—mainly rural, low-income, and public-sector based—rejected the CT, albeit often for reasons not associated with the EU. Three days later, Dutch voters also failed to offer their support for the CT: 61.1 per cent said *nee*. These popular rejections placed the future of the CT in doubt with opponents quick to declare the CT dead. A far-from-overwhelming endorsement in the Luxembourg referendum in July did little to create a sense that the CT was a text that commanded popular support even if, by then, national parliaments were voting in favour. Unsurprisingly, the UK government postponed its planned referendum, as did the Irish and Danes.

It was clear that the CT itself was only one of the reasons for the 'no' votes in France and the Netherlands and for the lack of overt enthusiasm for it elsewhere. Certainly, the text was problematic and, as a complicated compromise document, it was hard for its supporters to sell. The issues that it addressed were also poorly appreciated. Not that it had really mattered in France where detailed studies of the referendum make little reference to the CT's substantive content. Voters' worries were essentially national and social, seeing the EU as becoming too liberal. Paradoxically, the portions of the CT that seem to have motivated this were those that actually came straight from the existing treaties, suggesting that people were only now coming to realize what had been agreed in the original treaties, which had been rarely, if ever, read. Popular rejection of the CT was also part of a broader malaise that had at its

roots a general dissatisfaction and frustration with national governments as they struggled with unemployment, threats from **globalization**, and social welfare difficulties. However, some 'European' issues such as the **Bolkestein Directive** on services, Turkey's potential membership, and the increasing regularity and pace of treaty reform and the unsettling implications of **enlargement** in 2004 did feature (see Chapter 15).

KEY POINTS

- The 2003–04 IGC produced a slightly amended text.

- The CT was designed to replace all the existing treaties and become the single constitutional document of the EU.

- The CT attempted to establish a streamlined and more democratic EU.

- The constitutional dimension of the CT proved to be highly controversial.

- 'No' votes in the French and Dutch referendums reflected a range of concerns and was regarded as evidence of popular discontent with the EU.

3.4 From Constitutional Crisis to 'Negotiating' the Treaty of Lisbon

Although ratification continued well after the two 'no' votes, the CT was effectively dead, leaving the EU with a constitutional crisis. For much of 2005 and 2006, EU leaders were at a loss as to what to do. The UK Council presidency deliberately sought to avoid discussion; neither the French nor the Dutch could decide what they wanted in place of the rejected CT. The Austrian Council presidency in 2006 talked bravely of the CT's resuscitation, but was unable to overcome national disagreements. Many in Germany, including Chancellor Angela Merkel, made it clear that they supported the revival of the CT at the right time, but others preferred to see the text abandoned to history. Eurosceptic voices dominated debate. Not surprisingly, in June 2006, the reflection period announced the previous June was extended for a further year. The best that the Commission could come up with was the idea of a declaration for the fiftieth anniversary of the Treaty of Rome on 25 March 2007.

Some new ideas were, however, being proposed, notably the option of a *'mini-traité'* from France's soon-to-be President, Nicolas Sarkozy. Enquiries were also carried out into the cost of not having a constitution, and the Spanish and Luxembourgers began to rally ratifiers in an umbrella movement known as the '**Friends of the Constitution**'. More significantly, Germany was making preparations for its Council presidency during the first half of 2007. Chancellor Merkel felt the CT's reforms—which included an increase in Germany's voting power—were absolutely necessary for the EU. In October 2006, she declared that it would be the German Council presidency's

intention to produce a 'road map' for action by June 2007. Her underlying assumption seems to have been that the real problems lay with a select number of member states and, if identified, their issues could be settled confidentially. Discussions could take place between a very small group of nationally appointed 'focal points' and followed by a short 'technical' IGC (see Box 3.2).

Not everybody shared Merkel's enthusiasm. The UK was very cautious; Poland and the Czech Republic wished that the CT would simply go away. However,

---

BOX 3.2   BACKGROUND: KEY DATES IN EUROPEAN INTEGRATION: FROM REJECTION OF THE CONSTITUTIONAL TREATY TO THE TREATY OF LISBON

2005	29 May	French electorate reject the Constitutional Treaty (CT) in a referendum
	1 June	Dutch electorate reject the CT in a referendum
	16–17 June	European Council announces a 'pause' in ratification
2006	15–16 June	European Council agrees extension to the 'period of reflection'
2007	1 January	Germany assumes presidency of the Council
	1 January	Bulgaria and Romania join the EU
	25 March	Berlin Declaration adopted on fiftieth anniversary of the signing of the Treaties of Rome
	21–22 June	European Council adopts IGC mandate for new '**reform treaty**'
	23 July	IGC opens
	18–19 October	Informal European Council adopts Treaty of Lisbon
	13 December	Treaty of Lisbon signed
2008	12 June	Irish electorate reject Treaty of Lisbon in a referendum
	11–12 December	European Council agrees concessions to Irish government in exchange for commitment to complete ratification before 1 November 2009
2009	1 January	Original scheduled date for the entry into force of the Treaty of Lisbon
	18–19 June	European Council finalizes Irish 'guarantees'
	30 June	German Constitutional Court ruling on the Treaty of Lisbon
	2 October	Irish accept Treaty of Lisbon in a second referendum
	29 October	European Council agrees 'Czech Protocol'
	1 December	Treaty of Lisbon enters into force

a Berlin Declaration commemorating the fiftieth an-niversary of the signing of the Treaty of Rome, which was designed to reassure people about the EU's am-bitions and achievements, was adopted in March 2007 and provided an opportunity for the Germans to inten-sify discussions on how to proceed. A questionnaire on how certain issues might be addressed was soon being circulated and in May there were contacts with vari-ous EU leaders. The election of Sarkozy to the French presidency added political weight to Merkel's plans to push for more than simply a 'road map'. On 14 June a list of outstanding issues was circulated. Less than a week later, an unprecedentedly detailed IGC mandate envisioning the adoption of the bulk of the CT's re-forms in a new amending treaty was produced. This was then approved, along with a decision to launch an IGC, by the European Council on 21 June 2007 after last-minute concessions, notably to the UK and Poland.

The incoming Portuguese Council presidency made completing the negotiations on a new amending treaty its overriding objective. The IGC quickly commenced work. Foreign ministers, assisted by MEPs, considered progress at Viana do Castelo on 7–8 September and a final draft was produced in early October. Various loose ends were sorted, notably offering concessions to Bulgaria, the Czech Republic, Poland, and Italy, which threatened to veto a deal over the allocation of EP seats. An informal European Council in Lisbon on 18–19 October brought the negotiations to a close. Fol-lowing legal refinements to the text, a replacement to the CT was signed in Lisbon on 13 December. In less than a year the EU had moved from a forlorn period of unproductive reflection on what to do with the CT to a new 271-page text restating its essential content.

KEY POINTS

- The reflection period failed to produce any clear answer to the ongoing constitutional crisis.

- The German Council presidency followed a tightly controlled strategy to secure member state agreement on an IGC mandate to transfer much of the CT into a conventional amending treaty.

- Discussions about the new amending treaty occurred against the background of the fiftieth anniversary of the signing of the Treaty of Rome.

- Under the Portuguese presidency, a technical IGC rapidly produced the Treaty of Lisbon.

3.5 The main elements of the Treaty of Lisbon

The Treaty of Lisbon was an **amending treaty**. With its entry into force on 1 December 2009, it altered the existing TEU and TEC—renaming the latter the **Treaty on the Functioning of the European Union** (**TFEU**)—and then, in effect, disappeared from view, although commentators still mistakenly assume that it replaced existing treaties, hence erroneous references in the Brexit context to 'Article 50 of the Treaty of Lis-bon'. In one sense, the Treaty was a simple document with only seven articles. However, the first two were ex-tremely long, because they contained a whole series of amendments to the existing treaties. Article 1 contained 61 instructions on amending the TEU, while Article 2, amending the renamed TEC—now TFEU—contained eight horizontal changes and 286 individual amend-ments. The remaining articles made it clear that the Treaty of Lisbon had unlimited temporal effect, that ac-companying Protocols were also valid, and that the TEU and TFEU would be renumbered. In addition, there were 13 legally binding Protocols, an Annex, a Final Act, and 65 numbered Declarations. Five of the Protocols—covering the role of national parliaments, **subsidiarity** and **proportionality**, the **Eurogroup**, **permanent structured cooperation**, and the EU's planned acces-sion to the **European Convention on Human Rights** (**ECHR**)—were originally part of the CT. The remain-ing eight were new, including some dealing with the continuing significance of competition, the application of the Charter of Fundamental Rights in the UK and Poland, or interpreting **shared competences**, values, and public services. There were also various transi-tional institutional arrangements. These amendments and changes meant that the TEU and TFEU, in force from 1 December 2009, were significantly revised ver-sions of their immediate predecessors.

The resulting TEU provides a fairly succinct out-line of the purpose and structure of the EU, notably in terms of aims, objectives, principles, and institu-tions (see Box 3.3). It also now includes a good deal of detail on **enhanced cooperation** and, especially, on external action. It also has a more constitutional feel, since it deals with major facets of the EU, and has the same legal status as the TFEU and cannot be used to override it. The TFEU is even longer, with seven Parts and 358 Articles, and many Declarations (see Box 3.4). It starts with a set of common provisions and rules on **European citizenship**, which are followed by the

BOX 3.3   CASE STUDY: STRUCTURE OF THE CONSOLIDATED TREATY ON EUROPEAN UNION (TEU)

Preamble

Title I	Common Provisions
Title II	Provisions on Democratic Principles
Title III	Provisions on the Institutions
Title IV	Provisions on Enhanced Cooperation
Title V	General Provisions on the Union's External Action and Specific Provisions on the Common Foreign and Security Policy
Title VI	Final Provisions

BOX 3.4   CASE-STUDY: STRUCTURE OF THE TREATY ON THE FUNCTIONING OF THE EUROPEAN UNION (TFEU)

Preamble

Part One	**Principles**
Title I	Categories and Areas of Union Competence
Title II	Provisions having General Application
Part Two	**Non-Discrimination and Citizenship of the Union**
Part Three	**Union Policies and Internal Actions**
Title I	The Internal Market
Title II	Free Movement of Goods
Title III	Agriculture and Fisheries
Title IV	Free Movement of Persons, Services and Capital
Title V	Area of Freedom, Security and Justice
Title VI	Transport
Title VII	Common Rules on Competition, Taxation and Approximation of Laws
Title VIII	Economic and Monetary Policy
Title IX	Employment
Title X	Social Policy
Title XI	The European Social Fund
Title XII	Education, Vocational Training, Youth and Sport

(continued)

> **BOX 3.4   CASE-STUDY: STRUCTURE OF THE TREATY ON THE FUNCTIONING OF THE EUROPEAN UNION (TFEU)**   *(continued)*

Title XIII	Culture
Title XIV	Public Health
Title XV	Consumer Protection
Title XVI	Trans-European Networks
Title XVII	Industry
Title XVIII	Economic, Social and Territorial Cohesion
Title XIX	Research and Technological Development and Space
Title XX	Environment
Title XXI	Energy
Title XXII	Tourism
Title XXIII	Civil Protection
Title XXIV	Administrative Cooperation
Part Four	**Association of the Overseas Countries and Territories**
Part Five	**External Action by the Union**
Title I	General Provisions on the Union's External Action
Title II	Common Commercial Policy
Title III	Cooperation with Third Countries and Humanitarian Aid
Title IV	Restrictive Measures
Title V	International Agreements
Title VI	The Union's Relations with International Organizations and Third Countries and Union Delegations
Title VII	Solidarity Clause
Part Six	**Institutional and Financial Provisions**
Title I	Provisions Governing the Institutions
Title II	Financial Provisions
Title III	Enhanced Cooperation
Part Seven	**General and Financial Provisions**

longest section, Part III, which deals with policies. External relations, institutional, and budgetary provisions make up the bulk of the rest.

Together, the amended TEU and TFEU provide for a simplified and somewhat more efficient EU. First, in structural terms, the Treaty of Lisbon brought matters into line with common practice. Hence the Community disappeared, and the EU became the sole structure of integration, inheriting the Community's powers, legal personality, institutions, and policy mix. Apart from the Common Foreign and Security Policy (CFSP), everything now functions according to the basic **Community method**. Equally, there are still many opt-outs, while the facilities for enhanced cooperation were increased.

Second, despite the talk of a 'superstate', the Treaty of Lisbon made it abundantly clear that the EU is a body based on powers conferred by the member states, enshrined in the treaties, and subject to subsidiarity and proportionality. Member states have rights of action, **consultation**, recognition, support, and, significantly, **withdrawal**. The EU can also give up competences, and legal harmonization is subject to clear limits. Equally, the institutions can operate only within defined boundaries. The EU's powers are categorized as exclusive, shared, or supportive, which makes it clear that they are not all-embracing or self-generated (see Chapter 16).

Third, EU policies were not greatly expanded by the Treaty of Lisbon. Energy, tourism, and civil protection were written more clearly into the TFEU, while space, humanitarian aid, sport, and administrative operation were added for the first time. In energy, there is now specific reference to combating climate change and providing for energy solidarity. The main change concerned rules on justice and home affairs (JHA). These are no longer subject to special, largely intergovernmental arrangement, but governed by normal EU procedures. This is a significant development. And since 1 December 2014, all JHA activities have fallen under the jurisdiction of the Court (see Chapter 21).

Fourth, in terms of decision-making, the Treaty of Lisbon renamed **co-decision** as the **ordinary legislative procedure (OLP)** and established it as the default legislative process. The procedure was also extended to some 50 new areas. Inside the Council, QMV was extended to some 60 new instances with a new and simpler double-majority system replacing it from 1 November 2014. Under the new system, a majority of the member states (55 per cent) and the populations that they represent (65 per cent) is required. This has increased the proportional weight of larger member states. Member states have also retained unanimity or **emergency brakes** in areas such as tax harmonization, the CFSP, criminal matters, and social security—and, to satisfy the Poles, old-style QMV was available until 2017. Since then a form of the **Ioannina Compromise** applies.

Fifth, the Treaty of Lisbon introduced significant changes to institutional arrangements. The EP received extra powers, notably over the budget and treaty change. It also now has a virtual veto on the appointment of the Commission President. The European Council emerged strengthened and formalized as

an 'institution', meeting every three months, and with a new role in external relations and overall strategy, which points to the continuing influence of member states. Special arrangements for the Eurogroup were also provided. The Commission gained an expanded role in the area of freedom, security, and justice (AFSJ) and in foreign affairs. Thus, the **High Representative** of the Union for Foreign Affairs and Security Policy is now a 'double-hatted' Vice-President of the Commission as well as chair of the Foreign Affairs Council. The High Representative is assisted by an External Action Service. The General Affairs Council (GAC) as well as other Council formations continues to be chaired by the rotating Council presidency. The Courts' jurisdiction was extended, albeit not to the CFSP. Other institutions were largely unchanged.

A sixth facet was a new emphasis on values and rights. The former were expanded and given more prominence, while the latter were given a dual boost. Hence, the CFR was given legal status, subject to safeguards for national jurisdictions insisted on by the UK. Additionally, the EU can now sign up to the wider, independent, ECHR, although it has failed to do so. Lastly, the Treaty of Lisbon tried to make the EU more democratic. Thus, democracy was accorded a separate title in the TEU. This includes provision for a citizens' initiative. National parliaments also gained new rights to query proposed EU legislation on subsidiarity grounds, although these are not as extensive as some wished.

Not all the CT made its way into the revised TEU and TFEU. The constitutional language was dropped; so too was mention of the EU's symbols. Thus, EU acts are not called 'laws'. Equally, the term 'Minister for Foreign Affairs' was rejected. This abandonment of 'constitutional' language marked a significant change from the CT, but many critics preferred to ignore it.

KEY POINTS

- The Treaty of Lisbon was not designed to have a lasting existence of its own, since its function was to amend the two treaties—the TEU and TEC—on which the EU is based.

- The TEU and TEC were extensively altered and modernized, and, in the case of the latter, renamed as the TFEU.

- Together, the TEU and TFEU create one structure, the EU, with characteristics fairly close to those of the past.

- The Treaty of Lisbon introduced changes to institutional arrangements affecting all key institutions.

3.6 The Treaty of Lisbon: an appraisal

The first question is whether the Treaty of Lisbon succeeded in its intention of increasing the democratic legitimacy and the **efficiency** of the EU. Given it was initially rejected in a referendum in Ireland (see Section 3.7 'Ratification of the Treaty of Lisbon'), many would claim that it failed. However, this ignores the clear democratic improvements giving more powers to national parliaments and the EP, introducing the citizens' initiative, and commitment to the ECHR and the EU's own Charter. And, in the UK, the insistence on referring, incorrectly, to *Article 50 of the Lisbon Treaty* shows that it had become accepted even in the most hostile quarters. The more precise delimitation of EU powers and the insistence that these are 'conferred' by the member states underlines the role of national democracy in the EU. This was reinforced by the elevation of the European Council's role, equal status among member states, and their right to secede. The expansion of the Courts' jurisdiction can also be seen as reinforcing the legal and democratic nature of the EU, even if critics saw this as an example of competence creep. Conversely, some believed that the changes in the Common Foreign and Security Policy (CFSP) downgraded the Commission to the benefit of the member states. As to efficiency, the introduction of a European Council President, the linking of the High Representative with the Commission, the use of simpler voting procedures, and the extension of co-decision involving the European Parliament and the Council have all had an impact on the operation of the EU. However, such changes have hardly transformed the EU.

Thus, Lisbon introduced a wide-ranging series of changes, the actual importance of which is always difficult to determine in practice given the significance of the economic and political context in which reformed institutions function, new structures operate, and competences are used. Much of the decade or so since the Treaty of Lisbon entered into force has been one of almost perpetual crisis, at least as far as the **eurozone** is concerned, and so, given the need for leadership, has ensured a very high profile for the European Council. Merkel and others certainly intended the Treaty to shake things up. However, the new EU remained remarkably like the old one. And, if it failed to turn the world upside down, the Treaty did give the EU a new and surprising stability, enabling it to cope with crises which were soon to beset it.

KEY POINTS

- The Treaty of Lisbon was complex and difficult to understand.
- The Treaty of Lisbon sought to make the EU more democratic and efficient, but this has not always been acknowledged.
- Despite the range of changes introduced, and the criticisms made of it, its effects have not been revolutionary.
- Article 50 TEU sets out the procedure for a member state's exit from the EU.

3.7 Ratification of the Treaty of Lisbon

The Treaty of Lisbon entered into force in December 2009. It did so almost a year later than planned thanks to a protracted and contested ratification process. An initial period where member states completed the process relatively easily via parliamentary endorsements was interrupted in June 2008 by popular rejection in Ireland. However, ratification did not grind to a halt and, by the end of the year, very few approvals remained outstanding. This was in no small part owing to the nature of the Treaty of Lisbon. As a reworked version of the Constitutional Treaty, minus its constitutional and other symbolic trappings, the Treaty was deemed to be sufficiently far removed from its predecessor for member states previously committed to ratification via referendum to obviate the need for popular endorsement.

Much to the relief of Eurosceptic groups and other opponents of the Treaty, Ireland had to hold a referendum. Its result was very much to their liking. On a turnout of 53.1 per cent, a majority of 53.4 per cent voted against ratification, many signalling a lack of knowledge and understanding of the text and its significance. If the rejection was a bitter blow to the Treaty's supporters, it did not, however, bring the process of ratification to an end. Various non-ratifiers made a point of pushing ahead, notably the UK, which completed parliamentary ratification a week later. Others followed suit. By the end of 2008, only three countries, apart from Ireland, had still to complete ratification: Germany, Poland, and the Czech Republic.

On Ireland, EU leaders decided to leave it to Dublin to come up with a solution. A general assumption was that, if all other member states were to ratify, it would increase the pressure on Ireland and oblige voters to consider the possible threat to Irish membership when they voted again. Ratification therefore continued. Lisbon was far from dead. Nor was it open to further revision. However, the European Council in December 2008 did signal that concessions could be made and some 'legal guarantees' agreed if the Irish government committed itself to completing ratification before 1 November 2009. It did, and a second Irish referendum was held on 2 October 2009. The outcome was a clear 'yes'. On a turnout of 59 per cent, more than two thirds (67.1 per cent) of the 1,816,098 voters who cast their vote voted in favour of ratification. With the German Constitutional Court having ruled that there were 'no decisive constitutional objections' to ratification, provided that improvements were made to the *Bundestag*'s rights of scrutiny, all that stood in the way of the Treaty of Lisbon's entry into force was ratification in Poland and the Czech Republic. Polish President, Lech Kaczyński, soon penned his signature to Poland's Ratification Act, leaving only the objections of his counterpart, President Vaclav Klaus, in Prague to be overcome. Once a 'Czech' protocol with an 'exemption' from the Charter of Fundamental Rights had been agreed, Klaus finally signed off on Czech ratification. The Treaty of Lisbon then duly entered into force on 1 December 2009.

KEY POINTS

- Parliamentary ratification proceeded without undue difficulty into summer 2008.

- The main causes of the 'no' vote in Ireland were a lack of knowledge and understanding of the Treaty of Lisbon, together with specific national concerns.

- Ratification of the Treaty of Lisbon continued despite the 'no' vote in Ireland, with the Irish government committing itself to holding a second referendum before 31 October 2009.

- Irish voters' concerns were addressed through 'guarantees' and a dedicated 'Irish' protocol, thus paving the way for a 'yes' vote in a second Irish referendum.

3.8 The significance of the Treaty of Lisbon

The Treaty of Lisbon was a second attempt to realize reforms that many EU leaders thought necessary to make an enlarging EU fit for the world into which it was moving in the first decades of the 2000s, but in a format more acceptable to popular opinion. Critics, and not just Eurosceptics, have suggested that the determination to press on with reforms apparently rejected in 2005 was a piece of arrogance that was either mindless, or a deliberate attempt to foist a superstate on the nations and peoples of Europe. There may be something to this argument, but the Treaty of Lisbon was mostly a more pragmatic matter of ensuring that the EU changed in line with its expanding membership and policy challenges. That the idea was endorsed by those who actually have to work the system deserves to be remembered.

The Treaty of Lisbon substantively repeated that the Constitutional Treaty was its starting point and not something that needed be concealed. Pretending that this was not so was a peculiarly British phenomenon produced by the sulphurous nature of UK anti-Europeanism. It was also an argument that placed too much stress both on understanding the difference between a 'constitution' and a 'treaty', and on the importance attributed by opponents to the CT's constitutional status. Stripping off the constitutional element was seen as the way to defuse opposition. This overlooked the fact that opposition to the CT was based on a whole range of often contradictory stances and beliefs, many of them related more to the EU in general and the way in which Western European society had been developing than to the Treaty's actual terms. Another important factor was the way the 2005 'no' votes mobilized, deepened, and organized opposition to the EU. Hence the **ratification crisis** was again seen as symbolizing an underlying popular alienation from the EU, which was decreasingly being accepted as a wholly good thing. The crisis was also revelatory of governments' failure to give real attention to dealing with opposition concerns.

All this strengthened the argument that the EU was facing—and continues to face more than a decade on—a crisis of legitimacy. By the mid-2000s it was clear that there was a major problem in the old member states of Western Europe, the populations of which were now much less inclined to identify with the EU than they used to be. This was because of their economic unease, their lack of confidence in the future, and their feeling that their interests were not being taken into account by a distant 'Brussels'. Yet much of the opposition to Lisbon, as with the CT, came from people who described themselves as 'good Europeans'. Their objections were not to integration as such, but to the EU's style and strategy over the previous 15 years. Lisbon served as a symbolic surrogate for such doubts. However, if the Irish 'no' vote was a hammer blow for EU elites, it was not a death warrant for the Treaty of Lisbon. As in 2005, it opened a period of crisis, thanks in part to the way in which it revived anti-EU and Eurosceptic forces across Europe, which did well in the 2009 and 2014 European Parliament elections but less so in 2019. It certainly forced the EU to give more attention to institutional questions at the expense of the policy issues that both friends and foes alike believe should be its main concern. However, talk of the demise of the EU remained, and remains, much exaggerated. While there was clearly vocal and active opposition to the Treaty of Lisbon, this needed something special, such as a referendum, to make an impact. Ultimately, however, ratification was completed, and the new arrangements began to work with more effectiveness than many had expected, paradoxically sometimes to the benefit of some of those who had opposed the new Treaty.

KEY POINTS

- Abandoning the language of 'constitution' in the Treaty of Lisbon failed to pacify opponents.
- The Irish 'no' opened a new period of crisis over EU reform.
- Despite the success of Eurosceptic parties in European Parliament elections, talk of the demise of the EU remains much exaggerated.

3.9 Implementing the Treaty of Lisbon

It was never intended that the Treaty of Lisbon would transform the EU, so its actual entry into force on 1 December 2009 passed with very little fanfare. It nevertheless introduced some important institutional changes in the **European Council** President and the **High Representative of the Union for Foreign Affairs and Security Policy**. In both cases, EU leaders passed up the opportunity to appoint a prominent political leader with a view to them setting agendas, raising the EU's profile and challenging the member states, and instead opted for high profile fixers to oversee policy implementation and operate very much in line with instructions. So, Belgian Prime Minister, Herman Van Rompuy, became the first European Council President and Baroness Catherine Ashton, with just over a year's EU experience as Commissioner for trade, the first to hold the upgraded High Representative post.

Neither would have an easy ride in their new posts. Van Rompuy's time was soon being dominated by the eurozone crisis. This certainly ensured him a profile, but equally it involved much reactive firefighting and so limited his opportunities to define his new position, particularly given the central role that Germany was playing under Merkel. The barely known Ashton was meanwhile faced with not only taking on preparations for and chairing the Foreign Affairs Council and implementing its decisions, but also setting up the External Action Service. The latter was a tall order indeed and would prove to be a challenging and drawn-out process; the former demanded a sense of strategy and decisiveness not always evident.

Beyond these institutional appointments, the immediate impact of the Treaty of Lisbon was rather muted. This would soon change as the European Parliament, Council, and Commission came to terms with the realities of the ordinary legislative procedure's extension to most remaining areas of EU competence. For the first time, MEPs had a legislative role with regard to the Common Agricultural Policy (see Chapter 23); their budgetary powers were also increased. And so the voice of the EP on these as well as other issues was soon becoming louder, and it was a voice to which the Commission, and especially the Council, had to listen. The voice of citizens and national parliaments was also enhanced by the Treaty. The citizen's initiative was eventually launched in 2012 and national parliaments gained new opportunities to '**orange card**' Commission proposals. Few citizens' initiatives have, however, impacted on EU legislation and national parliaments have faced considerable logistical challenges in securing coordinated responses. All this, while well-intentioned, has done little to address the EU's democratic deficit and bring the EU closer to its citizens (see Chapters 9 and 12).

In advance of the 2014 and 2019 EP elections, the political groupings sought to personalize the process more. Exploiting the EP's enhanced role in the appointment of the Commission President, each grouping identified its own *Spitzenkandidat* ('lead candidate') who, it was expected, would be accepted by the European Council as the nominee for Commission President if that group secured the largest number of MEPs. The move failed to stimulate popular engagement and turnout in 2014 once again fell, this time to 42.6 per cent. It did, however, result in the candidate of the largest grouping, Jean-Claude Juncker from the European People's Party, being elected by MEPs as Commission President. As Luxembourg's Prime Minister from 1995 to 2013, Juncker was a veteran of European Councils and so very much part of the EU establishment rather than the youthful and fresh face that many critics of the EU thought it required.

The same could not be said for Ashton's replacement as High Representative. Here, the European Council opted for the much younger and relatively inexperienced Italian Foreign Minister, Federica Mogherini. The challenges she faced were no less daunting than those that Ashton had taken on, at least in policy terms. Once again, rather than appoint a 'big-hitter' the European Council had opted for a less high-profile appointment. Assuming an established role, however, Mogherini was able to engage in diplomatic initiatives more than her predecessor. Thanks to Juncker's reorganization of the Commission into Project Teams each led by a Vice-President, with the High Representative leading on 'A Stronger Global Actor', Mogherini was supported by a cluster of fellow Commissioners thus improving EEAS-Commission cooperation as responsibilities become clearer.

As for the European Council President, in replacing Van Rompuy with the former Polish Prime Minister, Donald Tusk, EU leaders made their first appointment to a senior position of a colleague from one of the 'new' member states in Central and Eastern Europe. Symbolically, at least, this was an important move. Unlike Van Rompuy, Tusk was spared the firefighting associated with the eurozone crisis, yet he too had only limited space to shape the still relatively new role owing to tensions and divisions over the migration crisis and the need to manage the protracted Brexit process. Both Mogherini and Tusk completed their terms of office without major incident. Their successors were appointed without controversy or fanfare in 2019, suggesting the posts were settled: Josep Borrell,

former EP President and Spanish Foreign Minister, became High Representative; former Belgian Prime Minister, Charles Michel, became European Council President. The same could not be said for the *Spitzenkandidat* process, which was effectively ignored after the 2019 EP elections when EU leaders nominated and MEPs elected Ursula von der Leyen as European Commission President (see Chapter 10).

KEY POINTS

- The implementation of the Treaty of Lisbon occurred against the background of the economic crisis.

- The new post of European Council President and the revised post of High Representative have been established and appear settled.

- MPs have seen their role in EU decision-making increase through the extension of the OLP.

- Whereas MPs in 2014 successfully used the *Spitzenkandidat* process to determine the next European Commission President, the process was effectively abandoned in 2019.

- Despite the measures introduced by the Treaty of Lisbon, the EU is still perceived as suffering from a democratic deficit.

3.10 Beyond the Treaty of Lisbon: crises, Brexit, and the future of the EU

When the Treaty of Lisbon was agreed, and later when it eventually entered into force, EU leaders appeared eager to call time on more than 20 years of seemingly interminable discussions about institutional reform and treaty change. Hence, on the day after the signing ceremony in Lisbon in December 2007, they declared that the new Treaty provided the EU with 'a stable and lasting institutional framework'. Furthermore, they expected 'no change in the foreseeable future' (Council of the European Union, 2008: point 6). Such sentiments were widely shared. The mood was that the days of treaty reform were now over. Ideally, there would be no major treaty for the next 25 years.

However, the Treaty of Lisbon was never conceived as a definitive text establishing the *finalité politique* of the EU. In fact, rather than limiting the options for treaty change and primarily in order to facilitate further treaty revision, it introduced two generally applicable '**simplified revision procedures**', and increased the number of provision-specific simplified revision procedures and so-called *passerelle* clauses in the TEU and TFEU. It therefore allowed simple, uncontentious changes to be made as needed without opening up to bigger and more contentious changes. It would not be long before these, as well as existing provisions, were being put to use. An initial change followed from the Spanish-led demand for the reallocation of seats originally planned for the 2009 European Parliament elections to be brought into effect post-haste. On 23 June 2010, a brief '15-minute' IGC was held to adopt the so-called 'MEP Protocol', allowing for a temporary raising of the cap on the size of the EP to 754 MEPs to accommodate 12 additional members. The Protocol entered into force on 1 December 2011 (see Box 3.5).

By then, two European Council Decisions amending the TFEU had also been introduced. The first—altering the status of Saint-Barthélemy, a French overseas collectivity—was a minor affair and barely attracted any attention. The second, coming in the midst of the deepening eurozone crisis, provoked far more debate. This was the amendment to Article 136 TFEU to enable the creation of a **European Stability Mechanism (ESM)** to provide financial assistance to eurozone countries in funding sovereign debts. Adopted on 25 March 2011, this entered into force on 1 May 2013. By then, an initial **Treaty Establishing the European Stability Mechanism (TESM)** had been signed by the 17 members of the eurozone on 11 July 2011. With eurozone leaders adopting additional decisions to strengthen the ESM in July and December 2011, this Treaty soon required modifications which were contained in a revised TESM signed on 2 February 2012. With Germany completing ratification in September, the ESM began operations on 8 October 2012 (see Chapter 25).

The TESM was not the only new treaty undergoing ratification. At Germany's insistence, a **Treaty on Stability, Coordination and Governance in the Economic and Monetary Union** had been drawn up following a fractious European Council in December 2011. Signed on 1 March 2012, its core purpose was to create between EU member states a 'Fiscal Compact' fostering budgetary discipline, greater coordination of economic policies, and improved governance of the euro area. However, in what was widely regarded as a portentous move, the Treaty created, thanks to the UK's obstinate refusal to countenance an agreement signed by all 27 member states, an intergovernmental, extra-EU arrangement to which neither the UK nor the Czech Republic were originally party, although the Czech Republic did subsequently sign up. This not only further marginalized the UK within the EU, but also raised questions about the position of the EU's **supranational institutions** within EMU, their influence over national economic policy, and general economic policy coordination. Such fears proved unfounded in practice (see Chapter 25), even if the substance of the Fiscal Compact has not been incorporated, as envisaged, into the TEU and TFEU.

Further treaty changes have also occurred, since March 2011, to alter the status of Mayotte, a French department (July 2012), and twice to adjust the organization of the Court of Justice (August 2012 and December 2015), the second adjustment providing for a staged increase in the number of judges at the General Court to 54 from 1 September 2019. The General Court does not require this many judges, but member states could not agree on an alternative to two judges per member state (see Chapter 13). A European Council decision has also been adopted (May 2013) reversing the reduction in the size of the Commission introduced by the Treaty of Lisbon and reinstating the principle of one Commissioner per member state (see Chapter 10). This was in line with the deal which saw Ireland hold its second 'Lisbon' referendum. Part of the package was the adoption of the 'Irish' Protocol which was agreed in a brief IGC in May 2012. Ratification took longer than anticipated owing to delays in Italy and so the Protocol failed to enter into force as planned when Croatia acceded to the EU on 1 July 2013. Entry into force eventually took place on 1 December 2014. By this time, a new Czech government had announced it was abandoning the goal of securing a 'Czech' Protocol. Croatia's accession therefore saw only a few minor adjustments to the TFEU.

The years since the Treaty of Lisbon entered into force have therefore seen only minor adjustments to the EU's treaty base. Things have proceeded quietly and efficiently, without rousing public ire, thus justifying the introduction of the new processes. In line with expectations, and in a context of popular apathy towards the EU, increasing populism, and Euroscepticism, there has been very little enthusiasm for further major treaty reform over the last decade. This is not to say that proponents of reform have remained silent.

BOX 3.5   BACKGROUND: KEY DATES IN EUROPEAN INTEGRATION: THE EU AND TREATY REFORM BEYOND THE TREATY OF LISBON

2010	23 June	'Fifteen-minute' IGC adopts 'MEP Protocol'
2011	25 March	European Council adopts treaty amendment to enable the creation of the **European Stability Mechanism (ESM)**
	11 July	17 eurozone member states sign **Treaty Establishing the European Stability Mechanism (TESM)**
	1 December	MEP Protocol enters into force
2012	2 February	17 eurozone member states sign modified TESM
	1–2 March	25 EU member states sign **Treaty on Stability, Coordination and Governance in the Economic and Monetary Union**—the **Fiscal Compact**
	16 May	IGC agrees Irish Protocol
	8 October	ESM becomes operational
2013	1 January	Fiscal Compact enters into force
	1 July	Croatia joins the EU
2014	March	Czech Government abandons Czech Protocol
	1 December	Jurisdiction of the Court of Justice of the European Union extended to outstanding areas of judicial and police cooperation
		Irish Protocol enters into force
2016	23 June	EU referendum in UK
2017	1 March	White Paper on the Future of Europe
	25 March	European Council adopts Rome Declaration
	29 March	UK government triggers Article 50 TEU
2017	19 June	Start of Withdrawal negotiations
2019	December	European Council agrees to Conference on the Future of Europe (CoFE) during 2020–2022
2020	31 January	UK withdraws from the EU
	24 June	Council agrees position for Conference on the Future of Europe
2021	9 June	The Conference on the Future of Europe is launched

Indeed, rarely was there a moment during the most intense phases of the eurozone crisis when EU leaders and officials were not being made desperately aware of the EU's limited capacity to respond effectively. Appropriate mechanisms and formal competences were often either inadequate or demonstratively absent.

Consequently, there was no shortage of calls for treaty reform to provide the EU with the necessary competences and improve the institutional framework for economic governance. For many observers and commentators, banking union, fiscal union, and effective economic governance have appeared vital to safeguard the future of at least the eurozone if not the EU; and each of them would require treaty reform.

Nothing came of the calls for treaty reform beyond the establishment of the ESM and Fiscal Compact. The preference was to exploit existing EU competences to the full. Equally, nothing came of the hopes of more federalist-minded MEPs for a new Convention following the 2014 EP elections. Instead, the prevailing sense of economic crisis during the first half of the 2010s—soon exacerbated by the worsening migration crisis from 2015 onwards—either curbed or muffled the political ambitions for the EU of many of its supporters. Even if they had been minded to pursue further reform, the prospect of facing electorates with further treaty reform simply did not appeal to EU leaders, particularly for those (e.g., France and the Netherlands) who would have come under enormous pressure to submit any text to a referendum for ratification. Others were simply opposed to any further deepening of integration. This was particularly so for the UK, although under David Cameron there was in 2014–15 a clear readiness to exploit any eurozone treaty reform to secure a major reform of the EU. Attention then turned to a renegotiation of the terms of UK membership. The agreement reached in February 2016 was much less far-reaching than Cameron had hoped and proved insufficient to prevent a 'leave' victory in the UK's EU referendum four months later.

Despite the eurozone and migration crises the EU continued to function. Responses to the eurozone crises, while often at least seemingly sub-optimal and tardy, nevertheless came, and primarily because of the commitment to maintaining the EU and European integration. A sense of existential crisis hung over many European Council and Council meetings during the 2010s, with no member state wishing to contemplate failure and a potential disintegration of the EU. The same was true in reaction to the UK government's decision to trigger Article 50, which was met with a remarkable sense of unity among the remaining 27 member states and an apparent determination to ensure that Brexit did not distract the EU unnecessarily (see Chapter 27). Also testing the EU was the state of democracy and the **rule of law** in Hungary and Poland where governments talked of tearing up the treaties when faced with accusations that they were failing to uphold core EU values. A far greater test was the COVID-19 pandemic, which stretched the EU's crisis response capabilities and posed major challenges to its free movement fundamentals. Collective action has, nevertheless, been pursued, as evidenced by the fiscal response and the coordinated approach to the procurement of vaccines, although these have not been without their tensions and problems (see Chapter 28).

The pandemic also, understandably, pushed less pressing issues to one side. Among these was whether there should be a further substantive debate on the future of the EU. Indeed, since 2017, there had been tentative signs of renewed confidence in integration, and even some suggestions that a further round of treaty reform and more integration might be in the offing. In the March 2017 Rome Declaration marking 60 years since the signing of the Treaty of Rome, the EU27 leaders spoke of making the EU 'stronger and more resilient, through even greater unity and solidarity'. And, parallel to this, the Commission produced a White Paper on the Future of Europe setting out possible future strategies for the Union.

No plans for any new convention or treaty reform were, however, agreed. A key purpose of the Rome Declaration was to demonstrate, at least at a rhetorical level, a sense of unity and commitment to shared values and solidarity as the UK government finally triggered Article 50 and began formally its withdrawal. However, some were keen to raise ambitions and breathe some new life into the EU. The new French President, Emmanuel Macron, eager to assert French leadership of the EU, launched an 'Initiative for Europe' and demanded a *'refondation d'une Europe souveraine, unie et démocratique'*. There were other calls too, with federalists, such as former EP President, Martin Schulz, and the MEP and former Belgian Prime Minister, Guy Verhofstadt, once again seeking progress towards a 'United States of Europe'. Other ideas circulating included those from the 'New Pact for Europe' network of prominent Brussels-based and national think tanks.

EU leaders generally responded hesitantly. The European Council in December 2019 did, however, discuss the idea of holding a Conference on the Future of Europe during 2020–2022, and agreed to engage the Commission and European Parliament. In June 2020, it was agreed that the conference would involve 'a large variety of different views and opinions—of EU institutions, Member States' governments, national parliaments, citizens, civil society, academia, social partners and other stakeholders' (Council of the EU, 2021). The focus would be on issues of concern to citizens and so include sustainability, societal challenges, innovation and competitiveness, fundamental values, and the EU's international role. It would be 'a broad and open-ended process' and report to the European Council in 2022 which would decide on the next steps. The CoFE was eventually launched on 9 May 2021, Europe Day.

Whether the CoFE will lead to any major reform of the EU remains to be seen. EU leaders continue to be cautious, and generally avoid any commitment to treaty change. For the present, the focus is on seeking to manage the COVID-19 pandemic and deal with the significant social and economic disruption this is causing. This could lead to a reconsideration of the role of the EU and reform, as was seen in the 2010s with the eurozone crisis. As then, however, further substantive treaty reform may not be necessary and cannot be assumed. Some tidying up of the TEU and TFEU will be needed at some point to remove the 30 plus references and provisions relating to the UK now that it has left the EU. This could end up being the limit of treaty of changes for the foreseeable future. Even amongst people like Chancellor Merkel, who has often spoken

of her openness to treaty change, there is immense caution. The likelihood is that the adapted treaties will continue to guide the Union for some more years yet.

KEY POINTS

- The Treaty of Lisbon was never intended to provide closure on EU treaty reform.

- The eurozone crisis led to calls for treaty reform to provide the EU with the necessary competences and improve the institutional framework for economic governance but only piecemeal, ad hoc treaty amendments were introduced.

- There continue to be calls for closer European integration. The CoFE aims to facilitate citizens' deliberation on the EU's priorities.

- Now that the UK has left the EU, the TEU, TFEU, and other treaty texts will need stylistic revision, but this is low on the EU agenda.

- There remains limited appetite to pursue reform, particularly given increased Euroscepticism.

3.11 Conclusion

Despite all of the talk of the Constitutional Treaty and the Treaty of Lisbon creating a superstate, what has emerged from the successive rounds of treaty reform over the last three decades or so is an EU dependent on its member states and defined by its treaties. There is no universally shared sense of 'Europe' on which to fall back as there is a Denmark, a Netherlands, or a Slovakia. It is because of this dependence on the treaties that amendments to them have been so sensitive and controversial. Treaty reform raises questions of what the EU is, what it should be, and where it might go. Given this, it should come as no surprise that the existing treaties have already been revised and supplemented as the EU has sought to deal first with the eurozone crisis, then with Brexit, and now with the pandemic. Further revisions will follow either out of a pragmatic need for minor change or because of new problems unforeseen back in 2007, or even as a result of idealists pushing for more integration. Pressure for reform, while somewhat muted for the last 15 years has not, and will not, go away. 'The Conference on the Future of Europe' will not be the last time when such ideas are floated.

However, as much as the EU might need or its leaders and engaged citizens desire reform, the process of effecting change is fraught with difficulties and so further treaty change, at least on the scale of past treaties, cannot be taken for granted. Essentially an elite-driven project, the question of 'more EU-rope' has become increasingly politicized as substantial levels of popular Euroscepticism and contention around EU policies and action continue to show. EU leaders were only able to secure many of the reforms contained in the Constitutional Treaty by ensuring that the Treaty of Lisbon was drafted in a secretive and technocratic manner and ratified almost exclusively through parliamentary processes. It would be unwise for such an approach to be repeated. Not only must any substantial treaty reform process now involve a convention, but the formal commitment of EU leaders and the EU institutions to greater transparency and citizen engagement mean that voters simply cannot be marginalized. A key challenge, however, is ensuring that debate is informed. As experience with the Constitutional Treaty and the Treaty of Lisbon amply demonstrated, many of the arguments deployed by their advocates and, especially, their opponents were decidedly inaccurate. Unfortunately, little by way of debate on the EU since the late 2010s appears to have narrowed the knowledge gap surrounding understanding of the EU, how it functions and what it does and does not do. This was amply reflected in the Brexit referendum. This all points, and certainly not for the first time, to the need for the EU's institutions and, more importantly, its member states to engage citizens in meaningful and informed debate on what the EU is, can, and should be.

It needs to be recognized, however, that the EU is far from static. Although the institutional and other reforms introduced by the Treaty of Lisbon have now bedded in, the EU remains a work-in-progress and therefore subject to, and often in need of, revision. This was amply demonstrated in the eurozone crisis where the EU was shown to lack any real fleetness of foot but rather a propensity simply to muddle through. Problems over vaccination strategies seem to have reinforced this. Given that it is ultimately a union of member states, each of which is committed to pursuing its own preferences, not infrequently with scant regard for the collective EU interest, reaching agreement on any increase in EU competence, institutional innovation, or change in the decision-making process will be slow if it can be achieved at all with such a sizeable membership.

UK withdrawal from the EU may change some of the dynamics of treaty reform. The EU will, after all, have lost one of its members least supportive of closer integration. However, other member states remain equally sceptical of lofty ambitions for the EU. Euroscepticism has become part of the political mainstream and, just as there are calls for more integration, so there are as many calls for reining in the powers of the EU if not abandoning the EU, and not just from populist politicians. The EU also faces challenges to fundamental principles as the clashes with Poland over judicial reform and the rule of law, and with Hungary demonstrate.

It cannot, therefore, be taken for granted that the unity of the EU27 expressed in the 2017 Rome Declaration and evident in the UK withdrawal process will translate into enthusiastic responses to calls for ambition from the likes of Macron. That said, as noted, the EU remains a work-in-progress and a far from perfect set-up for addressing the policy challenges that it and its member states face. Pressure for reform will continue, whether out of need or ambition; and adjustments and additions will be made to the imperfect 'union' that is the evolving EU. So, the Treaty of Lisbon was always unlikely to be the last chapter in the history of EU treaty reform.

? QUESTIONS

1. How and why did the EU move towards adopting the Treaty of Lisbon?

2. What were the main features of the consolidated TEU and TFEU?

3. How well have these consolidated treaties bedded down?

4. How has the EU's treaty base changed since the Treaty of Lisbon came into force?

5. Does Brexit necessitate further EU treaty change?

6. How well have the treaties coped with the eurozone crisis and the COVID-19 pandemic?

7. What are the prospects for future treaty revision?

8. What role do the treaties play in developing the EU?

GUIDE TO FURTHER READING

Craig, P. (2010) *The Lisbon Treaty: Law, Politics, and Treaty Reform* (Oxford: Oxford University Press). A comprehensive legal analysis of the Treaty of Lisbon.

Dinan, D., Nugent, N., and Paterson, W.E. (2017) *The European Union in Crisis* (Basingstoke: Macmillan). A collection of assessments of selected crisis and key challenges facing the EU.

Eriksen, E. O., Fossum, J. E., and Menéndez, A. J. (eds) (2005) *Developing a Constitution for Europe* (London: Routledge). An academic study of the rationale for a European constitution and the process that led to the adoption of the Constitutional Treaty.

Fabbrini, F. (ed.) (2017) *The Law and Politics of Brexit* (Oxford: Oxford University Press). An initial assessment of some of the constitutional and political implications for the UK and the EU of Brexit.

Phinnemore, D. (2013) *The Treaty of Lisbon: Origins and Negotiation* (Basingstoke: Palgrave). A comprehensive account of how the Treaty of Lisbon was negotiated and came into force.

Access the online resources to take your learning and understanding further, including extra multiple-choice questions with instant feedback, web links, answer guidance to end-of-chapter questions, and updates on new developments in EU politics.

www.oup.com/he/cini-borragan7e

PART 2
Theories and Conceptual Approaches

4

Neo-functionalism

Carsten Strøby Jensen

Chapter Contents

Reader's Guide

This chapter reviews a theoretical position, neo-functionalism, which was developed in the mid-1950s by scholars based in the United States. The fundamental argument of the theory is that states are not the only important actors on the international scene. As a consequence, neo-functionalists focus their attention on the role of supranational institutions and non-state actors, such as interest groups and political parties, who, they argue, are the real driving force behind integration efforts. The chapter that follows provides an introduction to the main features of neo-functionalist theory, its historical development since the 1950s and how neo-functionalism is used today.

4.1 Introduction

Neo-functionalism is often the first theory of **European integration** studied by students of the European Union. This is largely for historical reasons, because neo-functionalism was the first attempt at theorizing the new form of regional **cooperation** that emerged at the end of the Second World War. The chapter begins by asking: 'What is neo-functionalism?' The purpose of Section 4.2 is to outline the general characteristics of the theory. Section 4.3 then summarizes the rise and fall from grace of neo-functionalism between the 1950s and the 1970s. Section 4.4 examines three hypotheses that form the core of neo-functionalist thinking:

1. the spillover hypothesis;
2. the elite socialization hypothesis; and
3. the supranational interest group hypothesis.

These three arguments help to expose neo-functionalist beliefs about the dynamics of the European integration process. Section 4.5 reviews the main criticisms of the neo-functionalist school, while the final section turns to more recent adaptations of neo-functionalist ideas, accounting for the renewal of interest in this approach to the study of regional integration. The chapter concludes that neo-functionalism remains part of the mainstream theorizing of EU developments, even though there have been some major changes in the way in which neo-functionalism is used today compared to its original application in the 1950s.

4.2 What is neo-functionalism?

The story of neo-functionalism began in 1958 with the publication by Ernst B. Haas (1924–2003) of *The Uniting of Europe: Political, Social, and Economic Forces 1950–1957* (Haas, 1958). In this seminal book, Haas explained how six West European countries came to initiate a new form of supranational cooperation after the Second World War. Originally, Haas's main aim in formulating a theoretical account of the **European Coal and Steel Community (ECSC)** was to provide a scientific and objective explanation of regional cooperation, a **grand theory** that would explain similar processes elsewhere in the world (in Latin America, for example). However, neo-functionalism soon became very closely associated with the European Community (EC) case and, moreover, with a particular path of European integration.

Three characteristics of the theory help to explain what neo-functionalism is. First, neo-functionalism's core concept is spillover. It is important to note at this point, however, that neo-functionalism was mainly concerned with the process of integration and had little to say about end goals—that is, about what an integrated Europe would look like. As a consequence, the theory sought to explain the dynamics of change to which states were subject when they cooperated. Haas's theory was based on the assumption that cooperation in one policy area would create pressures in a neighbouring policy area, placing it on the political agenda, and ultimately leading to further integration. Thus 'spillover' refers to a situation in which cooperation in one field necessitates cooperation in another (Hooghe and Marks, 2007). Member states' willingness to cooperate, for example, on creating a common market for cars would spill over to cooperation on car safety equipment to establish a **common market**. Without common rules on safety equipment, car producers would face difficulties in selling their products in all member states because of differences in safety standards.

This might suggest that the integration process is automatic or beyond the control of political leaders, but when we look at the various forms of spillover identified by Haas, we will see how this 'automatic' process might be guided or manipulated by actors and institutions, the motives of which are unequivocally political.

A second, albeit related, point that helps to explain neo-functionalism concerns the role of societal groups in the process of integration. Haas argued that interest groups and political parties would be key actors in driving integration forward. While governments might be reluctant to engage in integration, transnational interest groups would see it as in their interest to push for further integration. This is because groups would see integration as a way of resolving the problems they faced. Although groups would invariably have different problems and, indeed, different ideological positions, they would all, according to neo-functionalists, see regional integration as a means to their desired ends. Multinational companies would argue for further economic integration in order to strengthen their market position and environmental organizations would argue for increased cooperation in order to handle cross-national problems with pollution. Thus one might see integration as a process driven by the self-interest of groups rather than by any ideological vision of a united Europe or by a shared sense of identity.

Finally, neo-functionalism is often characterized as a rather **elitist** approach. Although it sees a role for groups in the European integration process, integration tends to be driven by functional and technocratic needs. Although not apolitical, it sees only a minimal role for democratic and accountable **governance** at the level of the region. Rather, the '**benign elitism**' of neo-functionalists tends to assume the tacit support of the European peoples—a '**permissive consensus**'— upon which experts and **executives** rely when pushing for further European integration.

KEY POINTS

- Neo-functionalism is a theory of integration that seeks to explain the process of (European) integration.

- The theory was particularly influential in the 1950s and 1960s but is still widely used as a theoretical point of reference.

- Its main focus is on the 'factors' that drive integration: interest group activity at the European and national levels; political party activity; and the role of governments and supranational institutions.

- European integration is mostly seen as an elite-driven process—that is, as driven by national and international political and economic elites.

4.3 A brief history of neo-functionalism

Neo-functionalism is very much connected to the case of European integration. Indeed, most neo-functionalist writers have focused their attention on Europe (Lindberg, 1963; Lindberg and Scheingold, 1970, 1971). This was not their original intention. Rather, an early objective was to formulate a general or grand theory of international relations, based on observations of regional integration processes. Political and economic cooperation in Latin America was one of the cases investigated (Haas and Schmitter, 1964). It was in Europe, however, that political and economic integration was best developed and most suited to theoretical and empirical study. Therefore, Europe

and European integration became the major focus of neo-functionalism during the 1960s and 1970s.

With the benefit of hindsight, the success of neo-functionalism is understandable because it seemed that the theory explained well the reality of the European integration process at that time. Until the 1970s, neo-functionalism had wide support in academic circles. However, by the 1980s it had lost momentum as a credible theoretical and empirical position in the study of European integration. One reason for this is that the incremental political integration that neo-functionalism had predicted had not taken place. From the mid-1970s, political cooperation seemed less compelling and researchers became more interested in other kinds of theories, especially those that stressed the importance of the nation state. Even Haas was among those who recognized the limitations of neo-functionalism. On this point, he wrote that 'the prognoses often do not match the diagnostic sophistication, and patients die when they should recover, while others recover even though all the vital signs look bad' (Haas, 1975: 5).

After the early 1990s, neo-functionalism underwent a revival. The new dynamism of the EC/EU, a consequence of the **Single Market** programme (see Chapter 20), made theories that focused on processes of political integration relevant once again (Tranholm-Mikkelsen, 1991). Despite huge differences in interests among the member states and continuous crises in European cooperation—including Brexit—political integration somehow continues to develop in Europe. Neo-functionalism offers an explanation of why this is.

Since this revival of interest in neo-functionalism, a number of scholars have sought to adapt the theory to their own research agendas—whether on the European integration process writ large, on specific policy areas, or on the role of the supranational institutions. Correspondingly, there were, following Haas's death in 2003, several attempts to evaluate and re-evaluate the importance of the neo-functionalist contribution to our understanding of the development of the European Union (for example, in a special issue of the *Journal of European Public Policy* in 2005). Even trends towards disintegration in connection with Brexit have been analysed by taking neo-functionalism as a starting point (Schmitter and Lefkofridi, 2016); and, today, neo-functionalism—together with intergovernmentalism (see Chapter 5)—constitute one of the basic theoretical points of reference in European studies (Rosamond, 2016).

4.4 Supranationalism and spillover

The key questions asked by neo-functionalists are whether and how economic integration leads to political integration, and if it does, what kind of political unity will result? In this respect, neo-functionalism differs from other traditional approaches to international relations. **Realist** positions stress the **power** games that occur among states. By contrast, neo-functionalists believe that economic integration would strengthen all states involved and that this would lead to political integration. Economic integration leads to economic growth which in the long run implies increased welfare among EU citizens. The fundamental idea, therefore, was that international relations should not be considered a **zero-sum game**, and that everybody wins when countries become involved in economic and political integration.

Neo-functionalist theory also sheds light on the development of supranational institutions and organizations, which are likely to have their own political agendas. Over time, neo-functionalists predict, this supranational agenda will tend to triumph over member state interests. As an example, one might look at how the European Parliament (EP) operates. Members of the European Parliament (MEPs) are directly elected within the member states. One would therefore expect the EP to be an institution influenced very much by national interests. In the Parliament, however, MEPs are not divided into groups relating to their national origin; rather, they are organized along party-political and ideological lines (see Chapter 12). In other words, Social Democrats from Germany work together with

Labour members from the UK, and Liberals from Spain work with Liberals from Denmark. According to neo-functionalist theory, MEPs will tend to become more European in their outlook because of these working practices. This is often referred to as 'elite socialization'. The fact that MEPs work together across borders makes it difficult for them to focus solely on national interests. This also makes the EP a natural ally for the European Commission in its discussions with the EU Council, even if the institutions do not always agree on matters of policy (see Box 4.1).

Political integration is therefore a key concept for neo-functionalists, although it is possible to identify different understandings of this concept in neo-functionalist writings. Lindberg and Scheingold (1971: 59), for example, stressed that political integration involves governments doing together what they used to do individually. It is about setting up supranational and collective decision-making processes. Haas also saw political integration in terms of shifts in attitudes and loyalties among political actors. In 1958, he famously wrote:

Political integration is the process whereby political actors in several distinct national settings are persuaded to shift their loyalties, expectations and political activities toward a new center, whose institutions possess or demand jurisdiction over the pre-existing national states. The end result of a process of political integration is a new political community, superimposed over the pre-existing ones (Haas, 1958: 16).

Neo-functionalist writers developed at least three different arguments about the dynamics of the integration processes: the spillover hypothesis; the elite socialization hypothesis; and the hypothesis on supranational interest groups.

4.4.1 Spillover

Spillover is neo-functionalism's best-known concept. The concept of spillover refers to a process in which political cooperation conducted with a specific goal in mind leads to the formulation of new goals in order to assure the achievement of the original goal. What this means is that political cooperation, once initiated, is extended over time in a way that was not necessarily intended at the outset.

To fulfil certain goals, states cooperate on a specific issue. For example, the original aim may be the free

BOX 4.1   KEY DEBATES: LOYALTY SHIFT IN THE EUROPEAN PARLIAMENT

Although members of the European Parliament (MEPs) are elected at national level (in direct elections), their loyalty tends very often to be oriented towards the European level (Hix et al., 2005). This is also predicted by neo-functionalists when they talk about loyalty shifts among the participants of the European institutions. This 'shift in loyalty' among the parliamentarians could be observed in the election of a new President of the European Commission in 2014. The majority of MEPs decided that they would propose a candidate from the largest political party in the European Parliament (see also Chapter 12 on this procedure). After the election to the European Parliament in 2014, Jean-Claude Juncker was proposed as President of the Commission. After some debate, this was accepted by the member states. The process leading to the appointment of Juncker can be seen as a way of increasing the influence of the European Parliament at the expense of national governments (and national parliaments). Neo-functionalists argue that MEPs gradually shifted their loyalty preferences from the national level towards the European level. This happens partly because of changes in norms among the parliamentarians (with MEPs normatively influenced by the 'Brussels atmosphere') and partly because of their interest, once they become MEPs, in increasing the influence of the European Parliament on European politics. However, this neo-functionalist view has to a certain degree

been challenged in connection with the increasing number of explicitly Eurosceptic MEPs. After the 2014 election the Eurosceptic party groups in the European Parliament were strengthened (represented by Europe of Nations and Freedom (ENF) and European Conservatives and Reformists (ECR) (Whitaker et al., 2017)).

In the election to the European Parliament in 2019, and in connection with the nomination of a new President for the European Commission, Members of the Parliament expected that they could again force the Council to accept a President suggested by the Parliament (as in 2014). Candidates for the presidency of the Commission were even performing in debates similar to what is known from national election processes, and Manfred Weber from the European People's Party was one of the favourites. However, in the end the Council decided to elect Ursula von der Leyen as President for the European Commission, despite protests coming from the European Parliament. This indicates that the member states (and especially core member states like France and Germany) are still very central actors in the European Union. It also illustrates some of the weaknesses of neo-functionalism. Neo-functionalist theory would not predict nor expect this kind of roll back of the integration process.

---

movement of workers across EU borders, but it may soon become obvious that different national rules on certification prevent workers from gaining employment in other EU states. For example, nurses educated in one member state may not be allowed to work in another because of differences in national educational systems. As a consequence, new political goals in the field of education policy may be formulated so as to overcome this obstacle to the free movement of labour. This process of generating new political goals is the very essence of the neo-functionalist concept of spillover:

Spillover refers . . . to the process whereby members of an integration scheme—agreed on some collective goals for a variety of motives but unequally satisfied with their attainment of these goals—attempt to resolve their dissatisfaction by resorting to collaboration in another, related sector (expanding the scope of mutual commitment) or by intensifying their commitment to the original sector (increasing the level of mutual commitment), or both (Schmitter, 1969: 162).

Functional (or technical), political, and cultivated spillover constitute three different kinds of spillover process:

- An example of *functional spillover*—where one step towards cooperation functionally leads to another—can be seen in the case of the Single Market (see Chapter 20). The Single Market was functionally related to common rules governing the working environment. This meant that some of the trade barriers to be removed under the Single Market programme took the form of national **regulations** on health and safety, because the existence of different standards across the Community prevented free movement. The functional consequence of establishing a Single Market was, therefore, that the member states ended up accepting the regulation of certain aspects of the working environment at European level, even though this had not been their original objective (Jensen, 2000) (see Box 4.2).

BOX 4.2   CASE STUDY: FUNCTIONAL SPILLOVER: FROM THE SINGLE MARKET TO THE TREATY ON STABILITY, COORDINATION, AND GOVERNANCE

The Single Market has increased the opportunities for companies in Europe to trade across borders. This was intended to encourage a growth in trade among the countries of the European Community. However, the increased level of transnational trade in the EC caused companies and countries to be more exposed to exchange rate fluctuations, and this demonstrated the functional advantages inherent in a common European currency. From that perspective, economic and monetary union (EMU) embodies a functional logic connecting growth in trade across borders in the EU with the functional need for a common currency to reduce risks related to expanding trade. However, the 2008 financial crisis demonstrated the weakness of EMU. When the member states agreed to set up a monetary union, they chose not to give the EU the ability to influence directly national fiscal policies. When the financial crisis hit Europe, this serious institutional weakness was exposed. In that respect, the agreement of the Treaty on Stability, Coordination and Governance of 2012 can also be seen as an unintended consequence of functional spillover. The financial crisis revealed that if a group of countries has a common currency, there is a fundamental functional need to have a coordinated fiscal policy, even if it were not the original intention of the member states of the euro area when the common currency was first set up. In this sense, the establishment of supranational institutions such as the EU may be seen to be the result of unintended consequences of actions among the actors involved in decision-making.

- *Political spillover* occurs in situations characterized by a more deliberated political process, in which national political elites or interest groups argue that supranational cooperation is needed to solve specific problems. National interest groups focus more on European than on national solutions and tend to shift their loyalty towards the supranational level. Interest groups understand that their chances of success increase when they support European rather than national solutions (Turkina and Postnikov, 2012). This type of spillover is closely related to a theory that argues that European integration promotes shifts of loyalty among civil servants and other elite actors (see Box 4.3).

- *Cultivated spillover* refers to situations in which supranational actors—the European Commission in particular—push the process of political integration forward when they mediate between the member states (Tranholm-Mikkelsen, 1991; Niemann, 2006; Stephenson, 2010). For example, the Commission may take heed only of arguments that point towards further political integration ('more' Europe) during the negotiation process, while ignoring or rejecting arguments that are primarily based on national interests (see Box 4.4).

Supranational institutions may use special interests as a means of driving forward the integration process. These special interests may be promoted through so-called 'package deals', in which steps are taken to treat apparently discrete issues as a single (composite) item, enabling all (or the majority of) actors to safeguard their interests. For example, if a member state has an interest in a certain policy area, such as preventing cuts in agricultural spending, while another has interests in industrial policy, these member states may agree, formally or informally, to support each other

BOX 4.3   CASE STUDY: POLITICAL SPILLOVER IN THE BREXIT PROCESS

Although the UK's departure from the EU might be seen as a major setback for European integration, it may also encourage supranational actors to argue for increased political integration among the remaining member states. This might be interpreted as an example of political spillover. Supranational actors like the European Commission or pro-European interest groups might argue that Brexit and the underlying dissatisfaction with the EU is not a consequence of 'too much political integration', but of 'too little political integration' and that dissatisfaction among part of the British population with the free movement of labour (and with Eastern European workers coming to the UK) is a result of the EU's failure to introduce a developed social policy. A push for further social policy integration in the EU might therefore emerge from the Brexit process.

> **BOX 4.4   CASE STUDY: CULTIVATED SPILLOVER IN THE AREA OF HEALTH POLICY—THE USE OF ANTIBIOTICS IN THE VETERINARIAN SECTOR**
>
> Health policy is traditionally an area with no or very little EU involvement (Vollard et al., 2016). It is an area where the national interest prevails, and where member states have been reluctant to transfer competence to the EU. Increasingly, however, member states' health policies are influenced by the EU, especially when the policy is linked to the Single Market. Greer, for example, talks about spillover from Single Market to health policy (Greer, 2006: 143). The spillover effect can also be seen in the linkages that exist between the veterinarian area and health policy. The development of resistance to antibiotics is increasingly seen as a potential health problem both globally and in the EU (European Commission, 2011b). The overuse of antibiotics in both the human health sector and in the veterinary sector has led to resistance problems, which means that infections that used to be treated with antibiotics are increasingly non-treatable. The legal basis for EU regulation in the health area is rather weak, but in 2014 the Commission proposed a regulation on 'marketing authorizations' for veterinary medicine (European Commission, 2014). This proposal includes rules on the use of antibiotics in the veterinary sector, especially so-called critical antibiotics. Governing the use of antibiotics in the veterinarian sector for the sake of human health through a 'marketing authorization regulation' can be viewed as a case of cultivated spillover. Here the Commission has deliberately tried to create a new agenda to resolve a cross-border problem in an area where EU competences are weak. The lack of health policy has also been important in relations to the COVID-19 crisis.

in negotiations. As a result, the two policy areas can be easily linked within the bargaining process, particularly when an entrepreneurial actor such as the Commission takes the initiative.

Thus, spillover processes may be seen partly as the result of unintended consequences. Member states might deliberately accept political integration and the delegation of authority to supranational institutions on an issue. However, as a result of that decision, they may suddenly find themselves in a position where there is a need for even more delegation. As a result, Lindberg and Scheingold (1970) are right to stress that political integration need not be the declared end goal for member states engaging in this process. The latter have their own respective goals, which are likely to have more to do with policy issues than with integration. As Lindberg and Scheingold write:

> We do not assume that actors will be primarily or even at all interested in increasing the scope and capacities of the system per se. Some will be, but by and large most are concerned with achieving concrete economic and welfare goals and will view integration only as a means to these ends (Lindberg and Scheingold, 1970: 117).

The neo-functionalist concept of spillover has also recently been used to analyse possible EU-integrational effects of the so-called migrant/refugee crises, although this is an area often conceptualized as primarily being more related to intergovernmental dynamics (Niemann and Speyer, 2018; Börzel and Risse, 2018). The recent inflow of migrants and refugees to different EU countries put pressure on the Schengen agreements and the lack of border control between the Schengen countries. As Börzel and Risse write: 'Functional pressures to strengthen the common asylum and migration policy in order to preserve Schengen by establishing a centralized relocation mechanism or by creating a common border control have been strong' (Börzel and Risse, 2018: 93). Schengen makes it difficult to hinder movements among migrants and refugees across borders between the Schengen countries. Therefore, the need for a common asylum and migration policy in the EU increases. This can be seen as an example of (potential) functional spillover.

4.4.2 Elite socialization

The second aspect of neo-functionalist theory concerns the development of supranational loyalties by participants such as officials and politicians in the decision-making process. The theory here is that, over time, people involved on a regular basis in the supranational policy process will tend to develop European loyalties and preferences. For example, Commission officials are expected to hold a European perspective on problem-solving so that their loyalty may no longer be to any one national polity, but rather to the supranational level of governance (see Box 4.5). Even civil servants representing member states in Brussels will develop a more European perspective on how politics should develop. They will increasingly, according to the elite socialization theory, conceptualize their

> ### BOX 4.5   KEY DEBATES: 'ELITE SOCIALIZATION' AND 'LOYALTY TRANSFER'
>
> Neo-functionalism stresses the process of socialization and 'loyalty transfer'. In an analysis of political integration in the educational sector, Warleigh-Lack and Drachenberg (2011: 1006) quote a Director-General in the Commission who made the following observation: '[T]he typical socialization process would begin with the Member States' representatives being very hesitant at first. Then they call each other by first names, and then they want to change the world together' (see also Chapter 11). Socialization leads actors to look beyond their own roles, allowing them to leave behind the attitude that their own system is the best.

own role as being oriented towards mediating views at European level instead of primarily representing the narrow interests of the member state from which they come.

We can well imagine how participants engaged in an intensive ongoing decision-making process, which may extend over several years, bring them into frequent and close personal contact, and which engages them in a joint problem-solving and policy-making, might develop a special orientation to that process and to those interactions, especially if they are rewarding.

Participants may come to value the system and their role within it, either for itself, or for the concrete rewards and benefits it has produced or that it promises.

Thus, neo-functionalists predicted that the European integration process would lead to the establishment of elite groups loyal to the supranational institutions that hold pan-European norms and ideas (see Box 4.6). These elites would try to convince national elites of the advantages of supranational cooperation. At the same time, neo-functionalists also predicted that international negotiations would become less politicized and more technocratic. The institutionalization of the interactions between national actors and the continued negotiations between different member states would make it more and more difficult for states to adhere to their political arguments and retain their credibility (Haas, 1958: 291). As a result, it was expected that the agenda would tend to shift towards more technical problems upon which it was possible to forge agreement.

4.5 The formation of supranational interest groups

According to neo-functionalist theory, civil servants are not the only groups that develop a supranational orientation; organized interest groups are also expected to become more European as corporations and business groups formulate their own interests with an eye to the supranational institutions (see Chapter 14). In that respect neo-functionalism to a much higher

> ### BOX 4.6   KEY DEBATES: NEO-FUNCTIONALIST EXPECTATIONS ABOUT EUROPEAN INSTITUTIONS
>
> Neo-functionalists have formulated theories that they have used to predict the behaviour of the European institutions.
>
> - The European Commission is expected to act as a 'political entrepreneur' or a 'policy entrepreneur', as well as a mediator. The Commission will, according to neo-functionalist theory, try to push for greater cooperation between the member states in a direction that leads to more and more supranational decision-making.
>
> - The Court of Justice of the EU (CJEU) is expected not only to rule on the basis of legal arguments, but also to favour political integration. In this way, the Court will seek to expand the logic of Community law to new areas.
>
> - The European Parliament is expected to have a supranational orientation and to be the natural ally of the European Commission. Although MEPs are elected by the nationals of
>
> their home country, they are divided politically and ideologically in their daily work. Neo-functionalists expect MEPs to develop loyalties towards the EU and the 'European idea', so that they will often (although not always) defend European interests against national interests.
>
> - The EU Council is expected to be the institution in which national interests are defended. However, neo-functionalists would also expect member states to be influenced by the logic of spillover, which would lead them to argue for greater economic and political integration, despite their national interests. The member states are also expected to be influenced by the fact that they are involved in ongoing negotiations in a supranational context. This makes it difficult for a member state to resist proposals that lead to further political integration.

degree than intergovernmentalism stresses the importance of non-state actors in international relations and politics (see Chapter 5). As economic and political integration in a given region develops, interest groups will try to match this development by reorganizing at the supranational level. For example, national industrial and employers' organizations established a common European organization, the Confederation of European Business, BUSINESSEUROPE, in 1958 (originally called UNICE, the *Union des Industries de la Communauté Européenne*) at much the same time as the European Community was established. In so doing, their intention was to influence future Community policy. Early neo-functionalists also foresaw a similar role for political parties.

In a similar way, the financial crises also made some international organizations—like the Basel Committee—more visible. The Basel Committee is an international organization—situated in Basel—that develops global standards on prudential regulation of banks. The members are national Central Banks (including the European Central Bank). The importance of this kind of international financial organizations has increased, especially since the financial crises around 2007/08. The Basel Committee has, since the financial crises, developed international banking standards like Basel III and Basel IV in order to reduce uncertainty in the international financial system. The Basel Committee is a good example of the kind of international institution/organization that neo-functionalist theory predicts would develop. It is an international organization that creates international standards within the financial area without having any formal legal competence. However, the standards are to a high degree transformed into legislation in the EU and other countries.

Furthermore, neo-functionalists believed that interest groups would put pressure on governments to force them to speed up the integration process. These groups were expected to develop their own supranational interest in political and economic integration, which would ally them to supranational institutions, such as the European Commission. Thus, 'in the process of reformulating expectations and demands, the interest groups in question approach one another supranationally while their erstwhile ties with national friends undergo deterioration' (Haas, 1958: 313).

Transnational organized interests can also be observed in policy areas such as climate policy. Environmental organizations such as Greenpeace often try to influence policy-making, while cutting across national boundaries and national interests. They act as transnational organized interests in the way in which neo-functionalists predicted and argue that it is necessary to increase the **competences** of the EU in relation to climate issues to push forward the climate agenda.

> **KEY POINTS**
>
> - Neo-functionalists believe that there are different types of spillover.
> - Functional, political, and cultivated spillover account for different dynamics in the integration process.
> - Elite socialization implies that, over time, people involved in European affairs shift their loyalties to the European institutions and away from their nation state.
> - Neo-functionalists believe that interest groups also become **Europeanized**, placing demands on their national governments for more integration.

4.6 Critiques of neo-functionalism

Neo-functionalism has been criticized on both empirical and theoretical grounds. At an empirical level, the criticism focuses on the absence (or slow pace) of political integration in Western Europe during the 1970s and early 1980s. Neo-functionalism had predicted a pattern of development characterized by a gradual intensification of political integration—a development that, by the 1970s, had clearly not taken place. The French boycott of the European institutions in the mid-1960s had led to a more cautious phase in the evolution of the Community and recognition of the importance of political leaders as constraints on the process of integration. Indeed, with the European Community having suffered numerous crises, it could even be argued that the integration process had reversed. Moravcsik writes that:

Despite the richness of its insights, neo-functionalism is today widely regarded as having offered an unsatisfactory account of European integration... The most widely cited reason is empirical: neo-functionalism appears to mispredict both the trajectory and the process of EC evolution. Insofar as neo-functionalism advances a clear precondition about the trajectory in the EC over time, it was that the technocratic imperative would lead to a 'gradual', 'automatic' and 'incremental' progression toward deeper integration and greater supranational influence (Moravcsik, 1993: 476).

Haas even talked about the possibility that there might be a disintegrative equivalent to spillover: 'spillback'. In many ways, Brexit can be conceptualized as the prime example of a 'spillback' process in the EU. That a major country would choose to leave the EU was not foreseen among scholars advocating within a neo-functionalist framework. However, one could also use neo-functionalist theory to argue that spillback processes are often followed by processes of spillover. In that sense, it would not be a surprise if Brexit in the long run leads to increased political cooperation and integration among the remaining member states. The Brexit crisis also indicates that it is difficult for a country to break out of the European Union. The cost of disintegration is very high, for example if it implies leaving the common market (Cavlak, 2019). Therefore, the UK ended up accepting a deal that in many ways continues its close relationship with the EU. The Brexit deal can in that sense be seen as a process where the UK leaves and stays in the EU at the same time due to the functional ties that exists between the UK and the EU. The second set of objections was based on criticism of the theories formulated by Haas himself. By the late 1960s, Haas had accepted that his prediction—that regional organizations such as the European Union would develop incrementally, propelled forward by various dynamics such as spillover—had failed to encapsulate the reality of European cooperation (Haas, 1975, 1976). He recommended a different approach to regional integration, based on the theories of interdependence that were being developed in the mid-1970s by Keohane and Nye (1975, 1976), among others. This approach argued that institutions such as the EC/EU should be analysed against the background of the growth in international interdependence, rather than as regional political organizations. Referring to European integration, Haas (1975: 6) wrote that '[w]hat once appeared to be a distinctive "supranational" style now looks more like a huge regional bureaucratic appendage to an intergovernmental conference in permanent session'. In so arguing, Haas abandoned the theory that he had been so instrumental in developing.

In some later writings, Haas argued that neo-functionalism had a common ground with constructivist thinking (see Chapter 6). Constructivists argue that institutions, discourses, and intersubjectivity are important factors when international relations are analysed (Haas and Haas, 2002). It means that the way political problems are 'talked about' in itself influence

policy decisions made by the politicians. If tax fraud (as in the Panama case) is 'talked about' as a common European problem, it stimulates European political initatives. If it is 'talked about' as primarily a national problem for the single member state it stimulates national solutions and tends to hinder European initiatives. The importance of discourses also attracted major attention from neo-functionalists (although the vocabulary was different), especially with regard to how political elites are socialized. Socialization can be viewed as a process in which values and beliefs are constructed. Haas (2001: 22) writes: 'A case can easily be made that the Neo-functionalist approach, developed in order to give the study of European regional integration a theoretical basis, is a precursor of what has lately been called **Constructivism**.'

In the third group of objections to the theory, it was argued that neo-functionalism had placed undue emphasis on the supranational component of regional integration. Critics suggested that greater importance should be attached to the nation state and that regional forms of cooperation should be analysed as intergovernmental organizations. This line of attack was adopted by Moravcsik (1993, 1998, 2005), among others, under the rubric of **liberal intergovernmentalism** (see Chapter 5): 'Whereas neo-functionalism stresses the autonomy of supranational officials, liberal intergovernmentalism stresses the autonomy of national leaders' (Moravcsik, 1993: 491). Intergovernmentalists argue, for example, that although the President of the European Commission plays an important role in EU decision-making, it is the German Chancellor, who, together with other heads of government (or state) from the largest member states, has the decisive say.

Neo-functionalism first and foremost focused on political and administrative elites, and on the processes of cooperation among national elites (Risse, 2005: 297). The assumption was that if the elites started to cooperate, then the populations would follow. The experience of 'no' votes in national referendums on the EU treaties and on Brexit demonstrates that this focus on political elites is a major weakness in neo-functionalist theory. Although political and administrative elites at the national and European level agreed, for example, on the **Lisbon Treaty**, this did not mean that the voters followed them. And although the major political parties and the business and financial establishment in the UK argued for the UK to stay in the EU, the vote ended in a 'no'. In this respect, one could say that neo-functionalism as a theoretical tradition has a blind spot in its lack of understanding of the need for the EU to establish **legitimacy** among the peoples of Europe (see Chapter 9). This can especially be seen as a problem in times when EU policies are increasingly involved in most aspects of national policy and where identity policies are high on the agenda (Kuhn, 2019).

KEY POINTS

- Neo-functionalism has been criticized on both empirical and theoretical grounds.
- On empirical grounds, neo-functionalism has been criticized for failing to live up to the reality of the EC.
- On theoretical grounds, critics have denied the existence of elite socialization and have stressed the importance of the global dimension of integration.
- Critiques of neo-functionalism have also sought to reposition the nation state at the heart of the study of the European integration process.

4.7 The revival of neo-functionalism

After years of obsolescence, there was a revival in interest in neo-functionalism at the beginning of the 1990s. There are several reasons for the theory's renewed popularity. The first concerns general developments in the European Community. The **Single European Act (SEA)** and the creation of the Single Market (see Chapter 20) marked a new phase of economic and political cooperation in Western Europe in the mid-1980s. The processes of integration associated with these developments seemed very much in line with the sort of spillover predicted by neo-functionalist theory (Tranholm-Mikkelsen, 1991).

However, this renewed interest in neo-functionalism involved much more than just a step back to the 1960s. Rather than simply adopting the traditional or classical model, many of those who sought to reuse neo-functionalist theory accepted it only as a **partial theory** or as a middle range theory—that is, as a theory that explained some, but not all, of the European integration process. This contrasts with the earlier ambition of the neo-functionalists—to create a grand theory of European integration.

An important contribution to this new approach was made by Stone Sweet and Sandholtz (1998; see

also Stone Sweet, 2010, and Sandholtz and Stone Sweet, 2012). Although these authors are not neo-functionalists in any traditional sense, they claim that their theoretical considerations have 'important affinities with neo-functionalism' (Stone Sweet and Sandholtz, 1998: 5). They argue that the traditional distinction made in the theoretical literature on European integration—that it is either supranational or intergovernmental—is no longer sufficient. While both tendencies are represented in the real world of European politics, they appear differently in different policy areas within the Union, so that some are characterized by intergovernmentalism and others by supranationalism. However, Stone Sweet and Sandholtz do not use the spillover concept when they seek to explain processes of political integration and the formation of supranational institutions. Instead, they develop what they call a 'transaction-based' theory of integration (Sandholtz and Stone Sweet, 2012). This draws attention to the increasing levels of transactions (such as in the field of trade, communications, and travel) across EU borders, which in turn increases demands for European-level regulation. In time, these demands generate a process of institutionalization, leading to the establishment of what the authors call 'supranational governance'.

Along similar lines, references to neo-functionalist theory have increased dramatically since the beginning of the 1990s. In policy areas such as defence (Guay, 1996), social policy (Jensen, 2000), and telecommunications (Sandholtz, 1998), attitudes among European civil servants (Hooghe, 2001, 2012), regional economic integration in Asia (Sultan and Mehmood, 2020), competition policy (McGowan, 2007), **enlargement** (Macmillan, 2009), air transportation (Rauh and Schneider, 2013), health policy (Greer, 2006; Brooks, 2012), and transnational liberties (Newman, 2008), authors have discussed neo-functionalism as a possible frame for explaining specific forms of integration.

During the 2000s, there have also been some important attempts at further developing the original neo-functionalist framework. Arne Niemann (2006, 2015), for example, argues that the process of integration should not be seen as an inevitable process. Integration is no longer viewed as an automatic and exclusively dynamic process, but rather occurs under certain conditions and is better characterized as a dialectic process—that is, the product of both dynamics and countervailing forces. In addition, instead of a grand theory, the revisited approach is understood as a wide-ranging, but partial, theory. Thus, '[w]hile elites are still attributed a primary role for decision outcomes, the wider publics are assumed to impact on the evolution of the European integration process, too' (Niemann, 2006: 5). Niemann discusses the original neo-functionalist concepts of spillover and argues for the relevance of a new form of spillover: '**social spillover**' (Niemann, 2006: 37ff). Through this concept, he tries to combine the traditional spillover concept with the socialization theory discussed in section 4.4.2 on 'Elite socialization', arguing that this new concept of social spillover can capture processes that lead to a low level of European integration: 'In contrast to early neo-functionalism, which assumed constant learning and socialization, the revisited framework departs from the presumption and is concerned with delimiting the scope of social spillover' (Niemann, 2006: 42).

Philippe Schmitter—one of the 'old' neo-functionalists—has also argued that neo-functionalism is still useful. He has even talked about the need for developing a **neo-neo-functionalism** that can conceptualize the disintegrating logics of the European integration (Schmitter, 2004; Schmitter and Lefkofridi, 2016). One of the key points in Schmitter's concept of neo-neo-functionalism is that European integration tends to develop as a consequence of crises (Schmitter and Lefkofridi, 2016). Crises can be drivers for increased integration and can even speed up integration processes, as happened after the post-2008 financial crisis. One highly relevant question is the extent to which the COVID-19 crisis will lead to increased political integration, especially in relation to health policy. This crisis has shown that the member states are sometimes left very much to themselves, as was Italy in the early months of the pandemic. This may change, although political integration on health policy has traditionally—despite the spillover effects described above in relation to antimicrobial resistance—been hindered due to what Scharpf has called constitutional asymmetry (Scharpf, 2010). Constitutional asymmetry implies that only market integration within a policy area is covered by positive integration through the creation of market-regulating rules (Schmitter and Lefkofridi, 2016), while the non-market aspect is primarily an area of national competence with low levels of political integration and European coordination. While this situation has generally been observed in relation to health policy (Clemens et al., 2014; Jensen, 2020), it is seriously challenged by the COVID-19 crisis.

In specific areas, the COVID-19 crisis has already led to increased political integration in the EU. This is the case in relation to the handling of the economic impact of COVID-19. The EU recovery plan of 2020 (Council of the European Union 14310/20) implied, for example, that the European Union would have an extended right to revenue from direct tax (on non-recycled plastic packaging waste); and that the European Union on a collective basis would borrow money to finance the recovery. This initiative was heavily debated by the member states in mid-2020 because it implied that states collectively are liable for government debt. From a neo-functionalist perspective this can be seen as a major step forward in the political integration of the EU's economic policy.

> **KEY POINTS**
>
> - Interest in neo-functionalism re-emerged in the 1990s as the theory seemed to clearly describe key dynamics in the integration process such as the Single European Act and the Single Market.
> - The role of the CJEU as a typical example of supranational governance validates the relevance of neo-functionalism as an explanatory theory.
> - In more recent contributions neo-functionalists acknowledge that European integration is not an automatic and inevitable process.
> - Social spillover explains low levels of European integration.

4.8 Conclusion

Since the first writings of Haas in the 1950s, theories of regional integration, or 'neo-functionalism' as it is more popularly called, have had their ups and downs. As a means of explaining cooperation among states in the 1960s, neo-functionalism became very popular. New forms of cooperation developed after the Second World War, especially in Europe, and these demanded new research perspectives. Neo-functionalism was able to describe and explain these developments in a way that was novel and of its time. In the period after 1945, the fashion was for grand theorizing—that is, the construction of scientific theories that would explain the 'big picture'. Nowadays, most theorists (and particularly those working on the European Union) are content to devote their energies to the generation of less ambitious **middle-range theories** (see Chapters 6 and 7) that explain only part of the process.

Focusing on the supranational aspects of the new international organizations, neo-functionalism explained cooperation using concepts such as spillover and loyalty transfer. States were expected to cooperate on economic matters to realize the economic advantages that come with increased levels of trade. This would lead to demands for political coordination across state borders and, in some cases, to the establishment of supranational institutions. Cooperation in one policy area would involve cooperation in new areas, thereby initiating an incremental process of political integration. Over time, the supranational institutions would become more and more independent and better able to formulate their own agendas, forcing the national states to delegate further competences to the supranational level. Yet, by the mid-1970s, neo-functionalism was no longer a credible position to hold. States remained key actors and it became

hard to distinguish supranational institutions from more traditional international organizations.

Supranationalism did experience a revival, however, at the beginning of the 1990s and during the 2000s. The establishment of the Single Market, the creation of the European Union at Maastricht, and its enlargement opened the door to new interest in supranational developments and institutions. The EU suddenly began to look much more like the kind of institution that Haas and others had predicted would emerge out of regional economic and political integration. But although there was some interest in neo-functionalism at this time, most of the 'new' neo-functionalists felt free to pick and choose from those elements of the theory that best suited their research agendas. Today, neo-functionalism is not the most frequently used theoretical framework. It is, however, still an approach that contributes to the understanding of how EU institutions develop and of how political integration in the EU might be explained as the unintended consequence of cooperation among countries; and by introducing the concept of spillover, neo-functionalism has contributed to the understanding of the internal dynamics that have pushed political integration forward.

QUESTIONS

1. What do neo-functionalists mean by 'political integration'?

2. How can private interest groups influence the processes of political integration?

3. According to neo-functionalist theory, what role do the supranational institutions play in the European integration process?

4. What evidence is there that 'loyalty-transfer' among the civil servants in the supranational institutions occurs?

5. Does the conduct of the Court of Justice of the European Union support neo-functionalist theory?

6. Why is it very difficult for neo-functionalism to analyse and explain: (a) the rejection of the constitution by the French and Dutch voters in the 2005 referendums; or (b) the 2016 Brexit vote in the UK?

7. Can neo-functionalism be used to explain the Treaty on Stability, Coordination and Governance?

8. How, according to neo-functionalism, will the COVID-19 crisis influence health policy development in the EU?

GUIDE TO FURTHER READING

Journal of European Public Policy (2005) 'Special issue: The disparity of European integration: revisiting neo-functionalism in honour of Ernst Haas', 12/2. A special issue of this journal with contributions from Phillip C. Schmitter, Andrew Moravcsik, Ben Rosamond, Thomas Risse, and others. This is the best recent evaluation of neo-functionalism and its contribution to the study of European integration.

 Niemann, A and Ioannou, D. (2015) 'European economic integration in times of crisis: a case of neofunctionalism?', *Journal of European Public Policy*, 22/2: 196–218. This article discusses the financial crisis using a neo-functionalist perspective.

Sandholtz, W. and Stone Sweet, A. (eds) (1998) *European Integration and Supranational Governance* (Oxford: Oxford University Press). An edited volume that develops the notion of supranational governance, drawing on aspects of neo-functionalist theory.

 Schmitter, P.C. and Lefkofridi, Z. (2016) 'Neo-Functionalism as a Theory of Disintegration', *Chinese Political Science Review*, 1, 1–29. This article discusses how crisis can influence integration processes.

Tranholm-Mikkelsen, J. (1991) 'Neo-functionalism: obstinate or obsolete? A reappraisal in the light of the new dynamism of the EC', *Millennium: Journal of International Studies*, 20/1: 1–22. This is the key reference for examining the application of neo-functionalism to the post-1985 period.

Wolfe, J. D. (2011) 'Who rules the EU? Pragmatism and power in European integration theory', *Journal of Political Power*, 4/1: 127–44. This article provides a theoretical and methodological overview of the differences between neo-functionalism and realism.

Access the online resources to take your learning and understanding further, including extra multiple-choice questions with instant feedback, web links, answer guidance to end-of-chapter questions, and updates on new developments in EU politics.

www.oup.com/he/cini-borragan7e

5

Intergovernmentalism

Michelle Cini

Chapter Contents

Reader's Guide

This chapter provides an overview of intergovernmentalist integration theory, focusing on classical, liberal, and 'newer' variants. It first introduces the basic premises and assumptions of intergovernmentalism, identifying its realist origins and the state-centrism that provides the core of the approach, before examining in more detail the specific characteristics of the classical approach associated with the work of Stanley Hoffmann. The subsequent section also examines some of the ways in which intergovernmentalist thinking has contributed to different explanations of European integration. The topics covered in this section are: confederalism; the domestic politics approach; and institutional analyses that emphasize the 'locked-in' nature of nation states within the integration process. Next, the chapter introduces liberal intergovernmentalism, an approach developed by Andrew Moravcsik, which, since the mid-1990s, has become a focal point for intergovernmentalist research and addresses. This section also identifies some of the criticisms directed at the liberal intergovernmentalist approach. The chapter ends by introducing new intergovernmentalism, the most recent intergovernmentalist approach.

5.1 Introduction

From the mid-1960s to the present day, intergovernmentalism has continued to provide a useful way of studying the European integration process. For many years, students of European integration learnt about the two competing approaches that explained (and, in some cases, predicted) the course of European integration: **neo-functionalism** (covered in Chapter 4); and intergovernmentalism (the focus of this chapter). Although this dichotomy between these two ways of understanding European integration has been supplemented by alternative approaches (see Chapters 6 and 7), intergovernmentalism—or rather contemporary variants of intergovernmentalism—continue to resonate within the mainstream academic discourse on European integration. As such, it remains a dominant paradigm for explaining European integration.

This chapter provides a general introduction to the arguments and critiques of intergovernmentalist theory. It focuses on the works of Stanley Hoffmann, whose early writings date from the 1960s, and Andrew Moravcsik, who began to make an impact on the field in the early 1990s. It also examines some of the premises and assumptions underpinning intergovernmentalist thinking. The chapter begins by addressing the question, 'What is intergovernmentalism?' It then introduces classical intergovernmentalism and its main criticisms. Hoffmann's groundbreaking insights into the phenomenon of European integration, together with critiques of his work, led to new developments in European integration theory from the 1970s onwards. Although these might not always be termed 'intergovernmentalist' in any narrow sense of the word, they are premised upon a 'state-centrism' that owes much to Hoffmann's work. Important examples of these 'variants' of intergovernmentalism highlight the confederal characteristics of the European Union; the importance of domestic politics; and a more **institutionalist** kind of research agenda that shows how states, as central actors, become 'locked into' the European integration process. The following section discusses the 'liberal intergovernmentalist' (LI) theory of European integration and addresses criticisms of this approach. The final section covers the most recent form of intergovernmentalism, new intergovernmentalism.

5.2 What is intergovernmentalism?

Intergovernmentalism provides a state-centric explanation of the European integration process (see Box 5.1). In other words, intergovernmentalism privileges the role of states and state actors within European integration. The approach is drawn from classical theories of international relations and, loosely, from realist or **neo-realist** accounts of inter-state bargaining (Pollack, 2012). Realism views international politics as the interaction of self-interested states in an anarchic environment in which no global authority is capable of securing order (Morgenthau, 1985). States are rational, unitary actors that define their interests based on an evaluation of their position in the system of states (Dunne and Schmidt, 2011). State interest is therefore primarily about survival, with other concerns, such as economic growth, of secondary importance.

Neo-realism, like realism, sees states as self-regarding actors coexisting in an anarchical system (Waltz, 1979). According to neo-realists, **regimes** are arenas for the negotiation of zero-sum agreements, with the outcomes of those negotiations shaped by the distribution of state **power** within the regime. However, neo-realists also accept that there is some potential for order through international cooperation if only as a rational means to state survival (see Axelrod, 1984; Keohane, 1988). However, states' policy preferences (or interests) will often fail to converge, meaning that any attempt to build a community *beyond the state* is likely to be fraught with difficulties and may even intensify the sense of difference among states. Neo-realists accept that international institutions are established to reduce the level of anarchy within the states system and see the European Union as an example of this kind of institution, albeit within a highly institutionalized setting (de Grieco, 1995, 1996). Their influence on intergovernmentalism is clear, even if intergovernmentalism and (neo-)realism are not one and the same thing (Church, 1996: 25).

According to intergovernmentalists, there are costs and benefits attached to involvement in European integration (or 'cooperation'). Involvement in the EU will rest on a weighing up of the pros and cons of membership, and questioning the extent to which European integration improves the **efficiency** of bargains struck among its member states. The main aim in engaging in this qualitative cost–benefit analysis is

BOX 5.1   KEY DEBATES: INTERGOVERNMENTALISM AS DESCRIPTION, THEORY, AND METHOD

In this chapter, intergovernmentalism is a theory of European integration. This means that intergovernmentalism offers a plausible explanation of regional integration (or international **cooperation**). From a normative, political theory perspective, democratic intergovernmentalism argues that the EU ought to shift decision-making to arenas where democracy is most vibrant, namely national parliaments and national public spheres (Wolkenstein, 2020; Bellamy, 2019). Intergovernmentalism may also serve as a *description* of or as a *model* of European integration. The former simply describes the current state of the EU, its institutions or policies. The latter understanding of intergovernmentalism is prescriptive, in that it *advocates* a more central role for national governments and a reduction in the role of the **supranational institutions** (the European Commission, the European Parliament, and the Court of Justice of the European Union). It might also imply the repatriation of European policies to the EU's member states.

to protect national interests. This tendency becomes especially important at times of treaty change, where inter-state negotiations shape the future direction of the Union.

Cooperation within the EU is, therefore, conservative and pragmatic. It rests on the premise that common solutions are often needed to resolve common problems. To put it another way, cooperation has nothing to do with ideology or idealism, but is founded on the rational conduct of governments as they seek to deal with the policy issues that confront them in the modern world. For intergovernmentalists, European integration is normal or even 'mundane' (O'Neill, 1996: 57) behaviour on the part of state actors. There is nothing particularly special about it, other than the highly institutionalized form it has taken in the European context. As international cooperation occurs on a variety of levels, taking many different forms, cooperation within the EU is, therefore, deemed to be only one example of a more general phenomenon. This is why intergovernmentalists are reluctant to admit that there is a European integration *process*. Rather, they see cooperation occurring in fits and starts, sometimes less cooperation, sometimes more—and not as a trend heading inexorably in one direction towards some sort of political community or federal state.

As an institutionalized form of inter-state cooperation, European integration facilitated the survival of the Western European state after 1945 and during the subsequent Cold War (see Box 5.2). It is perhaps not surprising to find, therefore, that in the early 1990s some intergovernmentalists believed that European integration would not survive the end of communism in Central and Eastern Europe (CEE) (Mearsheimer, 1990).

At the heart of intergovernmentalism lies a particular conception of state **sovereignty**. Sovereignty is a very emotive word, particularly when used in the context of EU politics. It has various meanings, holding associations with power, authority, independence, and the exercise of will. One useful definition views sovereignty as the legal capacity of national decision-makers to take decisions without being subject to external restraints; another definition sees sovereignty as the right to hold and exercise authority. However, many use the word sovereignty as little more than a synonym for independence, and this is particularly the case in public discourse (for example, when journalists or politicians use the word). This was certainly the case in the campaign that led to the UK's **Brexit** referendum in early 2016, when the theme of 'taking back control' was used as a point of reference by Leave campaigners (see Chapter 27).

Intergovernmentalists claim that the EU member states, or national governments, are the most important actors by far, and that they remain very much in control of European-level decision-making. Accordingly, European integration implies at most a pooling or sharing of sovereignty, and not a transfer of sovereignty from the national to the supranational (European) level (Keohane and Hoffmann, 1991: 277).

Intergovernmental cooperation can also involve a **delegation** of sovereignty (Pollack, 2002; Maher et al., 2009). From this perspective, intergovernmentalists accept that European integration implies a transfer of functions from the state **executive** or from the parliaments of the member states, to the European institutions—to the Commission and the Court of

BOX 5.2   KEY DEBATES: THE EUROPEAN RESCUE OF THE NATION STATE

In his seminal book *The European Rescue of the Nation State* (1992), the economic historian Alan Milward analysed European integration in the 1940s and 1950s. He argued that the European integration process 'saved', rather than undermined, the nation state. Governments at this time had many difficult problems to resolve, arising out of increased **interdependence** and increased disaffection from social actors. The successful delivery of policy programmes was a matter of survival for the states of Western Europe. European integration became a means to this end. As Rosamond (2000: 139) notes: 'The idea of integration as a progressive transfer of power away from the state managed by emerging supranational elites is given little credence by this hypothesis' (see also Chapter 6). Rather, the key actors in European integration are governmental elites.

KEY POINTS

- Intergovernmentalism has been influenced by realist and neo-realist assumptions that privilege the role of the state and national interest in explaining European integration or cooperation.

- Intergovernmentalists believe that sovereignty rests with the EU member states.

- It may be in states' interests to cooperate and to delegate functions to European-level institutions to ensure that commitments made by states are taken seriously.

- The supranational institutions are usually considered servants or agents of the member states.

Justice of the EU (CJEU) in particular, but also to the European Central Bank (ECB) in the case of monetary policy for eurozone members. They argue that national governments find it in their interest to hand over certain (regulatory) functions in order to make cooperation work more effectively—that is, to make more credible the commitments they have entered into. This emphasis on delegation colours how intergovernmentalists understand the role of the EU institutions. Rather than assuming that these institutions are capable of playing an independent or autonomous role within the European integration process, intergovernmentalists tend to see European institutions, the Commission in particular, as little more than the servants or agents of the member states. Mark Pollack makes this point when he shows how member states delegate particular functions to the Commission to reduce transaction costs (Pollack, 1997). For example, the **European Semester**, the governance architecture for socioeconomic policy coordination in the EU, incorporates an *ex ante* review by the Commission of euro area national budgets (see Chapter 22). While these institutions may be permitted a more important role in less controversial areas of policy, the functions that they perform in more sensitive policy domains, such as foreign policy, will be severely circumscribed. The European institutions that really matter are, therefore, the EU Council (of national ministers) and the **European Council** (of heads of state and government), whereas other European institutions play a more peripheral role.

5.3 Classical intergovernmentalism and its critics

Intergovernmentalism, as a theory of or approach to the study of European integration, emerged in the mid-1960s, from a critique of neo-functionalist theory (see Chapter 4) and as a reaction to assumptions that the European Community (EC) would eventually transform itself into a fully fledged federal state. By the end of the 1960s, it had become a convincing explanation of European integration, more so than the neo-functionalist orthodoxy, as it reflected more accurately, it seemed, the practice of European integration at that time. After the French President General **Charles de Gaulle**'s 'boycott' of the European institutions in mid-1965, the so-called **'empty chair' crisis**, and the signing of the Accord that came to be known as the **Luxembourg Compromise** in early 1966 (see Chapter 2), a tide turned in the history of European integration. The persistence of the national veto after 1966, instability in the international political economy, and institutional changes that privileged the Council of Ministers (now the Council of the European Union or EU Council) and institutionalized the European Council as key decision-makers within the Community all suggested the limits of supranationalism, and the continued primacy of state actors in European politics. That the Commission began to play a more cautious role after 1966, as evidenced by the period of '**Eurosclerosis**' in the years that followed, was also an important factor supporting the intergovernmental hypothesis.

It was Stanley Hoffmann who laid the foundations of the intergovernmentalist approach to European integration. Most of the state-centric variants of integration theory in and after the 1970s drew upon his work. Hoffmann's intergovernmentalism, which is referred to as 'classical intergovernmentalism' in this chapter, began by rejecting neo-functionalist theory, claiming that, in concentrating on the *process* of European integration, neo-functionalists had forgotten the *context* within which it was taking place. This not only pointed to the importance of states, but also of other factors, such as the global context. More specifically, intergovernmentalism rejected neo-functionalist claims that European integration was driven by a sort of snowball effect known as 'spillover' (see Chapter 4), arguing that the neo-functionalists' attachment to spillover was more an act of faith than based on proven facts.

There was nothing inevitable about the path of European integration from this perspective; neither was there evidence of any political will to create a federal state in Europe (O'Neill, 1996: 63). If anything, the federalist rhetoric did little more than highlight the enduring qualities of the nation state which it sought to replicate on a European scale. As for neo-functionalism, not only did it ignore what was happening outside of Europe, notably the global nature of the Cold War, but it also missed the importance of cultural differences, such as attitudes to agriculture and the land, that were continuing to influence how states perceived their interests. The neo-functionalist idea of 'the logic of integration' was contrasted with a more intergovernmentalist 'logic of diversity', which saw European integration as a dialectic of fragmentation and unity (Hoffmann, 1966). This diversity was a consequence of the unique context of internal domestic politics and of global factors (that is, the situation of the state in the international system), both of which contributed to inexorable centrifugal forces placing limits on European integration (Rosamond, 2000: 76).

Intergovernmentalism therefore offered a 'systematic contextualization' (Rosamond, 2000: 75) of the situation as it was in the mid-1960s. It was much more than just an application of realist theory to the European Community case. In the post-1945 period, nation states were dealing with regional issues in very different ways than had earlier been the case. While traditional, exclusive notions of sovereignty now seemed obsolete, and there was a blurring of the boundaries between the national state and international

organizations (Hoffmann, 1966: 908), this did not mean that nation states and national governments had lost their significance. National sovereignty and the nation state were being tamed and altered, but not superseded (Hoffmann, 1966: 910–11). While the national dimension may well have seemed less important in the immediate post-1945 period than it had in earlier times, it had not taken long for states to reassert themselves. Indeed, national states had proven themselves extremely resilient actors in international politics. As Hoffmann (1966: 863) put it: 'The nation-state is still here, and the new Jerusalem has been postponed because the nations in Western Europe have not been able to stop time and to fragment space.' The nation state was said, famously, to be 'obstinate' not 'obsolete' (Hoffmann, 1966). Even though societal changes posed serious challenges for the nation state, state governments remained powerful for two reasons: first, because they held legal sovereignty over their own territory; and second, because they possessed political legitimacy (Bache et al., 2014: 14).

Although the successes of European cooperation, its distinctive characteristics, and the possibility that it was likely to produce more than zero-sum outcomes, were not to be underestimated (Hoffmann, 1995: 4), discord over the course of the 1960s, such as over UK accession to the EEC, highlighted the *differences* between member states as much as they pointed to their *common interests*. This was an important argument, since 'preference convergence' (Keohane and Nye, 1997) (the term itself was coined later) was earlier assumed to be a prerequisite for European integration. For intergovernmentalists, the starting point for explaining European integration was the political rather than the technocratic. Whereas high politics (the political sphere) touched on national sovereignty and issues of national identity, low politics (the economic sphere) was more technocratic and seemed much less controversial. There were said to be clear boundaries between the economic integration possible in areas of low politics, such as transport, and the 'impermeable' and very 'political' domain of high politics, foreign or economic policy for example, in which integration would not occur (O'Neill, 1996: 61). While intergovernmentalists conceded that functional spillover might occur in the former, there could be no assumption that states would allow it to transfer to the latter.

Although classical intergovernmentalism was based upon realist assumptions, it differed in its concept of the state. Thus, states are more than just 'black boxes' that contain no clear substantive content; rather, they represent communities of identity and belonging. They 'are constructs in which ideas and ideals, precedents and political experiences and domestic forces and rulers all play a role' (Hoffmann, 1995: 5). Hoffmann was particularly critical of the early theorists of European integration who had adopted a simplistic and unrealistic view of how governments defined their interests: interests were not reducible to power and place alone (Hoffmann, 1995: 5), but were calculated on the basis of various historical, cultural, and indeed political concerns.

However, this early form of intergovernmentalism has been subject to various critiques, which included rejecting Hoffmann's rigid demarcation between high and low politics. Even in the 1970s, **European political cooperation** (**EPC**), the forerunner to today's European foreign policy (see Chapter 19) and an area of 'high politics', seemed to disprove this particular aspect of his theory. Subsequently, the establishment of the euro and the Common Foreign and Security Policy (CFSP)—pointed in that direction as well. Indeed, after the 1960s, even Hoffmann softened his position on this issue.

Classical intergovernmentalism has also been criticized for playing down the constraints imposed on states resulting from their increasing 'interdependence'. One example of this phenomenon is the way in which business ownership across Europe became increasingly global or multinational, especially after the 1980s. Moreover, it was argued that intergovernmentalism failed to take into account the novelty and the complexity of the European integration project. European integration was about more than just the creation of a regional regime, and bargains struck at the European level could not simply be reduced to a set of national interests (Rosamond, 2000: 79).

At this stage, intergovernmentalism was also subject to the criticism that it was not a theory in any systematic sense (Church, 1996: 26), but was rather part of an approach that dealt with the wider phenomenon of regional cooperation. As such, it was extremely influential in shaping how scholars of European integration thought about the (then) European Community and set the agenda for future research undertaken in the field of integration theory from the 1970s onwards. Thus accepting the limits of intergovernmentalism as it was constructed in the 1960s did not mean opting for a supranational theory of integration; rather,

it allowed the door to be opened to new variants of intergovernmentalism, some examples of which are dealt with in the section that follows.

KEY POINTS

- Stanley Hoffmann was the originator and key proponent of intergovernmentalism in the mid-1960s.

- Hoffmann distinguished between high and low politics, arguing that, while functional integration (or spillover) might be possible in less controversial, technical areas of public policy, states would resist any incursion into areas of high politics.

- Critics have questioned Hoffmann's use of the high/low politics distinction and his failure to take into consideration the novelty and the complexity of the European integration project.

5.4 Variants of intergovernmentalism

This section presents some examples of how classical intergovernmentalism has been supplemented and adapted since the 1960s. While setting aside for the moment the most important example of this adaptation, liberal intergovernmentalism, and its newest version, new intergovernmentalism, this section deals with confederalism, the 'domestic politics approach', and with analyses that have sought to explain how states become 'locked into' the European integration process.

5.4.1 Confederalism

As a model or framework for European integration, the idea of '**confederation**' is closely allied to intergovernmentalism. A confederation may be viewed as a particular type of intergovernmental arrangement, in which national sovereignty remains intact despite the establishment of a common institutional framework as exemplified by the agreement in 1777 of the 13 original US states to work together in the hope of creating more effective government. This could be understood as a concert of sovereign states (O'Neill, 1996: 71; Laursen, 2012). However, despite the US experience, there can be no assumption that confederation will lead ultimately to greater unity, even if some authors like to talk of a 'confederal phase' within the integration process (Taylor, 1975; Chryssochoou, 2009). Rather, confederalism implies that the EU lies somewhere 'between sovereignty and integration' (Wallace, 1982: 65).

Confederal approaches draw attention to the institutionalized nature of the European integration process, recognizing (in contrast to intergovernmentalism) its distinctiveness. Confederalism is a helpful supplement to intergovernmentalism, moving it beyond its inherent constraints, while retaining its state-centric core. There are many different ways of differentiating between confederalism and intergovernmentalism, however. Confederalism may be more likely to involve supranational or international law. Alternatively, 'a confederalist approach may be said to apply where the scope of integration is extensive ... but the level of integration is low' (Taylor, 1975: 343). It may also be characterized by a defensive posture from national governments against the further extension of the powers of supranational actors, by an interpenetration of European politics into the domestic sphere, and by an oscillation between advanced proposals for integration and retreats into national independence. Much of this argument is state-centric, assuming that the nation state is likely to be strengthened through confederation. At the same time, it adds to intergovernmentalist understandings of European integration by defining the framework within which cooperation and integration take place.

5.4.2 The domestic politics approach

In the 1970s and 1980s, an approach that focused on domestic politics and policy-making became fashionable in the field of European integration studies. Although not a theory of European integration per se, the approach was critical of intergovernmentalism's failure to capture the transnational nature of the European policy process (Church, 1996: 26) and sought, as a consequence, to focus attention on the relationship between domestic politics and EC policy-making (Bulmer, 1983), for example, on party politics, or public opinion. In this, we can identify the origins of scholarly interest in **Europeanization** (see Chapter 8). We might also see this approach as one that links classical intergovernmentalism to later state-centric approaches—and to liberal intergovernmentalism in particular (Rosamond, 2000: 76).

Proponents of the domestic politics approach argued that it is impossible to understand the European

Community without taking domestic politics into consideration. It was therefore important to identify the domestic determinants of preference formation by undertaking in-depth case studies of the European policy process. This would allow researchers to identify variations in patterns of policy-making, emphasizing the linkages between the national and supranational dimensions of European politics. Two dimensions of domestic politics were deemed to be of particular interest: policy-making structures, such as those that govern parliamentary scrutiny; and attitudes towards the EC as expressed in opinion poll data (Bulmer, 1983).

There are several elements involved in this approach, which, when taken together, provide a framework for analysing the behaviour of member states. First, the national **polity** is considered the basic unit of the EC/EU. Second, each national polity differs in its unique socio-economic characteristics, and it is these differences that shape national interests. Third, European policy is only one facet of national political activity. Fourth, the national polity lies at the juncture of national and European politics. Finally, an important lens through which one might understand these elements is that of **policy style** (Bulmer, 1983: 360). The importance of the domestic politics approach, therefore, is that it demonstrated how intergovernmentalists had failed to look in any coherent way *within* the member states when analysing the European integration process.

5.4.3 The 'locking-in' of states

Several analyses explain how states have become *locked into* the European integration process. These draw heavily on an approach to the study of federalism originating in Germany, in which 'interlocking politics' (*Politikverflechtung*) characterizes interactions between different levels of government (Risse-Kappen, 1996). While these approaches rest on state-centric premises, they move quite far beyond classical intergovernmentalism and show how European integration is about much more than inter-state bargains. In the process, they emphasize the importance of institutional factors (see Chapter 6) and show how intergovernmentalist ideas may provide a starting point from which new arguments about and analyses of the European integration process develop.

An example of this kind of approach is the 'fusion hypothesis' (Wessels, 1997). This approach rests on state-centric premises in that it sees national interests as the primary driving force of integration, but it also links integration processes to the evolution of the state. It argues that, after 1945, Western European states became increasingly responsible for the welfare of their citizens, enhancing state legitimacy in the process. For the welfare state to persist, national economies had to be strong; and in order to maintain economic growth, states had to open up their markets. This tendency led governments to rely ever more on the joint management of shared policy problems, which amounted to much more than just a pooling of sovereignties. As states became more interdependent, they lost the ability to act autonomously, blurring the lines of **accountability** and responsibility that connected citizens to the state. These trends are increasingly difficult to reverse.

Also grounded in state-centrism is an approach that draws an analogy between German federalism and the European Union. This explains how European integration has become almost irreversible because of the intense institutionalization to which it has been subject. European decision-making offers states the ability to solve problems jointly; yet the outcomes of those decisions are likely to be suboptimal in that they do not emerge from any assessment of the best available solutions, but are reached through a process of bargaining that inevitably leads to the striking of compromises. In other words, as national interests determine policy positions, creative (and rational) problem-solving is not possible (Scharpf, 1988: 255). As such, no member state is likely to be entirely satisfied by what European integration has to offer. Over time, this will contribute to the slowing down of the integration process. However, the institutionalization of the decision-making process means that retreating from integration is not an option. As such, states are trapped in a European Union from which they cannot escape, in a paradox amounting to 'frustration without disintegration and resilience without progress' (Scharpf, 1988: 256)—that is, a '**joint decision trap**'.

Finally, historical institutionalists have sought to explain how states become locked into European integration through a process of path dependence. One element in this argument is that as states integrate, future options become ever more constrained by past decisions (Pierson, 2004; see Chapter 6). The only way of escaping this integration path is when there is a dramatic break with past practice, in the form of a so-called **critical juncture**.

> **KEY POINTS**
>
> - Confederalism complements and extends intergovernmentalism by acknowledging the institutionalized character of the European Union.
> - The domestic politics approach claims that it is impossible to study European integration without looking at policy-making *within* the member states.
> - Wessels's fusion hypothesis, Scharpf's joint decision trap, and Pierson's path dependence explain how states have, over time, become locked into the European integration process.

5.5 Liberal intergovernmentalism and its critics

In 1988, the scholar, Robert Putnam, published an influential journal article in which he explored the dynamics of domestic and international politics using the metaphor of 'two-level games' (Putnam, 1988). The first game deals with how states define their policy preferences (or national interest) at home within the domestic environment; the second is played on the international stage and involves the striking of interstate bargains. The insights from this study provided a framework for analysing the myriad entanglements involved in domestic–international interactions, as well as offering a starting point for understanding European integration.

5.5.1 Liberal intergovernmentalism

Since the early 1990s, liberal intergovernmentalism (LI) has been one of the most important theoretical approaches to European integration (Moravcsik, 1998). It has become a touchstone against which all integration theory has been judged, even for those who do not agree with its assumptions, its methods, or its conclusions (Kleine and Pollack, 2018). Drawing on and developing earlier intergovernmentalist insights, it offers an approach that is much more rigorous than those of its antecedents, incorporating within it both realist and neo-liberal elements, and dealing explicitly with the interface between domestic and international politics.

LI views the European Union as a successful intergovernmental regime designed to manage economic interdependence through negotiated policy coordination and which emphasizes the importance of both the *preferences* and the *power* of states. While national politicians advance state interests that reflect domestic policy preferences, decisions made by the EU are ultimately the result of bargaining among states. Agreements are usually reached on a 'lowest common denominator' basis, with clear limits placed on the transfer of sovereignty to supranational agents. Thus '[t]he broad lines of European integration since 1955 reflect three factors: patterns of commercial advantage, the relative bargaining power of important governments, and the incentives to enhance the credibility of inter-state commitment' (Moravcsik, 1998: 3). When economic or commercial concerns converge, integration takes place.

To begin with, there are two dimensions to LI: the supply side and the demand side. Both the *demand* for cooperation, which derives from the national polity, and the *supply* of integration, arising from inter-state negotiations, are important in understanding European integration. To explain the link between demand and supply, the theory is composed of three steps, each of which is explained by a different set of factors and each of which draws on complementary theories of economic interest, relative power, and credible commitments (Moravcsik, 1998: 4).

First, from liberal theories of *national preference formation*, the theory shows how state goals can be shaped by domestic pressures and interactions, which, in turn, are often conditioned by the constraints and opportunities that derive from economic interdependence (Moravcsik, 1998). Thus, underlying societal factors provoke an international demand for cooperation. National political institutions are subject to myriad pressures from domestic interests, leading to a process of preference formation. State preferences are formed, as groups compete for the attention of government elites and these feed into inter-state negotiations. To put it another way, national policy preferences are constrained by the interests of dominant, usually economic, groups within society, whether individual companies or sectors, such as the oil industry, or powerful representative bodies. Resting on a **pluralist** understanding of state–society relations, national governments represent these interests in international forums. Thus, national interests are derived from the domestic politics of the member states and not or rarely from the state's perception of its relative position in the states system—that is,

from **geopolitical** concerns. Thus 'the vital interest behind General de Gaulle's opposition to British membership in the EC . . . was not the pursuit of French *grandeur* but the price of French wheat' (Moravcsik, 1998: 7; see Box 5.3).

Second, the supply side in LI rests on *intergovernmentalist theories of inter-state relations*, with European integration supplied by intergovernmental bargains, such as revisions to the Treaty (Moravcsik, 1998: 7). More specifically, this stage 'draws on general theories of bargaining and negotiation to argue that relative power among states is shaped above all by asymmetrical interdependence, which dictates the relative value of agreement to different governments' (Moravcsik, 1998: 7). It emphasizes the centrality of strategic bargaining among states and the importance of governmental elites in shaping inter-state relations. States are considered to be unitary actors and supranational institutions are deemed to have a very limited impact on outcomes. This generally involves a two-stage process of negotiation: first, governments must resolve the policy problems that confront them; they do this by taking decisions, and only after these decisions are taken do they try to reach agreement on institutional mechanisms that would allow them to implement them. Various bargaining strategies and techniques, such as 'coalitional alternatives to agreement'—that is, the linking of issues and threats of exclusion and inclusion—shape outcomes. A bargaining space is formed out of the amalgamation of national interests, with the final agreement determining the distribution of gains and losses. This implies a limited range of possible integration outcomes, although inter-state

> ### ▶ BOX 5.3   CASE STUDY: LI AND DE GAULLE
>
> Moravcsik sought to apply his liberal intergovernmentalism to a number of cases. One such case was that of French agricultural policy. In line with the first element of LI, Moravcsik finds that 'the vital interest behind General de Gaulle's opposition to British membership in the EC … was not the pursuit of French grandeur but the price of French wheat' (Moravcsik, 1998: 7). In other words, French policy towards Europe in the 1960s was shaped by important commercial concerns, rather than by political factors. Critics have questioned whether such a sharp distinction between de Gaulle's economic objectives and his political goals is helpful given that his policy of French *grandeur* implied the use of economic ambitions for political ends (Trachtenberg, 2006).

bargains can also lead on occasion to **positive-sum outcomes**. Governments bargain hard to gain the upper hand. The power of individual states is crucial in determining whose interests win out in the end. This means that LI focuses most of its attention on the preferences of the largest and most powerful EU states: the UK (before Brexit), France, and Germany. In stressing the points that integration *benefits* states, that states face few constraints in the EU Council, and that inter-state negotiations enhance their domestic autonomy, this part of the theory addresses the question of why governments engage in European integration when it might otherwise appear irrational to do so (Rosamond, 2000: 138).

The third stage in LI is *institutional delegation*. The argument is that international (European) institutions are set up to improve the efficiency of inter-state bargaining, reflecting the desire for 'credible commitments'. Thus, governments delegate and pool sovereignty in these institutions to secure the substantive bargains that they have made by ensuring that all parties are obliged to commit to cooperation (Moravcsik, 1998: 3–4). For example, in the case of the EU, the European institutions create linkages and compromises across issues on which decisions have been made under conditions of uncertainty and in instances in which non-compliance would be a temptation. An example of this kind of behaviour can be found in the setting of environmental standards, particularly in the context of negotiation of international environmental agreements.

In this respect, LI has been influenced by liberal institutionalism (Keohane, 1989). That theory sees institutions as ways of facilitating positive-sum bargaining ('upgrading the common interest') among states, while denying that they undermine in any way the longer-term self-interest of the member states. From this perspective, then, '[t]he entrepreneurship of supranational officials . . . tends to be futile and redundant, even sometimes counterproductive' (Moravcsik, 1998: 8).

Supplementing the core of the theory, Moravcsik has developed three extensions: first, that the EU democratic deficit is defensible, and not as severe as critics make it out to be; that the EU is a stable constitutional settlement, and not threatened with disintegration (see Box 5.4); and that the EU is a global superpower. Like the core theory, these arguments are frequently criticized in the EU literature (Kleine and Pollack, 2018).

5.5.2 Critiques of liberal intergovernmentalism

LI remains an extremely useful way in which to organize data and to construct empirical studies, based on a deductive (theory-testing) methodology. As such, it is regarded as a baseline theory of regional integration (Kleine and Pollack, 2018). At the same time, it offers a framework for understanding European integration that some scholars find hard to accept. Criticism has come from various directions, such as from constructivists, institutionalists, and, more recently, post-functionalists. In the case of the latter, LI has been criticized for failing to take on board the impact of crises and the implications of the politicization of the EU, and for viewing the European Union too optimistically (Hix, 2018; Schimmelfennig, 2019; Hooghe and Marks, 2020; see also Box 5.5). Critics direct their attention to the component parts of the theory. LI's model of preference formation has been criticized for failing to acknowledge the relevance of EU norms and rules, and for failing to acknowledge the impact of identity in driving domestic preferences. LI's bargaining theory is challenged for ignoring the deliberative

---

↘ BOX 5.4   CASE STUDY: LI AND BREXIT

Andrew Moravcsik has described Brexit as 'the exception that proves the rule' (Moravcsik 2020). In his view, the UK's departure from the EU only occurred due to the combination of a set of specific circumstances that are unlikely to be reproduced elsewhere, namely: the UK 'is the only European country where Euroskepticism attracts more than a tiny fringe of the electorate'; David Cameron's call for an unnecessary referendum; and the intrinsic bias of the first past the post system that delivered a comfortable majority for Boris Johnson in 2019 on a promise 'to get Brexit done'. The UK's departure has not weakened the EU. In fact, the EU27 were able to take a 'tough stance' during the Brexit negotiations while the UK remains dependent on the EU for market access. At the same time, the EU has managed to navigate the COVID-19 crisis and retain its international influence.

Source: Moravcsik (2020)

> ### BOX 5.5   KEY DEBATES: LI AND REPRESENTATION
>
> In a 2018 article on Liberal Intergovernmentalism (LI), which was published in a special issue of *Journal of Common Market Studies*, Simon Hix addresses the assumptions made by LI regarding representation. If LI assumptions hold, he argues, voter–government relations will lead to policy gridlock. If they do not hold, there will be a growing gap between public and elites. This insight leads Hix to suggest that LI may not be as relevant in the highly politicised world of post-2010 EU politics in which the EU has become a more salient issue for EU voters, and in which populist anti-EU parties have gained substantial support. He concludes by acknowledging that governments are nowadays more constrained by public preferences than they were in the past, and that LI's optimism is misplaced.

nature of EU decision-making, and for ignoring the importance of EU institutions as actors in the EU policy process. LI's third core element is also criticized for ignoring the way in which internal (endogenous) feedback can destabilise the EU, creating pressure for reforms, whether in the direction of more or less integration (Kleine and Pollack, 2018: 1494).

Perhaps the most frequently repeated criticism of LI is a very basic one: that it simply does not fit the facts. In other words, LI is too selective with its empirical references. It was claimed by Scharpf (1999: 165), for example, that applying the theory to cases of *intergovernmental negotiation*, in which economic integration is the main concern and in which decisions were taken on the basis of unanimous voting in the Council, will invariably confirm the theory; 'Given this focus for his attention, it is hardly surprising that Moravcsik comes to the view that the EC is primarily motivated by the aggregation and **conciliation** of national interests' (Wincott, 1995: 602). The assumption is, therefore, that, in 'harder' cases, where international negotiations are not the primary form of decision-taking and where majority voting applies, which nowadays covers most policy fields, LI may not produce such clear-cut results. The criticism is often articulated in the following way: that liberal intergovernmentalism may explain the majority of 'history-making' decisions—that is, high-profile changes of constitutional significance, which often involve treaty change and which occur through inter-state negotiations—but it is much less able to explain how the EU works in matters of day-to-day politics.

A further criticism often directed at LI is that its conception of the state is too narrow. Liberal intergovernmentalism pays little attention to the way in which the state may be disaggregated into its component parts. Critics argue that understanding how governmental positions (or preferences) are determined requires a more nuanced analysis of domestic politics. Indeed, 'in some ways it [LI] was less sophisticated

in its account of domestic politics than Hoffmann's' (Bache et al., 2014: 15). In LI, the primary determinant of government preferences is *socio-economic* interests. In practice, however, diverse influences, including those that are identity-based, are likely to impinge on national preference formation.

Another critique of LI is that the theory understates the constraints faced by national policy-makers. The case of the **Single Market** programme is often used to back up this argument. As mentioned earlier, LI plays down the role of supranational actors within the European integration process. In other words, it does not provide a full enough account of the supply side of the model when focusing solely on inter-state negotiations. As the roles of the European Commission and the CJEU are deemed relatively unimportant, if not entirely irrelevant, in terms of policy outcomes, their interests and strategies do not figure particularly strongly in LI explanations.

The LI depiction of the Commission as little more than a facilitator in respect of significant decision-making has attracted particular criticism, with numerous empirical studies claiming to show that the Commission does exercise an independent and influential decision-making role, be it as *animateur*, a policy entrepreneur, or a motor force (Nugent, 2010: 135–7). A similar point also applies to non-state 'transnational' actors, such as European firms and European interest groups. Business groups in the 1980s, for example, were particularly important in influencing the Single Market (1992) project (Cowles, 1995; Armstrong and Bulmer, 1998; see also Chapter 14).

[I]ntergovernmental theory cannot explain the activities of the key non-state actors in the 1992 process. The single market programme was not merely the result of conventional statecraft. Nor were Member States' actions predicated solely on the basis of domestically defined interest group activity, as suggested by a recent version of intergovernmentalism [LI] . . . Indeed, the story of the ERT [European Round Table of Industrialists] points to the fact that non-state actors—and in particular, multinational enterprises—also play two-level games in EC policy-making (Cowles, 1995: 521–2).

This criticism concerns not just which actors and institutions matter in the process of European decision-making, it is also about how much weight can be placed on the more formal aspects of European decision-making at the expense of the informal, 'behind the scenes' dimension. If informal politics help to shape policy outcomes, this may mean that actors who appear to be responsible for decision-taking may not really be in control. As such, the substance of inter-state negotiations may already have been framed well before **intergovernmental conferences (IGCs)** and European summits meet to take their formal decisions.

Finally, LI has been criticized for not really being a theory at all (Wincott, 1995). This assumes that a rigorous theory ought to spell out the conditions under which it might be refuted or disproved. Some critics say that liberal intergovernmentalism does not do this but engages in an act of closure on certain types of argument about European integration. As such, LI should be considered an 'approach' rather than a theory, one that brings together three existing theories (preference formation, intergovernmental bargaining, and institutional delegation) to provide a 'pre-theory' or 'analytical framework' that can be applied to the European integration process (Forster, 1998: 365). Not surprisingly, many of these criticisms about LI are contested by advocates of the theory, and not least by Andrew Moravcsik himself (see, for example, Moravcsik, 2018).

KEY POINTS

- Liberal intergovernmentalism provides an explanation of European integration based on national preference formation, inter-state bargaining, and institutional delegation.

- Liberal intergovernmentalism supplements a rich account of bargaining inside the European and EU Councils, with a concern for how national interests (or preferences) are formed from the pressures placed on governments by domestic economic interests.

- Liberal intergovernmentalism is criticized for focusing only on 'history-making decisions' (treaty change in particular), and for ignoring day-to-day politics and the multilevel character of the European Union.

5.6 New intergovernmentalism

The new intergovernmentalism is the most recent attempt to re-theorize intergovernmentalism (see Bickerton et al., 2015a). Its advocates claim that the post-Maastricht period—that is, the period after 1991—opened a new phase in European integration, which has been characterized by both constitutional stability and an unrelenting expansion of EU activity, with the latter taking the form of intensified policy co-ordination among member states. This coordination has been possible because of the deliberative and consensual quality of EU decision-making (deliberative intergovernmentalism). Where policy functions have been delegated, the traditional supranational institutions have not gained from those decisions; rather, new bodies, such as agencies, set up to meet specific functional aims have been the beneficiaries (see Chapter 7). This, proponents argue, means that integration occurs without supranationalism: an integration paradox.

This integration paradox, the authors argue, is the result of changes in both Europe's political economy, and within the domestic political arena in the EU member states. In the former, an ideational convergence around neo-liberalism, greater institutional diversity, and an unravelling of post-war compacts (on the mixed economy, for example) have opened the door to a new phase in European integration. In the former, public disaffection with politics and the rise of Euroscepticism have led to a separation of politics (at the national level) from policy-making (at the European), and the promotion of more informal decision-making by elites in the case of the latter. With member states pressing ahead with integration, the divide between integrationist leaders and sceptical publics widens, casting doubt on the sustainability of the EU (Hodson and Puetter, 2019). This too has contributed to this new European integration phase.

The new intergovernmentalism is ambitious in its attempt to explain in very broad terms the latest phase in European integration. However, to its critics it remains at best a work-in-progress. Some even suggest that it might be better to adapt liberal intergovernmentalism to a new era of EU politics, rather than set up a new theory. Schimmelfennig (2015), for example, has remained unconvinced by new intergovernmentalism, to the extent of questioning whether it is entirely new or even intergovernmental. He argues that European integration in the post-Maastricht period is not that different from the earlier period; and that the new intergovernmentalists fail to demonstrate that the changes that have taken place since the early 1990s are—other than perhaps in certain policy areas—representative of a new form of intergovernmentalism. Others, however, identify weaknesses in the new intergovernmentalism that might be corrected with some modest adjustments or re-focusing (Baird, 2017 on non-state actors; Morillas, 2020 on EU external action).

KEY POINTS

- New intergovernmentalism aims to re-theorize European integration for the post-Maastricht period.

- This approach argues that there has been a dramatic expansion of EU activity in the form of policy coordination since the early 1990s.

- New intergovernmentalism seeks to explain this contemporary characteristic of European integration: the so-called 'integration paradox'.

- Critics of the new intergovernmentalism claim that it is a work-in-progress, and that adapting liberal intergovernmentalism might be a more productive way of addressing recent developments in European integration.

5.7 Conclusion

This chapter has reviewed the theory of European integration known as 'intergovernmentalism'. It has shown how intergovernmentalist premises (and, more specifically, state-centrism) have provided the foundations for a range of theories and models that have sought to explain the nature of EU decision-making and the European integration process. A particularly important variant, liberal intergovernmentalism, became dominant in the mid-1990s, and remains a touchstone for all researchers and students of European integration to this day (Kleine and Pollack, 2018). A more recent version—new intergovernmentalism—has sought to reinvent intergovernmentalism for the post-Maastricht era.

While intergovernmentalist approaches continue to provide inspiration for many scholars of European integration, new theories have tested the resilience of intergovernmentalist arguments. Intergovernmentalism has been flexible enough to adapt, however. It has increasingly been allied to rational institutionalist approaches (Puchala, 1999; Pollack, 2012; see Chapter 6), with the latter more able to account for day-to-day policy-making, while based on many of the same premises. Moravcsik and Schimmelfennig (2009) also say that it is in line with recent research on Europeanization (see Chapter 8). Even though there are many scholars who contest the (liberal) intergovernmentalist account of European integration, no student of the integration process can claim to be well informed without an understanding of the contribution that intergovernmentalism makes to past and to current debate on the European Union.

 QUESTIONS

1. How convincing are intergovernmentalist accounts of European integration?

2. Why has liberal intergovernmentalism been so influential?

3. What value does the 'domestic politics' approach add to classical intergovernmentalism?

4. How useful a model for explaining the EU is confederalism?

5. Is classical intergovernmentalism still a relevant approach to European integration?

6. How central is the state within the process of European integration?

7. What is new in new intergovernmentalism?

8. On what grounds do you find convincing critiques of liberal intergovernmentalism?

GUIDE TO FURTHER READING

Bickerton, C. J., Hodson, D., and Puetter, U. (eds) (2015) *The New Intergovernmentalism: States and Supranational Action in the Post-Maastricht Era* (Oxford: Oxford University Press). With contributions from many experts in the field, this edited book on new intergovernmentalism reflects on both the strengths and limits of this approach.

Fabbrini, S. (2015) *Which European Union? Europe after the Euro Crisis* (Cambridge: Cambridge University Press). Although this book is not explicitly on intergovernmental theory, it offers a fascinating, broadly intergovernmentalist, analysis of the EU, emphasizing the diverse interests and visions of the EU member states which will shape the EU's future as a compound democracy.

Hoffmann, S. (1995) *The European Sisyphus: Essays on Europe 1964–1994* (Oxford: Westview Press). An excellent collection of Stanley Hoffmann's work, showing how his ideas changed (or not) over the years. Includes seminal articles published in the 1960s, which set the scene for future intergovernmentalist writings.

Moravcsik, A. (1998) *The Choice for Europe: Social Purpose and State Power from Messina to Maastricht* (London: UCL Press). The seminal liberal intergovernmentalist book, by the founder of the approach. Chapter 1, 'Theorizing European integration', both covers a critique of neo-functionalism and sets out the characteristics of LI in some detail.

Moravcsik, A. and Schimmelfennig, F. (2018) 'Liberal intergovernmentalism', in A. Wiener, T.A. Börzel, and T. Risse (eds), *European Integration Theory*, 3rd edn (Oxford: Oxford University Press), pp. 67–90. An interesting chapter on liberal intergovernmentalism, which uses migration policy and the introduction of the euro as case studies to show how LI might be applied to contemporary European issues (see Chapter 7).

Access the online resources to take your learning and understanding further, including extra multiple-choice questions with instant feedback, web links, answer guidance to end-of-chapter questions, and updates on new developments in EU politics.

www.oup.com/he/cini-borragan7e

6

Theorizing the European Union after Integration Theory

Ben Rosamond

Reader's Guide

This chapter deals with recent theoretical work on the European Union. Three broad analytical pathways that depart from the classical debate are discussed in this chapter: comparative political science; a revitalized international relations (IR); and 'critical theories'. Two additional pathways—governance and normative political theory—are considered in other chapters (see Chapters 7 and 9). This chapter discusses in turn the contribution to EU studies of comparative political science in general and new institutionalist political science in particular, the emergence of social constructivist approaches to the EU, IR's contribution to the theorization of EU external action, together with approaches from the subfield of international political economy (IPE), and a variety of critical theoretical readings of the EU. The chapter also explores how IR theories might be brought back into EU studies. The purpose of the chapter is to show how the EU still raises significant questions about the nature of authority, statehood, and the organization of the international system. These questions are doubly significant in the present period of crisis, where the issue of 'disintegration' comes to the fore.

6.1 Introduction

It is still commonplace to introduce theoretical discussion of the European Union in terms of the classical debate between **neo-functionalism** and **intergovernmentalism** (see Chapters 4 and 5). There is a rationale for continuing to explore the opposition between these two schools (see Bickerton et al., 2015a). Thinking in this way forces us to address key issues of continuity versus change in European politics.

However, recent years have witnessed concerted attempts to 'think otherwise' about the EU. This chapter deals with some of these **new approaches** (see also Chapters 7 and 9). It is worth pausing for thought to consider what 'new' might mean in this context. The term implies, after all, that some theories are old—or perhaps redundant. In particular, many scholars who offer new theoretical prospectuses tend to begin with the proposition that the classical terms of debate—as represented by the rivalry between neo-functionalism and intergovernmentalism—fail to capture adequately what is going on in the contemporary EU. This chapter is attentive to this premise and begins with a deeper discussion of its soundness as a proposition for theoretical departure.

This discussion alerts us to the importance of thinking carefully about theoretical work. Theory is not simply a self-indulgent exercise, nor can it be sidestepped by any serious student of the EU. Being conscious about the theoretical propositions chosen by authors is important because alternative readings of the EU and **European integration** follow from alternative theoretical premises. That said, writers rarely (these days at least) attempt to construct 'grand theories' of integration. Instead, since the 1970s, they have tended to build theories to aid the understanding and explanation of elements of: (a) the integration process; and (b) EU governance (so-called 'mid-range' theorizing). Even the direct descendants of neo-functionalism and intergovernmentalism have limited ambitions. For example, Sandholtz and Stone Sweet's (1998) theory of **supranational governance** explicitly 'brackets' (that is, sets aside) the origins of the EU, because the theory has no way of explaining this (see Chapter 4). By implication, that job can be left to other theories. This suggests, in turn, an approach to the analysis of politics premised on the idea that different theories can explain different parts of the same phenomenon. Moreover, Moravcsik (2001) has emphasized that his **liberal intergovernmentalism** is not intended to be a comprehensive theory of European integration, but rather a theory of intergovernmental bargaining only (see Chapter 5).

These caveats still do not bypass the objection that the old neo-functionalist–intergovernmentalist debate fails to capture highly significant attributes of the present EU. The principal objection is that 'old' theories are rooted in an outdated conception of what the EU is. However, we need to be aware that the study of the EU is not something that simply ebbs and flows with the real-world development of European integration and the evolution of the European Union—what we might call the 'external drivers' of theoretical work (Rosamond, 2007). It is also—and perhaps more predominantly—bound up with developments in social scientific fashion, or 'internal drivers'. Many scholars think about this issue in terms of theoretical 'progress'—that is, as social science in general and political science in particular 'improve' their techniques and refine their theories, so we can expect objects of study such as the European Union to be treated more rigorously than previously. The alleged consequence is that theoretical advancement delivers more robust and reliable results, thereby advancing our empirical knowledge of the EU. In contrast to this upbeat account of theoretical progress, scholars approaching the history of academic fields via the sociology of knowledge / science tend to see theoretical choices as altogether more contingent and bound up with disciplinary **power** structures, and institutional practices and norms (see Rosamond, 2016).

In short, there are two overlapping meta-debates that help us to think about the development of theory in EU studies. The first discusses whether internal (academic) or external (real world) drivers account for the changing shape of theoretical work over time. The second involves a disagreement about whether theory development follows a logic of scientific progress, or whether instead it reflects the operation of disciplinary structures that enable some kinds of work, while marginalizing others. It is worth keeping these distinctions in mind as we examine the contemporary theoretical landscape of EU studies in this chapter.

6.2 The limits of the classical debate and five ways forward

The legacies of neo-functionalism and intergovernmentalism remain intact in much current writing about integration and the European Union. Even when analysts of the EU attempt to offer an alternative point of theoretical departure, they often set their coordinates with reference to the established neo-functionalist and intergovernmentalist positions. There is always a danger that the histories and trajectories of neo-functionalism and intergovernmentalism can end up being caricatured in such accounts; suffice to say that the early texts of **integration theory** repay careful reading by present-day students. This is not only because of the obviously useful legacies of ideas such as '**spillover**', but also because it is true to say that the ways in which these 'old' theories are criticized is open to contest. Indeed, the idea that there is a convenient and rigid division between 'new' and 'old' theories is open to considerable critical scrutiny (see Haas, 2001, 2004; Rosamond, 2005, 2016; Börzel, 2006; Niemann and Schmitter, 2009).

The 'old' debate has been criticized on at least three interrelated counts (discussed in Chapters 4 and 5): its alleged inability to capture the reality of integration and the EU; its supposed entrapment in the disciplinary wilderness of international relations; and its so-called 'scientific' limitations.

It would be a mistake to think that these criticisms have been completely decisive and have ushered EU studies into a new theoretical age. Each is contested and, even where scholars agree that there is some substance in the above argument, many argue that the theoretical landscape is more nuanced and complex than many of the critics of classical theory suggest. Yet not all critiques would take the failures of neo-functionalism and intergovernmentalism to match 'reality' as a legitimate starting point. Theorists working in what is sometimes called the 'constitutive' tradition regard the relationship between theory and reality as intimate and problematic, and would choose altogether different criteria for evaluating theories than their ability to correspond to and/or predict the 'real' world (see Jackson, 2011; Adler-Nissen and Kropp, 2015).

Moreover, the dismissal of international relations (IR) as a parent discipline has been taken to task by those who suggest that what goes on within IR departments and journals bears little resemblance to the grand theorizing and state-fixated area of study depicted by the critics. In any case, it is a bold claim that overstates the extent to which the study of European integration was ever cordoned off as a sub-field of IR. The likes of Ernst Haas, Karl Deutsch, Leon Lindberg, and Philippe Schmitter studied the early communities as self-conscious (and often pioneering) exponents of the latest political science (Haas, 2001, 2004; Ruggie et al., 2005). Integration theory's most obvious connection to IR was its contribution to the emergence of international political economy (IPE), a sub-area that explicitly emphasizes the fuzziness of the boundaries between domestic politics and international relations (Katzenstein et al., 1998). Others suggest that IR theories retain a valuable place in EU studies because they act as valuable tools for understanding the global environment within which the EU operates (Hurrell and Menon, 1996; Peterson and Bomberg, 2009).

The third point—the type of theorizing involved in the 'old' debate—is less a criticism than an observation about how the study of a phenomenon (in our case, the EU) is bound up with the ebbs and flows of social science, as much as it is related to the context supplied by that phenomenon. Markus Jachtenfuchs (2001) draws a distinction between a classical phase of integration theory, during which the 'Euro-**polity**' was the **dependent variable**, and the contemporary 'governance' phase, in which the 'Euro-polity' becomes the **independent variable**. In the other words, the EU has shifted from being a phenomenon that analysts seek to explain, to become a factor that contributes to the explanation of other phenomena. This amounts to moving from asking 'Why does integration occur?' to posing the question 'What effect does integration have?'

Dissatisfaction with established modes of theorizing the EU and European integration can be the starting premise for a number of alternative theoretical projects. Within conventional political science, research has tended to go in one of two broad directions. First, those who think of the EU as a conventional political system have tended to use EU studies as a space for the application and development of some of the tools of comparative political science (see Hix, 2007). Some of the key themes from this literature are discussed in this chapter. Second, those who prefer to see the EU as a newer type of political form are more inclined to align with the burgeoning literature on governance (see Jachtenfuchs, 2007; see also Chapter 7). A further trend has been the very significant expansion of work that brings the concerns of normative political theory to bear upon the analysis of the European Union (Føllesdal, 2007). Normative political theory is the consideration, using abstract philosophical techniques, of how political systems *should* be organized. Such questions have become especially urgent in the EU context with the decline of the so-called 'permissive consensus' on integration. Until the early 1990s, runs the argument, European integration was a project that was driven and settled by elites. European mass publics were compliant with, if not overly supportive of, the process. The troubled ratification of the Maastricht Treaty (1992) set the pattern for all subsequent treaty revisions as governments across the member states encountered intense societal and parliamentary opposition to the Treaty. The emerging disconnect between elites and masses and the consequent 'politicization' of integration was an obvious source of interest for those interested in questions of legitimacy and democracy. In addition, Maastricht deepened integration significantly, with explicit moves into areas of 'high' politics such as foreign and security policy and monetary union. The Treaty also created the legal category of EU citizenship (see Chapters 9 and 15). In other words, fundamental questions of sovereignty came to the fore, together with intriguing questions of how 'post-national' citizenship might work. In short, issues of direct concern to normative political theorists were now of core concern in EU studies (see also Bellamy and Attuci, 2009; Neyer and Wiener, 2011; Eriksen and Fossum, 2012).

There has also been, as this chapter will note, something of a revival in IR work on the EU. Internal and external drivers have been equally prominent. The growth of EU external action generally, and the evolution of the Common Foreign and Security Policy (CFSP) in particular, mean that the EU is an actor in world politics, while IR itself has brought forth approaches such as constructivism, which in turn have been exported to other subfields such as EU studies. We will discuss some of the most prominent themes in this new IR literature in this chapter.

Finally, beyond conventional analyses of politics and IR sit a range of self-consciously 'critical' approaches. In so far as the growing body of feminist, Foucauldian, post-structuralist, and neo-Marxist work has a unifying theme, then it is a commitment to using social science as a force for critique, social change, and human emancipation. Again, this chapter will address some of the ideas about the EU contained in such work.

There are several points of departure for such newer theories. Among the most important are the literatures on comparative political science, governance, and normative political theory (see Table 6.1). In addition, a revival of IR scholarship in the EU and a growing body of critical theoretical work has added to the substantial wealth of contemporary theoretical work on the EU.

> **KEY POINTS**
>
> - Recent years have seen renewed interest in theorizing the EU.
>
> - Most scholars accept that there has been a significant shift towards newer styles of theoretical work.
>
> - Critics of the classical debate regard neo-functionalism and intergovernmentalism as theories that ask the wrong sorts of question about the EU.
>
> - Discussion of the obsolescence of 'old' theories raises some interesting questions about the nature and purpose of theory.

6.3 Political science, the 'new institutionalism', and the European Union

It is often argued that the term 'integration' fails to capture a great deal of what actually matters in the European Union. This is because the EU is a source of authoritative policy outputs. A range of demands and supports are fed into that policy system, which means that the EU would seem to conform to a political system as defined in the classic work of David Easton (1965). The system that produces those policy outputs is institutionalized and those well-established institutions are assigned functions—executive, legislative, bureaucratic, and judicial—that resemble the classical design of all political systems. Moreover, the EU political system is full of actors pursuing their interests and looking to secure a close correspondence between their policy preferences and policy outputs. Interest groups and even political parties are visible to the academic observer of this system. In other words, the types of actors, institutions, and processes studied by political scientists are all in place within the EU system. If this is *empirically* valid, then it would seem to be *analytically* valid to draw upon the theoretical toolkit developed to study political systems.

The analytical case for moving towards the conceptual reservoir of political science is bolstered further by the claim that treating the EU as a political system solves the notorious n = 1 problem. This describes a situation in which the object under scholarly scrutiny cannot be compared to other cases. This renders generalization beyond the case impossible (because there are no other instances of what is being studied). For many scholars, this is a point at which social science

Table 6.1 Five pathways beyond integration theory

Approach	External drivers	Internal drivers
Comparative political science (this chapter)	EU as a source of authoritative policy outputs EU as a political system with identifiable **executive**, legislative, and judicial features	Rise of **rational choice** theory The '**new institutionalism(s)**'
Governance (Chapter 7)	EU as a source of **regulation** Hybrid/incomplete EU political system Multilevel character of the EU	Theories of governance New theories of public policy-making
Normative political theory (Chapter 9)	End of the 'permissive consensus' Emergence of EU citizenship Attempts to **constitutionalize** the EU	Revival of political philosophy Development of international political theory
International relations (this chapter)	Growth of EU foreign and security policy **competence** Growth of EU external action Reappearance of 'regionalism' as a feature of world politics	Emergence of constructivist IR theory Growth of international political economy (IPE) as a subfield of IR Appearance of scholarship on the 'new regionalism'
Critical theories (this chapter)	End of the 'permissive consensus' Rise of **neo-liberalism** as the EU's dominant policy mode Crises of the EU	Feminism Development of neo-marxist and neo-Gramscian political economy Critical and Habermasian political theory Post-structuralism

is no longer possible and, for some critics of integration theory, this is precisely the situation in which EU studies found itself by the 1980s. The European Communities had developed in such a distinctive way that it was meaningless to talk about the European case as an instance of a more general phenomenon ('regional integration') (Hix, 1994). However, by redefining the EC/EU as a political system, a move that seemed to have some prima facie empirical credibility, the analyst had available not only the 200 or so functioning contemporary political systems, but also every political system in recorded human history as comparators.

The move to comparative political science as EU studies' 'feeder' discipline has spawned much research and, naturally, draws upon a wide range of political science theories (see Hix, 2007; Hix and Høyland, 2011). By the standards of regional integration schemes worldwide, the EU is heavily institutionalized. It possesses a distinctive set of **supranational institutions**, as well as a number of intergovernmental bodies. The treaties define the roles of these various institutions, as well as the ways in which they are supposed to interact. Four points are worthy of

note. First, the founders of the European Communities sought to capture their desired balance between national and supranational forces through careful institutional design. Most accept that the balance has altered over time, but the formal institutional structure of European integration has remained remarkably resilient for over six decades. Second, close observers of the EU often note the growth of distinct cultures within the various institutions. It is not only that there is a particular **modus operandi** within the Commission, but also that individual Directorates-General (DGs) of the Commission possess distinct institutional cultures. The same is true of different Council formations. Third, scholarship has revealed the existence of various informalities within the formal institutional shape of the EU. This work suggests that much that is decisive within the policy process is the consequence of regularized practices that do not have formal status within the treaties. In spite of that, these established routines are frequently defined as institutions. Fourth, much recent scholarly effort has been directed at understanding the *multilevel* character of the EU's institutionalized polity (see Chapter 7). So much of the corpus of EU studies involves the analysis of formal and informal institutions, and the impact that institutionalized practices have upon policy outcomes. At the same time as studies of the EU have multiplied in recent years, so the wider world of political science became infused with the so-called 'new institutionalism' (Hall and Taylor, 1996).

It would be a mistake to regard the new institutionalism as a single theoretical perspective. Institutionalists agree, more or less, that 'institutions matter' (see Box 6.1). Institutions contain the bias that individual agents have built into their society over time, which in turn leads to important distributional consequences. They structure political actions and outcomes rather than simply mirror social activity and rational competition among disaggregated units (Aspinwall and Schneider, 2001: 2).

Importantly, institutionalists of different hues have alternative accounts of just *how much* institutions matter. Aspinwall and Schneider (2001) think about institutional political science as a spectrum. At one end of this spectrum sits an economistic-rationalist position that sees institutions as the consequence of long-run patterns of behaviour by self-seeking agents. Institutions in this account are both modifiers of the pursuit of self-interest and a medium through which actors may conduct their transactions with greater **efficiency**. At the opposite end of the spectrum is a

sociological position where actors' interests are actually constructed through processes of institutional interaction. Hall and Taylor's (1996) landmark discussion identifies three subspecies of institutionalism: rational choice; historical; and sociological. Each of these has a presence in EU studies (see Table 6.2).

Rational choice institutionalism is the most obvious way in which rational choice approaches to politics have infiltrated EU studies (Dowding, 2000; Pollack, 2007; see Box 6.2). This is a close relative—in terms of foundational theoretical premises—of Moravcsik's liberal intergovernmentalism. Rational choice theory—perhaps the dominant (although much criticized) strand in contemporary American political science—is based on the idea that human beings are self-seeking and behave rationally and strategically. The goals of political actors are organized hierarchically. They form their preferences on the basis of their interests. Institutions are important because they act as **intervening variables**. This means that institutions do not alter preference functions, but will have an impact upon the ways in which actors pursue those preferences. Consequently, changes in the institutional rules of the game, such as the introduction of the co-decision procedure (now known as the ordinary legislative procedure, or OLP), which gave the Council and the European Parliament co-legislative power in certain areas, or which altered the voting rules within the EU Council (from

> ### ⬊ BOX 6.1   KEY DEBATES: INSTITUTIONS AND THE NEW INSTITUTIONALISM
>
> For most students of politics, 'institution' brings to mind phenomena such as the legislative, executive, and judicial branches of government—what we might think of as ongoing or embedded sets of formalities, often underwritten or codified by constitutional prescription. Early political science dealt with the study of this sort of institution. Scholars explored how such bodies operated, how they interacted, and how they supplied sets of rules that helped to account for the ways in which political systems operated. Often, such studies concluded that institutional patterns reflected the character of a country's politics. This 'old' institutionalism was criticized—especially by behaviouralists—for an overemphasis on the formal, codified aspects of politics at the expense of looking at the nitty-gritty of politics: the interaction of groups in pursuit of their interests and the basis, form, and consequences of individual and collective political behaviour. However, classical institutional studies did
>
> bequeath a concern with the impact of rules upon the behaviour of actors and thus upon political outcomes more generally. 'New' institutionalism proceeds from the axiom that 'institutions matter' as shapers of, and influences upon, actor behaviour (rather than as mere expressions of political culture). This is combined with a broader definition of 'institution' to embrace not only formal rules, but also forms of ongoing social interaction that together make up the 'compliance procedures and standard operating practices' in the political economy, to borrow Peter Hall's well-established definition (Hall, 1986: 19). Thus, from the new institutionalist vantage point, we may be talking about anything from written constitutional rules through to norms, or even collectively recognized symbols, when we speak of 'institutions'. With this in mind, it is hardly surprising that the EU has become a favoured venue for the practice of new institutionalist political science.

BOX 6.2   KEY DEBATES: RATIONAL CHOICE AND THE SCIENCE OF EU STUDIES

Supporters of rational choice institutionalism believe that this approach to the EU is able to build knowledge in a systematic way. Scholars working under the auspices of rational choice subscribe to particular methods of theory-building. This usually involves the development of models capable of generating hypotheses, which can then be subjected to confirmation or disconfirmation through exposure to hard empirical evidence. Such work relies on the deployment of assumptions and the use of **game theory** as a tool of analysis. The substantial work of Geoffrey Garrett and George Tsebelis (for example, Tsebelis, 1994; Garrett and Tsebelis, 1996) yields the counter-intuitive claim that the co-decision/OLP procedure has strengthened the EU Council at the expense of the Commission and the European Parliament. The analysis is sophisticated, but relies on the assumption that institutions' preferences are arranged along a continuum according to the amount of integration that they favour. For critics, this type of work may produce intriguing results, but it relies too much on unrealistic assumptions and describes games that bear no relation to the complex interactions that take place between EU institutions on a day-to-day basis. Another dimension to this debate is that rational choice institutionalists often advance the view that theirs is a more rigorous form of political science than that offered by either EU studies 'traditionalists' or those of a more constructivist persuasion.

unanimity to qualified majority) will induce actors to recalculate the ways in which they need to behave in order to realize their preferences.

By and large, rational choice institutionalists have been interested in how their theory develops propositions about the changing relative power of institutional actors in the policy process. Scholars of this persuasion assume that institutional actors seek policy outcomes that correspond as closely as possible to their preferences. This is why institutions are created in the first place (the so-called 'functionalist' theory of institutional design). The construction of formal models, often deploying the type of reasoning found in economic analysis, allows for empirical research on specific cases to be mapped against formal decisions. A lively debate developed within EU studies about matters such as the **agenda-setting** power of the various institutions. Another key component of the rationalist argument has been the application of 'principal–agent analysis' to EU politics. Here, self-regarding actors ('principals') find that their preferences are best served by the **delegation** of certain authoritative tasks to common institutions ('agents'). In the EU case, this approach provides powerful explanations for member states' decisions to create and assign tasks to supranational institutions such as the Commission, the Court of Justice of the EU (CJEU), and the European Central Bank (ECB) (Pollack, 2002).

For their proponents, rational choice perspectives offer rigorous foundations for the development and testing of **falsifiable hypotheses** around a series of core shared propositions. This improves knowledge in a progressive and cumulative way. Scholars work from a set of (admittedly stylized) assumptions to produce progressively improved understandings of how the EU works. For their opponents, rational choice institutionalists miss the point: their focus on formal rules leads them to ignore the various informal processes that grow up around the codified practices, but it is these informalities that better explain policy outcomes. Moreover, rational choice accounts of actor preferences tend to leave these fixed rather than

Table 6.2 The 'new institutionalisms'

Type of institutionalism	Research objective
Rational choice institutionalism	The changing relative power of institutions
Historical institutionalism	The long-term effects of institutions
Sociological institutionalism	The role of culture OR persuasion and communicative action

Source: Hall and Taylor (1996).

recognize the ways in which processes of socialization can mould interests and identities.

Historical institutionalists are interested in how institutional choices have long-term effects. Institutions are designed for particular purposes, at particular times, in particular sets of circumstances. They are assigned tasks, and in this process acquire interests and ongoing agendas. If institutions interact with one another in a decision-making process, then patterns that are constitutionally prescribed or evolve in the early lifetime of the institutions concerned may 'lock in' and also become ongoing. This lock-in means that a 'path-dependent' logic may set in. The ongoing nature of institutional interests (their continuing bureau-shaping agendas and their preference for self-preservation) means that institutions become robust and may well outlive their creators. This also means that institutions may have an impact that their creators could not have foreseen, not least because they survive to confront new circumstances and new challenges. But these new challenges are met through the prism provided by pre-existing institutions; thus the range of possible action and policy choice is constrained. Policy entrepreneurs may attempt to redesign institutions to meet current needs, but they do so in the face of institutional agendas that are locked in and which are therefore potentially difficult to reform.

Like the other two variants of institutionalism, historical institutionalism is not exclusive to EU studies. But its applications are obvious. That said, scholars use this basic template in various ways. Paul Pierson's well-known discussion of path dependency (Pierson, 1998) looks at the problem of unintended consequences. He argues that the immediate concerns of the architects of the European Communities led them, at a critical juncture, into acts of institutional design that ultimately helped to erode the capacity of national governments to control the governance of their economies. So while the intention of Western European governments of the 1950s may have been to rescue the nation state (Milward, 1992), Pierson's work suggests that the long-term consequence of their deliberations may have been to engineer precisely the reverse. The implications for research from this theoretical insight are interesting. They push students of the EU to think about policy pathways—that is, how particular EU-level competences emerge over time as a result of specific decisions. We are asked to think about how rational acts at one point in time influence rational action in the future.

Less wedded to rational actor assumptions is other historical institutionalist work such as that of Kenneth Armstrong and Simon Bulmer (1998) in their classic study of the **Single Market**. Armstrong and Bulmer are more interested in the way in which institutions can become carriers of certain ideas, values, and norms over time. Once again, we are directed to think about how such normative and ideational 'matter' is loaded into institutions at their inception. But students of the EU are also invited to explore how institutional cultures (say, of the Commission generally, or of specific DGs) impact upon all stages of the policy process, influence action and policy choice, and (perhaps) assist in the conditioning of the interests of actors.

This last comment provides a link to sociological institutionalism, a strand of literature that is closely bound up with the constructivist 'turn' in international and European studies (discussed in Section 6.4, 'Social constructivist approaches to the European Union'; see also Wiener, 2006; Checkel, 2007; Risse, 2009). It is important to note that sociological institutionalists tend to reject the other institutionalisms because of their inherent '**rationalism**'. The meaning of this term is discussed in Section 6.4, but for now it is worth remembering that sociological institutionalists/constructivists operate with a quite distinct **ontology** (that is, an underlying conception of the world). This boils down to a very particular take on the nature of actors' interests. While rational choice and (most) historical institutionalists see interests as exogenous (external) to interaction, sociological institutionalists see them as endogenous (internal). In other words, interests are not pre-set, but rather they are the product of social interaction between actors.

This leads sociological institutionalists towards a concern with two broad issues: the 'culture' of institutions; and the role of persuasion and communicative action within institutional settings (Börzel and Risse, 2000). 'Culture' is used to mean the emergence of common frames of reference, norms governing behaviour, and 'cognitive filters'. In this account, 'institutions do not simply affect the strategic calculations of individuals, as rational choice institutionalists contend, but also their most basic preferences and very identity' (Hall and Taylor, 1996: 948). With this in mind, sociological institutionalist analysis of the EU looks at the ways in which ongoing patterns of interaction and 'normal' forms of behaviour emerge within institutional settings. As one writer puts it, 'institutions have theories about themselves' (Jachtenfuchs, 1997: 47). Thus institutions contribute to actors' understandings of who they are, what their context is, and what might be the motivations of other actors. This sort of work aims to add substance to often-heard claims such as the idea that different DGs of the European Commission function in quite distinct ways. Another area in which the application of this sort of thinking seems appropriate is the investigation of whether formally intergovernmental processes such as those associated with the Common Foreign and Security Policy (CFSP) conform to established patterns of inter-state interaction, or whether they bring about new norms of exchange between the envoys of member states, thereby transforming long-established norms of inter-state politics.

The roles of communication, argument, and persuasion are seen as particularly important in these contexts. This is likely to occur in settings in which norms have been established, but these deliberative processes also contribute to the establishment of common understandings. Thus sociological institutionalists often embark upon empirical quests for so-called 'norm entrepreneurs'—'well placed individual actors ... [who] ... can often turn their individual beliefs into broader, shared understandings' (Checkel, 2001: 31). Sociological institutionalism is not simply interested in the EU level of analysis. A lot of work is being done on the interaction of national and European-level norms, and in particular the ways in which 'European' norms filter into the existing political cultures of the member states.

KEY POINTS

- The EU has become a major venue for the application of 'new institutionalist' political science and for debates between its main strands.

- Rational choice institutionalists are interested in how the relative power of actors shifts in accordance with changes in institutional rules.

- Historical institutionalists focus on the long-term implications of institutional choices made at specific points in time.

- Sociological institutionalists pay attention to the 'culture' of institutions, and the ways in which patterns of communication and persuasion operate in institutional settings.

6.4 Social constructivist approaches to the European Union

The rise of constructivism has been the big news in international relations (IR) theory over the past two decades. The work of constructivist scholars such as Alexander Wendt (1999) has come to pose a serious challenge to the established schools of IR theory. Constructivists attack formalized, **rationalist** versions of IR—that is, the **neo-realist** and neo-liberal approaches that operate with a view of the world that sees interests as materially given, which adhere to a positivistic conception of how knowledge should be gathered, and which involve a commitment to 'scientific' method, the neutrality of facts, and the existence of observable realities (S. Smith, 2001: 227). Ranged against rationalism is a range of **reflectivist** and **interpretivist** approaches—such as postmodernism and critical theory—that begin from wholly different premises.

The appeal of constructivism—or at least the type of constructivism that has entered the IR mainstream in the last decade—is that it claims to offer a middle way between rationalism and reflectivism. Constructivists such as Wendt see interests as socially constructed rather than pre-given, which means that regularities in the international system are the consequence of shared (or 'intersubjective') meanings. Constructivists are interested in how these collective understandings emerge, and how institutions constitute the interests and identities of actors. However, some authors believe that constructivism can and should share the rationalist commitment to developing knowledge through clear research programmes, refutable hypotheses, and the specification of causal mechanisms that produce regularities (see Checkel, 2007). Many—although certainly not all—IR constructivists aspire to this ambition.

Various authors occupy different positions along the continuum between rationalism and reflectivism (Christiansen et al., 2001). Moreover, the commitment to 'break bread' with rationalist theories such as liberal intergovernmentalism varies from author to author. That said, constructivists argue that they are best placed to study integration as a *process*. While intergovernmentalists recommend that the European Union be studied as an instance of inter-state bargaining and comparativists think about the EU as a political system, constructivists purport to investigate the character of the move from a bargaining **regime** to a polity. Thus, if we think about European integration as a process bound up with change, then it makes sense to draw on a meta-theoretical position that treats reality as contested and problematic. This means that constructivist-inspired work should focus on 'social ontologies and social institutions, directing research at the origin and reconstruction of identities, the impact of rules and norms, the role of language and political discourse' (Christiansen et al., 2001: 12).

More concretely, as Risse (2009) notes, constructivists are predisposed to think about how human agents interact in ways that produce structures (be they norms, institutions, shared cultural understandings, or discourses) that simultaneously shape and influence social interaction, and the possibilities for action that follow. Constructivists endeavour to understand the constitution of interests and (thus) identities. Moreover, they are interested in the ways in which institutions act as arenas for communication, deliberation, argumentation, persuasion, and socialization. Constructivists also touch base with discourse analysts (Wæver, 2009) to emphasize the power resident in the capacity to create meaning and so to frame policy choices in often non-negotiable ways.

Perhaps the best way in which to present constructivism in EU studies is to mention a few examples of what constructivists actually work on. Many are interested in how European identities emerge. So the idea of a 'European economy', a 'European security community', or '**European citizenship**' should not be read as a consequence of actors' interests changing rationally in response to external material changes, such as the onset of **globalization** or the end of the Cold War. Rather, constructivists insist that we need to investigate the ways in which these identities are constructed through the use of language, the deployment of ideas, and the establishment of norms. We also need to pay attention to the ways in which these norms and ideas are communicated, and to the processes of learning and socialization that take place among actors. 'Norms' are particularly important in the constructivist vocabulary. These are defined as 'collective expectations for the proper behaviour of actors with a given identity' (Katzenstein, 1996: 5). It is through the internalization of norms that actors acquire their identities and establish what their interests are. This is what constructivists mean when they talk about the 'constitutive effects' of norms.

The constructivist research agenda in EU studies (which has much in common with that of sociological institutionalism) also pays attention to the ways in which European-level norms, ideas, and discourses penetrate into the various national polities that make up the EU (Börzel, 2002).

KEY POINTS

- Constructivism is not a theory of integration, but a position on the nature of social reality (that is, an ontology).

- There are many constructivist approaches and significant disagreement about the compatibility of constructivism with rationalist theories.

- Constructivists are interested in European integration as a process.

- Constructivists focus in particular on questions of identity, and the ways in which European norms are established and play out within the EU institutions and the member states.

6.5 International relations and international political economy revisited

In recent years, attempts have been made to 'bring international relations (IR) back in' to the study of the European Union, of which three in particular stand out:

1. the possibility that the EU can be studied as an instance of the so-called '**new regionalism**' that has emerged in recent years across the world as (perhaps) a response to globalization;

2. the growing significance of the EU as an actor on the world stage; and

3. the attempt to locate the analysis of the EU within burgeoning debates in international political economy (IPE).

6.5.1 **The EU and the 'new' regionalism**

Regional integration—especially in the form of **free trade areas (FTAs)** and **customs unions**—is not a new phenomenon. However, the period since the mid-1980s has been characterized by the growth of many regional economic blocs in the global political economy. Among the most conspicuous are the North American Free Trade Agreement (NAFTA), Asia Pacific Economic Co-operation (APEC), and the *Mercado Común del Sur* [Southern Common Market], or Mercosur, in South America.

The most obvious explanation for the revival of regional integration is the development of globalization. Globalization is a deeply contentious topic, but is usually thought of as a combination of things such as heightened capital mobility, intensified cross-border transactions, the transnationalization of production, and the spread of neo-liberal economic policy norms—in short, the growth of market authority at the expense of formal political authority. This debate is very complex, but one line of argument is that regionalism (as represented by NAFTA or Mercosur) is the primary way in which states have responded to globalization. The move to regionalism suggests that states have seen fit to pool resources in order to recapture some of the authority that globalization has taken away—a type of collective insurance against globalization.

Debate exists over the extent to which states actually and effectively lead the creation of regional integration schemes. This is where a distinction between regionalism and regionalization is important in the literature. While regionalism describes state-led projects of institution-building among groups of countries, regionalization is a term used to capture the emergence of a de facto regional economy, propelled by the cross-border activities of economic actors,

particularly firms. The question here is whether the formal institutions of regional integration are created to deal with and regulate this emergent transnational economic space, or whether the growth of cross-border activity is stimulated by the decisions of governments. These are empirical questions at one level, but the two positions in this particular debate emerge from two different theoretical accounts of the world—one largely **state-centric** and one not.

There is also a debate in international economics about the impact of regional agreements on the global economy. All of the foregoing instances mentioned are actual or aspirant FTAs. The question is whether the creation of regional FTAs creates or diverts trade on a global scale. Put another way, it asks whether we are heading for a regionalized world (of competing regional blocs) or a globalized world. Again, such matters can be measured empirically, but theoretical intervention is needed if we are to fully understand the meaning of a term such as 'globalization'. Notice also how much of the foregoing implies a particular type of relationship between globalization and statehood, and, it should be said, between structure and agency (see Box 6.3). Alternative accounts place differential emphasis upon the structural qualities of globalization—its ability to set imperatives and to shape the behaviour of actors.

The theoretical relevance of the questions raised in the preceding paragraphs becomes especially apparent when we think about their application to the EU. Thinking theoretically, as James Rosenau and Mary Durfee (1995) point out, involves asking 'Of what is

---

BOX 6.3   KEY DEBATES: THE EU AND STATEHOOD

Much of the routine political discourse on European integration engages with the question of whether the EU is becoming a 'federal **superstate**', which, by definition, is supplanting the powers of its constituent member states. Without doubt, the EU lacks some of the classical indices of 'statehood', as it has come to be understood (not least in Europe) over the past 350 years. For example, the EU lacks fixed territorial boundaries and does not possess monopolistic control over the legitimate means of violence. It does not engage in extensive programmes of redistribution, yet it does exercise meaningful and emphatic authority over the governance of its constituent economies, and by extension over the lives of hundreds of millions of Europeans. Moreover, the presumption of many current theorists is that the EU is

sufficiently similar to national political systems to allow the deployment of the tools of normal political science and policy analysis. But statehood also has external dimensions. Thus, world politics has developed into a game played between states with the notion of 'sovereignty' as the ultimate rule. Much contemporary IR literature debates the extent to which processes such as globalization have begun to transform this system. Yet the language of statehood, international politics, sovereignty, and diplomacy remains central to world politics. We might argue that the condition for admission to the world polity remains the achievement of statehood. So, the question becomes whether the EU is being constituted and shaped by the existing world system, or whether it is contributing to a radical reshaping of world politics.

this an instance?' The 'new regionalism' literature forces us to ask whether the EU is a comparable case with, say, NAFTA. If the answer is 'yes', then the study of comparative regional *integration* is brought back into play, with the EU as one of the primary cases.

Of course, the EU is at best a deviant case of regionalism. Its longevity rules out any claim that the EU was *created* as a response to global economic upheavals in the late 1970s and early 1980s. Moreover, compared with other cases of regionalism, the EU is considerably more institutionalized and much more deeply integrated. To use the EU as a **benchmark** case against which other regional projects should be measured is clearly a fallacy. Yet at the same time the acceleration of economic integration through the **Single Market programme** and progress towards monetary union has coincided with the growth of regional projects elsewhere.

There are two suggestions as to how the field of EU studies might be reunited with the study of comparative regional integration without the EU becoming the paradigm case. The first follows Warleigh-Lack's (2006) argument that EU studies offer a rich and fertile range of ideas for scholars interested in questions of governance beyond the nation state, the interplay between domestic politics and collective institutions, and the possibilities for post-national democracy and legitimacy. The second suggested strategy involves the rediscovery of some of the neglected themes of classical integration theory, particularly neo-functionalism, in which there was an overt emphasis on the study of the requisite material and cognitive background conditions for the formation and consolidation of regional projects (see Warleigh-Lack and Rosamond, 2010).

6.5.2 The EU as an international actor

What does the EU's maturing external policy competence mean for the ways in which we might conceptualize and theorize the EU's role in world politics? In addressing this question, it is important to consider whether we can conceptualize the EU as an *actor*—that is, is the EU a discernible entity with its own capacity to act on the basis of its own interests? Certainly, the EU possesses certain formal roles in world politics and in the management of the global economy. It speaks with a common voice in international trade negotiations, and has the makings of an embryonic foreign and security policy (Smith, 2008). On the other hand,

it consists of 27 member states, all of which operate as actors within the current international system (the very phrase—'inter-national system'—connotes an order founded on the interaction of authoritative national states).

That the EU is not a state (at least in the conventional modern sense of the term) is not really in dispute (Caporaso, 1996)—but is it becoming one? If this is the case, then we might want to argue that the EU is an embryonic state writ large, formed through the gradual merger of its component member states. This might then allow us to slot the EU—as a constituent unit of the international system—into long-established theories of IR, such as **realism**. This would construe the EU as an entity seeking to advance its own interests and, particularly, to render itself secure from external threat.

However, we might be reluctant to arrive at this conclusion. The EU might appear to be a unique entity, lacking those decisive authoritative attributes normally associated with modern (supposedly sovereign) nation states. If we think about the image of the EU that is described by the literature on **multi-level governance** (see Chapter 7) and then project outwards, students of integration will be confronted with something that seems to fit very badly with conventional theories of IR (Ruggie, 1998: 173–4). Indeed, rather than trying to fit the EU into IR theory, perhaps IR theorists need to look carefully at their established theoretical toolkits if they are to properly comprehend the EU. Theories such as neoliberal institutionalism (which dominates theoretical discourse in IR, especially in the US) are built around the idea of states as the dominant units of analysis in the world system. The EU might be a freak occurrence, specific to the peculiarities of Europe, but the ways in which the boundaries between domestic and international politics have become blurred, along with the styles of governance that have evolved, may well have a much wider application.

One caveat to this is that the EU's external action takes place, whether in terms of foreign policy or commercial policy, in conditions that still respond to the rules of state-centred international politics. Thus, for the EU to acquire legitimacy and recognition as a valid actor in the system, we might hypothesize that it has to conform to the rules of that system; this, in turn, would create pressures for the EU to become state-like. Therefore, the paradox is that while the EU may appear to transcend the international system, it is still in meaningful ways constituted (as constructivists would put it) by the norms of that very system.

6.5.3 **The EU and international political economy**

International political economy (IPE) is a well-established field of inquiry that explores the relationship between political and economic processes, and between states, markets, and international institutions in the establishment, maintenance, and transformation of world order. International political economy has been the venue for intense debate about the conditions under which liberal economic orders rise and fall. Economic order over the past 200 years is often depicted as vacillating between periods of economic openness (during which free trade ideology is underpinned by functioning international monetary institutions) and periods of growing protectionism, rising economic nationalism, and the spawning of international economic rivalries. Within IPE, several explanations are offered for the rise and decline of open liberal orders. The most popular focuses on state power, with the argument that liberal international trading and monetary orders are possible only when sponsored and underwritten by a hegemonic state. A second explanation focuses on the presence or absence of international institutions to create systems of rules for a market-based order. Neo-realists acknowledge that states will create cooperative institutions from time to time but point out that some states will benefit more than others from the existence of the institution. So even if every state is benefiting from the arrangements, the fact that some states are accumulating more power means that those states losing out in this pattern of 'relative gains' have a substantial incentive to defect from the institution. Neo-liberals, on the other hand, countenance the possibility that institutions can deliver 'absolute gains', which means that institutionalized **cooperation** will not exaggerate power asymmetries. Moreover, neo-liberals see institutions as places where relations of trust between states can be augmented and where the **transaction costs** associated with international interaction can be minimized. Neo-realists see a world in which the structural condition of 'anarchy' (the absence of authority beyond the state) cannot be overcome, whereas neo-liberals imagine the gradual replacement of anarchy by a rule-bound and (increasingly pacific) market order overseen by established institutions.

A third type of explanation emphasizes the power of ideas. From this vantage point, liberal orders emerge and consolidate because of the widespread acceptance of liberal narratives of how to organize the relationship between state, society, and market both domestically and internationally. For example, states come to believe in the technical and normative propriety of liberal free trade ideas. This means that both (a) the claim that allocative efficiency is best achieved by countries minimizing tariff barriers and specializing production in areas of comparative advantage, *and* (b) the moral case that free trade is ethically superior to other economic doctrines, become more or less commonsensical. The fall of liberal orders is associated with the increasing persuasiveness of other sets of ideas—in the twentieth century, left-wing and right-wing variants of the idea that national economic welfare should prevail over liberal notions of the universality of the market.

A fourth type of IPE explanation examines the relationship between economic order and domestic social purpose. In his famous account of the nineteenth and twentieth centuries written in 1944, Polanyi (2001) held that the successful rise of the doctrine of the 'self-regulating market' in the 1800s had created a situation in which society was increasingly subordinate to the market (rather than the market serving domestically negotiated social purposes). Polanyi saw such a situation as unsustainable and insisted that society would react in a counter-movement to the rise of the self-regulating market. Thus, he was able to explain increasing protectionism in the latter part of the nineteenth century and concrete governing projects—such as social democracy, communism, and fascism—in the twentieth century as instances of such societal counter-movements. This type of analysis inspired Ruggie's (1982) description of the post-war international order as one of '**embedded liberalism**'—a compromise under which the (desirable) goal of global economic liberalization was tempered by allowing governments very significant domestic policy autonomy. The product of this compromise was a regime known as the **Keynesian** welfare state, which was able to service domestic social purposes much more effectively.

How do these debates relate to the EU? The key to understanding the relevance of these IPE debates to European integration is to recognize that one of the main ways in which to read the EU is as a sustained project of liberal market-making. This means that the four IPE discussions just outlined can be applied to the EU in two broad ways. The first simply tries to understand the origins and **sustainability** of a pan-European liberal market order sitting above, yet feeding from and also shaping, the national economies of European states. The second revisits the question about the relationship between the creation of a distinctively European economic order, on the one hand, and the project of global market liberalization ('globalization'), on the other.

So, if we begin with the question of **hegemony**, IPE debates immediately force scholars to think about whether the construction of the European Single Market is dependent on a particular configuration of state power—both internally and globally. The status and importance of Germany as an internal hegemon and the USA as an external hegemon are obvious follow-up questions here, but the key from this perspective is to understand how much European **market integration** relies upon a permissive environment in which the most powerful states are prepared to bear the costs of maintaining liberal order.

In terms of debates about institutions, there are at least two lines of enquiry suggested by IPE debates. The first is to understand whether the EU is a durable institutional order. This, of course, is an especially pertinent question in times of economic crisis during which states might be expected to draw back from international commitments to liberalize markets and during which relative, rather than absolute, gains might become more visible. The second (following also from some strands of the new institutionalism) is to assess the degree to which institutions shape the conditions of possibility for addressing new challenges. A good example here is the financial crisis that has been affecting the EU in general and the **euro area** in particular since 2008. Did the **eurozone**'s intergovernmental decision rules hamper the search for effective solutions to the crisis? To what extent are solutions premised on austerity budgeting in debtor states (notably the so-called PIIGS group—Portugal, Ireland, Italy, Greece, and Spain) and the installation of technocratic governments direct consequences of institutional design choices that date back to Maastricht? To what extent has the drift of both EU decision-making in general and eurozone governance in particular facilitated the pursuit of neo-liberal policies (see Chapter 26)?

This last point bridges two questions about the relationship between the EU and the influence of certain economic ideas and particular conceptions of the economy. As we will note in Section 6.6, 'Critical theories and the European Union', a number of critical political economists have suggested that the EU represents a quasi-state form that is particularly useful for the '**constitutionalization**' of neo-liberal policy frameworks (Gill, 1998). This position would suggest that the institutionalization of European integration has been closely related to, if not fundamentally determined by, the growing legitimacy of neo-liberal ideas about the technical propriety and normative appropriateness of a free market order with minimal capacity for public authority to develop either welfare institutions or social policies to compensate for the effects of markets (Scharpf, 2002). This raises an interesting debate regarding whether the EU is ineluctably neo-liberal in character or whether it contains the potential for both market-making and market correction (see Jabko, 2006).

This type of debate is directly related to the final IPE debate mentioned here: the relationship between the construction of market orders and social purpose. Over the past 30 years, much official EU policy discourse has asserted that there is a 'social dimension' to market integration, that the EU embodies something called the 'European social model', and that the EU, both internally and externally, exists for the purpose of 'managing globalization'. While some analysts have broadly endorsed the idea that the EU is more than a crude institutional device for promoting the subordination of European society to the market (for example, Caporaso and Tarrow, 2009), there are interesting questions to be asked about how precisely the EU manages to 'embed' itself within European social purpose, especially given the problem of the **democratic deficit** (see Chapter 9). At the same time, there is an influential line of argument that insists that the EU should do no more than create the conditions for a free market order. This normative position is central to claims about the EU's status as a '**regulatory state**' (Majone, 2009). Moreover, it is the EU's status as a market regulator that spills over most conspicuously into the global political economy beyond Europe (Damro, 2012). So, the question of whether the EU represents a counterweight to the spread of neo-liberal market discipline is not only localized to Europe. If the EU is a major source of global market rules, or at least a major player in the negotiation of those rules, then it is difficult to study IPE and think about the world though the conceptual frames that it provides without bringing the EU squarely into the analytical frame.

KEY POINTS

- Much recent conceptual thinking in IR has been directed towards the analysis of the growth of regionalism in the global political economy, of which the EU may be a (peculiar) instance.

- Also important is recent thinking that challenges the state-centric vision of the world that has characterized much mainstream IR theory.

- The particular character of the EU as a presence in the global system confronts this traditional imagery by pointing to a number of ways in which structures of authority and patterns of politics may be changing.

- The important subfield of IPE raises a series of questions about the politics of international market orders which are of direct relevance for discussions of the EU.

6.6 Critical theories and the European Union

The term 'critical theories' is used here as an umbrella term to gather together some important reflections about 'alternative' or non-mainstream approaches to the European Union. We need to use the term with caution, since it does have a precise meaning in the history of ideas. The term is most associated with the neo-Marxist **Frankfurt School** of social theory. In one of the key founding texts of the Frankfurt School originally published in 1937, Max Horkheimer (1982) talked about 'critical theory' as a self-conscious attempt to theorize, in a non-dogmatic way, the conditions for human emancipation. Built into critical theory from the start, then, is a very clear commitment to unravelling the contradictions and injustices of the present social order, combined with an equally clear dedication to the pursuit of human freedom. This, of course, yields a distinctive understanding of the nature and purpose of social science, and one that is very different from most of the approaches to political analysis discussed in this and the previous two chapters. The critical theoretical position tends to see conventional social science as bound up with the object that it seeks to analyse and demystify. Modern economic theory, for example, is held to be complicit in the perpetuation of power structures. Robert Cox makes this point very effectively in a much-cited essay in which he writes that '[t]heory is always for someone and some purpose . . . there is no such thing as a theory in itself, divorced

from a standpoint in time and space' (Cox, 1981: 128). Cox goes on to distinguish between two types of theory: 'problem-solving'; and 'critical'. The former is the everyday matter of most social science. It consists of finding solutions to puzzles that are set by overarching and largely unquestioned frameworks for understanding social reality and social order. Such work, at a fundamental level, does not think about the possibilities for social transformation. It thereby contributes to the reproduction of existing social order. Thinking about EU studies in light of Cox's discussion, then, it is very likely that neo-functionalism, intergovernmentalism, comparative political science, a good portion of governance theory, much contemporary international relations (IR) and international political economy (IPE), and even a good chunk of normative political theory would be placed in the 'problem-solving' category. This point has been made forcefully by Ryner (2012) who asks why EU studies failed to anticipate the debilitating effects of the financial crisis. The answer, argues Ryner, lies in what he calls the 'orthodox codes' of integration theory. Key to these is the presumption that integration—whether economic, political, or social—is an expression of rationality and progress. This tendency does not rule out significant disagreement between theories about whether this promise will be realized (this is the essence of the debate between neo-functionalists and intergovernmentalists). But it also means that EU studies as a field (often separated into different disciplinary clusters) suffers from serious blind spots that prevent it from treating European integration in relation to the broader trajectories of capitalism and the social forces that both constitute and contest power structures in the political economy of the EU.

In contrast, for Cox, 'critical theory' does not take for granted the prevailing social order as if it were fixed. Indeed, the task of critical theory is to theorize the possibilities for change. A key step towards that goal is the realization that all social theories—even those purporting to be value-free and 'scientific'—emerge from and seek to reinforce particular perspectives, and, as such, can be tools of the powerful. One of the things to look for from a broadly critical theoretical perspective is silences in conventional academic work: what is *not* discussed, and why is it not discussed? (Manners and Whitman, 2016). An additional point, noted by Manners (2007), is the question of where to look for non-mainstream or critical work. If EU studies journals and book series are responsible for establishing, policing, and reproducing orthodox 'problem-solving' work, then we should hardly expect to find heterodox, critical work routinely showing up in such outlets.

In so far as it is possible to classify non-orthodox or critical work in EU studies, it seems to cluster around four broad approaches, all of which tend to begin by noting a missing component of the standard debate in EU studies. First, feminists have drawn attention to the highly gendered nature of EU theoretical and policy discourses. Kronsell's (2005) critique of integration theory provides a very good illustration of the extent to which standard political science approaches screen out gender relations from their analysis. The point is not simply to examine things such as the policy implications of European integration for gender equality (although that is very important, not least in the context of the UK's recent exit from the EU—see Guerrina and Masselot, 2018). A feminist-inspired reconstruction of EU studies must also think about the ways in which gendered practices are sustained and reproduced within both EU policy discourses and the academic analysis of EU politics (see also Locher and Prügl, 2009). The conception of politics that underpins most accounts of integration reduces the political to what happens in the public domain of the state. As such, it excludes most of those often private sites that feminists have identified as crucial to the practice of power relations. Moreover, most conventional political science theories rest upon heavily masculinist conceptions of rationality. As such, political science theories are actually affirming the gendered self-narrative of public institutions by assuming that they operate according to this very particular conception of rationality.

Second, there have been long-standing Marxist analyses of the EU. Marxists of various kinds insist on locating the EU's development within a broader analysis of the dynamics of capitalism. The earliest Marxist analyses of European integration understood the evolution of supranational institutions as a redesign of the capitalist state to take account of the changing nature of European relations of production. Thus Mandel (1970) saw European-level institutions as central to the process of capital concentration in Europe. Likewise, Cocks (1980) understood integration as crucial to the dynamic development of capitalist productive forces. More recently, neo-Gramscians (inspired by the Italian Marxist Antonio Gramsci) have been interested in the ways in which the EU has drifted towards treaty commitments and policy regimes (such as in corporate governance or competition policy) in which neo-liberal frameworks prevail and in which popular **accountability** is weak. Gill (1998) sees the EU as part and parcel of a global trend to lock in and constitutionalize neo-liberal conceptions of market society.

Third, writers inspired by Michel Foucault tend to think about the EU as a particular expression of liberal rationalities of government that seek to define the human subject in particular ways. This is interesting in the European context because the development of the Single Market regime requires the definition of the typical transnational human agent that inhabits and moves across that market space. Parker (2012) suggests that there are two potentially contradictory versions of the liberal European subject imagined in the treaties: one is a pure market actor—a 'subject of interest'—using European transnational space as an arena for economic transaction; the other is a political actor, a transnational citizen—a 'subject of right'—whose **cosmopolitanism** extends well beyond the arena of market transaction. Foucauldians are also interested in how governing actors, as part of the governing process, contribute to the statistical and discursive construction of the space over which they exercise authority. From this point of view, the outputs of **Eurostat** and **Eurobarometer** are not simply neutral data, but active constructions of Europe and Europeans designed to render the EU space governable from the European level.

Finally, post-structuralists (a category that usually embraces Foucauldians as well) have focused on the importance of linguistic constructions of Europe and its others, and the ways in which the supposed removal of borders of one kind is often accompanied by the imposition of bordering practices of other kinds. Diez (1999), for example, shows how the academic efforts trying to define the EU are not merely analytical moves, but active interventions in developing widespread understandings of Europe in wider political debates. Walters (2004) engages in a radical rethink of the EU's external borders—which we might think of straightforwardly as the point at which the EU ends and other jurisdictions begin—as objects of different types of governing strategy. As with all post-structuralist work, the emphasis is on problematizing a facet of the social world that may appear to be unambiguous and perhaps of little academic interest, and on showing how that facet (in this case, borders) can be rendered intelligible in different ways.

KEY POINTS

- A wide range of so-called critical theoretical traditions have been applied to the study of the EU.

- These include feminist, Marxist, Foucauldian, and post-structuralist perspectives.

- Critical theories of this kind point to the limited problem-solving qualities of conventional theory.

- They see a close relationship between orthodox academic work and the reproduction of power relations.

6.7 Conclusion

The revival of interest in theory in EU studies has occurred within the context of some serious thinking about the role of theory in political science. Some of the 'new' theories discussed in this chapter have emerged from a concern to render theoretical work more rigorously 'scientific'. Other approaches have emerged from positions that explicitly challenge the positivist mainstream in social science. Other theorists still—notably certain constructivists—try to occupy a middle position between positivism and reflectivism. These debates have begun to intrude into EU studies and have been played out more extensively in the broader international relations (IR) literature.

Theoretical reflection and debate simply bring out into the open assumptions that reside in any empirical discussion of the European Union. Alternative theories work from different accounts of social reality and sometimes lead to quite different strategies for acquiring valid knowledge about that world (Jackson, 2011). This translates eventually into a set of disagreements about fundamental matters: what sort of entity is the EU and how should it be studied?

Much of the 'new' theoretical work introduced in this chapter represents a self-conscious departure from thinking about the EU in terms of 'integration'. Its status as a supplier of authoritative policy outputs suggests that the toolkit of political science and policy analysis might be useful. At the same time, however, the fact that the EU is not a state as conventionally understood poses all sorts of challenges to those seeking to understand not only European integration, but also the nature of world order in the early twenty-first century. The EU may offer a clear indication of what a 'denationalized' world order might look like. It sits between nation states and the international system, and arguably transforms both through its very existence.

Nevertheless, we are now at a point where many see the EU as facing some sort of existential crisis. This is partly to do with the coincidence of several serious individual crises—such as those that have recently arisen as a consequence of the COVID-19 pandemic, and which earlier emerged in the eurozone and because of the governance of refugee flows into the EU—as well as the decision taken by one member state (the UK) to leave the EU. This raises two important questions that every student of the EU needs to consider. First, do our existing political science theories blind us to the full scope of these crises? Do they contain in-built assumptions about institutional continuity and resistance that yield both a complacency about the dangers facing the union and a neglect of the breakdown of governing norms that have prevailed in European integration for decades (Joerges and Kreuder-Sonnen, 2017)? The second question is whether it has now become necessary to develop a theory of disintegration (Jones, 2018; see also Chapter 29). 'Disintegration' implies the reversal of integration, although perhaps it needs to be best understood in terms of processes and tendencies that work against integrative processes and tendencies. The irony might be that to build such a theory successfully, scholars might well need to bring the concept of integration back in from the cold.

The facts that the EU is multidimensional, that integration is uneven, that the EU is faced with countervailing disintegrative tendencies and that EU governance is composed of multiple, coexisting policy modes all force us to think carefully about how the nature of authority is changing. The trick—as employers of the 'multilevel governance' metaphor remind us (see Chapter 7)—is to think about the EU as part and parcel of this changing pattern of governance. To treat the EU as a political system 'above' national political systems ignores the complex interpenetration of the domestic and the supranational in contemporary Europe. The task of theories—whether drawn from the formal disciplinary domains of 'international relations' or 'political science'—is to offer ways of organizing our thoughts about what is going on in this context. We might continue to be confused about the complexity of the EU, but the present vibrant theoretical culture in EU studies at least gives us a chance of being confused in a reasonably sophisticated way.

QUESTIONS

1. Is it fair to say that comparative politics provides a better disciplinary homeland for EU studies than international relations?

2. Can there be a single institutionalist research agenda in EU studies?

3. What added value do social constructivists bring to the study of the EU?

4. How might we go about theorizing the EU's role in the world?

5. To what extent is it possible to compare the EU with other instances of 'regionalism' in the global political economy?

6. How can we explain conventional integration theory's silence about gender?

7. How have the post-2008 global financial crisis and the subsequent euro crisis challenged standard theoretical approaches to European integration?

8. Do recent developments in the European Union imply that we need to develop a theory of disintegration? What would such a theory look like?

GUIDE TO FURTHER READING

Christiansen, T., Jørgensen, K. E., and Wiener, A. (eds) (2001) *The Social Construction of Europe* (London: Sage). A collection of constructivist-inspired readings of aspects of European integration, this contains critical responses and a notable late essay by Ernst Haas, the founder of neo-functionalism.

Cini, M. and Bourne, A. K. (eds) (2006) *Palgrave Advances in European Union Studies* (Basingstoke: Palgrave Macmillan). A collection on the state of the art in EU studies, with numerous theoretical insights.

Rosamond, B. (2000) *Theories of European Integration* (Basingstoke: Palgrave). A critical discussion of past and present theories of integration.

Saurugger, S. (2014) *Theoretical Approaches to European Integration* (London: Palgrave Macmillan). An up-to-date and thorough discussion of the theoretical landscape in EU studies.

Wiener, A. and Diez, T. (eds) (2009) *European Integration Theory*, 2nd edn (Oxford: Oxford University Press). Practitioners of a wide variety of theoretical perspectives discuss and apply their approaches to the EU.

Access the online resources to take your learning and understanding further, including extra multiple-choice questions with instant feedback, web links, answer guidance to end-of-chapter questions, and updates on new developments in EU politics.

www.oup.com/he/cini-borragan7e

7

Governance in the European Union

Thomas Christiansen

Chapter Contents

Reader's Guide

This chapter provides an overview of the 'governance turn' in the study of European integration. Opening with a discussion of the reasons why governance as a concept and as a practice has become so prevalent in Europe, the chapter goes on to discuss the various ways in which the governance approach has evolved. Two strands of this literature—'multilevel governance' and the 'regulatory state'—are examined in greater detail here. The chapter then introduces some of the important normative debates to which the 'governance turn' has given rise, before concluding with some observations about the relevance of the governance approach in the current phase of European integration.

7.1 Introduction

The concept of 'governance' has become ubiquitous over the past couple of decades. Looking at European Union politics, in particular, in terms of *governance*— that is, as a way of governing that does not assume the presence of a traditional, hierarchical *government* at the helm of the **polity**—is attractive from a conceptual point of view, not least because it promises a systematic way of studying the European Union (EU) that recognizes the particularities of the European construction. At the same time, as a concept, governance has shown itself to be rather open and flexible, facilitating a wide variety of usages. Taking as its starting point a rather vague agreement on what governance is *not*, it has been possible for scholars to find numerous applications for the governance concept in empirical research.

Beyond the academic community, the idea of governance also has political appeal in allowing policy-makers to talk about EU decision-making without invoking the idea that Europe is in the process of becoming a state (if not a '**superstate**'). The succession of crises that the EU experienced in the 2010s and early 2020s, requiring in their management the close cooperation of policy-makers at the national and European levels, of political and bureaucratic elites, and of the public and the private sector, has further enhanced the attraction of a concept that emphasizes the inclusive and non-hierarchical dimension of European Union decision-making.

At the same time, governance has also come to typify the de-politicized and technocratic aspects of EU policy-making often criticized by **Eurosceptics** and populists. As a result, talk of 'European governance' and the use of the governance concept has become extremely widespread, spawning a vast literature of policy papers, scholarly articles, and books on the subject. But the extensive and somewhat inflationary application of the concept has itself become a problem. It is applied to an increasingly broad range of phenomena and its diverse usage across different communities of scholars makes it difficult to identify what 'governance' seeks to describe (Kohler-Koch and Rittberger, 2009).

7.2 Conceptualizing governance in the European Union

In his seminal article, Jachtenfuchs (2001: 245) discussed the 'governance approach to European integration' in juxtaposition to 'classical **integration theory**' (see Chapters 4, 5, and 6). The governance approach, in this perspective, is distinctive because it treats the Euro-polity as an independent, not (as 'classical' theories have done) as a **dependent variable**. In other words, those studying governance are more interested in what the European Union does, rather than how the EU has come about. In charting the conceptual roots of the approach, Jachtenfuchs identified, inter alia, network governance, regulatory politics, and **Europeanization** research (see Chapter 8) as influential contributions to the governance literature.

Other authors have helped to clarify what governance is (see Box 7.1). Rhodes (1996: 652) defined governance as 'self-organising, inter-organisational networks

---

⇘ BOX 7.1   BACKGROUND: DEFINITIONS OF 'GOVERNANCE'

(European) Governance	'Self-organising, inter-organisational networks [which] complement markets and hierarchies as governing structures for authoritatively allocating resources and exercising control and coordination' (Rhodes, 1996: 652)
	'The development of governing styles in which boundaries between and within public and private sectors have become blurred [and a] focus on governing mechanisms which do not rest on recourse to the authority and sanctions of government' (Stoker, 1998: 17)
	'The intentional regulation of social relationships and the underlying conflicts by reliable and durable means and institutions, instead of the direct use of power and violence' (Jachtenfuchs, 2001: 246)
	'A process and a state whereby public and private actors engage in the intentional regulation of societal relationships and conflicts [and which] denotes the participation of public and private actors, as well as non-hierarchical forms of decision making' (Kohler-Koch and Rittberger, 2006: 28)
Multilevel governance	'The dispersion of authority to multi-task, territorially mutually exclusive jurisdictions in a relatively stable system with limited Jurisdictional levels and a limited number of units [as well as the presence of] specialized, territorially overlapping jurisdictions in a relatively flexible, non-tiered system with a large number of jurisdictions' (Hooghe and Marks, 2001a: 1)
Regulatory state	'Reliance on regulation—rather than public ownership, planning or centralised administration—characterizes the methods of the regulatory state' (Majone, 1994: 77)
	'Relies on extensive delegation of powers to independent institutions: regulatory agencies or commissions, but also the judiciary' (Majone, 1999:1)

[which] complement markets and hierarchies as governing structures for authoritatively allocating resources and exercising control and coordination'. Stoker (1998: 17) reminded us that while governance is seen increasingly in opposition to government, it does actually perform the same functions, 'creating the conditions for ordered rule and collective action'. This implies that its distinctive focus is not on outputs, as such, but on the *process* of achieving those outputs. Hix (1998: 343), in his important contribution to the debate, pointed out that the 'new governance conception of the EU emphasises the informal nature of the policy process, the non-hierarchical structure of the institutions and the non-**redistributive** nature of policy outputs'.

From Box 7.1 we can see that most authors identify as important the role of non-hierarchical networks; regulation rather than redistribution in policy-making; and the use of new instruments and procedures. However, contributors to the governance debate often privilege one of these aspects over the others and, as a result, the governance literature has mushroomed in a number of different directions. The reliance on, and relation to, research on **policy networks** and **epistemic communities** has been particularly strong (see, for example, Börzel, 1997; Zito, 2001; Knill and Tosun, 2009; Faleg, 2012).

Building on such insights, the governance approach has also been used to explore the way in which policy networks in the EU have become institutionalized, whether through committee structures (Christiansen and Kirchner, 2000) or through the growing number of regulatory agencies (Coen and Thatcher, 2007; Trondal and Jeppesen, 2008; Dehousse et al., 2010; Groenleer et al., 2010; Wonka and Rittberger, 2011). Others have focused on the informal dimension of governance (Christiansen and Piattoni, 2004; Kleine, 2013).

At the same time, governance research has also increasingly 'drilled down' into the specifics of particular sectors or policy fields. See, for example, the work done on European environmental governance (Lenschow, 1999; von Homeyer, 2004), on EU economic governance (Puetter, 2012), or on EU external governance (Lavenex, 2004; Schimmelfennig and Wagner, 2004). While this proliferation of sector-specific applications demonstrates the value of a governance perspective in guiding research in a multitude of different arenas, it contradicts the expectations of Jachtenfuchs (2001), for whom the governance approach was a welcome departure from the fragmentation of policy studies that had characterized EU research in the 1970s and 1980s.

Matters are somewhat complicated by the fact that one of the first and most important contributions on '**supranational governance**' (Sandholtz and Stone Sweet, 1997, 1999) did not depart from the use of traditional concepts and debates. Indeed, Sandholtz and Stone Sweet's theory positioned itself within the established theoretical arena of **intergovernmentalism** and **neo-functionalism**. Their main contribution was to re-evaluate the role of **supranational institutions** in the integration process, and in particular to emphasize the importance of judicial rule-making as one of the key drivers of this process.

What this example demonstrates is that, with respect to the expanding field of governance research, it is becoming increasingly difficult to identify it as a single, coherent approach. Beyond agreement on the basic elements of what constitutes governance (and what it is not), the selective focus of individual authors means that governance denotes rather different things to different people. Arguably, this suggests that the different strands of governance research deserve, or even require, their own distinctive label in order to maintain analytical clarity. An exercise in coming to grips with the way in which the concept of governance has been used to study the EU therefore needs to start by distinguishing some of the different usages of this concept.

It is possible to identify three approaches that have been especially important:

- the *multilevel governance approach*, which emphasizes the nature of EU policy-making as involving a multiplicity of actors on a variety of territorial levels beyond the nation state;

- the *new governance approach (or agenda)*, which views the EU as a 'regulatory state' using **non-majoritarian** decision-making to engage in problem-solving; and

- the study of *new modes of governance*, drawing on the use of non-binding instruments to make policies at the European level (with the open method of coordination, or OMC, as a prime example).

Each of these understandings of governance takes the view that there is something fundamentally 'new' in the way in which the EU operates that requires a departure from traditional approaches. As such, their application in the study of European integration has mainly been driven by external factors—that is, by perceived changes in the empirical object of study, rather than (internal) developments within integration theory (see also Chapter 6). A common feature of these governance approaches is their emphasis on non-hierarchical networks as a key aspect of EU policy-making and of the EU as a whole. The presence of such policy networks, bringing together EU officials, national administrators and regulators, business interests, non-governmental organization (NGO) representatives, and other **stakeholders**, is analytically relevant, because networks 'cut across' the formal boundaries that exist between institutions, territorial levels, and the public and private spheres.

However, despite such commonalities, there are also important differences within this field; these, however, are in danger of being overlooked. One difference lies in which 'classical' theory is being critiqued. For example, multilevel governance is best seen as part of the more established integration theory debate, and in particular as a response to the dominance of **liberal intergovernmentalism** in the 1990s. By contrast, the new governance agenda can be seen in opposition to the comparative politics approach to the EU. In other words, 'governance' is sometimes presented as an alternative to the view that the EU is an intergovernmental arrangement among sovereign states while on other occasions it is juxtaposed with the view that the EU itself should be studied as an emerging state, with its institutions and procedures comparable to those of nation states.

From this opposition to both (liberal) intergovernmentalist and comparative politics perspectives to European integration resulted in a perception that governance approaches could constitute some sort of 'third way' to the study of the EU, one that eschews the reliance on the **Westphalian** state as the underlying paradigm of EU politics (Pollack, 2005). This not only justified the original designation of governance as 'new' when it was first introduced during the 1990s, but it also underpinned its perception of the EU as a *sui generis* kind of polity—a new kind of political construct that departs from the way in which both international and domestic politics have operated in the past, or are operating elsewhere.

This presentation of governance as one corner of a triangular debate about integration theories involving international relations and comparative politics approaches might have helped to group together a variety of perspectives, presenting these as an 'approach'. But this has become more difficult in view of the way in which governance has also become widely used in the study of international and domestic politics. In this sense, governance, be it global, regional, or national,

appears to be a universal phenomenon, albeit one that has a strong and distinctive presence in the context of the EU. A consistent and comprehensive understanding of EU governance therefore also involves the recognition that technocratic decision-making at the EU level goes hand in hand with greater policization of European affairs at the national level, and that the 'new dynamics of EU governance' also involve the participation of parliamentary actors (Schmidt, 2018).

There is, also, an expanding literature on 'global governance'. The extent to which similar approaches and assumptions can be employed to study global politics *and* EU politics raises questions over the uniqueness of the EU as a political system (see Rosenau and Czempiel, 1992, for an early discussion of global governance, and Reilly, 2004, for a comparison of national, sub-national, and European understandings of the concept).

What this discussion shows is that, even though the governance approach has been seen by some as an argument for treating the EU as *sui generis* (see Hix, 1998), it has at the same time helped others to make a connection, if not a comparison, between research on the EU and on phenomena elsewhere. This has helped to overcome the **$n = 1$ problem** that arises when European integration is treated as unique (Krahmann, 2003; see also Chapter 6). In this vein, research on European governance can draw on insights from research in other areas, or on other territorial levels, while in turn work on the EU can inspire governance research elsewhere.

KEY POINTS

- The concept of governance has successfully described the transformation of policy-making in many parts of the world over the past few decades.

- Using the governance concept has been particularly useful in the context of the EU, given the difficulty involved in categorizing the Euro-polity in terms of the traditional distinction between international system and nation state.

- The governance approach is a broad concept, capturing a variety of different perspectives and applications. At its core, it involves the understanding that policy is made through non-hierarchical networks of both public and private actors located across different territorial levels.

- Multilevel governance, the new governance or regulatory state approach, and the study of new modes of governance are the main expressions of the 'governance turn' in EU studies.

7.3 Multilevel governance

Multilevel governance (MLG) was advanced in the 1990s as a particular take on governance in the European Union, challenging the **state-centric** nature view of the EU prevalent up to that point (Marks et al., 1996). In their account of European integration, the founders of MLG emphasized the independent role of supranational institutions, such as the Commission and the Court of Justice of the EU (CJEU), while also pointing out the internal differences that exist within member states and the inability of national **executives** to control how interests within individual states are represented. 'Multilevel' here referred primarily to the influence of EU-level actors and regional actors alongside the representatives of national executives (Marks, 1992). Whereas the former was very much in the mould of earlier neo-functionalist and more recent supranational governance accounts of integration, the addition of the regional level as part of the analytical frame was new and innovative. This aspect of MLG struck a chord with many researchers at the time, especially because it connected to the analysis of the EU conducted in federal systems such as Germany (Conzelmann, 1998; Benz and Eberlein, 1999; Eising and Kohler-Koch, 1999).

From the mid-1990s onwards, MLG quickly established itself as one of the main rivals to liberal intergovernmentalism. It starts from the observation that much of EU policy-making relies on networks of actors, but goes beyond this by emphasizing the significance of different territorial levels in this process. On the back of a critique of the liberal intergovernmentalist assumption that central governments aggregate national preferences, MLG points to the direct relations that have developed between EU actors and regional and local representatives within states. These relations bypass central governments and thereby prevent national executives maintaining a monopoly over the **representation** of territorial interests. Consequently, regions and municipalities become recognizable as actors independent of their central state. Moreover, their networking with the European Commission and among each other creates regional and local levels of interest representation within the EU. From this perspective, then, EU politics transforms itself from a 'two-level game' (Putnam, 1988) to one that involves multiple levels of government. Together with the incorporation of insights from the study of policy networks, this perspective constituted the basis of the MLG concept (see Box 7.2).

The appeal of this approach meant that its application, initially centred on the study of EU regional policy (Sutcliffe, 2000; Bache, 2008), eventually expanded to cover numerous other policy domains. Through the lens of MLG, authors have analysed the influence of regional actors in areas such as employment policy (Goetschy, 2003), research policy (Kaiser and Prange, 2002), environmental policy (Bulkeley et al., 2003), and even foreign policy (Smith, 2004; see also the expansive collection of sectoral case studies in Tömmel and Verdun, 2008).

What these policy studies have shown is that there is added value to incorporating actors beyond national executives and EU officials in accounts of EU policy-making. At the same time, these studies demonstrate the variation of such influence across different policy sectors and over different points in time (Schultze, 2003). Subsequently, MLG has also been applied to the implementation stage of the policy process, a logical move in view of the decentralized nature of the EU's administrative system (Thielemann, 1998; O'Toole and Hanf, 2003).

Multilevel governance has therefore succeeded not only as an effective critique of 'state-centric' integration theories, but also in **framing** a growing body of research on various aspects of the EU policy process; it addresses deeper questions about the potential for transformation in the Euro-polity (Eising and Kohler-Koch, 1999; Piattoni, 2009). However, while MLG has effectively exposed the weaknesses of liberal intergovernmentalism, it has not developed systematic and explicit statements about cause and effect, about **dependent** and **independent variables**, or about the scope conditions governing its explanatory power. In other words, it lacks the credentials of a theory such as liberal intergovernmentalism. As it stands, then, MLG constitutes an approach that has added valuable insights, which allow for a more comprehensive understanding of EU politics and policy-making, but it has not developed as a fully fledged theory.

More recent advances in the literature have nevertheless sought to advance MLG beyond the early claims that EU level and sub-state level actors matter in the European policy process. These aim to enhance its explanatory power and theoretical potential. Piattoni (2009), for example, building on the earlier work of Hooghe and Marks (2001a) and

BOX 7.2   CASE STUDY: THE REFORM OF EU REGIONAL POLICY AND THE DEVELOPMENT OF THE MULTILEVEL GOVERNANCE APPROACH

The EU has had a **European Regional Development Fund (ERDF)** since 1974, resulting from a deal done at the time of UK accession to ensure that the UK would receive further funds from the EU's budget, given that it did not stand to benefit that much from the Common Agricultural Policy (CAP). In subsequent years it became evident, however, that the disbursements from the ERDF often did not provide *additional* funding for regional development, but instead was used by national administrations merely to substitute domestic regional policy, effectively providing member state finance ministries with opportunities to spend more money elsewhere.

However, a tool that was originally designed to facilitate a *just retour* for some member states became the object of a major reform following the Southern enlargement and the agreement on the Single European Act (SEA) in the mid-1980s. Given the concerns about the further centralization of economic activity within the Single Market, there was an agreement that regional policy in the EU ought to deliver additional funding to lesser-developed and peripheral regions. In 1988, the EU's 'structural funds'—the ERDF plus certain elements of agricultural and social policy funds—were significantly increased and their management fundamentally reformed in order to ensure that EU spending would focus on specific territories defined according to EU-wide standards, that the money would actually arrive at the intended destination, and that local and regional stakeholders would be involved in the decision-making. This new approach was enshrined in EU regional policy through principles such as 'concentration', 'additionality', and 'partnership', respectively.

The 'partnership' principle, in particular, had a far-reaching relevance in governance terms, because it meant that for the first time local and regional authorities across the EU became legitimate actors in the policy process. This involved their participation in the programming committees that would oversee the implementation of specific regional policy projects. But it also led to a wider, political role for sub-state level actors in the EU, initially as members of a consultative committee convened by the Commission to provide general feedback on the direction of regional policy and the territorial impact of other European policies.

The reform of the **structural funds**, together with the regulatory impact of the Single Market programme, had demonstrated to regions across the EU that 'Europe Matters', and subsequently mobilized regional and local actors to campaign for a greater degree of involvement in EU decision-making. What followed was an explosion of offices set by regions, cities, and associations of municipalities in Brussels to represent their specific and general territorial interests, creating new channels of both vertical and horizontal networking for regional actors (Hooghe and Marks, 1996; Jeffery, 1996; Beyers and Donas, 2014). The creation of the **Committee of the Regions (CoR)** with the 1994 Maastricht Treaty was also a direct result of these dynamics (Christiansen, 1996).

The 1988 reform of the EU's structural funds, followed in the 1990s by further reforms, amounted to a 'Europeanisation of regional policy' (Benz and Eberlein, 1999) and brought a new 'third level' into the mix of EU policy-making (Jeffery, 1997). Scholars recognized that the nature of this Europeanized regional policy differed from the domestic experience of both unitary and **federal** states, and that a new conceptualization was needed in order to understand and study these dynamics. The multilevel governance approach was developed in response, and subsequently became a widely used tool not only in the study of EU regional policy, but also as more general approach to the study of European integration and a critique of liberal intergovernmentalism.

Skelcher (2005), has pointed out that territory in the emerging Euro-polity is not neatly separated into European, national, regional, and local levels, but that policies are often made within or for overlapping, interstitial, or loosely defined spaces that do not necessarily correspond to pre-existing territorial jurisdictions. This distinction between the older (territorially defined) 'type I' form of MLG and a more recently identified 'type II' approach helps scholars to engage with the tensions between different forms of MLG, while also bringing new normative dilemmas to light.

Although the initial statement of MLG was **rationalist** in its emphasis on cost–benefit calculations, informational asymmetries, and institutional self-interests, other contributions to the field have sought to demonstrate the **constructivist** potential of MLG (Christiansen, 1997). For example, in an interesting departure from the usual application of MLG, Aalberts (2004) employs a constructivist reading of the concept that seeks to reconcile the empirical observation that the significance of **sovereignty** in the Euro-polity has been declining with the apparent resilience of the nation state.

KEY POINTS

- Multilevel governance emphasizes the involvement and potential influence of actors from different territorial levels in the making of EU policy.
- Much of the literature making use of the insights of MLG has focused on the role of regions in the politics of the EU.
- Multilevel governance has demonstrated its usefulness above all in research on the **agenda-setting** and implementation phases of the EU policy process.
- Beyond the study of EU policy-making, MLG has also informed research on constitutive politics and the transformation of governance in the EU.

7.4 'New governance' and the European regulatory state

A rather different perspective on governance has been taken by authors who have conceptualized the European Union as a regulatory state. Rather than focusing on multiple levels of governance or on networks of actors, here the focus is on the kind of decisions being taken at the European level and the instruments that are being employed in order to achieve outcomes. The 'regulatory state' is seen in contrast to the traditional welfare state, interchangeably labelled also as the '**interventionist**', 'positive', or '*dirigiste*' state—that is, one that is heavily involved in the allocation of goods and the redistribution of wealth. The regulatory state, by contrast, does not involve classic decisions about spending and taxation, but is essentially concerned with socio-economic regulation (Majone, 1994, 1996; Caporaso, 1996; McGowan and Wallace, 1996).

While the rise of the regulatory function of the state has been part of a wider phenomenon both within states as well as globally (Moran, 2002), the argument about the EU as a regulatory state built on a number of factors that were specific to the EU. First, the EU's

Budget, in relation to the combined **gross domestic product (GDP)** of the member states' economies, is comparatively small and does not permit the kind of social expenditure that welfare states have at their disposal. At the same time, the EU has no practical tax-raising powers and cannot use taxes as an instrument of redistribution.

As a result, the EU has no choice but to intervene in the economy and in society through regulation. While regulatory activity at the European level was modest until the mid-1980s, hampered by the need for unanimous decision-making, a step-change occurred with the **Single European Act (SEA)** and the roll-out of the **1992 Programme**. The move to **qualified majority voting (QMV)** made the passage of European legislation much easier. Re-regulation at the European level, combined with the **mutual recognition** of technical and product standards at the national level, opened up member states' markets, and created the conditions for **regulatory competition** among national and regional jurisdictions (Young, 2006).

In terms of institutional foundations, scholars have focused on a number of particular arrangements in the EU through which regulatory activity takes place. Among these are the delegation of powers to the European Commission, the creation of a large number of decentralized agencies, and the growth of regulatory networks. What these mechanisms have in common, and what has been identified as a hallmark of the European regulatory state, is that decision-making through these institutional arrangements is both non-majoritarian and removed from the electoral process. This means that regulatory decisions are not taken through the 'normal' channels used by liberal democratic systems—majority votes by elected representatives in parliament or decisions by national executives accountable to voters—but by non-elected technocrats.

This departure from standard norms of parliamentary democracy has led to debate among scholars (see Section 7.5, 'Normative debates about governance' for a discussion). For proponents of regulatory governance, the immediate justification for this independence from politics has centred on the following argument: the kind of regulatory decisions that are taken in the EU are about the search for the best solution to a given regulatory problem. As such, they are about identifying what is called the 'Pareto optimal' outcome among a range of possible solutions—a

Pareto optimum being the outcome at which the greatest possible collective gain is reached. Setting technical standards for industrial goods, regulating financial services, preventing monopolistic tendencies and other forms of market abuse, or supervising safety standards and procedures for air travel and maritime transport, are all examples of the kind of activities that should, from this perspective, be better left to independent European regulators.

In the same vein, it is argued that it is not only right, but also indeed imperative to entrust technocrats and experts with the search for the best possible solutions. Equipped with access to information, possessing expertise in the particular area in which regulatory decisions are required, and insulated from political pressures, technocrats will have the best chances of identifying the right solution. Indeed, from the vantage point of the search for the Pareto-optimal outcome, **majoritarian** institutions, which tend to decide through voting on different options, cannot be trusted to come up with the *best* solutions. Consequently, regulatory governance arrangements involve the setting up of *independent* agencies that are removed from political interference so that they can do their work objectively.

The logic of non-majoritarian decision-making is most entrenched in the area of monetary policy in which the independence of **central banks** has become an article of faith. As long as the goal of stable money and low inflation is accepted as beneficial to society as a whole, it follows that the setting of **interest rates** and decisions about **money supply** should not be subject to the shifting preferences of electoral competition and party politics. Independent central bankers can ignore the short-term pressures of elections and instead can take decisions based on the long-term interests of monetary stability.

In line with the central bank analogy, the 'regulatory state' school of thought has identified a growing number of regulatory decisions that may (or should) be 'outsourced' to independent agencies. This has affected areas such as competition policy, utilities regulation, financial services oversight, and the implementation of public services more generally. The resulting rise of the regulatory state is seen as a global phenomenon, driven by competitive pressures in **globalized** markets, with the EU as a particular expression of this trend. In the EU, **negative integration**—the removal of domestic **non-tariff barriers**—has been accompanied, albeit to a more limited extent

by **positive integration**—the setting of minimum standards at the European level. Re-regulation—the creation of new standards applicable to the **Single Market**—has largely been left to networks of national regulators meeting at the European level, either informally through networks or in the more formalized settings of agencies and committees.

In addition, the European Commission has been entrusted with the centralized implementation of much of EU legislation through the delegation of powers (see also Chapter 10). This leads to the European Commission adopting thousands of implementing measures each year, with many of these being of a regulatory nature. Given that the Commission is exercising these delegated powers in the place of national administrations, member states have insisted on the setting up of a large number of advisory, management, and regulatory committees composed of national representatives. These committees oversee the adoption of implementing measures (Blom-Hansen, 2011). The resultant system is known as '**comitology**' and not only provides a framework for member state control over the Commission's use of delegated powers (Brandsma and Blom-Hansen, 2017), but also can be seen as a site for the systematic **cooperation**—indeed the 'fusion'—of national and EU-level administrations (Wessels, 1998; Christiansen, 2010).

A number of issues have been highlighted in the new governance literature. For example, the fact that European regulatory networks tend to be only loosely coupled, and essentially rely on national agencies to implement regulatory decisions agreed at the European level, has led Eberlein and Grande (2005) and others to point out that potential 'supranational regulatory gaps' may arise. The relative weakness of regulatory networks, lacking formal powers to sanction the uniform implementation of decisions, means that agreements might either fall victim to distributive conflict, or otherwise not be subject to democratic **accountability** (see also McGowan and Wallace, 1996).

This dilemma between effectiveness and accountability has been a common debating point among those studying the regulatory state. Indeed, Majone (1994) himself has been quick to point to the need for strong accountability structures that can go hand in hand with the empowerment of independent regulators. However, accountability is not understood in terms of political control in this case—something that, from the new governance perspective, carries with it the 'danger' of politicization—but rather relies on **judicial review**. In an accountability structure compatible with the tenets of the regulatory state, judicial control through courts, acting on behalf of political institutions, and enforcing established standards, constitutes the best way of ensuring compliance with agreed standards (Majone, 1999). Courts therefore, together with central banks and independent regulatory agencies, are the non-majoritarian backbone of the regulatory state.

KEY POINTS

- The literature on the 'European regulatory state' has developed from a wider recognition of the changing role of the state in society in the neo-liberal era.

- This variant of the new governance literature sees the EU as important in the shift from redistributive to regulatory politics in Europe.

- The regulatory state model advocates a de-politicization of regulatory decision-making through the setting up and strengthening of independent and non-majoritarian institutions.

- The proposition that regulatory decision-making constitutes the search for Pareto-optimal solutions that can best be left to technocrats has given rise to normative debates about the accountability of decision-makers.

7.5 Normative debates about governance

The previous sections have already alluded to the normative challenges that the governance turn confronts. The main debate in this regard has concerned the difficulties in reconciling the governance approach with the traditional form of liberal democracy, which is generally taken as the **benchmark** in this kind of normative assessment. This debate can be broken down into two distinct arguments in which scholars have engaged: first, do new forms of governance require legitimation in terms of traditional representative democracy; and second, does governance constitute a move towards an alternative kind of democracy, distinct from traditional models?

In terms of the first of these debates, the case 'against democracy' has already been presented in Section 7.4 '"New governance" and the European

regulatory state'. Advocates of the regulatory state approach argue that what matters here is not democratic **legitimacy** as expressed through the electoral process, but judicial means of holding independent regulators to account. The essence here is procedural control: ensuring that policy-makers have followed the required steps in the regulatory process (Majone, 1999). As long as that is ensured, the normatively desirable outcome of the policy process will be reached. While this initial argument has been applied to the delegation of power to the European Commission or the further 'outsourcing' of particular decisions from the Commission to independent agencies, others have taken this further, arguing that the European Union deals only with technocratic decisions and that, since it is not involved in 'high politics' of a kind that matters to citizens, there is no reason to worry about the putative **democratic deficit** (Moravcsik, 2002; see also Chapter 9).

This argument is in part based on the assumption that decision-making does not involve controversial choices and that, as such, there is no need for the politicization of decision-making. Against this assumption, critics have pointed to many regulatory decisions that have had significant societal implications and which have the potential to favour certain groups, sectors, or member states over others. Decisions of this kind, it has been argued, require legitimation in terms of representative democracy (Føllesdal and Hix, 2006). Take, for example, the regulation of genetically modified organisms (GMOs), which, in the EU, has been a highly contentious issue that has divided both societies and member states (see Box 7.3). The question of whether or not to permit the cultivation and use of GMOs in foodstuffs has shown itself to be more than a technocratic challenge to find the 'right' solution, and has been overlaid with ethical, emotional, and economic arguments that the EU's regulatory system has found difficult to integrate (Skogstad, 2003). The result is not only a perceived lack of legitimacy in this area of EU policy-making, but also problems with the effective regulation of this sector (Christiansen and Polak, 2009).

Authors have advanced many other examples of such 'loaded' decisions that, from a democratic theory point of view, would require legitimation through representative rather than non-majoritarian institutions. The EU's response to the 2008 banking crisis and the **eurozone**'s subsequent **sovereign debt crisis** have been further triggers for debates about the legitimacy

BOX 7.3   CASE STUDY: THE AUTHORIZATION OF GMOS: A CASE STUDY OF EUROPEAN REGULATORY GOVERNANCE

The authorization of GMOs in the EU can be seen as a good example of the challenges and difficulties of the European regulatory state. The need to regulate GMOs has arisen fairly recently and, within the EU's Single Market, requires the involvement of supranational institutions in order to ensure that such goods can be freely traded. In response to this challenge, the European Parliament and EU Council have adopted a number of regulations concerning both the cultivation of GMOs in Europe, and the bringing into the market of food and animal feed containing GMO ingredients.

Such legislation adopted under the ordinary legislative procedure (OLP), however, does not permit or prohibit the use of GMOs. Instead, these regulations delegate powers to the European Commission, which then has the responsibility of ruling on individual authorization applications from industry. The Commission itself is then obliged, under the procedural rules that have been adopted, to consult a number of other institutions before taking its decision. This includes primarily the scientific assessment of the proposed product by the European Food Safety Authority (EFSA) in Parma, as well as the approval of the Commission's intended decision by a **comitology committee** composed of representatives of member state administrations. In addition, the examination process also involves networks of national laboratories and committees of experts in bio-ethics. It is an exhaustive process that has frequently taken more than a year until the Commission was in a position to adopt its decision. In fact, on several occasions the process took so long that applicants have taken the Commission to court for inaction.

One reason for delay has been that the comitology committee overseeing the Commission's use of delegated powers is required, under the rules, to give its approval with a qualified majority. The problem is that attitudes among member states governments have usually been almost evenly divided between supporters and opponents of authorizing GMOs, so it has proven difficult for the Commission to achieve the necessary majority for approval. The absence of qualified majority voting (QMV) in favour of authorization has meant that applications are regularly referred to the EU Council, which can in theory

overrule the Commission by QMV. But given the foregoing situation, no such majority can be found here either, which means that, in the face of 'no decision' in the Council, the Commission has the final say after all. At the end of this process, the Commission has regularly found itself faced with (a) a favourable scientific report from EFSA, (b) no opinion either way emerging from internally divided comitology committees and Council meetings, and (c) threats of court cases for inaction looming. The usual end result has been the authorization of such GMO applications by the Commission, albeit in the face of strong opposition from a number of national governments (not to mention protests from NGOs and political parties), leading in some cases to domestic bans for GMOs in certain member states.

Opponents of GMOs have complained that the process lacks **transparency** and is biased in favour of GMOs, whereas industry has bemoaned the long delays in reaching a final decision, which is seen to leave Europe uncompetitive in the application of this new technology. By the early 2010s, the difficulties experienced with the delegation of these regulatory powers to the European Commission and EFSA led to the search for a new legislative framework that would allow for greater political input. In March 2015, an amendment of the GMO regulations was agreed that allowed member states to restrict or prohibit the cultivation of authorized GMOs (Directive 2015/412/EU), and soon afterwards the Commission proposed to extend this reform so that member states would be able to decide separately on the use of genetically modified food or feed on their territory.

In sum, the case of GMO authorization demonstrates amply the challenges to the delegation of regulatory powers to independent agencies when issues at stake are contested and carry the potential for **politicization**—something that has also become apparent with respect to other regulatory decisions in the EU, as highlighted by the controversies surrounding the authorization of the pesticide glyphosate. Decision-making through comitology also pitched the European Commission against the EP and NGOs, in the face of conflicting positions among the member states.

of European governance—and indeed have led scholars to highlight the 'crisis of EU governance' itself (Börzel, 2016). One observation made in this context has been that the alleged **flexibility** and adaptability of regulatory networks has been lacking (Mügge, 2011). In this reading, close cooperation among financial market regulators sharing a neo-liberal outlook has meant that financial regulations were devised by an

epistemic community based on a dogmatic worldview—a regulatory paradigm that was not adaptable to the changing requirements of the current crisis. This diagnosis echoes the earlier critique by Gill (1998) of the bias in what he called the 'new constitutionalism' of European economic governance.

From this perspective, regulatory decisions require democratic legitimation—if not through representative institutions, then at the very least through deliberative mechanisms. The presence of, or the need for, deliberation in the policy process takes us to the second of the normative debates. Some authors, focusing either on multilevel governance (MLG) or **new modes of governance (NMGs)** have explored the degree to which these forms of governance might meet the expectations of deliberative democracy (Steffek et al., 2007).

While research has demonstrated that such opportunities exist, it has also pointed out the limitations of such deliberation (Eriksen, 2011). The involvement of 'European **civil society**' is generally translated into the **consultation** of Brussels-based NGOs, casting doubts over the representativeness of such cooperation (Kohler-Koch, 2010; see also Chapter 14). Furthermore, observers have pointed out that many of the organizations representing civil society are, in fact, dependent on financial support from the European Commission, possibly resulting in their co-option within a sphere of 'approved' participants in the policy process (Bellamy and Castiglione, 2011). Authors have also pointed to the normative problems inherent in the way in which technocratic '**good governance**' has been 'exported' to third countries outside the EU (Karppi, 2005; Hout, 2010; Knio, 2010). At the extreme, critics have argued that 'far from laying the grounds for a more inclusive, participatory and democratic political order, the [European] Commission's model to governance represents a form of neoliberal governmentality that is actually undermining democratic government and promoting a politics of exclusion' (Shore, 2011: 287).

The normative debates about governance, technocracy, and the regulatory state in the EU have received new impulses from the recent rise of populism in Europe, and the critique of 'elitist rule' in the EU that has come with it (Abazi et al., 2021). Populist discourses—including statements such as 'Let the people decide' and 'we have had enough of experts' which featured in the 2016 **Brexit** referendum as well as in election campaigns in various European countries—are a way of linking scepticism of the nature of supranational governance to anti-European sentiments. As such, these discourses have proven powerful in mobilizing significant parts of the population against further integration or even, in the case of the UK, withdrawal from it (see also Chapter 27).

KEY POINTS

- The governance approach, as a departure from traditional liberal democratic procedures of decision-making, raises important normative questions.

- Some authors point to the normative benefits of governance, such as greater opportunities for deliberation, the potential of greater inclusiveness in the policy process, and the advantages of depoliticized regulatory activity producing the best result.

- Critics of the governance approach have pointed to the way in which theoretical advantages do not materialize in practice and have warned of the rigidity and dogmatism that may arise if policy-making is left to an exclusive community of experts.

7.6 Conclusion

In summarizing the main arguments advanced in this chapter, four points need to be emphasized. First, the 'governance turn' has been an important development in the literature on the European Union, signifying the changing nature of the integration process since the **Maastricht Treaty** and demonstrating the desire of scholars to adapt their research tools accordingly. Second, the study of European governance centres on the role of non-hierarchical networks in the policy process, emphasizing their relevance in a shift away from classic state-centric theories as developed in the subfields of international relations and comparative politics.

Third, governance has become a broad and internally highly diverse orientation, involving a range of different applications, based on a variety of underlying assumptions, making it increasingly difficult to talk of a single 'governance approach'. Fourth, the governance turn has raised, both explicitly and implicitly, a number of normative questions, leading to debates about the limitations of, and the need for, the democratic legitimation of EU governance arrangements (see Chapter 9).

These normative debates are ongoing and would seem all the more important as the study of governance has become part of the mainstream of approaches analysing EU politics (see Box 7.4). Indeed, the European Union's handling of the COVID-19 pandemic, involving both close cooperation among, but also disagreements between, EU institutions and member state governments, is likely to spawn yet more research from a governance perspective. Yet, while the 'governance turn' has certainly made its mark on the European Union, the debate about the way in which such governance can be legitimated remains as relevant as ever.

BOX 7.4   KEY DEBATES: MANAGING THE EUROZONE CRISIS: TECHNOCRATIC GOVERNANCE, REPRESENTATIVE DEMOCRACY, AND NORMATIVE DEBATE

An important site of normative debate has been the discussion about the future of economic governance in the EU. In view of the severe problems that the eurozone faced from 2010 onwards following the global financial crisis, the criticism levied at the weaknesses in both the financial services sector and the management of the single currency, and the calls for a tighter and more comprehensive *gouvernement économique*, the 2010s have demonstrated the tensions facing governance in this area.

The **Stability and Growth Pact (SGP)** adopted earlier, setting targets for member states in terms of permissible levels of **public debt** and budget deficits, is perhaps the most prominent example of the failure of the soft mode of governance, given that the non-compliance of member states with the SGP targets contributed to (if not caused) the crisis (see Chapter 22). Nevertheless, negative experiences of this kind do not mean that the EU will abandon this form of governance. Indeed, future plans with regard to economic governance include the tightening of the supranational oversight of **fiscal policies** through the introduction of a **'European semester'**, which permits the European Commission to monitor national budget plans more closely before their domestic adoption (Hacker and van Treeck, 2010). Other aspects of the response to the sovereign debt crisis—in particular the close cooperation between the European Commission, **European Central Bank (ECB)**, and **International Monetary Fund (IMF)** (what came to be known as the 'Troika') in negotiating and monitoring the **conditionality** of national bailouts—appear as further evidence of the significant role that technocrats are playing in the response to the crisis (see Chapter 25). At the same time, this shift towards technocracy at the European level frequently clashes with the operation of representative democracy at the national level, as the acrimonious relations between the Greek government and the EU institutions following the election of the *Syriza* government in January 2015 demonstrated. Critics of austerity, such as the then Greek finance minister Yannis Varoufakis, protested not only about the substance of what the creditors of Greece were demanding, but also about the undemocratic and non-transparent manner in which such demands were articulated. Accordingly, the Syriza-led government sought an end to the technocratic nature of structural reform negotiations through the Troika, and succeeded in elevating discussions to the political fora of the Eurogroup meeting of finance ministers and the European Council—a preference reflecting the belief that among elected politicians the Greek leadership would finally agree to the submitted terms.

The acrimony that played out during the spring and summer of 2015 therefore not only pitched one government against its creditors in other countries and institutions, it also reflected a wider debate about the relevance of representative democracy and the meaning of sovereignty in such circumstances. In one perspective, the Greek crisis of 2015 appeared to demonstrate the limitations of majoritarian decision-making: the impositions of structural reform requested by Greek creditors were rejected repeatedly at the ballot-box—first in the election in January 2015, and again, more explicitly, in July 2015 as a result of a hastily-called referendum on this issue. Yet despite such consistent popular opposition to the measures, the 'No' campaign won more than 60 per cent of the votes in the referendum; the Greek government ultimately agreed to a third bailout programme that did include many of the measures that had earlier been rejected.

From another perspective, representative democracy has prevailed, since, ultimately, Prime Minister Tsipras was re-elected at a second election in October 2015 and thereby received the democratic legitimation for the change of course that he had overseen.

In the second half of 2018 a new dispute arose between the European Commission objecting for the first time to the proposed budget from a member state and a populist government in Italy defying these demands. This demonstrated that the 2015 Greek crisis had not been a single event, but rather the product of persistent tensions in eurozone governance in which majoritarian democracy at the national level is confronting supranational authority. Given the severity of the crisis and the high stakes involved, the management of the eurozone crisis is a good example of both the relevance of, and the problems with, a greater reliance on governance in the European Union. At the same time, the experiences—positive and negative—from the management of the eurozone crisis also informed subsequent decisions taken by EU decision-makers in adopting a fiscal response to the COVID-19 pandemic which involved far-reaching reforms to the EU's finances.

QUESTIONS

1. How do you explain the success of the governance approach?

2. How different is European governance from traditional forms of governing?

3. Where can instances of non-hierarchical governing be identified in the EU context?

4. What are the main elements of the 'governance turn' in EU studies?

5. Does the governance approach constitute a convincing critique of liberal intergovernmentalism?

6. What is distinctive about multilevel governance?

7. What are the strengths and weaknesses of multilevel governance in analysing the process of European integration?

8. How is decision-making by unelected technocrats legitimized in the European regulatory state?

9. What are the main criticisms on normative grounds that can be advanced against new governance?

GUIDE TO FURTHER READING

Eising, R. and Kohler-Koch, B. (eds) (1999) *The Transformation of Governance in the European Union* (London: Routledge). Presenting the findings of a large-scale research project, this volume includes chapters on governance in a range of different sectors and member states.

Hooghe, L. and Marks, G. (2001a) *Multi-Level Governance and European Integration* (London: Rowman & Littlefield). This is the definitive statement of the key elements and findings of the multilevel governance approach by its founders.

Majone, G. (ed.) (1996) *Regulating Europe* (London: Routledge). A collection of contributions from the founder of the European regulatory state approach and others.

Marks, G., Scharpf, F. W., Schmitter, P. C., and Streeck, W. (1996) *Governance in the European Union* (London: Sage Publications). A collection of essays by senior scholars exploring different dimensions of the governance approach.

Scharpf, F. W. (1999) *Governing in Europe: Effective and Democratic?* (Oxford: Oxford University Press). A collection of essays exploring both the empirical and normative dimensions of governance in the EU.

Access the online resources to take your learning and understanding further, including extra multiple-choice questions with instant feedback, web links, answer guidance to end-of-chapter questions, and updates on new developments in EU politics.

www.oup.com/he/cini-borragan7e

8

Europeanization

Tanja A. Börzel and Diana Panke

Chapter Contents

Reader's Guide

The chapter first explains what Europeanization means and outlines the main approaches to studying this phenomenon. The second section describes why this concept has become so prominent in research on the European Union (EU) and its member states. In the third section, the chapter reviews the state of the art with particular reference to how the EU affects states ('top-down' Europeanization). It illustrates the theoretical arguments with empirical examples. Similarly, the fourth section examines how states can influence the EU ('bottom-up' Europeanization) and provides some theoretical explanations for the empirical patterns observed. This is followed by a section that presents an overview of research that looks at linkages between bottom-up and top-down Europeanization, and considers the future of Europeanization research with regard to the EU's recent and current crises and challenges. This chapter argues that Europeanization will remain an important field of EU research for the foreseeable future.

8.1 Introduction

Europeanization (see Box 8.1) has become a prominent concept in the study of the European Union and **European integration**. While Europeanization generally refers to interactions between the EU and its member states or third countries, the literature has defined the term in different ways. Broadly, one can distinguish between two different notions of Europeanization: 'bottom-up' and 'top-down' Europeanization.

The bottom-up perspective analyses how member states and other domestic actors shape EU policies, EU politics, and the European polity. For bottom-up Europeanization approaches, the phenomenon to be explained is the EU itself. This research analyses whether and how member states are able to upload their domestic interests to EU institutions and policies by, for example, giving the European Parliament (EP) more **powers**, increasing the areas in which the **ordinary legislative procedure (OLP)** applies, or extending the content and scope of EU policies (as is the case in the **liberalization of services**). European **integration** theories, such as **liberal intergovernmentalism**, **neo-functionalism**, and **supranational institutionalism**, complement bottom-up Europeanization approaches since they also address such uploading efforts by member state governments (see Chapters 4, 5, and 6).

The top-down perspective reverses the phenomenon to be explained and its plausible causes. Here, the focus is on how the EU shapes institutions, processes, and political outcomes in both member states and third countries (Ladrech, 1994; Sanders and Bellucci, 2012). The phenomenon of interest is whether and how states download EU policies and institutions that subsequently give rise to domestic change. Downloading EU policies presupposes that the EU has corresponding competencies to adopt them in the first place. This is, for instance, not the case with respect to pandemics, which explains why there was no immediate European response to the COVID-19 outbreak in the form of uniform measures across the member states to combat the pandemic (see Chapter 28).

Top-down Europeanization studies how the EU can impact domestic institutions, policies, or political processes. It raises questions, such as: to what extent, for example, has the shift of policy **competences** from the domestic to the EU level undermined the powers of national parliaments by reducing their function to that of merely transposing EU **directives** into national law? Is the EU responsible for a decline of public services by forcing France or Germany to liberalize telecommunications, postal services, or their energy markets? And to what extent has European integration empowered populist parties, such as the **Front National**, *Die Alternative für Deutschland* (**Alternative for Germany**), the **United Kingdom Independence Party (UKIP)**, or the *Movimento 5 Stelle*, which seek to mobilize those who feel that they have lost out because of the **single European market**, particularly since the economic and the migration crisis? With youth unemployment still above 35 per cent as of early 2021 (Trading Economics, 2001a, 2001b), citizens in Spain and Greece feel that EU policies and institutions are a major cause of their socio-economic grievances (see Box 8.2). The electoral success of populist movements, such as **Podemos** and Vox in Spain, or the Brexit referendum of 2016 testify to the increasing **politicization** of EU powers.

Top-down Europeanization approaches search for factors at the EU level that bring about domestic change. They share the assumption that the EU can (but does not always) cause adaptations of domestic policies, institutions, and political processes if there is a misfit between European and domestic ideas and institutions (Börzel et al., 2010). The incompatibility of European and domestic norms facilitates top-down changes only if it creates material costs or if it challenges collectively shared knowledge or beliefs about how to address societal problems. For example, it raises the question of whether it is more appropriate to protect the environment by preventing

---

> **BOX 8.1   KEY DEBATES: EUROPEANIZATION**
>
> Europeanization captures the interactions between the European Union and member states or third countries (including **candidate countries** and **neighbourhood countries**). One strand of Europeanization research analyses how member states shape EU policies, politics, and **polity**, while the other focuses on how the EU triggers change in member state policies, politics, and polity.

pollution (the German approach) or by fighting environmental pollution where it becomes too damaging (the British approach while the UK was an EU member state). Thus, top-down Europeanization approaches complement compliance theories which explain domestic change in the EU multilevel system, such as enforcement theory, management approaches, or legalization theories (Börzel et al., 2010, 2021), by combining EU- and domestic-level explanatory variables.

In addition to analysing separately bottom-up and top-down Europeanization, some scholars put forward a sequential perspective by examining policy cycles or long-term interactions between the EU and its members (Kohler-Koch and Eising, 1999; Radaelli, 2003). Member states are not merely passive takers of EU demands for domestic change; they proactively shape European policies, institutions, and processes, which they have to download and to which they later have to adapt. Moreover, the need to adapt domestically to European pressure may also have significant

effects at the European level, where member states seek to reduce the misfit between European and domestic arrangements by shaping EU decisions. For example, when Germany succeeded in turning its air pollution **regulations** into the Large Combustion Plant Directive adopted by the EU in 1988 (Directive 88/609/EEC), it did not have to introduce any major legal and administrative changes, and German industry had little difficulty in complying with EU air pollution standards. The UK, then an EU member state, was forced to overhaul its entire regulatory structure and British industry had to buy new abatement technologies for which German companies were the market leaders.

The sequential approach is not a new research avenue, but rather synthesizes the top-down and bottom-up Europeanization approaches. It analyses how member states shape the EU (uploading), how the EU feeds back into member states (downloading), and how the latter react in changing properties of the EU (uploading) (see Börzel and Risse, 2007).

BOX 8.2   CASE STUDY: TOP-DOWN AND BOTTOM-UP EUROPEANIZATION: THE CASE OF THE ECONOMIC CRISIS

Prior to the economic crisis, Ireland, Portugal, Greece, and Spain had benefited from the surge of cheap credit and domestic demand-driven booms in real estate and construction after the introduction of the euro. However, this made them particularly vulnerable to the credit crisis which started in 2007. The burst of the US housing bubble triggered chain reactions, which threw EU deficit countries into a systemic crisis that threatened the very existence of the **economic and monetary union (EMU)**. The rescue measures taken by the EU and its member states led to encroachment on a number of domestic policies that have been a classic domain of the democratic state: for example, pensions and wages, higher education, and healthcare, as well as other aspects of social policy.

The structural reforms the EU and its member states have demanded as a condition for financial bailouts have substantially reduced the economic well-being of the citizens in crisis countries, particularly among the middle class, young people, and women. Rocketing unemployment rates (over 35 per cent among young Greeks and Spaniards (Trading Economics 2021a, 2021b)) and the virtual breakdown of many social services (health, social welfare, pensions) transformed the financial crisis into a social crisis, which has undermined the legitimacy of

elected governments in Greece, Spain, Italy, Ireland, and France. The inability of these governments to respond to the pressing demands of their electorate for a different course in their economic policy fuelled the mobilization of protest by the most affected social groups. The EU has become the lender of last resort for member states in times of financial crisis. At the same time, Germany and some other Northern European member states managed to upload their austerity rules to the European level. The Stability and Growth Pact turned the EU into an agent of a particular type of economic and social policy, which, although highly contested at the domestic level, does not leave member state governments much possibility of deviating from the course of liberalism and fiscal restraint imposed by EU conditionality. Domestic opposition and political calculus led the Greek government to call for a referendum on the conditions of the European Commission, the European Central Bank, and the International Monetary Fund for a bailout to resolve the debt crisis of June 2015. In early July 2015, the Greek citizens rejected the bailout conditions by 61 per cent. Yet, since the vast majority of Greeks want to stay in the euro, Prime Minister Tsipras had to negotiate a third bailout in August 2015, which not only forced Greece to implement reforms rejected in the referendum, but imposed even stricter conditionality.

KEY POINTS

- Europeanization has become a key but disputed term in research on European integration.

- Top-down Europeanization seeks to explain how the European Union induces domestic change in member states or third countries.

- Bottom-up Europeanization analyses how member states and other domestic actors shape EU policies, EU politics, and the European polity.

- The sequential approach to Europeanization synthesizes the merits of top-down and bottom-up Europeanization.

8.2 Why does Europeanization matter?

The European Union has become ever more important for the daily lives of its citizens. The EU has gained more and more policy competences, which now range from market creation and trade liberalization policies, health, environmental research, and social policies, to **cooperation** in the fight against crime and foreign policy, to **no cooperation** in the relocation of refugees and migrants. The economic crisis has given rise to the establishment of a new architecture to better regulate the banking sector and coordinate national fiscal policy and the budgetary cycles of member states—without changing the EU Treaty (see Chapter 25). Similar attempts at delegating more power to supranational institutions failed in the case of the migration crisis. The member states ultimately rejected proposals for a semi-automated relocation of refugees. Nor did they approve plans for European Return Intervention Teams to repatriate illegally staying third-country nationals (see Chapter 26). How do we explain this variation in Europeanization? Which actors and which coalitions are active in shaping the EU? Why is it that we observe a general broadening and **widening** of integration where the member states have been willing to give the EU ever more power on regulating the banking sector, while resisting any significant **sovereignty** loss with regard to migration and asylum? Have France and Germany been in a better position to make their interests heard in the EU than Luxembourg, Ireland, Greece, or Malta? It is also very important to examine how the EU affects the domestic structures of its member states, because Europe has hit virtually

all policy areas penetrating the lives of its citizens in many respects. The EU not only regulates the quality of their drinking water, the length of parental leave, or roaming fees for mobile phones—Europeanization has also fundamentally affected core institutions and political processes of the member states and accession countries by, for example, disempowering national parliaments (Schmidt, 2006). What kind of domestic change (of policies, institutions, or political processes) does the EU trigger? Do Greece, Poland, Luxembourg, France, and Denmark all download EU policies in a similar way, or do national and sub-regional differences remain even after Europeanization? To what extent has the EU's crisis management to save the euro resulted in the dismantling of the European welfare state, not only undermining the democratic legitimacy of member state governments in Greece, Italy, Spain, and France, but also fuelling the politicization of the EU polity and the rise of nationalist, authoritarian populism to the extent that the future of European integration may be at stake because states such as the UK choose to exit the EU or block institutional reforms?

Another reason why research on Europeanization has been thriving is that European integration does not only affect member states, but can also have intended or unintended side effects on third countries. The EU is actively seeking to change the domestic structures of its neighbours and other third countries by exporting its own **governance** model. Examples of what is often referred to as 'external Europeanization' are the EU's **enlargement** policy with the famous **Copenhagen criteria**, which prescribe liberal democracy and a market economy for any country that seeks to join the club (see Chapter 18), and the **European Neighbourhood Policy (ENP)** that stipulates similar requirements (see Chapter 19). Both seek to induce third countries to implement parts of the *acquis communautaire*. Thus the EU has not only talked France, Germany, Spain, Greece, and the Central and Eastern European (CEE) countries into granting their citizens general access to environmental information. It has also asked Ukraine, Georgia, Armenia, and Azerbaijan to make data on the environmental impact of planned projects accessible to the public. **Conditionality** and capacity-building provide a major incentive for candidate and for neighbourhood countries to Europeanize their politics and institutions. Finally, Europeanization can have unintended effects on member states and third countries. Domestic actors can use the EU for their own ends and can induce domestic changes in the name of Europe

(Lavenex, 2001). For example, LGBT+ groups in Poland have used the EU to push for the rights of sexual minorities in the absence of any specific EU legislation. At the same time, the incumbent governments of the European **neighbourhood countries** have instrumentalized the EU's demands to fight corruption in return for accession to the Single Market and visa facilitations to undermine the power of the political opposition. Former Ukranian Prime Minister Julija Timoshenko was convicted of embezzlement and abuse of power, and sentenced to seven years in prison. Likewise, former President Mikheil Saakashvili of Georgia faced criminal charges filed by the Georgian prosecutor's office over allegedly exceeding official powers.

Countries that are not current or would-be members of the EU are subject to the indirect influence of the EU too (Börzel and Risse, 2012). Norway, for example, became part of the **Schengen Agreement** because it forms a passport union with the Scandinavian EU member states. The **Trade and Cooperation Agreement (TCA)** that governs the post-Brexit relationship between the EU and the UK requires checks on British goods entering the Single Market (see Chapter 27). Outside Europe, farmers in developing countries in Latin America and Africa suffer from consequences of the Common Agricultural Policy (CAP), which effectively shuts their products out of the **Single Market** (see Chapter 17). Finally, the EU's policies and institutions can also diffuse into other regional organizations, such as the Andean Community, the Southern African Development Community, the Association of South East Asian Nations, or the Eurasian Custom Union.

KEY POINTS

- Europeanization has become a key concept in the study of European integration.
- Europeanization research examines how the EU has obtained a broad array of policy competences over the course of more than 50 years of integration and also how this triggers changes in member states affecting various aspects of the daily lives of EU citizens.
- Students of Europeanization also investigate how the EU affects third countries, which may or may not want to become members, by pushing for market liberalization, democracy, human rights, and **good governance**.
- Europeanization research shows that European integration has had unintended effects on states both within and outside the EU.

8.3 Explaining top-down Europeanization

Top-down Europeanization seeks to uncover the conditions and causal mechanisms through which the European Union triggers domestic change in its member states and in third countries. It starts from the empirical puzzle that European policies, institutions, and political processes facilitate domestic change, but do not provoke the convergence of national polities, politics, or policies. It also posits that EU policies and institutions are a constant impetus of domestic change for all states (Cowles et al., 2001; Sanders and Bellucci, 2012). To solve the puzzle, the literature has drawn on two different strands of neo-institutionalism (see Chapter 6). While both assume that institutions mediate or filter the domestic impact of Europe, **rationalist** and **constructivist** approaches to top-down Europeanization differ in their assumptions about exactly how institutions matter. *Rational choice* institutionalism argues that the EU facilitates domestic adaptation by changing **opportunity structures** for domestic actors. In a first step, a misfit between the EU and domestic norms creates demands for domestic adaptation. In a second step, the downloading of EU policies and institutions by the member states is shaped by cost–benefit calculations of the strategic actors whose interests are at stake. Institutions constrain or enable certain actions by strategic rational actors by rendering some options more costly than others (Tsebelis, 1990; Scharpf, 1997). From this perspective, Europeanization is largely conceived of as an emerging **political opportunity structure** that offers some actors additional resources with which to exert influence, while severely constraining the ability of others to pursue their goals. Domestic change is facilitated where the institutions of the member states empower domestic actors to block change at veto points or to facilitate it through supporting formal institutions (Börzel and Risse, 2007). For example, the liberalization of the European transport sector (Regulations 96/1191 and 1893/91) empowered internationally operating road hauliers and liberal parties in highly regulated member states, such as Germany or the Netherlands, which had been unsuccessfully pushing for privatization and deregulation at home. But while the German reform coalition was able to exploit European policies to overcome domestic opposition to liberalization, Italian trade unions and sectoral associations successfully vetoed any reform attempt

(Héritier et al., 2001). Likewise, while the UK was still in the EU, British public agencies supported the appeal of women's organizations in support of the Equal Pay and Equal Treatment Directives (Directives 75/117/EEC and 76/107/EEC, respectively) to further gender equality by providing them with legal expertise and funding to take employers to court. In the absence of such formal institutions, French women were not able to overcome domestic resistance by employers and trade unions to implement EU equal pay and equal treatment policies (Caporaso and Jupille, 2001; Cowles et al., 2001).

Other research in the Europeanization literature draws on *sociological institutionalism*. This specifies change mechanisms based on the ideational and **normative** processes involved in top-down Europeanization. Sociological institutionalism is based on the 'logic of appropriateness' (March and Olsen, 1989), which argues that actors are guided by collectively shared understandings of what constitutes proper, socially accepted behaviour. These norms influence the way in which actors define their goals and what they perceive as rational action. Rather than maximizing egoistic self-interest, actors seek to meet social expectations. From this perspective, Europeanization is understood as the emergence of new rules, norms, practices, and structures of meaning to which member states are exposed and which they have to incorporate into their domestic structures. For example, consider a normative or cognitive misfit between what the Greek government believes or knows about managing public expenditure best and what EU policies prescribe is a necessary, but not sufficient, condition for domestic change in response to top-down Europeanization. If there is such a misfit, norm entrepreneurs, such as **epistemic communities** or **advocacy networks**, socialize domestic actors into new norms and rules of appropriateness through persuasion and social learning. Domestic actors then redefine their interests and identities accordingly (Börzel and Risse, 2007). The more active norm entrepreneurs are and the more they succeed in making EU policies resonate with domestic norms and beliefs, the more successful they will be in bringing about domestic change.

Moreover, collective understandings of appropriate behaviour strongly influence the ways in which domestic actors download EU requirements (see Box 8.3). First, a consensus-oriented or cooperative decision-making culture helps to overcome multiple veto points by rendering their use for actors inappropriate.

Cooperative **federalism** prevented the German *Länder* from vetoing any of the Treaty revisions that deprived them of core decision-making powers. Obstructing the **deepening** and widening of European integration would not have been acceptable to the political class (Börzel, 2002). Likewise, the litigious German culture encouraged German citizens to appeal to national courts against the deficient application of EU law, while such a culture was absent in France, where litigation is less common (Conant, 2002).

Second, a consensus-orientated political culture allows for a sharing of adaptation costs, which facilitate the accommodation of pressure for adaptation. Rather than shifting adaptation costs onto a social or political minority, the 'winners' of domestic change compensate the 'losers'. For example, the German government shared its decision powers in European policy-making with the *Länder* to make up for their EU-induced power losses. Likewise, the **consensual** corporatist decision-making culture in the Netherlands and Germany facilitated the liberalization of the transport sector by offering compensation to employees as the potential losers of domestic changes (Héritier et al., 2001). In short, the stronger informal cooperative institutions are in a member state, the more likely domestic change will be.

While Europeanization has affected the policies, politics, and polity, of all member states, the degree of change differs significantly. If we consider the example of environmental policy, the EU has promoted change towards a more precautionary problem-solving approach, particularly in the area of air and water pollution control. It also introduced procedural policy instruments such as the Access to Environmental Information and the Environmental Impact Directive (Directive 90/313/EEC). Equally, EU policies have led

BOX 8.3   KEY DEBATES: EXPLAINING 'DOWNLOADING' AND 'TAKING'

The top-down Europeanization literature uses the concepts of 'downloading' and 'taking' as synonyms. Both terms capture the response of member states and third countries to the European Union. States are good at taking or downloading policies if they are able to respond swiftly to impetuses for change coming, for example, from the EU in the form of EU law, EU neighbourhood policy, or EU development policy.

to tighter standards in virtually all areas of environmental policy. While the EU has affected the policy content of all member states, the environmental latecomers (Spain, Portugal, Greece, Ireland, the UK, and more recently the CEE countries) have been much more Europeanized than the environmentally progressive 'leader' states (Denmark, Sweden, Finland, the Netherlands, Germany, and Austria).

The Europeanization of administrative structures paints a similar picture, although domestic change has been more modest. In old and new member states, the domestic impact of Europe has fostered the centralization of environmental policy-making competences in the hands of central government departments and agencies at the expense of subordinate levels of government. While regional governments in highly decentralized states have, to some extent, been compensated by co-decision rights in the formulation and implementation of EU environmental policies, the main losers of Europeanization are the national and regional parliaments. Thus, the Europeanization of environmental policy-making has created new political opportunities, particularly for citizens and environmental groups, and has reinforced existing consensual and adversarial styles rather than changed them. The only exceptions are the three Northern countries that joined the EU in 1995. In Austria, Sweden, and to a lesser extent Finland, the need to implement EU environmental policies in a timely fashion has reduced the scope for extensive **consultation** with affected interests, thus undermining the traditionally consensual patterns of **interest intermediation**. Moreover, the legalistic approach of the Commission in the monitoring of compliance with EU law has constrained the discretion public authorities used to exercise in the implementation of environmental regulations in Ireland, and France.

External Europeanization also corroborates the differential impact of Europe. Europeanization has had a more of a similar effect on candidate and neighbourhood countries than it has on member states when it comes to the strengthening of core **executives** and increasing their autonomy from domestic, political, and societal pressures. It has also led to the development of a less politicized civil service and to a degree of decentralization and regionalization, at least when compared with the Communist legacy (Schimmelfennig and Sedelmeier, 2005). At the same time, however, Europeanization effects on institutions and politics vary considerably. EU political conditionality was successful only in cases of unstable democracy, in which it strengthened liberal politics (as in Slovakia or Serbia), while being irrelevant in those countries that already had strong democratic constituencies (most of the CEE countries) or in autocratically ruled states such as Belarus or Azerbaijan (Schimmelfennig et al., 2006). In general, there has been little institutional convergence around a single European model of governance.

Finally, some of the new member states show tendencies of **democratic back-sliding**. Attempts by the Hungarian Prime Minister, Viktor Orbán, and by Poland's Law and Justice Party (PiS) to undo some of the institutional changes introduced as a condition for EU membership indicate that Europeanization is not necessarily irreversible. The multiple crises the EU has been facing since 2008 including **Brexit** have reinforced concerns of de-Europeanization and disintegration (see Schimmelfennig, 2018a). Europeanization can analytically capture the reversing of domestic changes induced by EU policies and institutions. It is less equipped to account for such de-Europeanization. The opposite of Europeanization tends to be conceptualized as no Europeanization in terms of resistance and rejection. Domestic veto players and the absence of a cooperative institutional culture explain why the domestic status quo is not changed. They have less to say why change is undone (see Chapter 27).

In sum, the top-down impact of Europeanization is differential and reversible. EU policies and institutions are not downloaded in a uniform manner. Nor is their adoption and implementation equally (un)controversial. Denmark and Sweden are better takers than France, Italy, and Greece, because they have more efficient administrations (Börzel et al. 2010, 2021). At the same time, EU policies and institutions are politically more contested in Greece than in Spain, as the 2015 bailout debate and the subsequent referendum in Greece illustrates. Thus we should not be too surprised to find hardly any evidence of convergence towards an EU policy or institutional model: convergence is not synonymous with Europeanization. Member states can undergo significant domestic change without necessarily becoming similar.

By focusing on 'goodness of fit' and mediating factors, such as **veto players**, facilitating formal institutions, or norm entrepreneurs, we can account for the differential impact of Europe. These factors increasingly point to complementary rather than competing explanations of Europeanization. As such, students of

Europeanization primarily seek to identify scope conditions under which specific factors are more likely to influence the downloading of EU policies and institutions by the member states. Rather than lack of convergence, the challenges are recent tendencies of de-Europeanization with regard to the rule of law and the abolition of border controls.

KEY POINTS

- Top-down Europeanization explains how the EU triggers domestic change. A central concept in this regard is 'misfit'. Only if domestic policies, processes, or institutions are not already in line with what the EU requires can the latter causally induce domestic change.

- If misfit is present, the impact of the European Union can be explained through different theoretical approaches—namely, sociological or rational choice institutionalism.

- A frequent question of top-down Europeanization research is whether the policies, politics, and polity of states converge over time as an effect of membership, or whether states maintain distinct features.

- Academic research and empirical evidence show that convergence is not synonymous with Europeanization.

- The challenge for Europeanization is to explain the reversal of EU-induced domestic change.

8.4 Explaining bottom-up Europeanization

Bottom-up Europeanization research analyses how states upload their domestic preferences to the EU level. These preferences may involve EU policies, such as environmental standards; they may relate to European political processes, such as how far day-to-day decision-making should involve the European Parliament; or they can touch on issues of institutional design regarding, for example, whether the European Commission should get additional competences in fighting global pandemics or the EU's Cooperation in the Area of Freedom, Security, and Justice (AFSJ) matters (see Box 8.4). Bottom-up Europeanization studies can be divided into those that analyse **intergovernmental conferences (IGCs)** (Moravcsik, 1998) and those that examine the daily decision-making process (Thomson et al., 2006; Panke, 2010, 2012a; Thomson, 2011). In order to conceptualize how bottom-up

Europeanization works and how states are able to upload their preferences, students of the European Union have drawn on rationalist and constructivist approaches. Rationalist approaches assume that actors have fixed and predefined interests, and pursue them through recourse to their power resources (often economic strength or votes in the EU Council) strategically calculating the costs and benefits of different options. Constructivist approaches assume that actors are open to persuasion and change their flexible interests in the wake of good arguments.

One of the most prominent rationalist decision-making approaches is intergovernmentalism (Hoffmann, 1966, 1989) and its newer version, liberal intergovernmentalism (Moravcsik, 1998; see also Chapter 5). Intergovernmentalism assumes that states with many votes in the EU Council and strong bargaining power are in a better position to shape outcomes in EU negotiations than states with fewer votes. Moreover, powerful states are more likely to influence successfully the content of EU law if the policy at stake is very important for them and if they manage to form winning coalitions through concessions (**package deals** or side payments) or through threats, such as the disruption of further cooperation, stopping support on other issues, or reducing side payments. Hence the higher the bargaining power of a state and the higher the issue salience for that state, the more likely it is that this state will shape the content of the European policy (successful bottom-up Europeanization).

Quantitative studies of EU decision-making attribute different causal weight to formal rules, ranging from traditionally power-based studies to more **institutionalist** approaches (Panke, 2012a). The former assume that political and material power is the crucial explanatory factor governing EU negotiations (Widgren, 1994), whereas the latter put more emphasis

 BOX 8.4 KEY DEBATES: EXPLAINING 'UPLOADING' AND 'SHAPING'

The bottom-up Europeanization literature uses two concepts interchangeably in order to describe how states influence policies, politics, or institutions of the European Union: 'uploading' and 'shaping'. An EU member state is a successful shaper (or uploader) if it manages to make its preferences heard, so that an EU policy, political process, or institution reflects its interests.

on formal rules such as decision-making procedures or the share of votes (Tsebelis and Garrett, 1997). The collaborative research project 'The European Union Decides' showed that 'powerful actors who attach most salience to the issues receive the largest concessions from other negotiators' (Schneider et al., 2006: 305; see also Thomson et al., 2006). Hence, the voting weight that a member state has in the EU Council is an important negotiation resource, but does not determine outcomes. This is the result of an informally institutionalized consensus norm, according to which 'powerful and intense actors are conciliates, even when they might be legally ignored' (Achen, 2006: 297). Moreover, in order to influence policies successfully, states have to create coalitions. While there is evidence of the rationalist account of bottom-up Europeanization, a considerable amount of empirical variation is left unexplained.

Qualitative studies also demonstrate that bargaining and voting weight are very important for bottom-up Europeanization, because power influences the opportunities that states have to upload national preferences to the EU level (Liefferink and Andersen, 1998; Panke, 2012b). A study by Eugénia da Conceição-Heldt (2004) on the Common Fisheries Policy (CFP) highlights that power, preferences, and preference intensity influence the outcomes of complex, iterated negotiations under conditions of uncertainty (see Box 8.5). Another example of the importance of bargaining power in the shadow of votes is the **Working Time Directive** (Directive 2003/88/EC). During the two years of negotiations in the **Committee of Permanent Representatives (Coreper)** prior to an agreement, a potential compromise shifted the outcome towards the UK (then still an EU Member State) as a strong veto player. A majority of states favoured the Directive. Although member states could have voted according to **qualified majority voting (QMV)**, they abstained from proceeding in this way, seeking instead to bring the UK on board as well. As a result, the UK achieved key concessions before the Directive was passed (Lewis, 2003: 115–19). In line with the findings of the 'The European Union Decides' project, the bargaining power of a big state with high preference intensity mattered in the case of the Working Time Directive. Even though proceeding to vote could have secured support for the Directive against British interests, all large states' interests were accommodated. Therefore, it is clear that qualitative work lends support to major quantitative findings in showing that, when it comes to hard bargaining in the shadow of votes, the size of a member state matters in shaping its influence (Panke, 2010).

Constructivist approaches assume that the preferences of state and **non-state actors** are not completely fixed during interactions, but can change in the wake of good arguments (Risse, 2000). Actors have an idea of what they want when they start negotiating in the EU, but can change their preferences if another actor makes a convincing statement, for example, should new scientific insights be made available (Panke, 2011). According to this approach, policy outcomes and integration dynamics are shaped by processes of arguing among member states, typically involving

BOX 8.5   CASE STUDY: BOTTOM-UP EUROPEANIZATION: THE COMMON FISHERIES POLICY

The Common Fisheries Policy case is a good illustration of how states make use of their voting power and the threat of a negative vote in order to obtain better deals for themselves. Back in 1976, the European Commission proposed rules on fishing quotas and member states' access to fishing areas. This policy required **unanimity** among the member states. All member states agreed to the proposal, with Ireland and the UK opting for higher quotas and limitations of the equal access principle. Ireland and the UK had high bargaining power because their agreement was required to pass the policy. In the course of several years of bargaining, the Irish government accepted the Commission's modified proposal because it achieved concessions in the form of quota increases. The UK,

however, maintained its opposition and was brought back 'on board' only later, when the CFP was linked to the UK's budget contribution in a comprehensive package deal. At that point, however, Denmark turned into a veto player because it became dissatisfied with the quota system. Denmark demanded higher and more flexible fishing quotas, and created a stalemate by evoking the **Luxembourg Compromise**. To the threat of continued blockade, the Community responded with higher offers. Only after Denmark received higher quotas as side payments could the CFP finally come into existence in 1983.

Source: da Conceição-Heldt (2006).

supranational institutions such as the Commission, or policy experts and epistemic communities (Haas, 1970; Sandholtz and Zysman, 1989). Good arguments are the ones that resonate well with all interests. If an argument wins the competition of ideas, it influences outcomes. States are more successful in shaping policy outcomes (successful bottom-up Europeanization) the better their arguments resonate with the beliefs and norms of other actors.

While quantitative studies do not (yet) test the power of ideas and good arguments, qualitative studies can trace ideational processes. They demonstrate that the power of argument is highly important for influencing the opportunity that a member state has to influence the content of European laws, European institutions, or EU political processes. Concerning market creating and regulating policies, fewer than 15 per cent of all Council positions on a Commission proposal are actually decided at the ministerial level of the EU Council. Coreper and, especially, the working groups of the Council are the forums in which the vast majority of political decisions are taken (see Chapter 11). In both lower-level arenas, hard political bargaining, in which states resort to the threat of hierarchical delegation and voting, is rare (Panke and Haubrich Seco, 2016). The usual way of doing business is based on the exchange of arguments (Beyers and Dierickx, 1998; Elgström and Jönsson, 2000). A comprehensive study of negotiations within the EU Council shows, for example, that high-quality arguments can convince others even if the point is put forward by a small state with limited bargaining and voting power. For example, Luxembourg used its EU and issue-specific expertise to negotiate effectively in the Common Agricultural Policy health check negotiations of 2007 (Panke, 2011). Back then, a major cleavage ran between countries that favoured EU subsidies and countries that wanted to limit the EU budget spend on the CAP. Luxembourg belonged to the latter group. It had strong interests regarding land parcel transfer rules, minimum thresholds for direct payments, and in the correction scheme on milk quota. The Luxembourg expert had been dealing with the CAP regulations for much longer than most Commission staff, and knew the history of the files significantly well. Thus, from the very start of the negotiations, Luxembourg actively lobbied the Commission and the Council Presidency and circulated lengthy constructive reform proposals that reflected a high level of expertise. On this basis, Luxembourg successfully influenced the CAP. This and other cases illustrate that the possibility of persuading others with a convincing argument and norms of mutual responsiveness both work as great equalizers in Coreper negotiations. As a result—and in line with the constructivist hypothesis on bottom-up Europeanization—smaller member states can sometimes punch above their weight (Panke, 2011).

The two theoretical accounts of the shaping of European policies are compatible rather than mutually exclusive. We know empirically that, in EU institutions, actors sometimes engage in bargaining (as expected by the rationalist intergovernmental approach) and sometimes argue (as expected by the constructivist supranational approach). Therefore, both explanations of bottom-up Europeanization can account for different parts of social reality.

KEY POINTS

- Bottom-up Europeanization explains how states can trigger changes in the EU.

- Misfit is a necessary condition for EU-induced changes. If states' preferences are not already in accordance with EU policies, politics, or polity, states can induce European-level changes.

- Different theories focus on different means available to states to make their voices heard, such as economic and voting power, or argumentative and moral power.

- Two prominent questions of bottom-up Europeanization research ask whether large states, such as Germany, France, the UK, or Poland, are more successful in influencing European policies than smaller states, and under what conditions small states can punch above their weight.

8.5 Towards a sequential perspective on Europeanization?

As stated earlier, the sequential perspective on Europeanization seeks to explain both the shaping and taking of EU and state-level policies, procedures, and institutions. Few students of Europeanization have made an attempt to bring the two approaches together, although some studies consider 'shaping' as the cause of 'taking' or vice versa (Andersen and Liefferink, 1997; van Keulen, 1999; Börzel, 2021).

Member states that have the power and capacity to upload their preferences successfully, and to shape EU policies accordingly, have fewer difficulties in taking and downloading them. This explains why southern European member states are laggards in implementing EU environmental policies (Börzel, 2003). Portugal and Greece simply lack the capacity and power to strongly shape EU policy, and consequently face a higher 'misfit', incurring significant implementation costs. Problems in taking EU policies can provide member states with important incentives to engage in (re-)shaping in order to reduce the 'misfit'. France, for example, which had already deregulated its transport sector when it met the EU demands for liberalization, pushed for re-regulating the impact of liberalization in order to safeguard public interest goals (Héritier et al., 2001). The Greek referendum of 2015, by contrast, was a failed attempt of the Greek government to renegotiate painful reforms that previous governments had accepted in return for a bailout. Rather, Germany and other creditor countries have managed to upload their austerity policy to the EU level and impose it on the debtor states (see Chapter 25).

The more successful member states are in shaping EU policies, the fewer problems they are likely to face in taking these policies. For example, if a state with high regulatory standards in the environmental policy field, such as Denmark, manages to upload its environmental policy preferences to the European level, it has to invest fewer resources in implementing EU policies later on, which in turn reduces the risk of Denmark violating EU environmental law (Börzel, 2003). But are successful shaping and taking explained by the same factors, or do the two stages of the policy process require different explanations? Some factors might be more important to shaping than to taking, or vice versa; they could also have contradictory effects. However, so far only a small number of Europeanization studies have systematically combined and compared the causal influence of different factors in the two stages of the EU policy process (Börzel, 2021). Bringing the two together could help address the puzzle of de-Europeanization as in the case of Brexit (see Chapter 27) and differential outcomes. Reversing EU-induced domestic change and avoiding EU reforms are just as effective ways to reduce or avoid misfit as adjusting EU institutions and policies.

KEY POINTS

- The bulk of Europeanization research focuses either on top-down or on bottom-up processes.

- Sequential approaches analyse interactions between the shaping and the taking of European policies.

- There is limited research that identifies the interaction between unsuccessful uploading of preferences to the EU level and implementation problems at the national level.

- There is great potential for future research that seeks to integrate sequentially top-down and bottom-up Europeanization approaches which may help explain de-Europeanization processes such as Brexit.

8.6 Conclusion

This chapter has introduced the concept of Europeanization and has reviewed existing research on this topic. We have focused attention on the theoretical literature around the concepts of top-down and bottom-up Europeanization by identifying their explanatory quality and by contextualizing them in the wider political science literature. The empirical examples have shown how the European Union has contributed to changing structures, processes, and behaviour in national arenas, but also under what conditions member states are able to incorporate their preferences into EU policies, politics, and processes. Moreover, the chapter has addressed the external dimension of Europeanization as the EU is able to affect third countries by pushing for socio-economic and political reform. The chapter has also presented a sequential understanding of Europeanization that brings together the merits of top-down and bottom-up Europeanization approaches, and has outlined possible avenues for future research. Ultimately, the chapter concludes that Europeanization research will continue to be an important field of EU research for the foreseeable future.

QUESTIONS

1. What is Europeanization, and what are the differences between bottom-up and top-down Europeanization?

2. Why is Europeanization an important research field?

3. What is 'misfit'?

4. How can we explain why member states respond differently to Europeanization?

5. How can we explain member states' ability to shape EU policies and institutions successfully?

6. Are some states better equipped to shape EU policies than others?

7. What do the terms 'uploading' and 'downloading' mean?

8. Can states be subject to Europeanization without being members of the EU?

GUIDE TO FURTHER READING

Cowles, M. G., Caporaso, J. A., and Risse, T. (eds) (2011) *Transforming Europe: Europeanization and Domestic Change* (Ithaca NY, Cornell University Press). This edited volume gives a good overview of empirical studies on top-down Europeanization in the pre-accession EU 15.

Featherstone, K. and Radaelli, C. (eds) (2003) *The Politics of Europeanisation* (Oxford: Oxford University Press). This book gives a comprehensive overview of the various theoretical approaches and dimensions of top-down Europeanization.

Sanders, D. and Bellucci, P. (eds) (2012) *The Europeanization of National Polities? Citizenship and Support in a Post-Enlargement Union* (Oxford: Oxford University Press). This book offers interesting insights into top-down Europeanization.

Schimmelfennig, F. and Sedelmeier, U. (eds) (2005a) *The Europeanization of Central and Eastern Europe* (Ithaca, NY: Cornell University Press). This book provides an excellent account of top-down Europeanization in accession countries and new member states.

Thomson, R. (2011) *Resolving Controversy in the European Union: Legislative Decision-Making Before and After Enlargement* (Cambridge: Cambridge University Press). This book provides insights into bottom-up Europeanization with and without the new member states.

Access the online resources to take your learning and understanding further, including extra multiple-choice questions with instant feedback, web links, answer guidance to end-of-chapter questions, and updates on new developments in EU politics.

www.oup.com/he/cini-borragan7e

9

Democracy and Legitimacy in the European Union

Stijn Smismans

Reader's Guide

This chapter discusses the extent to which decision-making in the European Union can be considered democratic and legitimate. The chapter clarifies the concepts 'democracy' and 'legitimacy', and describes how, although initially the legitimacy of the European polity was not perceived as a problem, it became more problematic as the EU gained more competences. The European democratic deficit became an important issue of debate only during the 1990s after the Maastricht Treaty had transferred considerable powers to the EU. The main solution to the democratic deficit has been inspired by the parliamentary model of democracy and involves strengthening the European Parliament (EP), while also paying attention to the role of national parliaments and regional and local authorities. The chapter also shows how the governance debate at the start of the twenty-first century broadened the conceptual understanding of democracy in the EU by addressing the complexity of European governance (see also Chapter 7). By looking at different stages of policy-making and different modes of governance, while dealing with issues such as transparency and the role of civil society, the chapter discusses a wider range of issues associated with the democracy and legitimacy of the Union. It assesses the impact on EU democracy of the Constitutional Treaty and the Lisbon Treaty. The chapter concludes by warning that three crises, namely the economic, migration, and security crises, have revived nationalist and populist movements exacerbating the challenges to the EU's legitimacy.

9.1 Introduction

When one thinks about democracy, it is usually the political institutions of nation states that first come to mind. Yet democracy can also apply to the case of the European Union. Addressing this question in the EU is particularly challenging because the European Union is a **supranational** polity: it is less than a state, but more than an international organization.

To help to address this question, we first need to distinguish between two terms: democracy and legitimacy. According to Bobbio (1987: 19), 'a "democratic **regime**" is . . . a set of procedural rules arriving at collective decisions in a way which accommodates and facilitates the fullest possible participation of interested parties'. Therefore, democracy does not concern only states, but can also apply to any regime arriving at collective decisions. It can therefore also be applied to a supranational or multilevel polity such as the EU.

Whereas 'democracy' refers to a set of procedures guaranteeing the participation of the governed, 'legitimacy' refers to the generalized degree of trust that the governed have towards the political system. Broadly speaking, this generalized degree of trust can result from two elements. On the one hand, people might find a political system legitimate because they are sufficiently involved in the decision-making even if the outcome of those decisions is not always what they desire (**input legitimacy**). On the other hand, people might find a political system legitimate because they are satisfied with the policy outcomes produced by the political system (**output legitimacy**), even if they are not sufficiently involved in decision-making. The first aspect of legitimacy can be identified with the democratic process; the second with performance and **efficiency**. Input and output legitimacy are normally combined, but one may be emphasized more than the other. For example, it is often argued that the EU has primarily been built on output legitimacy. However, as the EU has become involved in more and more policy areas, it has become increasingly difficult to base the legitimacy of the European polity on policy outputs alone.

9.2 From 'permissive consensus' to 'democratic deficit'

Back in 1957 when the **European Economic Community (EEC)** was first set up, democratic **accountability** was not high on the Community's agenda. At that time, the European Community could be considered a 'special purpose association' to which a limited number of well-defined functions were **delegated**. The democratic nature of the Community was not a matter of serious concern and could, at this point, be guaranteed by the democratic credentials of the member states. The '**Monnet method**', the sector-by-sector approach to **European integration**, was based on the idea of a strong (technical) European Commission, composed of independent Commissioners representing the general interest of the Community. The Commission held the exclusive right of initiative and played a central role as the **executive** body (see Chapter 10), while the Council of Ministers acted as the final decision-maker (see Chapter 11). The Parliamentary Assembly was only indirectly elected and had only consultative powers. As such, it had only as much importance as the advisory Economic and Social Committee (ESC), which was composed of representatives from national **interest groups** and **stakeholders** in the areas of EEC competence (see Chapter 14).

This functional approach to European **integration** (see Chapter 4) was based on the idea of involving actors with particular expertise in the specific fields for which the EEC had been given competence. Functional expertise, rather than democratic participation, was the central issue of concern. The initial stages of European integration were thus said to be based on a '**permissive consensus**' (Lindberg and Scheingold, 1970: 41). There was little popular interest in this elite-driven and technocratic project, and this coincided with diffuse support for the idea of European integration—or, put differently, the legitimacy of the EEC was based on its output, without raising particular concerns about input legitimacy.

However, as the Court of Justice of the EU (CJEU) defined more clearly the features of the European legal order, based on principles such as supremacy and **direct effect** (see Chapter 13), and with the Community acting in new policy areas, the daily impact of the European integration process became ever more evident and the functionalist approach became insufficient as a way of addressing the legitimacy of the European project. In this context, the concept of the 'democratic deficit' refers above all to the idea that the transfer of policy-making power from the national level to the EU has not been accompanied by sufficient democratic control at the European level. At the national level, European integration had strengthened executives to the detriment of parliaments (Moravcsik,

1994) because European policy issues are decided and debated by the government (represented at EU level in the Council) rather than by national parliaments. At the same time, the European Parliament (EP) was institutionally too weak to ensure democratic accountability at the European level.

Framed in these parliamentary terms, there were two possible solutions to the EU's **democratic deficit**. Either one could democratize European decision-making by increasing parliamentary **representation** at the European level by way of the EP (the supranational or federal solution), or one could argue that democratic accountability can reside only in the national parliaments, in which case the priority had to be to limit the transfer of powers to the EU—and in as much as such transfer took place, national parliaments should have the means of ensuring the accountability of their minister in the Council (the **intergovernmental** solution).

As the EEC's influence grew during the 1970s and 1980s, political decision-makers opted for the first solution, and thus the further **parliamentarization** of the European level. In 1979, direct elections to the European Parliament (EP) were introduced to strengthen the direct democratic input at the European level. The Parliament subsequently received increasing powers in the budgetary and legislative process (see Chapter 12). In that way, the EU began to resemble a **bicameral** parliamentary democracy in which legislative power is shared by two branches: one representing the population of the Union (the Parliament), and the other its member states (the EU Council).

However, democratizing the EU by strengthening the role of the EP faces two main difficulties. First, the parliamentary model of democracy—in which government is accountable to the will of the people expressed in a directly elected parliament—does not see the role of parliament only as that of a legislature, but also expects a parliament to have control over the executive through its involvement in the appointment of the government and/or its use of a vote of censure. While the EP has gained important legislative powers, its control over the Commission is more limited. Although the **Treaty of Rome** already allowed the Commission to be dismissed by the then Assembly, this possibility remained theoretical because the Parliament was deprived of any real power in the appointment of a new Commission. The Commission is appointed by the Council from candidates proposed by the member states and thus tends to reflect the parliamentary majorities in power at the national level at the moment of appointment (see Chapters 10 and 11). As such, when European citizens vote in European elections, their opinion finds expression in parliamentary representation, but this does not automatically affect the composition of the Commission, which together with the Council forms the EU's 'executive'.

Second, the EU is neither a traditional international organization nor a state. It is a *sui generis* political system, which is best described as a supranational polity (see Chapter 7). Yet it has been repeatedly argued that this polity has no **demos**—that is, a 'people' with some common identity or shared values that might provide the basis for a parliamentary expression of democracy. The parliamentary model is based on the expression of the general will in parliament. The general will is (mostly) expressed by parliamentary decisions based on majority voting. In order to get these **majoritarian** decisions accepted by the minority, the governed represented in a parliament need to have a certain level of social unity, a common identity. However, it is argued that there is no such common identity in the EU, which, as Article 1 TEU states, is still based on a process of integration 'among the *peoples* of Europe'. Contrary to that, some have argued that there does exist a certain common cultural basis in Europe (Kaelble, 1994), that there is general acceptance of the 'idea of Europe' and 'a commitment to the shared values of the Union as expressed in its constituent documents' (Weiler, 1997: 270). This process could strengthen the loyalty of European citizens vis-à-vis the European polity in a similar way to that in which state action strengthens the loyalty of national citizens vis-à-vis the state, reinforcing the national demos. However, the shift in loyalty to the European level and the creation of some common identity seems to emerge very slowly (Risse, 2002). There is no European '**public sphere**' in which citizens are informed on, and take part in, political discussions. There are no European media. Communication on European issues is nationally coloured and split into different languages (see Chapter 15). Although interest groups have started to lobby and organize at the European level, their activities in Brussels remain rather invisible to the wider public and do not create broader debate on European issues (see Chapter 14). European political parties are weak and European parliamentary elections are '**second-order elections**', thus citizens do not participate and when they do most voters consider the

European political arena to be less important than the national one so they use their votes to express feelings of satisfaction or dissatisfaction with domestic parties or to bring about political change in their own country. Hence, despite the increased legislative powers of the EP, the Parliament struggles to engage European citizens in a political debate that they can understand as the democratic expression of their concerns and interests.

KEY POINTS

- The democratic character of the European Economic Community was not a major issue of concern at its creation, but became an issue of concern as more competences were transferred to the Community.

- The preferred solution to the European democratic deficit was to parliamentarize the European level by directly electing the European Parliament and increasing its powers.

- Parliamentarization faces two problems: the absence of a European demos and a weak European public sphere.

- European citizens do not participate in a shared debate about European politics and there is no direct connection between voting preferences in the EP elections and the composition of the Commission.

9.3 Maastricht and the debate during the 1990s

The debate on the European Union's democratic deficit over the course of the 1990s continued to be inspired by the parliamentary model. While this remained the conceptual reference point used to frame democracy in the EU it also included an additional dimension with the introduction of 'European citizenship'. Potentially, this could encourage the development of a common European identity and partially address the 'no demos' problem.

The **Maastricht Treaty** strengthened the legislative power of the European Parliament by introducing the **co-decision** procedure (now the **ordinary legislative procedure**, or **OLP**); the Maastricht, Amsterdam, and Nice Treaties attempted to create a better link between the EP election results and the composition of the Commission by ensuring that the Commission's term of office coincided with that of the Parliament. Moreover, although proposed by the European Council,

both the Commission President and subsequently the entire Commission have to be approved by the EP. The latter has used this new power to question and even oppose the appointment of new Commissioners (see Chapter 12). Parliamentary democracy at EU level has thus been strengthened, although the latter is still far from a system in which the government is the direct expression of the political majority in parliament.

The Maastricht Treaty also acknowledged the criticism of those arguing that democratic accountability is best guaranteed at the national level by introducing the principle of **subsidiarity**. This meant that, with the exception of areas for which it has **exclusive competence**, the EU can now act only if, and in so far as, the objectives of the proposed action cannot be sufficiently achieved by the member states. Moreover, the 1990s also saw attempts to strengthen the role of national parliaments in EU political decision-making. Member states tightened their domestic regulations to increase parliamentary control over their ministers in the Council, and the EU began to provide a better and more direct information flow to national parliaments so that they could fulfil this function effectively.

The Maastricht Treaty also addressed the role of regional and local authorities in European decision-making. While many European countries had witnessed a process of devolution of political power from the national to the regional level, some of these newly acquired competences were diluted as the EU began to operate in those policy areas. The member states agreed that regional and local actors also needed a place in European decision-making, and as such the Maastricht Treaty created an advisory **Committee of the Regions (CoR)**, representing both regional and local authorities. It also allowed member states to be represented in the Council by a regional minister in policy areas for which the regions held legislative competence.

Citizenship was also introduced in the Maastricht Treaty as a way of framing democracy. Citizenship has traditionally been defined in the context of the nation state, and built on three elements: a set of rights and duties; participation; and identity. By introducing the concept of 'European citizenship', the Maastricht Treaty made it clear that the EU provides citizens with a set of rights and duties that means that they belong to the same community. They can participate democratically in this community by voting in the EP elections, for example, and through acquiring rights that they would not otherwise be able to exercise, such as the right to reside in another member state. European citizenship is therefore expected to strengthen the feeling of a common European identity and to provide some extra fuel to make parliamentary democracy at the EU level work. However, the Maastricht Treaty and all subsequent treaties explicitly state that European citizenship is complementary to national citizenship, and is therefore not at odds with the idea that democratic legitimacy can reside at the same time in the European, national, or even sub-national parliaments.

The citizenship debate has focused primarily on output legitimacy rather than on input legitimacy (although European citizenship also provides participatory rights) (Smismans, 2009). The expectation is that if citizens are better aware of all of the benefits that the EU provides, they will identify more with the Union (see Chapter 15). This link between European rights and belonging to a European 'community' has also been exemplified in the debate at the end of the 1990s about the **Charter of Fundamental Rights** of the EU. With the adoption of the Charter, the EU wanted to make a clear statement of the fundamental rights and values for which it stands and with which its citizens can identify (Smismans, 2010). The way in which the Charter was drafted was also supposed to strengthen the sense of citizens' identification with the Union by making the drafting process more participatory. The latter took place in the first **European Convention**, which brought parliamentarians from the EP and national parliaments together with representatives from governments. Online **consultations** and debating activities made it not only a more parliamentary, but also a more open and participatory, process even if this mainly reached an elite of informed and interested citizens, and failed to witness the involvement of the broader citizenry.

KEY POINTS

- The European Union's democratic deficit was strongly debated during the 1990s. **Representative democracy** remained the central frame of reference.

- After the Maastricht Treaty, the European Parliament was further strengthened, and national, regional, and local authorities were given a role in European policy-making. At the same time, subsidiarity set a limit on the further transfer of powers to the EU.

- The introduction of European citizenship and the Charter of Fundamental Rights of the EU offered a way of developing a common European identity and thus partially addressed the 'no demos' problem.

9.4 EU democracy and the governance debate

Despite all previous efforts to strengthen European democracy on the basis of the parliamentary model, the European Union was still not perceived as more legitimate by European citizens. Events, such as the resignation of the Commission in 1999 (see Chapter 10) after it faced accusations of nepotism and financial management, made it ever more evident that democracy was not only about the role of parliament, but also about **good governance** and the parts played by other actors in policy-making (see Box 9.1). Thus, at the turn of the new century, the debate on democracy and legitimacy in the EU became more diversified.

Some scholars argued that the only way in which to resolve the EU's legitimacy problem was to strengthen the parliamentary model, further politicizing European decision-making. This could be achieved by creating a more direct link between the outcome of European parliamentary elections and the composition of the European Commission. European citizens could be offered a clear choice between different (ideological) policy positions, while at the same time the composition of the Commission could reflect the parliamentary majority and its ideological orientation. European citizens would therefore be able to elect their 'executive' on the basis of a European-wide public debate about policy choices. European decision-making would no longer be technocratic and ignored by European citizens.

This strategy was built on the assumption that if European elections were about clear ideological and political choices reflected in the composition of the Commission, European citizens would engage more with the European debate and identify themselves as active participants in the EU polity. However, what if European political choices were still translated into purely national interpretations through national media? If this were to happen, the effect could be the further delegitimization of the EU, which would be depicted as imposing European-level policies at the national level. This could be particularly problematic where the national government had a different ideological orientation from the parliamentary majority in the EP and the Commission. At the same time, this strategy would fundamentally change the role of the Commission from a motor driving European integration and representing 'the European interest' to an explicitly political body. If a European public sphere

BOX 9.1   BACKGROUND: GOOD GOVERNANCE ACCORDING TO THE EUROPEAN COMMISSION

The European Commission established its own concept of good governance in the White Paper on European Governance (WPEG). The WPEG was adopted in 2001 by the European Commission in order to improve both the efficiency and legitimacy of European governance. Five principles underpin good governance and the changes proposed: openness, participation, accountability, effectiveness, and coherence. Each

principle is important for establishing more democratic governance. The principles underpin democracy and the rule of law in the member states, but they apply to all levels of government—whether global, European, national, regional, or local.

Source: European Commission (2001a).

were not to emerge as a result of this strategy, such a supranational political body would be criticized on the basis of nationally defined interests and debates. As such, political leaders have been reluctant to adopt such a radical approach (see Section 9.5, 'The Constitutional Treaty and the Treaty of Lisbon').

Another argument is that framing EU democracy exclusively in terms of the role of parliament and parliamentary accountability is too much of a simplification and may even be misguided. First, when comparing the EU to a parliamentary democracy at the national level, the perfect functioning of the latter is too easily assumed. The EU is often criticized because the EP does not have the right of legislative initiative (which is the prerogative of the Commission), while assuming that this is always a central feature of parliamentary democracy. Yet, in many countries, legislative initiatives emerge de facto from the government.

Second, by focusing on representative democracy, the debate addresses only part of the problem and neglects other aspects of democratic accountability in European decision-making. The assumption is that democratic decision-making is guaranteed by means of parliamentary input, while the 'neutral' implementation of the parliamentary mandate is guaranteed by government and administration. However, this **normative** ideal has always been a fiction and is increasingly so in modern governance, in which the implementation of the parliamentary mandate is the result of the complex interaction of many actors deploying a multitude of policy instruments. If we want to conceptualize democratic accountability in modern governance, it is not enough to think in terms of parliamentary mandate; rather, we must address the question of who is involved in direct interaction with government and administration in the setting of the policy agenda and the drafting of new policy measures, as well as during the implementation process.

Third, there are multiple ways of conceptualizing democracy. While 'representative democracy' focuses on the electoral process and the representative role of parliament, theories of '**participatory democracy**' stress the importance of more regular and direct citizen involvement in collective decision-making. This could involve referendums or more decentralized governance mechanisms. Theories of '**deliberative democracy**' pay more attention to the quality of deliberative processes, rather than focus on who represents whom or ensuring direct citizen participation.

All of these arguments informed the debate on European governance that emerged at the end of the 1990s and the early twenty-first century. The so-called '**governance turn**' in EU studies (see Chapter 7) argued, among other things, that European policy-making is not only about intergovernmental bargaining among member states and power struggles among the European institutions, but also involves many different actors at different stages and in different modes of policy-making. This governance debate resets in several ways the terms of the discussion about legitimacy and democracy in the EU. First, it is attentive to the different stages of policy-making. Democracy and legitimacy are not only about the legislative process and the power of parliament in legislative decision-making; what happens at the initial stage of policy-making, when the European Commission consults widely and interacts with many actors when drafting legislative proposals, matters too. Moreover, once legislative acts have been adopted, the EU often adopts further regulatory measures by way of **delegated legislation** (see Chapter 16). If one wants to assess democracy and legitimacy in the EU, a closer look at this process is required, as it affects the majority of EU decisions (see Box 9.2).

Second, the governance debate has made clear that there are different modes of European governance,

---

BOX 9.2   CASE STUDY: DELEGATED LEGISLATION

Delegated legislation is a common feature of modern governance. Because adopting legislation often takes time, legislators may decide to delegate secondary or implementing decision-making to governments. While delegated legislation allows for speedier and more effective policy-making, it also takes decision-making out of the hands of the elected representatives in parliament; this may raise concerns about democratic accountability.

At the European level, delegated legislation occurs via the delegation by the EU Council and the EP (as co-legislators, in most cases) to the European Commission, as executive. This does not mean that the Commission can act in an uncontrolled way once it has been delegated the task to adopt further regulatory acts. The EU has developed a process referred to as 'comitology', requiring the Commission to interact with a 'comitology committee' composed of representatives from the member states when it adopts delegated legislation.

Comitology has often been criticized from a democratic point of view. It is a rather technocratic process driven by Commission officials and representatives from national administrations, normally without the involvement of elected politicians. Moreover, comitology is a rather opaque process, with few knowing where, how, and why the decisions have been taken. However, some scholars have described comitology as 'deliberative supranationalism' (Joerges and Neyer, 1997) indicating that it is not simply a technocratic process, but a process that allows for informed deliberation at the EU level on the basis of expertise and representation of interests in the comitology committees. The Commission has also taken initiatives that are intended to make the system less opaque by providing online information on comitology.

The Lisbon Treaty sought to strengthen the democratic character of further regulatory decision-making by creating a distinction between delegated acts and implementing acts. Legislative acts, which set out the most important provisions by way of the ordinary or special legislative procedures (thus involving the EP), now have two options to delegate to the Commission to take further action. One option is to give the Commission the power to adopt delegated acts, which can set out provisions of a general scope, but cannot define the most important provisions, which can only be set out in legislation. The Commission can adopt delegated acts on its own, but given that they are still rather important provisions, the EP and the Council have the right to oppose such a decision, thus allowing some democratic control over the process by elected politicians. The second option, is to give the Commission the power to adopt implementing acts, which are used for the less generic and more technical provisions. Such acts are still adopted through a (revised) comitology procedure, without involving the Council or the EP. Compared to the situation prior to the Lisbon Treaty, the new system of delegated regulation thus increases democratic control because of the new category of delegated acts. However, it can also be argued that, as far as the implementing acts are concerned, democratic control may actually have weakened, since neither the Council nor the EP can intervene any more in comitology, in situations in which they occasionally had a role under the previous system. In terms of reducing complexity and opaque governance, the new system is not exactly an improvement either, because although there are no formally empowered comitology committees any more for delegated acts, similar committees with member state representatives are still involved in an informal way.

---

and that democracy and legitimacy may be addressed differently for each of them. Traditionally, the legitimacy debate has focused on the 'Community method', based on legislative decision-making and a central role for the EP. However, many 'new modes of governance' (NMGs), such as the open method of coordination (OMC), hardly involve the European Parliament at all. The OMC was created in 2000 to allow the EU to coordinate the policies of the member states in particular policy fields, such as employment policy or macro-economic policy, but without adopting binding legislation at the European level. The OMC procedure is based on the adoption of guidelines by the Council, based on a proposal of the Commission, addressed to the member states. While such guidelines are not binding, the member states have to adopt national action plans to explain how they intend to reach the targets set in the guidelines. They have to report to the European Commission on their initiatives, after which the Commission and Council can propose new guidelines and (for some policy areas) send recommendations to the member states. It has been argued that the legitimacy of the OMC resides in its participatory and decentralized character. Since the EU only adopts guidelines and not binding measures in the OMC, the absence of the EP is regarded as non-controversial. In the end, it is up to the member states to take decisions to implement such guidelines and, in that case, democratic accountability is guaranteed by national parliaments. Moreover, the drafting of European guidelines and the national measures that implement them are said to be participatory, given the involvement of stakeholders. However, in reality, the stakeholder involvement is often patchy and national parliaments are not always well informed. By contrast, European guidelines, despite the fact that they are not binding, may have a decisive influence on policy options. Although there remain doubts about the impact of the OMC, the democratic claims made in relation to this mode of governance need to be nuanced (Smismans, 2008).

Third, three concepts have been particularly central to the debate on the legitimacy of European governance—namely, '**participation**', 'civil society', and 'transparency'. Democracy is not simply about participation in elections and representation through a parliament, but it is also about the participation of multiple actors, such as interest groups, experts, representatives from national administration, and individual citizens. These actors are involved in many different stages of policy-making, from the drafting of a new legislative proposal to participation in the implementation of the OMC at national level.

Since the end of the 1990s, the EU institutions have often encouraged the participation of civil society in European governance. The Economic and Social Committee (ESC) has presented itself as the ideal institutional form of representation for civil society, while the Commission has taken measures to ensure wider consultation at the initial stage of policy-making. The EU institutions have mainly sought the involvement of representatives from civil society organizations in policy-making, although the Commission has also taken initiatives to broaden general online consultations in which individual citizens can also participate. This has been referred to as '**participatory democracy**' or 'participatory governance'.

The way in which the EU provides consultative processes at the initial stage of policy-making is often more extensive than in many of its member states. However, talk of civil society and online consultations do not ensure equality of access to European decision-making, because those with most resources and money are bound to be the most effective lobbyists (see Chapter 14). The debate on participation and civil society is therefore linked to that on transparency. One can distinguish *ex post* and *ex ante* dimensions of transparency when talking about EU legitimacy. Thus, by ensuring the transparency of the activities of the EU's institutions, one can ensure

ex post democratic accountability. For example, this might involve the EP scrutinizing the Commission, national parliaments controlling the action of their ministers in the Council, or citizens voting for a particular party or group during EP elections. Many initiatives have been taken to increase transparency of this kind. For example, this has involved increasing the information sent by the Commission to both European and national parliaments, and by ensuring that Council meetings are public when dealing with legislative issues. Moreover, the EU institutions, and in particular the Commission, increasingly provide information during the drafting of policy measures. Such *ex ante* transparency allows for improved participation by civil society actors and stakeholders, and would thus also allow for better-informed policy-making (and thus increased output legitimacy). Compared again with the transparency provided at the national level by many countries, even within the EU, the EU's initiatives on transparency are relatively far-reaching. However, the EU governance system is so complex and remote that it remains the preserve of an informed elite. With the **European Transparency Initiative (ETI),** introduced by the Commission in 2005 to increase openness, transparency, and accountability of European governance, the EU also aims to shed some light on this elite when they participate in European policy-making. It does this by providing for a Transparency Register that contains information on interest groups' lobbying of the EU institutions (see Chapter 14).

KEY POINTS

- By 2000 the debate on democracy and legitimacy in the European Union had become more diversified.

- It was argued that a further parliamentarization and a politicization of the European Commission may not be a suitable or practicable response to the EU's democratic deficit.

- The governance debate broadened the conceptualization of democracy and legitimacy in the EU beyond the legislative process, the electoral process, and the power games that persist among the EU's institutions.

- Participation by multiple actors and civil society, as well as transparency, are key elements in the conceptualization of democracy.

9.5 The Constitutional Treaty and the Treaty of Lisbon

The debate surrounding the Constitutional Treaty (CT) between 2001 and 2005 added another layer to the conceptualization of EU democracy. This concerned the question of the 'constituent power' necessary to create and revise the constitutional rules of the EU. Democracy is not only about participation in European governance, but also raises questions about the initial design of the institutional framework. Before the CT, the constitutional rules of the European polity had always been drafted behind the closed doors of diplomatic meetings at **intergovernmental conferences (IGCs)**, leading to treaty reform. The European Convention charged with drafting the CT aimed at a more open and participatory debate on the constitutional design of the EU by also involving European and national parliamentarians, by using online consultations, and by hosting broader debating events. However, the French and Dutch 'no' votes in referendums on the proposed CT in 2005, which led to the demise of the CT, illustrate the difficulties involved in building the EU's legitimacy on the basis of a constitutional document.

Although not as innovative in democratic terms as the CT, the Lisbon Treaty subsequently provides some new ideas on EU democracy and legitimacy. First, and for the first time, the Treaty included an explicit title, 'Provisions on democratic principles'. In it, Article 10 clearly states that the Union 'shall be founded on representative democracy', indicating the representative role of the EP, stating that the Council and the **European Council** are accountable to the national parliaments, and mentioning the role of political parties. By contrast, Article 11 stresses elements that can be described as 'participatory democracy' (although the concept is not explicitly used)—namely, the importance of dialogue with citizens and civil society organizations (CSOs).

Second, the Treaty introduces the **'Citizens' Initiative'** as a new democratic instrument and form of direct participatory democracy (Article 11(4) TEU). This allows European citizens to gather a million signatures to ask the Commission to draft a proposal for a legal act on an issue on which they consider European action is required (as long as it falls within the competences of the EU). In order to launch a citizens' initiative, citizens must form a 'citizens' committee' composed of at least seven EU citizens being resident

in at least seven different member states. The citizens' committee must register its initiative before starting to collect statements of support from citizens. Once the registration is confirmed and checked on whether it falls within EU competence, organizers have one year in which to collect signatures. The Citizens' Initiative may stir up the European debate, and make the EU both more visible and bottom-up. However, it also entails risks if EU action does not live up to the expectations of those taking the initiative (see Box 9.3).

Third, the Lisbon Treaty has strengthened the principle of subsidiarity by giving national parliaments a way of controlling whether new proposals made by the Commission respect this principle. The new procedure allows control *ex ante*, before a decision is taken, which is more efficient than *ex post* control by the Court of Justice on whether a decision already taken respects subsidiarity. This is because the Court is reluctant to contradict a value judgement made by the European institutions. However, the success of this new procedure depends on whether national parliaments manage to collaborate within the short time span in which the procedure allows them to act. Since its creation, national parliaments only managed to trigger the subsidiarity control mechanism three times. In none of these cases did the Commission subsequently agree that subsidiarity had not been respected. In one of them it withdrew its proposal as the reasoned opinion by the national parliaments had made it clear that there was insufficient political support for the measure.

Finally, the Lisbon Treaty has further strengthened the role of the EP by turning the co-decision procedure into the ordinary legislative procedure and by giving the EP a controlling role over the adoption of a new type of delegated act. The Lisbon Treaty also contributes to further parliamentarization of EU decision-making by strengthening the links between EP elections and the Commission's composition: Article 17(7) TEU now requires the European Council to take into account the outcome of the EP elections before nominating a candidate for Commission President. To strengthen the link between EP election result and choice of Commission President the political groups in the EP each presented a candidate for Commission President (or '*spitzenkandidat*') during the campaign prior to the 2014 EP elections, arguing that the European Council should appoint the candidate of the party acquiring most votes in the election. The European Council did indeed appoint

BOX 9.3   CASE STUDY: THE EUROPEAN CITIZENS' INITIATIVE IN PRACTICE

Launched on 1 April 2012, the first years of practice of the Citizens' Initiative show the limitations of this new democratic instrument. The Citizens' Initiative has created limited debate and, above all, little impact. By July 2021, nearly a decade after its launch, 81 initiatives have been started but only six initiatives have reached the stage where the Commission has provided an answer, and none so far has led to the adoption of a legal act. Most initiatives failed to reach the number of signatures required to be submitted to the Commission, or were simply withdrawn by those launching the initiative. More problematic is the fact that many Citizens' Initiatives were refused by the Commission on the grounds that the topic was beyond its competence, sometimes on the basis of a very restrictive interpretation. This has created a lot of frustration among citizens who expected the Citizens' Initiative to provide them with a tool to set the EU's political agenda in a bottom-up way. A striking example of this was the Commission's refusal of a Citizens' Initiative asking the EU to withdraw from negotiating the Transatlantic Trade and Investment Partnership (TTIP) with the USA. The TTIP was highly controversial, with the EU being accused of secretly negotiating an agreement that only favoured business interests and undermined social and environmental standards (see Chapter 17).

Even in the case of the six Citizens' Initiatives for which all requirements were fulfilled and enough signatures were gathered, the Commission, which is not obliged to propose a new legal act, answered that the existing EU's legislative framework on the matter was sufficient. In one of the six cases the Commission argued that no new action was needed. In three other cases it promised that **soft law** measures and a new consultation would suffice, rather than legislative action. In the

initiative concerning the pesticide glyphosate the Commission did propose that it would take some legislative action but it declined taking up the initiative's key demand, namely banning glyphosate, and instead limited itself to developing new rules on transparency and quality of evidence studies used in EU regulation. Only in a recently answered initiative did the Commission live up to the expectation of introducing legislation in a similar way as asked by the initiative. The 'End the Cage Age' initiative aims to ban cages in animal farming, and the Commission has committed to introduce by the end of 2023 a legislative initiative to phase out cages for animals that are not already covered by such bans in European legislation.

One can conclude that there is clearly a wide gap between the initial expectations created by the introduction of the Citizens' Initiative, which was perceived as an opportunity for citizens to set the policy and legislative agenda of the EU, and the way this operates in practice. As a result, after the initial enthusiasm, the number of initiatives has gone down each year. However, more recently, several positive developments can be noted. The amount of Commission refusals has gone down. Moreover, in 2019, the EU set out a new framework for the Citizens' Initiative, by way of Regulation 2019/788, which facilitates the registration procedure and conditions for collecting signatures. That being said, the limits in legal competence of the EU will always frustrate many of those signing an initiative. Most importantly, with the exception of the 'End the Cage Age' initiative, practice so far shows that the European Commission is reluctant to revise the existing legal framework developed by the Council and European Parliament; or to put it differently, to allow that participatory democracy trumps representative democracy.

Jean-Claude Juncker, who was the candidate of the party that came out first in the elections, namely the European People's Party (EPP) (see Chapter 12). However, this new process remained modest in terms of politicizing the European Union and offering European citizens a clear choice between different politically orientated Commissions with clear and well-debated political programmes. The national debates on the role and impact of the different candidates remained limited. Moreover, while the role of the Commission President in selecting Commissioners has increased, it is still dependent on proposals made by the member states (and thus on the political majorities present at national level at the time of appointment). This limits the potential of any candidate proposed by a political party in the

EP to promise a clear electoral programme. At the same time, the member states have always remained reluctant about the *Spitzenkandidat* process and argued that it remained the prerogative of the European Council to nominate somebody else if they deemed that to be a better solution. In fact, following the 2019 EP elections, the European Council did not appoint the *Spitzenkandidat* of the EP party that obtained most votes, but rather Ursula von der Leyen, a national politician who belonged to the same political family but had not been campaigning for the role. While this did respect the logic of appointing a Commission President from the political group obtaining most votes, it clearly undermined the EU's capacity to make policy by way of clear electoral programmes presented by *Spitzenkandidaten*.

9.6 The output gap, populism, and EU legitimacy

Our analysis so far shows how the EU has gradually strengthened procedural mechanisms for democratic accountability, providing a complex governance structure of multiple checks and balances. Yet, at the same time it has faced increasing demands to deliver policy outputs for the major challenges of our time, which has often resulted in populist narratives using the EU as a scapegoat when policy intervention struggles.

Over the last decade, Europe has faced major challenges, in particular the economic crisis, the migration crisis, the terrorism crisis, and the public health crisis of **COVID-19**. All these are not as such 'EU problems', but they have amplified in an unprecedented fashion the main features of the EU's legitimacy challenge. As the EU's legitimacy is strongly based on 'output', not being able to deliver effective policy solutions to the crises above has put into question the legitimacy of the polity as a whole. While many people take the existence of the nation state for granted, any (perceived) policy failures by the EU quickly leads to questions about the *raison d'être* and viability of the EU (see de Búrca, 2013). Although the origins of the 2008 economic crisis do not lie in the European integration process, but in the lending and speculative practices of the banking sector and the lack of regulation of global financial transactions, it illustrated in a dramatic way the shortcomings of **economic and monetary union (EMU)** (see Chapter 22). EU institutions were not fit for purpose and policy reaction was delayed and patchy (see Chapter 25). Similarly, the migration and security crises introduced new external challenges to the EU, for which its institutional framework was ill-prepared and rather opened up the opportunity to

question one of the main achievements of European integration, namely the border-free **Schengen area** (see Chapter 26). Equally, as the COVID-19 pandemic unfolded, people were looking to the EU for coordinated action, and mutual support, for instance on protective medical equipment, but EU action took time to build up and was constrained by the EU's limited legal competence in the area of public health (see Chapter 28).

In fact, the expectations of what the EU should have done in relation to all the above challenges illustrate perfectly the double challenge at the core of the EU's legitimacy conundrum. Coordinated action to address these challenges requires 'more' rather than 'less Europe' but this faces two difficulties.

Firstly, further transfer of **sovereignty** from the member states to the EU exacerbates the European democratic deficit unless this is accompanied by sufficient democratic accountability of the EU's new policy-making powers. The EU's new **fiscal policy** governance, set up following the 2008 economic crisis, is most troublesome in this regard, as it limits member states' sovereignty to decide on their own budget without compensating with democratic input and control at the EU level. Although national parliaments retain their formal role in adopting the national budget, the budgetary margins and policy options set out in the budget are increasingly drafted at the European level, with the Commission in the lead, no intervention of the EP, and with the EU Council acting only as a potential (intergovernmental) blocking authority.

Secondly, appropriate EU action is only possible when the member states provide the EU with the legal and financial means for that, which requires that there is not only a sense of expectation of European action but also one of European solidarity, which brings us back to the question of a European demos and the deficient nature of the European public sphere. The adoption of a common European response has proved difficult because solidarity among European countries cannot be taken for granted, and political decision-makers tend to communicate with their own national electorate and media in terms of defending their national interest while blaming the other (see Chapter 15). Thus, efficient reaction to the economic crisis was undermined by lack of solidarity between 'credit' and 'defaulting' EU countries; while the EU's attempt to share some of the burden of immigration among all EU countries met with very hostile resistance in several countries, particularly in Central and Eastern Europe. Also in relation to the COVID-19 pandemic, the EU had to operate in a context of member states' (initial) reflex to act unilaterally, and the EU's limits in terms of legal capacity to act, while at the same time being faced with public expectations to deliver efficient policy and blame when the response did not immediately occur. In the end, the EU common vaccine procurement scheme can be considered a success. Particularly smaller EU countries, and those with no vaccine production, would have faced more substantial vaccine shortages had the EU been driven by the 'vaccine nationalism' shown by the British government, for example. Equally, the pandemic has led to the most extensive EU financial support scheme for those countries that most suffered from the crisis, showing that EU solidarity can and often does emerge in times of crisis.

The EU, though, has to operate in a context of rising populism, which is challenging for each level of government, but particularly so for a supranational polity as the EU. The causes of such general emergence of populism are broader than the EU, as exemplified by very similar developments in the USA with the presidency of Donald Trump. Yet, the EU is a particularly attractive target for such populist discourse; by depicting the EU as 'foreign' and an elitist 'creation of the establishment' populists aim to obtain the popular vote presenting themselves as the representatives of the homogenous single will of the people. Rising populism has gone hand in hand with an increase in **Euroscepticism**, as illustrated by the surge in support for anti-EU political parties in European elections and some national elections or **Brexit** (see Chapter 27). While these parties attack the EU for being undemocratic and inefficient, it is often due to their lack of solidarity that more efficient EU action is impeded. Moreover, criticizing the EU for being undemocratic is no guarantee of ensuring more democratic decision-making at the national level. Brexit has been the epitome of this.

Thus, Eurosceptic political parties and governments are themselves showing little respect for democracy and the rule of law at the national level. In fact, the biggest challenge to democracy in the EU lies in the democratic backsliding happening at the national level in some of its member states. In countries such as Hungary and Poland, the basic principles of democratic governance and the rule of law are being challenged, by governments undermining the independence of the judiciary, curtailing pluralism of the media, changing electoral systems to remain unchallenged in power, and undermining the fundamental rights of minorities, such as the LGBT+ community. Democratic backsliding and disrespect of

the rule of law in member states, is a problem for the EU for three reasons. Firstly, while the European Economic Communities were initially set up as a functional process of economic integration, the objective of ensuring peace has always been at its core. The initial design did not provide for the EEC to play a role in ensuring the respect of fundamental rights and the rule of law in European countries, as this role was to be played by the Council of Europe, and its **European Court of Human Rights** in particular. However, EEC/EU enlargement had a clear role in consolidating democracy in former dictatorships, such as Greece and Spain, and later in relation to the former communist countries of Central and Eastern Europe. Respect for fundamental rights and the rule of law became a key criteria for joining the EU, and is now solidly enshrined in Article 2 of the **Treaty on European Union**, which states that 'the Union is founded on the values of respect for human dignity, freedom, democracy, equality, the rule of law and respect for human rights, including the rights of persons belonging to minorities. These values are common to the Member States in a society in which pluralism, non-discrimination, tolerance, justice, solidarity and equality between women and men prevail'. Democratic backsliding at the national level thus puts into jeopardy the objectives and the legitimacy of the EU itself. Secondly, when autocrats rule at the national level, they will also have a seat in EU decision-making, from the (European) Council and the European Parliament, to the Commission and the Court of Justice. Hence disrespect of the rule of law at the national level thus has a direct impact on EU decision-making. Thirdly, the EU is built upon trust between member states. When some of these member states clearly disregard the rule of law, that trusts falls entirely away.

However, the EU has struggled to ensure that member states respect the rule of law. Since it was not created for that reason, it was not given the powers to exert such control. The Court of Justice has gradually built up case law on the respect of fundamental rights, but this was first to ensure that EU institutions and EU decision-making respect fundamental rights, and subsequently to ensure that member states do so *when they are implementing EU law*. Hence the Court of Justice has no general control over member states' governments not observing fundamental rights and the rule of law. Therefore, with the adoption of Article 7 of the Treaty of the European Union, the EU introduced a more political control mechanism to oversee the respect of the rule of law, but it has been proven to be insufficient to avoid democratic backsliding in several member states (see Box 9.4).

BOX 9.4   BACKGROUND: THE RULE OF LAW AND DEMOCRATIC BACKSLIDING

The Amsterdam Treaty introduced for the first time a sanction mechanism, now Article 7 of the Treaty on European Union, in case a member state does not respect the values of the EU, as set out in Article 2 of the Treaty on European Union, including democracy, the rule of law, and human rights. A member state found in serious and persistent breach may first be warned, and subsequently be suspended from certain of the rights deriving from the Treaties, including the voting rights of the representative of the government of that member state in the Council. However, it has proven difficult to put this article into practice. First, it is worth noting that Article 7 does not explicitly provide the opportunity to expel a member state. Secondly, to impose a sanction, the decision has to be taken unanimously by the European Council (minus the state under investigation). This is problematic when the EU faces several member states that do not respect the rule of law, as they tend to support each other in avoiding Article 7 sanctions. Imposing sanctions might also not be very effective if the sanction is not perceived as very painful by the disrespecting member state, and such (threat of) sanction is used nationally as a way to

further consolidate power by calling on sentiments of national pride against EU interference.

In order to improve the operability of Article 7, in 2014 the Commission introduced an early-warning tool allowing it to enter into dialogue with a member state to address systemic threats to the rule of law to prevent escalation. More importantly, in December 2020, the EU adopted Regulation (EU, Euratom) 2020/2092 on a general regime of conditionality for the protection of the Union budget. This Regulation finally provides a tool that allows the EU to adopt sanctions that really 'hurt' a member state not respecting the rule of law, namely limiting or blocking their receipt of EU funding. Governments not respecting the rule of law are generally also characterized by cronyism and paying off support via financial favours. The reduction of EU funding may therefore contribute to undermining national support for governments that do not respect the rule of law. With several countries, in particular Hungary and Poland, backsliding ever further, it is up to the EU to make it a priority to use this new tool appropriately.

KEY POINTS

- The European Union's output legitimacy has been called into question as a consequence of major challenges such as the financial, immigration, security, and pandemic crises.

- The EU's reaction to these crises was often seen as slow and debatable (as were many national policy reactions) and partially amplified the EU's democratic deficit when it involved a transfer of sovereignty from the member states to the EU with little democratic accountability; such as in the new financial governance mechanisms.

- The crises show a tension between, on the one hand, the ongoing expectations of many Europeans for the EU to address these major societal challenges; and on the other

hand, the reluctance of national politicians to support more European solutions, or to defend them publicly as the public debate remains mainly defined in national terms, given the weak nature of the European public sphere.

- Populism is on the rise in Europe. The EU is an easy target for populist discourse and politicians who want to retreat within national borders and look for an external scapegoat.

- When national retreat is combined with democratic backsliding, the EU is balanced on a tight rope, aiming to ensure the rule of law is respected while not creating a further Eurosceptic backlash that might favour disintegration.

9.7 Conclusion

As the European Union became involved in a broader range of policy areas, its legitimacy could no longer be taken for granted. Policy outputs were no longer deemed an adequate way of improving the EU's legitimacy. However, organizing democratic participation and accountability in a supranational polity is challenging, owing to the EU's distance from European citizens and the Union's complexity. The institutional set-up of the EU provides for some of the most important elements

needed to guarantee democracy—namely, that the EU is based on a division of powers guaranteed through respect for the rule of law. In a democracy, decision-making cannot be in the hands of a single authority, but has to be shared by several bodies in a system of **checks and balances**. Although the EU does not have a strict **separation of powers** across its legislative, executive, and judicial powers, it is based on a system of '**institutional balance**' in which the Commission represents the

Community interests, the Council, the member state interest, and the European Parliament, the European citizens' interests (Lenaerts and Verhoeven, 2002).

The Court of Justice guarantees respect for this institutional balance, so that none of the EU institutions can act beyond the powers that they have been afforded by the treaties. Within this institutional set-up, the body most directly representing Europe's citizens, the European Parliament, has gradually been given more powers. The EU has also tried to strengthen its democratic credentials by providing other checks and balances, for example, through the principle of subsidiarity, and by ensuring transparency and by institutionalizing consultation and participation. These initiatives have their shortcomings but on some procedural issues such as transparency and consultative practice they fare better than what many member states offer at the national level; while the overall design shows a system of checks and balances that definitely avoids an authoritarian concentration of power.

The main challenge for EU democracy remains the difficulty of linking European decision-making to a broad public debate across the member states, because national politicians and media either ignore European issues or address them from a particular national angle, while turnout in EP elections is in decline (see Chapter 15). Some therefore argue that the EU can never be democratic and that decision-making should remain national. However, such argumentation often builds on inaccurate assumptions. First, comparing the EU to an idealized idea of democracy at the national level is misinformed, since many of the difficulties of democracy in the EU are not unique to the European level, but are equally present at the national level.

Second, the fact that decision-making does not take place at the European level does not imply that it will 'return' to the national level. In today's **globalized** world, many issues, such as environmental protection or the regulation of new technologies, require decision-making beyond national borders, while the working of the global market has undermined the capacity of national governments to act on their own. From that perspective, the alternative to European decision-making does not look significantly more democratic, because decisions may simply be taken in less democratic settings such as the **World Trade Organization (WTO)**, or by big corporations acting on the global market. Brexit is a good case in point. Sold by its promoters as a way 'to take back control', the exit from the EU will require the UK to adopt many EU rules (while no longer

having a say) in order to have access to the Single Market, or it will have to accommodate the demands of other countries in trade negotiations in order to compensate for the lost trade with the EU; and respond to the deregulatory requests of foreign investors to compensate for the loss of its privileged competitive position within the Single Market. In a globalized world, the EU might be a 'democracy without a demos', but the national alternative looks increasingly like a *demos* without '*kratos*' (power). Moreover, 'renationalization' is no guarantee of more democratic decision-making, as illustrated by Brexit and those governments within the EU that are at the same time the most Eurosceptic and by undermining the rule of law nationally.

One may conclude that while the EU's democratic deficit debate has mainly focused on adjusting the EU's complex governance architecture, the two key questions of its legitimacy actually lie elsewhere; namely, the challenge of democratic backsliding at the national level, and how to translate EU citizens' expectations on what the EU should do about the major challenges of our time into support and into a participatory process for effective EU governance. The former would need to be addressed by a stronger governance infrastructure to apply the rule of law. For the second, an opportunity has been created by the **Conference for the Future of Europe**, set on track by Commission President Ursula von der Leyen, soon after her appointment. The Conference has similarities with the European Convention in its attempt to create a broad debate on the purpose and design of the EU. But it has two important different features. While the Convention already made use of online consultation with the wider public, the Conference pushes consultation further by making optimal use of technological opportunities and by creating bottom-up deliberative fora of individual citizens. Moreover, while the agenda of the Convention was defined by institutional questions, the agenda this time is fully open to bottom-up initiatives, affording the first opportunity to directly reflect on EU citizens' expectations about the core challenges of our time, and which role the EU ought to play. Such an approach, defining first, for instance, what citizens' expect from the EU in terms of climate change or tackling a pandemic, rather than another technical discussion on the nature of EU comitology, is likely to appeal more to EU citizens. It remains to be seen how (national) politicians engage with this opportunity, or whether national retreat or populism become more dominant.

QUESTIONS

1. Why was the democratic nature of the EEC not an issue of concern at its creation?

2. Why does the European Union suffer from a democratic deficit despite the gradual increase in the powers of the European Parliament?

3. Are national parliaments the source of legitimacy for the EU?

4. How did the governance debate change the EU's understanding of democracy and legitimacy?

5. What are the core features of 'participatory democracy' in the EU?

6. Has the Lisbon Treaty strengthened democracy in the EU?

7. Why do the economic, migration, security, and pandemic crises constitute a challenge to the legitimacy of the EU?

8. Would decision-making be more democratic if it took place at the national or international, rather than the European, level?

9. What can the EU do about a member state not respecting the rule of law, and what may happen if it does not intervene appropriately?

10. What is the relevance of the Conference for the future of Europe?

GUIDE TO FURTHER READING

Harlow, C. (2002) *Accountability in the European Union* (Oxford: Oxford University Press). Based on an analysis of the differing understandings of the concept of accountability in the member states, this book studies the mechanisms through which the EU attempts to hold policy-makers to account.

Kohler-Koch, B. and Rittberger, B. (eds) (2007) *Debating the Democratic Legitimacy of the European Union* (Lanham, MD: Rowman & Littlefield). This edited book discusses the role of parliamentary representation, the public sphere, participation, and deliberation in the EU.

Kröger, S. and Friedrich, D. (eds) (2012) *The Challenge of Democratic Representation in the European Union* (Basingstoke: Palgrave Macmillan). This book provides an analysis of the concept of democratic representation and its different meanings in the context of the EU.

Nanette, N. and Kovacs, C. (2021) 'Hungary and the EU's rule of law protection', *Journal of European Integration* 43/1: 17–32. This article reviews a national case study to illustrate the tools available to the EU in order to ensure the rule of law in its member states.

Piattoni, S. (ed.) (2015) *The European Union: Democratic Principles and Institutional Architectures in Times of Crisis* (Oxford: Oxford University Press). Taking into account the consequences of the economic crisis, this book studies both the democratic principles and the institutional architectures to reflect on democracy in the EU.

Smismans, S. (ed.) (2006) *Civil Society and Legitimate European Governance* (Cheltenham: Edward Elgar). This study provides both theoretical analysis and empirical assessment of the role of civil society and interest groups in European governance, addressing the potential and challenges in relation to the legitimacy of European decision-making.

Access the online resources to take your learning and understanding further, including extra multiple-choice questions with instant feedback, web links, answer guidance to end-of-chapter questions, and updates on new developments in EU politics.

www.oup.com/he/cini-borragan7e

PART 3

Institutions and Actors

10

The European Commission

Morten Egeberg

Chapter Contents

Reader's Guide

This chapter provides a general introduction to the European Commission, the main executive body of the European Union (EU). It argues that it is more productive to compare the Commission to national executives or to a government than to a secretariat of a traditional international organization. It begins with a summary of the Commission's functions within the EU's policy process. It then considers the question of Commission influence and autonomy, before moving on to look at the structure, demography, and decision behaviour within the organization—that is, at the role of the President of the Commission and the Commissioners, at the Commissioners' personal staffs, and at the Commission administration. It then examines the committees and administrative networks that link the Commission to national administrations and interest groups, and the recent growth of EU agencies. The chapter concludes by emphasizing that the Commission is much more of a European(ized) and supranational institution than it was at its inception.

10.1 Introduction

To many observers, the Commission is a unique institution. It is much more than an international secretariat, but not quite a government, although it has many governmental characteristics. The Commission encompasses elements of both intergovernmentalism (a national dimension) and **supranationalism** (a European dimension). It is the opposing pull of these two elements that forms the focal point of this chapter. By exploring the national and supranational features of the Commission's organization, the chapter restates the question: what sort of institution is the European Commission?

The Commission's origins lie in the **High Authority** of the **European Coal and Steel Community (ECSC)**. It represents a considerable institutional innovation if we compare the institutional arrangement of the European Union with international organizations around the world. Its most innovative aspect is that, for the first time in the history of international organizations, a separate executive body, with its own political leadership, had been set up *outside* the Ministers' Council. The concept of an Assembly, later the European Parliament (EP), was already known from the United Nations, the North Atlantic Treaty Organization (NATO), and the **Council of Europe**. An International Court of Justice (ICJ) had been in place in The Hague since the early twentieth century. An independent executive, on the other hand, was something quite new.

The chapter begins (Section 10.2) with a brief review of the Commission's main functions, which relate to its role in the EU policy process. These involve the Commission in **agenda-setting** and, more specifically, in the drafting of legislation and budgets; in the implementation of policies (albeit mainly at arm's length) and the management of programmes; and in the formulation and negotiation of certain aspects of the EU's external relations. Moreover, the Commission also has a role to play in mediating between the Parliament and Council, and among national governments and **non-state actors** involved in European policy-making, as well as in presenting its own, or a European, perspective on issues and events. Section 10.3 covers Commission influence and autonomy, viewing it through the lens of **integration theory** (see Chapters 4–9). In the sections that follow, attention turns to the organizational features of the Commission and their behavioural consequences, with

the focus first on the Commission President and College of Commissioners (Section 10.4); second, on the Commissioners' cabinets (their personal offices) (Section 10.5); third, on the Commission administration (departments and services) (Section 10.6); and finally, on the role of committees, external administrative networks, and EU agencies (Section 10.7). The conclusions to the chapter (Section 10.8) are that, even though some commentators on the Commission argue that it is becoming less influential (e.g., Bickerton et al., 2015b), the Commission is in many respects a more important and genuinely European institution than it ever was in the past (Becker et al., 2016; Nugent and Rhinard, 2016).

10.2 The functions of the Commission

The European Commission, like a government, is composed of a political executive wing (the Commissioners and their cabinets) and an administrative wing (the departments and services). It has a wide range of functions within the EU system: policy initiation and development, monitoring of policy implementation, management of European programmes, an important external relations role, and other functions that involve it as a mediator among the 27 member states, and between the EU Council and the European Parliament (EP), as well as asserting its own European identity (see Box 10.1). The Commission is clearly involved in the EU's policy process from start to finish. In much the same way as are national executives, the Commission is responsible for the initiation and formulation of policies, usually in the form of legislative, budgetary, or programme proposals. The Commission drafts the legislation that is passed on to the two legislative bodies, the EP and the Council. It is in this sense that, in the majority of policy areas, such as the **Single Market** (see Chapter 20) and Justice and Home Affairs (JHA) (see Chapter 21), the Commission performs an important agenda-setting role. Other actors, such as the **European Council** (the heads of state and government), the EP, national governments, and interest groups, may also take initiatives and advance policy proposals, but it is generally up to the Commission to decide whether these ideas will be picked up and subsequently passed on to the legislature in the form of a formal legislative proposal. A study shows that the Commission prioritizes policy issues that are deemed

BOX 10.1 BACKGROUND: THE COMMISSION AS A MULTI-SECTORAL AND MULTI-FUNCTIONAL ORGANIZATION

Although much media focus during autumn 2011 was on the euro crisis and thus on the Economic and Financial Affairs Commissioner as well as the Commission President, this does not mean that other Commission activities were in general put on ice. During two critical weeks (from 24 November to 7 December 2011), the former weekly *European Voice* (now *Politico*) reported, inter alia, that the Home Affairs Commissioner called on Members of the European Parliament (MEPs) to embrace an EU–US deal on passenger data; that the Transport Commissioner asked member states to speed up on implementing 'single European sky' legislation; that the Commissioner for Climate Action was trying to push others in the EU direction at the climate summit in Durban, South Africa; that the Research and Science Commissioner unveiled an €80 billion research programme; that the Internal Market Commissioner expected a deal on the single EU patent; that the Home Affairs Commissioner launched a new border-control proposal; and that the Commissioner for Health wanted the Commission to lead EU responses to health crises. All of these 'business as usual' activities illustrate very well the complex and compound nature of the Commission organization, and indeed the EU polity at large: a severe crisis within one policy area does not automatically hamper activities within other areas, since these are taken care of by their own organizational units and personnel.

particularly important by EU citizens according to Eurobarometer surveys (Koop et al. 2021). By contrast, the Commission does not enjoy such a privileged agenda-setting role in relation to the Common Foreign and Security Policy (CFSP) and the Common Security and Defence Policy (CSDP). It may be active in developing policy programmes in these policy areas, although this function is primarily shaped now by the European External Action Service (EEAS). Arguably, however, the **Lisbon Treaty**, which came into force in 2009, brought the head of the EEAS, the **High Representative** for Foreign Affairs and Security Policy closer to the Commission in the sense that the incumbent is no longer the Secretary-General of the Council, but rather a Vice-President of the Commission, and now physically located in the Commission headquarters (see Chapter 19). However, in CFSP matters, the High Representative is still mandated to act by the Council.

In line with the functions performed by national executives, the Commission also has an important role to play in the implementation of EU policies. What this means is that the Commission is responsible for the *monitoring* of implementation within the EU's member states. In much the same way as occurs in Germany, the execution or putting into effect of policy remains largely the responsibility of the EU's constituent states. However, before implementation can take place at the national or sub-national levels, it may be necessary for more detailed legislation to be agreed. This is because laws adopted by the Council and the EP sometimes take the form of frameworks rather than detailed steering instruments. Thus, it is up to the Commission, in close **cooperation** with the member states, to detail and fill in EP/Council legislation by agreeing more specific rules, often in the form of Commission **directives** or **regulations**, in what is called '**delegated legislation**' or 'implementing acts'. Only in very few policy areas, such as competition policy, is the Commission responsible for implementation in the sense of handling individual cases. Finally, the Commission has an external **representation** role, such as when it acts as the main negotiator for the Union in trade and cooperation negotiations (as in the case of Brexit), and within international bodies such as the **World Trade Organization (WTO)** (see Chapter 17). Moreover, the Commission acts as the guardian of the treaties. It proposes ways to sanction member states that are accused of neglecting the rule of law (e.g., Hungary and Poland).

The Commission also performs other less tangible and more diffuse functions within the EU. Important among these is its role as a mediator between the EU's member states, and between the EP and the EU Council. Thus, the Commission does its best, once it has produced a proposal, to ensure that agreement is reached within the Union's legislative bodies. After having agreed a policy proposal internally (see the section on 'The President and the Commissioners' for more on the internal functioning of the Commission), the officials who drafted the proposal may attend meetings of the relevant EP committee and plenary sessions (see Chapter 12), the relevant Council working party, the Council **Committee of Permanent Representatives (Coreper)**, and the relevant Council ministerial meetings (see Chapter 11), in order to defend their line and, if necessary, to mediate between conflicting parties.

The Commission also presents policy documents to heads of state and government at European Council meetings and at **intergovernmental conferences (IGCs)**. For example, much of the preparatory work related to crisis-packages, like the COVID-19 recovery fund, has to be done by the Commission. The Commission not only helps in the process of achieving a final agreement, but also has its own institutional position to advance, one that may involve the presentation of a more genuinely European picture of events than emerges from national quarters.

KEY POINTS

- The European Commission has a variety of functions to perform in the EU system, including agenda-setting, the implementation of policy and the management of programmes, and external relations.

- The Commission is involved at almost all stages of the European policy process.

- The Commission plays a more limited role in foreign, security, and defence policy.

10.3 Commission influence

It is all very well to state that the Commission is involved at almost all stages of the EU policy process, but to what extent does the Commission have any real influence? In studies of the European Commission, there is a great deal of dispute over whether Commission initiatives make a significant difference or not to EU outcomes (see Box 10.2).

On the one hand, intergovernmentalists believe that national governments are the real driving forces in the European project. In the *liberal* **intergovernmentalist** version of this theoretical stance (see Chapter 5), it is accepted that the Commission has an important role to play. However, liberal intergovernmentalists claim that the authority that the Commission exercises as an agenda-setter and overseer of implementation at the national level is merely a derived and delegated authority. According to this view, the Commission may facilitate intergovernmental cooperation, but it has no real **power** basis of its own, because the Commission's powers are decided upon and framed by the member states within treaty negotiations.

Intergovernmentalist thinking on the role of the Commission is countered by those whose approach might be labelled '**neo-functionalist**' (see Chapter 4) or '**institutionalist**' (see Chapter 6). Most of these institutionalists would argue that there is ample evidence that the Commission has displayed strong leadership and, on several occasions, has even had a profound effect on the outcomes of 'history-shaping' and frame-setting intergovernmental conferences (IGCs), and European Council meetings. For example, Armstrong and Bulmer (1998) assign a highly significant role to the Commission (and indeed to other EU institutions) in the process that led to the creation of the **Single Market**. The Single Market programme is one of the important frameworks within which the Commission operates. Since the **Amsterdam Treaty** came into force, policy development and executive functions within the area of Justice and Home Affairs have been gradually transferred from the EU Council to the Commission. Others have pointed to the increased role of the Commission in economic governance (see Box 10.2) and the Commission's influence on the EU's security and defence policies (Riddervold, 2016).

Another related scholarly dispute questions the extent to which the Commission can significantly affect decisions even within its own organizational boundaries. Not surprisingly perhaps, to many

---

 BOX 10.2 CASE STUDY: HAS THE COMMISSION BEEN WEAKENED BY THE FINANCIAL CRISIS?

At first glance, one might get the impression that since 2008, the Commission has been weakened by the financial and economic crisis. Important measures to deal with the crisis, such as the fiscal compact which further strengthens budgetary discipline in the euro area, or the stability mechanism which provides financial assistance to member states in financial difficulties (see Chapters 23 and 26 for the details), were created in an intergovernmental manner outside the EU Treaty framework (see Chapter 26). On the other hand, these measures add to the existing 'tool-kit' of the Commission. The Commission has been given new tasks, such as monitoring, commenting on, and possibly sanctioning member states' draft budgetary plans. It now has a key role in EU economic governance and policy coordination (in the so-called **European Semester**) as it is responsible for adopting the Annual Growth Survey, which sets out priorities and policy guidelines for the member states for the year ahead. This document then forms the basis of the Council discussions and of the final agreement ultimately adopted by the European Council (Szapiro, 2013; Bauer and Becker, 2014).

intergovernmentalists, the Commission appears very much as an arena permeated by national interests. From this perspective, Commissioners, their personal offices ('cabinets'), as well as officials in the Commission's departments (or services), are primarily pursuing the interests of their respective national governments. By contrast, institutionalists tend to emphasize that the Commission furnishes its leaders and staff with particular interests and beliefs that rise above national concerns, and that the Commission may even be able to re-socialize participants so that they gradually come to assume supranational identities (see Chapter 4). (On empirical evidence related to this dispute, see the next sections.)

KEY POINTS

- Although most intergovernmentalists consider the Commission to play an important role in the EU polity, it is seen as an agent acting on behalf of member states, thus without its own political will.

- Neo-functionalists and institutionalists argue that the Commission has an independent impact on policy outcomes.

- Intergovernmentalists and institutionalists hold different views on the extent to which the Commission is permeated by national interests.

10.4 The President and the Commissioners

The European Commission has both a political and an administrative dimension (see Figure 10.1). While there is no doubt that the actions of the administrative branch also have political significance, for example, by providing expertise and capacity for policy development, there is still a useful distinction to be made between the Commission's political leaders—the College of Commissioners—and the officials who sit in the Commission's departments and services.

The College consists of 27 Commissioners, including the President, three Executive Vice-Presidents, the Vice-President and High Representative for Foreign Policy and Security Policy, and four other Vice-Presidents. A new team of Commissioners is appointed every five years following the elections to the EP. Within the Commission's internal decision-making process, contentious issues that have not been resolved at the lower echelons of the Commission are lifted to this formally political level in the last instance. The College strives to achieve consensus through arguing and bargaining. If this does not result in a consensus, voting may take place, although this seems to be rare. When it does happen, all Commissioners, including the President, carry the same weight—one vote each—and a simple majority is necessary for a final decision to be reached. Since the College operates on the principle of **collegiality**—in other words, all Commissioners are collectively responsible for all decisions taken—it would be reasonable to assume that a relatively large proportion of all controversial decisions is referred to the College. However, owing to the considerable size of the College, more issues have of late been dealt with through direct interaction between the President and the particularly affected Commissioner(s). Thus, one might ask whether 'presidentialization' has taken place, that is, whether the President has moved from being a *primus inter pares* ('first among equals') to becoming a *primus super pares* ('first above equals') (Kurpas et al., 2008). It is now accepted that the work of the College is subject to the President's political leadership. And, like a national prime minister, the President also has at his disposal a permanent secretariat, the Secretariat-General, which has been strengthened since the mid-2000s. Moreover, much because of the considerable size of the College, the Juncker Commission (which began its work at the end of 2014) introduced a system of Vice-Presidents, each in charge of coordinating the work of other Commissioners in related policy fields, indicating a certain hierarchization within the College (see Figure 10.1).

'Ordinary' Commissioners have policy responsibilities (portfolios), which involve oversight of one or more Commission department (see Figure 10.1). These departments are known as Directorates-General (DGs) (see Box 10.4). Because DGs tend to be organized sectorally (for example, DG Agriculture) or functionally (for example, DG Budget), one might expect this to trigger conflicts among Commissioners along sectoral or functional lines more often than along territorial (national) lines (see Box 10.1).

Although Commissioners are supposed not to take instruction from outside the Commission and do not represent national governments in any formal sense, they are nevertheless nominated by them; one per member state. Before appointing Commissioners, however, the national governments must first agree on a candidate for the Commission presidency. This is

Figure 10.1 European Commission: Organization Structure (simplified)

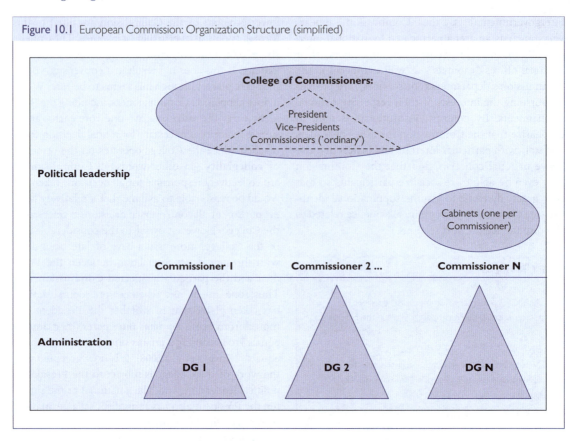

necessary if the new President is to be given an opportunity to influence the composition of the College. Over time, the President's role in selecting his or her colleagues has grown. In the treaty revisions agreed at Amsterdam in 1997, the President was able, for the first time, to reject candidates nominated by member governments. The President also has the final say in how portfolios are allocated and even has the right to reshuffle the team during the Commission's five-year term of office by redistributing dossiers or portfolios.

National governments have increasingly seen their role in the make-up of the College of Commissioners diminish. By contrast, the EP has gradually gained more of a stake in the process in a number of different ways, indicating that the EU has taken some steps in the direction of a parliamentary system. First, from the very start, the EP is able to dismiss the entire College by taking a vote of no confidence. Second, the term of office of the Commissioners was extended from four to five years, so as to bring it into close alignment with the term of the EP. This means that the

appointment of a new College takes place after the EP elections, to allow MEPs to have a say on the matter. Not only is the EP consulted on the European Council's choice of President, but it also has the right to approve the appointment. Steps have also been taken to render the Commission more directly accountable to the Parliament, as illustrated by the *Spitzenkandidat* procedure, and the fact that the EP committees now scrutinize nominated Commissioners as well as the political programme of the Commission President (see Box 10.3).

What kind of College does this create? First, it means that the political leadership of the Commission always has a fixed mix of nationals. Second, it tends to bring people into the College who have the same political party background as the national government nominating them. Over time, nominations to College posts have increasingly included people with impressive political experience and it is now quite usual to see former prominent national ministers in the list of nominees. Such a recruitment

BOX 10.3 KEY DEBATES: THE GROWING PARTY-POLITICIZATION OF THE COLLEGE OF COMMISSIONERS?

Historically, it has been the privilege of the member states to agree on the choice of Commission President. However, the European Parliament interpreted the Lisbon Treaty to mean that the result of the European elections (in and beyond those in 2014) should determine the choice of the leader of the EU executive, the Commission—that is, in much the same way as in a parliamentary system. Only in that way, they argued, could the executive be held to account for its activities. Therefore, the EP's main political groups each nominated a lead candidate, a so-called *Spitzenkandidat*, for the post of Commission President. The centre-right European People's Party (EPP) remained the largest political group in the EP after the 2014 elections, and its lead candidate, Jean-Claude Juncker, therefore stood out as the EP's candidate for the post. The UK, then an EU member state, and Hungary, which could not accept that the choice of Juncker necessarily followed from the Lisbon Treaty, tried unsuccessfully to prevent his appointment. Arguably, this move in the direction of a parliamentary system at the EU level constituted a step towards a more federal and supranational Union, with the EP having won an important victory on this occasion (Hobolt, 2014). However, the EP suffered a small set-back in 2019 when the European Council proposed EPP politician Ursula von der Leyen instead of the lead candidate nominated by the EPP, the largest political group.

BOX 10.4 BACKGROUND: SELECTED COMMISSION DEPARTMENTS/ DIRECTORATES-GENERAL (DGS)

Agriculture and Rural Development (AGRI)
Budget (BUDG)
Climate Action (CLIMA)
Communication (COMM)
Communications Networks, Content and Technology (CONNECT)
Competition (COMP)
Defence Industry and Space (DEFIS)
Economic and Financial Affairs (ECFIN)
Education, Youth, Sport and Culture (EAC)
Employment, Social Affairs and Inclusion (EMPL)
Energy (ENER)
Environment (ENV)
European Civil Protection and Humanitarian Aid Operations (ECHO)
European Neighbourhood and Enlargement Negotiations (NEAR)
Eurostat European Statistics (EUROSTAT)
Financial Stability, Financial Services and Capital Markets Union (FISMA)
Health and Food Safety (SANTE)
Human Resources and Security (HR)
Informatics (DIGIT)
Internal Market, Industry, Entrepreneurship and SMEs (GROW)
International Cooperation and Development (DEVCO)
Justice and Consumers (JUST)
Maritime Affairs and Fisheries (MARE)
Migration and Home Affairs (HOME)
Mobility and Transport (MOVE)
Regional and Urban Policy (REGIO)
Research and Innovation (RTD)
Secretariat-General (SG) ('Service department')
Taxation and Customs Union (TAXUD)
Trade (TRADE)

pattern obviously furnishes the College with political capital, although probably not so much in a strict party-political sense. A coherent party platform for the College is almost unthinkable under the current appointment procedure; instead, Commissioners' nationality is likely to be a more relevant background factor to take into account in explaining their conduct (Wonka, 2008). This is so since national governments, lobbyists, and the like tend to contact 'their' Commissioner as a first port of call when they want to obtain information or have a say at the very highest level of the Commission.

It should not be concluded from this, however, that Commissioners act primarily as agents of the national government that nominated them. In fact, a Commissioner's portfolio, or DG affiliation, may be more important in explaining his or her behaviour with regard to a particular decision. Like national ministers, Commissioners have multiple and often conflicting role expectations imposed upon them: at one and the same time, they are supposed to feel some allegiance, albeit informal, to the geographical area from which they originate, to champion Commission and EU interests, to advance their own portfolio, and to assume a party-political role (Egeberg, 2006). Balancing these diverse pressures is not always an easy task. Finally, what are described as the presidentialization and hierarchization of the College impose real constraints on the choice opportunities of individual commissioners (Bürgin, 2020).

10.5 Commissioners' cabinets

Like many national ministers in Europe, Commissioners have their own political secretariat or private office. The Commissioner's *cabinet* (note that the French pronunciation is sometimes used), as it is called, is organizationally separate from the administration of the Commission (see Figure 10.1). It is composed of people trusted by the Commissioner in question, who may be hired and fired at the Commissioner's discretion. Consequently, their tenure lasts only as long as the Commissioner's. A cabinet consists of about six or seven advisors, plus several clerical staff. Their role is to help to push Commissioners' ideas down to the departments, on the one hand, and, on the other, to edit and filter policy proposals coming up from the departments before they are referred to the Commissioner and the College. As an integral part of this 'editorial work', a Commissioner's cabinet frequently interacts with other Commissioners' cabinets to register disagreements and to pre-empt objections that might be raised at the level of the College. Because of the principle of collegiality, in essence a form of mutual responsibility, each of the 27 cabinets covers all Commission portfolios. Thus, a Commissioner's cabinet is vital as a source of information about issues beyond his or her own remit. Ahead of the weekly meeting of the College, the *chefs de cabinet* (cabinet heads) convene to ensure that the Commission acts as coherently and cohesively as possible.

In addition to the role played by cabinets in coordinating, both vertically and horizontally, decision processes within the Commission, they also have important functions at the interface between the Commission and the outside world. Cabinets are crucial points of access for governments, lobbyists, and other actors and institutions keen to influence the Commission (see Chapter 14). Their role is to assist Commissioners in this respect, with cabinet members responsible, among other things, for writing Commissioners' speeches, standing in for them, and representing them at conferences and meetings. Cabinets have also acted as a kind of liaison office between the Commissioners and 'their' respective governments, particularly via their permanent representations. Thus, they can inform the national governments about forthcoming Commission proposals that might become politically interesting from a national point of view, while at the same time acting as a conduit for information about national positions on policy initiatives under consideration in the Commission.

Cabinets have often been portrayed as national enclaves. This description was appropriate given that, in the past, the nationality of cabinet personnel almost directly reflected the nationality of the lead Commissioner. Since the Prodi Commission (1999–2004), however, at least three different nationalities must be represented in each cabinet and the head or the deputy head of the cabinet should be of a different nationality from that of the Commissioner. In 2004, at the start of the Barroso Commission, the formal requirements were clearly over-fulfilled: 96 per cent of the cabinets contained more nationalities than formally prescribed and 57 per cent of personnel were non-compatriots of their respective Commissioners (Egeberg and Heskestad, 2010). Moreover, at least half of cabinet members should be recruited from within the Commission services. This may also have interesting implications for the role of nationality in the cabinets since those coming from the Commission administration may have weaker ties to any national constituency (see the section on 'The Commission administration'). Those who have come to the cabinets from outside the Commission have, for the most part, served in national administrations, but some have also come from other kinds of organizations, such as from the political party to which the Commissioner belongs.

Before the Prodi Commission's reforms of the cabinet system in 1999, one would probably have concluded that these bodies foster kinds of intergovernmental patterns of behaviour within the Commission. However, this has changed. Since the Prodi reforms, the role of cabinets as the interface between national governments and the Commission is less important than it was in the past (Kassim et al., 2013).

10.6 The Commission administration

As is the case in national executives, the political leadership of the Commission is served by an administrative staff. These administrators provide organizational capacity and expertise that are essential for the Commission's ability to initiate and prepare policy proposals, as well as to monitor policy implementation. More precisely, the administration prepares legislative, budgetary, and other policy proposals for the College of Commisisoners as well as monitors implementation of EU policies after being finally adopted by the two legislative bodies: the Council and the EP. Key components of the Commission's administration are the departments or Directorates-General (DGs) which are roughly equivalent to national government departments and which now cover almost all possible policy fields (see Box 10.4). The basic principles of organizational specialization are also quite similar to those of national executives. While DG Agriculture and DG Energy reflect a sectorally structured Commission, DG Budget and DG Human Resources (personnel and administration) are organized around the functions that they perform ('horizontal services'). The Secretariat-General is another important horizontal service. As the permanent office of the Commission President, it plays an important role in shaping a coherent policy profile for the Commission as a whole and also has a crucial part to play in managing relationships between the Commission and other key institutions inside and outside the Union.

The role of Secretary-General, the head of the secretariat, parallels that of a permanent secretary within national prime ministers' offices, so that he or she may be identified as the first among equals of the administrative heads. Examples of other horizontal services are the European Statistical Office (**Eurostat**) and the Legal Service. The Legal Service provides much of the Commission's legal expertise, although lawyers are also found in large numbers in other parts of the Commission.

Headed by a Director-General, DGs usually consist of several directorates, with each of these led by a director. Each directorate is further split into 'units' (see Box 10.5). Obviously, some tasks and new policy initiatives do not fit well into this strictly specialized hierarchical structure. To meet such needs, special task forces or interdepartmental working groups are created. Sometimes, these temporary or ad hoc bodies become institutionalized and end up as new DGs or departments. The Commission employs approximately 30,000 officials. The most prestigious posts, requiring a university degree, belong to the so-called AD category, which consists of around 14,000 officials mainly engaged in policy-making and policy management. When the scholarly literature deals with 'Commission officials', it is referring to staff in this category rather than those performing executive, clerical, and manual tasks.

In addition to staff paid by the Commission, the administration also includes approximately 1,000 AD-category officials seconded from member governments. These seconded officials, or 'detached national experts', have their salaries paid by their national employer. In the early days of the High Authority of the European Coal and Steel Community (ECSC), the forerunner of the Commission (see Chapter 2), most officials were appointed on temporary contracts or seconded from the member states. Over time, this has changed: a clear majority of the posts are now permanent, while temporary jobs might be used for hiring personnel who might provide additional expertise on particular policy issues.

Recruitment of new AD-category candidates for a career in the Commission administration is based largely on the meritocratic principle. What this means is that appointments should be made based on what a person has achieved in his or her educational and professional career so far, rather than on any other criteria, such as a candidate's social or geographical background, or the extent to which

BOX 10.5   CASE STUDY: THE POLITICS OF ADMINISTRATIVE REORGANIZATION

In a political executive like the Commission, the setting up and arranging of organizational units is more than just a technical task. Even the moving of a unit (the smallest organizational component) from one DG to another may cause a change in the unit's policy focus. That happened in 2010 when the pharmaceutical unit was transferred from the (at that time) department for enterprise and industry to the department for health and consumers (DG SANCO at that time). The unit is involved in preparing the final authorization of medicines, based on a recommendation from the European Medicines Agency (EMA). After the reorganization, a study showed that the pharmaceutical unit assigned more weight to health and patient concerns and less weight to industry interests (Vestlund, 2015). In 2014, the incoming Commission President, Jean-Claude

Juncker, decided to move the unit back to the enterprise department (now merged with the internal market department (DG MARKT at that time)). However, the proposal met fierce criticism from healthcare organizations and Members of the European Parliament (MEPs), who argued that such a move would subordinate health to economics. Lobbyists working for the pharmaceuticals industry, on the other hand, were quite satisfied with the proposed reorganization: according to one of them, the move will 'make our life much easier' because DG MARKT is more 'pragmatic' about holding meetings with industry chiefs. 'Back when they were in DG Sanco, even setting a meeting with officials to explain our views to them, was impossible' (Pop, 2014). However, the result of the struggle was that Juncker scrapped his plan.

he or she has good contacts. This principle is inherently linked to an understanding of what a modern bureaucracy should look like if it is to avoid nepotism, favouritism, and corruption. Thus, in accordance with this principle, those who want to embark on a Commission career are normally required to hold a university degree. They also have to pass a competitive exam called the *concours*. The *concours* is modelled on the French standard entry route into the higher civil service, which means in practice that all applicants must pass written, as well as oral, tests. These tests are arranged in the member states on a regular basis and may involve thousands of applicants. A loose quota system (in the form of 'targets') regulates the intake of new recruits on a geographical basis. As a result, those hired should be drawn proportionately from all member states, so that larger countries provide more candidates than smaller ones. In a way, this sort of quota arrangement is at odds with the meritocratic principle, but the huge number of qualified applicants should nevertheless provide for a highly professional staff. This system does ensure that the Commission—or rather, the AD category—is not overpopulated by staff from only a few of the EU's member states.

An official's nationality has traditionally been a crucial factor, and increasingly so the more senior the level of the appointment. Obviously, the narrower the pyramid, the more complicated it becomes to manage the national quota system in a fair manner, while at the same time paying heed to merit as the basic norm for promotion. In these cases, national governments are often keen to look after their share of jobs, and it has conventionally been up to Commissioners and their cabinets to intervene if the 'balance' is deemed to be threatened. In addition to concerns about **proportionality**, a top official's immediate subordinate and superior should be of a different nationality. The argument goes that a multinational chain of command will prevent policy proposals from reflecting narrow national concerns.

It would seem that while the administration should continue to maintain a broad geographical balance, nationality is, subsequent to Prodi Commission reforms, no longer allowed to be the determining factor in appointing a new person to a particular post. The aim was clearly to abolish the convention of attaching national flags to senior positions. New and strict procedures now shape these processes by which top officials are appointed: senior Commission officials orchestrate such processes and Commissioners, who take the final decision, usually adhere to the shortlist of candidates presented to them (Fusacchia, 2009). New member states may claim a reasonable share of posts at all levels of the hierarchy and this has meant that highly experienced national officials have had to be brought into the senior ranks of the Commission administration. However, these officials also have to compete for vacant jobs and are subject to the same strict appointment procedures.

In accounting for the decision behaviour of Commission officials, how important is their national background? Given the enduring interest that national governments have shown towards recruitment and appointments, we are led to think that nationality matters very much indeed. However, the attention devoted to the issue does not necessarily correspond to the impact that national origins might have. There is little doubt that officials may bring to the Commission administrative styles and general *attitudes* that can be linked to their country of origin. For example, officials stemming from federal or decentralized states such as Germany or Belgium seem to view the prospect of a federal Europe more favourably than do those from unitary states, probably because the former are already more familiar with that kind of system (Hooghe, 2001; Kassim et al., 2013). A study also indicates that populism and public scepticism to the EU in Commission officials' home countries trigger legitimacy and subsidiarity concerns among the respective officials (Bes, 2017). Moreover, a common language and nationality facilitate interaction, so that Commission officials become points of access for compatriots keen to know and have a say on what is going on in the Commission. However, there is virtually no evidence of a clear link between officials' nationality, on the one hand, and their decision *behaviour* in the Commission, on the other, because organizational roles and decision-making procedures tend to diminish this sort of variation in conduct. In fact, the attachment of officials to particular DGs seems far more important than their national background as an explanation for the preferences and choices that they make in their daily work (Suvarierol, 2008; Kassim et al., 2013; Murdoch and Trondal, 2013).

KEY POINTS

- The Commission's administration is composed of sectoral and functional (horizontal) departments, called Directorates-General (DGs), and various Service Departments. Key tasks are to prepare policy proposals and to monitor policy implementation.

- Officials' decision behaviour is most often explained by their DG affiliation.

- Officials within the administration are recruited on a merit basis, with a view to maintaining an appropriate geographical balance among member states.

10.7 Committees, networks, and EU agencies

To assist the Commission in its preparatory work on new legislation and in other forms of policy-making, approximately 750 expert committees have been established. The practical work on a policy initiative often starts in such a committee, which may be composed of national officials (almost always), stakeholders, and independent experts. Committees of this sort are supposed to provide additional expertise on a particular subject and thus complement the work of the Commission's permanent staff. They may also serve as an arena for floating policy ideas and anticipating future reactions to them. Involving interest organizations that might ultimately be affected by a new proposal could make political support and **legitimacy** more likely. The Commission particularly welcomes European-level interest groups (see Chapter 14). Like the Commission itself, interest groups are organized primarily along functional and sectoral lines, rather than territorially. Thus, the Commission may see transnational interest groups as potential partners in an evolving EU **polity**.

Commission officials chair expert committees and advisory groups, calling officials from member governments to participate as experts. In line with the role expectations in this case, national officials participating in such committees assign considerably less weight to their role as government representative than those attending Council working parties (Egeberg et al., 2003). When committee work comes to an end, the policy proposal is processed in the administrative and political ranks of the Commission before it is submitted to the Council and the European Parliament for final decision. As mentioned earlier, some directives may need to be supplemented by rules of a more technical nature. This kind of legislative work is delegated to the Commission in the same way as national legislatures may let governments hammer out specific regulations. In order to monitor the Commission in this respect, however, the EU Council has set up about 250 so-called 'comitology committees' (also sometimes known as 'implementation committees'). The membership of these committees is composed of formal representatives of national governments, although it is the Commission that calls and chairs the meetings, sets the agenda, submits the proposals requiring discussion, and writes the protocols. Some comitology committees are entitled only to advise the Commission; others have **competence** to overrule the Commission's proposals under certain conditions. In practice, however, the Commission often gets its own way, although this is not to say that national representatives have no influence. It is, of course, also quite possible that the Commission deliberately chooses proposals that national governments are likely to endorse (see Christiansen and Larsson, 2007).

When it comes to the implementation of EU policies at the national level, the Commission has to rely on member state administrations, since the Commission does not itself possess agencies at this level. This may result in considerable variation in administrative practices across countries. However, there are signs that national regulatory authorities that often work at arm's length from ministries become a kind of 'partner' of the Commission in practical implementation, as well as in policy preparation processes. As a result of these authorities' 'semi-detached' status, they seem to be in a position in which they might be able to serve two masters simultaneously: both the national ministry *and* the Commission. Within a range of policy sectors (such as competition, telecommunications, environment, or food safety), there is evidence of transnational networks of national agencies in which the Commission and, increasingly, EU-level agencies constitute the hubs (Egeberg and Trondal, 2017; Mastenbroek and Martinsen, 2018).

Such Commission-led and, increasingly, EU agency-led networks of national agencies within most policy fields may contribute to more **harmonized** application of EU law and other EU policies across member countries. One might interpret the advent of EU (decentralized or regulatory) agencies from the 1990s on as one further step in the direction of ensuring a more uniform practice of EU policies. There are now more than 30 such administrative bodies across the EU, employing about 5,000 officials. Although they are all located outside Brussels, they are still EU-level agencies, meaning that their activities cover all member states. While member states might agree in general that more even application of EU legislation across countries is desirable, they may sometimes be hesitant to transfer more power to the Commission. A possible compromise was to establish these EU-level executive bodies outside the Commission—bodies that were planned to be under considerable member state control and which were, at the outset, assigned mainly 'soft regulatory power'. The first constraint (member state control) meant that such agencies became formally subordinated to management boards numerically dominated by government representatives. The second constraint ('soft power') meant that agencies should primarily deal with information exchange on 'best (implementation) practice' and the facilitation of transnational agency networks. In practice, however, governments' control over EU agencies seems more modest than originally envisaged and the Commission has become a pivotal partner of EU agencies. EU agencies tend to relate to their respective Commission DGs (that is, within the same issue area) in much the same way as national agencies connect to their 'parent ministries'. Moreover, over time, EU agencies have taken on tasks such as issuing guidelines on the application of EU law at the national level, and even involvement in individual decisions handled by national agencies. Such 'quasi-regulatory' tasks have been complemented by assigning some agencies the right to make authoritative decisions in individual cases (Busuioc et al., 2012). In addition to the Commission, national agencies make up the closest interlocutors in the daily life of EU agencies, indicating how EU agencies might become building blocks in a multilevel Union administration, partly bypassing national ministries (for an overview of the literature, see Egeberg and Trondal, 2017; Mastenbroek and Martinsen, 2018).

KEY POINTS

- Expert committees have an important role to play in the preparatory work of the Commission.

- Comitology committees monitor the Commission when it is issuing implementing acts.

- National officials behave less intergovernmentally in Commission expert committees than in Council committees and comitology.

- Issue-specific networks are emerging among the Commission, EU agencies, and semi-detached national agencies. Such agency networks play a key role in implementing EU policies, but they are also involved in developing new EU policies.

10.8 Conclusion

The Commission has often been portrayed as a hybrid and unique organization because of its mix of political and administrative functions. This is understandable if the Commission is compared to the secretariat of a traditional international organization, since such secretariats are not expected to have a political will of their own. However, the Commission is probably better compared to a national executive. Like governments, the Commission is headed by executive politicians who are responsible for various administrative services. In a similar way to national executives, the Commission is authorized to initiate and formulate policy proposals, and to monitor the implementation of policies. The Commission has not, however, achieved full control of all executive tasks at the EU level, sharing its executive function in foreign relations with the European External Action Service (EEAS). That said, the head of the EEAS, the High Representative, is also a Vice-President of the Commission.

This chapter has focused on how the various parts of the Commission are organized and staffed, and how these structural and demographic features might be related to the way in which decision-makers actually behave. Are these features mainly conducive to intergovernmental ways of behaving, or do they instead evoke patterns of decision-making that are more in line with what institutionalists would predict? At all levels—the College, the cabinets, the administration, and the committees—there have been components that may be more conducive to intergovernmental decision processes than to supranational behaviour. However, those organizational components that work in the opposite direction are becoming more and more important. These organizational components tend to focus decision-makers' attention on supranational concerns and along sectoral, functional, partisan, or institutional cleavages—that is, on lines of conflict and cooperation that cut *across* national boundaries, and which evoke non-national feelings of belonging among Commissioners and their officials. If these trends persist, the Commission is set to become much more of a genuinely European institution than it has been in the past, although one that will continue to exhibit a mix (albeit a different mix) of both intergovernmental and supranational characteristics.

 QUESTIONS

1. To what extent can the Commission be compared to national governments?

2. How influential is the Commission within the EU policy process?

3. How important is the national background of Commissioners in shaping their preferences and decisions?

4. What is the role of the Commissioners' cabinets?

5. How is the Commission administration organized, and what are the possible implications for patterns of conflict within the Commission?

6. What is 'comitology'?

7. Which roles do national officials evoke in EU committees?

8. What characterizes EU agency networks, and what are their tasks?

 GUIDE TO FURTHER READING

Ege, J., Bauer, M.W., and Becker, S. (eds.) (2018) *The European Commission in Turbulent Times* (Baden-Baden: Nomos). This book reviews literature on the Commission's power within the EU polity, both in general and within particular policy areas, such as economic governance and energy policy, as well as literature on in-house reforms.

Hartlapp, M., Metz, J., and Rauh, C. (2014) *Which Policy for Europe? Power and Conflict inside the European Commission* (Oxford: Oxford University Press). Based on new data, this book provides an encompassing perspective on day-to-day policy choices within the Commission.

Kassim, H., Peterson, J., Bauer, M. W., Connolly, S. J., Dehousse, R., Hooghe, L., and Thompson, A. (2013) *The European Commission of the Twenty-First Century* (Oxford: Oxford University Press). This book, based on extensive survey data, analyses Commission officials' backgrounds, careers, and attitudes.

Nugent, N. and Rhinard, M. (2015) *The European Commission*, 2nd edn (Basingstoke: Palgrave). This is a highly informative and well-balanced textbook on the European Commission.

Wille, A. (2013) *The Normalization of the European Commission: Politics and Bureaucracy in the EU Executive* (Oxford: Oxford University Press). Based on secondary and primary sources, this book argues that the Commission has gradually become more similar to national executives in its organization and decision processes.

 Access the online resources to take your learning and understanding further, including extra multiple-choice questions with instant feedback, web links, answer guidance to end-of-chapter questions, and updates on new developments in EU politics.

www.oup.com/he/cini-borragan7e

11

The European Council and the Council of the European Union

Jeffrey Lewis

Reader's Guide

This chapter examines the components that constitute the Council system: the European Council and the Council of the EU (henceforth 'the EU Council' or simply 'the Council'). Together, these institutions (the European Council and EU Council) form the part of the Union that unabashedly represents national interests in the European integration process. The EU Council is thus a site of intense negotiation, compromise-building, and at times acrimonious disagreement among the member states. Confusing to many academics and observers alike, the EU Council is not a single body, but rather a composite of national officials working at different levels of political seniority and policy specialization. From the heads of state and government to the ministers, and all the way down the ladder to the expert-level fonctionnaires (officials), the EU Council and the European Council embed governments of the EU into a networked club of collective decision-making that deeply penetrates into the national capitals and domestic politics of the member states. In authority, scope, and procedural methods, the Council system represents the most advanced, intensive forum of international cooperation between sovereign nation states in the modern world.

11.1 Introduction

The focus of this chapter is on the elements that make up the European Council and EU Council. This includes:

- The strategic, executive-like authority of the European Council.
- The formal legislative role of the national ministers who meet in the policy-specific formations of the EU Council.
- The preparatory and expert working committees involved in day-to-day negotiations.
- The supporting roles provided by a shared, rotating presidency and the Council bureaucracy, the General Secretariat of the Council (GSC).
- The post-Lisbon leadership posts including the European Council's President and the **High Representative of the Union for Foreign Affairs and Security Policy (HR)**.

Taken together, the Council system is at the epicentre of EU decision-making and plays a pivotal role in making Union policy. While ostensibly representing the national interests of the EU's 27 member states, the Council system is also composed of European-level institutions keyed to making collective decisions (mostly by consensus) and is not merely **intergovernmental** (de Schoutheete, 2017: 77).

The remainder of the chapter is organized as follows: Section 11.2 examines the Council system's structure through the different layers of authority and national officials involved in the EU's legislative process. This is followed by Section 11.3, which provides more detail on the elements that make up the Council system, including summits, the ministers' meetings, the preparatory work of the **Committee of Permanent Representatives (Coreper)**, and the technically minded working groups. Section 11.3 also considers the infrastructure of the Council system which includes the 'honest broker' role of the bureaucracy (the GSC) and the increased reliance on permanent leadership positions. Next, the chapter turns its attention to how the Council system actually works, including voting patterns, the rotating presidency, the 'closed door' nature of deliberations, and current challenges such as the wider implications of **enlargement**, **enhanced cooperation**, and Brexit. Section 11.7 will tie the main themes together, and argue that the EU Council and the European Council are best seen as a hybrid of intergovernmental and **supranational** elements.

11.2 The Council system's evolving hierarchy and enigmatic traits

The Council system is at the institutional heart of decision-making in the EU. It is composed of the EU Council (or 'Council of Ministers') and the European Council, comprising the heads of state and government of the EU member states. The European Council has gradually centralized executive-like functions as a result of increased politicization since the 1990s, and more recently, in the face of serial crises such as the **eurozone** crisis or the COVID-19 pandemic (De Wilde and Zürn, 2012; Werts, 2017; Riddervold et al., 2021). The regular practice of the European Council—that is, vetting decisions and defining 'general political directions and priorities'—now serves as a safety-valve to modulate the Union's perceived democratic deficit. The expansion of post-Maastricht policy areas—including, for example, economic governance and eurozone policy coordination, foreign affairs, employment and social policy, and internal security—has empowered the European Council as a 'new centre of political gravity' that coordinates policies and reacts to crises (Puetter, 2014). Some interpret this trend as a form of '**executive federalism**', comprising top-down centralized control by the EU leaders (Habermas, 2012). A good example would be the blockbuster four day and four night 'special meeting' of the European Council in July 2020 to finalize a new multiannual budget (€1,074 billion for 2021–27) and a novel economic recovery package in response to the COVID-19 pandemic (joint loans and grants worth another €750 billion) (see Box 11.3).

The legislative function of the Council system, which involves the adoption of legal acts into the EU's *acquis*, is fulfilled by national ministers meeting as the EU Council. The European Parliament's increased decision-making **power**, in the **ordinary legislative procedure (OLP)**, has not altered the basic fact that the Council remains at the core of the EU's legislative process. Technically the EU Council is a single legal entity, but this is misleading since, in reality, there are ten configurations organized by policy specialization (see Box 11.1). Each Council configuration manages a specialized policy sector and the participants authorized to adopt legislative acts are the national ministers

BOX 11.1   BACKGROUND: EU COUNCIL CONFIGURATIONS

General Affairs (GAC)

Foreign Affairs (FAC)

Economic and Financial Affairs (ECOFIN)

Justice and Home Affairs (JHA)

Employment, Social Policy, Health, and Consumer Affairs
  (EPSCO)

Competitiveness (including Internal Market, Industry, and
  Research) (COMPET)

Transport, Telecommunications, and Energy (TTE)

Agriculture and Fisheries (AGFISH)

Environment (ENV)

Education, Youth, Culture, and Sport (EYCS)

Source: Annex I, Council Decision of 1 December 2009 adopting the Council's Rules of Procedure, OJ L 325/35, 11.12.2009; Council of the European Union website (2021).

from each of the member states who hold domestic responsibility for that sector. Hence the 27 EU ministers of agriculture preside over the Agricultural and Fisheries Council (AGFISH), the environmental ministers over the Environment Council, and so on.

Historically, the 'senior' Council actors with general institutional responsibilities and overall policy coordination were the foreign affairs ministers, meeting as the General Affairs Council (GAC). However, general affairs and foreign affairs have become increasingly differentiated, with the latter Council now chaired by the High Representative for Foreign Affairs

and Security Policy (see Box 11.2). Today, the EU's GAC mirrors the domestic-level bureaucratic balance of power, which has generally seen a relative decline in the authority of foreign affairs ministries over EU policy. This is visible in the increasingly heterogeneous mix of job titles among participants in the GAC, which include foreign ministers as well as 'European affairs' ministers, who are often more closely attached to the office of the head of state or government. A further symbol of the decline in foreign ministries' seniority is since 2002, the EU foreign ministers are no longer invited to attend European Council meetings

BOX 11.2   BACKGROUND: RENOVATING THE GENERAL AFFAIRS COUNCIL

Following widespread agreement in the latter half of the 1990s that the Council's premier ministerial body—the General Affairs Council (GAC)—was impossibly over-tasked and increasingly dysfunctional, the European Council decided, at the 2002 Seville meeting, to split the GAC's work into two tracks: General Affairs and Foreign Affairs.

The 'new' General Affairs track is tasked to 'ensure consistency in the work of the different Council configurations'. This includes preparatory and follow-up work for European Council meetings. In addition, 'it shall be responsible for overall coordination of policies, institutional and administrative questions, horizontal dossiers which affect several of the European Union's policies, such as the multiannual financial framework and enlargement, and any dossier entrusted to it by the European Council' (Article 2(2), Rules of Procedure).

The Foreign Affairs track is assigned 'the whole of the European Union's external action, namely common foreign and security policy, common security and defence policy, common commercial policy, development cooperation and humanitarian aid' (Article 2(5), Rules of Procedure).

Technically, the two tracks operate independently, with their own meetings and agendas, but in practice, General Affairs and Foreign Affairs tend to meet on consecutive days or even back-to-back, with the foreign affairs ministers often attending both. However, each grouping now has a different chairperson: the new foreign policy chief is the 'permanent' chair of the Foreign Affairs track, while the member state holding the rotating presidency continues to chair the General Affairs track (see also Section 11.6.2, 'The role of the rotating presidency'). This certainly adds coherence to the substantive foreign policy work of the ministers within the Foreign Affairs track (which a new permanent chair is intended to enhance), but it does not guarantee a generalized leadership role for the General Affairs track as we have witnessed in decades past (see Gomez and Peterson, 2001 for a detailed study).

Sources: Presidency Conclusions, Seville European Council, 21–22 June 2002; Council Decision of 1 December 2009 adopting the Council's Rules of Procedure, OJ L 325/35, 11.12.2009; Consolidated Versions of the Treaty on European Union (TEU) and the Treaty on the Functioning of the European Union (TFEU), OJ C 83/53, 30 March 2010.

where, traditionally, they sat next to their head of state or government during negotiations.

Since the establishment of the euro, the finance and economics ministers have increased in stature through their work on the Economic and Financial Affairs Council, otherwise known as ECOFIN. A subset of ECOFIN, made up of those member states that subscribe to the euro, also meets in an informal body known as the **Eurogroup**, which internally selects its own permanent chair (see Chapters 22 and 25). Since the 1990s (post-Maastricht), there are also a number of newer Council configurations which include the interior/home affairs ministers, who meet in the Justice and Home Affairs (JHA) Council, and the defence ministers, who also regularly meet to discuss the Common Security and Defence Policy (CSDP).

The policy segmentation of the Council's work into distinct, compartmentalized formations is a hallmark of how the EU works. Each formation has its own pace and legislative agenda, with some meeting monthly (such as the GAC) and some barely twice per year (such as Education, Youth, Culture, and Sport (EYCS)). Each Council also has its own organizational culture, often including a set of informal (unwritten) rules and distinctive working habits. For example, some, such as Foreign Affairs, rely on highly restricted lunchtime sessions to discuss issues of particular importance or sensitivity. The GAC has institutionalized the right to meet on the day before European Council summits to conduct final preparations and adopt a definitive agenda for the heads of state and government (see Box 11.2). Another informal rule is for the eurozone finance ministers to avoid substantive macroeconomic policy discussions in the Eurogroup meetings that affect non-eurozone EU members without also holding those discussions in the ECOFIN Council. The Council is really a multifaceted decision-making system operating across a wide range of policy domains, with negotiations taking place concurrently. In one guise or another, the European Council and the EU Council are almost continually in session (see Table 11.1). For 2019, the yearly operating budget for the Council system was €582 million, including €79 million for interpreting costs.

The ministers are but the tip of the iceberg, however. The work of the Council system involves a much larger contingent of national officials. First, there are the EU permanent representatives who staff Coreper. Coreper, the Committee of Permanent Representatives, is responsible for preparing forthcoming Council meetings and this often involves intensive discussions to pave the way for agreement by the ministers. The EU permanent representatives (two per member state, each of which appoints its own EU ambassador and a deputy) live in Brussels, meet weekly, and 'eat, drink, and breathe EU issues seven days a week' (Barber, 1995). Each member state also maintains a **permanent representation** in Brussels run by the EU ambassador and deputy, and staffed by policy specialists from different national ministries.

But that is still not all. The bulk of day-to-day Council activity takes place at the expert working group level. At any point in time, the Council maintains around 150 standing working groups, although the number is significantly higher if you include ad hoc groups (such as the current eight configurations of the 'Friends of the Presidency Group' which report to Coreper) and all of the groups' sub-groups (such as the 'tax questions' and 'business taxation' groups, the veterinary experts, or intellectual property, which each have up to five sub-groups). Working group officials are tasked with examining proposals in the early stages of negotiation, and the groups serve as a clearing house for less controversial and more technical issues as well as an early warning system for complications that need attention at the level of Coreper or the ministers. In the context of Brexit, the Council began a new meeting format in 2017 to exclude the UK delegation from discussions among the remaining EU27, known as the 'Article 50 format' which extended to all levels from the European Council to the working group (see Box 11.4, Table 11.1).

In total, the Council system involves thousands of national officials meeting in dozens of working groups, Coreper, ministerial, and summitry settings each month to negotiate and decide on EU proposals. Today there are approximately 62,000 national officials who regularly meet and coordinate in Brussels (Genschel and Jachtenfuchs, 2015: 4). At base, this figure neatly captures the classic **neo-functionalist** term *engrenage* (meaning 'caught up in the gears') and what Ernst Haas insightfully forecast as the Council's 'concept of engagement' (Haas, 1958: 522–3).

Of all the EU institutions, the European Council and the EU Council are perhaps the least documented. Partly this stems from inaccessibility, but more fundamental is the Council system's enigmatic appearance. It is an institutional 'chameleon' (Wallace, 2002), because it blurs intergovernmental and

Table 11.1 European Council and EU Council meetings, 2009–19

Format	2009	2011	2013	2015	2016	2017	2018	2019
Institutional meetings								
Summits	7	9	6	12	9	11	15	17
(Article 50 Summits)						4	—	—
Councils	74	85	74	81	75	77	75	80
Coreper	140	135	140	138	109	105	117	124
(Article 50 Coreper)						22	29	28
Working groups	4,272	4,373	4,164	3,471	3,569	1,039	4,304	3,706
(Article 50 ad hoc Working groups)						32	61	28
Total	4,493	4,602	4,384	3,702	3,762	4,290	4,604	3,983
Other meetings*	2,021	2,075	2,027	2,271	2,034	3,030	3,129	3,685
Grand total	6,514	6,677	6,411	5,973	5,796	7,320	7,733	7,668

*Other meetings include training sessions, seminars, information sessions and briefings, and meetings with third countries.
Source: Council of the European Union (2020/C 266/01), Financial Activity Report 2019.

supranational organizational traits and behaviours. The standard, glossy image of the Council system is one of a stronghold of individualistically orientated national actors who focus more or less exclusively on their own self-interests rather than on the welfare of others or the group as a whole. This interpretation also forms a basic theoretical foundation for **intergovernmentalist** approaches. But the European Council and the EU Council constitute a more complex and variegated institutional construct which equals more than the sum of its parts (the member states). National actors in the Council system also act collectively, and many develop a shared sense of responsibility to produce results and reach consensual agreements. As a chamber of continuous negotiation across a wide range of issues, national actors often develop long-term relations of trust, mutual understanding, and obligations to try to help out colleagues with domestic political difficulties or requests for special consideration (Smeets, 2015). Participants in the Council system can also develop collective interests in the process of joint decision-making itself (Adler-Nissen, 2014: 157). In short, member states' officials' engagement with the work of the European Council and the EU Council involves socialization into a collective decision-making system.

KEY POINTS

- The Council system represents the member states and has both executive and legislative functions.

- The European Council is the Union's premier political authority and the heads of state and government who comprise it practise executive-like functions.

- The Council system involves 62,000 national officials who meet at the heads of state and government, ministerial, Coreper, and working-group levels, as well as those who coordinate EU policy positions back home.

- The Council system is enigmatic: it is both defender of the national interest and a collective system of decision-making, blurring the theoretical distinctions between intergovernmentalism and supranationalism.

11.3 The layers of the Council system

This section offers a synopsis of the main elements of the Council system and the division of labour between them.

11.3.1 **European Council summitry**

As the grouping that brings together the heads of state and government, no other EU body can match the political authority of the European Council. The prime ministers, chancellors, and presidents meeting in the high-profile summits practise executive-like collective leadership and supply overall strategic guidance for the Union. Historically, issues such as the Budget have been too politically charged for the ministers to settle themselves, and only the European Council is able to break deadlocks, overcome inter-ministerial discord (especially between finance and foreign affairs), and broker the big, interlocking **package deals** for which the EU's 'history-making' moments are famous (see Box 11.3).

The European Council meets formally at least twice a year, in June and December, and at least twice more as 'informal' gatherings typically organized around a specific topic or theme (such as economic growth and competitiveness). One outgrowth of the eurozone crisis is the decision to regularize a special **Euro Summit** among the eurozone leaders at least twice a year (see Chapter 25). The European Council can also convene on an emergency basis, as it did in 2015 on the migration crisis, or in 2014 on Russia's annexation of Crimea.

European Council summits attract intense public scrutiny. They are reported on by some 2,000 journalists (Council of the European Union, 2015) and increasingly attract a substantial number of protesters, ranging from farmers to anti-**globalization** activists. The European Commission President attends all summits, as does the HR, but, interestingly, not the EP President (see Section 11.6.3, 'Relations with other EU institutions'). Since 2009, the summits have been chaired by a permanent President whom the European Council selects by qualified majority for a two-and-a-half-year term (renewable once) (see Box 11.5). To give the President credible objectivity, the Treaty expressly prohibits him or her from wearing a 'double hat'—that is, they must not simultaneously hold a national office. All three European Council Presidents since 2009 were sitting Prime Ministers at the time of appointment, which meant they had to resign from domestic office to begin the EU-level job.

The European Council was created in the early 1970s and was informally institutionalized by 1974. Many EU scholars credit the European Council with holding the Union together during the nearly two decades of **Eurosclerosis**. This period covered the creation of the **European Monetary System (EMS)** in the late 1970s, the resolution of major budgetary

---

⬎ BOX 11.3   CASE STUDY: MAKING HISTORY: THE JULY 2020 MFF RULE OF LAW SUMMIT

After an epic four-day, four-night 'special meeting' of the European Council in July 2020, one of the longest on record and the first in-person meeting of the EU27 leaders since the onset of the COVID-19 pandemic, history was made. One of the priciest package deals ever had been accomplished: a new comprehensive seven-year budget (Multiannual Financial Framework, or MFF 2021–2027) combined with a novel economic recovery package (Next Generation EU, or NGEU) to combat the unprecedented impact of the pandemic. In total, new EU spending commitments exceed €1.8 trillion. What is more, the entire package is connected to a new 'regime of conditionality' that ties disbursement of EU funds with members' respect of the rule of law. EU spending is now explicitly linked to adherence with rule of law values enshrined in Article 2 (TEU). Such values include: public power acting within the constraints set out by law, in accord with the values of democracy and fundamental rights, and under the control of independent, impartial courts. In the event of rule of law 'breaches', the Commission makes recommendations that will be considered by the Council and adopted by qualified majority.

In such events, the Conclusions state, 'The European Council will revert rapidly to the matter' (Point 23). A concession to Hungary and Poland, who were adamantly against conditionality, includes a guarantee to allow legal appeals to the CJEU prior to any funding sanctions taking effect. But, unlike the extreme options of Article 7 proceedings to suspend a members' voting rights only after a unanimous vote (see Box 11.11), the **qualified majority voting (QMV)** basis for the new conditionality regime effectively means that aberrant behaviour under rule of law standards cannot be annulled by veto, but require a sufficient blocking minority to prevent sanctioning (at least four member-states representing at least 35 per cent of the EU population). Never before have such 'carrots' been paired with such 'sticks' under QMV, signalling the EU has evolved a more granular approach to sanctioning practices that contravene fundamental values like the rule of law.

Sources: European Council Conclusions, Special Meeting of the European Council, 17, 18, 19, 20, and 21 July 2020, EUCO 10/20, 21 July 2020; European Commission, 2020 Rule of Law Report, The Rule of Law Situation in the European Union, COM (2020) 580 final, 30.9.2020.

disputes in the early 1980s, and the launching of new intergovernmental conferences (IGCs) to revise the treaties. However, the European Council was not even mentioned in the treaties until the 1986 Single European Act (SEA). The Lisbon Treaty officially designated the European Council as an institution

BOX 11.4   CASE STUDY: THE COUNCIL'S BREXIT (ART. 50) FORMAT

The EU27 began to meet in 'special format' prior to official Article 50 notification by the UK on 29 March 2017. This includes the EU27 informal meeting of the European Council on 29 June 2016, less than one week after the UK referendum. The Bratislava summit on 16 September 2016 brought the 27 EU leaders together to discuss the EU's future without inviting the British. Preparations for this summit by Slovakia's Council presidency also began using the EU27 format to discuss strategic issues (Bilcik, 2017: 66). Council formations that have held an Article 50 configuration include:

- European Council (Art. 50)
- GAC (Art. 50)
- Coreper (Art. 50)
- Antici Group (Art. 50)
- Ad Hoc Working Party (Art. 50)

The Article 50 format standardized procedures to exclude the UK delegation from participating in Council discussions and

decision-making. By August 2019, the British government announced they would no longer attend Council meetings at all, entrusting Finland's rotating Council presidency to vote on behalf of the UK when needed, to prevent blocking the EU legislative process until Brexit became official on 31 January 2020. The Article 50 format is thus a dramatic formalization of 'outsiderness' in EU politics. On the gradual decline of 'diplomatic capital' and a growing outsider status from the 'social field' (Adler-Nissen's terms) for the British since 2010, see Rasmussen (2016). Post-Brexit, the Article 50 format has been converted into a new permanent special committee known as the 'Working Party on the UK' which is tasked with assisting Coreper and the Council 'in all matters pertaining to the relationship with the UK'.

Sources: General Secretariat of the Council, List of Council Preparatory Bodies, 10075/17 COR 1, 27 June 2017; Council Decision, 2020/121, 28 January 2020.

BOX 11.5   BACKGROUND: THE PRESIDENT OF THE EUROPEAN COUNCIL

In November 2009, Belgian Prime Minister Herman Van Rompuy was unanimously chosen by the EU heads of state and government to serve as the first permanent President of the European Council. In 2012, he was reappointed until November 2014. Formally, the Treaty enumerates the presidency job in ambiguous language (Article 15(6) TEU), although Van Rompuy's inaugural term had significant, if informal, precedent-setting implications. The European Council President is expected to:

- chair meetings of the European Council and the newer Euro summits, and drive forward its work;
- ensure the preparation and continuity of the work of the European Council;
- endeavour to facilitate cohesion and consensus; and
- issue a report to the Parliament after each summit.

According to a senior member of his cabinet, President Van Rompuy developed the practice of consulting each leader

before summits, either by telephone or in person, and as a result, when the European Council begins:

… he is the only one in the room that knows everything … It is not a very visible role, in finding agreement, cajoling, and pressuring, but it is essential to getting the European Council to function.
(Author's interview, 2 December 2011)

On 1 December 2014, the then Prime Minister of Poland, Donald Tusk, replaced Van Rompuy as President (see Box 11.6 on Tusk's 2017 reappointment—a curious moment where 'top-down' and 'bottom-up' Europeanization came to loggerheads, for more on the concepts see Chapter 8). Charles Michel, who was Belgian Prime Minister (2015–19), became the third European Council President on 1 December 2019. During the marathon budget negotiations during July 2020, President Michel's informal office terrace overlooking the European Quarter became the key site for brokering a milestone deal on EU spending (see Box 11.3).

of the EU, a formal acknowledgement of how regularized summits supply the EU with critical navigation. The usual output for a meeting is a lengthy *communiqué* (known as 'Conclusions'), which summarizes positions on issues and sets priorities for future EU policy-making that are then incorporated at the ministerial, Coreper, and working-group levels. As Puetter (2014: 76, 137) documents, in recent decades, European Council conclusions 'tasking' the Council and Commission have entailed an element of 'institutional engineering' in that they have made 'informal constitutional decisions' which have the power to modify existing treaty rules or create them *de novo*. Examples of the latter include the Eurogroup and Euro summits, and the creation of the **European Employment Strategy (EES)**. A new procedural coordination device is the European Council President's 'Leaders' Agenda' which contains a roll-out of summit topics over an 18-month period (see Box 11.7). Increasingly, what might look like a single summit could include a number of special meeting formats rolled into one: (1) regular summit meetings (formal or informal); (2) informal 'Leaders' Agenda' summits; (3) Euro summits; and/or (4) EU27 summits with non-members which the Brexit 'Article 50' format has pioneered.

11.4 The ministers' Council(s)

In terms of formal legislative authority, the ministers are the national representatives empowered to vote and commit member states to new EU laws (Article 16(2) TEU). While a good deal of informal decision-making takes place in Coreper and the working groups, the distinction between formal (legal) and informal (de facto) decision-making authority is important to understand, because the ministers are the elected officials who are accountable to their domestic constituencies for the policies adopted in Brussels.

Some EU Council formations have more work and meet more frequently than others. These include General Affairs, Foreign Affairs, ECOFIN/Eurogroup, and AGFISH. Each meets monthly, usually for one or two days. The types of legislative acts adopted by the ministers vary by policy area. In the traditional '**Community Method**' policy areas, legislation is typically in the form of **directives**, **regulations**, or decisions. For Justice and Home Affairs (JHA) (see Chapter 21) and Common Foreign and Security Policy (CFSP) (see Chapter 19), most legislative acts are made in the form of a **joint action** or a **common position**.

There are also rules for voting. Voting rules divide into two main categories—**unanimity** and **qualified**

BOX 11.6   KEY DEBATES: POLAND'S ISOLATION OVER PRESIDENT TUSK'S 2017 REAPPOINTMENT

Unusual theatrics surrounded the reappointment of President Tusk in March 2017, when the Polish government tried, unsuccessfully, to have him fired and replaced. Given Tusk's accomplishments in leading the European Council through serial crises concerning the eurozone, refugees, and Brexit, his reappointment until 30 November 2019 looked like a sure thing. Instead, for the first time in EU history, a top job was filled over the strenuous objections of the candidate's own home country. A long-simmering domestic political feud between the ruling Law and Justice (PiS) Party led by Jaroslaw Kaczynski and Tusk's own Civic Platform was the basis of the dispute, but the Polish government was not rewarded for attempting to upload the fight into the heartland of Council politics. Poland's Prime Minister Beata Szydlo sent a letter to her EU colleagues accusing Tusk of 'using his EU function to engage personally in a political dispute in Poland' (cited in *The Economist*, 18 March 2017: 57). She then nominated a rival candidate to replace him, a current Polish MEP, Jacek Saryusz-Wolski. By the eve of the summit on 9 March, Poland was considerably isolated yet

recalcitrant. The European Council responded by outvoting Poland 27–1, utilizing the formal procedure to select a President by qualified majority (Article 15(5) TEU). Prime Minister Szydlo reacted to the outcome with an angry and defiant tone to block the formal adoption of the summit's conclusions. The group rebuffed this too, by issuing them as 'Conclusions by the President of the European Council', stating the document was supported by 27 members although 'it did not gather consensus, for reasons unrelated to its substance' and hence, 'references to the European Council in the attached document should not be read as implying a formal endorsement by the European Council acting as an institution'. Afterwards, at a press conference, Belgian Prime Minister Charles Michel stated, 'This was more like … the export to the European level of an internal national political question. Nobody was duped by that' (cited in *Politico*, 10 March 2017). On the rarity of contested voting in the European Council, German Chancellor Angela Merkel stated, 'the search for consensus must not be used as a blockade' (ibid.).

↘
BOX 11.7 BACKGROUND: THE EUROPEAN COUNCIL PRESIDENT'S 'LEADERS' AGENDA'

In October 2017, President Tusk introduced his 'Leaders' Agenda' for the European Council—a new 18-month provisional calendar of the main topics and agendas for all upcoming summits. The 'Leaders' Agenda' is an attempt to balance ongoing thematic work (Social Europe, Climate Change, Defence, Budget) with 'issues that require discussions aimed at resolving deadlocks or finding solutions to key political dossiers' (Migration, *Spitzenkandidaten* process, EMU reform). The latter are treated as a special informal session where no notes are taken, allowing leaders to freely discuss divisive issues such as how to reform the controversial mandatory asylum quotas or what a European Monetary Fund might entail. Overall, this is a clear upgrade in agenda-setting power for the European Council president and one that mirrors the 18-month 'trio' planning now formalized for the Council's rotating presidency.

majority voting (QMV)—although some procedural issues are passed by a simple majority vote. With unanimity, any member state can block a proposal with a 'no' vote. Unanimity, in effect, gives each member a veto right. If a delegation wants to signal disagreement with some aspect of a proposal, but not block adoption by the others, he or she can abstain. Under unanimity, abstentions do not count as 'no' votes. Many policy areas are no longer subject to unanimity, although key areas that still are include foreign policy, defence, taxation, social security, judicial and police cooperation in criminal matters, and institutional reform. Qualified majority voting is now the default decision rule, which the Lisbon Treaty extended into about 40 new areas, thereby placing most Council negotiations under the so-called 'shadow of the vote'. How QMV works is tackled in Section 11.6, 'How does the Council system work?', but for now it is important to note that majority voting is one of the more distinctive traits of EU decision-making. Some scholars argue that only the most advanced and deeply integrated types of regional club operate by majority voting, since an outvoted minority is legally obligated to adopt a law against which it voted (Choi and Caporaso, 2002: 483). This is not friction-free, and at times can generate political pyrotechnics, such as the September 2015 JHA Council which adopted mandatory refugee 'relocation' quotas over the staunch objections of several member states who refused to accept the principle of a mandatory quota system (Council Decision (EU) 2015/1601, OJ L 248, 24.9.2015, p. 80) (see also Section 11.6.1, 'Voting and consensus patterns'). Qualified majority voting practices in the EU are all the more distinctive, as the EU does not impart a 'voting/veto' culture, but a **normative** environment of mutual accommodation and consensus-seeking (see Section 11.6, 'How does the Council system work?').

The ministers' meetings normally take place in Brussels, although during April, June, and October they are held in Luxembourg as part of an agreement dating from the 1960s over the location of the European institutions. The meetings take place in large rooms surrounded by interpreters' booths to provide simultaneous translation into the official EU languages. The meetings are far from intimate: typically, each delegation (and the Commission) will have three seats at the table (minister, permanent representative, assistant) and up to another half dozen who are waiting in the margins for a specific agenda point to be discussed. Normally, there are more than 100 people in the room at any one point, with lots of bilateral conversations, note passing, and strategizing going on at the same time as the individual who has the floor is speaking. Following the **Nice Treaty** decision to host all future European Council summits in Brussels, it was obvious that the existing building, Justus Lipsius, headquarters of the EU Council since 1995, could not handle the growing demand for meeting space. In 2004, the European Council decided to transform the neighbouring Résidence Palace, an art deco luxury apartment complex from the 1920s owned by the Belgian government, into a new headquarters for Council and European Council meetings. The new futuristic building is officially called 'Europa', blending historic and high-tech features such as solar roof panels with a massive urn-shaped meeting space that lights up at night to resemble a giant lantern. Unofficially, the building is referred to as the 'orb' or 'space egg' and was built at a cost of around €325 million. The largest meeting room can hold up to 330 people and 32 interpretation booths. The first meetings were held in 'Europa' in January 2017. Due to the ongoing COVID-19 pandemic, almost all Council meetings have been held by remote video conferencing since March 2020. The EU foreign ministers are a partial exception, and since January 2021 some FAC meetings have been held in-person to discuss diplomatically touchy topics such as Russian sanctions. Another exception, for reasons made clear in the next section, are the regular weekly meetings of Coreper, which still take place in Brussels and highlight the importance of face-to-face interactions in maintaining the Council's workflow and 'brand' of cooperation.

11.4.1 Coreper

Coreper, the Committee of Permanent Representatives, is the preparatory body of the EU Council, making it one of the most intense sites of negotiation in the EU. Whereas the ministers meet monthly at best, Coreper meets weekly. Wednesday 24 February 2021, for example, was the 2,797th meeting of Coreper (the first was in 1952). Officially, Coreper is charged with 'preparing the work of the Council', which reveals remarkably little about how important the Committee has become in making the Council run smoothly. Whereas any particular ministerial Council will be focused on a particular sectoral issue or set of policies, the members of Coreper negotiate across the entire gamut of EU affairs. In short, Coreper acts as a process manager in the Council system. While there are other Council preparatory bodies with a specialized purpose, such as the Special Committee on Agriculture (SCA) for AGFISH or the Economic and Finance Committee (EFC) for ECOFIN, none have the same seniority or density of issues as Coreper. As an institution, Coreper has a unique vantage point because it is vertically placed between the experts and the ministers, and horizontally situated with cross-sectoral policy responsibilities.

Because of the heavy workload in preparing Councils, since 1962 Coreper has split into two groups: Coreper I and Coreper II (see Box 11.8). Coreper I is made up of the deputy permanent representatives, responsible for preparing the so-called 'technical' Councils. The ambassadors, who hold the title of 'EU permanent representative', preside over Coreper II, and primarily work to prepare the monthly General Affairs and Foreign Affairs meetings, as well as issues with horizontal, institutional, or financial implications.

Coreper I and II are functionally independent bodies (responsible for different formations of the EU Council), even though the EU ambassadors in Coreper II have a more senior status with the national capitals. The permanent representatives live in Brussels and hold their positions for several years; some stay for a decade or longer, often outliving their political masters (ministers, prime ministers) and providing crucial continuity in the representation of national interests.

The most critical feature of Coreper is not discernible in the treaties—namely, the intensity of the negotiations that take place to prepare the ministers' meetings. At the start of Portugal's 2021 Council presidency, Prime Minister António Costa showed up at a regular weekly meeting of the EU ambassadors, announcing: 'Thank you for welcoming me at Europe's real power center' (*Politico*, Brussels Playbook, 21 January 2021). Aside from the weekly meetings, Coreper also holds restricted lunch sessions to sort out the most sensitive and tricky problems, during which not even the translators are allowed in the room. Recent invited guests to the Coreper lunch include many of the EU's top officials: the European Council President, Commission President, EP President, and High Representative all lunched with the EU ambassadors in January–February 2021. Permanent representatives also typically sit beside their minister at Council meetings and are often 'on call' in the wings of European Council summits. Putting a finger on the precise value added by Coreper is difficult, however, since the permanent representatives have no formal decision-making authority. It is clear that Coreper is an important de facto decision-making body, evident in the steady stream of pre-cooked agreements that are sent to the ministers for formal adoption. Over the years, Coreper has functioned under a fairly heavy cloak of confidentiality and insulation from domestic politics and domestic constituent pressures. This insulation enables the level of frankness in Coreper discussions that is essential for reaching a compromise across so many different subject areas.

Because of the intensity of negotiations and the long periods of tenure, Coreper officials often develop close personal relationships with one another based on mutual trust and a willingness to try to help each other. In this kind of normative environment and under the pressure to keep the Council moving forward, the permanent representatives are always on the lookout for ways in which to reach a compromise. The permanent representatives also exemplify the enigmatic identity of the Council: in order to succeed, they must at the same time represent a national set of interests and share a responsibility for finding collective solutions. Coreper illustrates how the Council does not only defend national interests, but is also a collective decision-making process embedded in

BOX 11.8   BACKGROUND: THE DIVISION OF LABOUR BETWEEN COREPER I AND II

Coreper I

Single European Market (Internal Market, Competitiveness)

Ordinary Legislative Procedure (OLP) (formerly co-decision) Negotiations with the EP (in relevant issue areas)

Environment

Employment, Social Policy, Health, and Consumer Affairs

Transport, Telecommunications, and Energy

Fisheries

Agriculture (veterinary and plant-health questions)

Education, Youth, Culture, and Sport

Coreper II

General Affairs

Foreign Affairs

Justice and Home Affairs

Multiannual Budget negotiations

Structural and Cohesion Funds

Institutional and horizontal questions

Development and association agreements

Accession

Ordinary Legislative Procedure (OLP) (formerly co-decision) Negotiations with the EP (in relevant issue areas) Inter-governmental conference (IGC) personal representatives (varies by member state and IGC)

---

social relations and informal norms of mutual responsiveness, empathy, and self-restraint.

11.4.2 Working groups

The expert group is the workhorse of the Council. Together, the working groups are a vast network of national officials who specialize in specific areas (such as food safety, the Western Balkans, business taxation, asylum, rural development, or combatting fraud) and form the initial starting point for negotiations on any new proposal or issue. The working group is also used in the later stages of negotiation to contemplate specific points of disagreement and can serve as a convenient way in which to place a proposal in 'cold storage' until the political climate is more favourable for an agreement. Some working groups are permanent, while others are ad hoc and disappear after tackling a specific question or issue. The FAC, AGFISH, and JHA Councils maintain the largest number of standing working groups, respectively 39, 26, and 30 each in 2021. Working groups are staffed with officials travelling from the capitals or from the Brussels-based permanent representations, depending on the issue area involved. The purpose of the working group is to pre-solve as much technical and fine detail as possible, while leaving areas in which there is disagreement or the need for political consideration to the permanent representatives or the ministers.

11.4.3 The General Secretariat of the Council

The Council employs a bureaucracy of approximately 3,000 officials known as the General Secretariat of the Council (GSC). Jobs are carefully allotted to each member state, such as the addition of 46 new posts for Croatia in 2013 following accession. The GSC Legal Service numbers around 200 employees, and is known for its deep knowledge of the treaties' legal bases and, at times, creative improvisation (such as the invention of the Danish 'opt-outs' after a domestic referendum rejected the initial Maastricht Treaty). The legal service acts as an impartial legal advisor to the Council on matters of precedent, in legislative negotiations with the EP (such as **trilogues**), and good drafting techniques. Good drafting is the remit of the legal services' 'Directorate for Quality of Legislation' (DQL) which reviewed close to 22,000 pages of legislative text in 2019 (Council of the European Union, 2020). The legal service also represents the Council in CJEU judicial proceedings, which typically involves the Council in 150–200 new cases per year. (For 2019, 139 court cases were closed, 256 were pending, and 167 new cases were initiated.) The GSC has more than 1,200 staff devoted to translation, document production, and managing the Council's archives. The top jobs are policy-making positions, which number about 300 in total. At the very top is the highly prestigious position

BOX 11.9   BACKGROUND: ORGANIZATION OF THE GENERAL SECRETARIAT OF THE COUNCIL

Office of the Secretary-General

Services attached to the Secretary-General (including Inter-institutional Relations, Communication and Digital Services)

Translation Service

Legal Service

Economic Affairs and Competitiveness (including Eurogroup)

General and Institutional Policy

Justice and Home Affairs

Agriculture, Fisheries, Social Affairs, and Health

External Relations

Transport, Energy, Environment, Education

of Secretary-General, a posting decided by the heads of state and government. The GSC is the administrative backbone and institutional memory of the Council system, which includes servicing newer organs such as the Eurogroup and the **European External Action Service (EEAS)**. Organizationally, it is divided into the Private Office of the Secretary-General, the Legal Service, and seven Directorates-General (DGs) for different policy areas (see Box 11.9).

The Secretariat is officially charged with keeping a record of all meetings, including: note taking (and producing the minutes of the meeting), vote calculating (including keeping up-to-date statistics on national population sizes, see Box 11.10), and translating all documents into the EU's 24 official languages. The GSC is also an important asset and ally of the presidency, providing logistical assistance, offering advice, and helping to find constructive solutions (the famous 'presidency compromise'). Over time, the GSC earned a reputation for being a dedicated, highly professional team, as well as for being 'honest brokers' helping to facilitate collective decisions.

Perhaps the key factor in the ascendance of the Secretariat in EU politics is the office of the Council Secretary-General. The position has changed hands only seven times. Historically, the long tenure of the job helped the Council impart a degree of continuity and leadership amidst the thousands of annual meetings. Under Niels Ersbøll, the long-serving Secretary-General (1980–94) from Denmark, the GSC was transformed from relative obscurity to a central position in Council negotiations—albeit a behind-the-scenes role that is not often credited in public (Hayes-Renshaw and Wallace, 2006: 103). The position of Secretary-General was granted new authority following the decision by the heads of state and government

at the 1999 Cologne European Council to upgrade the office to include the title of 'High Representative for Common Foreign and Security Policy', although the Lisbon Treaty hives off the chief foreign policy job, since renamed, (and the EEAS) and leaves coordination of European Council summits to the European Council President.

11.5 The High Representative of the Union for Foreign Affairs and Security Policy

One of the Council system's most significant internal developments in recent decades has been the consolidation of foreign policy authority in the Union's High Representative (see also Chapter 19). As noted above, the European Council elevated the GSC's top official, or Secretary-General, to the position unofficially dubbed 'Mr/Mrs CFSP' in 1999. Further upgrading the role and resources of the foreign policy post was an early consensus of the 2002–03 **Constitutional Convention**. While some members could not ultimately swallow the proposed title change—to 'EU Foreign Minister'—the agreed title, 'High Representative of the Union for Foreign Affairs and Security Policy', still carries with it a substantial enhancement of institutional clout as the EU's 'chief diplomat'. It is the area in which, practically speaking, the Union gains the most visible international legal personality. Lauded as Europe's answer to Henry Kissinger's alleged remark in the 1970s, 'I wouldn't know who to call if I wanted to talk to Europe' (Judt, 2005: 735), the political significance is to enhance the policy-making coherence of the Common Foreign and Security

Policy (CFSP) and the Common Security and Defence Policy (CSDP) (see Chapter 19). For EU scholars, the new position is intriguing, because it explicitly blurs the institutional boundaries between the Council and Commission in ways previously unthinkable (see also Chapter 10). To avoid organizational chaos in EU external relations, the new 'chief diplomat' is not only a top Council official, but also a vice-president of the Commission in charge of a sizeable external relations budget.

The European Council appoints the High Representative by qualified majority for a five-year term. The primary duties include:

- chairing the monthly Foreign Policy Council;

- attending European Council summits;

- serving as a Vice-President (VP) of the Commission and coordinating all External Relations portfolios;

- representing the EU externally (such as at the UN) and conducting high-level diplomacy through the European External Action Service (EEAS).

The first High Representative (HR/VP) to hold this position, Catherine Ashton, found herself in the difficult position of sorting out these institutional allegiances, managing a peripatetic travel schedule, and creating a new external diplomacy corps (the EEAS). A large contingent of officials from the GSC (over 400 in total) were transferred to the EEAS in 2010, which was given new responsibilities in preparing Foreign Policy Councils and managing over 120 EU delegations spread across the world. On 1 December 2014, Italy's Foreign Minister, Federica Mogherini, became the new HR whose five-year term led to the organization of the HR headquarters at the Commission and a Cabinet currently numbering about 30 officials including a Head of Cabinet (who services European Council meetings) and a Deputy Head (to coordinate monthly FAC meetings), as well as advisors, regional specialists, and press officials. Coordination of EU foreign policy is now aided by monthly meetings of a new Commission Group on External Action populated by relevant Commissioners and chaired by the HR. Gradually, these changes have upgraded the federal-like qualities of foreign policy in the Union, increasing the coherence of CFSP/CSDP and enhancing the EU as a credible global actor. In December 2019, Spain's Foreign Minister Josep Borrell became the new EU HR for a five-year term.

BOX 11.10   BACKGROUND: THE NEW QUALIFIED MAJORITY VOTING SYSTEM

Since 2014, the EU has followed a 'double majority' system of QMV that requires the support of at least 55 per cent of member states (at least 15 in an EU27), representing at least 65 per cent of the total EU population.

Member state	Percentage of total EU population
Germany	18.54
France	14.97
Italy	13.58
Spain	10.56
Poland	8.47
Romania	4.31
Netherlands	3.91
Belgium	2.58
Greece	2.39
Czech Republic	2.35
Portugal	2.30
Sweden	2.30
Hungary	2.18
Austria	1.98
Bulgaria	1.55
Denmark	1.30
Finland	1.23
Slovakia	1.22
Ireland	1.11
Croatia	0.91
Lithuania	0.62
Slovenia	0.47
Latvia	0.43
Estonia	0.30
Cyprus	0.20
Luxembourg	0.14
Malta	0.11
TOTAL	100

Sources: Lisbon Treaty; Council Decision 17116/11 of 8 December 2011 amending the Council's Rules of Procedure; Council of the European Union voting calculator, available at: https://www.consilium.europa.eu/en/council-eu/voting-system/voting-calculator/, accessed 8 February 2021.

11.6 How does the Council system work?

Having established how the Council system is organized, it is now possible to delve more deeply into how it works in practice. We begin by examining voting and consensus practices, including the Lisbon Treaty revisions of how qualified majority voting (QMV) is calculated. Next, we look at the rotating presidency, as well as at Council–Commission and Council–Parliament relations. Finally, the 'closed door' nature of the Council system is considered, along with the implications of enlargement, enhanced cooperation, and Brexit.

11.6.1 Voting and consensus patterns

A key procedural method for EU decision-making is the prospect of a vote under QMV. After the long shadow cast by the 1966 **Luxembourg Compromise**, QMV was reintroduced in the **Single European Act (SEA)** as a crucial precondition for establishing a **Single Market** by the 1992 deadline (see Chapter 20). Qualified majority voting has since gone from being the virtual exception to the rule to the Council's

default decision rule in the Lisbon Treaty (Article 16(3) TEU). Under QMV rules, each member state's vote is proportionate to national population size. Under the old system there was a complicated 'triple majority' design which required a minimum threshold of member states in favour (two-thirds), representing a minimum population threshold (62 per cent), and a fixed voting 'weight' allocation which created controversy during the Nice Treaty negotiations when France insisted on keeping a **parity** weighting with Germany, despite having 20 million or so fewer national citizens.

The new QMV rules simplify the procedure by dropping weighted votes entirely, and revising the thresholds for population and member state majorities. Thus, the new system for QMV is still a 'supermajoritarian' decision rule, but is now based on a **'double majority'** calculation that is arguably easier to understand and fairer to all (see Box 11.10). An additional clause requires at least four member states representing at least 35 per cent of the EU's population to form a **'blocking minority'**, a procedural safeguard against hypothetical big-state blocking coalitions.

But even where QMV applies, voting is a relatively uncommon event. Rarely is there ever a show of hands; typically, the presidency summarizes discussion and announces that a sufficient majority has been reached, or asks whether anyone remains opposed and, if not, notes the matter as closed. Voting is also unpopular in the EU because there is a highly ingrained culture of consensus and it is usually considered inappropriate to 'push for a vote' where there are one or more delegations with remaining objections or difficulties. Ironically, this culture grew out of the trauma of the 1965 **'empty chair crisis'** and the **Luxembourg Compromise**'s agreement to disagree on what constituted 'very important interests' (Ludlow, 2006; see also Chapter 2). Following this, as one participant recalls, 'the very fact of asking for a vote to be taken became an unusual step and endowed the calling of a vote with a solemn political significance' (Davignon, 2006: 18). As a result, actual voting and the use of votes to signal protest are fairly rare. We see this empirically in the low incidence of contested votes (that is, 'no' votes or abstentions) that occur in only about 20 per cent of all legislative acts (Hayes-Renshaw et al., 2006; Mattila, 2008; Van Acken, 2012). This affirms a deep-seated 'consensus-seeking' assumption in how negotiations should work. Consensus practices are reinforced by the shared benefit that consensual agreements mask who the actual winners and losers are, whereas public voting would broadcast it (Scharpf, 2006). New research documents how consensus patterns are not only about accommodation or reaching deals that make everyone happy with the outcome, but also act as a way for those opposed or isolated to avoid being on the losing side of a vote. In this way, consensus might not reflect 'general agreement' or the absence of opposition, but rather, a complex two-level game of 'blame avoidance' by ministers who do not want the loss of votes in Brussels to be displayed to domestic constituencies back home (Novak, 2013; Smeets 2015). For instance, in the Autumn 2015 JHA Council showdown over the EU refugee crisis, resulting in a divisive public vote under QMV, four member states voted against mandatory quotas (Hungary, Romania, Slovakia, and the Czech Republic) and one abstained (Finland), but up to 15 members were actually opposed to the idea of quotas (Zaun, 2018: 54). At the same time the *potential* recourse to the vote (the so-called 'shadow of the vote') is a powerful stimulus to delegations to avoid becoming isolated by simply saying 'no' and being unwilling to compromise. For this reason, EU Council participants claim that the fastest way in which to reach consensus is with the QMV decision rule.

11.6.2 The role of the rotating presidency

The EU Council presidency is held by member states for a six-month period. It is responsible for planning, scheduling, and chairing meetings of the ministers, permanent representatives, and working group experts. The Lisbon Treaty removes a number of roles from the rotating presidency with the creation of 'permanent' leadership jobs (including the European Council President and chairs for the Eurogroup and Foreign Affairs Council). In addition, a growing number of Council preparatory bodies have fixed, appointed chairs: the Economic and Financial Committee (EFC), the EU Military Committee (EUMC), and about 20 foreign policy-related committees and working groups that are chaired by the office of the HR (including the Political and Security Committee, PSC). This significant trend aside, the value of the rotating presidency lies in how it acts as a power equalizer between big and small states, giving tiny Luxembourg the same chance to run things as, say, Germany or France. The rotation is set to give variation between big and small, and newer and older member states (see Box 11.11).

Holding the rotating chair carries formidable logistical duties, and planning for the presidency typically begins 18 months prior to its start date. Poland, for example, began active planning in 2008 for their inaugural presidency in 2011. Preparations for Slovakia's 2016 presidency began five years in advance (Bilcik, 2017: 65). Despite the workload, the presidency is highly coveted, since the member state holding the presidency not only organizes meetings, but also helps to set the agenda and to find solutions by brokering deals, suggesting compromises, and drafting conclusions. This creates a **stakeholder** interest in overseeing a raft of successful legislative outcomes during the six-month rotation, which participants claim carry significant reputation and status concerns. Even the British, long considered an 'awkward partner' (George, 1998), earned a reputation for highly productive EU presidencies. A newer innovation, since 2007, is the institutionalization of greater coordination between presidencies into an 18-month work programme organized by a 'presidency trio'. The idea behind the 18-month programme is to enhance continuity and to formalize greater coordination in the Council's work. The 'trio's' programme is scrutinized and approved by the General Affairs Council (Article 2(6), Rules of Procedure).

The rotating presidency is a great example of the Council's enigmatic identity, since the country holding that position must simultaneously work to advance collective European solutions as well its own national interest. Member states that handle this balancing act with a deft touch can accumulate a great deal of political capital and respect. The Finnish presidency of 1999, for example, helped to earn that country a reputation for being very communitarian and skilful at compromise-building despite being a relative newcomer to the EU game.

11.6.3 Relations with other EU institutions

From the earliest days of the EU, interactions between the Council system and the Commission have constituted a key dynamic of European integration. But as the two were designed with a degree of inbuilt tension, with the Council representing individual member states and the Commission representing the 'European' interest, relations have at times been quite strained. The infamous 'empty chair' crisis of 1965 was prompted when French President de

BOX 11.11   BACKGROUND: EU COUNCIL PRESIDENCY ROTATIONS BY 'TRIO', 2019–30

Romania	January–June 2019
Finland	July–December 2019
Croatia	January–June 2020
Germany	July–December 2020
Portugal	January–June 2021
Slovenia	July–December 2021
France	January–June 2022
Czech Republic	July–December 2022
Sweden	January–June 2023
Spain	July–December 2023
Belgium	January–June 2024
Hungary	July–December 2024
Poland	January–June 2025
Denmark	July–December 2025
Cyprus	January–June 2026
Ireland	July–December 2026
Lithuania	January–June 2027
Greece	July–December 2027
Italy	January–June 2028
Latvia	July–December 2028
Luxembourg	January–June 2029
Netherlands	July–December 2029
Slovakia	January–June 2030
Malta	July–December 2030

Source: Council Decision 2016/1316 of 26 July 2016, amending Decision 2009/908/EU, OJ L 208/42, 2.8.2016.

history were very much at arm's length and mostly one-sided. Prior to the Maastricht Treaty, the Council merely had to consult the EP before adopting legislation and proposed EP amendments were not binding (see Chapter 12). This all changed when the co-decision procedure was introduced to selected issue areas, the essential feature of this procedure being that the EP is a co-legislator with the EU Council, since it is now much more difficult for the latter to ignore or overrule EP amendments. Since the 1990s, with each new treaty (Maastricht, Amsterdam, Nice, Lisbon), co-decision was introduced or extended to more issue areas. The Lisbon Treaty goes further, codifying co-decision as the EU's '**ordinary legislative procedure**' (OLP) rather than something exceptional (Article 289 TFEU). Under OLP rules, where the Council disagrees with EP amendments, there is a procedure known as '**conciliation**' in which the two sides meet to reach compromise on a final text. Conciliation meetings, and compromise-seeking negotiations to stave off conciliation with an 'early' (first or second reading) agreement, have dramatically intensified Council–EP relations since the mid-1990s. Working relations between the EU Council and EP have improved to the point at which the number of OLP files that are concluded by compromise (during the first or second reading) without the need for lengthy conciliation negotiations has steadily increased. Today, 85 per cent of all OLP agreements are reached without the need for conciliation. The growth of co-decision/OLP represents a new dynamic of inter-institutional networking in the EU and shows how the legislative process has evolved to become more like that of other **bicameral** federal political systems (see also Chapter 16).

Relations between the European Council and the EP have remained limited, driven mostly by the logic of limiting the scope and authority of the EP to shape 'history-making' decisions. The EP President does not participate in European Council summits (Article 235 (2) TFEU holds, 'The President of the EP may be invited by the European Council') and is only informed afterwards by a briefing from the European Council President. But as a sign of the times in the EU's evolving constitutional order, the EP has asserted new rights in areas where the European Council has traditionally acted alone, such as choosing the European Commission President (see Chapters 10 and 12).

Gaulle felt that the Commission had overstepped its authority in seeking to obtain its own sources of revenue (see Chapter 2). During other periods, relations between the Council and the Commission have been smoother, such as the period in the late 1980s when the bulk of legislation to create the Single Market was adopted in a steady stream by the Council (see Chapter 20). More recently, signs of strain have shown up again in areas of foreign policy, especially over who should represent the EU internationally (see Chapter 19).

In contrast to the Commission, relations with the European Parliament (EP) for most of the Union's

11.6.4 Transparency and accountability

Since the 1990s, the issue of the '**democratic deficit**' has been at the top of the EU's agenda (see Chapter 9). By contrast, the inner workings of the Council system have largely avoided scrutiny. Reducing the democratic deficit has centred on reforming the EU's decision-making procedures, increasing involvement by the EP, and introducing the **subsidiarity** principle to keep authority over decision-making as close to the citizen as possible. Every member government pays lip service to the need for the Union to be more transparent, more accessible, and more connected to EU citizens, but there is less agreement among them on how best to accomplish this task within deliberations.

One innovation is to hold 'public debates' by broadcasting select EU Council meetings on television and the Internet, but this has the perverse effect of stifling real dialogue, since the ministers start reading from set speeches. The Council's Rules of Procedure have become more detailed on requirements for broadcasting certain deliberations such as open sessions on the adoption of OLP acts, the 'first deliberation on important new legislative proposals' that do not involve OLP, and, within the GAC, an open 'public policy debate' on the 18-month presidency 'trio' programme (Article 8, Rules of Procedure). Yet researchers have shown that **transparency** has its limits in Council negotiations, as in the finding that more open deliberations can lead to bargaining breakdowns as national officials stick to positions that 'posture' and 'pander' to domestic audiences (Stasavage, 2004; Naurin, 2007).

11.6.5 Current challenges: 'absorption capacity', 'enhanced cooperation', and Brexit

There are several ongoing challenges facing the operation of the Council system that create institutional uncertainty and which could have future unintended consequences. The first issue is enlargement (see Chapter 18) and the ever-expanding size of the negotiating table. Some believe that, through enlargement, the Council system will become so unwieldy and heterogeneous that it will lose the deliberative and consensus-seeking capacities discussed earlier. Part of the perception of 'enlargement fatigue' in Brussels is the

strain on the decision-making structures—originally built for six members—by increasing '**transaction costs**', which will likely slow the pace and output of new legislation (Hertz and Leuffen, 2011). Enlargement also increases the workload on Coreper and the working groups, which hold greater responsibilities for discussing substantive issues and finding agreement.

The second challenge is known as **variable geometry**: how will the Council system change as the EU becomes more polycentric and differentiated? 'Enhanced' forms of cooperation, which were first introduced in the Nice Treaty, risk altering the very finely tuned mechanisms of exchange and consensus-seeking that have become a reflexive habit among Council participants. Treaty-based rights for enhanced cooperation are interpreted by many as the formalization and legitimation of an **à la carte** (or pick and choose) Europe. This was packaged as a way in which to 'further the objectives of the Union, protect its interests and reinforce its integration process', but a more cynical interpretation is that a vanguard of core members can no longer be held back in sensitive policy areas by the most reluctant integrationists. Enhanced cooperation is currently considered 'a last resort' when 'cooperation cannot be attained . . . by the Union as a whole' (Article 10(2) TEU). A recent example is the 2017 initiative for 'permanent structured cooperation' in security and defence ('PESCO') that includes 25 member states (but not Denmark, or Malta). Outsiders may still participate in deliberations, but they have no voting rights. Adopted acts bind only participating members and do not become part of the EU *acquis*. While many view **differentiation** as a method of promoting diversity and preventing the blockage of integration by reluctant members, others see it as setting a dangerous precedent for different 'classes' of membership that challenge the principle of equality.

A third challenge is the historic Brexit rupture and the ongoing 'future relationship' between the UK and the EU27. It is far too soon to know the full consequences of Brexit on European integration, but what is already apparent is the EU27's wilful effort to carry on without the UK. Within one month of the 'Leave' vote, the Council revised the order of the rotating presidency, effectively revoking the UK's upcoming rotation in 2017 and extending the new schedule through to 2030 (see Box 11.11). The use of the EU27 (Art. 50) format to restrict British participation was normalized months prior to the actual Article 50 notification in March 2017 (see Box 11.4). While scenarios for a 'hard' Brexit were averted, as significant is the question whether one member state's exit from the club will weaken or strengthen the remaining members' sense of joint enterprise and the 'doxa' of integration; that is, the undisputed and largely taken-for-granted truth of how 'Brussels' operates (Adler-Nissen, 2014: 57–8). There are also many future bumps in the road for the post-Brexit EU–UK relationship, with hardball bargaining and endless (re)negotiations clearly in the forecast. Current petty squabbles over diplomatic status pale in comparison to the stakes involved in determining 'equivalence' rules or the 'passporting rights' for sectors such as financial services.

KEY POINTS

- Most decisions are now made under QMV, which now has revised rules for calculating majorities, even though formal voting remains uncommon.
- Leadership is supplied by a rotating presidency, which alternates every six months and is coordinated by the 18-month work programme of the 'presidency trio'.
- Decision-making remains remote, opaque, and mysterious to EU citizens despite more formal efforts at deliberation 'open to the public'.
- Enlargement, enhanced forms of cooperation, and in-group/out-group dynamics such as Brexit could make negotiations more unwieldy, depersonalized, and unreceptive to compromise and consensus-based decision-making in the future.

11.7 Conclusion

The Council system is the core decision-making body of the European Union, representing national interests and power. It is also a collective system of governance that locks member states into permanent negotiations with one another. National officials who participate in this system have developed their own 'rules of the game', which include a culture of behaving consensually through compromise and mutual accommodation. The club rules also include group standards of (in)appropriateness, such as the opprobrium of Article 7 sanctions (see Box 11.12) or the newer rule of law conditionality attached to EU spending (see Box 11.3).

Thus, strictly speaking, the European Council and the EU Council are both institutions that represent national interests and bodies at the supranational level that make collective decisions. When examined closely, researchers often find evidence that the Council system blurs the traditional distinctions between the national and European levels, between intergovernmentalism and supranationalism. In organizational imagery, the actual operation of the Council system is perhaps closer to a network relationship of inter-organizational authority than to a corporate hierarchy, which is the typical portrayal.

Whether the Council system can continue to operate this way remains open to debate. There are signs of strain on decision-makers, as European Council agendas continue to balloon and the lines of coordination and coherence between Councils atrophy. There are also serious questions of democratic **accountability** that remain unanswered, as deliberations continue to be obscure and mysterious to EU citizens. Reform faces sharp trade-offs between greater transparency that is ineffective (public debates leading to set speeches) and more effective decision-making that takes place behind closed doors and out of the public spotlight (lunches, restricted sessions). An interesting new experiment was the November 2017 hybrid voting procedure to decide the post-Brexit relocation of the London-based European Medicines Agency (EMA) and European Banking Authority (EBA). The procedure combined an openly transparent application process evaluated with objective criteria developed by the Commission coupled with a drama-filled, multi-round secret ballot vote in a special session of the GAC.

Finally, the new focus on **differentiated integration** could have perverse effects on Council decision-making because some member states may find themselves excluded from certain discussions altogether, as we already see in areas of eurozone policy-making (see Chapters 22 and 25). This would have the unprecedented effect of institutionalizing different tiers or classes of membership. On the other hand, the EU has shown a remarkable capacity over the years to cope with crises and to innovate new solutions. The issue of 'institutional reform' is thus likely to be unresolved for some time and, in a governance system as advanced as the EU is, may even be an endemic feature of the EU's agenda.

BOX 11.12   KEY DEBATES: ARTICLE 7—WHAT WOULD IT TAKE?

Article 7 (TEU) covers sanctions on member states who violate fundamental EU values. These fundamental values are enshrined in Article 2 (TEU) and cover 'respect for human dignity, freedom, democracy, equality, the rule of law and respect for human rights'. Long considered a form of 'nuclear option', including the ultimate sanction—suspending voting rights—Article 7 has never been used. The deterrent effect of Article 7 lies in the group capacity to stigmatize aberrant behaviour such as Poland's reforms to politically control the judiciary that clashes with the EU's 'rule of law' values (Dinan, 2017). But formally invoking Article 7 is a dramatic event and suspending a member's rights would require the following steps:

• A four-fifths (80 per cent) majority of Council members (after obtaining the consent of the EP) would be required

to determine that a 'clear risk of a serious breach' of Article 2 values has occurred.

• The European Council would then need to determine 'a serious and persistent breach' of Article 2, acting by unanimity.

• Following this, by qualified majority, the Council 'may decide to suspend certain of the rights deriving from the application of the Treaties to the member state in question' and this might include voting rights in the Council.

Article 7's real power lies in the formalization of opprobrium by the EU over errant member state behaviour. More subtly, it is a clear example of the stigma management tools that advanced regional integration in Europe has evolved (see Adler-Nissen, 2014).

 QUESTIONS

1. Is the Council system intergovernmental or supranational?

2. How does the Council system perform both legislative and executive functions in the EU?

3. Does the Lisbon Treaty enhance the role of the European Council? If so, how?

4. Does the Council system resemble a hierarchy or/and a 'network'?

5. Do big states outweigh smaller states in power resources and influence in the Council system?

6. How do the member states coordinate the representation of national interests in EU Council negotiations?

7. What role does the rotating presidency play in EU governance?

8. How have Council–Parliament relations changed since the 1990s?

 GUIDE TO FURTHER READING

Hayes-Renshaw, F. and Wallace, H. (2006) *The Council of Ministers*, 2nd edn (New York: St Martin's Press). The *locus classicus* on the overall Council system, updated to reflect changes since the mid-1990s.

Naurin, D. and Wallace, H. (eds) (2008) *Unveiling the Council of the European Union: Games Governments Play in Brussels* (London and New York: Palgrave Macmillan). An edited volume that presents new data and contrasts different approaches to theorizing Council decision-making.

Puetter, U. (2014) *The European Council and the Council: New Intergovernmentalism and Institutional Change* (Oxford: Oxford University Press). The most thorough account of the European Council's centralizing tendencies, with detailed evidence of the practices that sustain consensus-seeking deliberations.

Van Middelaar, L. (2020) *Alarums & Excursions: Improvising Politics on the European Stage*. translated by Liz Waters (Newcastle upon Tyne: Agenda Publishing). An incomparable sweep of European Council summitry in today's era of 'EU crises' from a consummate Brussels insider.

Wessels, W. (2016) *The European Council* (London and New York: Palgrave Macmillan). A comprehensive history of EU summitry and the evolution of its role in the integration process.

 Access the online resources to take your learning and understanding further, including extra multiple-choice questions with instant feedback, web links, answer guidance to end-of-chapter questions, and updates on new developments in EU politics.

www.oup.com/he/cini-borragan7e

12

The European Parliament

Charlotte Burns

Chapter Contents

Reader's Guide

This chapter focuses upon the European Parliament (EP), an institution that has seen its power dramatically increase in recent times. The EP has been transformed from being a relatively powerless institution into one that is able to have a genuine say in the legislative process and hold the European Union's executive bodies (the Commission and Council, introduced in Chapters 10 and 11) to account in a range of policy areas. However, increases in the Parliament's formal powers have not been matched by an increase in popular legitimacy: turnout in European elections fell in successive elections up to 2014, and whilst turnout increased in 2019, an increasing share of the vote is going to populist Eurosceptic parties. Thus, while the EP's legislative power is comparable to that enjoyed by many national parliaments, it has struggled to connect with the wider European public and now has to find ways to accommodate populist Eurosceptic MEPs. The chapter explores these issues in detail. In the first section, the EP's evolution from talking shop to co-legislator is reviewed; its powers and influence are explained in the next section; the EP's internal structure and organization are then outlined with a focus upon the role and behaviour of the political groups, and finally, the European Parliament's representative function as the EU's only directly elected institution is discussed.

12.1 Introduction

The European Parliament (EP) is the only directly elected European Union institution. Until 1979, it was an unelected, weak, and marginalized body. However, the EP has gradually extended its legislative prerogatives so that under the terms of the **Treaty of Lisbon** it enjoys a range of powers comparable to those enjoyed by national legislatures. The extension of the EP's powers has led to a **parliamentarization** of the EU's political system. The EP has been an agent of deeper integration by pushing for increases in its powers, and a beneficiary of such processes as the EU has extended the range of competences upon which it legislates, and therefore upon which the EP can express its preferences. This chapter examines the development of the EP and its role within the EU's political system. In order to understand the function and operation of the Parliament, it examines three key areas of importance:

- the legislative work of the Parliament—namely, its role in shaping EU policies and laws;
- its internal politics, both in relation to the organization of the chamber and the nature of **cooperation** and competition between the political groups;
- the representative role of the Parliament, as a link between the electorate and EU decision-making processes.

While the EP has developed considerably as an institution, it still faces significant challenges in relation to its representative function, which weaken its claims to be the standard bearer for democracy within the EU's **governance** structures.

12.2 The evolving European Parliament

The European Parliament started life as the Common Assembly of the **European Coal and Steel Community (ECSC)**, and was introduced by the **founding fathers** to lend some democratic legitimacy to a set of institutions dominated by the unelected **High Authority** (later to become the European Commission) and national governments. The Assembly's original 78 members were appointed from national legislatures, thereby providing a link with national parliaments and an avenue for their input to and oversight of the ECSC's activities. The Assembly's powers were limited to dismissing the High Authority. Under the **Treaty**

of Rome, the Assembly became common to all three Communities—namely the ECSC, **European Economic Community (EEC)**, and the **European Atomic Energy Community (EAEC)** and was awarded the further right to be consulted on Commission proposals before they were adopted by the Council. Member state representatives were not, however, obliged to take the Assembly's position into account and, as members of the early Assembly were also national parliamentarians, they were effectively part-time. This dual mandate circumscribed the ability of the chamber to fulfil its limited legislative prerogatives. Thus, from its early days, the European Parliament gained the reputation of being little more than an ineffectual talking shop.

The Treaty of Rome included, however, the right for the Assembly to draw up proposals on elections by direct suffrage. This right was subject to **unanimity** in the Council and, because the member states were reluctant to support an elected Parliament, fearing a challenge to their own autonomy, the first direct elections were not held until 1979. Since those first elections, the Parliament has, as anticipated by the Council, used its status as the only directly elected EU institution to push for increases to its powers. The Parliament has exercised this strategy so effectively that today, its members are regarded as equal legislative and budgetary partners with the Council, and can scrutinize and hold the Commission to account (see Box 12.1).

KEY POINTS

- The European Parliament started life as an unelected Common Assembly to the ECSC.

- Its powers were limited to dismissing the High Authority and being consulted on legislative proposals, but the Council could ignore its suggestions.

- Until 1979, MEPs were national parliamentarians, hence the EP was a part-time institution, which, with its limited powers, led to it being dismissed as a powerless talking shop.

- Since 1979 direct elections have been held every five years and the EP has seen its powers increase, so that it is now regarded as an equal co-legislator with the Council.

12.3 The powers and influence of the European Parliament

The European Parliament's powers fall into three key areas: it enjoys considerable influence in relation to the EU Budget; it has the right to scrutinize, appoint,

BOX 12.1   BACKGROUND: THE EVOLVING EUROPEAN PARLIAMENT

Year	Event	Parliamentary powers
1952	ECSC Common Assembly created	78 nominated members take office. Right to dismiss High Authority.
1958	Becomes EC Common Assembly	142 nominated members take office. Right to be consulted on legislative proposals.
1975	Treaty changes on Budget	Greater budgetary powers for EP. Parliament given considerable influence over non-Common Agricultural Policy (CAP) spending.
1979	First direct elections	410 elected members. EP uses status as elected institution to push for greater powers.
1980	Isoglucose rulings by the Court of Justice of the EU (CJEU) (see Section 12.3.3, 'Legislative powers')	EP's right of **consultation** reinforced.
1987	**Single European Act (SEA)** enters into force	EP given greater scope to delay, amend, and block laws. **Assent** powers granted on some matters.
1993	Treaty of Maastricht enters into force	**Co-decision** procedure introduced for some areas. EP given approval power over nominated Commission.
1999	Treaty of Amsterdam enters into force	Co-decision procedure extended and amended in EP's favour. EP given formal right to veto Commission President.
2003	Treaty of Nice enters into force	Further extension of co-decision.
2009	Treaty of Lisbon enters into force	Co-decision renamed 'ordinary legislative procedure' (OLP) and extended to 85 policy areas. Special legislative procedures to be used for international treaties and accession agreements. EP given equal budgetary status with the Council, and division between compulsory and **non-compulsory spending** removed. EP political group leaders to be consulted on Commission President nominations and EP to elect Commission President. EP allowed to request treaty change.
2011	**Treaty on Stability, Coordination and Governance in Economic and Monetary Union** agreed	Four members of the European Parliament (MEPs) are included in the negotiations leading to the draft Treaty.
2012	**Citizens' initiative** is launched	EU citizens have the right to call for new legislation.
2014	Eighth European Elections	751 MEPs elected.
2016	UK votes to leave the EU	It is agreed that the size of the Parliament will be reduced and some UK seats redistributed to other states.
2019	Ninth European Elections	751 MEPs elected.
2020	Brexit	UK MEPs reallocated to other states and number of MEPs reduced to 705. The EP ratifies the **Withdrawal Agreement**.
2021	Brexit	The European Parliament ratifies the **Trade and Cooperation Agreement** between the UK and the European Union.
2023	EP Presidency	EP President Sassoli to step down to be replaced by a centre-right candidate.

and dismiss the Commission; and, in the context of EU law-making, the EP also has the right to amend and reject Commission proposals for legislation. These powers have expanded enormously in recent years largely as a result of the EP's proactive engagement with the process of treaty reform.

12.3.1 Budgetary powers

The first major increase in the EP's power came with the Budget Treaties of 1970 and 1975, under which the Parliament had limited powers to amend, reject, and sign off the EU budget, and be consulted on appointments to the **European Court of Auditors** (see Corbett et al., 2016). However, these powers were limited: the EP could request modifications to **compulsory spending** (largely agricultural policy), but could only insist on changes to non-compulsory spending, which comprised about 20 per cent of the budget. In order to extend its budgetary prerogative, the Parliament engaged in a series of battles with the Commission and Council in the early 1980s over spending levels and the allocation of funds between compulsory and non-compulsory expenditure. These persistent budgetary conflicts between the Council and EP were resolved in 1988 by a series of inter-institutional agreements that provided for annual Budgets within limits established by a multi-annual **financial perspective** that typically runs over six years.

The Treaty of Lisbon removed the distinction between compulsory and non-compulsory expenditure, thereby extending the EP's scope to amend the Budget across all areas, making it an equal budgetary partner. Today, the EP and Council act as a genuine **bicameral** budgetary authority, sharing a relationship based upon mutual respect and recognition of the need for stability and certainty when determining the EU's overall expenditure. Hence the EP has won a key democratic right to decide Europe's budgets and a long-standing cause of inter-institutional conflict has now been removed. Although agreeing the budget has continued to be challenging (see Box 12.2).

12.3.2 Holding the Commission to account

The EP has always enjoyed the right to dismiss the whole Commission, which it came close to doing in 1999, when the entire Santer Commission resigned (over a corruption scandal) in order to avoid a vote of censure from the Parliament. The EP had no powers of appointment under the original treaties but carved them out over time using its role as an elected institution to pressurize new Commission Presidents to submit themselves to a vote of approval by the Parliament. Formal recognition of the EP's right to appoint the Commission came in the Treaties of Maastricht and Amsterdam, which gave the EP a right to veto the Commission President-designate and the whole team of Commissioners. The Treaty of Lisbon went further by requiring the Council to take into account the outcome of the elections to the European Parliament

---

 BOX 12.2   CASE STUDY: AGREEING BUDGETS DURING CRISES

The EP's new budgetary powers came into force following the economic crisis at a time when European leaders were looking to cut spending, thus the Parliament had to balance the desire to achieve its broad policy aims against the wider need to behave responsibly in the face of widespread hardship across the EU. The negotiation of the 2014–20 multi-annual financial framework was consequently highly complex. Notably, the Budget was cut in real terms for the first time in the EU's history; however, the Parliament insisted upon the introduction of more flexibility over the allocation of spending, thereby making it easier to move funds to other areas as needed. The 2021–27 financial framework was similarly challenging due to the combined impact of Brexit, **COVID-19** (see Chapter 28) and the disputes over the **rule of law** in

Poland and Hungary. The UK was a net contributor to the EU budget and its exit meant that the EU had less money (see Chapter 27 on Brexit). COVID-19 made negotiating in person over the budget more challenging and had a profoundly negative impact upon growth in Europe. The EP agreed to a COVID-19 recovery package of €750 billion as part of the overall budget. However, negotiations over the final deal were protracted thanks to an ongoing row over the rule of law in Hungary and Poland. The Parliament and Commission introduced clauses to prevent states that do not observe the rule of law from accessing the recovery funds. Hungary and Poland at whom these measures were directed withheld their consent to the budget until the wording on the rule of law was changed (see Chapter 29).

and to consult the party leaders within the EP before nominating a candidate who is then elected by an absolute majority of all MEPs. If the MEPs reject that candidate, then the Council must propose a new one. The EP took advantage of this rule to pursue the so-called *spitzenkandidaten* process in 2014, by insisting, despite strong opposition from the UK, that the nominated candidate from the largest political grouping following the 2014 elections, Jean-Claude Juncker of the European People's Party (EPP), become the new Commission President. However, in 2019 the EP's *spitzenkandidat*, Manfred Weber failed to secure the support of the Council and a long-term ally of Angela Merkel, Ursula von der Leyen was eventually appointed as the new Commission President. Von der Leyen's appointment seemed to signal the death of the *spitzenkandidaten* process but in an effort to reassert its power the EP went on to apply considerable pressure on von der Leyen about the priorities for her term of office and the composition of the Commission.

Although the EP's right to approve the wider Commission does not allow for the dismissal of individuals, the Parliament has successfully used its rights of appointment to force individual candidates to step aside or to push for a reorganization of individual portfolios (see Box 12.3). However, an interesting anomaly has emerged under the terms of the Treaty of Lisbon in relation to the EP's rights of appointment. Under Article 17(8) TEU, if the Parliament decides to veto the appointment of the European Commission, the candidate for **High Representative** for Foreign Affairs, who sits as a vice-president in the Commission, can simply resign from the Commission, yet carry on with their duties as High Representative, thereby potentially sowing the seeds for future inter-institutional battles. That being said, it seems unlikely that the Council would insist on keeping a candidate in the post of High Representative who did not enjoy the support of the majority of the EP.

When it comes to scrutinizing the executive, the EP's scope is more limited. It can invite Commissioners, Commission officials, and Council presidency representatives to Committee meetings to explain and justify decisions. The Commission also submits its annual work programme to the EP. However, the main leverage that the Parliament possesses to hold the Commission to account is via its powers of appointment and dismissal, and members of the Council are held to account by their own national parliaments.

12.3.3 Legislative powers and policy-making

A key shift in the EU has been the increased parliamentarization of decision-making, which has primarily manifested itself in the increase in the EP's right to exercise a range of legislative powers. The Parliament has become increasingly involved in areas that are traditionally intergovernmental, especially since the entry into force of the **Lisbon Treaty**, so that it is now involved in nearly all policy areas.

The main vehicle through which the EP expresses its preferences and shapes legislation is the **ordinary legislative procedure (OLP)**. Originally introduced by the Treaty of Maastricht, the OLP only applied to 15 policy areas but following the entry into force of the **Lisbon Treaty** it now applies to 85 areas, including the traditionally intergovernmental arenas of

---

BOX 12.3   BACKGROUND: APPOINTING THE COMMISSION

Officially, the EP is limited to endorsing the whole Commission. However, the Parliament has made clear over the years that it is prepared to veto the entire team rather than accept an inappropriate candidate. The EP's committees hold hearings with the relevant Commissioners-designate in order to determine their suitability, and there are usually some casualties. In 2019 three nominees were rejected by the Parliament. Rovana Plum from Romania and László Trócsányi from Hungary were rejected by the Legal Affairs Committee over conflicts of interest. French nominee, Sylvia Goulard, was also rejected because she used her European Parliament assistant to carry out political work, in clear contravention of EP rules. The rejection of Goulard was the first time the EP had rejected a nominee from one of the larger states and reflects an increasing confidence on the part of the Parliament to deploy its powers.

international trade, migration, fisheries, and agriculture. The OLP makes the EP a genuine co-legislator with the Council: the Parliament's agreement is required before a proposal can become law. The OLP consists of three readings of legislation and introduced a formal conciliation process between the EP and Council after the second reading if the two sides cannot agree. Conciliation involves a committee comprised of equal-sized delegations from the Council and EP negotiating a compromise text, which the Commission seeks to facilitate. If the two sides cannot agree the legislation falls, or the EP can veto the proposal, although it rarely exercises this veto power (see Chapter 16).

The right to conciliation was a significant step forward in putting the EP on an equal legislative footing with the Council. However, the numbers involved in meetings make reaching agreement difficult, so since the early days of the OLP in the 1990s a system of informal meetings (**trilogues**) has been used to facilitate negotiation. Decisions are also increasingly taken in even smaller informal meetings at first- or second-reading via a procedure known as early agreements. The evolution of this way of working with small informal meetings between select personnel from the EP and Council has enabled the process to function effectively and reduced the need for the larger conciliation meetings so successfully that there were no formal conciliations between 2014 and 2019 (European Parliament, 2019).

This shift to informal decision-making has enhanced the inter-institutional relationship between the Council and Parliament as they have become genuine co-legislators. However, while this informality facilitates agreement and the building of inter-institutional trust, it has also come at a price as it involves a trade-off between efficiency and transparency. Increasing concerns have been raised about small groups meeting behind closed doors with limited opportunity for input from the relevant EP committee or the wider plenary, which undermines the EP's claim to be the standard bearer for democracy in the EU. In response to these concerns the Parliament has amended its own rules of procedure to ensure that the EP's negotiating team is acting on a mandate from the parent committee or the plenary as a whole. Nevertheless, the **European Ombudsman** launched an own-initiative enquiry into the transparency of trilogues, which made a series of

recommendations as to how transparency could be improved. These included making the dates, personnel, and paperwork associated with the meetings publicly available, which the ombudsman suggested should also be held in a joint database. Many of these issues, as well as the operation of relationships between the institutions, are covered in a new inter-institutional agreement on Better Law-making. This document brings together a range of pre-existing inter-institutional agreements into one document and has updated them in the light of new institutional challenges and processes. It spells out clearly the prerogatives of each institution and the way in which they should cooperate with each other to produce clear and transparent legislation (European Parliament, European Council, and European Commission, 2016a). Overall, the introduction of OLP has ushered in a more cooperative set of working arrangements between the Council and EP. However, its extension to new, traditionally intergovernmental policy areas has seen a series of disputes emerge between the two co-legislators over fisheries and the Council has also struggled to accommodate the Parliament's greater inclusion in agricultural policy.

The other key procedures of decision-making the EP has at its disposal are termed special legislative procedures under which the EP can consent to, or is consulted on, legislation (see Table 12.1 for detail). The most significant aspect of these is the EP's right to consent to (or veto) international agreements and trade agreements, as well as a country's Withdrawal Agreement from the EU. The Parliament has used these veto powers sparingly to ensure it is not ignored during the process. This restraint reflects a long-standing strategy employed by the Parliament to balance its right to use its veto powers against its desire to be seen as a responsible legislative partner.

12.3.4 An advocate for constitutional change

The Parliament has been proactive in seeking to enhance its power through advocating constitutional reform under which the EP and the wider European citizenry would be given an enhanced role in determining the shape and function of the EU (Corbett, 1998; see Chapter 9). In the 1980s the EP's Institutional Affairs Committee prepared a draft Treaty of European Union, which was part of a wider set of

Table 12.1 Special legislative procedures

Special legislative procedures	
Consent procedure	Consultation procedure
EP can accept or reject proposal but CANNOT amend	EP can accept, amend, or reject proposal. Following CJEU *Isoglucose judgment* of 1979 Council cannot act without EP opinion.
Legislative Consent Covers new legislation on: • combatting discrimination • the establishment of a Public Prosecutor's Office • the adoption of a system of own resources and of the multi-annual financial framework • any legislation adopted under the 'subsidiary' legal basis (Article 352 TFEU), otherwise known as the catch-all article of the Treaty, which allows the institutions to act in areas not explicitly covered by the Treaties	**Legislative Consultation** Covers: • internal market exemptions • competition law
Non-Legislative Consent Covers: • international agreements to which the OLP applies • cases of a serious breach of fundamental rights (Article 7 of the Treaty on European Union) • accession of new EU members • withdrawal from the EU	**Non-Legislative Consultation** Covers: • international agreements adopted under common foreign and security policy

factors promoting the adoption of the Single European Act. In subsequent treaty negotiations, the Committee again prepared detailed reports, and advanced the case for further reform with lobbyists, non-governmental organizations (NGOs), and national governments. As a consequence of this activity, MEPs were formally included in the **intergovernmental conference (IGC) reflection groups** preparing the Amsterdam and Nice Summits, and under the Treaty of Lisbon the EP has gained the formal right to request treaty changes (see Chapter 3). In recognition of this new role, the EP was asked to assent to changes to the Treaty of Lisbon allowing for the creation of the **European Stability Mechanism (ESM)** in 2011. Later that same year, the President of the **European Council** requested that a delegation from the Parliament be involved in the negotiations and drafting of the new Fiscal Treaty for the **euro area**. Thus, the EP has a growing role in drafting treaty changes and can therefore bring more democratic accountability to the process. Moreover, the empowerment of the EP in this area allows for greater involvement of **supranational** actors in what were traditionally intergovernmental arenas, despite claims that the EU has become more intergovernmental since the eurozone crisis (see Chapters 5 and 25).

KEY POINTS

• The European Parliament gained significant budgetary powers in the 1970s and acts as one half of the EU's bicameral budgetary authority.

• The EP can appoint and dismiss the Commission President and College of Commissioners.

• The EP's powers have extended furthest in the legislative realm. It acts as a co-legislator with the EU Council in 85 policy areas. However, the use of informal meetings raises questions about the wider transparency of EU decision-making.

• The EP has long pressed for constitutional change to bring Europe closer to its citizens; many of its goals were realized in the Treaty of Lisbon. The EP itself is now more closely involved in the process of treaty change.

12.4 The internal politics of the European Parliament

The European Parliament has been characterized as an institution composed of strong committees and weak parties. The committees allow the EP to exercise its legislative prerogatives and hold the EU executive to account. However, as the Parliament's powers have expanded, the political groups rather than the national political parties, have emerged as important actors, for they hold the power of patronage within the Parliament, and act as a conduit between Brussels and national political parties. The EP's political groups are cross-national: they are composed of members from different countries who share the same broad ideological convictions. To form a political group requires 23 MEPs representing a quarter of the member states. There are currently seven political groupings and a cohort of MEPs who have chosen not to affiliate themselves (see Table 12.2). The two largest groups are the European People's Party (EPP), a centre-right political group, and the Progressive Alliance of Socialists and Democrats (S&D), a centre-left political group.

The groups play a central role within the EP because they control appointments to positions of responsibility and set the EP's calendar and agenda. It therefore makes sense for MEPs to affiliate themselves with large groups but forming them can be challenging. For example, in the 2014 elections, the far-right did well in several states, including France, where the *Front National* (**FN**) (now *Rassemblement National*) came first overall, securing 24 seats, which in theory should have placed its leader, Marine Le Pen, in a powerful position to form a political group within the Parliament. However, it was a year before Le Pen was able to persuade enough MEPs from seven states to form a group, the Europe of Nations and Freedom (ENF). This delay was due to other right-wing parties, most notably the **UK Independence Party** (UKIP) one of the largest of the **Eurosceptic** national delegations, being reluctant to partner with Le Pen, as association with the FN was seen by many as politically toxic.

The Group to which UKIP was affiliated in the 2014–19 Parliament, the Europe of Freedom and Direct Democracy (EFDD), ceased to exist following Brexit, which saw a reallocation of the UK's seats to other countries and a reduction in the number of MEPs from 751 to 705 (see Chapter 27). A new far-right grouping, Identity and Democracy, was created following the 2019 elections and is composed of MEPs from ten countries, with the two largest delegations drawn from the Italian **Lega** party and the French *Rassemblement National*.

As the allocation of posts within the EP is determined by group size and, within the groups, by the size of each national delegation, there are strong

Table 12.2 Composition of the European Parliament post-Brexit (2020)

Political group	Political orientation	Number of MEPs
European People's Party (EPP)	Centre-right Christian Democrat and Conservatives	187
Progressive Alliance of Socialists and Democrats (S&D)	Centre-left	145
Renew	Liberal	98
Identity and Democracy (ID)	Far-right	75
Greens and European Free Alliance (Greens/EFA)	Environmentalist and regionalist	73
European Conservative and Reformists	Right-wing and Eurosceptic	62
European United Left/Nordic Green Left (EUL/NGL)	Left-wing	39
Non-affiliated Members (NA)	Various	26
Total		705

incentives to keep the groups together. But allotting posts requires intensive intra- and inter-group negotiation and coordination. The most important positions within the Parliament are:

- the President, who acts as the EP's figurehead, chairing the Plenary and representing the Parliament in external negotiations and meetings;
- the Vice-Presidents who support the President and help to run the Parliament;
- the committee chairs, who organize and run committee meetings.

The negotiations between the parties over these posts are typically conducted by party elites behind closed doors, a process that has attracted opprobrium for its lack of transparency. In 2019 the EP presidency nomination was made after protracted negotiations behind closed doors in the Council over who would get the top EU jobs. Eventually, the EP Presidency went to Italian centre-left MEP, David-Maria Sassoli, with an agreement that he would step down after two and half years to make way for a representative from the centre-right European People's Party. This kind of horse-trading for posts within the Parliament undermines the EP's claim to be the standard bearer for transparency within the EU's institutional structures.

A key position within the EP is the role of committee chair, who is responsible for organizing the calendar and agenda of meetings, chairing meetings, and participating in inter-institutional negotiations under the OLP. Chairs are important as committees are the locus for the majority of parliamentary work, and they play a key role in enabling the Parliament to exercise legislative power and hold the EU's executive to account. In the 2019–24 Parliament, there are 20 standing committees divided functionally into different policy areas. The membership of each committee roughly mirrors the ideological balance of the wider Parliament. The committees are the repositories of policy expertise and are responsible for appointing teams of negotiators who can engage in intra- and inter-institutional negotiations.

The EP also appoints two further types of temporary committees. Special committees, which usually have a twelve-month mandate, report on topical or urgent issues. Recent examples include those on Beating Cancer; on Foreign Interference in Democratic Processes of the EU; and on Artificial Intelligence in a Digital Age. Committees of inquiry investigate breaches or maladministration of EU law. Recent inquiries have covered the Protection of Animals during Transport, and Emission Measurements in the Automotive Sector (see Chapter 24).

Within the committees, MEPs are selected as *rapporteurs* to draft reports and their work is aided by 'shadow' *rapporteurs*, who are drawn from another political group and can feed in alternative political perspectives to the *rapporteur* and committee, as well as keeping their own party and the wider EP informed about the positions being developed. The *rapporteurs* and shadow *rapporteurs* are central members of the team responsible for negotiating with the Council under the OLP. They also play an important role in shaping the position adopted by their political groups as a result of their policy expertise.

Once committees have crafted their reports, they are subject to amendment and adoption by the EP's Plenary (the meeting of all MEPs), which, normally meets in Strasbourg and Brussels (see Box 12.4). During the Plenary, MEPs vote on the various reports and motions for resolution, and adopt amendments to legislation. The MEPs must secure the support of a majority, and because the largest political group, currently the EPP, cannot on its own command a majority, the adoption of amendments and resolutions requires cooperation between the political groups. Thus, securing the support of a majority both in the committees and in Plenary requires inter-group negotiation.

 BOX 12.4   CASE STUDY: THE SEATS OF THE EUROPEAN PARLIAMENT

The EP was originally located in Strasbourg on the Franco-German border as a symbol of the new European unity. The EP also has offices in Luxembourg, which were originally established there to allow it to work alongside the ECSC High Authority (see Chapter 2). However, the Parliament does most of its work in Brussels, where the other EU institutions are located. Some administrative staff are still based in Luxembourg and, once a month, MEPs, their staff, and representatives from the Commission and EU Council decamp to Strasbourg for the EP's Plenary session. Although the majority of MEPs would far rather conduct all of their business in Brussels, French opposition to losing the Strasbourg EP seat led to a commitment in the Treaty of Lisbon to maintaining it. Thus, outside of pandemic times the monthly adjournment to Strasbourg will continue despite the cost and inconvenience to MEPs and the European taxpayer.

Cooperation between the two largest groups to secure majorities has long been the norm in the Parliament, although as smaller parties have done well that coalition has increasingly had to draw upon other groups to secure majorities. In the 2014–19 Parliament the EPP and S&D had to work with the liberal group to secure stable majorities. A similar type of grand coalition will be required in the 2019–24 Parliament, as for the first time in the EP's history the two largest groups cannot command an absolute majority between them. Moreover, MEPs from populist right-wing Eurosceptic parties have been able to form the fourth largest political group with implications for the functioning of the Parliament as some MEPs from these groups are committed to disrupting EU policy-making (See Box 12.5).

It might be expected that MEPs would vote according to national preferences, forming national blocs regardless of ideological differences. While there are occasional instances of such national defections, studies of the Parliament's voting behaviour show that, as a general rule, the MEPs behave ideologically (Hix et al., 2007): they vote with their political groups, not with their fellow nationals. Even when the EU enlarged to take in 12 new states, MEPs from the accession states quickly acclimatized to these EP norms to vote according to ideological preferences (Scully et al., 2012). Hence while the EP is unique as a parliamentary chamber, given its multinational and multilingual composition (it has 24 official languages compared with the UN's six), in practice it behaves like an ordinary parliament, organizing and voting along classic left–right ideological lines (Ripoll Servent and Roederer-Rynning, 2018).

A significant challenge that emerged early on in the ninth Parliament was responding to the COVID-19 pandemic and setting up systems to allow scrutiny, debates, and voting to continue under lockdown conditions (see Chapter 28). The European Parliament has largely been regarded as an example of best practice globally in its rapid response to the COVID-19 pandemic. The EP moved quickly to introduce social distancing, ban visitors, introduce face masks, and to encourage MEPs to work from home where possible to reduce travel-related transmission. The Bureau of the Parliament agreed to temporary change to the EP's rules of procedure to allow MEPs to participate and vote remotely. An electronic system was introduced to allow for online multilingual meetings of up to 1,000 participants (bear in mind the EP has 24 official languages). The EP also supported local communities in the cities in which the Parliament buildings are based. For example, in Brussels the EP kitchens were used to prepare meals for those in need during lockdown and a building was turned into a refuge for women who needed help and support. In Strasbourg an EP building was turned into a screening centre for COVID-19.

> **BOX 12.5   KEY DEBATES: ACCOMMODATING EUROSCEPTIC MEPS**
>
> In both the eighth (2014–19) and ninth (2019–24) Parliamentary elections, Eurosceptic parties performed well, raising the prospect that MEPs from these groups would seek to undermine parliamentary business. The larger mainstream political groups sought to prevent this eventuality by putting in place a **cordon sanitaire**, which has limited the access of Eurosceptic parties to positions of responsibility in the Parliament. For example, the radical right group, Identity and Democracy (ID) should have received two vice-presidencies of the EP and two committee chair positions following the 2019 elections. However, the other political groups ignored the informal rules to allow the election of ID members to positions of responsibility (Brack, 2020). Whilst this move reduced the opportunity for Eurosceptic groups to disrupt parliamentary processes it also exemplified behaviour that Eurosceptic parties were challenging and disenfranchised MEPs who were democratically elected to pursue Eurosceptic policies. The rise of Eurosceptic parties underlines the challenge raised for the EP about how it should accommodate MEPs who have been democratically elected but whose main purpose is to undermine the effective operation of EU policy processes.

> **KEY POINTS**
>
> - Members of the European Parliament sit and vote in cross-national political groups, which control appointment to important posts.
>
> - Detailed policy work in the EP is carried out by its committees. Committee rapporteurs play a key role in shaping group opinions and in representing the Parliament in inter-institutional negotiations under the OLP.
>
> - The Parliament votes along ideological, rather than national, lines and the voting behaviour of MEPs is increasingly cohesive.
>
> - The EP moved rapidly to address the challenge of the COVID-19 pandemic by adapting its working practices.

12.5 Elections, the people, and the European Parliament

Elections to the European Parliament are held every five years. The rules governing European elections are different from those that typically apply to national elections, because EU citizens resident in another EU state (for example, Bulgarians living in Germany) are entitled to vote in local and European elections, but not in national elections. Citizens resident in an EU state can also stand for election even if they are a non-national, thus Danny Cohn-Bendit, a German citizen, was elected as an MEP in both Germany (1994–9, 2004–09) and France (1999–2004, 2009–14). Since 1999, European elections have been conducted on the basis of **proportional representation (PR)** across the whole EU, although there are differences between the member states in the systems that they use. For example, in France, European elections are decided by a regionally based **list system**, but in Germany a national list is used. An inevitable consequence of this disparity is that the number of constituents whom each MEP represents can vary enormously. Where MEPs represent a large constituency, it is challenging to build a relationship between the elected politician and the citizen, which may provide a partial explanation for the EP's ongoing struggle to connect with EU citizens, as

indicated by the fall in turnout at successive European elections up to 2014 (see Figure 12.1).

How can we explain the trends in turnout, which fell in successive European elections and then stabilized in 2014 and increased in 2019? One potential explanation is that European elections are second-order, so they are viewed as less important than national elections, so voters do not turn out to vote. A side-effect of the second-order nature of EP elections is that as voters think that their preferences do not count they can use the election to express dissatisfaction with the governing party of their member state (Reif and Schmitt, 1980), which may explain why smaller parties such as the greens and populist parties have done well, especially in 2014 and 2019. An alternative explanation for the increasingly successful performance of smaller parties is that voters do care about EU issues and a party's position as being pro- or anti-European shapes how citizens vote (Hobolt and Spoon, 2012). The 2014 and 2019 elections were both contested with the assumption that the Commission President selection would be linked to the outcome of the election, which could explain why turnout did not fall in these two elections and indeed increased in 2019. Another credible explanation for voting behaviour is the fact that EU election campaigns are organized and financed by domestic political parties rather than by the European political

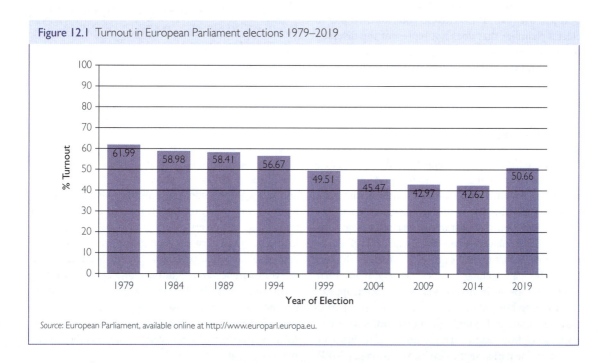

Figure 12.1 Turnout in European Parliament elections 1979–2019

Source: European Parliament, available online at http://www.europarl.europa.eu.

groups. Thus, candidates do not seek re-election as a member of the S&D or EPP, but as a French Socialist or a German Christian Democrat. Moreover, the parties often campaign on national, rather than genuinely European, platforms. So both turnout and voting choices maybe shaped by domestic rather than European political factors, which helps to explain the variation in voting behaviour across the EU.

The EP faces a key challenge: it has predicated its calls for empowerment upon its status as a democratically elected body that can bring the voice of Europe's citizens to the heart of the EU's decision-making processes, but its legitimacy is undermined by the relatively poor turnout for European elections and the increasing popularity of Eurosceptic parties. Moreover, the EP is still largely white and male. In 2019, 41 per cent of the MEPs elected were female (European Parliament, 2020) and 5 five per cent came from ethnic minority groups, comparing poorly with an EU minority population of at least ten per cent (European Network Against Racism, 2019). Whilst the Parliament can take some comfort from the fact that it is not suffering alone as many parliaments struggle to secure appropriately balanced representation and turnout is low in many elections across the EU, nevertheless elections legitimate political systems and executives. The EP has argued that it can act as a corrective to the EU's **democratic deficit** by holding the executive to account and participating in policy-making. Yet if only just over half of EU citizens vote, and in doing so elect a chamber that does not represent the diversity of EU communities, not only is the legitimacy of the EP undermined, but so too is that of the wider system

of EU governance (see Chapter 9). The Lisbon Treaty sought to address concerns over democratic accountability by further extending the EP's powers and by including a greater role for national parliaments in decision-making. Thus, under the '**yellow card system**' (Protocols 1 and 2 of the Treaty of Lisbon), if a third (or a quarter in relation to freedom, security, and justice) of national parliaments feel that draft legislation could be better achieved by domestic legislation, the Commission must review the act. Between 2012 and 2016, three yellow cards were issued by national parliaments on the establishment of common EU rules on the right to strike, the creation of a European Public Prosecutors' Office, and the posting of workers (European Commission, 2013, 2014, 2016), demonstrating that national parliaments are now more able to exercise their prerogatives under the principle of **subsidiarity**.

KEY POINTS

- The European Parliament is directly elected every five years. The number of constituents represented by each MEP varies widely.

- European elections are typically regarded as being less important than national elections, both by the electorate and by national political parties, which fail to campaign on European issues; this has contributed to low turnout.

- The EP is still largely white and male and therefore fails to reflect the more diverse nature of the EU's population.

- National parliaments are now able to block proposed EU legislation.

12.6 Conclusion

The European Parliament has been the major beneficiary of treaty change in the European Union, being transformed from a marginalized institution into a key policy actor within the system of EU governance. The EP has developed a set of transnational political groups, which behave cohesively and vote along ideological left–right lines. Whist the EP's power has increased, there has not been a matching increase in its legitimacy: turnout for European elections has stabilized, but it appears to have been buoyed by the rise of Eurosceptic parties that are committed to undermining the EU's system of governance from within. The response of mainstream groups in the parliament to exclude Eurosceptic MEPs

from positions of power and responsibility exemplifies the types of behaviour criticized by populist parties and raises some important questions about the wider legitimacy of the European project. MEPs now enjoy a wide range of powers covering most policy areas, and, in order to enhance decision-making efficiency, they engage in informal practices that further undermine the transparency and legitimacy of EU policy-making processes. Thus, the EP now faces three interlinked challenges: how to increase its appeal to the wider European electorate; managing the presence of Eurosceptic MEPs within its midst; and contributing to efficient *and* open governance in the EU.

QUESTIONS

1. Why was the European Parliament created?

2. How and why have the EP's power increased?

3. Do MEPs vote according to nationality or ideology? To what extent are MEPs free from national control?

4. What impact has the empowerment of the European Parliament had upon inter- and intra-institutional relations?

5. How is it possible to account for the turnout in European elections?

6. What impact does the emergence of a larger bloc of Eurosceptic parties have upon the operation of the Parliament? What, if any, impact has Brexit had in this regard?

7. What are the principal challenges facing the EP and how should it address them?

8. What function does the European Parliament serve in the EU system of governance?

GUIDE TO FURTHER READING

Corbett, R., Jacobs, F., and Neville, D. (2016) *The European Parliament*, 9th edn (London: John Harper). An excellent and comprehensive guide to the history and day-to-day operation of the European Parliament, written by practitioners.

Hix, S., Noury, A. G., and Roland, G. (2007) *Democratic Politics in the European Parliament* (Cambridge: Cambridge University Press). A study of the internal politics of the European Parliament that draws upon an extensive dataset of voting behaviour in the Plenary.

Ripoll Servent, A. (2018) *The European Parliament* (Basingstoke: Palgrave Macmillan). An advanced textbook outlining the organization and powers of the Parliament.

Ripoll Servent, A. and Roederer-Rynning, C. (2018) 'The European Parliament: A Normal Parliament in a Polity of a Different Kind' in *Oxford Research Encyclopaedias, Politics* (New York: Oxford University Press USA). An advanced essay that reviews the debates over whether the EP can be considered a normal parliament.

Access the online resources to take your learning and understanding further, including extra multiple-choice questions with instant feedback, web links, answer guidance to end-of-chapter questions, and updates on new developments in EU politics.

www.oup.com/he/cini-borragan7e

13

The Court of Justice of the European Union

Paul James Cardwell

Chapter Contents

Reader's Guide

This chapter provides an overview of the Court of Justice of the EU. The Court has emerged as a powerful player in the history and development of the European integration process. Its contribution to the workings of the EU and our understanding of it are central to both legal and political accounts, while its decision-making has at times been controversial. This chapter explores the history of the Court as an institution of the EU, how it has developed its role and how we can understand the 'politics' of the judicial arm of the EU's institutional framework.

13.1 Introduction

As an institution of the European Union, the Court of Justice of the European Union (CJEU) is a curious beast. On the one hand, it is a court much like any other: it makes decisions, which can be enforced, it resolves disputes between parties and it offers opinions on contested points of law. It makes interpretations of the law and, depending on one's viewpoint, creates, furthers, or at least recognizes legal principles. It has a defined remit for its caseload and has a structural relationship with other courts from which

↘ BOX 13.1 BACKGROUND: THE DISTINCTIVENESS OF THE COURT OF JUSTICE

Trying to understand the EU's institutional framework via the prism of a nation state is problematic. In a democratic a state, power is exercised by the executive, the legislature, and the judiciary. However, the Commission is not the same as a national executive (government), and neither can the Parliament's composition or role be seen as directly comparable to that of a state. For the Court, although it shares common features with courts in nation states—its role in resolving different kinds of disputes and its power to grand remedies—there is an important distinction. This distinction lies in the fact that the Court is a product of the Treaties that have been put in place by the EU member state—and the purpose of the Court is to ensure that the law of the Treaties is respected. The purpose of the EU is, as we are told right at the start of the Treaty on European Union (TEU) 'the process of creating an ever closer union among the peoples of Europe' (Article 1 TEU). Understanding the Court of Justice and the other institutions must therefore be seen in this context.

The Court of Justice is a multi-national court, with its judges drawn from each of the member states, but who must act independently. Its composition resembles other courts in multi-national settings (such as the **European Court of Human Rights (ECHR)** or International Court of Justice (ICJ)). But comparisons with international courts only go part way in understanding what the Court of Justice does, how and why. For instance, unlike international courts, the Court is equipped under the Treaty with remedies to ensure that its decisions are enforceable and that the law of the EU is thus upheld. It does not therefore only rely on member states to do this on its behalf.

---

it receives cases. Like many other courts with a cross-border scope, it is made up of judges nominated by different countries, but it makes its decisions as an independent institution.

On the other hand, the Court is unlike any other court, whether in a national or international setting (see Box 13.1). In the historical development of the European Union, the role of the Court in the process of European integration has not merely been one which has been secondary to other institutions. Whether the account is by political scientists, legal scholars, or economists, understanding the role that the Court has played cannot be considered separately from the other institutions. Since the creation of the institution at the outset of European integration, the Court has developed constitutional principles that have a far-reaching effect and enabled the process of integration to move forward, especially when the other institutions were unable to.

Discussing the 'politics' of courts and judicial decision-making has a number of different dimensions. A substantial body of scholarship has drawn on the different theoretical and methodological tools to try to understand the role of courts in general, and the Court of Justice is no exception. The work and decisions of the Court have at times been controversial, and a vigorous debate about where the limits of the Court's decision-making power (should) lie continues to this day. The politics of the Court of Justice also speak to its relationships with the other EU institutions

and national courts. As the EU has developed, the Court has been faced with an increasingly diverse set of questions to answer—and such questions are often related to key political moments in the trajectory of European integration.

This chapter explores the set-up of the Court and its role, before assessing its contribution to the EU, its relations with the other institutions, and some of the key debates about the Court and its work.

13.2 The history and development of the Court of Justice

The Court of Justice of the European Union, to give its full official title as specified in the **Treaty on European Union (TEU)** (Article 13(1)), was one of the original institutions created by the **European Coal and Steel Community** in 1952. With the signing of the **Treaty of Rome** in 1957, the Court became a fully-fledged *institution* of the Community.

Unlike other institutions, most notably the Parliament, the Court's formal powers and role have changed little in the text of the Treaty from 1957 until the present day (Craig and de Búrca, 2020: 92). The Court fulfils, on paper, many of the same tasks it was originally set up to do and many of those that we would expect a court to do. However, over time its status has been enhanced in ways that were not foreseen when the original Treaties were drafted.

For instance, the Court has made a series of 'constitutional' decisions in the 1960s and 1970s which have consolidated its position as a key player in European integration. Such decisions included recognizing 'general principles of EU law' (C-29/69 *Stauder v City of Ulm* ECLI:EU:C:1969:57). This allowed the Court to develop principles on the protection of human rights within the EU's legal order, at the same time as confirming the status of EU law as supreme over national constitutional law (C-11/70 *Internationale Handelsgesellschaft* ECLI:EU:C:1970:114).

So, although we will start by looking at what the Treaty says about the Court in terms of its composition and role, it is in the decisions made by the Court that we can evaluate how significant its contribution has been and uncovering why the Court's 'political' role has courted controversy.

KEY POINTS

- The Court of Justice is a significant institution of the European Union.
- The Court's formal role has changed little since the creation of the EU in 1957.
- However, the Court has been vigorous in developing and applying legal principles that have enhanced its role and status.

13.3 Composition and status

The Court of Justice sits in Luxembourg. We refer to the Court in the singular, but in fact the institution has several courts within it: the Court of Justice itself, plus the General Court and other 'specialized courts' (Article 19 TEU). The General Court (originally created under the name of the 'Court of First Instance') was created as a means of lightening the workload of the Court of Justice and deals with certain types of cases (defined in Article 256 TFEU). Although Article 19 refers to specialized *courts* (plural), there is only one: the Civil Service Tribunal for individuals who work for the EU institutions. Further courts can be created in the future (Article 257 TFEU) if needs arise.

13.3.1 Judges of the Court of Justice

As per Article 19(2) of the Treaty on European Union, one judge is nominated per member state 'from persons whose independence is beyond doubt'. In this respect, the Court is similar to the Commission: although there is a national of each member state amongst the judges or Commissioners, they do not *represent* their home state or government and must act with complete independence. So, for example, 'the Croatian judge at the CJEU' refers to the nationality of the judge and does not mean they represent, put forward, or defend the views of that country or government. What is does mean is that the diverse national legal systems and legal traditions across Europe are represented amongst the judges of the Court as well as geographical balance.

Judges nominated to the Court must 'possess the qualifications required for appointment to the highest judicial offices in their respective countries or who are jurisconsults of recognised competence' (Article 253 TFEU). Some CJEU and General Court appointees are career judges in their own member state, and others might have been lawyers or academics. The condition is that they have the professional status and experience that makes them *eligible* for appointment to the highest national court. This might be a Supreme Court, Constitutional Court or similar but there is no requirement for the judges to have actually sat in the highest national court before appointment to the CJEU. Judges in CJEU do not sit on cases individually, but sit either as a full Court of 27 (although this is rare) or in groups of three or five as 'Chambers' (Statute of the Court of Justice, Article 16(1)), which helps spread the workload more evenly. For each case, the Court only gives one decision and the reasons for that decision. Unlike some national legal systems, there are no 'dissenting' views expressed by judges of the Court. Therefore, it is not possible to 'work out' what the individual judges' views on any particular issues are. The decisions are written in a way which represents a compromise between the views of the judges, and so are very carefully drafted. All of the deliberations between the judges are strictly private. Great care is taken over the precise wording since even slight variations in linguistic meanings can have important legal effects (see McAuliffe, 2011).

13.3.2 Advocates-General of the Court of Justice

Other key actors in the Court are the Advocates-General. The Treaty (again, Article 19 TEU) states that Advocates-General 'assist' the Court of Justice. There is no comparable position of Advocates-General in many legal systems of EU member states and their

BOX 13.2   CASE STUDY: THE BREXIT EFFECT ON THE COURT OF JUSTICE

Judges and Advocates-General are appointed 'by common accord of the governments of the member states after consultation of a panel responsible for assessing candidates' suitability' (Article 255 TFEU). As a result of the UK's withdrawal from the EU, the last UK nominated judge, Christopher Vajda, ended his functions on 31 January 2021. The term of the British Advocate General, Eleanor Sharpston, was due to end in October 2021. However, the governments of the 27 member states stated in a Declaration on 29 January 2020 that as a consequence of the UK leaving the EU, the post of Advocate General would become vacant. This was confirmed by the President of the Court of Justice several days later, and thus the Advocate-General was effectively removed from office.

Sharpston challenged her removal from office before her period of appointment ended and her replacement by a new Advocate General. Her challenge was on the basis that removal was not included within the reasons provided for in the Treaty or the Statute of the Court of Justice, which contains more details about the workings and procedures of the Court. As such, she claimed that it infringed 'the constitutional principle of the independence of the judiciary in EU law'. The General Court found that it had no legal powers to review the Declaration of the member states, and dismissed the action. This decision has received academic criticism (Kochenov and Butler 2020). Her appeals to the Court of Justice were dismissed in June 2021.

(T184/20 Sharpston v CJEU ECLI:EU:T:2020:474 and T180/20 Sharpston v Council ECLI:EU:T:2020:474).

creation is the result of the early influence of the French legal system (Arnull, 2020: 3). The role of the Advocate General in the CJEU is to give an independent and impartial 'opinion' that is then considered by the judges when deciding the case (Article 253 TFEU). The opinion will set out the various legal questions, the legal background to the points of law and give a view on what the Court should decide and on what basis. As such, the Opinion is a valuable source of analysis of the law but it does not bind the Court when making its decision. The Court may come to the same outcome, but it may be on the basis of different reasoning put forward by the Advocate General. Usually, the Court does arrive at the same outcome as the Advocate General but this is by no means always the case (see Box 13.2).

13.3.3 A 'supreme court for the EU'?

The main role of the Court is to 'ensure that in the interpretation and application of the Treaties the law is observed' (Article 19(1) TEU). In this respect, it has the final say on matters of interpretation of EU law. But, it is not the only Court to apply EU law: all Courts in the member states are also required to apply EU law, from the Supreme or Constitutional Courts down to specialized financial courts, social security tribunals and so on. In this respect, national courts are 'decentralised "European" courts' (Schütze, 2016: 198). The reason for this is that EU law is integrated within the legal systems of the member states—if all questions arising from the considerable body of EU law were

left to a single Court of Justice then it would be instantly overwhelmed and there would be too much legal uncertainty across the EU.

Therefore, is the Court a 'supreme court for the EU'? Yes and no. It is in the sense that it has the final say on matters of EU law. This is for logical reasons: if the same piece of EU law was interpreted differently in different courts in member states then the law would apply unevenly, which would be a major problem given that the purpose of EU law is *integration*. But, the jurisdiction of the Court of Justice *only* extends to matters of EU law. EU law is extensive and there are few areas of law in the member states where there is no role for EU law at all. It is also perhaps true that the Court has established for itself a reputation which means that it cannot be ignored or sidelined, and that goes beyond the judicial arena. But the Court has no competence to hear cases which do not relate to EU law. As such, unlike most Courts that sit at the top of a (national) hierarchy, it does not cover all areas of law but only those over which it is given power by the Treaties. As will be seen below through the preliminary reference procedure (Section 13.4.3), many of the cases that the Court deals with are referred to it but then sent 'back' to the national courts which may have non-EU law aspects to consider when giving a final ruling. It might more reasonably be argued that the Court of Justice is a type of *Constitutional* Court, given that the Court has developed very important legal principles which were not (and are still not, in some cases) mentioned in the Treaty. This is explored via the Court's work further in Section 13.5.

The Court cannot also be considered to be sitting at the top of Europe's legal hierarchy due to the views of some national courts themselves. Largely for historical reasons, the debate about hierarchy has focused on Germany and the protection of the rights and freedoms in the German Constitution. A decision of the German Constitutional Court (*BVERFG*) in 1974 that the supremacy of EU law was not unconditional triggered a long-running debate triggered via the 'Solange' cases. 'Solange' means 'so long as' and refers to the formulation by the German Constitutional Court (in 1986) that it would accept the jurisdiction of the Court of Justice 'so long as' it respected fundamental rights (as protected in the German Constitution). In other words, EU law is supreme because courts such as the German Constitutional Court accept it being so, but with the possibility that they will reverse this if they perceive that rights are not respected (Craig and de Búrca, 2020: 331–2).

One last point to make here is that the Court is often confused with the European Court of Human Rights, which sits in Strasbourg and is *not* an institution of the EU but the (separate, but confusingly named) **Council of Europe**. However, the **Charter of Fundamental Rights of the European Union** was given equal legal status with the Treaties in the **Treaty of Lisbon** and so the CJEU is empowered to interpret and apply it (see Sarmiento 2013; Peers et. al. 2014). Human rights do therefore figure amongst the extensive case-law of the Court. Furthermore, the **Treaty of Lisbon** (Protocol No. 8) foresaw that the EU itself would become a party to the **European Convention on Human Rights (ECHR)**, as all the member states are—though this has not yet occurred (for further, see Eckes 2013).

KEY POINTS

- The Court of Justice shares similarities with national courts found in member states, and in international contexts, but it has many important differences and needs to be understood on its own terms.

- The Court cannot be accurately described as a 'supreme court' for the EU, since it only deals with matters of EU law and not general law, even though the scope of EU law has grown over time.

- EU law must be applied by all courts in the member states but the Court of Justice remains the final arbiter on questions of EU law. The General Court is part of the Court of Justice as an EU institution but deals with certain specific cases, including those brought by individuals against legislation or decisions of the institutions.

13.4 Roles of the Court of Justice

Article 19 TEU tells us that the Court has three roles: (a) to rule on actions brought by a member state, an institution, or a natural or legal person; (b) give **preliminary rulings**, on the interpretation of EU law or the validity of acts adopted by the institutions; (c) rule in other cases provided for in the Treaties. The roles in (a) and (b) can be categorized as direct and indirect actions respectively, although in terms of legal principles the outcomes of both are the same.

13.4.1 Direct actions

Direct actions are when a matter is first brought before the Court of Justice rather than before a national court. These include **infringement actions**: if the Commission (or another member state, though this is very rare) considers that a member state is breaching EU law then it may bring the matter before the Court of Justice (Articles 258 and 259 TFEU). The member states have obliged themselves, via Art 4(3) TEU, to 'take any appropriate measure, general or particular, to ensure fulfilment of the obligations arising out of the Treaties'. All member states have found themselves on the receiving end of this procedure, for example in cases where **directives** (see Chapter 16) have not been transposed (implemented) fully, properly, within the prescribed time period or where there has been a breach of procedure or practice. In 2019, the Court completed 25 cases of failures to fulfil obligations by 15 member states, which is much lower than the approximately 200 per year between 2000 and 2009 (Court of Justice 2020). Nevertheless, in recent years the Court has been asked to rule on matters which go far beyond the technical application of the law and whether instances of 'democratic backsliding' in member states constitute a breach of EU law (see Box 13.3). The Court of Justice did so twice in 2019, where Poland's reforms to its domestic courts (lowering the retirement ages of judges, and setting different retirement ages for male and female judges) were found to be a failure to respect both EU law on equal treatment and the right to ensure effective legal protection.

Since it was introduced by the **Treaty of Maastricht**, if a member state does not abide by the Court's decision, then a further action before the Court can result in the imposition of financial penalties to be paid by the member state (Article 260 TFEU). This was used for the first time in 2000 against Greece, and has gradually increased over time, although the Court is

BOX 13.3   CASE STUDY: INFRINGEMENT ACTIONS DECIDED BY THE COURT OF JUSTICE IN 2019

Infringement actions brought before the Court by the Commission against a member state, such as the example of Poland above, can be headline-grabbing. Most, however, are not. *Commission v Austria* is a more representative example of this type of case.

Freedom to provide services in other member states is stipulated in the Treaty (Article 56 TFEU). A 2006 Directive gives the general provisions of the law, and also the exceptions to the general freedom or conditions which may be applied by the member states. Existing Austrian law on companies of civil engineers and veterinary surgeons made several stipulations, such as the requirement to have the company seat in Austria and how different branches could operate. The Commission considered that these breached EU law. The Austrian laws had not been changed after the Directive was passed.

The Commission's view was that the provisions of Austrian law restricted the exercise of these professions by those from other

member states in Austria by creating hindrances, and that the relevant Austrian legal provisions did not fall within the exceptions allowed under the Directive.

The Court stated that exceptions to the Directive must be interpreted narrowly, and rejected Austria's argument that an exception for 'civil servants' or professions in 'public health' applied to civil engineers (who are not specifically mentioned in the Directive) or veterinary surgeons (as 'public health' applies to humans only). The Court also rejected Austria's arguments that its domestic law protected consumers or would apply only in narrow circumstances. As a result, the Court of Justice found that maintaining the legal requirements on these professions in its law, Austria had failed to fulfil its obligations under the 2006 Directive.

Source: Case C-209/18 *Commission v Austria* ECLI:EU:C:2019:632

not obliged to follow the Commission's suggestion if a penalty is warranted. There is also the question of whether the 'carrot or stick' approach is effective (see Jack, 2013). Member states do respect the Court's decisions, but more recently attention has been paid to how the Commission decides which actions to pursue on a strategic basis, given that the EU has grown in size and there are limited resources at the Commission's disposal (see Falkner, 2018; Börzel and Buzogány, 2019).

13.4.2 Actions in annulment

The Court is also able to hear actions in annulment, where an EU institution or a member state attempts to find a piece of EU legislation to be unlawful and therefore invalid (Article 263 TFEU). This is commonly referred to as 'judicial review' and is a common (though varied) legal tool in the national legal systems of the member states (Castillo Ortiz, 2020). This action might be invoked on the grounds of the wrong procedure being used, or a lack of competence of the EU institutions. The European Parliament has used this power when it feels that a law-making procedure has been used that has sidelined its own role (Sánchez-Barrueco, 2020). It is possible for a natural or a legal person (such as a company) to bring an action in annulment against a piece of legislation, but the test for

doing so is highly restrictive (for recent commentary, see Bogojević, 2015). The rationale for such a restrictive test is that if it were not so, then the Court would be potentially facing countless claims—an argument that has been strongly criticized but which the member states have not sought to change via the provisions of the Treaty as the highest source of EU law.

Courts in member states are not able to declare EU legislation to be invalid—if this were possible, then EU law could apply in some states and not others, thus defeating the purpose of EU integration. However, they might refer a question of validity to the CJEU under the preliminary reference procedure. Nevertheless, actions in annulment account for around 50 per cent of cases brought before the General Court by natural or legal persons (Court of Justice, 2020). This is because the challenge is to a decision taken by one of the EU institutions which is directly addressed to that individual or company, or where they have a particular interest. Such decisions usually relate to state aid (where the Commission has approved the granting of financial aid to a particular company, and a rival company or body attempts to contest it, such as T-894/17 *Air France v Commission* EU:T:2019:508), where a company has been fined by the Commission for a breach of competition rules (for example, T-1/16 *Hitachi-LG v Commission* ECLI:EU:T:2019:514) or where individuals or groups have been subjected to sanctions for suspected involvement in terrorism (for example, T-289/15 *Hamas v Council* ECLI:EU:T:2019:138, appealed to the Court of Justice in C-386/19 *Hamas v Council* ECLI:EU:C:2020:691) or suspected criminal activity (for example, the former President of Ukraine in T-244/16 *Yanukovych v Council* ECLI:EU:T:2019:502).

13.4.3 Preliminary references

Preliminary references are *indirect* actions as they are not brought to the Court of Justice by the parties to the case, but are rather referred to the Court by a national court or tribunal. A total of 601 such cases were referred to the Court of Justice in 2019, which is double the total from ten years previously. A preliminary reference occurs when the national court is faced with an issue of EU law it is unable to answer (Article 267 TFEU). Therefore, this does not happen for every question of EU law—as explained above, all courts in the EU are bound to apply to EU law. But if there is a question of interpretation or validity that only the CJEU can answer, then the Court may make a preliminary reference in terms of a question or questions to the CJEU. The Brexit-related case of *Wightman* is a good example (see Box 13.4). Since any court

---

 BOX 13.4   CASE STUDY: THE *WIGHTMAN* DECISION (2018)

The process for a member state to leave the EU is set out in Article 50 TEU. This was a new provision inserted in the **Treaty of Lisbon** and, of course, it had never been used until Brexit. According to Article 50, the member state that wishes to leave informs the European Council and there will then be negotiations for an exit agreement. The Treaties cease to apply to the departing member state on the date agreed in the exit agreement, or if there is no exit agreement, then two years after the notification.

As per this procedure, the UK notified the European Council, on 29 March 2017, of its intention to leave the EU. Six Members of the European Parliament, Scottish Parliament, and UK Parliament—from three different political parties—brought a joint case against the UK government in the **Court of Session in Scotland**. The question was whether the UK could retract its notification to the European Council if it decided that it no longer wanted to leave the EU, or whether the notification could only be withdrawn if the European Council (i.e. the member states) gave their approval. Article 50 itself gave no help—it talks about notification, but not about withdrawal. The Scottish Court referred the following question to the Court of Justice:

> Where, in accordance with Article 50 [TEU], a member state has notified the European Council of its intention to withdraw from the European Union, does EU law permit that notice to be revoked unilaterally by the notifying member state; and, if so, subject to what conditions and with what effect relative to the member state remaining within the European Union?

The process was expedited: the preliminary reference was made on 21 September, the AG Opinion was delivered on 4 December 2018 and the decision of the full Court on 10 December 2018. Such speed is highly unusual.

At the heart of the matter was a largely hypothetical question: the UK had not *actually* asked to withdraw its intention to leave the EU. But the case was to establish if the UK could have the option to do so if (for example) a change of government or public opinion forced the issue. The Court does not generally answer hypothetical questions, but recognized that this was a real dispute and an important (and urgent) question to be answered.

As the Advocate General Campos Sánchez-Bordona recognized in his Opinion (para. 59), the views in legal academia on the question were divided. On the one hand, if there was a possibility of retraction, that this would have been stated in the Treaty. The Council and Commission supported this view. On the other, since the leaving state made the notification, then it could withdraw it too. The question is a legal one but has political consequences: a state could threaten to leave, only to revoke later, and therefore this could be used as a political tool.

The Court decided that notification could be withdrawn. It noted that the Treaty referred to the states' 'intention' to withdraw, which is therefore not definitive or irrevocable (para. 49). Rather than referring to international law which governs how Treaties work (as the Advocate General had done), the Court underlined the specific legal order of the EU and the fact that it is composed of member states with sovereign rights to withdraw—or not. Therefore, should the UK wish to remain a member state before the two-year period or entry into force of the exit agreement, then it could since—to quote the Court—'a State cannot be forced to accede to the European Union against its will, neither can it be forced to withdraw from the European Union against its will' (para. 65).

Source: C-621/18 Wightman and Others v Secretary of State for Exiting the European Union ECLI:EU:C:2018:999 (judgment) ECLI:EU:C:2018:978 (AG Opinion)

or tribunal in a member state may make a preliminary reference, the enlargement of the EU and the development of law and policy in a growing number of areas have contributed to the consistent growth in the number of cases referred.

13.4.4 Preliminary reference versus 'appeal'

The CJEU answers those questions of EU law asked of it in a judgment and returns the matter to the national court. This makes it different to an 'appeal' because the CJEU is not resolving the case (although, as in *Wightman*, the decision of the Scottish court it was returned to was more a formality). To ensure that the CJEU is not over-burdened with preliminary references, Courts in member states cannot ask questions on points of law where the CJEU has already given a ruling, nor should theoretical or hypothetical questions be referred. Some of the most important points of EU law set out by the CJEU (such as the cases of *Cassis de Dijon* and *Francovich*, below) have originated in the references from national Courts, and the decisions of the Court—as in all other cases—are made publicly and published (see Hübner, 2018). For individuals who want to challenge EU law, the preliminary references procedure is a much more useful tool than the 'direct' challenge route with its restrictive test. The relationship between the CJEU and national courts has been termed a 'partnership' rather than a hierarchy since, as mentioned above, the CJEU is not a supreme court in the way we understand it in a national context.

KEY POINTS

- The Court of Justice has a variety of roles, all of which relate to upholding and protecting the legal order of the EU. These roles are defined in the Treaty.

- The Court has the final say on matters of EU law brought before it, and a great deal of EU law has developed as courts in member states have referred questions to it under the preliminary reference procedure.

- The Court is responsible for hearing actions brought against the member states or EU institutions for breaching EU law and has dealt with an increasing number of cases which have strong legal *and* political ramifications.

13.5 The work of the Court of Justice

The workload of the Court of Justice has increased year on year. Partly this is due to the expanded scope of the EU's **competences** and the amount of legal instruments and decisions that can be contested. But it is also because the Court itself has expanded its role and with it the potential scope of EU law. Therefore, it is less about the number of decisions the Court has made that explain its significance and more about the principles of EU law that it has recognized or established over the past 60 years. Recalling that the role of the Court is essentially to settle disputes, and that in the early days most of these disputes related to matters of goods crossing borders, the way in which the Court has developed its case law has come from some surprising (and also mundane) cases (Cardwell and Hervey, 2015). Few decisions have been as headline-grabbing or overtly 'political' as *Wightman* (see Box 13.4) but nevertheless the importance of many and their impact on EU politics should not be underestimated.

13.5.1 The Court and the Single Market

The case law of the Court also tells us about the extent to which establishing the **Single Market** and the free movement of goods, services, capital, and workers has been a lengthy and complex process; working out the contours of European citizenship; deciding on matters of law that are sensitive in terms of national cultures and also on the EU's international agreements which touch on issues even beyond Europe. As the EU's competence has grown to include justice and home affairs, the Court has become more involved in ruling on aspects of fundamental rights and in areas which were not foreseen at the outset of the European **integration** process, such as criminal procedure. So, cases brought to the Court of Justice have included the extent to which types of pornography are included within free movement of goods (C-34/79 *Henn and Darby* ECLI:EU:C:1979:295); whether abortion is a 'service' under EU law (C-159/90 *SPUC v Grogan* ECLI:EU:C:1991:378); if a member state can prevent the entry of a Scientologist on the grounds of public policy (C-41/74 *Van Duyn v Home Office* ECLI:EU:C:1974:133); if an EU trade agreement with Israel covers products made in the occupied territories (C386/08 *Brita* ECLI:EU:C:2010:91; C-363/18 *Organisation juive européenne and Vignoble Psagot Ltd v Ministre de l'Économie et des Finances* ECLI:EU:C:2019:954) and the lawfulness of a regulation on trade in seal products from Canada (C-583/11 *Inuit Tapiriit Kanatami* ECLI:EU:C:2013:625).

13.5.2 The Court and the 'new legal order' of the EU

Some of the most significant decisions came very early on in the history of the EU. In 1962, a dispute involving the import of chemicals from (West) Germany to the Netherlands and customs charges resulted in one of the most ground-breaking decisions of the Court (C-26/62 *van Gend en Loos* ECLI:EU:C:1963:1). Although this appeared to be a relatively minor dispute about recovering customs charges, the way in which Court made its decision has structured EU legal thinking ever since. The Court stated that the parties to the Treaty (i.e. the member states) had created a 'new legal order' in the EU and that the Treaty created rights that had 'direct effect' in the member states. In other words, every company and citizen could use EU law against the state.

The consequence of this powerful decision meant that from a very early stage, EU law was characterized as something which was neither akin to national nor international law, since the latter would not have 'direct effect'. Two years later, in the case of C-6/64 *Costa v ENEL* ECLI:EU:C:1964:66—where the facts were also not particularly illuminating—the Court stated that EU law was supreme over provisions of national law and, in cases of conflict between the two, then EU law prevails. The Court went further in 1971 by saying that this included national constitutional law too (C-11/70 *Internationale Handelsgesellschaft* ECLI:EU:C:1970:114). What is remarkable about *Costa v ENEL* is that the Treaty—which was written by the member states only several years previously—did not mention supremacy. Rather, the Court inferred that the intention of the drafters and signatories of the Treaty was to ensure the effectiveness of EU law via supremacy.

These early decisions have set the tone for the most longstanding debate over whether the CJEU was right or justified in coming to this characterization, or whether it overstepped the mark and has allowed itself to be 'activist' in terms of creating law rather than simply interpreting and applying it. This debate is returned to below.

The Court can also be seen as responsible for facilitating the European **integration** process, especially during the 1970s. In the Treaty, the emphasis on legislation (**regulations** and **directives**) as a means to integrate the different systems of the EU was not matched by a practical ability of the institutions to pass such legislation. In other words, facilitating cross-border trade relied on the agreement to create common standards on a particular product or group of products (such as chemicals, children's toys, or any goods requiring specific labelling). Such common standards require the passing of detailed pieces of legislation via the Commission, Council, and the Parliament. Since extensive legislation was not forthcoming in the 1970s, it fell to the Court of Justice to take the major step of interpreting the Treaty terms on free movement widely. The important cases of C-8/74 *Dassonville* ECLI:EU:C:1974:82 and *Cassis de Dijon* (see Box 13.5) show the extent to which the Court removed barriers to free movement of goods and gave the completion of the Single Market in the 1980s a boost.

13.5.3 The Court and 'gap filling': the *Francovich* decision

A further important innovation of the Court related to the harm caused by breaches of EU law. There was nothing in the Treaty to cover the situation where an individual suffered harm due to the breach of EU law by a member state. In the case of C-6/90 *Francovich v Italy* ECLI:EU:C:1991:428, it was established that Italy had failed to transpose (implement) a Directive (80/987) that would have given employees a minimum level of protection in case of the insolvency of the employer. When the firm Francovich and others worked for became insolvent, they were thus not protected, but would have been in another member state where the Directive had been properly transposed. They therefore brought an action against Italy for the harm suffered due to Italy's breach of EU law (i.e. failure to transpose the Directive). In the absence of Treaty provisions, the Court of Justice established the principle of state liability for harm caused to individuals by breaches of EU law. It did so on the basis that 'the full effectiveness [of EU law] would be impaired and the protection of the rights which they grant would be weakened if individuals were unable to obtain compensation when their rights are infringed' (para. 33) and that there was a general stipulation in the Treaty that member states are 'required to take

BOX 13.5   CASE STUDY: THE *CASSIS DE DIJON* DECISION

To allow the free movement of goods, the Treaty forbids member states from imposing quotas on goods that can be imported from other member states or 'measures having equivalent effect' (now Article 34 TFEU). Cassis de Dijon is a French alcoholic liqueur that the producers were trying to export to the German market. There were no common rules on the marketing and sale of alcoholic drinks. A German law stated that the minimum alcohol level for liqueurs was 25 per cent, which was higher than Cassis de Dijon (15–20 per cent), meaning that it could not be sold in Germany. So, although this rule applied to drinks produced in Germany as well as outside of it, the effect of the rule was to hinder the free movement of goods as there was no way for the French producer to comply (unless they made a completely different product for the German market).

The Court did not accept Germany's arguments that the rule was necessary to protect public health (by the proliferation of more, weaker alcoholic drinks on the market) or consumer choice (so that consumers are not 'cheated' by producers)—the display of where the product was from and the alcohol

percentage should suffice. Since this law had the practical effect of 'excluding from the national market products of other member states' (para. 14), the Court found that it fell foul of the Treaty. In doing so, the Court adopted a broad interpretation of 'measures having equivalent effect' and stated that rules about products (such as size, weight) that hinder free movement must be set aside. Therefore, if a product is lawfully made and marketed in one member state, it should be allowed to enter and be sold in other member states.

The decision in Cassis de Dijon was fundamental in shifting the balance in moving the single market forward: instead of having to wait for the institutions to agree common standards via legislation, member states could be challenged and have to justify national rules that hindered trade between the member states. (see further, on the politics of the decision Alter and Meunier-Aitsahalia, 1994 and for more recent comment Snell, 2019).

Source: C-120/78 Rewe-Zentral AG v Bundesmonopolverwaltung für Branntwein ('Cassis de Dijon') ECLI:EU:C:1979:42

---

all appropriate measures, whether general or particular, to ensure fulfilment of their obligations "under EU law"' (para. 36; now Article 10 TEU) (for a recent re-evaluation of this principle see Dougan, 2017; Granger, 2017).

These decisions are some of the Court's most well-known, although there are many others which established principles that have underlined the importance of EU law in the member states, and the distinctiveness of EU law. As early as 1981, Eric Stein (1981: 1) aptly characterized the Court as 'Tucked away in the fairyland Duchy of Luxembourg and blessed, until recently, with benign neglect by the powers that be and the mass media, the Court of Justice . . . has fashioned a constitutional framework for a federal-type structure in Europe.' Stein's words have captured the work of the Court as representing a 'new species' of law beyond that of the nation state, which underpinned the emerging political order of the EU (Shaw and Hunt, 2009: 94). As such, the importance of the role of the Court for both EU law and politics cannot be understated. The main debate that has permeated these developments is whether the Court of Justice's '**activism**' has been justified in doing so, to which discussion now turns.

KEY POINTS

- The Court was originally not assumed to play a major role in the EU's institutional framework or the development of the law at the outset of the European integration process in the 1950s.

- However, in a number of key areas including the single market, the Court's decisions have had a greater substantive effect than legislation in breaking down barriers between the member states.

- The Court has developed legal principles, such as remedies for breaches of EU law, even where the Treaty was silent.

13.6 'Activism' of the Court?

The above decisions are a testament to the way in which the Court of Justice has sought to uphold the commitments made by the member states in the Treaty. In looking beyond what the Treaty explicitly says (or does not say), the Court has engaged in what is known as '**teleological**' interpretation. That is to say, the Court has looked at the broad terms in which the Treaty has been drafted in and interpreted them in light of the objectives of the Treaty. In the words of one former judge at the Court of Justice, to do otherwise would be a denial of justice (Lenaerts and Gutierrez-Fons, 2014: 32). Therefore, the Court's decisions can be seen not just as filling in the gaps left by the drafters of the Treaty but relying on the intentions behind them. In other words, in the *Francovich* case, for example, if there was a clear intention for EU law to be effective as expressed in the Treaty (albeit vaguely), then the Court was justified in turning that commitment into a workable solution. This has not required the explicit consent of the member states but has required the Court to work in partnership with national courts (see Alter, 2001). In practical terms, *Francovich* set out the principle of state liability (harm caused by the state for breaches of EU law) but it would be the national courts—Italy in that case—to actually deal with the case for compensation.

Furthermore, although the Commission is the 'motor of integration'(see Chapter 10), the Court of Justice is also an institution created by the Treaty to uphold the law. Therefore, as Poiares Maduro (2007) has written, the 'dynamic character of the process of integration' is guided by the overall objective of creating 'an ever closer union among the peoples of Europe' (Article 1 TEU). This explains why the Court, although acting independently, tends to favour a solution which lies on the side of more European **integration**, not less. The Court has been unimpressed with arguments which would harm integration. For example, the Treaty allows for member states to make exceptions to free movement law in some circumstances, such as the protection of public health (Article 36 TFEU). But it has interpreted this very narrowly to avoid the temptation for member states to widen these exceptions, perhaps as a means to 'protect' domestic industries. Therefore, the Court would require evidence if a member state claims that a measure is justified on these grounds (C-174/82 *Sandoz* ECLI:EU:C:1983:213).

As one might expect, the way in which the Court has gone about its business has attracted robust critique. Within the UK legal academy, Professors Hartley and Arnull debated in the 1990s the nature of judicial objectivity in the CJEU. Over 20 years later, their respective points remain valid in terms of understanding the history of the Court's decision-making and why the Court has attracted the reputation for '**activism**'(see Box 13.6).

13.6.1 The work of the Court and the Treaties

The Hartley–Arnull debate remains a very useful way to understand the role of the Court as an institution of the Union. It is important to recall, however, that the important constitutional principles of direct effect and supremacy, as well as all the other significant decisions that the Court has taken, could be reversed by the member states if they so wished (although it would need all of them to agree).

BOX 13.6   KEY DEBATES: THE HARTLEY AND ARNULL DEBATE

According to Hartley (1996: 107), the Treaties 'are not static instruments but were intended from the beginning to be dynamic: they are "genetically coded" . . . to develop into the constitution of a fully-fledged federation. . . . If the Treaties are indeed so coded, the judges are doing no more than their duty in developing the law in the desired direction, even if some laggard member states are reluctant to accept such developments. According to this approach, by joining the Community, member states accept not only the obligations written into the Treaties as they exist at the time, but also undertake to assist in their development into the constitution of a European federation.' He points therefore to the existence of a 'higher law' above the Treaties in which the 'embryonic federation' is the goals. The problem, Hartley says, is that there are two models of the EU—one as a Treaty-based organisation

founded by sovereign states, and the other which is a nascent federation—and that these are incompatible (1996: 109).

Arnull's response to Hartley's points is that this analysis is oversimplistic, and not all of the Court's decisions can be read in this way (p. 411). Although he notes that the Court has at times been 'creative' (p. 420), this is within the spirit of the Treaty and its overall objectives which must be given due regard. As such, 'it would be quite wrong to suggest that the Court pursues some hidden agenda of its own: the Court looks for guidance to the preamble to the Treaty, its introductory provisions and overall structure. If there is an agenda pursued by the Court, it is therefore one set by the Treaty's authors. The Court can hardly be criticised for striving to construe the Treaty in a way which gives effect to its authors' overall design.'

The main mechanism to do so would be to change the text of the Treaty. On occasion, Treaty reforms have incorporated decisions of the Court (such as, on equal treatment in pensions, C-262/88 *Barber* ECLI:EU:C:1990:209). Despite its fundamental importance, the member states have not done so with supremacy—though neither have they attempted to remove it either. The failed Constitutional Treaty would have included a provision about the supremacy of EU law in the main text, to give it the full recognition that (as a fundamental principle) it deserves, but the Treaty of Lisbon attached it as a Declaration (no. 17) to the Treaty instead:

The Conference recalls that, in accordance with well settled case law of the Court of Justice of the European Union, the Treaties and the law adopted by the Union on the basis of the Treaties have primacy over the law of member states, under the conditions laid down by the said case law.

Therefore, we can assume that the member states accept the principles as laid down by the Court, but do not want to give them prominence within the Treaty. A Treaty is an outcome of diplomatic negotiations, where member state interests are present and brought to the fore. Negotiating governments are aware that the treaty must be 'sold' (including via referendums in some cases) to the general public at home, and compromises made where necessary. This would fit the liberal intergovernmentalist view of the member states being in control of the EU, but only so far as they do not control the CJEU.

13.6.2 Does the Court always favour 'more' integration?

The assumption that the Court of Justice always favours a solution which results in more **integration** and powers of the Union continues to be debated (see Terpan and Saurugger, 2020: 33). One area where the Court has been active is in recognizing rights in the Treaty relating to free movement of persons and EU citizenship. This is a complex area, since the original focus of the EU was on the free movement of workers. Citizenship is entwined with powers retained by the member states, such as social welfare law, and where third-country nationals, that is those who come from outside the EU but who may have a family link to an EU citizen, are involved (see Strumia, 2016).

For instance, in C-85/96 *Martínez Sala* ECLI:EU:C:1998:217 a Spanish woman who was resident in Germany had not been working for some time and was receiving social benefits. Her application for an additional child-raising allowance was refused by the German authorities. The Court of Justice stated that so long as she was lawfully resident, a general principle of non-discrimination applied and it was not possible to refuse her application simply because she was no longer working. Free movement is not an absolute right, but the Court has found that when member states impose limitations (for example, to avoid individuals being a financial burden on the state), they must do so in a proportionate way that does not overly limit the exercise of Treaty rights (C-413/99 *Baumbast* ECLI:EU:C:2002:493; C-200/02 *Zhu and Chen* ECLI:EU:C:2004:639).

However, more recent cases have cast doubt on whether the court is 'hard-wired' to always maximise the effect of EU law. The case of *Dano* (C-333/13 *Elisabeta Dano and Florin Dano v Jobcenter Leipzig* ECLI:EU:C:2014:2358) touched on the sensitive issue of access to benefits of EU citizens who are not 'economically active', that is working. In this case, a non-economically active Romanian woman living in Germany with her son was refused a particular benefit, which she challenged on the basis of discrimination. The Court of Justice emphasized that member states do have the right to require individuals to have sufficient resources to live in that state, and that the Treaty free movement rights cannot be used 'solely in order to obtain another member state's social assistance' (para. 78). This judgment was interpreted as a move away from the previous line of case law in so far as it focuses on the entitlement of member states to impose restrictions rather than expanding the rights on the basis of Treaty goals and the Charter of Fundamental Rights (Thym, 2015; Zahn, 2015).

> **KEY POINTS**
>
> - The proper role and purpose of the Court of Justice has been a constant debate since its early decisions in the 1960s.
> - Legal scholars have been divided on the question of whether the Court has been justified in developing its own competence and the reach of EU law, or overreached.
> - The Court is generally assumed to favour solutions which support EU integration, but more recent analysis has cast doubt on some of these assumptions.

13.7 Conclusion

Through its many judgments, the Court of Justice can be understood as an institution whose contribution to the integration of the EU goes far beyond that of a merely technical body responsible for settling disputes. For this reason alone, accounts of the history, development, and future of the EU which do not consider how the judicial body within the institutional framework fits in are likely to be inadequate.

Few would have predicted that a Court would have taken on and developed the status which it has gained today. Hence, analysis of the Court, what it does, and what effect it has on the other institutions as well as the member states is not limited to legal scholars. From the early 1990s in particular, political scientists have approached what Stone Sweet (2000) has referred to as the 'judicialization of politics' and how judicial law-making influences the behaviour of other actors. The impact of the Court's work in setting the boundaries of definitions of free movement and citizenship, amongst other areas, has been argued by Schmidt (2018) to constitute a direct constraint on the policy-making abilities of the other institutions and the member states. The Court's work in settling disputes between the institutions goes to the heart of some of the key institutional questions about where power lies, and should lie, in an organization with no direct parallel anywhere in the world. The way in which the European Parliament has strategically used actions before the Court of Justice as a means of bolstering its own power and influence is a testament to the institutional and political role of the Court (Sanchez Barrueco, 2020).

Therefore, it was almost to be expected that the Court of Justice would eventually have a strongly influential role to play in the Brexit process, and very likely too the eventual consequences of the COVID-19 pandemic. The decisions of the Court in relation to the Brexit process, as well as its findings that domestic institutional reforms in Poland and Hungary have breached EU law, have thrust the Court into the public spotlight. This has not previously been the experience of the Court of Justice, save perhaps in isolated examples. As an evolving institution, the Court is not immune from the wider context of the European integration process and how we understand it. It may be that the age of grand decisions moving the integration process forward is now over, but there is little doubt that the role the Court has developed for itself in the governance arrangements of the EU will not diminish as the polity evolves. At the same time, the Court is faced with the same challenges, such as the risk of institutional overload and the need for timely decision-making, but only has limited opportunity to do anything itself. If the Court is to be reformed, either in terms of its structure, composition, or its role, then this can only be fully achieved with the member states via changes to the Treaties. The history of the Court tells us that incremental changes, such as the creation of the General Court, are generally found to be the answer rathr than wholescale reform.

? **QUESTIONS**

1. What was the original purpose of the Court of Justice and how has its role changed?

2. What is the difference between a judge of the Court of Justice and an Advocate General?

3. What are preliminary references?

4. Do all questions of EU law go to the Court of Justice?

5. What is meant by the Court of Justice being an 'activist' court? Is this a justified label?

6. How does the Court often approach legal problems when there is no clear-cut answer?

7. How and why did the Court establish the principles of direct effect, supremacy, and state liability?

8. Does the Court always pursue solutions which further EU integration?

GUIDE TO FURTHER READING

Arnull, A. (2020) *The Many Ages of the Court of Justice of the European Union*. EUI Working Papers AEL2020/02. Available from: https://cadmus.eui.eu/bitstream/handle/1814/67273/AEL_2020_02.pdf?sequence=1&isAllowed=y. This study offers a thorough and accessible review of the Court of Justice's influence on European integration through its case-law.

Blauberger, M. and Sindbjerg Martinsen, D. (2020) 'The Court of Justice in times of politicisation: "law as a mask and shield" revisited', *Journal of European Public Policy*, 27/3, 382–99. This article analyses if and under what conditions bottom-up pressures constrain the Court of Justice of the European Union. The article develops a typology of four constellations depending on whether CJEU jurisprudence is subject to bottom-up pressures stemming from member state governments and/or politicization.

Lenaerts, K., (2019) 'The Court of Justice of the European Union as the guardian of the authority of EU law: a networking exercise', in W. Heusel and J.P. Rageade (eds), *The Authority of EU Law* (Berlin: Springer), pp. 21–30. This chapter, by the President of the Court of Justice, discusses the dialogue that exists between the courts of the Member States and the Court of Justice of the European Union and among national courts themselves.

Schmidt, S.K. (2018) *The European Court of Justice and the Policy Process* (Oxford: Oxford University Press). This excellent monograph demonstrates the importance of judicial policy-making through case law development and codification.

Terpan, F., and Saurugger, S. (2020) 'The Politics of the Court of Justice of the European Union', in P.J. Cardwell and M.-P. Granger (eds), *Research Handbook on the Politics of EU Law* (Cheltenham: Edward Elgar), pp. 31–49. This chapter offers a comprehensive understanding of the Court of Justice of the EU by arguing that the Court is better understood through a combination of law and politics. And that, although constrained by law, the Court is not isolated from politics.

Access the online resources to take your learning and understanding further, including extra multiple-choice questions with instant feedback, web links, answer guidance to end-of-chapter questions, and updates on new developments in EU politics.

www.oup.com/he/cini-borragan7e

14

Interest Groups and the European Union

Rainer Eising and Julia Sollik

Research for this chapter has been supported by the Ministry of Economic Affairs, Innovation, Digitalisation and Energy of the State of North Rhine-Westphalia (MDWIDE NRW)

Chapter Contents

Reader's Guide

This chapter examines the role of interest groups in European Union (EU) politics. It also considers the way in which the EU institutions influence interest group structures and activities. The chapter begins with an overview of the relationship between the EU institutions and interest groups and examines the steps taken thus far to regulate that relationship. It then looks at the evolution and the structure of the interest group system, focusing in particular on two salient aspects: the difference between national and EU organizations; and the difference between specific and diffuse interests.

14.1   Introduction

The EU institutions have developed many links with interest groups that can impact on the EU's political agenda, the formulation of EU policies addressing problems already on the agenda, provide feedback on the implementation of EU policies and, more generally, affect the legitimacy of EU politics. Interest groups (see Box 14.1) have a particularly important role to play in connecting European-level institutions with the citizens of the European Union, as well as in mediating between them. Frequently, they are expected to socialize their members into democratic politics, to give a voice to citizens

↘ BOX 14.1   KEY DEBATES: LOBBIES AND INTEREST GROUPS

The literature on the European Union's interest groups rests largely on a body of research in the field of comparative politics. In this literature, interest groups have been labelled and defined in a variety of ways which, in turn, reflect specific approaches and normative assessments. Lobbies, pressure groups, non-governmental organizations (NGOs), social movement organizations, and interest organizations are the most common terms used to characterize interest groups in this literature.

- The term 'lobbyist' originated in the nineteenth century, when individuals waiting in the British parliamentary lobby exerted influence on members of legislatures to pass bills on behalf of unknown customers. Lobbying was then almost exclusively regarded as a commercial activity. Later, attempts by organizations to influence public bodies were also included in this narrow definition.

- Since the 1920s, the term 'pressure group' has increasingly been used in the political science literature as a term that is considered familiar and therefore needing little explanation. Its meaning comes close to that of a lobby group in that it centres on the functions of these groups to influence—or put pressure on—a parliament or government.

- The term 'interest group' refers to the underlying rationale of these groups and has less negative connotation. Members join groups as they share common attitudes, or interests (Truman, 1951: 34).

- 'Interest organizations' refers to interest groups that are highly formalized. This highlights the continuity of organiza-

tions as well as their ability to cope with complexity via differentiation. It also draws attention away from particular leaders and members, and towards the effects of the organizational form.

- The term 'non-governmental organization' (NGO) connotes a **normative** outlook and is often used by diffuse interests to avoid the 'interest group' label that is frequently associated with selfish lobbying for material interests.

- Similarly, the term 'civil society organizations' (CSOs) is frequently meant to imply that such organizations act and speak for the citizenry at large, or at least for large segments of society.

Beyers et al. (2008) propose three factors that define an actor as an interest group: organization (which excludes broad movements and waves of public opinion), political interests (also called political advocacy), and informality (no aspiration to public offices and no competition in elections, but the pursuit of goals through frequent informal interactions with politicians and bureaucrats). Note that not only interest groups (as membership groups) voice their positions in public policy-making but also a wide array of other organizations such as firms, institutions (e.g., hospitals), law firms, and consultants. Jordan et al. (2004) label these organizations 'policy participants' because they do not have members and are not primarily dedicated to political activities. They distinguish policy participants from 'interest groups' as membership organizations.

---

between elections, to participate in constructing a general will out of the specific concerns of groups, and, as Tocqueville (1835) pointed out, to serve as schools for democracy.

Interest group scholars distinguish between two main modes of interest intermediation: **pluralism** and **corporatism**. At first glance, the EU interest group system looks broadly **pluralist** (see Streeck and Schmitter, 1991). Both the large number of groups and their huge variety suggest that many interests are represented in the EU institutions. Usually no interest group enjoys a clear monopoly of representation in any one policy area. Of the EU groups present in the agricultural sector, for example, many reflect particular product specializations. Some of these compete and bargain not only with groups across policy areas, such as with environmental or consumer groups, but also with groups within the

agricultural domain. Yet examples such as the **European Social Dialogue** question the notion of free competition between interests, because here only certain actors, in this case the cross-sectoral social partners (employers' associations and trade unions), have a guaranteed, monopolistic, access to the policy process which points towards a **neo-corporatist** practice. The multilevel character of the EU **polity** that offers interest groups many access points and opportunities, the differing interest representation practices across policy areas and institutions, and the diversity of interests point towards a distinct and dynamic EU system of interest mediation (see Beyers et al., 2008).

The following sections set out the broad terrain of EU interest mediation. Section 14.2 highlights the impact of the EU institutional setting on interest representation. Section 14.3 describes the measures that the EU institutions have implemented to regulate lobbying activities. Section 14.4 summarizes the structure of the EU interest group system, focusing on different types of interest organizations. The conclusion (Section 14.5) reflects on the effect of European integration on interest representation in Europe and the contribution that interest groups can make to the quality of democracy in the EU.

14.2 The EU institutions and interest groups

Political institutions, such as the EU, have important effects on interest organizations. Classic interest group studies highlighted that they form the primary 'target structure' of interest groups (Almond, 1958: 279). Social movement scholars (e.g. Kitschelt, 1986) stress that they are an important element of the 'political opportunity structure' that shapes the strategic options of social movements and impacts on their success. And more recent studies maintain that the EU's political institutions embody the 'institutional venues in which interest group lobbying takes place' (Klüver et al., 2015: 453).

However, the EU institutions are not merely a set of access points for interest groups. They can themselves shape the interest group system by providing finance, organizational help, and granting privileged access (Pollack, 1997; Smismans, 2004); devising procedures, committees, and bodies to incorporate groups into policy-making (Mazey and Richardson, 2002). They also enjoy considerable discretion about whose opinion they take into account (and whose they do not) when formulating EU policies and may pursue their own policy preferences in alliances with groups that are supportive of their case (Eising, 2009). In particular, four characteristics of the EU as a political system affect how interest groups seek to influence the European institutions as well as the ways in which these institutions incorporate interest groups into EU policy-making: first, its treaty foundations characterize the EU as a representative democracy; second, the EU is a system that favours consensus building; third, the EU is a highly dynamic system; finally, the EU system is horizontally and vertically differentiated.

First, the EU is committed to ensuring the participation of citizens and interest groups in the policy process as a principle of **good governance**. Title II

of the Treaty on European Union includes provisions on democratic principles. Article 10 characterizes the European Union as a 'representative democracy'. According to Article 11(2), the EU institutions 'shall maintain an open, transparent and regular dialogue with representative associations and civil society'. Furthermore, Article 11(3) stipulates that the 'European Commission shall carry out broad **consultations** with parties concerned in order to ensure that the Union's actions are coherent and transparent'. Representatives of the EU institutions acknowledge the importance of contacts with interest groups for the formulation of EU policies. Frans Timmermans, then First Vice-President of the European Commission, put it this way: 'Making laws requires engaging with many different stakeholders—from NGOs to companies,—and lobbying is a normal part of the policy process' (EURACTIV, 2019b). Danuta Hübner, former Chair of the Constitutional Affairs Committee in the European Parliament, adds: 'When we decide to regulate in a specific field, lobbyists are there to complete the picture . . . we are getting from the expertise of the Commission, member states, consultative bodies and research carried out within our institutions' (EURACTIV, 2017: 15).

The openness of the EU towards interest groups is also promoted by its second institutional feature, the preference of its politicians and high-level bureaucrats for **consensus**-building. This is a consequence of the dynamic EU policy agenda as well as the complexity of its institutional setting with the many veto points (Kohler-Koch, 1999). For member states, consensual decision-making guarantees some protection against being outvoted in the EU Council when vital interests are at stake. Decision-making by consensus, rather than on the basis of a **qualified majority voting (QMV)**, implies that EU institutions and the national governments need to take the opinions of relevant interest groups into account to prevent groups opposed to the legislation from ultimately blocking the agreement.

Second, over time, the European Community (EC) (and after 1993, the European Union (EU)) has significantly extended its **competences** and its territorial scope. The dynamic accretion of powers through and between treaty changes has had important consequences for interest groups. From a short-term perspective, it is difficult for interest organizations to forecast the development of the EU's political agenda, particularly in the early phases of the EU policy process. This forces them to devote considerable resources to monitoring EU developments. From a long-term perspective, the number and variety of groups operating at the European level has steadily increased in response to European institution-building. Due to the EC's initial focus on market integration, initially the interest group system consisted mostly of business interest groups. Groups representing diffuse interests, such as environmental groups or development NGOs, have become more vocal since the 1970s and 1980s when the EU began to engage to a greater extent in social **regulation**. And while only groups from the six founding members were initially present in the European arena, nowadays EU policies attract the attention of organizations in 27 member states and beyond, including groups from **candidate countries**. This means that the EU interest group system is marked by both functional and territorial demarcations.

The EU's third relevant characteristic with regard to interest groups is the distribution of political responsibilities between and within the EU institutions as well as between EU and national institutions. The European Commission is still the most important point of contact for interest groups at the European level. The supranational bureaucracy has a monopoly over policy initiation in EU legislation (see Chapter 10), which grants it a crucial role in agenda-setting and policy formulation. The Commission's services are also much sought contacts due to their administration of the agricultural and fisheries markets as well as of EU funding programmes such as those in external aid, structural and cohesion policy, and research and technology policy. As 'guardian of the treaties' the Commission also plays an important role in monitoring member states' and non-state (or private) actors' compliance with Community law. Interest groups providing policy information tend to maintain relations with one or several Directorates-General (DGs) that are responsible for specific policy areas and proposals. They also prefer relations with DGs that are proximate to their own policy outlook and positions.

As the second legislative chamber of the EU, the EU Council is a highly relevant contact for interest groups, especially if EU policy proposals are salient to the national actors. The European Council is also an important actor as it sets the EU's general political direction and priorities, and deals with sensitive issues that cannot be resolved at a lower level of intergovernmental cooperation. Unlike the Commission, the EU Council and the European Council are more difficult targets for interest groups because both institutions do not tend to be so readily accessible with regard to regular lobbying. Because it is composed of national representatives, the EU Council and its administrative machinery, the **Committee of Permanent Representatives (Coreper)** and the Council working groups (see Chapter 11), are rarely lobbied as collective actors, although there is some evidence that the Councils are opening up gradually to interest representation (Hayes-Renshaw, 2009: 79). The European Council is even more removed from interest group pressure.

The co-legislative role of the EU's first legislative chamber, the European Parliament (EP), has been gradually expanded in EU governance since the **Single European Act**. The **Lisbon Treaty** established the **ordinary legislative procedure** (OLP) as the main procedure for adopting legislation in the European Union, making the EP a highly relevant lobbying target for interest groups (see Chapter 12). Within the Parliament, the *rapporteurs* (and shadow-rapporteurs) who draft the parliamentary committees' positions and amendments on particular dossiers and the heads of the Standing Committees are the most important addressees for interest group demands. Since Members of the European Parliament (MEPs) are elected by national voters, they are more amenable to demands raised by national interest groups than the Commission (Bouwen, 2004).

As the EU's judiciary, the Court of Justice of the European Union (CJEU), which, since Lisbon entered into force, includes the European Court of Justice (ECJ) and the General Court, formally interprets EU law and monitors compliance with it. European law takes precedence over national law and grants rights to individual citizens that national courts must uphold and that national and European actors can employ in strategic litigation. Notably, the **preliminary rulings** procedure (see Chapter 13) allows national courts to refer questions of European law to the CJEU and enables national actors to challenge the compatibility of domestic and EU law. However, in practice, to take a case to the CJEU usually demands that a body of EU law already exists. Even when this is the case, the outcome of such action is uncertain, the financial costs are heavy, and the duration of the case is generally lengthy, which means that this avenue is not available to all citizens and organizations and will be worthwhile only when the stakes are perceived to be especially high. Usually, it is not interest groups themselves but individual members or stakeholders that engage in such legal action.

Set up to channel the opinions of organized interests into European politics, the advisory **European Economic and Social Committee (EESC)** is a tripartite body composed of individual members who are nominated by the EU member states and who represent employers, workers, and other interests. Interest groups consider the EESC to be of much less importance for the representation of interests within the EU than direct contacts with the EU institutions. Nonetheless, during the debate about the role of civil society in European democracy (see Chapter 9), the EESC sought to establish itself as an important voice of European civil society and has developed several proposals for strengthening its participation in EU policy formation and institution-building (Smismans, 2004).

In EU legislation, the EU institutions exchange information with interest groups (Bouwen, 2004; De Bruycker, 2016). While all policy-makers require information about the pertinence of problems, the effects of the proposed solutions, and how policy choices may affect re-election prospects (Burstein and Hirsh, 2007: 177) and institutional legitimacy, the emphasis they place on different types of information may vary. Given its central role in EU policy-making and its remoteness from European voters, the Commission is said to depend highly on **technical information** (economic, legal, administrative, and other aspects) about the EU-wide effects of its policy proposals (Bouwen, 2004) and less so on **political information**; that is, information about the levels of opposition and support EU policy proposals are facing (De Bruycker, 2016). In contrast, the European Parliament, whose members are subject to re-nomination and re-election in the member states, are in greater need of political information than technical information. As a corollary, MEPs seem to be more responsive to diffuse interests (see Section 14.4, 'The variety of European interest groups'), including those representing the environment, consumers, and large groups such as the unemployed and pensioners (Pollack, 1997). Furthermore, lower-level units or the policy officers in the EU institutions (desk officers in the Commission, EP rapporteurs and shadow rapporteurs, members of Council working groups) place a higher emphasis on technical rather than political information which is different for higher-level units (Commissioners and cabinets, leadership of EP's political parties, permanent representatives, and ministers in the EU Council).

Policy-making in the EU is not confined to the European institutions, however. *Vertically*, the EU institutions share powers with the member states. Agenda setting and policy formulation in the policy cycle are concentrated at the European level whereas implementation (excluding competition policy and agricultural policy) is reserved extensively to the member states. Accordingly, the European Union is often regarded as a multilevel system (Marks and Hooghe, 2001; Eising, 2015; see also Chapter 7), implying that multiple points of access at EU level and in the member states are open to interest organizations (Pollack, 1997). In this multilevel system, the European Commission tends to be more open to EU-wide interest groups than to national interest groups (Bouwen, 2004), which is not the case for the European Parliament and exactly the other way around for the EU Council. Regarding the latter, national interest groups tend to address their positions on EU policies to politicians and bureaucrats of the national government departments. Given the increased use of the qualified majority voting rule in the Council since the SEA, national groups opposing Commission proposals can no longer rely on a veto of 'their' governments to defend their interests and need to engage in EU level activities or to be represented at EU level. Accordingly, close interactions and a pronounced division of labour have emerged between EU level interest groups and national interest groups (see Section 14.4, 'The variety of European interest groups').

KEY POINTS

- Political institutions, such as the EU, form a political opportunity structure that influences the formation and behaviour of interest groups.

- The EU's institutional setting (its dynamic political agenda, its complexity and multilevel character, and its reliance on consensus) shapes the interest group system and interest mediation within the EU.

- There are multiple points of access to the policy process available to interest groups.

14.3 Regulating EU lobbying: the long road towards a mandatory register of interest groups

The EU has significantly increased the regulation of interest groups since the 1990s. These efforts have centred on the design of consultation procedures and on the registration of individuals and organizations that want to contact the EU institutions. The development of better-defined frameworks to institutionalize consultations with interest groups aims to ensure both pluralism and transparency. It has been embedded in EU-wide debates on the EU's democratic deficit and lack of transparency, as well as the quality of EU regulation. Potentially affecting the institutional balance among the Commission, the EP, and the Council, the debate on the regulation of lobbying made evident the different viewpoints of these institutions on the role of interest groups in EU governance. The main differences among the institutions centre on the contribution of interest groups to mitigate the EU's democratic deficit, on the voluntary or mandatory nature of interest group registration, and on the institutional scope of the interest group register.

The European Commission has traditionally preferred not to regulate consultative practices, but to apply general administrative rules and to let interest groups operate on the basis of self-regulatory principles. In 1992, it proposed 'an open and structured dialogue' that aimed mostly at making the access of interest groups more transparent (European Commission 1992b). During the 1990s, when it became clear that there was no longer a **permissive consensus** among European citizens on European integration, the participation of interest groups in EU governance was increasingly framed as a mechanism to reduce the EU's widely debated **democratic deficit**. Therefore, in its 2001 White Paper on European Governance (WPEG), the Commission made recommendations on how to enhance democracy in Europe and increase the **legitimacy** of the institutions (European Commission, 2001a). A series of measures aimed at raising the **input legitimacy** of the EU by incorporating expert advice into EU policy-making. These measures introduced web-based registers of experts and committees, and a comprehensive code of practice on expert advice, as well as legislative impact assessments (Greenwood, 2011; Kohler-Koch and Quittkat, 2013). Furthermore, the Commission signed protocols with the EESC and the **Committee of the Regions** to involve interest groups earlier in the policy process, and to enhance their function as intermediaries between the EU, on the one hand, and civil society and the regions, on the other. Interest groups could register in the voluntary 'Consultation, the European Commission and Civil Society' (CONECCS) database.

In the follow-up to the WPEG, the Commission adopted a set of general principles and minimum standards for consulting interest groups (European Commission 2002: 15). These standards expected the Commission to ensure clear and concise communications, to announce open public consultations on a single online access point, to ensure an adequate coverage of the target groups, to provide sufficient time for responses, and to acknowledge the receipt of comments by reporting on the results of the open public consultations (European Commission, 2002: 19–22). These standards should enhance the **transparency** and **accountability** of consultations, and ensure that all interested parties are properly consulted. Regarding **output legitimacy**, the standards aimed to enhance the effectiveness and coherence of EU policies.

In 2005, and in the context of the **European Transparency Initiative** (ETI), the Commission started a further reform of lobbying regulation arguing that 'lobbyists can have a considerable influence on legislation, in particular on proposals of a technical nature' but that 'their transparency is too deficient in comparison to the impact of their activities' (Kallas, 2005: 6). The ETI sought to enhance the accountability of EU funding, to strengthen the integrity of the EU institutions, and to impose stricter controls on lobbying (European Commission, 2006). It also served to meet the criticism that the previously adopted standards on consultations were insufficient to streamline interest group participation, given their non-binding character and the omission of some established modes of consultation. Thus, the Commission proposed the voluntary registration of organizations and their compliance with a 'Code of Conduct for Interest Representatives' (European Commission, 2008). The Commission launched its voluntary register for lobbyists in 2008. This register replaced the CONNECS database. In an evaluation in 2009, the Commission highlighted that the register enhanced transparency and provided a reasonable level of financial disclosure. The Commission also noted the relatively high number of registrations despite the voluntary nature of the scheme. In 2011, the register listed 3,900 interest groups.

Furthermore, the European Commission introduced a new code of conduct for Commissioners in 2011 and set out new guidelines on whistleblowing at the end of 2012, to encourage staff to report corruption and other serious irregularities. Article 11 of the EU Staff Regulations set out their obligations in relation to outside interest groups (European Parliament, 2013a). In its **Better Regulation** agenda that was put centre-stage by the Juncker Commission in 2015, the European Commission (2015: 70–1) restated the principles and minimum standards that applied to stakeholder consultations, and elaborated further aspects of consultation procedures. Mandatory, open online consultations became mandatory for initiatives with impact assessments, evaluations, and fitness checks of existing legislation, and for green papers preparing political initiatives. Furthermore, it introduced the requirement that stakeholders be given the opportunity to comment on roadmaps for evaluations and fitness checks, on draft **delegated acts** and certain **implementing acts**, and on legislative proposals adopted by the College of Commissioners (see Chapter 16). Thus, the requirement to consult has been extended across the entire range of the policy-making cycle of the EU, even though several EU fora are still being exempted from these obligations or governed by other rules.

As directly elected representatives of the European citizens, MEPs have been more sceptical of interest group participation as a cure to the democratic deficit than the Commission. Given their electoral mandate to speak for European citizens, they maintained that 'the European and national parliaments' rather than civil society groups 'constitute the basis for a European system with democratic legitimacy'. Because of it being 'inevitably sectoral' and therefore lacking 'democratic legitimacy' (European Parliament, 2001: points 8, 11a), the MEPs did not consider functional representation by interest groups to be equivalent to territorial representation by parliamentarians. Concerns about a lack of transparency and a desire to ensure the integrity of its members explain the EP's preference for stricter lobbying regulation. In 1995, the EP launched a register of interest groups. After registration and upon acceptance of a code of conduct, interest representatives would receive a door pass that allows them access to the EP for a year. Under the rules of parliamentary procedures, the MEPs and their assistants were also obliged to indicate their paid activities and the donations they receive, clarifying any relationship that they might have with groups outside the EP.

In response to the Commission's introduction of its voluntary register in 2008, the EP issued a resolution to establish a single mandatory register of lobbyists for all EU institutions. It also established a new code of conduct for MEPs in 2012. Implementing measures were adopted in April 2013, laying out the provisions for accepting gifts and invitations offered to the parliamentarians (European Parliament, 2013a). On 31 January 2019, the European Parliament adopted binding rules on transparency in lobbying. In a revision of its Rules of Procedure (European Parliament, 2018), the EP stipulated the online publication of meetings with lobbyists by MEPs involved in the drafting and negotiation of legislation (EURACTIV, 2019a).

The Commission's and the Parliament's initiatives resulted in the creation of the **Joint Transparency Register** (JTR)—that is, a joint register of interest groups for the EP and the Commission. In May 2011, the EP and the Commission concluded an inter-institutional agreement (IIA) to establish the Joint Transparency Register (European Parliament, 2011a). The register was soon critized for being inaccurate and incomplete. According to early academic critics, the register misclassified several groups and had only an incomplete coverage of interest groups (Greenwood and Dreger, 2013). These critics claimed that 15 per cent of the NGOs registered in the JTR in January 2013 should be reclassified as trade, business, or professional interest groups. The authors also estimated that, at that time, the JTR missed about 27 per cent of the firms in the relevant population of EU level actors, 25 per cent of the consultants, and 41 per cent of the NGOs. Internal evaluations by an inter-institutional high-level working group of the European Parliament and the European Commission in 2013 led to a revised IIA (European Parliament and the European Commission, 2014). The revised IIA introduced several changes to the register and the obligatory code of conduct. However, it maintained the voluntary nature of registration.

There was considerable contention among the EU institutions about the JTR's mandatory or voluntary character and on the inclusion of the EU Council in the register. Against the position of the European Parliament, registration was not made mandatory because, according to the EU's legal services, that would have raised 'a great number of complex legal issues'. The introduction of a mandatory register required not only unanimity in the EU Council (which refused to take part in the register) but also the consent of

Figure 14.1 Number of registrations in the Transparency Register, 2011–20

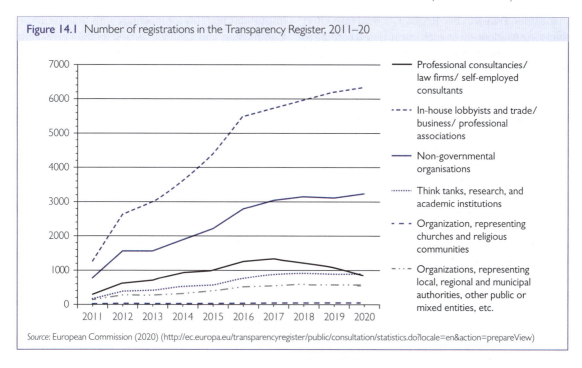

Source: European Commission (2020) (http://ec.europa.eu/transparencyregister/public/consultation/statistics.do?locale=en&action=prepareView)

national parliaments in some member states (European Commission, 2014b: 1). Nonetheless, the EP expected the Commission to create a legal basis allowing for the introduction of a mandatory register at a later stage (European Parliament CCA, 2014: 29–30) and called upon the Commission to introduce a compulsory register by the end of 2016.

The window of opportunity for a mandatory register opened up with the incoming Commission in 2014. In his political guidelines for the next European Commission, then Candidate for President of the European Commission Jean-Claude Juncker had committed to 'enhanced transparency when it comes to contact with stakeholders and lobbyists' as well as to the creation of 'a mandatory lobby register covering all three institutions' (Juncker, 2014: 11). Following up on these promises, the Commission decided to publish information on meetings of Commissioners, members of Cabinets, and Directors-General with lobbyists from 1 December 2014 onwards. Only interest groups registered in the JTR were eligible to meet with this senior staff of the Commission. Furthermore, after setting up an open public consultation on the Transparency Register in 2016 the Commission put forward a proposal for a mandatory register covering the EU Council, the European Parliament, and the European Commission (European Commission, 2016). Faced with high-level

support in both EP and Commission, the Committee of Permanent Representatives agreed on a Council's position increasing transparency regarding EU interest representation in December 2017 (Council of the EU, 2017a). This requires interest representatives to register in order to meet with senior staff of the General Secretariat of the Council as well as to take part in thematic briefings, public events, and access to Council premises. But the Council also emphasized that 'interaction between interest representatives and national officials, like the diplomats working the Permanent Representations to the EU, is the sole responsibility of the member state concerned' (Council of the EU, 2017b). Hence, such interactions fall outside the scope of the register even though member states are encouraged to make certain interactions of their ambassadors and their deputy ambassadors 'conditional upon registration of such representatives in the Transparency Register, when holding the Presidency of the Council' (Council of the EU, 2017a: Article 13). After further negotiations had been put on hold ahead of the European elections and the appointment of the new Commission in 2019, the European Parliament, the Council of the EU, and the European Commission resumed their negotiations in 2020. On 15 December 2020, the three institutions endorsed a compromise package for a joint inter-institutional agreement on a mandatory Transparency Register. It shall take effect following its adoption by each institution according to its internal procedures and its publication in the Official Journal.

In sum, interest group participation in EU policy-making and implementation in the past 15 years has been increasingly formalized as it was tied to general concerns about EU democracy, legitimacy, transparency, and accountability. While, at first sight, 'better regulation' and 'increased transparency' may be goals 'that no one could object to' (Pachl, 2015: 375), the institutional developments derived from them can impact on the institutional balance and autonomy of the European Commission, the European Parliament, and the EU Council (Alemanno, 2015). Therefore, the Commission and the EP have different opinions about the legitimacy-enhancing effects of functional as compared to territorial representation on the EU's legitimacy, and the Council members stated their reservations extending the remit of the Transparency Register to contacts between interest groups and Coreper members. These institutional developments have also been assessed differently by the diverse range of interest groups. Several interest groups stated their concern that the aim of the better regulation agenda to cut red tape in order to promote jobs, investment, and growth in the EU (Juncker, 2014: 6) might weaken the pursuit of substantial goals such as consumer protection, environmental protection, or public health. In fact, more than 50 non-governmental organizations formed a network called the Better Regulation Watchdog in order to promote and defend the rights of citizens to high social, labour, environmental, consumer, and public health standards. NGOs fear also that the extension of consultation procedures along the entire policy-making cycle could benefit business interests perhaps more than non-business groups because the former have more resources at their disposal and can provide detailed technical information along the policy cycle whereas 'the latter direct their overstretched resources to the most relevant moments in the decision-making process for maximum input' (Pachl, 2015: 376–7). Business groups, in turn, complained that procedural instruments such as impact assessments often merely serve to justify the EU's 'pre-defined political decisions' (Delogu, 2016: 226). Finally, ALTER-EU and other organizations engaged in the promotion of lobbying transparency argued that interest group registration should not just be required for meetings with the senior staff in the EU institutions but also for meetings with officials in the Commission and Council, as well as the permanent representatives who work out the details of EU legislation (ALTER-EU, 2016: 5).

KEY POINTS

- The EU institutions initially avoided regulating interest groups.
- In 2011 the European Commission and European Parliament set up a Joint Transparency Register.
- Over time the European institutions have agreed to regulate interest group behaviour even though there are still significant variations among and within institutions in the handling of interest representation.

14.4 The variety of European interest groups

The number and variety of interest organizations operating at the EU level are vast, although it is difficult to quote an accurate number of interest groups. A number of factors explain this difficulty, including complexities in identifying and classifying actors (Beyers et al., 2008), differing data sources (Berkhout and Lowery, 2008), as well as the lack of transparency. While different sources do not yield a common figure, they do at least provide consistent indications of growth over time, with the two high growth periods appearing to be the late 1950s to early 1960s and the mid-1980s to the early 1990s. Also, the mixture of represented interests has changed over time. Figure 14.1 indicates the increase in the number of registrations in the Commission and the EP's joint Transparency Register from its beginnings in June 2011 until 21 September 2020. The register counts now 11,970 entries. This is more than a threefold increase compared to the Commission register's listing of 3,900 organizations in 2011. The entries include not only European interest organizations, but also national associations, think tanks, professional consultancies, law firms, institutions, and organizations representing local, regional, and municipal authorities (see Figure 14.1).

Many studies suggest that organizational characteristics matter greatly to the actors' adaptation to the EU multilevel system. Various typologies have been developed to capture the main features of interest organizations. One might classify interest groups according to type, number, or the homogeneity of their members, the kind of interests that they represent, or whether they operate at a national or European level, or both. In the next section, whether groups operate at the national or European level and the types of interests that they represent (business and non-business interests) will be considered in greater detail. The former is important because the EU is a multilevel system and the latter has consequences for the mobilization of interests and strategies of groups.

14.4.1 EU and national groups

As already indicated, it is important to distinguish between national and EU interest groups (the latter are sometimes called **Eurogroups**), because their organizations and constituencies differ and also because they tend to pursue different strategies when representing their interests.

Over time, EU regulation has triggered the emergence of an EU layer of interest organizations. Many EU interest organizations are **federations** of national interest groups, even though the portion of Eurogroups comprising either the direct membership of other organizations (such as firms or institutions) or combining the two elements (Aspinwall and Greenwood, 1998) has steadily increased. An example of the latter is the European Chemical Industry Council (CEFIC), which brings together both national associations and individual firms. Generally, EU associations have fewer functions than their national members (Eising, 2009; Berkhout et al., 2017) and their resources tend to be smaller. To different degrees they create links among their members, provide and distribute information on EU activities, develop **common positions**, and promote the interests of their members by presenting expertise and arguments to the EU institutions (Lindberg, 1963: 98). Compared with national associations, they concentrate on the representation of interests rather than on the provision of services to their members. Owing to their multinational membership and the heterogeneity of the national settings in which their members are placed, EU groups often have real difficulty in reaching agreement on important policy questions as well as in ensuring their members' compliance with these agreements (see Haas, 1958).

National groups are composed of individuals, firms, institutions, or non-profit organizations, but can also operate as federations that aggregate other sectoral or regional associations. For example, the Federation of German Industry (BDI) brings together 40 sectoral business associations. Among them is the German Chemical Industry Association (VCI), which has a mixed membership of firms and associations: it represents 1,700 chemical firms as well as 22 subsectoral associations. Given the impact of EU regulation on their members, national groups must take heed of political developments at the European and the national levels. They may also feel the need to *adapt* to the EU's multilevel system through organizational change and through change in their relations with other groups (see Grote and Lang, 2003). Many national groups need to coordinate interest representation at different levels of the EU multilevel system and decide which roles the Brussels route, the national route, EU level interest groups, their own direct lobbying, coalition formation, media campaigns, protests, and professional consultants are supposed to play in their strategies. Only a minority of them are able to pursue multilevel strategies in the sense of establishing routine contacts with political institutions at each level. This is because they are tied to their national membership in one form or another, and must also make efficient use of scarce resources. Therefore, in EU legislation, EU level interest groups focus their activities mostly on EU level institutions, whereas most national groups concentrate more on the domestic institutional settings and, particularly, on the national governments, underlining the national importance of their interests (Eising, 2004; Eising et al., 2017). Nonetheless, a sizeable number of national interest groups are present at both the national and the European level. To give an example, according to the EU's Transparency Register, The Investment Association, a trade body representing investment managers and asset management firms in the UK (see Box 14.2), has 38 staff members (10.5 full-time equivalents [FTE]). One staff member is accredited for access to the premises of the European Parliament. In 2019, The Investment Association spent between €1,250,000 and €1,499,999 on EU lobbying.

A fairly elaborate division of labour has evolved between the EU associations and their national counterparts. European interest groups have become important intermediaries between their national members and the EU institutions. This particularly holds true when the EU political agenda is set and when policies are being formulated by the EU institutions. In contrast, national associations are more vocal than EU associations when EU policies are being transposed into domestic law or being implemented by the national public administration. European integration need not necessarily weaken relations among domestic groups and domestic institutions; it may even contribute to a strengthening of existing ties among actors (Benz, 1998: 583). For example, when there is uncertainty over new EU legislation, this can prompt national actors to exchange information or reinforce domestic alliances. The degree of impact seems to be down to organizational factors, issue-contexts, as well as domestic institutional contexts.

Domestic interest organizations that are situated in an unfavourable domestic opportunity structure have an important incentive to act at the EU level to pursue their interests. The closure of the national route to them increases the likelihood of EU level activities (Poloni-Staudinger, 2008). Increased conflict between them and national governments are also an incentive for domestic interests to 'exit' to EU level consultations (Marshall and Bernhagen, 2017), whereas common positions between them and national governments lead to joint domestic mobilization against EU legislative proposals (Eising et al., 2017). Correspondingly, those interests that are located in a favourable domestic context may feel less need to follow the Brussels route, since the national venue is open to them. However, according to several empirical studies, strong ties with national politicians and bureaucrats can enable domestic interests to also act at EU level (Eising, 2009).

14.4.2 Business interests

Historically, business interest organizations formed the largest share of interest groups in the EU. Among the 6,357 in house lobbyists and trade/business/professional associations in Figure 14.1, there are 2,512 trade and business associations. This category of interests was quick to respond to **European integration**. The confederation of European Business (BUSINESSEUROPE), which is the primary European producers' and employers' association, was set up as early as 1958. The equivalent public sector association, the European Centre for Public Sector Firms (CEEP), followed soon after in 1961. The Federation of the Chambers of Commerce (EUROCHAMBRES), which represents small and medium-sized enterprises (SMEs), was also founded in 1958. Alongside these EU federations, there are a number of cross-sectoral associations that have a direct membership of firms. For example, the American Chamber of Commerce

EU (AmCham EU) comprises more than 150 large companies. It collaborates with the European Council of American Chambers of Commerce (AmChams in Europe) that unites 45 American Chambers of Commerce (or equivalent organizations) in Europe and Israel and represents more than 17,000 European and American corporate members. The European Round Table of Industrialists (ERT) is composed of 55 executives of large European firms and was particularly influential in pushing for acceptance of the **Single Market** programme in the mid-1980s (Cowles, 1997; see also Chapter 20).

Large firms have also become increasingly important in the interest group landscape as individual actors (Coen, 2009; Marshall and Bernhagen, 2017). They can easily afford to be present in both the domestic and the European arenas. Among the 6,357 in house lobbyists and trade/business/professional associations shown in Figure 14.1, there are 2,569 firms (and groups of firms). They lobby EU institutions directly, have formed direct membership organizations (rather than federations), and have also been important in the restructuring of business associations since the 1980s. Within BUSINESSEUROPE, for example, large firms were able to secure top positions in the standing committees, giving them a key role in the formulation of policy positions (Cowles, 1997). In several sectors, such as automobiles, chemicals, and biotechnology, large firms, by acting outside the framework of established interest organizations or by forming new direct membership organizations, have acquired greater influence than either the national or the EU federations. Individual lobbying by large firms often secures better access to both EU and domestic political institutions than that of the European and national associations. The EU institutions in particular may prefer to cooperate with large firms and direct membership organizations, because these are able to agree on common positions more easily than the EU federations. This can have a detrimental effect on European federations, which find it more difficult to aggregate interests along national lines.

14.4.3 The social partners and the social dialogue

The social partners take part in the genesis of any Commission initiative in the social policy field through the European Social Dialogue. The term 'European social partner' refers to those organizations at

BOX 14.2   CASE STUDY: UK FINANCIAL SECTOR LOBBYING DURING BREXIT NEGOTIATIONS

In 2013, Prime Minister David Cameron announced a referendum on the EU membership of the United Kingdon (UK) during his 'Bloomberg' speech. The referendum was held on 23 June 2016 and, with 51.9 per cent votes in favour of leaving the EU, resulted in the withdrawal of the UK from the EU on 31 January 2020 (see Chapter 27).

In Brexit negotiations, the British government as well as interest groups strived to establish beneficial conditions and arrangements for UK businesses with the EU, for example by reshaping regulatory processes and trying to establish cooperative arrangements. The UK's financial services sector, often referred to as 'the City (of London)', profited from banking regulation, hedge fund regulation, and beneficial rules for derivatives and other financial products in the EU while the UK was a member state. After Brexit, these advantages no longer apply. Also, market access is more complicated and London's position as the European financial centre may be weakened (CEO et al., 2019).

A study by Corporate European Observatory (CEO) based on data from the EU lobby register shows the great importance the UK financial sector ascribed to lobbying the EU: it indicates annual lobby expenditures of at least €34 million and the employment of more than 140 staff members engaged in lobbying the EU. Lobbyists were granted 71 access passes to the

European Parliament and took part in 228 high-level meetings with Commission representatives between December 2014 and May 2016. Participation in MEP industry forums such as the European Parliamentary Financial Services Forum (EPFSF) or Financial Future, lobbying meetings with UK (conservative) MEPs or participation in consultative bodies of European supervisory agencies—for example, the European Securities Markets Authority (ESMA), the European Banking Authority (EBA), and the European Insurance and Occupational Pensions Authority—complement their lobbying activities (CEO, 2016).

Finance was the most lobbied issue the Department for Exiting the EU (DExEU) handled during the Brexit negotiation —46 meetings on that subject were held within six months. Corporate lobbyists, among them financial interests, had privileged access to meetings of the DExEU and the **EU Brexit Task Force**. DExEU consulted smaller businesses and civil society groups affected by the socio-economic consequences of Brexit much less frequently than businesses. For instance, 70 per cent of DExEU meetings were with large business representatives, whereas only 12 per cent were with NGOs, trade unions, or think tanks. NGOs were even less well represented in meetings of the team of Chief EU Brexit Negotiator Michel Barnier as well as in the meetings of ministers from the UK Department for International Trade (DIT) (CEO and Global Justice Now, 2017a, b).

EU level that are engaged in the European Social Dialogue as provided for under Articles 151 to 155 of the Treaty on the Functioning of the EU (TFEU). Social partners may decide on how they wish to implement an agreement. Article 155(2) TFEU provides two ways to ensure its implementation: the 'autonomous route' relying on national procedures and practices specific to management and labour and the member states; or the route via 'implementation by Council decision', which leads in practice to implementation by Council Directive including all legal consequences specific to the instrument of a directive. Social partners may decide on autonomous agreements in all social policy fields—even those not falling under the competences of the EU as defined in Article 153 TFEU.

Hence, the European social dialogue is a quasi-corporatist arrangement at EU level. It involves large, encompassing EU-level associations that tend to have representational monopolies for their domains and gives them some policy-making and implementation rights. Along with CEEP and BUSINESSEUROPE,

the European Trade Union Confederation (ETUC) is the most important cross-sectoral **social partner** in the EU. CEC (European Confederation of Executives and Managers Staff), EUROCADRES (Council of European Professional and Managerial Staff), and UEAPME (*Union Européenne de l'Artisanat et des Petites et Moyennes Entreprises*) are further cross-sectoral social partners that represent certain categories of employees or undertakings (see Chapter 21). According to a study on their representativeness for the employers and workers in the 27 EU member states, these organizations 'affiliate the great majority of national organizations, which have a role in cross-industry industrial relations in the EU27 Member states and cover about 90% of member employees and firms' (European Foundation for the Improvement of Living and Working Conditions, 2014).

The social dialogue arose in the mid-1980s as part of the drive by former Commission President, Jacques Delors, to build a social dimension into the Single Market. In 1991, the Maastricht Treaty included a

Social Agreement, which provided the **legal basis** for this mechanism. In 1997, the social dialogue was incorporated into the Amsterdam Treaty. The competences of the social partners in the social field are extensive: they are allowed to provide technical information, to indicate the position of their members, or to suggest alternative courses of action, and they also have the right to formulate and/or implement the policies themselves. Under these legal provisions, four framework agreements were implemented via Council Directives (on parental leave, in 1996; on part-time work, in 1997; on fixed-term contracts, in 1999; on parental leave (revised), in 2009). Also, four autonomous agreements were concluded (on telework, in 2002; on work-related stress, in 2004; on harassment and violence at work, in 2007; and on inclusive labour markets, in 2010). It is common to argue that the threat of EU legislation has prompted the social partners to reach these agreements. For the four framework agreements, they also depended on the EU institutions to get them implemented. According to a recent study, the social partners concluded their autonomous agreements in areas which were not yet the subject of 'comprehensive national regulation' enabling them to save transaction costs and to avoid parallel national negotiations and regulations (Keune and Marginson, 2013: 486). Moreover, the first autonomous agreement of the social partners on telework also seems to reflect their aspirations to become more autonomous from the European Commission (Larsen and Andersen, 2007: 184).

14.4.4 **Non-business interests**

Non-business interests include those pursued by religious, social, human rights, consumer, and environmental groups, and are typically recognized under the umbrella label of 'non-governmental organizations' (NGOs) or 'civil society organizations' (CSOs) (see Box 14.1). They are characterized by the broad scope of their policy goals and the absence of a well-defined group membership, which is why they are often also considered to be **diffuse interest groups**. Due to their advocacy of ideas and values, they are also often labelled promotional groups or cause groups (Lieber, 1972). Diffuse interests have faced two key challenges that initially constrained their mobilization at the EU level—namely, collective action problems and a relative absence of EU regulation till the 1980s. A first reason for the presence of fewer diffuse interest

organizations is their collective action problems. The broad scope of their policy goals and the absence of a well-defined group membership encourage free-riding and the suboptimal provision of **collective goods** (Olson, 1965), constraining the ability of diffuse interests to aggregate the concerns of their constituencies and organize effectively. This problem, however, is less prevalent among EU-level interest groups because many of them can build on prior domestic interest organizations. For diffuse interests, it is also particularly difficult to mobilize their constituencies and supporters in different countries (see Box 14.3).

Second, as argued under Section 14.4.2, 'Business interests', the expanding policy competences of the European institutions were accompanied by the mobilization of interests at the European level wanting to influence policy outcomes. However, in the early years of the integration process, the absence of regulatory activity in areas such as welfare and social policy resulted in the absence of incentives for diffuse interests to mobilize at the European level, because their key concerns were still regulated at the domestic level. Even well into the 1970s, welfare and social policy groups were conspicuously absent from Brussels (Harvey, 1993: 189–90). But the numbers of non-business interests started to significantly increase in the 1980s as a response to new European programmes. The EU's increasing regulatory activity has mobilized diffuse interest groups at the EU level. The vast majority of non-business interests responded to new European programmes. Thus, the growth of anti-poverty groups in the second half of the 1980s was a direct consequence of new EU programmes in this policy area (Harvey, 1993). The foundation of the European Environmental Bureau (EEB) came about as a consequence of the EC's first environmental programme in 1974. Today the EEB is the most comprehensive European environmental organization, bringing together 138 national environmental organizations and 23 European networks. An early example of the impact of the EU institutions on the evolution of diffuse interest groups is the European Consumer Union Bureau (BEUC). Domestic consumer organizations formed the BEUC in 1962, with the support of the European Commission and as a response to market integration (Young, 1997: 157–8). There are now more diffuse interest organizations than business associations listed in the transparency register (see Figure 14.1). The proportion of diffuse interests among all interests has significantly increased in the EU in the past two decades (Greenwood, 2011).

An important reason is that the Commission and the European Parliament have sponsored the formation of diffuse interest groups. They offer them financial support through EU budget lines. While many NGOs obtain relatively short-term action grants to implement EU policies, others, such as the European Environmental Bureau, obtain longer-term operating grants because they pursue an aim that is of EU interest. According to a study of the European Court of Auditors (2018), the Commission has implemented an estimated 1.7 per cent of the EU budget and 6.8 per cent of the European Development Funds (EDFs) through NGOs between 2014 and 2017, amounting to €11.3 billion for implementation by NGOs. Most funds allocated to NGOs were for external action. This suggests that the relevance of NGOs in EU policy implementation has increased over time, particularly when regarding the EU's external policies. For instance, in 2013, NGOs obtained 33.8 per cent of the EU funds allocated to EuropeAid and 21.3 per cent of the funds allocated to humanitarian funds. In their analysis of the financial disclosure information included in the JTR in January 2013, Greenwood and Dreger (2013: 154) found that 19.3 per cent or 405 out of 2,095 EU groups had received a grant from at least one of the EU institutions in the year preceding their registration. Among them, 41.2 per cent (169) of NGOs and 31 per cent (31) of the trade unions had received a grant. In addition, 17.5 per cent of companies (53) and 10.7 per cent (84) trade/business/professional associations had received substantial EU grants. These related mostly to their participation in the EU's research and technology development programmes. To the NGOs, EU funding can be very important: it contributed an average of 42.9 per cent of the total budget among the population of 330 NGOs which provided budget information in the JTR (Greenwood and Dreger, 2013: 154).

There is a perceived risk that the EU institutions use NGOs for window dressing in social policy and that interest organizations become highly dependent on the EU institutions, thus influencing the organizations' political positions and activities. Financial support might allow the EU institutions to co-opt interest organizations, limiting their opposition to European initiatives. For such reasons, some associations, such as Greenpeace or ALTER-EU, do not accept public funding. Previous studies denied that the Commission attempts to steer actors towards or 'away from, particular policy positions' (Harvey, 1993: 191; Mahoney and Beckstrand, 2011). Recent studies of the Commission's consultations confirm that the Commission reaches out to a great variety of actors (Kohler-Koch and Quittkat, 2013). In sum, financial support enables diffuse interest organizations to participate in EU decision-making, while simultaneously allowing the Commission to broaden its support base, to improve its expertise on the divergent arguments of different groups, and to claim that the legitimacy of EU policies has increased. However, the EU's funding of NGOs has become much more controversial in the recent past with its opponents in the European Parliament arguing that the EU's funding of NGOs can change the general climate of EU policy debates and may even be against its own strategic interests (see EP PDBA, 2017c).

14.4.5 The influence of business and diffuse interests

The previous sections point out that business interests (firms and business associations) outnumber diffuse interests in the EU interest group population. However, in general, the extent to which the business community is able to pursue its interests effectively varies enormously across time and issues. For example, within the Single Market programme from the late 1980s, many economic sectors such as transport, electricity and gas, and telecommunications were liberalized despite strong resistance from incumbent firms. In the case of electricity liberalization, even Europe's largest utility, *Electricité de France* (EdF), had to accept the loss of its monopoly position on the French market, despite its best attempts to defend that position. Moreover, business is far from being a unitary actor. Large electricity consumers take a different stance on sectoral liberalization and regulation than the incumbent utilities, and these, in turn, also differ from renewable energy producers. Nonetheless, it remains relevant to ask whether the strong presence of the business community is a result of the greater variety of business interests needing representation, or whether it has more to do with firms being better able to form interest groups based on specific interests than are the more diffuse, non-economic interest groups. Interest group theories have predominantly focused on the latter reason, raising important questions about the democratic implications of interest group activity. These developments have led scholars to characterize EU interest mediation as a form of '**elite pluralism**' (Coen, 2009: 160).

BOX 14.3   CASE STUDY: INTEREST REPRESENTATION DURING THE COVID-19 CRISIS

Initially reported in Wuhan, China, **COVID-19**, an infectious disease caused by the newly discovered coronavirus, spread rapidly to over 200 countries worldwide in early 2020. It was declared a pandemic by the World Health Organization on 11 March 2020 (see Chapter 28). Besides health issues, environmental, social, and economic impacts have been increasingly addressed by interest groups and other actors to influence crisis response policies which aim at managing the impacts of the pandemic (Jones and Comfort, 2020). In fact, political advocacy has focused more on economic measures and rescue packages than on health and safety measures or on the easing of restrictions (Junk et al., 2020: 12–14). At the same time, governments are specifically seeking expertise by setting up advisory boards such as the Commission's advisory panel on COVID-19 (E03719). This panel, established on 16 March 2020, aims at formulating coordinated response measures and fostering exchange across member states. It is composed of seven regular members (individual experts from member states) and three EU agencies and bodies as observers.

Within the scope of the Interest Representation during the Coronavirus Crisis (InterCov) Project, Junk et al. (2020) have examined the interest representation of organizations and large firms during the COVID-19 crisis in ten European countries and at the EU level. Their preliminary findings indicated that the access of interest groups during the crisis has remained relatively stable across venues in all European countries (Junk et al., 2020: 5–7, cf. Rasmussen, 2020). However, access to the EU institutions in general and the European Parliament in particular decreased for a large share of actors. The authors explain this change as follows: first, as decision-making on travel restrictions and economic restrictions takes place at the national level, national institutions become more pivotal targets for interest representation. Second, interest representation at the EU level might experience practical difficulties due to international travel restrictions (Junk et al., 2020: 7–8). Regarding types of actors, the authors find a decrease in the access of NGOs and an increase in the access of business organizations and professional groups during the crisis (Junk et al., 2020: 8–10).

In her study on the access of interest groups and businesses to the European Commission, based on data by Transparency International, Anne Rasmussen (2020) found that the use of digital lobbying strategies in particular expanded during the COVID-19 crisis. While before, digital interest representation was not the norm—fewer than 1 per cent of participating actors took part in digital meetings with the Commission—its share rose to 38 per cent for all meetings and to 84 per cent for COVID-19 related meetings during the period February to May 2020. In line with previous findings, Rasmussen (2020) found a dominance of business representatives in high-level meetings with the European Commission: two thirds of all participating actors represented business interests. For digital meetings on COVID-19 related subjects, business dominance was especially high. While companies and business associations represented 33 per cent in non-digital meetings, compared to a share of 56 per cent of non-governmental organizations, in digital meetings their share rose up to 70 per cent. NGOs accounted for only 19 per cent of the participants in digital meetings with the Commission. Further, Rasmussen (2020) suggests that social distance measures and the discontinuation of physical events and face-to-face meetings put NGOs at a disadvantage because they typically find it more difficult to mobilize resources and organize themselves (see also Junk et al., 2020: 10–12). Another alarming observation Rasmussen (2020) points to is 'corona washing', a strategy companies and business associations use to legitimize their demands by relating to the virus and by using the crisis to postpone legislation or reduce obligations in areas such as taxation, greenhouse gas reduction, agriculture, and others.

These preliminary results must be carefully interpreted at this very early stage, and the lobbying activities and the eventual impact of interest groups on legislation have to be evaluated in their entirety. Junk et al. (2020) indicate that in comparison to the national level, interest groups rate their impact as rather low at the EU level. Also, NGOs perceive their influence as lower than do business organizations and professional groups (Junk et al., 2020: 15–16).

However, research conducted within a comprehensive study of interest group politics in the EU, the INTEREURO project (Beyers et al., 2014), on more than 70 EU regulation or directive proposals that were put forward by the European Commission between 2008 and 2010, do not corroborate these assessments. Thus, one study found that the policy frames (the understandings of what the essence of a policy proposal

is) of European Commission officials were frequently closer to the frames of diffuse interest groups than to those of business interest groups (Boräng and Naurin, 2015). Another INTEREURO study measured the *success* of interest groups in EU legislation (Dür et al., 2015: 963) defining success as the absolute distance of the actor's preferred outcome from the so-called reversion point (the hypothetical outcome if no EU directive or regulation had come about, which is often the status quo before EU legislation) minus the absolute distance of an actor's preferred position from the final outcome. The study shows that diffuse interests were more *successful* than business interests in pulling the EU policy outcome away from the reversion point towards their preferred outcome (Dür et al., 2015: 969). On issues that were more technical and did not involve a wider political debate, business interests' *success* increased. This corroborates the general argument that business tends to be more successful when politics is quiet (Culpepper, 2011) and that diffuse interests are more successful when issues are amenable to public debate (Dür and Mateo, 2016). However, the findings demonstrate not only that business is usually not able to block forthcoming EU legislation entirely but they (Dür et al., 2015) also imply that business does rather well when settling for its second-best option, the promotion of less rigid rather than more rigid standards in forthcoming legislation. The distance of business actors from the median outcome in EU legislation is much smaller than that of citizen groups. While any interpretation of these findings must take into account that the proposals were tabled in a period of stronger economic and social regulation in the aftermath of the global financial crisis as well as the crisis in the euro area, these findings indicate nonetheless that diffuse interests are not necessarily on the losing side in EU politics. However, they depend critically on allies within the EU institutions, notably in the European Parliament and the European Commission.

> ### KEY POINTS
>
> - Interest groups in the EU are not a consistent unitary actor. EU level interest groups focus their activities on the European level and national interest groups concentrate on the domestic level. Only a limited portion of interest groups acts at both levels as multilevel players.
>
> - Diffuse interests tend to rely to a greater extent on so-called voice strategies that mobilize the media and the public than specific interests that rely relatively more on access strategies, that is on direct contact with policy-makers.
>
> - The social partners have extensive rights, such as the right to formulate and/or implement European policies themselves. They are co-legislators in EU social policy-making.
>
> - The Commission and the EP provide material and procedural support in order to enable 'diffuse' interest organizations to participate in decision-making.
>
> - Empirical studies indicate that EU policy outcomes are not inevitably biased in favour of business interests even though these constitute the majority of European interest organizations.

14.5 Conclusion

European integration has left its mark on interest representation in Europe. A new multi-layered interest group system has emerged to reflect the multilevel institutional set-up of the EU. The EU offers interest groups numerous points of access and it also grants interest groups an important say in the European policy process because of its disposition towards consensual decision-making. The EU institutions actively promote the formation of European-level groups, by providing funds for weaker, more diffuse interests and supporting those involved in implementing European policy. Over time, the perspective on interest groups has changed. While they are still important contributors to EU policy-making, they are increasingly regarded as representatives of civil society in the EU.

Some observers even argue that interest groups have the potential to remedy the EU's democratic deficit (see Chapter 9), as they allow for greater political participation. However, this kind of argument has to recognize that there is a potential bias built into the system of EU interest representation. The system is asymmetric, with a simple majority of all organizations representing business and professional interests, and only a minority representing more diffuse social interests. While EU policy-making does, nonetheless, often work to the advantage of diffuse interests, it is important to recognize that these are highly dependent on support from the European institutions. Moreover, interest groups offer a different sort of representation than that of bodies such as national parliaments. It is therefore questionable whether the institutionalization of interest group participation offers an appropriate remedy to the problems of democracy and accountability from which the European Union suffers.

QUESTIONS

1. How does the institutional setting of the EU impact upon interest mediation?

2. How have the European institutions sought to regulate and structure interest group activity?

3. In what way and to what extent does the EU support interest groups? Why does it do this?

4. In what way do interest organizations benefit the European Union?

5. How important is each European institution as an addressee of interest group demands?

6. What are the similarities and differences between national and EU groups?

7. Why are there still more business than non-business interests present in the EU?

8. On what type of issues are diffuse interests more likely to succeed as lobbyists than business interests?

 GUIDE TO FURTHER READING

Dür, A. and Mateo, G. (2016) *Insiders versus Outsiders. Interest Group Politics in Multilevel Europe* (Oxford: Oxford University Press). This book is a comprehensive empirical study of how business and diffuse interest groups in Austria, Germany, Ireland, Latvia, and Spain adapted to European integration.

Eising, R., Rasch, D., and Rozbicka, P. (2017) 'Multilevel Interest Representation in the European Union: The Role of National Interest Organisations', *West European Politics* Special Issue 40/5: 939–1152. This special issue analyses the role of national interest groups in the EU multilevel system, focusing on their alignments with political institutions, their Europeanization, and the bias inherent in the EU interest group population.

Greenwood, J. (2017) *Interest Representation in the European Union*, 4th edn (New York: Palgrave Macmillan). This textbook provides a very useful introduction to the role of interest groups in the EU.

Klüver, H., Beyers, J., and Braun C. (2015) 'Legislative lobbying in context: the policy and polity determinants of interest group politics in the European Union', *Journal of European Public Policy* 22/4: 447–587. This special issue highlights the relevance of institutional contexts and issue contexts for the representation of interests in EU legislation.

Kohler-Koch, B. and Quittkat, C. (eds) (2013) *De-Mystification of Participatory Democracy. EU-Governance and Civil Society* (Oxford: Oxford University Press). This study provides an in-depth and critical analysis of participatory democracy through interest group involvement in EU decision-making.

Access the online resources to take your learning and understanding further, including extra multiple-choice questions with instant feedback, web links, answer guidance to end-of-chapter questions, and updates on new developments in EU politics.

www.oup.com/he/cini-borragan7e

15

Citizens and Public Opinion in the European Union

Simona Guerra and Hans-Jörg Trenz

Chapter Contents

Reader's Guide

This chapter provides an overview of trends in public opinion towards the European Union (EU). The chapter also discusses the key factors thought to explain differences in mass opinion regarding the EU. These include political economy and rationality; that is, opinions stemming from calculations about the costs and benefits of the EU; perceptions of the national government (domestic proxies); the influence of political elites; political psychology, including cognitive mobilization (attentiveness to politics) and concerns about the loss of national identity; and, finally, the role of the mass media in driving opinions regarding the EU.

15.1 Introduction

The European Union began primarily as an elite-driven process. The early days of agreements and negotiations were seen as too complicated for the ordinary citizen and so most decisions were taken outside of the public limelight. Hence early observers of public opinion towards the European project remarked on what was perceived as a 'permissive consensus' of public opinion (Lindberg and Scheingold, 1970), whereby citizens generally held neutral opinions regarding what their governments were doing in Brussels, giving these governments considerable leeway to pursue policies outside of the purview of an attentive public. It was only after the addition of Eurosceptic member states (particularly Denmark and the UK, that left the EU on 31 January 2020) in the first enlargement (1973) that the European Community (EC) began to consult with mass publics on issues related to European integration (see Box 15.1). Even then, such consultation tended to be limited and was primarily focused around referenda campaigns. In general, through the mid-1980s, EU member governments and bureaucrats were interested in limited public involvement in the integration process. The Single European Act (SEA) first and later the Constitutional Treaty (CT) and the Lisbon Treaty later began selling their varying visions of a renewed European project that would contribute to the further economic and political development of the EU integration process. The 2005 referendums in France and the Netherlands on the CT and the subsequent rejection of the Lisbon Treaty in Ireland in 2008 highlight the important role that the mass public increasingly plays in the integration project. The June 2016 Brexit referendum is a turning point in EU integration history, representing the first referendum vote to leave the EU.

Nowadays, it would be difficult to argue that mass European publics are providing a permissive consensus for EU-level policy-making. Moreover, it is clear that public opinion is important in constraining integration outside of referenda settings as well. Research (Caiani and Guerra, 2017) shows that there is a growing salience of the European integration issue in the public discourse, which does not necessarily lead to increasing consensus on the EU polity or policies. A rational utilitarian dimension, when explaining public attitudes, is at stake when looking at citizens' position towards the current Europe (Conti and Memoli, 2017). EU attachment is affected by expectations towards future life and a general loss of confidence in the performance of democratic politics (Guerra, 2018a; Guerra and Serricchio, 2014). Scholars in the field of social sciences are, thus, starting to study Euroscepticism through the lens of a crisis of trust and solidarity (Trenz, 2018), as the EU is confronted by numerous challenges.

This chapter outlines the leading explanations for public opinion formation regarding the EU. It begins with an overview of general trends in the perception of the European Union and differences between European member states. It then provides an overview of the main traditions of attitudinal research and media and public sphere research that explain public opinion formation at the level of individual attitudes and collective behaviour. The chapter concludes by outlining the post-Brexit scenario of a 'constraining dissensus' (Hooghe and Marks, 2009) that has emerged in the

---

↘ BOX 15.1   BACKGROUND: EUROSCEPTICISM

The term 'Euroscepticism' was first used in 1986 to describe the position of British Prime Minister Margaret Thatcher (*The Times*, 30 June 1986) and was later used in the 26 December 1992 issue of *The Economist* with regard to the increasingly negative German public opinion on European integration after Germany was ordered to adjust its rules on beer purity to conform with the internal market (Hooghe and Marks, 2007). In academic discourse, the term has tended to refer to 'doubt and distrust on the subject of European integration' (Flood, 2002: 73). The terms 'hard Euroscepticism' and 'soft Euroscepticism' have been used to describe the varying types and degrees of Euroscepticism.

Hard Euroscepticism exists where there is a principled opposition to the EU and European integration. It is therefore associated with parties who believe that their countries should withdraw from EU membership, or whose policies towards the EU are tantamount to opposition to the entire project of European integration.

Soft Euroscepticism arises when there is not a principled objection to European integration or EU membership, but rather concerns about one (or a number) of policy areas, leading to the expression of qualified opposition to the EU, or a sense that the 'national interest' is at odds with the EU's trajectory (Taggart and Szczerbiak, 2002: 7).

Euroscepticism can be also interpreted as a 'healthy' phenomenon (Milner, 2000; Vasilopoulou, 2013), showing the public's awareness of the relationship between the EU and the national institutions, and engagement with the EU integration process. A 'Euroneutral' category reflects high levels of neutrality regarding the image of the EU among citizens and a lack of knowledge about the EU. In 2020 only 63 per cent of EU citizens knew that Members of the European Parliament (MEPs) are directly elected (EB 93, 2020).

The concept of 'Euroalternativism' has been put forward by FitzGibbon (2013) to distinguish between outright opposition to European integration and 'pro-systemic opposition' that suggests alternative policies and institutional reforms. Thus, drawing on the 'No' campaigns in the 2005 French EU Constitutional Treaty referendum (see also Startin and Krouwel, 2013) and the 2012 Irish Fiscal Compact referendum, FitzGibbon proposes a contestation focused on the idea of EU integration in the Treaties, while campaign leaders argued that 'another Europe (was) possible'.

course of the **politicization** of the EU and that jeopardizes the substantive legitimacy of the EU and its available options for future integration.

15.2 General perceptions of the European Union

Since the early 1970s, the European Commission has sponsored regular opinion polls that monitor public support for various aspects of the European project (along with a whole host of other topics). The reports—known as **Eurobarometer** polls—are

published by the Commission and are freely available online. One of the key questions that has been used to determine levels of support for European integration is: 'Generally speaking, do you think that [our country's] membership of the European Union is a good thing, a bad thing, or neither good nor bad?', but since 2012 this question has been discontinued and only asked in candidate countries. In 2014, Eurobarometer still asked about general future expectations; although in 1995 the closest comparable question was whether EU citizens were hopeful or fearful regarding the completion of the **Single Market** or about the image of the EU (see Table 15.1).

Table 15.1 Image of the EU

Country	Total positive (Sum. 2020)	Total positive (Spr. 2015)	Difference	Neutral (Sum. 2020)	Neutral (Spr. 2015)	Difference	Total negative (Sum. 2020)	Total negative (Spr. 2015)	Difference
EU27	40	41	−1	40	38	+2	19	19	=
EU28 (UK)	40			40			19		
IE	71	57	+14	20	29	−9	9	12	−3
HR	47	47	=	40	40	=	13	12	+1
PL	55	53	+2	37	38	−1	5	7	-2
SK	36	38	−2	42	43	−1	22	18	+4
LT	51	55	−4	43	40	+3	5	5	=
LV	43	39	+4	48	49	−1	8	11	-3
RO	51	62	−11	37	27	+10	11	10	+1
CY	36	24	+12	43	34	+9	21	42	+21
CZ	30	37	−7	41	42	−1	29	20	+9
SI	42	37	+5	48	46	+2	10	16	-6
IT	31	38	−7	39	34	−5	29	25	+4
DE	47	45	+2	37	37	=	16	17	−1
EE	46	49	−3	37	41	−4	17	8	+9
BE	37	43	−6	37	35	+2	26	21	+5
FR	33	37	−4	43	40	+3	24	21	+3
PT	55	42	+13	35	39	−4	9	17	−8
HU	49	43	+6	39	43	−4	12	13	−1
ES	35	34	+1	48	47	+1	15	13	+2
AT	34	29	+5	36	35	+1	29	36	−7
EL	27	25	+2	41	38	+3	32	37	+5
NL	36	42	−6	43	37	-6	21	21	=

(continued)

Table 15.1 *(continued)*

Country	Total positive (Sum. 2020)	Total positive (Spr. 2015)	Difference	Neutral (Sum. 2020)	Neutral (Spr. 2015)	Difference	Total negative (Sum. 2020)	Total negative (Spr. 2015)	Difference
BG	53	55	−2	27	29	−2	20	14	+6
SE	41	42	−1	38	36	+2	21	22	+1
DK	45	39	+6	40	44	−4	14	16	−2
FI	35	37	+2	40	47	−7	25	16	+9
LU	41	52	−11	32	30	+2	27	17	+10
MT	25	51	−26	56	39	+16	10	8	+2

Sources: Eurobarometer 83, Autumn 2015, and Eurobarometer 93, Summer 2020, available at: https://europa.eu/eurobarometer/screen/home.

In the period leading up to the Maastricht Treaty ratification, there was a marked increase in levels of Euroenthusiasm (see McLaren, 2006). By 1991, more than 70 per cent of Europeans were claiming that their country's membership of the then Community was a good thing and the completion of the Single Market made 59 per cent of citizens hopeful. The most fearful countries towards the Single Market were Germany and France (37 per cent), but overall European integration was embraced by the population.

Since the early 1990s, and thus with the completion of the Single Market and the creation of the EU, public support of European integration has been in decline, with some fluctuations and with a quite dramatic drop of support in recent years in response to the eurozone crisis, between 2008 and 2010 (see Table 15.1). Perhaps most surprisingly, public opinion regarding the EU among the member states that joined the EU in May 2004 and January 2007 has also been fairly lukewarm (see McLaren, 2006). The cross-time trends in the Central and East European (CEE) Candidate Barometers—that is, polls conducted by the European Commission prior to the entry of these countries into the EU—indicated that, even in the early 1990s, the image of the EU in the CEE countries was not all that positive (Guerra, 2013). By 2018 there seemed to be a lack of positive or neutral narratives around the EU with critical voices reflecting increasingly Eurosceptic views or highlighting the EU's inability to deliver on behalf of its citizens (see Box 15.2).

BOX 15.2   KEY DEBATES: PUBLIC OPINION: BEYOND POLITICAL PARTIES, ACROSS CIVIL SOCIETY

There are common patterns and new trends that characterize opposition towards the EU among citizens (Guerra, 2018b). First, there seems to be a lack of positive or neutral narratives, with persistent predominantly critical voices exemplified by the Euroscepticism phenomenon. John FitzGibbon (2013) already noted this, by pointing to pro-systemic attitudes opposing the current direction of the EU integration process, defining this phenomenon as **Euroalternativism** (see Caiani and Guerra, 2017). Second, there is an emotional dimension in EU opposition that becomes salient, in particular, in its more extreme and negative positioning at times of hardship or crisis such as in Greece (in the context of the eurozone crisis) or in the aftermath of the Brexit referendum in the UK (Michailidou,

2017; Startin, 2018). Third, there is a new possible cleavage, conceptualized as the rise of the well educated (Zürn and de Wilde, 2016), emerging across Europe, which generally correlates with a cosmopolitan/liberal category of citizens who are moderately in favour of the EU. Fourth, in post-communist countries, there is evidence of a mismatch between high expectations about the EU and what the EU can actually deliver for its citizens. This is accentuated by double talk from political elites in Brussels and in the domestic context that embeds Euroscepticism across the EU. At the EU level, they typically adopt a 'save national interests' narrative', whereas domestically they adopt the 'blame the EU' narrative (particularly to justify unpopular measures such as reduction in public expenditure)

(continued)

BOX 15.2   KEY DEBATES: PUBLIC OPINION: BEYOND POLITICAL PARTIES, ACROSS CIVIL SOCIETY   *(continued)*

(Batory, 2018). Fifth, member states tend to blame 'the other' (member state) when faced with challenging economic, social, and political situations. For example, in the new member states, research shows not just Euroscepticism or Euro-apathy, but Euro-conflicted-ness around questions of fair distribution. Citizens complain that the country diligently implements any reform or EU requirements, and still needs to pay or show solidarity for countries like Greece (in the context of the eurozone crisis), 'that always abused the system' (Guerra, 2017). Sixth, there are some common narratives, that point to the loss of shared core values and lack of solidarity such as the 'us vs. them' dichotomy in Greece (Stavrakakis and Katsambekis, 2014) or 'is this the Union of 28 or what?' narrative reflecting a perception in Germany that rules are not applied equally across the EU. Seventh, remote governance (from Brussels) is

extremely difficult to communicate (Guerra, 2013), and possibly communication needs to start locally to then move towards the EU. Recent comparative analysis between Western and Eastern member states shows that the utilitarian model helps explain citizens' attitudes towards the EU in Central and Eastern Europe. Conversely, in Western Europe, identity and political cues are the determinants of attitudes towards the EU. The analysis indicates that the only significant factor across all cases is EU identity. This not just about feeling 'European', being born in the EU, or being a Christian. Instead, support for the EU is explained by specific expectations, such as (i) to respect European Union's laws and institutions; (ii) to master any European language; and (iii) to exercise citizens' rights, like being active in politics of the European Union, by voting in European elections (Guerra and Serricchio, 2014).

Despite these trends, citizens have recently become more positive and the image of the EU has improved across all EU member states, in particular in Ireland and Portugal (see Table 15.1).

KEY POINTS

- Trends in public opinion towards the European Union are collected through regular opinion surveys known as 'Eurobarometer' polls.

- Enthusiasm for the European integration project was generally on the rise until 1991.

- Although there is a general lack of positive or neutral narratives around the EU, with persistent critical voices, since 2016 the image of the EU has been increasingly more positive across the EU member states.

- Being born in the EU is not a sufficient factor to support the EU, rather support develops when one is able to benefit from the rights and opportunities afforded by European integration.

15.3 Explaining public attitudes towards European integration

Ever since the rejection of the permissive consensus on the part of European publics, theories have been developed to try to explain why some Europeans tend to be more positive about the European integration

process, while others tend to be more negative. These theories generally fall into the following groups: political economy and rationality; attitudes to the national government (domestic proxies); the influence of political elites; political psychology (including cognitive mobilization and identity); and media effects. We discuss each of these in turn.

15.3.1 **Political economy and rationality**

In the mid-1980s, the discipline of political science was becoming heavily influenced by rational, utilitarian approaches to the study of politics. More specifically, models of political behaviour were being developed around the assumption that individuals rationally pursue their self-interests. This approach has had a considerable impact on the study of attitudes to European integration. Some of these theories have been egocentric in nature—that is, individuals support or oppose the integration project because they have personally benefited (or will benefit) from it or have been harmed (or will be harmed) by it. Other approaches that would fit within this context are more sociotropic in nature: citizens of some of the EU member states are said to be more supportive of the European project because their countries have benefited from the European project.

With regard to the egocentric utilitarian theories, the contention is that individuals from certain socioeconomic backgrounds are doing far better economically than individuals of other backgrounds as a result of European integration. In particular, the opening up of the Single Market and the introduction of the common currency are thought to benefit top-level business executives, who no longer face trade barriers and exchange rate differences across most of the EU. Similarly, individuals with higher levels of education will be more likely than those with little education to feel that their knowledge and skills will serve them well in a wider EU market.

These theories are generally supported empirically. For example, analysis of Eurobarometer 93, conducted in the summer of 2020, indicates that the image of the EU is still very negative in Greece (32 per cent), Austria, the Czech Republic, and Italy (29 per cent). This lack of positive attitudes towards the EU does not necessarily translate into negativity; in general, those who are not thought to do very well from an expanded market lean towards neutral responses more heavily than groups such as professionals and executives. Thus, the potential losers of EU integration do not appear to perceive themselves as such and instead tend to be generally neutral about the project, although the social costs of the economic crisis are clear in particular in the case of Greece (see Chapter 25). Similarly, the outcome of the 2016 Brexit referendum in the UK reflects individual worries about immigration, a lack

of economic opportunities, and anger with the political class (see Box 15.3 and Chapter 27).

15.3.2 Domestic proxies and attitudes to the national government

The arguments presented in Section 15.3.2, 'Political economy and rationality' assume that EU citizens are able to consider rationally the impact of economic costs and benefits of EU membership on their own personal lives or on their countries. The approaches discussed in this section and the next argue that support for or opposition to integration may have very little to do with perceived economic gains or losses. This is because it is unlikely that most Europeans are able to calculate whether they have indeed benefited or not from European integration: the egocentric utilitarian models demand a great deal of knowledge of both the integration process and the economy, and for the ordinary European to come to any conclusion about whether he or she is going to be harmed by the process is likely to be extraordinarily difficult. Thus, many researchers have argued that, because of the complexity of the integration process and the EU institutions, the EU is often perceived in terms of national issues rather than European-level ones. This

---

▼ BOX 15.3   CASE STUDY: EMOTIONS AND THE 2016 BREXIT REFERENDUM

The campaign ahead of the referendum on British membership of the EU, leading to the vote of 23 June 2016, was highly charged. The rhetoric deployed by both camps sought to generate anxiety uncertainty, anger, and fear. According to a YouGov study carried out two weeks after the referendum (6–7 July 2016), emotions are likely to affect attitudes towards the EU and the development of the process of European integration (Guerrina et al., 2016). The study found that both supporters of Brexit and supporters of remaining in the EU cited immigration, the economy (or economic stability), and sovereignty as the reason for their voting preference. Both campaigns had an influence in increasing citizens' anxieties and uncertainties, with uncertainty quite widespread among those who voted Remain and with a gender and age-group cleavage. While women and young people tended to be more anxious or uncertain, men were likely to feel angry and disappointed. Additionally, the study found that emotions can affect different attitudes and behaviours. For example, uncertainty can make some voters more risk-averse. Finally, positive feelings were almost completely absent from the answers offered by voters. Uncertainty ('towards the

future', 'towards economic stability') affected those who voted Remain, and anger was more common among Leave voters ('taking back control'). The analysis shows that we can safely assert that uncertainty played a major affective role in the voters' choice in the Brexit referendum thus highlighting an increasing polarization of emotions. UKIP voters were definitely the most hopeful (56 per cent) and proud of their vote (39 per cent). The Leave voter is typically male, is 65 years old or older, belongs to a lower social status, and is likely to live in the Midlands, Wales, or the North of England. This is also the group of voters who were most likely to feel 'relief' at the result of the referendum. The feelings of uncertainty, anxiety, and apprehension were mostly shared by Scottish citizens, Londoners, and very young people. Repeating the survey three years after, in May 2019, only 5 people out of almost 2,000 felt 'content' about Brexit. While two weeks after the referendum, in July 2016, 31 per cent felt 'hopeful', with time less and less British citizens felt positive about Brexit and the percentage of those feeling hopeful dropped to about 4 per cent in 2019, with 41 per cent feeling 'disappointed', and 195 people feeling 'sad' (Guerra, 2020).

effect is seen most clearly in the context of referendums on European issues (Franklin et al., 1994) in that referendums often turn into a vote on the national government's popularity. For example, the French nearly voted against the Maastricht Treaty in 1992, not because of opposition to the contents of that treaty (for example, monetary integration), but because of unhappiness with the government of the day. Further, it is likely that the French and Dutch votes in the 2005 Constitutional Treaty referendums were also driven to some extent by unhappiness with the government of the day (see Box 15.4). Moreover, European elections are generally fought on national issues rather than European-level issues (van der Eijk and Franklin, 1996).

Even outside of the context of referendums and elections, general feelings about the EU are also driven in part by feelings about the national government. As argued by Christopher Anderson (1998), surveys show that few Europeans know much about the details of the European project; so they must be formulating their opinions towards this project from something other than their own knowledge and experience. Anderson's contention is that such attitudes are in part projections of feelings about the national government—that is, hostility to the national government is projected onto the EU level, while positive feelings about one's national government also translate into positive feelings about the EU.

BOX 15.4   KEY DEBATES: THE CONSTRAINING DISSENSUS THROUGH REFERENDUMS ON EUROPE

In 2001, EU member states established a European Convention for the purpose of drafting a Constitutional Treaty (CT) for the EU. While the majority of EU member states ratified the CT, in 2005 French and Dutch voters put a brake on the process by voting 'no' in referenda held 29 May 2005 and 1 June 2005, respectively. Why?

While the French are not overly Eurosceptic, trends in support for the EU indicate that positive feelings about the EU have been in decline since the early 1990s. Thus, in considerable contrast to the Netherlands, the French 'no' vote was perhaps less of a surprise. Indeed, previous experience indicates that even when feelings about the EU are generally positive, votes in EU referenda in France can be very close indeed. This was the case with the vote on the Maastricht Treaty, in which a bare majority of 51.05 per cent voted to support the Treaty. The 'no' vote in France in 2005 appears to be the product of two key issues: first, the state of the French economy in particular, unemployment, fears about the relocation of business and the decline of the small business sector; anxiety about undermining the French 'social model' and the failure of the CT to address the issue of social Europe. Second, opposition to the incumbent government—which was becoming increasingly unpopular, so that for many French voters the referendum became a confidence vote. Thus, on 29 May 2005, 54.7 per cent voted against the CT (with 70 per cent voter turnout).

In the case of the Netherlands, the constitutional referendum held on 1 June 2005 was the first such referendum in modern Dutch history. The Dutch are generally amongst the most enthusiastic EU supporters, and so it was widely predicted that they would provide resounding support for the CT. However,

with a relatively high turnout of 62 per cent, 61.8 per cent voted against the treaty. While the referendum was to be consultative only, most major parties had pledged to respect the voters' wishes, whatever the outcome.

Given the widespread support for the EU in the Netherlands, why did the vote go the way it did? One of the key explanations seems to be that Dutch citizens were unclear as to what they were being asked to approve. The referendum campaign had got off to a very slow start, and media and politicians had struggled to find ways to frame the debate about the Treaty. Moreover, in the absence of clear information as to what that Constitution meant for the EU and for the Netherlands, many Dutch citizens relied on the sorts of cues discussed in this chapter—especially opposition to the government. There may have been some EU-related reasons for the 'no' vote as well, however. One of these relates to the budget contribution made by the Netherlands; another is connected to unhappiness with the way in which the Dutch government had adopted the euro, as many commentators at the time had argued that it had led to the Dutch guilder being devalued against the euro. It was also perceived that the introduction of the euro had led to an increase in prices. The prospect of Turkish EU membership contributed in part to the 'no' vote too, both because of the threat of cheap labour and because of the perceived threat to Dutch culture (see Chapter 18). Finally, with EU enlargement, two fears have subsequently developed in the Netherlands. One is whether this small founding member state can continue to wield influence in the new Europe, and the other is whether Dutch interests can still be protected within the EU. Ultimately, however, the 'no' vote may have been in great part a result of the disorganization of the 'yes' campaign.

On the other hand, and somewhat confusingly, other research has argued the opposite. Specifically, when the national political system is functioning well, when there is little corruption, a strong rule of law, and a well-developed welfare state, individuals are less positive about the EU than when they live in countries in which there is a high level of corruption, weak enforcement of the rule of law, and a weak welfare state. In the case of the former, it is thought that some individuals may see little need for an additional level of government when the national government is functioning so well, while in the case of the latter, individuals may look to the EU to counterbalance weak national political institutions.

15.3.3 Mass publics and political elites

Another approach to studying EU attitudes examines mass–elite linkages. These linkages can mainly be structured in two forms:

- *political elites* can be instrumental in helping to determine citizens' attitudes in a top-down approach, which views the **cueing** process as a form of information flowing from elites to citizens (Zaller, 1992);

- *mass opinion* can also cue elites, in that elites can assume a position on European integration that reflects citizens' views in a bottom-up manner (Carubba, 2001).

Both of these approaches have been found to be correct, but the former has been more widely examined and supported (Franklin et al., 1994; Ray 2003a, 2003b). For example, early research shows that negative attitudes in countries such as the UK, Norway, and Denmark follow the negative connotation of discourse about the EU emerging from the political elites in these countries (Slater, 1982). Some research suggests that there might be different outcomes in the top-down approach, depending on which political parties are doing the cueing and which political party a citizen generally supports (Feld and Wildgen, 1976). Other evidence indicates that, when political parties are united in their position on the EU (Siune and Svensson, 1993), they can further strengthen their influence on mass publics. Thus, consensus across political parties emerges as an important factor explaining public support or opposition to European integration.

Moving away from this top-down approach, Marco Steenbergen and his colleagues (2007) show that both the top-down and bottom-up approaches seem to be correct: political parties are responsive to mass opinions, and mass opinions are shaped also by parties' cues. However, public opinion can cue parties in systems that use **proportional representation (PR)**, but not in **plurality systems**, while in the run-up to national elections, political parties may be less responsive towards the masses on the EU issue. Finally, leadership is a significant factor (Ray, 2003a): mainstream parties seem to have less mobilizing ability than parties on the fringes of the political system, and there is a stronger disconnection between citizens and mainstream parties with regard to the EU issue. This means that the electorate is more likely to be mobilized by protest parties that frame the EU in Eurosceptic terms.

Political parties have a weak mobilizing force in post-communist countries, where trust towards political parties is often very low (Klingemann et al., 2006). The EU is highly salient in these countries (Tilley and Garry, 2007), but because of the deep distrust of political parties, the latter tend to be less credible on international issues related to the EU. Consequently, there tends to be far less top-down elite cueing of citizens on the issue of European integration in these countries.

15.3.4 Political psychology: cognitive mobilization and identity

Early studies of attitudes to European integration conceptualized the project in terms of '**cosmopolitanism**' and contended that those who were more 'cognitively mobilized', specifically those who think about and discuss political issues, would gravitate towards the new supranational organization. It was also contended that differences in opinion regarding the European Community were likely to stem from familiarity with the project itself—that is, the more people knew about it, the less fearful, and thus the more supportive, they would be of it. Evidence indicates that those who talk about politics with their friends and family—the 'cognitively mobilized'—are indeed more supportive of the European integration project (Inglehart, 1970). Moreover, knowledge of the EU appears to have positive implications for public opinion: those who can pass a 'knowledge quiz' about the history and institutions of the EU are, overall, more enthusiastic about the project than those who know very little about the EU (Karp et al., 2003).

The quest for rational explanations of individual-level feelings towards the EU was motivated by the assumption that the European project was mostly economic in nature. Such an assumption is not unreasonable, in that much of the integration that has occurred has indeed been in various sectors of the economy. However, the overriding goal of such integration has always been political—namely, the prevention of war on the European continent. Because the Second World War is often perceived as having been motivated in part by nationalist expansion, thwarting it anchored European integration. Thus, while the project has mostly been sold to Europeans as an economic one, particularly through the 1980s and 1990s, some are likely to perceive it not in economic terms, but instead as a threat to one of their key identities.

The body of work known as 'social identity theory' leads us to the firm conclusion that identities are extremely important for people and that protectiveness of 'in-groups' (social groups to which an individual belongs and with which he or she identifies) can develop even in the context of seemingly meaningless laboratory experiments and even when individuals expect no material gain for themselves by maintaining such an identity (Tajfel, 1970). The major explanations for this behaviour are that many people use in-group identity and protectiveness to bolster their self-esteem, while others use identity to help them to simplify and understand the world (Turner, 1985). European integration may be perceived by Europeans as a potential threat to their *national* identities.

As argued by Liesbet Hooghe and Gary Marks (2004), however, what may be important is the *exclusiveness* of national identity. Thus, the important distinction may be between those who hold multiple territorial identities and those who feel themselves to identify only with their nationality. In fact, exclusively national identity seems to vary widely across the EU. In the original six member states, as well as Spain and Ireland, fewer than half of those surveyed by Eurobarometer tend to see themselves in exclusively national terms, while clear majorities of the samples in Lithuania, Hungary, and Estonia claim to identify exclusively as nationals. Evidence also indicates that this factor is important in explaining general feelings about the EU.

15.3.5 The media: framing the EU

In the tradition of European media and public sphere research, an important conceptual distinction has been introduced between public opinion in its latent form as it is aggregated from individual attitudes (e.g. through Eurobarometer), and public opinion in its manifest form as it is activated through engagement in public and media discourse (Duchesne et al., 2013). As only few citizens experience the EU directly, the way media and journalists select and interpret European news can be held responsible for the formation of public opinion about European integration. By providing a shared communicative infrastructure through which information can be transmitted and opinions exchanged, the mass media further play a key role for EU democracy that depends on: (1) the transparency of EU decision-making processes and the general availability of information about the EU and its activities; (2) the inclusion of the citizens and possibilities to participate in the political process; and (3) principled support of European integration and legitimacy of its main actors and institutions. Below we discuss the role of the news media as facilitators of information about the EU, as providers of an arena for contestation as shapers of value judgements about European integration.

First, the news media traditionally provide citizens with critical knowledge and information about the EU, yet the role of the written press as a provider of reliable news is in decline. According to Eurobarometer (2019), 47 per cent of the Europeans use television as their preferred medium to seek information about the EU, followed by the Internet (43 per cent) and by newspapers (21 per cent). Social media sites especially have become established as alternative news sources for being informed about the EU. The way the news media fill the gaps in information about the EU varies, however, according to the type of media source with quality newspapers giving more prominence to the EU than, for instance, tabloids or regional newspapers. The Internet further increases the risk for European citziens to be confronted with unreliable and biased news about the EU (Michailidou et al. 2014).

Second, the news media constitute an arena of contestation where political actors compete for the attention of the audience. In the so-called claims-making tradition, the news media are analysed in their function of giving voice to both political representatives and citizens allowing them to participate in public debates that are made salient to a larger audience (Koopmans and Statham, 2010). Instead of amplifying the plurality of voice that finds expression in the public sphere and contributing to open and inclusive debates, the news media are found to apply a selective bias in their coverage of EU affairs. Most journalists still focus primarily on the prominence of national actors as protagonists of EU news stories, whereas the role of EU actors and institutions as well as of civil society actors is often downplayed or misrepresented. This leads to a segmentation of national arenas, in which the EU is contested according to different logics and in response to different salient issues.

Third, the news media transmit basic values and identities and engage citizens in normative debates about the benefits of European integration, support of European institutions, and their own attachment to the EU. In the tradition of media frame analysis, it is investigated how media debates shape perceptions of legitimacy of the EU, its policies, and institutions (Diez Medrano and Gray, 2010). Comparative analysis of media discourse shows that journalists frequently express their concerns with manifestations of the EU democratic deficit but overall are rather hesitant to support the deepening and widening of European integration (Wessler et al., 2008). Instead of highlighting a common European perspective, EU news coverage is often framed in instrumental terms with an emphasis on national interests (Statham, 2008). EU financial policies are, for instance, typically framed in terms of costs and benefits for national taxpayers, and EU foreign and security policies are framed in terms of risks and opportunities for the nation state (de Vreese and Kandyla, 2009). Especially during the last crisis years, media debates have become more confrontational giving high salience to Eurosceptic parties and their re-nationalized visions of Europe (Michailidou and Trenz, 2015; Galpin, 2017). Apart from debating democratic legitimacy, the news media are also an important arena for the mobilization of collective identities. Traditional newspapers and television often appear as the 'voice of the nation' and thus can be held responsible for defending nationally exclusive notions of collective identity (Billig, 1995). The European public sphere is distinguished, instead, by debates that emphasize the multilayered and overlapping forms of belonging and thus reflect the socialization of EU citizens in an increasingly Europeanized social and political environment (Risse, 2010). Shared European value frames have been mobilized, above all, in debates about the EU constitutional settlement and in EU foreign policies with a vision of Europe as a 'civilizing force' that promotes democracy, human rights, or sustainable development at a global scale (Manners, 2006; Trenz, 2010; Eriksen, 2014). In more recent years, we observe, however, the re-emergence of more popular and exclusive notions of national or regional belonging. Evidence for a re-nationalized identity discourse can be found in the case of Brexit (Adler-Nissen et al., 2017), in the case of the national stereotypes and resentments that fuelled public debates on accountability during the European sovereign debt crisis since 2008 (Michailidou, 2017), and in the press coverage of the migrant and refugee crisis in 2015 (Triandafyllidou, 2017; Cinalli et al. 2021).

In the tradition of comparative media studies, attempts have been made to map the European **public sphere** in relation to different media outlets (e.g., quality newspapers, tabloids, television, or the Internet) and in relation to different traditions of journalism. So-called media system theory distinguishes the tradition of public service media in the North of Europe (Germany, the Netherlands, and the Nordic countries) with high professionalization of journalists dedicated to community value; the liberal tradition in the UK based on the commercialization of news; and the tradition of a polarized media in Mediterranean countries with a strong elite orientation of the press and frequent state interventions (Hallin and Mancini, 2004). In view of this fragmented media landscape in Europe, pan-European media debates that are received by a cross-national audience are at best amplified by some elitist newspapers like the *Financial Times* or by niche TV channels like *Euronews*. Instead of the unlikely emergence of a unitary European public sphere, the expectation has been that national public spheres would gradually Europeanize with quality newspapers and public service television functioning as a regular supplier of EU news (Trenz, 2004). The production of EU news is supported by the corps of EU correspondents, who face the increasingly difficult task to act as a critical watchdog of EU governance and to translate the complexity generated by EU differentiated integration into public parlance (Michailidou and Trenz 2020a; 2020b).

The debate on the role of the media in EU public opinion has further developed around questions of media biases in the application of news values that frame European news stories in particular ways. One consistent finding across different media sectors is the existence of a negativity bias in journalistic news coverage of the EU (de Vreese and Kandyla, 2009; Galpin and Trenz, 2016). Attention to distant events in Brussels is more easily drawn when they convey drama and conflict, when serious repercussions can be emphasized, when the integrity of EU actors and institutions can be undermined or when the news can be related to feelings of fear and scepticism. In EU news coverage, the objectivity rule of journalism is further often found to be violated in the way news stories are built around the defence of national interest, sovereignty, or identity, which are seen to be at stake in the discussion of EU policies. This comes at the price of a more balanced analysis of EU policies and their potential benefits as well as the role of EU actors and institutions in shaping these policies.

Finally, the news media are held responsible for introducing a conflict dimension into EU politics and turning the permissive consensus, which has characterized European integration for the first three decades into a new 'constraining dissensus' (Hooghe and Marks, 2009). The so-called politicization of the EU is not driven by policy debates among political elites and experts but by public debates involving a wider mass audience and the media (De Wilde, 2011; Hurrelmann et al., 2015). EU politicization as expressed in a new form of 'mass identity politics' is considered by some as a motor of the renationalization of the public sphere. It polarizes the European population along a pro-European and anti-European dividing line and leads to populist backlashes against globalization and open liberal markets (Fligstein, 2008; Kriesi et al., 2012). EU politicization can, however, also promote further Europeanization; for instance, the recent events of contesting crisis-related austerity policies that are rather framed in terms of new class divisions and redistributive conflicts and their transnational repercussions (Statham and Trenz, 2014). Last but not least, it needs to be reminded that there is no linear development towards further and intensified politicization of the EU. In the EU differentiated system of governance, politicization remains exceptional; depoliticized governance the rule (Kauppi and Trenz, 2021).

Apart from questioning how the media impact on public opinion, there is also a tradition of studying the more direct interactions between media, journalism, and EU institutions. This regards, in particular, the question of media effects on EU governance and the formulation of a more active information and communication policy by EU actors and institutions. From a normative perspective, the news media and journalism can be considered as a motor of the democratization of the EU; for instance, in the way journalists perform as a control agency of EU-institutions and decision-making processes (Trenz, 2008). From a more institutional perspective, the mediatization of EU institutions can be measured in the way EU actors become themselves professional media players, investing in new tools of public communication management; for instance, through social media, such as the Facebook pages of the European Parliament (Meyer, 2009; Tarta, 2017). Selective framing of EU news is, in this sense, not the sole responsibility of journalists working within media organizations but is also carried forward by spin doctors and public relations officers within the EU.

The increased politicization and mediatization of the EU has offered new opportunities for raising public awareness about the EU and the relevance of its policies for the citizens, yet it also offers more opportunities for Euroscepticism to become visible. Most recent trends point at the growing role of the Internet for communicating about Europe. Online participatory media are used by citizens, above all to express their discontent and debates on blogs and social media often reflect a climate of hostility towards the EU (Galpin and Trenz, 2018). Social media campaigning in the political battle over Brexit, for instance, intensified the fractures in British politics along ideological and also increasingly along identitarian lines around questions of EU membership (Brändle et al., 2021). Instead of grassroots mobilization, anti-EU campaigns are often run by 'astroturf', or fake grassroots organisations funded by alt-right groups and companies (Bennett and Livingston, 2018).

The **COVID-19** pandemic has brought into sharp relief precisely the vulnerabilities of European journalism and news media systems, facing an existential crisis not only for the loss of revenue but also in light of increasing political pressures and restrictions of the freedom of the press in some member states. While fake news and conspiracies mainly spread through social networks and digital platforms, quality journalism and public media proved essential to reach out to the populations with necessary information about the pandemic and to guarantee levels of trust in governments and the EU during lockdown. During the first months of the pandemic in 2020, polls from different countries indicated that trust in scientific expertise was on the rise and that people were more likely to listen to expert advice in the media. The debate among experts however also brings up new controversy and popularises scientific debate which opens up news space for misinterpretation and conspiracies (Trenz et al., 2020).

15.4 Conclusion

Public opinion about the European Union ranges widely from open hostility to ambivalence and support. Despite the more recent contestation, only small numbers across the EU are openly hostile to the EU. After Brexit, the political turbulences around the COVID-19 crisis led to a strong call for more EU competences to coordinate the health crisis and re-distribute funding (see Chapter 28). European funding contributed to a recovery of the lost public support in countries that were hit particularly hard by the eurozone crisis or the migration crisis, such as Greece and Italy (see Chapters 25 and 26). Surprisingly, despite the many crises affecting the EU, high numbers of citizens remain relatively positive about the Union while expressing their dissatisfaction with the lack of sufficient inter-state solidarity (Eurobarometer 2020).

This chapter has outlined the explanations for differences of opinion regarding the EU, how Euroscepticism is spreading beyond political parties, rising emotional contestation, and the role of the media. First, some of this difference in opinion was argued to be utilitarian in nature. Thus, egocentric utilitarians support the EU because it has brought them economic benefits or is likely to bring them such benefits; others in this category are ambivalent towards the project because they have not received any benefits themselves. Sociotropic utilitarians support or oppose the project because of the budgetary outlays that they have received from the EU, which have presumably increased economic development and growth, or because of the large amount that their country contributes to the EU budget.

Second, some of the differences in attitudes to the EU are thought to be related to perceptions of the national government—that is, some individuals project their feelings about their own government onto the EU level: when they feel positively about the national government, the EU gets an extra boost of support, but when they feel negatively about the national government, the EU is punished.

Third, the chapter has introduced the emotional dimension of Euroscepticism that has emerged in the context of the Brexit referendum campaign and that is increasingly persistent in social and political debates.

Finally, recent research on the role of the media finds that news matters and becomes the strongest factor impacting on citizens' attitudes, while online media generally show more contested debates. Because news coverage can be framed strategically, this has implications for what information citizens receive regarding the EU.

Overall, then, we have a fairly good idea as to why some individuals are positive about the EU, some are negative, and many others are simply ambivalent. Still, research in this field is continually evolving, with further studies emerging offering an updated view on the EU after Brexit, on the effect of EU multiple (financial, economic, migration, and most recently public health) crises, or the impact of EU differentiated integration on public support (Leuffen et al., 2020). In particular, more comparative and long-term research designs are needed to explain the relationship between public opinion, the media, and EU integration beyond the crisis.

QUESTIONS

1. What is Euroscepticism?

2. How can we explain contemporary forms of opposition towards EU integration?

3. What explains drops in the level of support for EU integration in the last ten years, with recent more positive views of the EU across member states?

4. What role did the economic and financial crisis have on attitudes towards the EU?

5. Why did Britain vote Leave in the 2016 EU membership referendum?

6. How do emotions affect citizens' perceptions of the EU?

7. How can the different media shape citizens' attitude towards the EU?

8. Are the new media facilitators an obstacle to European democracy?

GUIDE TO FURTHER READING

Caiani, M. and Guerra, S. (eds) (2017) *Euroscepticism, Democracy and the Media. Communicating Europe, Contesting Europe* (Basingstoke: Palgrave Studies in European Political Sociology). This book focuses on the relationship between the media and European democracy, as important factors of EU legitimacy.

De Vries, C. E. (2018) *Euroscepticism and the Future of European Integration* (Oxford: Oxford University Press). This book examines the role of public opinion in the European integration process. It suggests that public opinion cannot simply be characterized as either Eurosceptic or not, but rather that it consists of different types.

Koopmans, R. and Statham, P. (eds) (2010) *The Making of a European Public Sphere. Media Discourse and Political Contention* (Cambridge: Cambridge University Press). This book investigates an important source of the EU's recent legitimacy problems. It shows how European integration is debated in mass media, and how this affects democratic inclusiveness.

Leconte, C. (2010) *Understanding Euroscepticism* (Basingstoke: Palgrave Macmillan). This book examines the process of European integration, and how different actors can engage with the process and oppose it.

Sanders, D., Magalhaes, P., and Toka, G. (eds) (2012) *Citizens and the European Polity: Mass Attitudes towards the European and National Politics* (Oxford: Oxford University Press). This book presents an overview of mass attitudes in the EU from the 1970s.

Access the online resources to take your learning and understanding further, including extra multiple-choice questions with instant feedback, web links, answer guidance to end-of-chapter questions, and updates on new developments in EU politics.

www.oup.com/he/cini-borragan7e

PART 4
Policies and Policy-making

16

Policy-making in the European Union

Edward Best

Reader's Guide

This chapter provides an overview of how policy is made in the European Union (EU), focusing on the main procedures involved and the varying roles of the EU institutions. It begins by describing the range of powers that have been given to the EU by the member states in different policy areas, and the multiple modes of governance that are involved. The concept of the policy cycle is used as a framework to explain the stages in EU law-making. The ordinary legislative procedure is presented in some detail, and a case study illustrates the whole cycle from problem definition to implementation. The roles of the institutions in other kinds of policy process are then presented. Policy coordination is explained, with particular attention to economic governance and the European Semester. Finally, the chapter looks at external relations and the common foreign and security policy.

16.1 Introduction

Policy-making in the European Union (EU) works in many different ways. There is no single 'Union method' today that we can neatly identify and contrast with other forms of policy-making, either within or between countries. According to the policy area concerned, the EU has different powers, the EU institutions follow different procedures, and the outcome ranges from the harmonization of national laws to the financing of student exchanges. The key question is how far the member states have chosen to limit their own autonomy in policy-making in order to benefit from collective action, and to delegate powers to common bodies to help make the system work. At one end of the spectrum, member states have agreed to act as the EU or not at all. At the other end, the EU only supports or coordinates what member states do. This chapter compares the different kinds of policy-making in the EU in this light. How far have the EU member states agreed in each case to limit their own powers and discretion? How do the EU institutions and member states work together in the different policy areas according to the kind of competence that the EU has been given?

16.2 EU competences and modes of governance

The Treaty on the Functioning of the European Union (TFEU) lists the categories of EU **competences**—that is, the powers that have been given to the EU—and indicates the policy areas in which these apply (see Table 16.1). In the case of 'exclusive' competences, autonomous action has been renounced completely and irreversibly: member states act together or not at all. Member states cannot conclude bilateral trade agreements with a non-EU country, for example, even if there is no agreement in place between the EU and that country. When decisions are taken on monetary policy for the euro area, moreover, it is the independent European Central Bank that decides.

By contrast, where competence is 'shared', member states agree that the EU may act to help achieve common objectives. This action may take the form of supranational law, including harmonization of national laws and regulations. However, EU decisions to act are not automatic; they have to be justified in terms of **subsidiarity** (the principle that the EU should only act where this is necessary, either because of the nature of the issue or because the objectives can be better achieved at the level of the EU than by the member states) and must be negotiated among the EU institutions before they affect the freedom to act of the member states. For example, different national policies in transport continued to operate until common measures were taken at EU level. While member states are required to stand back so long as the EU is acting, moreover, they would recover their freedom of action were the EU to cease exercising competence. The treaty states that this principle, known as 'pre-emption' does not apply, however, in the areas of research, technological development, space, development cooperation, and humanitarian assistance. In these policy areas the fact that the EU is acting does not prevent member states from doing so. These areas are often referred to as 'parallel competences'.

In the case of 'supporting, coordinating, and supplementary' competences, the EU only provides finance or 'incentive measures' to support what member states do. In these cases, member states retain full legislative competence, and the harmonization of national laws and regulations is explicitly excluded. For example, the EU cannot adopt measures that would oblige member states to shape their national cultural policy in any particular way.

Finally, 'policy coordination' means that the EU provides the arrangements by which member states coordinate their national policies around common objectives and guidelines, for example, in employment policy.

The operation of the common foreign and security policy is indicated separately in the TEU (see Chapter 19).

Starting with the EU's formal competences does not prevent us from looking at how things work in other terms. In the first place, it should be borne in mind that, in this untidy EU system, the same procedures and even the same instruments can be used for quite different purposes.

EU laws have different degrees of precision. At one extreme, a law may create a rule that is directly applicable (it comes into force in all member states without any action on the part of member states), uniform (it must be applied in the same way in all member states), and exhaustive (it covers all possible aspects of the matter concerned). For example, an EU regulation may explicitly lay down 'identical rules'

Table 16.1 EU competences category

	Definition	Areas of application
Exclusive competences	Only the EU may legislate and adopt legally binding acts.	• customs union • common commercial policy • competition (for internal market) • monetary policy (euro area) • protection of marine biological resources • international agreements
Shared competences	Member states shall exercise their competence to the extent that the Union is not exercising its competence. * Member states may exercise their competences even if the EU is acting.	• internal market • social policy • economic, social, and territorial cohesion • agriculture and fisheries • environment • consumer protection • transport • trans-European networks • energy • area of freedom, security, and justice • common safety concerns in public health • research * • technological development * • space * • development policy * • humanitarian aid *
Supporting, coordinating, or supplementary competences	The Union may act without superseding member states' competences. Harmonization of national laws and regulations is excluded.	• protection and improvement of human health • industry • culture • tourism • education, vocational training, youth, and sport • civil protection • administrative cooperation
Policy coordination		• economic policy • employment policy • some social policy

for, say, determining the characteristics of EU fishing vessels in order to 'unify conditions' for fishing under the Common Fisheries Policy. However, EU law may also take the form of a framework law, typically in the form of a directive, which allows some diversity in the national measures that are adopted to ensure the effectiveness of the specific results that are legally binding. Harmonization is often limited to 'essential requirements' of health and safety with which manufacturers must comply by adhering to some recognized standard, while other product characteristics are subject to **mutual recognition** of national norms.

Some instruments that we refer to as 'laws' (because it is a legal requirement to put them into effect) do not create specific duties that can be enforced by courts. A regulation may serve as the legal basis for EU financing of common programmes in areas in which the EU does not have the power to harmonize member states' laws or regulations (for example the '**Erasmus+**' regulation in the area of education). Or it may shape a general legislative framework for other methods, such as policy coordination, that do not employ legally binding instruments for their operation.

There have been multiple proposals for classifying EU policy-making in terms of different modes of governance. Wallace and Reh (2020) identify five 'policy modes': the classical Community method, the EU regulatory mode, the EU distributional mode, policy coordination, and intensive transgovernmentalism. Others categorize different modes as being hierarchical as compared to comprising bargaining or learning; as having different levels of discretion and obligation; or as reflecting different combinations of binding or non-binding legal instruments with rigid or flexible implementation (see Treib et al., 2007). It is not always possible to make simple distinctions between '**hard law**', defined as legal obligations that can be enforced by courts, and '**soft law**', in the sense of measures such as guidelines that are purely indicative. It may now be more appropriate to think of a matrix with different combinations of hardness and softness with respect to the two dimensions of 'obligation' and 'enforcement' (Terpan, 2015). This chapter will use many of these concepts to describe policy-making in the different spheres.

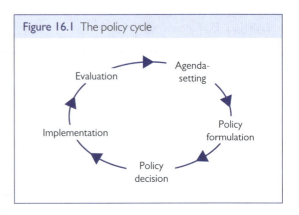

Figure 16.1 The policy cycle

be the final stage and/or the beginning of a new cycle.

The centrepiece of the *agenda-setting* process when it comes to legislation is the Commission Work Programme (CWP). The Commission has the last word in deciding whether or not to present a proposal. However, its programme is based on prior consultation with the other institutions, as well as on the political priorities of the Commission itself. Since the 2016 Interinstitutional Agreement on Better Law-Making (IIABL), an agreement involving the European Parliament (EP), the Council, and the Commission, the annual cycle is as follows: first, the Commission President gives the State of the Union speech in the EP in mid-September and presents to the President of the EP and the Council Presidency a Letter of Intent for the following year. Next, the CWP is presented in the EP in late October. The three institutions then agree on a Joint Declaration of legislative priorities for the following year.

Policy formulation, in the context of EU law, mainly refers to the elaboration of proposals for legislative acts. This is almost always in the hands of the European Commission as part of that institution's 'right of initiative'.

Decision in this context means the adoption of basic rules affecting a particular policy area. These are '**legislative acts**' adopted on the basis of treaty articles by the Council and the EP, usually acting jointly under the '**ordinary legislative procedure**'. Legislative acts may take the form of regulations that are directly applicable in all member states following publication; directives that have to be transposed by a deadline into national laws and regulations; or decisions that are used for individual purposes and for specific cases.

Implementation of EU policies has to be seen on (at least) two levels and involves several forms of interaction between the European Commission and the

> ## KEY POINTS
>
> - The EU only has powers that have been given to it by the member states.
> - The EU's powers vary greatly: at one extreme, only the EU can act; at the other, the EU only supports or coordinates what member states do.
> - The different forms of EU policy-making can also be analysed in terms of the modes of governance that are involved.

16.3 The policy cycle and EU law

The 'policy cycle' is a useful framework for understanding how EU law-making works. Five stages are often identified in a typical public policy cycle (see Figure 16.1 and Box 16.1).

- *agenda-setting*: identifying a problem and agreeing to do something to address it;
- *policy formulation*: defining the problem and its drivers, assessing options and elaborating specific proposals;
- *decision*: adopting the final decision;
- *implementation*: putting the decision into effect;
- *evaluation*: reviewing actual outcomes and identifying possible modifications, which may

member states. National authorities are primarily responsible for doing what is necessary to make things work through practical implementation in terms of resources, surveillance, and enforcement, as well as by means of the **transposition** of EU directives into national laws where appropriate. The task of the Commission is to assist member states and stakeholders. It is only as a last resort that the Commission will initiate infringement proceedings before the Court of Justice, if it concludes that a member state is not applying or enforcing legal obligations, for example by failing to notify measures incorporating directives into national law, or transposing directives incompletely or incorrectly. That said, EU policies often require 'uniform conditions' of application across the EU in order to be effective: for example, they may require EU-wide marketing authorizations for food additives; financing decisions for EU research programmes; or common data-reporting formats for accidents in the offshore oil and gas industry. In such cases, the Commission is empowered in an individual legislative act to adopt binding decisions which apply the basic rules laid down in the legislative act (which is therefore often referred to as the 'basic act'). Since the Lisbon Treaty came into force, these decisions of the Commission are known as '**implementing acts**'. These acts also take the form of regulations, directives, or decisions. The Commission must first consult the member states in what are known as '**comitology** committees'. These committees (around 320 active in early 2021) are created by the 'EU legislator' (that is, the institutions that adopt an EU legislative act, which usually means the Parliament and Council acting jointly, and sometimes only the Council) in the basic act and are chaired by the Commission. Implementing acts have no impact on the basic act itself, unlike 'delegated acts' (see Box 16.2; see also Chapter 10).

The importance of the *evaluation* of EU policies has been increasingly recognized across the EU institutions and has acquired ever greater importance in the Commission's Better Regulation agenda, which seeks to ensure that new initiatives are prepared on the basis of the best evidence available and with ample stakeholder consultation, and that existing rules are reviewed to check whether they are still 'fit for purpose'. In late 2017, the Commission could indeed assert that 'its approach . . . is based on the "evaluate first principle". Before revising legislation or introducing new legislation the Commission has made a commitment to evaluate what already exists to identify the potential for simplification and cost reduction' (European Commission, 2017b: 8).

KEY POINTS

- There are five stages in a typical policy cycle.
- Agenda-setting, policy formulation, and decision involve the proposal, elaboration, and adoption of legislation.
- Implementation and evaluation entail putting the legislation into effect as well as assessing it.

16.4 Legislative procedures

This section explains how 'legislative acts' are adopted in the EU.

16.4.1 The Commission's proposal

The first stage in the adoption of legislative acts is the elaboration of a proposal by the European Commission. Stakeholder consultation is carried out in various ways, including through Commission expert groups, public online consultations, and targeted stakeholder meetings. These feed into the **impact assessment** that must be carried out in most cases. The Commission has to explain why there is a problem that requires an intervention; why this is a problem that the EU should address, as compared to member states or international bodies (subsidiarity); what objectives the Commission hopes to achieve; which options are available to pursue those objectives, in terms of both forms of action and policy mixes; the impact that those options can be expected to have, particularly in economic, social, and environmental terms; how those options compare and which option is recommended; and how monitoring and evaluation is to be assured. The final version of the proposal is adopted by the College of Commissioners after a final round of interservice consultation (see also Chapter 10).

16.4.2 Examination of the proposal in Council and Parliament

The second stage in the adoption of a legislative act is the examination of the proposal in parallel within each of the EU's two co-legislators: the EU Council and the European Parliament.

Inside the Council, files are dealt with in one of the 150 or so Working Parties. Working Parties are mostly chaired by the rotating presidency of the Council (see Chapter 11), and bring together representatives of the member states (usually the attachés posted in

Brussels and specialists who come in from the home governments as required) for technical discussion of the proposal. The Commission is represented by the lead department responsible for the file. The Working Party reports to the respective part of the Committee of Permanent Representatives (Coreper), which is made up of the top national officials based in Brussels, who prepare Council decisions.

Inside the European Parliament, one of the 20 standing committees is usually recognized as the 'committee responsible' for the file. Other committees may be invited to give an opinion on the text. Committees may also be 'associated', which means they should agree on a division of labour over different parts of the proposal that come under their respective competences. In some cases, committees act jointly. Within the committee, the file is given to one of the political groups (each committee is composed of members from each political group in the same proportions as the whole, each set of group members being led by a Coordinator) (see Chapter 12). That group nominates the rapporteur (the MEP responsible for the committee Report) for that file. The other groups nominate shadow rapporteurs.

16.4.3 Other actors

All legislative initiatives must be submitted to the national parliaments at the same time as to the Council and the EP for 'subsidiarity control'. Within eight weeks a national chamber may send a 'reasoned opinion' to the Commission if it believes the proposal does not respect the principle of subsidiarity—in other words, they consider that this matter does not need to be dealt with at EU level. If one third of the total votes (two per country) are against the initiative, a 'yellow card' of warning is held to have been issued, and the Commission must review its proposal.

The two Advisory Bodies, the European Economic and Social Committee (EESC) and the European Committee of the Regions (CoR), are also usually consulted, though their opinions are not binding.

16.4.4 Decision by the legislator

The way in which decisions are taken depends on which kind of legislative procedure is specified in the treaty article that is being used as the legal basis. In most cases the treaty now states that the 'ordinary

legislative procedure', under which the Council and the EP have to agree, should be used. This procedure was first introduced by the Maastricht Treaty in 1993 and has now become the dominant method for adopting EU legislation. It was followed in 434 of the 494 legislative acts that were published between July 2014 and June 2020.

The other 'special legislative procedures' are set out in the treaty. The main procedure of this type, known as 'the consultation procedure', reflects the way in which legislative decisions were taken when the Community was set up—the original 'Community method'. The Council must request, and wait for, an Opinion from the EP before acting, but that Opinion is not binding. In most cases, the Council must act by unanimity. This procedure is mainly used in the area of tax, and in a few other areas of high sensitivity such as family law with cross-border implications or consular protection of EU citizens in third countries. In a very few cases the Council must request the EP's 'consent' before it can adopt a legislative act. This procedure, usually required for ratification of international agreements, was used for the EU's seven-year 'multiannual financial framework' in 2020 and the creation of the European Public Prosecutor's Office in 2017. The annual budget is approved using an ad hoc special legislative procedure.

16.4.5 The ordinary legislative procedure

The ordinary legislative procedure can be summed up through the following twin principles: the Council acts by qualified majority (see Box 16.3), and the EP and the Council have to agree. There are up to three readings of legislation in this procedure, meaning that there are four successive moments at which the two institutions can come to an agreement.

'First reading agreements' are reached when the EP and the Council find a compromise through informal negotiations (trilogues) (see Box 16.4) on the basis of the Commission's proposal. The mandate on the Council side may be given by Coreper to the (Council) Presidency or take the form of a General Approach endorsed by ministers. The Council is normally represented by the Chair of Coreper, supported by the Chair of the Working Party and officials from the Council Secretariat. The EP team is under the authority of the relevant Committee Chair, who may be represented

Table 16.2 Trilogues: how compromises are reached

Commission Proposal doc. 5899/13	EP Amendments (first reading)	Council's General Approach doc. 17004/13	Comments
	AMD 65 Article 3—para 6		
6. The Commission shall evaluate the national policy frameworks and ensure that there is coherence at EU level. It shall forward to the European Parliament the report on the evaluation on the national policy frameworks within one year from the reception of the national policy frameworks.	6. The Commission shall evaluate the national policy frameworks, *especially in terms of their efficacy for the achievement of the national targets referred to in paragraph 1*, and ensure that there is coherence at **Union** level. It shall forward to the European Parliament the report on the evaluation on the national policy frameworks within one year from **receipt** of the national policy frameworks.	6. The Commission shall *assist Member States through the reporting on* the national policy frameworks *with a view to assess their* coherence *and in the cooperation process set out in paragraph 2*.	*Presidency compromise proposal acceptable to EP:* 6. The Commission shall assist Member States in the reporting on the national policy frameworks by means of guidelines referred to in Article 10(3), assess their coherence at EU level and assist Member States in the cooperation process set out in paragraph 2.

Source: Report from General Secretariat of the Council to Permanent Representatives Committee (Part 1), Proposal for a Directive of the European Parliament and of the Council on the deployment of alternative fuels infrastructure, Preparation for the third informal trilogue. Council document 6649/14 of 25 February 2014.

 BOX 16.1   CASE STUDY: THE ALTERNATIVE FUELS INFRASTRUCTURE DIRECTIVE

The EU's 2014 Directive on the Deployment of Alternative Fuels Infrastructure (European Parliament and Council, 2014a) illustrates the way in which the EU's ordinary legislative procedure operates, relating the steps involved in the actual practice of policy-making to the stages in the classic policy cycle. The case goes round the whole cycle from problem definition in 2011, through adoption of the directive in 2014 and assessment of its implementation, to evaluation in 2019 and a revision starting in 2021.

The problem

The strategic goals of reducing Europe's dependence on imported oil and cutting carbon emissions in transport have been proclaimed since 2010. The increased use of vehicles powered by 'alternative fuels' (especially electricity, hydrogen, Compressed Natural Gas (CNG), and Liquified Natural Gas (LNG)) is a specific objective intended to contribute to that goal. One obstacle, however, has been identified as low consumer confidence in the distance range of 'green vehicles' as

well as in the availability and technical compatibility of recharging facilities. The result is a 'chicken-and-egg' problem: 'alternative fuel infrastructure is not built as there is an insufficient number of vehicles and vessels; the manufacturing industry does not produce them at competitive prices as there is insufficient consumer demand; and consumers in consequence do not purchase them' (European Commission, 2013). How could EU action help to break this deadlock?

Agenda setting

In line with the **Europe 2020** strategy for jobs and smart, sustainable, and inclusive growth adopted by the European Council, the Commission in March 2011 presented a new White Paper on Transport. The list of specific initiatives within that document included a sustainable alternative fuels strategy comprising the appropriate infrastructure and guidelines and standards for refuelling infrastructures. The Commission had also submitted a separate Communication on clean and energy-efficient vehicles. These plans were generally endorsed in EU

(continued)

BOX 16.1 CASE STUDY: THE ALTERNATIVE FUELS INFRASTRUCTURE DIRECTIVE   *(continued)*

Council Conclusions and a Resolution of the European Parliament.

Policy formulation

Within the Commission the process was led by DG MOVE (Transport and Mobility), which chaired an inter-service group together with the Commission's Secretariat-General. Expert Groups were consulted and online consultation also took place. The Commission's impact assessment identified three main policy options alongside the baseline scenario of 'no change': recommendations setting out only basic criteria and indicative targets in all cases; basic criteria plus binding targets for electricity and LNG for waterborne transport and indicative targets for the rest; and basic criteria plus binding targets for all fuels. The Commission preferred the third option mainly on the grounds that only binding targets would provide the kind of credible commitment that was required for consumers and producers to change their behaviour. The Commission adopted its legislative proposal on 24 January 2013. It would mean that each member state would have to adopt a national policy framework (NPF) through which it would guarantee minimum levels of coverage for all fuels by the end of 2020.

National parliaments received the draft and the EU advisory bodies were consulted.

Policy decision

In the EP the file was sent to the Committee on Transport and Tourism (TRAN) as the committee responsible. The Committee on Industry, Research and Energy (ITRE) gave an opinion. Within TRAN, the file went to the European People's Party (EPP) Group, the centre-right political group in Parliament. On 26 November 2013, TRAN voted on the report and on the decision to enter into negotiations ahead of the first reading.

Meanwhile, in the Council the file went to the Working Party on Transport, Intermodal Questions and Networks. The Council Presidency submitted a compromise text to Coreper on 27 November 2013. The Council endorsed an amended version as a General Approach on 5 December 2013.

Four trilogues, as well as technical meetings, took place. A provisional agreement was reached on 26 March. This was confirmed in Coreper and in TRAN, adopted by the EP and the Council, and signed on 22 October 2014.

The result was a typical compromise package of trade-offs between dates, figures, review clauses, and supporting measures, facilitated by creative drafting. In the case of electricity, the Commission's proposal was that each member state would have to assure a specified minimum number of

recharging points by the end of 2020, of which 10 per cent would have to be publicly accessible. The EP considered that only the publicly accessible recharging points should be subject to EU law, and also reduced the minimum numbers of these points that would be mandatory. The Council preferred only to stipulate 'an appropriate number' of recharging points (in other words, each member state would decide what was required), and to extend the deadline to the end of 2030. The final compromise followed the Council in referring to an 'appropriate number' but the deadline was kept as 2020. The numbers included in the national plans would be justified by each member state with regard to the number of electric vehicles estimated (by each member state) to be registered by the end of 2020, as well as in best practices and recommendations issued by the Commission. The level of attainment of these targets by the member states would be subject to evaluation by the Commission, which would submit a report on application of the directive to the EP and Council by November 2020. If progress was insufficient, the Commission could submit a proposal to amend the directive, taking into account the development of the market in order to ensure that an additional number of recharging points accessible to the public would be put in place in each member state by 2025. In other words, the proposal had been significantly watered down by the Council, but the directive held out the possibility of a process of review and an eventual proposal which was more stringent.

The excerpt in Table 16.2 from the four-column document used in the third trilogue illustrates how compromises are drafted. The Commission's ambition to exercise influence over the national plans is strengthened by the EP, while the reluctance of a majority of member states to be subjected to Commission pressure leads to a rather weak compromise.

Implementation

The Commission promoted various measures to assist in the implementation of the directive. The Commission provided templates for national plans and a study with 'good practice examples', set up a European Alternative Fuels Observatory, and created a Sustainable Transport Forum (STF) with representatives of member states, the transport sector, and civil society. Yet the response by the member states was less than hoped for. On 8 November 2017 the Commission presented its report. It noted that 'greater efforts' were required and that the level of ambition varied significantly.

In addition to some infringement proceedings, the Commission now presented an Action Plan to assist member states through EU financing support and capacity-building. This was part of a new Clean Mobility Package including other measures to address the infrastructure problem from different angles,

(continued)

BOX 16.1 CASE STUDY: THE ALTERNATIVE FUELS INFRASTRUCTURE DIRECTIVE *(continued)*

including new requirements for public procurement of clean vehicles, and proposed new CO_2 emission performance standards for new passenger cars and light commercial vehicles.

Evaluation and back to agenda setting

In parallel with the assessment of national implementation, the Commission launched a formal evaluation of the directive itself in early 2019, including a public consultation, as well as a survey of stakeholders through the Sustainable Transport Forum. Meanwhile, in October 2018, the European Parliament had adopted a resolution calling on the Commission to accelerate revision of the directive, and an informal meeting of transport and environment ministers under the Austrian Presidency expressed support for a review.

The first lap round the legislative policy cycle was complete and the second had begun. Many of the problem drivers and possible responses identified in the 2020 inception impact assessment were similar to those of 2012. However, the policy context had changed significantly. Notably, the 2019 regulation on CO_2 emission performance standards obliged carmakers to reduce the average emissions from new cars and vans, which meant increasing the share of zero- and low-emission vehicles according to benchmarks for 2020, 2021, and 2025. The effect was to increase not only the offer of electric vehicles but also pressure from carmakers for measures to ensure that there would be adequate infrastructure to support them, including binding targets for member states.

In 2019 the new Commission made the issue a legislative priority within the European Green Deal. The proposed revision was included in the dialogue with the EP and the Council in 2020, and formally announced in the Commission Work Programme for 2021. A Proposal to replace the Directive by a new Regulation was presented on 14 July 2021.

 BOX 16.2 KEY DEBATES: THE TROUBLED INTRODUCTION OF DELEGATED ACTS

Basic rules may need to be updated in the light of scientific and technical progress, adapted to changes in the market or to new policy preferences. General rules may need to be followed by rules for specific product groups. In such cases, in order to avoid lengthy legislative procedures, the EU legislator (normally the Council and the Parliament) may choose to empower the Commission to adopt binding acts that 'supplement or amend' 'non-essential elements' of the basic legislative act. Since the Lisbon Treaty came into force, these are known as '**delegated acts**', in contrast to the 'implementing acts' discussed earlier in this chapter.

There were two main reasons for splitting the pre-Lisbon world of comitology into these two new categories. First, where the Commission is asked to make minor changes to the law, it should be accountable to the actors responsible for adopting the law, namely the EP and Council, rather than to the actors responsible for implementing it, namely the member states. Second, this new procedure would make it possible to recognize the EP as a co-legislator exercising oversight of the Commission's executive rule-making, while maintaining the system of member state control over the Commission for implementing acts.

The Commission thus drafts, consults and adopts an act, and then notifies the Parliament and the Council. The latter institutions have a deadline, normally two months extendable by another two months, during which they can 'object to'—that is, veto—an individual delegated act. As of February 2021, the Council had objected six times and the EP ten times using this procedure. For example, the EP has objected over the allowable levels of sugar in baby food, over the continued exemption for cadmium in display and lighting applications, and over the identification of high-risk third countries with regard to money laundering and terrorist financing. In principle, either Parliament or Council can also cancel the whole procedure and 'revoke' the delegation of powers to the Commission in a particular field. This had not happened as of early 2021.

Introducing this new system was not straightforward. Two main issues of contention emerged. One concerned 'delineation': whether there was any overlap between delegated and implementing acts, and any discretion for the EU legislator in choosing which kind of act to use in particular cases. The Commission argued that there was not, while the Council thought there was. After two rulings by the Court of Justice (*Biocides* in 2014 and *Visa* in 2015), the institutions have now agreed in the new Common Understanding attached to the 2016 IIABL that 'It is the competence of the legislator to decide whether and to what extent to use delegated or implementing acts, within the limits of the Treaties'. In many cases the choice will be clearly dictated by what the treaty articles say, but in some cases there is room for discretion. The other issue was how the Commission would carry out consultations before adopting a delegated act. The first Common Understanding only committed the Commission to 'carry out appropriate consultations during its preparatory work, including at expert level'. Commission expert groups cannot exert control over the Commission and do not vote on drafts, in contrast to

(continued)

BOX 16.2 KEY DEBATES: THE TROUBLED INTRODUCTION OF DELEGATED ACTS   *(continued)*

'comitology committees'. The Council became concerned that there were not sufficient guarantees that all member states' experts would be systematically consulted before delegated acts are adopted that they will have to implement or transpose. The new Common Understanding clearly states that the Commission 'will consult experts designated by each Member State in the preparation of draft delegated acts'. Moreover, both Council and EP may be represented by their secretariats in Commission expert groups that prepare delegated acts. A basic interinstitutional agreement on non-binding criteria was reached in 2019. However, the extent to which the Commission may be empowered to adopt delegated acts continues to be one of the main sources of discussion in negotiations over new EU legislation.

 BOX 16.3   BACKGROUND: QUALIFIED MAJORITY VOTING

The internal market and the core policies that complement it require some binding rules that are applied uniformly if there is to be fair competition and legal certainty. Until the early 1980s progress was held back by the requirement for unanimity in the Council. The introduction of qualified majority voting (QMV) in these areas made it possible to 'complete the internal market' in terms of the basic legislative framework by the end of 1992.

Unanimity is still required to change the treaties and in most of the 'special legislative procedures', as well as the common foreign and security policy. Simple majority continues to be used for procedural purposes but is not used for the adoption of general norms. Since the Lisbon Treaty came into force, however, QMV is the default setting. Since 1 November 2014, a qualified majority has required satisfaction of two criteria: 55 per cent of the member states ('at least 15', which means 15 out of 27 after Brexit) as well as 65 per cent of the total population of the EU. Conversely, a 'blocking minority' can be formed by either 45 per cent of the member states or at least 35 per cent of the population (representing at least four member states).

The ethos of Council decision-making, however, remains consensus-building. The implicit threat of a vote is meant to encourage compromise. As many national concerns as reasonably possible should be accommodated in order to come up with a text that almost all delegations can live with. In most cases, the pressure of qualified majority is felt mainly during the earlier stages of negotiation, including indicative votes which are not usually made public. Once the compromise is agreed, the final result is very often registered as unanimous.

Member states do record negative votes or abstentions in some 20–25 per cent of cases, and indeed have come to do so more often since around 2009. These generally reflect statements of principle or required responses to a domestic mandate. However, very sensitive decisions are now sometimes taken in a majority vote that reflects deep splits among the member states.

by a Vice-Chair, but the negotiations are led by the rapporteur, who is accompanied by the shadow rapporteurs, and supported by officials from the EP Secretariat, policy advisors from the political groups, and assistants. The process is supported by a four-column document at first reading. The first column contains the Commission's proposal, the second and third columns normally show the EP and Council's respective mandates, while the fourth column is gradually filled with comments, compromise proposals, and eventually the complete agreement. The text is voted upon by the EP as its 'position'. This is approved by the Council, and the act can then be adopted and signed. Around 90 per cent of concluded files end here.

'Early second readings' account for most of the rest of the files that are concluded under the ordinary legislative procedure. In these cases, the compromise is reached after the Parliament's first reading. It is adopted as the Council's 'position' and approved by the Parliament without change.

'Second readings' mean that the Council's position at first reading had not been pre-agreed with Parliament. Subject to time limits of three, extendable to four months, the Parliament may adopt amendments to the Council's position that are agreed in advance and approved by the Council. Between July 2014 and June 2019, only four out of a total 401 files were concluded at this stage.

'Third readings' represent the last chance to agree. A 'conciliation committee' is convened between Council and Parliament delegations with short deadlines to agree on a 'Joint Text'. This then has to be ratified by the two institutions. There was no case of conciliation between July 2014 and June 2020.

BOX 16.4   KEY DEBATES: TRILOGUES AND TRANSPARENCY

Most EU legislative acts are agreed between representatives of the EU institutions in informal meetings known as 'trilogues'. The documents supporting these meetings are not made public while negotiations are taking place. This has led to debate as to whether this practice satisfies norms of transparency, participation and accountability, especially at first reading.

Critics argue that the process is opaque and secretive. Why should citizens and other stakeholders not have the right to know what is going on, and perhaps be able to offer their input as positions change? Moreover, it does not seem to be a very 'parliamentary' way of acting. Where is the public deliberation and open confrontation of ideas? Discussions seem to take place between a small number of people behind closed doors, while the plenary does no more than formally ratify the provisional agreement by a single vote.

Others, in contrast, consider that a reasonable balance has now been found. They argue that such meetings represent the only efficient way to manage negotiations between a 705-member Parliament and 27 member states. The arrangements have now been semi-formalized. Negotiations cannot take place without formal mandates that can be identified by citizens, and the teams are accountable to their political principals throughout the process. The Council Presidency reports back to the member states through Coreper after each meeting and the mandate

may be changed; likewise, the EP team reports back to the political groups in the committee.

The European Ombudsman conducted an inquiry in this respect in 2016. She emphasized the importance of proactively providing full information before and after the negotiations. However, she also identified the need: 'to balance the interest in having a transparent process with the legitimate need to ensure a privileged negotiating space. . . . It is arguable that the interest in well-functioning Trilogue negotiations temporarily outweighs the interest in transparency for as long as the Trilogue negotiations are ongoing' (European Ombudsman, 2016: paras 30, 54).

The matter was also dealt with by the Court of Justice of the EU (General Court) in its 2018 *De Capitani* ruling concerning the right of access to the compromise proposals contained in the fourth column of trilogue tables while negotiations were still ongoing. The Court ruled that there can be 'no general presumption of non-disclosure' in relation to the four-column documents. If someone requests access to a trilogue table, it will now usually be granted. However, the institutions may refuse access 'in duly justified cases'. The Court also recognized the need for 'a free exchange of views' in preparatory meetings before compromise texts are inserted into the table. The ruling only concerned access to the documents drawn up in trilogues (CJEU, 2018: paras 112, 106).

16.5 Policy coordination and economic governance

The EU's economic and monetary union has developed on the basis of an unstable combination of different modes of governance. Monetary policy is an exclusive competence of the EU for the euro area and decisions are taken by an independent European Central Bank. Economic policy, on the other hand, remains a matter

of national legislative competence, even for countries in the euro area. EU policy-making in matters of 'economic governance' mainly involves a set of EU frameworks for shaping national policies, usually referred to as forms of 'policy coordination' (see Chapter 22).

Since the Maastricht Treaty, the EU member states have agreed on some common goals and guidelines in economic policy and submit their programmes and their performance to review at the EU level. This has evolved on two dimensions.

One process aims to prevent the negative consequences for growth and stability across the EU that can be caused by fiscal imbalances such as excessive deficits and levels of public debt, and **macro-economic imbalances** such as large current account deficits and housing bubbles. The first goal has been to ensure sound public finances and price stability. This approach is embodied in the Stability and Growth Pact (SGP), originally adopted in 1997, which provides a set of rules for the coordination of national fiscal policies in the EU. Each country in the euro area must submit a 'stability programme'. The others submit a 'convergence programme'. To prevent excessive deficits, the Council may adopt recommendations to the member state concerned, which are not legally binding. However, member states are in theory subject to financial penalties if they persist in failing to put into practice Council decisions adopted in the 'corrective' stage. The SGP was reinforced in 2011 and 2013. For a euro area member state, this has meant that failure to control deficits could result in the imposition of sanctions in the form of a fine of 0.2 per cent of GDP. Euro area countries also became obliged to submit their draft budgetary plans for comment by the Commission. A new procedure was also added to cover macroeconomic imbalances, since the origins of the global financial crisis of 2007–08 had been more than fiscal in nature. Under this Macroeconomic Imbalance Procedure (MIP) member states would be subject to surveillance using a 'scoreboard' of indicators concerning possible internal imbalances (including private indebtedness and housing markets) as well as external imbalances. Euro area countries would be subject to possible sanctions here as well.

The other dimension of economic policy coordination aimed to achieve more positive results through cooperation, peer review, and mutual learning. The Europe 2020 strategy was adopted by the European Council in 2010. It defined EU targets concerning employment, research and development, climate change and energy, education, and poverty and social exclusion. This was explicitly referred to as a 'reference framework' against which member states set their own national targets. Each country submits a 'national reform programme' every year.

The two dimensions were brought together in an annual cycle known as the 'European Semester'.

The roles of the EU institutions, the instruments used, and the modalities of obligation and enforcement, are quite different from those in the policy cycle described above. The leading role in policy coordination is that of the Council, exercising its policy-making and coordinating functions as laid down in the treaties. The Commission is the main actor responsible for analysis, coordination, and assessment. The policy coordination cycle starts in November. The Annual Sustainable Growth Survey outlines what the Commission sees as the most pressing economic and social priorities, on which the EU and its member states need to focus their attention. The Alert Mechanism Report identifies member states that require In-Depth Reviews to assess whether they are affected by macroeconomic imbalances and are in need of policy action. At the same time, the Commission gives its comments on the Draft Budgetary Plans submitted by each euro area member state. Member states submit

their plans and programmes for assessment by the Commission and by committees in the Council framework. The Commission submits its own recommendations as the basis for the Council's final recommendations. The Council adopts Country-Specific Recommendations addressed to each member state each year and may adopt measures to enforce its recommendations. The European Council must endorse first the priorities in March, and then the draft recommendations in June.

This has been an area of experimentation in EU governance, combining elements of hard and soft law. By 2020, however, the accumulation of threads in the annual cycle, and the multiplicity of rules and indicators, had produced a process that was highly complex and of questionable effectiveness.

The supposedly 'hard' elements of the SGP had come to seem inappropriate and to lack credibility. In 2015 and 2016 the Commission showed flexibility for France (and Italy), provoking comments that the Commission looked as though it was treating big countries differently from small countries. In July 2016, the Council concluded that Spain and Portugal had failed to take effective action to correct their excessive deficits and were therefore subject to sanctions. Yet the Commission then proposed dropping the fines.

The 'soft' parts, on the other hand, were seen as largely ineffectual. In 2012–19, the proportion of recommendations on which member states made 'at least some progress' declined from 71 per cent in 2012 to 39.8 per cent in 2019, and the share with 'full/substantial progress' gradually decreased from 11 per cent in 2012 to about 1 per cent in 2019 (Angerer et al., 2020: 5).

In February 2020, the Commission opened a review of economic governance, although this was overtaken by the COVID-19 pandemic. Moreover, outside the European Semester as such, the Commission had also already been introducing new governance strategies to achieve EU goals in particular sectors where there is limited EU competence and disagreement among member states. This approach has been characterized as a distinct 'harder soft' mode of governance (HSG) (Schoenefeld and Knodt, 2020). In the case of the Energy Union, this resulted in the 2018 'Governance Regulation', designed 'to help ensure that the Union meets its energy policy goals, while fully respecting Member States' freedom to determine their energy mix' (European Parliament and Council, 2018: recital 12). The EU's goals, and its commitments under the Paris Agreement, were included as binding targets. However, depending on the specific legal bases, some national targets would be binding (greenhouse gas emission reductions and renewable energy) and others would not (energy efficiency, energy security, internal energy market, research). For these 'soft' targets, various 'hardening' elements were included. Drafts of the National Energy and Climate Plans (NECPs) would be made public in order to increase peer pressure and the involvement of civil society. The regulation obliges member states to take into account Commission recommendations and increases opportunities for 'blaming and shaming'. Mandatory templates and Commission review would exert pressure through concrete implementation practices (Knodt et al., 2020).

Second, various new steps of a broader nature had also already been taken to increase the incentives and pressures for member states to shape their national policies to EU policy objectives, and to implement national reforms in line with EU recommendations. This has not only concerned resources, with stronger links between the EU budget and the European Semester, as well as an increasingly important role for cohesion policy. It has also relied on the direct involvement of the Commission in assisting implementation on the ground through the structural reform support programme set up in 2017.

The EU's Recovery plan will see a deepening of these approaches. The EU's Recovery and Resilience Facility increases the incentives for national reforms, through its conditional offer of €312.5 billion in grants and €360 billion in loans. National plans must align with EU priorities (for example, at least 37 per cent of projects must support the Green Transition and 20 per cent the Digital Transformation) as well as address country-specific challenges in line with the recommendations made in the European Semester.

This, together with the momentous agreement in 2020 to engage in collective borrowing, may represent a critical juncture in the evolution of European economic governance, and the ways in which the EU tries to pursue European goals through national policies.

KEY POINTS

- In some areas EU member states retain legislative competence but agree to coordinate their national policies.

- EU member states are committed to respecting common objectives and guidelines in their economic policies to ensure sound finances, and to promote growth and jobs.

- There is an annual cycle known as the European Semester in which the plans and performance of member states are subject to review and recommendations at EU level.

16.6 Policy-making in external relations

Since the coming into force of the Lisbon Treaty, the EU's various forms of external relations, which range from trade and development cooperation to foreign and security policy, are all considered to fall under the umbrella of 'external action', and as such are obliged to respect the same basic objectives and values. Several steps have been taken to improve coherence and consistency between external relations policies, such as the introduction of the figure of a High Representative for Foreign Affairs and Security Policy who is now also a Vice-President in the Commission (hence the common abbreviation 'HR/VP') as well as head of the European External Action Service (EEAS). However, there continue to be important differences in the institutional roles, procedures, and instruments.

External action encompasses some areas of EU exclusive competence, notably trade and international agreements, and other areas of shared competence that are managed under EU law and often through legislative procedures set out in the Treaty on the Functioning of the European Union (TFEU) (see Chapter 17). Where the EU has exclusive competence, the Commission represents the EU on the basis of negotiating directives from the Council, but it is the Council that will conclude agreements on behalf of the EU. The Commission is also responsible for the practical management of international development cooperation and humanitarian aid. The Parliament has co-decision powers over framework decisions on trade policy and is to be kept informed about the state of negotiations in international agreements. It must also now give its 'consent' to the Council before agreements are concluded (see Box 16.5), as well as exercising indirect influence by virtue of its role as joint budget authority on development cooperation. In both trade and development policy the EP can play an important role in the EU's external relations, even if its formal powers appear more limited.

External action also covers the common foreign and security policy (CFSP), including the common security and defence policy. This area is based in the provisions of the Treaty on European Union (TEU) and does not operate through legislative acts. The main actors in these policy areas are the European Council, which defines the EU's 'strategic interests and objectives'; the Council, which takes the decisions necessary for defining and implementing the CFSP on that basis; and the High Representative. CFSP business is managed in the Council by

BOX 16.5   THE EU AND CUBA

On 1 November 2017, a Political Dialogue and Cooperation Agreement (PDCA) provisionally came into effect between the EU and Cuba. The Agreement includes chapters on political dialogue, cooperation, and sector policy dialogue as well as trade. This document was a turning point. From 1996 until 2016, EU–Cuba relations had been limited by a **common position** that made full cooperation with the EU conditional upon improvements in human rights and political freedom in Cuba. The EU had even imposed sanctions in 2003 in response to the arrest of 75 prominent dissidents.

The Agreement covers not only EU exclusive competences (such as trade) and shared competences, for which the European Commission would normally represent the EU and which could be adopted in the Council by qualified majority, but also the common foreign and security policy (CFSP), for which the High Representative is responsible. Since CFSP is a field in which unanimity is required for adoption of a Union act, a unanimous agreement was required before the Agreement could be signed. Moreover, this is a mixed agreement, which means it involves both EU and member state competences and has to be ratified in all EU countries.

The 1996 common position had been strongly supported by the conservative Spanish government, which favoured a policy of isolation. At the beginning of the Spanish Presidency in the first half of 2010, the socialist government proposed changing EU policy towards dialogue and even a bilateral agreement. Most countries did not favour changing the common position, however, while the European Parliament continued to be highly critical of Cuba's performance in human rights and political freedom. The EP's Sakharov prize was awarded to Cuban human rights activists in 2002, 2005, and again in October 2010. Yet, in a decision that also reflected the shift in leadership in external relations away from the rotating Council Presidency after the Lisbon Treaty, the Foreign Affairs Council in October 2010 asked the High Representative to explore possibilities on the way forward for relations with Cuba.

The High Representative held a first meeting with the Cuban Foreign Minister in February 2011. In spring 2011 the Cuban government released the last of the political prisoners sentenced in the 2003 crackdown that saw the rift with the EU. It approved economic reforms in late 2011 aimed at encouraging private enterprise and recognizing a right to private property. It also freed 2,500 prisoners in December 2011 in advance of the visit by Pope Benedict XVI planned for the following March. Meanwhile, 16 EU member states had signed bilateral statements, agreements, or memoranda of understanding with Cuba (and by 2017 that figure numbered 20).

In April 2013, the Commission submitted a Recommendation to the Council to authorize the Commission and the High Representative to open negotiations. By January 2014, the Council Working Party on Latin America and the Caribbean was able to endorse three texts: a Council Decision authorizing the Commission and the High Representative to open negotiations on provisions within the EU's competences; a 'Decision of the Representatives of the Governments of the Member States, meeting within the Council', authorizing the Commission to open negotiations on provisions within the competence of the member states; and 'negotiating directives'.

Negotiations took place between April 2014 and March 2016, at which point the agreement was initialled. The EU delegations were led by the European External Action Service (EEAS) and included representatives of the Commission. In September 2016, the Commission and the High Representative submitted a 'Joint Proposal' for a Council Decision on the signing and provisional application of the Agreement. The Council adopted the Decision on 6 December, and the agreement was signed on 16 December 2016 in Brussels.

The final stage at EU level was the 'consent' of the EP, where concern had continued to be expressed about human rights and political freedom. The file was examined in the Committee on Foreign Affairs (AFET). A draft recommendation for the EP's consent was accompanied by a separate draft report on the Council decision in which the political concerns were reaffirmed. These were adopted with some amendments in April. On 5 July 2017 the EP adopted the two resolutions in plenary by a large majority. The PDCA could now come into effect 'provisionally' for all areas under EU competence, which covered the bulk of the agreement. However, it would only apply after ratification by all member states for a detailed list of areas specified as coming under member state competence: anti-money laundering, consular protection, maritime transport, border security, international cooperation in taxation, and non-agricultural geographical indications.

the Political and Security Committee (PSC). The PSC is chaired by a representative of the High Representative, as is the Committee on the Civilian Aspects of Crisis Management and around half of the Council Working Parties dealing with external relations.

The Council adopts decisions by unanimity under the CFSP that are binding on the member states. However, they cannot be enforced by the EU. As a result, measures may be adopted in two parallel forms, CFSP and EU. For example, in May 2016, the Council adopted a 'Decision (CFSP)' concerning restrictive measures against North Korea, based on a proposal from the High Representative under the TEU. This decision is updated by Council implementing acts. In

May 2020, for example, an entry was added to the list of persons and entities subject to restrictive measures in a fresh UN Security Council resolution. The annex to the 2016 Decision was consequently amended in June 2020 by a 'Council Implementing Decision (CFSP)'. To ensure that the measures can be directly enforced, the same list was also adopted simultaneously in a parallel 'Council Implementing Regulation (EU)'.

KEY POINTS

- EU external action combines those areas in which the EU has competence and in which the Commission represents the EU, with the Common Foreign and Security Policy (CFSP).
- There are no legislative acts in CFSP.

- The Council adopts the basic decisions in CFSP and the leading role is played by the High Representative and the European External Action Service.

16.7 Conclusion

As it has expanded both its scope of action and its membership, the EU has come to use a variety of methods of policy-making. The original 'Community method' rested on a hierarchical mode of governance. Member states chose to limit the exercise of their sovereign rights in order to achieve certain common objectives, mainly to do with market integration. In some cases, such as trade, they would act together or not at all. In most cases they agreed eventually also to pool sovereignty through qualified majority voting in the Council. They accepted that some enforceable common rules were necessary for the sake of credibility and legal certainty, and that these should in principle be uniformly applied. And the member states saw that it would make it easier to manage the process over time if they were to delegate powers of agenda-setting and control to two supranational bodies, the European Commission and the Court of Justice. The European Parliament played a secondary role in interest aggregation and policy legitimation. Other forms of cooperation emerged among the same member states, notably in foreign policy and internal security, but these were kept outside the Community as such.

The Maastricht Treaty brought these more intergovernmental forms of cooperation, as well as deeper forms of supranational policy-making, together under the umbrella of the new Union.

In the internal market and related policies, there has been more pooling of sovereignty and a deepening of the role of EU institutions, resulting in what one may think of as a 'Community method 2.0'. Qualified majority voting in the Council has become the rule in most areas, and the European Parliament has acquired equal powers in most legislative procedures.

Around this core, policy-making has developed in opposing directions. On the one hand, there have been moves towards a reinforcement of policy-making at Union level. Monetary policy for the euro area is in the hands of an independent European Central Bank. Some EU agencies and supervisory authorities have also been given stronger powers in decision-making. On the other hand, most of the post-Maastricht innovations have neither followed the hierarchical mode of governance nor reinforced Union capacities for policy management. Economic policy remains a matter of national competence, subject to loose coordination under the European Semester. Likewise, foreign and security policy remains a matter of deep cooperation between national governments with no direct enforceability of CFSP measures.

This diversity may be seen as necessary in order to assure the stability of the European integration process. A hard core of uniform commitments around a common project (the 'internal market plus'), protected by a strong legal and institutional system, can hold things together. Around this, controlled flexibility in methods and in participation may be desirable in order to manage the pressures that arise when some member states face political or constitutional obstacles to joining new common arrangements.

Even this approach has come under strain, however, as the EU has faced successive crises. Acceptance of a hard and uniform core has been challenged not only by Brexit but by the deep splits that have emerged in the enlarged EU over key aspects of the internal market, as well as by the search for common responses to the migration crisis. Brexit may foster some fresh interest among the 27 to reinforce integration, and the changing international environment may also push the EU in the direction of deeper common approaches to key issues such as climate change and security. Although initial responses to the COVID-19 pandemic seemed to show an alarmingly low level of both agreement between EU governments and solidarity between EU peoples, by early 2021 the Recovery Plan seemed to promise a net positive impact on the 'resilience' of EU governance. Yet the public mood across the EU remains mixed and troubled; whatever they are, the next steps in EU policy-making will not come easily.

QUESTIONS

1. What are the main differences between the EU's competences?

2. What role do national parliaments play in EU policy-making?

3. How does the role of the European Parliament in policy-making vary?

4. How might the ordinary legislative procedure be simplified in the light of practice?

5. Is it acceptable that many compromises over EU law are reached through informal interinstitutional negotiations?

6. What are the main inputs and outputs of the European Semester?

7. Which entities take the lead in the common foreign and security policy?

8. How may European crises affect EU policy-making?

GUIDE TO FURTHER READING

Bergstrom, C.F. and Ritleng, D. (eds) (2016) *Rulemaking by the European Commission. The New System for Delegation of Powers* (Oxford: Oxford University Press). A thorough discussion from different perspectives of the system of delegated and implementing acts introduced by the Lisbon Treaty.

Buonanno, L. and Nugent, N. (2020) *Policies and Policy Processes of the European Union*, 2nd edn (Basingstoke: Palgrave Macmillan). A comprehensive overview of the main areas of EU policy-making.

European Parliament (2020) *Handbook on the Ordinary Legislative Procedure*. http://www.epgenpro.europarl.europa.eu/static/ordinary-legislative-procedure/en/ordinary-legislative-procedure/handbook-on-the-ordinary-legislative-procedure.html. How the main EU legislative procedure works, with references and links to key documents.

Falkner, G. and Müller, P. (eds) (2014) *EU Policies in a Global Perspective. Shaping or taking international regimes?* (Abingdon: Routledge). A helpful discussion of how EU policy-making in many sectors has to be seen in the context of broader international frameworks.

Wallace, H., Pollack, M.A., Roederer-Rynning, C., and Young, A.R. (eds) (2020) *Policy-Making in the European Union*, 8th edn (Oxford: Oxford University Press). An excellent review of the different modes of EU policy-making, set in a theoretical and comparative perspective, but providing detailed discussion of a range of key policy areas with extensive case studies.

Access the online resources to take your learning and understanding further, including extra multiple-choice questions with instant feedback, web links, answer guidance to end-of-chapter questions, and updates on new developments in EU politics.

www.oup.com/he/cini-borragan7e

17

Trade and Development Policies

Michael Smith

Chapter Contents

Reader's Guide

This chapter focuses on the external economic relations of the European Union—the longest-established area of collective European international policy-making and action—and specifically on trade and development policy. The chapter begins by examining institutions and policy-making for trade, in which the Commission plays a central role in initiating and conducting policy, and looks especially at the Common Commercial Policy (CCP). It goes on to examine development policy—an area of mixed competence, in which policy responsibility is shared between the EU institutions and national governments. The chapter then proceeds to explore the substance and impact of EU trade and development policies, and to assess the linkages between the two areas. The conclusions draw attention to a number of tensions and contradictions in EU trade and development policy, including those arising from the departure of the United Kingdom.

17.1 Introduction

The European Union is unquestionably one of the largest concentrations of economic power in the global arena. As can be seen from Table 17.1, the Union possesses 'assets' in the form of economic resources, human resources, and territory that put it at least on a par with the United States, Japan, China, Russia, and other leading economic actors, and well ahead of several of them. Equally, in trade, investment, and other forms of international production and exchange, the EU can be seen as a potential economic superpower, not least because it constitutes the largest integrated market in the world. It is rich, it is stable, and it is skilled, and thus it inevitably occupies a prominent position in the handling of global economic issues. This fact of international economic life has only been underlined by the **accession** of the 13 new member states between 2004 and 2013 (see Chapter 18).

Basic to the conversion of this economic potential into economic power and influence, as in so many other areas of EU policy-making, is the institutional context for the conduct of external economic policy. From the very outset in the 1950s, with the establishment of the **customs union**, the then **European Economic Community (EEC)** had to develop a Common Commercial Policy (CCP) with which to handle its relations with partners and rivals in the world economy. During the 1960s, the Community also initiated what was to become a wide-ranging and complex development assistance policy, primarily to manage relations with the ex-colonies of Community members. Each of these key areas of external economic policy presented the EU with distinct institutional problems and with distinct opportunities for the exertion of international influence. Not only this, but they have also developed in ways that are linked, both with each other and with the broader pursuit of the EU's international 'actorness'.

The purpose of this chapter is to explore these areas of external economic policy, to link them with the institutions and policy-making processes that they generate within the EU, and to explore the ways in which these policies create challenges and opportunities for the EU in the global arena. By doing this, the chapter will expose a number of areas in which there are tensions and contradictions within EU policies, as well as linkages between them; it will also enable us to evaluate EU policies towards major partners and rivals in the global arena, and the extent to which the EU

Table 17.1 The European Union and its major rivals in the global political economy

	Population (m)	Area (m km2)	GDP (€ bn)	Share of world trade (%) Exports Imports
China	1,400	9.6	12,631	13.5 12.6
India	1,352	3.3	2,622	2.6 3.2
Japan	126	0.4	4,604	4.5 4.7
Russia	147	17.1	1,463	2.4 1.7
United States	329	9.8	19,151	12.2 15.1
EU 27	448	4.4	13,900	17.3 15.6

Note: All figures for 2019.
Source: DG Trade, http://ec.europa.eu/trade/en/.

has been able to establish itself as a global 'economic power' through its trade and development policies.

17.2 Institutions and policy-making: the Common Commercial Policy

The core of the European Union's external economic relations is the Common Commercial Policy (CCP). Established by the **Treaty of Rome**, but not fully implemented until the late 1960s, the CCP is the means by which the EU manages the complex range of partnerships, negotiations, agreements, and disputes that emerge through the operation of the customs union and the **Single Market** (see Chapter 20). It is important to understand the core principles and policy-making procedures of the CCP as the basis for understanding the whole of the Union's external economic policies.

As established in the Treaty of Rome, the CCP was based on Article 113 of the Treaty—since amended to become Article 133 of the **consolidated treaties** in the late 1990s, and now Article 207 TFEU. Article 207 sets out not only the principles on which the CCP is to be pursued, but also the policy-making processes through which it is to be implemented. In terms of principles, as set out in Box 17.1, the CCP embodies not only a set of aims for the external policies of the

BOX 17.1   BACKGROUND: THE COMMON COMMERCIAL POLICY

1. The Common Commercial Policy shall be based on uniform principles, particularly in regard to changes in tariff rates, the conclusion of tariff and trade agreements relating to trade in goods and services, and the commercial aspects of intellectual property, foreign direct investment, the achievement of uniformity in measures of liberalization, export policy and measures to protect trade such as those to be taken in the event of dumping or subsidies. The common commercial policy shall be conducted in the context of the principles and objectives of the Union's external action.

2. The European Parliament and the Council, acting by means of regulations in accordance with the ordinary legislative procedure, shall adopt the measures defining the framework for implementing the common commercial policy.

3. Where agreements with one or more states or international organizations need to be negotiated . . . the Commission shall make recommendations to the Council, which shall authorize the Commission to open the necessary negotiations . . . The Commission shall conduct these negotiations in consultation with a special committee appointed by the Council to assist the Commission in this task and within the framework of such directives as the Council may issue to it. The Commission shall report regularly to the special committee and to the European Parliament on the progress of negotiations.

Source: Article 207 TFEU.

Union, but also a set of far broader aims in relation to the operation of the world trade system. This key tension is at the heart of the successes registered and the difficulties encountered by the CCP, since it sets up a series of contradictions: is the EU to achieve the aim of prosperity and stability for Europeans at the cost of international stability and development? Or is it to privilege the aim of global prosperity and development at the expense of the EU's citizens and their welfare? The reality, of course, is that there is a complex balancing process for policy-makers as they utilize the instruments of the CCP.

Essentially, these instruments fall into two broad areas. The first deals with what might be called 'trade promotion': the activities that develop the EU's international activities and organize them around certain core practices. These instruments fall partly within the control of the EU itself, but are also to be found in the broader global institutions and rules established in the world arena. Thus the EU has developed a complex range of trade and commercial agreements, covering almost every corner of the globe. Some of these are bilateral, with individual countries such as Russia or China; others are inter-regional, covering relations with groupings such as the Association of Southeast Asian Nations (ASEAN); others still are multilateral, with the prime example being the World Trade Organization (WTO). In all of these areas of trade promotion, the EU aims to establish stable partnerships and relationships, often with a set of formal rules, which enable trade to develop and diversify.

A second set of CCP instruments is that relating to 'trade defence'. Here, the EU is concerned to counter perceived unfair trade practices by its key partners, such as the **dumping** of goods at unrealistically low prices on the EU market, the subsidization of goods, or the creation of barriers to EU exports. To support it in these areas, the Union has developed a battery of trade tools, including anti-dumping and anti-subsidy measures, rules of origin, sanctions, and other punishments. But it does not exercise these powers in isolation; frequently, the Union works through the WTO to counter what are seen as unfair practices, using the WTO dispute settlement procedures to defend itself at the global level. Trade and partnership agreements also include procedures for dealing with trade disputes, as a matter of routine, and sometimes linkages are made with other areas of external policy such as those on human rights and development assistance (see Section 17.3).

In the post-**Lisbon Treaty** context, the policy processes through which the CCP is implemented still make use of what historically was known as the '**Community method**' (see Chapter 16). In practical terms, this means that the Commission has the power of initiative, conduct, and implementation of commercial policy agreements. In many cases, the Commission will propose '**negotiating directives**' in which its negotiating mandate is set out; where this is the case, the Council has to approve the mandate as well as any changes in it, and the Commission is monitored by a special Council committee, the Trade

Policy Committee of member state representatives. In other areas, the Commission has **delegated** powers to apply **regulations** (for example, in anti-dumping cases), subject to monitoring and approval by the Council. The Commission has developed a sophisticated apparatus for the conduct of trade negotiations and the conduct of 'commercial diplomacy' through the Union's delegations and specialist missions, such as that to the WTO in Geneva. It might be argued on this basis that, in this area, the EU has effectively displaced the national trade policies of the member states. As a result of the Lisbon Treaty, the European Parliament has also been given a more active role in the CCP, especially in relation to the framework for trade policy-making and to the approval of trade agreements once they have been negotiated.

As time has passed, the Union has also had to respond to the changing nature of world trade and exchange, and the CCP has been reshaped to reflect the key trends. In a number of instances, this has exposed the continuing tension between the national preferences of the member states and the European perspective of the Commission, thus raising questions about the extent to which the EU has really undermined the independence of national commercial policies. A key issue here is that of competence: in the Treaty of Rome and for a long time afterwards, the CCP was assumed to be about trade in manufactured goods, but the changing global economy has given a much more prominent role to trade in services (for example, aviation services or financial services) and to related questions such as that of 'intellectual property' (the trade in ideas, such as those embodied in computer software) or foreign investment. In order to cater for these changes, the scope of Article 113 and then Article 133 had to be expanded during the 1990s, and this was not always a simple process, because member states found reasons to resist the expansion of the Commission's role.

The Lisbon Treaty effectively resolved these tensions, and the Union now has competence not only in trade in goods and services, but also in issues relating to intellectual property and foreign investment. In these areas, the Union's use of its new or expanded powers raises interesting questions—for example, the member states have a very wide range of existing bilateral investment treaties, and the EU's exercise of its post-Lisbon competences entails the modification or elimination of such treaties (for example, in the Union's pursuit of a bilateral investment treaty with China, the negotiations for which started in 2014, resulting in signature of a Comprehensive Agreement on Investment in early 2021). Another area of tension, which has existed from the earliest days of the European Community, reflects the linkage (or the gap) between 'internal' EU policies and the Union's external relations. As internal **integration** reaches new areas, it is inevitably found that these have external policy consequences. Thus, in the early days of the Community, the Common Agricultural Policy (CAP) was recognized to be not only a policy about what went on within the Community, but also a policy about the regulation of food imports and the promotion of exports, and so it has remained ever since (see Chapter 24). More recently, the completion of the 'single European airline market' during the late 1990s raised questions about who was to negotiate with countries such as the USA about the regulation of international air routes. Only after a prolonged struggle was it agreed that the Community (and thus the Commission) could exercise this power. A large number of other 'internal' policy areas, such as competition policy, environmental policy, and industrial policy, are inevitably linked to trade and the global economy, and this will continue to be an issue for the conduct of the CCP and related policies. This has been borne out by the recent negotiation of 'deep and comprehensive' free trade agreements between the EU and a range of significant partners. The most ambitious of these, the negotiations between the EU and the United States for a wide-ranging **Transatlantic Trade and Investment Partnership** (TTIP), had provided a major case-study in the move from negotiations based on trade in goods to talks which were set to encompass a host of areas in both domestic and international commercial policy (see also Chapter 20). The advent of the Trump Administration in the USA effectively 'froze' the TTIP negotiations, and it was unclear in early 2021 whether they would be resuscitated by the incoming Biden Administration. December 2020 saw agreement on an even more complex set of agreements, the Trade and Cooperation Agreement with the United Kingdom, which set a framework for future relations after the UK's departure from the Union. Although it centred on arrangements for trade in goods, it encompassed other areas such as regulatory policy and security, and left many others for subsequent negotiation and development.

As a result of these trends and processes, the CCP has, in a sense, 'spread' to encompass new areas of external commercial policy, especially in the area of regulatory policy but also now in foreign investment and related areas. The EU has become engaged with a very large number of international institutions in the conduct of these policies and has developed a complex web of agreements with which to manage them. Not all of the EU's international economic policies fall into this framework, and we will now turn to look at one of the most important of these—development policy.

17.3 Institutions and policy-making: development assistance policy

Historically, there has been pressure for the Community, and now the Union, to expand the scope of its international economic policies. Thus, from the 1960s onwards, there has been a continuing concern with development assistance policy, stimulated originally by the process of decolonization in the French empire. In contrast to the trade and commercial policy area, though, this area has never been subject to the full Community method and thus to the leading role of the Commission. As a result, it demonstrates distinctive patterns of institutions and policy-making.

Starting in the early 1960s, a series of increasingly ambitious agreements between the EEC, its member states, and a growing range of ex-colonies created a unique system for the multilateral management of development assistance issues. Box 17.2 summarizes progression from the 'Yaoundé system' to the 'Lomé system', and then to the present 'Cotonou system' (each taking its name from the place where the agreements were finalized). It can be seen from this summary that the successive conventions have set progressively larger ambitions for the scope of the activities that they cover and also that they have covered an increasing number of partners. As a result, the 'Cotonou system' now covers well over half of all countries in the international system, including some of the very richest and a large number of the very poorest. At the time of writing, negotiations for a new agreement to run from 2021 onwards are in progress. The EU's key aims in these negotiations are firstly to extend linkages to a number of key issues, including environmental policies and migration, and secondly to conclude three wide-ranging regional agreements with African, Caribbean, and Pacific partners under the Cotonou 'umbrella' as the basis for further evolution of the framework.

The initiation of the Lomé system in the 1970s was widely felt, especially by EC member states, to herald a revolution in development assistance policy by setting up an institutionalized partnership between the EEC and the **African, Caribbean, and Pacific (ACP) countries**. Processes were established to create and maintain a stable partnership, in which the ACP group would have its own collective voice, and to underpin the development of the poorest economies in the face of an unstable world economy. As time passed, however, there was criticism that the Lomé framework was increasingly irrelevant to the development of a global economy. As a result, the Cotonou system places a much greater emphasis on what might be called 'bottom-up' processes of development, in which individual ACP countries or groups of them produced their own plans for **sustainable development** to be negotiated with the EU. The Cotonou system also contains markedly more in the way of what has come to be called 'conditionality'—in other words, provisions that make the granting of EU aid conditional on **good governance**, observance of human rights, and the introduction of market economics. As such, it parallels broader developments in the provision of aid on the global scale and the United Nations' **Millennium Development Goals (MDGs**, revised in 2015 as the Sustainable Development Goals). It has also been accompanied by special measures relating to the very poorest countries, especially the Union's 2001

'Everything but Arms' Regulation, which allows free access for all products—except those with a military use—from the 40 poorest countries, and by a global scheme, the Generalised System of Preferences, which grants trade concessions to a wide range of countries as long as they meet certain conditions. The Cotonou system is thus a part of a broader and comprehensive approach to development assistance and cooperation, based on an agreed European Consensus on Development, which in turn is an integral part of the EU's Global Strategy, adopted in 2016. The Global Strategy explicitly links development assistance with broader foreign policy and external economic policy goals.

The EU's development assistance policies have thus had to respond to the changing nature of the global economy while taking account of new linkages (for example, between trade and development, environment and development, and so on), and to balance the needs of the developing countries against those of the EU and its member states. The most acute tensions come in the area of agricultural policy: the Common Agricultural Policy (CAP) does demonstrable damage to the economies of some of the poorest countries, by depressing commodity prices, preventing free access to the European market, and subsidizing EU exports. Here, again, we can see that external economic policy is closely connected to internal policy processes, and it is not always a profitable linkage (see Chapter 24).

Central to the problems encountered by the EU's development assistance policies are two factors. The first is an internal institutional problem: the mixture of policy competences between the EU and its member states, and (in the post-Lisbon context) between the new array of EU institutions. For example, the

---

BOX 17.2 BACKGROUND: KEY STAGES IN THE EVOLUTION OF THE EU'S RELATIONS WITH AFRICAN, CARIBBEAN, AND PACIFIC (ACP) COUNTRIES

1963	First Yaoundé Agreement (renewed 1969)
	Reciprocal preferential trade access between EEC member states and associated states (former colonies of member states)
	European Development Fund
	Joint Council of Ministers, Joint Parliamentary Assembly, and Committee of Ambassadors
1974	Lomé Convention (renewed 1979, 1984, 1990, and 1995)
	Includes former British colonies
	ACP group established, with Secretariat in Brussels
	ACP partners increase from 46 (1974) to 68 (1995)
	Non-reciprocal trade preferences
	Schemes to support ACP agricultural prices (System for the Stabilization of ACP and OCT Export Earnings, or STABEX, in 1979) and mineral export prices (System for the Promotion of Mineral Production and Exports, or MINEX, in 1984)
2000	Cotonou Agreement
	20-year agreement (entered into force April 2003; revised in 2005, 2010, and 2015)
	79 ACP partners (2017)
	Multilateral agreement to be supplemented by bilateral or minilateral economic partnership agreements (EPAs) by December 2007 (by the end of 2017, all seven such EPAs were in application, covering 32 of the 79 Cotonou partner countries; another 21 partner countries had concluded negotiations but not yet implemented the agreements).
	From 2018 onwards, negotiations for a new agreement to run from 2021 were in progress, but had not been concluded by the end of 2020.

Source: European Commission, available at: https://ec.europa.eu/info/aid-development-cooperation-fundamental-rights_en.

post-Lisbon arrangements gave the European External Action Service (EEAS) responsibility for overall development strategy, while the financial and other resources needed to implement the strategy at the European level remained with the Commission and with the Directorate-General for Development and Cooperation (DG DEVCO). The second is an external factor: the ways in which development assistance policies have become increasingly politicized in the contemporary global arena. In terms of the EU's institutional make-up, development assistance policy remains an area of 'mixed competence' in which policies proposed and implemented at the EU level coexist with national policies for international development. Thus, although the EU claims to be the world's largest donor of development aid, the majority of that figure consists of aid given by member states as part of their national programmes (see Table 17.2). The complex programmes that have evolved at the European level are also, unlike the CCP, the result of a complex division of powers between the European institutions and the national governments represented in the Council. As a result, the Commission and the Union cannot claim to speak with one exclusive voice in this area, although their policies and initiatives have had considerable influence on the ways in which development assistance is targeted and allocated. The departure of the UK in 2020 meant that a powerful voice was also lost in the area of EU development policy, as well as one of the world's largest bilateral donors.

Agreements such as the Lomé and Cotonou conventions are mixed agreements, and the Council collectively and the member states individually have the power to ratify or not to ratify them. As with trade policy, this is also an area in which the European Parliament has a stronger and more assertive voice after the Lisbon Treaty. The major institutional innovations made by the Treaty lie elsewhere, however—namely, as noted above, the establishment of the EEAS and the reshaping of the Commission's services into DG DEVCO, which created significant uncertainties about who controls the policy framework and (perhaps most importantly) the funding for development assistance programmes. For several years after the implementation of the Lisbon Treaty, there remained areas of tension and competition in these policy domains.

In addition to the problems created by internal institutional factors, EU development assistance policies have to contend with the fact that issues of economic and social development have become intensely

Table 17.2 EU27 net bilateral and multilateral overseas development assistance (ODA), 2019

Country	Amount (US$ m)
France	12,176
Germany	23,806
Netherlands	5,292
Sweden	5,397
Spain	2,896
Italy	4,900
Denmark	2,546
Belgium	2,177
Finland	1,126
Austria	1,211
Ireland	935
Greece	308
Portugal	373
Poland	684
Luxembourg	474
Czech Republic	306
Slovenia	86
Hungary	317
Slovak Republic	129
DAC EU 27 Members, Total	65,139
EU Institutions	14,827
EU total (EU DAC members + EU institutions)	86,908
US	34,615
Japan	15,507

Note: OECD Development Assistance Committee (DAC) members only. Excludes United Kingdom, which in 2019 committed over $19 billion of ODA; also excludes Estonia, Latvia, Lithuania, Bulgaria, Romania, Cyprus, and Malta, which together gave $535 million in 2019.
Source: OECD Development Assistance Committee, 'Aid by DAC members increases in 2019 with more aid to the poorest countries', 2020, available at: https://www.oecd.org/dac/financing-sustainable-development/development-finance-data/ODA-2019-detailed-summary.pdf

politicized within the global arena. This means that aid is not simply an economic matter; it has become linked to problems of human rights, of good governance, and of **statehood** in the less developed countries, and the EU has had to develop mechanisms to deal with this. There has been an increasing tendency to concentrate the EU's development assistance policies, especially through the EuropeAid development office and now through DG DEVCO, and to link them with the operation of agencies such as the European Community Humanitarian Office (ECHO). Since the end of the Cold War, there has also been a series of conflicts, for example, in the former **Yugoslavia**, and in Afghanistan, in which the EU has played a key role in coordinating reconstruction and post-conflict economic assistance; more recently, conflicts in the Middle East and elsewhere have created major challenges in terms of reconstruction, humanitarian assistance, and the management of major movements of refugees. As a result, the EU's development assistance policies have moved away from their primary focus on the ACP countries and a far wider range of recipients has been identified. Among these, post-communist **regimes** and those involved in conflict form a key focus, as do the poorest countries, which as noted above are granted additional concessions in terms of free access to the European market for their goods.

Development assistance policy thus represents a long-established, yet continually changing, focus in the EU's external economic relations. EU development assistance, as an area of mixed competences and challenges associated with political change and conflict, is also increasingly subject to processes of politicization and securitization, some of which create major tensions. Not only this, but the relationship between EU development assistance policies and trade policies, as noted at several points in this chapter, is also a complex and often contested one.

KEY POINTS

- Development assistance is a key area of 'mixed competence' in EU external relations.

- Development assistance policy is an area in which the EU can claim global leadership; but there are tensions between the EU's policy framework, global rules, and the needs of developing countries.

- Key problems in development assistance include those caused by the emergence of new issues, such as those concerning the environment or human rights, and the increasing politicization of the area. The departure of the UK has removed a significant contributor to EU development policies, both in political and in financial terms, of which the effects are only beginning to be felt.

17.4 The European Union's policy objectives in trade and development

As noted, the European Union is nothing if not explicit about many of its external economic policy objectives. The tone was initially set by the provisions of Article 113 of the Treaty of Rome, in which the Common Commercial Policy (CCP) is established according to explicit principles, applying not only to the EEC and then to the EU, but also to the broader management of international commercial relations. Perhaps significantly, this set of principles has not been absorbed within the general principles and objectives of the EU's external action (see Box 17.1). This has been backed up over the years by an extremely wide-ranging and sophisticated series of trade agreements with a wide range of partners, which go into great detail about the privileges and concessions to be given to specific partners. This can be seen as establishing an elaborate hierarchy, or 'pyramid of privilege', in which the EU manages and adjusts its relations to individual partners. From time to time, this set of arrangements raises questions about exactly how particular partners should be dealt with: for example, in the case of China, the EU has had to change its approach as the country has developed economically, and as it has increasingly become integrated into the global economy through membership of the World Trade Organization (WTO) and other international bodies. Likewise, commercial relationships with Russia have been significantly affected by the conflicts of the past few years in Ukraine and elsewhere, which have also led to the imposition of economic sanctions by the Union.

At the same time, the EU has to balance its external obligations against the internal needs of the member states and of European producers and consumers. We have already noted that the Common Agricultural Policy provides extensive safeguards (often said to be discriminatory) for EU farmers, but this is frequently at the expense of consumers whose food bills are higher because of the protectionism built into the Common Agricultural Policy (CAP). Likewise, some of the key disputes between the EU and China over such areas as textiles and solar panels, have revealed severe tensions between the aims of EU trade policies and the interests of distributors and consumers (see Box 17.3). A large number of the disputes between the EU and the United States (which, between them,

BOX 17.3   CASE STUDY: EU–CHINA TRADE DISPUTES: TEXTILES, SOLAR PANELS, STEEL, AND CYBER-SECURITY

During the early 2000s, the rapid growth of Chinese exports created a challenging situation for the EU (as it did for other major importers, such as the USA). In particular, the phasing out of the Multi-Fibre Arrangement (MFA), an international agreement that allowed importers to impose quotas if they were threatened with a surge of cheap imports, led to a major increase in Chinese penetration of the European market for cheap textiles and clothing. The EU was faced with a dilemma: on the one hand, the remaining European textile producers, concentrated in southern member states such as Italy, Portugal, and Greece, demanded protection; on the other hand, northern member states with rapidly growing markets for cheap T-shirts and other products felt the heat from their consumer and retail lobbies. The Commission was faced with an almost impossible choice: whether to live up to its international obligations and thus offend powerful internal groups, or to impose restrictions and thus potentially renege on its international commitments. The climax of the problem was reached in 2005, when frantic negotiations produced a set of compromise agreements based on voluntary restraints by China, whilst shiploads of clothing products were trapped in European ports. More recently, a dispute with China over the alleged 'dumping' of solar panels raised many of the same issues: European solar panel manufacturers complained

about the prices at which Chinese products were imported into the EU, but installers and consumers were equally adamant in support of continued imports. Again, a compromise agreement was made, in 2012–13, which saw some restraints on Chinese exports but no punitive EU measures. In contrast, the case of Chinese steel exports to the EU raised a more 'traditional' type of trade dispute in 2014–15, with the EU imposing anti-dumping measures and EU member state governments concerned with the protection of employment and 'strategic industries' threatened by a surge of imports. By 2018, the focus of concerns with China had shifted towards a new problem-area: that of cyber-security and its links to new information technologies. Several EU member states had incorporated into their next-generation IT systems products made by the Chinese company Huawei, but concerns grew in the USA and elsewhere that this made those systems vulnerable to Chinese government infiltration and that this posed a growing security risk. Whilst some EU member states resisted pressure from Washington, others responded more positively and followed the UK in trying to phase out Chinese-originated equipment—whilst network providers focused on the relative costs and efficiency of Huawei and competing European products. This was a foretaste of what may well be continuing tensions.

still account for a significant proportion of disputes brought before the WTO) have been exacerbated by the lobbying of producer groups both in the EU and the USA, which has created political problems around disputes that might, in earlier times, have been managed in a technocratic manner by officials and experts.

The net result of these cross-cutting tensions and pressures is a complicated picture in which the EU professes its commitment to the global management of trade issues, but often acts as though it wishes to pursue its own interests in a unilateral manner. Some of the same sorts of tensions emerge in relation to development assistance: the EU trumpets its commitment to international development and claims to be a pioneer of new types of development assistance policy, but there is always a balance to be struck between the broader international aims, those of the EU as a collective, and those of individual member states. This is institutionalized in the EU, thanks to the mixed nature of the institutional framework and the need to get agreement from the member states on major policy initiatives, and also reflects a number

of powerful historical and cultural forces arising from the history of the European empires. In recent years, the EU's leading role in development assistance policy has been challenged by the emergence of new 'models', especially those promoted by China in Africa and elsewhere, which place a lower burden of conditionality on aid recipients.

The EU thus has to face up to a number of tensions emerging from its pursuit of its trade and development policies. These have become more significant as the EU (either as a whole, or through major subgroups such as the euro area countries) has expanded its role in the global economy, and as the linkages between economic, political, and security activities have become more pronounced. One way of stating these tensions is in terms of the competing demands of multilateralism, inter-regionalism, bilateralism, and unilateralism in EU external economic policies. Each of these patterns can be seen in current EU policies, and they have to be held in a complex and fluctuating balance by a set of collective institutions and individual member states with competing interests.

The impact of the financial and economic crisis since 2008 must also be factored into this balance, since it has created pressures for greater protectionism in trade and for reductions in overseas development assistance. On the whole, the EU has maintained its general stance in favour of trade liberalization and a major commitment to overseas aid, but the pressures persist, and have been underlined by the rise of populism and nationalism in a number of EU member states.

KEY POINTS

- The EU has a general aim of 'organizing' its external environment through commercial agreements and of creating a 'pyramid' of partners in the global economy.

- The demands of external commitments can come into conflict with internal pressures from different interests within the EU.

- This is part of a general problem created by the need for responses to a changing global environment, but can express itself in concentrated disputes and crises for the EU.

- The EU also faces the need to balance between different types of relationship: multilateral; inter-regional; and bilateral. In addition, internal pressures can lead to unilateral behaviour by the Union.

17.5 The European Union as a power through trade and development

The European Union has enormous potential for influence and activity in the global economy, but it is equally clear that it faces a number of important constraints on its capacity to turn potential into reality. We have already noted that a series of complex balances have to be struck in the making and implementation of EU trade and development policies, between:

- the collective interests of the EU as a whole and those of individual member states or groups of member states;

- the claims and competences of specific institutions and the pressures generated by different sectors of trade and development policy;

- the claims of different partners and rivals in the global arena, which demand different patterns of incentives and resources from the EU;

- the changing nature of the EU's involvement in the global arena and the increasing levels of politicization that accompany international trade and development policies; and

- the competing claims of multilateralism, inter-regionalism, bilateralism, and unilateralism in the pursuit of EU policies, often within cross-cutting institutional frameworks with complex patterns of demands.

In some ways, these are no more demanding than the problems confronting any national government in the **globalizing** world economy. In the case of the EU, though, they are compounded by the fact that the EU itself is founded on a series of institutional compromises and a process of continuous negotiation. This makes the competing claims more obvious and, in some ways, less manageable than they might be for a national government, no matter what its size or complexity. As noted above, these competing claims and pressures were intensified by the impact of the post-2008 financial and economic crisis, which has often had uneven effects on EU member states. Another major factor with uncertain long-term consequences is the impact of the departure of the UK from the Union (see Box 17.4).

Against this background of challenges, the EU has considerable assets and opportunities. We have already noted that the EU is the world's 'champion trader', with a key position in the exchange of goods, services, and ideas, and its position as manager of the world's largest integrated market provides it with opportunities as well as with challenges. In recent years, the Union, through the Commission, has sought to exploit a number of these opportunities and to establish itself as a key player in the emerging global economy. Thus it has become increasingly active in leading global trade negotiations, with varying levels of success; it has taken a leading role in the handling of international environmental issues such as those dealt with by the Kyoto Protocol and later the Paris Accords on global warming (see Chapter 25); and it has pursued its claim to be a leader in the provision of international development assistance, and increasingly of humanitarian aid and disaster relief.

This means that the EU is increasingly acknowledged as a power in the global economy. It has acquired the legal and institutional apparatus with which to pursue this ambition, and this legal and institutional framework gives it the capacity to carry

BOX 17.4   KEY DEBATES: BREXIT AND THE EU'S TRADE AND DEVELOPMENT POLICIES

The decision by the UK government to negotiate departure from the EU, following the referendum in June 2016, created a number of potential issues for EU trade and development policies. The UK was one of the three largest trading countries in the Union, and its second largest donor of overseas development assistance (see Table 17.2). It was historically part of the 'liberal' free trading group in the Union, along with countries such as Sweden, Denmark, and the Netherlands. From the UK perspective, it also gained through the 'multiplier effect' of EU membership; for example, through the EU's weight in trade negotiations and in overall development assistance.

In relation to trade, the UK government sought to create a new deep and comprehensive relationship with the EU, but to retain the freedom to pursue its own trade agreements in the global arena. The departure of the UK clearly changes the internal balance between free traders and more protectionist countries within the EU, and thus might change the nature of EU trade policy more generally, especially in relation to the handling of trade disputes. In absolute terms, the UK's departure would have affected only about 4 per cent of EU GDP, even if no trade carried on between the two, and about 2 per cent of EU GDP in relation to trade in services. It was always likely, though, that a new form of trade agreement would be negotiated, so the key question was what type of agreement this would be. At one end of the spectrum, the UK could simply have left, and its trade with the EU would then be regulated by WTO rules, with tariffs rising in key areas (e.g. to 15 per cent in some agricultural products). At the other end, the UK could have adopted the 'Norway solution' entailing membership of the European Economic Area and the need to comply with most of the EU acquis despite not being a member state. The outcome,

encapsulated in the Trade and Cooperation Agreement of December 2020, is somewhere in between these two extremes, coupling a free trade agreement largely centred on trade in goods with a range of agreements relating to regulatory policies, security and other matters. This process means that the EU has acquired a new and significant trade partner (or rival) in its immediate neighbourhood, and that there will be uneven economic (and political) impacts on EU member states depending on their closeness to the UK. In relation to EU development policy, the UK has always been a major influence— indeed, the current system of relations with the ACP countries derives from the need to set up a framework able to deal with the ex-colonies of the UK when it joined in 1973. The UK's departure subtracts significant resources from collective EU development programmes, and will also affect the internal balance between 'northern' countries with large commitments to development assistance and those with less of a commitment, for example in Eastern Europe. It might also reinforce one of the trends noted in this chapter, towards a more 'geopolitical' or 'securitized' approach to development assistance, although that trend was established long before 'Brexit' became an issue. The EU will be faced with decisions about how far to continue to assist the UK's ex-colonies, while the UK is faced with the actual or potential loss of the benefits from EU collective action and information-gathering. The task of disentangling the UK from development policy, while complex, is not of the same order as the challenges faced in trade policy, but it will nonetheless be a potential distraction and entail time-consuming negotiations (for example, about contributions to the European Development Fund and about the development of mechanisms for coordination in future development activities).

out a number of important 'state functions' to preserve and enhance the prosperity of its citizens in a changing world economy. It has been able to establish itself as a key participant in global economic processes, both in formal institutional terms and in less formal terms of engagement in fundamental processes of trade, production, and exchange. In this, it has had to cope with challenges created by a number of other international economic powers, such as the USA, Japan, and (increasingly) China and India. It has created an impressive network of international trade and development partnerships and has, in many cases, been able to link these with increasingly political conditions or requirements, for example, through the use of economic sanctions. It has also taken an increasing role in global governance

through its support for multilateral action on trade and development.

It remains unclear in some respects what the EU as a global power in trade and development is for or against. As we have seen, this is a reflection of the complex institutional and other forces operating on its external economic policies, and the cross-cutting pressures to which its policy-making processes are subject. The result is a constant disparity between the EU's claims to global distinctiveness and the reality of its untidy policy-making processes. One thing that is clear, however, is that the enlarged EU of 27 members will continue to pursue ambitious trade and development policies and through them will continue to have a significant global impact.

17.6 Conclusion

This chapter has dealt with the core elements of the European Union's trade and development policies: institutions and policy-making; aims and objectives; constraints and opportunities; and the impact of the EU's activities. Each of these areas of policy has its own characteristic history in terms of the evolution of institutions and in terms of the EU's international engagement. We have seen that the Common Commercial Policy was almost built into the foundations of the EEC because of the need to manage the customs union, while the development assistance policy responded to the need to deal with the ex-colonies of the EU's member states. In each of these cases, the history matters, because it situates the external policy in a certain framework of institutional development and also because it locates the policy in terms of the development of the global economy.

It is also clear that, in each of the policy areas that we have explored, there is a complex and shifting array of pressures and demands to which the EU has more or less successfully responded. The internal pressures—from member state governments, from producer or consumer groups, and from competition between the institutions—intersect with the external pressures created by globalization, by competition from major established and emerging economies, and by the pursuit of the EU's sizeable ambitions in a changing world. In these areas, the EU has for a long time had to deal with real and pressing policy dilemmas, which are a natural product of its assumption of major 'state functions'.

Despite these contradictory pressures and the difficulties of constructing policy in a changing global economy, the EU can claim in its trade and development policies to have gone some distance 'beyond the nation state'. This does not mean that the member states are redundant: far from it, they are a major source of policy pressures and challenges for the Union's institutions, and they are a key source of the **legitimacy** that has been acquired by those institutions in the context of global governance. But there is also the legitimacy that has been acquired by decades of steadily **deepening** involvement in the global economy, and the acquisition of the knowledge and skills that go with it. These are what give the EU's trade and development policies a distinctive significance and impact, and make them a key subject for study.

 QUESTIONS

1.   What are the key sources of the EU's power in trade and development?

2.   How have the sources of EU power changed in importance during the course of European integration?

3.   What are the key features of the distribution of power between the EU institutions in issues of trade and commercial policy?

4.   Has the balance of power between the EU institutions changed, and if so, how and why?

5.   How has the changing nature of world trade affected the EU's Common Commercial Policy?

6.   What does it mean to say that development policy is an area of 'mixed competence' in the EU, and how does that affect processes of policy-making?

7.   Why is it appropriate to describe the EU's development policies in terms of a 'pyramid of privilege'?

8.   What are the key differences between the Lomé and Cotonou systems of EU development policy?

GUIDE TO FURTHER READING

Gstöhl, S. and de Bièvre, D. (2018) *The Trade Policy of the European Union* (Basingstoke: Palgrave Macmillan). Most recent comprehensive study, including chapters on development policy as well as trade.

Hill, C. and Smith, M. (eds) (2017) *International Relations and the European Union*, 3rd edn (Oxford: Oxford University Press). Several chapters deal with various aspects of policy-making and implementation in the EU's external economic relations; Chapter 10 deals specifically with trade policy, and Chapter 13 with development policy.

Holland, M. and Doidge, M. (2012) *Development Policy of the European Union* (Basingstoke: Palgrave Macmillan). The best and most recent general treatment of the aid and development issue, including the negotiation of the Lomé and Cotonou Agreements.

Kuiper, P., Wouters, J., Hoffmeister, F., de Baere, G., and Ramopoulos, T. (2013) *The Law of EU External Relations: Cases, Materials, and Commentary on the EU as an International Legal Actor* (Oxford: Oxford University Press). This is a major study of the legal aspects of EU external relations, including many areas covered in this chapter.

McGuire, S. and Smith, M. (2008) *The European Union and the United States: Competition and Convergence in the Global Arena* (Basingstoke: Palgrave). Chapters 3–7 cover a number of dimensions of EU–US economic relations. New edition scheduled for 2022.

Woolcock, S. (2012) *European Union Economic Diplomacy: The Role of the EU in External Economic Relations* (Farnham: Ashgate). This is a wide-ranging study of the effectiveness of EU external economic action; in particular, trade policy and its associated diplomacy, with detailed case studies.

 Access the online resources to take your learning and understanding further, including extra multiple-choice questions with instant feedback, web links, answer guidance to end-of-chapter questions, and updates on new developments in EU politics.

www.oup.com/he/cini-borragan7e

18

Enlargement

Ana E. Juncos and Nieves Pérez-Solórzano Borragán

Chapter Contents

Reader's Guide

The process of enlargement has transformed the European Union. It has had far-reaching implications for the shape and definition of Europe, and for the institutional set-up and the major policies of the Union. This has been accomplished through a number of enlargement rounds, which Section 18.2 analyses in detail. This is followed by a review of the enlargement process itself, with a focus on the use of conditionality and the role of the main actors involved. The contributions of neo-functionalism, liberal intergovernmentalism, and social constructivism to explaining the EU's geographical expansion are evaluated in the third section of the chapter. The success and prospect of future enlargement are discussed in the context of wider EU developments, especially the effect of the external crises and increasing geopolitical competition, 'enlargement fatigue', the domestic context in the candidate countries, and Brexit.

18.1 Introduction

Membership of the European Union has increased over time from the **original six** to the current 27 (after Brexit). Through a series of enlargement rounds, the territory of the Union has been expanded to stretch from the Mediterranean shores to the Baltic Sea, and from the Atlantic to the Black Sea, in just over four decades. The **accession** of new member states to the EU is generally considered a success of **European integration**, because it has proven to promote stability across the continent, while the willingness of countries to join the EU remains undeterred despite the often cumbersome processes attached to adapting to the Union's accession requirements and despite the challenging times resulting from the eurozone and migration crises, Brexit, and more recently, the **COVID-19** pandemic (see Chapters 25, 26, 27, and 28).

EU enlargement is best understood as both a process and a policy. As a process, it involves the gradual and incremental adaptation undertaken by countries wishing to join the EU to meet its membership criteria. This process became more complicated after the end of the Cold War, when the Union had to respond to the accession applications of the newly democratizing countries from Central and Eastern Europe (CEE). With time, the EU's membership requirements have been expanded, and the number and diversity of countries wanting to join the Union have increased, thus the EU has adapted its decision-making, policies, and institutional set-up to an ever-increasing and diverse membership. As a policy, enlargement refers to the principles, goals, and instruments defined by the EU with the aim of incorporating new member states. It is a typically intergovernmental policy under which member states retain the monopoly over decision-making, and the Commission plays a **delegated** role monitoring the suitability of countries to join and acting as a key point of contact during the accession negotiations. The European Parliament (EP) must approve the accession of new members through the **consent** procedure.

The accession of new member states poses interesting and challenging questions, such as why do countries want to join the EU? How and why does the EU support the accession of new member states? How has EU enlargement developed over time? How can European integration theories explain enlargement? And what is the future of enlargement? This chapter will address each of these questions in turn. The first part

of the chapter briefly traces the evolution of enlargement from the first round of accession in 1973 to the latest round in 2013. The second section outlines the process of enlargement from a country's application for membership to accession, and the policy instruments devised by the EU to support applicant countries in their endeavours. The ability of **integration theory** to explain the EU's geographical expansion is evaluated in Section 18.3. The future of enlargement is assessed in the context of wider developments both within and beyond the European Union. The chapter closes with a brief conclusion.

18.2 The history of enlargement

The European Union has been involved in five rounds of accession adding 22 members to the original six (although the UK left in 2020) and bringing the Union's overall population to 448 million people. These rounds tend to group countries under geographical labels—namely, the 'Northern enlargement', the 'Mediterranean enlargement', the 'EFTA enlargement' (referring to Austria, Finland, and Sweden's membership of the European Free Trade Area), the 'Eastern enlargement', and 'the Balkan enlargement' (see Table 18.1). Each round of enlargement faced the European Community (and later the Union) and the new member states with different sets of challenges;

Table 18.1 Enlargement rounds

Enlargement round	Member states acceding	Accession date
Northern enlargement	Denmark, Ireland, UK	1973
Mediterranean enlargement	Greece	1981
	Portugal, Spain	1986
EFTA enlargement	Austria, Finland, Sweden	1995
Eastern enlargement	Cyprus, Czech Republic, Estonia, Hungary, Latvia, Lithuania, Malta, Poland, Slovakia, Slovenia	2004
	Bulgaria, Romania	2007
Balkan enlargement	Croatia	2013

each was informed by different sets of political and economic interests, and had diverse effects on both the EU and its members. It is widely agreed that the Eastern enlargement brought about the most extensive change for all parties concerned. What follows is a brief review of each enlargement round, explaining key challenges and patterns.

The 1973 Northern enlargement featured the accession to the then **European Economic Community (EEC)** of Denmark, Ireland, and the UK. Norway had also applied for membership in April 1962, but accession was rejected in a 1972 referendum. The negotiations between the EEC and the applicant countries were characterized by two French vetoes to the accession of the UK, which affected the destiny of the other two countries. This first enlargement illustrated a characteristic that would define subsequent accession rounds—namely, the asymmetrical relationship between the EU and the applicant country, which places the latter in a weaker position, meaning that it has to adapt to the accession requirements or risk the negative effect of exclusion. It also illustrated how an enlarging membership brings about more diverse

national preferences. The accession of two more **Eurosceptic** member states, the UK and Denmark, challenged the typically pro-integration approach of the original six. The UK's political significance unsettled the bargaining influence of the **Franco-German axis** until the country's departure in 2020. The institutionalization of the **European Council** in 1974 was, to a large extent, the pragmatic Franco-German response to this challenge (see Chapter 11).

The Mediterranean enlargement took place in two stages: Greece joined in 1981, and Portugal and Spain in 1986. Turkey had also applied in 1959, but negotiations were suspended in light of the military intervention in 1970 (see Box 18.1). This round of enlargement was characterized by the political and symbolic significance that membership had for three countries that had just completed transitions to democracy. Accession to an organization that required a commitment to democracy was regarded as a guarantee for democratic consolidation. For Spain, it also signified a return to Europe after Franco's self-imposed isolation. This enlargement round also featured an asymmetric relationship between candidates and the Union, and

 BOX 18.1   CASE STUDY: THE ACCESSION OF TURKEY TO THE EU

Turkey is the longest-standing EU candidate. An Association Agreement was signed in 1964 and a Customs Union established in 1996. Turkey's membership application was filed in 1987, but the Commission did not recommend the opening of accession negotiations at that point. It was not until 1999 that Turkey was granted candidate status, with formal accession negotiations opening in October 2005. However, since then, not much progress has been achieved: out of 35, only 16 negotiating chapters have been opened, and one chapter has been provisionally closed. There are a number of reasons for this lack of progress. First, increasing geopolitical tensions between Turkey and EU member states in the Eastern Mediterranean, including issues such as the Cyprus conflict, maritime disputes between Turkey and Greece, the involvement of Turkey in regional conflicts (Libya, Nagorno-Karabakh), and competition over the exploitation of gas resources. In July 2019 the EU's Foreign Affairs Council agreed to adopt sanctions against Turkey because of its refusal to stop gas drilling activities off the coast of Cyprus. Second, there are serious concerns about the state of democracy in Turkey, due to President Recep Tayyip Erdogan's authoritarian style. For instance, the clampdown on human rights, the rule of law, oppositions parties, and media freedom after the attempted

coup in July 2016; constitutional changes that further centralize powers in the office of the President; and Turkey's withdrawal from the Istanbul Convention, a treaty on preventing and combating violence against women, in 2021, have been met by condemnation across the EU. The European Parliament called for a suspension of Turkey's membership negotiations in July 2017. Third, increasing support for populist parties in European elections on a typically anti-migration and anti-Muslim ticket challenge the accession of a new member state with a predominantly Muslim population and which is geopolitically placed at the forefront of a migration crisis that the EU has been unable to solve. This largely explains why the controversial 2016 **EU–Turkey Statement** (better known as the EU–Turkey refugee deal) was arrived at outside the accession negotiation framework. Fourth, Turkey's sheer size (more than 79 million inhabitants), its poverty (GDP per capita about a quarter of the EU average), and its contested European credentials also raise concerns that will have to be assuaged before an accession treaty is agreed. Finally, the EU's own absorption capacity, enlargement fatigue, increasing opposition to Turkey's membership across the EU, member states' domestic preferences, the EU's travails post-Brexit and post-COVID-19 pandemic will also shape any further progress.

the shifting in bargaining coalitions between member states, which explains the introduction of the **Single European Act (SEA)** and **qualified majority voting (QMV)** in the EU Council (see Chapters 2 and 11). The main effect of the Mediterranean enlargement was economic. Greece, Portugal, and Spain were not **net contributors** to the EU Budget, but rather required financial support to rebuild their lagging economies. The EU's **cohesion** policy was the EU's response to this challenge (see Chapter 21).

The 1995 EFTA enlargement saw the accession of Austria, Finland, and Sweden to the EU. Norway also negotiated accession, but EU membership was rejected again in a 1994 referendum. This was the least controversial round of enlargement because the three countries were wealthy established democracies that became net contributors to the EU Budget. For the EU, the accession of three new member states affected the formation of coalitions in the EU Council, with the clear emergence of a Nordic pro-environmental block that supported the entrepreneurial role of the Commission in strengthening the EU's environmental policy.

The Eastern enlargement took place in two stages: Cyprus, the Czech Republic, Estonia, Hungary, Latvia, Lithuania, Malta, Poland, Slovakia, and Slovenia joined the EU in 2004; and Bulgaria and Romania in 2007. This round of enlargement was the most complex for the EU. The Union had to respond to the effect of the collapse of communism, the eagerness of the newly established democracies to 'return to Europe', and the new security concerns posed by the end of the Cold War. The symbolic dimension of EU membership was heightened in the early 1990s, as the Union regarded enlargement as a tool with which to implement its commitment to democracy and stability promotion to the east of its borders. This symbolism derived from a 'rhetorical entrapment' which prevented member states from either openly opposing or threatening to veto enlargement without damaging their credibility (Schimmelfennig, 2001; and see Section 18.4.3, 'Social Constructivism'). This, however, did not diminish the strong asymmetrical **power** relationship between the EU and the candidates. The EU was prompted to set up a comprehensive list of accession requirements, the so-called '**Copenhagen criteria**' (see Box 18.3), and a better-defined staging of the process of accession, as well as a toolkit of policy instruments to support the extensive domestic reforms requested from the **candidate countries** in

preparation for EU membership. The sheer number and variety of potential new member states, combined with their economic underdevelopment, presented the EU with the challenge of institutional and policy reform to ensure its own readiness for a larger membership. This often-difficult reform was initiated at the 1996 **intergovernmental conference (IGC)** and its effects were still felt during the negotiations leading up to the **Lisbon Treaty ratification** in 2009 (see Chapters 2 and 3). The member states had to agree a new weighting of votes in the EU Council under an extended QMV and a new distribution of seats in the EP, as well as a reform of the size of the Commission. Strict transitional arrangements were negotiated, particularly on the free movement of people, direct payments to farmers, and restrictions to agricultural exports from the new member states. While these are clear evidence of the candidate countries' weak position, they are also evidence of the very diverging preferences that individual member states had about the Eastern enlargement (see Section 18.4.2, 'Liberal intergovernmentalism'). Suffice to say that while security and economic benefits were obvious to countries such as Germany or the UK, and a sincere Baltic identity explained Danish, Swedish, and Finnish support, countries such as Spain and Portugal feared the shift of EU financial support to help struggling economies in the east. Moreover, the accession of Cyprus was a particularly sensitive issue. The EU faced the additional challenge of importing into its borders the unresolved conflict between the Greek Cypriot community in the south of the island and the Turkish occupied territory in the north; while Turkey had finally been awarded candidate country status in 1999 (see Box 18.1).

The Balkan enlargement started in 2013 when Croatia joined the EU. By 2017, negotiations were ongoing with Montenegro and Serbia and in 2020 the EU Council agreed to start accession negotiations with Albania and the Republic of North Macedonia. This round of enlargement is different from the others in three respects. First, the Western Balkans is a more unstable region as democratic governance is still challenged by years of ethnic conflict and political polarization, and corruption and organized crime are still rife. Second, the EU is being challenged on different fronts by the aftermath of the economic crisis, the rise of **Eurosceptic** populist parties, the refugee crisis, Brexit, and a difficult coordinated response to the COVID-19 pandemic. These challenges, coupled with an 'enlargement fatigue', that is a less enthusiastic narrative around the desirability of future enlargements and the EU's capacity to accommodate a larger and more diverse membership, explain the hesitant support for more EU territorial expansion. Third, the experience of the previous enlargement rounds clearly informs how the EU manages further expansion. Therefore, the EU has become more cautious to the point that EU enlargement is no longer a priority. And as a process, enlargement has become more asymmetrical, more politicized, more technical, and more focused on the monitoring of compliance with EU requirements.

KEY POINTS

- Through successive enlargements, the EU has expanded its membership from the original six to 27.

- Each enlargement round has been characterized by an asymmetrical relationship between member states and the countries wishing to join, the internal adaptation of the EU to cope with a larger membership, and differing national preferences among member states.

- The Eastern enlargement has been the most challenging of all enlargements to date.

- Turkish EU membership is controversial and it is unlikely that the country will join the EU in the near future.

- The Balkan enlargement is shaped by the impact of the previous enlargements, the crises affecting the EU, and the challenging circumstances in the region.

18.3 Enlargement: the process and actors

Although the main actors have remained the same, the process through which a country becomes a member of the EU has become more complex over time. This section provides an overview of the changes to the process of accession, the key principles and provisions guiding enlargement, the role of the different actors involved (member states, candidate countries, the Commission, and the European Parliament), and the main stages in the process. Originally, Article 237 of the Rome Treaty required the applicant country only be a 'European state'. For example, Morocco applied for EU membership in 1987, but its application was turned down because it was not considered to be a European country. By contrast, Turkey, which had applied for membership in the same year as Morocco,

was officially recognized as a candidate country by the Helsinki European Council in December 1999, despite the fact that Turkey's European identity had been questioned by some member states (see Box 18.1). Before the Eastern enlargement, the enlargement procedure was also simpler: the application was dealt with by the EU Council after receiving an opinion from the Commission and subject to the approval of the member states. But this does not mean that the process was less politicized. For example, French President **Charles de Gaulle** vetoed the British membership application in 1963 and 1967 because of fears that the UK would undermine the EC; the UK would join the EC only in 1973 after the French veto was lifted. Also, despite the Commission's negative *avis* (opinion), the member states decided to start accession negotiations with Greece, with the country joining the EU in 1981. Hence, from the beginning, enlargement has been an intergovernmental policy, in the hands of the member states (see Box 18.2).

Conditionality, that is, the requirement that candidates must comply with EU conditions to progress in the accession process, has been the key principle driving enlargement. The use of political conditionality and the subsequent establishment of a complex monitoring procedure by the Commission were only

---

 BOX 18.2   BACKGROUND: ACCESSION PROCESS FOR A NEW MEMBER STATE

According to Article 49 TEU:

'Any European State which respects the values referred to in Article 2 and is committed to promoting them may apply to become a member of the Union. The European Parliament and national Parliaments shall be notified of this application. The applicant State shall address its application to the Council, which shall act unanimously after consulting the Commission and after receiving the consent of the European Parliament, which shall act by a majority of its component members. The conditions of eligibility agreed upon by the European Council shall be taken into account.'

'The conditions of admission and the adjustments to the Treaties on which the Union is founded, which such admission entails, shall be the subject of an agreement between the Member States and the applicant State. This agreement shall be submitted for ratification by all the contracting States in accordance with their respective constitutional requirements.'

Source: Treaty on the European Union. © European Union.

BOX 18.3   BACKGROUND: THE COPENHAGEN CRITERIA

To join the European Union, a candidate country must have achieved:

- stability of institutions guaranteeing democracy, the rule of law, human rights, and respect for and protection of minorities;

- the existence of a functioning market economy, as well as the capacity to cope with competitive pressure and market forces within the Union; and

- the ability to take on the obligations of membership, including adherence to the aims of political, economic, and monetary union.

At the 1993 Madrid European Council, an additional administrative criterion was introduced: that the candidate country must have created the conditions for its integration through the adjustment of its administrative structures.

introduced with the Eastern enlargement round in the early 1990s. The 1993 Copenhagen European Council adopted a set of political and economic conditions with which countries willing to become EU members had to comply (see Box 18.3). According to the so-called 'Copenhagen criteria', applicant countries must have stable institutions guaranteeing democracy, the rule of law, respect for human rights, and the protection of minorities; a functioning market economy capable of coping with the competitive pressures and market forces within the Union; and the ability to take on the obligations of membership, including adherence to the aims of political, economic, and **monetary union**, and adopt the *acquis communautaire*. The establishment of clear membership conditions satisfied both pro- and anti-enlargement camps. On the one hand, it reassured reluctant member states such as France by increasing the hurdle for enlargement since applicant countries would be admitted to the EU only once these conditions had been met. On the other hand, those in favour of enlargement, such as the UK and Germany, saw the adoption of the Copenhagen criteria as a way to provide some certainty about the process, reducing—although not eliminating—the possibilities for politically motivated decisions (Menon and Sedelmeier, 2010: 84–6).

The identification of this set of criteria led to the establishment of a complex monitoring mechanism currently managed by the Commission's European Neighbourhood Policy and Enlargement Negotiations Directorate-General (DG NEAR), which acts as a 'gatekeeper', deciding when countries have fulfilled these criteria and whether they are ready to move to the next stage (Grabbe, 2001: 1020). This monitoring process takes place following the **benchmarks** set by the Commission in different documents—in the case

of the Western Balkans, the **stabilization and association agreements (SAAs)** and the **European partnership** agreements (EPAs); and the **Europe agreements** in the case of the Eastern enlargement. Compliance is also monitored in the regular annual reports produced by the Commission. This monitoring means that the enlargement process follows a merit-based approach (Vachudova, 2005: 112–13), yet political considerations have also played a part in this process.

Linked to the use of conditionality is the principle of **differentiation** and a preference for bilateralism in the EU's relations with candidate countries. During the Eastern enlargement, a regional approach was rejected in favour of a meritocratic approach according to which each country would proceed towards membership on its own merits and at its own speed. The expectation was that this method would spur the adoption of reforms in the candidate countries. The downside was that it could lead to a **multi-speed** process, with some countries being left behind. For example, the decision made at the Luxembourg Council in December 1997 to start negotiations with a selected group of applicant countries (Cyprus, the Czech Republic, Estonia, Hungary, Poland, and Slovenia) raised fears among those left out (Slovakia, Lithuania, Latvia, Estonia, Romania, and Bulgaria). For this reason, accession negotiations were opened with the remaining Central and Eastern European (CEE) applicant countries (in addition to Malta) at the Helsinki European Council in December 1999 and efforts were made to include as many countries as possible in the 'big bang' enlargement of 1 May 2004, which saw the accession of ten new member states (see Table 18.2). Romania and Bulgaria were not deemed ready to join the EU yet. At the 2002 Copenhagen European Council, it was agreed that these two countries could join

Table 18.2 Applications for EU membership (since 1987)

Applicant country	Date of application	Date of accession
Turkey	14 April 1987	—
Austria	17 July 1989	1 January 1995
Cyprus	3 July 1990	1 May 2004
Malta	16 July 1990	1 May 2004
Sweden	1 July 1991	1 January 1995
Finland	18 March 1992	1 January 1995
Switzerland	26 May 1992	—
Norway	25 November 1992	—
Hungary	31 March 1994	1 May 2004
Poland	5 April 1994	1 May 2004
Romania	22 June 1995	1 January 2007
Slovakia	27 June 1995	1 May 2004
Latvia	13 October 1995	1 May 2004
Estonia	24 November 1995	1 May 2004
Lithuania	8 December 1995	1 May 2004
Bulgaria	14 December 1995	1 January 2007
Czech Republic	17 January 1996	1 May 2004
Slovenia	10 June 1996	1 May 2004
Croatia	21 February 2003	1 July 2013
North Macedonia	22 March 2004	—
Montenegro	15 December 2008	—
Albania	28 April 2009	—
Iceland	17 July 2009	(Iceland withdrew candidacy in 2015)
Serbia	22 December 2009	—
Bosnia and Herzegovina	15 February 2016	—

in 2007 provided that they had met the membership criteria. On 1 January 2007, Bulgaria and Romania became EU members despite evidence that they had not fully met their obligations, in particular in the area of

BOX 18.4   DEBATE: ENLARGEMENT, STATE-BUILDING, AND PEACE-BUILDING IN THE BALKANS

The power of attraction of EU membership has been hailed as one of the most powerful tools of EU foreign policy. Enlargement is said to have extended peace and security to other areas of the continent through the democratization processes fostered by the adoption of the *acquis communautaire*. EU enlargement is thus seen as a peace-building project. However, despite significant financial and technical assistance and wide domestic support for EU accession, progress towards membership in the Balkans has remained limited. In the case of Bosnia and Herzegovina, this state of affairs can be explained as a result of a number of contradictions that have undermined the EU's member state-building strategy (Juncos, 2012). First, the EU's strategy has been perceived as an attempt to impose particular reforms externally—that is, a reform 'from above'. Despite a commitment to promote 'local ownership', in practice this has hardly implied an involvement of civil society and the domestic public, undermining the legitimacy of the enlargement process. Moreover, the EU has continued to portray the reforms as mere technical changes despite the highly politicized nature of state-building and peace-building: EU reforms promote specific models of political and economic re-organization. This 'technocratic approach' has only served to increase distrust and conflict among the ethnic parties. Furthermore, while all nationalist parties still support the wider goal of European integration, they have increasingly redefined the project to suit their political goals. Overall, the EU needs to recognize that the main problems in Bosnia are linked to unresolved statehood issues which are intrinsically political. Until this is acknowledged by the EU, sustainable progress towards accession will remain fragile.

rule of law (including judicial reform, corruption, and organized crime). A special '**cooperation** and verification mechanism' was thus established by the Commission to monitor progress in these areas and to help the countries to address the outstanding shortcomings.

Conditionality has also been actively used in the EU's enlargement to the Western Balkans as a means to stabilize the region (see Box 18.4). This new phase in the EU's intervention also sought to restore the Union's reputation after its failure to stop the war in the former **Yugoslavia** at the beginning of the 1990s (see Chapter 19). The prospect of future membership for the Western Balkans was first brought to the table during the Kosovo crisis, and led to the establishment of the Stability Pact and the Stabilization and Association Process (SAP). The membership perspective for the Western Balkans was reconfirmed by the European Council in Feira in 2000 and in Thessaloniki in June 2003. Since then, most Western Balkan countries have applied for membership; North Macedonia, Montenegro, Serbia, and Albania have been given candidate status (see Table 18.2).

The Commission and the Council have repeatedly reminded applicant countries of the meritocratic nature of the process: 'Each country's progress towards the European Union must be based on individual merits and rigorous conditionality, guiding the necessary political and economic reforms' (Presidency of the EU, 2009). However, some candidate and potential candidate countries expressed their disappointment with what seemed like privileged treatment for Iceland, whose membership application was referred to the Commission by the Council in a matter of days. By contrast, Montenegro's application was referred only after five months and Albania's application took even longer. In the case of North Macedonia in 2009, although the Commission has repeatedly recommended the opening of accession negotiations, the European Council has delayed the process due to the name dispute with Greece, and more recently, a language dispute with Bulgaria. As Schimmelfennig and Sedelmeier (2004: 664) put it, the effectiveness of EU conditionality depends on the 'credibility of the threats and rewards'. Further, the authors argue that 'a lack of credibility has undermined the effectiveness of pre-accession conditionality in SEE and of post-accession sanctions against democratic backsliding in CEE' (Schimmelfennig and Sedelmeier 2020: 816). The perceived domestic politicization of enlargement in the member states sends the wrong message to the applicant countries, which are also concerned about high adoption costs, and weakens the Commission's emphasis on a transparent and a merit-based process.

The lessons learnt from the 2004 enlargement, and, in particular, problems with the adoption of the *acquis communautaire* in the cases of Bulgaria and Romania, have led to a stricter application of conditionality by the EU. For example, the 'new approach' to enlargement pays more attention to issues related to the rule of law, so the rule of law chapters are opened first in the negotiation process. The hurdles for accession have also been raised because new legislation has

been added to the *acquis*. As a result, the number of chapters has increased from 31 to 35. Another concern, that of the 'absorption capacity' of the Union, has also become more salient as new member states have joined the EU, and the commitment for enlargement among member states and citizens has waned. Although it was part of the Copenhagen criteria, references to the need to take into account the capacity of the EU to integrate new members increased after the 2004 enlargement.

In its current version in the Lisbon Treaty, Article 49 outlines the conditions and the main stages in the enlargement process (see Figure 18.1 and Box 18.2). It states that any European state can apply for membership as long as it respects the foundational values of the EU (freedom, democracy, equality, the rule of law, and respect for human rights). Apart from the role attributed to the EU Council and the Commission, this article also requires the consent of the European Parliament and, since the Treaty of Lisbon, that national parliaments be informed of membership applications. Once an application for membership is successful, the Commission is invited to prepare an opinion (*avis*) on the preparedness of applicant countries to meet the membership criteria. The Commission forwards a questionnaire to the concerned government requesting information. On the basis of the responses to this questionnaire and other information gathered by the Commission in its annual reports about the candidate and potential candidate countries, the Commission might recommend to the European Council the opening of accession negotiations, on which the latter then decides under **unanimity**. The accession negotiations between the EU and the applicant country begin with the adoption of a negotiating framework and the opening of an intergovernmental conference (IGC). The content of the negotiations is broken down into chapters, each of which covers a policy area of the *acquis* (for example, competition policy, fisheries, or economic and monetary policy). Prior to the negotiation of a specific chapter, the Commission carries out a 'screening' of the *acquis* to familiarize the candidate with its content, as well as to evaluate its degree of preparedness.

The Commission plays a key role during the accession process, in particular through the monitoring of candidate countries' compliance and in drafting the EU's negotiating position. However, the process remains decidedly intergovernmental, as the opening

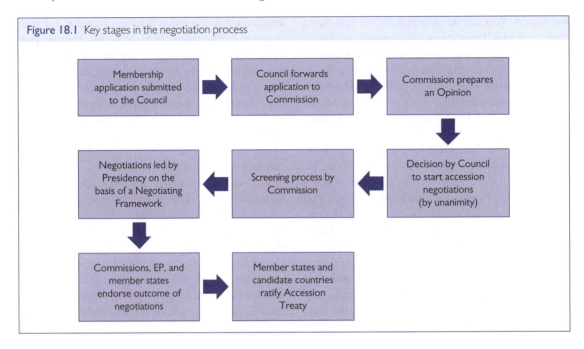

Figure 18.1 Key stages in the negotiation process

and closing of each of the negotiating chapters requires the unanimous agreement of the 27 member states. The term 'negotiations' is actually a misnomer: candidate countries cannot affect the substance of the negotiations, but only the timing of the implementation of the *acquis*. It is possible for candidate states to negotiate some transition periods, but also for the EU to impose some transitional measures or to withhold some benefits (such as financial disbursements) until a later date. For example, in the Eastern enlargement, a transitional period of up to seven years was agreed during which restrictions on the free movement of workers could be applied to workers from the new member states.

Once all of the chapters have been negotiated, the **accession treaty** must be approved by the European Parliament and needs to be ratified by each member state and the candidate country in accordance with their respective constitutional requirements. In most cases, candidate countries have held a referendum prior to joining the EU. The most recent referendum was held by Croatia in January 2012, with 66 per cent of the voters supporting EU membership (33 per cent voted against). However, as was the case with the referendums held by the CEEs, the turnout was very low (at 44 per cent).

KEY POINTS

- Compliance with the political conditions set out in the Copenhagen criteria is at the heart of the enlargement process.

- Conditionality remains the key mechanism guiding the accession of new members to the EU.

- The meritocratic nature of the enlargement process is an essential aspect in maintaining the credibility of the process.

- Enlargement remains an essentially intergovernmental process, firmly in the hands of the member states. The Commission plays a key role managing the accession negotiations and monitoring compliance with the accession criteria.

18.4 Explaining enlargement

EU enlargement is a complex process that challenges the explanatory power of European Studies' conceptual and theoretical toolkit. The academic scholarship discusses key aspects of enlargement as a process and accession as an outcome, their effect on power asymmetries, and on the adaptation capacity of the new member states and the EU. This section summarizes the contributions of neo-functionalism (see Chapter 4), liberal intergovernmentalism (see Chapter 5), and constructivism (see Chapter 6) towards explaining the geographical expansion of the EU, as well as those of Europeanization (see Chapter 8) and differentiated integration theories. We draw mainly on the case of the Eastern enlargement given its extensive implications for both the EU and the candidate countries.

18.4.1 Neo-functionalism

While neo-functionalism was the first attempt at theorizing European integration, initially, it did not pay much attention to enlargement. Two interrelated reasons explain this: first, early neo-functionalism was too closely related to the empirical reality that it was trying to explain. In the 1960s, French President Charles de Gaulle's two vetoes of British membership did not suit the conceptual toolkit of neo-functionalism, which, like other theories of regional integration, analysed the establishment and stabilization of regional organizations, a process that precedes studying their territorial expansion (Schimmelfennig and Sedelmeier, 2002: 501). Second, at the time of the first enlargement (1973), neo-functionalism had already lost appeal among scholars of European integration (see Chapter 4). In the 1990s, the revived interest in the theory among scholars, and the research dynamism surrounding the Eastern enlargement provided the appropriate context for the theory's attempt to explain the geographical expansion of the EU. Neo-functionalism explains three dimensions of enlargement—namely, enlargement as a process, the role of **supranational institutions**, and functional integration. First, enlargement as a gradual process that involves several incremental stages from the point of membership application, through the association and pre-accession stages, leading to accession, reflects the neo-functionalist logic of the irreversibility of a process in which, as a result of successful negotiations, the full *acquis* is imposed upon the new members (Schmitter, 2004: 70). Second, during enlargement negotiations, the Commission plays a major role in managing the process and its entrepreneurial role is evident, for example, in its promotion of the **European Social Dialogue** in the Central and Eastern European (CEE) countries, which is not strictly a criterion for accession (Pérez-Solórzano Borragán and Smismans, 2012). The Commission has traditionally supported the enlargement process to protect its leading role in this policy

area. Third, neo-functionalism accounts for the role of European **interest groups** supporting enlargement and coordinating their role transnationally, particularly by welcoming members from the new member states and by engaging in Commission-funded programmes to promote and support interest groups in the new member states (Blavoukos and Pagoulatos, 2008). Neo-functionalism, however, does not explain the role of domestic actors and structures in either the member states or the candidate countries; nor does it explain the effects of enlargement or its normative dimension (Niemann and Schmitter, 2009: 63).

18.4.2 Liberal intergovernmentalism

Rationalist approaches, such as liberal intergovernmentalism, see enlargement through the lens of national interests and state power, and regard the member states' promotion of accession as being in their long-term economic and geopolitical interest (Moravcsik and Vachudova, 2003). The contribution of liberal intergovernmentalism is twofold: on the one hand, it shows how 'the costs and benefits of socio-economic **interdependence**' (Moravcsik and Schimmelfennig, 2009: 80) inform whether member states and candidate countries support enlargement—and on the other hand, it focuses on how states bargain with each other in this typically intergovernmental policy. In the case of the Eastern enlargement, socio-economic factors informed preference formation in the member states to some extent, because countries that benefited the most from market expansion as a result of the accession of new member states, such as Germany or the UK, were supportive of a rapid and all-inclusive enlargement, while countries competing for EU funds with the new arrivals had a more conservative approach and thus preferred a more gradual and less inclusive geographical expansion (Moravcsik and Schimmelfennig, 2009: 83). Similarly, the bargaining process was an asymmetrical relationship between the member states, which could behave as 'an exclusive club dictating the terms of accession to new members' (Risse, 2009: 157), and a set of candidate countries, which accepted such demanding accession criteria in addition to temporary restrictions to the free movements of people, for example, to avoid exclusion from the EU (Vachudova, 2005: 65–79). What liberal intergovernmentalism is unable to explain is why the member states decided to go ahead with negotiating EU accession when, given their stronger position in this asymmetrical relationship, they could have framed their advantageous relationship with their Eastern neighbours, plus Malta and Cyprus, in the context of an association or preferential status agreement, thus avoiding the costs resulting from enlargement.

18.4.3 Social constructivism

Social constructivism turns its attention to two questions unanswered by neo-functionalism and liberal intergovernmentalism: why did member states accept the Eastern enlargement? and why did candidate countries agree to transpose the *acquis communautaire*? The answers to these questions lie in three complementary propositions. First, as Schimmelfennig points out, the constitutive liberal values and norms of the European international community, which are at the basis of the membership criteria, commit member states to the accession of 'states that share the collective identity of an international community and adhere to its constituent values and norms' (Schimmelfennig, 2001: 58–9). In other words, the closer a country is to adhering to these norms, the closer it is to joining the EU. Thus 'rhetorical commitment to community values entrapped EU member states into offering accession negotiations . . . despite the initial preferences against enlargement' (Risse, 2009: 157). Second, Sedelmeier and Schimmelfennig stress this point by focusing on the discursive creation of a particular identity of the EU towards the new member states, which asserted 'a "special responsibility" of the EU for the reintegration of the peoples who had been involuntarily excluded from the integration project' (Schimmelfennig and Sedelmeier, 2002: 522). Third, Jacoby (2004) used the language of social learning and norm diffusion (see Chapter 8) to explain how institutional reform to adapt to EU accession requirements took place in the new member states. He placed elites at the core of a process characterized by the emulation of institutional models offered by the EU and the member states in the candidate countries. At a time of profound domestic change following the demise of the communist system, elites wished to 'accelerate their country's embrace of successful Western ways', but also had to cope with very specific norms propagated by the EU (Jacoby, 2004: 35), and a very detailed monitoring process aimed at checking the **transposition** of an extensive *acquis* and the country's administrative ability to implement it.

18.4.4 Europeanization

Europeanization is useful in explaining how, prior to EU accession, candidate and potential candidate countries are mainly 'takers' of EU policy thus illustrating the power asymmetry of the negotiation process. Top-down Europeanization helps explain the impact and costs of EU enlargement on a candidate's domestic environment including policies, politics, norms, and actors (see Chapter 8). Similarly, a discreet section of the Europeanization literature has devoted some attention to whether Europeanization is an irreversible process (Featherstone, 2003). Featherstone suggests that not only can the effects of Europeanization be differentiated over time, but also its systemic effects are not necessarily permanent or irreversible. Research on democratic backsliding in Hungary, Poland, and Romania further illustrates the reversibility and impermanent nature of Europeanization and the (limited) ability of conditionality to promote democracy and governance effectiveness in non-member and new member states (Sedelmeier, 2008, 2014; Börzel and Schimmelfennig, 2017; Schimmelfennig and Sedelmeier, 2020).

18.4.5 Differentiated integration

The concept of differentiated or flexible integration—that is, a series of strategies to reconcile heterogeneity within the EU (Stubb, 1996: 2)—helps explain how enlargement has been a driver of internal differentiation in the EU and whether that differentiation is taking place along the divide between 'old' and 'new' member states. Enlargement means the accession of a more diverse set of countries with different capacities to adopt the entire *acquis communautaire*. Differentiated integration explains the phasing of the negotiation process, the use of conditionality, and the bespoke nature of each accession treaty that contains transitional arrangements with derogations from the full implementation of the *acquis* (Schimmelfennig and Winzen, 2017: 240). The withering of the initial differentiating between old and new member states is explained by the EU's capacity to integrate new and more diverse members and is reflected in the split between euro and non-euro area countries or Schengen and non-Schengen countries as key divides between member states. The focus of this chapter is the accession of new member states rather than a country's withdrawal from the EU, as in the case of Brexit. However, the Trade and Cooperation Agreement signed between the EU and the UK is an association agreement whose content and negotiation owe much to the EU's experience negotiating similar agreements with candidates and other third countries. Thus the external differentiated integration literature (Gstöhl, 2015; Schimmelfennig 2018) and the metaphor of concentric circles of flexible European integration (Lavenex, 2011) shed light on the EU's political and economic strategies and templates to accommodate third countries, which, while not wishing to become member states, aspire to a close relationship with the Union. These models of external differentiated integration have been labelled as 'quasi-colonialism' to illustrate the EU's relationship with countries in the European Economic Area (EEA); 'pragmatic bilateralism' exemplified by the EU's relationship with Switzerland; 'association', such as the relationship under negotiation with **Mercosur** countries (Argentina, Brazil, Paraguay, and Uruguay); and 'external governance', such as the Cotonou Agreement or the **Comprehensive Economic and Trade Agreement (CETA)** between Canada and the EU (see Gstöhl and Phinnemore 2019 and Chapters 17 and 27).

KEY POINTS

- It is possible to explain aspects of enlargement from more than one theoretical perspective.

- Neo-functionalism explains the entrepreneurial role of the Commission, the role of European interest groups, and the gradual and incremental nature of enlargement.

- Liberal intergovernmentalism explains the socio-economic preferences behind member states' support for enlargement.

- Social constructivist approaches explain member states' commitment to enlargement despite the availability of alternative and less demanding options, such as association agreements.

- Europeanization helps explain the impact of EU enlargement on candidates' domestic environment and draws attention to the reversibility and impermanent nature of EU influence.

- Differentiated integration explains the strategies to reconcile heterogeneity within the EU.

18.5 The future of enlargement: key challenges

EU membership continues to be an attractive incentive for countries in the Union's neighbourhood. Accession negotiations were opened with Turkey in 2005 (see Box 18.1), Montenegro in 2012, Serbia in 2013, and Albania and North Macedonia in 2020. Bosnia and Herzegovina applied for EU membership in February 2016, but remains to date a 'potential candidate country', as is the case with Kosovo. Ukraine, Moldova, and Georgia have repeatedly expressed their desire to become EU members one day. Despite the continuing attraction of the prospect of membership among its neighbours, and the fact that enlargement has been deemed the EU's most successful foreign policy, several challenges affect the enlargement project in the medium and long term. We deal with them in turn in the remainder of this chapter.

First, more than a decade after the Eastern enlargement, enlargement fatigue is very much evident in EU member states. EU citizens are very much split on the issue of 'further enlargement of the EU', although a small majority of 44 per cent support the process, while 42 per cent oppose it. (Eurobarometer, 2019: 95). Support for EU membership also varies across candidate countries. While Albanian, Macedonian, and Montenegrin citizens are still pro-EU membership (87 per cent, 57 per cent, and 54 per cent respectively), support for membership has continued to decline in Serbia (26 per cent) (Balkan Barometer, 2020: 40), and especially in Turkey, where only 28 per cent consider accession to the EU a 'good thing' (Eurobarometer, 2016: 78). Enlargement fatigue has also developed in the context of and fuelled by increasing support for populist Eurosceptic parties in the majority of EU member states who see enlargement as a source of insecurity, putting further pressure on migration and crippled welfare systems across the EU. While the exit of the UK from the EU has not led to an exit domino effect, it has removed one of the most fervent supporters of territorial expansion and, in the medium and long term, it might also have an impact on the EU's willingness and capacity to accommodate a larger and more heterogeneous membership.

Second, despite some positive signs, progress in the candidate countries has generally been disappointing. This results from three main factors: democratic backsliding; the legacies of the conflicts; and standing bilateral issues. European integration imposes high adoption costs for politicians in the candidate countries (Schimmelfennig and Sedelmeier, 2019). In some cases, EU integration not only threatens the power base of local elites, but also their private economic interests, because many of them profit from weak legal and regulatory frameworks and are involved in organized crime. The Commission has identified problems in the candidate and potential candidate countries that have hindered reforms in relation to the independence of the judiciary, the fight against corruption and organized crime, a highly confrontational political climate, and ethnic-related tensions. Particularly worrying is democratic backsliding. Observers have accused the EU of turning a blind eye to the so-called 'stabilitocrats' in the region (Vučič in Serbia or Djukanović in Montenegro) by favouring stability over democratic reforms in a context of increased geopolitical competition and security challenges in the neighbourhood. Problems of compliance with the rule of law within the EU (e.g., in the cases of Hungary or Poland) have also sent the wrong signal to candidate countries. In fact, some scholars have argued that EU conditionality has contributed to processes of state capture in the Western Balkans. The economic liberalization, top-down, and elitist processes that characterize the enlargement process have consolidated powerful clientelist networks in the region (Richter and Wunsch, 2019).

Many of these problems are also linked to the legacies of the conflicts that affected the Western Balkans region in the 1990s and 2000s. The effectiveness of EU conditionality remains low in countries in which the legacies of ethnic conflict make compliance with EU criteria very costly, especially in Serbia and Bosnia and Herzegovina. Political, economic, and social reforms have fallen hostage to recalcitrant nationalist politicians in Bosnia and threaten the European perspective of Serbia, Montenegro, Kosovo, and North Macedonia. Bilateral disputes, and in particular the Kosovo issue, remain a significant obstacle to regional cooperation.

Third, there is evidence of the increasing politicization or 'creeping nationalization' of enlargement (Hillion, 2010). EU member states have sought to strengthen their influence over the EU's enlargement policy by insisting on the use of benchmarks before the opening of negotiating chapters and the inclusion of new conditions in every step of the process. In recent years, Germany has emerged as the 'reluctant hegemon' in the Western Balkans by taking the lead in different initiatives, while other countries have followed German leadership (e.g., Austria, Slovenia with the Berlin Process, or the UK in the case of Bosnia). For Germany, leading in the case of enlargement provides it with an opportunity to control the process to ensure that candidate countries meet the accession criteria before membership is granted. For its part, a French veto of the opening of membership talks for Albania and North Macedonia in 2019 was justified by French President Emmanuel Macron as a way to ensure that the process remains politically driven. The veto was lifted when the European Commission presented a new enlargement strategy in March 2020 (entitled 'a credible EU perspective for the Western Balkans'), which foresees a stronger input from the member states throughout the process, while strengthening the monitoring mechanisms. On the plus side, candidate countries will receive more rewards and incentives along the way and it is expected that clearer conditions will make the process more predictable.

The rising number of bilateral disputes holding up the enlargement process also constitutes another indication of a stronger role of the member states in the enlargement process. For example, some member states have used their privileged position inside the EU to put pressure on candidate countries in the hope that they will make concessions (Geddes and Taylor, 2016). Thus, Turkey's accession has been delayed over the conflict with Cyprus (see Box 18.1), the adoption of a negotiating framework for North Macedonia has been blocked by Bulgaria since 2020 because of a dispute over the 'Macedonian language', and last, but not least, Kosovo's independence remains a divisive issue among member states.

Fourth, the enlargement process has also been regularly impacted by external crises. The 2008 economic crisis had a major impact on enlargement by slowing down the process of economic convergence between the new and old member states, and between the EU and the candidate and potential candidate countries. The economic crisis resulted in an increase of unemployment, which was already very high in some candidate countries, and worsened the fiscal position of many of these countries. Moreover, the crisis continued to erode the EU's attraction power—its so-called 'soft power'—in particular vis-à-vis countries such as Turkey and neighbouring countries under Russia's sphere of influence. For many candidate countries, the way the EU has handled the 'refugee crisis' caused by the Syrian civil war also contributed to weakening the EU's image as a soft or normative power (see Chapter 26). The health, social, and economic effects of the COVID-19 pandemic have only added to these problems as the EU has been criticized in the region for failing to show solidarity during the early stages of the pandemic and the vaccine rollout (see Chapter 28 and Juncos, 2021).

Fifth, the EU's enlargement policy is taking place in an increasingly competitive geopolitical context. In particular, the annexation of Crimea, the civil war in Ukraine, and Russia's treatment of opposition figures such as Alexei Navalni have strained EU–Russia relations, as illustrated by the EU's imposition of economic sanctions on Russia and the latter's retaliation by limiting food imports from the EU member states. Hence, in the medium term, and despite the EU's view that Moscow cannot veto EU expansion, the EU's approach to enlargement in the Balkans and to its Eastern neighbours is likely to be shaped by an increasingly belligerent Russian Federation, which regards Ukraine, Moldova, and Georgia as part of its sphere of influence. While China's approach has been subtler so far and focused on strengthening of bilateral economic relations, its presence in the neighborhood also challenges the EU's attraction power by deploying an alternative narrative of economic growth without political conditionality. For instance, China has used the vaccine rollout to strengthen its role in the Western Balkan region. The disinformation, fake news, and 'battle of narratives' witnessed during the COVID-19 pandemic also illustrate the geopolitical games that are being played out in the region.

KEY POINTS

- The prospect of EU membership continues to attract countries in the EU's neighbourhood.

- Despite the continuing potential of EU membership to promote political and economic reforms in candidate countries, the enlargement project faces significant internal and external challenges.

- Enlargement to the Western Balkans and Turkey faces domestic obstacles in the form of high adoption costs, the legacies of the conflicts, and ongoing bilateral issues.

- A growing enlargement fatigue, Euroscepticism, the increasing politicization of this policy, the aftermath of the economic and COVID-19 crises, and geopolitical competition risk undermining the credibility of EU enlargement.

18.6 Conclusion

The enlargement project has remained intrinsically linked to the project of European integration. Enlargement has both shaped and been shaped by the development of the European Union over time. A more complex EU has meant that the conditions of membership have also become tighter and more technical in nature. Different enlargement waves have also been affected by the internal dynamics within the EU. As the Union has extended its borders and increased its membership from six to 27, questions have also been raised about the ability of an enlarged Union to be able to function effectively. Thus each enlargement has required numerous institutional and policy reforms in order to allow the Union to incorporate the new member states. Undoubtedly, the most significant decision for the EU was to expand to Central and Eastern Europe in the 1990s, because of the number and diversity of applicant countries. The **Europeanization** of the candidate countries has had a significant impact on their institutions, politics, and policies, and has generally been seen as a key incentive in promoting political and economic reforms and fostering stability despite some evidence of democratic backsliding. Yet, in a context where Brexit has, for the first time, led to the contraction of the EU, and given other significant internal and external challenges, how the EU will ensure the incorporation of new members, while continuing to further integrate in new areas such as economic and fiscal **governance**, will thus remain crucial.

QUESTIONS

1. How is it possible to explain the decision of the European Union to enlarge?

2. How similar are the different rounds of enlargement?

3. To what extent has the enlargement process become increasingly politicized over time?

4. What roles do the Commission, European Parliament, and member states play in the process of enlargement?

5. How important is conditionality in the enlargement process?

6. How successful has EU enlargement been to date?

7. What internal and external challenges is the enlargement process likely to face in the coming years?

8. What is the likely impact of Brexit on the enlargement process?

 GUIDE TO FURTHER READING

Börzel, T.A., Dimitrova, A., and Schimmelfennig, F. (2017) 'European Union Enlargement and Integration Capacity', *Journal of European Public Policy*, Special Issue 24/2, 157–315. An excellent in-depth analysis of the consequences of the EU's Eastern enlargement.

Grabbe, H. (2006) *The EU's Transformative Power: Europeanization through Conditionality in Central and Eastern Europe* (Basingstoke: Palgrave Macmillan). An excellent account of the impact of the EU's conditionality on the candidate countries during the Eastern enlargement.

Kelemen, R.D., Menon, A., and Slapin, J. (2015) *The European Union: Integration and Enlargement* (London: Routledge). This book examines the debate of widening versus deepening by looking at the impact of enlargement on EU integration.

Noutcheva, G. (2012) *European Foreign Policy and the Challenges of Balkan Accession: Conditionality, Legitimacy, and Compliance* (London: Routledge). This book offers an in-depth analysis of why the Western Balkan states have varied so much in their compliance with the EU's accession requirements.

Schimmelfennig, F. and Sedelmeier, U. (2020) 'The Europeanization of Eastern Europe: The External Incentives Model Revisited', *Journal of European Public Policy* 27/6 : 814–33. An application of the external incentives model to different stages and waves of enlargement.

Solveig R. and Wunsch, N. (2020) 'Money, power, glory: the linkages between EU conditionality and state capture in the Western Balkans', *Journal of European Public Policy*, 27/1, 41–62. A discussion relating to the challenges relating to conditionality and the rule of law in the Western Balkans.

Vollaard, H. (2014) 'Explaining European Disintegration', *Journal of Common Market Studies*, 52: 1142–59. This article offers a useful explanation of European disintegration as a multi-causal phenomenon.

 Access the online resources to take your learning and understanding further, including extra multiple-choice questions with instant feedback, web links, answer guidance to end-of-chapter questions, and updates on new developments in EU politics.

www.oup.com/he/cini-borragan7e

19

The European Union's Foreign, Security, and Defence Policies

Ana E. Juncos and Anna Maria Friis

Chapter Contents

Reader's Guide

EU cooperation in foreign, security, and defence policy has developed rapidly since the launch of the Common Foreign and Security Policy (CFSP) in the early 1990s. Section 19.1 charts the first steps towards a common policy in this area, including the development of the Common Security and Defence Policy (CSDP) and the gradual militarization of the EU. Section 19.2 then reviews the key theoretical debates on the EU's role as a foreign and security actor. Sections 19.3 and 19.4 analyse the main actors involved in the CFSP, focusing in particular on the role of the member states and EU institutions in the development of the policy. Section 19.5 evaluates the range of military and civilian CSDP operations and missions that the EU has undertaken to date, before examining the key challenges that the EU faces in this area in Section 19.6.

19.1 Introduction

The Common Foreign and Security Policy of the European Union (EU) covers all aspects relating to foreign policy, security, and defence cooperation among EU member states, including diplomatic cooperation with other third countries and international organizations, the use of sanctions as a foreign policy tool, and the promotion of peace and security around the world. A constituent part of the CFSP, the Common Security and Defence Policy (CSDP) focuses specifically on enabling EU member states to deploy military and civilian missions in conflict areas and to cooperate on the development of their defence capabilities. The CFSP is one of the most popular EU policies with European electorates. Since its inception in 1993, popular support for the CFSP has ranged from 68 to 79 per cent, and in the last decade it has never fallen below 70 per cent (Eurobarometer, 2019: 96). Despite this overwhelming public support, the CFSP has also been a controversial and contentious policy area, fraught with tensions.

First, there exists a tension between intergovernmentalist and integrationist perspectives. Traditionally, the former view international relations as a system of independent sovereign states, with foreign, security, and defence policy linked to state sovereignty. Close security and defence cooperation is often seen as undermining state independence and vital national interests. Thus, permanent and institutionalized EU cooperation through the CFSP and CSDP is seen as anathema to EU member states' national interests. By contrast, the more integrationist view understands the development and institutionalization of the CFSP and CSDP as a natural extension of the EU's function as an international actor, combining its economic soft power with military means in order to shoulder its responsibilities on the international stage.

Second, a further source of tension is the split between Atlanticist and Europeanist states. On the one side are EU states committed to a strong NATO and US presence in European security, such as the Central and Eastern European states, who fear that the development of the CSDP might undermine NATO. On the other side are states like France that promote an independent European security and defence structure as an alternative to NATO, and as a way of balancing US international influence (Keukeleire and Delreux, 2014).

Finally, there is a tension between more interventionist states, such as France, and those member states that have a tradition of non-intervention, such as Germany. With the development of the CSDP and the launch of CSDP missions in 2003, this has become a key issue. It has become clear that a minority of member states have shouldered the responsibility and cost for the majority of the operations undertaken under the EU flag. Moreover, the EU member states differ in the importance they attach to military instruments. In particular, the **post-neutral states**, such as Sweden and Finland, have traditionally supported a civilian dimension and a tradition of strong attachment to UN primacy in peacekeeping as a counterbalance to the militarization of the EU. Despite these underlying tensions, the EU has rapidly developed agency in the area of foreign, security, and defence policy since the early 1990s. The following section will look more closely at this development.

19.2 The emergence of the EU as a foreign and security actor

At the end of the Cold War, calls for the EU to play a leading role in the new world order increased. The forerunner to the CFSP, the so-called **European Political Cooperation (EPC)**, a loose coordinating network of European foreign ministries, had proved unable to deliver a proactive European foreign policy. Moreover, previous attempts at establishing cooperation in security and defence in Europe, including a failed initiative to establish a **European Defence Community**, had been unsuccessful. The **Western European Union (WEU)**, established in the 1950s outside of Community structures, had also had a very limited impact on European security. The collapse of the Soviet Union removed the need for a security 'buffer zone' between Russia and 'the West', which allowed neutral states Sweden, Finland, and Austria to join the EU. With the fall of communism, and the gradual US withdrawal from the European theatre, questions arose over NATO's future role in the European security architecture.

In this context, the Maastricht Treaty would provide the basis for developing the EU's Common Foreign and Security Policy (CFSP). It stated that the CFSP should cover 'all areas of foreign and security policy' and that, in time, the EU should work towards creating a common defence policy and eventually a common defence, if the member states so wish (Article J.4.1, title V, TEU). The main CFSP objectives, outlined in the Treaty, included: to safeguard the common values, fundamental interests, independence, and integrity of the Union; to strengthen the security of the Union; to promote international cooperation and strengthen international security; and, finally, to develop and consolidate democracy, the rule-of-law, and respect for human rights. The Treaty also established the **three-pillar structure** of the EU to accommodate and safeguard the intergovernmental character of the CFSP. The second intergovernmental pillar placed the CFSP under the control of the Council (and hence the member states) and involved minimal input from the Commission and the European Parliament. Moreover, the CFSP's decision-making was based on member state **unanimity**, giving each government the ability to veto any policy initiative or operation.

During its early years, the CFSP seemed to achieve little. **Common positions** agreed among the member states were often weak, reflecting lowest-common-denominator politics. Therefore, further institutional change was deemed necessary to improve coherence and effectiveness. The Amsterdam Treaty (1997) introduced two significant changes to the CFSP. First, it created a new institution, the **High Representative (HR) for the CFSP**, which was to represent the EU on the international stage and to act as the Secretary-General of the Council. Second, the Treaty incorporated the Western European Union's '**Petersberg tasks**' into the Treaty, namely humanitarian and rescue tasks, peacekeeping, and crisis management, including peacemaking, raising expectations about an operational role for the EU. These tasks were further expanded in the **Lisbon Treaty (LT)** (2009) to include conflict prevention, joint disarmament operations, military advice and assistance tasks, and post-conflict stabilization tasks (see Box 19.1).

The activities of the early years of the CFSP did not include a defence dimension. However, against the backdrop of the Yugoslav civil wars in the 1990s and the EU's inability to respond effectively to conflicts in its neighborhood, the need for further policy development became clear. The Yugoslav experience provided the political will necessary to increase the ambitions and capacities of EU foreign policy, leading to a slow militarization of the Union. In the context of the Kosovo crisis, a window of opportunity opened at a summit between France and the UK in St Malo in December 1998. Over the years, disagreements between France and the UK had made progress on a security and defence policy at the EU level impossible. However, in 1998, Tony Blair's Labour government saw EU defence cooperation as a means and symbol of British EU leadership after years of outsider status. Moreover, it represented a possibility to shape military and security policy in line with British interests (Dover, 2007). For the French government and Jacques Chirac, St Malo was an unexpected

opportunity, fitting well with its traditional position of support for a European security architecture independent from NATO (Howorth, 2014). The St Malo summit resulted in a joint declaration that stated that 'the Union must have the capacity for autonomous action, backed up by credible military forces, the means to decide to use them, and a readiness to do so, in order to respond to international crises'.

In subsequent European Council meetings in Cologne (1999) and Helsinki (1999), these proposals were developed and a European Security and Defence Policy (ESDP) was established. The member states also agreed on the establishment of a Political and Security Committee (PSC), which was to be assisted by a committee for civilian aspects of crisis management, as well as the European Union Military Committee (EUMC) and the European Union Military Staff (EUMS) and which were institutionalized in the **Nice Treaty** (see Section 19.3, 'CFSP institutions and actors'). Of particular significance was the adoption of a '**headline goal**' at the Helsinki Council, foreseeing that by 2003, the EU would be able to deploy 60,000 troops, in 60 days, sustainable for up to a year (Merlingen, 2012). This and other capability-development initiatives sought to make the ESDP operational, and not just a 'paper policy'. Moreover, to enable the EU to undertake military operations, it was necessary to ensure that the EU had access to NATO assets, such as planning and surveillance. The 'Berlin Plus' arrangements securing this access were agreed between the EU and NATO in 2002, allowing the Union to launch certain operations in the Balkans. However, the EU was also able to undertake autonomous military missions without recourse to 'Berlin Plus', such as Operation Artemis in the Democratic Republic of Congo (DRC). While St Malo resulted in the emergence of a military dimension, Sweden and Finland were keen to broaden this framework to include non-military security instruments and civilian crisis management missions, including policing, rule of law, civil protection, and civilian administration (the so-called Feira priorities). As with the military headline goals discussed earlier, a civilian capability catalogue was assembled to allow civilian personnel to be deployed rapidly.

With the entry into force of the Lisbon Treaty (LT) in 2009, the *European* Security and Defence Policy was renamed as the *Common* Security and Defence Policy (CSDP). This change might seem a minor issue of semantics; however, it has great symbolic value as it demonstrates an ambition for closer cooperation and potential integration. Furthermore, the Treaty

BOX 19.1   BACKGROUND: A CHRONOLOGY OF THE CFSP

1949   **NATO** is founded by the USA, Britain, France, Belgium, Netherlands, Denmark, Norway, Italy, and Luxembourg.

1954   Rejection of the proposal for a **European Defence Community** by the French National Assembly.
        The **Western European Union (WEU)** is created outside of European Community structures as an attempt to encourage European security cooperation.

1970   **European Political Cooperation (EPC)** is instituted and members agree to cooperate more fully on foreign policy matters.

1993   The **Maastricht Treaty** establishes the CFSP as the successor to the EPC and the second pillar of the EU.

1998   The December **St Malo summit** between France and Britain sets in motion the establishment of a European Security and Defence Policy.

1999   The **Amsterdam Treaty** institutes the post of High Representative for the CFSP and incorporates the Petersberg tasks.
        In December, the Helsinki **Headline Goal** is adopted.

2002   EU and NATO formalize the 'Berlin-plus' arrangement, providing the EU with access to NATO assets.

2003   In January, the ESDP launches its first civilian police mission to Bosnia Herzegovina.
        In February, the **Nice Treaty** formally establishes the ESDP and its politico-military structures.
        In December, the **European Security Strategy** is published.

2007   EU battlegroups become fully operational. These are 1,500 standby rapid-reaction forces rotating every six months between EU framework states.

2009   In December, the **Treaty of Lisbon** takes full effect: the CFSP is no longer a separate **pillar**. The role of High Representative is extended. The ESDP is renamed Common Security and Defence Policy (CSDP).

2011   In January, the **European External Action Service (EEAS)** becomes fully operational.
        In June, the WEU is formally dissolved.

2016   In June, the EU Global Strategy is presented by the High Representative.
        In November, the Council adopts the Implementation Plan on Security and Defence.

2017   In December, the Council establishes **Permanent Structured Cooperation** (PESCO) with 25 participating member states.

2020   The Council and the European Parliament agree on the launch of a European Defence Fund.

---

abolished the EU's pillar system. The CFSP is still formally intergovernmental and Council decisions continue to be taken by unanimity. However, coupled with institutional developments introduced in the Treaty, such as the new position of the Permanent President of the European Council, the extended powers of the High Representative, and the establishment of the European External Action Service (see Section 19.3, 'CFSP institutions and actors'), the LT signals a further 'Brusselization' of the CFSP. Moreover, the Lisbon Treaty incorporates two related and significant clauses guiding the CSDP. It includes the Solidarity clause, which confirms that EU states are obliged to act together when another member state is the victim of a terrorist attack or a natural or man-made disaster (Article 222 TFEU); and

it also includes the mutual assistance clause that states that if an EU state is a victim of armed aggression, other EU states have an 'obligation of aid and assistance by all the means in their power'. This clause is binding for all EU states, but does not affect the neutrality of member states where relevant, nor member states' membership of NATO (Article 42.7 TEU). While these clauses seem to take the EU into a new mutual defence agreement, military capacities remain in the hands of the individual member states, leaving obligations voluntary and intergovernmental.

Despite these institutional improvements, important challenges remain. In particular, EU civilian and military capabilities are still weak. The financial crisis of 2008 and the austerity policies that followed reduced what were already very small defence budgets (for instance, in 2016 only three EU member states met the NATO target of 2 per cent of defence expenditure as a percentage of GDP). The problem is not only the level of spending on defence, but also the quality of European armed forces. Of a total of around 1.5 million troops, fewer than 20 per cent are deployable abroad. Other capability shortfalls relate to intelligence, surveillance, and reconnaissance (ISR) systems, strategic air-lift and air-refuelling capabilities, and remotely piloted aircraft systems. Moreover, the increase in geopolitical competition, tensions during the Donald Trump Presidency, and the effects of the COVID-19 pandemic have highlighted the need for the EU to become strategically autonomous, including in the areas of security and defence. Over the past few years, further initiatives, such as the Implementation Plan on Security and Defence (2016) and the establishment of Permanent Structured Cooperation (2017)—with over 46 joint defence cooperation projects launched until the end of 2020—have sought to remedy some of these shortfalls (EEAS, 2020).

KEY POINTS

- At the end of the Cold War, the Maastricht Treaty established the intergovernmental Common Foreign and Security Policy.

- Following repeated failures to deal with conflicts in the EU's neighbourhood, the St Malo summit created momentum towards a European Security and Defence Policy.

- In 2003, the EU undertook its first civilian and military ESDP missions. Throughout the 2000s, the EU attempted to increase its military capabilities.

- With the Lisbon Treaty, the European Security and Defence Policy became the Common Security and Defence Policy.

19.3 CFSP institutions and actors

Since the inception of the CFSP, intense institutional development or 'Brusselization' has taken place (Allen, 1998). That said, the CFSP is still formally an intergovernmental policy area where EU member states continue to be the key actors and drivers through their right of initiative, their veto power, and the high profile of security and defence policy. To a large extent, this

influence is exerted through the European Council and the Foreign Affairs Council.

19.3.1 The European Council and the Foreign Affairs Council (FAC)

The Lisbon Treaty considerably enhanced the European Council's and thus the member states' role in shaping the EU's international agency. The European Council defines the strategic outlook for the EU, adopts common strategies, and provides guidelines for the Foreign Affairs Council (FAC) on how to translate CFSP treaty provisions and strategies into policies and practice.

The FAC is the Council formation concerned with the CFSP/CSDP. The FAC is the principal decision-maker in this policy area, and the national foreign ministers meet at least monthly. Prior to the entry into force of the Lisbon Treaty (2009), this Council formation was chaired by the rotating Presidency (see Chapter 11). Since 2009, this has been replaced with a permanent chair held by the High Representative, thus limiting the agenda-setting and implementation powers of member states. The FAC makes formal decisions on external action including on sanctions and the launch of civilian and military operations. So far, the attempted militarization of the EU has not meant the establishment of a Council of defence ministers, though defence ministers do participate in the FAC when needed. The responsibility for the implementation of Council decisions falls mainly on the HR. In recent years, there has been an increase in informal FAC meetings, especially in the aftermath of international crises. These tend to facilitate frank discussions and consensus-building between ministers.

19.3.2 The Political and Security Committee and its sub-committees

The Political and Security Committee (PSC) occupies a central position in the CFSP and the CSDP, and is one of the main channels for the member states to control the CFSP. The Committee consists of high-ranking national representatives at the ambassador level. It manages and directs a network of committees and working groups responsible for preparing foreign policy decisions relating to particular countries, regions, or issues of interest to the EU. Moreover, the PSC is the main advisor to the Foreign Affairs Council on CFSP. The Committee monitors and analyses the security context in which the EU operates, drafting common policies; and, once these have been adopted by the FAC, the Committee also oversees policy implementation (Merlingen, 2012). The EU Military Committee (EUMC) is the main military body of the EU and is composed of the national chiefs of staff, supported by the EU Military Staff (EUMS). On the civilian side, the Committee for Civilian Crisis Management (CivCom) provides information and drafts recommendations to the PSC on civilian aspects of crisis management.

19.3.3 The High Representative and the European External Action Service

With the coming into force of the Lisbon Treaty, the office of the High Representative (HR) was extended and renamed the 'High Representative of the Union for Foreign Affairs and Security Policy'. The Lisbon Treaty established the HR as both chair of the Foreign Affairs Council (FAC) and vice-president of the Commission, with responsibility for EU external action. The job was to be 'double-hatted' in order to improve consistency in the EU's external policies between the Council and the Commission. Furthermore, the extended role of the HR was intended to improve the visibility of the CFSP and the EU around the world. The HR has a particularly important role in agenda-setting as he or she has the right to submit joint proposals in all areas of external action.

The job of the HR is complex and the different responsibilities difficult to merge. It is a potentially powerful job, with three functions merged into one: the continuing job of the HR; the performance of the duties of the External Affairs Commissioner; and, finally, fulfilling the role previously undertaken by the rotating Presidency in the CFSP area. On top of this, the HR is also the Head of the **European Defence Agency**, in charge of supporting the development of member state defence capabilities. This pivotal position brings with it opportunities to influence the future of the CFSP and CSDP. However, the office also harbours inherent difficulties. There are tensions between the need to exert leadership and the need to mediate between member states. EU states tend to be suspicious about HR leadership and often strive to limit the influence of the HR in shaping EU foreign policy (see Box 19.2). Furthermore, there are conflicts between the Council and the Commission over the ownership of the CFSP, although the double-hat of the HR as Vice-President of the Commission has helped eased tensions.

The 'Brusselization' of the CFSP is further deepened by the creation under Article 27 TEU of the **European External Action Service (EEAS)**, which assists the HR. The EEAS became fully functional in 2011. It manages the EU's diplomatic relations and responses to crises, much like a national foreign service. The workforce of the EEAS consists of seconded staff from the member states, the Commission, and the Council Secretariat. Moreover, the EEAS acts as the diplomatic corps of the EU. It has 140 Union

---

 BOX 19.2   BACKGROUND: THE POLITICS OF THE HIGH REPRESENTATIVE

When the office of HR was first established in 1999, the European Council appointed a well-connected, experienced, and high-profile figure to the post: the former NATO General-Secretary, Javier Solana. Solana and his small office were a driving force in the development and institutionalization of the ESDP in the 2000s, and in mediating in international crises, such as Ukraine's Orange Revolution in 2004 and the Georgian war in 2008. The Lisbon Treaty gave the office of the HR extensive powers over the CFSP. However, the member states were reluctant to allow the new HR the means to use these powers. Considerations such as political affiliation, geographic origin, and lack of foreign policy experience and influence seemed important in appointing a new HR. As a result, the first post-Lisbon HR was a little-known British Labour politician and civil servant, Catherine Ashton. Her most important task was to negotiate the European External Action Service (EEAS) mandate and remit, and to get the EEAS fully functional as quickly as possible. This was a huge task, and gave Ashton an introverted focus, resulting in a lack of visibility, which raised criticism (Howorth, 2014). However, she was widely commended for her role in the negotiations that led to the deal with Iran regarding its nuclear energy programme and a historic agreement between Serbia and Kosovo, the so-called Brussels Agreement. At the end of 2014, when the EEAS was up and running, the European Council appointed a new HR, the former Italian Foreign Minister, Federica Mogherini. Mogherini was actively involved in shaping the EU's foreign policy, including the drafting and implementation of the new EU Global Strategy. She raised the profile and visibility of EU foreign, security, and defence policy considerably during her years in office. In November 2019, she was replaced by the Spaniard, also former Minister of Foreign Affairs, Josep Borrell, who has expressed his commitment to strengthening the international role of the EU, ensuring the EU embraces the 'language of power' in a more geopolitical world (Borrell, 2020).

Delegations or embassies around the world. These represent both the EU and its member states in third countries, and in international organizations. While it is possible for member states to merge their national representations with that of the EU, this possibility has not yet materialized in practice as most EU member states want to keep their own embassies and international presence (Howorth, 2014).

The EEAS has a rather challenging mandate; to coordinate the diplomatic and foreign policies of the member states and, at the same time, to produce new and common positions and policies. Moreover, the EEAS needs to do this without infringing on the members' national interests and sensitivities. Against this backdrop, it was initially hard for the newly established EEAS and the HR to live up to expectations, but over the past decade both the HR and the EEAS have become more active in leading and producing EU foreign and security policy such as in the case of the implementation of the EU Global Strategy (see also Box 19.6).

19.3.4 The Commission and the European Parliament

The Commission lives in the shadow of the Council in the CFSP area and has very limited powers and influence over the CFSP/CSDP, despite its broader role in the area of external relations, trade, and development. The implications of the Lisbon Treaty on the Commission in this regard are ambivalent. The Commission used to have the right to put forward CFSP policy proposals. However, this right has now been transferred to the HR, who is also a Commission Vice-President. Moreover, the EEAS has taken over the Union Delegations that used to be under the Commission's responsibility. The Commission has also limited influence regarding the military dimension of CSDP. However, when it comes to civilian CSDP missions, the Commission has more input, as these are included in the EU budget over which the Commission has a say. This being said, in recent years, the Commission has played a more proactive role in security and defence with the launch of a European Defence Fund, a multiannual financial programme to support defence industrial cooperation among EU member states (Haroche, 2019). Moreover, the engagement of the Commission in conflict prevention and its role in the provision of development and humanitarian aid is important for the EU to be able to deliver its integrated approach to security (see Box 19.3), drawing on the many instruments available to it.

The European Parliament (EP) has even more limited influence on the CFSP than the Commission. However, the Parliament is kept informed and consulted on CFSP issues. Furthermore, through its role in the EU budget process, the EP has a say in the budget allocated to civilian CSDP missions and policies. Since the Lisbon Treaty, the EP has had indirect influence over the appointment of the High Representative, as the EP must consent to the appointment of the Commission, including its Vice-President (the HR). MEPs have also been very keen to engage in foreign policy issues, continually pushing their case for an enhanced parliamentary role in external relations.

KEY POINTS

- Over the years, the CFSP has undergone an increasing 'Brusselization' with the establishment of new policy structures in Brussels.

- As an intergovernmental policy area, EU member states remain the key drivers in CFSP through their right of initiative, their veto power, and the implementation of EU security and defence policies.

- The key institutional actors in CFSP/CSDP are the European Council, which sets the main policy guidelines, and the Foreign Affairs Council, which acts as the main decision-making body, supported by the Political Security Committee and its working groups.

- The Lisbon Treaty extended the remit of the High Representative and established the European External Action Service (EEAS), the foreign and diplomatic service of the EU.

- Traditional supranational actors like the Commission and the European Parliament play a more limited role in the CFSP area.

19.4 Explaining the EU as an international actor

The emergence of the EU as an actor with security and defence ambitions on the international arena has presented EU and International Relations (IR) scholars alike with a theoretical puzzle and challenge. Traditional IR and EU theories have struggled to both define the EU as an international actor and explain why the EU ventured into the field of security and defence policy. This is particularly so for mainstream rationalist IR theories, such as (neo)realism and (neo)liberalism. Other theoretical approaches, such as social constructivism, have been

BOX 19.3   KEY DEBATES: THE EU'S INTEGRATED APPROACH

The EU embraces an integrated approach to external conflicts and crises. This entails a coherent and strategic use of all the EU's available tools and instruments in order to increase security and stability for the EU and the wider world. The EU's integrated approach is based on a holistic view of peace and security that takes into account the root causes of insecurity, such as poverty, state failure, and lack of development and good governance, as well as the more immediate security issues and crises. The EU is particularly well placed to deal with both long-term root causes of insecurity and their immediate effects as it has a wide range of policies, tools, and instruments at its disposal covering diplomatic efforts, security, trade policies, development cooperation, and humanitarian aid. The EU's integrated approach also refers to the need to coordinate policy instruments throughout the conflict cycle (from conflict prevention to crisis management to peace-building), at different levels (local, national, regional, and international) and with the member states and other international actors.

better placed to embrace the emergence of the CSFP/CSDP. This is because they focus on the development of common foreign, security, and defence norms, practices, and identity at the European level as a result of increased cooperation and integration.

During the early years of the CFSP, (neo)realists tended to ignore the development of this policy area, seeing it as a policy of rhetoric rather than substance, without any major impact on the ground (Hoffmann, 2000). Both (neo)realism and (neo)liberalism understand the CSFP as a formally and substantially intergovernmental policy, thus resting firmly in the hands of sovereign member states. The two theories do vary in how much value they attach to EU level cooperation in the realm of security and defence. (Neo)realism privileges the state as the only actor on the anarchical international arena, characterized as a zero-sum self-help system where each state's main obligation, and interest, is to secure its own survival in competition with other states. In such a system, the potential for trust and cooperation between actors is low. Inasmuch as there is a common EU security and defence policy, (neo)realists would see this as a temporary and precarious alliance that will only last as long as the member states' own security benefits from it, and which does not impinge on their own security situation (Mearsheimer, 2010). **Neo-realists** would expect to see two forms of intergovernmental cooperation in this area: balancing or bandwagoning the USA, the only remaining superpower after the end of the Cold War (Cladi and Locatelli, 2012). On the one hand, CSDP can be seen as balancing; that is, an attempt by EU member states to enhance their military capacities through cooperation in order to balance US hegemony and power. On the other hand, CSDP can be understood in (neo) realist terms as bandwagoning; that is, as an attempt by EU member states to contribute more substantially to European security thus complementing the US and NATO and strengthening the transatlantic link.

(Neo)liberals and liberal intergovernmentalists share realist assumptions that EU foreign, security, and defence policy is a fundamentally intergovernmental policy area, where the member states are the key actors. However, both neo-liberals and liberal intergovernmentalists see much more potential for positive cooperation at the EU level (Pohl, 2013). For liberal scholars, the international arena, while anarchic, is understood as a positive-sum system, where actors can better their security and increase their prosperity without threatening other actors. Furthermore, they posit economic cooperation as key, alongside defence capacity, to international security. Rather than a form of deeper integration, the liberal intergovernmental approach understands CFSP as an arena for interstate bargaining where EU member states can upload their preferences to shape the policy outcome. Cooperation at this level adds value: bargaining between states produces better security and prosperity outcomes for all (Moravcsik, 2009).

In contrast, constructivism, which focuses on actors' social construction of shared and common values, norms, practices, and identity (Christiansen et al., 2001), does not posit or privilege any particular actor on the international arena. Constructivism instead seeks to identify the values and norms embraced at the EU level, and how processes of socialization impact on member states' norms and identities. Social constructivists have, therefore, been well placed to study the emergent foreign, security, and defence policy of the EU, and the possible birth of a new, and even unique, form of international security agent. For instance, constructivist studies have focused on the concept and development of a potentially shared, common strategic culture across the member states, through, for example, the production of common strategic documents, such as the European Security Strategy (2003) and the deployment of EU missions on the ground (Meyer, 2006).

Similarly, constructivists have also made a contribution to the debate about the EU's international identity. According to Ian Manners (2002), the EU can be understood as a **Normative Power Europe** (NPE) which promotes its core values of peace, liberty, democracy, rule of law, and respect for human rights in its foreign, security, and defence policy, thus presenting itself as a model for other actors to follow. The NPE concept and idea has been very influential in European foreign policy studies. The NPE school of thought not only emphasizes the normative-driven content and practice of the CFSP/CSDP, but also understands the EU as normative and unique in another way. It is normative by virtue of its hybrid character, as a new kind of international actor, comprising both common institutions and policy at the EU level and, as such, sets new standards for how an international actor can and should be understood (Manners and Whitman, 2003). One often-cited successful example of a promotion of normative values by the EU is the advancement of the abolition of the death penalty within and beyond Europe. However, the NPE concept has been criticized from a realist perspective as hypocritical, as the EU applies its normative principles selectively if and when they clash with other economic or military concerns (Hyde-Price, 2008). The next section moves from theory to practice, by examining the implementation of this policy and specifically CSDP missions and operations.

19.5 CSDP operations and missions: policy in action

The first ever CSDP missions were launched in 2003, only four years after the establishment of the then ESDP (see Box 19.4). The first two missions were deployed in the Western Balkans: a civilian police mission—EUPM—to Bosnia Herzegovina; and a military operation—Operation Concordia—in the form of a peacekeeping force deployed in the Former Yugoslav Republic of Macedonia (FYROM). When the CSDP became operational it was thought that the focus was going to be on the EU's close neighbourhood, on conflict management and state-building in the Western Balkans. However, that same year, the second military operation took place outside Europe, on the African continent: the autonomous Operation Artemis in the Democratic Republic of Congo (DRC). Moreover, there was an expectation that

these overseas deployments would be first and foremost military in character, as the EU quickly demonstrated a willingness and some autonomous capacity to undertake military operations. However, the majority of the CSDP missions to date have been civilian (see Box 19.4), with a particular focus on security sector reform (SSR), and police and rule of law missions (Juncos, 2020).

Approximately one-third of the CSDP missions so far have been either military, or have had a military component. The EU has thus demonstrated that it can deploy a wide range of military missions from low-key operations involving military training in Mali, to high-intensity combat against military insurgents in DR Congo, to maritime operations such as Operation Atalanta (see Box 19.5). Eight of these have seen the deployment of military troops on the ground in a peacekeeping or crisis management capacity in the Balkans and on the African continent. A further five missions to Africa have included military training and advisory missions to Somalia, Mali, and the Central African Republic (CAR).

The size and scope of EU missions and operations vary widely, from very small-scale civilian and training missions employing a dozen personnel, to larger-scale military missions such as EUFOR Althea in Bosnia Herzegovina that in 2004 included 7,000 peacekeeping troops. However, by and large, the size and the scope of their mandates have been rather modest. The length of a mission can vary substantially from missions covering a few months, to decade long missions such as the ongoing border assistance mission—EUBAM—to Ukraine and Moldova, which was launched in 2005. Decisions on the scope, length, and size of a mission are provided for in the mission mandate decided by the Foreign Affairs Council, but a mission's mandate can be amended. For example, the mandate of EUNAVFOR was extended several times between 2008 and July 2018.

While the geographical focus of the CSDP missions has been on Europe, including the Caucasus, and on the African continent, the EU has also undertaken missions outside these areas: for example, in the form of a police mission in Afghanistan. Moreover, the EU has sent civilian missions to the Middle East, including to Iraq and the Palestine territories.

The early years of the CSDP were surprisingly hectic, with the EU launching more than 20 missions during the period 2003–09. This rather intense activity was followed by a period of 'mission fatigue' especially with regard to military missions and coincided with the coming into force of the Lisbon Treaty in 2009. Since 2011, however, there has been a re-ignition of the EU's enthusiasm

BOX 19.4   BACKGROUND: CSDP MISSIONS AND OPERATIONS

Name	Location	Nature	Type	Duration
EUPM	Bosnia	Civilian	Police	2003–12
Concordia	FYROM	Military	Military	2003
Artemis	RD Congo	Military	Military	2003
EUPOL Proxima	FYROM	Civilian	Police	2004–05
EUJUST Themis	Georgia	Civilian	Rule of law	2004–05
EUFOR Althea	Bosnia	Military	Military	Since 2004
EUPOL Kinshasa	RD Congo	Civilian	Police	2005–07
EUSEC RD	RD Congo	Civil-Military	Security sector reform	2005–16
EUJUST LEX	Iraq/Brussels	Civilian	Rule of law	2005–13
AMM	Aceh/Indonesia	Civilian	Monitoring	2005–06
EUBAM Rafah	Palestinian Territories	Civilian	Border	Since 2005
EUBAM	Ukraine-Moldova	Civilian	Border	Since 2005
EUPOL COPPS	Palestinian Territories	Civilian	Police	Since 2006
EUPAT	FYROM	Civilian	Police	2006
EUPT	Kosovo	Civilian	Planning	2006–08
EUFOR	RD Congo	Military	Military	2006
EUPOL	RD Congo	Civilian	Police	2007–14
EUPOL	Afghanistan	Civilian	Police	2007–17
EUFOR	Tchad/RCA	Military	Military	2008–09
EU SSR	Guinea-Bissau	Civil-Military	Security sector reform	2008–10
EULEX	Kosovo	Civilian	Rule of law	Since 2008
EUMM	Georgia	Civilian	Monitoring	Since 2008
EUNAVFOR	Somalia	Military	Maritime	Since 2008
EUTM	Somalia	Military	Capacity-building	Since 2010
EUAVSEC	South Sudan	Civilian	Security sector reform	2012–14
EUCAP NESTOR/ Somalia	Horn of Africa	Civilian	Capacity-building	Since 2012
EUCAP Sahel Niger	Niger	Civilian	Capacity-building	Since 2012
EUBAM Libya	Libya	Civilian	Border	Since 2013
EUTM Mali	Mali	Military	Capacity-building	Since 2013

(continued)

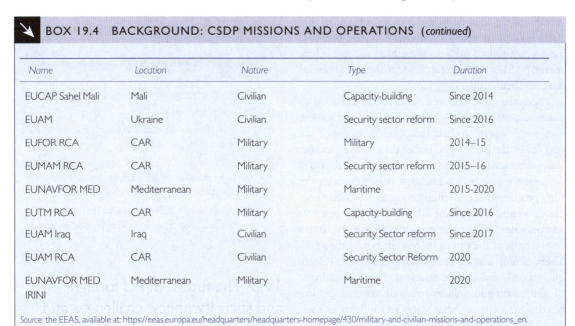

 BOX 19.4   BACKGROUND: CSDP MISSIONS AND OPERATIONS (*continued*)

Name	Location	Nature	Type	Duration
EUCAP Sahel Mali	Mali	Civilian	Capacity-building	Since 2014
EUAM	Ukraine	Civilian	Security sector reform	Since 2016
EUFOR RCA	CAR	Military	Military	2014–15
EUMAM RCA	CAR	Military	Security sector reform	2015–16
EUNAVFOR MED	Mediterranean	Military	Maritime	2015-2020
EUTM RCA	CAR	Military	Capacity-building	Since 2016
EUAM Iraq	Iraq	Civilian	Security Sector reform	Since 2017
EUAM RCA	CAR	Civilian	Security Sector Reform	2020
EUNAVFOR MED IRINI	Mediterranean	Military	Maritime	2020

Source: the EEAS, available at: https://eeas.europa.eu/headquarters/headquarters-homepage/430/military-and-civilian-missions-and-operations_en.

for CSDP operations, in particular with regard to Africa, with several missions and operations being deployed in the Sahel region, in the CAR, and in the Horn of Africa (see Box 19.5).

The EU's military missions have often acquired the role of a rapid-reaction force that is sent into a crisis, and that will then be relieved by a larger UN or African Union force. This was the case with the CSDP mission to Chad/RAC in 2008, where 3,700 troops were sent to protect refugee camps until a larger UN force took over in 2009. The pattern was repeated in 2014 in the same area when the EU sent a military mission to the CAR to stabilize the crisis until an African Union force could take over. It is

BOX 19.5   CASE STUDY: OPERATION ATALANTA: FIGHTING PIRACY OFF THE HORN OF AFRICA

Operation Atalanta, or EUNAVFOR Somalia, is an ongoing (as of April 2021), autonomous, military, anti-piracy operation in the Gulf of Aden off the coast of Somalia. It was launched in December 2008 and forms part of a comprehensive EU security strategy for the Horn of Africa (HoA). The EU's strategy for the HoA aims to tackle both current symptoms and root causes of the insecurity, instability, and piracy in the region. Operation Atalanta is one of three CSDP missions in the HoA. The other two are EUCAP Somalia (formerly known as EUCAP Nestor), a mission that works to support maritime capacity building in Somalia, and EUTM Somalia, a military training mission.

EUNAVFOR Atalanta was the first naval CSDP operation outside of Europe, deploying up to 2,000 personnel; since then the EU has deployed two more maritime operations: EUNAVFOR Med and its successor, EUNAVFOR MED Irini. The aim of Atalanta's vessels is to secure the strategically important

trade routes from Europe to the Asia-Pacific area; 20 per cent of the world's trade passes through the area covered by Operation Atalanta, an area one-and-a-half times the size of the European continent. It aims in particular to protect the World Food Programme's (WFP) shipments of food aid to Somali refugees, and similar transports for the African Union.

The EU has proclaimed its mission a great success and gives it a 100 per cent success rate in the protection of WFP shipments. Moreover, the number of piracy incidents has dropped massively, from 736 hostages and 32 ships being held by pirates in 2011 to no hostages and ships being held by April 2021 (EUNAVFOR, 2021). Despite being hailed as a success by the EU, there have also been criticisms of Atalanta, including the EU's inability to stabilize Somalia, its failure to end piracy for good, and its lack of CSDP protection for the most vulnerable vessels (Howorth, 2014).

worth noting that despite the development of EU Battlegroups in 2007, all military CSDP missions have consisted of ad hoc assembled troops volunteered by EU member states; so far the battlegroups have not been called into use.

There are some important differences between civilian and military CSDP missions with regard to how they are financed and staffed. Civilian missions are covered by the EU budget, rather than by the member states themselves. However, this often means delays in deployment as a mission request passes through the EU's procurement system. By contrast, in military operations, most of the financial burden for military assets and personnel falls on the participating member states on the basis of the principle 'costs lie where they fall'. There is only a small budget for shared costs (Headquarters, IT, and communication). The financial cost of participating in military missions can thus be prohibitive for some member states and influences their decision to make troops available. Furthermore, in civilian missions further delays can be caused by staffing problems. This is because civilian personnel, such as police officers and judges, do not remain on standby to be deployed like their military counterparts, but they need to be seconded (i.e. nominated) by their national authorities in order to participate in EU missions.

How can we judge the success or failure of the CSDP missions and operations? The EU works in very complex theatres, often with multiple actors involved. It is therefore difficult to discern and isolate EU influence and achievement. As all EU operations are by invitation from the host country, and/or with the backing of a UN mandate, they tend to be uncontroversial. It could also be said that the EU avoids the most difficult conflict situations. However, the demand for EU CSDP missions vastly exceeds the EU's capacity and the number of missions launched. This demonstrates that there is a perception that the EU can and should do something to help. According to the EU's own assessment, and judged on the mission mandates, CSDP missions have been successful in achieving their goals. However, the EU missions and operations have been criticized for their often narrow mandates and limited ambitions (Menon, 2009; Juncos, 2020). Moreover, they are said to have 'built-in success' in their mandate. By contrast, if we instead look at the need to deal with the root causes of insecurity and instability, the EU's activities have fallen short of their ambitions (Juncos, 2013; Rodt, 2014).

KEY POINTS

- In 2003, the EU undertook its first civilian and military CSDP missions.

- Two-thirds of CSDP missions have been civilian and one-third have been military.

- The EU has focused geographically on Europe and Africa, but has also undertaken missions in Asia and the Middle East.

- The EU embraces a comprehensive approach to security which involves the use of all available instruments.

- CSDP missions have been relatively successful, although they have also been criticized for their modest and limited mandates.

19.6 The future of EU foreign and security policy: challenges and opportunities

The European Security Strategy, the first strategic reflection at the EU level adopted in 2003, opened with the sentence 'Europe has never been so prosperous, so secure nor so free' (European Council, 2003). The optimism contained in this statement contrasts starkly with the opening remarks of the EU Global Strategy adopted in 2016 (see Box 19.6), which states: 'We live in times of existential crisis, within and beyond the European Union. Our Union is under threat. Our European project, which has brought unprecedented peace, prosperity and democracy, is being questioned' (High Representative, 2016). This shift in strategic thinking was linked, among other things, to the problems encountered by the EU in its neighbourhood.

Externally, the EU's foreign policies have been thwarted by the emergence of an 'arc of instability' from the East to the South (EEAS, 2015). The deterioration of the situation in Libya and Yemen, the civil war in Syria, and the refugee crisis all point to the inability of the EU's foreign policy to shape developments in the Southern neighbourhood. In the East, the deterioration of the political situation in Ukraine, ultimately leading to Russia's annexation of the Crimean peninsula in March 2014 and the ongoing conflict in the Donbass region, have also challenged EU foreign policy.

In many cases, this undesirable state of affairs reflects the absolute and relative decline in the power of

BOX 19.6   KEY DEBATES: THE EU GLOBAL STRATEGY

In 2003, the EU, under the auspices of Javier Solana, the then High Representative for the CFSP, published its first ever European Security Strategy (ESS), entitled 'A secure Europe in a better world'. The ESS was drafted against the backdrop of the events of 9/11, the subsequent war on terror, and the US-led invasion of Iraq in March 2003. The occupation of Iraq divided the EU member states along the traditional lines of Atlanticists–Europeanists and gave rise to intense speculation over the future of and potential demise of the EU's security and defence policy. However, the European Security Strategy, approved unanimously by the member states in December 2003, was intended to demonstrate that the EU, despite disagreement over Iraq, was an international actor with a coherent strategic vision and common ambitions on the world stage (Biscop and Andersson, 2008). The ESS called on the EU to be a more active, more coherent, and more capable international actor and to develop a 'strategic culture that fosters early, rapid, and when necessary, robust intervention'.

Since the adoption of the ESS, the EU's international context has changed drastically. In the aftermath of the wars in Afghanistan and Iraq, Russia is emerging as a security concern in the East, the rise of China has continued, the effects of the global economic crisis have been felt, and the power transition from US unipolarity towards a potentially more unstable multipolar world has been witnessed. These new circumstances led to calls for a new EU Global Strategy, which was presented by High Representative Federica Mogherini to the member states in June 2016. The EU Global Strategy identified the following key priorities for the EU's external action: to protect the security of the Union; to foster state and societal resilience in the Eastern and Southern neighbourhood; to implement an integrated approach to conflicts and crises; to promote cooperative regional orders; and to advance a rules-based global order. The EUGS has firmly put the need to achieve 'strategic autonomy' at the centre of the policy agenda. Moreover, by proclaiming the notion of 'principled pragmatism', the EU Global Strategy of 2016 emphasized the fact that EU foreign policy should be not only about the promotion of values, but also about protecting the security and the interests to the Union in a world where geopolitics still matter.

Europe. In other cases, the problems are self-inflicted, as a result of a failure to invest in security and defence capabilities, or of the continuing disagreements among the EU member states, which prevent it from speaking with one voice. The exit of the UK from the EU in January 2020 is likely to exacerbate some of these problems; for instance, by reducing the total resources available for EU foreign policy initiatives. This is particularly true in matters of security and defence, since the UK's defence budget was the largest among the EU member states. Moreover, it is still unclear what institutional shape EU–UK foreign policy cooperation will take in the years to come. Despite the signing of a Trade and Cooperation Agreement between the EU and the UK at the end of 2020, matters relating to foreign and security cooperation were left outside the agreement, with most initiatives currently relying on ad hoc cooperation, including on issues relating to sanctions against Russia or China.

Yet, current challenges can also be seen in a more positive light as providing momentum for further integration in the area of foreign and security policies. Renewed concerns among some EU member states about territorial defence linked to external crises (Ukraine, Syria), a more assertive Russia, the refugee crises, and mixed signals from the Trump Presidency accelerated calls for strategic autonomy and the development of an autonomous defence capability at the EU level. Cooperation has also been propelled by growing security challenges in the EU's neighbourhood and the outcome of the Brexit referendum. Hence, with the exit of the UK and the removal of a major veto player in defence, the EU has been able to agree on some steps for further security integration. These include the implementation of the EU Global Strategy (see Box 19.6), and plans to move forward in the area of defence with a Commission initiative to support a European Defence Fund, the establishment of a Military Planning and Conduct Capability (MPCC), the implementation of Permanent Structure Cooperation (PESCO) initiatives, the adoption of a Civilian CSDP Compact, and ways to make better use of the EU battlegroups. Although the economic downturn resulting from the COVID-19 pandemic is likely to put more strain on the resources available to EU member states for security and defence purposes, the crisis has also demonstrated the importance of ensuring strategic autonomy (e.g., regarding critical supplies and infrastructures) and to be able to act alone when necessary.

19.7 Conclusion

Opinions on the impact and importance of the CFSP and CSDP differ, and there are uncertainties over the future development of the policy, especially in the aftermath of Brexit and the COVID-19 pandemic. In the face of current geopolitical challenges, will it return to lowest-common-denomination (intergovernmentalist) politics or even to European inter-state security competition, as some neo-realist observers predict; or will the coordination and integration of the member states' foreign, security, and defence policies continue to deepen as exemplified by recent initiatives such as the EU Global Strategy? Despite its shortcomings, the CFSP represents an impressive institutional, normative, and identity-building policy, which has turned the EU into a veritable international security actor able to deploy crisis management operations on the ground. However, as this chapter has made clear, the member states continue to be the key actors in this policy area, and as such, future progress will be inextricably linked to the willingness and ability of the member states to sustain this cooperation.

QUESTIONS

1. How can we explain the emergence of the EU as a security and defence actor?

2. Is the EU a fully fledged foreign policy and security actor on the world stage? If so, why and how?

3. Is the CFSP still intergovernmental or has 'Brusselization' introduced supranational elements?

4. How helpful are mainstream IR theories in explaining the development of EU security and defence policies?

5. How do CSDP missions and operations contribute to international security?

6. How should we measure the success of CSDP missions and operations?

7. Does the EU Global Strategy provide the EU with a comprehensive and up-to-date strategic document?

8. What will be the likely impact of the COVID-19 pandemic on the EU's foreign and security policy?

GUIDE TO FURTHER READING

Hill, C., Smith, M., and Vanhoonacker, S. (2017) *International Relations and the European Union* (Oxford: Oxford University Press). A comprehensive collection on the main aspects of the EU as an international actor.

Howorth, J. (2014) *Security and Defence Policy in the European Union* (Basingstoke: Palgrave Macmillan). An interesting and informative book on the CSDP, its development, key actors, and implementation. It provides useful information on the political games behind the policies.

Fiott, D. (ed.) (2020) The CSDP in 2020. The EU's legacy and ambition in security and defence, Paris: EU-ISS, available at https://www.iss.europa.eu/sites/default/files/EUISSFiles/CSDP%20in%202020_0.pdf. An up-to-date discussion of the historical evolution and current challenges faced by the CSDP.

Keukeleire, S. and Delreux, T. (2014) *The Foreign Policy of the European Union* (Basingstoke, Palgrave Macmillan). A useful introduction to the topic of European foreign policy.

Wong, R. and Hill, C. (eds) (2011) *National and European Foreign Policy: Towards Europeanization* (London: Routledge). A strong edited collection that is particularly useful for its comparative perspective.

 Access the online resources to take your learning and understanding further, including extra multiple-choice questions with instant feedback, web links, answer guidance to end-of-chapter questions, and updates on new developments in EU politics.

www.oup.com/he/cini-borragan7e

20

The Single Market

Michelle Egan

Chapter Contents

Reader's Guide

This chapter charts the evolution of the Single Market project, from its original conception in the 1950s, beginning with the Treaty of Rome through to efforts to expand and enforce Single Market commitments in a climate of unfair trade practices and rising economic nationalism. The chapter highlights the tensions and trade-offs between legal and regulatory strategies to integrate markets; the challenges of creating a social market due to internal asymmetries between market integration at supranational level and social protection at national level; and the efforts to facilitate the free movement of goods, capital, services, and labour. The chapter highlights the importance of the Single Market in seeking to promote competitiveness and growth as well as the diffusion of its regulations beyond its borders. It concludes by demonstrating how both traditional international relations theories of integration and newer approaches in comparative politics and international relations, can be used to shed light on the governance of the Single Market.

20.1 Introduction

The Single Market is a core element of the European integration process. Within the Single Market project, the EU has sought to promote the free movement of goods, capital, services, and factors of production to ease cross-border trade among member states to try and achieve 'an ever-closer economic union'. Yet the Single Market has evolved considerably in ambition and scope since early efforts to address tariffs and quotas in the 1950s and 1960s. At the same time the European economy has undergone profound structural changes. Yet even though the European Union continues to use the Single Market as a platform for economic renewal, to project international influence, and to address unfair trade distortions and market practices, critics argue that European firms are now less anchored than ever before to the European continent as they prefer to invest in emerging markets so they have shifted their energies outside of the European Union. The result is that European firms are losing ground as banks have retrenched to their home markets so that innovation is hampered by a lack of a unified capital market as differences in bankruptcy rules or tax regimes create structural barriers for many small and medium firms that impede their ability to engage in cross-border trade. While there has been sustained effort to deepen the single market in areas closely linked to the single market through new proposals in, for example, energy, digital, technology, and banking, where member states have often shielded their domestic markets, there are still persistent gaps in achieving the single market (Howarth and Sadeh, 2010; Camisão and Guimarães, 2017; *The Economist*, 24 September 2019; Egan, 2020).

In taking stock of what the European Union (EU) has accomplished in terms of internal trade liberalization, this chapter assesses the legal, political, and economic dynamics that have shaped Single Market integration. It focuses on the tensions within the Single Market, the promotion of Single Market rules externally, and the increased salience of the Single Market to address rising economic nationalism and to advance foreign economic priorities. This chapter reviews the state of the Single Market, from its historical origins to more recent efforts, recognizing its economic imperatives as well as its political rationale by highlighting different theoretical efforts to understand and explain the dynamics of market integration.

20.2 Market integration in historical perspective

In the space of one year, from the **Messina Conference** in June 1955 to the **Venice Conference** in May 1956, the idea of economic unification among six West European states took root. After months of discussion, what became known as the **Spaak Report** (after its principal author) generated the idea of a new kind of inter-state economic relationship as the basis for treaty negotiations (Bertrand, 1956: 569). This report provided a blueprint for a Single Market in Western Europe, with three main elements:

- the establishment of normal standards of competition through the elimination of protective barriers;
- the curtailing of state intervention and monopolistic conditions; and
- measures to prevent distortions of competition, including the possible **harmonization** of legislation at the European level.

The economic intent of such proposals dovetailed with the **federalist** agenda (Laurent, 1970). Initially, there were visible benefits as the creation of the common market initially boosted European growth and increased intra-European trade in the European Economic Community (EEC) (Egan, 2020). Despite the economic benefits of integration, the single market is also a political project aimed at scaling up political authority to unify diverse markets which can be viewed in terms of power struggles over the rightful locus of authority and the nature of governance (McNamara, 2019). Based on the Spaak Report, the Treaty of Rome (1957) aimed for a **common market** by coordinating economic activities, ensuring stability and economic development, and raising living standards. At the core of the proposed European common market was the creation of a **customs union** (see Box 20.1). This meant that member states would not only abolish all their customs duties on mutual trade, but also apply a uniform tariff on trade with non-European Community (EC) countries. The other measures proposed to promote internal trade liberalization, including free movement of labour, services, and capital, and a limited number of sectoral policies (agriculture, transport, and trade or commercial policy), were to be regulated and managed at the European level.

> ### ⬊ BOX 20.1   BACKGROUND: STAGES IN ECONOMIC INTEGRATION
>
> | | |
> |---|---|
> | Free trade area (FTA) | Reduces tariffs to zero between members |
> | Customs union | Reduces tariffs to zero between members and establishes a common external tariff |
> | Single market | Establishes a free flow of factors of production (labour and capital, as well as goods and services) |
> | Economic union | Involves an agreement to harmonize economic policies |

The transformation of the Community into a common market was to take place over a period of 12 to 15 years, starting with the elimination of customs duties and quantitative restrictions in 1958, and a **common external tariff** in 1968. Internal tariff reductions were also frequently extended to third countries to limit the discriminatory effects of the customs union, which was politically important in the formative period of the EC (Egan, 2001: 41). Membership of the EC meant more than simply a customs union, however, as the 'four freedoms'—the free movement of goods, services, capital, and labour—were viewed as central features of the Single Market. However, the requirements for each freedom varied according to the political circumstances at the time that the Treaty was drafted and were dependent on the willingness of states to incur adjustments so that their domestic market structures and regulatory styles dovetailed with European policies and legal obligations.

Initially, the removal of trade barriers for *goods* focused on the removal of tariffs and quantitative restrictions, and then on the removal of **non-tariff barriers**. This meant dismantling quotas, subsidies, and **voluntary export restraints**, and measures such as national product **regulations** and standards, public purchasing, and licensing practices, which sometimes reflected legitimate public policy concerns, but were often a thinly disguised form of protectionism designed to suppress foreign competition (Egan, 2001: 42). For the free movement of *capital*, the goal was freedom of investment to enable capital to go where it would be most productive. Yet vivid memories of currency speculation in the interwar period meant that liberalization was subject to particular '**safeguard clauses**', frequently used during **recessions**. Free movement of *services* meant the freedom of establishment for industrial and commercial activity—that is, the right to set up

in business anywhere in the Community, on a temporary or permanent basis. However, the Treaty provisions on services contained virtually no detail on what should be liberalized (Pelkmans, 1997). For *labour*, the provisions for free movement meant the abolition of restrictions on labour mobility which was originally designed for workers to take up employment in another EU member state, something that generated concerns about 'guest workers' and whether this policy would be sustainable during a recession and high domestic unemployment.

National governments were receptive to early efforts to eliminate trade barriers and to create a customs union because they were able to use domestic social welfare policies to compensate for the increased competition stemming from market integration. Favourable starting conditions for the European trade liberalization effort were set against the backdrop of the mixed economy and welfare state, which were central components of the post-war settlement to create a 'social contract' that allowed for the creation of an open and integrated system of economic exchange (Tsoukalis, 1997). Yet even with these national policies, it was still politically necessary to provide some sort of financial aid at the European level to ease the effects of competition through basic investment in underdeveloped regions, the suppression of large-scale unemployment, and the coordination of economic policies (see Bertrand, 1956; Spaak, 1956).

Despite post-war economic growth and increased trade among the member states, the prevalence of domestic **barriers to trade** reflected the continued tensions between import- and export-oriented industries as proponents of protectionism wanted to shelter industries while opponents wanted greater market access and internal liberalization. As such the diverse growth models and institutional architectures within the European Union have influenced how member states regulate production, investment, industrial relations, and exchange. The tension across these distinct political economies began in the earliest years of the European Community around the implied commitment to market liberalization. In the 1960s and 1970s, this meant, on the one hand, stressing the virtues of increased competition and greater efficiencies through reduced transaction costs and economies of scale and, on the other hand, promoting *dirigisme* and intervention by state agencies and nationalized monopolies, resulting in a tension between 'regulated capitalism' and '**neo-liberalism**' (Hooghe and Marks, 1997; see Box 20.2). Such different 'varieties of capitalism' across Europe can provide a comparative institutional advantage, for the more export growth models have fared better than domestic consumption growth models in the single market in responding to increased competition and opportunities in the EU (Hall and Soskice, 2001: 15). As a result, from the 1980s onwards, neo-liberal ideas have proved resilient as competitive market institutions were promoted in the Single Market, and member states were pushed to reform labour and product markets to better deal with rapid technological change, integrated supply chains and increased global competition. But under recent pressure of rising economic nationalism, trade tensions with the United States and Chinese distortive market practices, the proposed European response—to push European champions and promote resilient value chains within the EU— again reflects tensions over economic strategies—and the balance between interventionism and competition in the single market.

KEY POINTS

- The objective of creating a single European market can be traced to the 1956 Spaak Report and the 1957 Treaty of Rome.

- The Treaty of Rome sought to establish a customs union in Europe.

- The Treaty also sought to dismantle trade barriers among the six original members of the European Economic Community (EEC).

- Distinctive forms of capitalism persist given strong institutionally embedded practices and norms that foster different preferences on market integration.

20.3 What is a Single Market?

While Article 26(2) TFEU defines an internal market as an area without internal frontiers for goods, capital, services, and labour, it is a legally ambiguous concept (Weatherill, 2017). Internal markets vary in terms of their scope and composition (Egan, 2015). As such, the nature and governance of the European Single Market depends on the scope of legal and political competences allocated to the central level as well as the degree to which constituent units are permitted to pursue different regulatory policies. To achieve its ambitions, the functional requirements for an internal market include some type of policy coordination or mode of governance (Armstrong and Bulmer, 1998). Two important governance changes took place that helped to set the scene for the creation of a Single Market. The first was

---

 BOX 20.2   BACKGROUND: CHARACTERISTICS OF CAPITALISM

Neo-liberalism

Market liberalization removes restrictions to trade and market access; it provides a regulatory climate attractive to business and investment.

Regulatory competition among member states leads to competition among different national regulatory policies and pressure for domestic structural reform.

The rejection of greater regulatory **power** for institutions at EU level; the insulation of the market from political interference; the retention of political authority at the national level.

Regulated capitalism

Market intervention: government intervention in market.

Social market economy and social solidarity places emphasis on the welfare state and distributive compensatory politics.

Increased capacity to regulate at European level; the mobilization of particular social groups; the reform institutions to generate greater use of **qualified majority voting (QMV)**; the enhancement of legislative **legitimacy** and **social inclusion objectives**.

Source: adapted from Hooghe and Marks (1997).

the emergence of **mutual recognition** as a key principle; the second, the increasing **judicial activism** of the Court of Justice of the EU (CJEU).

Initially, the European mode of governance was **harmonization**. This was to provide a lightning rod for public opposition to efforts to regulate what many felt were long-standing national customs, traditions, and practices (Dashwood, 1983; see Box 20.3). The years of fruitless arguments over noise limits on lawn-mowers, the composition of bread and beer, or tractor rear-view mirrors were amplified by a **unanimity** requirement which allowed individual governments to veto specific legislative proposals. This changed when the principle of mutual recognition was introduced. This new mode of governance simplified the rules for Single Market access. Mutual recognition allows member states to recognize regulations as equivalent (Schmidt, 2007). Member states do not unconditionally accept such mutual equivalence of rules, as they reserve the right to enforce their own regulations on the basis of 'general interest' considerations. Mutual recognition and harmonization reduce the barriers created by national regulations, but at the same time provide a necessary level playing field. Without this, the absence of regulations for product and process standards might lead to a 'race to the bottom' in social and environment standards, as states seek to reduce their domestic measures to attract foreign direct investment and gain significant competitive advantage through **social dumping** where suppression of worker's rights and decreased labour costs creates unfair competition.

The problems associated with addressing trade restrictions through harmonization did not go unnoticed by the CJEU, which has often used its judicial power for the purposes of fostering an integrated economy (see Chapter 13). Indeed, a large measure of the credit for creating the Single Market belongs to the CJEU's judicial

---

BOX 20.3   BACKGROUND: THE SINGLE MARKET PROGRAMME

The Single Market programme involved the removal of three kinds of trade barrier, as follows.

Physical barriers	The removal of internal barriers and frontiers for goods and people
	The simplification of border controls (including the creation of a single administrative document for border entry)
Technical barriers	The coordination of product standards, testing, and certification (under the so-called **new approach**)
	The liberalization of public procurement
	The free movement of capital (by reducing capital exchange controls)
	The free movement of services (covering financial services, such as banking and insurance, to operate under home country control)
	The liberalization of the transport sector (rail, road, and air; rights of *cabotage*; the liberalization of markets and removal of monopolies, state subsidies, and quotas or market-sharing arrangements)
	The free movement of labour and the mutual recognition of professional qualifications (including non-discrimination in employment)
	The Europeanization of company law, intellectual property, and company taxation (including the freedom of establishment for enterprises, a **European Company Statute**, and rules on trademarks, copyright, and legal protection)
Fiscal barriers	The harmonization of divergent tax **regimes**, including sales tax
	The agreement of standard rates and special exemptions from sales tax
	Other indirect taxes aimed at reducing restrictions on cross-border sales

activism. Confronted by restrictions on their ability to operate across national borders, firms began to seek redress through the Community legal system. The Court was asked to determine whether the restrictions on imports imposed by member states were legitimate under the Treaty. Member states' restrictions included Italy's prohibition on the sale of pasta not made with durum wheat, Germany's 'beer purity' regulations prohibiting the sale of any product as 'beer' that was not brewed with specific ingredients, and Belgian regulations that required margarine to be sold only in cube-shaped containers to prevent confusion with butter, sold in round-shaped containers. As a result, the Court had the task of balancing the demands of market integration with the pursuit of legitimate regulatory objectives advanced by member states.

Several landmark cases limited the scope and applicability of national legislation. One of the most important cases in this regard was Case 8/74 *Procureur du Roi v Dassonville* [1974] ECR 837. Dassonville imported whisky into Belgium purchased from a French supplier. It was prosecuted by Belgian authorities for violating national customs rules that prohibited importation from a third country without the correct documentation. Dassonville argued that the whisky had entered the French market legally, that it must therefore be allowed to circulate freely, and that restrictions on imports within the EC were illegal. In a sweeping judgment, the Court argued that 'all trading rules that hinder trade, whether directly or indirectly, actually or potentially, were inadmissible'.

National measures that impact trade negatively were therefore prohibited (Stone Sweet and Caporaso, 1998: 118). This was softened by the recognition that reasonable regulations made by member states for legitimate public interests like health, safety, and environment policies were acceptable if there were no European rules in place. The judgment was predicated on the belief that the European Commission should adopt harmonized standards to allow free movement across markets, while at the same time giving the CJEU the opportunity to monitor member states' behaviour and scrutinize permissible exceptions.

In what is probably its best-known case, Case 120/78 *Rewe-Zentral AG v Bundesmonopolverwaltung für Branntwein (Cassis de Dijon)* [1978] ECR 649, the Court ruled on a German ban on the sale of a French blackcurrant liqueur because it did not conform to German standards regarding alcoholic content (see Egan, 2001: 95 and Chapter 13). The Court rejected German arguments that Cassis, with its lower alcoholic content, posed health risks, but noted that the protection of the consumer could occur by labelling alcohol content. Most importantly, it clearly defined what national measures were deemed permissible. The most-cited part of the ruling suggested 'there was no valid reason why products produced and marketed in one member state could not be introduced into another member state'.

The notion of equivalence of national regulations, which this ruling introduced, crucially meant that harmonization would not always be necessary for the construction of a Single Market. Mutual recognition as a new mode of governance implies that it is only in areas that are not mutually equivalent that member states can invoke national restrictions, practices, and traditions, and restrict free trade in the Community.

In fact, the Court argued that **derogations** from (exceptions to) the free trade rule for the purposes of public health, fair competition, and consumer protection were possible, but that they had to be based upon reasonable grounds. Governments, whether national, local, or sub-national, had to demonstrate that any measure restricting trade was not simply disguised protectionism. Anxious to safeguard the Community-wide market, the Court has continued to determine on a case-by-case basis whether specific laws are valid under the Treaty. However, faced with a growing number of cases, the Court, in Joined Cases C-267/91 and 2-268/91 *Keck and Mithouard* [1993] ECR I-6097, reduced the scope of judicial scrutiny in cases that applied to all traders operating in specific national territory, under certain conditions. Thus, the Court would not examine issues such as Sunday trading, mandatory closing hours, or other issues that had a limited effect on cross-border trade and which reflected national moral, social, and cultural norms.

Case law relating to the free movement of services and rights of establishment is now at the centre of recent legal developments because the 'country of origin' principle is the starting point in assessing restrictions to free movement. In the seminal Case C-438/05 *International Transport Workers' Federation and anor v Viking Line ABP* [2008] IRLR 143, Case C-341/05 *Laval* [2007] ECR I-11767, and Case C-346/06 *Rüffert v Land Niedersachsen* [2008] IRLR 467, the importance of freedom of establishment and services is prioritized over social and collective labour rights in economic integration.

Judicial activism has thus allowed companies the right to choose the least restrictive regulatory environment to allow for more home-country control rules. Scharpf (2010) highlights the constitutional asymmetry that this creates, as these judgments involving efforts to liberalize services challenge national socio-economic models. This results from the predominance of market-based treaty obligations promoting economic freedoms and legal obligations to safeguard against protectionism. The constitutive role of law is crucial in understanding the consolidation of markets. The CJEU has placed state and local laws under its purview to determine whether they are discriminatory or not, balancing the different policy objectives to determine the locus of regulatory authority as well as the extent to which states can differentiate and provide asymmetrical market access due to specific legitimate exemptions and exceptions.

KEY POINTS

- The *dirigiste* strategy of harmonization of rules to integrate national markets in the 1960s and 1970s achieved limited results.

- Mutual recognition provided a new mechanism for regulatory coordination and the possibility of mutual equivalence of member state rules.

- Seminal rulings by the Court of Justice have played a key role in challenging non-tariff trade barriers.

- More recent cases, *Viking*, *Laval*, and *Rüffert*, have raised questions about the balance between economic freedoms and social and labour rights.

20.4 The politics of neo-liberalism and '1992'

Throughout the 1970s and early 1980s, member state efforts to maintain import restrictions and discriminatory trade practices had thwarted attempts to create a Single Market. By the mid-1980s, however, things began to change. Growing recognition of a competitiveness gap vis-à-vis the USA, Japan, and newly industrializing countries, led to strenuous efforts to maintain overall levels of market activity and provide conditions for viable markets (Pelkmans and Winters, 1988: 6). While past economic policies, notably **neo-corporatist** class

compromises and **consensual** incomes policies, had successfully promoted growth, these national policies were unable to cope with changes in the international economy as trade deficits soared and stagflation increased.

Assessments were so bleak that, on the 25th anniversary of the Treaty of Rome, *The Economist* put a tombstone on its cover to proclaim the EC dead and buried. A growing consensus among business and political leaders that a collective strategy was needed to stop an 'escalating trade war' (*Financial Times*, 25 July 1980) led the European Round Table, the heads of Europe's largest companies, to put forward numerous proposals to improve European competitiveness. Other trade associations flagged problems of industry standards, border formalities, and export licences, France and Italy being the worst offenders. Industry began a campaign of proactive lobbying, ambitious proposals, and visible political engagement (*Financial Times*, 20 March 2001). Responding to this groundswell, the European Commission proposed addressing the most problematic barriers in the member states (*Financial Times*, 23 September 1980; *The Economist*, 22 October 1983).

Governments, cognizant that their efforts to create national champions, protect labour markets, and maintain public spending were not stemming rising trade imbalances and deficits, sought new solutions. Efforts to contain import competition and stabilize industries had failed, shifting strategies from **Keynesian** demand management towards market liberalization. This did not mean a common consensus around neo-liberalism, because different conceptions of the agenda for European integration emerged. While the British advocated a genuine common market in goods and services, and promoted a radically neo-liberal agenda, the French argued for the creation of a common industrial space wherein trade barriers could be reduced internally, provided that external trade protection would compensate for increased internal competition (Pearce and Sutton, 1983). Major steps taken at the 1984 **European Council** meeting in Fontainebleau broke the impasse, as agreement on the long-running disputes over the UK's contribution to the Community Budget and the pending Iberian **enlargement** were reached. The **Dooge Committee** was also established to reform the institutional and decision-making structure of the Community.

Agreement at the 1985 **Intergovernmental Conference (IGC)** in Milan to 'study the institutional conditions under which the internal market could be achieved within a time limit' proved critical for market integration. This built on several earlier developments, including the **Spinelli Report**, which focused on the need to link national regulations and institutional reform, and the parliamentary draft Treaty on European Union on institutional reform, which included increased parliamentary powers and greater use of qualified majority voting (QMV) in the Council. At the subsequent IGC, the proposed treaty reforms were assembled to become the **Single European Act (SEA)** (see also Chapter 2).

The SEA endorsed the Single Market and altered the decision-making rules for Single Market measures (with exceptions such as taxation and rights of workers) from unanimity to QMV. This linked institutional reforms to substantive goals and made it more difficult for recalcitrant member states to veto legislative action, as had been the case under harmonization. The SEA also strengthened the powers of the European Parliament with respect to Single Market measures by allowing for the rejection or amendment of proposals under the **cooperation procedure**.

20.4.1 **A strategic blueprint and agenda: The 1992 programme**

By early 1985, newly appointed Commission President Jacques Delors and Internal Market Commissioner Lord Cockfield, a British former Secretary of State for Industry, put together a package of proposals that aimed to complete the Single Market by 1992. The 300 proposals—subsequently modified and amended to become 283 proposals—became a Commission White Paper entitled *Completing the Internal Market*. The final product became known as the '**1992 Programme**'.

The White Paper grouped remaining trade obstacles as physical, technical, and fiscal barriers. Lord Cockfield used this simple categorization to introduce legislative proposals across goods, services, capital, and labour markets to improve market access and prevent distortions to competition and restrictive business practices. The European Commission bolstered support by commissioning a series of economic evaluations on the 'costs of non-Europe' (the **Cecchini Report**, 1988), which was revived in the European Parliament's 2014 report *Mapping the Cost of Non-Europe*. This concept, first pioneered in the 1980s, emphasized trade and welfare gains from removing trade

barriers, as well as efficiency gains achieved through market enlargement, intensified competition, and industrial restructuring. The new Parliament report suggests the European economy could be boosted by some €800 billlion—or 6 per cent of current GDP, as the Single Market has yet to achieve its full potential, which could be achieved by more effective application of existing legislation and a deepening of the Single Market.

At the core of the Single Market project is mutual recognition, the consequence of which would be increased competition among intra-EU firms, as well as different national regulatory systems (see Sun and Pelkmans, 1995). Governments sponsoring regulations that restricted market access would be pressured since firms from other member states would not be required to abide by them, putting their local firms at a disadvantage. The European Commission sought to apply this innovative strategy to the service sector as well. The concept of 'home country control' was to allow banks, insurance companies, and dealers in securities to offer elsewhere in the Community the same services as those they offered at home. A single licence would operate, so that these sectors would be licensed, regulated, and supervised mostly by their home country.

Building on the legal decisions outlining the doctrine of mutual recognition as a broad free trade principle and with reference to standard-setting as a more flexible regulatory strategy, the Commission drafted a proposal on harmonization and standards in 1985 (Pelkmans, 1997). This 'new approach' reflected a critical effort to address trade barriers by sharing regulatory functions between the public and private sectors. Where possible, there was to be mutual recognition of regulations and standards, and Community-level regulation was to be restricted to essential health and safety requirements with delegation to European standards bodies as a means of allowing private sector governance to provide business with the standards to comply with European legislation.

The White Paper gained widespread political support by providing a target date for the completion of the Single Market, emphasizing the merits of economic liberalism. It included measures across the four freedoms, such as the abolition of frontier and capital exchange controls, mutual recognition of goods and services, and rights of establishment for professional workers. While the White Paper focused mostly on market access or **negative**

integration measures, such as removing technical trade barriers, dismantling quotas, and removing licensing restrictions for cross-border banking and insurance services, they were complemented by market-correcting or **positive integration** measures, such as health and safety standards, rules for trademarks and deposit insurance, and solvency ratios for banks and insurance (see Box 20.4).

Despite its 1992 deadline, the Single Market remained incomplete. The White Paper avoided a number of issues, such as the social dimension, politically sensitive sectors including textiles and clothing, and taxation of savings and investment income, despite these areas' evident distortions and restrictions. Completion of the Single Market meant tackling politically difficult dossiers and ensuring legislation was implemented in all member states; otherwise consumers' and producers' confidence in realizing economic benefits would be undermined. Nationally important sectors like utilities (for example, gas and postal services) were given special exemptions in the Single Market due to social and economic arguments that 'universal services' must be provided, resulting in natural monopolies and limited competition. With rapid liberalization and technological changes, the traditional economic rationale for such *dirigiste* policies was being undermined. Pressure to open telecommunications, electricity, and gas markets resulted in the Commission forcing liberalization of these basic services through its competition powers. The competition policy pursued by the Commission has reinforced a liberalizing bias within the Single Market—because specific features of restrictive practices, monopolies, rules governing state aid to industry, and merger policy have played a substantial role in reducing market distortions.

> ### KEY POINTS
>
> - Business supports the Single Market and continues to lobby for measures to improve European competitiveness.
>
> - The White Paper on the Single Market created a package of measures to liberalize trade that became the 1992 Programme.
>
> - The Single Market is a 'work in progress', with efforts underway to deepen and widen the internal market in new areas such as the Digital Single Market, artificial intelligence (AI), and the collaborative economy.

20.5 Compensatory measures and regulatory adjustment in the Single Market

The pressures of increased competition and liberalization brought pressures for ancillary policies along social democratic lines (Scharpf, 1999). Fearful that excessive competition would increase social conflict, proponents of regulated capitalism (see Box 20.2) recommended various inclusive mechanisms to generate broad-based support for the Single Market. These included **structural policy** for poorer regions to promote economic and social **cohesion**, consumer and

---

BOX 20.4   CASE STUDY: UPDATING THE SINGLE MARKET: THE DIGITAL ECONOMY

The rapid growth and diffusion of digital technologies are fast changing global trade. The Digital Single Market represents the latest effort to provide rules for digital content, e-commerce, and online services as restrictions on watching movies online, mobile phone roaming charges, and delivery fees for online purchases hamper cross-border activities. Data localization rules require information held by companies to be held on servers in their home country which restricts data flows, undermining cross-border e-trade in goods and services. The transformation of European economies means that traditional means of market integration through the removal of trade barriers and sector harmonization appears outdated in the context of changes in production, technology, and innovation, and the growth of tradable services.

Take, for example, the collaborative economy which allows users to enjoy cheaper access to a wider variety of goods and services whenever they need them. While existing European regulations were devised for traditional business-to-business transactions, these new platforms impact a wide array of Single Market issues from consumer and labour protection to service and tax provisions. The lack of a Single Market in services has generated increased uncertainty and market fragmentation in the collaborative platforms, with outright bans or burdensome limits to market access in some member states. Thus, *Uber*, the collaborative platform providing alternative urban transportation, has been banned in European cities such as Sofia, Barcelona, or Budapest, but is available in Sheffield, Birmingham, and Madrid.

environmental protection, and rural development. **Fiscal transfers** spread the burden of adjustment and assisted the adversely affected countries. They signalled a willingness to accept further trade liberalization but only in exchange for compensatory measures.

These initiatives acknowledged that the domestic political pressures on national welfare states meant that they could no longer compensate for the effects of integration as they had done in the past (Scharpf, 1999). The goal of regulating markets, redistributing resources, and shaping partnership among public and private actors led advocates of regulated capitalism to propose provisions for transport and communications infrastructure, information networks, workforce skills, and research and development (Hooghe and Marks, 1997). The progressive expansion of activities at the European level brought into focus the two long-standing opposing views about the economic role of governments.

Some have argued that the Single Market has progressively increased the level of statism or interventionism in Europe especially in the aftermath of the economic crisis (Messerlin, 2001; Schmidt, 2007). It is argued that the economic consensus favourable to market forces and neo-liberalism under the 1980s Single Market programme has been offset by increased intervention or regulated capitalism in labour markets (minimum wage and working time), and new provisions for culture (broadcast quotas), industry (ship-building, textiles, and clothing), and technology (new energy resources, biotechnology, and broadband networks) in the 1990s and loosening of state aid rules in the 2000s.

Yet these forms of **embedded liberalism** have partly been overshadowed by a growing emphasis on competitiveness in the 1990s, in terms of increased market competition and discipline through the **Lisbon Process**, a collective strategy across different policies wherein the Single Market is central to delivering the goals of growth, jobs, innovation, and competition, and to drive European recovery and the **Europe 2020** strategy. The **Monti Report** sought to frame the Single Market as a mechanism to bolster the social market economy, to help address serious problems related to inequality, productivity, and growth (Monti, 2010). And more recently, this has led to increased intervention as central banks have purchased government debt to assist with liquidity and solvency problems and pandemic aid has cushioned workers and businesses from a severe recession.

KEY POINTS

- Proponents of regulated capitalism have advocated policies to generate support for the EU, including structural policies and social dialogue.

- The disjuncture between market integration at **supranational** level and social protection at national level has become increasingly contentious due to concerns that the socio-political legitimacy of the Single Market project has been undermined by the adverse consequences of globalization.

- Fears about the socio-political legitimacy of market outcomes were echoed in the 2010 Monti Report which argued that the social dimensions of the market economy needed to be strengthened in order to strengthen public support.

20.6 Swings and roundabouts: the revival of the Single Market

As Europe faces the challenges of making the Single Market deliver, greater attention has been given to enforcement and compliance, as well as promoting growth (European Council, 2020). The European institutions have continuously promoted regulatory reform and more flexible modes of governance, in part motivated by business requests for an easing of regulatory burdens as a prerequisite for the achievement of a Europe-wide Single Market (European Commission, 1992a; Molitor, 1995; Mandelkern Group, 2001). Specific initiatives have included 'Simpler Legislation for a Single Market' (1996), the Action Plan for the Single Market (1997), a scoreboard to generate peer pressure to enhance regulatory compliance (European Report, 28 November 1997), and **regulatory impact assessments**. Yet there remain compliance problems with Single Market obligations in both new and old member states, generating a range of formal and informal mechanisms with which to address the situation (Falkner et al., 2004). While the Commission has actively pursued **infringement proceedings** (under Article 226 of the Treaty), whereby it formally notifies member states of their legal obligations, it has also sought to address the slow pace of standardization, and misunderstandings with the application of mutual recognition in practice (Nicolaïdis and Schmidt, 2007). This involves out-of-court informal solutions to complaints by consumers and businesses regarding the incorrect application of internal market laws, notification of new national laws and standards to prevent new trade barriers, and the new goods package, all aimed at better market surveillance. Business surveys indicate that firms still face obstacles that prevent them from realizing the full benefits of the Single Market (Egan and Guimarães, 2011, 2017).

Recognizing that the Single Market constitutes a key driver for European economic growth, Mario Monti, a former Commissioner and Italian Prime Minister, was commissioned to write a report on how to improve the Single Market in a time of economic crisis. Facing concerns about 'internal market fatigue' and growing nationalist pressures (see Box 20.5), Monti advocated deepening and widening the Single Market, using social benefits to generate public support and renewed momentum, as well as adaptation to new technologies, business models, and market practices (Pelkmans, 2010). Seeking to generate a momentum, the timing of the Monti Report, entitled *A New Strategy for the Single Market: At the Service of Europe's Economy and Society*, coincided with the start of the **eurozone** crisis and was thus largely ignored. The European Commission persisted, however, promoting 12 key areas that ultimately became the **Single Market Act I** (2011), which was subsequently complemented by the **Single Market Act II** (2012).

While Europe has identified the digital economy, patents, the coordination of tax policies, copyright, and electronic commerce, and deepening services liberalization, the goal of delivering on this agenda was, from the outset, very ambitious given Europe's economic and political climate. The acceleration of economic integration has generated more anti-system politics, driven by the acute financial crisis and economic austerity of the late 2000s that has led to a surge in economic nationalism as the sources of economic and social stress have fostered a protective countermovement to subordinate the market to political constraints (Hopkin, 2017). Pressure was placed on the Single Market during the financial crisis, as cross-border financial markets disintegrated, and investment was repatriated, creating a credit crunch for some member states, and stringent austerity measures. Though the Commission saw the crisis as an opportunity to put the Single Market at the top of the agenda, as part of a two-tiered response that would promote economic governance and financial market supervision, there was less interest in viewing the Single Market as a response to promote growth and efficiency gains in the aftermath of the economic slowdown and sovereign debt crisis in Europe (Camisão, and Guimarães, 2017).

And with competition rules now being quietly shelved as Europe grapples with the pandemic, the large bailouts can impact the functioning of the Single Market. The vision for Europe has again shifted as France and Germany argue that the real answer

---

 BOX 20.5   CASE STUDY: BREXIT AND THE IMPORTANCE OF THE UK SINGLE MARKET

On 29 March 2017, the UK formally notified the EU of its intention to leave the world's largest trade bloc. Attention focused heavily on the options about the future relationship between the UK and EU leading eventually to a Trade and Cooperation Agreement (TCA) in December 2020. The EU stressed the indivisibility of the Single Market. Economic assessments have highlighted the largest impact will be on pharmaceuticals, automotive, engineering, financial, and chemical sectors in the UK due to the loss of Single Market access. Coupled with the prospect of customs checks, rules of origin requirements, and the imposition of levies or tariffs for nearly three million small businesses that are currently exempt, the withdrawal from the Single Market requires multiple new arrangements. The regulation of internal UK trade was not considered a significant issue until Brexit. The British government was concerned that the four nations would have different rules leading to regulatory divergence and market fragmentation within the UK. The introduction of an Internal Market Bill generated intense controversy as it rode roughshod over the expectations that there would be devolution of specific competences post-Brexit that had previously been managed by the EU. This generated significant pushback from the EU. This is because it violated the terms of the Withdrawal Bill in which Northern Ireland was to be governed by regulatory arrangements that were subject to joint approval by the EU and the UK. The impact of these developments on the domestic market is important as any resultant legislative divergences could create barriers to trade and competitive distortions of competition. Just like the European Single Market, the British government was faced with determining how it would ensure non-discrimination while deciding between harmonization, regulatory competition, or mutual recognition.

is dirigiste industrial policy as open and competitive markets are under pressure. Even though there are efforts to ensure that the Single Market works more effectively on the ground without unnecessary burdens and restrictions, with scorecards, dispute resolutions mechanisms, and now a joint Single Market Enforcement Task Force (SMET) established in 2020, concerns about the uneven application of the four freedoms across member states are not new. The Single Market is not a static process but a continuous system of internal trade liberalization that shapes and transforms both markets and polities. Yet it is a nominal 'single' market as it remains incomplete, subject to the vagaries of politics, even as it has eliminated many barriers to cross-border trade and commerce. Across the four freedoms—of goods, capital, service, and labor—the Single Market demonstrates a pattern of selective liberalization, leading to deep integration of capital and good markets, while lagging in services and labor markets.

KEY POINTS

- There has been continued emphasis on improving compliance with Single Market regulations as well as with easing the overall business climate through regulatory reform.

- There have also been ongoing efforts to revive the Single Market such as through the Monti Report and Single Market Acts I and II, which provide a range of initiatives to enhance general macroeconomic performance against a difficult climate of austerity and populist pressures.

- The salience of the Single Market has been enhanced by the Brexit referendum as the UK is faced with the indivisibility of the four freedoms, and the future economic relationship with the EU, against the backdrop of highly integrated supply chains and trade relations.

20.7 Globalization, external governance, and the Single Market

Some scholars argue that European integration contributes to globalization because increased intra-European flow of goods, services, capital, and people generate economic opportunities and market openness. Others argue that globalization threatens the European social model, and that the direct impact on national economies requires

coordinated action to manage the tensions and challenges created by increased global competition (see Box 20.6). While much attention within the European Union has been focused on the need to manage the consequences of rising protectionism, while promoting efficiency to ensure greater productivity and ease intra-European transaction costs, debates about managing economic liberalization have now been transferred to the global level. While there are discussions underway about how the EU can generate economic growth through industrial policy efforts, the EU is linking rules on competition, public procurement, and trade defence instruments to ensure fair conditions for domestic European companies operating in the Single Market (European Commission, 2021).

The size of the Single Market has also enabled the European Union to exercise its authority in multilateral trade negotiations and use market access as a 'soft power' instrument to promote economic and political reform in Central and Eastern Europe and the Balkans through **stabilization and association agreements (SAAs)** to, in many cases, eventual EU membership (see Chapter 18). The European Union has allowed non-members through the European Economic Area (EEA) access to its internal market via regulatory alignment and judicial enforcement (Gstöhl, 2015).

As the largest trade bloc in the world, the EU has a leading role to play in international trade negotiations and liberalization, promoting a new generation of FTAs. These cover goods and some services, promoting liberalization through rule making rather than exchange of tariff concessions (Baldwin, 2011). While many argue that across a broad range of sectors, the EU is increasingly shaping global markets through the transfer of its Single Market rules and standards, others point to a limited export of regulatory rules through new FTAs, focusing on regulatory equivalence with international rather than European standards (Damro, 2012; but see Young, 2015). In select cases, the EU has sought to play a leading role by promoting key concepts of its internal market strategy in areas like competition policy, environmental management standards, and food safety leading to what is known as the 'Brussels effect'. For example, the EU pushes its protection of specific food products in trade agreements, known as geographical indicators which protect certain regional products, with

BOX 20.6   KEY DEBATES: THEORIZING THE SINGLE MARKET

There are different theoretical approaches from various disciplinary perspectives that can explain the causes, content, and consequences of the Single Market (see Pelkmans et al., 2008).

Intergovernmentalists (see Chapter 5) claim that the institutional dynamics that underpin the Single Market project were the result of a convergence of policy preferences in the early 1980s between the UK, Germany, and France (Moravcsik, 1991). National interests and policies are expected to constrain integrationist impulses, because state resources, power, and bargaining are the driving factors of economic integration. Garrett (1992) furthers this, arguing that, in important areas of legal activity, the Court was constrained by member states' governments and serves their interests (especially those of the most powerful member states) in rendering its judgments.

By comparison, **neo-functionalists** (see Chapter 4) stress the importance of supranational actors in shaping the Single Market. Sandholtz and Zysman (1989) point to the Commission as an innovative policy entrepreneur shaping the European agenda, supported by business interests seeking to reap the benefits of an enlarged market. Burley and Mattli (1993) argue that Court rulings have resulted in interactions between national and European courts, creating a distinctive legal regime that shapes rules and procedures governing markets. When political attempts to create a common market stalled, the Court advanced its supranational authority over national courts, expanding its jurisdictional authority in order to make a pivotal contribution to the promotion of free trade (see Shapiro, 1992; Egan, 2001; Scheutze, 2017). Cameron (1992) seeks to blend these different theoretical perspectives by arguing that the 1992 Programme was the result of the complex interaction of different actors and institutions, simultaneously accelerating economic integration and **supranational institution**-building, while also representing intergovernmental bargaining among states. By contrast, van Apeldoorn (1992) argues that market outcomes are the result of struggles between contending transnational forces, and that economic integration reflects the economic interests of transnational capital strengthened by deepening globalization processes and the rise of a neo-liberal market ideology within the European political economy. Conversely, Jabko (2006) focuses on the role of ideas in **framing** the Single Market project, drawing on **constructivist** premises (see Chapter 6) that the market can be strategically used as a political strategy to appeal to various constituencies at different times.

Subsequently, the Single Market process has been examined through the lens of comparative policy analysis. Empirical studies have shown that European policies are a patchwork of different **policy styles**, instruments, and institutional arrangements (Héritier, 1996). Majone (1996) described such changes in European governance (see Chapter 7), as generating an increasing transfer of regulatory authority to the EU level to reduce **transaction costs** and to resolve problems of heterogeneity through collective action and coordination. The need to ensure credible commitments has led to burgeoning scholarship on implementation and compliance with European laws and norms (Adam et al., 2020). For Majone (1995), European governance is increasingly delegated to **non-majoritarian** institutions, such as independent banks, regulatory agencies, and courts, to foster such collective regulatory outcomes, because they are better suited than traditional political bodies, such as parties, legislatures, and **interest groups**, to achieve the independence and credibility necessary to govern the market. Bradford (2020)—building on Majone's work—claims that the rules governing the internal market create a 'Brussels' effect which shapes global product and consumer markets that ties into the earlier work on 'external governance' (Lavenex and Schimmelfennig, 2009).

Other scholars have sought to demonstrate that the Single Market may not be entirely benign in its consequences as embedding states in transnational markets and regulatory regimes weakens state capacity to govern their national economies (Scharpf, 1999, 2002; Streeck, 1999). While political economists have illustrated how the European **polity**'s activism has increased market competition in sectors hitherto shielded from the discipline of the market (Scharpf, 1999), there has been growing attention in comparative politics to the role of public opinion and party politics in intensifying conflict around European policies as the distributional consequences across member states have become increasingly salient (Hooghe and Marks, 2009). Few subjects have generated more debate than the effects of economic integration and globalization on the policy autonomy of governments. Opponents argue that the increasing constraints on national policy choices, especially regarding immigration, increased economic competition and pressures on the welfare states, have, in fact, contributed to the growing opposition among the populace towards further European integration. As Hooghe and Marks (2009) have argued, as important as economic imperatives are, market integration is also the product of politics—most notably, but not exclusively, tensions and conflicts about **sovereignty**, identity, and governance in a multilevel polity. There is a strong relationship between economic and political developments, as the Single Market and its ancillary policies require political support and legitimacy, as well as institutional capabilities and effectiveness (Egan, 2015). While EU capacities have increased in fiscal, administrative, and tax powers through coordination rather than displacement of national powers (Genschel and Jachtenfuchs, 2015), the politicization of core state powers generates conflict and bargaining over institutional power and authority, resulting in growing economic insecurity among domestic publics about the effects of a broader breakdown of economic barriers on national identity, culture, and values (see Chapter 15).

Canada, across Latin America, Australasia, and China. Yet European integration also takes place in a situation of global sourcing of goods and services, increased tradability of goods and services, and changing patterns of trade and investment as other regional arrangements are evolving.

20.8 Conclusion

While the Single Market is the backbone of European integration, it is still incomplete or even non-existent in some areas, so it has fallen short of its potential. Amid continued efforts to promote productivity and growth, the salience of the Single Market has been enhanced by the negotiations on the UK's exit from the EU, and its insistence on withdrawal from the Single Market and customs union. Nonetheless, the Single Market remains a key component of the European project as the digital economy, collaborative economy, or capital markets union reflect contemporary efforts to address changes in the global economy. In some areas, the Single Market has underperformed, while in other areas it has promoted highly efficient cross-border supply chains. Thus, the Single Market is a differentiated model of integration, with varying modes of governance, and different levels of liberalization across the four freedoms.

Although the Single Market is now well entrenched, its feasibility and effectiveness depend on two conditions. First, it requires well-defined legal and judicial mechanisms to guarantee **enforcement** and compliance with Single Market rules. Second, it also needs to generate political support and legitimacy for further economic integration. In this respect, the relationship between economic and social rights needs to be re-examined, since viable and sustainable integration is likely to be more successful if economic growth is fairly distributed. For some, the extensive European case law bolsters equity, economic development, and social welfare, expanding social rights to match market rights (Caporaso and Tarrow, 2009). Others stress the primacy of neo-liberalism in generating a populist backlash against the dominance of the market. Most agree however with the need to update Single Market rules to keep pace with the European service-led business economy, and to address the unfair competitive practices from foreign subsidies that cause distortions in the Single Market.

6. What new initiatives have been undertaken to further promote the single market? How crucial is enforcement and compliance of single market rules?

7. What are the possible consequences of a British exit ('Brexit') for the UK's own Internal Market?

8. Is globalization a threat or an opportunity for the EU?

GUIDE TO FURTHER READING

Anderson, G. (ed.) (2012) *Internal Markets and Multi-level Governance: The Experience of the European Union, Australia, Canada, Switzerland, and the United States* (Oxford: Oxford University Press). This book considers the concept of the Single Market in a comparative perspective.

Egan, M. (2015) *Single Markets: Economic Integration in Europe & the United States* (Oxford: Oxford University Press). Offers insights on the consolidation of the EU Single Market by comparing it to nineteenth-century American market integration.

Egan, M. (2020) 'The Internal Market of the European Union: From Indivisibility to Differentiated Integration', in F. Laursen (ed.), *The Oxford Encyclopedia of European Union Politics* (Oxford: Oxford University Press).

Egan, M and Guimareas M.H. (2017) 'The Single Market: Trade Barriers and Trade Remedies', *Journal of Common Market Studies* 55/2: 294–311. Assesses the Single Market in terms of barriers to trade and effective implementation.

Weatherill S. (2017) *The Internal Market as a Legal Concept* (Oxford: Oxford University Press). Examines what the concept of the 'internal market' means from a legal perspective.

Access the online resources to take your learning and understanding further, including extra multiple-choice questions with instant feedback, web links, answer guidance to end-of-chapter questions, and updates on new developments in EU politics.

www.oup.com/he/cini-borragan7e

21

The Area of Freedom, Security, and Justice

Emek M. Uçarer

Chapter Contents

Reader's Guide

This chapter looks at one of the most recent European policies, Justice and Home Affairs (JHA), and its subsequent transformation into the Area of Freedom, Security, and Justice (AFSJ). The AFSJ comprises the policy areas immigration and asylum, and police and judicial cooperation, some elements of which were found prior to the Lisbon Treaty in the EU's third pillar. This chapter focuses first on the early years of cooperation in this policy area, providing an introduction to the Schengen Agreement. It then reviews the procedural steps taken first by the Maastricht Treaty (1993), then at Amsterdam (1999), and subsequent institutional developments culminating in the Lisbon Treaty. The latter half of the chapter concentrates on policy output, again looking at steps taken with Maastricht, Amsterdam, and Lisbon, but also in the landmark Tampere European Council meeting, the Hague Programme, and most recently the Stockholm Programme. The chapter argues that, although some progress has already been made towards Europeanizing AFSJ policy, this field continues to be laced with intergovernmentalism and numerous challenges remain to be resolved, especially in light of broader challenges facing the Union.

21.1 Introduction

Cooperation in the Area of Freedom, Security, and Justice (AFSJ) has undergone a remarkable ascent from humble beginnings to a vibrant European Union (EU) policy. One of the newest additions to the EU mandate, AFSJ tasks the EU in the fields of immigration and asylum policy, and police and judicial cooperation. Because of the sensitive nature of the issues involved, cooperation has been slow and difficult. However, it has resulted in a body of policies that apply across the EU's internal and external borders, and which have locked previously inward-looking national authorities into a multilateral process. This has involved significant political compromise, which led to the introduction of a complicated mix of **Communitarized** and intergovernmental institutional procedures peculiar to this field. The EU is now developing a complex immigration and asylum **regime**, albeit one severely challenged recently, and is also making progress on police and judicial cooperation. Particularly after the conclusion of the **Amsterdam Treaty**, the EU's capacity to reach collectively binding decisions in this field has improved considerably, creating momentum towards further cooperation and increasing concerns about the creation of a '**Fortress Europe**' into which access is increasingly restricted. However, many challenges and tensions remain to be resolved.

21.2 Preludes to cooperation

If, in the late 1960s, government ministers responsible for home affairs and justice were told that they would soon need to consult with fellow European ministers while formulating policies on immigration, asylum, judicial, and police matters, they would no doubt have found this a very unlikely and undesirable prospect. Yet, during the 1980s and 1990s, issues falling within their mandates were increasingly of collective EU concern, inviting efforts to deal with them at the European, rather than exclusively at the national, level. Beginning in the mid-1970s and accelerating in the 1980s, these clusters were increasingly incorporated into the collective political agenda, leading to the creation of new, overlapping forums (see Box 21.1).

There were two broad sets of catalysts that drove this development. The first was the consequence of increased cross-border movements into and across Europe. After the Second World War, Western Europe became an area of immigration. Cross-border movements increased, straining border patrols and causing delays at points of entry. With this came growing concerns about transnational crime because of weak border controls and a lack of effective communication among European national law **enforcement** agencies. The second catalyst was the revitalization of the European integration agenda after the **Single European Act** (**SEA**) in 1986 (see Chapter 20). The removal of internal EU border controls was written into the 1957 **Treaty of Rome**, even though this had not been fully realized by the early 1980s. With this goal back on the agenda, attention turned to the need to create external Community borders, and to develop coherent and common rules on access. Early efforts targeted three groups: the citizens of the European Community, and then Union, whose freedom of movement within the EC/EU was to be secured; long-term EU residents of third countries—that is, non-EU citizens who had relocated to the EU and who held residence and work permits; and **third-country nationals** (**TCNs**), including labour migrants and asylum seekers seeking to enter the collective territory of the EC/EU. Early efforts to cooperate were launched not by the EU, but by the **Council of Europe** (CoE), the membership of which comprised both East and West European countries. Judicial matters were raised often at CoE meetings. While the CoE's work was significant, the drawbacks of its processes, including slow and 'lowest common denominator' policy output, were also clear.

Given these shortcomings of the CoE, member states set up the '**Trevi Group**' in 1975 as an informal assembly to deal with cross-border terrorism through **closer cooperation** among EC law enforcement authorities. Trevi was a loose network rather than an institution, and the meetings concluded in non-binding **consultations** on organized international crime, including drug and arms trafficking. Subsequently, several other groups were established, including the Judicial Cooperation Group, the Customs Mutual Assistance Group, and the Ad Hoc Groups on Immigration and Organized Crime. These groups spanned the four JHA policy clusters that were gradually becoming Europeanized: immigration policy; asylum policy; police cooperation; and judicial cooperation.

BOX 21.1   BACKGROUND: CATALYSTS FOR EARLY COOPERATION IN JUSTICE AND HOME AFFAIRS (JHA) MATTERS

Linked to immigration	Increase in cross-border movements between Western European countries
	Increase in labour and family unification migration into Western European countries
	Increase in applications for asylum
	Concerns about cross-border organized crime
Linked to the **European integration** project	Undesirable impacts of delays at borders on economic activities
	Desire to complete the creation of the **Single Market** by gradually removing controls at the Union's internal borders
	Recognition of the necessity to develop common measures to apply to the external borders before doing away with controls at the internal borders

KEY POINTS

- Cooperation in Justice and Home Affairs was not foreseen in the Treaty of Rome.

- The Council of Europe (a non-EC institution) was the main forum for the discussion of JHA issues, but it worked slowly and its output was meagre.

- The Trevi Group was created in 1975 as a loose network within which terrorism might be discussed at the European level.

- The Trevi Group led to the setting up of similar groups in related areas.

21.3 The Schengen experiment

Perhaps the most ambitious project of these early years was Schengen. In 1985, a number of EC member states decided to do away with border controls, formalized in the 1985 Schengen Agreement and later the 1990 Schengen Implementation Convention. Belgium, the Netherlands, and Luxembourg (the 'Benelux' countries), along with Germany, France, and Italy, created a new system that would connect their police forces and customs authorities. They also created the **Schengen Information System (SIS)**, an innovative, shared database that stored important information (such as criminal records and asylum applications), and which was accessible by national law enforcement authorities. Schengen's primary objective was to develop policies for the Community's external borders that would eventually remove the EC's internal borders. This was an ambitious goal of which the UK, Ireland, and Denmark remained sceptical. Despite Schengen involving only some member states, it became a model for the EC (and later the Union) as a whole.

Within the Schengen framework, significant progress was made in each of the four emergent areas of cooperation. With respect to asylum, Schengen instituted a new system for assigning responsibility to review asylum claims to one state to stop multiple asylum applications and reduce the administrative costs of processing duplicate asylum claims. It also provided the groundwork for an EU-wide visa policy through a common list of countries the citizens of which would need an entry visa, also introducing uniform Schengen visas. There was more modest output in judicial cooperation, with the easing of extradition procedures between member states. Finally, Schengen involved cooperation on law enforcement. However, since most of this work fell outside the EC decision-making structure, it was conducted away from the scrutiny of the general public and their elected representatives (see Box 21.2).

> ↘ **BOX 21.2   BACKGROUND: WHAT IS SCHENGEN?**
>
> Named after the small Luxembourg border town where a subset of the member states of the EC resolved to lift border controls, the Schengen system is a path-breaking initiative to provide for ease of travel between member states. In 1985, France, Germany, Italy, and the Benelux countries signed the first Schengen Agreement and were later joined by nine other EU members, bringing the total number of participating states to 15. The Schengen accords sought to remove controls on persons, including TCNs, at their internal borders while allowing member states to reintroduce them only under limited circumstances. Member states agreed to develop common entry policies for their collective territory, to issue common entry visas, to designate a responsible state for reviewing asylum claims, and to combat transnational crime jointly. They also created a novel database—the Schengen Information System (SIS)—to exchange information between the member states on certain categories of individual and property. Because the
>
> original SIS was designed to interlink at most 18 countries, a new version, SIS II, was launched, made necessary by the enlarged EU. In 2021 the 26 Schengen countries are: Austria; Belgium; Czech Republic; Denmark; Estonia; Finland; France; Germany; Greece; Hungary; Iceland; Italy; Latvia; Liechtenstein; Lithuania; Luxembourg; Malta; the Netherlands; Norway; Poland; Portugal; Slovakia; Slovenia; Spain; Sweden; and Switzerland. Four of these countries (Iceland, Liechtenstein, Norway, and Switzerland) are not members of the EU.
>
> Ireland is not part of the Schengen system, choosing to **opt in** on an issue-by-issue basis. The UK, which held an opt-in prior to Brexit, is now fully outside the framework, their citizens becoming TCNs. Starting in 2022, UK citizens will need to register with the European Travel Information and Authorization System to obtain a visa waiver for EU/Schengen territory.

KEY POINTS

- The 1985 Schengen Agreement was a commitment by a subset of EC member states to remove controls at their internal borders.

- Steps were taken by the Schengen members to agree on common rules on their external borders, for example, on visa policy.

- For those countries involved, Schengen allowed national civil servants in these fields to become accustomed to European-level cooperation.

- Significant progress was made in each of the four emergent areas of cooperation within Schengen.

21.4 Maastricht and the 'third pillar'

Efforts intensified in the early 1990s to shift decision-making towards the European institutions. With the implementation of the Treaty on European Union (TEU) in 1993, JHA was incorporated into the European Union, forming its third pillar. The TEU identified the following areas of 'common interest': asylum policy rules applicable to the crossing of the Union's external borders; immigration policy and the handling of TCNs; combating drug addiction and drug trafficking; tackling international fraud; judicial cooperation in civil and criminal matters; customs cooperation; police cooperation to combat and prevent terrorism; and police cooperation in tackling international organized crime. The Treaty also created a new institutional home for the groups that had been set up in earlier decades and created a decision-making framework. However, this new JHA pillar was the product of an awkward inter-state compromise. In the run-up to Maastricht, while most member states supported bringing JHA matters into the Union, they remained divided over how this should be done. Some argued that JHA should be handled within the first pillar, as a **supranational** policy; others preferred to keep this sensitive field as a largely intergovernmental dialogue.

The TEU reflected the institutional consequences of this political compromise. With the third pillar, the Treaty established an intergovernmental negotiating sphere that marginalized the Community institutions, particularly the European Commission, within the JHA decision-making process, thus diverging significantly from standard decision-making in the EC. The key decision-taking body became the JHA Council. The European Commission's usual function as the initiator of European legislation (see Chapter 10) was diminished by its shared right of initiative in JHA. The role of the European Parliament (EP) did not extend beyond consultation, a situation that led to accusations that JHA exemplified the Union's **democratic deficit** (Geddes, 2008; Uçarer, 2014; Bache et al., 2014; see also Chapter 9). The Court of Justice of the EU (CJEU), the body that might have enhanced the **accountability** and judicial oversight of policy, was excluded from jurisdiction in JHA matters (see Chapter 13).

Although bringing JHA into the EU was an important step, critics of the third pillar abounded. Two sets of interrelated criticisms were advanced. Some lamented the lack of policy progress in the post-Maastricht period. The problem was that the post-Maastricht institutional arrangements were ill equipped to handle the projected, or indeed the existing, workload falling under JHA. Decision-making was cumbersome, with often non-binding policy instruments necessitating drawn-out (and potentially inconclusive) negotiations. All decisions in the third pillar had to be reached unanimously, leading to deadlock. When **unanimity** was achieved, the result was often a lowest-common-denominator compromise that pleased few. Negotiations were secretive and the EP remained marginalized, particularly problematic at a time when the Union was trying hard to improve its democratic image.

> **KEY POINTS**
>
> - The Maastricht Treaty, which came into effect in 1993, created a 'third pillar' for Justice and Home Affairs.
> - The institutional framework put in place for JHA was intergovernmental and cumbersome.
> - Key institutions such as the EP and the Court were marginalized in JHA decision-making.
> - The JHA framework was subject to much criticism in the mid-1990s.

21.5 Absorbing the third pillar: from Amsterdam to Lisbon

In the run-up to the 1999 Amsterdam Treaty, proposals for reforming JHA included: enhanced roles for the Commission, EP, and Court of Justice; the elimination of the unanimity rule; and the incorporation of the Schengen system into the European Union. As with Maastricht, there was a fierce political debate over these issues.

The challenge was to make the Union 'more relevant to its citizens and more responsive to their concerns', by creating an 'area of freedom, security and justice' (AFSJ) (Council of the European Union, 1996). Within such an area, barriers to the free movement of people across borders would be minimized without

jeopardizing the safety, security, and human rights of EU citizens. The Amsterdam compromise led to three important changes. First, parts of the Maastricht third pillar were transferred to the first pillar, or 'Communitarized'. Second, the institutional framework for issues that remained within the third pillar was streamlined. And third, the Schengen framework was incorporated into the Union's *acquis communautaire*.

21.5.1 New first-pillar issues under Amsterdam

The Communitarization of parts of the third pillar was the most significant JHA development at Amsterdam. These provisions called for the EU Council to adopt policies to ensure the free movement of persons within the Union, while concurrently implementing security measures with respect to immigration, asylum, and external border controls. The Treaty also specified new decision-making rules. A transition period of five years was foreseen, during which unanimity was required in the JHA Council following consultations with the EP. After five years, however, the Commission would gain an exclusive right of initiative, with member states losing their right to launch policy instruments. While the EP's access to the decision-making procedure would still be limited to consultation in most cases, an automatic shift to the **co-decision** procedure (now the **ordinary legislative procedure**, or OLP), which would give the EP much more of a say, was foreseen for uniform visa rules and the procedures for issuing visas. The Court would receive a mandate for the first time, allowing it to undertake **preliminary rulings** in policy areas falling within the first pillar in response to requests by national courts (see Chapter 13). Despite these improvements, however, the new Amsterdam architecture turned out to still be a formidable maze created through masterful 'legal engineering' for political ends and opaque even for seasoned experts.

21.5.2 The left-over third pillar: cooperation in criminal matters

The Amsterdam reforms left the following criminal matters in the third pillar: combating crime, terrorism, trafficking in persons and offences against children, illicit drugs and arms trafficking, corruption, and fraud. Closer cooperation between police forces, customs, and judicial authorities, and with **Europol**, the European Police Office (see Section 21.6.1, 'Post-Maastricht developments in policy') was envisaged through an approximation of the criminal justice systems of the member states as necessary.

While Amsterdam essentially retained the intergovernmental framework created at Maastricht, the Commission obtained a shared right of initiative for the first time—an improvement over its pre-Amsterdam position. The EP gained the right to be consulted, but that was all. The Treaty constrained the Court in a similar fashion in that it recognized its jurisdiction to issue **preliminary rulings** (see Chapter 13) on the instruments adopted under Title VI, but importantly made this dependent on the **assent** of the member states. While the Commission, Parliament, and Court were to continue to struggle to play an active role in the third pillar, the Council retained its dominant decision-making function and unanimity remained the decision rule used in third-pillar legislation.

21.5.3 **Absorbing Schengen**

After much debate, Schengen was incorporated into the EU by means of a protocol appended to the Amsterdam Treaty. The Protocol provided for the closer cooperation of the Schengen 13 (that is, the EU15 minus Ireland and the UK prior to Brexit) within the EU framework. With this development, cooperation on JHA matters became even more complicated, involving various overlapping groupings. These include EU members fully in the Schengen area, EU members with **opt outs** (Denmark) and **opt ins** (Ireland and pre-Brexit UK), EU members who plan to join Schengen (Bulgaria, Croatia, Cyprus, and Romania), non-EU members who are officially part of Schengen (Iceland, Liechtenstein, Norway, and Switzerland), and non-EU microstates that are de facto part of Schengen (Monaco, San Marino, and the Holy See) because they maintain open borders with their Schengen neighbors (See Box 21.2). One could argue that the incorporation of Schengen into the *acquis communautaire* did not result in the desired simplification, but rather maintained, if not amplified, the convoluted system of the early 1990s. Not surprisingly, some now regard this particular aspect of the AFSJ as the ultimate example of a **multi-speed**, or 'à la carte', Europe.

The Treaty of Nice made few substantial changes to these institutional developments, but extended the shared right of initiative for the Commission in the otherwise intergovernmental (residual) third pillar.

21.5.4 **'Normalizing' AFSJ: the Constitutional Treaty and the Lisbon Treaty**

The **Convention on the Future of Europe** and the 2003–04 intergovernmental conference (IGC), culminating in the October 2004 signing of the **Constitutional Treaty (CT)**, marked the next, if incomplete, stage in JHA reform. The CT provided for the 'normalization' of JHA by abolishing the pillar structure, greater use of **qualified majority voting (QMV)** except for judicial and police cooperation in criminal matters (JPCCM). It retained the shared right of initiative for the Commission and the member states in judicial cooperation in criminal matters, but foresaw proposals coming from coalitions composed of at least 25 per cent of the membership of the Union. These were all efforts to streamline decision-making while preserving a diminished capacity for member states to block decisions. The CT further provided for a role for national parliaments to monitor the implementation of JHA policies and for a **judicial review** of compliance by the ECJ. Finally, the Constitution retained the UK and Irish opt-ins, and the Danish opt-out. However, the CT was rejected in referendums in France and the Netherlands, and the CT was abandoned.

The AFSJ provisions in the CT were later given a new life in the Lisbon Treaty, signed in December 2007. The Lisbon Treaty contains all of the major innovations pertaining to JHA, now called AFSJ, that were present in the CT, and underscores its salience by placing it ahead of **economic and monetary union (EMU)** and the Common Foreign and Security Policy (CFSP) in the Union's fundamental objectives. The Lisbon Treaty also incorporates the 2005 Prüm Convention, a law enforcement treaty that allows signatories to share data and cooperate to combat terrorism into the *acquis communautaire*. It foresees jurisdiction for the CJEU to enforce all AFSJ decisions apart from provisions adopted under the post-Amsterdam third pillar. Since 1 December 2014, the normal powers of the Commission and the CJEU now extend to all areas of AFSJ. The EP will operate with OLP (formerly co-decision) authority in almost all cases. However, the Lisbon Treaty's transformative provisions were also brought about by compromises. Opt-outs and opt-ins remain for Denmark, the UK, and Ireland (see Table 21.1), now complicated further by Brexit, and further signalling a multi-speed Europe (see Box 21.5).

Table 21.1 JHA/AFSJ cooperation: from Trevi to Lisbon

	Pre-Maastricht JHA	Post-Maastricht third pillar (Title VI TEU, Article K)	Post-Amsterdam first pillar (Communitarized areas of former third pillar) Immigration; asylum; Police and Judicial Cooperation in Civil Matters (Title IV TEC, Articles 61–69)	Post-Amsterdam third pillar Police and judicial cooperation in criminal matters (Title VI TEU, Articles 29–42)	Lisbon Treaty (Title IV TEC, Articles 61–69 Consolidated pillars)
European Parliament	No role	Limited role, consultation	1999–2004 Co-decision; Post-2004 Consultation	Consultation	Ordinary legislative procedure
European Court of Justice	No jurisdiction	No jurisdiction	Referral for an obligatory first ruling for national last-instance courts	Preliminary rulings for framework decisions and decisions, conventions established under Title VI and measures implementing them	Jurisdiction to enforce all AFSJ decisions after 1 December 2014
Council	No direct role	Dominant actor	Dominant but Commission and EP ascendant	Shared power position in decision-making	Shared power position 'Enhanced cooperation' possible
Commission	Consultative Occasional observer at intergovernmental meetings	Shared right of initiative with member states except judicial and police cooperation (no right of initiative)	Shared right of initiative (member states asked the Commission to assume an exclusive right for asylum issues)	Shared right of initiative (previously impossible)	Exclusive right of initiative
Decision-making mechanisms	Intergovernmental negotiations Non-binding decisions in the form of resolutions Binding decisions in the form of treaties	Unanimity rule on all issues	Council acts unanimously on proposals from Commission and member states for the first five years Move to QMV (except legal migration) Opt-in (UK*, Ireland), opt-out (Denmark)	Council acts unanimously on proposals from Commission and member states	QMV for most decisions Opt-out (Denmark on judicial cooperation) Opt-ins (UK* and Ireland)

*Brexit terminated UK opt-ins.

Nonetheless, the Lisbon Treaty represents the most significant reform of AFSJ to rectify vexing institutional problems that were created by Maastricht.

> **KEY POINTS**
>
> - The Amsterdam Treaty sought to address the shortcomings of the third pillar by bringing immigration and asylum, as well as judicial and police cooperation in civil matters, into the first pillar. The third pillar, cooperation in criminal matters (police and judicial cooperation), remained intergovernmental.
> - Schengen was incorporated into the Treaty, but this did not result in simplification given the overlapping memberships involved in this agreement.
> - The **Nice Treaty** added a few changes to the Amsterdam set-up and extended a right of shared initiative to the Commission in the third pillar.
> - The **Lisbon Treaty** entailed the most significant reform of JHA to date. It made important strides in normalizing this policy domain in the aftermath of the failed Constitutional Treaty.

21.6 Policy output: baby steps to bold agendas

There have been several spurts of policy since the beginnings of cooperation on Justice and Home Affairs (JHA), building on the early pre-Maastricht efforts, but gathering momentum after Maastricht and Amsterdam. More recently, in addition to making progress on the four main dossiers (immigration, asylum, police cooperation, and judicial cooperation), the European Union has acknowledged the importance of the external dimension of JHA and has embarked on attempts to export its emergent policies beyond the Union.

21.6.1 **Post-Maastricht developments in policy**

After Maastricht, member states first focused on rules to apply to third-country nationals (TCNs) entering the Union territory. The Council formulated common rules in this area for employment and education, and recommended common rules for the expulsion of TCNs. It also recommended a common format for 'bilateral readmission agreements' (which would allow

for the deportation of TCNs) between member states and third countries. Agreement was also reached on the format of a uniform visa, as well as on a list of countries the nationals of which required a visa to enter EU territory. These relatively unambitious agreements sought to develop comparable procedural steps for the entry, sojourn, and expulsion of TCNs.

The most notable development in asylum was the conclusion of the 1990 Dublin Convention, which designated one member state as responsible for the handling of an asylum claim, resting on the concepts of safe countries of origin and transit into the EU, rejecting applications lodged by the nationals of countries deemed safe or by those who had passed through safe countries en route to EU territory. Refugee rights activists frowned upon these policies as dangerously restrictive and warned that such rules could potentially weaken refugee protection.

Work also began on the European Dactyloscopy (EURODAC)—that is, fingerprinting—system, which would allow member states to keep track of asylum seekers, as well as on the negotiation of a common framework for the reception of individuals seeking temporary protection status in Union territory. The Maastricht Treaty launched the ambitious agenda to create a European Police Office (Europol, now called the EU Agency for Law Enforcement Cooperation) to enhance police cooperation and information exchange in combating terrorism and the trafficking of drugs and human beings. Based in The Hague, Europol became operational in October 1998. Ministers of the member states also signed an agreement to create a Europol Drug Unit to assist in criminal investigations.

21.6.2 **Amsterdam and beyond**

Following Amsterdam, progress accelerated, aided by a European Council dedicated exclusively to JHA. The goal of this summit, which was convened in Tampere (Finland) in October 1999, was to evaluate the impact of Amsterdam and to discuss the future direction of cooperation. There was a reiterated commitment to the freedom of movement, development of common rules for the fair treatment of TCNs, including guidelines for dealing with racism and xenophobia, the convergence of judicial systems, and the fostering of **transparency** and democratic control. Among the more far-reaching goals were better controls on, and management of, migration and the deterrence of trafficking in human beings.

On matters of immigration and asylum, Tampere advocated a 'comprehensive approach', closely linked to the combating of poverty, and the removal of the political and economic conditions that compel individuals to leave their homes. It was argued that JHA policies should be linked closely to tools of foreign policy, including development cooperation and economic relations. This called for intensified cooperation between countries of origin and transit to address the causes of flight, empowering neighbouring countries to offer adequate protection to those in flight and speeding up the removal of undocumented immigrants from Union territory.

EU member states also committed to creating a Common European Asylum System (CEAS), including standards for reviewing claims and caring for asylum applicants, and comparable rules for refugee recognition. The Commission was designated as the coordinator of policy proposals dealing with asylum and soon introduced numerous proposals, including on reception conditions for refugees, and a common set of minimum standards for the review of asylum claims, as well as common family reunification schemes for refugees. The Union also approved the creation of the European Refugee Fund, designed to aid EU recipient states during times of significant refugee arrivals, such as those experienced during the fallout from Bosnia and Kosovo. By this point, the Dublin Convention had taken effect, and the EURODAC system was now functioning. The creation of the CEAS was in progress.

In matters of judicial and police cooperation, still third pillar issues, a European Judicial Area (EJA) was foreseen in which the **mutual recognition** of judicial decisions and cross-border information exchange for prosecutions, as well as minimum standards for civil procedural law, would be ensured. Furthermore, the EU's Judicial Cooperation Unit (Eurojust), composed of national prosecutors, magistrates, and police officers, was created. Eurojust would aid national prosecuting authorities in their criminal investigations of organized crime. A European Police College (CEPOL), which would also admit officers from the **candidate countries**, and a European Police Chiefs Task Force (PCTF) were also planned. Priorities were established for fighting money laundering, corruption, euro counterfeiting, drug trafficking, trafficking in human beings, the exploitation of women, the sexual exploitation of children, and high-tech and environmental crime, designating Europol as the lead agency in these efforts. Importantly, Tampere also

established **benchmarks** and set deadlines, which enlivened the policy process. The Commission tabled new and revised initiatives relating to asylum procedures: on reception conditions for asylum seekers; on the definition and status of refugees; and on a first-pillar instrument to replace the Dublin Convention.

The next phase of cooperation involved creating an integrated border management system and visa policy, complete with a Visa Information System (VIS) database to store the biometric data of visa applicants, a common policy on the management of migration flows to meet economic and demographic needs, and the creation of the EJA. The Hague Programme that was adopted in November 2004 called for the implementation of the CEAS and the gradual expansion of the European Refugee Fund. The Council Secretariat's Situation Centre (SitCen), which would provide strategic analyses of terrorist threats, was endorsed and **Frontex**, responsible for securing the external borders of the EU, was created. The Hague Programme invited greater coordination on the integration of existing migrants, and, for the external dimension, stressed partnership with countries of origin and/or transit, and the conclusion of further readmission agreements as necessary. The Hague Programme arguably gave policy-making a push, resulting in the adoption of hundreds of texts in 2007 alone.

The subsequent Stockholm Programme guided AFSJ cooperation for 2010–14, echoing the political priorities of its predecessors: promoting **European citizenship** and fundamental rights; an internal security strategy to protect against organized crime and terrorism; integrated border management; a comprehensive Union migration policy; completing the CEAS; and integrating these priorities into the external policies of the EU. It foresees an expansion of Europol, as well as several other measures in the police cooperation realm, and further empowers Frontex.

As the 1990s progressed, the planned **enlargements** projected the collective territory outwards, making it necessary to discuss JHA/AFSJ matters with the Union's *future* borders in mind. Member states began to involve certain third countries in some of their initiatives, attempting to solidify EU border controls by recruiting other countries to tighten their own controls (Lavenex and Uçarer, 2002). This involved entering into **collective agreements** with countries of origin and transit. These attempts to recruit neighbouring countries to adopt close variations of the EU's emergent border management regime were particularly pronounced in Central and Eastern Europe (CEE), the **Maghreb**, and the Mediterranean basin, because of the proximity of these areas to the EU. North African, Mediterranean, and **African, Caribbean, and Pacific (ACP) countries** were also steered towards adopting policies to ease migratory pressures into the Union. In addition to the readmission agreements negotiated by its member states, by 2015, the EU itself implemented 17 readmission agreements with third countries ranging from Albania, Cape Verde, Russia, to Turkey and Ukraine. Frontex also played a crucial role by engaging countries that are on the EU's land borders in the southeast and the Western Balkans, and on its maritime borders in the Mediterranean. Such deployments, with operational names such as 'Hermes', 'Triton', and 'Poseidon', frequently occur in the Mediterranean, particularly near Malta, Italy,

and Greece. Securing and maintaining these processes have been difficult, frequently intertwining the domestic politics of the affected countries with those of the EU (see Box 21.3).

KEY POINTS

- Activity in the field of Justice and Home Affairs (JHA) gathered momentum after Maastricht and Amsterdam.

- Post-Maastricht, the emphasis was on third country nationals (TCNs) entering the EU.

- The Tampere summer in late 1999 renewed the EU commitment to JHA and included a commitment to set up a Common European Asylum System.

- In the 2000s the EU placed greater emphasis than in the past on the external dimension of JHA.

BOX 21.3   CASE STUDY: STRAINS ON SCHENGEN AND THE FREEDOM OF MOVEMENT: POPULISM, THE REFUGEE 'CRISIS,' AND THE PANDEMIC

Schengen is arguably the most important multilateral mechanism that jump-started the AFSJ. However, it came under strain as a result of the **Arab Spring**. In May 2011, Schengen's provisions were temporarily suspended between Italy and France, and border checks were reinstated when Italy issued travel documents to arrivals from North Africa. Despite the principle of mutual recognition, France refused to recognize these documents as valid, reinstated border checks, and started sending individuals with these documents back to Italy. Unrelatedly, Denmark, citing a perceived increase in cross-border crime, also briefly reinstated controls at its Schengen borders as a concession to the anti-immigration **Danish People's Party**, on the cooperation of which the government relied in the legislative process. Meanwhile, while the initial stand-off de-escalated between France and Italy, President Sarkozy announced in March 2012, from the campaign trail (a month before critical national elections in France), that France might pull out of Schengen unless the EU stemmed undocumented migration. As with Denmark, this was in an effort to curry favour with nationalist, anti-immigration, and far-right electorate and political parties. Developments in the UK were likewise an example of populist backlash, with Brexit a prime example of tensions in EU and migration governance. In addition to populism, a second challenge emerged during the summer of 2015, just as Schengen was marking its 30th anniversary, hundreds of thousands of asylum seekers, mainly from Syria, entered the EU. Many EU states temporarily reintroduced border controls either completely or partially (see Chapter 27).

Finally, the COVID-19 pandemic presented a third wave of challenges to Schengen in less than a decade. Border closures,

quarantines, lock-downs, and a pivot to national efforts during the pandemic put significant strains on the Schengen system and the freedom of movement in the EU. In March 2020, 17 member states unilaterally and temporarily closed their national borders to suppress transmission of COVID-19, effectively suspending Schengen in much of its territory. The 2020 suspensions were unprecedented and caused massive disruptions at the affected borders, uncertainty for individual travellers, and negative impacts on the right to freedom of movement. Member states also responded in a divergent manner to the pandemic. The European Commission and the European Parliament spearheaded efforts to work together to 'return to normal', even when individual member states were going it alone at a time that clearly required cooperation. Problems associated with the Europe-wide rollout of a vaccination programme, and the resulting prospects of delays in opening up in individual countries frustrated efforts and underscored deficits in governance. To hasten the re-opening of the EU, the European Commission launched several efforts to collect and disseminate pandemic data. As summer 2021 approached, EU leaders supported the introduction of a 'Digital Green Certificate' (essentially a COVID vaccine passport) that would enable their holders to travel across all 27 member states (and potentially also to Schengen members Norway, Iceland, and Switzerland), restoring the opportunity to travel to vaccinated people. As of November 2021, 6 Schengen members are maintaining border controls until Spring 2022. These waves of difficulties further highlight the strains on the collective management of the Schengen area (see also Chapter 28).

21.7 EU migration and asylum policy before and after the migration crisis

The Common European Asylum System (CEAS) was the product of the aforementioned 1999 Tampere summit. It is the EU's response to its international obligations to provide humanitarian protection to refugees and a functioning asylum system across the EU (see Section 21.6.2, 'Amsterdam and beyond'; see also Chapter 26). CEAS seeks to address three challenges. First, it addresses the practice which leads asylum seekers whose application for asylum is denied in one member state to apply for asylum in another EU country. This is often termed 'forum shopping'. Second, it addresses the problem of differential asylum outcomes in different member states, leading asylum seekers to gravitate towards those countries where their application is more likely to be approved. Third, it addresses the variety of social benefits for asylum seekers that exist across EU member states, which also draws refugees to gravitate towards one particular jurisdiction.

Tampere foresaw CEAS implementation in two phases: in the first phase, the adoption of common minimum standards in the short term should lead to a common procedure and a uniform status for those granted asylum, which would be valid throughout the Union in the longer term. Thus this 'first phase' of the CEAS, which lasted from 1999 to 2004, established the criteria and mechanisms for determining the member state responsible for examining asylum applications. This replaced the earlier regime governed by the 1990 Dublin Convention, and which included the establishment of the EURODAC database for storing and comparing fingerprint data; the definition of common minimum standards to which member states had to adhere regarding the reception of asylum seekers; rules on international protection and the nature of the protection granted; and procedures for granting and withdrawing refugee status (see Box 21.4).

In the 2004 Hague Programme, second-phase instruments and measures were foreseen by the end of 2010, highlighting the EU's ambition to go beyond minimum standards and develop a single asylum procedure with common guarantees and a uniform status for those granted protection. In the 2008 European Pact on Immigration and Asylum, this deadline was postponed to 2012. The Lisbon Treaty, which entered into force in December 2009, changed the situation by transforming the measures on asylum from establishing minimum standards to creating a common system comprising a uniform status and uniform procedures. Since Lisbon, Article 80 TFEU has also introduced the principle of solidarity and has provided for the fair sharing of responsibility among member states. EU asylum actions should, where relevant, contain appropriate measures to give effect to the solidarity principle. The new treaty also significantly altered the decision-making procedure on asylum matters by introducing the ordinary legislative procedure (OLP) as the standard procedure. Although the Commission had tabled its proposals for the second phase of CEAS as early as 2008–09, negotiations progressed slowly. Accordingly, the 'second' phase of the CEAS was adopted only after the entry into force of the Lisbon Treaty.

BOX 21.4   KEY DEBATES: THE DUBLIN CONVENTION

The Dublin Convention was first agreed in January 1990. Now in its third incarnation, the so-called Dublin III Convention entered into force in July 2013, with the aim of establishing a common framework for determining which member state decides an asylum seeker's application. This is intended to ensure that only one member state processes each asylum application. The criteria for establishing responsibility runs, in hierarchical order, from family considerations, to recent possession of a visa or residence permit in a member state, to whether the applicant has entered the EU irregularly or regularly. The arrival of numerous migrants and asylum seekers in the EU since 2013 and their concentration in particular geographical areas, has exposed the weaknesses of the Dublin System, however, since it establishes that the member state responsible for examining an asylum application will tend to be the country of the first point of irregular entry. In May 2016, the Commission presented a draft proposal—the Dublin IV Regulation—to make the Dublin System more transparent and to enhance its effectiveness, while providing a mechanism to deal with the disproportionate pressure placed on countries on Europe's southern borders, such as Greece, Italy, Malta, and Spain. The proposal has been controversial and remains deadlocked.

Set up in 2005 and revised in 2012, the Global Approach to Migration and Mobility (GAMM) is the external dimension of the EU's migration policy. It is based on a partnership with third countries and is designed to address the management of legal migration from outside the EU, the prevention and reduction of irregular migration, enhancing international protection and asylum policy, and the relationship between migration and development. The GAMM's primary focus is the Southern Mediterranean and the Eastern Partnership. Under the 'more for more' mechanism, the EU tries to persuade third countries to strengthen their border controls, restrict their visa policy, and readmit irregular migrants with incentives such as trade benefits, visa facilitation, or financial support. This is a controversial approach, and the GAMM has been criticized for omitting criteria on human rights in the selection of partner countries and for the absence of a mechanism for monitoring or suspending cooperation.

The origins of the EU migration crisis can be traced back to the events of 3 October 2013 when a boat sank near the Italian island of Lampedusa with the loss of more than 360 lives. By 2015 the EU started to see larger numbers of migrant flows resulting from the war in Syria. There are several ways to interpret this as a 'crisis', though not everyone would interpret it as such (see Chapter 26). For example, the dominant narrative provided by the EU institutions sees this issue as both a security and humanitarian crisis, presenting the EU and its member states with a challenge to its inadequate common migration and asylum policies, focusing more on issues of security and less on humanitarian responses (please refer to Chapter 26 on the Migration and Refugee Crisis for a full discussion of the crisis). In the UK, the 'crisis' became entangled with the issue of Brexit (see Box 21.5). From 2015 most member states sought to strengthen and militarize their borders. The Commission launched the European Agenda on Migration in May 2015, which included several measures including an emergency relocation mechanism for a total of 160,000 people in need of international protection to assist Italy and Greece in particular. However, relocation rates were very low and the policy proved unsuccessful (see Chapter 26). In September 2020 the Commission launched a New Pact on Migration and Asylum, focusing on strengthened partnerships with countries of origin and transit, robust management of external borders, and internal rules to achieve solidarity and a

---

 BOX 21.5   KEY DEBATES: BREXIT AND AFSJ

When Schengen was incorporated into the EU with the Amsterdam Treaty in 1999, the UK, along with Ireland, secured an opt out but reserved the right to opt into immigration and asylum-related policies as it saw fit. Brexit was itself driven by a desire for the UK to remove itself from the jurisdiction of the CJEU and not give up control over immigration, one of the UK Prime Minister (PM) Theresa May's red lines. When he took over as PM, Boris Johnson's negotiations retained this hard line, even at the risk of undermining the 1998 Good Friday agreement (see Chapter 27). This agreement ended the conflict in Northern Ireland and provided for avoiding a hard border between Northern Ireland and the Republic of Ireland, which was threatened by the Brexit stance of the UK government. Given this hard-line stance, Brexit has rendered the UK a third country and its citizens TCNs, less along the lines of Norway which has a close relationship with the EU, and more along the lines of Canada. Brexit was poised to impact the status of UK citizens living and working in the EU and EU citizens living and working in the UK. This was resolved by making it possible for impacted EU citizens to apply for EU Settled Status by 30 June 2020 before the end of the transition period. UK citizens already resident in

EU territory would seek similar relief in their countries of residence. A different regime applies to individuals who arrived after the end of the transition period on 1 January 2021, leaving their entry up to the discretion of the countries concerned. With respect to asylum and refugees, the UK was still bound by a number of CEAS measures after Brexit and could seek guidance from the CJEU until the end of the transition period. Since 1 January 2021, the UK has withdrawn from the EU's Common European Asylum System, including the Dublin system and its associated databases. With this withdrawal, the UK is now free to set standards lower than what was possible under CEAS. At the same time, it is no longer able to transfer asylum seekers to other member states under the Dublin system. The end of the transition period also occasions changes to criminal law cooperation, rolling back cooperation between the EU and the UK. The UK now has limited access to the EU's relevant databases, causing an important data gap for the UK. The April 2021 protests in Belfast, Northern Ireland, some of which turned violent, foreshadow feared adverse consequences of Brexit, which complicates freedom of movement between Northern Ireland and the Republic of Ireland.

balanced distribution of responsibilities while allowing sceptical countries (such as Hungary, Poland, and Slovakia) to opt out of relocation mechanisms. Given its restrictive tenor, however, the Pact has drawn sharp criticism (see Chapter 26).

21.8 Towards a Security Union?

'Europeans need to feel confident that, wherever they move within Europe, their freedom and their security are well protected, in full compliance with the Union's values, including the rule of law and fundamental rights', opined the European Commission in its 2015 communication to the Council and the Parliament on the 'European Agenda on Security' for 2015–20. In less than a year after its adoption, the March 2016 coordinated suicide attacks in Brussels prompted Commission President Juncker to insist that the EU needed a genuine Security Union by improving information exchange and strengthening external borders. A good deal of police cooperation is necessary to achieve these ends. At the same time, such cooperation has its drawbacks and critics, even within the EU institutions, and certainly within civil liberties circles. For instance, the EU, while it now has broader powers in this arena, has simultaneously lamented the loss of a genuinely common approach to internal security, and the data protection hazards that accompany such initiatives. The Passenger Name Record (PNR) system is a case in point. In 2016, the EU adopted a directive on the use of PNR within the context of its counter-terrorism efforts. PNR collects data such as personal information and itinerary on international passengers and, as such, could be helpful in flagging potential threats. At

the same time, in order to collect information on potential threats, non-threatening individuals would also see their information compiled, and possibly shared within and outside the European Union as the EU has PNR agreements with the United States, Canada, and Australia. The European Parliament resisted this European Commission initiative long and hard until it was satisfied that adequate data protection measures were incorporated into it. Ultimately, although the institutional framework on police cooperation has become simpler since the TFEU, police cooperation (along with judicial cooperation in criminal matters) remains more loosely incorporated into the EU than the other planks of AFSJ.

The European Agenda on Security identifies three key priorities and challenges for the near future: fighting terrorism, disrupting organized cross-border crime, and tackling cybercrime. This takes us all the way back to the beginning of this chapter. JHA/AFSJ cooperation owes its genesis partly to the efforts of the Trevi Group, the main goal of which was to establish cross-border cooperation in the fight against organized crime and terrorism. These matters were subsequently incorporated into the Union. Europol was created to facilitate the apprehension and prosecution of transborder criminals, and established jointly accessible databases to enhance police cooperation. The Commission began work in late 1999 to develop an instrument that would outline the Union's position on terrorism, covering terrorist acts directed against member states, the Union itself, and international terrorism.

The EU's focus on terrorism heightened following the 11 September 2001 ('9/11') attacks. The events in the USA prompted the EU to move speedily towards adopting anti-terrorist policies already in preparation. In October 2001, the Council committed the Union to adopting a common definition of terrorist offences, a common decision on the freezing of assets with links to suspected terrorists, and establishing the **European Arrest Warrant (EAW)** designed to replace the protracted extradition procedures between EU member states with an automatic transfer of suspected persons from one EU country to another. The Council urged better coordination between Europol, Eurojust, intelligence units, police corps, and judicial authorities, and announced work on a list of terrorist organizations. The Union called for increased vigilance for possible biological and chemical attacks, even though such attacks had never previously occurred in the EU.

Finally, linking the fight against terrorism to effective border controls, the European Council insisted on the intensification of efforts to combat falsified and forged travel documents and visas (European Council, 2001). The focus on anti-terrorism measures intensified yet further after the 11 March 2004 attacks in Madrid. While no stranger to terrorist attacks from separatist Basque militants, Spain's trauma sharpened the attention to terrorism. The EU and its member states subsequently negotiated a number of cross-border initiatives to enhance their collective capabilities to combat terrorism. Among these was the Prüm Convention of 2005 which enabled signatories to exchange DNA, fingerprint, and vehicle registration data to combat terrorism. The possibility that violent acts could be perpetrated by poorly integrated migrants—highlighted by the widely publicized murder of Theo van Gogh, a prominent Dutch film director, at the hands of a Muslim who held dual Dutch and Moroccan citizenship—rekindled the integration debate. Fears about 'home-grown' terrorism hit another high with the 7 July 2005 ('7/7') London bombings and later with the attack on the French satirical weekly *Charlie Hebdo* on 7 January 2015, some of the perpetrators of which were also thought to be involved in the March 2016 Brussels attacks.

The Union is now working on improving its information exchange infrastructure to help with its anti-terrorism efforts. Along with a second-generation Schengen Information System (SIS II), a new EU Visa Information System (VIS) is now operational all over the world. Possessing interactive capabilities, SIS II includes additional information on 'violent troublemakers' (including football hooligans, but potentially also political protesters) and suspected terrorists, and also stores biometric information (digital pictures and fingerprints) and EAW entries. In turn, the VIS collects and stores data from all visa applications in all member states, including biometric data such as digital photos and all ten fingerprints—something that is criticized for potentially falling foul of data protection measures.

The EU also now has a directive on combating terrorism, which was adopted in 2017 and replaces previous post-9/11 framework decisions. This directive offers a common definition of terrorist offences and criminalizes undertakings to prepare for terrorist acts, such as travelling abroad for training or aiding and abetting terrorist activities. The Commission also prepared, in consultation with national experts, EU

agencies and Interpol, a set of common risk indicators for foreign terrorists in an effort to assist in the work of national border personnel. A European Counter Terrorism Center (ECTC) launched in January 2016 within Europol to assist member states in fighting terrorism and radicalization. In 2016, the Commission also put forth an action plan for measures against financing terrorism, including asset freezing, anti-money laundering measures, and cooperation between financial intelligence units from member states. These measures can also be used to combat other types of transnational organized crime. In the coming years, the Commission, as spelled out in its 2020–25 EU Security Union Strategy, envisions EU legislation on, for example, stemming illicit cash movements, counterfeiting, and the movement and sale of cultural goods to achieve financing of terrorist activities. The European Public Prosecutor's Office (EPPO) will be helpful in this regard. With respect to radicalization, in 2016, the Commission identified areas of cooperation between member states, including countering online terrorist propaganda and hate speech, addressing radicalization in prisons, and promoting inclusive education and inclusive societies. The Commission also set up financial assistance to support rehabilitation, de-radicalization, and training programmes. Finally, the Commission proposed cooperation with the External Action Service, cooperation with third countries in matters of security, and counter-terrorism, deploying experts to the EU delegations of a number of Middle-East and North African (MENA) countries as well as Nigeria. To address the third realm of priorities, namely cybersecurity, the EU adopted a Cybersecurity Strategy in 2013 and also created several institutions to enhance cooperation between member states. The 2020–25 strategy also focuses on securing and protecting critical infrastructure. These efforts have also yielded some policy instruments creating a common European criminal law framework against cyber-attacks.

While the attention directed towards anti-terrorist, organized crime, and cybercrime measures is certainly warranted, the EU's efforts in this field have already attracted criticism from civil liberties and migrants' rights advocates (Statewatch, 2011). Activists caution against a possible backlash against migrants of Arab descent and argue against closing the EU's outer doors even more tightly. Anti-Islam and xenophobic rhetoric displayed by various groups, such as **Pegida (Patriotic Europeans against the Islamisation of the West)** in

Germany, and political parties such as the **Rassemblement Nationale (National Rally)** in France, capitalize on violence that can be linked to persons of migrant origin and raise concerns about further securitization of migration and asylum in Europe. As in the post-9/11 USA, European anti-terrorism measures have attracted sharp criticism from civil libertarians in Europe, who also remain sceptical about closer anti-terrorism cooperation between the USA and the EU for data protection reasons. In terms of academic analysis, it is highly inadvisable to conflate migration, security, and terrorism, even though all three are areas that fall under the mandate of AFSJ. In essence, the challenge in Europe is similar to that in the USA: developing policy instruments that meet security needs while protecting the civil liberties of individuals residing in the EU territory. The events of 11 September 2001, 11 March 2004, 7 July 2005, 7 January 2015, and 22 March 2016, and more seem to have brought JHA/AFSJ cooperation full circle to its Trevi origins. It is certain that this dossier will remain very lively, if controversial, in the future, preserving the security narrative that sits uneasily in a multi-religion, multi-ethnic, and multi-origin Europe. At the same time, while we can chart quite a bit of progress in these highly sensitive and sovereignty-inspiring fields, the security union of which the Commission speaks is still far off.

> **KEY POINTS**
>
> - Cooperation in the Area of Freedom, Security, and Justice (AFSJ) has developed a significant external dimension, particularly vis-à-vis the EU's neighbours.
>
> - The enlargement of the Union not only pushes its borders (and therefore the AFSJ) eastwards, but also commits applicant countries to adopt Justice and Home Affairs (JHA) rules before their accession.
>
> - AFSJ policy output also has an impact on countries that are not part of the enlargement process.
>
> - How to respond to terrorism is a key challenge facing the EU and its member states.

21.9 Conclusion

Cooperation in Justice and Home Affairs has come a long way since its obscure beginnings in the 1970s. It currently occupies a prominent and permanent position in EU **governance**. The European Commission now has a more active role, facilitated by the creation within it of two new Directorates-General. The status of the European Parliament and the Court of Justice of the EU has also improved since Amsterdam and Lisbon. Matters discussed in this field continue to strain the sovereign sensibilities of the EU member states and the policy remains intrinsically intergovernmental. However, few believe that the European Union can achieve its **common market** goals without making significant progress in the Area of Freedom, Security, and Justice (AFSJ). As the events of 11 September 2001 in the USA and the attacks in Madrid, London, Paris, Brussels, and the summer of 2015 clearly demonstrate, the tackling of transborder issues so typical of this dossier demands coordination and cooperation beyond the state. AFSJ is still a young field compared to the other more established **competences** of the EU. And yet, it demonstrates significant institutional change over time while maintaining consistent policy thrusts.

The EU must contend with a number of important, and sometimes conflicting, challenges specific to AFSJ cooperation. In order to lift internal border controls on people moving within the EU, the Union must articulate and implement policies to manage its *external* borders. These policies should foster the freedom of movement of EU citizens and third-country nationals within the Union. They should also spell out common rules on the entry of TCNs. To demonstrate its commitment to basic human rights and democratic principles, the EU must protect TCNs against arbitrary actions, uphold their civil liberties, encourage inclusiveness, and deter acts of violence against them. To maintain the rule of law, the Union must press forward with judicial and police cooperation, while ensuring the privacy and civil liberties of those living in the EU. To live up to its international obligations, the EU must keep its policies in line with its pre-existing treaty obligations, particularly in the field of refugee protection. To protect its **legitimacy** and to improve its public image, the EU must take pains to address issues of transparency and democratic deficit. Finally, it must undertake these endeavours without raising the spectre of an impenetrable 'Fortress Europe', which some argue already exists. The challenges facing the policy remain substantial.

QUESTIONS

1. What are the catalysts that have led to the Europeanization of Justice and Home Affairs/Area of Freedom, Security, and Justice policy?

2. What have been the impediments to effective cooperation in JHA/AFSJ matters?

3. If the issues dealt with in JHA/AFSJ can also be addressed through unilateral decisions by individual countries, or by bilateral agreements concluded with interested parties, why is there such an effort to develop multilateral and collective responses in this field?

4. What are some of the lingering shortcomings of JHA/AFSJ cooperation?

5. What is meant by 'normalizing' JHA/AFSJ and how does the Lisbon Treaty contribute to such 'normalization'?

6. How effective has the EU's response to the migration crisis been? What does this tell us about migration governance in the EU?

7. How is the European Union dealing with terrorism?

8. What has prompted work towards a European security union? What are some of the opportunities and challenges for such efforts?

 GUIDE TO FURTHER READING

Geddes, A. and Scholten, Peter (2016) *Politics of Migration and Immigration in Europe* (London: Sage). A very accessible and well-informed book on the EU's immigration regime.

Kaunert, C. (2011) *European Internal Security: Towards Supranational Governance in the Area of Freedom, Security, and Justice* (Manchester: Manchester University Press). A comprehensive recent volume that assesses European internal security and integration.

Peers, S. 'Legislative updates', *European Journal of Migration and Law*—various issues (for example, (2012) 'Legislative update, The Recast Qualifications Directive', *European Journal of Migration and Law*, 14/2: 199–221). These legislative updates capture the policy output, as well as providing insightful discussions of the decision-making process.

Ripoll Servent, A. and Trauner, F. (eds) (2018) *The Routledge Handbook of Justice and Home Affairs Research* (New York: Routledge). A comprehensive edited volume that offers theoretical, institutional, and substantive analyses of the developments in AFSJ.

Trauner, F. and Ripoll Servent, A. (eds) (2015) *Policy Change in the Area of Freedom, Security and Justice: How EU Institutions Matter* (New York: Routledge). An edited volume that explores the role of EU institutions in the making of policy in various AFSJ issue areas.

Access the online resources to take your learning and understanding further, including extra multiple-choice questions with instant feedback, web links, answer guidance to end-of-chapter questions, and updates on new developments in EU politics.

www.oup.com/he/cini-borragan7e

22

Economic and Monetary Union

Amy Verdun

Chapter Contents

Reader's Guide

This chapter introduces **economic and monetary union (EMU)**. It describes the key components of EMU and what happens when countries join. EMU was the result of decades of collaboration and learning, which have been subdivided here into three periods: 1969–91, from the agreement to creation to its inclusion in the Treaty on European Union (TEU); 1992–2002, from having the plans for EMU to the irrevocable fixing of exchange rates; and 2002 onwards, when EMU had been established, and euro banknotes and coins were circulating in member states. Next, the chapter reviews various theoretical explanations, both economic and political, accounting for why EMU was created and looks at some criticisms of EMU. Finally, the chapter discusses how EMU has fared under the global financial crisis, the **sovereign debt crisis** and the COVID-19 pandemic. These crises brought to the fore various imperfections in the design of EMU and provided opportunities for further development. This section discusses what changes have been made since 2009 to address those flaws and looks at what may be yet to come.

22.1 Introduction

Euro banknotes and coins were introduced on 1 January 2002. On that date, the euro became legal tender in 12 EU member states, among a total of more than 300 million people. Denmark, Sweden, and the United Kingdom (UK) did not participate. This event signalled the start of a new era in the history of the EU not least because, at this point, the majority of EU citizens were in daily contact with a concrete symbol of **European integration**. What was the path that led to the euro?

The goal to create an **economic and monetary union (EMU)** had been an integral part of European **integration** since the early 1970s, although those early plans were derailed. Once back on track in the late 1980s and 1990s, supporters of the idea of economic and monetary union wanted to make sure that the process was done properly. Member states agreed that there should be economic and monetary convergence prior to starting EMU. But at the same time, some member states did not want to join EMU.

22.2 What is economic and monetary policy?

Having a common currency among distinct European nations has occurred before: the Roman empire had a single currency two thousand years ago. From 1865 to 1927 Belgium, France, Italy, Switzerland, and others were part of a Latin monetary union (LMU). They minted francs that were of equal value across their union. In 1872, the Danes, Norwegians, and Swedes launched a single currency, the Scandinavian krona, used until 1914. Although the nineteenth-century European monetary unions were significant, the scale and scope of EMU in the EU was further reaching, because these earlier unions only **harmonized** coinage and did not introduce a **single monetary policy** or a **central bank**. Furthermore, the financial system has since undergone a major transformation and the role of the state has expanded enormously over the past century. EMU is thus the most ambitious monetary union to date.

22.2.1 The component parts of EMU

EMU, as set out in the **Maastricht Treaty,** refers to a union of participating countries which have agreed to a single monetary policy, a single monetary authority, a single currency, and coordinated macroeconomic policies. Central banks formulate and implement monetary policy, in some cases in collaboration with the government—that is, with the ministry of finance and sometimes also with the economics ministry. In EMU, monetary policy is no longer formulated at the national but at the European level by a single monetary authority: the **European Central Bank (ECB)**.

The December 1991 Maastricht European Council agreed to create a **European System of Central Banks (ESCB)**, consisting of the ECB and the national central banks of all EU member states. By mid-2021 19 EU member states had adopted the euro in what is officially called the '**euro area**' (informally '**eurozone**'). The term '**Eurosystem**' denotes the ECB plus the national central banks—the latter becoming merely 'branches' of the ECB. The Governing Council is the ECB's main decision-making body. The ECB is responsible for the single currency. It sets monetary policy: sets a key **interest rate**, monitors the **money supply** and **credit conditions**. To facilitate coordination of economic and financial policies, an informal ministerial group has been set up: the so-called '**Eurogroup**'. It consists of the euro area member states' ministers of finance, and sometimes economics, to coordinate policies. The formal body to deal with EU level economic and financial matters is called the Ecofin Council and all EU member states take part.

To have a successful mix of monetary policy and fiscal policy (taxing and spending), EMU envisages the coordination of economic policies (Article 121 TFEU). The euro was geared to be a low-inflation currency, its primary objective being price stability. To secure that objective there are rules in the Treaty on **public debts** and **budgetary deficits**. Member states must avoid budget deficits in excess of a so-called **reference value** of 3 per cent of **gross domestic product (GDP)** and general government debt should be at or below 60 per cent of GDP. Furthermore, monetary financing is not permitted: euro area countries may not use the printing press to create money to service their debt. This so-called 'no-bailout clause' was put in place to reduce the likelihood of one member state assuming the debt of another or for the EU as a whole (for example through the ECB) to take over some of the debt of a member state should it be unable to pay its debts (Article 125 TFEU). Prior to EMU, a member state that ran high budget deficits or debt would have been 'punished' by the market, because it would have needed to pay higher interest rates than other member states to attract funds in the market. In EMU this mechanism was expected to disappear (which indeed occurred as long-term interest rates of EMU countries converged right after the start of EMU until the sovereign debt crisis). The rules on debts and deficits and the no-bailout clause were to be put in its place to ensure that no country would take advantage of being in EMU and issue too much debt.

Finally, a central bank may aim to target a particular value of the currency vis-à-vis other currencies. The ECB has mostly considered the external value of the euro as subordinate to its primary aim, which is to achieve price stability (set as close to, but not more than, 2 per cent inflation). Furthermore, because of a situation dubbed by Tomasso Padoa-Schioppa as an 'inconsistent quartet', the euro has typically been left to market forces and thus floats freely against other major currencies. The inconsistent quartet means that under conditions of free trade, free capital markets, and fixed exchange rates one cannot also have autonomous monetary policy.

The acronym 'EMU' consists of two components, 'economic' and 'monetary', with the latter the most prominent component. The term *economic and monetary union* can be traced back to the discussions in the late 1960s and early 1970s. The policy-makers at the time were not sure how best to create EMU. To have fixed exchange rates—and ultimately a single currency—required some coordination of economic policies. Belgium, Luxembourg, and France thought that, by fixing the exchange rate, the necessary **cooperation** of the adjacent economic policies would naturally start to occur (the '**Monetarists**'). West Germany and the Netherlands held the opposite position. They argued that economic policies needed to be coordinated *before* fixing exchange rates or introducing a single currency (the '**Economists**'). This debate is referred to as the dispute between the 'Monetarists and the Economists'. (Note that the term 'Monetarists' used in this context does not have the same meaning as the term 'monetarists' referring to the followers of the ideas of Milton Friedman.)

The question of how to reach EMU had already been discussed in some detail by economic thinkers of the 1960s such as Bela Balassa and Jan Tinbergen. According to these and others, economic integration can be subdivided into a number of stages (see also Chapter 20) that range from more minimal to more extensive integration. The least far-reaching form of integration is a **free trade area** (FTA). In an FTA, participating members remove **barriers to trade** among themselves, but maintain the right to levy tariffs on third countries. The next stage of integration is a **customs union**. In addition to the free trade among members, a customs union has **common external tariffs** on goods and services from third countries. A **common market**—since 1985, renamed **Single Market**—is characterized by the free movement of goods, services, labour, and capital among the participating states, and common rules, tariffs, and so on vis-à-vis third countries. An **economic union** implies not only a common or Single Market, but also a high degree of coordination of the most important areas of economic policy and market **regulation**, as well as monetary policies and income redistribution policies. A **monetary union** contains a common or Single Market, but also further integration in the area of currency cooperation. Historically, deeper integration has not always been part of a monetary union: the Scandinavian monetary union did not contain a customs union. A monetary union either has irrevocably fixed exchange rates and full **convertibility** of currencies, or a common or single currency circulating within the monetary union. It also requires integration of budgetary and monetary policies. An EMU combines elements of both economic and monetary union (which is what the EU Council in 1969 and in the late 1980s envisaged). A **full economic union** (FEU) implies the complete unification of the economies of the participating member states and common policies for most economic matters. **Full political union** (FPU) is when, in addition to the FEU, much of the political governance and policy-making has transferred to the **supranational** level. Effectively, political unification occurs when the final stage of integration has taken place and a new **confederation** or federation has been created.

The eventual institutional design of EMU in the 1980s and 1990s was an asymmetrical one (Verdun, 1996, 2000). It featured a relatively well-developed monetary union, but a much less developed economic union. Monetary policy was to be transferred to a new **supranational institution** (the ECB), whereas in the area of economic policy-making decisions remained the full responsibility of national governments. To some extent, one observes here the difference between positive and negative integration. **Positive integration** refers to the creation of common rules, norms, and policies. **Negative integration** is all about taking away obstacles—eliminating rules and procedures that are an obstruction to integration.

KEY POINTS

- Economic and monetary union consists of a single monetary policy, a single monetary authority, a single currency, a Single Market (including free movement of capital), and coordinated macroeconomic policies.

- The 'Monetarists' and the 'Economists' differed in opinion as to how best to create EMU.

- There are various stages of integration, ranging from a free trade area to a full political union. The stages are an analytical device.

- EMU can be characterized as asymmetrical.

22.3 From The Hague to Maastricht (1969–91)

At the 1969 Hague Summit, the heads of state and government decided to explore a path to economic and monetary union. A group of experts, headed by Pierre Werner, prime minister and finance minister of Luxembourg, drafted the blueprint. The 1970 **Werner Plan** proposed three stages to reach EMU by 1980. It recommended setting up two supranational bodies: a Community System for the Central Banks and a Centre of Decision for Economic Policy. The former would conduct monetary policies, while the latter would coordinate macroeconomic policies (including some tax policies). Although most of the recommendations of the Werner Plan were adopted, the process stalled in the 1970s. Circumstances changed dramatically and member states had different ideas about how to deal with them. For example, the **Bretton Woods agreement** that had facilitated stable exchange rates in Western Europe since 1945 ended in August 1971. West European countries responded to its demise by setting up their own **exchange rate mechanism (ERM),** the so-called **'snake'**. However, it only functioned with moderate success throughout the 1970s, and not all member states participated, although several non-members were involved.

22.3.1 Developments leading to the relaunch of EMU in the late 1980s

The **European Monetary System (EMS)** was set up in 1979. Not all European Community (EC) member states were immediately part of its most important feature, the exchange rate mechanism or 'ERM'—a system of fixed, but adjustable, exchange rates. For instance, the UK was not part of the ERM during the 1980s, but its currency was part of the **European currency unit (ecu)**—the unit of account at the heart of the EMS. In 1991, the British pound sterling did join the ERM, but it was forced to leave on 16 September 1992 ('**Black Wednesday**') following a period of intense selling of sterling in the financial markets, which the British government was unable to bring to a halt. Italy participated in the ERM from the outset, but was initially given more leeway. The rules stipulated that most currencies could not fluctuate more than ± 2.25 per cent from an agreed **parity**, whereas the bandwidth for those who needed more leeway (for example, Italy) was set at ± 6 per cent from the parity. If a currency threatened to move outside the agreed band, central banks would intervene by buying or selling currencies in order to keep the currency from leaving the band. If an imbalance were persistent, the so-called EC Monetary Committee (MC), an informal advisory body created by the **Treaty of Rome** to discuss monetary policy and exchange rate matters, would decide whether or not to adjust the parities. In 1999, the MC was renamed the Economic and Financial Committee (EFC).

The ERM needed some time to become successful. The first four years (1979–83) were learning years, with numerous exchange rates fluctuations and parity adjustments. The participating currencies became more stable in the interim period (1983–7). In 1987 the Basel–Nyborg accord stipulated closer cooperation so that early intervention would be possible to offset the chances of realignment. Indeed, until summer 1992, the ERM witnessed no realignments. The EMS had finally become an important 'symbol' of successful European integration. In the 1980s, the West German currency, the Deutschmark, was a **strong currency**, and became the *de facto* 'anchor currency'. Monetary authorities in ERM countries took German monetary policies as their point of reference and closely followed the decisions of the German central bank (the *Bundesbank*).

A few other developments in the 1980s helped to revive the EMU process. The 1986 **Single European Act (SEA)** facilitated the completion of the Single Market and mentioned the need to relaunch EMU. The 1988 Hanover European Council mandated Commission President Jacques Delors to head a committee composed of the 12 central bank presidents, another

> **BOX 22.1   BACKGROUND: THREE STAGES TO ECONOMIC AND MONETARY UNION**
>
> | First stage | 1 July 1990–31 December 1993 | Free movement of capital among member states |
> |---|---|---|
> | | | Closer coordination of economic policies |
> | | | Closer cooperation among central banks |
> | Second stage | 1 January 1994–31 December 1998 | Convergence of the economic and monetary policies of the member states (to ensure stability of prices and sound public finances) |
> | Third stage | 1 January 1999–to date | Establishment of the European Central Bank |
> | | | Fixing of exchange rates |
> | | | Introduction of the single currency |

Commissioner, and a few experts to draft a blueprint for EMU. Just as the earlier **Werner Report**, the **Delors Report** (April 1989) proposed a road to EMU in three stages (see Box 22.1), including the creation of a European System of Central Banks (ESCB). In contrast to the Werner Report, it did not find it necessary to set up a similar supranational institution in the economic sphere. The Delors Report had the same objectives as the earlier report: full freedom of goods, services, capital, and labour, and, if possible and if the political will was there, the introduction of a single currency. On the basis of the Delors Report, the June 1989 Madrid European Council adopted the EMU blueprint, with the first stage of EMU (the **liberalization of capital markets**) starting on 1 July 1990. An **intergovernmental conference (IGC)** opened in Rome in October 1990 and closed in Maastricht in 1991 to discuss the next stages (see Chapter 2). To join EMU, countries would have to meet the '**convergence criteria**' (see Box 22.2): good performance in the area of inflation rates, interest rates, and exchange rates. Moreover, it was agreed that participating countries should not have excessive budgetary deficits or public debts. National central banks needed to be politically independent, and no monetary financing was to be allowed. It is important to note that, right from the outset, there were 'escape clauses' built into the legal provisions. The criteria had leeway with regard to the debt criterion, because countries, such as Belgium and Italy, would not be able to meet the reference value in less than a decade, so language was included to allow

> **BOX 22.2   BACKGROUND: THE MAASTRICHT CONVERGENCE CRITERIA**
>
> - Budget deficits should be no more than 3 per cent of gross domestic product (GDP).
> - Accumulated public debt should be no more than 60 per cent of GDP.
> - Exchange rates should have participated without devaluation or severe tensions in the exchange rate mechanism (ERM-2) for at least the previous two years.
> - Inflation should not be more than one and a half percentage points above the rate of the three best-performing member states.
> - Long-term interest rates should be not be more than two percentage points above the rate of the three best-performing member states.
>
> *Source:* Article 140 TFEU and Protocol 12.

for continuous and downward development of the level of public debt. As for the budgetary criterion, however, this one *had* to be met.

Many have argued that the creation of EMU was assisted by the fall of the Berlin Wall in 1989, and the end of communist **regimes** in Central and Eastern Europe (CEE) in 1990. The observant reader will have noted, however, that the Delors Report had already been commissioned in June 1988 and was completed by April 1989 and therefore preceded these turbulent political developments. Nevertheless, the political determination of German Chancellor Helmut Kohl to secure EMU was connected to his eagerness to move ahead quickly with German unification. The IGCs were completed in December 1991, and the European Council in Maastricht agreed to revise the Treaty of Rome and accept a new Treaty on European Union (TEU). It was signed on 7 February 1992 and came into force on 1 November 1993, after the national parliaments of all 12 member states ratified it.

KEY POINTS

- In the 1970s, EMU stalled because of differences among member states and changing international circumstances.

- The European Monetary System and the Single European Act contributed to the relaunch of EMU in the late 1980s.

- The 1989 Delors Report offered a blueprint for EMU.

- The treaty changes necessary for acceptance and implementation of EMU were negotiated in an intergovernmental conference, which was completed in Maastricht in 1991. Member states need to meet the 'Maastricht convergence criteria' to join EMU.

22.4 From treaty to reality (1992–2002)

The period from 1992 to 2002 posed numerous challenges for EMU, most notably over the **ratification** of the Maastricht Treaty, the issue of what would happen post-EMU, and the 'real' criteria for membership of the monetary union.

22.4.1 Ratification problems and the 'real' convergence criteria

The ratification process of the Maastricht Treaty turned out to be challenging. Only months after the Treaty was signed, on 2 June 1992, Danish citizens voted against it in a referendum. A razor-thin majority rejected the Treaty (50.7 per cent against; 49.3 per cent in favour). A French referendum was held on 20 September 1992. Against the background of major speculation in the financial markets, which had resulted in the British pound sterling and the Italian lira leaving the ERM days before the referendum, the

French referendum resulted in a very slim majority in favour of the Treaty (51 per cent in favour; 49 per cent against). The period from late 1992 through to early 1994 was characterized as one of continued exchange rate turbulence, placing the ERM under further pressure and casting a shadow on the run-up to EMU. In August 1993, the ERM exchange rate bands were widened from ± 2.25 per cent to ± 15 per cent. After the introduction of the euro, a new system, the ERM II, was set up to succeed the previous ERM. It officially maintained the ± 15 per cent bands.

In May 1998, the European Council decided that 11 countries would participate in EMU from 1 January 1999—the day on which exchange rates would be irrevocably fixed between the participating member states. However, Denmark, Sweden, and the UK did not want to join, whereas Greece was judged ready in June 2000 and joined the euro area as the twelfth member on 1 January 2001.

When eight Central and Eastern European (CEE) countries and two very small Mediterranean countries joined the EU on 1 May 2004, the **accession treaty** stipulated that these countries would eventually join EMU. However, they had to wait at least two years and fulfil the convergence criteria before they could adopt the euro. In 2007, Slovenia became the first new member state to join EMU. In 2008, Cyprus and Malta joined; in 2009, Slovakia became the sixteenth member of the euro area. The three Baltic States (Estonia, Latvia, and Lithuania) joined in respectively 2011, 2014, and 2015.

22.4.2 Managing EMU: the Stability and Growth Pact (SGP) before the sovereign debt crisis

In the mid-1990s, the then German Finance Minister, Theo Waigel, proposed rules for countries once in EMU. The **Stability and Growth Pact (SGP)** was put in place to ensure that no single member state, in EMU, could **freeride**, for example, by incurring high debts and deficits. Under the SGP, member states that violate the rules to keep their public debt and budgetary deficit low can be penalized, and may have to pay a fine. The SGP was designed primarily to work as a deterrent.

The SGP involves **multilateral budgetary surveillance** (a 'preventive arm'), as well as specifying a deficit limit, the **excessive deficit procedure (EDP)** (a 'corrective arm') (see Box 22.3). When, on the basis of

> **BOX 22.3   BACKGROUND: THE STABILITY AND GROWTH PACT**
>
> The Stability and Growth Pact aims to ensure that member states continue their budgetary discipline efforts after the introduction of the euro.
>
> | Dates | Decisions |
> | --- | --- |
> | The SGP comprised a European Council Resolution (adopted at Amsterdam on 17 June 1997) and Regulations of 7 July 1997 The Council Regulations were revised on 27 June 2005 The rules were further strengthened in 2010 and 2011 ('six pack'), in 2012 (the **Treaty on Stability, Coordination and Governance**) and in 2013 (**'two pack'**) | The surveillance of budgetary positions and coordination of economic policies Implementation of the excessive deficit procedure (EDP) |
> | Annually since 1999 | Member states have undertaken to pursue the objective of a balanced, or nearly balanced, budget, and to present the Council and the Commission with a stability programme Euro-outs (member states not taking part in the third stage of EMU) are also required to submit a convergence programme Opening and closing (where appropriate) of an excessive deficit procedure for EU member states |
> | Since 2010, procedures strengthened, streamlined, and formalized with the **European Semester** | The European Commission analyses the fiscal and structural reform policies of each member state, provides recommendations, and monitors their implementation; the member states implement the commonly agreed policies |
> | **COVID-19** pandemic | Activation of the 'General Escape Clause'. Does not suspend the procedures of the SGP, but allows the Commission and the Council to depart from the budgetary requirements that would normally apply |

a Commission recommendation, the Council decides that an excessive deficit indeed exists, the member state concerned is obliged to reduce its deficit below the Treaty's reference value of 3 per cent of GDP; otherwise financial sanctions can be levied against the member state in question.

In 2002, France, Germany, and Portugal were given an 'early warning' that they were in breach of the SGP. Portugal made the necessary corrections so the EDP was abrogated in 2004. But France and Germany failed to make the necessary adjustments to reduce their budgetary deficits and were coming closer to the financial sanctions set out in the SGP. At a November 2003 ECOFIN meeting a proposal by the Commission to move closer to sanctions against France and Germany was defeated. The result was that the SGP was interrupted for the cases of France and Germany. The crisis atmosphere prompted the European Commission to ask the Court of Justice of the EU (CJEU) whether this Council decision was legal. In July 2004,

the CJEU ruled that the November 2003 Council decision was, in fact, *illegal* because the Council had adopted its own text outside the context of the Treaty. The Court ruled that the Council has the right not to follow the recommendations of the Commission. By spring 2005, the SGP formal rules were revised to provide more **flexibility** over the circumstances under which member states could temporarily run deficits in excess of the 3 per cent reference value, and small adjustments were made to the time schedule.

The preventive arm of the SGP was strengthened by a more differentiated medium-term orientation of the rules. The new provisions ensured that due attention was to be given to the fundamentals of fiscal **sustainability** when setting budgetary objectives. Going forward the medium-term budgetary objective of a country had to be based on debt ratio and potential growth. In practice, this meant that countries with a combination of low debt and high potential growth would be able to run a small deficit over the medium term, whereas a balanced budget or a surplus is required for countries with a combination of high debt and low potential growth. The preventive arm of the SGP was strengthened because member states committed to consolidate further their public finances when facing favourable economic conditions and accepted that, failing this, the Commission would give them 'policy advice' to correct the situation. The new agreement was also more sensitive to the effects of member state efforts to make structural reforms. The SGP's corrective arm also allowed more room for economic judgements and left open the possibility that the one-year deadline for the correction of an excessive deficit could be increased to two years.

The first test of the new SGP came in the second half of 2008 when the global financial crisis upset markets and challenged the survival of the banking sector. Member state governments in the EU responded by guaranteeing the savings of consumers, buying out banks, and offering other stimulus packages. Due to their sheer size, public finances were affected by these national rescue operations. The rules of the SGP still applied, however, even if, because of the economic crisis, these countries were allowed to overshoot the reference value for the duration of the downturn. Once growth returned, they needed to satisfy the rules of a budgetary deficit of 3 per cent and there are stricter rules if member states have a public debt in excess of 60 per cent.

The global financial crisis, the economic **recession**, and the sovereign debt crisis changed the perceived importance of the role of the SGP in guiding EMU. Some of the rules were strengthened (see Chapter 25 and Section 22.7, 'The global financial crisis and the sovereign debt crisis').

KEY POINTS

- The aftermath of the signing of the Maastricht Treaty posed challenges to creating economic and monetary union, including treaty ratification difficulties, the exchange rate mechanism crisis, and difficulties meeting the convergence criteria.

- Some member states have had difficulties avoiding excessive deficits.

- Difficulties implementing the Stability and Growth Pact led to a crisis, and subsequently to its revision.

- Government spending led to an increase in debts and deficits in the EU, which had to be addressed.

22.5 Explaining economic and monetary union

This section considers two ways in which economic and monetary union can be explained: from an economics and from a political science perspective.

22.5.1 An economics perspective

In the field of economics, there are two schools of thought that offer analytical tools with which to determine whether or not it made sense for the EU to create an EMU. The first argues that countries should create an EMU only if they constitute a so-called **optimum currency area** (OCA). Countries should adopt a single currency only when they are sufficiently integrated economically, when they have **mechanisms** in place that can deal with **transfer payments** if one part of the currency union is affected by an economic downturn and the other part is not, and when they no longer need the exchange rate instrument to make those adjustments. Most analysts claim, however, that the EU is not an OCA, although a few think that a small number of its members come close to it. OCA theory states that if countries do not form an OCA, they should not give up their exchange rate instrument, but use it to make adjustments as the economic situation dictates. These analysts argue that the EU should not have moved to EMU. Others who judge that the EU does indeed constitute an OCA are less critical of this situation. They see the current group of countries as being well integrated. Furthermore, they use a broader definition of an OCA, claiming that original OCA theory is too rigid and pointing out that, following the original definition, no federation (including Canada, Germany, or the USA) would constitute an OCA. Finally, some argue, following Frankel and Rose (1998), that once countries join EMU, they could become an OCA over time ('endogenous' OCA theory). Other developments that have influenced recent thinking about the role of exchange rates are the effects of financial markets on exchange rate policies—particularly on smaller open economies. Foreign exchange markets can create their own disturbances, which can be irrational. This effect is worse for smaller open economies than for larger established countries. The original OCA theorists did not take the destabilizing effects of exchange rate freedom into consideration.

A second school of thought focuses on central bank credibility. It argues that the EU witnessed long periods of collaboration in central banking prior to EMU. Central banks can be effective only if financial markets have confidence in their policies. In the case of the exchange rate mechanism, participating countries had to keep their exchange rates stable. They focused on the monetary policy of the strongest currency, the German Deutschmark. Many individual central banks, by choice, followed the policies of the leader (the *Bundesbank*). The most credible way in which to secure monetary policy is to commit firmly to it in a treaty. That is, in fact, what happened with the Maastricht Treaty. A regime was set up that envisaged full central bank independence and gave the ECB a clear single mandate to maintain price stability.

22.5.2 **A political science perspective**

Political science has drawn on European integration theories (see Chapters 4–6) to explain EMU. It is noteworthy that scholars from opposing schools of thought have argued that EMU can be explained using different theoretical approaches. For reasons of simplicity, this section focuses on the two opposing schools in order to capture a larger set of arguments.

A **neo-functionalist** explanation (see Chapter 4) claims that EMU can best be explained as the result of **spillover** and incremental policy-making. The success of the exchange rate mechanism and the completion of the Single Market necessitated further collaboration in the area of monetary integration. EMU was needed to maximize the benefits of these developments. Significant monetary **policy convergence** had occurred, arising out of the collaboration within the framework of the ERM and the tracking of German policies by other member states. Hence EMU could be seen as a natural step forward. Moreover, it is argued that supranational actors were instrumental in creating EMU—which is another characteristic of the neo-functionalist explanation of European integration. Not only were the Commission President and the services of the Commission (such as the Directorate-General for Economic and Financial Affairs) involved, but also various committees, such as the EC Monetary Committee (created by the Treaty of Rome), and they each proved influential.

An **intergovernmentalist** explanation (see Chapter 5) argues that EMU can best be understood by examining the interests and bargaining behaviour of the largest member states. This approach sees the European Council meetings and meetings of the EU Council as crucial for decisions such as the creation of EMU and for follow up regulations. By examining the interests of the largest member states, one is able to see why EMU happened. France was in favour of EMU as a way of containing German **hegemony**. Germany, in turn, was able to secure a monetary policy regime that was sufficiently close to its domestic regime. Some argue that Germany was in favour of EMU in the early 1990s to signal its full commitment to European integration, following German unification. The UK was not in favour of EMU, but was aware that it was likely to happen. The UK wanted to be involved in **agenda-setting**, in shaping the process, and in ensuring EMU would not create a more federal political union at the same time. It has also been argued that EMU served the economic interests of the business communities within these countries, which subsequently led governments to be more supportive of the project.

KEY POINTS

- It is possible to explain economic and monetary union from different perspectives.

- Economists and political scientists have tried to explain economic and monetary union.

- Economists often use optimum currency area theory to assess EMU.

- Political scientists use theories of European integration to explain EMU.

22.6 Criticisms of economic and monetary union

Economic and monetary union is not without its critics, however. Criticisms may involve distinctive national perspectives but can also rest on institutional grounds.

22.6.1 **Countries outside the euro area**

The Danes and Swedes have not joined the euro. In both countries, a referendum on EMU was held (in Denmark, in 2000; in Sweden, in 2003) and in both cases the majority of those who voted were against joining EMU. Denmark has an opt-out agreed at Maastricht and thus can choose to stay outside the euro area. Although the Swedish government does not have an opt-out, it pursues policies that guarantee that it does not qualify for EMU.

The global financial crisis, the economic recession, and the sovereign debt crisis have had varying effects on member state perception of EMU. Initially, in 2007 until summer 2008, various currencies of EU member states that had remained outside the euro area did better than the euro. Yet, in the autumn of 2008 and the first months of 2009 the euro strengthened against currencies such as the Czech koruna, the Polish zloty, or the Hungarian forint. But as currencies weakened, this benefited the export sector and was regarded as a factor that could assist in a speedier recovery following the economic downturn or recession after the financial crisis. Some have criticized the design of the euro as being too much focused on price stability, meaning that the mandate of the ECB is to consider first and foremost the internal management of the euro (to ensure price stability) rather than, for example, at what exchange rate the euro area might be more competitive at the global level. Especially in the early 2000s, when the euro area countries were growing more slowly than countries outside the euro area (and again during the sovereign debt crisis), the criticism was often that the ECB could only consider growth as a secondary consideration. All in all, support for the euro has been varied. Roughly 70 per cent of both the Danish and Swedish populations are still against adopting the euro as their national currency (Eurobarometer 94, 2021). The ten member states that joined the EU in 2004 have also had varying attitudes to euro adoption. The seven that have joined to date (Slovenia, Cyprus, Malta, Slovakia, Estonia, Latvia, and Lithuania) have been keen to do so. In 2021, 79 per cent of those in the euro area support EMU (Eurobarometer 94, 2021). Those that have remained outside have done so for a variety of reasons. The three CEE member states that are still outside the euro area, as of 2021, have a government and population that are reluctant to join even if they are currently not too far removed from meeting the criteria for entry, which focus on inflation, deficit, debt, and long-term interest rates. None of them, however, participate in the exchange rate mechanism and will mostly likely only start doing so if and when they become more supportive of the idea of joining EMU. In all cases, these countries have the formal requirement that they are obliged to join EMU once they meet the criteria. It should be noted that this is a formality because countries, such as Sweden, can stay outside the euro area simply by having their currencies not enter the ERM in the first place.

22.6.2 Criticism of EMU's institutional design

EMU has also been criticized for its poor institutional design. Critics argue that the extreme independence of the European Central Bank may lead to problems of **legitimacy** and **accountability**. The argument is developed in four steps. First, the ECB is more independent than any other central bank in the world. Its independence and its primary mandate (to secure price stability—in effect, low inflation) are firmly anchored in the Treaty. The Treaty also stipulates that no one is allowed to give instructions to the European Central Bank, nor should it take instruction from anyone. Second, it is difficult to change the ECB mandate, because it requires a treaty change, which means that all EU member states would have to sign and ratify the changed treaty. Third, there are very few **checks and balances** in place to ensure that the policies pursued by the ECB are those that the member states would have chosen—except for the one clear one, to secure price stability (low inflation). Even on that issue there is not much control: the ECB President gives quarterly reports to the European Parliament, but the EP cannot give instructions to the ECB. Thus, in fulfilling its low inflation mandate the hope is that ECB policies benefit the EU as a whole. Fourth, there is no EU level Ministry of Finance, or 'Treasury' (as there is in a member state) that can correct imbalances using fiscal policy at the EU level.

Let us clarify this fourth issue a little further. Compared to mature federations, the institutional design of EMU is incomplete: the ECB decides monetary policies for the entire euro area, yet there is no equivalent supranational economic institution that sets economic policies for that same area. Budgetary and **fiscal policies** remain in the hands of national governments. Although countries such as France argued strongly in favour of creating such a *gouvernement économique* ('economic government'), in the early days the choice was made not to go down that route.

National fiscal policies differ significantly across the EU 27. Some member states have a high income tax burden whereas others have a much lower income tax burden; the same holds for the levels of corporate taxation, which is much higher in some countries than in others. To give an example, in 2019, total tax revenues in France, Denmark, and Belgium were just under 50 per cent of GDP, double that of Ireland—which collected less than 25 per cent in tax. In terms of spending, here too some member state governments spend a much larger percentage of the country's GDP than others. On the whole, member states may pick their preference for how much they tax and spend but the outcome of their choices should not exceed the so-called public debt (60 per cent of GDP) and budgetary deficit targets (3 per cent of GDP). In a similar vein there is an expectation about other macroeconomic factors that can be deemed out of balance (e.g., current account balance, net international investment position, cost of labour, house prices, and unemployment). If national policy choices lead to what is referred to as **macroeconomic imbalances**, the EU deals with these divergences through the so-called **European Semester** (see Box 22.4). The European Commission provides so-called '**country-specific recommendations**' (**CSRs**) with suggestions as to which imbalances to address. Member states, in turn, obtain the opportunity to respond to these recommendations.

What are the advantages and disadvantages of having a European economic government? The advantages would be that EU level policies could possibly correct imbalances. However, an economic government would make sense only if a majority of the citizens of the euro area were to feel comfortable with it. If it were not to have that support, then a decision by such a body would be deemed illegitimate. The current situation in the EU is that most citizens feel most comfortable with their national government taking on the role of taxing and spending.

KEY POINTS

- The Czech Republic, Hungary, Poland, and Sweden are not planning to join the euro area in the near future, nor is Denmark—the latter has a formal opt-out from EMU.

- There has been criticism of the institutional design of EMU.

- Some concerns relate to the independence of the European Central Bank and how this raises questions about legitimacy and accountability.

- Fiscal policies in the EU differ considerably from country to country which leads to difficulties in adjusting in a coherent fashion to the challenges posed by the global financial crisis and the sovereign debt crisis.

- The institutional design of EMU has been criticized for being incomplete and falling short of 'an economic government'.

⬊ BOX 22.4   BACKGROUND: THE EUROPEAN SEMESTER

The 'European Semester' is a governance architecture for socioeconomic policy coordination in the EU that was created in 2010 during the financial and sovereign debt crises and revamped in 2015. Its procedures build on, but also reformulate, the EU's pre-existing processes of fiscal, economic, employment, and social policy coordination, as these had developed during the 1990s and 2000s, including the Stability and Growth Pact (SGP), the **Broad Economic Policy Guidelines (BEPGs)**, the **European Employment Strategy (EES)**, the Lisbon Strategy and the Social Open Method of Co-ordination (OMC). The Semester was introduced as part of a panoply of far-reaching measures aimed at reinforcing EU economic governance in response to the euro crisis: the so-called 'Six-Pack', 'Two-Pack', and 'Fiscal Compact'. These measures included stronger and more 'automatic' sanctions for the SGP's Excessive Deficit Procedure (EDP); a new Macroeconomic Imbalance Procedure (MIP) for detecting and correcting non-fiscal imbalances (e.g., in the housing market or current account) that could negatively affect other member states, based on a scoreboard of economic indicators, in-depth country reviews and recommendations, with financial sanctions for persistent non-compliance; *ex ante* review by the Commission of euro area national budgets; and Reverse Qualified Majority Voting (RQMV) for overturning Commission proposals under the excessive deficit and imbalance procedures. The Semester was also intended to serve as the governance architecture for 'thematic co-ordination' of member state policies towards the 'smart, sustainable and inclusive growth' objectives of the **Europe 2020** strategy, which was explicitly designed to have a stronger social dimension than the preceding Lisbon Strategy, including specific guidelines and targets on poverty and social inclusion.

Source: Verdun and Zeitlin (2018)

22.7 The global financial crisis and the sovereign debt crisis

In 2007–08, a major financial crisis hit the global economy. The crisis was caused by a series of problems, many of them originating in the USA. However, the financial crisis and its aftermath affected the EU even more than it did the USA. After the collapse of investment bank Lehman Brothers in September 2008, stock exchanges crashed, credit dried up, and many banks were at risk of collapse. National governments responded by guaranteeing deposits, (partially) nationalizing banks, and by putting together rescue packages. In 2009, the real economy shrank. In the EU, almost all countries were showing negative growth or were in recession (defined as two successive quarters of negative growth). As the economic recession took hold of the EU, many member state governments chose to spend considerably more than they taxed, leaving them with high deficits and public debt. Some countries experienced problems in securing money in capital markets to refinance their debt (see Chapter 25). This situation posed immense challenges for the euro area, through pressures on financial markets, pressure on interest rates for governments to attract funds in capital markets, and vicious circles of lack of confidence in markets and government policies. The result was a major crisis in the EU and a need to create new tools and mechanisms, such as the **European Financial Stability Facility (EFSF)**—which was eventually replaced by the permanent **European Stability Mechanism (ESM)** that became operational in September 2012.

On 11 December 2011, 'reinforced' SGP rules entered into force. The so-called 'six pack' (five **regulations** and one **directive**) includes rules that kick in if member states fail to comply with the 3 per cent deficit and/or the 60 per cent debt criteria. Some of the changes include that the role of the debt is now taken to be as important as the deficit. In the past, the debt criterion was largely ignored. Another 'reinforced rule' is that it requires a qualified majority vote (QMV) to *stop* the sanctions (whereas before it required a QMV to *impose* sanctions on a member state that was facing financial sanctions). The changes to the SGP also provided the European Commission with a larger supervisory role in guiding member states through the fiscal year and ensuring sound policies over the medium term.

In 2012, two further regulations were introduced to strengthen euro area budgetary surveillance. These entered into force in May 2013, and both increased the coordination of budgetary policies in the euro area starting with the 2014 budgetary cycle. The Treaty on Stability, Coordination and Governance (informally referred to as the '**Fiscal Compact**'), came into effect in January 2013. The Fiscal Compact is an intergovernmental treaty that was put in place to ensure even stricter compliance with SGP rules. The Treaty envisaged what were called 'balanced budgets provisions' (no more than 3 per cent budgetary deficit and other rules related to the debt-to-GDP-ratios) which were incorporated in domestic constitutions. The Treaty also envisaged fines if member states failed to comply with these rules. The above-mentioned 'European Semester', introduced in 2010, sought to capture this process of European Commission supervision of member state public finance over a six-month period. Finally, a so-called **Banking Union** was created to strengthen and extend the regulation of the banking sector. Its aim was to ensure that there was centralized supervision and resolution of banks in the euro area. Its four aims are a single rulebook for regulation of banks in the 27 member states; a **Single Supervisory Mechanism (SSM)**; a harmonized system of deposit guarantee schemes; and a **Single Resolution Mechanism (SRM)**, to provide a framework for banks in danger of failing. The rules were put in place to prevent bank crises, for example, by increasing the amount of funds that banks were required to hold (recapitalization). It also ensured that consumers' deposits across the EU were guaranteed up to €100,000 in case of a bank failure (see Chapter 25).

In 2015, five presidents of EU institutions (European Commission, European Parliament, European Central Bank, European Council, and finally the Eurogroup) put forward a roadmap to deepen EMU. This Five Presidents' Report envisaged two stages to complete EMU by 2025. Stage one, 'Deepening by Doing', was to be completed by summer 2017. It focused on using existing instruments to achieve further structural convergence and work towards fiscal coordination, enhancing democratic accountability, and seeking to complete the financial union (i.e. complete the Banking Union, launch what was known as the Capital Markets Union, and Reinforce the European Systemic Risk Board (see Chapter 25)). Stage two, 'Completing EMU', would require more far-reaching steps and envisaged making the convergence process more binding (via benchmarks for convergence). It also foresees the creation of a euro area treasury which would enhance coordination but also accountability at the EU level. In March 2017 the European Commission published a **White Paper on the Future of Europe**. By the end of May the Commission issued a reflection paper that examined the way forward for EMU by 2025. It effectively served as a clarification of the steps to take that had been set out in the Five Presidents' Report. It emphasized the need to reduce social and economic divergences among euro area members, in view of the fact that the 'economic' part of EMU was still not as well developed as the 'monetary' part of EMU. Furthermore, the reflection paper recognized that stronger governance was possible. Rather than providing a single path, four principles were spelled out for deepening EMU. It stipulated that EMU should first of all ensure 'jobs, growth, social fairness, economic convergence and financial stability'. Second, it stated that 'responsibility and solidarity' as well as 'risk reduction or risk-sharing' should go together. A third point (something reinforced by President Juncker in his State of the Union speech of September 2017) was that the EMU should at all times remain accessible to all member states. Fourth and finally, the decision-making process had to be further democratically enhanced so as to ensure better democratic accountability. The reflection paper indicated that it was going to be necessary to share more competences and decisions about euro matters within a common legal framework. It pointed to the need to complete the Banking Union; in particular, the Single Resolution Fund and the European Deposit Insurance Scheme (EDIS) (see Chapter 25). This reflection paper envisaged the next stage to end in 2019 and achieve the final objectives by 2025.

KEY POINTS

- The global financial crisis posed major challenges to the euro area.

- Most countries in the EU faced a recession following the global financial crisis.

- The EU's reaction to the crisis involved new institutions, including changes to the Stability and Growth Pact, which increased the supervisory role of the Commission.

- The European Council agreed to the creation of a Banking Union in June 2012.

- The 2015 Five Presidents' Report and the 2017 Reflection Paper offer further insights into steps to take to deepen EMU.

22.8 A new European Commission, Parliament, and the COVID-19 crisis

The year 2019 was an important year for the European Union: it was a year that was dominated by the Brexit negotiations, European Parliament elections, and a new European Commission. The EP elections held in May 2019 saw a significant increase in voter turnout and a slight decline in the support for the two largest parties (See Chapter 11). The new Commission, presided over by Ursula von der Leyen, came into office on 1 December 2019. Its six priorities were a European Green Deal, preparing for the digital age, improving the economy, a stronger Europe in the world, promoting the rule of law, and enhancing democracy. It was also responsible for the final stages of the Brexit negotiations. The formal departure of the UK from the EU was on 31 January 2020.

These events were occurring as an unprecedented health crisis hit the EU member states: the COVID-19 crisis. The EU had been notified by the World Health Organization (WHO) at the end of December 2019 about the virus. EU health experts responded immediately through the European Centre of Disease Prevention and Control. Yet, the sheer size and shape of the COVID-19 crisis took the EU by surprise. Christine Lagarde, who had taken over from Mario Draghi as the President of the ECB, chose her words poorly when, on 12 March 2020, she announced that she was 'not here to close spreads'. On the eve of WHO declaring the coronavirus a pandemic and Europe its epicentre, what she had meant to say was that EU governments would need to take responsibility for fiscal policy. Unintentionally, her words sent the financial markets sharply down. The ECB quickly corrected the situation by providing a pandemic emergency purchase programme (PEPP): a temporary asset purchase programme of private and public sector securities. Initially, in March 2020, 750 billion euros were earmarked for this fund, but in June 2020 this was increased by 600 billion and again by another 500 billion in December, adding up to a total of 1,850 billion euros.

The European Commission agreed to take action to support, coordinate, and supplement national policy. The challenge posed by the COVID-19 crisis was in the realm of economic policy and provided an opportunity for EU member states to act in concert. Following various initiatives by member states and by the Commission, the European Council decided in

July 2020 to make available to member states grants and loans to help them overcome the likely economic downturn that was to occur as member states dealt with the pandemic through lockdowns and border closures. Member states provided their citizens and companies with financial support. The European Commission announced that the SGP rules were temporarily abandoned as were rules on state aid and banking regulations. The EU also sought to put in place a system for sharing medical supplies, as a mark of solidarity; and sought to use its size to negotiate on behalf of all EU member states over the cost of vaccines whilst also serving as a clearing house to obtain vaccines. EU member states also exchanged expertise. Although not all of these actions were equally successful (for instance vaccine delivery dates and availability were a challenge for some months), the EU member states did manage to collaborate. The use of the EU budget and providing funds through a Recovery and Resilience Facility was seen by many as an important marker of solidarity and collaboration. A temporary measure was made available to draw funds from financial markets, issuing joint debt. Some have argued that issuing joint debt would be a major step towards deeper integration—towards Full Political Union (FPU). The steps taken in the EU are temporary but important lessons will be learnt from the experience—not unlike those that occurred in the past with temporary measures.

> **KEY POINTS**
>
> - After a shaky start, the ECB quickly set up an asset purchase programme to respond to the COVID-19 crisis.
>
> - The European Council agreed to various initiatives offering grants and loans to member states in July 2020, and relaxing rules associated with the SGP, state aid, and banking.
>
> - Although not all initiatives were successful, the EU played an important role in the sharing of medical supplies and the procurement and distribution of vaccines.

22.9 Conclusion

It has taken more than 30 years to create economic and monetary union. It was a long and slow process that ultimately led to the creation of a single monetary policy, the European Central Bank, and rules on budgetary policies and public debts. The introduction of the euro was based on a lengthy and gradual process of learning about economic and monetary cooperation. Not only was it necessary for countries to have met the convergence criteria, but also it was crucial that member states maintain stable exchange rates and that they agree on common goals for EMU.

Economic and political motivations lay behind EMU. Although one can make a case for a purely economic rationale for monetary union, its ultimate creation cannot be understood without an appreciation of its political dimension. EMU is a new stage in European integration. It signals the capability of EU member states to take firm action together and it places the EU more clearly on the international map. Nevertheless, a number of issues remain unresolved. In discussing the asymmetrical EMU, the chapter has indicated how fragile the balance is between 'economic' and 'monetary' union. The sovereign debt crisis has also unearthed challenges in EMU institutional design. Facilities were put in place to deal with some of the problems created by the euro area crisis, such as the European Stability Mechanism and the Banking Union. The COVID-19 crisis awarded the EU an opportunity to act in concert, which on the whole it did. Yet it is not unthinkable that, in the future, further integration might be needed in the area of 'economic union' or that steps will have to be taken towards further political unification, if only to redistribute more evenly the costs and benefits of EMU. At the same time, we have seen that European integration is a gradual process, which lacks legitimacy if pushed ahead too quickly (see Chapters 9 and 15).

What is the impact of the euro on the future of the EU? The continuing presence of the euro may well give the EU a stronger position in world politics, if only because it might offer an alternative to the US dollar (but see Chapter 15 on this point). As such, the euro contributes to the symbolism of European integration. It offers a concrete token representing the rapid and far-reaching process of integration taking place in the EU.

The regional use of the euro has increased quite rapidly from being legal tender in 11 member states in 1999 to 19 member states two decades hence. Furthermore, it is conceivable that more countries (e.g., Bulgaria) may want to be ready to join the euro area in the not-so-distant future, thereby adding further to the euro area's credibility and strength. Others, such as the Czech Republic, Hungary, and Poland, are still reluctant to join. Yet not all monetary unions in the past have lasted; EMU will survive only if it continues to be supported by the citizens, and by national and European politicians. Leaders will have to keep listening to the needs of their citizens. If they do so satisfactorily, the euro may well continue to have a very promising future.

 QUESTIONS

1. Why was the term 'economic' and 'monetary' union used? What is an 'asymmetrical EMU'?

2. What are the 'convergence criteria' and why were they invented?

3. Why has the Stability and Growth Pact been difficult to implement?

4. What are two opposing political science theories explaining why EMU happened? Do you agree that they are opposing theories or are they complementary?

5. What are the main criticisms of EMU?

6. Discuss how the creation of EMU was both an economic and politically driven process.

7. How have the global financial crisis, the economic recession that followed, and the sovereign debt crisis impacted EMU governance?

8. How has the COVID-19 crisis advanced EMU?

GUIDE TO FURTHER READING

Brunnermeier, M.K., James, H., and Landau J-P. (2016), *The Euro and the Battle of Ideas* (Princeton, NJ: Princeton University Press). Addresses how philosophical differences between euro area member states contributed to the euro crisis, and how to move beyond these challenges.

Dyson, K. and Featherstone, K. (1999) *The Road to Maastricht: Negotiating Economic and Monetary Union* (Oxford: Oxford University Press). An influential political science volume based on 280 interviews and documents.

Heipertz, M. and Verdun. A. (2010) *Ruling Europe: The Politics of the Stability and Growth Pact* (Cambridge: Cambridge University Press). A comprehensive account of the genesis of the Stability and Growth Pact, the 2003 crisis, and 2005 reform.

Hodson, D. (2011a) *Governing the Euro Area in Good Times and Bad* (Oxford: Oxford University Press). A short book that offers an oversight into the past, present, and future of governance of the euro area, written in language accessible to the non-specialist.

Verdun, A. (2000) *European Responses to Globalization and Financial Market Integration: Perceptions of Economic and Monetary Union in Britain, France, and Germany* (Basingstoke: Palgrave Macmillan). A volume examining perceptions of EMU from the perspective of the member states. It includes insights on how actors (monetary authorities and employers' and trade unions) use EMU to serve or frustrate their interests.

 Access the online resources to take your learning and understanding further, including extra multiple-choice questions with instant feedback, web links, answer guidance to end-of-chapter questions, and updates on new developments in EU politics.

www.oup.com/he/cini-borragan7e

23

The Common Agricultural Policy

Ève Fouilleux and Viviane Gravey

Chapter Contents

Reader's Guide

This chapter examines one of the first European policies, the Common Agricultural Policy (CAP). It does so by focusing on the policy's objectives, instruments, actors, and debates. It looks at the way in which the CAP has evolved since the 1960s, and attempts to explain this evolution by asking and answering a number of important questions: why has the CAP been so problematic for European policy-makers? Why has it proven so resistant to change? Given the constraints identified, how has reform come about? This chapter also looks at some of the challenges facing agricultural policy, as new debates emerge among citizens on the place and the functions performed by agriculture. The chapter grants particular attention to the way the CAP tackles issues such as rural development, relations between agriculture, food and the environment, transparency, and social equity.

23.1 Introduction

The Common Agricultural Policy (CAP) has long been of symbolic importance to the European integration process and has been subject to calls for reform since the 1960s. This chapter begins with a brief introduction to the principles underpinning the CAP and then provides an explanation of why it has taken (or is taking) so long to reform this policy. In Section 23.3, attention turns to the long reform process that has taken place step by step since 1992. Understanding the original policy and how it has progressively changed over time helps us to better understand the contemporary debates on the CAP that are explained in Section 23.4.

23.2 The early days of the Common Agricultural Policy and the issue of CAP reform

This section presents the main principles and instruments of the early Common Agricultural Policy and provides an overview of the CAP's brake mechanisms at national and European levels.

23.2.1 The early days of the policy

The objectives of the CAP, which came into force from 1962, were laid down in the **Treaty of Rome** in 1957 (Article 39) and subsequently at the **Stresa Conference** in July 1958. Three general principles underpinned the policy: **market unity**; **Community preference**; and **financial solidarity**. The initial move in establishing a European agricultural market (applying the so-called market unity principle) was the setting up of **common market organizations (CMOs)** for all agricultural products, most notably for wheat, barley, rye, corn, rice, sugar, dairy products, beef, pork, lamb, wine, and some fruits and vegetables. The idea was to allow free trade internally within the Community, but also to erect barriers to the outside world, to protect the income of European farmers.

The CMOs usually operated on the basis of three complementary policy tools: a **guaranteed price**; a public intervention system; and some **variable levies** at the Community's border. First, the notion of a guaranteed price is crucial to understanding how the CAP operated. The idea was that the specificities of the farming sector (dependence on climatic conditions and vulnerability to natural disasters) and the consequent structural instabilities of agricultural markets made some public intervention necessary to guarantee decent living conditions for farmers. This is why, instead of allowing the market to determine price levels, the prices that farmers received for their produce were administrative prices—that is, they were fixed centrally by Community civil servants and politicians. Such a system had the objective of

both supporting farmers' incomes and boosting agricultural production: the more farmers produced, the more money they earned. Indeed, with the food shortages of the post-1945 period and the security concerns of the Cold War in mind, the aim of self-sufficiency in foodstuffs was presented as one of the major objectives of the policy. In practice, the level of guaranteed prices was initially set on the basis of a political compromise between France and Germany. In the early 1960s, the Germans had a very inefficient cereal sector, but numerous politically powerful farmers, who asked for a high level of support for cereals. Although the French were more efficient and had a lower national price for cereals, they did not mind setting guaranteed prices higher under the CAP, as long as they did not have to pay for them. It is for this reason that Germany has ended up as the primary contributor to the CAP since 1962, while France has always been among the main financial beneficiaries.

Second, if the price began to fall due, for example, to an excessive internal supply, which would have had the effect of depressing farmers' incomes, intervention agencies would step in when the price reached a certain level (the **intervention price**) to buy up the surplus and store it until the market was balanced again, thus keeping prices high.

Third, if the price fixed inside the Community was to be high enough to support farmers' incomes, it was imperative to prevent cheap imports from flooding the **common market**. Therefore, to achieve the second CAP principle (community preference), a system of variable levies was set up for each product. Produce could generally only enter the common market if it was priced at or above the internal price; if not, the importer had to pay a tariff equalling the difference to the European Budget and thus had to sell their product at the European price. Moreover, a system of 're-imbursements' (refunds), similar to export subsidies, was also put in place, enabling European producers to sell their products on the world market at world prices without losing income. These subsidies covered the difference in cost between the world and the higher European prices.

Finally, to promote the principle of financial solidarity, a common fund was set up to cover the financing of the CAP. This fund, the **European Agricultural Guidance and Guarantee Fund (EAGGF)**, comprised two parts: guidance and guarantee. While the guarantee section covered costs attached to the operation of the market system, such as the costs of intervention and export refunds, the much smaller guidance section was responsible for funding **structural policies**. The EAGGF originally comprised almost the entire European Community (EC) Budget.

23.2.2 Problems arising and the first incremental reforms

Initially, the policy was very successful in that it very quickly met its initial objectives of increasing productivity, supporting farmers' revenues, and achieving European self-sufficiency. However, by the 1970s, *overproduction* had become a political issue, with the first surpluses having appeared in the form of the famous 'butter mountains' and 'wine lakes' of this period. These problems of overproduction, caused when the supply of agricultural produce outstrips demand, increased throughout the 1980s. As an ever-increasing volume of products surplus to internal requirements was being paid for at the guaranteed price, stored at high cost, and exported out of the Community, and with support from the agricultural budget compensating for lower prices on the world market, the CAP was becoming ever more costly to operate. It is far from surprising, therefore, that the CAP was frequently criticized during this time for being too expensive and for taking up too many EC resources, thereby preventing the development of other potentially important political priorities. From the late 1980s onwards, the CAP also began to be criticized internationally for depreciating and destabilizing world market prices with negative consequences for farmers in the rest of the world. As a consequence, agricultural policy began to be a major concern for European policy-makers and the issue of CAP reform appeared on the European political agenda.

Some reforms took place from the late 1970s to the end of the 1980s, but these were marginal and incremental. The economic policy tools that were used during this first period of reform were mainly directed towards controlling the supply of produce by imposing quantitative restrictions on production. These took the form of 'guaranteed ceilings' for crops in 1981, milk quotas in 1984, and a **regime** imposing maximum guaranteed quantities (MGQs) for cereals in 1987–88, generalized to other commodities in 1988–89. Despite these changes, the principle of guaranteed prices for agricultural products remained the core element of the CAP.

23.2.3 Why is it so difficult to reform the CAP?

The modest changes made to the policy at this time can be explained by institutional factors rooted in the workings of CAP decision-making, which still apply today. Beyond the formal rules of the process (see Box 23.1), decision-taking in this policy area is based on what might be termed an 'inflationist bargaining dynamic'. Because the CAP is a **redistributive** policy, each member state's minister of agriculture is under pressure to bring home the maximum that they can get from that part of the EU budget dedicated to agriculture. As a consequence of the number of member states involved in the negotiations (all of them trying to increase their CAP budgetary return), the range of products involved, and the rules that have long governed the CAP, there is an inbuilt inflationary tendency. For example, each minister in the Council would agree to price increases in his or her neighbour's favoured products in order to get the increases that they want. As a consequence, decisions that would lead to a reduction in agricultural costs, or that would change the redistributive effects of the policy, are more than likely to be rejected by the Agricultural Council. This makes it very difficult for a body such as the Commission to propose reforms that cut costs. The CAP is also an excellent example of what happens when there is no real link between the EU authorities and EU citizens. In such circumstances, it is easy for governments to use the European Commission as a scapegoat for decisions that they really do not want to take or that they have taken collectively in the Council but do not want to be held accountable for. The Commission is restricted in what it can do when this happens and often ends up taking the blame for a policy that it would like to see reformed.

Second, the incremental character of CAP reform can also be explained by national political pressures, which are exported to the European level through the agriculture ministers of each member state in the Agricultural Council. Owing to their ability to mobilize support in many European countries, farmers' organizations are able to exert pressure on governments to support their line on the CAP. Political influence of this kind was particularly intense in France and Germany in the 1970s, 1980s, and 1990s (and it is still quite important despite the ever-decreasing number of farmers). In both countries, farmers were important in electoral terms because public opinion, influenced

BOX 23.1   BACKGROUND: THE FORMAL CAP DECISION-MAKING PROCESS

For much of the CAP's history, the main actors in the CAP decision-making process have been the European Commission, responsible for drafting legislation, and the EU Council, more specifically, the Agricultural Council, responsible for taking decisions. The European Parliament (EP) has had only a very limited consultative role. CAP decision-making usually began with a proposal from the Commission, most often in response to a broadly defined request from the **European Council**. Since 1991, the Commission got used to launching reform proposals on its own decision, as the Treaties allow. Once formulated, the Commission's proposal is then submitted to the EP for **consultation** and the Agricultural Council for decision. It is also transmitted to the Committee of Professional Agricultural Organizations (COPA), the main **interest group** representing European farmers, and to other institutions as appropriate, such as the **Committee of the Regions (CoR)**. The Agricultural Council might reject the Commission's proposal or ask for modifications. Alternatively, it might begin to negotiate on the

basis of what the Commission has proposed, resulting ultimately in a decision. Although the formal rule was **qualified majority voting (QMV)** within the Agricultural Council, it was not applied. More often than not a consensus was sought across all member states. This meant de facto that each member could veto any decision. Decision rules such as this have had important consequences for the CAP, especially with regard to the pace of reforms and their incremental nature.

In the last two decades, two major changes have taken place with regard to CAP decision-making. First, after the **Nice Treaty** came into force in 2003, the Agricultural Council began to take decisions as a matter of course using the qualified majority rule. Second, since 2009, the EP has used the ordinary legislative procedure (OLP) in agricultural policy-making under the **Lisbon Treaty**. Although the former has certainly fuelled a more vigorous reform process, the consequences of the latter are still uncertain.

by a deep-rooted affinity for rural life, viewed farmers' interests favourably. In the French case, close links were established from the late 1950s between the government and the main farmers' representative organizations, the *Fédération Nationale des Syndicats d'Exploitants Agricoles* (FNSEA, or 'National Federation of Farmers' Unions') and the *Centre National des Jeunes Agriculteurs* (CNJA, or 'Young Farmers' Association'). Thanks to their capacity for collective action and the threat of public disorder, these organizations were able to impose their views on both right-wing governments (their traditional allies) and, after 1981, on successive socialist incumbents. Although the left-supporting farmers managed to get organized during the 1980s with the establishment of the farming union *Confédération Paysanne* in 1987, which had a rather different position, they were still too weak to challenge the power of the right-leaning FNSEA. Consequently, despite an increased pluralism in the representation of farmers since the 1980s, the French position on the CAP still remains very close to that of the FNSEA.

Farmers' opposition to CAP reform is usually explained simply with reference to their economic interests. However, the conservatism of farmers' associations has also had much to do with deep-rooted symbolic issues linked to the identity of the farming community. In the French case, for example, the FNSEA has vehemently refused to replace the

guaranteed price system with direct payments, even if the latter were calculated to provide a higher income than the former for farmers. Such a position can be explained by certain ethical and professional values that have been inherited by CNJA and FNSEA leaders, arising out of their early experiences in the 1950s with the *Jeunesse Agricole Chrétienne* (JAC, or 'Young Christian Movement'). Farmers were considered to be individual entrepreneurs, actively working the land and selling the products that they had grown in order to earn their living. It is for this reason that they could not tolerate the idea of living and supporting their families on the back of direct income payments, which were viewed either as salaries or, even worse, as a form of social security/welfare payment. Another explanation relates directly to the nature of CAP instruments at that time. In upholding the idea that all farmers should get the same rewards, guaranteed prices had been feeding the myth of farmer unity. This was something of a paradox, because in practice they provided very different levels of support across the EU, across farmers, and across products. For example, the bigger the farm, the more financial support available for the farmer. However, as it was hidden by the guaranteed price system, such inequity did not disrupt farmers' unity. Indeed, after three decades of successive reforms, the CAP remains profoundly marked by these historic disparities.

KEY POINTS

- The Common Agricultural Policy was based on three fundamental principles: market unity; Community preference; and financial solidarity.

- The original CAP comprised the administrative guaranteed price, a public intervention system, and variable levies at EU borders.

- The CAP began to pose problems in the 1970s: agricultural surpluses began to grow and the cost of the CAP increased dramatically, but an inflationary bias in decision-making prevented major reform.

- Farmers' reluctance to change is not only rooted in economic interests, but also reflects identity and symbolic dimensions.

23.3 After 1992: the long reform process

An important shift in the instruments of the Common Agricultural Policy took place in 1992, which opened the way for a long reform process.

23.3.1 External pressures and the MacSharry reform of 1992

World agricultural markets in the early 1980s were affected by massive instabilities. In 1982, member countries invited the **Organization for Economic Co-operation and Development** (OECD) Secretariat-General to undertake a review of agricultural policies to analyse their effects on international trade. With the help of academic economists working in the paradigm of welfare economics, the officials in charge constructed an economic model and tools that enabled estimates to be made of the impact of domestic policies on world prices and trade. These studies were initially used to classify the trade-distorting effects of national policies, and later to rank policies, demonstrating which of them were in most serious need of reform. This process engendered a learning process within the international agricultural policy community and induced a profound change in the way in which agricultural policy issues were defined and discussed. Most notably, it was concluded that, to be less trade distorting, instruments used within an agricultural policy had to be 'decoupled' from agricultural

production so that they would have no direct impact on the type and quantity of commodity produced by the farmer. This conclusion spoke directly to the CAP's **price support** system.

A very important concrete decision followed this international ideational shift. This was the end of the so-called 'agricultural exception' in international trade negotiations. In 1986, the **Uruguay Round** of the **General Agreement on Tariffs and Trade** (GATT) opened. For the first time, the negotiations included agriculture. As is often the case in GATT rounds, the main players were the USA and its allies, the Cairns Group (a group of 14 net exporters of agricultural produce, notably including Argentina, Australia, New Zealand, Uruguay, and Thailand). They were on the offensive from the start, denouncing the CAP as a system that allowed European farmers to eschew competition with the rest of the world, and calling for an end to all trade-distorting domestic subsidies and tariff barriers on agricultural products. The EU, with traditionally more protectionist countries such as Norway and Japan, found itself on the defensive. At the Heysel Ministerial Conference in December 1990, the USA and EU positions were still at odds, leading to a stalemate in the negotiations and threatening the entire process. To put additional pressure on the Europeans, the Americans and their allies took the decision not to negotiate on any other aspect of the round until the agricultural issue was resolved.

Such a crisis in the GATT arena provided a window of opportunity for European reformers. A radical CAP reform was seen as the only solution. At this point, the Commission launched a project that it had been preparing secretly for some months. Using its right of initiative (for the first time in the history of the CAP), the Commission delivered its radical CAP reform proposal to the Agricultural Council in February 1991. The spirit of the reform was in line with international requirements, in that it would partly replace the system of agricultural price support with a system of **individual direct payments** to farmers aimed at compensating their loss of income.

The political decision to implement such a radical shift in policy instruments, agreed by the Council in May 1992, was taken initially by Helmut Kohl and François Mitterrand, the then leaders of Germany and France. Both were very keen to conclude the Uruguay Round. Germany had important interests in the non-agricultural part of the negotiations and the German industrial policy community put intense pressure on the German government to resolve the impasse. In France, the pressures came—secretly—from the biggest cereal growers, who had a direct interest in the reform. Thanks to the agreed price decreases, they would be able to gain an upper hand in the European animal food market over US cereal substitutes. Such **freeriding** behaviour by the—very influential—cereal lobby explains why the idea of reform was immediately accepted by the French government (although not officially), against the advice of the *Fédération Nationale des Syndicats d'Exploitants Agricoles* (FNSEA), which was totally opposed to it. The French government immediately decided to accept the reform (in part due to the cereal growers' influence) but they kept their decision secret almost until the end of the decision process (due to their fear of the FNSEA which was able to threaten public order by putting farmers in the streets and paralyse the country by blocking main roads etc.). In addition, in order to benefit from the reform at two levels, cereal growers together with large landowners—who were organized and powerful in the UK for example, lobbied actively for full compensation of the price decreases for all (contrary to the Commission proposal of a sliding scale compensatory scheme making individual direct payments dependent on the size of the farm).

The negotiations on the Commission's proposal took place in the Agricultural Council over a period of 18 months, resulting in the rewriting of the Commission's original proposal. At the end of this process, the outcome of the 1992 reform was not quite as innovative as it might have been. The deal that was finally concluded on 21 May 1992 (known as the 'MacSharry reform', deriving from the name of the agriculture commissioner at that time) was still regarded, however, as historic (see *Financial Times*, 22 May 1992).

23.3.2 An ongoing reform process

The MacSharry reform marked the start of a new trend for CAP reform which continues to this day. Reforms since the early 1990s have been structured around a central motto: '**decoupling**' public support from the market—which increasingly has gone hand in hand with discursive innovations attempting to reconnect (or recouple) CAP payments with societal concerns, such as environmental protection and social equity.

The first post-MacSharry reform was agreed in March 1999 at the Berlin European Council and was incorporated into the Commission's **Agenda 2000** plans.

It was prepared and issued in the broader context of the Eastern **enlargement** of the EU (see Box 23.2). Alongside a number of **subsidiarity**/decentralization initiatives, the 1999 reform was remarkable in that it placed a new emphasis on the environment. Three possible options were presented to the member states, to be implemented on a voluntary basis. This was also the case for a proposal allowing maximum levels of direct aid received by farmers to be set. But these optional social and environmental measures were rarely implemented.

The Agenda 2000 reform also endorsed two important discursive innovations. First, the term '**multifunctionality**' was introduced to signal that agriculture is not only about production, but also incorporated 'non-production' aspects of farming—that is, its social, cultural, territorial, and environmental dimensions. With this concept, European policy-makers were not only seeking new ways in which to legitimize the CAP within the EU, but also had the forthcoming **World Trade Organization (WTO)** Round in mind. When the Uruguay Round was concluded in 1994, the Agreement on Agriculture (AoA) defined three 'boxes' used to distinguish between support for agricultural policy programmes that directly stimulated production and consequently distorted trade, and those that were considered to have no **direct effect** on production and trade.

- Domestic measures with a direct effect on production were placed in the 'amber box': they had to be cut.

- Measures considered to be 'decoupled from production', with no linkage between the amount of payment and the production process, agricultural prices, or factors of production, were placed in the 'green box' and could be freely used.

- Payments linked to programmes aiming at limiting production went into the 'blue box' and did not need to be reduced, as long as certain conditions were met.

In the AoA, the post-1992 CAP compensatory payments were classified in the blue box—but, in view of the forthcoming WTO negotiations, their future was seen as uncertain. In that context, the strategy decided by the Agricultural Council in October 1999 involved 'securing' CAP payments in the blue box by arguing that the CAP could not be challenged because it pursued multifunctionality, meaning non-production, as well as production, goals.

The second discursive innovation of the Agenda 2000 reform was to distinguish between two 'pillars' of the CAP. In addition to a first pillar dedicated to market support, rural development became the 'second pillar' of the CAP. This was presented as a way of enhancing the 'multifunctionality' of European agriculture in line with a subsidiarity-based approach. However, Agenda 2000 was, in fact, only one small step in this direction, with a small percentage of total CAP expenditure allocated to the second pillar. Thirty years later, actors involved in the policy still talk about the 'two pillars' of the CAP; however, the concept of multifunctionality has almost disappeared from their discourse, to be replaced progressively by the concept of 'public good'.

A new CAP reform plan was issued by the European Commission in July 2002, one year after the opening of a new WTO Round, the so-called **Doha Development Round** (see Box 23.3). This plan was largely driven by these new WTO negotiations, within which the fate of the blue box became more and more uncertain, making it clear that the EU could not secure CAP payments to European farmers only by transferring them to the green box, requiring further 'decoupling' from production. While initially supported by the UK, Germany, and other 'northern' governments, the new CAP reform proposal faced very strong French opposition. The French government refused to see the support to its larger cereal growers reduced and wanted the reform to be postponed until 2006.

BOX 23.2   CASE STUDY: EASTERN ENLARGEMENT AND THE CAP

A first crucial issue regarding EU enlargement and agriculture at the end of the 1990s was the extent to which the CAP was to be applied to the ten member states that were to join the EU in 2004, and whether the CAP instruments would have to be adapted. This raised questions about the economic consequences of applying CAP to the new members in respect of the general structure of farming. In addition, there were serious concerns about how the CAP would be financed in the future.

The European Commission presented its strategy for dealing with these questions at the beginning of 2002. Its proposal involved offering direct payments to farmers and introducing production quotas for new member countries after they joined. To ease transitional problems in rural areas and to encourage the restructuring of agricultural sectors, the Commission also proposed complementing its financial support with an enhanced **rural development policy**. Given that the immediate introduction of 100 per cent direct payments would have bankrupted the EU, the Commission favoured its gradual introduction over a transition period of ten years, covering 25 per cent in 2004, 30 per cent in 2005, and 35 per cent in 2006, ultimately reaching 100 per cent in 2013.

For existing member states, the northern Europeans argued that the proposal was too costly, and that there should be no direct aid to the Central and East European (CEE) countries in the first few years after accession. The Dutch government pointed out that no direct aid for new members was assumed in the Agenda 2000 agreement in 1997. The Swedes argued that direct aid for the new member states would actually discourage much-needed agricultural restructuring. Germany was more concerned about predictions that its net contribution to the

agricultural budget would grow after enlargement and that, as a result, its budgetary returns would decrease. France, always aiming to keep its own budgetary returns on CAP as high as possible, also expressed concern about the cost of the Commission's strategy, but firmly opposed the suggestion by some members that a more profound reform of the CAP was needed before enlargement. For their part, most of the candidate countries reacted by saying that the Commission's proposal did not offer them enough and that they needed 100 per cent of direct aid paid from year one. This was not only for sectoral, but also for political reasons, in order to convince their publics to agree to EU membership in the first place.

At the Brussels European Council on 25 October 2002, the EU heads of state and government finally adopted the main lines of the Commission's proposal. To address some national concerns (from Germany in particular), they placed their decision in a framework of financial stability from 2007 to 2013. This meant that total annual expenditure on CAP direct payments and market-related expenditure for a Union of—at that time—25 members would not exceed the corresponding combined ceilings for 2006.

One important aspect of the 'CAP and EU enlargement' debate was the concern that CEE countries would not have the capacity to implement CAP legislation and control expenditures. Bulgaria and Romania were at the core of especially important debates in this respect in the years before their accession in 2007. In addition to more general concerns about their judicial systems and high-level corruption, the control of agricultural funds and food safety issues (animal disease control and bovine spongiform encephalopathy, or BSE, regulations, in particular) were seen as major areas of concern.

Figure 23.1 CAP annual expenditure (1980–2019)

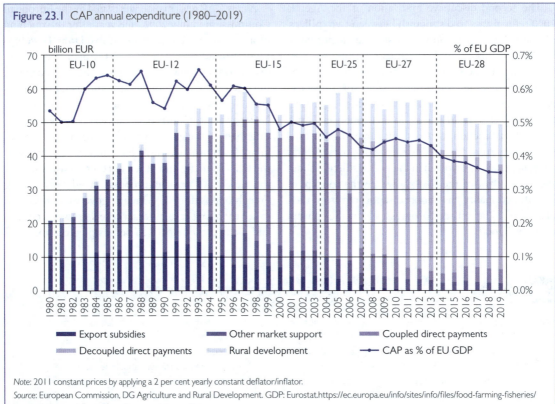

Export subsidies   Other market support   Coupled direct payments

Decoupled direct payments   Rural development   CAP as % of EU GDP

Note: 2011 constant prices by applying a 2 per cent yearly constant deflator/inflator.

Source: European Commission, DG Agriculture and Rural Development. GDP: Eurostat.https://ec.europa.eu/info/sites/info/files/food-farming-fisheries/farming/documents/cap-expenditure-graph2_en.pdf

The Agricultural Council finally reached a compromise in June 2003. The 2003 'mid-term review' (MTR) of the CAP (so-called because it was foreseen in the 1999 Berlin Agreement as a simple reviewing exercise) is considered by some commentators as a second revolution in CAP reform after the 'historic' 1992 reform. It introduced a new element, the **Single Farm Payment (SFP)**, a unique CAP direct payment aimed at achieving a complete decoupling of support from production (see Figure 23.1). Under this system, even a farmer who decides to grow nothing is eligible to receive the SFP, as long as they comply with EU environmental, food safety, animal welfare, and occupational safety standards. Finally, another important measure called '**modulation**' was set up to transfer funds from the first CAP pillar (market support) to the second (rural development).

With no direct international pressure this time, a further reform (the so-called **health check**) was approved in November 2008. This was primarily concerned with budgets, further decoupling and

efficiency. As usual, the Commission made ambitious initial proposals, which were considerably eroded in the negotiation process. For example, in the field of modulation, in order to increase both fairness in the distribution of CAP support among farmers and available budgets for rural development, the Commission had proposed a basic rate of 13 per cent transfer from the first to the second pillar by 2013, rising to 23 per cent on individual payments over €100,000, 38 per cent above €200,000, and 58 per cent above €300,000. Owing to (among others) German pressure in the Council—since reunification, Germany has had some very big farms—the final agreement included a much lower modulation scheme, with a basic rate of 10 per cent in 2013 and only an additional 4 per cent for individual payments above €300,000. This reform also led to the end of the quota system for milk in 2015.

Another CAP reform was adopted in June 2013. The reform process was launched in April 2010 with an innovative wide-ranging public consultation

⬊ BOX 23.3   KEY DEBATE: THE CAP AND DEVELOPING COUNTRIES

Since the 1980s, the CAP has often been criticized for its effects on developing countries. Through its system of export refunds (payments given to the exporter to compensate for the difference between the European guaranteed price and the much lower world price), the EU was exporting agricultural products at prices much below their costs of production, contributing to the ruin of producers in the global South. For example, cans of Italian concentrated tomatoes, and millions of tons of frozen chicken and wheat from Northern Europe, regularly arrived on African markets at very low prices and caused local production to collapse.

Step by step, the various CAP reforms have reduced the level of internal prices and consequently phased out most export refunds (which now represent only 1 per cent of the CAP budget, see Figure 23.1). This has reduced trade distortions considerably. However, although they are quantitatively much less important, some actors claim that the CAP continues to produce negative effects on developing countries. Although most CAP payments have been shifted to the 'green' box of the WTO, many development non-governmental organizations (NGOs) argue that European products are highly subsidized and are thus exported below their costs of production. As such, they potentially compete unfairly with domestic products in less-developed countries. Others argue, however, that EU agricultural exports mainly target developed and emerging countries rather than less developed ones, and that, under the present circumstances, the problem is not whether to support

European agriculture or not, but whether to support less-developed countries' agriculture (through developing countries' national budgets or through cooperation policies, or even through tariffs that protect internal markets).

Another issue is formulated in terms of 'market access'. Some actors criticize the European Union for being too protectionist owing to its 'non-trade barriers' (such as EU environmental rules, animal welfare standards, and labelling legislation). However, these arguments tend to come from the minority of countries with large producers who export, or who would like to export, their products to the EU with fewer constraints.

By contrast, the European food system is highly dependent upon a number of imports from the global South. This is the case for soybeans, a major input used in industrial animal production processes. Due to the implementation of a zero import tariff on soybeans since 1967, the EU's production of poultry and pig meat, milk, and eggs has developed based on massive imports of soybeans from the USA and, later on, Brazil, Argentina, and Uruguay. In these regions, the intensive industrial production of soybeans causes major social and environmental damage. In order to decrease this problematic dependency, many actors have called on the Commission to support actively the production of protein crops in the EU. Palm oil, which is massively imported from South East Asia to be used in the food industry, raises similar social and environmental issues highlighting how EU agri-food systems continue to fuel deforestation in the global South.

---

aimed at assessing the opinions of European citizens and stakeholders regarding the CAP. The result showed a clear desire by the public for a fairer and a greener CAP (European Commission, 2010a). To a large extent echoing these views, the Commission presented its first formal reform proposal in November 2011, with the aim of building 'a new partnership between the CAP and the society and achieving three long-term goals: viable food production, sustainable management of natural resources and climate action, and balanced territorial development' (Cioloç, 2011). The proposal proposed the introduction of a new architecture of direct payments based on a green payment scheme: at least 30 per cent of each national direct payment envelope should reward good environmental practice by farmers. The Commission also suggested the removal of all production constraints (the remaining quotas in wine for example) and the introduction

of new market mechanisms (that is, an enhanced safety net), as well as some measures aimed at strengthening rural development. Once again, the initial Commission proposal was significantly diluted in the three years of intense negotiations. The **co-decision** procedure, which included the European Parliament (EP) as a co-legislator in a large agricultural policy reform for the first time, seems to have weakened the Commission and favoured the Council, which traditionally voices dominant agricultural interests (Greer, 2017). The EP and the Council's positions converged on many issues and particularly on the core issue of direct payments, and greening measures were considerably watered down (Hart, 2015). Modulation was maintained, but a reverse modality was introduced authorizing member states to transfer funds from pillar 2 to pillar 1. Consequently, and to a certain extent paradoxically, despite a more democratic decision-process, the outcome of the 2013 CAP reform failed to match public expectations as expressed in the initial public consultation. A report by the European Court of Auditors found that the 2013 CAP flagship **green payment** only changed farming practices in 5 per cent of all EU farmland and was, overall, not environmentally effective (ECA, 2017).

Facing a systematic watering down of its proposals in the negotiation process while being accused of being responsible for all of CAP's failures (the so-called scapegoat syndrome), the European Commission has adopted a strategy of progressive strategic disengagement, with the idea of defining a common frame and giving to the member states responsibility for defining their own political priorities and preferences. This strategy was explicit in the new CAP reform that was proposed in the summer 2018 and agreed in June 2021, which aimed for 'simpler rules and a more flexible approach'. The proposal was built around national CAP Strategic Plans to allow national and regional authorities to design agricultural policies better fitting to local circumstances. For many commentators, this opened the way for the most radical renationalization that has ever taken place in the history of the CAP (with member states allowed to decide how and to whom to allocate CAP support). Many feared that the divergent policies that would result could impede fair competition among European producers, and lead to an uneven playing field for environmental rules to be met by farmers. Once more, the level of environmental ambition was one of the most debated parts of the reform. Green payments were discontinued, replaced by **eco-schemes**—compulsory for member states to offer as part of direct payments, but voluntary for farmers. As with green payments before them, both Council and Parliament were intent on widening the number of practices that could qualify for these new payments—but the Commission's intent was for these to be focused on delivering environment and climate objectives.

While only a small number of stakeholders engaged with the CAP reform process historically, the 2021 CAP reform occurred under much more intense scrutiny, as environmental groups and climate campaigner Greta Thunberg argued that the CAP proposal, inherited from the Juncker Commission, undermined the von der Leyen Commission's flagship proposal for a European Green Deal (EGD). Commission Vice-President,

Frans Timmermans, assured environmentalists that the CAP could still deliver on the EGD, if and only if the two legislators increased the proposal's ambition during trilogues—which did not happen. The EU institutions were divided on both ambition and priorities for reform, but so were stakeholders, as the CAP reform process revealsed once more the heterogeneity of the EU farming community. For COPA-COGECA, farmers are 'climakers', and 'climate and biodiversity are very much at the heart of [their] action'. The new CAP and EGD should simply support existing farmer-led efforts: 'we are already on the move across Europe' (COPA-COGECA, 2020). Conversely, European Coordination Via Campesina, the organization which represents small agriculture and 'family farming' is critical of the reform for underdelivering on the environment and letting down small farms: 'the focus of eco-schemes on environmentally friendly "practices" (rather than environmentally friendly "systems") may mean that large farms with strong financial resources will be able to comply with these practices via investment, while excluding small and medium farmers who can make a move towards sustainability and agroecology in this period'. They are cautiously optimistic however that the European Parliament is starting to take social conditionality seriously, that is, the idea of considering good social conditions on farms, such as farm workers' conditions, as pre-requisite for receiving CAP funding, similar to the role of cross-compliance for environmental standards (ECVC, 2020).

After decades of reform, the core of the CAP remains productivist, prioritizing production and productivity over other objectives. Over time, new instruments have been layered upon pre-existing instruments, retaining broadly the same distributive policy effects (which favour larger farms and older member states). The way the CAP is justified has changed—with a growing importance of public goods and ecosystem services—but this has not gone hand in hand with a profound greening of the CAP, and agriculture remains one of the main drivers of biodiversity loss and air and water pollution in Europe (European Environment Agency, 2019). The recent 2021 reform marks a step change in the governance of the CAP: with renationalization at its heart, it risks further undermining the level playing field between farmers from different member states, and leading to growing divergence in meeting the CAP's environmental and social aims.

23.4 Past and present debates on the CAP and EU agriculture

For decades the agricultural reform debate has been focused mainly on the budgetary, economic, and trade distortive effects of Common Agricultural Policy instruments conducive to a progressive liberalization of the policy. However, although they have not been the main engine for change, other important issues have emerged and have progressively found their way into discussions about the future of the CAP; rural development, environment protection, food quality, and equity fall into this category.

23.4.1 The long road to rural development

Since the early years of the CAP, the lack of a socio-economic dimension in the policy has been criticized. This is why in the late 1960s (European Economic Community, 1969), Dutch Agricultural Commissioner, Sicco Mansholt, proposed a radical revision of the CAP's market measures, together with an active structural agricultural policy. Strongly rejected by the

Council, the proposal gave birth to a very timid **structural policy** in 1972, providing funds for such things as new techniques and equipment as means to foster the modernization of farms. Differing from other CAP measures, these structural measures were co-financed by member states through fixed, multi-annual budgetary 'envelopes'. Despite an increase in allocations since the mid-1980s, only an extremely small part of the European agricultural budget has ever been devoted to structural measures. In the following decades, structural measures were merged with social, forestry, and agri-environment measures to create a rural development policy within the framework of the CAP.

The European Commission has made various attempts to promote rural development as a parallel approach to agricultural policy since the beginning of the 1990s. Its Directorate-General for Agriculture was renamed 'Agriculture and Rural Development' at that time, and it published numerous documents promoting its 'sustainable rural development' strategy. An important event organized in this perspective was the European Conference on Rural Development (in Cork, Ireland, November 1996), initially planned as a way of building an ambitious approach to the countryside within the CAP. The Cork Declaration invited European policy-makers to switch their public support from financing market measures to assisting rural development programmes (including agro-environmental measures). Again, however, the member states were very reluctant to adopt such an approach. Consequently, the Commission decided to separate the issue of rural development policy from the overall reform of the CAP, which is how the second pillar of the CAP was born in 1999.

Since its earlier incarnation, rural development policy has attracted two main sets of critics. First, for many, this new 'pillar' remains too marginal both from a budgetary point of view (see Figure 23.1) and from a political perspective, considering that the measures in the second pillar must be co-financed by the member states (whereas the first pillar is entirely funded by the EU). Second, rural development policy is criticized as being too 'farming'-orientated, the measures of the second pillar being essentially designed for farmers rather than other members of the rural community. As a consequence, while agriculture is no longer the sole engine for rural development, it still consumes almost all available funds, with rural development actors outside the farming sector benefiting from only very scarce resources. In order to address these issues better, commentators have argued for a shift in rural development from the CAP to regional policy, a proposal strongly resisted by the agricultural policy community. In response, the 'modulation' measure was decided in 2003 and reinforced in 2008. A new regulatory framework was adopted for the period 2007–13 which notably reinforced innovative policy tools such as so-called LEADER programmes (highly specific projects designed and implemented through local partnerships). Subsequent CAP reforms have confirmed this fragility of Rural Development funding: for the 2014–20 period and the 2021–27 period, pillar two suffered greater cuts compared to pillar one, and 'reverse modulation' allowed member states with low levels of direct payments to top these up from the rural development budget (see Henke et al., 2017).

23.4.2 Beyond agriculture? Environment and food

The environment and, more broadly, issues of **sustainable development** have progressively found their way into the agricultural policy debate since the 1980s. The negative effects of modern farming were initially denounced by environmental groups. Problems identified included soil degradation in areas of intensive crop production, pollution by pesticides, water pollution caused by nitrate fertilizers in areas of intensive livestock production, and the homogenization of the rural landscape. Until the 1990s, however, due to the opacity of the guaranteed price mechanism, it was not easy to appreciate how the CAP affected the environment in rural areas by prompting farmers to intensify their practices, thereby exacerbating environmental degradation. With CAP support becoming gradually more transparent through the introduction of direct payments, the situation became clearer and environmentalists could enter the agricultural policy debate more directly.

Among the various environmental organizations in Brussels, one has gained an increasing influence on the debate in the last decades: Birdlife International. Since the early 1990s, this organization has emerged as the main representative of the 'CAP and the environment'. Strongly influenced by the UK's Royal Society for the Protection of Birds (RSPB), Birdlife International has diffused a market-orientated vision of the relationship between agriculture and the environment in the CAP. They call for the dismantling of traditional market regulations, seen as most harmful for the environment, and they argue that the CAP should limit its scope to market failures, that is, the provision of environmental public goods by agriculture (Birdlife International, 2008). They ask for a 'new contract' between society and farmers drawing on a land-based approach: 'appropriate land management is crucial for the conservation of a range of ecosystem services, a critical one of which is food production for the human population and underpinning this, the long-term capacity of land for food production' (Birdlife International/European Landowners' Organization, 2010). They require that 'all payments . . . be based on a clear contract between the contractor and society, spelling out the public goods that the contractor is expected to deliver in exchange for the payments'.

Contrasting Birdlife's market-based vision of the relationship between agriculture policy and the environment, other actors put the environment at the core of their agriculture model. Organic farmers, for example, reject the use of chemicals in farming and support the use of ecological processes instead. However, their organization (the European branch of the International Federation of Organic Agriculture Movement) completely failed to push their more holistic vision of agriculture and the environment within the CAP debate (Gibbon, 2008). The European organic sector thus remains subject to EU regulation (since 1992) based only on market-based mechanisms (Fouilleux and Loconto, 2017), and quite separately from the CAP, although the newly proposed eco-schemes could see support for organic farming at the heart of pillar one. Other actors are calling for radical changes in the CAP on both environmental and social grounds. This is the case of ARC2020, a multi-stakeholder platform that has involved over 150 civil society networks and organizations from 22 EU member states since its creation in 2010 and claims for a 'paradigm shift in agriculture and a rural renaissance' through radical CAP reforms. New actors have also entered the CAP debate in relation to animals and animal production models. Organizations opposing cruelty to animals and/or defending animal welfare are increasingly active, as well as actors warning against the role of livestock in global warming and climate change, and those advocating lower meat consumption levels and less intensive animal production methods.

Finally, voices calling for the better integration of food and diets in CAP related debates are becoming louder. They have even argued for a Common Food Policy (IPES, 2019). Agricultural production as supported by the CAP has underpinned the development of an industrial food system, which is currently facing multiple challenges. In addition to European-wide sanitary crises, massive waste in the food chain, food culture loss, and increasing anxiety of the consumers, it also results in massive consumption of junk food, with important effects on diets and consequently on health (De Schutter et al., 2020). Most of these actors, whose positions contrast with an exclusively market-based approach to environmental issues, converge in the defence of agroecology as an alternative model that should underpin the CAP. Using the recent framework proposed by the Food and Agriculture Organization (FAO) in that field (Loconto and Fouilleux, 2019), they propose mainstreaming agroecology into all policies governing EU food systems, including the CAP (ARC2020 et al., 2021).

Research projects have tried to test the feasibility of such approaches, such as the *Ten Years for Agroecology* forecasting exercise (Poux and Aubert, 2018). This exercise shows that a fully agroecological Europe, free from synthetic inputs and favouring natural grasslands and agroecological infrastructures (hedges, trees, ponds, stony habitats) could sustainably feed 530 million Europeans by 2050. Despite an induced decline in production of 35 per cent compared to 2010 (in kcal), this scenario feeds Europeans healthily (with less meat) while maintaining export capacity; reduces Europe's global food footprint; results in a 40 per cent reduction in agricultural GHG emissions; and helps to restore biodiversity and to protect natural resources.

Will agroecology succeed where 'Public money for public goods' failed? Environmental public goods, central to the 'green-liberal' pact for CAP reform (Lumbroso and Gravey, 2013), have been hegemonic in CAP related discussions and decision-making regarding the environment in the last decades. However, this principle was hollowed out and only a few changes occurred in practice, resulting in a greenwashing of the CAP (Pe'er et al., 2020). The growing evidence base of the need for urgent action to tackle the twin climate and biodiversity emergencies (European Environment Agency, 2019) seems to have been taken more seriously by the von der Leyen Commission's proposal for a European Green Deal, which appears as doubly important for European agriculture. First, contrary to previous European Commission flagship projects (see for example, the **Lisbon Strategy**) it has a clear agriculture component. Second, the agricultural component, the Farm to Fork Strategy, challenges the CAP by prioritizing food, setting an objective of at least 25 per cent of the EU's agricultural land under organic farming by 2030 and by taking clear and ambitious commitments

to reduce the risk and use of pesticides by 50 per cent, mineral fertilizers by 20 per cent, and antibiotics use by 50 per cent in 2030, and mentioning agroecology as one of the rationales for eco-schemes. Yet once more the 2021 reform saw the Commission proposal weakened by the co-legislators. This makes it likely agroecology will also be hollowed out and that the CAP will undermine, not support delivery of the EGD.

23.4.3 On budgets and equity: where does the money go?

The debate on CAP expenditure has always been very lively. Beyond the general issue of the share of expenditure on the Common Agricultural Policy (CAP) in the total EU budget (which has dropped from 74 per cent in 1985 to 37.4 per cent in 2019), critics have traditionally pointed to the inequitable distribution of support across member states and, more recently, among types of farmers.

A first feature of the debate set countries such as the UK, Sweden, and Denmark against countries such as France, Spain, and most of the Eastern member states. The former three supported cuts in CAP budgetary expenditure, if not the dismantling of the overall policy. The latter have defended a significant CAP budget. The debate was very lively during the 2013 CAP reform, with countries such as the UK claiming that the EU must secure more funds for 'growth' policies (research, education, innovation), rather than agricultural policy (seemingly viewed as a backward policy area). Behind these arguments for and against the CAP is a debate among member states about 'budgetary return'—namely, the benefits gained by a given country from the CAP *less* the contribution of that country to the EU budget. This issue, which recalls Margaret Thatcher's demands for a **budget rebate** for the UK back in 1984, continues to be present in all Agriculture Council negotiations. This was also raised in the context of the Eastern enlargement (see Box 23.2) and since they joined the EU, East and Central European member states have continued to ask for a more equitable distribution of the CAP budget. The departure of the UK re-opened the CAP budget debate, with concerns it would lead to major gaps in the budget unless the remaining member states agreed to pay more (see Box 23.4).

The distribution of support among types of farmers is a second feature of the CAP equity debate. This is an old issue, which has been much less formally and publicly discussed than the latter, due to the reluctance of the most influential member states involved in CAP decision-making. Since the 2013 reform, this issue has been re-qualified by the Commission in terms of the 'internal' convergence issue (among farmers), as contrasting with the 'external' convergence issue (among member states) (Cioloç, 2011).

Since the early 1980s, 'small farmers', championed by European Coordination Via Campesina, were arguing for 'differentiated prices'—that is, a guaranteed price system based on both production and social parameters. With the direct payment system, CAP support became more transparent, as did its inherent inequities, and the debate opened up to a larger public. Although data on individual payments were initially kept secret, some lists of the main beneficiaries of the CAP were published after 2004. It came as a surprise when citizens discovered that huge CAP payments were made to the late Queen Mother in the UK, to Prince Rainier of Monaco, to big companies and food industries, and political figures (including the Agriculture Commissioner, Mariann Fischer Boel). Following an intense lobbying campaign by transparency activists (in particular those of farmsubsidy.org), the Council agreed in October 2007 to the full disclosure of all recipients of financial support under the CAP. However, since 2011, after farmers' organizations argued against it on privacy grounds, data on legal persons (individual farmers) are no longer published.

Since any potential change in CAP instruments can substantially modify the distribution of EU budgetary support among the member states, external convergence is back on the agenda each time a new CAP reform is discussed, and strongly constrains the decision-making process. Internal convergence is a more fundamental issue, which directly talks to the political objectives of the policy. The distribution of CAP support is still very unequally spread. For example, on average, 80 per cent of CAP beneficiaries (88 per cent in Bulgaria and Romania) received around 20 per cent of the payments in 2015. In the UK, prior to Brexit, 42.1 per cent of the UK farmers were sharing 4.5 per cent of total UK CAP payments (and were paid less than €5,000 each), while 8 per cent of them (paid between €50,000 and €200,000 each) were sharing 37 per cent of the total amount of CAP payments allocated to the UK. How this imbalance is addressed varies widely between, and sometimes within, member states. The 2013 CAP reform offered states the ability to cap payments for the highest beneficiaries, redistributing this funding to small farmers. Some countries opted to cap, others did not. At the other end of the spectrum, some countries have minimum claim size, others do not. For example,

---

BOX 23.4 KEY DEBATE: THE CAP AND BREXIT

Although farming unions across the UK—especially the National Farmers' Union (NFU)—advocated for a 'Remain' position at the time of the 2016 referendum (British agriculture gets around £3 bn subsidies a year from the CAP), a majority of their members voted 'Leave'.

Although negotiations are still in progress as of mid-2021, it is likely that Brexit will have some major impacts on the CAP. First, it might reshuffle power relationships among actors. In the 1990s, UK-rooted Brussels-based interest groups such as RSPB/Birdlife and the Country Landowners Association (CLA)/European Landowners Organization (ELO) had built alliances with reformists in the European Commission, forming a 'green-liberal' pact, to liberalize the CAP and reduce its negative environmental outcomes (Lumbroso and Gravey, 2013). Brexit, which weakens the standing of these powerful actors in the EU arena, leaves the floor to, on the one hand, the traditional sector-based productivist farming unions and, on the other, more radical critics of the CAP, in the small farmers movement (Via Campesina) and proponents of agroecology and system change. Second, the loss of the UK budgetary contribution raised concerns about

CAP funding. The adoption of a COVID recovery fund (Next Generation EU) (see Chapter 26), in addition to the new Multiannual Financial Framework offset these cuts in part—while the CAP will make do with 40 billion euro less during 2021–28, at 344 it is still 20 more than what the Commission originally offered in 2018.

On the UK side, Brexit implies replacing the CAP by domestic policy, an endeavour further complicated by the devolved nature of agriculture in the UK. England, Wales, Scotland, and Northern Ireland are each developing their own national policies, with few common rules. For some, this creates unique opportunities to trial new agri-environment instruments and focus on public goods to improve the environmental impact of farming (Hart and Baldock, 2019), for others it opens the door to divergence in use of chemicals, gene editing, or genetically modified organisms. Intra-UK differentiation is further increased by the terms of the UK–EU agreements. While Northern Ireland remains aligned with the EU sanitary and phytosanitary rules and can freely export its agri-food goods to the EU, GB producers are facing new barriers making trade with the EU difficult, especially for small companies.

before it left the EU, within the UK during the 2014–21 CAP, England had no cap but Northern Ireland, Wales, and Scotland did, at a maximum of €150,000, €300,000, and €500,000 respectively. England and Wales had minimum claim sizes of 5 ha, Northern Ireland and Scotland only 3 ha, while neighbouring Ireland elected to have no minimum claim sizes.

The last CAP reform has been overshadowed by two still unfolding scandals. The first, one of political corruption, and how CAP funding is used to support the political allies of some EU leaders—if not EU leaders themselves. The second concerns the working conditions of farm workers. In a series of articles in 2019, the *New York Times* exposed how in the Czech Republic, where in 2015 2.7 per cent of Czech farmers shared 46.8 per cent of the country's CAP budget and were paid more than €200,000 each, the highest recipient was actually the Prime Minister, Andrej Babis. This led the European Parliament to demand that Babis abstain from voting on the EU budget deal when it was agreed in July 2020. The *New York Times* further revealed how Babis' Hungarian counterpart, Viktor Orbán, used CAP subsidies to fuel a system of patronage, enriching friends and family, while punishing his rivals. But conflict of interests go well beyond EU leaders, and many Members of the European Parliament (MEPs) on the influential EP Agriculture Committee themselves come from a farming background, and are either recipients of CAP funding themselves, or have family members and business partners receiving funding. The second scandal is one of working conditions on farms and in the agri-food sector. Investigative journalists from *Euronews*, *Der Spiegel*, and *Mediapart* revealed during Summer 2020 how the rights of seasonal workers, often migrants, were routinely abused on European farms (Borges and Huet, 2020). The COVID-19 pandemic further shed a spotlight on working conditions as outbreaks happened repeatedly in meat factories across the EU. This has fuelled calls for social conditionality of CAP payments, with an open letter signed by more than 300 international and national organizations and individuals (EFFAT et al., 2021), and the European Parliament voting an amendment to include social conditionality in the future CAP.

KEY POINTS

- Although arising early in the Common Agricultural Policy debate, the issue of rural development has experienced a number of difficulties. The second pillar of the CAP now makes rural development policy within the CAP more legitimate, but the budget allocated to it remains small.

- With the shift to direct payments, the distribution of CAP support suddenly became more visible. This turned transparency into a core element of the debate in the 2000s.

- More transparency in the CAP does not mean more equity and social justice in the distribution of CAP support among different type of farmers; huge disparities still remain.

- The environmental issue is becoming a key element of the CAP debate.

23.5 Conclusion

Originally intended to make Western Europe self-sufficient in food, the Common Agricultural Policy was equipped with 'productivist' instruments that led to an overproduction of agricultural produce, serious budgetary problems for the European Community and important environmental and social issues on the ground. In the 1980s, the first reforms introduced supply control measures, such as quotas. At the beginning of the 1990s, as a consequence of international developments, neo-liberal policy beliefs inspired the 'decoupling' of farm support from production. A first reform of the CAP was launched in 1992, which shifted policy instruments from market or price support to direct income support. A series of further reforms followed during the 1990s and 2000s adopting a process of policy-layering (Daugbjerg and Swinbank, 2016), with further 'decoupling' and increasing attention paid to new dimensions of the policy. However, changes were very slow to be implemented, and although these items have been under discussion for decades, the CAP still suffers from major environmental gaps, poor links to rural development, unequal distribution of support among farmers, and no clear consideration of the food and health issues related to agriculture.

The evolution of the CAP is an excellent illustration of the complexity of the links that exist between national, European, and international political arenas. Inter-sectoral deals that are not easily understood at national level become even more complicated when various governments, coalitions of interests, and European and international institutions enter the game. Caught in the crossfire between national interests and international bargains, the EU's political system is complex, intricate, and competitive. The growing involvement of local government in the implementation of the CAP further increases this complexity. The CAP also illustrates another type of contemporary complexity, which points to the sociotechnical models that are favoured explicitly or implicitly by a policy and its instruments and related controversies. The only way in which to deconstruct this complexity is to examine the actors involved in the policy process, the visions of agriculture and agricultural policy that they support, the nature of the political exchanges that take place among them, and the resources that they are able to invest to defend their position and influence the policy process.

 ## QUESTIONS

1. Why did the Common Agricultural Policy originally seek to maintain high prices for agricultural produce?

2. What were the negative consequences of the CAP's price support mechanism?

3. Why did the 1992 reform take place?

4. What do the 1992, 1999, 2003, 2008, and 2013 CAP reforms have in common?

5. Which new issues entered the agricultural policy debate from the late 1990s and why?

6. Why do some actors consider that the greening of the CAP has been a failure?

7. To what extent are developing countries affected by the CAP?

8. What are the three main contrasting discourses regarding the future of agriculture in the EU, especially in relation to the environmental issue?

GUIDE TO FURTHER READING

Daugbjerg, C. and Feindt, P. (2018) *Transforming Food and Agricultural Policy: Post-exceptionalism in Public Policy* (London: Routledge). This book gives an overview of current trends in the field of food and agricultural policy, and engages with contemporary debates on related issues.

Greer, A. (2005) *Agricultural Policy in Europe* (Manchester: Manchester University Press). This book provides a unique comparative analysis of agricultural policies, and shows that, despite the existence of the CAP, substantial agricultural policy variation exists across the EU.

Patel, K. K. (2009) *Fertile Ground for Europe? The History of European Integration and the Common Agricultural Policy since 1945* (Baden-Baden: Nomos). An overview of the historic development of the Common Agricultural Policy and its implications for European integration.

Skogstad, G. and Verdun A. (eds) (2012) *The Common Agricultural Policy: Policy Dynamics in a Changing Context* (London: Routledge). This book gathers contributions by some of the best specialists of agricultural policy analysis worldwide, and provides an excellent overview of a number of CAP-related issues and debates.

Swinnen, J. (ed.) (2015) *The Political Economy of the 2014–2020 Reforms of the Common Agricultural Policy: an Imperfect Storm* (Brussels & London: Centre for European Policy Studies/Rowman & Littlefield International). This book discusses the outcome of the 2013 CAP reform and the factors that influenced the policy choices and decisions made at that time.

 Access the online resources to take your learning and understanding further, including extra multiple-choice questions with instant feedback, web links, answer guidance to end-of-chapter questions, and updates on new developments in EU politics.

www.oup.com/he/cini-borragan7e

24

Environmental Policy

Viviane Gravey, Andrew Jordan, and David Benson

Chapter Contents

Reader's Guide

Despite its very strong economic roots, the European Union has nonetheless become an international leader in environmental protection and sustainable development policy. Environmental concerns have consequently shifted from being a marginal aspect of the European integration process to one that routinely grabs news headlines and, unlike many other EU policy areas, generates relatively strong political support from EU citizens. In the past, these policies, which now impinge on most sectors and areas of the economy, have proven resilient to economic and deregulatory pressures. This chapter documents and explores the reasons behind the relatively rapid transformation in the EU's governing capabilities in this policy area, explores the main dynamics of policy-making from different analytical perspectives, and assesses the impact of challenges such as climate change, Brexit, and the COVID-19 pandemic.

24.1 Introduction

At its founding in 1957, the then **European Economic Community (EEC)** had no environmental policy, no environmental bureaucracy, and no environmental laws. The word 'environment' was not even mentioned in the **Treaty of Rome**. Over 60 years later, EU environmental policy is 'broad in scope, extensive in detail and stringent in effect' (Weale et al., 2000: 1). It conforms to a set of guiding principles, has its

> ↘ **BOX 24.1   BACKGROUND: THE EVOLUTION OF EU ENVIRONMENTAL POLICY**
>
> | | |
> |---|---|
> | 1972 | Heads of state and government, meeting in Paris, request the Commission to prepare an environmental strategy. |
> | 1973 | Commission adopts First **Environmental Action Programme (EAP)**. |
> | 1987 | Single European Act provides a more secure **legal basis**. |
> | 1993 | Publication of Fifth EAP: pursuit of a new goal—**sustainable development**. |
> | 1997 | Treaty of Amsterdam: makes promotion of sustainable development and environmental policy integration central objectives. |
> | 2002 | A Sixth, more binding, EAP is adopted. |
> | 2008 | EU adopts a climate and energy package of policies committing member states, inter alia, to a 20% reduction in greenhouse gas emissions by 2020. |
> | 2012 | Conflicts erupt between the EU and its trading partners over the **regulation** of new energy sources such as biofuels and shale gas, and the proposed inclusion of international aviation in the EU **Emissions Trading System**. |
> | 2013 | A Seventh EAP is adopted with an emphasis on natural capital and resource efficiency. |
> | 2014 | The Juncker Commission targets existing environmental laws for simplification. |
> | 2015 | The EU leads the 'high ambition coalition' during the **Paris Climate Conference**, but the **Dieselgate** scandal reveals that car manufacturers are evading EU air pollution rules. |
> | 2016 | More than 500,000 European citizens ask the Commission to safeguard the Birds and Habitats directives against deregulatory pressures. |
> | 2019 | The von der Leyen Commission proposes a **European Green Deal** centred on making the EU climate neutral by 2050 ('**net zero**'). |
> | 2020 | The UK is the first EU member state to leave the bloc, raising questions about future EU–UK environmental relations. |

own terminology, is the focus of significant activity amongst a dedicated network of policy actors, is underpinned by a binding framework of laws which have an explicit basis in the founding treaties, and has deeply affected the policies of its member states. In short, it has successfully evolved from a set of 'incidental measures' (Hildebrand, 2005: 16) to a mature system of multilevel environmental **governance**. Consequently, virtually all environmental policy-making within the member states now involves the European Union.

What is especially striking about this transformation is how quickly the EU assumed control over policy **powers** 'that in a federal state would have been ceded to the centre only grudgingly, if at all' (Sbragia, 1993: 337). Moreover, as a sector, environmental policy has shown itself to be relatively resilient to ongoing deregulatory pressures. This chapter documents the reasons behind this relatively rapid transformation (see Box 24.1), identifies the main dynamics of policy-making, and discusses the resilience of EU environmental policy to new and/or ongoing challenges such as the post-COVID economic crisis (see Chapter 28), austerity, and Brexit (see Chapter 27). It concludes by exploring future challenges as environmental policy enters its middle age.

24.2 The development of environmental policy: different perspectives

There are several ways to comprehend the evolution of EU environmental policy: one is to explore the content of the EU's environmental action programmes (EAPs); a second is to examine the main policy outputs; a third is to scrutinize the periodic amendments to the founding treaties; and finally, the dynamic interplay between actors at the international, EU, and national levels can be examined. The remainder of this section is structured around these four perspectives.

24.2.1 The Environmental Action Programmes

Seven EAPs have been adopted by the Commission since the early 1970s, with an eighth expected to be adopted in 2021 that will guide European environmental policy until 2030. Initially, these were essentially 'wish lists' of new legislation, but they gradually became more comprehensive and programmatic. The First (1973–76), identified pressing priorities— namely, pollution and other threats to human health. It also established several key principles (see Box 24.2), which were subsequently enshrined in the founding treaties (see Section 24.2.3, 'The evolution of the treaties'). They were not particularly novel—many derived from national and/or **Organisation for Economic Co-operation and Development (OECD)** best practices—but they represented an innovative

attempt to apply them via regulatory means in a new, **supranational** setting.

The Second EAP (1977–81) followed the same approach, but emphasized the need for scientifically informed decision-making, through procedures such as environmental impact assessment (EIA) for proposed developments, and underlined the Commission's desire to become more involved in international-level policy-making (see Section 24.2.2, 'Key items of policy').

By contrast, the Third (1982–86) and Fourth (1987–92) EAPs were more programmatic, setting out ambitious strategies for protecting the environment before problems occurred (Weale et al., 2000: 59). They also underscored the benefits of preventing problems by fitting the best available abatement technology to factories and vehicles.

The Fifth (1993–2000) and Sixth (2002–12) EAPs accelerated the shift to a more strategic and cross-cutting approach, with a new focus on sustainable development (Fifth) and over-arching thematic strategies (Sixth). The introduction of the seventh EAP in 2013 was continually delayed due to political arguments over its contents, and whether such a programme was even needed. It followed the Sixth EAP approach in adopting strategic themes (notably on natural capital

---

⬊ BOX 24.2   BACKGROUND: KEY PRINCIPLES OF EU ENVIRONMENTAL POLICY

Environmental management	Prevention (preventing problems is cheaper and fairer than paying to remedy them afterwards)
	Action at source (using the best available technology to minimize polluting emissions)
	Integrated pollution control (ensuring that, for example, attempts to remedy water pollution are not transformed into air or land pollution problems)
Specification of environmental standards	Resource conservation (environmental protection as a goal in its own right)
	High level of protection (aiming for the highest level of protection possible)
	Precaution (acting to protect the environment even when cause–effect relationships are not fully understood)
Allocation of authority	Appropriate level of action (acting at the 'right' level):
	Subsidiarity (only acting at EU level when problems cannot be tackled nationally)
Policy integration	Polluter pays (the polluter, rather than society as a whole, should pay to address problems)
	Environmental policy integration (integrating an environmental dimension into the development of sectoral policies such as agriculture and transport)

BOX 24.3   KEY DEBATES: THE EIGHTH ENVIRONMENTAL ACTION PROGRAMME

Traditionally, Environmental Action Programmes have comprised long lists of legislation that the EU hopes to adopt at some point in the future. The seventh almost succumbed to deregulatory pressure and was even at risk of never being published. But the proposed Eighth programme arguably constitutes a step change. It is nothing less than the main monitoring mechanism for the entire European Green Deal (EGD), while also supporting the implementation of the UN's Sustainable Development Goals (SDGs) and 2030 Agenda. It features six thematic priorities including the achievement of EU-wide climate neutrality by 2050, advancing a 'regenerative growth model' of resource use and the circular economy, and protecting biodiversity (European Commission, 2020a: 8). These high-level policy commitments to

sustainability are matched by a sharper focus on monitoring and implementation, the latter being a persistent problem area for the EU.

So given its greater ambition than previous EAPs, why did the Eighth EAP garner wide support from Council and Parliament? The answer probably lies in the rising levels of public concern over the climate crisis and deepening worries over the scale and speed of global biodiversity loss. These pushed the Council to request the Commission to produce proposals for a new programme in 2019 which was commensurate with the scale of the challenges laid out in the European Environment Agency's 2020 state of the environment report (European Environment Agency, 2019).

and resource efficiency), but also placed a greater emphasis on addressing the underlying (that is, systemic) causes of problems such as mass consumption and globalization. In many ways, it illustrates the sector's transition into a more mature—although contested—area of policy-making. When adopted, the eighth EAP will represent another marked shift: not only is it much more ambitious, but it also incorporates stronger monitoring powers (See Box 24.3).

24.2.2 **Key items of policy**

Looking back at the content of the EAPs, a steady trend is visible away from a rather ad hoc, reactive approach driven by the Commission, to a more strategic framework, co-developed by multiple **stakeholders**. A similar picture emerges when considering legislative output. In the 1960s and 1970s, this output was relatively limited, but then it rocketed in the 1980s and 1990s, tailing off again in the 2000s. By the late 1990s, more effort was devoted to consolidating, streamlining, and reforming the environmental *acquis communautaire* via less prescriptive framework legislation, including **directives** on air quality (1996), water (2000), chemicals (2006), and marine issues (2008). In the 2010s, growing bureaucratic centralization within the Commission led to the adoption of a narrower political agenda focused on the Commission President's political priorities. For the environment, this meant fewer, but more influential initiatives such as the Plastics Strategy in 2018 and the European Green Deal (EGD) in 2019.

As the environmental *acquis* grew, its purpose changed. Thus, the first environmental directives addressed very specific traded products such as cars and chemicals. In the 1980s and particularly the 1990s, the EU diversified into new areas including access to environmental information, genetically modified organisms (GMOs), and even zoos, exemplifying rising political demands for environmental protection 'for its own sake'. Since the 2000s the EU has further diversified by responding to global environmental challenges such as climate change, biodiversity loss, plastics pollution, and, via the 2015 UN Sustainable Development Goals, sustainable development. Nonetheless, the EU continues to favour 'command and control' regulation, confirming its position as a **'regulatory state'** (Majone, 1996) in the environmental sphere.

24.2.3 **The evolution of the treaties**

Another way to comprehend EU environmental policy is to analyse the environmental provisions of the EU treaties. The legal codification of the environmental *acquis communautaire* has followed the same gradual, but ever increasing, pattern noted above. Thus, the original Treaty of Rome contained no reference to environmental matters. New environmental measures consequently had to rely either on Article 100 EC (now 115 TFEU), relating to the internal market, or on Article 235 EC (now 352 TFEU), which allowed the EU to move into new policy areas to accomplish its goals. Arguments emerged as actors fought over the legal basis of environmental policies. For the

Commission, Article 100 proved to be legally more secure and hence politically less contested than Article 235, hence the tendency (noted in Section 24.2.2, 'Key items of policy') for early Commission proposals to target traded products.

In one sense, the **Single European Act (SEA)** established a more secure legal basis, with qualified majority voting (QMV) for issues with a **Single Market** dimension. This undoubtedly allowed the EU to enter new and less 'obvious', areas such as access to environmental information and ecosystem conservation (the Natura 2000 network and the Habitats Directive, for example)—all somewhat removed from the EU's internal market. In another sense, it simply codified the status quo: over one hundred items of policy had already been adopted when it was ratified in 1987 (Wurzel, 2008: 66). The Maastricht (1992) and Amsterdam (1997) Treaties introduced new policy principles (such as sustainable development, precaution, and environmental policy integration—see Box 24.2) into the founding treaties. Crucially, they also extended QMV to almost all areas and greatly increased the European Parliament's powers. By the late 1990s, most environmental policy followed one decision-making route, QMV in the Council plus **co-decision** (now the ordinary legislative procedure, or OLP) with the Parliament. Because the legal underpinnings of environmental policy were already embedded, there was little need for new environmental content in the Nice (2001) (Jordan and Fairbrass, 2005) and Lisbon (2007) Treaties (Benson and Adelle, 2012).

24.2.4 Actor dynamics

The development of environmental policy has not followed a single pattern. There have been periods of continuity, and sudden and very significant policy change. Furthermore, some aspects (for example, the action programmes) have evolved in a fairly gradual and systematic manner, whereas others (for example, the main types of policy) have emerged much more unpredictably and opportunistically. In order to understand these similarities and differences, we must look at the main actors and the evolving constraints under which they operate.

The European Commission deserves the bulk of the credit for developing an EU-wide environmental policy. Initially, it worked hard to establish a case for EU involvement. Undaunted by the absence of high-level political support (no Commission President has consistently championed environmental policy), a weak treaty basis, and limited administrative capacities (there was no designated environmental Directorate-General until 1981), it realized that it had to be creative and opportunistic to thrive. This approach strongly reflected Monnet's **neo-functionalist** method of integrating 'by stealth' (Weale, 2005; see also Chapter 4). But as the political and legal basis of EU policy became more secure, the Commission focused more efforts on governing instead of continually expanding protection to new areas.

Until the 1980s, the chief policy-making body was the Council (see Chapter 11). The first meeting of the Environment Council took place in 1972. Pushed hard by a '**troika**' of environmental 'leader' states comprising the Netherlands, Denmark, and West Germany, it adopted increasingly ambitious legislation. After 1982, West Germany strongly advocated new EU policies based on the philosophy of 'ecological modernization' that suggests high levels of environmental protection are reconcilable with, and can even promote, economic growth. Less ambitious or 'laggard' states (typically from the Mediterranean region, but also including Ireland and the UK), were rather slow to recognize what was happening, adopting some policies almost 'absent-mindedly' (Weale et al., 2000: 359). Sbragia (1996: 237) has argued that the outcome of these actor constellations was a 'push–pull' dynamic (See Box 24.4). The stark division between 'leaders' that set the policy agenda and 'laggards' seeking to wield their veto power began to dissolve in the 2000s. New member states had entered the fray (for example, after 2004) and some existing participants (the UK, for example) had changed their preferences and bargaining tactics as a result of EU membership (Jordan, 2002). Debates around the EGD and achieving a just transition for European societies is rekindling this earlier divide, with Poland emerging as the main cheer leader of the Visegrad Group of more reluctant states.

The European Parliament (see Chapter 12) is often described as the 'greenest' EU institution (Burns, 2021), although it did not actually establish its own dedicated environment body—a committee—until 1979. During the 1970s and 1980s, it highlighted new environmental issues such as animal protection and policy implementation, which were subsequently taken up by actors within formal policy-making processes. With the appearance, first, of the **cooperation** and then later the co-decision/OLP procedures, its formal influence grew. However, enlargement coupled with the electoral success of centre-right parties

BOX 24.4   CASE STUDY: PLASTIC POLLUTION POLICY

A good example of how the 'push–pull' dynamic still plays out in EU policy making is action on plastic pollution. The EU had originally regulated plastic wastes via the Packaging and Packaging Waste Directive 1994, which set mandatory targets for their recovery and recycling. However, national level policy innovation has since rebounded back on the EU, stimulating a new round of EU action (see Section 24.3.1, 'Europeanization'), with several states taking the lead. Denmark introduced a pioneering levy on plastic bags in 1994. However, it was Ireland's 'plastax' on bag sales, adopted in 2002, which persuaded the UK and other member states to adopt similar market-based instruments. To ensure regulatory harmonization within the single market, the Commission subsequently amended the 1994 Directive in 2015 with the aim of achieving reductions in lightweight plastic carrier bag use, allowing flexibility in its implementation through the use of national target setting, economic measures or marketing controls. As a result, a patchwork of differing policy responses is now visible across the EU. In addition to national levies, states such as France ban specific plastic bags, while Luxembourg and Sweden promote industry-led voluntary approaches to waste reduction (Monciardini and Benson, 2019).

reduced the Parliament's environmental ambitions after 2004 (Burns et al., 2012). Today, its influence remains largely reactive. It certainly struggles to hold the Council to account in environmentally important areas (such as land use planning, energy use, and taxation) in which unanimous voting remains the norm (Burns, 2021), and struggles to monitor the Commission's growing reliance on secondary legislation, which on occasions has a lower policy ambition (Pollex and Lenschow, 2020).

The Court of Justice of the EU (CJEU) played a pivotal role in establishing the legal importance (and hence **legitimacy**) of EU environmental policy via rulings on the **direct effect** of directives (see Chapter 13). During the 1970s and 1980s, the Court was drawn into adjudicating on the legal basis of EU laws, often resolving them in favour of the Commission (Krämer, 2021). Earlier rulings also supported the Commission's right to participate in international environmental policy-making (Sbragia, 2005). As the legal basis of EU policy was established, the CJEU's focus shifted to resolving disputes over policy implementation. By 2019, there were more ongoing infringement cases in the environmental area (337 out of 1564) than any other sector (European Commission, 2020b), but most will be dealt with in informal, or formal stages of infringement proceedings overseen by the Commission and very few reaching the CJEU (71 out of 164 at the end of 2020) (European Commission, 2020c).

Interest groups constitute the final type of actor. National-level environmental pressure groups established a Europe-wide **federation** (in 1974) to coordinate their efforts. The European Environment Bureau (EEB) now has more than 140 member organizations, ranging from large, well-established national bodies to much smaller and more local ones. In the 1980s and 1990s, environmental pressure groups lobbying directly in Brussels mushroomed—another indicator of how far **European integration** has proceeded in this sector (Berny and Moore, 2021). Although these organizations are highly motivated, they are comprehensively out-resourced by business interests that can hire the very best public relations firms to lobby EU policy-makers. Nonetheless, they are drawn to Brussels because they perceive that they can achieve things there and internationally that would be unattainable back home (see Chapter 14). They also play a key role in informing the European Commission of suspected cases of non-compliance.

KEY POINTS

- At its inception in 1957, the EU had no environmental policy. Environmental issues were not even explicitly mentioned in the Treaty of Rome.

- Nonetheless, over the last 50 years, the EU has developed a wide-ranging environmental *acquis communautaire*.

- Environmental policy development can be understood by examining, inter alia, the different Environmental Action Programmes, the content of key policy outputs, EU treaty amendments, and the interplay between different policy actors across multiple levels.

- Several actors vie for influence within this system. The Commission has been instrumental in driving policy development. Other influential actors include the Council of the EU, the European Parliament, the Court of Justice of the EU (CJEU), and interest groups.

24.3 Linking different perspectives: the underlying dynamics of environmental policy

Having now introduced the main actors, policies, and legal frameworks, we are better placed to explore the underlying dynamics of EU policy-making. In the past, EU environmental policy could be explained through one main dynamic (for example, the **regulatory competition** between member states) and/or in binary terms (leaders vs laggards; EU institutions vs member states; economy vs environment). But as the sector has matured and become more deeply entangled with others, these binary constructs no longer suffice (Lenschow, 2021). Indeed the nature of specific policy outputs (Directives, Regulations, etc.) and their differentiated impact on the ground within the member states are far too complex to be explained by a single model or framework (Sbragia, 1996: 241). To understand better how policy is made, analysts therefore started to explore policy developments in particular sub-areas of environment policy using multiple approaches and more systematic empirical data (Lenschow, 2021). These studies have revealed the salience of three interacting dynamics: **Europeanization**; internationalization; and cross-sectoral policy integration.

24.3.1 **Europeanization**

Europeanization is the process through which EU-level policies affect domestic systems (see Chapter 8). As analysts started to investigate the domestic implications of more multilevel environmental governance, the picture that emerged was one of differential Europeanization. Thus, every state has been affected by EU membership, even the greenest 'leader' states. Moreover, states have been affected by the EU in different ways: studies show that the content of their policies has been more deeply affected than their style of operation (for example, anticipatory or reactive, **consensual** or adversarial) or their internal administrative structures (Jordan and Liefferink, 2004). The EU has therefore introduced entirely new policy instruments in some countries and altered the manner in which existing instruments are applied in all countries. Moreover, the EU has tightened the level at which these instruments are formally calibrated or 'set'. The overall extent of domestic adaptation to

these new policy settings has been relatively limited in some countries (e.g., the Netherlands, Austria, Sweden, and Germany), whereas in others it has been dramatic (namely Greece, Ireland, and Spain).

In summary, while some aspects of national policy have become more similar, no long-term convergence towards a common 'European' model is apparent (Jordan and Liefferink, 2004). But national politics (as distinct from policy) have undoubtedly been very deeply affected by EU membership. Europeanization has been an unpredictable and, at times, rather chaotic process, casting doubt on claims made by intergovernmentalists that states are remote from (and largely in firm control of) the European integration process. With Brexit, the UK is engaging in the first systematic attempt at what could be termed de-Europeanization (see Chapter 27). Brexit is raising fundamental questions regarding environmental policies (will UK standards increase, decrease, or be maintained outside the EU?) and environmental governance, (how will UK policy be implemented and enforced?) (Burns et al., 2019).

24.3.2 **Internationalization**

International-level drivers are far more important in EU environmental policy than is sometimes assumed. After all, it was the 1972 UN Stockholm Conference that first gave EU actors an impetus to discuss their respective approaches, to build new institutions, and, eventually, to develop common policies. An internal–external dynamic has therefore been apparent since the dawn of EU policy.

What does this particular dynamic entail? First and foremost it involves different EU-level actors (chiefly the Commission and the EU Council Presidency) working alongside the member states in international-level discussions. However, in practice, the point at which member state control ends and EU control begins varies across issue areas, engendering highly complex debates about who exactly should take the negotiating lead. In the 1970s and 1980s, 'laggard' states prevented the EU from developing a more progressive collective position at the international level in emerging global issue areas such as stratospheric ozone depletion (Sbragia, 2005). In the 1990s, changing internal political and legal conditions facilitated quicker internal agreement, allowing the EU to adopt a more ambitious international position on global climate change, biodiversity protection, and sustainable development (Jordan et al., 2010). The EU has since increasingly operated as a 'soft power' actor by promoting its environmental norms to third countries through its trade relations and development assistance (Fritsch et al., 2017). Environmental policy has therefore assumed a greater role in the development of a broader EU foreign policy (see Chapters 17 and 19), despite continuing internal disagreements between the Commission and the Council over who should 'speak for Europe'.

The EU's position as the self-styled global environmental 'leader' (see Zito, 2005) was, however, severely dented at the chaotic Copenhagen Conference of the United Nations Framework Convention on Climate Change (UNFCCC) in 2009, when EU negotiators openly disagreed with one another. The EU eventually found itself side-lined by the USA and China, and forced to accept a weakened deal on reducing global greenhouse gas emissions. Since the UNFCCC Paris Summit in 2015, the EU has resumed its climate leadership by building alliances with developing states, upgrading its internal coordination systems and adopting more ambitious policy goals.

This takes us to the second dimension of internationalization: the drive to give the EU an external environmental face has, in turn, boomeranged back and affected internal EU policies via a process that is analogous to Europeanization. For example, the EU developed internal policies to control chemicals (such as chlorofluorocarbons, or CFCs) that deplete the ozone layer—a policy area originally formalized and transformed by two important UN agreements brokered in Vienna (1985) and Montreal (1987). As discussed in Section 24.3.4, 'Policy dynamics in practice', the EU's participation in the UNFCCC Kyoto Protocol negotiations (1997) were subsequently to influence European and, in turn, national-level climate policy (Jordan et al., 2010). In recent years, international climate commitments entered into in 2015 at New York (the 17 UN Sustainable Development Goals) and Paris (via the UNFCCC) have started to similarly rebound back into established areas of internal EU policy-making, as witnessed by the discussions about how far to align the Common Agricultural Policy with the EGD (which aims to deliver on the Paris Agreement and the SDGs).

24.3.3 Policy integration

Environmental policy integration is a long-standing goal of EU policy (see Box 24.2), linked to the achievement of sustainable development. In practice, integration means ensuring that economically powerful sectors, such as transport, agriculture, and energy, routinely build an environmental dimension into their policy design activities. In the past, DG Environment approached integration from a somewhat weaker and more defensive position—that is, by issuing regulations to compel these non-environmental sectors to take environmental issues into account. The obvious benefit of this rather segmented approach was that a large amount of ambitious environmental legislation could be adopted relatively quickly. The drawback was that much of it was either watered down in the Council or systematically ignored by the sectors and/or reluctant states during the implementation stage.

In the 1990s, the environmental sector moved towards a more systematic form of integration via the Fifth and Sixth Environmental Action Programmes (EAPs), the post-1998 Cardiff Process of integrating environmental considerations into all policy sectors (Jordan and Schout, 2006), and the 2001 Sustainable Development Strategy. Moving out of the environmental 'policy ghetto' (Sbragia, 1993: 340) was always going to be fraught with difficulty, given the inherently expansive nature of environmental issues. But it seemed to offer the tantalizing prospect that the sectors might eventually bear more responsibility for adopting strong and implementable environmental policies. At the time, some environmentalists wondered whether this approach could even, if pushed to its logical end point, make environmental policy-makers redundant. Other commentators, such as Liberatore (1993: 295), however, warned of 'policy dilution', under which sectors adopted and implemented new environmental measures but in a greatly 'diluted and piecemeal' form. Section 24.3.4 examines the accuracy of these predictions.

24.3.4 Policy dynamics in practice

Since 2000, the interplay between these three dynamics moved centre-stage, shaping the EU's response to many new issues including climate change and energy insecurity. Today, these two are the most dynamic and high-profile foci not only of environmental policy, but also of cross-sectoral integration generally (Jordan et al., 2010). In a bid to achieve international leadership at the 1997 UN Kyoto Conference on climate change ('internationalization'), the EU consequently pledged the most far-reaching policy targets of any party (an 8 per cent reduction from 1990 levels by 2008–12). The progressive and proactive stance adopted by the EU resulted from simultaneous pushing by greener member states and the Commission. However, the EU struggled to implement this commitment within its borders ('Europeanization'), while engaged in negotiating a 'post-Kyoto' agreement ('internationalization') in the run-up to the 2015 Paris climate summit. Given that all sectors of the EU generate greenhouse gas emissions (and hence need to mitigate them) and/or stand to be affected by rising temperatures, it is apparent that achieving net zero emissions by 2050 will require unprecedented levels of cross-sectoral policy coordination ('policy integration'). In this respect, all three perspectives shed light on past dynamics, but also hint at significant challenges to the sector's future development.

KEY POINTS

- EU environmental policy now exhibits several features that do not conform to a single analytical perspective. More governance-centred approaches reveal the salience of three interacting dynamics: Europeanization; internationalization; and policy integration.

- Member states have been Europeanized by the EU in a non-uniform manner. However, Brexit will provide a very stern test of the EU's ability to cope with de-Europeanization.

- The EU has shaped, and in turn been shaped by, international-level environmental politics via a process known as 'internationalization'.

- The integration of the environment into sectoral policies has become a key EU objective, but its implementation remains patchy.

- One high-profile area in which these three interacting dynamics are now especially prominent is climate change.

24.4 Policy challenges: new and continuing

In spite of the undoubted achievements of EU policy, new and important challenges repeatedly emerge—namely improving integration, strengthening policy implementation, coping with **enlargement**

and **Brexit**, and expanding the toolbox of policy instruments.

24.4.1 Policy integration: consolidation or dilution?

In the late 1990s, environmental policy integration leading to more sustainable forms of development was the 'big idea' in the environmental sector. Various strategic processes were initiated (see Section 24.3.3, 'Policy integration'), but the results thus far have proven rather mixed. The institutional and cognitive barriers to better coordination in the EU multilevel system are daunting (Jordan and Schout, 2006). So it is hardly surprising to discover that non-environmental sectors did not willingly accept responsibility for 'greening' their activities. On the contrary, they used some of the new integrating systems to 'reverse integrate' economic and social factors into environmental policy-making, as predicted by Liberatore (1993). However, the worsening economic climate in the 2000s and growing fears that Europe was falling behind emerging economic powers in Asia was what really blunted the Commission's enthusiasm for integration. The Barroso I Commission (2005–09) pointedly identified the delivery of the **Lisbon Agenda** of more 'jobs and growth' as its overriding strategic priority. The Cardiff Process of environmental policy integration was disbanded, the thematic strategies envisaged in the Sixth Environmental Action Programme (EAP) were repeatedly delayed, and the 2001 Sustainable Development Strategy eviscerated of binding targets and new implementing structures.

Under the Barroso II Commission (2009–14), environmental policy adopted an even more 'back to basics' approach. Integration remained a rhetorical objective, but this time it was organized around, and implemented through, binding climate change targets on emissions and the increased use of renewable energy. In other words, it corresponds to the more tightly framed aim of achieving greater *climate* (not environmental) policy integration (Dupont, 2016).

In the post-2008 'age of austerity', the EU's commitment to these legal commitments appeared rather more uncertain. The Juncker Commission's (2014–19) decision to merge the Environment and Fisheries portfolios and the Climate Action and Energy portfolios reawakened long-standing concerns that integration could lead to policy dilution. Under Juncker, the EU struggled to agree a new long-term mitigation target (eventually, 40 per cent by 2030) and sharply reduced the adoption of new environmental policies (Kassim et al., 2017). If EU environmental policy hit a plateau under Juncker, in the early days of the von der Leyen Commission it shot back up the political agenda, propelled by the findings of the European Environment Agency's State of the European Environment 2020 report (European Environment Agency, 2019) which highlighted the need for rapid and systemic changes in order to deliver sustainability. Von der Leyen set out her EGD package shortly after taking office, subsequently reinforced by the publication of a proposal for a brand new (eighth) EAP. Whether the EGD will deliver on this ambitious agenda is still uncertain. Internally, barriers to environmental policy integration remain, and the reform of the Common Agricultural Policy has been decried as being at odds with the EGD. Externally the EU, along with the rest of the world, had to grapple with the COVID-19 pandemic, which disrupted normal policy-making and raised new questions about how to 'build back' better and greener (Dupont et al., 2020).

24.4.2 Turning policy process into environmental outcomes

Agreeing environmental policies is one thing, but implementing them is an entirely different challenge. Policy implementation was effectively a 'non-issue' until the Parliament politicized it in the 1980s after the Seveso industrial accident (see Box 24.5). Poor implementation is endemic across many EU policy areas. But in contrast to the competition and fisheries sectors, DG Environment lacks inspection powers, being reliant on other actors (for example, interest groups and EU citizens) to bring cases of non-compliance to its attention.

The exact size of the implementation 'gap' remains a matter of intense academic and policy debate (Zhelyazkova and Thomann, 2021). Some of the earliest and most analytically novel work on implementation was done in the environmental sector but it tended to focus on specific directives (Treib, 2014) and contributed to a common assumption that implementation was mostly a 'Southern problem' (Börzel, 2003). More recent work has employed larger databases to compare many sectors and explored a number of sub-stages of the implementation process, such as legal **transposition** and enforcement. The finding that *all* states experience implementation problems at some point and in relation to certain (sub)types of policies has helped to undermine the view that implementation followed a binary, North vs South pattern (see Figure 24.1).

The responses to inadequate implementation have tended to follow two main approaches (Tallberg, 2002). One approach focuses on increasing national administrative capacities to implement EU law. The other follows a more coercive mentality whereby states that fail to comply are subjected to financial penalties and reputational damage ('naming and shaming'). Since the early 1990s the EU has followed a mixture of both approaches. A good example of the former is the IMPEL (European Union Network for the Implementation and Enforcement of Environmental Law) network of national regulators. Started in 1992, it shares good practices among officials. The

 BOX 24.5   CASE STUDY: THE SEVESO ACCIDENT

Poor implementation became a live political issue in the environmental sector following a serious industrial accident in Seveso, Italy in 1976. An explosion at a factory, in which clouds of highly toxic dioxin gas contaminated the surrounding area, necessitated a major clean-up operation. Drums of dioxin waste recovered from the site should have been incinerated under existing EU legislation, but instead were stored on site until public pressure finally forced the company to deal with them. In 1982, en route to their incineration, the drums disappeared. The subsequent political uproar and public concern sparked a hunt for the waste, which was eventually found abandoned in a disused abattoir in Northern France. Unhappy over the generally lax state of waste policy implementation, the European Parliament heavily censured the Commission. New legal measures on preventing industrial accidents (named the Seveso Directive) and transboundary shipments of waste were subsequently introduced but incredibly, implementation still remains problematic. In 2019, waste was the sub area of environmental protection in which the Commission initiated the most infringement procedures (71 waste cases out of 171 new infringement procedures) (European Commission, 2020d).

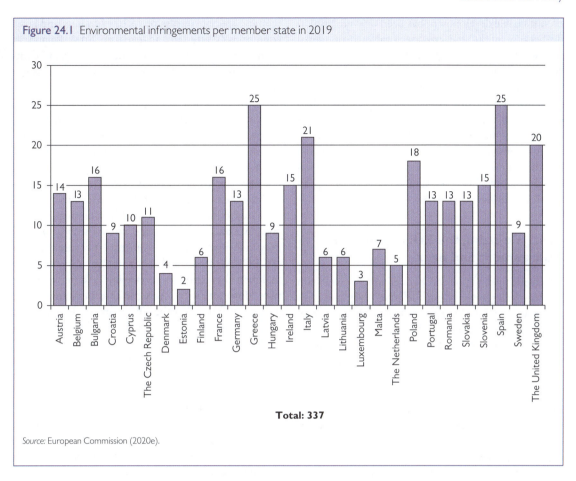

Figure 24.1 Environmental infringements per member state in 2019

Total: 337

Source: European Commission (2020e).

European Commission has also repeatedly reviewed the *acquis* in order to simplify it. In the 1990s this was dubbed 'better lawmaking' but in the 2010s it was recast as 'Fitness Checking' (Gravey and Jordan, 2016). But these attempts at 'better regulation' have nonetheless raised concerns among civil society that the EU is intent on deregulation. For example, when the Commission announced plans to merge two long-standing nature directives on wild birds (1979) and habitats (1991), environmental NGOs mobilized their massive memberships to generate a petition with more than 500,000 signatures on it. Eventually, the Commission published research showing that both laws were fit for purpose but just needed better implementation.

Meanwhile, the EU has also partly followed a more coercive approach. Enforcement capacities have been increased—first, in 1992 when the CJEU was given the power to financially sanction member states and second, in 2009, when the Lisbon Treaty granted it the power to financially sanction a member state that repeatedly flouts a particular law. But the infringement procedure that the Commission follows is not really that coercive. It can take many years, and is dependent both on the European Commission being alerted to an infraction—which is bound to be uneven, as the environmental movement is not as developed across all parts of the EU—and deciding to act—as it has no legal obligation to start infringement proceedings (see Chapter 13).

According to the European Environment Agency, the continuing presence of poor implementation is an important factor affecting levels of environmental quality across Europe (European Environment Agency, 2015). Many pollutants such as acid rain have been reduced, due mainly to effective national application of laws such as the Large Combustion Plant Directive. But data from Eurostat consistently show that progress in relation to the more interconnected challenge of sustainable development has been uneven, primarily because of limited cross-sectoral environmental policy integration (European Environment Agency, 2019). So while many economic indicators show positive trends over time, some environmental criteria have moved in the other direction. Of concern is that, despite a raft of regulatory countermeasures, there are systemic pressures (e.g., urbanization, mass mobility, and consumption) that are accelerating habitat destruction, urban air pollution, and the contamination of water sources by agricultural pollutants (European Environment Agency, 2019).

24.4.3 Re-sizing the EU: coping with enlargement and Brexit

EU environmental policy coped remarkably well with previous enlargements, but the 2004, 2007, and 2013 **accessions** were always expected to weigh more heavily on the policy process in Brussels, as well as in the new entrant states (see Chapter 18). The underlying issues were their size, number (13 in total), and relatively poor economic performance.

Fears that the new entrants would work together to impose a brake on the development of new environmental policies have not been borne out (Burns et al., 2012). Indeed, new member states have overall been found to implement environmental policy more swiftly (Zhelyazkova and Thomann, 2021). However, on specific issues—such as climate change—they have worked together to fight their corner. During the adoption of the climate–energy package in late 2008, Poland led a group of eight Eastern European states that called for concessions to be built into the policy designs. This was the first occasion on which the new entrants had acted as a coherent negotiating bloc in the environmental sector, although existing states were also active in demanding concessions. This episode adds weight to the argument (outlined in Section 24.3, 'Linking different perspectives: the underlying dynamics of environmental policy') that binary analytical categories are no longer significant.

The more immediate practical problem for the Commission, however, was that, having resisted once and succeeded, the newer members would do so again. Repeated attempts by the Commission to boost the low carbon prices within the emissions trading system were blocked by the **Visegrad group** led by Poland (Jordan and Moore, 2020). As well as slowing down the pace of reform, they were also highly effective at

winning special concessions, extra funding, and laxer conditions (Wettestad and Jevnaker, 2016). Poland, in particular, sought to resist the EU's attempts to commit to and try to implement net zero greenhouse gas emissions by 2050.

As the EU still adapts to its 'new' member states, further enlargement remains possible—with five candidate countries at various stages of the long enlargement process. But Brexit showed that enlargement, European integration, and Europeanization are not necessarily one-way processes. During the Brexit withdrawal process a great deal of attention was devoted to exploring how national environmental policy and governance could change within the UK. 'Non regression' provisions were subsequently inserted into the EU–UK Trade and Cooperation Agreement to maintain the existing level-playing field between the two. However, as the Agreement is implemented, it is also likely to affect the EU. In areas where the UK was a leader, such as climate change, Brexit could significantly impact upon the EU's ability to adopt ambitious internal targets and push the international climate regime to a higher level of ambition (Burns et al., 2019). A first test of how the UK and the EU are able to work together will come in the shape of the 2021 UN COP 26 Climate Conference in Glasgow. Finally, beyond government, the importance of UK charities and NGOs in setting up, funding, and supporting the environmental movement in Brussels could leave a gap in environmental advocacy within Brussels (Haigh, 2016).

24.4.4 Enlarging the toolbox

In principle, the available toolbox of environmental policy instruments is relatively full. There has been an active technical debate over the (de)merits of selecting more 'new' instruments from the toolbox since the late 1960s (Jordan et al., 2005). These include voluntaristic instruments, including informal management standards, **voluntary agreements** (among polluters, but also between polluters and the state), and market-based instruments, such as environmental taxes and emissions trading. Nonetheless, despite significant learning and borrowing interactions between states, not many have been selected and deployed: regulation remains the EU's main instrument of choice (Jordan et al., 2005). The lack of a sound legal **treaty base** for fiscal measures has certainly retarded the use of environmental taxes, but so has resistance from large

BOX 24.6   CASE STUDY: EMISSIONS TRADING

In the 1990s, the EU tried—unsuccessfully—to adopt an EU-level carbon energy tax, but was thwarted by a blocking coalition of member states backed by business interests. However, EU influence over climate policy has grown since the late 1990s, resulting in large part from the emergence of the Emissions Trading Scheme (ETS). Based on the trading of greenhouse gas emissions allowances, it is not a fiscal instrument and therefore did not fall foul of the **unanimity** requirement in the Council. Spotting a political opportunity to exploit this legal loophole in the treaties and noting that several member states had already adopted trading schemes, the Commission proposed an EU-wide emissions trading system. When this proposal was debated, the UK and Germany strongly endorsed a voluntary approach, whereas most other member states accepted the Commission's plan for a mandatory scheme (van Asselt, 2010). After concessions were made to the UK and Germany, an emissions trading directive was adopted with amazing speed, quickly becoming the keystone of the EU's climate policy. But while a globally significant climate policy innovation, the ETS has been beset with problems. After a bright start when allowance prices rose, repeated over-allocation of allowances caused trading prices to slump, prompting political demands for the Commission to overhaul and possibly even scrap the scheme. However, the system has arguably generated powerful political supporters in the form of the large energy suppliers and thus has remained immune from dismantling (Jordan and Moore, 2020). In fact, the system has been identified as a new source of revenue to allow the EU to pay back some of the costs of dealing with COVID-19. Nevertheless, it has proven immensely difficult to secure agreement amongst the various participants on how to reform the ETS (Wettestad and Jevnaker, 2016). When relatively incremental reforms were eventually implemented, they slowly raised allowance prices but only to around the same level as they had originally been in 2005/6 (Jordan and Moore, 2020). Recent commitments in the EGD to net zero by 2050 have seen prices rise further.

polluters. Meanwhile, voluntary agreements have been trialled, but not extensively employed. However, an increasing trend has been to bundle multiple instrument types together within single policy 'packages' such as the EU Strategy for Plastics in the Circular Economy 2018.

In relation to climate change, the international and scientific pressure to reduce emissions has encouraged the EU to dip deeper into its environmental toolbox, but with rather mixed success. The most prominent example of a voluntary agreement at EU level aimed to reduce CO_2 emissions from new cars, but after failing to meet expectations has now been replaced by a (2010) regulation (Jordan and Matt, 2014). In contrast, the EU has managed to pioneer an entirely new kind of instrument—emissions trading (see Box 24.6)—but it has been beset with problems. Finally, the Commission has pledged to explore the feasibility of a carbon border adjustment tax that protects EU businesses from unfair competition.

KEY POINTS

- The addition of new **competences** in the environmental sector has become harder to sustain, primarily owing to fears over international competitiveness.

- Recent enlargement of the EU has presented new problems for environmental policy-making, with some accession states in Eastern Europe prioritizing economic development over environmental protection.

- The poor implementation of environmental policies is likely to become an increasingly significant challenge in an expanding EU.

- EU policy is likely to remain heavily reliant on regulation despite repeated rhetorical commitments to employ 'new' instruments and being host to the world's largest supranational emissions trading scheme.

24.5 Conclusion

An active EU role in areas such as the environment is entirely unsurprising. Because the EU is comprised of very affluent states, it was obvious that it would eventually be drawn into ensuring differing national standards did not disrupt free trade. Where problems spanned borders or involved a strong trade dimension, the 'value added' of EU involvement seemed self-evident. Yet many issues now governed by the EU do not exhibit these characteristics: zoos, bathing and drinking water quality, waste water treatment, birds, habitats, and renewable energy supplies, to name just a few. Nor does a functional–economic rationale completely explain why the EU possesses such stringent and wide-ranging environmental powers, particularly when compared to other multilevel systems such as the USA.

Putting aside these legal and administrative constraints, the underlying reason for this rapid transformation is probably political: once the basic idea had been accepted that the environment should be protected 'for its own sake, it was but a relatively short step to the regulation' of these and other apparently 'local' issues (Sbragia, 1996: 253). The absence of a fixed constitutional blueprint and relatively weak policy coordination structures, in addition to strong support from environmental interest groups and the public, allowed (and perhaps even tacitly encouraged) DG Environment to behave opportunistically.

The focus of EU environmental policy has significantly shifted over time, from remedying problems to 'designing them out' of sectoral policies in accordance with the **sustainability** and environmental integration principles. But as the policy's focus has become more diffuse, effectively targeting the whole of society rather than single factories and farms, opportunities have grown for the sectors to 'reverse integrate'

their concerns into environmental policy. Thinking about EU policy in terms of the intersecting processes of Europeanization, internationalization, and integration helps to explain its current characteristics, while also pointing to several future challenges.

The 2000s witnessed a shift 'back to basics' centring on the production of new regulations that address climate change and energy security concerns. Environmental policy integration and sustainable development have been sidelined as national governments struggled to save both their own economies and the euro area. But the environmental *acquis communautaire* has endured, with limited evidence (at least thus far) of significant dismantling (Gravey and Jordan, 2016). Indeed, the late 2010s arguably marked the beginning of a new area of policy expansion, through the adoption of ambitious packages covering the Circular Economy, Plastic Pollution, and the European Green Deal.

To conclude, the political embedding of environmental policy and its continued popularity among ordinary citizens means that it should be considered one of the EU's greatest 'success stories'. However, important challenges remain, not least that of rapidly scaling up policy to deliver net zero emissions by 2050 and addressing the root causes of unsustainable development (European Environment Agency, 2019). EU environmental policy has come a very long way in a relatively short space of time but it still remains a 'work in progress'.

? QUESTIONS

1. Why did the EU first become involved in environmental policy-making in the late 1960s and what kinds of obstacles stood in its way in the early years?

2. What roles do the Council, the Commission, and the European Parliament play in environmental policy-making at EU level, and how have these changed over time?

3. In what ways does EU environmental policy interact with and affect national policies?

4. How 'effective' has EU environmental policy been in the context of systemic pressures such as urbanization, globalization, and rising consumption?

5. How might Brexit affect the main dynamics of environmental policy in the EU and within the UK?

6. Why is the implementation of EU policy such an important, continuing challenge?

7. What challenges are EU environmental policy-makers likely to face in the future?

8. In what ways does EU environmental policy interact with and affect international policies?

GUIDE TO FURTHER READING

Haigh, N. (2015) *EU Environmental Policy: Its Journey to Centre Stage* (London: Routledge). A practitioner's perspective on the development of EU policy since the 1970s.

Jordan, A. and Gravey, V. (eds) (2021) *Environmental Policy in the European Union*, 4th edn (London: Routledge). A textbook summarizing the main actors, institutions, and processes of environmental policy-making.

Knill, C. and Liefferink, D. (2007) *Environmental Politics in the European Union* (Manchester: Manchester University Press). A concise analysis of the evolution of EU environmental politics.

Weale, A., Pridham, G., Cini, M., Konstadakopulos, D., Porter, M., and Flynn, B. (2000) *Environmental Governance in Europe* (Oxford: Oxford University Press). A detailed empirical analysis of how and why the EU created such a complex and multilevel system of environmental governance.

Zito, A., Burns, C., and Lenschow, A. (eds) (2020) *The Future of European Environmental Politics and Policy* (London: Routledge). An expert analysis of the challenges facing EU policy as it reaches maturity. It is also available as a special issue of the journal of *Environmental Politics* (2019, 28(2)).

 Access the online resources to take your learning and understanding further, including extra multiple-choice questions with instant feedback, web links, answer guidance to end-of-chapter questions, and updates on new developments in EU politics.

www.oup.com/he/cini-borragan7e

PART 5

Issues and Debates

25

The Euro Crisis and European Integration

Dermot Hodson and Uwe Puetter

Chapter Contents

Reader's Guide

This chapter discusses the European Union's (EU) response to the euro crisis that emerged in late 2009, two years after the global financial crisis struck. It identifies the challenges this crisis has posed to the existing institutional set-up of **economic and monetary union (EMU)** and shows that it had a lasting impact on discussions over the EU's future well beyond its most dramatic moments. A timeline of the euro crisis is provided and the main changes to the institutional framework of European economic **governance** at the time of writing are reviewed. The chapter considers whether the crisis was caused by a deficit of centralized decision-making and whether it has served, in turn, as a catalyst for deeper economic and political integration in the euro area and the Union more generally. The consequences of the crisis for the EU's legitimacy are also explored from competing theoretical perspectives.

25.1 Introduction

Looking back on the history of European integration, it is difficult to remember a time when the EU or its predecessors were not facing a crisis of one sort or another. The 1950s were marred by the political fallout from the failure of the **European Defence Community** Treaty, just as the **'empty chair' crisis** came to dominate the 1960s (see Chapter 2). The 1970s saw initial plans for economic and monetary union (EMU) abandoned following the collapse of the **Bretton Woods** system and the first oil shock. The side-effects of this economic turmoil lingered on in several member states in the 1980s, with the 1990s witnessing exchange rate crises, as well as a crisis of **legitimacy** for European integration after Denmark's 'no' vote against the **Maastricht Treaty**. Concerns over the EU's legitimacy merely intensified in the 2000s, with plans for a **Constitutional Treaty** rejected by voters in France and the Netherlands, and the **Lisbon Treaty** passed only after a second referendum in Ireland (see Chapters 3, 9, and 15).

In spite of these successive crises, European integration has stumbled onwards. The EU of the Lisbon Treaty is an altogether different animal than the **European Economic Community** (EEC) of the Rome Treaty. Indeed, major advances in European integration have often followed periods of profound crisis. The **Single Market** programme came after the economic malaise of the 1970s and early 1980s and progress towards EMU in the 1990s intensified after a series of crises in the functioning of the **European Monetary System** (EMS). Some politicians have even sought to portray crises as the principal opportunity for further cooperation between member states. **Jean Monnet** memorably wrote that 'Europe will be forged in crises, and will be the sum of the solutions adopted for those crises' (Monnet, 1976: 488).

Scholars are more circumspect on the causal relationship between crises and European integration. Lindberg and Scheingold (1970)—two pioneers of the neo-functionalist school of European integration—saw crises as drivers of integration, but only under certain conditions. Large crises may be more conducive to integration than small ones, they conjectured, because the latter are more likely to disrupt some rather than all of the Community's decision-making structures (Lindberg and Scheingold, 1970: 217). Crises can also blunt opportunities for supranational institutions to show leadership, they suggest, because of the tendency of national leaders to close ranks during periods of economic and political turmoil. Supranationalism, which emerged in the 1990s as the intellectual successor to neo-functionalism (cf. Fligstein and McNichol, 1998), even views crises as symptoms of how integration has not gone far enough. Mattli and Stone Sweet (2012), for example, see the euro crisis as 'revealing the striking absence of what Europe needs most: strong political leadership capable of forging a more federal EU' (Mattli and Stone Sweet, 2012: 14).

The euro crisis, which emerged in late 2009, was arguably the worst economic calamity to befall the EU with the exception of the economic and financial consequences of the more recent COVID-19 pandemic (see Chapter 28). Following two years of chaos on international financial markets after the collapse of the US **subprime mortgage** market, the member states that share the single currency found themselves facing deep recessions and burgeoning budget deficits. No euro area member was immune from these developments, but Greece, Ireland, Portugal, Spain, and Cyprus proved particularly vulnerable. That this crisis served as a trigger for institutional change in the EU in an attempt to save the euro is also self-evident. The heads of state and government have never met so frequently as during the crisis, with summits taking place on average every two months, and finance ministers meeting often more than once per month. In addition to a far-reaching reform of the **Stability and Growth Pact** (SGP) and other elements of euro area governance, EU leaders pledged up to €2 trillion to revive European banks and around €1 trillion to contain the **fiscal crisis** in Cyprus, Greece, Ireland, Portugal, Spain, and other euro area members. Financial support was not offered lightly to these member states who had little choice but to accept swingeing budgetary cuts and emergency revenue-raising measures, as well as unprecedented surveillance of their economic policies by the EU and the **International Monetary Fund** (IMF).

The euro crisis also triggered changes to the Lisbon Treaty, which now contains a legal basis for a permanent euro area assistance fund, the **European Stability Mechanism** (ESM). The 'Fiscal Compact', which provided for closer economic policy coordination and a binding commitment to **fiscal discipline** in national law, was concluded in the form of an **intergovernmental treaty** because of the refusal of the United Kingdom (UK) to agree to these measures in December 2011. The EU has also agreed to a **Banking Union**, which includes a single supervisory regime and a single resolution mechanism for struggling financial institutions. A euro area-wide deposit insurance scheme to protect savers is envisaged too but it remains to be implemented as of early 2021. Member states finally agreed in June 2019 on the creation of a so-called euro area budget instrument, but it fell short of initial plans by French president Emmanuel Macron for a stabilization instrument that could help member states to adjust to economic shocks.

How much the euro crisis has changed EU integration was forcefully felt when the EU was hit by

COVID-19 in 2020. The pandemic caused the economic and financial shock policy-makers had sought to hedge against unsuccessfully in their earlier crisis-led reforms. COVID-19 was clearly a different sort of crisis, but the speed with which the European Central Bank (ECB) engaged in large-scale bond purchases and with which member states in the European Council agreed to an unprecedent stabilization fund, referred to as Next Generation EU, showed how keen policy-makers were to learn from the euro crisis and to avoid its recurrence.

This chapter explores how the EU has responded to the euro crisis and how the crisis has shaped EMU and European integration. We argue that the crisis has served as a spur for integration, but it has done so in ways that rest uneasily with existing theoretical approaches to the delegation of sovereignty in the EU. Whereas integration scholars have traditionally thought of integration in terms of the empowerment of the Community institutions, it is the heads of state or government and *de novo* institutions—that is, bespoke bodies that operate at one remove from the Commission and the Court of Justice—that are the real institutional winners from this crisis. This **new intergovernmentalism** (Bickerton et al., 2015a, 2015b; see Chapter 5) did not begin with the euro area crisis but rather characterizes European integration since the Maastricht Treaty was signed in 1992. Yet, new intergovernmentalism's grip on the EU has been reinforced as a result of the crisis because of the determination of member states to press ahead with collective solutions to shared policy problems but without being seen to cede new powers to old Community institutions along traditional lines. The chapter begins by discussing why the euro crisis arose and how it unfolded, followed by a discussion of its impact on EU institutions. The penultimate section explores competing perspectives on what the crisis means for the EU's legitimacy and, finally, the chapter concludes by highlighting its main findings.

25.2 From global financial crisis to euro crisis

The global financial crisis, by some reckonings, struck the EU on 9 August 2007. The first sign of trouble was a press release from French financial institution BNP Paribas, which suspended trading on three investment funds as a result of difficulties in the US subprime mortgage market. Trouble had been brewing in this market for months, with the second biggest provider of subprime mortgages in the USA (that is, home loans offered to individuals with poor credit ratings) filing for bankruptcy in February 2007. Such difficulties were related, in turn, to a sharp slowdown in the US housing market in 2006, leaving many subprime mortgage holders unable to make their loan repayments. This turmoil soon spread to the country's financial sector at large, with the US investment bank Bear Stearns announcing large subprime-related losses in July 2007. Within weeks of BNP Paribas's press release, it was clear that several European banks were badly exposed to the subprime crisis. In Germany, in August 2007, Landesbank Sachsen was hastily bought by Landesbank Baden-Württemberg after an Irish-based subsidiary of the former had incurred large subprime-related losses. In the UK, Northern Rock fell victim to the first **run on a bank** in Britain for 150 years after struggling to meet its own borrowing needs in increasingly nervous financial markets.

In March 2008, the US **Federal Reserve** negotiated the sale of Bear Stearns to another US investment bank, JP Morgan, after the former had incurred in excess of US$3 billion in subprime-related losses. No such solution could be found for Lehman Brothers, another troubled US investment bank, forcing this financial institution into bankruptcy in September 2008. The result of this decision was pandemonium in international markets, as speculation mounted about which large financial institutions would be next to fail. EU member states' initial response to this escalation of the global financial crisis was ineffective and uncoordinated (see Box 25.1). A case in point was Ireland's unexpected decision in September 2008 to guarantee Irish banks. This move posed problems for the UK financial system, as British savers switched to Irish bank accounts on the understanding that their savings would be safer. Fearful of such 'beggar thy neighbour' policies, several EU member states moved quickly to guarantee bank deposits, ignoring calls for a more coordinated approach. The Irish guarantee had fateful consequences and brought the country from a position of budget balance and low government debt after two decades of impressive economic growth to the brink of sovereign default in a matter of months. A centralized system of EU bank deposit insurance and a common system for dealing with troubled financial institutions would have helped to manage the crisis better and the realization of this fact was a key driver behind the later plans for an EU Banking Union.

The euro area entered a recession—a prolonged period of falling real **gross domestic product (GDP)**—in the first quarter of 2008 due to a dramatic downturn in global trade and a credit crunch at home, as euro area banks grew less willing and able to lend to consumers and businesses. In an attempt to counteract these developments, EU leaders agreed in December 2008 on a **fiscal stimulus package** under which national governments committed themselves to tax cuts and expenditure increases valued at 1.5 per cent of GDP. This stimulus was relatively small compared to similar efforts in the USA and Japan, for example, with some commentators suggesting that EMU paid a price for not having a common budget instrument (Henning and Kessler, 2012). The macroeconomic effects of fiscal federations are a matter of debate, however. On the one hand, such an instrument would have encouraged growth, especially in member states

---

⬛ BOX 25.1   BACKGROUND: THE GLOBAL FINANCIAL AND EURO CRISES

The euro crisis followed the global financial crisis, but the relationship between the two is complex. Economists are divided as to the precise causes of this global crisis, but most emphasize excessive risk-taking in financial markets in the early 2000s (see Financial Services Authority, 2009). Symptomatic of such risk-taking is the increasing importance of **securitization** since the mid-1980s. 'Securitization' refers here to a financial practice that allows banks to sell on the risks associated with loans to other financial institutions. Initially, it was hoped that securitization would diversify risk should borrowers fail to meet repayments on these loans. In the event, it served only to amplify risk by imposing worldwide losses when US house prices started to fall in 2006. Globalization was the key driver of such financial innovation. In this regard, the EU's efforts to create a single financial market under the Financial Services Action Plan launched in 1999 arguably left member states more rather than less vulnerable to the events of 2007–08. The Capital Requirements Directives adopted in 2006, for example, failed to prevent some financial institutions in the EU from being woefully undercapitalized once the global financial crisis struck.

Supervisory failures were a general feature of the global financial crisis rather than one that was specific to the euro area, as the failure of authorities in the UK and the USA to prevent financial institutions from taking excessive risks showed. Neither of the latter two countries had ready-made instruments to help distressed financial institutions once the crisis struck. The UK lacked a permanent resolution mechanism for taking control of insolvent banks until 2009.

Many economists also see a link between the global financial crisis and the problem of **global imbalances** (Obstfeld and Rogoff, 2009). This problem refers to the accumulation of large **current account surpluses** in Asia and in oil-exporting countries since the mid-1990s, mirrored by the largest **current account deficit** in the history of the USA. The causes of these imbalances include high levels of savings in Asian countries, high oil prices, the reluctance of the USA to reduce domestic consumption, and the tendency of some surplus countries to peg their currencies to the dollar. The consequences of global imbalances are more straightforward; the savings glut in Asia and in the oil-exporting countries fuelled low **interest rates** in the USA and, by making it cheaper for homeowners to secure loans, contributed to the US **housing bubble**, which burst to such spectacular effect in 2006.

The euro area had a current account position of 'close to balance' or 'in surplus' during the first decade of the single currency and so was only indirectly exposed to the problem of global imbalances. However, it faced its own problem of internal balances, in part, because the falling interest rates experienced by some member states upon joining the single currency fuelled **credit booms** and housing bubbles. Portugal was an early victim of these imbalances, experiencing an inflationary boom between 1999 and 2002, followed by a prolonged period of low growth. The Portuguese economy's failure to recover from this prior shock is one reason why it proved so vulnerable once the global financial crisis struck. Ireland, Spain, and Greece, on the other hand, saw credit booms and housing bubbles cut short by the crisis—facts that might explain why the **fiscal hangover** from the crisis was so strong in these countries.

Falling interest rates associated with joining a single currency is only one source of **macroeconomic imbalances** in the euro area; another is the failure of these countries to monitor excessive risk-taking by banks through a robust system of financial supervision. Such failures were acute in Ireland, where the Central Bank of Ireland and the Financial Regulator failed to sound the alarm over excessive risk-taking by borrowers and lenders alike. Problematic too was the failure of some peripheral euro area countries to prevent sustained losses of competitiveness during the first decade of EMU. This situation was acute, for example, in Portugal, which saw its unit labour costs relative to other euro area countries continue to rise even after economic conditions slowed in 2002. For some economists, this situation was simply the corollary of developments in Germany, which experienced a sustained fall in relative unit labour costs after 1999 in an effort to restore competitiveness and to shake off a decade of economic underperformance following the country's unification in 1990.

that had limited room for national stimulus packages. On the other hand, foreknowledge of such fiscal help may have created a problem of moral hazard (Persson and Tabellini, 1996) by encouraging even riskier policy choices from member states such as Greece in advance of the global financial crisis.

The coordinated fiscal stimulus package agreed by EU member states in 2008 provided a small but valuable lifeline to consumers and businesses, contributing towards a resumption of real GDP growth in the third quarter of 2009. Although the euro area had by then exited recession, concerns over the state of public finances in the euro area intensified after all members experienced a sharp increase in government borrowing. Those countries that had witnessed an end to prolonged housing booms at the outset of the economic crisis were particularly hard hit, with Spain and Ireland posting budget deficits in excess of 10 per cent of GDP in 2009, as the stamp duties associated with buoyant housing sales evaporated and the effects of a very steep recession hit. The rush to cut expenditure in these and other member states has been criticized in retrospect but national governments faced considerable pressure from financial markets at the time to get government borrowing under control. A common budget instrument would have helped to ease the burden of such austerity in the short run but it might have made matters worse in the long run for the reasons discussed above.

Whereas Ireland and Spain began the euro crisis with levels of government debt below 40 per cent of GDP, government debt was in excess of 100 per cent for Greece. This debt level alone provided grounds for pessimism about the state of Greek public finances once the recession hit. Matters were made considerably worse, however, when new Prime Minister George Papandreou announced in October 2009 that previous administrations had concealed the true scale of government borrowing. As a result of this announcement, Greece's budget deficit was revised from 3.7 per cent of GDP to 12.5 per cent, leading to a sudden loss of faith by financial markets in the country's ability to repay its national debt without outside assistance.

Had Greece not been a member of the euro area, then it would presumably have been offered assistance without delay; an EU–IMF financial support package was, after all, agreed with three non-euro area EU members, Hungary, Latvia, and Romania, in late 2008 and early 2009 with a minimum of fuss. That Greece was a member of the euro area complicated matters both legally and politically. Legally, the EU could not offer the same type of financial assistance to Greece as that to Hungary, Latvia, and Romania, since the latter was carried out under Article 143 TFEU, which applies only to non-euro area members. Politically, member states were divided on the decision to involve the IMF in the affairs of a euro area country. After several long months of procrastination—a period in which Greece's fiscal problems went from bad to worse—the heads of state or government finally agreed, in May 2010, on a €110 billion financial support package. The EU contribution to this package took place outside the Treaty, with individual member states putting up €80 billion in bilateral loans. In exchange for this financial support, Greece signed up to a detailed programme of economic policies designed to get its public finances under control. A **troika** of representatives from the Commission, ECB, and IMF assumed responsibility for negotiating this programme and monitoring its implementation, thus ensuring that key decisions over Greece's economy would, in principle, be jointly decided by the EU and IMF.

Why member states were so slow to provide financial support for Greece is a key question for understanding the politics of the euro crisis. For some economists, politicians simply failed to understand the magnitude of the crisis and the complexity of the policy responses required (De Grauwe, 2013) but this answer is not satisfactory from a political science perspective. The euro crisis was undoubtedly complex but dealing with complexities is part of what politicians do on a daily basis. A more plausible explanation is that the policy options for dealing with the crisis were costly, that such costs were unevenly distributed across the EU and that those member states that were disproportionately exposed to such costs withheld support until they secured concessions. Take EU member states' foot-dragging over involving the IMF in financial support for Greece. Some heads of state or government, including Spanish Prime Minister José Luis Rodríguez Zapatero, were wary of involving the Fund in the affairs of a euro area member, but others, including German Chancellor Angela Merkel, were in favour. These differences had little to do with these individuals' grasp of economics but instead reflected national interests over involving the Fund (see Hodson, 2015). For Zapatero, any deal over Greece would set a precedent in the event of financial support for Spain, which had become a distinct possibility by early 2010. Since Spain has more influence in the EU than it has in the Fund, Zapatero had a strong interest in pushing for an EU solution to the sovereign debt crisis. Angela Merkel had a different set of interests because Germany stood to contribute the most to any financial support package and so had a strong interest in ensuring credible oversight of the conditions attached to any loans. Involving the IMF alongside the EU in support for Greece came to be seen as a more credible course of action because of the Fund's track record in crisis management and perceived independence from EU member states. Given the urgency of the crisis and the impossibility of finding a solution without the EU's largest member states, Merkel eventually convinced other heads of state or government on a joint EU–IMF package for Greece.

By May 2010, financial market concern about the sustainability of public finances in other euro area members had intensified. In response, euro area leaders pledged €60 billion via a newly created European Financial Stabilization Mechanism (EFSM) and €440 billion via a new **European Financial Stability Facility (EFSF)** to provide financial support to any euro area member state that might need it. Ireland became the first member state to access these funds in November 2010. Portugal was next in line, securing €78 billion in loans from the EU and IMF in May 2011. By this point, the nightmare scenario was that the sovereign debt crisis would spread to Spain, Italy, and other large euro area members and so require financial support that went well beyond the resources available via the EFSM, EFSF, and the ESM, a €500 billion permanent crisis resolution mechanism that started operating in September 2012 (see below). Although the combined weight of these funds was €1 trillion, some economists estimated that at least twice this amount might be required if large euro area members got sucked into the crisis (Buiter and Rahbari, 2010). In the end, the euro area rode its luck during this phase of the crisis. Further financial assistance was channelled to Greece via the EFSF and, since 2015, via the ESM. Spain negotiated a loan from the EU of €100 billion, of which only €41.3 billion were disbursed in December 2012 and February 2013, to recapitalize its financial institutions after its housing bubble burst. Italy managed to restore confidence by jettisoning Prime Minister Silvio Berlusconi in November 2011, a politician who had lost the confidence of financial markets, and installing Mario Monti, a former European Commissioner, as head of a caretaker government. Monti's time as Prime Minister was not an unqualified success

but until he left office in April 2013 he took decisions that his predecessor did not and brought Italy back from the brink in the process.

Euro area members can claim credit here for doing just enough before it was too late to survive this stage of the sovereign debt crisis, but it is doubtful that the policies pursued would have been sufficient without the intervention of the ECB. The ECB was a reluctant hero in this instance, having responded with a combination of decisiveness and caution to the unfolding crisis. When it came to providing **liquidity** to European banks in the early stages of the global financial crisis, the ECB generally acted decisively. A case in point was the Bank's decision to allocate €94 billion in overnight loans on the day on which BNP Paribas sounded the alarm over problems in the US subprime market. The ECB was altogether more hesitant about cutting interest rates, waiting until November 2008 to reduce the cost of borrowing in the euro area. The US Federal Reserve, in contrast, had embarked on a similar course of action in September 2008.

Between November 2008 and May 2009, the ECB's **base rate** fell from 3.75 per cent to 1.0 per cent. Fearful that these historically low interest rates would be insufficient to prevent the threat of deflation—sustained falls in the overall level of prices—the Bank launched a new so-called 'covered bond scheme' in June 2009. This scheme committed the Bank to spend €60 billion on covered bonds, that is long-term debt securities issued by private financial institutions and backed by collateral. Investors who purchase covered bonds effectively lend money to the issuing institution and receive a stream of interest payments until the loan is repaid or the bond is sold on to other investors. If things go wrong and the issuer cannot repay, the investor is protected by the collateral pool. With this intervention the ECB sought to drive up lending by financial institutions and drive down long-term interest rates.

Under the **European Securities Markets Programme (SMP)**, which was launched in May 2010, the ECB finally agreed to purchase bonds issued by euro area governments, albeit from investors who purchased government bonds rather than directly from the governments themselves. The scale of bond purchases under the programme was modest, and so it failed to convince financial markets that the ECB was doing all that it could to help member states. In July 2012, ECB President Mario Draghi finally bit the bullet by publicly announcing that he was prepared to do whatever it would take to save the euro. This move had an almost instantaneous impact on financial markets, which came to believe, rightly or wrongly, that the worst of the crisis was over now that the unlimited bond purchases from the ECB was a possibility (see Box 25.2).

In 2013, Cyprus became the fifth and also the last euro area member to receive emergency financial support from the EU. Most importantly, Ireland exited from its EU–IMF programme in December 2013, with Spain and Portugal following suit soon after. It was around the same time that a series of crisis-driven institutional reforms were adopted and implemented.

EMU's tightened framework for economic policy co-ordination became fully operational by mid-2013 and key elements of Banking Union were implemented by the end of 2014 (see Section 25.3, 'EU institutions and the euro crisis' and Box 25.3). Moreover, progress was reported with regard to the overall stability of the financial system. An ECB stress test of the euro area's 130 largest banks in October 2014 suggested that just 13 financial institutions required further re-capitalization. Finally, after recession and a period of only sluggish growth, the euro area rebounded in 2013. Employment levels had reached an all time low by mid-2013 but they too recovered strongly.

BOX 25.2   CASE STUDY: THE ECB AND THE CRISIS

'Within our mandate, the ECB is ready to do whatever it takes to preserve the euro. And believe me, it will be enough' (Draghi, 2012). With these 23 words, delivered in a speech in London in July 2012, ECB President Mario Draghi finally gave financial markets what they had been looking for since the euro crisis began in 2009. Draghi's intervention meant, in effect, that the ECB was ready to play the role of **lender of last resort** vis-à-vis member states to save the single currency. This commitment gave rise to the so-called **Outright Monetary Transactions (OMT)**, under which the ECB agreed, in principle, to the unlimited purchase of government bonds on secondary markets for member states facing fiscal crises. This meant that the bank was ready to buy government bonds from private investors and banks rather than from governments directly, thus providing investors with confidence that these financial instruments remain tradeable at attractive market rates. Draghi's move was a major success in the short run, as evidenced by the falling risk premiums on government debt issued by Spain and Italy in the second half of 2012. Risk premiums capture the difference between interest rates on government bonds issued by member states with higher debt compared to the interest rates on German government bonds, which are treated by investors as a safe and stable benchmark.

All of this raises the question of why the ECB did not act sooner. The answer is institutional. The ECB's reluctance to ride to the rescue reflected internal tensions within the Bank between those who were open to unconventional monetary policies and those who feared that such measures violated the Treaty's prohibition of monetary financing of member states' debt and the Bank's mandate to maintain price stability above all other goals. There was also a concern that bond purchases would take the pressure off member states to reform their economies and so get to the root causes of the euro crisis, such as a lack of competitiveness and weaknesses in financial supervision.

Draghi won out thanks to his skilful chairing of the ECB Governing Council and his position was bolstered by the tacit support of German Chancellor Angela Merkel. Whereas the Bundesbank was critical of ECB bond purchases, the German Chancellor gave her country's central bank limited backing in such debates and so left German monetary authorities politically isolated. Although it took time to work through these internal tensions, the ECB's commitment to unlimited bond purchases was probably the single most important step in deescalating this stage of the crisis. This is a crucial point in the debate about whether the euro crisis was amplified because of a lack of centralized decision-making under EMU because it confirms that the EU had the policy instruments at its disposal to act earlier but chose not to because politics got in the way. EMU is hardly unique here. In the USA, for example, policy-makers faced deep divisions over how to handle the global financial crisis that they overcame only slowly and with varying degrees of success.

Even though the OMT was never deployed, serious economic and legal doubts surrounded it. Regarding economic doubts, the ECB's decision to make access to the OMT conditional on compliance with a strict programme of economic and fiscal adjustment is problematic. This is so because member states most in need of OMT could well struggle to meet such conditions. Regarding legal doubts, the compatibility of the OMT with EU and German law was challenged before Germany's Federal Constitutional Court in June 2013. In its judgment on this case in February 2014, the Court raised concerns that the ECB had exceeded its mandate by launching the OMT and referred this matter to the Court of Justice of the European Union (CJEU) (see Gerner-Beuerle et al., 2014). The CJEU ruled in June 2015 that the ECB's announcement of the OMT programme was in line with EU law and within the Bank's mandate to take measures ensuring price stability in the euro zone.

Allowing the bank to purchase €2.6 trillion in government and private sector bonds (Hammermann et al., 2019), the ECB's asset purchase programme helped to reduce borrowing costs for euro area members with high levels of public debt. Here, again, the ECB's intervention was aimed at driving down long-term interest rates. Without bond purchases on this scale, the demand for, and price of, government bonds would have remained low because of investor uncertainty and with that long-term interest rates would have remained high.

Greece remained a worry despite the ECBs efforts because of its exceptionally high debt levels and slow return to economic growth. The election of a new Greek government led by Syriza, a populist left-wing party, in January 2015, reflected Greek voters' deep frustation over the euro crisis. It also prolonged the euro crisis after relations between Greece and its international creditors broke down and Syriza called an anti-austerity referendum. The results of this referendum were never in doubt but the country remained in need of additional financial assistance, which it duly received from the EU in July 2015 subject to even stricter conditions. Greece exited its final ESM programme in August 2018, a date that is widely seen as marking the end of the euro crisis. And yet, concerns remained over Italy's fragile banking system, high public debt levels, and the commitment of its populist governing parties, the League and the **Five Star Movement**, to remain in the single currency. The collapse of this coalition in August 2019 helped to defuse political tensions over this issue, but Italy's economic problems remained and became a crucial factor when the euro zone and the entire EU intervened to counter the consequences of COVID-19.

KEY POINTS

- Problems in the US subprime mortgage market triggered a banking crisis in the European Union which in turn paved the way for a steep recession, fiscal turmoil, and political instability.

- The EU's stop–start response to the economic crisis included a coordinated rescue of banks, a modest fiscal stimulus package, and, in cooperation with the International Monetary Fund, emergency loans for member states, which have proved politically contentious.

- The ECB's commitment in 2012 to engage in unlimited bond purchases to save the euro area marked a turning point in the crisis, but not the end.

- Some scholars blame the euro crisis on a lack of more centralized policy instruments, but this is open to debate given the downsides associated with some centralized solutions and the instruments already available to euro area authorities.

25.3 EU institutions and the euro crisis

For those who posit a link between crises and European integration, the euro crisis might have provided the perfect opportunity for a further transfer of powers to traditional supranational actors. In spite of claims to the contrary, the evidence thus far suggests that such transfers have been limited (for a contrasting argument, see Chapter 10). This section shows that there has indeed been no shortage of institutional reforms in response to the euro crisis, but that the changes implemented chime with the **new intergovernmentalism** (Bickerton et al., 2015a, 2015b) rather than ringing the bell for a new era of supranationalization. This section provides an overview of these reforms, discussing the changing role of the European Commission in euro area governance since 2009, before exploring the prominent part played by euro area finance ministers in the Eurogroup and by heads of state or government through the **European Council** and the **Euro Summit**.

25.3.1 The role of the Commission

The euro crisis revealed the **importance** of the Commission as a supranational actor in EMU. The EU executive was present in all major debates over how to handle the crisis and it was given a more prominent role in economic and fiscal surveillance through the '**six pack**' and '**two pack**' reforms (see Box 25.3). However, in spite of these changes, there is little evidence to suggest that the Commission played the role of a supranational entrepreneur by pushing through proposals to empower itself at the expense of member states (Hodson, 2013). The muscular role played by the European Council and the Eurogroup in crisis management is part of the explanation because it limited the room for Commission leadership. Yet, the Commission did not openly challenge this division of labour, but worked, often behind the scenes, to support European Council and Eurogroup decision-making and implementation. The Commission's administrative resources were key in monitoring the implementation of the financial assistance packages—next to the ECB and the IMF, the Commission was a member of the so-called **troika missions**. It also provided administrative support to the Greek authorities. In the context of institutional reform, the Commission essentially worked towards implementing political agreements reached within the European Council. Although it formally issued the legislative proposals which provided the basis for the six- and two-pack reforms as well as for the Banking Union (see Box 25.3), the Commission took its political cue here from EU member states.

Some scholars see the Commission's role as having been significantly strengthened as a result of these changes (cf. for example, Majone, 2014; Chapter 10) but this assessment is open to question. A review of the major crisis-related institutional reforms (see Box 25.3) shows few instances in which the Commission gained significant new competences in the light of the crisis. Both the 'six pack' and the 'two pack' have essentially reinforced the role played by the Commission before the crisis: that of delegated monitoring with the power to sound the alarm when national

BOX 25.3   BACKGROUND: 'SIX PACK', 'TWO PACK', FISCAL COMPACT, AND BANKING UNION

Two major institutional reforms were adopted in the form of new secondary legislation introduced under Articles 121, 126, and 136 TFEU. The six pack, which entered into force in November 2011, reforms existing reprimand and surveillance mechanisms so far regulated by the Stability and Growth Pact (SGP) in the following way:

- greater emphasis on total government debt in excess of 60 per cent of GDP in EU fiscal surveillance;

- more frequent and earlier use of pecuniary sanctions under the excessive deficit procedure;

- 'reverse voting' according to which Commission recommendations for corrective action in relation to the SGP will take effect unless they are opposed by a qualified majority of finance ministers;

- the creation of an excessive imbalance procedure; and

- changes to national budgetary rules so as to establish agreed minimum standards for, inter alia, public accounting and statistics, forecasts, and fiscal rules.

The two pack, which took effect in May 2013, tightens budgetary surveillance in a similar vein by requiring euro area member states to submit national draft budgets for the coming calendar year prior to their adoption for review by the Commission and the Eurogroup in October each year. Moreover, the new regulations stipulate specific conditions for the monitoring of countries receiving euro area financial assistance.

The Fiscal Compact, or in full, the Treaty on Stability, Coordination and Governance in the EMU, which entered into force in January 2013, contains both a statement of broader political commitment and novel definitions of the roles of individual institutional actors and the member states. Under this intergovernmental treaty, which was signed by all EU member states except the Czech Republic and the UK, though the Czechs signed later, governments have committed themselves to support the Commission when it issues recommendations and proposes sanctions under the excessive deficit procedure, and pledged to introduce national-level legislation which implements the EU budget rules in domestic constitutional or budgetary legislation. The Court of Justice for the first time is given a potential role in the excessive deficit procedure as member states—not the Commission—can now call on the Court should governments fail to implement recommendations under the excessive deficit procedure. Finally, the lead role of the Euro Summit, which brings together euro area heads of state or government in an informal setting which was not foreseen by the Lisbon Treaty, is codified.

A Banking Union—or, at any rate, key elements of it—were agreed by the European Council in December 2012. The project is based on a comprehensive set of legal provisions which stipulate that the financial industry in the EU is regulated according to a single rulebook and is subject to a Single Supervisory Mechanism. In November 2014 the role of the single supervisor was taken over by the ECB. A Single Resolution Mechanism will apply in case of bank resolution and the build-up of a Single Resolution Fund began in 2016 on the basis of private sector contributions. It is supposed to reach its full size by 2023. A European deposit insurance scheme, which is envisaged to protect individual savers up to €100,000, is yet to be implemented. It is modelled on existing national insurance schemes, while offering protection regardless of potential asymmetric shocks.

governments fail to meet certain criteria, rather than an agent empowered to formulate and implement economic policies on behalf of member states (Hodson, 2009). Both reform packages give the Commission a wider range of criteria to monitor and increase the potential scope and intrusiveness of policy recommendations. Similarly, a new reverse majority rule strengthens the agenda setting powers of the Commission by ensuring that proposals for corrective action against member states that breach the excessive deficit and excessive imbalance procedures will be carried (in some cases) unless a qualified majority of member states disagree.

The real test of the Commission's role in the light of the crisis will occur if and when it finds itself on a collision course with member states over their economic policies. The EU executive can appeal under such circumstances to its independence and technocratic expertise but its perceived problems of legitimacy are also an easy target for national politicians seeking to deflect blame for their policy mistakes to Brussels. Moreover, in the past the Eurogroup did not find it difficult to unite when it came to fending off Commission recommendations which were not seen to be appropriate; a practice which suggests that the new reverse majority rule may be a much less powerful instrument for the Commission than it seems. Because of this tension, the Commission is likely to rely even more on the tacit support of the Eurogroup and, in cases of highly controversial decisions such as financial sanctions, the European Council. The political sensitivity of the euro area economic governance portfolio was also reflected in the allocation of portfolios under the Juncker Commission, which took office in November 2014. Juncker's team included the former French finance minister and Eurogroup member Pierre Moscovici as the Commissioner for Economic and Financial Affairs but also put the portfolio under the close oversight of the Commission President and a dedicated Vice President.

The 'six pack' and 'two pack' reforms show EU member states' willingness to reinforce the Commission's role as an economic watchdog by increasing its bark if not its bite. Other reforms show an even more marked reluctance by national governments to give new competences to the Commission. The most clear-cut case here concerns the EU's role in crisis management. The European Council of December 2010 agreed on a limited revision to Article 136 TFEU to allow for the activation of a stability mechanism

'if indispensable to safeguard the stability of the euro area as a whole'. It was on this legal basis that the ESM was created in July 2011 with the signing of a special intergovernmental treaty setting out the statutes of the ESM and authorizing it to lend up to €500 billion to euro area members. Euro area member states act as shareholders of the fund and have contributed the base capital, which is in turn used to lend capital on international financial markets so as to finance ESM assistance packages. The ESM Board of Governors is composed of the euro area finance ministers and the Eurogroup president as its chair. The ESM is a *de novo* institutional structure, which is based on pooled member state resources rather than on the EU budget. The Commission is given a key role in negotiating and monitoring the conditions attached to ESM loans—alongside the ECB and IMF—but it attends meetings of the ESM Governing Council in an observer capacity only and has no say over ESM resources.

The ECB, rather than the Commission, is arguably the key winner from Banking Union. Under the single supervisory mechanism, the first pillar of Banking Union, which began operating in November 2014, the ECB has assumed overall responsibility for the supervision of over 3,000 banks in the 18 members of the euro area. To this end, a new Supervisory Board has been established within the ECB and given responsibility for, inter alia, assessing the stability of these financial institutions and licensing them. The second pillar of Banking Union is a Single Resolution Mechanism to deal with failing banks. Initially, the Commission proposed in July 2013 that it should have lead responsiblity for deciding whether a failing bank should be resolved and envisaged the creation of a board of representatives of the Commission, the ECB, and national authorities. Cautious though this proposal was in some respects it went too far for the Economic and Financial Affairs (ECOFIN) Council, which decided that decisions on whether to resolve a bank should rest with the ECB and national representatives but not the Commission (see Howarth and Quaglia, 2014).

25.3.2 The Eurogroup

Already prior to the euro crisis, the **Eurogroup** was the lead forum for economic policy coordination and decision-making under EMU. The informal forum comprising euro area finance ministers, the Commissioner for economic and financial affairs, and the

ECB president, which was created by the European Council in December 1997, assumed an important role right from the start of the final phase of EMU, with the **ECOFIN** devoting less and less time to EMU matters (Puetter, 2006). The Eurogroup has been busier than ever in response to the euro crisis. It was the Eurogroup which negotiated the allocation of capital and loan guarantees to the EFSF and now effectively exercises political oversight powers over the ESM. The Eurogroup has also been in charge of implementing and assessing compliance with the economic policy programmes accompanying all financial support packages adopted so far. Euro area finance ministers play the central political role in the newly adopted surveillance, reprimand, and sanctioning mechanisms (see Box 25.3). The intensification of Eurogroup activity has been reflected in the fact that the group, since the beginning of the crisis, has been convened repeatedly more than once per month. Moreover, the Eurogroup's preparatory infrastructure has been expanded in the wake of the crisis. It is led by the Eurogroup Working Group (EWG), a high-level coordination committee of senior finance ministry officials from the member states, the Commission, the ECB, and a full-time president. The EWG itself is now supported by a committee of Brussels-based EWG alternates. Although already an important political body before the crisis, the Eurogroup has gained substantial new responsibilities and has become one of, if not the, most powerful and most frequently convened group of ministers in Brussels. The group and its preparatory infrastructure is at the heart of a dense web of day-to-day coordination activities involving the finance ministries of euro area member states and the Commission's Directorate-General for Economic and Financial Affairs.

25.3.3 European Council leadership

Another major indication of how new intergovernmentalist institutional dynamics were triggered as a result of the euro crisis is the direct and frequent involvement of the European Council in aspects of day-to-day euro area decision-making. Whereas the heads of state and government have already played an increased role in overseeing EMU economic governance and various related coordination instruments such as the **Lisbon Agenda** since the end of the 1990s, the crisis was a catalyst for closer top-level coordination. Never before in the history of EU decision-making

have the heads of state or government met so often as during the euro crisis. While the European Council was convened on average three times a year before the launch of EMU, it now meets at least seven times. Economic governance issues constitute by far the most important agenda item of the forum (Puetter, 2014. 91–7). In 2011, the heads gathered for a total of 11 summit meetings—some of them held for all EU member states, some exclusively for the euro area. The practice of convening additional summit meetings only for euro area heads was first introduced in October 2008 when an emergency summit in Paris discussed the unfolding banking crisis. In October 2011, the euro area heads decided to further institutionalize this meeting format by referring to it as the Euro Summit and charged the Eurogroup to act as its preparatory forum.

These institutional developments were further helped by the entering into force of the Lisbon Treaty, which created the position of a full-time European Council president by the end of 2009. In this capacity the former Belgian Prime Minister Herman Van Rompuy quickly began to call additional meetings of the euro area members of the European Council and to coordinate political agreement among the heads. The reason for the growing involvement of the heads was mainly that many crisis management decisions cut deep into domestic politics and would not have been possible without strong political backing. Often decision-making was tied to the political fate of individual member state governments. Moreover, crisis management involved a number of institutional decisions which had been unprecedented so far and for which the existing legal basis was partially contested, as the example of the first financial support package for Greece in 2010 illustrated. Except for the financial assistance package for Cyprus, the heads insisted on finalizing all financial aid decisions themselves and only left implementation to the Eurogroup. The July 2015 meeting of the Euro Summit was one of the most controversial in the EU's history, as the heads met to agree on a third ESM programme for Greece with even stricter conditions attached in spite of the country's anti-austerity referendum. Yet this agreement held the euro area together against the odds.

The heads of state or government also played a key role in euro crisis reforms. The European Council president chaired the preparatory work of EU finance ministers on institutional reform between May

BOX 25.4   KEY DEBATE: THE EURO CRISIS AND THE EU'S PROBLEMS OF LEGITIMACY

The euro crisis followed a period of comparative economic calm—2008 was the first time since the single currency had been launched that the euro area experienced a recession—but it was just the latest in a series of political shocks to hit the EU over the last two decades. Others terms in this series include Denmark's rejection of the Maastricht Treaty in 1992, the resignation of the Santer Commission in 1999, Ireland's 'no' votes against the Nice Treaty in 2001 and the Lisbon Treaty in 2008, and the abandonment of the European Constitution after failed referendums in France and the Netherlands. Together, these and other events mark the end of what Lindberg and Scheingold (1970) called 'the **permissive consensus**' over European integration. One manifestation of this trend is rising public scepticism about the benefits of EU membership. In 1991, 71 per cent of EU citizens agreed that membership was a good thing. By the time that the global financial crisis struck in 2007, this figure had fallen to 56 per cent, and by the end of 2013, it had reached 50 per cent (Eurobarometer Interactive Search System).

The meaning of the euro crisis for the EU's legitimacy is the subject of an ongoing and lively debate in the academic literature. For Moravcsik (2012), national governments acted with 'remarkable flexibility' to stabilize the single currency even if doubts remain over its long-term viability. Challenging the idea that Germany did too little too late to prevent the crisis from escalating, he praises Angela Merkel's government for showing leadership over the euro crisis and bearing significant costs in dealing with it. In keeping with his liberal intergovernmentalist approach, he sees Germany and other member states as acting not for reasons of ideology or altruism but because the economic costs of seeing the euro dissolve would have been catastrophic. While acknowledging that EMU's problems are far from over, Moravcsik (2012) concludes that 'Europeans should trust in the essentially democratic nature of the EU, which will encourage them to distribute the costs of convergence more fairly within and among countries'.

Scharpf (2011) offers an altogether darker reading of the euro crisis, which he sees as fuelling a 'crisis of democratic legitimacy' in the EU. He reserves harsh criticism for the troika, which he describes as a form of 'economic receivership' that has foisted painful economic policy adjustment on Greece and other member states rather than allowing national politicians and voters to reach a consensus on what had to be done. For Majone (2014), concerns over legitimacy go beyond the terms of emergency financial support to the reforms to euro area governance enacted in the light of the crisis. The crux of his argument is that the crisis has taken the EU yet further away from its roots as a regulatory regime. The new powers of economic surveillance entrusted to the European Commission under the 'six pack' and other reforms, he argues, go well beyond the kinds of functions that are and, more importantly, should be delegated

to non-majoritarian institutions. Majone (2014) points the finger both at the European Commission and at a subset of Germany and other member states, which he sees as being driven by a liberalizing zeal and which insist on reforms as a quid pro quo for providing financial support.

Implicit in the debate between these authors is the age-old question of whether the EU answers to its member states. It does for Moravcsik, who thus sees concerns over the EU's legitimacy as overblown, but does not for Scharpf (2011) and Majone (2014), who thus cry foul over how the euro crisis has been handled. Bickerton et al. (2015a, 2015b) offer a different take on this issue and argue that member states were in the driving seat of the European integration process while questioning the legitimacy of the choices they made. This new intergovernmentalist approach sees the EU's response to the euro crisis as symptomatic of national governments' commitment to cooperative solutions but reluctance to delegate new powers to old supranational institutions along traditional lines. This explains the dominance of the Eurogroup and European Council in dealing with the crisis and member states' preference for empowering *de novo* institutions such as the ESM rather than the Commission. Yet national governments themselves cannot be sure of representing societal interests when acting at the EU-level as their ability and willingness to accommodate and represent these interests has become increasingly contested. The result is a dangerous discord between elite and popular preferences which has taken hold in the EU since the early 1990s, but which has intensified as a result of the euro crisis.

The euro crisis can also be seen as a test case as to whether and to what extent closer euro area integration is compatible with the EU's original pledge to operate a broad socio-economic governance agenda for all its member states. The euro crisis was a test for the integration of economic governance with the EU's social and employment policy coordination portfolios in the sense that the latter dimension was almost absent from crisis management. Attempts by the European Council to reinstate this link through new initiatives in 2012 and 2013 speak to this point but came very late in the crisis management cycle. There is little doubt that the euro crisis has strained relations between the euro area and non-euro member states. This became plain as the European Council started to meet in the configuration of the Euro Summit, but it was also revealed by fundamental opposition from UK Prime Minister David Cameron, who used the prospect of deeper integration among euro area members as a pretext for holding a referendum in 2016 on whether the UK should remain a member of the EU. Moreover, member states which are eager to join the euro area in the future, or are in favour of closer EU-wide socio-economic policy coordination, have criticized crisis management procedures for excluding them from far reaching decisions on institutional reform.

and October 2010—the so-called **Van Rompuy Task Force**. From then on, until December 2012, the European Council and its euro area formation met frequently to decide on all major institutional reforms (see Box 25.3). In each case, the European Council set the political agenda and provided detailed instructions for other institutional actors—notably the Commission, the ECOFIN Council, and the Eurogroup—to work towards the implementation of specific institutional reforms. Legislative proposals were issued and adopted at a high pace and also found approval from the European Parliament (EP). How determined (most) heads of state or government were to press ahead with institutional reforms became clear in December 2011 when the British Prime Minister, David Cameron, refused to support plans for further changes to the Lisbon Treaty to facilitate closer cooperation between the euro area and other willing member states. In response to this impasse, the European Council moved quickly and negotiated the so-called **Fiscal Compact** (see Box 25.3) in the form of an intergovernmental treaty. The fact that this treaty was negotiated outside EU law, but still impinged on the work of EU institutions and their relations with each other and the member states, showed how much the European Council was willing and able to bend existing constitutional principles.

In other words, the episode showed once again how much weight direct agreement between the heads of state and government within the European Council carried within the context of euro crisis management politics. Even though agreement often proved cumbersome, once adopted, European Council decisions had far reaching consequences for how the EU currently operates. It thus can be said that the European Council has become the 'new centre of political gravity' (Puetter, 2014) in euro area economic governance. This institutional development reflects both the deepening and the widening of economic policy coordination as collective EU-level decision-making has become far more important for domestic politics than it ever was. Moreover, both increased Eurogroup and European Council activity showed how much EMU economic governance relies on permanent consensus generation among the EU's most senior decision-makers. The further institutionalization of these bodies as forums for face-to-face policy deliberation which allow policy-makers to collectively react to unforeseen crisis situations and novel policy challenges can be understood as a new

deliberative intergovernmentalism among euro area leaders (Puetter, 2012).

KEY POINTS

- The euro crisis triggered a number of major institutional reforms and EMU economic governance is now wider in scope and cuts deeper into domestic politics than it has ever done before.

- Integration has been deepened but without major new transfers of powers to the supranational level; instead intergovernmental policy coordination has been intensified substantially.

- The European Council and the Euro Summit, assisted by the Eurogroup, have played a lead role in the EU's response to the euro crisis and this role has been further institutionalized by the Fiscal Compact.

- The Commission has been given new responsibilities under reforms agreed in the light of the euro crisis, but the Eurogroup and the European Council remain in the driving seat.

KEY POINTS

- EU scholars are engaged in a debate on what the euro crisis meant for the EU's perceived problems of legitimacy.

- Opinion is divided over whether the EU's response to the euro crisis reflected the collective will of the member states and what this means for legitimacy.

- The crisis was a test of the EU's commitment to economic as well as social integration.

25.4 The euro crisis and the future of the EU

The euro crisis had a profound and lasting impact on European integration. This impact has reached well beyond questions of immediate crisis management such as emergency financial assistance and institutional adjustment. Most importantly, it showed how closely the fate of the Union has become intertwined with that of the single currency and how the fate of the euro rests on the ability of national governments to achieve consensus on difficult and unpopular choices under considerable time pressure. An indicator for this is how citizens think about EU integration.

In 2007, before the global financial crisis was fully felt in the EU, the Eurobarometer recorded that 62 per cent of the citizens of the newly enlarged Union felt very or fairly attached to the EU. During the crisis this support dropped markedly. By 2012, when several financial aid packages had been adopted and the conditionality of the adjustment programmes was felt in the euro area's most affected member states, the Eurobarometer recorded a post-enlargement record low of 45 per cent of citizens who felt attached to the EU. By 2018 levels of positive attachment to the EU had risen to 56 per cent, a level maintained since then. While support in countries like France, Germany, and Spain had come back strongly and was partially even above the 2007 levels, it was just 37 per cent in Greece. Low attachment levels have persisted there since then.

The euro's status as a bellwether for the Union can also be seen in domestic developments in some of the euro area's most important member states. In France, Marine Le Pen saw her electoral prospects increase in advance of the 2017 presidential election as the euro crisis deepened and she campaigned for an 'orderly' exit from the single currency. In Germany, it is no coincidence that Alternative für Deutschland (AfD), with its brand of German euroscepticism, was founded at the height of the euro crisis in 2012. Next to its anti-migration policy stance, opposition to the ESM has been a crucial element in its campaigns.

When COVID-19 hit the EU in the first semester of 2020, policy-makers understood that the pandemic's devastating impact on economic growth and public finances, because of the significant strains placed on healthcare and social security costs, had the potential to reignite the euro crisis. This was nowhere clearer than in Italy, which was hard hit by the pandemic but fearful of its ability to borrow massively on international financial markets for a longer period of time. Determined to avoid another sovereign debt crisis, the ECB launched its Pandemic Emergency Purchase

Programme in March 2020, while a month later the Eurogroup cleared the way for a novel ESM Pandemic Crisis Support instrument with lowered conditionality. Italy's prime minister Giuseppe Conte still strongly opposed using ESM loans, mistrusting possible conditionality and demanded an alternative solution for fighting a public health crisis.

As during the euro crisis, the EU witnessed a new intergovernmentalist scenario. It was for the European Council to resolve the impasse in the context of a four-day meeting in July 2020. The heads reached principled agreement on the rescue fund Next Generation EU, which allowed the Commission to borrow up to €750 billion to help member states with the costs of the crisis. A substantial part of the funding comes in the form of transfers rather than loans; thus constituting an alternative to existing ESM stabilization efforts. Member states' willingness to put the Commission rather than a *de novo* institution in charge of this new instrument marked a departure from euro crisis solutions. The relatively swift consensus on the part of member states constituted another difference. Whether used again in the future or not the new stabilization instrument reflects the euro area's dependency on consensus among member state governments, as highlighted by the new intergovernmentalism. Only the member states, not the Commission, can pave the way for collective borrowing and EU stabilization efforts.

KEY POINTS

- The euro crisis has had an impact on how citizens think about Europe.
- COVID-19 has the potential to reignite the euro crisis.
- The European Council took the lead in seeking to respond to the economic impact of the pandemic.

25.5 Conclusion

In 2008, the euro area marked the tenth anniversary of the EU member states' decision to press ahead with the third and final stage of EMU. These celebrations were low key but infused with a sense of relief that EMU's first decade was not the disaster that some of its critics had predicted. Fireworks of a different sort were to come, however, when the global financial

crisis that had begun the previous year led to a sovereign debt crisis that came close to tearing the single currency asunder. This scenario would have been a major catastrophe for the EU and, indeed, the world economy. The fact that it was avoided was due to good fortune and a set of policy responses that did just enough before it was too late to regain the confidence of financial markets. The euro area members at the epicentre of this crisis—Cyprus, Greece, Ireland, Portugal, and Spain—received emergency financial support from the EU and IMF, but paid a devastating price in view of the austerity measures that they had to endure. This combination of financial support and fiscal austerity allowed these member states to weather the storm—although some would argue that there were better places to take shelter—but in the end it was the ECB's commitment to do whatever it takes to preserve the single currency that prevented the sovereign debt crisis from spreading further in 2012. This commitment was a balm rather than a cure and serious concerns remained over the economic outlook for the euro area several years later.

Opinion is divided on whether a lack of European integration is to blame for the euro crisis and whether deeper integration is likely to be its legacy. The answer to these questions depends, of course, on how integration is defined. Scholars have traditionally equated integration with supranationalization, with some suggesting that a centralization of powers would have helped to mitigate the euro crisis and others seeing centralization to come. This chapter has challenged these views. A more centralized approach to fiscal policy and financial supervision would not have inoculated the euro area against the global financial crisis, it was argued, and may even have made matters worse. The ECB's belated decision to commit to unlimited bond purchases, moreover, relied on the belated use of an existing policy competence rather than the acquisition of a new one. Turning from cause to consequence, this chapter sees the EU as tending not towards a supranational system of policy-making following the euro crisis, but as reinforcing the new intergovernmentalism which prevails within the field of EMU economic governance. This trend can be seen most clearly in member states' reluctance to empower the Commission in the light of the crisis, in their preferences for deliberation through bodies such as the Eurogroup and European Council and delegation to *de novo* bodies such as the ESM, and in the worrying disconnect between politicians and the people as European integration intensifies in unfamiliar ways. The experience of the euro crisis undoubtedly shaped the EU's financial reaction to COVID-19, as can be seen by the speed with which EU institutions and member states acted to avoid another sovereign debt crisis. Yet, with the unprecedented mobilization of stabilization funds, the EU once more may have failed to liberate itself from its own disequilibrium (Hodson and Puetter, 2019). Crisis-hit Italy recorded a record 8 per cent year-on-year drop in attachment to the EU sentiment levels in the autumn 2020 Eurobarometer, leaving a minority of 42 per cent of Italians who feel attached to the EU. Anxiety over whether EU financial assistance would come with more intrusive policy interventions on the part of the EU probably persisted in this country. While the outgoing grand coalition government of Angela Merkel had supported the swift consensus with France's Emmanuel Macron on the COVID-19 recovery fund, Germany's former finance minister, Wolfgang Schäuble, known for his tough stance during the euro crisis, spoke sceptically about the lack of conditionality and control over the spending of EU money in the context of Next Generation EU (Chazan 2021). Policy-makers across the euro zone, including Schäuble, have by now acknowledged in principle that the euro depends on a greater EU-level stabilization capacity. Yet, many national leaders have still not been able to resolve domestic political conflicts about this reform step, which would involve greater financial resources at the EU-level. Thus, it can be concluded that the aftershock of the euro crisis is being felt up until today. This aftershock has become manifest in sustained political conflict about burden-sharing and the location of political authority in the EU.

QUESTIONS

1. What are the key characteristics of the EU's response to the euro crisis?

2. Why and how are the heads of state and government seeking closer control over EU economic governance in view of the euro crisis?

3. Did the Commission acquire new powers as a result of the euro crisis?

4. Can closer integration be achieved through intergovernmental policy coordination within the euro area and, if so, how does it happen?

5. To what extent does the EU develop through crises?

6. Why did the euro crisis affect euro area member states differently?

7. How has the euro crisis affected the relationship between euro area members and other EU member states?

8. How has the EU's response to COVID-19 differed to its handling of the euro crisis?

 GUIDE TO FURTHER READING

Bickerton, C. J., Hodson, D., and Puetter, U. (2015a) 'The new intergovernmentalism: European integration in the post-Maastricht era'. *Journal of Common Market Studies*, 53/4: 703–22. This article identifies six broad hypotheses for understanding European integration in the post-Maastricht era. It is a helpful background reading to the explanation of what impact the euro crisis had on integration as outlined in this chapter.

Hodson, D. (2011) *Governing the Euro Area in Good Times and Bad* (Oxford: Oxford University Press). This book discusses the evolution of euro area governance, from the launch of the single currency in 1999 to the beginning of the sovereign debt crisis in 2010.

Hooghe, L., Laffan, B., and Marks, G. (eds) (2018) 'Special Issue: Theory Meets Crisis' *Journal of European Public Policy* 25/1. This special issue offers competing perspectives on the EU's crises from some of the leading theorists of European politics.

Matthijs, M. and Blyth, M. (eds) (2015) *The Future of the Euro* (Oxford: Oxford University Press). This edited collection contains essays on the euro crisis from leading scholars in the field of international political economy.

Puetter, U. (2012) 'Europe's deliberative intergovernmentalism: the role of the Council and European Council in EU economic governance', *Journal of European Public Policy*, 19/2: 161–78. This article explores intergovernmental responses to the euro crisis and the emerging role of euro area heads of state and government in the governance of EMU.

Schelkle, W. (2017) *The Political Economy of Monetary Solidarity: Understanding the Euro Experiment* (Oxford: Oxford University Press). This important book challenges the idea that economic differences between euro area members is necessarily a problem for the smooth functioning of EMU, viewing the single currency instead as a clever but contested form of risk sharing.

Schmidt, V. (2020) *Europe's crisis of legitimacy: Governing by Rules and Ruling by Numbers in the Eurozone* (Oxford: Oxford University Press). This book offers a state-of-the-art treatment of how the euro crisis and the reforms it inspired added to the EU's legitimacy challenges.

 Access the online resources to take your learning and understanding further, including extra multiple-choice questions with instant feedback, web links, answer guidance to end-of-chapter questions, and updates on new developments in EU politics.

www.oup.com/he/cini-borragan7e

26

The Migration and Refugee Crisis

Andrew Geddes

Chapter Contents

Reader's Guide

This chapter explores the intersection of three key migration and asylum dynamics: the reasons why people migrate internationally to (and from) EU member states; the responses to non-EU migration and asylum that have developed both at member state and EU level; and the political 'framing' of migration as an issue or challenge. We begin by asking why, how, and with what effects migration and asylum became salient political issues after the so-called 'migration crisis' of 2015, but contextualize these more recent developments by showing how responses after 2015 actually emerged from patterns of cooperation established since the 1980s.

26.1 | Introduction

This chapter aims to explain the specific forms that EU actions on migration and asylum have taken and to consider what these forms tell us about EU politics. As will be seen, this is a not a straightforward study of the steady development of a common EU migration and asylum policy. Rather, the picture is less linear, more contingent, and also politically contested. While there are transnational and transboundary concerns, migration and asylum cannot be represented as technical matters alone because these issues resonate at state level where they can be intensely political.

To help understand the development of EU actions on migration and asylum, we begin by thinking about the events of 2015 that were labelled as a 'migration crisis'. While we can look at the events themselves, it is also crucial to think about the ideas that informed EU responses. By doing so, we can see that events after 2015 actually drew from longer-standing patterns of cooperation on migration and the ideas that have informed them that can be traced to the late 1980s. To do this, we examine two sets of proposals from the European Commission that sought to plot a path forward for the EU. The first of these, the European Agenda on Migration (EAM) of May 2015, was not successful. How do we know it was not successful? Because it was followed in September 2020 by a New Pact on Migration and Asylum that sought to make progress in areas where the EAM had been blocked. Having looked at these more recent post-2015 developments, we then extract four key analytical themes and use them to show how they draw quite directly from approaches evident since the 1980s.

Since the late 1980s, EU-level cooperation has been driven by concern in key member states about the potential for large scale and potentially uncontrollable migration. In the 1990s, the focus was on central and eastern Europe, but since at least the 2000s has been particularly focused on migration from the Middle East and Africa. This necessarily connects with a wider set of debates and issues. For example, the effects of military interventions by some European countries have exacerbated the underlying conditions that can cause refugee flows, as well as the broader patterns of economic inequality and unequal development that can also cause people to migrate. Looking more deeply, inescapable legacies of colonization and decolonization continue to shape migration in a number of ways, including the migration networks that continue

to link colonial and once-colonized states, as well as discussion of 'good migration governance' that can be seen as requiring countries in Africa and the Middle East to adapt to the requirements of European countries in relation to border control and security. The wider point is that migration is not something that simply 'happens' to European governments and the EU. The EU and its member states through their actions and inactions are a potential cause of the migration that they then seek to 'manage'.

Organizing the chapter to contextualize current events also shows the ambiguity about the EU's final destination on migration and asylum. It should not be assumed that this is a common migration and asylum policy because the member states themselves are not in agreement about the measures and priorities around which they could converge, their effects on migration as well as their social and political effects in EU member states.

The chapter also considers two key conceptual questions. The first is the balance between what could be called 'liberal' and 'restrictive' approaches to migration and asylum. Liberal in this context means approaches that are more accommodating of the arrival of migrants and of the rights that are extended to migrants. The chapter shows that the EU has tended to focus on restricting rather than facilitating migration. The EU does not do this independently from the member states, of course. Rather, efforts to restrict migration—particularly from the Middle East and Africa—reflect the policy preferences of the member states that retain the upper hand in EU decision-making on migration and asylum. Importantly, the EU Treaty makes it very clear that the numbers of migrants to be admitted is a matter for the member states. Put differently, the EU's main efforts are aimed at stopping those types of migration that the member states have defined as 'unwanted', meaning asylum-seekers and 'irregular' migrants (a term we define in Box 26.1).

The second conceptual issue is the relationship between **intergovernmentalism** and **supranationalism** which poses the question of who is in charge: are **supranational institutions** such as the Commission in the driving seat or do the member states retain control? What we can see both before and after 2015 is a 'transgovernmental' dynamic. This means regular interactions between national level political leaders and officials at EU level where engagement also occurs with EU institutions and important EU agencies such as the European Border and Coast Guard Agency (known as **Frontex**) and the European Asylum Agency. Transgovernmentalism creates habits of working together, but does not necessarily mean a common and shared viewpoint on the issues between the member states.

26.2 Setting the scene

What do we actually mean by migration and asylum? The United Nations (UN) provides a standard definition of international migration as movement from one country to another for a period of more than one year. In addition, temporary migration lasts for periods of less than a year and there is also shorter term mobility such as tourism. A key point is that international migration comes in many forms and the boundaries between different types of migration can become blurred.

Media coverage could give the misleading impression that most people migrating to Europe do so in small boats across the Mediterranean. Most people coming to Europe actually enter via regular channels to work, study, or join with family members (see Box 26.1). As we see, however, the EU response to migration and asylum has been very focused on asylum-seekers, refugees, and 'irregular' migrants.

The EU does not have its own borders because EU borders are in fact the borders of the EU's member states. Nor does the EU have any competence over the numbers of migrants to be admitted to the Union as this is also a matter for the member states to decide. That said, increased powers have been granted to Frontex, the European Border and Coast Guard Agency, to coordinate border controls. In 2021, for the first time, Frontex will have uniformed officials whose numbers are projected to grow to 10,000 by 2027 from the 1,000 in place in 2021. There have, however, been concerns expressed about Frontex involvement in illegal pushbacks, where migrants moving to Europe with a potentially viable claim to seek asylum were being returned to countries such as Libya where their safety and even their lives could be at risk. This is in contravention of international legal standards that prohibit **refoulement**, that is, returning asylum seekers or refugees to a country where they may face persecution.

While territorial borders are important, there are also other borders that are internal to EU member states that play a crucial role in migration and asylum policy. An important role is played by organizational borders, meaning rules governing access to welfare states and labour markets. Taken together, these play a crucial role in mediating the relationship between migrants and the societies to which they move and their 'integration' into these societies. These relations are complex because there are very different ways of organizing welfare states in the EU while labour markets are also very diverse in their form and organization.

 BOX 26.1   KEY DEBATES: MIGRATION FLOWS TO THE EU

To understand more about non-EU migration to the EU we can look more closely at the three million residence permits issued to non-EU citizens by an EU member state in 2019. The reason why these permits were issued shows us the main reasons why people migrate.

- 41 per cent of these permits were issued for employment reasons;
- 27 per cent for family reasons;
- 14 per cent for education;
- 18 per cent for international protection (e.g., refugees).

This demonstrates the main reasons why people migrate: for employment, to join with family, to seek protection, and to study. Each of these categories can be broken down into sub-categories (migration into higher- and lower-skilled employment, for example), but these are the forms of migration that are potentially the subjects for EU migration and asylum policies, although labour and family migration remain largely in the domain of the member states with weaker EU competencies.

Missing from this list is 'irregular' or 'illegal' immigration which occurs when someone either overstays their original permission to reside in an EU member state or when they cross a border without permission to enter an EU member state (overstaying is actually much more common than irregular border crossing). It is very hard to know the number of irregular migrants and estimates are controversial. The Pew Research Institute estimated that there were between 3.9 million and 4.8 million irregular migrants in the EU in 2017, or around 0.5 per cent of the EU's total population.

To these territorial and organizational borders can also be added 'conceptual' borders of belonging and identity. The issue of 'who belongs' and, by extension, who does not run through the politics of migration and asylum and are associated with powerful forms of inclusion and exclusion that can also reinforce racialized distinctions and boundaries within the EU.

KEY POINTS

- International migration comes in many forms.
- Most people who migrate to the EU arrive for work via regular channels.
- EU borders are the borders of EU member states.
- EU borders are territorial, organizational, and conceptual.

26.3 Problematizing the policy approaches

EU member states play a very powerful role in defining the migration issue because it is at their borders (territorial, organizational, and conceptual) that decisions are made about who can enter, for what purpose, and for what duration. The categories and classifications into which migrants are placed are essential components of migration governance. The migration systems of EU member states can look very different from the perspective of a migrant moving into high-skilled and high-paid employment when compared to a person seeking asylum. For migrants who do not have a 'regular' or 'legal' pathway to the EU, then an alternative can be to seek irregular entry.

Type the words 'EU migration crisis' into a search engine and look at the associated images. It is likely that a dominant image of migration is of people crossing by boat trying to get to Greece or Italy. Yet, as a way of understanding migration to Europe, this is a very distorted image. As we have seen, most people entering Europe do so via regular channels to work, study, or for family reasons. Even those who are classed as irregular migrants, are more likely to have overstayed their original permission than to have entered the EU by boat. This is not to downplay the importance of boat crossings and of the terrible loss of life at the EU's external borders, but it is to suggest that images of migration can have powerful effects on

the understanding of the issue or challenge and feed into a fear or concern that Europe faces large-scale and uncontrollable flows that require ever more stringent border controls.

This kind of understanding focused on border controls can be contested in four main ways. First, it can be argued that 'irregular migration' is a consequence of the narrowing of channels for regular or legal migration to the EU, which creates demand for irregular entry. Second, there are opportunities for people in an irregular situation to find work in the EU in sectors such as agriculture and food production or social care, meaning that migrant workers are needed. Unscrupulous employers may prefer migrant workers in an irregular situation who can be exploited because of their precarity. The COVID-19 pandemic revealed across Europe that migrants in both regular and irregular situations were involved in what was labelled as 'essential work' in the face of the massive public health emergency that faced the EU. Third, irregular migration and asylum are entwined with a much broader debate about development, under-development, peace, and security that is necessarily tied to the actions of EU member states that can destabilize countries as a result of, for example, military interventions, and cause migration and refugee flows. Fourthly, and perhaps most importantly, despite all the focus on asylum and irregular migration in the EU, it is a fact that the vast majority of people in the world who have been displaced live in lower income countries and do not move to Europe. It would be entirely mistaken to imagine that Europe is the epicentre of a global migration or refugee crisis. The protection of displaced people is a hugely important global issue, but, of the world's 34 million refugees and asylum seekers in 2020, around only 10 per cent were in Europe, and those refugees amounted to 0.6 per cent of the EU's total population.

We can identify four reasons why events after 2015 were labelled as a 'migration crisis':

- More than 1 million people entered the EU in 2015, mainly from Syria, seeking refuge from civil war and conflict.
- There were longer standing concerns among EU governments about the perceived potential for large-scale and uncontrollable migration to the EU that has been a key driver of policy cooperation.

- An EU policy framework has developed that has focused on border controls, asylum, refugees, and irregular migration and within which member states and their concerns about border control remain very much to the fore.

- The heightened political salience of migration and asylum with its consolidation is part of a new dividing line or cleavage in EU politics and increased support for right-wing anti-immigration political parties across the EU.

The timeline in Box 26.2 shows that EU policies are partial because they focus mainly on border controls, irregular migration, and asylum while they also have differential effects on the member states because of their differing exposure to migration flows. After 2015, because of their geographical position, Greece and Italy were embarkation points within the EU for hundreds of thousands of migrant. ers, with Germany the preferred dest The balance of responsibility betwee states and EU institutions is also comp. been a growth in the role of supranat. tions with, for example, the **Lisbon Trea** the **Ordinary Legislative Procedure** to ˌ,ʃation and asylum and giving the Court of Justice jurisdiction over the migration and asylum provisions of the Treaty. Member states, however, retain a key role, in so far as they have ensured that the Treaty precludes EU involvement in decisions on the numbers of migrants to be admitted to the Union, and also in policies affecting the 'integration' of these migrants in member state societies. To use a phrase coined in the UK's Brexit campaign, EU governments seem not to want to be seen by their citizens to 'lose control' of migration.

BOX 26.2   BACKGROUND: TIMELINE OF KEY DEVELOPMENTS

1985   The Schengen Agreement commits to the abolition of internal border controls within the EU with compensating internal security measures to include migrants from outside the EU (implemented via the Schengen Implementing Convention of 1990).

1990   The Dublin Convention (formally ratified in 1997) established the core principle that an asylum application be made in the first EU state of arrival with the decision valid for all member states. Initially an agreement in international law outside the formal Treaty framework, the Dublin Convention maintained the core principle and was subsequently developed by two EU Regulations agreed in 2003 and 2013.

1992   The Maastricht Treaty creates an intergovernmental 'pillar' outside the EU's formal Treaty framework dealing with Justice and Home Affairs, including provisions on immigration and asylum.

1997   The Treaty of Amsterdam moves migration and asylum from the intergovernmental pillar into a new Title IV of the EU Treaty covering free movement, migration, and asylum, and imports the Schengen framework into the EU Treaty system.

2009   The Treaty of Lisbon makes migration and asylum subject to the EU's 'ordinary legislative procedure' meaning co-decision between member states and the European Parliament on legislation and jurisdiction for the Court of Justice.

2011   The Commission proposes a Global Approach to Migration and Mobility that will involve trying to work more closely with non-member states (EU Council) on migration issues.

2015   The European Agenda on Migration published by the European Commission with proposals for further development of EU migration/asylum framework in the wake of the 'refugee crisis'.

2020   The New Pact on Migration and Asylum is proposed by the European Commission after failure to secure agreement on the European Agenda on Migration and with a focus on asylum, border controls, irregular migration, and cooperation with non-EU member states.

26.4 The impact of crisis

In 2015, more than one million people, mostly Syrians, made perilous crossings by boat across the Aegean Sea from Turkey to Greece. These flows did not start in 2015. There had been irregular movement by sea towards Europe before then and also terrible losses of life. This was the case in October 2013 when a boat sailing from Libya towards Italy sank just off the coast of the island of Lampedusa. The exact death toll is not known, but was put by the Italian authorities at 'more than 360'. Table 26.1 shows the increase in Mediterranean crossings that occurred in 2015, but also the significant fall in numbers since then.

In 2015, the reason why people were seeking refuge in Europe was very clear: they were fleeing a brutal

and bloody civil war in Syria that began in 2011 and intensified during 2015, and they were seeking protection in Europe. The vast majority of those displaced from Syria did not move to Europe. Most sought refuge in the neighbouring states of Jordan, Lebanon, and Turkey. By 2021, of the 5.6 million people estimated to have fled from Syria, around 3.5 million were in Turkey with just under one million in Lebanon and 650,000 in Jordan. If most of those displaced from Syria did not move to Europe then why did this come to be seen as a European crisis?

The first reason is that the numbers of people arriving overwhelmed the authorities in member states, particularly in Greece, and was also a dominant component of media coverage. People were moving by boat to small Greek islands, such as Lesbos, where the local authorities were unable to cope with the numbers of people who were arriving. They effectively waved them through to the Greek mainland and, from there, many sought to move by whatever means possible to other EU member states, particularly Germany. The impression given by media coverage of the response to arrivals was of chaos as thousands of people moved, often by foot, across Europe. This was compounded by the terrible loss of life. As Table 26.1 shows, in 2015 alone, 3,771 people were reported by the United Nations High Commissioner for Refugees (UNHCR) as dead or missing. This contributed to a perception that this was a European crisis.

The events of 2015 were framed by EU member states as a security and border control crisis, but this 'crisis of control' from the perspective of the member states also became a political crisis centred on the perceived failings of policy responses at both member state and EU level. The wider point here is that crises always have a subjective component. Some would dispute that the events after 2015 can accurately be referred to as a crisis because the numbers of arrivals were small compared to other countries and the rich and powerful EU member states should have been able to cope; labelling these events as a crisis only served to stigmatize migrants and refugees.

Facing events that were framed by the member states as a crisis of control, the issue became whether the EU and its member states could come up with a plan to deal collectively with the challenges they faced. The immediate, unilateral response in August 2015 by the German government led by Angela Merkel was to open German borders to Syrian refugees. With the words *wir schaffen das* (we can do this) Chancellor

Table 26.1 Mediterranean sea crossings

Year	Arrivals	People reported dead or missing
2014	225,455	3,538
2015	1,032,408	3,771
2016	373,652	5,096
2017	185,139	3,139
2018	141,472	2,270
2019	123,663	1,335
2020	94,950	1,166
TOTAL 2014–2020	2,176,739	40,630

Source: United Nations High Commissioner for Refugees (CC BY 3.0), available at: https://data2.unhcr.org/en/situations/mediterranean

Merkel said that any Syrian asylum-seeker could make their claim for refugee status in Germany. This ran counter to the mechanism for allocating responsibility for assessing the claims of asylum seekers that the EU had put in place in the early 1990s known as the **Dublin system** (see Box 26.2). The basic principle of the Dublin system was that the country of first arrival for an asylum applicant would be the member state in which they made their claim for refugee status and that any decision would be valid for the whole EU. This would prevent applications being made in more than one member state. Even before 2015, it was clear that countries such as Greece and Italy were experiencing relatively high inflows of migrants and asylum seekers because of their geographical location nearer to areas of conflict. Not surprisingly their governments were advocates of EU solidarity and the sharing of responsibility.

The catalyst for EU action—and marking the effective collapse of the Dublin system, as it turned out—was the decision taken by the German government in August 2015 to temporarily disregard the Dublin system. The problem was that other member states were not prepared to adopt the same stance as the German government and share responsibility for asylum seekers and refugees. In September 2015, EU leaders did actually agree to a system, in the form of two EU Council decisions, whereby there would be a relocation of up to 160,000 asylum applicants between the member states; fewer than 28,000 were actually relocated. Particular opposition came from Visegrád (the name of the cultural and political alliance) governments of the Czech Republic, Hungary, Poland, and Slovakia. There was a distinct reluctance to support forms of solidarity that would involve relocating asylum seekers and refugees between member states. The Dublin system appeared to be broken and major revisions to the EU policy framework seemed necessary (see Section 26.5).

After 2015 migration and asylum became highly salient political issues across the EU, but this is not the same as saying that there was increased opposition to immigration among the general public. Right-wing, populist, nationalist, and anti-immigration political parties did make advances in key member states, but, at the same time, attitudes to migration

---

 BOX 26.3   KEY DEBATES: ASYLUM SEEKERS AND REFUGEES

An international legal framework—the Geneva Convention of 1951—specifies the obligations of states to asylum applicants who are seeking refugee status. People can claim asylum in another country on the basis of 'a well-founded fear of being persecuted for reasons of race, religion, nationality, membership of a particular social group or political opinion'. If a claim is justified then an applicant can be granted refugee status. All EU member states have ratified the Geneva Convention.

There have been two main components of the debate about asylum in the EU.

1. *The obligations of EU states to asylum seekers.* Advocates for the protection of refugees argue that the objective causes of people seeking refugee status have remained very real and, if anything have worsened. The Syrian conflict was one example of a factor that can cause displacement. As rich and developed countries, EU member states have a duty and an obligation to protect people. This duty can be more present when some EU member states through their actions such as military interventions caused the conditions that lead people to be displaced and to seek protection. Opponents argue that the current asylum system is broken and that many of those seeking asylum are not genuine refugees, but rather are people moving for economic reasons (not a reason for protection covered by the Geneva convention). This argument surfaced as long ago as the early 1990s and has become associated with the notion of the 'bogus asylum seeker'.

2. *Where should people be protected?* If it is accepted that there are people in need of protection, then where should this occur? On one side are those who argue that the EU and its member states have a duty to protect and that this means that they should be prepared to admit greater numbers of refugees to their territory. In contrast are those who argue that protection can be offered in places that are closer to the countries from which people are displaced so long as educational and economic opportunities are offered. Opponents of this idea argue that this is simply a way for richer EU countries to avoid their responsibilities and, instead, offload asylum seekers and refugees to (usually) poorer countries that are neighbouring to states where there is conflict. In response to this, advocates of protection closer to the countries from which people are displaced argue that they are political realists who recognize the political constraints on large-scale protection in EU member states and seek practical solutions that can deliver protection.

BOX 26.4   CASE STUDY: THE COVID-19 CRISIS AND MIGRATION

The COVID-19 crisis had a very immediate and powerful effect as all EU member states imposed travel restrictions, entry bans, and quarantine measures. There was also a dramatic fall in the numbers of people travelling with once busy airports eerily quiet while levels of air pollution linked to mass transportation also fell.

The crisis also turned attention to 'essential work'. The COVID-19 crisis showed how the presence and roles of migrant workers had become very important to life during a pandemic in sectors such as health care, agriculture, food production, and food delivery. While now viewed as essential,

these were also forms of employment where pay could be low and working conditions precarious. For other migrants and asylum seekers, COVID-19 meant further misery as many were housed in camps or in detention centres in often terrible conditions with the risk of an increased exposure to the virus.

As of mid-2021, the route out of the pandemic also raises questions for immigration and asylum. For example, will vaccine passports be needed? Also, for those from lower income countries, vaccine rollout may well be slower with the result that migration becomes more difficult.

have been relatively stable and have actually become more favourable, even since the crisis of 2015. The point is that the salience of the issue—its prominence as a political issue in citizens' minds—had powerful effects because it activated latent anti-immigration sentiment among sections of the European electorate that were channelled towards support for anti-immigration political parties. Thus, while general attitudes among European citizens were not turning against migrants and refugees, the high salience of the issue had powerful effects on the representation of anti-immigration political parties and meant that their voices were loudly present in debate and had an influence on the types of policies that were adopted. The views of these anti-immigration parties became more mainstream components of debate about migration in Europe and contributed to an emphasis on restrictive measures.

KEY POINTS

- There was large-scale movement by asylum seekers and refugees towards EU member states after 2015.

- Understandings of these flows as a crisis in Europe was influenced by representations of human distress and by the disorder associated with boat arrivals.

- The crisis also became a wider crisis of member state and EU politics and institutions.

- After 2015 migration and asylum became more salient political issues which fuelled the rise of radical right, populist, and anti-immigration political parties.

26.5 A new agenda after 2015?

We now assess EU efforts to set a new course for migration and asylum policy after 2015 by asking what was actually 'new' about it? Some aspects were novel such as the level of political attention on these issues and also the significantly increased resources in terms of both personnel and finances that were devoted to them. Frontex, the European Border and Coast Guard, saw its budget grow from €142 million in 2015 to €460 million in 2020.

26.5.1 The European Agenda on Migration

In relation to both immediate responses to events and to thinking about the longer-term the EU has experienced major difficulties. An important statement of the EU's intent was the European Agenda on Migration (EAM) agreed in September 2015, which, unsuccessfully as it turned out, sought greater solidarity between member states. By September 2020, the EAM had been superseded by the Commission's proposals for a new Pact on Migration and Asylum.

The European Agenda for Migration (EAM) sought to define the EU's response to the 2015 migration and refugee crisis. While the EAM was an immediate response to the inflow of mainly Syrian refugees in 2015, it also built on 25 years of cooperation on migration and asylum and the associated policies and practices that have been focused on asylum, refugees, border controls, and irregular migration. It was not so much a change in direction as an attempt to marshal

EU resources to pursue more effectively longer standing objectives.

Of particular relevance is that the EAM dealt with both the 'internal' and 'external' dimensions of policy. The 'internal dimension' includes measures that affect the migration and asylum policies of the member states and is where the EU has more direct reach because of its own institutional and legal system. This does not impinge on member states' admissions policies, but it does affect issues such as cooperation on border controls. It also impinges on an EU legal framework for asylum policy that sets minimum standards for the ways in which asylum seekers will be received and their claims processed as well as establishing the Dublin system for the allocation of responsibility.

The external dimension is where the EU tries to affect the behaviour of non-member states, particularly those in neighbouring states to the east and south but also migrant-origin countries in regions such as the Middle East and sub-Saharan Africa. The development of 'external' governance has been an important feature of EU policy, with roots that can be traced to the 1990s when, prior to their accession, countries in Central Europe were included in EU migration and asylum provisions as a requirement for their eventual membership. A rather obvious challenge is that the EU's institutional and legal processes do not reach directly into non-member states, which means that different kinds of instruments and measures need to be used.

In response to the crisis of 2015, the EU sought agreement with the Turkish government which resulted in the EU–Turkey Statement of April 2016. The Statement provided for: the return of all irregularly arriving Syrian nationals from Greek Islands to Turkey; a mechanism for one vulnerable Syrian to move to the EU for every Syrian returned to Turkey; a €6 billion Facility for Refugees in Turkey; and designation of Turkey as a 'safe third country' to allow the return of asylum applicants from the EU who had passed through Turkey. The numbers of migrants moving along the 'Eastern Mediterranean' route from Turkey to Greece fell from 176,000 in 2016 to 35,000 in 2017. The agreement also increased the importance of EU–Turkish relations while giving Turkish President Erdoğan leverage over the EU.

Non-EU member states may well not share the concern of EU member states about migration and border security and may seek wider issue linkages connecting migration to, for example, trade, aid, development, and security or to exploit migrants as pawns in a wider political conflict, as happened with Belarus's President Lukashenko in November 2021. A reason for these linkages is that non-member states are likely to need some encouragement in the form of incentives to agree to measures and instruments that are designed to allow the EU to achieve its objectives. An example is the EU's Emergency Trust Fund for Africa established at the Valletta summit meeting of EU and African Union leaders held in November 2015. The Fund has made available around €4.5 billion, 89 per cent of which comes from the EU and 11 per cent from the member states and other donors. In an assessment of the Fund, Oxfam reported that funding targeted at border controls and associated security measures in African countries could be contrary to efforts to promote economic development with potentially harmful effects on peoples' livelihoods.

The EAM rests on four pillars that remain centred on stemming or deterring migration flows, particularly from Africa and the Middle East.

1. Reducing the incentives for irregular migration with a focus on 'root causes behind irregular migration in non-EU countries' on 'dismantling smuggling and trafficking networks' and on 'the better application of return policies'. This demonstrates a tension between short term fixes and longer-term solutions. The kinds of interventions that could deal with the 'root causes' of migration are likely to require long periods of time and have uncertain outcomes. There can be a more immediate political pressure to get results, which has led, for example, to a lot of talk from EU political leaders about 'disrupting the business model' of people smugglers. Smugglers can be thought of as illicit facilitators of migration for which they are paid by migrants. Human trafficking, in contrast, typically involves coercion. The basic issue here is that smugglers and traffickers are a symptom of border controls and not the cause of irregular migration. Smugglers provide a service that would-be migrants could use if they want to evade border controls. Making border controls stricter can actually mean that more migrants seek to use the services of smugglers. In the aftermath of the EAM there was also an active targeting of non-governmental organizations (NGOs), most notably by the Italian government when the leader of the *Lega* political

party, Matteo Salvini, served as Interior Minister in the Italian coalition government between 2018 and 2019. Rather than being seen as humanitarian organizations involved in rescuing migrants, NGOs were targeted as a 'pull' factor bringing irregular migrants to Italy as though they were ferries rather than rescue ships. Salvini introduced punitive fines for smugglers and tried to prevent NGO boats with rescued migrants on board from docking at Italian ports. While harsh and punitive, Italian government measures have been largely consistent with an EU approach that, since the 1990s, had sought to combat irregular migration as a key policy priority.

2. This focus on irregular migration leads us to the EAM's second pillar, which is 'better management' of the external border through 'solidarity' towards member states such as Greece and Italy that have been the particular focus of arrivals via Mediterranean routes. The creation of 'hotspots' in Greece and Italy was an emergency response to the registration and processing of new arrivals. The Commission identified solidarity as an element of future migration and asylum policy but the Commission sought an EU-led and more 'vertical' form of convergence centred on EU institutions and processes. As noted above, the Council decision to relocate up to 160,000 asylum applicants were unsuccessful. The risk was that, instead of vertical coordination around EU institutions and convergence around policy measures and instruments, there would instead be forms of horizonal convergence where groups of more likeminded member states would work together in ways that would not necessarily be consistent with EU objectives. Cooperation with non-EU member states—the external dimension—is also identified as central to border management.

3. The EAM's third pillar was a strengthening of the EU's common asylum policy. A key issue, as we have already seen, was reform of the Dublin system. Rather than solidarity, an effect of the crisis of 2015 was a 'reverse domino effect' with new fencing and border controls introduced within the EU's Schengen area of free movement that were designed to stop the onwards movement of asylum seekers. Asylum seekers and migrants found themselves consigned to camps either on the borders of Europe in countries such as Bosnia or in the EU in locations such as the Greek island of Lesbos. In these camps were people who could not or did not want to go back, could not move on because of controls and restrictions on what the EU calls 'secondary movement' and were consigned to live in terrible conditions that got even worse after the onset of the COVID-19 pandemic in 2019 when they were exposed to the risk of infection because of often terrible and dehumanising living conditions.

4. The final and least developed pillar of the EAM is 'regular' migration. It is less developed because EU competencies are limited. In 2009, for example, the EU agreed a Directive to create a 'Blue Card' targeted at migration into high-skilled employment, but this was limited in its effects. Member states still determined the numbers of people to be admitted and had very different rules on, for example, salary thresholds and the duration of permits. While EU institutions have actively sought to develop a stronger EU role with some modest achievements such as the Blue Card, member states remain unconvinced that this is an area that requires EU action because they tend to be of the view that they can achieve their migration objectives without a common EU approach to admissions and would probably be reluctant to be bound by common rules that might mean they lost control over the numbers of migrants to be admitted.

At the core of the EAM was the idea that the EU should seek to build greater solidarity between member states as a cornerstone of the Common European Asylum System. Emblematic of this failure was the fire at the Moria refugee camp on the Greek island of Lesbos in September 2020 that left thousands of people homeless. In the same month the Commission proposed a New Pact on Migration and Asylum. Just in case there was any doubt, not only was the Pact 'new', it was also labelled as 'a fresh start on migration and asylum'.

26.5.2 The New Pact on Migration and Asylum

In promoting the New Pact on Migration and Asylum, the basic dilemma faced by the Commission was how to get the member states on board and promote a more vertical form of convergence centred on EU institutions and shared priorities. Solidarity, in the form of compulsory relocation of asylum seekers, had not worked. This time, the Commission came up with a different idea. It kept the idea of relocation and solidarity but also allowed member states that did not want to take relocated asylum applicants to 'sponsor' the return (meaning expulsion) of failed asylum applicants from other member states.

The Pact was a set of ideas that would need to be turned into concrete legislative proposals, but there are reasons to doubt that it is entirely new and distinctive. It maintains a focus on border security, asylum, refugees, and irregular migration and also lowers the bar through the idea of sponsoring return as a way to try to appease those member states that refuse to countenance solidarity in the form of relocation of asylum applicants.

KEY POINTS

- The EU's response to the migration and refugee crisis after 2015 was the European Agenda on Migration.

- A key issue was whether member states could reach agreement on sharing responsibility for asylum applicants.

- The failure to implement a solidarity mechanism to relocate asylum seekers raised questions about the EU's common asylum system.

- The 2020 Pact on Migration and Asylum was presented as a fresh start, but still, as of mid-2021, requires agreement between member states.

26.6 Four key themes

Having explored the impact of events after 2015 on EU migration and asylum policy and politics, we now identify four analytical themes that show how responses drew from earlier approaches that can be traced to the origins of European cooperation on migration and asylum in the late 1980s.

26.6.1 Migration flows

The first concern is about large and potentially uncontrollable migration flows. This is a dynamic that was clearly present at the origin of cooperation on migration and asylum in the late 1980s. The setting up of the

Single Market had already created an impetus to cooperation on 'compensating' internal security measures. The end of the Cold War led to concern about the potential for large scale migration to the EU from the former Soviet bloc. Most notably, this led to increased asylum-seeking with people fleeing the civil war in Yugoslavia heading mainly towards the newly reunited Germany. This meant that the German government was a leading advocate of a common approach to asylum and of the principles that became the foundation stones of the common EU asylum policy. This included the Dublin principle allocating responsibility for assessment of a claim to an asylum seeker's first country of arrival in the EU or to a 'safe third country'. Essentially, the German government 'Europeanized' migration and asylum policy as a way to reduce inflows of asylum applicants onto German territory in the early 1990s. However, concern among member states about the potential for large-scale flows to the EU has remained a fairly constant factor among EU member states and has impelled policies that seek to deter migration to the EU by making it more and more difficult. This has led, as we have seen, to cooperation on border security, asylum, and irregular migration as well as efforts to develop an external dimension to EU migration and asylum policy. Whether well-founded or not, these concerns about large-scale migration have been a key driving factor in EU migration and asylum policy and politics. They are now clearly manifest in responses to migration from African countries. Given wealth differences and also the much younger age profile of African populations there is migration potential from that continent, but, at the same time, there is ample research that shows that most African migration takes place within the African continent. It is also the case that migration from Africa to Europe is likely to be very expensive and also risky because of the controls that EU member states have put in place. Fear or concern in Europe about large scale migration flows may be accurate or not; but fears or concerns themselves can have very real effects on the direction of policy. It can lead to efforts to reinforce controls and to deter migrants from trying to get to Europe.

26.6.2 Policy emphasis

The second theme that emerges from our assessment of events after 2015 is the focus of EU migration and asylum policy on some forms of migration and not others. This was evident in the early stages of EU cooperation that led to the Maastricht Treaty that created an intergovernmental pillar on Justice and Home Affairs, including provisions on immigration and asylum. The emphasis then, as now, was to address flows of asylum seekers to the EU, to develop stronger cooperation on border control and border security and to tackle irregular migration. These are consistent themes that are still evident in the EU treaties that focus on border controls and the intention to move towards integrated border management (Article 77), the aim to create a common European asylum system (Article 78) and measures to promote effective management of migration and 'to combat illegal immigration and the trafficking in human beings' (Article 79). Article 79.5 makes it clear that none of these provisions affects the right of member states to determine the numbers of migrants seeking work to be admitted to their territory. There is only very limited capacity for the EU to shape admissions policy. The EU Blue Card, referred to above, creates structures for cooperation but there remains considerable variation between member states in rules governing salary thresholds and duration. There is a family reunification directive, agreed in 2003, that seeks common standards but also allowed for significant discretion by member states and also did not affect their ability to decide on the numbers of family migrants to be admitted.

26.6.3 Hybrid institutional responses

The third theme that emerges is the hybrid character of the institutional response that seems to correspond with a transgovernmental dynamic. Nascent cooperation in the 1980s and 1990s was strongly intergovernmental in the Schengen framework and the Justice and Home Affairs 'pillar' of the Maastricht Treaty (1992) (see Chapter 21). Migration and asylum were brought within the Treaty framework by the Amsterdam Treaty (1997) albeit with limits on the role of the Court of Justice (see Box 26.2). Amsterdam also imported the Schengen framework as it had developed since the mid 1980s into the Treaty framework. Since the Lisbon Treaty in 2009 there has been full application of the Ordinary Legislative Procedure and jurisdiction for the Court of Justice. This represents a greater role for supranational institutions, but corresponds more closely to a dynamic of 'intensive transgovernmentalism' whereby national level officials interact on a frequent basis on migration and asylum issues where they also interact with EU institutions, particularly the Commission and the European Parliament. Importantly, the subject of these interactions is very focused on border security, asylum, refugees, and irregular migration while the numbers of migrants to be admitted remains largely beyond the purview of the EU institutions. Events after 2015 revealed disagreement among member states and a more horizonal dynamic with groups of likeminded member states, such as the anti-immigration Visegrád group comprising the Czech Republic, Hungary, Poland, and Slovakia. The New Pact of 2020 was an attempt to find some common ground with the idea of sponsorship for return/expulsion that would allow those states that refused to accept relocated asylum applicants to incur the financial costs associated with expulsion from other member states.

26.6.4 The political nature of migration and asylum

Fourth and finally, after 2015 migration and asylum became a highly salient political issue in the EU. Again, this was not new. In the early 1990s asylum had become an important domestic political concern in Germany and motivated the development of cooperation on asylum. What was distinctive after 2015 was the way in which anti-immigration, populist, and nationalist political parties profited from this salience either to enter governments, as happened in Austria and Italy, or to have a major influence on governing coalitions. In the UK, the Brexit vote was driven by concerns about immigration that were mobilized by the anti-EU UKIP political party (see Box 26.5). Research has shown how attitudes to both immigration and European integration have now coalesced into a new dividing line or cleavage in European politics. This means that political conflict centred on issues such as immigration and European integration that connect to the idea of sovereignty have become stable components of European party politics. This presents considerable challenges for the EU because, while migration and asylum are clearly transboundary and transnational issues, they also raise political questions that strike at the heart of states and their identity.

BOX 26.5   KEY DEBATES: MIGRATION AND BREXIT

Opposition to immigration and 'taking back control' played an important part in the Brexit vote.

The anti-immigration and anti-EU political party, UKIP, with its bedrock of support in England, plus the Eurosceptic wing of the Conservative Party, were able to attach longer standing Euroscepticism in the UK, which was typically higher than in other EU member states, to specific concerns about immigration.

These 'immigration' concerns were actually centred on free movement by EU citizens, which had been a key flow into the UK since 2004 when the UK government, along with those of Ireland and Sweden, agreed to allow immediate access for citizens of the 10 new member states into their labour markets, while other member states imposed restrictions for up to 7

years. Anti-migration sentiment was exacerbated by the decision of the Conservative-led coalition government after 2010 to impose a 'net migration target' which it failed to achieve and which was updated on a quarterly basis as an indicator of policy failure.

While these concerns animated political debate, it is also the case that the UK had managed to establish for itself a semi-detached position in relation to EU migration and asylum policy since the 1980s. It was not part of the Schengen agreement (see Chapter 21) and had maintained the right to exercise its own border controls while also having an opt-out from key migration and asylum provisions of the EU treaty. Prime Minister Tony Blair called this getting 'the best of both worlds' but this pragmatic approach was not enough to satisfy the anti-EU Brexit campaign.

KEY POINTS

- Since their inception in the early 1990s, EU actions have focused on asylum, refugees, border security, and irregular migration.
- Migration and asylum have been powerfully framed by the EU as issues requiring more effective border controls, although this view can be challenged.
- Institutional structures are hybrid with both

intergovernmental and supranational elements that can be understood as 'intensive transgovernmentalism'.

- Migration has been a controversial political issue but support for or opposition to immigration now forms part of a new dividing line or cleavage that structures political systems.

26.7 Conclusion

This chapter addressed two questions. The first was about the presence of liberal and restrictive tendencies in EU migration policy. It was argued that the main drive behind EU cooperation since the 1980s has been to reduce and prevent flows of asylum seekers, refugees, and irregular migrants. This has meant a strong focus on border security and on cooperation with non-EU member states as a way to try to attain EU objectives. The EU has, through common rules on asylum and other relevant policy areas such as family migration, tried to create a common framework of rules by which member states should abide, but the numbers of migrants to be admitted remains a member state competence and this is unlikely to change.

The second question was about the balance between intergovernmental and supranational

authority. While the initial impetus was intergovernmental, there has been a growing role for supranational institutions. This can be understood as a form of intensive transgovernmentalism that brings together national political leaders and officials in regular interaction with their colleagues from other member states and with EU institutions and agencies. The key question that remains open is whether this will lead to greater vertical convergence around common priorities and the EU institutions or whether the dynamics will be more horizontal with groups of likeminded states working together within the general framework of the EU Treaty. The fate of the New Pact on Migration and Asylum is likely to provide the answers to that question.

QUESTIONS

1.   What are the main reasons for migration to the EU from non-EU countries?

2.   What policy areas have been the main focus for EU actions on migration and asylum?

3.   Is a common EU policy on labour migration either likely or desirable?

4.   Should the EU do more to protect the rights of asylum seekers and refugees?

5.   What are the implications for human rights of cooperation on migration and asylum by EU member states with non-member states?

6.   Has the European Commission been the driving force for EU cooperation on migration and asylum?

7.   Why did some member states oppose the implementation of the 2015 decision by EU member states to have mandatory relocation of asylum seekers?

8.   Is the populist, anti-immigration trend in European and EU politics here to stay?

GUIDE TO FURTHER READING

Andersson, R. (2014) *Illegality Inc: Clandestine Migration and the Business of Bordering Europe* (Oakland: University of California Press). This work shows how border security in Europe and neighbouring states has become big business.

Dennison, J. and Geddes, A. (2019) 'A rising tide? The salience of immigration and the rise of anti-immigration political parties in Europe', *Political Quarterly* 90/1: 107–16. This article looks at attitudes to immigration in Europe and their effect on support for anti-immigration political parties.

Geddes, A., Hadj-Abdou, L., and Brumat L. (2020) *Migration and Mobility in the European Union*, 2nd edition (London: Palgrave Macmillan). This book provides a comprehensive and accessible overview of EU actions on migration and asylum.

Kingsley, P. (2016) *The New Odyssey: The Story of Europe's Refugee Crisis* (London: Faber and Faber). A book that provides a powerful account of the events in 2015 and 2016 that were labelled as Europe's refugee crisis.

Léonard, S. and Kaunert, C. (2019) *Refugees, Security and the European Union* (London: Routledge). This book assesses EU measures on asylum.

Access the online resources to take your learning and understanding further, including extra multiple-choice questions with instant feedback, web links, answer guidance to end-of-chapter questions, and updates on new developments in EU politics.

www.oup.com/he/cini-borragan7e

27

Brexit

Nieves Pérez-Solórzano Borragán and Michelle Cini

Chapter Contents

Reader's Guide

This chapter analyses the United Kingdom's departure from the European Union (EU), commonly known as Brexit. The chapter examines the historical context that shaped the UK's decision to join the European Economic Community (EEC) and its subsequent relationship with the EU. It charts the events leading to the 2016 EU referendum, including the campaign, and explains the reasons for the narrow Leave vote. The **Withdrawal Agreement (WA)** negotiations under Article 50 are discussed by focusing on process, actors, and outcomes. This is followed by an evaluation of the negotiations leading to the signing of the **Trade and Cooperation Agreement (TCA)** and its implications. The chapter ends by discussing the impact and implications of the UK's departure from the EU.

27.1 Introduction

On 31 January 2020 the United Kingdom left the European Union (EU). This event, and the process leading up to it, is commonly known as **Brexit**. To understand Brexit it is important to look not only to the short-term factors explaining the outcome of the 2016 EU membership referendum, but also to longer-term trends informing the UK's engagement with the European integration project. This is because the UK's involvement in the EU has been shaped by the UK's history and culture. Indeed, stories from the past combine with pragmatic economics, short-term (party) political and media interests, social and economic cleavages, and broader global issues to form a base-line for understanding why, in the 1950s, European states decided to work together to forge a common market; why the UK decided first to stay out and then applied to join this venture; and why after 47 years the UK left the EU.

This chapter offers an introductory overview of Brexit as an unprecedented process for both the EU and the UK. It starts by examining the historical context shaping the UK's post-1945 relationship with its European neighbours. It then charts the events leading to the EU referendum, including the campaign, and explains the reasons for the narrow Leave vote in the referendum. The Withdrawal Agreement (WA) negotiations under Article 50 are discussed by focusing on process, actors, and outcomes. This is followed by a review of the Trade and Cooperation Agreement (TCA) that frames the post-Brexit UK–EU relationship. The chapter concludes by discussing the implications of the UK's departure from the EU.

27.2 The UK in Europe between 1945 and 2016

In the 1950s, six West European states agreed to co-ordinate first their coal and steel industries and later other economic sectors to form a European community. By 1958, the European Economic Community (EEC) was up-and-running (see Chapter 2). The British government was invited to participate but declined. There was little enthusiasm in the UK for **supranational integration** because of concerns over its implications for national sovereignty. By the end of the 1950s, however, the UK's position had altered. The British economy was stagnant and the **Suez crisis** had put paid to the view that the UK could retain its status as a first-order world power. After toying with an alternative free trade arrangement, the UK government applied to join the EEC in 1961.

The road to accession was far from smooth. Notwithstanding opposition within the UK, it was French president Charles de Gaulle who created the biggest barrier to the UK's EEC membership, vetoing British membership twice, in 1963 and 1967. It was only after he left office in 1969 that negotiations could proceed, led in the UK by the pro-European Conservative Prime Minister, Edward Heath. The negotiations were completed quickly, and the UK joined the EEC on 1 January 1973.

The 'anti-marketeers' opposed to EEC membership argued that the UK had conceded too much in the accession negotiations. The opposition Labour Party leader, Harold Wilson, facing elections in 1974 with his party divided over EEC membership, sought a pragmatic solution. Foreshadowing Prime Minister David Cameron's actions more than four decades later, Wilson agreed, if elected, to renegotiate the UK's EEC deal and to hold a UK-wide referendum on EEC membership. Once elected, and with little enthusiasm, Wilson engaged in a rather limited renegotiation. The referendum to decide whether the UK would leave the EEC was held less than 18 months after the UK had joined, in June 1975. A clear majority of 67 per cent supported membership. The fact that all political parties, aside from the Communist Party, wanted to stay in the EEC, as did all national newspapers aside from the Communist *Morning Star*, no doubt helped the pro-EEC campaign, which was also well-funded and well-organized. The 'outs', by contrast, comprised a rather ill-assorted group of politicians, including Tony Benn on the far left and Enoch Powell on the far right.

Wilson's renegotiation had ignored several tricky questions, however, including the UK's contribution to the European budget. This was one of several issues, which provoked tensions throughout the 1970s, coming to a head after Margaret Thatcher took office as Prime Minister in 1979. At the Fontainebleau summit in 1984, European leaders struck a deal on this issue, which was heralded in the British media as a great victory. However, the aggressive way in which the discussions had taken place left European leaders bruised.

While Thatcher continued to adopt an adversarial approach to European issues, she was nevertheless willing to bargain when in the UK's interest. She was supportive of plans to create a Single Market, which was in line with her domestic deregulatory agenda and could benefit the UK economy, even if it was likely to have long-term institutional and political ramifications. Ultimately, despite or perhaps because of Thatcher's tough stance, the European issue ended up playing a part in her downfall. It also plagued her successor, John Major, in his struggles to negotiate the Maastricht Treaty (see Chapter 2). Although he managed to gain opt-outs for the UK on euro membership and social policy, these concessions were not enough to quell the opposition of Conservative backbenchers who, in 1993, came close to bringing down the government. The legacy of this period influenced British European policy in the decades that followed.

Meanwhile, by the early 1980s, the Labour Party in opposition had moved substantially to the left, so much so that the 1983 election manifesto included a commitment to withdraw from the EEC. After electoral defeats in 1983 and 1987, the Labour Party began to adopt a pro-European position. With a new Prime Minister, Tony Blair, in office from 1997, the tone of the UK's relationship with the EU seemed to improve. Indeed, the first Blair government opted back into the EU's social 'chapter' and negotiated an important deal with France on defence cooperation. However, while Blair favoured euro membership, his Chancellor, Gordon Brown, was hostile. The demanding criteria was established to judge whether the time was right for the UK to join the euro, but as public opinion proved unsupportive, the issue of euro membership was eventually dropped.

Although the **United Kingdom Independence Party (UKIP)** had emerged onto the British political scene in the mid-1980s, it was only in the 2000s that it had its first substantial electoral gains. These culminated in their lead position in the 2014 European Parliament elections, and successes—albeit to a lesser extent—in the 2015 UK general election. UKIP was also able to influence the mainstream political parties, especially the Conservative Party. While UKIP campaigned on a range of issues, its *raison d'être* had from the start been withdrawal from the EU via an in/out referendum. During the Major and Blair governments there had been frequent calls for European referendums on specific European issues and in 2007 David Cameron, then leader of the opposition, gave an 'iron-clad guarantee' that a Conservative government would hold a referendum on the Lisbon Treaty. Thus the referendum issue had entered public discourse.

In office, Cameron's back-tracking on his referendum pledge angered Eurosceptic Conservative backbenchers, turning Europe into the defining issue of his premiership. Cameron had a reputation as soft Eurosceptic (see Chapter 15) who had not wanted Europe to dominate his government. He had already told his Party in 2006 that politicians alienated the public by 'banging on about Europe'. Refusing to hold a referendum on a treaty that had already come into force made sense but simmering tension on this issue required action. Cameron therefore supported legislation (the 2011 European Union Act) to prevent Parliament agreeing any major *future* treaty reform without first holding a referendum, a so-called 'referendum lock'.

In his January 2013 'Bloomberg' Speech, Cameron outlined his vision for a reformed EU and the UK's place within it. He outlined the British agenda for EU reform around four proposals. He acknowledged the gap between the EU and its citizens and the need to address the EU's lack of democratic accountability and consent; he gave an assurance that developments in the eurozone would not prejudice those outside the single currency; he proposed a limit to welfare incentives encouraging EU citizens to seek work in the UK; and emphasized the need to maintain competitiveness, jobs, growth, and innovation. He also confirmed that a referendum that would be held before the end of 2017 to settle the European question, was contingent on the negotiation of a 'new settlement' for the UK in the EU (Cameron, 2013). The Conservative Party subsequently fought and won the 2015 general election on the basis of this promise to change the UK's relationship with the EU and to reclaim power from Brussels; and with a commitment to hold an in/out referendum before the end of 2017.

KEY POINTS

- Although there was initially little enthusiasm in the UK, by the early 1960s, the economic rationale for joining the EEC had become more convincing. The UK joined in 1973.

- A post-membership referendum in 1975 resulted in 67 per cent of the electorate voting to stay in the Community.

- The UK supported European initiatives where they were perceived to be in the national interest.

- After 2010, the Prime Minister David Cameron addressed the rise of UKIP and ongoing parliamentary hostility to the EU by calling a referendum on membership of the Union.

27.3 The 2016 Brexit Referendum

After unexpectedly winning an overall Conservative majority in the 2015 general election, David Cameron confirmed that an in/out referendum would take place in June 2016. From the end of February to the official start of the campaign on 15 April 2016, the Leave and Remain camps rallied to attract supporters from the worlds of politics, business, and entertainment. Their challenge was to translate a generic question: 'Should the United Kingdom remain a member of the European Union or leave the European Union?' into meaningful issues that would engage and mobilize voters.

The key message put forward by the Leave campaign was 'take back control'. This slogan referred to control over borders and immigration and the reinstatement of British sovereignty in key policy areas. The Leave side argued that the UK could retain the benefits of access to the EU Single Market without the obligation to allow free movement of people. The call for referendum day to become 'independence day' and the promise that the country would be made 'great again', reflected the ability of the Leave campaign to appeal with skill to national pride and sentiment. The Leave campaign also stressed the vast trading and economic opportunities available to the UK outside the EU, arguing that as one of the largest economies in the world, the UK would thrive.

The Remain campaign made the economy its key theme, arguing that Brexit would have a devastating effect on UK growth. It stressed that as well as creating short-term instability, a decision to leave the EU would plunge the country into recession. These negative predictions led the Leave campaign to claim that the Remain camp was engaged in 'Project Fear'. Meanwhile, the Remain campaign avoided confronting the immigration and border control issue. It failed to recognize the fears and misconceptions of those worst hit by the effects of globalization and government austerity policies; that is, those who regarded EU immigration as a challenge to their national identity, a cause of unemployment, and an unsustainable burden on the country's healthcare, housing, and education systems.

The issue of the UK's territorial integrity emerged during the campaign as opinion polls highlighted an enhanced level of support for a Remain vote in both Northern Ireland (NI) and Scotland. Wales was an outlier, with the UKIP vote in the Welsh elections in May 2015 already having shown evidence of discontent in traditionally Labour working-class areas over job losses.

The Leave campaign could dismiss Remain's 'doom-and-gloom' narrative by discrediting the expert advice on which it was based as elitist. This reaction wrong-footed the Remain campaign, which seemed unable or unwilling to develop a progressive and positive narrative about EU membership. As the referendum drew closer, the tone of the campaign became more abrasive despite a public outcry over the murder of Jo Cox MP by a far-right terrorist. The 'Leave' campaign strengthened and normalized its anti-immigration narrative and framed the debate as one of 'us' (the decent, ordinary people passionate for our country) against 'them' (the uncaring disconnected elites in both Westminster and in Brussels). At this point, efforts by the Remain campaign to challenge Leave's narrative based on untrue messages about Turkey's imminent EU membership, the possibility of staying in the Single Market without free movement, and the instant transfer of funds from the UK's EU budget contribution to the National Health Service (NHS), became fruitless.

On 23 June 2016, the UK electorate voted to leave the EU. In total 17,410,742 people voted to leave and 16,141,241 voted to remain. That amounted to 51.9 per cent for Leave and 48.1 per cent for Remain, on a turnout of 72.16 per cent (See Box 27.1).

The referendum showed the UK to be a divided country both regionally and ideologically. Scotland and Northern Ireland voted to stay in the EU, while England and Wales voted to leave (see Figure 27.1).

↘ BOX 27.1   KEY DEBATES: WHY DID THE UK VOTE TO LEAVE THE EU?

There is no single explanation that accounts for the UK's decision to leave the European Union.

The anti-politics literature argues that 'anti-political sentiment was a critical underlying factor in explaining the decision to leave the EU' (see Flinders, 2018). In other words, the Brexit referendum offered a window of opportunity to channel frustration around the issue of EU membership. That frustration was fuelled by 'drivers of dissatisfaction' (Flinders, 2018: 183) namely, economic inequality revealed in declining living standards, economic insecurity, and decreasing levels of social protection (Halikiopoulou and Vlandas, 2017). Thus, the poorest households, with incomes of less than £20,000 per year, people

in low-skilled employment, and those left behind by rapid economic change were more likely to support Brexit (Goodwin and Heath, 2016). Second, there was a cultural backlash against progressive, post-materialist values and in favour of authoritarian nativism, demonstrated in the successful anti-migration and 'taking back control' narratives. The Leave campaign, and UKIP in particular, successfully tapped into this dissatisfaction. Third, Britain is a deeply divided society along age, class, and level of education. These divisions cut across the left/right ideological divide creating a realignment in British politics that allowed the Conservative Party to gain support in Labour's working class areas, thus confirming the Labour Party's weakening relationship with working class Britain (Cutts et al., 2020).

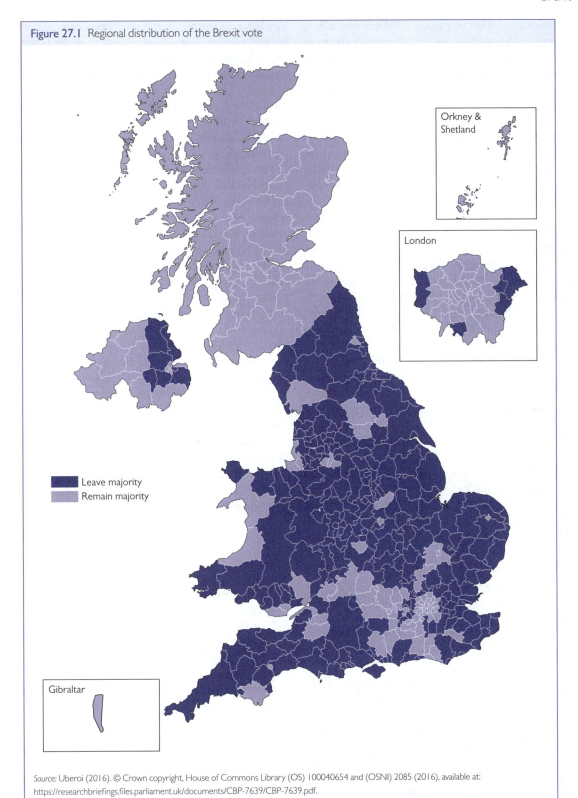

Figure 27.1 Regional distribution of the Brexit vote

Leave majority
Remain majority

Orkney & Shetland

London

Gibraltar

Source: Uberoi (2016). © Crown copyright, House of Commons Library (OS) 100040654 and (OSNI) 2085 (2016), available at: https://researchbriefings.files.parliament.uk/documents/CBP-7639/CBP-7639.pdf.

Ideologically, the country was divided into two tribes. Leavers, older socially conservative voters living in villages, towns, and smaller cities; and Remainers, younger, urban, university-educated voters. (Surridge et al., 2021). Thus, the best indicator of whether someone would vote Leave or Remain (other than in Scotland) was whether they had a university degree or not. Areas with a large preponderance of working-class voters tended to have higher levels of support for Leave. This divide marked a realignment of the British electorate than has characterized voting preferences since 2016.

Over the summer of 2016 there was a lull in Brexit activity. After Theresa May was appointed as Prime Minister in July, beyond the assertion of 'Brexit means Brexit', there was little evidence of a plan. It was not until the Conservative Party Conference on 2 October, that May gave her first full-length speech on the way forward. In it, she announced that Article 50, the **Lisbon Treaty** provision that set out the process by which EU member states might leave the Union, would be invoked by the end of March 2017. May also confirmed that she would commit to a hard Brexit; namely, the UK would leave the EU, the EU's **Single Market** (of which non-EU countries are also members), and even the EU **Customs Union** (of which non-EU countries are also members) if necessary.

The Prime Minister's decision to exclude Parliament from the invocation of Article 50 led a coalition of civil society actors, including a concerned citizen, Gina Miller, to launch a legal challenge in the UK High Court. The Court ruled on 3 November that Parliament had to legislate before Article 50 could be invoked. The judgment led to a media frenzy with the government taking the case to the UK Supreme Court, which on 24 January 2017 ruled against the government. However, it was evident that Parliament—neither the House of Commons nor the House of Lords—would not vote against the government.

Despite splits during the referendum campaign, the Conservative Party presented a united front behind the new Prime Minister. May proved her Brexit credentials by appointing hardline Brexiters, David Davis and Liam Fox, to key ministerial positions. At the same time the Labour Party did not offer much opposition to Brexit. The Labour leader, Jeremy Corbyn, stuck with the argument that the outcome of the referendum should not be contested.

The Liberal Democrats and the Green Party threw themselves into their role as defenders of the 48 per cent who had voted to remain in the EU. UKIP, by contrast, found itself in a more difficult position. Arguably, its *raison d'être* was fast disappearing, and with its high-profile leader, Nigel Farage, stepping down after the referendum, UKIP entered—and not for the first time—a period of contentious leadership wrangling.

The political parties representing Scotland, Northern Ireland, and Wales, responded in different ways to the government's Brexit plans. The Scottish National Party (SNP) reflected Scotland's majority Remain position by arguing for a soft Brexit, for more involvement in the Brexit process, and subsequently for a second Independence Referendum. In Northern Ireland, which also supported Remain, there was serious concern about the land border with the Republic of Ireland. The failure of power-sharing after the March 2017 election meant that even as Article 50 was triggered, there was relatively little attention being paid to Brexit. Finally, with a majority vote for Leave, with Labour the largest party in the Welsh government and no talk of independence, there was little controversy in Wales.

In many respects, the interim period between the 2016 referendum and the British government's triggering of Article 50 on 29 March 2017 was marked by many of the same themes that affected the campaign itself. There is a good reason for that. For both camps there was still a great deal to play for.

KEY POINTS

- The Leave campaign focused on 'taking back control' while the Remain campaign emphasized the impact on the UK economy.

- The result of the 2016 referendum was 51.9 per cent in favour of leaving the EU.

- The referendum result showed clear evidence of the UK being a divided country. These divisions remained evident in the aftermath of the referendum and in the period prior to the triggering of Article 50.

- Theresa May's Conservative government favoured a hard Brexit scenario with the UK leaving both the Single Market and the Customs Union.

27.4 The Withdrawal Agreement

This section discusses the lengthy negotiations that led to the 2019 Withdrawal Agreement (WA) and Political Declaration (PD). It focuses on the negotiating positions and areas of agreement and disagreement between the British government and the EU and on the arduous negotiation process. It concludes by discussing the content and ratification of the WA and the PD.

27.4.1 The negotiating positions

The EU's negotiating position was outlined in the European Council's successive mandates and acted upon by the European Commission. The EU approached the Brexit negotiations as an exercise in damage limitation. While accepting the democratic choice of the British electorate, the EU27 made it clear that there were no winners in the Brexit process and that their main concerns were to protect the EU Single Market, citizens, and businesses, to avoid a domino effect, and ensure an orderly British departure. These goals translated into a negotiating position defined by the following principles:

- Unity. The EU27 were to act with one voice. Thus, the Brexit negotiations were to take place as a single package with no room for informal talks or bilateral negotiations between the UK government and any individual member state.

- A phased approach to the negotiations. Phase one would be completed once sufficient progress had been achieved on the following issues: citizens rights, the border on the island of Ireland, and the UK's financial settlement. Phase two would include other aspects of the UK's departure including transitional arrangements and the terms of a future UK–EU relationship. The EU made it clear that if the UK government wanted to ensure free movement of goods and services post-Brexit, this could only be achieved by accepting the free movement of people. The UK would not be allowed to cherry-pick and enjoy the same rights and benefits as a member state.

- A commitment to the **Good Friday Agreement** and peace in Northern Ireland. The EU27 committed to a solution avoiding the erection of a border on the island of Ireland and to respect the priorities of the Irish government.

- A commitment to a Brexit agreement. The EU27's goal was to avoid a disorderly British departure. This commitment also translated into the principle of 'nothing is agreed until everything is agreed', that is, that there would be one single agreement with one single governance architecture, rather than multiple agreements.

- A broad ranging future relationship. The EU was ready to consider establishing an ambitious partnership with the UK post-Brexit to include trade but also the fight against terrorism and international crime, and security and defence.

- Sincere cooperation between the UK and the EU during the negotiations. Negotiating in good faith was at the core of the EU's approach to the Brexit negotiations. This principle was also included in the WA to ensure that obligations arising from it were fulfilled by both parties. This translated into an unprecedented and regular publication of negotiating documents. This was not matched on the UK's side as the British government established early in the negotiations that it 'would not provide a running commentary on the process'.

The EU's strategy had an internal (within the EU) and an external (in relation to the UK) dimension. Internally, the EU managed to retain its unity. Laffan argues that the shock of the UK's departure mobilized a survival instinct in the EU that led to unprecedented unity built on the need to protect the achievements of European integration and a framing of the UK as an 'embryonic other', that is, as a soon-to-be third country (Laffan, 2019:2). Externally, the EU effectively and strategically deployed its legal and technical expertise in intergovernmental negotiations to deliver a coordinated response.

The UK's negotiating position was formally outlined in a White Paper in February 2017 and in key speeches delivered by the Prime Minister in 2017 and 2018. Informed by slogans such as 'Brexit means Brexit' and 'we are all Brexiters now', the British government committed to repatriate powers from Brussels, to end free movement of people, and to put an end to the CJEU's jurisdiction. These commitments translated into the following negotiating goals:

- A commitment to engage constructively and respectfully in the negotiations with the EU, in a spirit of sincere cooperation.

- Repatriation of powers from Brussels. This would be achieved through domestic legislation by repealing the 1972 European Communities Act via the 2018 EU Withdrawal Act.

- Control of the number of people coming to the UK from the EU by ending free movement of people.

- Leaving the Single Market but ensuring unfettered access. The British government aimed to achieve 'a bold and ambitious free trade agreement' that would ensure an independent trade policy at the same time as free trade in goods and services, including financial services, with the EU. The UK government was also ready to cooperate on cyber security and the fight against terrorism.

- Ending the jurisdiction of the CJEU in the UK but honouring international commitments and following international law.

- Ensuring certainty for citizens and business. The British government sought a transition period and mutually beneficial transitional arrangements.

- A commitment to peace in Northern Ireland. The British government committed to maintain the Common Travel Area with the Republic of Ireland and to avoid a hard border on the island while protecting the integrity of the United Kingdom. To this end the British government proposed the creation of a customs union between the UK and the European Union. This proposal was ultimately withdrawn when the government was unable to ensure sufficient parliamentary support for it (see Box 27.3).

- No payments into the EU budget unless beneficial to the UK, such as to facilitate access to EU research programmes.

- A preference for negotiating the WA and the future partnership alongside each other.

- No deal is better than a bad deal. While the UK wanted to avoid a no-deal scenario, it made it clear that it would walk away from the negotiations without an agreement if the outcome was not satisfactory. This proved to be an empty threat.

The UK's strategy on the Brexit negotiations also had an internal (within the UK) and an external (in relation to the EU) dimension. Internally, the British government faced three key challenges. First, after the referendum, the UK was a divided country lacking a clear consensus on Brexit. The country also suffered from Brexit fatigue as the negotiations endured beyond the expected two years. The May and, from July 2019, the Johnson governments' preference for a hard Brexit was not unanimously supported in the country. The business community expressed concerns about post-Brexit barriers to trade, and increased bureaucratic processes and constraints. The devolved administrations in Scotland, Wales, and NI were concerned about how the repatriation of powers from Brussels might facilitate centralization rather than further devolution. A divided British parliament mirrored the lack of consensus over what Brexit ought to look like as the three votes against the agreed WA text demonstrated. It took another general election in December 2019 and a Conservative majority to ensure the ratification of the WA.

Second, the British government displayed an unexpected lack of readiness in the face of complex Brexit negotiations. Limited administrative capacity was exacerbated by a problematic Whitehall reorganization that created a new Department for Exiting the European Union (DexEU) and a Department of International Trade. This reform dispersed the UK's government administrative and policy expertise on the EU. Similarly, the government found it difficult to match the negotiating expertise of the European Commission and was often reactive and unable to articulate the technical details behind its negotiating aspirations such as ensuring a solution to the Irish border or retaining the benefits of EU membership after becoming a third country.

Finally, Theresa May exhibited weak leadership. She had started her premiership by demonstrating her Brexit credentials after having supported Remain in the 2016 referendum. But an absence of deliberation with the constituencies that she had to accommodate ultimately led to her demise. She was unable to ensure sufficient support for the negotiated WA draft in 2019 because she failed to build bridges with the opposition parties in Parliament while appeasing, to no avail, the Brexiteers in her party.

Externally, the British government adopted a three-pronged strategy. First, it attempted to divide the EU by seeking bilateral political contacts with key national leaders such as Macron, Merkel or Leo Varadkar, and by presenting the European Commission as inflexible, too focused on technical detail and acting beyond the mandate of the EU27. This strategy did not work. Second, the option of a 'no deal Brexit' was never off the table. While this was largely a tactic for domestic consumption, the intended threat turned into weak posturing as the government's own analysis demonstrated the catastrophic effects of exiting the EU without an agreement. Finally, in its commitment to run the WA negotiations in parallel to negotiations on the future relationship, the British government achieved some success as talks about a future UK–EU relationship started in 2018 and the UK's main aspirations were included in the Political Declaration attached to the WA.

27.4.2 The negotiation process

The process by which a member state leaves the European Union is governed by Article 50 TEU (see Box 27.2). This treaty provision sets out the time-frame, scope, and broad negotiating procedure. It also identifies the key actors and the balance of power between the EU and the exiting member state.

The UK government initiated the Brexit process under Article 50 on 29 March 2017 when it communicated to the European Council its intention to leave the Union. However, the Brexit negotiations did not start until 19 June 2017. Between March and June, the EU published its negotiating guidelines and appointed Michel Barnier as the EU's negotiator. British PM, Theresa May, called a general election which was held on 8 June 2017 with the purpose of strengthening

the Conservative Party's position. However, while the Tory party won the majority of parliamentary seats, it did not manage to gain an overall majority, making the Conservative government dependent on the support of the Democratic Unionist Party (DUP), a unionist and loyalist Northern Irish political party. This dependence further weakened May's leadership and shaped future proposals on the solution to the island of Ireland post-Brexit, as the DUP rejected any scenario that differentiated Northern Ireland from the rest of the United Kingdom.

The key actors in the negotiation process were, on the British side, the Prime Minister and the Secretary of State for Exiting the European Union who negotiated on behalf of the British government. This latter role was performed, in turn, by David Davies and Dominic Raab and then by Stephen Barclay (from November 2018). Each led the Department for Exiting the European Union (DExEU). Parliament, under the **EU Withdrawal Bill**, was afforded a vote to ratify any agreement with the EU. Parliament made use of this right by opposing ratification three times.

On the EU side the Brexit negotiations were firmly intergovernmental. The EU's negotiating guidelines were drafted by the European Council, acting on the advice of the EU Council via the General Affairs Council (Article 50 formation, thus not including the UK). Donald Tusk, president of the European

---

 BOX 27.2   BACKGROUND: ARTICLE 50 TEU

1. Any Member State may decide to withdraw from the Union in accordance with its own constitutional requirements.

2. A Member State which decides to withdraw shall notify the European Council of its intention. In the light of the guidelines provided by the European Council, the Union shall negotiate and conclude an agreement with that State, setting out the arrangements for its withdrawal, taking account of the framework for its future relationship with the Union. That agreement shall be negotiated in accordance with Article 218(3) of the Treaty on the Functioning of the European Union. It shall be concluded on behalf of the Union by the Council, acting by a qualified majority, after obtaining the consent of the European Parliament.

3. The Treaties shall cease to apply to the State in question from the date of entry into force of the Withdrawal Agreement or, failing that, two years after the notification

referred to in paragraph 2, unless the European Council, in agreement with the Member State concerned, unanimously decides to extend this period.

4. For the purposes of paragraphs 2 and 3, the member of the European Council or of the Council representing the withdrawing Member State shall not participate in the discussions of the European Council or Council or in decisions concerning it.

5. A qualified majority shall be defined in accordance with Article 238(3)(b) of the Treaty on the Functioning of the European Union.

6. If a State which has withdrawn from the Union asks to rejoin, its request shall be subject to the procedure referred to in Article 49.

Source: Article 50 TEU.

Council, became the face the of EU27 governments. It was the European Council that agreed by unanimity the three requests from the UK to extend the negotiation period. These extensions were not taken lightly and they included conditions such as the UK holding European elections in May 2019.

The European Commission negotiated on behalf of the EU27. Michel Barnier, the EU's Chief Negotiator, was supported by an Article 50 Taskforce in the European Commission. The Commission informed the EU27 weekly on the progress of the negotiations, liaised with the European Parliament and national parliaments, and drafted the EU negotiating positions. When the negotiations concluded, the EU Council decided on the Withdrawal Agreement by qualified majority voting. The European Parliament (EP) created a Brexit Steering Group and appointed its own Brexit coordinator, Guy Verhofstadt. In line with Article 50 TEU, the EP had to provide its consent (by a simple majority of voting members) to the final agreement.

At the start of the negotiations in June 2017, the British government and the European Union agreed the principles that were to shape the Brexit negotiations. These included a commitment to transparency and to negotiate in good faith. The two negotiating parties also agreed to a phased approach to negotiations. Phase one focused on the withdrawal issues: the status of UK citizens in the EU and EU citizens in the UK; the border between the Republic of Ireland and Northern Ireland; and the settlement of the UK's financial obligations. This phase concluded on 15 December 2017 when the parties agreed that sufficient progress had been achieved.

This agreement in principle included. (1) Protecting the rights of Union citizens in the UK and UK citizens in the EU. Crucially on this issue the UK and the EU agreed to provide reciprocal protection for EU and UK citizens exercising free movement rights by the date of the UK's departure. (2) A framework for addressing the unique circumstances in Northern Ireland (NI) that respected the Good Friday Agreement and avoided the reinstatement of a hard border between the Irish Republic and NI (see Box 27.3), and to maintain full alignment with those rules of the Internal Market and the Customs Union which support North–South cooperation, the all-island economy, and the protection of the Good Friday Agreement. (3) On the financial settlement, the methodology for working out the final bill (estimated to be between

€40 bn and €60 bn) was settled but the final figure and the payment schedule were not. Both the UK and the EU agreed that the commitments made in phase one of the negotiations would be maintained in phase two.

Phase two of the negotiations started formally on 6 February 2018 with a focus on the governance of the agreement, the border on the island of Ireland, the transition period, and the framework for future EU–UK relations. This phase lasted until the UK's departure from the EU on 31 January 2020 and involved more frequent and intense negotiating rounds.

On 19 March 2018 the UK and the EU agreed a Draft Withdrawal Agreement that established the terms of the UK's departure from the EU planned for 29 March 2019. The subsequent negotiations tweaked the terms of the solution to the Irish border and tried to achieve common ground on the future UK–EU relationship. The political situation in the UK was complicated by the resignation in July of the Brexit Secretary and the Foreign Secretary, Boris Johnson, due to disagreements with the Prime Minister, while the DUP did not agree with the proposal on the Irish border. By 17 October 2018 the EU27 confirmed the absence of sufficient progress in the negotiations on the Irish border and the future economic relationship and warned of a no-deal Brexit. However, on 14 November the negotiating teams agreed on a Withdrawal Agreement text as well as on the outline of a Political Declaration defining the framework for a future UK–EU relationship. This was endorsed on 25 November 2018.

However, the ratification of the WA text would prove impossible on the British side. Parliament was divided on the terms of the departure as well as on the framework for the future relationship. On 15 January 2019, British MPs voted against the WA by 432 to 202 votes. On 12 March 2019 they once again voted against the WA by 391 to 242 votes. And in a desperate attempt to get the WA through parliament, on 29 March 2019 (the day the UK should have left the EU) a vote was held to approve the WA without the PD. MPs rejected this agreement too by 344 to 286 votes. Faced with this lack of parliamentary support and to avoid a no-deal Brexit, the Conservative government had to request three successive extensions of the negotiation period.

A revised Withdrawal Agreement and Political Declaration were the result of a limited renegotiation of the original text agreed between Theresa May and the EU

BOX 27.3   CASE STUDY: THE IRISH BORDER

How to square the commitment by the UK government and the EU27 not to introduce a border between the Republic of Ireland (an EU member state after Brexit) and Northern Ireland (NI) (part of the UK and thus outside the EU after Brexit) while respecting the terms of the 1998 Good Friday Agreement, was one of the most difficult stumbling blocks in the WA negotiations, and an issue of contention that shaped UK–EU relations in subsequent years. While a range of scenarios was discussed during the negotiations (such as a 'backstop' creating a temporary customs area for the EU and the whole of the UK) the final treaty text incorporates a Protocol on Ireland/Northern Ireland. The Protocol ensures the absence of a physical border between NI and the Republic of Ireland but creates a complex solution that erects a regulatory border in the Irish Sea thus de facto recognizing the special status of Northern Ireland within the UK internal market. In practice this means that Northern Ireland follows EU regulatory and customs rules to ensure free movement of goods (particularly agri-food and industrial goods) across the island of Ireland and that regulatory controls on goods moving from Great Britain to Northern Ireland need to be implemented so that they can then freely circulate within the EU's Single Market. The complex implementation of this solution and relevant dispute mechanisms are overseen by a UK–EU Joint Committee.

The Protocol also incorporates a section on 'democratic consent' that affords the Northern Ireland Assembly the possibility to vote on whether to maintain the provisions of the Protocol, with a requirement to have cross-community support. This provision reflected a shift in the EU's position and the attempt by the British government to give voice to the devolved administration while recognizing the effect of the Protocol on community relations in NI. Article 16 of the Protocol allows Protocol provisions to be overridden in the event of 'serious economic, societal or environmental difficulties'.

The implementation of the Protocol has been controversial. On the UK side, the Democratic Unionist Party and some members of the Conservative Party oppose it on the grounds that it creates a de facto border in the Irish Sea between NI and the rest of the UK. In June 2021, the High Court in Belfast dismissed a legal challenge that argued that the Protocol undermined the UK's constitutional integrity. Earlier that year, rioting erupted in some protestant areas of Belfast in protest against the regulatory border in the Irish Sea. Second, the British government knowingly challenged the commitment entered into under the Protocol by unilaterally proposing changes to its terms through domestic legislation (see Section 27.5, 'The Trade and Cooperation Agreement'). While these changes were subsequently dropped, this unilateral action clearly meant a departure from the good faith approach to the Protocol's implementation. Third, the British government showed an incomprehensible lack of readiness to implement the Protocol. Thus after heavily politicized exchanges, in June 2021, the European Commission agreed a temporary (until September 2021) easing of rules governing the movement of chilled meats and livestock as well as the provision of medicines from the rest of the UK into NI. On the EU side, Commission President, Ursula von der Leyen, had to backtrack on her attempt to invoke Article 16 of the Protocol to limit the export of **COVID-19** vaccines beyond the EU. The political sensitivities in Northern Ireland, the difficult implementation of the Protocol, and calls for its revision or even suspension are likely to shape the UK–EU relationship in the years to come.

in November 2018. When Boris Johnson became PM in July 2019 he promised to oversee the UK's departure from the EU by 31 October, to abolish the Irish backstop (see Box 27.3) and to include the Irish border in the negotiation of a future UK–EU relationship. The EU preferred to agree an Irish border solution as part of the WA. Negotiations intensified to avoid a no-deal Brexit. Finally, a new Irish Protocol was agreed (see Box 27.4). The text of the Political Declaration was also re-drafted to reflect the new British government's preference for a looser future UK–EU relationship based on a free trade agreement. On 17 October 2019 the United Kingdom and the European Union reached an agreement on a revised Withdrawal Agreement and Political Declaration, setting in motion a new ratification process.

27.4.3 Content of the Withdrawal Agreement and Ratification

In line with Article 50, the WA outlines the terms of the British departure from the EU and defines the framework for a future UK–EU relationship in an accompanying Political Declaration. These are lengthy and detailed documents. The WA is structured as follows:

- Part One—Common Provisions: this section sets out definitions to be used in the remainder of the WA including the objective of the agreement, territorial scope and the principle of good faith.

- Part Two—Citizens' Rights: all EU citizens arriving in the UK during the transition period should have exactly the same rights as EU citizens who arrived before the UK's withdrawal. UK citizens who arrive in an EU Member State after withdrawal but before the end of the transition period, should be covered by the WA. An independent Authority should be created in the UK to monitor the implementation and application of the citizens' rights part of the Agreement.

- Part Three—Separation Provisions: this part of the agreement outlines rules applicable to procedures that are ongoing when EU law ceases to apply to the United Kingdom ranging from European Arrest Warrants to Geographical Indicators, VAT, intellectual property, public procurement, and EURATOM. It protects EU officials, judges, and politicians' immunity from prosecution and taxpaying obligations in the UK until the end of the transition period.

- Part Four—Transition: this section provides for a transition period lasting until 31 December 2020 that can be extended once by up to one or two years. During this time, the UK benefits from the Single Market and Customs Union and is bound by the same obligations, even new ones acquired during the transition period, while being a third country. However, during the transition, the UK loses all voting rights and decision-making power. The CJEU has full jurisdiction over the United Kingdom with regard to all matters in the Withdrawal Agreement during the transition period.

- Part Five—Financial Settlement: this section outlines how the UK and the EU will honour the financial obligations undertaken while the UK was an EU member state. It includes the methodology to calculate the final obligations and additional details such as payment deadlines.

- Part Six—Governance Structure: this section envisages the creation of a Joint Committee responsible for supervising and facilitating the implementation and application of the WA. It will comprise representatives of the EU and the UK. It also sets out the dispute resolution mechanisms (an arbitration committee) and the CJEU's role in adjudicating on any question of EU law. This part also includes the mechanisms to address non-compliance including the partial suspension of the application of the Withdrawal Agreement itself, except for citizens' rights.

- Protocol on Ireland/Northern Ireland: the protocol includes the agreed solution to the border on the island of Ireland that recognizes the unique circumstances on the island of Ireland and the joint aim of protecting peace and stability (see Box 27.4).

- Protocol on the Sovereign Base Areas in Cyprus: this protocol sets the general framework for the implementation of applicable EU law in relation to the Sovereign Base Areas in Cyprus after Brexit.

- Protocol on Gibraltar: this Protocol provides the framework for cooperation on Gibraltar between Spain and the UK in relation to key policy areas (such as environment, police, and customs) during the transition period, and on the implementation of the citizens' rights section of the WA.

- The Political Declaration on the Future Relationship outlines the shared UK–EU ambition to have a Free Trade Agreement with zero tariffs and quotas between the EU and the UK post-Brexit. It commits the two parties to a level playing field (see Section 27.5, 'The Trade and Cooperation Agreement') and to enforcement and dispute settlement mechanisms.

The ratification of the WA and Political Declaration was finalized in January 2020. The WA entered into force on 31 January 2020 at midnight, when the UK finally left the EU. This also marked the beginning of the transition period.

KEY POINTS

- Article 50 establishes the timing and scope of the exit negotiations as well as the key actors and decision-making procedures. It was drafted to ensure the orderly withdrawal of the exiting member state.

- The Brexit negotiations under Article 50 started on 29 March 2017 and continued until 31 January 2020, thus beyond the two years afforded by the exit procedure, and requiring three successive extensions.

- The negotiation of the Withdrawal Agreement was structured around two phases. A first phase focused on withdrawal issues with a second phase focused on the terms of exit, the transition period and the future UK–EU relationship.

- These were difficult negotiations that demonstrated the EU's ability to speak with one voice and protect the Single Market and the UK government's lack of preparedness. The solution to the border between the Irish Republic and Northern Ireland as well as the framework of the future UK–EU relationship were key points of disagreement.

27.5 The Trade and Cooperation Agreement

The Trade and Cooperation Agreement (TCA) was negotiated in a record eight-month period between 31 March and 24 December 2020. This section outlines the dynamics informing the negotiating positions, the negotiation process, the content of the agreement, and its challenging implementation.

27.5.1 The negotiating positions

After the difficult Brexit negotiations and as the COVID-19 pandemic started to take hold in the UK and the European Union, the parties began 2020 by setting out the key principles informing their negotiating positions, building on the Political Declaration attached to the WA. On 25 February 2020, the EU published its mandate for negotiations on its future relationship with the UK, with the UK government publishing its own mandate two days later. On 18 March the European Commission published its draft texts for negotiation. The British government published its draft texts for negotiation on 19 June.

The EU's negotiating position envisaged a free trade agreement (FTA) with the UK that would apply zero tariffs and zero quotas to trade in goods. The agreement would reflect the areas outlined in the Political Declaration, namely trade and economic cooperation, law enforcement and judicial cooperation in criminal matters, foreign policy, security and defence, and other areas of cooperation such as science and innovation, youth, culture and education, participation of the United Kingdom in the European Research Infrastructure Consortiums (ERICs), and a PEACE PLUS programme to sustain reconciliation in Northern Ireland. On fisheries, the EU expected the future partnership to uphold the existing reciprocal access to waters as well as stable quota shares. The EU committed to ensure that the FTA 'should be underpinned by robust commitments to ensure a level playing field for open and fair competition' (European Council, 2020) and to include effective management and supervision, dispute settlement, and enforcement arrangements.

The British government aimed for:

A comprehensive free trade agreement covering substantially all trade, an agreement on fisheries, and an agreement to cooperate in the area of internal security, together with a number of more technical agreements covering areas such as aviation or civil nuclear cooperation. These should all have governance and dispute settlement arrangements appropriate to a relationship of sovereign equals (Johnson, 2020).

The UK government made it clear that it could not agree to 'any regulatory alignment, any jurisdiction for the CJEU over the UK's laws, or any supranational control in any area, including the UK's borders and immigration policy' (Johnson, 2020).

There were four key areas that were not agreed until the autumn and winter of 2020 when negotiations intensified as the end of the transition period approached. These were: governance of the future relationship including treaty architecture and dispute resolution mechanisms; the establishment of a level playing field (LPF) to ensure open and fair competition; fisheries; and police and judicial cooperation in criminal matters (see Box 27.4).

27.5.2 The negotiation process

On 28 February 2020 just before the negotiations started, the UK and the EU published their terms of reference informing the process. Two further addendums were published on 11 June and 21 October.

On the EU side, the negotiations were led by the European Commission mandated by the EU27. Michel Barnier was again appointed chief negotiator and head of the Task Force for Relations with the United Kingdom (UKTF), the successor to the Article 50 Task Force. Negotiations were based on negotiating directives set by the EU Council, taking into account the resolutions of the European Parliament. On the UK side, negotiations were led by David Frost, head of Task Force Europe (TFE), the successor to the Department for Exiting the European Union (DeXEU).

There were a total of nine rounds of negotiations followed by an intensive negotiating phase between 15 October and 24 December. The negotiations took place against the backdrop of the COVID-19 pandemic. This affected progress, with the negotiations suspended shortly after they started on 31 March and conducted remotely via videoconference from April to early June 2020. Negotiations returned to face-to-face meetings from June until 24 December alternating their location between London and Brussels.

The negotiations were structured vertically along two levels: plenary negotiating sessions co-chaired by the chief negotiators or their deputies, and technical

BOX 27.4   KEY DEBATES: THE STICKING POINTS DURING THE TCA NEGOTIATIONS

The UK and the EU disagreed on a number of substantive issues during the TCA negotiations:

- *Governance of the future relationship*. The EU preferred a single treaty and overarching governance structure to deal with the issues included in the FTA. Furthermore, the EU envisaged a dispute resolution system that protected the CJEU's right to interpret questions of EU law. Conversely, the British government preferred a set of independent agreements on fishing, aviation, nuclear cooperation, and law enforcement and judicial cooperation with independent governance arrangements separate from the FTA. The TCA was concluded as a single treaty with a single governance structure.

- *Fair competition, or a 'level playing field' (LPF)*, was a principle already included in the Political Declaration. It was a precondition of the EU to protect the Single Market from the UK government's lowering of labour, environmental, tax, and state aid standards. The UK made it clear that it would not agree to be bound by level playing field obligations and that it would not accept any regulatory alignment with the EU, or any CJEU jurisdiction over any dispute mechanisms. The TCA includes LPF provisions to cover six fields: competition, subsidy control (state aid), state-owned enterprises

and designated monopolies, taxation, labour and social standards, environment and climate, and a complex bilateral procedure to assess divergence and arbitration mechanisms in the event of a lack of agreement (see Barnard, 2020).

- *Fisheries*. This was a highly political and symbolic issue even though fisheries only amount to around 0.1 per cent of GDP of both parties' economies. The EU expected to retain unrestricted access to British waters and unchanged fishing quotas. In turn, the British government made it clear that any loss of sovereignty over its ability to control access to its own waters and fisheries quotas was unacceptable. Both parties had to give ground. The TCA allows EU vessels to maintain their access to UK waters for only five years and requires a gradual reduction in catches from EU vessels.

- *Police and judicial cooperation in criminal matters*. For the EU, cooperation in this area was conditional on the enforcement of data protection and human rights standards in the UK, as well as CJEU jurisdiction. For the UK, any alignment with the EU Charter of Fundamental Rights and CJEU jurisdiction were in clear opposition to its recently regained sovereignty. In the end, the positions in this area did converge quite effectively, although it reduces the UK's access to EU databases and excludes the CJEU and mutual recognition of standards.

---

level negotiations across 11 negotiating groups focusing on the key issues for negotiation such as trade, the level playing field (LPF), fisheries, energy, transport, and governance. Between March and June 2020, the negotiations faltered for want of common ground on the LPF, fisheries, the governance of the agreement, and judicial and police cooperation. As face-to-face negotiations started in June, Michel Barnier spoke of slight progress. Nevertheless, by 5 June the EU's chief negotiator's frustration and sense of urgency was clear when he confirmed that an agreement would not be ready by July and that the British government was backtracking on the commitments it had undertaken in the PD (Barnier, 2020). At a High-Level Meeting on 15 June, all leaders agreed to intensify negotiations while Johnson restated the British red lines: no role for the CJEU in the UK; the right to determine future UK laws without constraints; and a new agreement on fisheries.

By the end of July the two parties agreed that their positions were still far apart and that there was a need to intensify negotiations to ensure an agreement by

the end of the transition period, which the UK had decided not to extend. This intensification was translated into specific roundtables on fishing rights and the level playing field. By the end of August, Barnier confirmed his worry and disappointment at the lack of sufficient progress and the unlikelihood of an agreement. As the eighth round of negotiations ended in London on 10 September, the negotiating climate had soured: the British government proposed measures in the UK Internal Market Bill that would allow the UK unilaterally to override elements of the Northern Ireland Protocol, thus knowingly breaking international law. On 1 October, the European Commission initiated infringement proceedings against the UK for violating the good faith provisions included in the WA.

By early October, fisheries had moved up the agenda as French President Macron requested that the TCA allowed French fishermen the same access to British waters as before the UK's departure from the EU. He was concerned that Barnier would sacrifice the French fishing industry's interests to achieve an agreement. Macron's request could not be further from that of the British government which sought to replace the pre-Brexit status quo with a series of annual negotiations on quotas and access that would favour the British fishing industry. At the European Council on 15–16 October, the EU27 confirmed their unity, the lack of sufficient progress on an agreement, the need for the UK to move its negotiating positions to respect the terms of the WA, and the preparations for all scenarios after the end of the transition period including that of no agreement. In a rather dramatic move, the British government suspended negotiations, albeit only for a couple of days.

The period from October to 24 December 2020 was defined by a further intensification of talks in London and in Brussels with the aim of reaching an agreement that could be ratified before the end of the transition period. On 17 December the EU–UK Joint Committee agreed a set of solutions which included the UK's withdrawal of the contentious text in the UK Internal Market Bill.

By early December, while agreement had been reached on law enforcement and judicial cooperation, social security coordination, goods, services, and transport, disagreements persisted over governance, the LPF, and fisheries. Whereas the EU remained committed to the integrity of the Single Market, and to robust enforcement and governance mechanisms, concerns about UK sovereignty over its territorial waters remained. In the final weeks of the negotiations, positions converged, however, allowing for certain concessions to be made, particularly on fisheries by the EU27, and on the level playing field and governance by the British government. The prospect of no agreement by the end of December; queues of lorries approaching the Channel ports due to the closure of EU borders to UK freight and passenger transport to limit the spread of the so-called alpha COVID-19 variant; and concerns about stockpiling and shortages of food in British supermarkets helped concentrate minds; so much so that on 24 December the TCA was agreed.

In some ways, the dynamics shaping the negotiation of the TCA were distinct from those shaping the WA negotiations. First, the negotiations leading to the TCA took place as the COVID-19 pandemic developed. This limited the ability of the negotiating teams to meet in person. Towards the end of 2020 there were long queues at the ports, a shortage of storage space, and spikes of panic-buying in British supermarkets. These dynamics helped to concentrate the political

effort to agree a trade agreement before the end of the transition period. Second, as a non-EU member state, the UK was no longer bound by EU procedures or the need to abide by the commitments acquired during EU membership. This presented an opportunity for the British government to overcome some of the advantages enjoyed by the European Union during the negotiation of the WA. Third, drawing on the experience of previous trade negotiations, there was an expectation that the EU27 would be unable to retain the unity that they had so effectively displayed during the WA negotiation. Fourth, the ability to engage in informal negotiations between the formal rounds of negotiations was limited. This might have allowed the British government to use its soft diplomacy to drive agendas and create trust. In practice, this did not happen. Fifth, with a comfortable majority in Parliament, the Conservative Government was able to ratify the TCA without delay.

27.5.3 The content and ratification of the TCA

The TCA is a free trade agreement, which affords wide scope for cooperation in other policy areas (transport, research, judicial cooperation). Within the EU it is defined as an association agreement governed by Article 217 of the Treaty on the Functioning of the European Union (TFEU). The TCA is a long and detailed document. It has seven parts that span 1,200 pages. It is structured as follows:

- Part One—Common and institutional provisions: the object and purpose of the agreement, the creation of a Partnership Council and the independence of the two parties are outlined.

- Part Two—Trade (goods and services), transport, fisheries, and other arrangements (other arrangements covered include intellectual property, public procurement, aviation, road transport, energy, social security, and visas for short-term visits): the Agreement establishes zero tariffs and quotas on trade between the UK and the EU, where goods meet the relevant **rules of origin**. The level playing field conditions and their implementation are outlined in this part, including dispute resolution and commitments not to lower standards on competition law, taxation transparency, labour and social standards, and environmental and climate protection. On fisheries, the Agreement provides for a gradual change of quota-sharing arrangements including the reduction of the quota available to the EU fishing industry.

- Part Three—Law enforcement and judicial cooperation in criminal matters: this part creates a new framework for law enforcement and judicial cooperation in criminal matters that allows for cooperation between national police and judicial authorities, including extradition arrangements, and the exchange of data.

- Part Four—Thematic co-operation (including health security and cybersecurity): this section includes cooperation in the field of health security, in particular the possibility that the UK be invited to participate on a temporary basis in a set of EU structures (for example to fight a pandemic). The structures for cooperation on cybersecurity have a similar pattern, but the UK and the EU have signed a separate Security of Information Agreement on the exchange of classified information.

- Part Five—Participation in EU programmes: this part sets out the arrangements for the UK's participation in EU programmes and access to programme services. These include the terms for the UK's financial contribution towards the programmes, fair treatment of UK participants, and sound financial management of programme funding and governance arrangements. Programmes include Horizon Europe, the Euratom Research and Training programme, the International Thermonuclear Experimental Reactor (ITER), and Copernicus. **Erasmus** is excluded.

- Part Six—Dispute settlement and horizontal provisions (governance): this section outlines the creation of a Joint Partnership Council to manage the TCA. The Council is co-chaired by a member of the European Commission and a UK representative at ministerial level. The EP and the UK Parliament can create a joint parliamentary assembly to exchange views on the TCA and make recommendations to the Partnership Council. There are also provisions for consultation with civil society and dispute settlement mechanisms.

- Part Seven—Final provisions: this section provides for a review of the TCA every five years, the procedure to be followed should a new country join the EU, and the terms of the unilateral termination of the agreement. Regarding its territorial scope this part makes it clear that the TCA applies to the UK but that it does not apply to the overseas countries and territories of the EU or to the UK's Overseas Territories. The UK, Gibraltar, and Spain would negotiate separate arrangements.

The TCA was ratified separately in the UK and in the EU between December 2020 and April 2021. In the United Kingdom, the legislation that allowed the TCA to enter into UK law, that is the European Union (Future Relationship) Act 2020, was passed by Parliament on 30 December 2020 soon after Prime Minister Boris Johnson signed the agreement. On the EU side, the process was more complicated. Agreeing the TCA so late in the day meant that the European Parliament could not be afforded sufficient time to scrutinize the text. Thus, on 29 December 2020, the EU Council adopted the decision on the signing of the TCA and its provisional application as of 1 January 2021 pending ratification by the European Parliament. The EU signed the agreement on 30 December 2020 and on the 28 April 2021, the European Parliament ratified the TCA by 578 votes, with 51 against and 68 abstentions.

KEY POINTS

- The TCA is the comprehensive Free Trade Agreement that frames the relationship between the UK and the EU after Brexit.

- The TCA was negotiated in a record time. The negotiations were complex and politically charged. They were affected by the difficult experience of negotiating the WA, the effects of the COVID-19 pandemic, the complex implementation of the Northern Ireland Protocol, and the need to ensure agreement before the end of the transition period in December 2020.

- The TCA affords zero quota and zero tariff trade in goods as well as wide scope for cooperation in other policy areas such as transport, research, and judicial cooperation.

- The TCA was temporarily ratified in December 2020. The EP was afforded time to scrutinize the text and finally delivered its consent on 28 April 2021.

27.6 Conclusion

This chapter has contextualized Brexit by reviewing the uneasy involvement of the United Kingdom in the European integration process, while accounting for the 2016 referendum, the negotiation of the 2019 WA and PD, and the negotiation and implementation of the 2020 TCA. In so doing, the chapter has reflected on the divisions in British society and their effect on the outcome of the referendum, the politically sensitive situation in Northern Ireland, the relevance of the COVID-19 pandemic and the distinct approaches of the EU27 and the British government as they negotiated the terms of the UK's departure from the EU and the future UK–EU relationship. While it is still too early to fully understand the effect of the UK's exit from the EU, it is possible to identify four ways in which this historic event might affect European integration and UK–EU relations in the years to come.

First, Brexit could weaken the EU (see Chapter 29). While the EU27 displayed unprecedented unity in the face of an existential crisis, this is unlikely to last as disagreements over the rule of law (see Chapter 9) and the COVID-19 pandemic (see Chapter 28) have demonstrated. Being able to respond to the disintegration challenges posed by populist parties from the left and the right, and to the demands of EU citizens for a more democratic Union, would go a long way to protect the robustness of the integration process.

Second, Brexit is a failure of European integration. While the absence of a Brexit dividend and the negative effect of the COVID-19 pandemic on trade flows between the UK and the EU have halted a domino effect in the Union, the UK's exit offers an opportunity to reform the EU. Some national leaders may regard the UK's exit as an opportunity to strengthen EU integration to address key challenges; others are more likely to see Brexit as an opportunity to enhance the use of opt-outs and calls for exceptionalism. As the Commission White Paper on the Future of Europe (European Commission, 2017) acknowledged, a more agile Union, less integration, and more flexibility are the way forward.

Third, Brexit may weaken the international standing of both the UK and the EU. Viewed from China, India, and the USA, Brexit may suggest a weak and divided Europe. For the first time, the EU has shrunk in size, a prospect that goes against conventional wisdoms that see progress bound up with forward steps in integration and enlargement. Some may find it hard to imagine that the EU will be taken seriously in matters of global economy and politics under these circumstances. The prospect of global EU leadership on issues ranging from environmental protection to the exchange of anti-terrorist intelligence seems perhaps less likely; and despite its robust standing within the United Nations Security Council (UNSC), the G7, the G20 groupings of nations, the Commonwealth, and NATO, the UK will need to ensure that it does not become marginalized in the international arena.

Finally, Brexit affects short-term and long-term EU–UK relations. Both partners are learning to operate in this new context in which barriers are erected rather than removed, and policy goals diverge rather than converge, while the legacy of tense years of negotiation and the contested implementation of parts of the agreements (Ireland and Northern Ireland Protocol or the UK's financial commitments) are taking their toll. The WA and TCA do not solve all issues pertaining to UK–EU relations and new ways of working together will have to be developed to address wider challenges such as climate change, security concerns, upholding the universal values of democracy and the rule of law, or a public health crisis such as the COVID-19 pandemic. Equally, the good faith framing the negotiations needs to be sustained as the UK and the EU share a commitment to peace in Northern Ireland and prosperity across Europe. As the effects of Brexit sink in, it has become obvious that the UK's departure from the EU is not just a matter of high politics; rather it affects the lives of individuals whether businesspeople, students, musicians, or private citizens whose experiences of travelling and working across Europe have been fundamentally changed.

QUESTIONS

1. What factors led to the UK joining the EEC in 1973?

2. In what senses did membership of the EU change the UK?

3. Why did the UK hold a referendum on EU membership in 2016?

4. What factors explain the vote to leave the EU in June 2016?

5. Why was the border on the island of Ireland such a controversial issue in the negotiation of the Withdrawal Agreement and the Trade and Cooperation Agreement?

6. How successful has the UK been in negotiating Brexit and its future relationship with the EU?

7. How successful has the EU been in negotiating Brexit and its future relationship with the UK?

8. What are the likely effects of Brexit on UK–EU relations?

 GUIDE TO FURTHER READING

Diamond, P., Nedergaard, P., and Rosamond, B. (eds) (2018) *Routledge Handbook of the Politics of Brexit* (London: Routledge). An excellent collection that offers an insightful analysis of the political, economic, regulatory, theoretical, and policy-oriented dimensions of Brexit.

Evans, G. and Menon, A. (2017) *Brexit and British Politics* (Cambridge: Polity Press). A short, but well-informed overview of both long- and short-term factors leading to the British decision to leave the EU, covering in more detail many of the themes discussed in this chapter.

Fabbrini, F. (ed.) (2017) *The Law & Politics of Brexit* (Oxford: Oxford University Press). A serious academic collection of essays by leading voices on Brexit, covering a range of questions but with a particular focus on the constitutional change dimension of Brexit.

Fabbrini, F. (ed.) (2021) *The Law & Politics of Brexit: Volume III. The Framework of New EU–UK Relations* (Oxford: Oxford University Press). A collection of academic essays analysing the Trade and Cooperation Agreement and the future UK–EU relationship.

O'Toole, F. (2018) *Heroic Failure: Brexit and the Politics of Pain* (London: Head of Zeus Ltd). A lively journalistic account of the early stages of the Brexit process from a respected Irish commentator.

Access the online resources to take your learning and understanding further, including extra multiple-choice questions with instant feedback, web links, answer guidance to end-of-chapter questions, and updates on new developments in EU politics.

www.oup.com/he/cini-borragan7e

28

COVID-19 and EU Health Policy

Eleanor Brooks, Sarah Rozenblum, Scott L. Greer,
and Anniek de Ruijter

Chapter Contents

Reader's Guide

This chapter explores the implications of the COVID-19 pandemic for the EU's health policy. Health is an area in which member states have historically been reluctant to cede powers. Consequently, the EU's treaty competences in health are limited. The chapter first introduces the extent and parameters of the EU's role and the resulting patchwork of health policy and law which exists at European level. The narrow mandate available to the EU when COVID-19 emerged precluded a comprehensive response, whilst the scale of the emergency put pressure on norms of solidarity and free movement. Section 28.3 describes the initial period of the pandemic and reviews the EU's response within six different areas of (health and non-health) policy. It highlights the strengths and weaknesses of the EU's efforts to fight and mitigate the pandemic using the public health, internal market, and fiscal governance dimensions of its health powers. Section 28.4 discusses the implications of the pandemic and the EU's response to it for the future of cooperation and integration in the area of health.

28.1 Introduction: from egotism to integration

On 24 January 2020 the first European case of COVID-19, a disease caused by a novel coronavirus known as SARS-CoV-2, was reported in France (Box 28.1). A month later, clusters of cases were confirmed in Italy and by 25 March, COVID-19 cases had been reported in all EU/EEA member states and more than 150 countries worldwide (ECDC, 2020). The initial response within the EU was uncoordinated and threatened core Union principles, such as free movement and solidarity.

National governments' first response was to look after their own. They introduced export bans, imposed border restrictions and adopted contrasting policies in an effort to contain the virus. For example, Germany, France, and Italy quickly banned the export of face masks and other personal protective equipment (PPE), and Germany introduced new checks on people crossing its Southern border. Moreover, governments made little use of EU structures, beyond sharing information and data, which raised questions about the purpose and added value of these structures in a public health emergency. Much of the difficulty reflected the EU's limited competence and capacity in the field of health; the founding treaties reserve health as a national competence and grant the EU a narrow, supporting role. However, the initial period of

protectionist national responses soon passed. Export bans were lifted, collective purchasing and stockpiling of supplies was organized and, by the end of summer, proposals to expand and strengthen various elements of the EU's health policy were under discussion. This culminated, in late 2020, in a proposal to build a European Health Union in which the European Commission and the EU's key agencies have a more robust mandate. It seems possible, therefore, that the COVID-19 pandemic could underpin further integration in health policy.

This chapter offers an introductory overview of the EU's response to COVID-19, from its emergence through to the end of 2020, and the potential impact of the pandemic on the EU's health law and policy. It starts by introducing EU health policy, reviewing the emergence and development of the EU's limited competence in the health field, and describing the tools, mechanisms, and competences that were consequently available to it when the pandemic first emerged. It introduces the 'three faces' framework, which understands EU health policy to have distinct public health, internal market, and fiscal governance dimensions. It then uses these three faces to chart the EU's response to COVID-19. Here, it explores a series of specific policy areas and institutions—health security, the European Centre for Disease Prevention and Control (ECDC), the EU4Health programme, borders and free movement, vaccines and pharmaceuticals, and the fiscal governance framework—drawing out case studies of the EU's response and of subsequent changes to EU health law and policy. The chapter closes by reflecting on the changes afoot in EU health law and policy. It posits that, despite difficult beginnings, COVID-19 may prove to be yet another crisis-catalyst of greater cooperation and more expansive EU action in the field of health.

28.2 What is EU health policy?

The beginnings of EU health policy can be traced back to the first disease programmes for steel and mineworkers in the context of the Coal and Steel Communities (Hervey and McHale, 2015). As the communities expanded to other 'markets', new EU health provisions were needed to support these regimes. The creation of common agricultural markets, for example, required cooperation on food safety protections, as made clear and accelerated by the

> **BOX 28.1   BACKGROUND: COVID-19 AS A PUBLIC HEALTH EMERGENCY OF INTERNATIONAL CONCERN**
>
> On 30 January 2020, the World Health Organization (WHO) declared the global outbreak of novel coronavirus to be a Public Health Emergency of International Concern (PHEIC). This declaration is the highest level of alert that the WHO can issue and it is provided for within the International Health Regulations (IHRs). The IHRs set out countries' responsibilities regarding international cooperation when handling public health emergencies that might spread across borders. If such an emergency is deemed to constitute an 'extraordinary event' with a risk of international spread and implications for other states, the WHO can declare a PHEIC to galvanise prevention and response activities by governments and other actors (such as the EU). Recent examples of PHEICs include the 2015/16 Zika virus epidemic in the Americas, the 2014 Ebola outbreak in West Africa, and the global H1N1 (swine flu) outbreak in 2009.

outbreak of bovine spongiform encephalopathy (BSE, also known as 'mad cow disease') in the 1990s. It is for this reason that the development of EU health policy can be understood using the theory of neo-functionalism. Neo-functionalism describes a dynamic whereby the need for regulation in one area creates pressure for regulation in functionally related areas, resulting in 'spillover', with the potential to create EU policy even when the governments of the member states do not necessarily want or plan for it (see Chapter 4). The EU's regulation of how tobacco products are manufactured and sold on the internal market, for instance, has led to common rules on tobacco advertising, warning labels, and ingredients, all of which shape health; the integration of agricultural markets led to demand for an integrated food safety regime after the vCJD ('mad cow') crisis showed the divergence of regulatory systems. These and countless other examples illustrate the crucial role of neo-functional spillover as a driver of the EU's growing role in health.

EU health policy has historically advanced through crises that create a window of opportunity for further regulatory and policy development. The 1965 Thalidomide disaster formed the backdrop of the first harmonizing regulations in the area of pharmaceuticals, whilst the first EU public health programmes can be traced back to the HIV/AIDS crisis in the 1980s. Similarly, it was the first severe acute respiratory syndrome (SARS) coronavirus which put the creation of the ECDC on the agenda in 2003. This second, crisis-driven dynamic has the potential to push health, usually a low-priority item, high up the EU agenda.

The expansion of the EU's role in health has not been comprehensive, or without opposition, however. In an effort to curtail the EU's influence, member states have attributed it limited powers. Health is a general aim of the EU and thus Article 9 TFEU states that the protection of human health should be considered in all EU policies and activities. In terms of attributed power, Article 168 TFEU outlines the specific competences of the EU in health. They are far more limited and can be thought of as falling into two contrasting categories, reflecting a division between the willingness of member states to work together on 'public health' and on 'health care'. Public health refers to the health of the population as a whole. In policies adopted to protect the *public* from health risks—such as safety standards for pharmaceuticals and children's toys, for example—member states have agreed to cooperate and have assigned the

EU the necessary competences. By contrast, health care refers to policies that ensure *individual* access to medical care and the financing, organization, and distribution of resources to achieve this. The EU's role here is explicitly—above and beyond the general rules on subsidiarity—curtailed in Article 168 (7) TFEU, a provision intended to safeguard the autonomy of the member states in sensitive areas of national policy. To illustrate, this means that, whilst the EU is the sole regulator of the safety of medicines, the Treaties make clear that it has no role in national decisions about how medicines are purchased, allocated, or distributed.

The extent to which these efforts to bound the EU's health powers have been successful is limited. Although member states have used Article 168 TFEU to restrict the EU's direct access to the field of health, the health-relevance of so many other policies (agriculture, trade, internal market, competition, etc.) has made it impossible to prevent indirect, and often powerful, influence from elsewhere. Health issues find their way into legislation in areas where the EU has strong powers (such as agriculture or the internal market) whilst national public health policies that present a barrier to the free movement of goods or services are prohibited (the introduction of Minimum Unit Pricing of alcohol is a good example here). The development of health using these indirect and disparate legal bases, however, has led to a fragmented patchwork of EU health law and policy. Some initiatives are based on the direct, public health mandate; others rest on mandates from, inter alia, internal market, competition, or internal trade policy. Wider EU influence on health derives from high-level governance frameworks such as the EU's fiscal governance regime. As such, whilst the distinction between public health and health care is useful for understanding the formal allocation of health powers in the EU (de Ruijter, 2019), the reality of policy development is better understood as having three faces (Greer, 2014; Table 28.1).

The *first face*, representing the EU's public health dimension, is signified by the objective to safeguard the EU population as a whole and protect it from health risks. These efforts include binding regulation in the areas of food safety, plant and animal health, blood products, medical devices, and pharmaceuticals. They also include softer initiatives, such as the EU health programmes (see section on EU4Health), which support action on specific diseases, such as cancer and

Table 28.1 The three faces of health policy

	First face: public health	Second face: internal market	Third face: fiscal governance
Legal basis for EU action	Article 168 TFEU	Article 114 TFEU	Article 121/126 TFEU
Key EU policies and institutions	Europe Against Cancer, Quality and Safety of Blood Products, European Centre for Disease Prevention and Control	Working Time Directive, Air Quality Directives, Cross-border Healthcare Directive, Tobacco Products Directive	European Semester
Dominant policy logic	Subsidiarity, coordinating measures	Harmonization, free movement	Macroeconomic stability

HIV/AIDS. The first face of health policy is where coordination to protect against infectious disease outbreaks takes place, rooted in the ECDC, the Health Security Committee (HSC) and corresponding networks of surveillance and information sharing. Actions in the first face are generally led by DG SANTE (the Directorate General for Health and Food Safety) and are based on a logic of subsidiarity, wherein the EU seeks to support and coordinate national approaches.

The *second face* of EU health policy is connected to the public health dimension, but only to the extent that it touches on health as a side issue of market regulation. Here EU health policy has developed in interaction with market-making and regulation. Using its powers to create an internal market where goods, services, people, and capital can move freely, the EU has introduced regulations on (healthcare) professional qualifications, medicines (including vaccine approval), tobacco manufacturing and advertising, and cross-border healthcare provision. Furthermore, its wide-ranging regulations on workplace safety, the application of competition law to health care, and the right to establish services, to use just three examples, affect the working conditions of doctors, the financing of health service delivery, and the provision of health care. The second face has been the main way that the EU has shaped health and health care. In some instances, tobacco control being a good example, this has had positive outcomes for health. However, second face health policies are rarely made with health as their primary objective and this risks the development of policies which prioritize the deepening of the market and pay only 'lip service' to health concerns.

The *third face* of EU health policy takes us even further away from the immediate field of health, to the governance of fiscal policy. This involves the surveillance of member states' taxing, spending, and policies affecting their economic stability. Although it has a long history, EU fiscal governance policy accelerated in the aftermath of the euro crisis in the late 2000s (see Chapter 25) and seeks to regulate member states' fiscal policies to ensure that they do not destabilize the Eurozone or risk another crisis. Health is a large and expensive item in national budgets and so was naturally of interest to EU actors seeking to keep member states' spending under control. Its inclusion in the main fiscal governance framework—the **European Semester**—enables the EU to encourage, or even require, national governments to alter particular health policies. For example, in 2015 the EU recommended that France amend its policy on health professional education, with the theoretical power to punish in the event of noncompliance (Baeten and Vanhercke, 2017). Although the potential scope of the third face is considerable, in practice it has not been as influential as first feared (Greer and Brooks, 2021).

KEY POINTS

- EU health policy has always been fragmented, developing into a patchwork of laws and policies.
- It is possible to think of EU health policy as having three faces: public health, internal market, and fiscal governance.
- The existing tools and actors that developed within these three faces shaped the COVID-19 response.

28.3 The EU's response to COVID-19

In responding to the pandemic, the EU utilized a variety of existing policy mechanisms and adopted new measures across a number of policy areas. This section offers a short overview of the actions that were taken in the context of the three faces of EU health policy.

28.3.1 The public health face of the COVID-19 response

The EU's public health response to COVID-19 drew on the health security framework, the European Centre for Disease Prevention and Control, and the EU health programme, each of which is explored in this section.

Health security

The primary instrument of the EU's health security regime is the Decision on Serious Cross Border Threats to Health (Decision 1082/2013/EU). The Health Threats Decision was born out of a series of coordination failures in response to epidemics of SARS (2002), Bird flu (2005), Swine flu (2009), and E-Coli (2011), and its subsequent amendments established a range of instruments for responding to infectious disease outbreaks, most of which were relatively new when COVID-19 emerged (de Ruijter, 2017; Bengtsson and Rhinard, 2019). The older ones, such as communicable disease networks for the surveillance and notification of outbreaks, merged with newer elements, such as a formalized HSC representing member state health ministries, and a voluntary joint procurement mechanism for medical countermeasures for health emergencies.

Communicable disease surveillance networks are operated by the ECDC (discussed below) and, in an emergency situation, feed into the HSC. The HSC functions a little differently to most other EU committees. Committees are generally installed as an accountability mechanism to ensure Council (co-legislator) control over the Commission's (executive) implementing and delegation powers. However, the HSC is more political than most committees and aims to represent the national capitals directly, in the case of an emergency, via high level health ministry representation. During the early months of the COVID-19 outbreak, the HSC struggled to coordinate smooth information transfer but eventually served as a stable platform for coordination of national responses (Brooks et al., 2021). The Health Threats Decision also underpinned the joint procurement of vaccines and medical equipment, led by the DG SANTE. The success of this mechanism was not wholesale—its voluntary nature quickly faced challenges, and it struggled to address the sharp shortages of medical equipment, and act on mounting pressure to secure contractual agreements with pharmaceutical companies.

The Health Threats Decision is linked to the Union Civil Protection Mechanism (UCPM; Article 11 (4) Decision 1082/2013/EU), which is managed by the directorate for civil protection and humanitarian operations (DG ECHO), and both frameworks share a commitment to the 'solidarity clause' in Article 222 TFEU. The UCPM is a more generalist response mechanism, designed to foster cooperation in preventing and protecting against natural or man-made disasters, and normally used when a situation affects one or a handful of member states at one time (Box 28.2). During the COVID-19 pandemic, however, the UCPM and the HSC worked in parallel, exploiting complementary mechanisms for procurement and distribution of critical supplies. The UCPM was used to repatriate citizens and deploy medical teams, whilst RescEU, a stockpile facility within the UCPM, was used to create a supply of medical equipment. Separately from these activities, the joint procurement mechanism was used to obtain medical supplies, PPE and pharmaceuticals. Each mechanism—DG ECHO's UCPM and DG SANTE's joint procurement system—has strengths and weaknesses. Funded directly by member states, the joint procurement mechanism is intergovernmental in nature, enjoying a far higher budget but lacking centralized control over distribution. By contrast, the more supranational UCPM has a smaller budget (from central EU funds) but is more quickly activated and easily coordinated. In the months that followed the onset of the pandemic, steps were taken to maximize the benefits from both models by boosting the budget of the UCPM and strengthening coordination of the joint procurement mechanism via the HSC, with new legislation for the procurement of COVID-19 vaccines (European Commission, 2020e).

BOX 28.2   CASE STUDY: THE UNION CIVIL PROTECTION MECHANISM

EU cooperation in the area of civil protection began in the 1980s, with mutual assistance in response to natural disasters. A formal framework for coordination—the UCPM—was adopted in 2001 and subsequently strengthened to give the EU a role in certifying, coordinating, and deploying critical resources, as well as supporting preparedness and prevention activities. In addition to EU member states, the UCPM has six 'participating states' (Iceland, Norway, Serbia, North Macedonia, Montenegro, and Turkey). It works by match-making countries 'in need' with countries that have available resources. The EU maintains a list of states' available strategic resources (expert rescue teams, medical personnel, fire-fighting equipment, etc.), certifies the quality and standard of these nominated resources, and coordinates various training and simulation exercises. Should a disaster occur, a state can make a request and activate the UCPM, at which point the Emergency Response Coordination Centre identifies the needed resources and coordinates their deployment from the 'host' to the country in need. Over time, the UCPM has been upgraded to include RescEU, a common, European pool of resource; that is, owned collectively rather than reliant on states. In 2019, a reserve of RescEU aeroplanes and helicopters was created and, in March 2020, a stockpile of medical equipment and field hospital resources was added.

Whilst the UCPM has successfully provided resources to tackle forest fires, earthquakes, and similar emergencies, it is less well positioned to respond to a situation in which all member states require the same resources at the same time. As COVID-19 unfolded, national governments were either already facing the pandemic or fearful that it would soon reach their territories, and thus reluctant to volunteer resources for deployment elsewhere. It performed well in some areas—for example, the UCPM was used to coordinate transport for the repatriation of EU citizens stranded abroad when travel restrictions were introduced. The new RescEU medical stockpile was used to distribute PPE, ventilators, and laboratory supplies, and medical teams were also dispatched to regions heavily affected by the virus. However, several of these elements were slow and limited. The medical stockpile, for instance, was only created after the pandemic had started and global demand for these supplies had increased, which limited its impact in 2020 and 2021. These experiences contributed to a broader sense that the existing EU structures were not sufficient to address a large-scale emergency and could not play a central role in response to the crisis.

The European Centre for Disease Prevention and Control (ECDC)

Established in 2004, the ECDC is a decentralized EU health agency based in Stockholm whose mission involves identifying, assessing, and communicating emerging health threats (Regulation 851/2004). It works in partnership with the European Commission, national experts nominated by member states, and other EU agencies, including the European Medicines Agency (EMA) and the European Food Safety Authority (EFSA). However, its powers and resources are limited. The ECDC has no binding authority outside its own staff and, due to its lack of executive and operational powers, it is weaker than other EU agencies such as the EMA. The ECDC's budget for 2020 was €60.4 million and it had just 286 employees (compare to, for example, the $6 billion and approximately 20,000 staff assigned to the Centers for Disease Control, the ECDC's US-equivalent; see European Parliament, 2020; Jordana and Trivino-Salazar, 2020). Consequently, the ECDC has been described as a 'hollow core' rather than a 'hub of communicable disease control in the EU' (Greer, 2012).

During the COVID-19 pandemic, the ECDC's primary role was to release periodically updated 'rapid risk assessments' and provide scientific advice on public health responses to member states and the Commission. Additionally, it set up a COVID-19 website and produced technical guidelines to support national responses on topics such as the use of face masks, contact tracing, control measures in public transport, and surveillance at long-term care facilities. The limits of its capacities were soon made apparent, however, and it was criticized for lacking data-sharing capacity, legal authority, and executive power (European Parliament, 2020). Criticism was also directed at ECDC's initial risk assessment—which understated the likelihood of spread to Europe—as well as its position on both laboratory capacity and the use of face masks.

The ECDC is constrained on two fronts. Firstly, its mandate is only to *assess* risk, whilst responsibility for *managing* risk rests with member states (Pacces and Weimer, 2020). In practice, this meant that when COVID-19 emerged, the agency played an important role in assessing the risk of the disease reaching other states, of transmission between people and of the threat from new variants, for example. Its authority was much more curtailed when it came to prescribing appropriate actions and responses from national leaders (for example in asserting whether governments should make face masks mandatory outdoors). Secondly, implementation of its advice relies upon national public health capacities, infrastructure, and resources, which vary considerably between member states. To take a simple (if crude) example, the number of organizations listed as 'competent' for communicable disease control originally ranged from one (as in, for instance, Spain) to seven (as in Poland), suggesting quite different approaches to organizing and coordinating responses to disease outbreaks (Elliott et al., 2012). Subsequent rationalization of competent bodies might have simply made the system look neater by obscuring the complexity rather than actually making surveillance and reporting more coherent—all member states have a single competent body now, but how competent are those competent bodies (Mätzke 2012)? The pandemic thus highlighted the need for an empowered ECDC, equipped with a stronger mandate to address and coordinate the response to cross-national health threats and support communicable disease capacity-building within member states. Responding to this, and to proposals from the French and German governments in May 2020, the Commission proposed in November 2020 to expand the ECDC's legal mandate and give the Centre a stronger role in coordinating surveillance, preparedness, and responses to health crises.

Public health programmes: The EU4Health Programme

The 2021–27 health programme was originally intended to be smaller than its predecessor and to be subsumed, for the first time, within the much broader umbrella of the European Social Fund Plus. However, COVID-19 highlighted the importance of cooperation in health and the value of EU health policy. In response to this increased salience, the European Commission proposed a new, stand-alone version of the 2021–27 health programme, known as the EU4Health programme. After much negotiation (see the paragraph on the third face response to COVID-19, above) a budget of €5.1 billion was agreed, more than ten times the budget of the previous health programme, and the scope of the new plans is ambitious. Programmes to date have contained similar sets of objectives, such as preventing disease, improving health security and generating health knowledge, and have been proposed in documents of between 10 and

15 pages. By contrast, the EU4Health proposal is 56 pages long and retains the 'traditional' objectives, as well as adding new ones (for instance to improve the availability of medicines) and widening the scope of the EU's health policy (to encompass health system strengthening, for example) (see Box 28.3).

The health programme is a **soft law** tool, meaning that it does not compel or require member states to act in a particular way or change national policies. Rather, it provides funds for collaborative projects and facilitates voluntary cooperation, exchange of best practices and sharing of information between health officials, civil society actors and health professionals. Its scope, however, is still determined by the health mandate given to the EU in the founding treaties. What makes the EU4Health programme significant is the potential to extend EU activity into areas that are ostensibly reserved for national governments and where the EU has previously played a lesser role. Health systems strengthening is a good example here. The strength of a health system depends upon many factors, including the physical infrastructure of hospitals and clinics, the recruitment and training of a skilled health workforce, the procurement and distribution of medicines and therapies, and the existence of a sustainable system of financing. Article 168 (7) TFEU states that 'the organisation and delivery of health services and medical care', under which most of these factors fall, are responsibilities of member states. The EU4Health programme does not transfer legal power in this area to the EU, but it does establish a significant 'carrot' to encourage cooperation and engagement with common capacity-building actions. For example, it envisages the provision of training and temporary exchange programmes for medical and healthcare staff. The extent to which the EU will be able to encourage, support, and bring about change to strengthen national health systems will depend upon the willingness of national governments to engage with these efforts but the EU4Health programme presents the potential for a Europeanization of health systems, as well as of vaccine policy, emergency preparedness planning, health data reporting and surveillance, and many other aspects of health policy.

28.3.2 The internal market face of the COVID-19 response

In addition to its direct, public health responses to the pandemic, the EU took action using the various internal market tools at its disposal. This section reviews

BOX 28.3   CASE STUDY: THE EU4HEALTH PROGRAMME

The EU's fourth health programme (2021–27) has ten specific objectives.

1. Strengthen the capability of the Union for prevention, preparedness, and response to serious cross-border threats to health, and the management of health crises, including through coordination, provision, and deployment of emergency health care capacity, data gathering, and surveillance.

2. Ensure the availability in the Union of reserves or stockpiles of crisis relevant products, and a reserve of medical, health-care, and support staff to be mobilized in case of a crisis.

3. Support actions to ensure appropriate availability, accessibility, and affordability of crisis relevant products and other necessary health supplies.

4. Strengthen the effectiveness, accessibility, sustainability, and resilience of health systems, including by supporting digital transformation, the uptake of digital tools and services, systemic reforms, implementation of new care models and universal health coverage, and address inequalities in health.

5. Support actions aimed at strengthening the health system's ability to foster disease prevention and health promotion, patient rights and cross-border healthcare, and promote the excellence of medical and healthcare professionals.

6. Support action for the surveillance, prevention, diagnosis, and treatment and care of non-communicable diseases, and notably of cancer.

7. Foster and support the prudent and efficient use of medicines, and in particular of antimicrobials, and more environmentally friendly production and disposal of medicines and medical devices.

8. Support the development, implementation, and enforcement of Union health legislation and provide high-quality, comparable, and reliable data to underpin policy making and monitoring, and promote the use of health impact assessments of relevant policies.

9. Support integrated work among Member States, and in particular their health systems, including the implementation of high-impact prevention practices, and scaling up networking through the European Reference Networks and other transnational networks.

10. Support the Union's contribution to international and global health initiatives.

Source: European Commission (2020c).

the Commission's response to early border closures and challenges to free movement, as well specific measures within the markets for vaccines and pharmaceutical products.

Borders and free movement

As described in the introduction, one of the immediate policy reflexes to the announcement of a new and highly contagious pathogen in Europe was the closure of borders, for people and for exports. As shortages of medical grade masks, respirators, and other supplies became apparent, a number of EU member states enacted prohibitions on the export of these goods. This reflex touched the core of the European project—the four freedoms—and threatened the norm of solidarity (see Chapter 20). The EU response was quick and multi-faceted.

An initial threat of infringement proceedings against offending governments was followed by statements reiterating the importance of the free movement of goods as a countermeasure to combat COVID-19, and outlining that the EU should stand together to ensure that goods and equipment are 'channelled to those who need them most' (European Commission, 2020b). This call to use the internal market as an instrument of solidarity was complemented by a diplomatic approach to seeking the reopening of borders. Ordinarily, when a member state creates a barrier to the free movement of goods or persons, or otherwise hinders the internal market, this decision is communicated to all other member states and the Commission. During the pandemic, the Commission set up a specific task force which drew on this information to compile a list of the essential goods that were needed to fight COVID-19 and pinpoint the disruptions they faced. This was used to negotiate the reopening of borders and the creation of 'Green Lanes' for expedited movement of critical supplies.

Some interesting legal developments have followed these events. Formally speaking, during an infectious disease outbreak member states are permitted to use the public health exception contained in Article 36 TFEU, which allows governments to violate the rules of free movement in Article 35 TFEU, in order to protect health. In this instance, a member state is allowed to restrict the import or export of a particular good, such as contaminated foods, so long as they do this in a proportionate and non-discriminatory manner. A proportional measure, in this setting, has traditionally been interpreted with reference to the objective of protecting *national* public health. However, in the face of numerous export bans of face masks and other PPE, the Commission has proposed a different legal analysis:

[The measures need to be] appropriate, necessary and proportionate to achieve such [health] objective, by ensuring an adequate supply to the persons who need the most while preventing any occurrence or aggravation of shortages of goods, considered as essential—such as individual protective equipment, medical devices or medicinal products—throughout the EU. (European Commission, 2020a: annex 2)

The new interpretation on the Commission's side goes on to state that:

A simple export ban alone . . . would therefore prove unsuitable to reach the objective of protecting the health of people living in Europe. (European Commission, 2020a: annex 2)

There are two innovations in this approach. The first is that proportionality should be understood with reference to the protection of *European* public health—that is, the health of the EU population as a whole—and not just national public health. The second is that the Commission's interpretation essentially turns the internal market face of EU health policy on its head, by assuming that health is the objective and the market exists as an instrument to ensure health, rather than the traditional, reverse understanding of health as ancillary to the market. On this basis, the Commission deemed the national bans on the export of critical health supplies to be disproportionate and, via the diplomatic channels that had been opened, ensured their removal without the involvement of the Court of Justice of the EU. However, if the Court were to adopt a similar interpretation, this would mark a significant redefinition of the proportionality of the public health exception to the prohibition to hamper intra-EU trade, with the potential to underpin expansion of the influence of EU law on national health policies.

Vaccines and medicines

The market for pharmaceutical products has been at the core of the EU's COVID-19 response and two important measures have been adopted to strengthen

it: the EU Vaccine Strategy and the EU Pharmaceutical Strategy.

The Commission presented its Vaccine Strategy in June 2020, with the objective of catalyzing the manufacture of vaccines to combat COVID-19 and coordinating their distribution across Europe (European Commission, 2020d). The Strategy aims to ensure equitable access for all member states to an affordable vaccine, as well as establishing the EU's contribution to global vaccine equity (see Box 28.4). In addition to adapting the regulations that govern vaccine development and approval to speed up these processes, it provides for European authorities to forge agreements with individual vaccine producers on behalf of interested member states, using advance purchase agreements (APAs). By the end of 2020, the Commission had signed APAs with six pharmaceutical companies: Pfizer-BioNTech, Moderna, AstraZeneca, Johnson & Johnson, Sanofi-GSK, and CureVac. As of April 2021, €2.8 billion had been used to secure production and supply, and four vaccines have been authorized by the EMA: the vaccine developed by BioNTech and Pfizer was granted a conditional marketing authorization on 21 December 2020, the Moderna vaccine was authorized on 6 January 2021, the AstraZeneca vaccine was authorized on 29 January 2021, and the Johnson & Johnson vaccine was given conditional authorization on 11 March 2021.

The regulatory basis for the Vaccine Strategy gives the EU more centralized power in the purchasing and distribution of vaccines than the joint procurement agreement under the Health Threats Decision (discussed in the Health Security section), foreseeing distribution on a per-capita basis to ensure fair access and support from a platform to monitor the effectiveness of national vaccination strategies. However, its operation has been far from coordinated. Challenges emerged as soon as contract negotiation began. Although the APAs theoretically prevent member states from engaging in parallel negotiations, several EU countries purchased more vaccine doses on their own. Germany, for instance, bought an additional 30 million doses of the Pfizer-BioNTech and CureVac vaccines in the autumn of 2020. Moreover, as time passed and shortages of vaccines became more apparent, several member states began to seek vaccines from beyond the EU, namely in Russia and China. Hungary has led this initiative but Poland, Austria, Slovakia, Denmark, and the Czech Republic are all reported to have engaged in discussions about procuring Russian 'Sputnik V' or Chinese 'Sinovac' doses.

Even where vaccines have been successfully secured by the EU, difficulties have beset their supply and rollout. At the end of January 2021 it became clear that the contract negotiated with AstraZeneca was not going to be fulfilled as promised; by the end of March 2021, the EU had received only a third of the AstraZeneca doses that it was expecting. Concerns soon emerged that doses of the vaccine were being diverted from the EU to fulfil other contracts (namely that with the UK); Europe is a leading producer of vaccines and yet it seemed to be exporting most of what it made to other countries. This led to criticism of the Commission's approach to negotiating the APA contracts, which lacked detail on how supply would be ensured and precise timelines for delivery. After a public battle with AstraZeneca and facing mounting pressure over the turn to Russian and Chinese vaccines in several member states, the EU announced that it would empower member states to block exports of vaccines. An initial framework for this narrowly avoided disaster when it activated an emergency override provision in the Brexit Withdrawal Agreement and introduced border checks between the Republic of Ireland and Northern Ireland (see Chapter 27). This was quickly rescinded and, in its place, in March 2021, new rules were adopted that allow the EU to withhold the export of vaccines to countries which have higher vaccination rates than Europe, or which have blocked exports to the EU. Although softer than an outright ban, these rules have been criticized as restricting access to vaccines in other countries (see Box 28.4).

In understanding the controversies about vaccines in 2021, two things are worth bearing in mind. The first is that delays in acquiring vaccines create a politics of blame avoidance. Member state politicians will routinely blame the EU for any policy failure, and vaccines are no exception. Absorbing blame is a major function of the EU. The second is that while governments chose to procure vaccines through the EU, they are responsible for turning vaccines into vaccinations—for getting shots into arms. The EU's role is minimal once the vaccines are purchased and delivered. Once the vaccine supply is adequate, we can expect different countries to have very different success in vaccinating their population, with challenging public health problems and perhaps recriminations as a result.

At the root of the EU's vaccine problems is a lack of capacity for production on a large scale and at speed, and broader, systematic weaknesses in the supply chains of pharmaceutical manufacturing. In the short term, the EU sought to mitigate these issues by temporarily relaxing relevant aspects of the regulatory regime, and delaying entry into force of new legislation, for instance on medical devices (Box 28.5). For the longer term, these issues are the subject of the EU Pharmaceutical Strategy, published in November 2020 (European Commission, 2020g). The Strategy aims to amend the current pharmaceutical

---

BOX 28.4   KEY DEBATES: EQUITABLE ACCESS TO COVID-19 VACCINES

Since the start of the crisis, the EU has pledged its commitment to ensuring global vaccine equity and opposed any obstruction of relevant global supply chains. It has been one of the leading donors to the COVAX Facility (a global platform for coordinating equitable and affordable access to COVID-19 vaccines) and committed to creating a vaccine sharing mechanism at EU level, through which it will donate a portion of its purchased vaccines to non-EU countries. The veracity of its commitment can be challenged, however, not least given that its tighter export rules (discussed above) have already seen it refuse an export request to Australia. Moreover, having announced the sharing mechanism in January 2021, this had yet (as of April 2021), to take form.

The uncertainties over the EU's commitment to vaccine equity mirror those in the international system. The COVAX facility projects that it might be able to cover 3.3 per cent of the population in the countries which depend upon it, in the first half of 2021, and just 20 per cent by the end of 2020 (del Rio et al., 2021). These figures stand in stark contrast to the vaccination rates in wealthier states like the UK, which has led vaccination and aims to give its whole population a first dose of vaccine by mid-2021. Lack of donations is accompanied by obstructions to national vaccine production efforts in the form of intellectual property rules which prevent countries that could produce vaccines—like those in Africa, Asia, and Latin America—from doing so. The EU is a strong actor on the global stage, particularly as regards pharmaceuticals, but it has, so far, failed to use its political influence to affect such barriers and ensure a more equitable global rollout of vaccinations.

BOX 28.5   CASE STUDY: MEDICAL DEVICES REGULATION IN THE EU

The COVID-19 pandemic increased the demand for vital medical devices, such as ventilators, in vitro diagnostics, and PPE. It also disrupted the application of two important new EU regulations for medical devices and in vitro diagnostic devices, initiated in 2017 and intended to come into effect in 2020 and 2022 respectively. These new regulations were adopted to address significant shortcomings in the existing regime. The requirements for commercializing medical devices in the EU vary according to the level of risk that different devices present. For low-risk (Class I) medical devices, companies may simply declare that their devices meet relevant standards. For high-risk (Class III) products, private companies known as notified bodies (NBs) must be involved throughout the design and manufacture stages. Designated by their member states, NBs—rather than public authorities—carry out tasks related to conformity assessment before devices are put on the market. Importantly, unlike pharmaceuticals (and medical devices in the USA) medical devices are not evaluated for their safety and effectiveness in the EU regime. Rather, a narrower assessment is made of their safety and whether they function as intended. Several defective medical devices—including the PIP breast implants manufactured in France—exposed the weaknesses of a framework relying on private bodies to conduct pre-market safety assessment (Jarman et al., 2020). This pre-2017 framework was not protective of a high level of human health (Jarman et al., 2020).

In 2017, the EU passed two new laws intended to address these issues. The new regulations will expand the EU's centralized database (EUDAMED) to collect new data on post-market surveillance, create a central register of supply chain operators and NBs, centralize serious incident reports, and ensure life-cycle traceability. Despite representing a significant improvement to some elements of the previous regulatory framework, NBs and supply chain operators remain almost entirely responsible for pre-market control, leaving the pre-2017 framework intact in these areas (Jarman et al., 2020). Regulation 2017/745 (the Medical Devices Regulation, MDR) was due to be applied from 26 May 2020, whilst Regulation 2017/746 (the In Vitro Diagnostic Medical Devices Regulation) was to be fully effective in 2022. However, in April 2020 the Commission announced the postponement of the application of the MDR for one year and introduced a new derogation from existing conformity assessment procedures, to expedite the production of PPEs, containers for intravenous injections, and to alter requirements for ventilators. These initiatives were intended to counter the risk of potential equipment shortages due to the pandemic and give manufacturers more time to conform to the new regulatory regime, offering a good example of how the market face of EU health policy has responded to COVID-19.

governance system to make medicines more affordable and innovative. Elements which respond directly to COVID-19 and the threat of pandemics include the creation of a Health Emergency preparedness and Response Authority (HERA), tasked with monitoring raw material availability, addressing supply chain vulnerabilities, developing strategic investments for research, development, manufacturing, and distribution of medical countermeasures. HERA will act as a 'horizon scanning' facility, anticipating new threats, like a potential outbreak of influenza, and identifying any weaknesses in the supply chain that might hinder the development, production, and distribution of an appropriate vaccine. Among its wider actions, the Strategy will create a European Health Data Space to facilitate interoperable cross-border analysis of health data. This would mean, for instance, that patients moving from one EU country to another would be able to bring their health data with them, rather than having to re-do tests just because the data cannot be transferred between systems. More sources and

interoperability of health data will also support health research, giving researchers access to a larger pool of cases to study and better evidence with which to map inequalities in health between Europeans.

Finally, the Pharmaceutical Strategy provides for a revision of EU pharmaceutical legislation to improve access to affordable medicines. Currently, whilst the EU has a unified regime for market access, regimes for pricing and reimbursement remain fragmented. This means, for example, that whilst a new cancer medicine may be evaluated and approved for sale in a centralized, EU system, the negotiation of its price and the conditions under which (and whether) it will be reimbursed happens separately in each member state. The EU requires transparency about the nature of the pricing regime and the provision of information about the decisions that are made, but pricing remains the purview of national governments. The Pharmaceutical Strategy does not fundamentally challenge this status quo but provides for the Commission to launch a group to steer cooperation between national pricing and reimbursement authorities and healthcare payers. The aim is to foster cooperation on the affordability and cost-effectiveness of medicines, extending coordination into areas of health policy that are currently outside of the EU's formal competence. As it develops, the Pharmaceutical Strategy will therefore offer a good indication of whether COVID-19, as a public health crisis, has been 'enough' to prompt an expansion of the EU's role in health and greater EU health integration.

28.3.3 The fiscal policy face of the COVID-19 response

Fiscal policy might not seem like a health policy, but the third face of the EU has had powerful consequences for health and health systems before and during the crisis. A core pillar of the EU's response to COVID-19 has been the adaptation of the existing fiscal policy framework and the mobilization of funds to help member states mitigate the effects of the crisis and repair their economies (see Chapter 22). With each of these measures, the EU institutions and national governments have been careful to avoid repeating the mistakes made in the aftermath of the financial and economic crises of 2010/11. Two particularly important decisions have been taken. The first was to activate the 'general escape clause' and temporarily suspend the limits on national deficits and debt that are applied by the EU's fiscal governance framework (see Chapter 22). This decision, taken in early 2020, recognizes that restricting government spending during the pandemic is infeasible and that the approach taken in 2011—where Germany and others urged (and enforced) balanced budgets despite the ongoing recession—caused further damage, including damage to health systems (Stuckler et al., 2017). Part of the weakness of health systems in the face of COVID-19 could be clearly attributed to the previous decade's austerity measures (Dubin, 2021; Falkenbach and Caiani, 2021). Meeting in March 2021, leaders agreed to continue this suspension until at least the end of 2022.

A second key decision was the adoption of an amended long-term budget for the EU, supplemented by a dedicated recovery package, known as Next Generation EU (NGEU). NGEU provides €750 billion of additional funding to support recovery from the pandemic and mitigation of its economic impact. Its largest component is the Recovery and Resilience Facility (RRF), a fund to support reforms and investment.

Of the €672.5 billion available to member states under the RRF, €360 billion will be issued as loans and €312.5 billion will be issued as grants. This immediately marks a change from the approach taken in 2011, when assistance was offered only in the form of loans and, at the behest of the 'creditor' states, these loans came with conditions attached. The provisions for funding the RRF also mark a step-change—for the first time, member states have agreed that the EU should raise funds itself, directly, on the capital markets, and play a role in distributing them. This is new territory for the EU and represents perhaps the most significant change to result from the crisis.

The impact of these new instruments on health will be determined by the administrative structure through which they are applied. The approach here has been to adapt key elements of the existing fiscal governance framework—the **European Semester**—to the RRF, so as to integrate the two. Governments will submit Recovery and Resilience Plans (RRPs) in which they will outline the investment projects and reforms that they intended to undertake with funds from the RRF. Reflecting the usual Semester process, the Commission will assess these plans and they will be signed off by the Council, before funds are disbursed. Crucially for health, the documents and objectives guiding the RRPs are different to those which usually guide national input into the Semester process. Prior to 2020, governments submitted national reform programmes which outlined their intended investments and reforms in response to the Annual Growth Survey (AGS), a set of economic priorities for Europe. The AGS is published by the Commission and has historically referred to health in terms of fiscal sustainability and the relevance of initiatives on climate change, data and artificial intelligence, and taxation; it has rarely addressed health as an objective in its own right. By contrast, the 2021 Annual Sustainable Growth Survey (now renamed), explicitly recognizes the need to invest in health and health systems and outlines how RRF funds can support this. Moreover, the RRPs, which governments will submit in April 2021, are guided by a set of templates and flagship areas identified by the Commission. The templates list examples of health investments that can be supported and health features as part of the fifth flagship, which urges governments to target the modernization of healthcare and other public administration systems with their reforms. In sum, whereas health used to be either ignored, or framed in relation to other priorities within the Semester, is it now a core objective, raising the potential for greater, EU-financed investment in national health systems and pandemic preparedness (Renda and Castro, 2020).

The decisions that underpin these developments in fiscal governance were politically fraught ones. EU leaders clashed during the second-longest ever European Council summit and the resulting agreement re-balanced the loan and grant components and stripped much of the funding proposed for health and other programmes. The European Parliament fought back strongly and much of the funding was restored but the battle continued, through early 2021, as national parliaments began to play their role in ratifying the agreement. In order to raise funds on the capital markets and launch the RRF, the Commission needs national parliaments in all 27 member states to ratify the relevant legislative instrument (the Own Resources Decision). Several states have failed to timetable ratification, delaying the timetable for disbursing the funds, and the German constitutional

court complicated matters further by pausing German ratification to review an (unsuccessful) challenge to the RRFs legality under the EU treaties. As of April 2021, it remained unclear when the decision would be ratified and national governments would submit their RRPs.

The EU's fiscal policy response to COVID-19 and the impact of these changes upon health policy is thus a story of significant integrative steps and deep political contention. Much of what has been agreed—the RRF, the Commission's role in raising and distributing funds, amendments to the Semester process—is temporary in nature, designed to apply only in the context of the pandemic and to be removed/reverted once this is over. However, important precedents are being set and it remains possible that the benefits of a more integrated, coherent EU fiscal policy will become both apparent and appealing. It is not clear, if this is the case, whether those who wish to revert to the old, flawed model of EU fiscal governance will be easily able to do so.

KEY POINTS

- The EU's immediate public health response drew on its health security and civil protection regimes, supported by the ECDC. These functioned relatively well, within the confines of their mandates and capacities.

- Early border closures and acts of national protectionism were resolved quickly, but the EU Vaccine Strategy has been beset by difficulties, both logistical and political.

- Weaknesses revealed by the pandemic prompted the adoption of a new public health programme, with a significantly increased budget, and a new Pharmaceutical Strategy. These have the potential to underpin a greater EU role in health in the future.

- Some of the most significant changes have been brought about in the third face of health policy, but most of these are both temporary and highly political.

28.4 Conclusion: investing in EU health policy?

Advocates for a European Union health policy entered 2020 relieved that the EU would continue to have a public health Directorate-General, but well aware of their marginality in an EU that influences health in many ways. A year later, the EU had committed to invest in public health in a way that they would have found unimaginable.

Much was still recognizable: the change was in the political salience and funds associated with EU health policy, in particular in its first face of explicit public health action. The basic architecture, comprised of DG SANTE, the ECDC, the Health Programme, the

EMA, and civil protection, remains recognizably the same, just far better funded and politically visible. The Treaty bases also remain the same, showing just how much was legally possible under Article 168 TFEU once member states became politically supportive (Purnhagen et al., 2020). Yet under the surface of this largely unchanged architecture, important developments are afoot. The strategies on vaccines and pharmaceuticals are novel and wide-ranging, the content of the EU4Health Programme broadens the scope of the EU's health activity, and proposals under the European Health Union would see the mandates of the ECDC and EMA expanded, and new agencies (like HERA) created.

In the second and third faces we see developments that are less obviously relevant to health but just as, if not more, influential. The potential legal redefinition of public health—as an EU-level goal rather than a reason to avoid EU regulation—might mark a significant change in EU regulatory politics and law for the future. The powers of the EU over health care systems remain limited but the adaptation of the European Semester and the guidance that accompanies its 2021 cycle has the potential to reframe the way in which health is addressed within the fiscal governance framework. These initiatives have been heavily contested and their roll-out has been far from smooth in some cases. The Vaccine Strategy has been one site of criticism, which bodes ill for its longer-term companion, the Pharmaceutical Strategy, whilst the RRF has been another, still yet to be implemented two months after entering into force. On balance, however, the decisions that have been taken are ambitious, often unprecedented and significant in their potential to change the nature of EU health policy. As a result the EU should, in the future, enjoy considerable normative and directive public health force through its increased fiscal and intellectual resources. The risk is that the EU is blamed, however justifiably, for public health and vaccination failures, and its legitimacy to act erodes again.

There was a brief moment in the spring of 2020 when narratives of failure and disintegration were everywhere, based on member states' egotism and border closures. Similar narratives of failure arose early in 2021 with vaccination programmes. Health policy has been one of the most contentious and difficult areas for member states to collaborate, even after earlier communicable disease scares, such as SARS and Swine flu. What should impress us is how quickly EU member states realized that they were all in it together—that the EU was too integrated, and its component countries too small, to fragment. Fragmentation and disunion was manifestly too costly, and so its member states took a leap ahead. Was it the right answer, and are the EU institutions and procedures up to the tasks they have been given? Will the EU gain legitimacy in the eyes of voters and governments? Time will tell. But the logic of integration is powerful. Shared good public health was always part of a viable European Union; in 2020, member states realized that this would take investment. And invest they did.

? QUESTIONS

1. Should the EU have a greater role in health policy?

2. Why have member states supported the involvement of the EU in some areas of health policy but not others?

3. Which theory or theories are more successful in explaining the development of EU health law and policy?

4. Should the ECDC have a role in risk management, as well as risk regulation?

5. How might the EU4Health programme change member states' health policies?

6. How could the EU regulatory regime for pharmaceuticals and medical devices be improved in light of lessons from the pandemic?

7. Does the response to COVID-19 suggest that EU member states feel solidarity with each other?

8. How might the Commission's reinterpretation of the public health derogation affect the future of EU health policy?

9. What is the potential relevance of the Recovery and Resilience Facility for health policy?

10. In which of the three faces of EU health policy is the most significant change being seen?

 ## GUIDE TO FURTHER READING

de Ruijter, A. (2019) *EU Health Law & Policy: The Expansion of EU Power in Public Health and Health Care* (Oxford: Oxford University Press). Describes how the EU's power in healthcare and public health has expanded, and discusses what this power means for EU health values and rights.

Greer, S.L. et al. (2nd edition 2019; 3rd edition forthcoming 2021) *Everything You always Wanted to Know about European Union Health Policies but Were Afraid to Ask* (Copenhagen: WHO Europe). Provides a detailed overview of the EU's health laws and policies; forthcoming 2021 edition includes account of COVID-19 and relevant changes to EU health governance.

Greer, S.L., King, E.J., Perlata, A., and Massard de Fonseca, E. (eds) (forthcoming 2021) *Coronavirus Politics: The Comparative Politics and Policy of COVID-19* (Michigan: University of Michigan Press). A global comparative study of how COVID-19 has been addressed in different countries, with a dedicated chapter on the EU's response.

Health Economics, Policy and Law (2021) Special issue on the future of EU health law and policy, 16(1). A special issue on the politics and law of EU health policy when the pandemic struck, including discussions of the ECDC, regulation and pricing of medical devices and pharmaceuticals, and fiscal governance.

Journal of Health Politics, Policy and Law (2021) Special issue on health care and the fate of social Europe, 46(1). A special issue bringing together research on the state of EU health policy as it was when the COVID-19 pandemic struck. Assessments of the fiscal governance framework, public health competence, and health technology assessment case study are particularly relevant to the subsequent COVID-19 response.

 Access the online resources to take your learning and understanding further, including extra multiple-choice questions with instant feedback, web links, answer guidance to end-of-chapter questions, and updates on new developments in EU politics.

www.oup.com/he/cini-borragan7e

29

The Future of the EU

Brigid Laffan

Chapter Contents

Reader's Guide

This chapter is structured around four scenarios on the future of the European Union (EU): 'Disinte-gration', 'Piecemeal Adjustment', 'Functional Federalism', and 'A European Sovereignty'. The political battle concerning the future of the Union is a battle that cuts across all four scenarios. The second decade of the twenty-first century will be a formative one for the EU because of the immense chal-lenges of climate change, the accelerating digital transformation, Europe's unstable neighborhood and the impact on Europe's role in the world arising from the return of Great Power competition. After a decade of crises, the EU finds itself again in testing times against the backdrop of the COVID-19 pan-demic and its consequences for European societies and economies. In 2021 it embarked on one of its periodic deliberations about its future with a Conference on the Future of Europe (CoFE), launched on 9 May 2021. The perennial questions about the EU remain—how does it collectively amass suf-ficient political authority to address Europe's challenges while maintaining its legitimacy? How can it be resilient as a Union while managing the deep diversity that characterizes Europe? European inte-gration has to manage the ties and tensions between the Union and its component parts, between its character as a Union of states and peoples. The four scenarios are a heuristic device to explore the future of the Union at a time of extraordinary uncertainty and structural change. Disintegrative fissures should not be ignored. The United Kingdom (UK), a significant member state, departed the EU on 31 January 2020 and left the Single Market at the end of the transition period on 31 December 2020. Piecemeal Adjustment, the dominant response to the EU crisis and to events on Europe's bor-ders, continues to have resonance, as does Functional Federalism, defined as further integration but in specific fields. The fourth scenario, 'A European Sovereignty', sometimes defined as 'strategic au-tonomy', emerged on the political agenda with the election of French President Macron in May 2017.

29.1 Introduction

Debate and discussion on the future of the European Union (EU) never abates because the EU is not a stable polity and the political project to build an 'ever closer union' continues. The EU, which is tangible and visible in daily life, remains indeterminate and ambiguous, as captured by the idea that European integration is *A Journey to an Unknown Destination* (Schonfeld, 1973). The **Lisbon Treaty** supplies the Union's overarching constitutional framework in the second decade of the twenty-first century; it specifies the decision rules and institutional roles that govern how policies are made and administered and it establishes the competences of the Union in different spheres. In addition, it encapsulates the values and goals that underpin the EU (see Chapter 3).

The Union is in a period of transition, a **critical juncture**, and is subject to multiple, and not necessarily convergent, trends and pressures. Europe's Union was tested and contested during the troubled times it faced since 2009. Two exogenous shocks, the eurozone crisis and the migration crisis, generated internal economic, political, and social turbulence in the Union (Laffan, 2018). Ursula von der Leyen, Commission President nominee when she outlined her key political priorities at the European Parliament (EP) in July 2019 prior to her election, aimed to take the Union beyond crisis politics to a focus on key strategic goals. The von der Leyen agenda was bold; it included four transformative projects—a European Green Deal, Digital, strengthening Europe's role in the world, and a European economy that works for the people (von der Leyen, 2019). These priorities converged with the European Council's Strategic Agenda. Within three months of assuming office, Europe was again in crisis mode as the COVID-19 pandemic swept across the continent. Crises are 'open moments' or 'moments of truth' that impact on rulers and ruled (Laffan, 2018: 2). They generate uncertainty and threat and may act as a focal point for major change (Gourevitch, 1992). Once again Europe has to prove its resilience.

Four important developments are likely to have a major impact on the Union by 2030. The first is the continuing legacy of the **eurozone** crisis, a crisis that tested the Union's legal, institutional, economic, and political fabric, and although the acute phase of the crisis has ended, the single currency regime is neither fully stable nor complete. The divergence of economic performance between the core eurozone countries and those on the periphery create deep tensions at the heart of the currency union that resurfaced during the pandemic. An incomplete Banking Union remains a source of potential stress (see Chapter 25). Second, Europe's borderlands and neighbourhood continue to be unstable, and the consequences of this may be seen in the continuous migratory flows across the Mediterranean, conflict, and the failed or failing states in the MENA (Middle East and North Africa) region. Relations between Turkey and the EU have deteriorated as President Erdogan adopted an increasingly hostile posture in the Eastern Mediterranean. To the Union's east, member states are faced with major threats given Russia's growing assertiveness in territories that once formed part of the Soviet Union. Not content with its disruptive role in the neighbourhood, Russia has actively engaged in hostile cyberattacks against the member states and seeks to foster opposition to European integration (see Chapter 19). Instability on the EU's borders is not just a matter of foreign policy, because war and dislocation lead to strong migratory pressures that confront the Union and particularly the Mediterranean member states with major political and security dilemmas (see Chapter 26). The combined effects of the economic crisis and instability in the neighbourhood have further weakened the prospect of enlargement beyond the Balkans (see Chapter 18).

Third, there is far more contention in and about the EU and more pronounced fragmentation and volatility in domestic politics than in the past. The Union is no longer just a system of multilevel governance but has become a multilevel political system characterized by vertical and horizontal political dynamics (see Chapter 7). The rise of radical right-wing parties in the member states, motivated by deep **Euroscepticism**, has politicized the Union and this is unlikely to abate. Left-wing radicalism is also Eurosceptic but seeks a different more socially oriented and interventionist EU. Populism is stronger in Europe than it has been at any stage in the post-war period. The interaction of populism and European integration is multi-faceted. The EU is political arena for populists and a target of populists. Moreover, EU supported policies of austerity during the financial crisis exacerbated political tensions in the member states (see Chapter 15). The 2019 EP elections resulted in gains for the radical right and left and also the Greens and Liberals who are generally supportive of the EU. Although populist parties won 29 per cent of the seats in the EP elections, their political impact is circumscribed because they are split across party groupings. The most significant outcome of the elections was that the European People's Party (EPP) and the Social and Democratic Party (S&D) could no longer command a majority and needed support from the Liberals or Greens to fashion majorities (Youngs, 2019). Significantly, **Brexit** appears to have led to a revival in support for the EU in the remaining states as the shock of the UK's departure galvanized pro-EU forces across the continent; Emmanuel Macron campaigned in 2017 on a strong pro-EU platform and, in the 2021 Dutch election, the pro-European **Democrats 66 (D66)** performed strongly. Eurosceptic parties on the continent toned down their opposition to the EU and no longer advocate leaving the Union or the euro.

Fourth, the international system is in a period of profound structural transformation. The election of Donald Trump as US President on an 'America First' ticket in November 2016 undermined the post-war liberal international settlement, founded by the USA, when he privileged unilateralism over multilateralism. Moreover, President Trump was the first postwar US President who was openly hostile to European Integration. The Trump administration saw the rise of a more assertive China under the leadership of President Xi Jinping. The election of Joe Biden in November 2020, when he defeated Donald Trump in both the popular vote and electoral college, offers an opportunity to re-set global politics. President Biden brought the USA back into the **Paris Agreement** and is significantly more multilateralist than his predecessor. Unlike President Trump, the Biden Administration seeks a close cooperative relationship with the EU underlined by his virtual participation in a European Council meeting in March 2021, just months after taking office, and his presence at the June 2021 European Council in Brussels. Forging the Transatlantic relationship for the future is not without challenges even under a Biden administration. President Biden and his Secretary of State Antony Blinken have adopted a strong assertive stance vis-à-vis China, signalling an era of Great Power competition. The EU does not want to have to take sides between the USA and China although the Union has classified China as both a co-operation partner, competitor, and a systemic rival. The Transatlantic Alliance remains the cornerstone of European security policy. Growing authoritarianism in China and the repression of the **Uighurs** may leave the EU with little choice but to support the USA.

How Europe positions itself in a multipolar, although not necessarily multilateral, world will have a major bearing on its future.

29.2 Four scenarios on the future of the EU

Given the impossibility of predicting with any accuracy the future of the Union, and given the conflicts and struggles identified above, this chapter presents a number of scenarios in order to underline the different considerations and pressures that have a bearing on the future of the EU. Scenarios enable us to think about the future in a structured manner by providing a framework for addressing uncertainty and contingency. Four scenarios on the future of the EU are presented: (1) Disintegration (Section 29.2.1); (2) Piecemeal Adjustment (Section 29.2.2); (3) Functional Federalism (Section 29.2.3); and (4) a European Sovereignty (Section 29.2.4). The scenarios are presented as a two-by-two matrix with the vertical line representing 'more' or 'less' Europe and the horizontal line representing 'transformation' and 'adaptation' (see Figure 29.1). We argue that although systemic disintegration is unlikely, partial disintegration is occurring because of the exit of the UK, and the battle about European values in a number of member states. In analysing the pressures and tensions characteristic of European integration, it is possible to trace elements of all scenarios in the likely future trajectory of the Union. The political battle revolves around those forces that are committed to more Europe, those that want to return power to the member states, and those that are content with muddling through or incremental change. As we will see in this chapter, Europe's future will not be determined in Europe alone but by wider forces in global geopolitics and geo-economics.

29.2.1 Scenario 1: Disintegration

In the past, scholars of European integration focused attention on how and why the EU and European integration developed. Little consideration was given in the theoretical literature to processes of disintegration. Following the collapse of communism and the end of the Cold War, the realist scholar, John Mearsheimer, predicted a return to the dark forces of nationalism in Europe and to heightened distrust among states. His portrayal of Europe was a

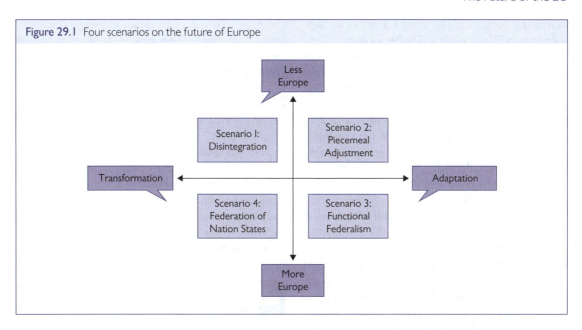

Figure 29.1 Four scenarios on the future of Europe

Europe of hyper-nationalism, insecurity, and conflict (Mearsheimer, 1990). Although an extreme version of Mearsheimer's vision did not materialize, nationalism and identity politics have gained traction in Europe. Moreover, the return of authoritarianism in Russia under Putin is a stark reminder that democratic transition is demanding and remains uncertain in many states on the Union's borders. In the post-Cold War era, the EU became a powerful source of stability as it prepared to become continental in size. The success of the Big Bang enlargement in May 2004 was, and remains, a major achievement for the Union (see Chapter 18). From autumn 2009 onwards, however, the EU has been subject to a series of interrelated crises—eurozone, migration crisis, Brexit, and the rise of authoritarian governments and leaders such as Viktor Orbán in Hungary and the **Law and Justice Party (PiS)** in Poland that have generated deep fissures in the Union (see Chapters 25, 26, and 27). How seriously should the prospect of disintegration be taken? In addressing this question, it is helpful to distinguish between disintegration as 'fragmentation' and disintegration as 'system collapse'. The argument here is that further fragmentation is likely but that the EU appears sufficiently robust to resist system collapse.

The eurozone crisis engendered a sustained discussion about the prospect of disintegration in the euro area and the EU more generally. The crisis, in its early phase, was labelled *The Euro's Existential Crisis* by

Barry Eichengreen (2010), a view shared by numerous political actors in Europe. Speaking in May 2010, following the first Greek bailout, German Chancellor Angela Merkel claimed that 'The current crisis facing the euro is the biggest test Europe has faced in decades. It is an existential test and it must be overcome . . . if the euro fails, then Europe fails' (Merkel, 2010). The then European Council President, Herman Van Rompuy, agreed that Europe was 'in the middle of a crisis which affects the material and symbolic heart of the European Union—the euro. An existential crisis and we mean to overcome it' (Van Rompuy, 2011). Scholars too began to ask what were the prospects of an EU collapse, and disintegration was identified as 'a clear and present danger' (Krastev, 2012; Wright, 2012). There is no doubt that there have been times since 2010 when the exit of a eurozone member state was highly plausible and the collapse of the euro itself was not inconceivable. At each critical juncture, however, the eurozone states and the **European Central Bank (ECB)** found the capacity and the instruments to stabilize the crisis (see Chapters 22 and 25). Europe's political actors and institutions have shown a determination to ensure that the euro survives. The then President of the ECB, Mario Draghi, speaking at Lancaster House in the heart of the City of London in July 2012, boldly stated that 'Within our mandate, the ECB is ready to do whatever it takes to preserve the euro' and, pausing for effect, he went on to say 'And believe me, it will be enough' (Draghi, 2012). The eurozone crisis highlighted both EU resilience and vulnerability.

The presence of the ECB as the eurozone's indispensable institution provided the EU with the fire power to bring the euro crisis under control. The migration crisis, which reached its height in summer 2015, proved much more difficult. The war in Syria and instability in the region created the conditions for the arrival of over a million refugees, double the previous numbers, fleeing to Europe across the Mediterranean. The crisis exposed the severe limitations of the EU's Common European Asylum System (CEAS), which has as its centrepiece the **Dublin Regulation**. This regulation places the onus on the first country of entry to register and process the asylum request. Given the numbers arriving in Greece and Italy, these two countries bore the weight of the crisis. Throughout the summer of 2015, hundreds of thousands of refugees were attempting to get to Germany and beyond through the Balkan route. The Union, in an attempt to foster burden sharing, agreed measures on the distribution of migrants throughout the member states. The countries of Central Europe vehemently opposed this and began building walls to cut off the Balkan route. Under the pressure of events, Chancellor Merkel waived the Dublin Regulation, leading to a significant influx of refugees into Germany. The number of refugees entering Europe was significantly reduced when Germany took the lead in an EU-brokered deal with Turkey in March 2016. The arrangement with Turkey was a deliberate EU strategy to externalize the migration challenge given the deep and unresolved cleavages within the Union. The migration crisis and the Union's struggle to manage it had an impact on politics in Europe (see Chapter 26). It fuelled anti-migrant sentiment and support for the far right, as the far-right **Die Alternative Für Deutschland (AfD)** entered parliament following the September 2017 German election.

The cleavage between the eastern and western half of the continent worsened because of the migration crisis but the East–West divide had additional ingredients. The rise of illiberal democracies in the Eastern half of the continent poses a major challenge to the Union. Hungarian Prime Minister Orbán and his **Fidesz** party, in power since 2010, gradually morphed from a centre right conservative party into an authoritarian party that is undermining the rule of law and the values of the EU. The election of the Law and Justice Party (PiS) in Poland in 2015 further

challenged the rule of law and European values with direct attacks on Polish judicial institutions and media freedoms. Developments in these countries, together with other member states in the region, pose acute functional and normative challenges to the EU which it struggles to address. The EU is built on law and relies on the **rule of law** to cement the Union as stated in Article 2 TEU (see Box 29.1).

The Commission began Article 7 proceedings against both states in the Court of Justice of the EU (CJEU) but this has not proved sufficient to protect the fabric of law and independent institutions in Poland and Hungary (see Box 29.2). The assault on the independence of the media and the judiciary is relentless. In addition to triggering Article 7 proceedings, the

BOX 29.1   BACKGROUND: ARTICLE 2 TEU

The Union is founded on the values of respect for human dignity, freedom, democracy, equality, the rule of law, and respect for human rights, including the rights of persons belonging to minorities. These values are common to the Member States in a society in which pluralism, non-discrimination, tolerance, justice, solidarity, and equality between women and men prevail.

BOX 29.2   CASE STUDY: ARTICLE 7 PROCEEDINGS AGAINST POLAND AND HUNGARY

Article 7 TEU is the main Treaty mechanism to deal with member states that breach the values outlined in Article 2 TEU. It ultimately allows for the suspension of certain Treaty rights, including voting rights in the Council. The EU's rule of law problem has been primarily concerned with the challenge to the independence of the judiciary in Poland and Hungary.

The European Commission has been reluctant to invoke Article 7 TEU because the threshold to trigger the article is very high, both in terms of its activation in case of 'clear risk of a serious breach' and in terms of the sanctioning mechanisms: to be used only in cases of 'serious and persistent breach by a Member State'. Thus the European Commission has favoured other mechanisms such as the 2014 EU Rule of Law Framework. The framework involves a three-stage process: assessment, recommendation, and follow up. In the case of no satisfactory follow up of the recommendations by the member state, the Commission can decide to trigger Article 7.

Commission has taken four cases to the CJEU on aspects of Polish law governing the judiciary and in all completed cases the CJEU found against Poland (EU, 2021). Neither country would have achieved membership of the EU whilst following these policies and practices. Freedom House concluded in its 2020 report that 'Hungary today can no longer be regarded as a democracy but belongs to the growing group of hybrid regimes, sitting in the "grey zone" between democracies and pure autocracies' (Freedom House, 2020). It took the European People's Party (EPP) until 2021 to finally push Fidesz out of the political grouping. The assault on democratic institutions in some member states undermines the values of the Union and brings the Union's vulnerability sharply into focus.

The UK's exit from the EU on the 31 January 2020 transformed it from member state to third country, the first state ever to leave the Union. There was deep shock and emotion in Brussels on 24 June 2016 as the outcome of the referendum sank in, but shock quickly turned to determination. Within one week, the EU had framed its response to Brexit and made a commitment to unity of purpose when negotiating with a departing state. The reflex was to aim for an orderly exit by using Article 50 as the shaper of process. Added to this the EU informed London that there would be no negotiation without notification and signalled that there would be no special deals for a former member state. The UK was left in no doubt that the integrity of the Single Market and the indivisibility of the four freedoms were EU red lines. EU leaders were acutely conscious that the EU27, acting in a unified manner, was far more powerful than a state acting on its own. That said, the EU sought as 'close a relationship as possible' with the UK although how close would be determined by the UK's trade-off between market access and freedom to diverge. The UK declared its intention to leave the Single Market, customs union, and the jurisdiction of the CJEU and when Boris Johnson took office in July 2019, he was determined to pursue a sovereignty first Brexit. The outcome of this preference was a very hard Brexit encapsulated both in the Withdrawal Agreement (agreed on 17 October 2019) and in the Trade and Cooperation Agreement (TCA) agreed just six days before the end of the UK's transition period on 31 December 2020 (see Chapter 27). The EU demonstrated its resolve to protect the Union and its major geopolitical asset, the Single Market. Speaking in March 2021, Michel Barnier, the Union's chief negotiator, reflected that Brexit has not triggered the

demise of the EU but its reawakening and had highlighted that it was Europe's unity, Single Market, and common policies that gave it clout on the world stage (Barnier, 2021). Moreover, he emphasized the strength that flows from the pooling of sovereignty (Barnier, 2021). In essence Brexit was a clash not about sovereignty but its practice. The UK sought a return to a more absolutist practice of sovereignty but as Mario Draghi said in an address to the Italian Senate 'there is no sovereignty in solitude' (Draghi, 2021).

The disintegration scenario points to fissures that characterize the EU as it struggles to address a range of challenging issues. There is little evidence of systemic disintegration. The rule of law challenges undermine the EU from the inside but do not represent system collapse. The departure of the UK, which appeared existential at the outset, saw the EU consciously build its political and institutional capacity to minimize the dangers of geographic disintegration. During a decade of crises, the EU proved resilient because it offers European states the scale and anchor to deal with deep interdependence.

29.2.2 Scenario 2: Piecemeal Adjustment

Piecemeal Adjustment implies small steps rather than transformative change. The response to Europe's multiple crises was described as 'muddling through', an approach to decision-making that was developed by Charles Lindblom as an antidote to dominant rationalist approaches (Lindblom, 1959). Muddling through is characterized by incrementalism and satisficing rather than the search for comprehensive solutions. As the euro crisis gathered pace in the first half of 2010, the eurozone lacked the instruments and tool kit to address the multiplicity and severity of the problems that were emerging (see Chapter 25). Nor was there a convergence of preferences across the member states on the nature of the problem and what should be done. In fact, there was a deep cleavage between the creditor and debtor states, with the latter finding themselves in a very vulnerable position. Led by Germany, crisis management and resolution was driven by the creditor countries, on the one hand, and the ECB, on the other. The debtor countries were seeking salvation and support whereas the creditor countries wanted to do the minimum necessary to sustain the euro. Public opinion in the creditor states did not want to bail out the troubled countries and in turn the wave of austerity that swept across the southern countries and Ireland meant that incumbent governments paid a high price in crisis elections (see Chapter 15). An incremental response that bought time was the most palatable political approach to the crisis but one that was not designed to engender confidence in the markets or provide the optimal support to the debtor countries. Every time the crisis became acute for sovereigns or banks, the leading politicians of the eurozone and the ECB acted. Crisis management was characterized by rescue programmes for specific vulnerable countries, the development of a set of crisis management instruments and a ratcheting up of regulations on economic governance (see Chapter 25).

The crisis exposed dangerous design faults in the euro; centralized monetary policy, accompanied by decentralized fiscal and financial supervisory regimes, left the system vulnerable to imprudent fiscal policy in one or more countries and to an unsustainable rise of private debt in others (see Chapter 22). As the EU attempted to come to terms with the onset of a eurozone crisis in spring 2010, the question of economic governance became central to the agenda. The focus was on the collective co-responsibility of the member states within the euro area. Beginning with the Van Rompuy Task Force on Economic Governance in 2010, the euro area states agreed to a new regulatory regime for domestic budgetary and economic policy consisting of a **'six pack'**, **'two pack'**, and a **Fiscal Compact**. The clear policy direction is towards more stringent surveillance, reinforced penalties, and constraint (see Chapter 25). EU intrusion and surveillance was designed to ensure that euro states put their public finances in order and once order has been restored, maintain them within the rules. This, however, was considered insufficient for the future sustainability of the euro. A more ambitious road-map was crafted that led the euro area towards a higher level of functional federalism.

Muddling through also characterized the approach to the migration crisis as the Union adopted piecemeal measures in their response. The Commission drafted a burden-sharing agreement to ease the burden on those states experiencing the largest flows but was unable to achieve member states' compliance or reform the regulatory framework. When it became apparent that European publics were concerned about the apparent un-governability of the refugee flows, the EU moved to stop the flows via a strategy of externalization; the 2016 Turkey Agreement, training of Libyan

coast guards, actions in the Niger Sahel region, and the creation of a European Border and Coast Guard Agency in 2016. The objective was to stem the flow of irregular migration and all measures point to a progressive strengthening of the Union's external borders. Attempts by the Union to adopt a long-term strategic approach to migration have faltered because of deep divisions across the member states and the sensitivity of the issue (see Chapter 26).

29.2.3 Scenario 3: Functional Federalism

Functional Federalism implies centralization but on a sectoral rather than on a polity basis. A focus on the long-term architecture of EMU going beyond economic governance began to surface on the agenda of the European Council in 2012. The European Council president at the time, Herman Van Rompuy, was mandated by the Council to prepare a time-bound road-map for the creation of what has been termed a genuine economic and monetary union (GEMU), a euro mark 2. The Van Rompuy report, which was drafted in cooperation with the Presidents of the Commission, the ECB, and the **Eurogroup**, was submitted to the European Council in draft form in June 2012 and in final form in December 2012. The report was designed to set the agenda and frame the issues for the European Council, which had the power to agree a programme of work and timeframe for action. In other words, the presidents of the supranational institutions laid out what they considered desirable and the heads of state and government decided what they would agree to over what timeframe.

The use of the term 'genuine' in the title of the report was to underline the incompleteness of the original euro design. The Van Rompuy report identified four pillars or building blocks of a future EMU, namely:

- an integrated financial framework (Banking Union);
- an integrated budgetary framework (Fiscal Integration);
- an integrated economic policy framework (Economic Policy Coordination); and
- ensuring the necessary democratic legitimacy and accountability of decision-making within EMU, based on the joint exercise of sovereignty for common policies and solidarity (Van Rompuy report, 5 December 2012)

The immediate task was ensuring fiscal sustainability and breaking the link between sovereigns and banks, to be achieved in 2012–13. This placed Banking Union as the key priority agenda item in the redesign of the eurozone. Following intensive and difficult negotiations on bank supervision and resolution, the ECB took over responsibility for the supervision of Europe's banking system in November 2014. This represented a further strengthening of the power of the ECB and its place in the Union's institutional landscape because Banking Union was the most significant centralization of power since the establishment of the single currency. Going beyond Banking Union to further fiscal integration remained a major challenge for the member states as it would bring the Union even further into core state functions.

It took the COVID-19 crisis in 2020 to open up a window of opportunity on EU public finances. As the economic consequences of the pandemic became evident and the need for massive public expenditure to maintain health systems and the flow of funding to business, workers, and families, demands grew for a collective EU response. The context for negotiating the Multi-Annual Financial Framework (MFF, 2021–27) was transformed. The EU leveraged its financial capacity for both short- and long-term measures. For the short term, the Commission proposed and got agreement to a €100 billion loan fund known as SURE (the European instrument for temporary Support to mitigate Unemployment Risks in an Emergency) to support employment related expenditure in the member states. When political attention turned to the recovery, there were calls from the hardest hit member states for sizeable financial support given the scale of the problem and their limited fiscal space given the overall stock of debt. The April European Council mandated the Commission to prepare a proposal in the context of the EU budget and the MFF. By mid-May the German Government signalled a major shift in policy when Chancellor Merkel and President Macron called for a €500 billion recovery fund, some of which would be issued to member states as grants not loans. The taboo on common debt issuance began to weaken although a group of states known as the 'frugals'—the Netherlands, Denmark, Sweden, Austria with some support from Finland—continued their opposition. This will be a key political battle in the decade ahead. Moreover, common debt may help build a European Capital Union and create a safe asset for the euro. This points towards a deepening of functional integration over the next decade (see Box 29.3).

BOX 29.3   KEY DEBATE: SOLUTIONS TO THE ECONOMIC EFFECTS OF THE COVID-19 PANDEMIC

Following the April 2020 European Council, the Commission proposals consisted of two elements, the MFF 2021–27 amounting to €1.1 trillion over seven years, and the *Next Generation EU* instrument of €750 billion funded completely by borrowing from the capital markets (European Commission 2020a and 2020b). The key elements of the *Next Generation EU* proposals were: a Recovery and Resilience Facility (RRF) of €560 billion to be dispersed as both grants and loans; a further €55 billion for cohesion policy; and a Just Transition Fund of up to €40 billion to support the green agenda (European Commission, 2020). This was a remarkable proposal in the budgetary politics of the Union. It took a four-day European Council marathon in July 2020 to reach political agreement. The opposition of the frugals had to be overcome and there were also tense negotiations on the demand for 'rule of law' conditionality in EU funding. The latter was trenchantly opposed by Poland and Hungary. The RFF requires ratification by national parliaments. The July 2020 financial package represented a major breakthrough, although to call it the EU's 'Hamiltonian' moment exaggerates. Its salience lies not just in the breaking of the common debt taboo but also in its potential longer-term impact. The RFF has to be repaid from the EU budget, which inevitably raises the question of resources and the prospect of EU level taxation.

29.2.4 Scenario 4: A European Sovereignty

From the outset there have always been political actors who favoured a **federal** outcome to the process of European integration. Jacques Delors, then Commission President, was the first European politician to use the term Federation of Nation States in the 1990s. It was deliberately ambiguous and an attempt to square the circle by emphasizing the collective, the Federation, but also the Nation States. In other words, a European Federation could be reconciled with the member states as nation states. The term **federation** would not necessarily imply a federal state. Rather it could be a **polity**, a compound political system without declaring itself a state. Whenever political actors invoke the 'federal' word and advocate further centralization of power and competence in the EU, they grapple with the challenge of reconciling the embedded nature of Europe's nation states with their advocacy of further integration. This leads them towards ideas of federalism as a method and labels that fall short of a United States of Europe, a federal state. Joschka Fischer, in his Humboldt speech of 12 May 2000 entitled 'From confederacy to federation—thoughts on the finality of European integration', launched an intense debate among Europe's political leaders on the future of the European Union. The debate led to the Convention on the Future of Europe but died with the failed ratification of the **Constitutional Treaty** (see Chapter 3). The acute nature of the crises facing the EU since the late 2000s left little political room for grand visions on the future of the Union. The election of Emmanuel Macron in 2017 altered the context and dynamic of debate. In September 2017, President Macron delivered a major speech to students at the Sorbonne, a speech he began with the words, 'I have come to talk to you about Europe' (Macron, 2017). The speech was lengthy and full of prescriptions on all areas of EU policy and institutions. Rather than deploying terms such as 'federal' or 'federation', President Macron used the term 'European sovereignty' and argued that it must be constructed in areas such as security and defence, border control and preserving Europe's values, the ecological transition, digital technology, Europe's social model, and taxation (Macron, 2017). The Macron speech demonstrated that those supporting deeper integration were fighting back against the constraints of crisis and **Euroscepticism**. President Macron said that those supporting deeper integration should not be held back by those unable or unwilling to participate. Paradoxically, Brexit followed closely by the election of President Trump in the USA helped make the case for Europe in an uncertain and unsettled world.

Two of von der Leyen's policy priorities are transformational in nature: the Green Deal and addressing the digital transformation. Although the pandemic influenced the rollout of EU policies in these areas, they remain core to the agenda and are projects for the future. Both require agency not just in Europe but intensive engagement with international players. Macron's concept of 'European Sovereignty' has morphed into 'strategic autonomy', which is usually accompanied with the words 'open' and 'effective'. Sabine Weyand, Director General of DG Trade and former senior member of the Brexit negotiating team, defines open strategic autonomy as an analytical prism or aspirational goal for the EU as it seeks to 'chart our own course in world affairs, the world economy, and the world trade in line with our interests and values' (Weyand, 2020). The addition of 'open' is to dispel fears of a protectionist EU.

The ambition to chart the EU's own course is leading to the emergence of new approaches to trade, industrial policy, competition, supply chains, and the prospect of a carbon levy. It points to the deployment of the collective capacity of the Union and represents the EU's strategy for dealing with the challenges of the twenty-first century. There are strong pressures on Europe to be more united and integrated in an increasingly competitive world characterized by deep structural change.

Given the politicization of integration since the 1990s and the impact of the crisis on democratic politics in Europe, Europe's elites will not be able to achieve a federation even of nation states without the active engagement and consent of their citizen electorates (see Chapter 15). The challenge is not so much about building a federation with the member states but building one with their citizens. That said, the EU did not collapse under the weight of its multiple crises over the last ten years and the shifts and shocks of global and European politics highlight the role of the EU as a protective holding space for its member states and their peoples.

> ### KEY POINTS
>
> - Understanding the EU's future challenges requires a systematic approach around four possible scenarios.
>
> - As a future scenario, Disintegration is useful in highlighting the possibility of fragmentation of the Union rather than the complete collapse of the system.
>
> - The Piecemeal Adjustment scenario reflects the EU's incremental response to the crisis.
>
> - The Functional Federalism scenario focuses on the creation of centralized institutions and policy capacity in limited functional areas to address the financial crisis.
>
> - In the European Sovereignty scenario, the EU would need to bridge the gap between the grand plans of political actors and citizens in the member states.

29.3 Intervening factors shaping the future of the EU

The scenarios presented in this chapter are developed as if the Union had complete control over its destiny and was not subject to immense pressures from the international system. The contemporary world is characterized by an intensification of linkages and connections across regions, countries, and societies driven by technology, the ICT (Information and Communications Technology) revolution, trade, international business, security threats, aid, mobility of people, and ideas. This section assesses the impact of these two factors in the EU's immediate future.

29.3.1 The Union's external environment

Originally classified as 'complex interdependence', the growth of transnational relationships and dynamics are best subsumed under the label of globalization, one of the strongest forces in twenty-first-century international politics. Accompanying globalization, international power distributions have dramatically shifted since the end of the Cold War with its strategic **bipolarity**. The period of contested American unipolarity, defined by US economic, political, and military preponderance has ended. Multi-polarity now seems an increasingly pronounced feature of the international system, underlined by the transcendence of the G8 of Western powers by the G20. The growing weight of China and others, notably India, Brazil, and Russia, points to a relative decline in the power of the USA and Europe, especially within the international political economy.

China is no longer an emergent power but an increasingly assertive global power in its own right. This is evident in its deployment of its economic power, the ambition of the **Silk Road**, its growing presence in international regulatory bodies, and the growth of its military power and reach. USA–China rivalry is the major driver of twenty-first century global politics. Unlike the Cold War when the advantages of the Western capitalist model and democracy were evident, an 'undemocratic capitalist' China is much better placed to rival the USA than the former USSR, which remained technologically inferior. The Biden Administration sees China as it top geopolitical rival and concludes that 'It is the only competitor potentially capable of combining its economic, diplomatic, military, and technological power to mount a sustained challenge to a stable and open international system' (USA, 2021). The USA will seek to contain China and will make demands on the EU in this regard.

Europe's capacity to shape global forces and the emerging systems of global governance will be influenced by its power resources, the manner in which it deploys that power, and its coherence on international issues. The fragmented nature of the Union and the diversity of member state preferences on major international issues make it extremely difficult for the Union to act consistently with one voice in a strategic manner. Europe's role in global governance and as a player in the contemporary international system may be viewed through the lens of 'Europe as Model' and 'Europe as Actor'. The first lens points to the EU as a testing ground for governance beyond national borders, to its role as an exemplar of peaceful reconciliation among warring states, and to its successful advancement of a highly developed form of transnational integration. If it can successfully drive the European Green deal and carbon transformation, the Union will gain considerable 'soft power' and validate the EU model. That said, it is Europe as international actor, a player in global politics, that is under considerable pressure. Across a wide a range of foreign policy fields such as international trade, investment, development cooperation, international services and the promotion of human rights, and democratization, and, increasingly, security and defence, there are pressures on Europe to strengthen its collective capacity. The debate on strategic autonomy is a response to these pressures. The future of the EU will be greatly influenced by its ability to act in concert, to be strategic, to influence its neighbourhood, and to shape the pattern and substance of global governance—in brief, by Europe's ability to find its role and place in the world of twenty-first-century global politics. It must seize the 'multilateral moment' that the Biden administration offers to strengthen the rule bound institutionalized international order that is best suited to its model. It must find a way to navigate USA–China rivalry without having to side always with the USA but it must also protect itself and the Single Market from unfair Chinese subsidies and stand up to China's human rights record. It must defend itself against an authoritarian Russia intent on sowing division within its borders. If the EU fails to act and to influence, non-decisions come with consequences for Europe's place in the world and its ability to shape its future (see Chapters 17 and 19).

29.3.2 The challenge of heterogeneity and leadership

The European Union is characterized by deep diversity in levels of wealth, geography, state tradition and capacity, language, and culture. Managing diversity is a perennial challenge to the EU. Added to this are the varying preferences of the member states about the

European project; what the EU should be and what it should do. In response to growing heterogeneity, the EU evolved as a system of **differentiated integration (DI)** whereby not all member states participate in all EU policy regimes. The eurozone, **Banking Union**, **Schengen**, aspects of Justice and Home Affairs, and **Permanent Structured Cooperation (PESCO)** represent different forms of DI. The treaties provide for a form of **enhanced cooperation** whereby member states may act as an *avant garde* and go ahead without all member states within specified institutional rules. These treaty provisions have been used sparingly as a last resort. However, every time there is a discussion about the Future of Europe, differentiated integration is on the agenda as a strategy for those member states that want to forge ahead. Yet it rarely gains traction beyond the existing areas of differentiated integration. The EU will remain a system characterized by DI and DI may expand to some additional areas but the big EU issues such as, the COVID-19 recovery, Green Deal, and the digital agenda, are important to all 27 member states and unlikely to be candidates for further DI.

All political systems need leadership and given the nature of the EU as a multilevel policy, leadership is distributed across the Brussels institutions and the member states (see Chapter 7). The reconciliation of France and Germany was at the core of the EU project from the outset and the Franco-German tandem has played a central role in the development of Union as the 'motor of integration' (see Chapters 2 and 3). German power, highlighted by Chancellor Merkel's omniscient presence, was to come to the fore during the eurozone crisis. Effectively, Germany had a veto over the management of the crisis and the design of policy instruments to address it. The concept of Germany as a hegemon, albeit a reluctant one, gained traction in political and scholarly discourse. However reluctantly, Germany gave leadership during the crisis, even if it tended to act at the last minute and within a very narrow policy frame. The forthcoming departure of Chancellor Merkel, a longstanding member of the European Council, ushers in a new era in German and EU politics. The next German chancellor faces

difficult choices arising from the instability on Europe's borders to the East, especially German policy on Russia and more generally its approach to European security and foreign policy. Germany is unlikely to escape the fact that it is a regional power and that regional powers carry particular responsibilities.

The election of Emmanuel Macron as President of France in 2017 posed a challenge to Germany's newly found leadership of the EU. President Macron, as discussed earlier in this chapter, is willing to lead on Europe and wants to do so with Germany. There was recognition in Germany that the election of a pro-European President in France offered a window of opportunity that was important for the sustainability of the Union. It took until the COVID-19 pandemic for the Macron vision of the EU to make progress and arguably the Recovery and Resilience Fund (RRF), especially the EU's issuance of common debt, could not have happened without strong pressure from President Macron and a change of core preferences in Berlin. President Macron faces a testing re-election battle in 2022. The severity of the COVID-19 crisis given the legacy of the eurozone crisis prompted Italy and Spain to play a very active role in ensuring that the EU would respond in a bolder and speedier manner to the pandemic. The installation of Mario Draghi (February 2021) as Italian Prime Minister points to stronger Italian presence in EU leadership for however long his technocratic government lasts.

KEY POINTS

- The EU's external environment will influence its future development.

- The future of the EU will be determined by its ability to become an influential actor in the new global environment.

- Germany, together with France, has been traditionally regarded as one of the engines of European integration. The election of President Macron offers an opportunity for the renewal of the Franco-German relationship.

29.4 Conclusion

Although it is impossible to predict the shape of the European Union in all of its complexity in the coming years, the Union is undoubtedly undergoing a

period of change and transition as it grapples with the legacies of the eurozone crisis, the departure of the UK, and the shifting power balances and turbulence of global politics. The Union proved that it had considerable resilience and decision-making capacity during the various crises, but at a high political cost. Politics in Europe is displaying heightened levels of volatility, which make it more difficult for governments to govern when faced with challenger parties and public disenchantment with politics and the European Union. Euroscepticism and opposition to migration have proved a potent electoral platform for the radical right in many, although not all, member states. Brexit was a wake-up call for pro-EU forces across the continent and both traditional parties and progressive forces such as the Greens have taken the argument to the radical right. How the tensions and conflicts evident within and across the member states will play out will depend on post-pandemic recovery, particularly in Europe's vulnerable economies, on the EU's ability to address the authoritarian governments at the table in Poland and Hungary, and make progress on the transformative projects in climate and digital.

All of the four scenarios presented in this chapter offer a lens on how the Union might evolve. Scenario one, if defined as systemic failure, appears unlikely at this stage. The EU managed Brexit in a way that protected its core preferences and the UK was not able to pick and choose the bits of integration it wanted to maintain. The challenge to Europe's values from within has the potential to fragment the Union as it has struggled to prevent the deterioration of democratic norms and standards in some member states. What can certainly be said is that differentiated integration, which as argued above is not the solution to internal EU policies, is likely to become an even more pronounced feature of EU relations to its neighbourhood in future. Muddling through with incremental piecemeal change (Section 29.2.2) was the predominant approach during Europe's multiple crises, until Brexit and the COVID-19 pandemic. The establishment of Banking Union and a strengthening of European capacity in defence and security pointed to Scenario 3 (Section 29.2.3). This scenario was strengthened by the response to the COVID-19 pandemic and the evidence of learning from the eurozone crisis. The July 2020 financial agreement is historic in the politics of EU public finance and contains further transformative capacity.

The fourth scenario, a European Sovereignty or what might be described as 'collective power Europe', was evident in the management of the Brexit negotiations, during which the EU acted in a seamless and unified manner from the beginning of the negotiations to the end, and deployed its collective capacity to protect the Union given the disintegrative potential of the UK's departure. The EU's strategic agenda-climate, digital, and Europe's role in the world requires the deployment of collective capacity and there are strong global pressures on the EU to do so. The climate crisis in particular will exert pressure for public power and resources at national, EU, and global levels. Europe has a window of opportunity to forge the next phase of European integration and to build on the Union's robustness. The transformative agenda compels the EU to build collective capacity and commit to a strategic turn. Developments in domestic politics in the member states will have a major bearing on this, as will wider international developments.

? QUESTIONS

1. Why did the eurozone crisis prove so divisive and challenging to the EU and its member states?

2. Which of the scenarios outlined in this chapter are the most plausible?

3. Has Germany become a hegemon in the EU or will the Franco-German tandem reassert itself?

4. What are the implications for the EU of the UK's withdrawal from the Union?

5. How can the EU deploy its power more effectively in its neighbourhood?

6. What kind of actor is the EU in the international system?

7. Why have the Union and its future become more politicized over time?

8. Can the EU achieve further integration without a federation?

GUIDE TO FURTHER READING

Krastev, I. (2012) 'European disintegration? A fraying Union', *Journal of Democracy*, 23/4: 23–30. This reading reviews the pressures on the EU system and asks if the reversal and rupture of the integration process is possible. Given the depth of the crisis in the EU since 2010, it is important to consider disintegration and not just integration.

Laffan, B, (2018) *Europe's Union in Crisis: Tested and Contested* (London: Routledge), 1–208. This volume, which first appeared as a Special Issue of West European Politics, offers a wide ranging analysis of how the EU responded to multiple crises over the past decade.

Paterson, W. E. (2011) 'The reluctant hegemon? Germany moves centre stage in the European Union', *Journal of Common Market Studies*, 49/1: 57–75. This article highlights the growing role of Germany in the Union and the dilemmas it faces as a reluctant hegemon.

Schimmelfennig, F. (2014) 'European integration in the euro crisis: the limits of postfunctionalism', *Journal of European Integration*, 36/3: 321–37. This article explores and offers an explanation of why, despite the turmoil of the crisis and growing opposition to the EU, the Union managed to deepen economic governance.

Sjursen, H. (2006) 'The EU as a "normative" power: how can this be?', *Journal of European Public Policy*, 13/2: 235–51. The idea that the EU is a normative power in world politics is one of the main claims in the literature on the international role of the Union. This article explores this claim.

Access the online resources to take your learning and understanding further, including extra multiple-choice questions with instant feedback, web links, answer guidance to end-of-chapter questions, and updates on new developments in EU politics.

www.oup.com/he/cini-borragan7e

Glossary

1992 Programme The Commission's programme and timetable for implementation of the internal market. In its 1985 White Paper, the Commission listed some 300 legislative measures to be taken to implement the single market programme. These included the elimination of physical, technical, and tax frontiers. *See* single market (programme); Single European Act.

à la carte A non-uniform method of integration that would allow member states to select policies as if from a menu.

accession The process of joining the EU.

accession treaty An international agreement concluded between the EU member states and the acceding country. It defines the accession conditions of the new member state, and the subsequent adaptations and adjustments of the EU Treaty.

accountability The requirement for representatives to answer to the represented on how they have performed their duties and powers, and for them to act upon criticisms and accept responsibility for failure, incompetence, or deceit.

acquis communautaire A French term that refers literally to the Community patrimony. It is the cumulative body of the objectives, substantive rules, policies, and, in particular, the primary and secondary legislation and case law—all of which form part of the legal order of the EU. It includes the content of the treaties, legislation, judgments by the Court of Justice of the European Union, and international agreements. All member states are bound to comply with the *acquis communautaire*.

Activism *See* judicial activism.

advocacy coalition (or advocacy network) A network of institutional and non-institutional actors that interact together to defend a common cause.

African, Caribbean, and Pacific (ACP) countries Those developing countries in Sub-Saharan Africa, the Caribbean, and the Pacific that have entered into partnership with the EU through the Lomé and Cotonou Conventions.

Agenda 2000 An influential action programme adopted by the Commission on 15 July 1987, which set out the reforms needed for the EU to enlarge in 2004 and in 2007.

agenda-setting The process by which an issue or problem emerges onto the political scene and is framed for subsequent debate.

Alternative für Deutschland (Alternative for Germany) A Eurosceptic and conservative political party in Germany founded in 2013. The party won 4.7 per cent of the vote in the 2013 federal election, narrowly missing the 5 per cent electoral threshold, and won seven seats in the 2014 European election, joining the European Conservatives and Reformists (ECR) group in the chamber.

Altiero Spinelli An important federalist thinker and politician (1907–86), responsible for the influential Ventotene Manifesto of 1941 and for the European Parliament's Draft Treaty on European Union (1984), which helped to shape the European political agenda of the late 1980s.

amending treaty *See* reform treaty.

Amsterdam Treaty Signed in October 1997 and in force from 1 May 1999, the Treaty amended certain provisions of the Treaty on European Union (TEU) and the European Community treaties.

Arab Spring A series of anti-government uprisings in various countries in North Africa and the Middle East, beginning in Tunisia in December 2010.

Assent (procedure) *See* consent procedure.

Association Agreement An agreement between the EU and a third country that creates a framework for cooperation in several policy fields such as trade, socio-economic issues, and security, as well as the creation of joint institutional structures.

avis A French term that literally means 'opinion'. In the context of EU enlargement, once a country has formally submitted an application for membership to the Council of the European Union, the Commission is invited to submit its so-called *avis* (or opinion) to the Council. In its *avis*, the Commission presents recommendations about the process, including any conditions for immediate accession talks.

Banking Union At the Euro area summit in June 2012, the European Council agreed to 'break the vicious circle between banks and sovereigns' and decided to create a banking union that would allow for centralized supervision and resolution for banks in the euro area. It is made up of the Single Supervisory Mechanism (SSM) and the Single Resolution Mechanism (SRM), both of which are mandatory for all euro area member states and open to all other countries in the EU.

barrier(s) to trade One of the protectionist technical and fiscal rules, and physical constraints, that carve up or prevent the creation of the internal market.

base rate The rate of interest used by banks as a basis on which to make loans to their customers.

benchmarking One of the mechanisms of the open method of coordination (OMC) that allows for the comparison and adjustment of the policies of member states on the basis of common objectives.

Benelux An economic and political union composed of Belgium, the Netherlands, and Luxembourg, signed in 1944.

benign elitism The neo-functionalist characteristic tendency to assume the tacit support of the European peoples upon which experts and executives rely when pushing for further European integration.

Berlin Republic Is a term that refers to the strengthened and newly defined Germany after the fall of the Berlin Wall and reunification.

best practice exchange One of the OMC mechanisms to encourage member states to pool information, to compare themselves to one another, and to reassess policies against their relative performance.

bicameral Involving two chambers. Usually refers to parliaments divided into an upper and lower house.

bipolarity The understanding of the international system before the end of the Cold War as being structured around the two major superpowers—namely, the United States and the Soviet Union.

Black Wednesday Refers to 16 September 1992 when the British Conservative government was forced to withdraw the pound sterling from the European Exchange Rate Mechanism (ERM) after it was unable to keep the pound above its agreed lower limit in the ERM.

blocking minority Is the number of votes needed on the EU Council to block a decision needing to be made by qualified majority voting (QMV). In the context of the new system of QMV introduced by the Lisbon Treaty, a blocking minority must be composed of at least four member states representing over 35 per cent of the EU population. *See* dual majority or double majority system of voting.

Bolkestein Directive Directive 2006/123/EC on Services in the Internal Market, which aims to break down barriers to trade in services across the EU. It was controversial because while some believe that it will boost European competitiveness, critics feel that it promotes social dumping.

Bologna Process A series of reforms aimed to make European higher education more compatible and comparable, more competitive, and more attractive for Europeans, and for students and scholars from other continents. It was agreed in the Bologna Declaration of June 1999 by the ministers responsible for higher education in the member states.

Bonn Republic Is a label commonly used to refer to the Federal Republic of Germany or in the period between its creation on 23 May 1949 to German reunification on 3 October 1990.

brake clause One of a number of clauses that have been created in order to enable the ordinary legislative procedure (OLP) to be applied to the measures for coordinating social security systems for migrant workers, judicial cooperation in criminal matters, and the establishment of common rules for certain criminal offences. The OLP is restrained by a braking mechanism: a member state may submit an appeal to the European Council if it considers that the fundamental principles of its social security system or its criminal justice system are threatened by the draft legislation being proposed.

Bretton Woods agreement Signed by 44 countries in July 1944, this agreement was set up to support an international monetary system of stable exchange rates. Its aim was to make national currencies convertible on current account, to encourage multilateral world trade, and to avoid disruptive devaluations and financial crashes. The Bretton Woods system itself collapsed in 1971, when President Richard Nixon severed the link between the dollar and gold. By 1973, most major world economies had allowed their currencies to float freely against the dollar.

Brexit An abbreviation of 'British exit' and it refers to the withdrawal of the United Kingdom from the EU.

Broad Economic Policy Guidelines (BEPGs) The 1993 Treaty of Maastricht first introduced a system for coordinating the economic policies of EU member states. Article 121 TFEU states: 'Member States shall regard their economic policies as a matter of common concern and shall co-ordinate them within the Council.' The BEPGs are adopted by the Council as a reference document guiding the conduct of the whole range of economic policies in the member states. They play a central role in the system of economic policy coordination, setting out economic policy recommendations that give a basis for economic policy in both the member states and the EU as a whole in the current year, and which take into account the particular circumstances of each member state and the different degree of urgency of measures.

Budget rebate (or British rebate) The refund that the UK received on its contribution to the EU Budget, which was negotiated by UK Prime Minister Margaret Thatcher in 1984. The main reason for the rebate was that a high proportion of the EU Budget was spent on the Common Agricultural Policy (CAP), which benefited the UK much less than other countries.

budgetary deficit A governmental shortfall of current revenue over current expenditure.

bureau-shaping An approach to public sector organization, which originates in the work of Patrick Dunleavy. The approach contends that public officials have preferences for the type of work that they handle, and thus they will develop individual and collective strategies to pursue these preferences. Collective bureau-shaping strategies are likely to be pursued to shape organizations by a variety of means.

cabotage In road haulage, the transport of loads that have both their origin and their destination in a foreign country.

candidate countries Countries that have applied for membership of the EU and whose application has been accepted by the European Council. (*See* potential candidate country.)

capabilities catalogue A pool of personnel, expertise, and military equipment pledged by member governments, to be used in EU-led military actions.

Cecchini Report One of the reports published in 1988 in response to the European Commission's 1985 White Paper Completing the Internal Market. The report was drafted by a group of experts, chaired by Paolo Cecchini. The report examined the benefits and costs of creating a single market in Europe. According to the report, the single market would lead to lower trade costs and greater economies of scale, as firms exploited increased opportunities; it was also expected that there would be greater production efficiency achieved through market enlargement, intensified competition, and industrial restructuring.

central bank A national bank that provides services for the country's government and commercial banking system. It manages public debt, controls the money supply, and regulates the monetary and credit system.

Charles de Gaulle President of France 1959–69, de Gaulle was responsible for keeping the UK out of the EEC in the 1960s and for the 'empty chair' crisis, which is said to have slowed down the European integration process after 1966. See 'empty chair' crisis.

Charter of Fundamental Rights of the European Union The first formal EU document to combine and declare all of the values and fundamental rights (economic and social, as well as civil and political) to which EU citizens should be entitled. The text of the Charter does not establish new rights, but assembles existing rights that were previously scattered over a range of international sources. It was drafted through a convention and proclaimed at the 2000 Nice European Council. It became binding in December 2009 when the Lisbon Treaty entered into force.

checks and balances The system of building safety mechanisms into government that stems from the idea that no one branch of government should be able do something without another branch of government reviewing that action and, if necessary, halting it.

citizens' initiative One of the new democratic instruments incorporated into the Lisbon Treaty to enhance democracy and transparency in the EU. The initiative allows 1 million EU citizens to participate directly in the development of EU policies, by calling on the European Commission to make a legislative proposal. The first initiative was registered on 9 May 2012.

civil society An intermediate realm between the state and the individual or family; a particular type of political society rooted in principles of citizenship.

closer cooperation *See* enhanced cooperation procedure.

co-decision *See* ordinary legislative procedure (OLP).

co-determination The process by which employees participate in company decision-making through, for example, works councils.

cognitive mobilization The ability of voters to deal with the complexities of politics and to make their own political decisions thanks to the advance of education and the information explosion through the mass media.

cohesion A principle that favours the reduction of regional and social disparities across the EU.

Cohesion Fund An EU fund aimed at member states with a gross national income per inhabitant that is less than 90 per cent of the EU average. It aims to reduce their economic and social shortfall, as well as to stabilize their economies. It is now subject to the same rules of programming, management, and monitoring as the European Social Fund (ESF) and the European Regional Development Fund (ERDF).

collective agreement An agreement reached through collective bargaining between an employer and one or more trade unions, or between employers' associations and trade union confederations. It is normal to divide collective agreements into *procedural agreements*, which regulate the relationships between the parties and the treatment of individual workers (such as disciplinary procedures), and *substantive agreements*, which cover the wages and conditions of the workers

affected, although in practice the distinction between the two is not always clear-cut.

collective bargaining The process of negotiating an agreement on pay or on the working conditions of employees between trade unions and employers or employer associations.

collective good A shared good that cannot be withheld from those who have not paid for its use (such as 'clean air').

collegiality A principle that implies that decisions taken by one are the collective responsibility of all.

comitology (or 'committee procedure') The procedure under which the European Commission executes its implementing powers delegated to it by the legislative branch—that is, the European Parliament and the Council of the European Union—with the assistance of so called 'comitology committees' consisting of member state representatives. This delegation of power is now based on Article 290 TFEU.

comitology committee *See* comitology.

Committee of Permanent Representatives (Coreper) Committee responsible for preparing the work of the Council of the European Union. It consists of the member states' ambassadors to the European Union ('permanent representatives') and is chaired by the member state that holds the EU Council presidency.

Committee of the Regions (CoR) A Committee set up by the Maastricht Treaty as an advisory body composed of nominated representatives of Europe's regional and local authorities, to ensure that regional and local identities and interests are respected within the EU.

Common Commercial Policy (CCP) The set of principles, procedures, and rules that govern the EU's involvement in international trade and commercial negotiations.

common external tariff A central element of any customs union: a set of common tariffs, agreed by all members, imposed on goods coming into the union from outside its borders.

common market An economic agreement that extends cooperation beyond a customs union, to provide for the free movement of goods, services, capital, and labour.

common market organization (CMO) An organization operating for individual items of agricultural produce that involves public intervention, a price guaranteed for farmers, and levies at the EU's borders.

common position In the context of the EU's CFSP/CSDP, common positions allow member states to define European foreign policy towards a particular third-country or on a particular issue. A common position, once agreed, is binding on all EU states.

common strategy Overall policy guidelines for EU activities within individual non-member countries.

Communitarization The shift of policy activity from the intergovernmental pillars to the Community pillar.

Community method The use of the 'established' process of decision-making, which involves a Commission legislative initiative being agreed by the Council, and now usually the European Parliament. It also implies that the Court of Justice of the EU will have jurisdiction over any decision taken.

Community preference The preference and price advantage from which EU agricultural products benefit in comparison with imported products.

competence The legal capacity to deal with a matter.

Comprehensive Economic and Trade Agreement (CETA) Is a free trade agreement between the EU and Canada. The objective of CETA is to increase bilateral trade and investment flows and contribute to growth through the removal of customs duties, the end of limitations in access to public contracts, the creation of predictable conditions for investors, and the prevention of illegal copying of EU innovations and traditional products, amongst other measures. The negotiations ended in August 2014 but the agreement still has to be ratified, so it is not yet binding under international law.

Comprehensive security actor Is an international actor that typically combines a wide range of means to achieve its aims of a fairer, safer world characterized by multilateralism and governed by international law. The EU has been defined as such by the European Security Strategy (ESS). See European Security Strategy.

compulsory spending That part of the EU's Budget on which only the EU Council could make a decision. The Lisbon Treaty has done away with the distinction between compulsory and non-compulsory spending.

In the post-Lisbon context, the European Parliament and the EU Council decide together on the whole EU Budget. The underlying principle and the amount are legally determined by the treaties, secondary legislation, conventions, international treaties, or private contracts. In addition, the Lisbon Treaty simplifies the decision-taking procedure and makes the long-term Budget plan, or financial perspectives, legally binding.

conciliation (procedure) The third stage of the ordinary legislative procedure (OLP), at which point an equal number of representatives of the Parliament and Council get together to try to work out an agreement acceptable to all. The conciliation procedure always applies if the EU Council does not approve all of the amendments of the European Parliament adopted at its second reading.

conciliation committee A committee that, as part of the conciliation procedure, brings together equal numbers of representatives from the European Parliament and the EU Council to broker an inter-institutional agreement on outstanding problems with the proposed legislation. The committee has to be convened within six weeks (which may be extended by two weeks on the initiative of either institution) of the Council's second reading. The Committee has six (or eight) weeks in which to draw up a 'joint text' from the date of its first meeting. Within a period of six (or eight) weeks, the joint text is submitted by the presidents of the Parliament and Council delegations for approval, without any possibility of amendment. If the conciliation committee does not reach an agreement or if the 'joint text' is not approved by the Parliament or the Council, the act is deemed not to have been adopted.

conditionality (EU enlargement) The principle that applicant states must meet certain conditions before they can become EU member states; (EU external relations) provisions that make the granting of EU aid conditional on good governance, observance of human rights, and the introduction of market economics.

confederation A political model that involves a loose grouping of states, characterized by the fact that the centre has fewer powers than the states or regions.

Conference on the Future of Europe (CoFE) Launched on 9 May 2021 by the European Parliament, the Commission, and the Council, the Conference on the future of Europe aims to give citizens a greater role in shaping EU policies and ambitions, improving the Union's resilience to crises, be it economic or health-related. It will create a new public forum for an open, inclusive, transparent, and structured debate with Europeans around the issues that matter to them and affect their everyday lives.

consensual (decision-making) A type of decision-making that involves the agreement of all, even where this is no formal requirement.

consent (procedure) Was initially introduced by the Single European Act (1986) as the assent procedure. It requires the EU Council to obtain the European Parliament's agreement before certain important decisions are taken. The assent principle is based on a single reading. Parliament may accept or reject a proposal but cannot amend it. If Parliament does not give its assent, the act in question cannot be adopted. As a non-legislative procedure, it usually applies to the ratification of certain agreements negotiated by the European Union, or is applicable most notably in the cases of serious breach of fundamental rights under Article 7 Treaty on European Union (TEU) or for the accession of new EU members or arrangements for the withdrawal from the EU. As a legislative procedure, it is to be used also when new legislation on combating discrimination is being adopted and it now gives the European Parliament a veto when the subsidiary general legal basis is applied in line with Article 352 TFEU.

consolidated treaty A treaty that incorporates all of the amendments made since the original Treaty of Rome.

Constitutional Convention *See* Convention (on the Future of Europe).

Constitutional Treaty (CT) Sometimes known as the 'EU Constitution', a treaty signed on 24 October 2004. It was not ratified due to negative referenda in France and the Netherlands in 2005.

constitutionalization The formalization of the rules of the game, which, in an EU context, might involve a process whereby the treaties become over time—de jure or only de facto—a constitution.

constructive abstention A provision that allows member states to abstain in the Council on Common Foreign and Security Policy (CFSP) decisions, without blocking a unanimous agreement. This was replaced by the 'enhanced cooperation' provision in the Lisbon Treaty. *See* enhanced cooperation.

constructivism A theoretical approach that claims that politics is affected as much by ideas as by power. It argues that the fundamental structures of political life are social rather than material.

Constructivist *See* constructivism.

consultation (procedure) A special legislative procedure, under Article 289 TFEU, whereby the European Parliament is asked for its opinion on proposed legislation before the Council adopts it. The Parliament may approve or reject a legislative proposal, or propose amendments to it. The Council is not legally obliged to take account of Parliament's opinion, but in line with the case law of the Court of Justice of the EU, it must not take a decision without having received it.

Convention (on the Future of Europe) A body set up in 2002 to debate alternative models and visions of the EU, and to prepare a draft constitution that could be used as the basis of discussion in the intergovernmental conference of 2004.

convergence criteria The rules that member states have to meet before they could join economic and monetary union (EMU) in 1999.

convertibility (of currencies) The extent to which one currency is freely exchangeable into other currencies.

cooperation Usually implies government-to-government relations (with little supranational involvement).

cooperation procedure A legislative procedure introduced in the Single European Act (Article 252, ex 198c EC), which allowed the European Parliament a second reading of draft legislation. Since Amsterdam, it had been hardly used, because most policies originally falling under cooperation came under the then co-decision procedure (now ordinary legislative procedure, or OLP); the Lisbon Treaty repealed the cooperation procedure.

Copenhagen criteria The criteria that applicant states have to meet in order to join the EU. It was agreed at the Copenhagen European Council meeting in 1993.

cordon sanitaire The refusals to cooperate with other parties politically. Used in the EU to refer to shutting the far-right out of influential positions.

core Europe (or 'hard core') The idea that a small group of countries able and willing to enter into closer cooperation with one another might 'leave behind' the less enthusiastically integrationist members of the EU.

co-regulation The mechanism whereby an EU legal act entrusts the attainment of the objectives defined by the legislative authority to parties that are recognized in the field, such as economic operators, the social partners, non-governmental organizations (NGOs), or associations. It is one of the modes of governance developed in the context of the Lisbon Strategy to simplify and improve regulation in the EU.

corporatism A system of interest representation in which the constituent units are organized into a limited number of singular, compulsory, non-competitive, hierarchically ordered, and functionally differentiated categories, recognized or licensed (if not created) by the state and granted a deliberate representational monopoly within their respective categories, in exchange for observing certain controls on their selection of leaders and articulation of demands and supports.

cosmopolitanism The idea that citizens are 'citizens of the world'.

Council of Europe (CoE) A European political organization founded on 5 May 1949 by ten countries and distinct from the EU. The Council of Europe, based in Strasbourg, has 47 member countries. It seeks to develop, throughout Europe, common and democratic principles based on the European Convention on Human Rights (ECHR) and other reference texts on the protection of individuals.

Court of Session in Scotland The Court of Session is Scotland's supreme civil court. It sits in Parliament House, Edinburgh, and is presided over by the Lord President, Scotland's most senior judge.

covered bond scheme Under such a scheme, bonds are issued to free up cash tied up in assets, such as mortgages, for on-lending. Covered bonds allow the issuing bank to raise funds at a lower cost. They are generally fixed-interest instruments, thus the interest rate risk for the issuing bank is known and can be suitably managed.

COVID-19 Infectious coronavirus that led to a global pandemic with national lockdowns from early 2020.

credit boom Part of the credit boom–bust cycle, an episode characterized by a sustained increase in several economic indicators usually followed by a sharp and rapid contraction.

credit condition One of the criteria used for the grant of credit by banks.

critical juncture A period of institutional flux within the historical institutionalist model of institutional development. This literature assumes a dual model characterized by relatively long periods of path-dependent institutional stability and reproduction that are punctuated occasionally by brief phases of institutional flux (the 'critical junctures'), during which more dramatic change is possible. Junctures are critical because they place institutional arrangements on paths or trajectories that are then very difficult to alter.

cueing A form of information flowing from elites to citizens to illustrate mass–elite linkages. These linkages can mainly be structured in two forms. Political elites can be instrumental in helping to determine citizens' attitudes in a top-down approach, or elites can assume a position on European integration that reflects citizens' views, in a bottom-up manner.

current account deficit A negative difference between a country's savings and its investment.

current account surplus A positive difference between a country's savings and its investment.

customs union An economic association of states based on an agreement to eliminate tariffs and other obstacles to trade, and which also includes a common trade policy vis-à-vis third countries, usually by establishing a common external tariff on goods imported into the union.

Danish People's Party (DPP) or *Dansk Folkeparti (DF)* The DPP is a Danish right-wing populist and Eurosceptic party that won the 2014 European Parliament elections in Denmark with 26.6 per cent of the vote. It joined the European Conservatives and Reformists Group in the European Parliament. It received 21.1 per cent of the vote in the June 2015 Danish general election, but did not join the government as part of a coalition but rather agreed to provide tacit parliamentary support to the new Liberal Prime Minister, Lars Løkke Rasmussen.

Davignon Report A document issued by EC foreign ministers in 1970, outlining how the Community might develop its own foreign policy and setting out some initial steps to that end.

decoupling The divorcing of the grant of direct aid to farmers from production in the context of the Common Agricultural Policy (CAP).

deepening An intensification of integration processes and structures.

delegated act A new category of legal act created under the Treaty of Lisbon in which the legislator delegates the power to adopt acts amending non-essential elements of a legislative act to the Commission. Delegated acts may specify certain technical details or they may consist of a subsequent amendment to certain elements of a legislative act. The legislator can therefore concentrate on policy direction and objectives without entering into overly technical debates.

delegated legislation Legislation made usually by executive bodies on behalf of legislatures. It often involves the making of administrative rules and the filling in of gaps in existing legislation.

delegation The handing over of powers by a legitimate political institution to a body that then acts on its behalf.

deliberative democracy A school of thought in political theory that claims that political decisions should be the product of fair and reasonable discussion and debate among citizens. In deliberation, citizens exchange arguments and consider different claims that are designed to secure the public good. Through this conversation, citizens can come to an agreement about what procedure, action, or policy will best produce the public good. Deliberation is a necessary precondition for the legitimacy of democratic political decisions.

deliberative intergovernmentalism A version of contemporary EU intergovernmentalism that stresses the relevance of policy deliberation. It refers to two different dimensions regarding the analysis of intergovernmentalism; the first concerns the question of what makes intergovernmental relations dependent on deliberative processes; the second relates to the question of under what conditions we should expect policy deliberation to flourish in an intergovernmental context and what this would imply.

deliberative supranationalism 'Deliberative supranationalism', a term coined by Christian Joerges and

Jürgen Neyer, is concerned with the interaction of democratic nation states. It is neither the successor of the nation state nor does it aim to establish a democratic polity above it. Its aim is to improve the democratic nation state by adding a supranational layer of governance which helps to correct the functional deficiencies of national governance under conditions of complex interdependence.

Delors Report The report drafted by central bankers in 1989, which later formed the basis of the monetary union section of the Treaty on European Union. The Committee that produced the report was chaired by Jacques Delors, then Commission President.

democratic back sliding This term refers to the possibility of an EU member state reneging its democratic commitments (as defined by the Copenhagen Criteria) and points to the fact that democracy cannot be simply assumed.

democratic deficit The loss of democracy caused by the transfer of powers to the European institutions and to member state executives arising out of European integration. It implies that representative institutions (parliaments) lose out in this process.

Democrats 66 (D66) Is an internationalist and liberal Dutch political party founded in 1966. In the European Party it is part of the liberal Renew Europe Group.

demos The people of a nation as a political unit; a politically defined public community.

dependent variable The object of study; the phenomenon that one is trying to explain.

derogation A temporary exception to legislation.

Die Linke Literally, 'The Left', a democratic socialist political party in Germany, founded in 2007.

differentiated integration *See* differentiation.

differentiation The idea that subsets of member states might engage in European integration projects that do not involve all existing members; contrasts with the notion of the EU as a uniform Community.

diffuse interest group A type of interest group that is characterized by its broad scope and lack of clear membership. These include, for example, religious, social, human rights, consumer, and environmental groups.

direct action A case brought directly before the Court of Justice of the EU.

direct effect A principle of EU law by which provisions of EU law are to be enforced in national courts, and which imposes obligations on those against whom they are enforced.

direct implementation The putting into effect of European legislation by the European institutions rather than by national governments.

direct support In the context of the Common Agricultural Policy (CAP), the agricultural subsidies given directly to farmers, decoupled from production.

directive A legislative instrument that lays down certain end results that must be achieved in every member state. National authorities have to adapt their laws to meet these goals, but are free to decide how to do so. Directives may concern one or more member states, or all of them.

dirigiste *See* interventionist.

Doha Development Round The latest round of trade negotiations among the World Trade Organization (WTO) membership, aiming to achieve major reform of the international trading system through the introduction of lower trade barriers and revised trade rules. The work programme covers some 20 areas of trade and its agenda is fundamentally to improve the trading prospects of developing countries.

domestic proxy A representative or an agent authorized to act on behalf of others. In the political context, a national government is authorized to act on behalf of citizens.

Dooge Committee A committee set up after the Fontainebleau European Council in 1984 to discuss the institutional reforms required to complete the internal market and to solve the paralysis provoked by the excessive use of unanimity in the Council. It submitted its final report to the European Council in March 1985, which identified a number of priority objectives necessary to deepen integration, such as restricting the use of unanimity in the Council, strengthening the legislative role of the European Parliament, and giving more executive power to the Commission. The Committee conclusions paved the way to the Single European Act.

dual majority (or double majority) (system of voting) A voting system that takes into consideration the number of votes and population necessary to achieve a majority. The Treaty of Lisbon simplifies the system with a view to improving its efficiency. It abolishes the weighting of votes and establishes a dual majority system for adopting decisions. Thus a qualified majority is achieved if it covers at least 55 per cent of member states representing at least 65 per cent of the population of the EU. Where the Council does not act on a proposal from the Commission, the qualified majority should cover at least 72 per cent of member states representing at least 65 per cent of the population. The Treaty of Lisbon also provides for a blocking minority composed of at least four member states representing over 35 per cent of the EU population. This new system of qualified majority voting (QMV) applied with effect from 1 November 2014. However, until 31 March 2017, any member state could request, on a case-by-case basis, that a decision is taken in accordance with the rules in force before 1 November 2014 (that is, in accordance with the qualified majority, as defined by the Treaty of Nice).

Dublin Regulation The Dublin Regulation (sometimes referred to as Dublin III) determines which EU country is responsible for examining an asylum application (*see* Dublin system).

Dublin system The EU agreement which helps identify which country is responsible for processing the asylum application of a non-EU or stateless person. Introduced in the early 1990s, the basic principle of the Dublin system was that the country of first arrival for an asylum applicant would be the member state in which they made their claim for refugee status and that any decision would be valid for the whole EU. This would prevent applications being made in more than one member state. Member states' disagreement over forms of solidarity that would involve relocating asylum seekers required reforming the system. Thus it was replaced by the Dublin II Regulation in 2003; that Regulation was in turn replaced by the Dublin III Regulation in 2013. The Commission proposed a new Regulation in 2016, but it has not been agreed yet (*see also* Dublin Regulation).

dumping Selling at below cost, often to force competition out of the market.

economic and monetary union (EMU) A form of integration that combines the features of the economic union (which implies the existence of a single market, but also a high degree of coordination of the most important areas of economic policy and market regulation, as well as monetary policies and income redistribution policies) and the monetary union, which implies further integration in the area of currency cooperation. The process involves three stages and the fulfilment of the so-called 'convergence criteria' by all participating countries.

economic union A form of integration that implies the existence of a single market (and therefore free movement of goods, services, labour, and capital among the participating states and common rules, tariffs, and so on, vis-à-vis third countries), but also a high degree of coordination of the most important areas of economic policy and market regulation, as well as monetary policies and income redistribution policies.

Economist An advocate of one of the possible economic strategies with which to achieve economic and monetary union (EMU); in the 1960s and 1970s, the Economist camp postulated that economic policies needed to be coordinated before fixing exchange rates or introducing a single currency. *See* Monetarist.

efficiency The ratio of output to input of any system.

elite pluralism A system of interest mediation in which access to the EU consultative institutions is open, but competitive, resulting in biased access patterns.

elite socialization Closely related to the neo-functionalist idea of political spillover, this theory posits that European integration promotes shifts of loyalty among civil servants and other elite actors; thus members of the European Parliament (MEPs) will tend to become more European in their outlook, although this may be disputed empirically.

elitist A characteristic describing the tendency of neo-functionalists to see European integration as driven by functional and technocratic needs. Although not apolitical, it sees little role for democratic and accountable governance.

embedded liberalism A term introduced by John Ruggie to describe the policy orientation of the interwar international economic order and to explain the social conditions upon which it rested. This order was based on two doctrines: the first is that states should cooperate in devising and implementing international economic institutions to facilitate international market integration and to preserve international

economic stability; the second is that states should retain sufficient autonomy to pursue economic and social objectives domestically.

emergency brake *See* brake clause.

'empty chair' crisis The crisis that affected the European Community after July 1965 when France boycotted the meetings of the Council in opposition to Commission proposals addressing the financing of the Common Agricultural Policy (CAP). France insisted on a political agreement that would clarify the role of the Commission and majority voting if it were to participate again. This crisis was resolved in the Luxembourg Compromise in January 1966. *See* Luxembourg Compromise.

enforcement The process of ensuring that EU rules are implemented. It may involve taking action in the Court of Justice of the EU.

engrenage The enmeshing of EU elites, which may arise out of a process of socialization in Brussels.

enhanced cooperation (procedure) Initially established by the Amsterdam Treaty as 'closer cooperation' and renamed 'enhanced cooperation' by the Lisbon Treaty, a procedure that allows groups of member states that wish to integrate further than provided for in the treaties to do so, with the exception of areas of exclusive Union competence. The Commission will assess the request and it may submit a proposal to the Council in this respect. If the Commission decides not to present a proposal, it will explain its reasons to the member states concerned.

enlargement The process of expanding the EU geographically to include new member states.

Environmental Action Programme (EAP) Since 1973, a document defining the future orientation of EU policy in the environmental field and suggesting specific proposals that the Commission intends to put forward over the coming years.

epistemic community A network of knowledge-based experts or groups with an authoritative claim to policy-relevant knowledge within the domain of their expertise.

epistemology The theory of knowledge, which accounts for the way in which knowledge about the world is acquired.

Erasmus The European Commission's flagship programme for higher education students, teachers, and institutions, intending to encourage student and staff mobility for work and study, and promoting trans-national cooperation projects among universities across Europe.

euro area (or eurozone) The economic area that covers those countries that have so far joined the EU's single currency.

euro bond A government bond issued in euros jointly by all of the euro area member states. This is a debt investment whereby an investor loans a certain amount of money, for a certain amount of time, with a certain interest rate, to the eurozone as a whole, which then forwards the money to individual governments. Euro bonds were suggested as an effective way in which to tackle the sovereign debt crisis, and later the COVID-19 crisis, although they remain controversial.

Euro Plus Pact As agreed by the euro area heads of state or government, and joined by Bulgaria, Denmark, Latvia, Lithuania, Poland, and Romania, this agreement further strengthens the economic pillar of economic and monetary union (EMU) and achieves a new quality of economic policy coordination, with the objective of improving competitiveness and thereby leading to a higher degree of convergence, reinforcing the EU's social market economy. The Pact remains open for other member states to join. The Pact fully respects the integrity of the Single Market.

Euro Summit Under the Fiscal Compact signed in March 2010, it was agreed that the heads of state or government would meet informally at least twice a year to discuss issues related to economic and monetary union (EMU) and to provide 'strategic orientations for the conduct of economic policies'. Euro summits, it was further agreed, would be chaired by a president, who would be elected by simple majority for a two-and-a-half-year term of office. The new Euro Summits reign supreme over the Eurogroup.

Euroalternativism Term coined by John FitzGibbon that refers to pro European Union views that contest integration and offer alternative policies or institutional reform.

Eurobarometer A European Commission publication and website monitoring and analysing public opinion in the member states since 1973.

Eurogroup An informal group comprising those member states of ECOFIN that are members of the single currency; (also) an interest group operating at the EU level, typically organized as a federation of national interest groups.

Europe 2020 The EU's growth strategy for the coming decade. It has five objectives on employment, innovation, education, social inclusion, and climate/energy to be reached by 2020. Each member state has adopted its own national targets in each of these areas. Concrete actions at EU and national levels underpin the strategy.

Europe agreement One of the agreements that constituted the legal framework of relations between the EU and the Central and Eastern European (CEE) countries, adapted to the specific situation of each partner state while setting common political, economic, and commercial objectives. In the context of accession to the EU, they formed the framework for implementation of the accession process.

European Agency for the Management of Operational Cooperation at the External Borders of the Member States of the European Union (Frontex) Set up in 2004 to reinforce and streamline cooperation between national border authorities, Frontex has several operational areas of activity, including training, risk analysis, research, and rapid response capability via the European Border Guard Teams (EBGT). It also helps member states in joint return operations involving foreign nationals staying illegally, and provides information systems and an information-sharing environment regarding the current state of affairs at the external borders.

European Agricultural Guidance and Guarantee Fund (EAGGF) One of the funds supporting the Common Agricultural Policy (CAP). The EAGGF is composed of two sections, the guidance section and the guarantee section. Within the framework of European economic and social cohesion policy, the EAGGF supports rural development and the improvement of agricultural structures.

European Arrest Warrant (EAW) A system that replaces the lengthier extradition procedures among EU member states, simplifying the arrest and return of suspected criminals across the Union; introduced after the terrorist attacks on the USA of 11 September 2001 ('9/11').

European Atomic Energy Community (Euratom, or EAEC) The Euratom Treaty was signed on

25 March 1957 by six states—namely, Belgium, France, Italy, Luxembourg, the Netherlands, and West Germany—to coordinate their research programmes for the peaceful use of nuclear energy. The Treaty today helps in the pooling of knowledge, infrastructure, and funding of nuclear energy. It ensures the security of atomic energy supply within the framework of a centralized monitoring system.

European Central Bank (ECB) Established in Frankfurt in 1999, the central bank is responsible for the single monetary policy of the euro area.

European (or EU) citizenship A status conferred directly on every EU citizen under the Treaty on the Functioning of the European Union (TFEU)—that is, any person who holds the nationality of an EU country is automatically also an EU citizen. EU citizenship is additional to, and does not replace, national citizenship.

European Coal and Steel Community (ECSC) Established by six states in April 1951 by the Treaty of Paris, the ECSC allowed for the pooling of authority over coal and steel industries. Because it was based on a 50-year treaty, the ECSC ceased to exist on 23 July 2002.

European Committee for Electrotechnical Standardization (CENELEC) The body responsible for standardization in the electro-technical engineering field, it prepares voluntary standards, which help to facilitate trade between countries, to create new markets, to cut compliance costs, and to support the development of a single European market.

European Committee for Standardization (CEN) Officially created as an international non-profit association based in Brussels on 30 October 1975, CEN is a business facilitator in Europe, removing trade barriers for European industry and consumers. Its mission is to foster the European economy in global trading, and the welfare of European citizens and the environment. It provides a platform for the development of European standards and other technical specifications.

European Company Statute A statute that refers to a regulatory framework aiming to create a 'European company' with its own legislative framework, which will allow companies incorporated in different member states to merge or to form a holding company or joint subsidiary, while avoiding the legal and practical constraints arising from the existence of different legal systems. This legislative framework also provides for the involvement of employees in European companies, giving due recognition to their place and role in the business.

European Convention *See* Convention (on the Future of Europe).

European Convention on Human Rights (ECHR) An international treaty to protect human rights and fundamental freedoms in Europe. Drafted in 1950 by the then newly formed Council of Europe, the Convention entered into force on 3 September 1953. All Council of Europe member states are party to the Convention and new members are expected to ratify the Convention at the earliest opportunity. The Convention established the European Court of Human Rights (ECtHR). *See* European Court of Human Rights (ECtHR).

European Council A body that defines the general political direction and priorities of the EU. With the entry into force of the Treaty of Lisbon on 1 December 2009, it became an institution, with its own president.

European Council of Economics and Finance Ministers (ECOFIN) Composed of the economics and finance ministers of the member states, as well as budget ministers when budgetary issues are discussed, ECOFIN meets once a month to discuss EU policy in a number of areas, including economic policy coordination, economic surveillance, monitoring of member states' budgetary policy and public finances, the euro (legal, practical, and international aspects), financial markets and capital movements, and economic relations with third countries. ECOFIN also prepares and adopts every year, together with the European Parliament, the Budget of the European Union. *See* Eurogroup.

European Court of Auditors (ECA) Established by the Treaty of Brussels of 1975, the Court carries out the audit of EU finances. Thus it assesses the collection and spending of EU funds, it examines whether financial operations have been properly recorded and disclosed, and legally and regularly executed and managed, and it assists the European Parliament and the EU Council in overseeing the implementation of the EU Budget.

European Court of Human Rights (ECtHR) An international court set up in 1959, which rules on individual or state applications alleging violations of the civil and political rights set out in the European Convention on Human Rights (ECHR). Since 1998, it has sat as a full-time court and individuals can apply to it directly. *See* European Convention on Human Rights (ECHR).

European currency unit (ecu) The unit of account under the European Monetary System (EMS), composed of a 'basket of currencies'; replaced by the euro.

European Defence Agency (EDA) Is an agency of the EU assisting the member states in their efforts to improve European defence capabilities in support of the Common Security and Defence Policy of the Union. The EDA was set up in 2004 and is based in Brussels.

European Defence Community (EDC) The first attempt by western European powers, with United States support, to counterbalance the overwhelming conventional military ascendancy of the Soviet Union in Europe by creating a European army, with the eventual involvement of German units, to be placed under a single military and political European authority. This proposal sparked fierce debate in France. Although it was accepted by most Western countries, the plan for a European Defence Community was rejected by the French National Assembly in August 1954.

European Economic and Social Committee (EESC) A tripartite advisory body composed of individual members, who are nominated by the EU member states and who represent employers, workers, and other interests, such as environmental organizations or farmers.

European Economic Community (EEC) A body created by the 1957 Treaty of Rome, its aim being to bring about economic integration, including a common market, among its six founding members: Belgium, France, Germany, Italy, Luxembourg, and the Netherlands.

European Employment Strategy (EES) A 'soft' law mechanism designed to coordinate the employment policies of the EU member states. While the objectives, priorities, and targets are agreed at EU level, the national governments are fully responsible for formulating and implementing the necessary policies.

European External Action Service (EEAS) A body formed to assist the High Representative, comprising staff from the European Commission, the General Secretariat of the Council (GSC), and the diplomatic services of EU member states.

European Financial Stability Facility (EFSF) A facility created by the euro area member states following the decisions taken on 9 May 2010 within the framework of ECOFIN, with a mandate to safeguard financial stability in Europe by providing financial assistance to the euro area. The EFSF is a part of the wider safety net, alongside the European Financial Stability Mechanism (EFSM). The EFSM and the EFSF can be activated only after a request for financial assistance has been made by the concerned member state and a macroeconomic adjustment programme, incorporating strict conditionality, has been agreed with the Commission, in liaison with the European Central Bank (ECB).

European Financial Stability Mechanism (EFSM) This mechanism provides financial assistance to EU member states in financial difficulties. The EFSM reproduces for the EU27 the basic mechanics of the existing balance-of-payments regulation for non-euro area member states. The EFSM is a part of the wider safety net alongside the European Financial Stability Facility (EFSF). The EFSM and the EFSF can be activated only after a request for financial assistance has been made by the concerned member state and a macroeconomic adjustment programme, incorporating strict conditionality, has been agreed with the Commission, in liaison with the European Central Bank (ECB).

European Free Trade Association (EFTA) An international organization set up in 1960 to promote free trade among its members. Most of its original members have since joined the European Union.

European Globalization Adjustment Fund (EGF) A financial tool aiming towards the effective re-entry into the labour market of those workers who have lost their jobs. The EGF provides individual support for a limited period of time to workers who are affected by trade-adjustment redundancies. All member states can apply for support according to specific criteria.

European integration The process of political and economic (and possibly also cultural and social) integration of the states of Europe into a unified bloc.

European Investment Bank (EIB) Created by the Treaty of Rome in 1958 as the long-term lending bank of the EU, its task is to contribute towards the integration, balanced development, and economic and social cohesion of the EU member states.

European Monetary System (EMS) A regulated exchange rate system established in the EC in 1979 after failures to set up economic and monetary union earlier in the decade, the EMS aimed to promote monetary cooperation and exchange rate stability.

European Neighbourhood Policy (ENP) Developed in 2004 by the European Commission to frame the bilateral policy between the EU and each partner country, the policy aims to avoid the emergence of new dividing lines between the enlarged EU and its neighbours, and to strengthen prosperity, stability, and security.

European Ombudsman An independent body that investigates complaints about maladministration in the institutions and agencies of the European Union.

European partnership Within the framework of the stabilization and association process with the countries of the Western Balkans, the European Union has set up such partnerships with Albania, Bosnia and Herzegovina, North Macedonia, Montenegro, and Serbia, including Kosovo, as defined by United Nations Security Council Resolution 1244 of 10 June 1999. The partnership establishes a framework of priority action and a financial structure to improve the stability and prosperity of the country, with a view to greater integration with the EU, because the state is recognized as a potential candidate for membership.

European Police Office (Europol) The European law enforcement agency, which aims to make Europe safer by assisting EU member states in their fight against serious international crime and terrorism.

European Political Community (EPC) The idea of a European Political Community was developed in parallel with negotiations on the shape of the European Defence Community (EDC). The original Six sought to develop a political statute affording leadership and democratic control over the future European army. With a clear federalist goal, the plan proposed the establishment of a bicameral parliament, comprising a Chamber of the Peoples elected by direct universal suffrage, and a European Senate appointed by the national parliaments. It also proposed the establishment of an Executive Council, which would effectively be the government of the Community, a Court of Justice and an Economic and Social Council. The refusal of the French National Assembly on 30 August 1954 to ratify the Treaty establishing the EDC led to the plan for a European Political Community being abandoned. *See* European Defence Community (EDC).

European political cooperation (EPC) A form of foreign policy cooperation prior to Maastricht, set up after 1970 and formalized by the Single European Act.

European Regional Development Fund (ERDF) A fund that aims to strengthen economic and social cohesion in the EU by correcting imbalances between its regions. The ERDF finances: direct aid to investments in companies (in particular small and medium-sized enterprises, or SMEs) to create sustainable jobs; infrastructures linked notably to research and innovation, telecommunications, environment, energy, and transport; financial instruments to support regional and local development, and to foster cooperation between towns and regions; and technical assistance measures. The ERDF can intervene in the three objectives of regional policy—namely, convergence, regional competitiveness and employment, and European territorial cooperation.

European Securities Markets Programme (SMP) One of the programmes of the European Central Bank (ECB) that correspond to the strategies that it pursues on a temporary basis to deal with specific monetary problems, often concerned with liquidity shortages in the inter-banking market and their negative impact on the transmission of monetary policy. Through the SMP, the ECB purchases government bonds, in secondary markets, in order to provide liquidity to alleviate pressures from sovereign debt risk.

European Security Strategy (ESS) Is a comprehensive document that analyses and defines the EU's security environment, identifying key security challenges and subsequent political implications for the EU. It was adopted by the European Council on 12–13 December 2003.

European Semester A cycle of economic policy coordination, this is an additional instrument for the EU's preventive surveillance of the economic and fiscal policies of its member states. The main new aspect is that the enforcement of economic policy coordination is now extended right through to the budgetary process of every member state. The European semester is based on a coordination process lasting several months, with fixed calendar deadlines.

European Social Dialogue A joint consultation procedure involving social partners at EU level, aiming to discuss and negotiate agreements where relevant.

European Social Fund (ESF) Set up in 1957, a fund that aims to sustain and improve mobility in the European labour market through education and requalification initiatives for workers in areas experiencing industrial decline.

European Stability Mechanism (ESM) A permanent rescue funding programme to succeed the temporary European Financial Stability Facility (EFSF) and European Financial Stabilization Mechanism. The European Stability Mechanism (ESM) came into force on 8 October 2012, following an amendment to the Treaty on the Functioning of the European Union (TFEU) and the signing of an ESM Treaty by the euro area countries.

European System of Central Banks (ESCB) A system that brings together the national central banks, together with the European Central Bank (ECB).

European Telecommunications Standards Institute (ETSI) Recognized as an official European standards organization by the EU, a body that produces globally applicable standards for information and communications technology (ICT).

European Transparency Initiative (ETI) Launched by the European Commission in 2005, the ETI aimed to increase the financial accountability of EU funding, strengthen the personal integrity and independence of the EU institutions, and impose stricter controls on lobbying.

European Working Time Directive (EWTD) A directive aiming to protect the health and safety of workers in the European Union. It lays down minimum requirements in relation to working hours, rest periods, annual leave, and working arrangements for night workers.

Europeanization The process of European integration itself, or a shorthand for the incorporation of European characteristics into domestic institutions, politics, and identities (*see* Chapter 8).

Eurosceptic Someone who is opposed to European integration, or is sceptical about the EU and its aims.

Euroscepticism Indicates opposition to the process of European integration. According to Taggart and Szczerbiak, whereas policy Euroscepticism refers to opposition to specific policies and extension of EU competences, national interest Euroscepticism involves employing the rhetoric of defending or standing up for the national interest in the context of debates about the EU.

Eurosclerosis A word used to characterize the period of EC history between 1966 and the early 1980s, during which the process of integration appeared to have slowed down and the common market objective was not implemented.

Eurostat Established in 1953, the statistical office of the European Union. Its task is to provide the EU with statistics at the European level that enable comparisons between countries and regions.

Eurosystem Is the collection of national central banks of countries that have adopted the euro plus the European Central Bank (ECB). Those national central banks are merely 'branches' of the new ECB.

eurozone *See* euro area.

EU–Turkey Statement Signed on 18 March 2016, this intergovernmental agreement between the EU member states and Turkey aims to end the flow of irregular migration from Turkey to the EU. Under the agreement, all new irregular migrants or asylum seekers crossing from Turkey to the Greek islands will be returned to Turkey after their asylum claims have been assessed. For every Syrian returned to Turkey, another Syrian will be resettled to the EU from Turkey directly. Through a new financial tool, the Facility for Refugees in Turkey, the EU supported Syrian refugees and host communities in Turkey with €3 bn between 2016 and 2017.

EU Withdrawal Bill A bill to repeal the European Communities Act 1972 and make other provision in connection with the withdrawal of the United Kingdom from the EU. The bill became the European Union (Withdrawal) Act 2018, having been given royal assent on 26 June 2018.

excessive deficit procedure (EDP) The procedure under monetary union (EMU) that can be used to sanction those member states who fail to control their budget deficits.

exchange rate mechanism (ERM) The main element of the European monetary system, a mechanism that aimed to create a zone of monetary stability within Western Europe.

exclusive competence or exclusive Union competence One of the specific areas in which only the EU is able to legislate and adopt legally binding acts. The member states may intervene in the areas concerned only if empowered to do so by the Union or in order to implement Union acts (*see* shared competence).

executive The branch of government responsible for implementing laws made by parliament.

executive federalism Decision-making in the European Union has been described as being multi-layered and federal in structure and thus constituting a system of executive federalism. This system is characterized by three elements: (i) interwoven competencies: making laws is the domain of the supranational level, but implementing these laws is the domain of the national level; (ii) the Council as federal chamber: a central institution of this federal system a meeting point for actors from the national and supranational level, a meeting point for politicians and bureaucrats, a place to negotiate, legislate, and implement, and the consensual form of decision-making; (iii) consensual decision-making—solutions are sought through ongoing negotiations, openness to compromise, and the incorporation of as many parties as possible. This method is based on mutual trust and the expectation of gaining more by giving in to a certain extent, and being repaid in another round. And based on the secrecy and confidentiality of the negotiations in the Council.

extraordinary rendition The handing over or surrender of a fugitive from one state to another, in contravention of national and international law, such as when a suspect is handed over without the permission of a judicial authority or, after the transfer, that person is tortured or held in breach of his or her human rights.

falsifiable hypothesis A hypothesis that can be tested and which may thus be proven false. It is relatively easy to gather evidence for just about any idea, but a hypothesis is essentially worthless unless it makes predictions that evidence could contradict.

Federal *See* federalism and federation.

Federal Reserve (the Fed) The United States' central bank.

federalism An ideological position that suggests that everyone can be satisfied by combining national and regional/territorial interests in a complex web of checks and balances between a central government and a multiplicity of regional governments. In an EU context, it tends to imply an ideological approach that advocates the creation of a federal state in Europe.

federation A way of organizing a political system, which involves the constitutionally defined sharing of functions between a federal centre and the states. A federation will usually have a bicameral parliament, a constitutional court, and a constitution.

Fidesz The Federation of Young Democrats–Hungarian Civic Alliance is a Hungarian populist centre-right political party founded in 1988. Since 2006 and under the leadership of Viktor Orbán, Fidesz has governed Hungary with the support of the Christian Democratic People's Party. In 2021 Fidesz left the European People's Party in the European Parliament as the Hungarian party was about to be suspended over breaches of rule of law and media freedom, and democratic backsliding in Hungary.

finalité politique The EU's final constitutional settlement.

Financial Instrument for Fisheries Guidance (FIFG) An instrument that aims to contribute to achieving the objectives of the Common Fisheries Policy (CFP). It supports structural measures in fisheries, aquaculture, and the processing and marketing of fishery and aquaculture products. It aims to promote the restructuring of the sector by putting in place the right conditions for its development and modernization.

financial perspective The EU's multi-annual spending (budget) plan.

financial solidarity The sharing of financial burdens across the EU members.

Fiscal Compact *See* Treaty on Stability, Coordination and Governance in the Economic and Monetary Union.

fiscal crisis An inability of the state to raise enough tax revenue to pay for its expenditure.

fiscal discipline A notion dealing with the specific externalities associated to the adverse spillover effects of excessive deficits leading to potentially unsustainable debt accumulation in member countries. Among economists and policy-makers, there is not much disagreement either on the risk that irresponsible fiscal behaviour creates for monetary union, or on the need for common rules or mechanisms that ensure fiscal discipline. There is, however, disagreement on the proper design of those rules and mechanisms. Hence, the discussion focuses on issues of design rather than of principle.

fiscal hangover An expression referring to the end of the happy days of economic and monetary union (EMU) and how the financial crisis has to change the rules of the game regarding financial transactions, the regulation of banks, and how states manage their debts.

fiscal policy The means by which a government adjusts its levels of spending in order to monitor and influence a nation's economy.

fiscal stimulus package An energizing plan that provides tax rebates directly to taxpayers.

fiscal transfer A financial transfer from a central authority to a subsidiary in a federal system, or to a member of a fiscal union. *See* fiscal union.

fiscal union The integration of the fiscal policy of nations or states, under which decisions about the collection and expenditure of taxes are taken by common institutions and shared by the participating governments.

Five Star Movement (M5S) An anti-establishment, populist, Eurosceptic and environmentalist political party set up by Beppe Grillo in Italy. At the 2013 general election, M5S was the third largest political party with 25.6 per cent of the vote in the Chamber of Deputies and obtained 109 deputies. In the European Parliament it is part of the Europe of Freedom and Direct Democracy (EFDD) group.

flexibility One of the mechanisms, first introduced in the Amsterdam Treaty, which allows the EU to pursue differentiated integration. The Lisbon Treaty incorporates changes to its application under the enhanced cooperation procedure. *See* enhanced cooperation procedure.

fonctionnaire A French term that means 'civil servant'. In the EU context, this term is used to refer to the civil servants working for the EU institutions.

'Fortress Europe' In the context of the EU, the strengthening of the EU's external borders to promote the territorial integrity and security of the Union, and the effect that it has on limiting the access of migrants into the EU.

Fouchet Plan A plan proposed in 1961 and pushed by the French government, which would have led to the creation of a European intergovernmental defence organization, but which was rejected by the EC's member states.

founding fathers The principal male architects of European integration following the end of the Second World War, including Konrad Adenauer, Winston Churchill, Alcide de Gasperi, Walter Hallstein, Jean Monnet, Robert Schuman, Paul-Henri Spaak, and Altiero Spinelli.

framework directive Incorporated into the 2001 White Paper on European Governance (WPEG) as part of the Commission's strategy for better and faster regulation, these are legal instruments that offer flexible implementation, and which tend to be agreed more quickly by the EU Council and the European Parliament.

framework-type legislation Legislation that does not involve legally enforceable rules, but which rests on mechanisms such as sharing ideas, benchmarking, and naming and shaming.

framing An important component of how the media can affect public opinion. A frame is an emphasis in salience of certain aspects of a topic.

Franco-German axis The relationship between France and Germany that is often said to lie at the heart of the European integration process.

Frankfurt School The Frankfurt School was set up by a group of Marxist intellectuals in Germany in 1923, affiliated to the University of Frankfurt and independently of the Communist Party, which has been influential in the development of Marxist theory ever since.

free trade area (FTA) A group of countries that agree progressively to reduce barriers to trade, such as quotas and tariffs, which are often imposed at borders.

freeriding Reaping the benefits of a collective agreement without having participated in efforts to forge the agreement or to implement it. *See* collective good.

Friends of the Constitution In January 2007, the Spanish and Luxembourg governments convened a ministerial-level meeting of member states that had ratified the Constitution to discuss how the EU might proceed on the basis of the 2004 Constitution.

Front National *See Rassemblement Nationale*

Frontex *See* European Agency for the Management of Operational Cooperation at the External Borders of the Member States of the European Union

full economic union (FEU) The complete unification of the economies of the participating member states and common policies for most economic matters.

full political union (FPU) The term used when, in addition to full economic union (FEU), political governance and policy-making have moved to the supranational level. Effectively, political union occurs when the final stage of integration has taken place and a new confederation or federation has been created.

functional spillover The knock-on effect of integration in one sector, which is said by neo-functionalists to provoke integration in neighbouring sectors.

G20 The group of 20 leading industrialized nations.

game theory An interdisciplinary rational approach to the study of human behaviour in which 'games' are a metaphor for a wide range of human interactions. It analyses the strategic interaction among a group of rational players (or agents) who behave strategically. A strategy of a player is the predetermined rule by which a player decides his or her course of action during the game. Each player tries to maximize his or her pay-off irrespective of what other players are doing.

General Agreement on Tariffs and Trade (GATT) First signed in 1947, the agreement was designed to provide an international forum that encouraged free trade between member states by regulating and reducing tariffs on traded goods, and by providing a common mechanism for resolving trade disputes. It lasted until the creation of the World Trade Organization (WTO) on 1 January 1995.

geopolitical A characteristic referring to the relationship between geography, politics, and international relations.

global imbalance A situation in which there are large trade deficits and large trade surpluses in different parts of the world, which is perceived to be unsustainable and in need of rebalancing.

globalization A contested concept that usually refers to the growing economic interdependence of states and non-state actors worldwide. Often associated with increased capital mobility and the spread of neo-liberal ideas, it implies that market authority is enhanced at the cost of formal political authority.

Golden Dawn Populist far-right Greek political party that in the 2015 parliamentary elections managed to secure 18 seats in the Greek parliament.

Good Friday Agreement Signed on 10 April 1998, the Good Friday Agreement brought to an end the 30 years of sectarian conflict in Northern Ireland. The agreement set up a power-sharing assembly to govern Northern Ireland by cross-community consent.

the Six *See* original six.

good governance A concept that encompasses the role of public authorities in establishing the environment in which economic operators function and in determining the distribution of benefits, as well as the relationship between the ruler and the ruled. It is typically defined in terms of the mechanisms thought to be needed to promote it. Thus governance is associated with democracy and civil rights, with transparency, with the rule of law, and with efficient public services.

governance The intentional regulation of social relationships and the underlying conflicts by reliable and durable means and institutions, instead of the direct use of power and violence.

governance turn The shift in interest in EU studies that included the increased application of theories of governance, comparative politics, and public policy, as well as the study of the EU as a political system in its own right.

grand theory A theory that tries to explain the entirety of a political process, such as European integration.

gross domestic product (GDP) The market value of all officially recognized final goods and services produced within a country in a given period.

gross national product (GNP) A measure of the country's total economic activity.

guarantee price (or intervention price) In the context of the Common Agricultural Policy (CAP), the (agricultural) price at which member states intervene in the market to buy up produce.

Hague Programme Adopted at the November 2004 Brussels European Council, the Hague Programme was an ambitious five-year plan aimed at strengthening freedom, security, and justice within the, then, 25 member states of the EU.

hard ecu proposal One of the alternatives to introduce a single currency into the EU, this proposal foresaw the introduction of a common currency in parallel to the existing national currencies. This suggestion was not implemented.

hard law Another way of saying 'the law', emphasizing its enforceability (*see* soft law).

harmonization The act of setting common European standards from which states are unable to deviate (either upwards or downwards).

headline goal(s) Initially, a political commitment agreed at the Helsinki European Council in 1999 to deploy, by 2003, 50,000–60,000 troops in 60 days, sustainable for a year (a 'Rapid Reaction Force') to meet the requirements of the Petersberg tasks. It has since been superseded by a new headline goal.

health check A review of the Common Agricultural Policy (CAP) as part of the overall review of the EU Budget. The reason for doing this in parallel is that the CAP forms a significant part of the EU Budget and, without looking at this policy, there is significantly less scope for reforms in the overall Budget.

hegemony Power, control, or influence exercised by a leading state over other states.

High Authority The original name given to the (now) European Commission in the 1950 Schumann Declaration and subsequently incorporated into the European Coal and Steel Community (ECSC) Treaty.

High Representative (HR) for the CFSP or High Representative of the Union for Foreign Affairs and Security Policy The Amsterdam Treaty created the post of 'High Representative for the Common Foreign and Security Policy'; the Lisbon Treaty renames the position the 'High Representative of the Union for Foreign Affairs and Security Policy' and extends his or her responsibilities by assigning the High Representative

the functions of Council presidency in matters of foreign affairs, of Commissioner responsible for External Relations, and of High Representative for the Common Foreign and Security Policy (CFSP). The High Representative is one of the five vice-presidents of the European Commission and presides over the Foreign Affairs Council (FAC). The role was renamed 'High Representative of the Union for Foreign Affairs and Security Policy' by the Lisbon Treaty.

housing bubble An increase in housing prices fuelled by demand and speculation. The bubble is said to burst when demand decreases or stagnates while supply increases, resulting in a sharp drop in prices.

impact assessment An evaluation intended to provide a detailed and systematic appraisal of the potential impacts of a new regulation in order to assess whether the regulation is likely to achieve the desired objectives.

implementing acts The Treaty of Lisbon authorizes the Commission to adopt implementing acts relating to the carrying out of European measures that require uniform implementation across the EU (*see* also comitology).

independent variable A factor contributing to an explanation of a phenomenon (a dependent variable).

individual direct payment An agricultural subsidy paid directly to individual farmers.

infringement actions An action for breach of European law that may result in a court case.

infringement proceedings *See* infringement actions.

input legitimacy One part of a concept that follows Scharpf's distinction between input-oriented and output-oriented legitimacy. On the input side, democratic legitimacy requires mechanisms or procedures to link political decisions with citizens' preferences. In modern democracies, these mechanisms are reflected in representative institutions in which political decision-makers can be held accountable by the means of elections. *See* legitimacy; output legitimacy.

institutional balance In the EU context, a concept meaning that each institution has to act in accordance with the powers conferred on it by the treaties.

institutional isomorphism A term used by DiMaggio and Powell (1991) to denote the tendency for institutions within a similar environment to come to resemble each other.

institutionalist *See* new institutionalism.

integration The combination of parts of a unified whole—that is, a dynamic process of change. European integration is usually associated with the intensely institutionalized form of cooperation found in Europe after 1951.

integration theory Sometimes used generally as a shorthand for all theoretical and conceptual approaches that discuss European integration; otherwise it refers more specifically to supranational (especially neo-functionalist) theories of European integration.

interdependence The extent to which the actions of one state impact upon others.

interest group Any group of individuals or associations that is organized, with shared political interests and informality, and which does not aspire to public office or to compete in elections, but rather to the pursuit of goals through frequent informal interactions with politicians and bureaucrats.

interest intermediation The process of translating interests into policy, through the medium of interest organizations.

interest rate The rate of return on savings, or the rate paid on borrowings.

intergovernmental (cooperation) Cooperation that involves sovereign states and which occurs on a government-to-government basis, without the extensive involvement of supranational actors.

intergovernmental conference (IGC) A structured negotiation among the EU's member states, which usually leads to treaty revision. *See* simplified revision procedure.

intergovernmental treaty A treaty that formally sits outside of the EU framework (in other words, not an EU Treaty), such as the Treaty on Stability, Coordination and Governance.

intergovernmentalism A theory of European integration that privileges the role of states. When conceptualizing decision-making mechanisms in the context of the EU, this refers to decisions being made by the member states only, without involvement of the supranational institutions.

International Monetary Fund (IMF) Conceived in 1994, an organization of 188 countries, working to foster global monetary cooperation, to secure financial stability, to facilitate international trade, to promote high employment and sustainable economic growth, and to reduce poverty around the world. *See* Bretton Woods agreement.

interpretivism A tradition that developed largely as a criticism of the dominant theory of positivism. Interpretivists argue that the positivist idea of a chain of causation is quite logical in the natural world, where a particular stimulus consistently produces a given effect, but does not apply in the social world. People do not merely react to stimuli; rather, they actively interpret the situations in which they find themselves and act on the basis of these interpretations.

intervening variable A variable that explains the relationships between independent and dependent variables.

intervention price *See* guarantee price.

interventionism/interventionist The concept that governments involve themselves in the regulation of markets, through policy, rather than leave markets to regulate themselves.

Ioannina Compromise A negotiated compromise that took its name from an informal meeting of foreign ministers in the Greek city of Ioannina on 29 March 1994. The resulting compromise lay down that if members of the Council representing between 23 votes (the old blocking minority threshold) and 26 votes (the new threshold) expressed their intention to oppose the taking of a decision by the Council by qualified majority, the Council would do all within its power, within a reasonable space of time, to reach a satisfactory solution that could be adopted by at least 68 votes out of 87. The Lisbon Treaty (Article 16 TEU) introduces a new definition of the rule of qualified majority that applied from 1 November 2014 onwards. *See* dual majority (voting); qualified majority voting.

Jean Monnet One of the founders of the European integration project. The driving force behind the 1950 Schuman Plan, which led to the establishment of the European Coal and Steel Community (ECSC), Monnet became the first head of the ECSC's High Authority. He continued to play an active role in European integration throughout his life, although often behind the scenes.

joint action Coordinated action by member states to commit resources for an agreed (foreign policy) objective. They require a unanimous vote in the Council.

joint-decision trap The idea promoted by Fritz Scharpf in 1988 that while it might be increasingly difficult in future for further integration to take place, it will also be impossible for states to go back on agreements already made; as such, states are 'trapped' within the European integration process.

Joint Transparency Register (JTR) The JTR has been set up by the European Parliament and the European Commission as a 'one-stop shop' where organizations representing particular interests at EU level register and provide up-to-date information about who or what they represent as well as their budgets. The JTR also incorporates a code of conduct governing relations of interest representatives with the EU institutions and a mechanism for complaints.

judicial activism In the context of the Court of Justice of the European Union (CJEU), this refers to the way in which the Court exploits the gaps and vagueness existing in areas of EU law so as to expand its powers and role. The Court has been criticized on the basis that its activism exceeds its judicial powers and falls into the area of policy-making.

judicial review The right of a court to review a law or other act for constitutionality or its violation of some fundamental principle.

Keynesian A position that supports J. M. Keynes' economic theory and which has as its starting point the assumption that state finances should be used to counteract cyclical economic downturns. The argument implies that governments should focus on issues of employment and economic growth, rather on variables such as inflation.

Konrad Adenauer The first Chancellor of the Federal Republic of Germany after the end of the Second World War, Adenauer held office for 14 years and was responsible for overseeing the reconstruction of Germany in the 1950s, particularly in the context of European integration, of which he was a key supporter.

Laeken Declaration Adopted by the European Council in December 2001, the Laeken Declaration provided the parameters for the next stage of treaty reform. It contained more than 50 questions for consideration as part of the 'Future of Europe' debate.

The topics covered included the democratic legitimacy of the EU, the future of the pillar structure and cooperation in the area of social exclusion.

laissez-faire An economic position that argues that the state (governments) should play only a minimal regulatory role in economic affairs, with decisions left mainly to the market.

Law and Justice Party (PiS) *Prawo i Sprawiedliwość (PiS)* is a Polish right-wing populist party. It has been in power since 2015, winning re-election in 2019. Over time it has been accused of authoritarian tendencies because of its disregard for the constitution, the rule of law, parliamentary procedures, and citizens' rights.

LEADER This EU programme is designed to support local businesses, farmers, foresters, community groups, those involved in tourism, and a range of rural enterprises. The fund can cover 50 per cent of the cost of a project. If the project is a farm diversification, the programme may be able to offer a grant covering up to 100 per cent of costs.

League of Nations An international organization set up in 1922 that had as its rationale the maintenance of peace in Europe.

Lega Populist, Eurosceptic, radical right-wing Italian political party.

legal basis *See* treaty base.

legitimacy The extent to which a regime's procedures for making and enforcing laws are acceptable to all of its subjects; the right to rule. *See* input legitimacy; output legitimacy.

lender of last resort An institution, usually a country's central bank, that lends money to commercial banks and other financial institutions when they have no other means to raise funds.

Leo Tindemans A former Belgian prime minister who in 1975 wrote the influential Tindemans Report. The report advocated consolidation of the existing institutions and the development of common policies. The report also called for a 'people's Europe' and advocated European economic and monetary integration and greater coordination of Europe's foreign and defence policies.

liberal intergovernmentalism Andrew Moravcsik's update on classical intergovernmentalism (*see* Chapter 5).

liberal-democratic A system of representative government that is characterized by universal adult suffrage, political equality, majority rule, and a constitutional check on the power of rulers.

liberalization of capital markets The removal of exchange controls by states, allowing capital to flow freely across state borders.

liberalization of services The removal of barriers to the establishment and provision of services across state borders.

liquidity The ability to convert an asset to cash quickly.

Lisbon Agenda (or Lisbon Process, or Lisbon Strategy) The EU strategy intended to turn the Union into the most competitive and dynamic economy in the world by 2010.

Lisbon Treaty Revising the Nice version of the TEU, the Lisbon Treaty was signed in 2007 and entered into force in December 2009 after a protracted ratification. *See* Treaty on the European Union (TEU); Treaty on the Functioning of the EU (TFEU).

list system A method of voting for several electoral candidates, usually members of the same political party, with one mark of the ballot. Electors vote for one of several lists of candidates usually prepared by the political parties.

lock-out A situation in which employers lock employees out of their place of work as a consequence of a labour dispute.

Luxembourg Compromise An intergovernmental agreement arrived at in January 1966 between the member states that solved the 'empty chair' crisis. It states that when vital interests of one or more countries are at stake, members of the Council will endeavour to reach solutions that can be adopted by all, while respecting their mutual interests.

Maastricht Treaty *See* Treaty on the European Union (TEU).

Maastricht Treaty ratification The process that lead to the approval—in both national parliaments and in some cases in referenda—of the Treaty on the European Union (TEU), which came into force in 1993.

macro-economic imbalance (procedure) A new tool that helps to detect and correct risky economic developments as part of the 'macro-economic surveillance' leg of the EU's new rules on economic governance (the so-called 'six pack'). *See* 'six pack'.

macro-economic policy An economic policy that deals with aggregates such as national income and investment in the economy.

Maghreb A region of North Africa bordering the Mediterranean Sea that comprises the Atlas Mountains and the coastal plain of Morocco, Algeria, Tunisia, and Libya.

majoritarian Characterized by the application of majority rule; the principle that the majority should be allowed to rule the minority.

market citizenship The concept introduced to the EC in the 1950s whereby citizens of member states became endowed with certain rights as workers within the European Community.

market integration The breaking down of barriers to trade among the EU's member states, plus any regulation necessary to ensure the smooth running of the single market. It does not involve an explicitly political dimension.

market unity The removal of protection across the Union, allowing agricultural produce to move freely across borders.

market-making measure A measure that involves the prohibition of certain types of market behaviour.

market-shaping measure A measure that lays down an institutional model that shapes market behaviour.

Mercosur An economic and political bloc comprising Argentina, Brazil, Paraguay, Uruguay, and Venezuela. It was created in 1991 with the signing of the Treaty of Asuncion, an accord calling for the free movement of goods, services, and factors of production between countries. The Mercosur countries have eliminated customs duties and set up a common external tariff (CET).

Messina conference Attended by the foreign ministers of the six member states of the European Coal and Steel Community (ECSC), the Messina conference took place from 1 to 3 June 1955. The six ministers agreed on '*une rélance européenne*', a re-launch of the integration process, through a customs union as well as integration in specific economic sectors.

middle-range theory A theory that aims to explain only part of a political process and which does not have totalizing ambitions.

Millennium Development Goals (MDG) The Millennium Development Goals are the world's time-bound and quantified targets for addressing extreme poverty in its many dimensions by 2015. The eight goals were agreed by world leaders at the Millennium Summit in September 2000 and range from halving extreme poverty rates to halting the spread of HIV/AIDS and providing universal primary education.

modulation The transfer of agricultural subsidies to agri-environmental and other rural development projects.

modus operandi A Latin expression meaning 'method of operating or proceeding'.

Monetarist An advocate of one of the possible economic strategies with which to achieve economic and monetary union (EMU); in the 1960s and 1970s, the Monetarist camp postulated that, by fixing the exchange rate, the necessary cooperation of the adjacent economic policies would naturally start to occur (*see* Economist).

monetary union A form of integration that usually contains a single market (and therefore free movement of goods, services, labour, and capital among the participating states and common rules, tariffs, and so on, vis-à-vis third countries) and has further integration in the area of currency cooperation. A monetary union either has irrevocably fixed exchange rates and full convertibility of currencies, or a common or single currency circulating within the monetary union. It also requires integration of budgetary and monetary policies.

money supply The stock of liquid assets in an economy that can be freely exchanged for goods and services.

Monnet method *See* Community method.

Monti Report On the invitation of Commission President Barroso, Mario Monti delivered on 9 May 2010 a report concluding that the economic crisis had opened a window of opportunity for Europe to become more pragmatic and in which it could relaunch the Single Market.

Movimento 5 Stelle *See* Five Star Movement (M5S).

multifunctionality The notion in agricultural policy that the policy can be used to serve a range of functions, including environmental protection and rural development.

multilateral budgetary surveillance Against the background of the Stability and Growth Pact (SGP), a monitoring mechanism that aims to ensure that national economic policy is broadly consistent with the SGP and thus with the proper functioning of economic and monetary union (EMU).

multilevel governance An approach to the study of EU politics that emphasizes the interaction of the many different actors who influence European policy outcomes.

multi-speed (Europe/EU) A characteristic of differentiated integration whereby common objectives are pursued by a group of member states able and willing to advance further than others in the integration process.

mutual recognition The principle that an economic product sold in one member state should not be prohibited from sale anywhere in the EU. This was upheld in the famous *Cassis de Dijon* (1979) case brought to the Court of Justice of the EU. Exceptions can be made in cases of public health and safety, however.

n=1 problem The situation in which the object under scholarly scrutiny cannot be compared to other cases. This renders generalization beyond the case impossible (because there are no other instances of what is being studied).

national action plan (NAP) A key element of the European Employment Strategy, an annual report supplied by each member state to the Commission and the Council on the principal measures taken to implement its employment policy in the light of the guidelines for employment drawn up each year by the Council under Article 148 (3) TFEU.

national envelope In the context of the Common Agricultural Policy (CAP), a de facto national allocation paid to a member state from the EU Budget, and which each state can distribute to its farmers to target specific national and/or regional priorities.

National Front *See Rassemblement Nationale.*

National Rally *See Rassemblement Nationale.*

national sovereignty The doctrine that sovereignty belongs to and derives from the nation, an abstract entity normally linked to a physical territory, and its past, present, and future citizens.

NATO The North Atlantic Treaty Organization.

negative integration A form of integration that involves the removal of barriers between the member states.

negotiating directive A directive that sets out the terms on which the Commission negotiates in international trade and other contexts, establishing the boundaries of the negotiating mandate and providing for monitoring of the negotiations and their outcomes.

neighbourhood country (countries) This term refers to the EU's immediate neighbours by land or sea whose relationship with the EU is governed by the European Neighbourhood Policy. *See* European Neighbourhood Policy.

neo-corporatism A model of policy-making that links producer interests to the state and in which interest organizations are incorporated into the system. The 'neo-' prefix was added in the 1970s to distinguish this from corporatism in the past—particularly in the fascist era.

neo-functionalism A theory of European integration that views integration as an incremental process, involving the spillover of integration in one sector to others, ultimately leading to some kind of political community. *See* spillover.

neo-liberalism An economic school that advocates the reduction of state influence in the market, the liberalization of the economy, the privatization of state-owned firms, and the tight control of money supply, and which supports a general trend towards deregulation.

neo-neo-functionalism Through the concept of neo-neo-functionalism, Philippe Schmitter revises some of the neo-fuctionalist assumptions and adapts them to recent development in the integration process. This revised version of the theory acknowledges that integration does not happen 'automatically', as in the original model, and that it requires a considerable amount of political action that is usually associated with a crisis in the integration process. It also recognizes that there might be instances of 'spill back' whereby national actors can decide to withdraw from joint obligations.

neo-realism An international relations theory, associated with the work of Kenneth Waltz, which claims that the international state system is anarchic and that, as such, state uncertainty is a given. States will want to maintain their independence and survival will be their primary objective, but they may nonetheless engage in European integration if this serves their ends.

neo-realist *See* neo-realism.

net contributor A country that receives less from the EU Budget than it contributes.

net recipient A country that receives more from the EU Budget than it contributes.

new approach A novel approach to regulating internal market rules, as established in the Commission's White Paper on Completing the Internal Market (1985) in which legislative acts would set out only the main objectives and detailed rules would be adopted through private standardization bodies.

new institutionalism A conceptual approach to the study of politics that restates the importance of institutional factors in political life. It takes a number of very different forms, from rational institutionalism and historical institutionalism, to sociological institutionalism.

new intergovernmentalism A recent attempt to re-theorize intergovernmentalism that tries to explain in very broad terms the latest phase in European integration by identifying the causal mechanisms that mediate between political economy, domestic politics changes, and the EU.

new mode of governance (NMG) In contrast to the traditional Community method, which relies on the proposal, adoption, and implementation of legislation by the EU's main institutions, the policy goals of an NMG are achieved through a novel mechanism that involves explicit, but not legally binding, commitments from the member states. In a formalized process, each government commits itself to certain goals in areas such as education policy, innovation, or labour market reform. The European Commission is involved both in the design stage of specific policies and in a monitoring function overseeing subsequent implementation.

new regionalism Is a broad, open-ended framework for analysing regionalization in a multilevel and comparative perspective.

Nice Treaty A treaty revision agreed at Nice in December 2000, signed in February 2001, and ratified in 2002. It introduced a number of institutional reforms that paved the way for the enlargement of the Union in 2004 and afterwards.

no cooperation Implies the absence of government-to-government collaboration or coordination on a particular policy.

non-compulsory spending *See* compulsory spending.

non-majoritarian (institution) A governmental entity that possesses and exercises specialized public authority, separate from that of other institutions, but is neither directly elected by the people nor directly managed by elected officials.

non-state actor Usually, any actor that is not a national government; often refers to transnational actors, such as interest groups (rather than to international organizations).

non-tariff barriers *See* barrier to trade.

normative Of value judgements—that is, 'what ought to be', as opposed to positive statements about 'what is'.

Normative Power Europe (NPE) An approach that understands the EU as normative in two ways. It is normative by virtue of its hybrid character, and as such it sets new standards for what an international actor can and should be. And second, it is normative in its outlook as its foreign and security policy is driven by principles, such as universal human rights, democracy, and international law.

Ombudsman *See* European Ombudsman.

ontology An underlying conception of the world—that is, of the nature of being; that which is being presupposed by a theory.

open method of coordination (OMC) An approach to EU policy-making that is an alternative to regulation and which involves more informal means of encouraging compliance than 'hard' legislation.

opportunity structure *See* political opportunity structure.

opt in The practice whereby one or more member state, having opted out of a particular policy area, decide at a later date to cooperate with those other member states that have proceeded despite the earlier opt-out(s) (*see* opt out).

opt out The practice whereby one or more member states refuse to cooperate in a particular policy area despite the fact that the majority of member states wish to commit themselves to do so. To allow for progress among those who wish to proceed, the reluctant member states may 'opt out', which usually occurs in the context of a treaty revision. Member states that opt out may opt in at a later stage (*see* opt in).

optimum currency area (OCA) A theoretical notion that implies that monetary union will work effectively only when the states participating are economically very similar.

orange card (system) After the yellow card system has been set in motion and the European Commission has proposed a law again, national parliaments can still block the law if half of the national parliaments oppose it (rather than just the one third required for a yellow card). For the law to be repealed, 29 reasoned opinions from national parliaments are required, as well as either a majority of government or MEPs agreeing that the orange card wielded by the national parliaments is justified. *See* subsidiarity and yellow card system.

ordinary legislative procedure (OLP) The main procedure for adopting legislation in the European Union, known before the Lisbon Treaty entered into force as 'co-decision'. The OLP makes the Parliament an equal co-legislative partner with the Council. While agreement is normally concluded at first reading following informal negotiations, under the OLP the EP has the right to hold up to three readings of legislation, to reject the legislation, and to hold conciliation meetings with the Council to negotiate a compromise agreement (Article 294 TFEU).

Organisation for Economic Co-operation and Development (OECD) Established in 1961 and based in Paris, the mission of this body is to promote policies that will improve the economic and social well-being of people around the world.

Organisation for European Economic Cooperation (OEEC) Forerunner to the Organisation for Economic Co-operation and Development (OECD), it was established in 1948 to run the US-financed Marshall Plan for European reconstruction. By making individual governments recognize the interdependence of their economies, it paved the way for a new era of cooperation that was to change the face of Europe.

Encouraged by its success and the prospect of carrying its work forward on a global stage, Canada and the USA joined OEEC members in signing the new OECD Convention on 14 December 1960. *See* Organisation for Economic Co-operation and Development (OECD).

original six The original signatories of the Treaty of Rome—namely, France, Germany, Italy, Belgium, Luxembourg, and the Netherlands.

output legitimacy Following Scharpf, democratic legitimacy is a two-dimensional concept, which refers to both the inputs as well as the outputs of a political system. Scharpf argues that democracy would be an empty ritual if the democratic procedure were not able to produce effective outcomes—that is, to achieve the goals about which citizens care collectively. *See* legitimacy; input legitimacy.

Outright Monetary Transactions (OMT) OMT is a bond-buying programme that was announced by Mario Draghi, president of the European Central Bank (ECB), in September 2012. Under the OMT programme the ECB would offer to purchase euro area countries' short-term bonds to bring down the market interest rates faced by countries subject to speculation that they might leave the euro.

package deal The exchange of loss in some issues for benefits in others, resulting in mutual overall gain between actors with different interests. EU decision-making presents legislators with multiple issues for consideration, and their repeated interactions in the EU legislative process create opportunities for package deals and exchange of support.

Paris Agreement The Paris Agreement is a legally binding international treaty on climate change. It was adopted by 196 Parties in Paris, on 12 December 2015 and entered into force on 4 November 2016. Its goal is to limit global warming to well below 2, preferably to 1.5 degrees Celsius, compared to pre-industrial levels (*see also* Paris UN meeting).

Paris UN meeting The governments of more than 190 nations gathered in Paris from 30 November to 12 December 2015 and agreed the Paris Agreement, a new global agreement on climate change, aimed at reducing global greenhouse gas emissions and thus avoiding the threat of dangerous climate change (*see also* Paris Agreement).

parity Equality in amount, status, or character.

parliamentarization In the EU, parliamentarization of decision-making primarily manifests itself in the increase in the EP's right to exercise a range of legislative powers. The EP has become increasingly involved in areas that are traditionally intergovernmental, especially since the entry into force of the Lisbon Treaty, so that it is now involved in nearly all policy areas.

parsimony The characteristic of a theory that provides an extremely simplified depiction of reality.

partial theory A theory that only purports to address or explain an aspect of a specific political phenomenon.

participation *See* participatory democracy.

participatory democracy A theory of democracy that stresses the importance of more regular and direct citizen involvement in collective decision-making, such as via referenda or via more decentralized governance mechanisms.

Passerelle clause A clause that allows for derogation from the legislative procedures initially specified under the treaties. Specifically, and under certain conditions, a Passerelle clause makes it possible to switch from the special legislative procedure to the ordinary legislative procedure (OLP) in order to adopt an act, and to switch from voting by unanimity to qualified majority voting (QMV) in a given policy area. Activating a Passerelle clause depends on a decision being adopted unanimously by the Committee or by the European Council.

path-dependence The idea that decisions taken in the past limit the scope of decisions in the present (and future).

Pegida (Patriotic Europeans against the Islamisation of the West) in German *Patriotische Europäer Gegen die Islamisierung des Abendlandes* An anti-Muslim group initially set up in Dresden in the Autumn of 2014 that claims to defend Judeo-Christian values and refuses to allow the spread of activities by groups such as ISIS and al-Qaeda in Europe.

permanent representation The diplomatic delegation of any member state vis-à-vis the EU in Brussels.

permanent structured cooperation (PESCO) According to Article 42 TEU, the cooperation that must be established within the Union framework by those member states with military capabilities that fulfil higher criteria and which have made more binding commitments to one another in this area. *See* enhanced cooperation.

permissive consensus The political context that allowed elites in the post-1945 period to engage in European integration, without involving Europe's citizens.

Petersberg tasks An integral part of the then European Security and Defence Policy (ESDP)/Common Security and Defence Policy (CSDP). They define the spectrum of military actions and functions that the European Union can undertake in its crisis management operations.

pillars Prior to the Treaty of Lisbon, the structure of the European Union was akin to a Greek temple consisting of three pillars—namely Pillar 1, Pillar 2, and Pillar 3. With the entry into force of the Treaty of Lisbon on 1 December 2009, the pillars disappeared. *Pillar 1* comprised the original communities and was typically supranational. *Pillar 2* comprised intergovernmental cooperation in foreign and security policy. *Pillar 3* comprised intergovernmental cooperation in police and judicial cooperation in criminal matters (PJCCM).

Plan 'D' Commissioner Margot Wallstrom's communication strategy, emphasizing democracy, dialogue, and debate.

pluralism A general approach that implies that organized groups play an important role in the political process.

plurality system A type of electoral system that awards the seat to the candidate who receives the most votes regardless of whether the candidate receives a majority of votes.

Podemos Meaning 'we can' in English, *Podemos* is a left-wing, populist, anti-system Spanish political party founded in 2014. It became the fourth most voted political party in the 2014 European elections in Spain.

policy convergence The tendency for policies (in different countries) to begin to take on similar forms over time.

policy network A set of actors who are linked by relatively stable relationships of a non-hierarchical and interdependent nature. These actors share common interests with regard to a policy and exchange resources to pursue these shared interests, acknowledging that cooperation is the best way in which to achieve common goals.

policy style A set of characteristics that describe different ways of policy-making (for example, in a particular sector or across a particular country).

policy transfer The replication of policies pursued in one context (country, sector) to others.

political codetermination A political model of codetermination in which a complex set of legal and social institutions shape employee participation in company decision-making through works councils and representation in the supervisory boards of large firms.

political opportunity structure The various characteristics of a political system, such as political institutions, political culture, and the structure of opponents and allies, which influence elements within it, such as social movements, organizational forms, and the way in which political actors behave.

politicization Is the process that manifests itself in (a) the growing salience of European politics, involving (b) a polarization of opinion, and (c) an expansion of actors and audiences engaged in monitoring EU affairs.

polity A politically organized society.

pooling and sharing The concept refers to initiatives and projects to pool and share more military capabilities among EU Member States. In November 2011 the European Defence Agency (EDA) proposed and Defence Ministers adopted an initial list of 11 pooling and sharing priorities. Among these projects are Air-to-Air Refuelling, the Helicopter Training Programme, maritime surveillance, and the European Satellite Communications Procurement Cell.

positive integration A form of integration that involves the construction of policies and/or institutions.

positive-sum outcome An outcome that constitutes more than the sum of its parts. It is often talked of in EU terms as an 'upgrading of the common interest'.

post-national A form of governance beyond the nation state.

post-neutral states Some European states such as Sweden and Switzerland, have a long tradition of neutrality during conflict, and stayed neutral during the Second World War, as did Ireland. After the Second World War Austria and Finland joined these countries pursuing a policy of neutrality. The states refrained from aligning with neither the West/NATO nor the

East/Warsaw pact. Since then Ireland, Austria, Finland, and Sweden have joined the EU, retained their non-aligned status, but are no longer regarded as neutral, but rather as post-neutrals, as they are part of the EU's security and defence policy.

potential candidate country A country that has been promised the prospect of joining the EU when it is ready (*see* candidate countries).

power The ability to control outcomes; the capacity of A to force B to do something in A's interest.

Praesidium In the context of the 2002 Convention on the Future of Europe, the Praesidium was the steering group responsible for setting the Convention's agenda and overseeing its progress. *See* Convention on the Future of Europe.

preliminary ruling (procedure) A judgment of the Court of Justice of the EU that arises as a response to a question of European law posed in a domestic court.

presidency of the EU Council A leadership position that is held on a six-monthly basis by member states in rotation. Since the Lisbon Treaty entered into force, the European Council has its own appointed President.

price support The system of agricultural support that involves keeping food prices higher than the market price, to give farmers a higher and more stable income.

primus inter pares A Latin expression meaning 'first among equals'.

primus super pares A Latin expression that means 'first above equals'.

proportional representation (PR) A form of electoral system that attempts to match the proportion of seats won by a political party with the proportion of the total vote for that party.

proportionality A principle that implies that the means should not exceed the ends; applies to decision-making and the legislative process.

pro-systemic opposition In the context of conceptual debates about Euroscepticism, this term has been used by FitzGibbon to refer to critiques of the integration process that, rather than being sceptical about it, propose alternative models of integration.

public debt The amount of money owed by the state.

public goods theory A branch of economics that studies, from the perspective of economic theory, how voters, politicians, and government officials behave.

public sphere A space or arena for broad public deliberation, discussion, and engagement in societal issues. According to Habermas, the democratic deficit can be eliminated only if a European public sphere comes into existence in which the democratic process is incorporated.

qualified majority voting (QMV) A system of voting based on the qualified majority, which is the number of votes required in the Council for a decision to be adopted when issues are being debated on the basis of Article 16 TEU and Article 238 TFEU. Under the ordinary legislative procedure (OLP), the Council acts by qualified majority in combination with the European Parliament. With the entry into force of the Treaty of Lisbon, a new system known as 'double majority' was introduced. *See* dual majority; ordinary legislative procedure (OLP).

quantitative easing The process whereby, when lower interest rates have been used to encourage people to spend, not save, and interest rates can go no lower, a central bank pumps money into the economy directly, by buying assets or simply by printing money.

Rapid Reaction Force A transnational military force managed by the European Union.

rapporteur A member of the European Parliament (MEP) responsible for drafting legislative opinions.

Rassemblement Nationale Populist, Eurosceptic, radical right-wing French political party. Until June 2018 it was known as the *Front National* or National Front.

ratification Formal approval. In the EU context, it implies approval of Treaty revisions by national parliaments and sometimes also by popular referendum.

ratification crisis (1992) The crisis provoked by the Danish 'no' vote in their 1992 referendum on the Maastricht Treaty (2005). The crisis provoked by the negative referendums on the Constitutional Treaty in France and the Netherlands in May and June 2005.

rational choice *See* rationalism.

rational utilitarianism The idea that opinions stem from calculations involving the weighing up of costs and benefits.

rationalism A theory that assumes that individuals (or states) are able to rank options in order of preference and to choose the best available preference.

realism A rationalist theory of international relations.

recession A temporary depression in economic activity or prosperity, which is, specifically, three consecutive quarters of negative growth.

redistributive The characteristic of a policy that transfers wealth from one group to another.

reference *See* preliminary ruling.

reference currency A tool for settling trade transactions.

reference value A baseline measure against which economic progress can be assessed.

reflection group A group established prior to an intergovernmental conference (ICG) to prepare preliminary papers on relevant issues.

reflectivism A perspective that centres on ontological and epistemological questions not answered to a satisfactory degree by the rationalist, behaviourist, or positivist perspectives, such as the nature of knowledge, its objectivity or subjectivity, and the nature of international politics. Reflectivism questions the existence of objective truth and our ability to discover such truths.

reform treaty A Treaty that amends the provisions of existing EU treaties. The difference between a reform treaty (operating within the framework of existing treaties) and a constitution (which would consolidate all of the rules governing the EU and give rise to a new set of legal principles) shaped the debates over the ratification of the Lisbon Treaty and member states' justification not to hold referenda.

refoulement The act of forcing a refugee or asylum seeker from a place where they can claim asylum to a country or territory where he or she is likely to face persecution or other threats.

regime The framework of principles, norms, rules, and decision-making procedures around which actors' expectations occur. An international regime is usually considered to take the form of an international organization. It is a concept associated with neo-realism.

regulation The rules or legislation made in order to provoke certain policy outcomes; one of the legislative instruments used by the EU. EU regulations are directly effective, spelling out not only the aims of legislation, but also what must be done and how (*see* directive).

regulatory competition A situation in which a country tries to offer a regulatory environment that will attract business from abroad. This may involve deregulation.

regulatory impact assessment (RIA) An evaluation intended to provide a detailed and systematic appraisal of the potential impacts of a new regulation in order to assess whether the regulation is likely to achieve the desired objectives.

regulatory state The expansion in the use of rule-making, monitoring. and enforcement techniques and institutions by the state, and a parallel change in the way in which its positive functions in society are being carried out.

representation The principle by which delegates are chosen to act for a particular constituency (group of electors).

representative democracy A form of democracy founded on the principle of elected individuals representing the people. People allow representatives who form an independent ruling body to represent them in the various forms of democratic process such as legislating.

res public composita A composite union comprising diverse publics.

right of association The democratic right of people to form groups such as trades unions.

Robert Schuman Former French Foreign Minister and one of the 'founding fathers' of the European Coal and Steel Community (ECSC), through his Schuman Plan of 1950.

rule of law Refers to the independence, quality and efficiency of national justice systems. The rule of law is one of the fundamental values of the Union, enshrined in Article 2 of the Treaty on European Union.

run on a bank Crisis that occurs when a large number of customers withdraw their deposits from a financial institution and either demand cash, or transfer those funds into government bonds or a safer institution, because they believe that financial institution is, or might become, insolvent.

rural development policy The EU's common rural development policy aims to address the challenges faced by rural areas and to unlock their potential. Rural development addresses three key areas: improving the competitiveness of the agricultural and forestry sector; improving the environment and the countryside; and improving the quality of life in rural areas and encouraging diversification of the rural economy.

safeguard clause A traditional trade liberalization measure which protects against future problems.

Schengen Agreement An agreement to create a border-free European Community. It was originally outside the treaties, but was incorporated at Amsterdam.

Schengen Area The border-free Schengen Area guarantees free movement across most EU states, except for Bulgaria, Croatia, Cyprus, Ireland, and Romania. However, Bulgaria and Romania are currently in the process of joining the Schengen Area. Of non-EU states, Iceland, Norway, Switzerland, and Liechtenstein have joined the Schengen Area.

Schengen Information System (SIS) The largest shared database on maintaining public security, supporting police and judicial cooperation, and managing external border control in Europe. Participating states provide entries ('alerts') on wanted and missing persons, lost and stolen property, and entry bans. It is immediately and directly accessible to all police officers at street level, and other law enforcement officials and authorities who need the information to carry out their roles in protecting law and order and fighting crime.

Schuman Plan Signed on 9 May 1950, it led to the setting up of the European Coal and Steel Community (ECSC).

secession The act of withdrawing from an organization, union, or a political entity.

secessionist movement See secession.

second-order elections European elections are often said to be second-order in character (Reif and Schmitt, 1980). This means that most electors consider the European political arena to be less important than the national one and that they, accordingly, use their votes in EP elections to express feelings of satisfaction or dissatisfaction with domestic parties or to bring about political change in their own country.

sectoral integration A description of, or strategy for, integration that involves an incremental sector-by-sector approach. See spillover.

securitization The financial practice of pooling various types of contractual debt, such as residential mortgages, commercial mortgages, auto loans, or credit card debt obligations, and selling that consolidated debt as bonds to various investors.

separation of powers A condition of democratic political systems under which the executive, legislature, and judiciary are separate, providing a system of checks and balances that serve to prevent abuses of power.

set-aside A characteristic of land, which farmers are not allowed to use for any agricultural purpose. It was introduced by the EU in 1992 as part of a package of reforms of the Common Agricultural Policy (CAP) to prevent over-production. It applies only to farmers growing crops.

shared competence A specific area in which the member states and the EU have powers to legislate and adopt legally binding acts. The member states exercise their powers in so far as the Union has not exercised, or has decided to stop exercising, its competence. Most of the EU's competences fall into this category. See exclusive competence.

Silk Road China's Belt and Road Initiative, reminiscent of the Silk Road, was launched in 2013 by President Xi Jinping. It incorporates a vast collection of development and investment initiatives that would stretch from East Asia to Europe, significantly expanding China's economic and political influence.

simplified revision procedure The Treaty of Lisbon creates a simplified procedure for the amendment of policies and internal actions of the EU. The government of any member state, the Commission, or the European Parliament can submit proposals for amendments to the European Council. The European Council then adopts a decision laying down the amendments made to the treaties. The European Council acts by unanimity after consulting the Commission, the Parliament, and the European Central Bank (ECB) if the amendment concerns monetary matters. New provisions of the treaties enter into force only after they have been ratified by all member states pursuant to their respective constitutional requirements. This procedure avoids the convening of a convention and an IGC. However, the competences of the EU may not be extended by means of a simplified revision procedure.

Single European Act (SEA) The first of the large-scale Treaty revisions, signed in 1986. It came into force in 1987 and served as a 'vehicle' for the single market programme.

single European market *See* single market (programme).

Single Farm Payment (SFP) A unique direct payment under the Common Agricultural Policy (CAP), aimed at achieving a complete decoupling of support and production. Under this system, even a farmer who decides to grow nothing is eligible to receive this payment, as long as he or she complies with environmental, food safety, animal welfare, and occupational safety standards.

single market (programme) The goal of one unified internal EU market, free of (national) barriers to trade. While the idea was included in the Treaty of Rome, the Single Market is usually associated with the revitalization of the Community from the mid-1980s.

Single Market Act I and II Adopted by the European Commission in April 2011, the Single Market Act I aimed to deliver 12 instruments to relaunch the Single Market for 2012. These 12 instruments of growth, competitiveness, and social progress ranged from worker mobility, to small and medium-sized enterprise (SME) finance and consumer protection, via digital content, taxation, and trans-European networks. In October 2012 the Commission proposed a second set of actions (Single Market Act II) to further develop the Single Market and exploit its untapped potential as an engine for growth. It included actions on transport and energy networks; citizens and business mobility; the digital economy and social entrepreneurship, cohesion and consumer confidence.

single monetary policy Common monetary policy across the euro area. *See* economic and monetary union (EMU).

Single Resolution Mechanism (SRM) One of the components of the Banking Union in the eurozone. Its purpose is to ensure an orderly resolution of failing banks with minimal costs for taxpayers and to the real economy. It applies to banks covered by the SSM. In the cases when banks fail despite stronger supervision, the mechanism will allow bank resolution to be managed effectively through a Single Resolution Board and a Single Resolution Fund, financed by the banking sector. *See* Banking Union.

Single Supervisory Mechanism (SSM) One of the components of the Banking Union in the eurozone. Under the SSM, which became operational in November 2014, the European Central Bank (ECB) has become the banking supervisor for all banks in the euro area, directly responsible for supervising the approximately 123 largest banking groups. *See* Banking Union.

Sinn Féin An Irish Republican party seeking to end British rule in Northern Ireland.

'six pack' The five regulations and one directive that entered into force on 13 December 2011. It applies to all member states with some specific rules for euro area member states, especially regarding financial sanctions. Not only does it cover fiscal surveillance, it also includes macro-economic surveillance under the new macro-economic imbalance procedure.

'snake' A system aimed to stabilize exchange rates within the EC in the 1970s.

Social Chapter Agreed at Maastricht, the Social Chapter establishes minimum social conditions within the EU.

social constructivism *See* constructivism.

social dumping The undercutting of social standards in order to improve competitiveness.

social partner(s) The social partners are the bodies representing the two sides of industry: the employers and the employees.

social partnership The partnership of labour (the unions) and capital (employers) acting together and enjoying a privileged position in the EU policy process.

social spillover A recent neo-functionalist concept that explains the learning and socialization processes that help to drive European integration.

soft law Those documents that are not formally or legally binding, but which may still produce political effects. *See* hard law.

sovereign debt crisis A crisis that arises when national governments are unable to guarantee repayment of debt that they have issued—even though sovereign debt is theoretically considered to be risk-free, because the government can employ different measures to guarantee repayment, by increasing taxes or printing money.

sovereignty The supremacy of a state, which is not subject to any higher authority; supreme, unrestricted power (of a state).

Spaak Report Following the Messina Conference, Belgian socialist politician Paul-Henri Spaak was appointed to prepare a report on the creation of a common European market. The 1956 Spaak Report recommended greater economic union and the union of nuclear energy production. *See* also Venice conference.

'special legislative procedures' There are two types of special legislative procedures. Consent: the European Parliament has the power to accept or reject a legislative proposal by an absolute majority vote, but cannot amend it. And consultation: the European Parliament may approve, reject, or propose amendments to a legislative proposal.

specific interest group A type of interest group that is characterized by its broad scope and lack of clear membership. These include, for example, religious, social, human rights, consumer, and environmental groups (*see also* diffuse interest group).

spillback A mechanism identified by neo-functionalist theorists. According to Schmitter, spillback occurs in regional integration when, in response to tensions, actors withdraw from their original objective, downgrading their commitment to mutual cooperation. *See* spillover.

spillover A mechanism identified by neo-functionalist theorists who claimed that sectoral integration in one area would have knock-on effects in others and would 'spill over', thereby increasing the scope of European integration. *See* neo-functionalism.

Spinelli Report On 14 February 1984, the European Parliament adopted a draft Treaty on European Union (TEU), also known as the 'Spinelli Report' because it was written by Altiero Spinelli. The aim of the report was to bring about a reform of the Community institutions. The report was soon buried by the governments of the member states, but it provided an impetus for the negotiations that led to the Single European Act and the Maastricht Treaty. *See* Altiero Spinelli.

Spitzenkandidat/Spitzenkandidaten is a German word that means top candidate or party list leader. The term refers to the European Parliament's interpretation of the Lisbon Treaty's provision that stipulates that the European Council shall nominate a candidate for European Commission President 'taking into account the elections to the European Parliament', by qualified majority, and the parliament in turn must 'elect' the nominee with an absolute majority (Article 17 TEU). Thus for the 2014 European elections European-level political parties proposed rival candidates for the post of Commission President.

St Malo summit At the Franco–British Summit held in St Malo on 3 and 4 December 1998, the Heads of State or Government of the United Kingdom and France agreed on the need to give the European Union (EU) the capacity for autonomous decision-making and action, backed up by credible military forces, in order to respond to international crises when the Atlantic Alliance is not involved. To avoid unnecessary duplication, it was decided that the EU should take into account the assets of Western European Union (WEU).

Stability and Growth Pact (SGP) An agreement of the EU member states concerning conduct over their fiscal policy, which aimed to ensure that the constraints on member states prior to the introduction of the single currency would continue after economic and monetary union (EMU) was in place.

Stabilization and Association Agreement (SAA) A framework for the implementation of the stabilization and association process between the EU and the Western Balkan countries. Each agreement is adapted to the specific situation of each partner country, while establishing common political, economic, and commercial objectives and encouraging regional cooperation. *See* Stabilization and Association Process (SAP).

Stabilization and Association Process (SAP) The main framework for EU relations with the Western Balkan region (Albania, Bosnia and Herzegovina, Croatia, North Macedonia, Montenegro, Serbia, and Kosovo under UN Security Council Resolution 1244). In addition to the political, economic, and institutional criteria established at the Copenhagen European Council in 1993, the SAP added five further specific criteria for the Western Balkans: full cooperation with the International Criminal Tribunal for the former Yugoslavia (ICTY), respect for human and minority rights, the creation of real opportunities for refugees and internally displaced persons to return, and a visible commitment to regional cooperation.

stakeholder A person, group, organization, member, or system who affects or can be affected by an organization's actions.

state-centrism A conceptual approach to understanding European integration that gives primacy to the role of state actors within the process.

statehood The condition of being a state. *See* stateness.

stateness The quality of being a state—that is, a legal territorial entity with a stable population and a government.

Stockholm Programme As the follow-up to the Hague Programme, the Stockholm Programme provided the guidelines for cooperation in the Area of Freedom, Security and Justice for the period 2010–14. It gave policymaking a push by calling for the implementation of a common asylum system, and stressed partnership with countries of origin and/or transit. *See* Hague Programme.

Stresa Conference From 3 to 12 July 1958, the delegations of the six founding member states met in Stresa (Italy) with Walter Hallstein, President of the European Commission, and Sicco Mansholt, Commissioner with special responsibility for Agriculture, to discuss the introduction of a common agricultural policy (CAP).

strong currency A situation arising out of relative levels of exchange rate whereby the value of national money is increased. This has the effect of lowering the price of imports (making imported goods cheaper), but also of increasing the price of exports, making exports less competitive in international markets.

Structural Fund(s) A financial instrument aimed at fostering economic and social cohesion in the EU by part-financing regional and horizontal operations in the member states. There are four types of Structural Fund: the European Regional Development Fund (ERDF); the European Social Fund (ESF); the European Agricultural Guidance and Guarantee Fund (EAGGF) Guidance section; and the Financial Instrument for Fisheries Guidance (FIFG).

structural policy The EU's framework to maintain a sufficient level of economic and social cohesion among member states. It incorporates a number of programmes and financial instruments, including the Structural Fund, with which to achieve its aims.

subprime mortgage market The market comprising mortgage loans to people who were perceived to be at high risk of defaulting on the repayment schedule. These loans are characterized by higher interest rates and less favourable terms in order to compensate for the higher credit risk. The subprime mortgage crisis arose in the USA as a result of the bundling together of subprime and regular mortgages.

subsidiarity The principle that tries to ensure that decisions are taken as close as possible to the citizen. *See* yellow card system and orange card system.

Suez crisis The 1956 Suez crisis erupted when Britain, France, and Israel responded to the nationalization of the Suez Canal Company by Egyptian President Nasser (thus potentially threatening the flow of primarily oil from the Persian Gulf to Western Europe) with a combined military operation. This was a key moment in the Cold War period as Nasser's triumph strengthened Arab nationalism, while it demonstrated the decline in French and British international influence as the two countries and Israel were heavily criticized for their invasion of Egyptian territory by the UN, the USA, and the Soviet Union.

superstate A political term that implies that the aim of supporters of European integration is to turn the EU into a state, with connotations of the detachment of elites and the European institutions from ordinary citizens.

supranational Above the national level. It may refer to institutions, policies, or a particular 'type' of cooperation/integration.

supranational integration An intensely institutionalized form of cooperation that may involve institutions or policy-making above the national level.

supranational governance A theory of European integration proposed by Wayne Sandholtz and Alec Stone Sweet, which draws on neo-functionalism and provides an alternative approach to Moravcsik's liberal intergovernmentalism.

supranational institution An institution in the EU system of governance to which the member states have delegated sovereignty, such as the European Commission, the European Parliament, the European Central Bank (ECB), or the Court of Justice of the European Union.

supranationalism An approach to the study of the EU that emphasizes the autonomy of the European institutions and the importance of common European policies.

sustainability (or 'sustainable development') The ability to meet the needs of the present without compromising the needs of future generations.

Syriza or Coalition of the Radical Left A left-wing, anti-establishment political party in Greece, originally founded in 2004 as a coalition of left-wing and radical left parties. The party twice won the 2015 parliamentary elections in Greece.

Tampere A city in Finland at which a summit meeting in 1999 agreed to create an 'area of freedom, security and justice' (AFSJ) in Europe.

Tampere European Council At the 1999 Tampere European Council the member state governments agreed to create an 'area of freedom, security and justice' (AFSJ) in Europe.

technical information Refers to economic, legal, administrative, and scientific expertise informing the European Commission about the EU wide effects of its policy proposals (_see also_ political information).

teleological In the context of the EU's legal doctrine, the characteristic of an argument drawn from the objectives or purpose of EU law, rather than its causes. A typical teleological argument is the reference to the need to achieve a single European market.

third-country national (TCN) A citizen of a country outside the European Union.

three-pillar structure _See_ pillars.

Trade and Cooperation Agreement between the UK and the European Union (TCA) The EU–UK Trade and Cooperation Agreement concluded between the EU and the UK sets out preferential arrangements in areas such as trade in goods and in services, digital trade, intellectual property, public procurement, aviation and road transport, energy, fisheries, social security coordination, law enforcement and judicial cooperation in criminal matters, thematic cooperation, and participation in Union programmes. It is underpinned by provisions ensuring a level playing field and respect for fundamental rights. The TCA was signed on 30 December 2020, was applied provisionally as of 1 January 2021, and entered into force on 1 May 2021.

transaction costs The costs related to the exchange of money.

Transatlantic Trade and Investment Partnership (TTIP) A proposed trade agreement that is being negotiated between the EU and USA. It is aimed at creating the world's biggest free trade zone by reducing regulatory barriers to trade in areas ranging from food safety law to environmental rules and banking regulations.

transfer payment A payment not made in return for any contribution to current output. Usually refers to agricultural subsidies.

transparency Used in the EU to refer to the extent of openness within the EU institutions.

transposition The translation of European law into domestic law.

treaty base The treaty provision that underpins a particular piece of European legislation.

treaty base game The act of selecting a treaty base (in a 'grey area') for political ends.

Treaty Establishing the European Stability Mechanism A treaty signed by euro area member states on 2 February 2012. The European Stability Mechanism (ESM) is constituted as an international financial institution based in Luxembourg. Its purpose is to provide financial assistance to euro area member states experiencing or being threatened by severe financing problems. _See_ European Stability Mechanism (ESM).

Treaty of Brussels Signed on 17 March 1948 between Belgium, France, Luxembourg, the Netherlands, and the UK, the Treaty of Brussels (or 'Brussels Pact') aimed to set out terms for economic, social, and cultural cooperation, and especially collective self-defence. It provided for the establishment of an international organization that led to the creation of the Western European Union (WEU). _See_ Western European Union (WEU).

Treaty of Dunkirk A treaty signed on 4 March 1947, between France and the UK in Dunkirk (France), as a treaty of alliance and mutual assistance against a possible German attack.

Treaty of Lisbon _See_ Lisbon Treaty.

Treaty of Nice _See_ Nice Treaty.

Treaty of Rome Signed in 1957, the Rome Treaty formally established the European Economic

Community (EEC) and the European Atomic Energy Community (Euratom, or EAEC).

Treaty on Stability, Coordination and Governance in the Economic and Monetary Union (or the Fiscal Compact) Agreed on 30 January 2012 by the informal European Council, the only really substantive binding provision of this treaty is that the member states undertake to adopt, at the national level, rules that limit their structural deficit to 0.5 per cent of gross domestic product (GDP). This should be done 'preferably at the constitutional level'.

Treaty on the European Union (TEU) (or Maastricht Treaty) The TEU established the European Union, prepared for economic and monetary union (EMU), and introduced elements of a political union (citizenship, and common foreign and internal affairs policy). It has been amended by the Amsterdam, Nice, and Lisbon Treaties.

Treaty on the Functioning of the European Union (TFEU) The Lisbon Treaty amended the EU's two core treaties, the Treaty on European Union (TEU) and the Treaty establishing the European Community (TEC), renaming the latter as the TFEU. The TFEU organizes the functioning of the Union and determines the areas of, delimitation of, and arrangements for exercising its competences.

Trevi (Group) A forum for internal security cooperation, which operated from the mid-1970s until 1993.

Trilogue(s) or Trialogue(s) Informal meetings of representatives of the EP, Council, and Commission which aim to facilitate compromises on legislative matters. The trialogue process starts as soon as the institutions agree an initial position on a law.

troika (i) The country holding the presidency of the EU Council together with the previous presidency and the forthcoming presidency; (ii) in Common Foreign and Security Policy (CFSP), it traditionally referred to the presidency of the EU Council, the High Representative for CFSP, and the Commission, but since the Lisbon Treaty entered into force, the High Representative of the Union for Foreign Affairs and Security Policy functions as Council President in matters of foreign affairs, as Commissioner for External Relations, and as High Representative for the Common Foreign and Security Policy; (iii) The group of international lenders, namely, the European Commission, the International Monetary Fund (IMF), and the European Central

Bank (ECB) that have provided bailouts, or promises of bailouts, for indebted euro area countries, subject to stringent austerity conditions. *See* High Representative (HR) for the CFSP or High Representative of the Union for Foreign Affairs and Security Policy.

troika missions This term refers to the group of representatives from the European Commission, the International Monetary Fund (IMF), and the European Central Bank (ECB), also known as the troika, that visit countries who have received loans from the EU and the IMF to monitor that the relevant governments are meeting the conditions under which the money has been lent to them. These conditions are established in a sort of contract, called a Memorandum of Understanding (MoU). If a troika mission concludes that a country has not done enough in exchange for the money, it can decide to postpone payment of the next tranche. *See* troika.

'two pack' In November 2011, the Commission proposed two further Regulations to strengthen euro area budgetary surveillance (in addition to the 'six pack'). This reform package provides increased transparency on the member states' budgetary decisions, stronger coordination in the euro area starting with the 2014 budgetary cycle, and the recognition of the special needs of euro area member states under severe financial pressure. The 'two pack' entered into force on 30 May 2013 in all euro area member states.

Uighurs The Uighurs are a mostly Muslim minority living in north-western China in the region the Xinjiang Uyghur Autonomous Region (XUAR). The Uighurs speak their own language, similar to Turkish, and see themselves as culturally and ethnically close to Central Asian nations. The Chinese government is accused of committing genocide and crimes against humanity through its repression of the Uighurs.

UK Independence Party (UKIP) Is a Eurosceptic and right-wing populist political party in the United Kingdom. The party won the 2014 European elections in the UK. In the European Parliament it belongs to the Europe of Freedom and Direct Democracy Group.

unanimity The principle that all member states must vote in favour for an agreement to be reached. It implies that each member state holds a potential veto.

Uruguay Round The eighth round of multilateral trade negotiations (MTN) conducted within the framework of the General Agreement on Tariffs and Trade (GATT), spanning from 1986 to 1994 and embracing 123 countries. The Round transformed the GATT into the World Trade Organization (WTO). The Uruguay Round Agreement on Agriculture provides for converting quantitative restrictions to tariffs and for a phased reduction of tariffs. The agreement also imposes rules and disciplines on agricultural export subsidies, domestic subsidies, and sanitary and phytosanitary measures.

utilitarian theory A theory that relates to choosing the greatest good for the greatest number of people.

Van Rompuy Task Force Set up in June 2010 by the then President of the European Council, Herman Van Rompuy, this high-level group was created to explore the EU's economic governance and identify ideas on how to achieve closer harmonization of European economies.

variable geometry An image of the European Union that foresees the breakdown of a unified form of co-operation, and the introduction of a 'pick and choose' approach to further integration.

variable levy In the context of the Common Agricultural Policy (CAP), a levy raised on produce before it enters the common market, so that it is priced at or above the internal price. A system of 'reimbursements' (refunds) enables European producers to sell their products on the world market at world prices without losing income.

vassal state This expression typically refers to a state that is subordinate to another. This term has been used to describe the United Kingdom's status during the so-called 'transition period' lasting from Brexit day on 29 March 2019 to 31 December 2020. During this period, the EU expected the UK to continue to apply EU law and policies but without being involved in any decision-making process.

Venice conference On 29 and 30 May 1956, the Foreign Ministers of the six member states of the European Coal and Steel Community (ECSC) met in Venice to consider the implications of the Spaak Report and the plans for a common market and for Euratom. *See also* Spaak Report.

Ventotene Manifesto Was written by Altiero Spinelli and Ernesto Rossi, while prisoners on the Italian island of Ventotene in 1941. The Manifesto encouraged a federation of European states, which was meant to keep the countries of Europe close, thus preventing war. *See also* Altiero Spinelli.

veto player According to Tsebelis, for policy change to occur, a certain number of individual or collective actors (veto players) have to agree to the proposed change.

Visegrad group Founded on 15 February 1991, the Visegrad group aims to promote cooperation between the Czech Republic, Hungary, Poland, and Slovakia.

voluntary agreement An agreement resulting from the autonomous European Social Dialogue, which proceeds without the initiative or participation of the Commission and, as such, its implementation is not subject to legal enforcement. *See* European Social Dialogue.

voluntary export restraint (VER) A trade restriction on the quantity of goods that are exported to another state.

Walter Hallstein The first president of the European Commission from 1958 to 1969, a committed European, and a decisive proponent of European integration. In his opinion, the most important prerequisite for a successful political integration of Europe was the creation of common economic institutions. As president of the European Commission, Hallstein worked towards a rapid realization of the common market.

Warsaw Pact Signed on 14 May 1955 by the USSR, Poland, East Germany, Czechoslovakia, Hungary, Romania, Bulgaria, and Albania, the 'Warsaw Treaty of Friendship, Cooperation, and Mutual Assistance' aimed to ensure the close integration of military, economic, and cultural policy between these communist nations. The democratic revolutions of 1989 in Eastern Europe heralded the end of the Warsaw Pact and the Cold War between East and West.

Werner Plan This 1970 blueprint for economic and monetary union (EMU) proposed three stages with which to reach EMU by 1980. On the institutional side, it recommended setting up two supranational bodies: 'a Community System for the Central Banks' and a 'Centre of Decision for Economic Policy'. The former would pursue monetary policies, whereas the latter would coordinate macro-economic policies (including some tax policies). Most of the recommendations of the Werner Plan were adopted.

Werner Report The first report on Monetary Union dating from 1970 and named after the Prime Minister of Luxembourg, Pierre Werner. *See* Werner Plan.

Western European Union (WEU) A collaborative defence agreement and extension of the 1948 Treaty of Brussels, signed in 1955. It was designed to allow for the rearmament of West Germany. It was revitalized in the 1980s, and subsequently served as a bridge between the North Atlantic Treaty Organization (NATO) and the EU. Its functions have lately been subsumed within the European Union. *See* Treaty of Brussels.

Westphalian Refers to a specific view of international relations rooted in the Westphalian system of sovereign states, which was established in 1648 as part of the Peace of Westphalia. This approach is defined by three key characteristics: the principle of state sovereignty; the equality of states; and the non-intervention of one state in the international affairs of another.

White Paper on the Future of Europe The White paper presented by the European Commission on 1 March 2017 set out five possible scenarios for the future of Europe depending on how the EU decides to address challenges such as globalization, the impact of new technologies on society and jobs, security concerns, and the rise of populism.

widening Generally refers to the enlargement of the EU, but may also be used to denote the increasing scope of Community or Union competences.

Withdrawal Agreement (WA) The EU–UK Withdrawal Agreement concluded between the European Union and the United Kingdom establishes the terms of the United Kingdom's orderly withdrawal from the EU, in accordance with Article 50 of the Treaty of the European Union. The WA entered into force on 1 February 2020, after having been agreed in October 2019.

Working Time Directive *See* European Working Time Directive.

World Trade Organization (WTO) An international organization that oversees the global trade in goods and services.

yellow card (system) If a draft legislative act's compliance with the subsidiarity principle is contested by a third of the votes allocated to national parliaments (the yellow card), the Commission has to review the proposal and decide to maintain, amend, or withdraw the act, also motivating its decision. This threshold is a quarter in the case of a draft submitted on the basis of Article 76 TFEU on the Area of Freedom, Security, and Justice (AFSJ). A yellow card requires 19 reasoned opinions provided by national chambers explaining why the EU law in question impinges upon the principle of subsidiarity. The Commission can get around a yellow card by giving clearer justifications for its actions and proposing the law again. National parliaments may still block this second attempt via an orange card. *See* Orange card and Subsidiarity.

Yugoslavia A country in the Western Balkans that existed during most of the twentieth century. In 1963, it was renamed the Socialist Federal Republic of Yugoslavia, which included six republics—namely, Bosnia and Herzegovina, Croatia, SR Macedonia, Montenegro, Slovenia, and Serbia—and two autonomous provinces (Vojvodina and Kosovo). After the 1991 Balkan Wars, which followed the secession of most of the country's constituent entities, the Federal Republic of Yugoslavia existed until 2003, when it was renamed Serbia and Montenegro. On the basis of a referendum held on 21 May 2006, Montenegro declared independence on 3 June of that year.

zero-sum game A game played (by states) in which the victory of one group implies the loss of another.

Zollverein A customs union between German states in the eighteenth century under Bismarck; the economic basis for German unification.

References

Aalberts, T. A. (2004) 'The future of sovereignty in multilevel governance in Europe: a constructivist reading', *Journal of Common Market Studies* 42/1: 23–46.

Abazi, V., Adriaensen, J., and Christiansen, T. (eds) (2021) *The Contestation of Expertise in the European Union* (London: Palgrave).

Achen, C. H. (2006) 'Evaluating political decision-making models', in R. Thomson, F. N. Stokman, C. H. Achen, and T. Koenig (eds), *The European Union Decides* (Cambridge: Cambridge University Press), pp. 264–98.

Adams, M., De Waele H., Meeusen H., and Straetmans G. (eds) (2014) *Judging Europe's Judges: The Legitimacy of the Case Law of the European Court of Justice* (Oxford and Portland, OR: Hart).

Adelle, C. and Anderson, J. (2012) 'Lobby groups', in A. Jordan and C. Adelle (eds), *Environmental Policy in the European Union*, 3rd edn (London: Routledge), pp. 152–69.

Adelle, C., Jordan, A., and Benson, D. (2015) 'The role of policy networks in the coordination of the European Union's economic and environmental interests: the case of EU mercury policy', *Journal of European Integration* 37/4: 471–89.

Adler-Nissen, R. (2014) *Opting Out of the European Union: Diplomacy, Sovereignty and European Integration* (Oxford: Oxford University Press).

Adler-Nissen, R. and Kropp, K. (2015) 'A sociology of knowledge approach to European Integration: four analytical principles', *Journal of European Integration* 37/2: 155–73.

Adler-Nissen, R., Galpin, C., and Rosamond, B. (2017) 'Performing Brexit: How a post-Brexit world is imagined outside the United Kingdom', *The British Journal of Politics and International Relations* 19/3: 573–91.

Agence Europe, daily news service on EU matters, edited by Agence Europe S.A. Brussels.

Albors-Llorens, A. (1999) 'The European Court of Justice, more than a teleological court' *Cambridge Yearbook of European Legal Studies* 2: 373–98.

Alemanno, A. (2015) 'How much better is better regulation?', *European Journal of Risk Regulation* 6/3: 344–56.

Allen, D. (1998) 'Who speaks for Europe? The search for an effective and coherent external policy', in Peterson J. and Sjursen, H. (eds), *A Common Foreign Policy for Europe? Competing Visions of CFSP* (London and New York: Routledge), pp. 41–58.

Almond, G.A. (1958) 'A comparative study of interest groups in the political process', *American Political Science Review* 52/1: 270–82.

ALTER-EU (2016) EU lobby transparency: time for a stronger lobby register. Brussels.

Alter, K. (2001) *Establishing the Supremacy of European Law* (Oxford: Oxford University Press).

Alter, K. J, and S. Meunier-Aitsahalia (1994) 'Judicial politics in the European Community: European integration and the pathbreaking Cassis de Dijon decision', *Comparative Political Studies* 26/4: 535–56.

Andersen, M. S. and Liefferink, D. (eds) (1997) *European Environmental Policy: The Pioneers* (Manchester: Manchester University Press).

Anderson, C. J. (1998) 'When in doubt, use proxies. Attitudes toward domestic politics and support for European integration', *Comparative Political Studies* 31/5: 569–601.

Anderson, G. (ed.) (2012) *Internal Markets and Multilevel Governance: The Experience of the European Union, Australia, Canada, Switzerland, and the United States* (Oxford: Oxford University Press).

Anderson, J. J. (1995) 'The state of the (European) Union: from the single market to Maastricht, from singular events to general theories', *World Politics* 47/2: 441–65.

Angerer, J., Grigaitė, K. and Turcu, O. (2020), *Country-specific recommendations: An overview - September 2020*, European Parliament, Directorate-General for Internal Policies, Economic Governance Support Unit (EGOV), September 2020.

ARC2020 et al. (2021) 'A 10+13 Agroecology approach to shape policies and transform EU food System', https://www.arc2020.eu/wp-content/uploads/2021/01/Policy-paper_mainstreaming-agroecology-in-EU-policies.pdf

Archer, C. (2000) 'Euroscepticism in the Nordic region', *Journal of European Integration* 22/1: 87–114.

Armstrong, K. and Bulmer, S. (1998) *The Governance of the Single European Market* (Manchester: Manchester University Press).

Arnull, A. (1996) 'The European Court of Justice and judicial objectivity: A reply to Professor Hartley' *Law Quarterly Review* 112: 411.

Arnull, A. (2006) *The European Union and its Court of Justice*, 2nd edn (Oxford: Oxford University Press).

Arnull, A. (2020) 'The Many Ages of the Court of Justice of the European Union' EUI Working Papers AEL2020/02. Available at: https://cadmus.eui.eu/bitstream/handle/1814/67273/AEL_2020_02.pdf.

Arnull, A. and Wincott, D. (eds) (2002) *Accountability and Legitimacy in the European Union* (Oxford: Oxford University Press).

Aspinwall, M. and Greenwood, J. (1998) 'Conceptualising collective action in the European Union: an introduction', in J. Greenwood and M. Aspinwall (eds), *Collective Action in the European Union: Interests and the New Politics of Associability* (London: Routledge), pp. 1–30.

Aspinwall, M. and Schneider, G. (2001) 'Institutional research on the European Union: mapping the field', in M. Aspinwall and G. Schneider (eds), *The Rules of Integration: Institutionalist Approaches to the Study of Europe* (Manchester: Manchester University Press), pp. 1–18.

Axelrod, R. (1984) *The Evolution of Co-operation* (New York: Basic Books).

Bache, I. (2008) *Europeanization and Multilevel Governance: Cohesion Policy in the European Union and Britain* (London: Rowman & Littlefield).

Bache, I., Bulmer, S., George, S., and Parker, O. (2014) *Politics in the European Union*, 4th edn (Oxford: Oxford University Press).

Baeten, R. and Vanhercke, B. (2017) 'Inside the black box: the EU's economic surveillance of national health care systems', *Comparative European Politics* 15/3: 478–97.

Baird, T. (2017) 'Research note. Non-State actors and the New Intergovernmentalism', *Journal of Common Market Studies* 55/6: 1192–202.

Baldwin, R. (2011) '21st Century Regionalism: Filling the gap between 21st century trade and 20th century trade rules', World Trade Organization Economic Research and Statistics Division, Staff Working Paper, ERSD-2011–08, 2011 Geneva.

Balkan Barometer (2020) 'Balkan Barometer 2020, Public Opinion, Analytical Report', available at https://www.rcc.int/pubs/95/balkan-barometer-2020-public-opinion-survey

Balme, R. and Chabanet, D. (eds) (2008) *European Governance and Democracy: Power and Protest in the EU* (Lanham, MD: Rowman & Littlefield).

Barber, L. (1995) 'The men who run Europe', *Financial Times*, 11–12 March, section 2: 1–2.

Barbier, J.-C. (ed.) (2012) 'EU law, governance and social policy', *European Integration online Papers* (EIoP), 16/1.

Barents, R. (2010) 'The Court of Justice after the Treaty of Lisbon', *Common Market Law Review* 47/3: 709–28.

Barisione, M. and Michailidou, A. (eds) (2017) *Social Media and European Politics. Rethinking Power and Legitimacy in the Digital Era* (London: Palgrave).

Barnard, C. (2020) 'The wonky level playing field: The heart of the trade talks disagreement: The UK in a changing Europe', available at https://ukandeu.ac.uk/level-playing-field/

Barnier, M. (2020) 'Statement by Michel Barnier following Round 4 of negotiations for a new partnership between the European Union and the United Kingdom' available at https://ec.europa.eu/commission/presscorner/detail/en/speech_20_1017

Barroso, J. M. (2012) 'State of the Union', Speech, 12 September, available at http://europa.eu/rapid/press-release_SPEECH-12-596_en.htm.

Batory, A. (2018) 'EU referendums in the "new" member states: politicisation after a decade of support?', in B. Leruth, N. Startin, and S. Usherwood (eds), *Routledge Handbook of Euroscepticism* (Abingdon: Routledge), pp. 256–68.

Bauer, M. (2016) 'Manufacturing discontent: The rise to power of anti-TTIP groups'. ECIPE (European Centre for International Political Economy) Occasional Paper 02/16. Brussels.

Bauer, M. W. and Becker, S. (2014) 'The unexpected winner of the crisis: The European Commission's strengthened role in economic governance', *Journal of European Integration* 36/3: 213–29.

Baumgartner, F. and Leech, B. (1998) *Basic Interests: The Importance of Groups in Politics and Political Science* (Princeton, NJ: Princeton University Press).

Bayliss, J., Smith, S., and Owens, P. (2010) *The Globalization of World Politics*, 5th edn (Oxford: Oxford University Press).

Beck, G. (2014) 'ECJ legal rulings designed to help the Eurozone are threatening the accountability of European governance', LSE EUROPP Blog, 10 December, available online at https://blogs.lse.ac.uk/europpblog/2014/12/10/ecj-legal-rulings-designed-to-help-the-eurozone-are-threatening-the-accountability-of-european-governance/.

Becker, S., Bauer, M. W., Connolly, S., and Kassim, H. (2016) 'The Commission: boxed in and constrained but still an engine of integration', *West European Politics* 39/5: 1011–31.

Bellamy, A. (2002) *Kosovo and the International Society* (New York: Palgrave).

Bellamy, R. (2019) *A Republican Europe of States. Cosmopolitanism, Intergovernmentalism and Democracy in the EU* (Cambridge: Cambridge University Press).

Bellamy, R. and Attuci, C. (2009) 'Normative theory and the EU: between contract and community', in A. Wiener and T. Diez (eds), *European Integration Theory*, 2nd edn (Oxford: Oxford University Press), pp. 198–220.

Bellamy, R. and Castiglione, D. (2011) 'Democracy by delegation? Who represents whom and how in European governance', *Government and Opposition* 46/1: 101–25.

Bellamy, R., Castiglione, D., and Shaw, J. (eds) (2006) *Making European Citizens: Civic Inclusion in a Transnational Context* (Basingstoke: Palgrave).

Bengtsson, L. and M. Rhinard (2019) 'Securitisation across borders: The case of "Health Security" cooperation in the European Union', *West European Politics* 42/2: 346–68.

Bennett, W. L. and Livingston, S. (2018) 'The disinformation order: Disruptive communication and the decline of democratic institutions', *European Journal of Communication* 33/2: 122–39.

Benson, D. and Adelle, C. (2012) 'Re-assessing European Union environmental policy after the Lisbon Treaty', in A. Jordan and C. Adelle (eds), *Environmental Policy in the European Union*, 3rd edn (London: Routledge), pp. 32–48.

Benson, D. and Jordan, A. (2013) 'Environment policy', in M. Cini and N. Pérez-Solórzano Borragán (eds), *European Union Politics* (Oxford: Oxford University Press).

Benson, D. and Jordan, A. (2014) 'Explaining task allocation in the EU: "retooling" federalism for comparative analysis', *Journal of Common Market Studies* 52/4: 794–809.

Benz, A. (1998) 'Politikverflechtung ohne Politikverflechtungsfalle: Koordination und Strukturdynamik im europäischen Mehrebenensystem', *Politische Viertelja.hresschrift* 39/4: 558–89.

Benz, A. and Eberlein, B. (1999) 'The Europeanization of regional policies: patterns of multi-level governance', *Journal of European Public Policy* 6/2: 329–48.

Berger, S. and Dore, R. (1996) *National Diversity and Global Capitalism* (Ithaca, NY: Cornell University Press).

Berkhout, J. and Lowery, D. (2008) 'Counting organized interests in the European Union: a comparison of data sources', *Journal of European Public Policy* 15/4: 489–513.

Berkhout, J., Hanegraaff, M., and Braun C. (2017) 'Is the EU different? Comparing the diversity of national and EU-level systems of interest organisations', *West European Politics* 40/5: 1109–31.

Bernard, C. and Peers, S. (eds) (2017) *European Union Law*, 2nd edn (Oxford: Oxford University Press).

Berny, N. and Moore, B. (2021) 'Interest groups', in A. J. Jordan. and V. Gravey, (eds) (2021) *Environmental Policy in the European Union*, 4th edn (London: Routledge).

Bertelsmann Stiftung (2016) 'Brexit has raised support for the European Union', available at https://www.bertelsmann-stiftung.de/en/publications/publication/did/flashlight-europe-022016-brexit-has-raised-support-for-the-european-union/(last accessed 13 May 2017).

Bertrand, R. (1956) 'The European common market proposal', *International Organization*, 10/4: 559–74.

Bes, B. J. (2017) 'Europe's executive in stormy weather: How does politicization affect Commission officials' attitudes?', *Comparative European Politics* 15/4: 533–56.

Best, E. (2016) *Understanding EU Decision-Making* (Cham: Springer).

Best, E., Christiansen, T., and Settembri, P. (eds) (2008) *The Institutions of the Enlarged European Union: Continuity and Change* (Cheltenham: Edward Elgar).

Beyers, J. (2002) 'Gaining and seeking access: the European adaptation of domestic interest associations', *European Journal of Political Research* 41/5: 585–612.

Beyers, J. and Dierickx, G. (1998) 'The working groups of the Council of the European Union: supranational or intergovernmental negotiations?', *Journal of Common Market Studies* 36/3: 289–317.

Beyers, J. and Donas, T. (2014) 'Inter-regional networks in Brussels: analyzing the information exchanges among regional offices', *European Union Politics* 15(4): 547–71.

Beyers, J. and Kerremans, B. (2012) 'Domestic embeddedness and the dynamics of multilevel venue shopping in four EU member states', *Governance* 25/2: 263–90.

Beyers, J., Eising, R., and Maloney, W. (eds) (2008) *West European Politics*, 31/6 (special issue entitled 'The politics of organised interests in Europe: lessons from EU studies and comparative politics').

Beyers, J., Chaqués Bonafont, L., Dür, A., Eising, R., Fink-Hafner, D., Lowery, D., Maloney, W., and Naurin, D. (2014) 'The INTEREURO Project: logic and structure', *Interest Groups and Advocacy* 3/2: 126–40.

Beyers, J., de Bruycker, I., and Baller, I. (2015) 'The alignment of parties and interest groups in EU legislative politics: a tale of two different worlds?', *Journal of European Public Policy* 22/4: 534–51.

Bickerton, C. J., Hodson, D., and Puetter, U. (2015a) 'The new intergovernmentalism: European integration in the post-Maastricht era', *Journal of Common Market Studies* 53/4: 703–22.

Bickerton, C., Hodson, D., and Puetter, U. (eds) (2015b) *The New Intergovernmentalism: States and Supranational Actors in the Post-Maastricht Era* (Oxford: Oxford University Press).

Bijsmans, P. (2017) 'Varieties of Euroscepticm and opposition to the EU in the European press', in S. Usherwood, N. Startin, and S. Guerra (eds), *Euroscepticism in the EU: New Dimensions in Opposition to European Integration* (Cheltenham: Edward Elgar).

Bilcik, V. (2017) 'The Slovak EU Council Presidency: in defence of post-Brexit EU', *Journal of Common Market Studies Annual Review* 55/si, March.

Billig, M. (1995) *Banal Nationalism* (London: Sage).

Birdlife International (2008) 'Europe's farmland birds continue to suffer from agricultural policy', 2 December, available online at http://www.birdlife.org/news/news/2008/12/monitoring.html.

Birdlife International/European Landowners' Association (2010) 'Proposals for the future CAP: a joint position from the European Landowners' Organization and Birdlife International', available online at http://www.birdlife.org/sites/default/files/attachments/Proposal_for_the_future_cap_FINAL_21_01_2010_0.pdf.

Birdlife International, European Environmental Bureau (EEB), European Forum on Nature Conservation and Pastoralism (EFNCP), International Federation of Organic Agriculture Movements (IFOAM), and World Wide Fund for Nature (WWF) (2009) 'Proposal for a new EU Common Agricultural Policy', available online at http://cap2020.ieep.eu/vision/NGO-CAP-proposal.pdf.

Biscop, S. and Andersson, J. J. (2008) *The EU and the European Security Strategy* (London: Routledge).

Biscop, S. and Whitman, R. (eds) (2012) *The Routledge Handbook of European Security* (London: Routledge).

Blauberger, M. and Schmidt, S. K. (2017) 'The European Court of Justice and its political impact', *West European Politics* 40/4: 907–18.

Blavoukos, S. and Pagoulatos, G. (2008) 'Enlargement waves and interest group participation in the EU policymaking system: establishing a framework of analysis', *West European Politics* 31/6: 1147–65.

Blom-Hansen, J. (2005) 'Principals, agents and the implementation of EU cohesion policy', *Journal of European Public Policy* 12/4: 624–48.

Blom-Hansen, J. (2011) 'The EU comitology system: taking stock before the new Lisbon regime', *Journal of European Public Policy* 18/4: 607–17.

Bobbio, N. (1987) *The Future of Democracy* (Cambridge: Polity Press).

Bogojević, S, (2015) 'Judicial protection of individual applicants revisited: access to justice through the prism of judicial subsidiarity' *Yearbook of European Law* 34/1: 5–25.

Boräng, F. and Naurin, D. (2015) '"Try to see it my way". Frame congruence between lobbyists and European Commission officials', *Journal of European Public Policy* 22/4: 499–515.

Borges, A., Huet, N. (2020) 'Invisible workers: Underpaid, exploited and put at risk on Europe's farms', *Euronews* 22 July, https://www.euronews.com/2020/07/17/invisible-workers-underpaid-exploited-and-put-at-risk-on-europe-s-farms

Borrás, S. and Jacobsson, K. (2004) 'The open method of co-ordination and new governance patterns', *Journal of European Public Policy* 11/2: 185–208.

Borrás, S. and Radaelli, C. M. (2010) *Recalibrating the Open Method of Coordination: Towards Diverse and More Effective Usages* (Stockholm: Swedish Institute for European Policy Studies).

Borrell, J. (2020) 'Embracing Europe's power, Project Syndicate', available at https://www.project-syndicate.org/commentary/embracing-europe-s-power-by-josep-borrell-2020-02?barrier=accesspaylog

Börzel, T. A. (1997) 'What's so special about policy networks? An exploration of the concept and its usefulness in studying European governance', *European Integration online Papers (EIoP)* 16/1.

Börzel, T. A. (2002) 'Pace-setting, foot-dragging and fence-sitting: member state responses to Europeanisation', *Journal of Common Market Studies* 40/2: 193–214.

Börzel, T. A. (2003) *Environmental Leaders and Laggards in the European Union: Why There is (not) a Southern Problem* (London: Ashgate).

Börzel, T. A. (ed.) (2006) *The Disparity of European Integration: Revisiting Neofunctionalism in Honor of Ernst Haas* (London: Routledge).

Börzel, T. A. (2016) 'From EU governance of crisis to crisis of EU governance: regulatory failure, redistributive conflict and Eurosceptic publics', *Journal of Common Market Studies* 54: 8–31.

Börzel, T. A. (2021) *Why Noncompliance. The Politics of Law in the European Union* (Ithaca, NY: Cornell University Press).

Börzel, T. A. and Buzogány, A. (2019) 'Compliance with EU environmental law. The iceberg is melting', *Environmental Politics* 28/2: 315–41.

Börzel, T. A. and Risse, T. (2000) 'When Europe hits home: Europeanization and domestic change', *European Integration online Papers (EIoP)* 15/4.

Börzel, T. A. and Risse, T. (2007) 'Europeanization: the domestic impact of EU politics', in K. E. Jorgensen, M. A. Pollack, and B. Rosamond (eds), *Handbook of European Union Politics* (London: Sage), pp. 483–504.

Börzel, T. A. and Risse, T. (2012) 'From Europeanization to Diffusion', special issue of *West European Politics* 35/1.

Börzel, T. A. and Risse, T. (2018) 'From the euro to the Schengen crises: European integration theories, politicization, and identity politics', *Journal of European Public Policy*, 25/1: 83–108.

Börzel, T. A. and Schimmelfennig, F. (2017) 'Coming together or drifting apart? The EU's political integration capacity in Eastern Europe', *Journal of European Public Policy* 24/2: 278–96.

Börzel, T. A., Hofmann, T., Panke, D., and Sprungk, C. (2010) 'Obstinate and inefficient: why member states do not comply with European law', *Comparative Political Studies* 43/11: 1363–90.

Bossong, R. (2012) 'Assessing the EU's Added Value in the Area of Terrorism Prevention and Radicalisation', Economics of Security Working Paper 60, available online at https://www.econstor.eu/bitstream/10419/119386/1/diw_econsec0060.pdf.

Bouwen, P. (2004) 'Exchanging access goods for access: A comparative study of business lobbying in the European Union institutions', *European Journal of Political Research* 43/2: 337–69.

Brack, N. (2020) 'Towards a unified anti-Europe narrative on the right and left? The challenge of Euroscepticism in the 2019 European elections', *Research & Politics* 7/2: 1–8.

Brändle, V. K., Galpin, C. and Trenz, H. J. (2021) 'Brexit as "politics of division": social media campaigning in the aftermath of the referendum', *Social Movement Studies* https://doi.org/10.1080/14742837.2021.1928484

Brandsma, G. J. and Blom-Hansen, J. (2017) *Controlling the EU Executive?: the Politics of Delegation in the European Union* (Oxford: Oxford University Press).

Breuer, F. and Kurowska, X. (eds) (2012) *Explaining the EU's Common Security and Defence Policy: Theory in Action* (Basingstoke: Palgrave Macmillan).

Brooks, E. (2012) 'Crossing borders: A critical review of the role of the European Court of Justice in EU health policy', *Health Policy* 105/1: 33–7.

Brooks, E., de Ruijter, A., and Greer, S. L. (2021) 'Covid-19 and European Union health policy: from crisis to collective action', in B, Vanhercke, S. Spasova, and B. Fronteddu (eds), *Social Policy in the European Union: State of Play 2020, Facing the Pandemic* (Brussels: ETUI), pp. 33–48.

Buiter, W. H. and Rahbari, E. (2010) 'Greece and the fiscal crisis in the EMU', Policy Insight No. 51 (Brussels: Centre for Policy Research Paper).

Buoanno, L. and Nugent, N. (2013) *Politics and Policy Processes of the European Union* (Basingstoke: Palgrave Macmillan).

Bulkeley, H. Davies, A., Evans, B., Gibbs, D., Kern, K., and Theobald, K. (2003) 'Environmental governance and transnational municipal networks in Europe', *Journal of Environmental Policy and Planning* 5/3: 235–54.

Bulmer, S. (1983) 'Domestic politics and European Community policy-making', *Journal of Common Market Studies* 21/4: 349–63.

Bulmer, S. and Lequesne, C. (eds) (2005) *The Member States of the European Union* (Oxford: Oxford University Press).

Bürgin, A. (2020): 'The impact of Juncker's reorganization of the European Commission on the internal policy-making process: Evidence from the Energy Union project', *Public Administration* 98: 378–91.

Burns, C. (2012) 'The European Parliament', in A. Jordan and C. Adelle (eds), *Environmental Policy in the European Union*, 3rd edn (London: Routledge), pp. 132–51.

Burns, C. (2021) 'The European Parliament', in A. J. Jordan and V. Gravey (eds) *Environmental Policy in the European Union*, 4th edn (London: Routledge).

Burns, C., Carter, N., and Worsfold, N. (2012) 'Enlargement and the environment: the changing behaviour of the European Parliament', *Journal of Common Market Studies* 50/1: 54–70.

Burns, C., Jordan, A., Gravey, V., et al. (2016) 'How has EU membership affected the UK and what might change in the event of a vote to Remain or Leave?', UK in a Changing Europe, available at https://www.brexitenvironment.co.uk/policy-briefs/.

Burns, C., Gravey, V., Jordan, A., and Zito, A. (2019) 'De-Europeanising or disengaging? EU environmental policy and Brexit', *Environmental Politics* 28/2: 271–92.

Burstein, P. and Hirsh, C. E. (2007) 'Interest organizations, information, and policy innovation in the U.S. Congress', *Sociological Forum* 22/2: 174–99.

Busch, K. (1988) *The Corridor Model: A Concept for Further Development of an EU Social Policy* (Brussels: European Trade Union Institute).

Busuioc, M., Groenleer, M., and Trondal, J. (eds) (2012) *The Agency Phenomenon in the European Union* (Manchester: Manchester University Press).

Caiani, M. and Guerra, S. (eds) (2017) *Euroscepticism, Democracy and the Media. Communicating Europe, Contesting Europe* (Basingstoke: Palgrave).

Cavlak, H. (2019) 'The cost of Brexit: neo-functionalism strikes back', *Romanian Journal of European Affairs* 19: 65–78.

Cameron, D. (1992) 'The 1992 initiative: causes and consequences', in A. Sbragia (ed.), *Europolitics: Institutions and Policy-making in the 'New' European Community* (Washington, DC: Brookings), pp. 23–74.

Cameron, D. (2013) EU speech at Bloomberg, available at https://www.gov.uk/government/speeches/eu-speech-at-bloomberg, accessed on 15 June 2016.

Cameron, D. (2015) Letter to Donald Tusk, available at https://www.gov.uk/government/uploads/system/uploads/attachment_data/file/475679/Donald_Tusk_letter.pdf, accessed on 15th June 2016.

Cameron, F. (2012) *An Introduction to European Foreign Policy* (London: Routledge).

Camisão, I. and Guimarães, M. H. (2017) 'The Commission, the Single Market and the crisis: The limits of purposeful opportunism', *Journal of Common Market Studies* 55: 223–39.

Capelos, T. and Exadaktylos, T. (2017) 'Feeling the pulse of the Greek Debt Crisis: emotional reactions on the web of blame', *National Identities* 19/1: 73–90.

Caporaso, J. A. (1996) 'The European Union and forms of state: Westphalian, regulatory or post-modern?', *Journal of Common Market Studies* 34/1: 29–52.

Caporaso, J. A. and Jupille, J. (2001) 'The Europeanization of gender equality policy and domestic structural change', in M. G. Cowles, J. A. Caporaso, and T. Risse (eds), *Transforming Europe: Europeanization and Domestic Change* (Ithaca, NY: Cornell University Press), pp. 21–43.

Caporaso, J. A. and Tarrow, S. (2009) 'Polanyi in Brussels: supranational institutions and the transnational embedding of markets', *International Organization* 63/4: 593–620.

Cardwell, P. J. (2013) 'On "ring-fencing" the Common Foreign and Security Policy in the legal order of the European Union' *Northern Ireland Legal Quarterly* 64: 443–63.

Cardwell, P. J. (2019) 'The role of law and legal integration in the European Union post-Brexit', *JCMS: Journal of Common Market Studies* 57/6: 1407–18.

Cardwell, P. J. and Hervey, T. (2015) 'The metaphors of law and legal scholarship of a 21st Century European Union: bringing the technical into the socio-legal', in D. Cowan and D. Wincott (eds), *Exploring the Legal in Socio-Legal Studies* (Basingstoke: Palgrave Macmillan), pp. 157–82.

Carubba, C. J. (2001) 'The electoral connection in European Union politics', *Journal of Politics* 63/1: 141–58.

Castillo Ortiz, P. (2020) 'Constitutional Review in the Member States of the EU28: a political analysis of institutional choices' *Journal of Law and Society* 47/1: 87–120.

Centre for European Policy Studies (2014) 'The first CAP reform under ordinary legislative procedure: a political economy perspective', Centre for European Policy Studies, Brussels.

Chalmers, D. (2012) 'The European Court of Justice has taken on huge new powers as "enforcer" of the Treaty on Stability, Coordination and Governance. Yet its record as a judicial institution has been little scrutinised', LSE EUROPP Blog, 7 March, at http://blogs.lse.ac.uk/europpblog/2014/12/10/ecj-legal-rulings-designed-to-help-the-eurozone-are-threatening-the-accountability-of-european-governance/.

Chalmers, D. and Tomkins, A. (2007) *European Union Public Law* (Cambridge: Cambridge University Press).

Chazan, G. (2021) 'Wolfgang Schäuble issues warning on EU recovery fund', *Financial Times*, 26 January.

Checkel, J. T. (2001) 'A constructivist research programme in EU studies', *European Union Politics* 2/2: 219–49.

Checkel, J. T. (2007) 'Constructivism and EU politics', in K. E. Jørgensen, M. A. Pollack, and B. Rosamond (eds), *Handbook of European Union Politics* (London: Sage), pp. 57–76.

Checkel, J. T. and Katzenstein, P. J. (eds) (2009) *European Identity* (Cambridge: Cambridge University Press).

Choi, Y. J. and Caporaso, J. (2002) 'Comparative regional integration', in W. Carlsnaes, T. Risse, and B. Simmons (eds), *Handbook of International Relations* (London: Sage), pp. 480–99.

Christiansen, T. (1996) 'Second thoughts on Europe's "Third Level": the European Union's Committee of the Regions', *Publius: The Journal of Federalism* 26(1): 93–116.

Christiansen, T. (1997) 'Reconstructing European space: from territorial politics to multi-level governance', in K. E. Jørgensen (ed.), *Reflective Approaches to European Governance* (London: Macmillan), pp. 51–68.

Christiansen, T. (2010) 'Administrative fusion in the European Union—reviewing 10 years of comitology reform', in U. Diedrichs, A. Faber, F. Tekin, and G. Umbach (eds), *Europe Reloaded: Differentiation or Fusion?* (Baden-Baden: Nomos).

Christiansen, T. and Kirchner, E. (eds) (2000) *Committee Governance in the European Union* (Manchester: Manchester University Press).

Christiansen, T. and Larsson, T. (eds) (2007) *The Role of Committees in the Policy Process of the European Union* (Cheltenham: Edward Elgar).

Christiansen, T. and Piattoni, S. (eds) (2004) *Informal Governance in the European Union* (Cheltenham: Edward Elgar).

Christiansen, T. and Polak, J. (2009) 'Comitology between political decision-making and technocratic governance: regulating GMOs in the European Union', *EIPASCOPE* 1: 5–11.

Christiansen, T., Jørgensen, K. E., and Wiener, A. (eds) (2001) *The Social Construction of Europe* (London: Sage).

Chryssochoou, D. N. (2009) *Theorizing European Integration*, 2nd edn (London and New York: Routledge).

Church, C. H. (1996) *European Integration Theory in the 1990s*, European Dossier Series (London: University of North London).

Church, C. H. and Phinnemore, D. (2002) *The Penguin Guide to the European Treaties: From Rome to Maastricht, Amsterdam, Nice and Beyond* (London: Penguin).

Church, C. H. and Phinnemore, D. (2006) *Understanding the European Constitution: An Introduction to the EU Constitutional Treaty* (London: Routledge).

Cinalli, M., Trenz, H.J., Brändle, V.K., Eisele, O. and Lahusen, C. (2021) *Solidarity in the Media and Public Contention over Refugees in Europe* (London: Routledge).

Cini, M. and Bourne, A. K. (eds) (2006) *Palgrave Advances in European Union Studies* (Basingstoke: Palgrave Macmillan).

Cioloş, D. (2011) 'A new partnership between Europe and its farmers', Speech presenting the legislative proposals on the reform of the common agricultural policy to the European Parliament, SPEECH/11/653, 12 October, Brussels.

Cladi, L and Locatelli, A. (2012) 'Bandwagoning, not Balancing: Why Europe Confounds Realism', *Contemporary Security Studies* 33/2: 264–88.

Clemens, T, Michelsen, K., and Brand, H. (2014) 'Supporting health systems in Europe: added value of EU actions?' *Health Economic Policy Law* 9: 49–69.

Cocks, P. (1980) 'Towards a Marxist theory of European integration', *International Organization* 34/1: 1–40.

Coen, D. (2009) 'Business lobbying in the European Union', in D. Coen and J. Richardson (eds), *Lobbying the European Union: Institutions, Actors, and Issues* (New York: Oxford University Press), pp. 145–68.

Coen, D. and Richardson, J. (eds) (2009) *Lobbying the European Union: Institutions, Actors, and Issues* (New York: Oxford University Press).

Coen, D. and Thatcher, M. (2007) 'Network governance and multi-level delegation: European networks of regulatory agencies', *Journal of Public Policy* 28/1: 49–71.

Cohen, B. (2008) 'The euro in a global context: challenges and capacities', in K. Dyson (ed.), *The Euro at 10: Europeanization, Power, and Convergence* (Oxford: Oxford University Press), pp. 37–53.

Cohen, B. J. (1971) *The Future of Sterling as an International Currency* (London: Macmillan).

Collett, E. (2017) 'New EU Partnerships in North Africa: Potential to Backfire?' Migration Policy Institute, Commentary, February. At https://www.migrationpolicy.org/news/new-eu-partnerships-north-africa-potential-backfire, accessed 26/06/2018.

Committee of Professional Agricultural Organization—General Committee for Agricultural Cooperation in the European Union (COPA-COGECA) (2011) 'The future of the CAP after 2013: The reaction of EU farmers and agri-cooperatives to the Commission's legislative proposals', PAC(11) 7038, Brussels.

Conant, L. J. (2002) *Justice Contained: Law And Politics in the European Union* (Ithaca, NY: Cornell University Press).

Conti, N. and Memoli, V. (2017) 'How the media make European citizens more Eurosceptical', in M. Caiani and S. Guerra (eds), *Euroscepticism, Democracy and the Media. Communicating Europe, Contesting Europe* (Basingstoke: Palgrave), pp. 121–40.

Conzelmann, T. (1998) '"Europeanization" of regional development policies? Linking the multi-level approach with theories of policy learning and policy change', *European Integration online Papers (EIoP)* 4/2.

Coombes, D. (1970) *Politics and Bureaucracy in the European Community: A Portrait of the Commission of the EEC* (London: George Allen & Unwin).

COPA-COGECA (2020) 'European farmers and agri-cooperatives asked Vice-President Timmermans for clarification around the Commission's position on CAP negotiations', Press release, 3 December 2020. https://copa-cogeca.eu/Archive/Download?id=3843207&fmt=pdf

Corbett, R. (1998) *The European Parliament's Role in Closer EU Integration* (London: Macmillan).

Corbett, R., Jacobs, F., and Shackleton, M. (2011) *The European Parliament*, 8th edn (London: John Harper).

Corbett, R., Jacobs, F., and Neville, D. (2016) *The European Parliament*, 9th edn (London: John Harper).

Corporate Europe Observatory (CEO) and Global Justice Now (2017a) Big Business Britain. 'How corporate lobbyists are dominating meetings with trade ministers', available at https://corporateeurope.org/sites/default/files/big_business_britain_2_0.pdf.

Corporate Europe Observatory (CEO) and Global Justice Now (2017b) 'Big Business Britain. Part Two. How corporate lobbyists dominate secret meetings with Brexit negotiators in London and Brussels', available at https://corporateeurope.org/sites/default/files/analysis_of_dexeu_and_brexit_task-force_august_2017_final_2.pdf.

Corporate Europe Observatory (CEO), LobbyControl, Observatoire des Multinationales, Spinwatch (2019) 'Brexit, finance sector lobbying and regulatory cooperation', available at https://www.lobbycontrol.de/wp-content/uploads/brexit-finance-sector-lobbying-and-regulatory-cooperation.pdf.

Council of the European Union (1996) *The European Union Today and Tomorrow: Adapting the European Union for the Benefit of its Peoples and Preparing it for the Future—A General Outline for a Draft Revision of the Treaties* (Brussels: EU Council).

Council of the European Union (2007) 'Accession of Bulgaria and Romania: EU appointments and changes to Council procedures', Press release 5002/07, available online at http://www.consilium.europa.eu/ueDocs/cms_Data/docs/pressData/en/misc/92310.pdf.

Council of the European Union (2008) Brussels European Council: Presidency Conclusions, 14 February, Brussels, available online at http://www.consilium.europa.eu/ueDocs/cms_Data/docs/pressData/en/ec/97669.pdf.

Council of the European Union (2009) *Council Conclusions on a Strategic Framework for European Cooperation in Education and Training* ('ET 2020'), 12 May, Brussels.

Council of the European Union (2010) Lisbon European Council: Presidency Conclusions, 23–24 March, Lisbon, available online at https://www.consilium.europa.eu/uedocs/cms_data/docs/pressdata/en/ec/00100-r1.en0.htm.

Council of the European Union (2011) 'Financial Activity Report 2010: Section II—European Council and Council', 30 June, Brussels, available online at http://www.consilium.europa.eu/media/1250609/st11598.en11.pdf.

Council of the European Union (2015) 'The European Council: The Strategic Body of the EU', General Secretariat of the Council.

Council of the European Union (2017) General Secretariat, Legal Service, The Director-General, '2016 Annual Activity Report of the Authorising Officer by Delegation', 23 March.

Council of the European Union (2017a) Proposal for an Inter-Institutional Agreement on a mandatory Transparency Register. Approval of a negotiating mandate, Brussels, 15173/17.

Council of the European Union (2017b) Transparency register: Council agrees mandate for negotiations. Press office. General Secretariat of the Council. Brussels, 744/17.

Council of the European Union (2017c), 2016 Annual Activity Report of the Authorising Officer by Delegation. General Secretariat of the Council, Legal Service. 23 March.

Council of the European Union (2020) 'Council Decision authorising the opening of negotiations with the United Kingdom of Great Britain and Northern Ireland for a new partnership agreement', 5870/20, Brussels, 13 February, available at https://www.consilium.europa.eu/media/42737/st05870-en20.pdf

Council of the European Union (2020a) Proposal for a Regulation of the European Parliament and of the Council establishing a Recovery and Resilience Facility—Confirmation of the final compromise text with a view to agreement, Brussels, 14310/221.

Council of the European Union (2020b) Council Regulation (EU) 2020/521 of 14 April 2020 activating the emergency support under Regulation (EU) 2016/369, and amending its provisions taking into account the COVID-19 outbreak (OJ L 117, 15.4.2020, p. 3–8)

Council of the EU (2021) Conference on the Future of Europe—revised Council position, 911/21, 3 February, Brussels, point 6.

Court of Justice of the European Union (2016) C-299/14, García-Nieto and others

Court of Justice of the European Union (2018), Judgment of the General Court (Seventh Chamber, Extended Composition) of 22 March 2018. *Emilio De Capitani v European Parliament*. Case T-540/15.

Court of Justice of the European Union (2018), Judgment of the General Court (Seventh Chamber, Extended Composition) of 22 March 2018. *Emilio De Capitani v European Parliament*. Case T-540/15.

Cowles, M. G. (1995) 'Seizing the agenda for the new Europe: the ERT and EC 1992', *Journal of Common Market Studies* 33/4: 501–26.

Cowles, M. G. (1997) 'Organizing industrial coalitions: a challenge for the future?', in H. Wallace and A. R. Young (eds), *Participation and Policy-making in the European Union* (Oxford: Clarendon Press), pp. 116–40.

Cowles, M. G., Caporaso, J. A., and Risse, T. (eds) (2001) *Transforming Europe: Europeanization and Domestic Change* (Ithaca, NY: Cornell University Press).

Cox, R. (1981) 'Social forces, states and world orders: beyond international relations theory', *Millennium: Journal of International Studies*, 10/2: 126–55.

Craig, P. (2010) *The Lisbon Treaty: Law, Politics, and Treaty Reform* (Oxford: Oxford University Press).

Craig, P. and de Búrca, G. (2011) *EU Law: Text, Cases and Materials*, 5th edn (Oxford: Oxford University Press).

Craig, P. and de Búrca, G. (2015) *EU Law: Texts, Cases and Materials*, 6th edn (Oxford: Oxford University Press).

Crespy, A. and Gajewska, K. (2010) 'New Parliament, new cleavages after the Eastern enlargement? The conflict over the Services Directive as an opposition between the liberals and the regulators', *Journal of Common Market Studies*, 48/5: 1185–208.

Crespy, A. and Schmidt V. A. (2017) 'The EU's economic governance in 2016: beyond austerity?', in B. Vanhercke, S. Sabato, and D. Bouget (eds), *Social Policy in the European Union: State of Play 2017*. Eighteenth annual report (Brussels: ETUI), pp. 99–114.

Culpepper, Pepper (2011) *Quiet Politics and Business Power: Corporate Control in Europe and Japan.* (New York: Cambridge University Press).

Cunha, A. and Swinbank, A. (2011) *An Inside View of the CAP Reform Process: Explaining the MacSharry, Agenda 2000, and the Fischler Reforms* (Oxford: Oxford University Press).

Curtin, D. (1993) 'The constitutional structure of the Union: a Europe of bits and pieces', *Common Market Law Review* 30/1: 17–69.

Cutts, D., Goodwin, M., Heath, O., and Surridge, P. (2020) 'Brexit, the 2019 General Election and the Realignment of British Politics', *The Political Quarterly* 91/1: 7–23.

d'Oultremont, C. (2011) 'The CAP post-2013: more equitable, green and market oriented?', *European Policy Brief, 5.*

da Conceição-Heldt, E. (2004) *The Common Fisheries Policy of the European Union: A Study of Integrative and Distributive Bargaining* (London: Routledge).

da Conceição-Heldt, E. (2006) 'Taking actors' preferences and the institutional setting seriously: the EU Common Fisheries Policy', *Journal of Public Policy* 26/3: 279–99.

De Bruycker, I. (2016) 'Pressure and expertise: explaining the information supply of interest groups in EU legislative lobbying', *Journal of Common Market Studies*, 54/3: 599–616.

de Búrca, G., de Witte, B., and Ogertschnig, L. (eds) (2005) *Social Rights in Europe* (Oxford: Oxford University Press).

de Búrca, G. (2013) *Europe's raison d'être*, Working Paper, EUI AEL, 2013/02, Distinguished Lectures of the Academy.

De Grauwe, P. (2013) 'The political economy of the Euro', *Annual Review of Political Science* 1: 153–70.

de Grieco, J. M. (1995) 'The Maastricht Treaty, economic and monetary union and the neo-realist research programme', *Review of International Studies*, 21/1: 21–40.

de Grieco, J. M. (1996) 'State interests and international rule trajectories: a neorealist interpretation of the Maastricht Treaty and European economic and monetary union', *Security Studies* 5/2: 176–222.

de Ruijter, A. (2017) 'Mixing EU security and public health expertise in the Health Threats Decision', in M. Weimar and A. de Ruijter (eds), *Regulating Risks in the European Union: The Co-production of Expert and Executive Power* (Oxford: Hart Publishing), pp. 101–20.

de Ruijter, A. (2018) 'EU external health security policy and law', in S. Blockmans and P. Koutrakos (eds), *Research Handbook on the EU's Common Foreign and Security Policy* (Cheltenham: Edward Elgar), pp. 374–92.

de Ruijter, A. (2019) *EU Health Law & Policy: The Expansion of EU Power in Public Health and Health Care* (Oxford: Oxford University Press).

de Ruijter A., Beetsma, R., Burgoon, B., Nicoli, F., and Vandenbroucke, F. (2020) 'EU solidarity and policy in fighting infectious diseases: state of play, obstacles, citizen preferences and ways forward', research paper 2020–06 Amsterdam Centre for European Studies, http://dx.doi.org/10.2139/ssrn.3570550.

De Schoutheete, P. (2017) 'The European Council: A formidable locus of power', in D. Hodson and J. Peterson (eds), *The Institutions of the European Union*, 4th edn (Oxford: Oxford University Press), pp. 55–79.

De Tocqueville, A. (1862) *Democracy in America*, translated by Henry Reeve (London: Longman, Green, Longman, & Roberts).

De Vreese, C. H. and Kandyla, A. (2009) 'News framing and public support for a Common Foreign and Security Policy', *Journal of Common Market Studies* 47/3: 453–81.

De Wilde, P. (2011) 'No polity for old politics? A framework for analyzing politicization of European integration', *Journal of European Integration*, 33/5: 559–75.

De Wilde, P. and Zürn, M. (2012) 'Can the politicization of European integration be reversed?', *Journal of Common Market Studies*, 50/S1: 137–53.

Damro, C. (2012) 'Market power Europe', *Journal of European Public Policy* 19/5: 682–99.

Dashwood, A. (1983) 'Hastening slowly the Community's path towards harmonisation', in H. Wallace, W. Wallace, and C. Webb (eds), *Policy-making in the European Community*, 2nd edn (Chichester: John Wiley), pp. 273–99.

Dashwood, A., Dougan, M., Rodger, B., Spaventa, E., and Wyatt, D. (2011) *Wyatt and Dashwood's European Union law*, 6th edn (Oxford: Hart Publishing).

Daugbjerg, C. and Swinbank, A. (2016) 'Three decades of policy layering and politically sustainable reform in the European Union's agricultural policy', *Governance* 29/x: 265–80.

Davies, A. C. L. (2008) 'One step forward, two steps back? The *Viking* and *Laval* cases in the ECJ', *Industrial Law Journal* 37/2: 126–48.

Davies, G. (2018) 'Does the Court of Justice own the Treaties? Interpretative pluralism as a solution to over-constitutionalisation', *European Law Journal* 24: 358–37.

Davignon, E. (2006) 'Foreword', in J.-M. Palayret, H. Wallace, and P. Winand (eds), *Visions, Votes and Vetoes: The Empty Chair Crisis and the Luxembourg Compromise Forty Years on* (Brussels: P.I.E. Peter Lang), pp. 15–19.

Deakin, S. (2017) 'What follows austerity? From social pillar to New Deal', in F. Vandenbroucke, C. Barnard, and G. de Baere (eds), *A European Social Union after the Crisis* (Cambridge: Cambridge University Press), pp. 192–210.

Dedman, M. (2009) *The Origins and Development of the European Union: A History of European Integration* (London: Routledge).

Degryse, C. (2017) 'The relaunch of European social dialogue: what has been achieved up to now?', in B. Vanhercke, S. Sabato, and D. Bouget (eds), *Social Policy in the European Union: State of Play 2017*. Eighteenth annual report (Brussels: ETUI), pp. 115–32.

Dehousse, R., Boussaguet, L., and Jacquot, S. (2010) 'Change and continuity in European governance', *Les Cahiers Européens de Sciences Po.*, 6, available online at http://www.cee.sciences-po.fr/erpa/docs/wp_2010_6.pdf.

del Rio, C., Gonsalves, G., Hassan, F., and Kavanagh, M. (2021) 'COVID-19: A call for global vaccine equity', *British Medical Journal* 17 March.

Delgado, J. (2006) 'Single market trails home bias', *Bruegel Policy Brief* 5, 7 October, Brussels.

Delogu, B. (2016) *Risk Analysis and Governance in EU Policy Making and Regulation. An Introductory Guide* (Berlin: Springer).

Department for Environment, Food and Rural Affairs (Defra) (2011) CAP Reform Post 2013: DEFRA Discussion Paper on the Impact in England of EU Commission Regulatory Proposals for Common Agricultural Policy Reform, Post 2013, available online at http://www.defra.gov.uk/consult/2011/12/12/cap-reform-1112/.

DG Enlargement (2006) *Twinning: A Tested Experience in a Broader European Context* (Brussels: European Commission).

Diez, T. (1999) '"Speaking Europe": the politics of integration discourse', *Journal of European Public Policy* 6/4: 598–613.

Diez Medrano, J. and Gray, E. (2010) 'Framing the European Union in national public spheres', in R. Koopmans and P. Statham (eds), *The Making of a European Public Sphere. Media Discourse and Political Contention* (Cambridge: Cambridge University Press), pp. 195–219.

Dinan, D. (2009) 'Institutions and governance: a new treaty, a newly elected parliament and a new

Commission', *Journal of Common Market Studies Annual Review* 48: 95–118.

Dinan, D. (2011) 'Governance and institutions: implementing the Lisbon Treaty in the shadow of the euro crisis', *Journal of Common Market Studies* 49/SI: 103–21.

Dinan, D. (2014) *Origins and Evolution of the European Union*, 2nd edn (Oxford: Oxford University Press).

Dinan, D. (2017) 'Governance and institutions: the insidious effect of chronic crisis', *Journal of Common Market Studies Annual Review* 55/si: September: 73–87.

Dispersyn, M., Vandervorst, P., de Falleur, M., and Meulders, D. (1990) 'La construction d'un serpent social européen', *Revue Belge de Sécurité Sociale* 12: 889–979.

Dods (2011) *European Public Affairs Directory (EPAD) 2011* (London: Dods Parliamentary Communications).

Dølvik, J. E. (1997) *Redrawing Boundaries of Solidarity? ETUC, Social Dialogue and the Europeanization of Trade Unions in the 1990s*, ARENA Report No. 5, Oslo.

Dougan, M. (2017) 'Addressing issues of protective scope within the Francovich right to reparation', *European Constitutional Law Review* 13: 124–65.

Dover, R. (2007) 'For Queen and company: the role of intelligence in the UK arms trade', *Political Studies* 55/4: 683–708.

Dowding, K. (2000) 'Institutional research on the European Union: a critical review', *European Union Politics* 1/1: 125–44.

Draghi, M. (2012) 'Verbatim remarks made by Mario Draghi', speech at the Global Investment Conference, London, 26 July, http://www.ecb.europa.eu/press/key/date/2012/html/sp120726.en.html.

Draghi M., (2021) Speech to the Italian Senate, reported in Irish Times, February 21, https://www.irishtimes.com/opinion/editorial/the-irish-times-view-on-the-new-italian-government-draghi-s-moment-1.4491171.

Dubin, K. A. (2021) 'Spain's Response to Covid-19', in S. L. Greer, E. J. King, A. Peralta-Santos, and E. Massard da Fonsa (eds), *Coronavirus Politics: The Comparative Politics and Policy of Covid-19* (Ann Arbor: University of Michigan Press), pp. 339–60.

Duchesne, S., Frazer, E., Haegel, F., and Van Ingelgom, V. (2013) *Citizens' Reactions to European Integration Compared: Overlooking Europe* (Basingstoke: Palgrave Macmillan).

Dudek, C. M. (2018) 'Changing governance of cohesion policy', in N. Zahariadis and L. Buonanno (eds), *The Routledge Handbook of European Public Policy* (London: Routledge), pp. 83–93.

Dunne, T. and Schmidt, B. C. (2011) 'Realism', in J. Baylis and S. Smith (eds), *The Globalization of World Politics*, 2nd edn (Oxford: Oxford University Press), pp. 162–83.

Dupont, C. (2016) *Climate Policy Integration into EU Energy Policy: Progress and Prospects* (London: Routledge).

Dür, A. and Mateo, G. (2016) *Insiders versus Outsiders. Interest Group Politics in Multilevel Europe* (Oxford: Oxford University Press).

Dür, A., Bernhagen., P., and Marshall, D. (2015) 'Interest group success in the European Union: when (and why) does business lose?', *Comparative Political Studies*, published online, 20 January, DOI: 10.1177/0010414014565890.

Dyson, K. and Featherstone, K. (1999) *The Road to Maastricht: Negotiating Economic and Monetary Union* (Oxford: Oxford University Press).

Dyson, K. and Quaglia, L. (eds) (2010) *European Economic Governance and Policies, Vol. I: Commentary on Key Historical and Institutional Documents* (Oxford: Oxford University Press).

Dyson, K. and Quaglia, L. (eds) (2011) *European Economic Governance and Policies, Vol. II: Commentary on Key Policy Documents* (Oxford: Oxford University Press).

Easton, D. (1965) *A Systems Analysis of Political Life* (New York: John Wiley & Sons).

Eberlein, B. and Grande, W. (2005) 'Beyond delegation: transnational regulatory regimes and the EU regulatory state', *Journal of European Public Policy*, 12/1: 89–112.

Eberlein, B. and Kerwer, D. (2002) 'Theorising the new modes of European Union governance', *European Integration Online Papers (EIoP)* 6/5: 1–21.

Eberlein, B. and Kerwer, D. (2004) 'New governance in the European Union: a theoretical perspective', *Journal of Common Market Studies* 42/1: 121–42.

ECDC (2020) 'Timeline of ECDC's response to COVID-19', available at https://www.ecdc.europa.eu/en/covid-19/timeline-ecdc-response.

Eckes, C. (2013) 'EU accession to the ECHR: between autonomy and adaptation', *Modern Law Review* 76/2: 254–85.

The Economist (2019) 'Why Europe's single market is at risk', 24 September.

ECVC (2020) 'Cap Reform: good objectives, insufficient measures, says ECVC', Press Release, 22 October,

EEAS (2020) 'Permanent Structured Cooperation—PESCO', available https://eeas.europa.eu/sites/default/files/pesco_factsheet_2021-05-version-2.pdf

EESC (European Economic and Social Committee) (2004) *Final Report of the Ad Hoc Group on Structured Cooperation with European Civil Society Organisations and Networks*, CESE 1498/2003, February, Brussels.

EFFAT et al. (2021) 'Open Letter: The new CAP needs social conditionality—End exploitation and raise labour standards in European agriculture', https://effat.org/wp-content/uploads/2021/02/Open-Letter-The-new-CAP-needs-Social-Conditionality-With-signatories-1.pdf

Egan, M. (2001) *Constructing a European Market: Standards, Regulation and Governance* (Oxford: Oxford University Press).

Egan, M. (2015) *Single Markets: Economic Integration in Europe and the United States* (Oxford: Oxford University Press).

Egan, M. and Guimarães, M. H. (2011) 'Compliance in the single market', Paper prepared for the EUSA Biennial Conference, 3–5 March, Boston.

Egan, M. and Guimarães, M. H. (2017) 'The Single Market: trade barriers and trade remedies', *Journal of Common Market Studies* 55/2: 294–311.

Egeberg, M. (2006) 'Executive politics as usual: role behaviour and conflict dimensions in the college of European commissioners', *Journal of European Public Policy* 13/1: 1–15.

Egeberg, M. and Heskestad, A. (2010) 'The denationalisation of *cabinets* in the European Commission', *Journal of Common Market Studies* 48/4: 775–86.

Egeberg, M. and Trondal, J. (2017) 'Researching European Union agencies: what have we learnt (and where do we go from here)?', *Journal of Common Market Studies* 55/4: 675–90.

Egeberg, M., Schaefer, G. F., and Trondal, J. (2003) 'The many faces of EU committee governance', *West European Politics* 26/3: 19–40.

Eichengreen, B. (2010) 'The Euro's existential crisis', *The Milken Institute Review* 12/3: 32–43.

Eichengreen, B., Jung, N., Moch, S., and Mody, A. (2014) 'The Eurozone crisis: Phoenix miracle or lost decade?', *Journal of Macroeconomics* 39: 288–308.

Eising, R. (2004) 'Multi-level governance and business interests in the European Union', *Governance* 17/2: 211–46.

Eising, R. (2009) *The Political Economy of State–Business Relations in Europe: Capitalism, Interest Intermediation, and EU Policy-making* (London: Routledge).

Eising, R. (2015a) 'Multilevel governance in Europe' in J. M. Magone (ed.), *Routledge Handbook on European Politics* (London: Routledge), pp. 165–83.

Eising, R. (2015b) 'Outnumbered but not outgunned? The participation of citizen groups and business interests in national and EU level consultations on EU policies', in P. Shotton and P. G. Nixon (eds), *Interest Groups in the European Union: Changing Times, Changing Minds* (Farnham: Ashgate).

Eising, R. and Kohler-Koch, B. (eds) (1999) *The Transformation of Governance in the European Union* (London: Routledge).

Eising, R., Rasch, D., and Rozbicka, P. (2017) 'Who says what to whom? Alignments and arguments in EU policy-making', *West European Politics* 40/5: 957–80.

Elgström, O. and Jönsson, C. (2000) 'Negotiating in the European Union: bargaining or problem-solving?', *Journal of European Public Policy* 7/5: 684–704.

Elgström, O. and Smith, M. (eds) (2006) *The European Union's Role in International Politics* (London: Routledge).

Ellinas, A. and Suleiman, E. (2012) *The European Commission and Bureaucratic Autonomy: Europe's Custodians* (Cambridge: Cambridge University Press).

Elliott, H., Jones, D. K., and Greer, S. L. (2012) 'Mapping communicable disease control in the European Union', *Journal of Health Politics, Policy and Law* 37/6: 935–54.

ENDS Europe (2008) 'EU climate change plans survive summit test', 16 October.

Epstein, R. A. and Jacoby, W. (2014) 'Eastern enlargement ten years on: transcending the East-West divide?', *Journal of Common Market Studies* 52/1: 1–16.

Eriksen, E. O. (2011) 'Governance between expertise and democracy: the case of European security', *Journal of European Public Policy* 18/8: 1169–89.

Eriksen, E. O. (2014) *The Normativity of the European Union* (Basingstoke: Palgrave Macmillan).

Eriksen, E. O and Fossum, J. E. (eds) (2012) *Rethinking Democracy in the European Union* (London: Routledge).

Eriksen, E. O., Fossum, J. E., and Menéndez, A. J. (eds) (2005) *Developing a Constitution for Europe* (London: Routledge).

EU (2021) Conference on the Future of Europe, https://ec.europa.eu/info/strategy/priorities-2019-2024/new-push-european-democracy/conference-future-europe_en accessed 30 April 2021.

EU Commission (2017) A Roadmap for Deepening Europe's Economic and Monetary Union. https://eunavfor.eu/mission.

EU Commission (2017a) White Paper on the Future of Europe, 1 March, https://ec.europa.eu/commission/publications/white-paper-future-europe_en.

EUNAVFOR (2017) Mission, available at http://eunavfor.eu/mission. https://eunavfor.eu/mission.

EUNAVFOR (2020) 'Mission', available at https://eunavfor.eu/mission/.

EURACTIV (2017a) 'Greens denounce "Hungary-style" attack against EU-funded NGOs', EURACTIV 19 April 2017.

EURACTIV (2017b) Lawmaking in the dark. Special report. EURACTIV, 23 Nov—1 Dec 2017.

EURACTIV (2019a) Meetings between MEPs and lobbyists to be made public, 1 January 2019.

EURACTIV (2019b) Make lobbying in the EU truly transparent, 11 February 2019.

Eurobarometer (2004) *Eurobarometer 62: Public Opinion in the European Union*, available online at https://europa.eu/eurobarometer/surveys/detail/455.

Eurobarometer (2007) *Eurobarometer 67: Public Opinion in the European Union*, available online at https://europa.eu/eurobarometer/surveys/detail/617.

Eurobarometer (2011a) *Eurobarometer 74: Public Opinion in the European Union*, available online at https://europa.eu/eurobarometer/surveys/detail/918.

Eurobarometer (2011b) *Eurobarometer 76: Public Opinion in the European Union* available online at https://europa.eu/eurobarometer/surveys/detail/1020.

Eurobarometer (2013a) *Eurobarometer 79: Public Opinion in the European Union*, available online https://europa.eu/eurobarometer/surveys/detail/1120.

Eurobarometer (2013b) *Eurobarometer 80: Public Opinion in the European Union*, available online at https://europa.eu/eurobarometer/surveys/detail/1123.

Eurobarometer (2013c) *Eurobarometer 79: Public Opinion in the European Union* (Brussels: European Commission), available online at http://ec.europa.eu/commfrontoffice/publicopinion/index.cfm/Survey/getSurveyDetail/instruments/STANDARD/surveyKy/1120.

Eurobarometer (2014) *Eurobarometer 81: Public Opinion in the European Union*, available online at https://europa.eu/eurobarometer/surveys/detail/2040.

Eurobarometer (2016) *Eurobarometer 86: Public Opinion in the European Union*, available online at https://europa.eu/eurobarometer/surveys/detail/2137.

Eurobarometer (2016a) *Standard Eurobarometer 86. Public Opinion in the European Union*, available online at https://europa.eu/eurobarometer/surveys/detail/2137.

Eurobarometer (2016b) Flash Eurobarometer 440, Introduction of the euro in the Member States that have not yet adopted the common currency, May.

Eurobarometer (2017a) *Standard Eurobarometer 87. Public Opinion in the European Union*, Spring, available online at https://europa.eu/eurobarometer/surveys/detail/2142.

Eurobarometer (2017b) *Eurobarometer 88: Public Opinion in the European Union* (Brussels: European Commission), available online at https://europa.eu/eurobarometer/surveys/detail/2143.

Eurobarometer (2018) *Eurobarometer Survey 89.2 of the European Parliament*, A Public Opinion Monitoring Study, May 2018 available at https://www.europarl.europa.eu/at-your-service/files/be-heard/eurobarometer/2018/eurobarometer-2018-democracy-on-the-move/report/en-one-year-before-2019-eurobarometer-report.pdf.

Eurobarometer (2019) *Standard Eurobarometer 92 Autumn 2019, Europeans' Opinions about the European Union's Priorities*, available at https://europa.eu/eurobarometer/surveys/detail/2255

Eurobarometer (2021) *Standard Eurobarometer 94*, https://europa.eu/eurobarometer/surveys/detail/2355

European Central Bank (2018) 'Asset purchase programmes, Frankfurt' available at https://europa.eu/eurobarometer/surveys/detail/2255.

European Citizens Initiative (2012) 'Basic facts', available online at http://ec.europa.eu/citizens-initiative/public/basic-facts.

European Commission (1992a) The Internal Market after 1992: Meeting the Challenge, SEC(92)2044, October, Brussels.

European Commission (1992b) An Open and Structured Dialogue between the Commission and Special Interest Groups, SEC(92)2272 final, December, Brussels.

European Commission (2001a) European Governance: A White Paper, COM(2001)428 final, July, Brussels.

European Commission (2001b) Proposal for a Council Framework Decision on Combating Terrorism, COM(2001)521 final, February, Brussels.

European Commission (2002a) Towards a Reinforced Culture of Consultation and Dialogue: General Principles and Minimum Standards for Consultation of Interested Parties by the Commission, COM(2002)704 final, December, Brussels.

European Commission (2002b) The Mid-Term Review of the Common Agricultural Policy, COM(2002)294 final, March, Brussels.

European Commission (2002c) A Project for the European Union, COM(2002)394 final, July, Brussels.

European Commission (2004) Area of Freedom, Security and Justice: Assessment of the Tampere Programme and Future Orientations, COM(2004) 4002 final, June, Brussels.

European Commission (2005) 'European Roadmap towards a Zero Victim Target: The EC Mine Action Strategy and Multiannual Indicative Programming 2005–2007', available online at http://eeas.europa.eu/anti_landmines/docs/strategy_0507_en.pdf.

European Commission (2006) Green Paper: European Transparency Initiative, COM(2006)194 final, May, Brussels.

European Commission (2008a) '"Education & Training 2010": Main Policy Initiatives and Outputs in Education and Training since the Year 2000', Communication from the Commission, February.

European Commission (2008b) Communication from the Commission: An updated strategic framework for European cooperation in education and training, COM(2008)865 final, 16 December.

European Commission (2008c) Communication from the Commission: European Transparency Initiative. A framework for relations with interest representatives (Register and Code of Conduct), COM(2008) 323 final, Brussels, 27 May.

European Commission (2008d) Report from the Commission to the European Parliament and the Council on the Activities of the European Globalisation Adjustment Fund in 2007, COM(2008)421 final, July, Brussels.

European Commission (2009) Report from the Commission to the European Parliament and the Council on the Activities of the European Globalisation Adjustment Fund in 2008, COM(2009)394 final, July, Brussels.

European Commission (2010a) 'The CAP after 2013 public debate', summary report.

European Commission (2010b) Report from the Commission to the European Parliament and the Council on the Activities of the European Globalisation Adjustment Fund in 2009, COM(2010)464 final, Brussels.

European Commission (2011a) Communication from the Commission to the European Parliament and the Council: Enlargement Strategy and Main Challenges 2011–2012, COM(2011)666 final, October, Brussels.

European Commission (2011b) Communication from the Commission to the European Parliament and the Council Action Plan against the Rising Threats from Antimicrobial Resistance, COM(2011)748, Brussels.

European Commission (2013) Clean Power for Transport: A European alternative fuels strategy, COM(2013)17, Brussels, 24 January 2013.

European Commission (2013a) Annual Report 2012 on Relations between the European Commission and National Parliaments, COM(2014)507 final, Brussels, 30 July 2014.

European Commission (2013b) 'Overview of the CAP Reform 2014–2020', available online at http://ec.europa.eu/agriculture/policy-perspectives/policy-briefs/05_en.pdf.

European Commission (2014) Proposal for a Regulation of the European Parliament and of the Council on the manufacture, placing on the market and use of medicated feed and repealing Council Directive 90/167/EEC (Brussels, 10 September 2014 COM(2014) 556 final), Brussels: European Commission.

European Commission (2014a) Annual Report 2013 on Relations between the European Commission and National Parliaments, COM(2014)507 final, Brussels, 5 August 2014.

European Commission (2014b) Proposal for a Regulation of the European Parliament and of the Council on veterinary medicinal products, COM(2014)558 final, September, Brussels.

European Commission (2014c) 'European and Training Monitor 2014.

European Commission (2014d) 'The revised Transparency Register: more information, more incentives, tougher on those who break the rules', Memo 14/302, Brussels, 15 April.

European Commission (2014e), Budgetary Impact of NGO Funding in the last 10 Years. Speech by Manfred Kraff, Deputy Director-General of DG at the EP Hearing on 'Implementation of EU policies by NGOs', Brussels, 30 January 2014.

European Commission (2015a) 'A new state for social dialogue', available online at http://ec.europa.eu/social/main.jsp?langId=en&catId=329.

European Commission (2015b) 'Strategic framework—Education & Training 2020.

European Commission (2015c) 'Better regulation "Toolbox"', Brussels (http://ec.europa.eu/smart-regulation/guidelines/docs/br_toolbox_en.pdf).

European Commission (2016a) Proposal for a Directive of the European Parliament and of the Council amending Directive 96/71/EC of the European Parliament and of the Council of 16 December 1996 concerning the posting of workers in the framework of the provision of services, COM(2016) 128 final, Brussels.

European Commission (2016b) Proposal for an Interinstitutional Agreement on a mandatory Transparency Register, Brussels, 28 Sept. 2016: COM(2016) 627 final.

European Commission (2017) 'Monitoring the application of European Union law 2016 Annual Report', Brussels: European Commission, available at http://eur-lex.europa.eu/legal-content/EN/TXT/PDF/?uri=COM%3A2017%3A370%3AFIN&from=EN.

European Commission (2017a) Better Regulation Guidelines, SWD (2017) 350, 7 July.

European Commission (2017b) Completing the Better Regulation Agenda: Better Solutions for Better Results. COM(2017) 651 final, 24 October.

European Commission (2017c) 'A Roadmap for Deepening Europe's Economic and Monetary Union.

European Commission (2017d) 'White Paper on the Future of Europe', 1 March, https://ec.europa.eu/commission/publications/white-paper-future-europe_en.

European Commission (2017e) 'Monitoring the application of European Union law 2016 Annual Report', Brussels: European Commission, available at http://eur-lex.europa.eu/legal-content/EN/TXT/PDF/?uri=COM%3A2017%3A370%3AFIN&from=EN.

European Commission (2017f) Completing the Better Regulation Agenda: Better solutions for better results. COM(2017) 651 final, 24 October.

European Commission (2018a) Transparency Register: Statistics—Evolution of Registrations. Brussels, 9 January 2018.

European Commission (2018b) 'Member States' Support to Emergency Relocation Mechanism (As of 9 July 2018).

European Commission (2020), *Economic governance review*. COM(2020) 55 final, 5 February 2020.

European Commission (2020) Statistics for the Transparency Register. Brussels, 21 September 2020.

European Commission (2020a) Economic governance review. COM(2020) 55 final, 5 February.

European Commission (2020b) Communication on a coordinated economic response to the COVID-19 outbreak, COM(2020) 112 final, 13 March 2020.

European Commission (2020c) COVID-19 Guidelines for border management measures to protect health and ensure the availability of goods and essential services, 2020/C 86 I/01, 16 March 2020.

European Commission (2020d) Proposal for a Regulation on the establishment of a Programme for the Union's action in the field of health—for the period 2021–2027 and repealing Regulation (EU) No 282/2014 ('EU4Health Programme'), COM(2020) 405 final, 28 May 2020.

European Commission (2020e) Communication on the EU Strategy for COVID-19 vaccines, COM(2020) 245 final, 17 June 2020.

European Commission (2020f) Commission Decision approving the agreement with Member States on procuring COVID-19 vaccines on behalf of the Member States and related procedures, C(2020) 4192 final, 18 June 20.

European Commission (2020g) Press release: Commission presents next steps for €672.5 billion Recovery and Resilience Facility in 2021 Annual Sustainable Growth Strategy, Brussels, 17 September 2020.

European Commission (2020h),Communication on the Pharmaceutical Strategy for Europe, COM(2020) 761 final, 25 November 2020.

European Commission (2020i) Proposal for a Decision of the European Parliament and of the on a General Union Environment Action Programme to 2030. Brussels: European Commission.

European Commission (2020j) 'Commission staff working document part I: General statistical overview accompanying the document monitoring the application of European Union Law 2019 Annual Report', available at https://ec.europa.eu/info/sites/info/files/file_import/report-2019-commission-staff-working-document-monitoring-application-eu-law-general-statistical-overview-part1_en.pdf, accessed 27 January 2021.

European Commission (2020k) 'Records of active cases in infringement decisions database for policy area "environment"', Available at https://ec.europa.eu/atwork/applying-eu-law/infringements-proceedings/infringement_decisions/Accessed 27 January 2021.

European Commission (2020l) 'Commission Staff Working Document part II: Policy areas accompanying the document monitoring the Application of European Union Law 2019 Annual Report', available at https://ec.europa.eu/info/sites/info/files/file_import/report-2019-commission-staff-working-document-monitoring-application-eu-law-policy-areas-part2_en.pdf accessed 27 January 2021.

European Commission (2020m) 'DG Environment :statistics on environmental infringement', Available at https://ec.europa.eu/environment/legal/law/statistics.htm, accessed 27 January 2021.

European Commission/Organisation for Economic Co-operation and Development (OECD) (2010) 'EU Donor Atlas', Vol. 1, January, available online at http://ec.europa.eu./development/index.en.cfmp.

European Council (1999) *Cologne European Council, Conclusions of the Presidency*, Annex IV—European Council Decision on the Drawing Up of a Charter of Fundamental Rights of the European Union, 3–9 June.

European Council (2000) 'Presidency Conclusions, Lisbon European Council', available online at http://www.europarl.europa.eu/summits/lis1_en.htm.

European Council (2001) Declaration by the Heads of State and Government of the European Union and the President of the Commission: Follow-up to the September 11 Attacks and the Fight against Terrorism, SN 4296/2/01, October, Brussels.

European Council (2002) 'Presidency Conclusions 21–22 June', 13463/02 POLGEN 52.

European Council (2003) 'A Secure Europe in a Better World. European Security Strategy', Brussels, 12–13 December, available online at www.eeas.europa.eu/csdp/about-csdp/european-security-strategy.

European Council (2009) 'Council Decision 2009/937/EU of 1 December 2009 adopting the Council's Rules of Procedure', 2009 OJ L 325/35, 11.12.2009.

European Council (2010) 'Consolidated Versions of the Treaty on European Union (TEU) and the Treaty on the Functioning of the European Union (TFEU)', OJ C 83/53, 30 March 2010.

European Council (2012) 'Conclusions of the European Council (1–2 March)', EUCO 4/3/12 REV 3, 8 May, Brussels.

European Court of Auditors (2017) 'Greening: a more complex income support scheme, not yet environmentally effective', Special Report 21/2017, https://op.europa.eu/webpub/eca/special-reports/greening-21-2017/en/

European Court of Auditors (2018) Transparency of EU funds implemented by NGOs: more effort needed. Special Report No. 35. Luxembourg.

European Economic Community (1969) *Le Plan Mansholt: Un Memorandum de la Commission sur la Réforme de l'Agriculture de la CEE* (Paris: SECLAF).

European Environment Agency (2015) 'The European environment—state and outlook', available at https://www.eea.europa.eu/soer.

European Environment Agency (2019) *The European Environment—state and outlook 2020* (Copenhagen: EEA)

European External Action Service (EEAS) (2015) 'The European Union in a Changing Global Environment. A More Connected, Contested and Complex World', Brussels, June 2015.

European Foundation (2014) 'Representativeness of the Social Partners in the European Cross-Industry Social Dialogue', Dublin.

European Movement for Food Sovereignty and another Common Agricultural Policy (FoodSovCAP) (2012) 'FoodSocCAP Position on CAP Reform', March, Brussels.

European Network Against Racism (2020) 'Ethnic minorities in the new European Parliament 2019–2024', available at: https://www.enar-eu.org/ENAR-s-Election-Analysis-Ethnic-minorities-in-the-new-European-Parliament-2019 Accessed 13 December 2020.

European Ombudsman (2016) 'Decision of the European Ombudsman concerning the transparency of Trilogues', available online at https://www.ombudsman.europa.eu/en/cases/decision.faces/en/69206/html.bookmark.

European Parliament (2001) 'EP Resolution on the Commission White Paper on European Governance', C5–0454/2001.

European Parliament (2011a) Agreement between the European Parliament and the European Commission on the Establishment of a Transparency Register for Organisations and Self-Employed Individuals Engaged in EU Policy-making and Policy Implementation, PE446.932/CPG/GT.

European Parliament (2011b) 'The EU Protein Deficit: What Solution for a Long-standing Problem?', A7-0026/2011.

European Parliament (2013a) 'Lobbying the EU Institutions', European Parliament Library, Library Briefing 130538REV1, 18 June 2013.

European Parliament (2013b) Review of the European Transparency Register. European Parliament Library. Library Briefing 130538REV1, Brussels 18 June 2013 5pp (author: Nic Copeland).

European Parliament (2014) 'Gold-plating in EAFRD: To What Extent do National Rules Unnecessarily Add to Complexity, and, As a Result, Increase the Risk of Errors?', PE 490.684, Brussels.

European Parliament (2015) 'The Ordinary Legislative Procedure', available online at http://www.europarl.europa.eu/aboutparliament/en/20150201PVL00004/Legislative-powers.

European Parliament (EP) (2018) A8-0462/2018. 'Report on amendments to Parliament's Rules of Procedure' affecting Chapters 1 and 4 of Title I; Chapter 3 of Title V; Chapters 4 and 5 of Title VII; Chapter 1 of Title VIII; Title XII; Title XIV and Annex II(2018/2170 (REG)), available at https://www.europarl.europa.eu/doceo/document/A-8-2018-0462_EN.pdf.

European Parliament (2019) 'Activity Report, Developments and Trends of the Ordinary

Legislative Procedure 1st July 2014 to 1st July 2019 (8th parliamentary term)', available at: https://www.europarl.europa.eu/cmsdata/198024/activity-report-2014-2019_en.pdf Accessed 10 December 2020.

European Parliament (2020) European Parliamentary Research Service briefing 'The European Centre for Disease Prevention and Control: During the pandemic and beyond', PE 651.973 18 June 2020.

European Parliament (2020a) 'MEPs' gender balance 2019–2024', available at: https://www.europarl.europa.eu/election-results-2019/en/mep-gender-balance/2019-2024/ Accessed 13 December 2020.

European Parliament (2020b) 'Mandatory Transparency Register: political meeting to restart negotiations'. Press Releases, 16 June 2020, available at https://www.europarl.europa.eu/news/en/press-room/20200615IPR81216/mandatory-transparency-register-political-meeting-to-restart-negotiations.

European Parliament, Committee on Budgetary Control [CBC] (2017) *Draft report on budgetary control of financing NGOs from the EU budget.* (Rapporteur Markus Pieper). Brussels: PE589.138v01-00, 16 March 2017.

European Parliament, Committee on Constitutional Affairs [CCA] (2014) Report on the modification of the interinstitutional agreement on the Transparency Register (Rapporteur Roberto Gualtieri). Brussels: PE528.034v02-00, 28 March.

European Parliament, Committee on Constitutional Affairs [CCA] (2017b) Report on transparency, accountability, and integrity in the EU institutions (2015/2041(INI), (Rapporteur: Sven Giegold). Brussels: PE567.666v02-00, 30 March 2017.

European Parliament, Policy Department on Budgetary Affairs [PDBA] (2017c) Democratic accountability and budgetary control of non-governmental organisations funded by the EU budget (study commissioned to Blomeyer & Sanz Ltd on request of the European Parliament's Committee on Budgetary Control), Brussels: PE 572.704, 24 January.

European Parliament and Council (2004) Regulation (EC) No 851/2004 of the European Parliament and of the Council of 21 April 2004 establishing a

European Centre for Disease Prevention and Control.

European Parliament and Council (2013) Decisions No. 1082/2013/EU of the European Parliament and of the Council of 22 October 2013 on serious cross-border threats to health and repealing Decision No 2119/98/EC.

European Parliament and Council (2014) 'Directive 2014/94/EU of 22 October 2014 on the deployment of alternative fuels infrastructure', Official Journal L 307 of 28 October.

European Parliament and Council (2017a) Regulation (EU) 2017/745 of the European Parliament and of the Council of 5 April 2017 on medical devices, amending Directive 2001/83/EC, Regulation (EC) No 178/2002 and Regulation (EC) No 1223/2009, and repealing Council Directives 90/385/EEC and 93/42/EEC.

European Parliament and Council (2017b) Regulation (EU) 2017/746 of the European Parliament and of the Council of 5 April 2017 on in vitro diagnostic medical devices and repealing Directive 98/79/EC and Commission Decision 2010/227/EU.

European Parliament and Council of the EU (2018), *Regulation (EU) 2018/1999 of 11 December 2018 on the Governance of the Energy Union and Climate Action*, Official Journal L 328 of 21 December 2018.

European Parliament and Council of the EU (2021), *Regulation (EU) 2021/241 of 12 February 2021 establishing the Recovery and Resilience Facility*, Official Journal L 57 of 18 February 2021.

European Parliament, European Council and European Commission (2016) 'Interinstitutional Agreement on Better Law-Making', Official Journal L123, Vol 59, 12 May, Brussels. available at, http://eur-lex.europa.eu/legal-content/EN/TXT/PDF/?uri=OJ:L:2016:123:FULL&from=EN.

European Parliament and European Commission (2014) 'Agreement between the European Parliament and the European Commission on the transparency register for organisations and self-employed individuals engaged in EU policy-making and policy implementation', OJ L 277/11- L 277/24, 19 September 2014.

European Parliamentary Research Service Blog (2016) 'EU Migratory Challenge: Possible Responses To The Refugee Crisis', available at https://epthinktank. eu/2015/09/07/eu-migratory-challenge-possible-responses-to-the-refugee-crisis/fig-1-detections-of-illegal-border-crossing-in-the-eu/

European Union (2015) 'Completing Europe's Economic and Monetary Union', issued on 15 June 2015, http://ec.europa.eu/priorities/economic-monetary-union/docs/5-presidents-report_en.pdf.

Eurostat (2015) 'Unemployment statistics', available online at http://ec.europa.eu/eurostat/statistics-explained/index.php/Unemployment_statistics (last accessed 8 August 2018).

Exiting the European Union Committee (2017) The progress of the UK's negotiations on EU withdrawal. Second Report of Session 2017–19 - HC 372.

Fabbrini, F. (ed.) (2017) The Law and Politics of Brexit (Oxford: Oxford University Press).

Fabbrini, F. (ed.) (2021) The Law & Politics of Brexit: Volume III. The Framework of New EU-UK Relations (Oxford: Oxford University Press).

Faleg, G. (2012) 'Between knowledge and power: epistemic communities and the emergence of security sector reform in the EU security architecture', European Security 21: 1–24.

Falkenbach, M and Caiani, M. (2021) 'Italy's Response to Covid-19', in S. L. Greer, E. J. King, E. Massard da Fonseca, and A Peralta-Santos (eds), Coronavirus Poliitcs: The Comparative Politics and Policy of Covid-19 (Ann Arbor: University of Michigan Press), pp. 320–38.

Falkner, G. (1998) EU Social Policy in the 1990s: Towards a Corporatist Policy Community (London: Routledge).

Falkner, G. (ed.) (2016) 'EU policies in times of crisis', Journal of European Integration Special Issue, 38/3.

Falkner, G. (2018) 'A causal loop? The Commission's new enforcement approach in the context of non-compliance with EU law even after CJEU judgments', Journal of European Integration 40/6: 769–84.

Falkner, G. and Treib, O. (2008) 'Three worlds of compliance or four? The EU-15 compared to new member states', Journal of Common Market Studies 46/2: 293–313.

Falkner, G., Hartlapp, M., Leiber, S., and Treib, O. (2004) 'Non-compliance with EU directives in the member states: opposition through the backdoor?', West European Politics 27/3: 452–73.

Falkner, G., Hartlapp, M., Leiber, S., and Treib, O. (2005) 'Die Kooperation der Sozialpartner im Arbeitsrecht: Ein europaïscher Weg?', in R. Eising and B. Kohler-Koch (eds), Interessenpolitik in Europa (Baden-Baden: Nomos), pp. 341–62.

Falkner, G., Treib, O., Hartlapp, M., and Leiber, S. (2005) Complying with Europe: EU Minimum Harmonisation and Soft Law in the Member States (Cambridge: Cambridge University Press).

Falkner, G., Hartlapp, M., and Treib, O. (2007) 'Worlds of compliance: why leading approaches to the implementation of EU legislation are only "sometimes-true theories"', European Journal of Political Research 463: 395–416.

Falkner, G., Treib, O., Holzleithner, E., Causse, E., Furtlehner, P., Schulze, M., and Wiedermann, C. (2008) Compliance in the Enlarged European Union: Living Rights or Dead Letters? (Aldershot: Ashgate).

Featherstone, K. (2003) 'Introduction: in the name of "Europe"', in K. Featherstone and C. Radaelli (eds), The Politics of Europeanization (Oxford: Oxford University Press), pp. 1–32.

Featherstone, K. (2015) 'External conditionality and the debt crisis: the "Troika" and public administration reform in Greece', Journal of European Public Policy 22/3: 295–314.

Featherstone, K. and Radaelli, C. (eds) (2003) The Politics of Europeanisation (Oxford: Oxford University Press).

Feld, W. and Wildgen. J. (1976) Domestic Political Realities and European Unification: A Study of Mass Publics and Elites in the European Community Countries (Boulder, CO: Westview Press).

Fennelly, N. (1998) 'Preserving the legal coherence within the new treaty: the ECJ after the Treaty of Amsterdam', Maastricht Journal of European and Comparative Law 5/2: 185–99.

Financial Services Authority (FSA) (2009) The Turner Review: A Regulatory Response to the Global Banking Crisis (London: HMSO).

Finke, D. (2009) 'Challenges to intergovernmentalism: an empirical analysis of EU treaty negotiations since Maastricht', West European Politics 32/3: 466–95.

Fischer, J. (2000) 'From confederacy to federation—thoughts on the finality of European integration', speech at Humboldt University, Berlin, 12 May, available online at http://www.cvce.eu/obj/speech_by_joschka_fischer_on_the_ultimate_objective_of_european_integration_berlin_12_may_2000-en-4cd02fa7-d9d0-4cd2-91c9-2746a3297773.html.

FitzGibbon, J. (2013) '"Another Europe is possible" and the end of Euroscepticism? Addressing the fine-line between opposing Europe and offering a Euro-alternative', paper presented to the 'Studying Euroscepticism' conference, Annual Conference for Research on the European Matrix (CRonEM), 2–3 July.

Fjellner, B. (2017) 'To register or not to register? Lobby registration in the European Parliament', Working Paper. Strasbourg.

Fligstein, N. (2008) *Euro-Clash. The EU, European Identity, and the Future of Europe* (Oxford: Oxford University Press).

Fligstein, N. and McNichol, J. (1998) 'The institutional terrain of the European Union', in W. Sandholtz and A. Stone Sweet (eds), *European Integration and Supranational Governance* (Oxford: Oxford University Press), pp. 59–91.

Flood, C. (2002) 'The challenge of Euroscepticism', in J. Gower (ed.), *The European Union Handbook*, 2nd edn (London: Fitzroy Dearborn), pp. 73–84.

Føllesdal, A. (2007) 'Normative political theory and the European Union', in K. E. Jørgensen, M. A. Pollack, and B. Rosamond (eds), *Handbook of European Union Politics* (London: Sage), pp. 317–35.

Føllesdal, A. and Hix, S. (2006) 'Why there is a demo-cratic deficit in the EU: a response to Majone and Moravcsik', *Journal of Common Market Studies* 44/3: 533–62.

FoodSovCAPb (2012) 'FoodSovCAP Position on CAP Reform', March, Brussels.

Fouilleux, E. and Loconto, A. (2017) 'Voluntary stand-ards, certification, and accreditation in the global organic agriculture field: a tripartite model of techno-politics', *Agriculture and Human Values* 34/1: 1–14.

Frankel, J. A. and Rose, A. K. (1998) 'The endogeneity of the optimum currency area criteria', *Economic Journal* 108/499: 1009–25.

Franklin, M. N., Marsh, M., and McLaren, L. (1994) 'Uncorking the bottle: popular opposition to European unification in the wake of Maastricht', *Journal of Common Market Studies* 32/4: 455–72.

Freedom House (2020) 'Hungary: Nations in Transit 2020', https://freedomhouse.org/country/hungary/nations-transit/2020, accessed 30 April 2021

Friis, L. and Murphy, A. (2001) 'Enlargement of the European Union: impacts on the EU, the candi-dates and the "next neighbours"', *The ECSA Review* 14/1.

Fritsch, O., Adelle, C., and Benson, D. (2017) 'The EU Water Initiative at 15: origins, processes and assess-ment', *Water International* 42/4: 425–42.

Frost, D. (2020) 'David Frost's statement following the conclusion of round 4 negotiations with the EU', available at https://no10media.blog.gov.uk/2020/06/05/david-frosts-statement-following-the-conclusion-of-round-4-negotiations-with-the-eu/

Fusacchia, A. (2009) 'Selection, appointment, and redeployment of senior Commission officials', PhD thesis, European University Institute, Florence.

Galloway, D. (2001) *The Treaty of Nice and Beyond* (Sheffield: Sheffield Academic Press).

Galpin, C. (2017) *The Euro Crisis and European Identities: Political and Media Discourse in Germany, Ireland and Poland* (London: Palgrave).

Galpin, C. and Trenz, H. J. (2016) 'The spiral of Euroscepticism: media negativity, framing and oppo-sition to the EU', in M. Caiani and S. Guerra (eds), *Euroscepticism, Democracy and the Media. Communicating Europe, Contesting Europe* (Basingstoke: Palgrave), pp. 49–71.

Galpin, C. and Trenz, H. J. (2018) 'Die Euroskeptizismus Spirale: EU-Berichterstattung und Medien-Negativität', *Österreichische Zeitschrift für Soziologie* 43/1, 147–72.

Garman, J. and Hilditch, L. (1998) 'Behind the scenes: an examination of the informal processes at work in conciliation', *Journal of European Public Policy* 5/2: 271–84.

Garrett, G. (1992) 'International cooperation and institutional choice: the European Community's internal market', *International Organization* 46/2: 533–60.

Garrett, G. and Tsebelis, G. (1996) 'An institutional critique of intergovernmentalism', *International Organization* 50/2: 269–99.

Geddes, A. (2008) *Immigration and European Integration: Beyond Fortress Europe?*, 2nd edn (Manchester: Manchester University Press).

Geddes, A. and Taylor, A. (2016) 'Those who knock on Europe's door must repent? Bilateral border disputes and EU enlargement', *Political Studies* 64/4: 930–47.

Genschel, P. and Jachtenfuchs, M. (2015) 'More integration, less federation: the European integration of core state powers', *Journal of European Public Policy*: 1–18.

George, S. (1998) *An Awkward Partner: Britain in the European Community*, 3rd edn (Oxford: Oxford University Press).

Gerner-Beuerle, C., Kücük, E., and Schuster, E. (2014) 'Law meets economics in the German Federal Constitutional Court', London School of Economics, unpublished manuscript.

Gibbon, P. (2008) 'An analysis of standards-based regulation in the EU organic sector, 1991–2007', *Journal of Agrarian Change* 8/4: 553–82.

Gilbert, M. F. (2003) *Surpassing Realism: The Politics of European Integration since 1945* (Lanham, MD: Rowman & Littlefield).

Gilbert, M. (2020) *European Integration: A Political History*, 2nd edn (Lanham, MD: Rowman & Littlefield).

Gill, S. (1998) 'European governance and new constitutionalism: economic and monetary union and alternatives to disciplinary neoliberalism in Europe', *New Political Economy* 3/1: 5–26.

Gillespie, P. (2015) 'News media as actors in European foreign policy-making', in K. E. Jorgensen, A. K. Aarstad, E. Drieskens, K. Laatikainen, and B. Tonra (eds), *The SAGE Handbook of European Foreign Policy* (London: Sage), pp. 413–28.

Gillingham, J. R. (2016) *The EU: An Obituary* (London and New York: Verso).

Goetschy, J. (2003) 'The European employment strategy, multi-level governance and policy coordination: past, present and future', in J. Zeitlin and D. Trubek (eds), *Governing Work and Welfare in a New Economy: European and American Experiments* (Oxford: Oxford University Press).

Gomez, R. and Peterson, J. (2001) 'The EU's impossibly busy foreign ministers: "No one is in control"', *European Foreign Affairs Review* 6: 53–74.

Gorges, M. J. (1996) *Euro-corporatism? Interest Intermediation in the European Community* (London: University Press of America).

Gourevitch, P. (1986) *Politics in Hard Times: Comparative Responses to International Economic Crises* (Ithaca, NY: Cornell University Press), pp. 1–272.

Grabbe, H. (2001) 'How does Europeanization affect CEE governance? Conditionality, diffusion and diversity', *Journal of European Public Policy* 8/6: 1013–31.

Grabbe, H. (2006) *The EU's Transformative Power: Europeanization through Conditionality in Central and Eastern Europe* (Basingstoke: Palgrave Macmillan).

Grande, E. (1994) 'Vom Nationalstaat zur Europäischen Politikverflechtung: Expansion und Transformation moderner Staatlichkeit—undersucht am Beispiel der Forschungs—und Technologiepolitik', PhD thesis, Universität Konstanz.

Granger, M.-P. F. (2017) 'Francovich liability before national courts: 25 years on, has anything changed?' in P. Gilliker (ed) *Research Handbook on EU Tort Law* (Cheltenham: Edward Elgar), pp. 93–127.

Gravey, V. and Jordan, A. (2016) 'Does the European Union have a reverse gear? Policy dismantling in a hyperconsensual polity', *Journal of European Public Policy* 23/8: 1180–98.

Graziano, P. and Vink, M. (eds) (2007) *Europeanization: New Research Agendas* (Basingstoke: Palgrave).

Greenwood, J. (2011) *Interest Representation in the European Union*, 3rd edn (New York: Palgrave Macmillan).

Greenwood, J. and Dreger, J. (2013) 'The Transparency Register: a European vanguard of strong lobby regulation?', *Interest Groups and Advocacy* 2/2: 139–62.

Greer, A. (2005) *Agricultural Policy in Europe* (Manchester: Manchester University Press).

Greer, A. (2017) 'Post-exceptional politics in agriculture: an examination of the 2013 CAP reform', *Journal of European Public Policy* 24/11: 1585–603.

Greer, S. L. (2006) 'Uninvited Europeanization: neofunctionalism and the EU in health policy', *Journal of European Public Policy* 13/1: 134–52.

Greer, S. L. (2012) 'The European Centre for Disease Prevention and Control: Hub or hollow core?', *Journal of Health Politics, Policy and Law* 37/6: 1001–30.

Greer, S. L. (2014) 'The three faces of European Union health policy: Policy, markets, and austerity', *Policy and Society* 33/1: 13–24.

Greer, S. L. (2020) 'National, European, and global solidarity: Covid-19, public health and vaccines', *Eurohealth* 26/2: 104–8.

Greer, S. L. and Brooks, E. (2021) 'Termites of solidarity in the house of austerity: Undermining fiscal governance in the European Union', *Journal of Health Politics, Policy and Law* doi: 10.1215/03616878-8706615.

Greer, S.L., Fahy, N., Rozenblum, S., Jarman, H., Palm, W., Elliot, H., and Wismar, M. (2019) *Everything You always Wanted to Know about European Union Health Policies but Were too Afraid to Ask*, 2nd edn (Copenhagen: WHO European Observatory on Health Systems and Policies).

Grin, G. (2003) *Battle of the Single European Market: Achievements And Economic Thought 1985–2000* (London: Kegan Paul).

Groenleer, M., Kaeding, M., and Versluis, E. (2010) 'Regulatory governance through agencies of the European Union? The role of the European agencies for maritime and aviation safety in the implementation of European transport legislation', *Journal of European Public Policy* 17/8: 1212–30.

Grote, J. R. and Lang, A. (2003) 'Europeanization and organizational change in national trade associations: an organizational ecology perspective', in K. Featherstone and C. M. Radaelli (eds), *The Politics of Europeanization* (Oxford: Oxford University Press), pp. 225–54.

Gstöhl, S. (2015) 'Models of external differentiation in the EU's neighbourhood: an expanding economic community?', *Journal of European Public Policy* 22/6: 854–70.

Gstöhl, S. and Phinnemore, D. (2019) *The Proliferation of Privileged Partnerships between the European Union and its Neighbours* (Routledge, London).

Guay, T. R. (1996) 'Integration and Europe's defence industry: a "reactive spillover" approach', *Political Studies Journal* 24/3: 404–16.

Guerra, S. (2013) *Central and Eastern European Attitudes in the Face of the Union: A Comparative Perspective* (Basingstoke: Palgrave Macmillan).

Guerra, S. (2017) 'What is public Euroscepticism?', *Think: Leicester*, 20 December, University of Leicester, Leicester, available online at https://www2.le.ac.uk/offices/press/think-leicester/arts-and-culture/2017/what-is-public-euroscepticism.

Guerra, S. (2018a) 'Young People and the EU at Times of Crisis' in B. Leruth, N. Startin, and S. Usherwood (eds), *The Routledge Handbook of Euroscepticism* (Abingdon: Routledge).

Guerra, S. (2018b) 'What Euroscepticism looks like in Central and Eastern Europe', LSE Brexit Blog, 4 January 2018.

Guerra, S. (2020) 'Understanding public Euroscepticism', *Quaderni dell'Osservatorio elettorale—Italian Journal of Electoral Studies* 83/2: 45–56.

Guerrina, R. and Masselot, A. (2018) 'Walking into the footprint of EU Law: Unpacking the gendered consequences of Brexit', *Social Policy and Society*, 17/2: 319–30.

Guerra, S. and Serricchio, F. (2014) 'Identity and economic rationality: explaining attitudes towards the EU in times of crisis', in B. M. Stefanova (ed.), *The European Union beyond the Crisis: Evolving Governance, Contested Politics, Disenchanted Publics* (Lanham, MD: Lexington Books), pp. 269–94.

Guerrina, R., Exadaktylos, T., and Guerra, S. (2016) 'Brexit or Bremain: Britain and the 2016 British Referendum', Research Project, University of Surrey and University of Leicester, June–July 2016.

Haas, E. B. (1958) *The Uniting of Europe: Political, Social and Economic Forces, 1950–1957* (Stanford, CA: Stanford University Press).

Haas, E. B. (1970) 'The study of regional integration: reflections on the joy and anguish of pretheorizing', *International Organization* 24/4: 607–46.

Haas, E. B. (1975) *The Obsolescence of Regional Integration Theory*, Research Studies 25 (Berkeley, CA: Institute of International Studies).

Haas, E. B. (1976) 'Turbulent fields and the theory of regional integration', *International Organization* 30/2: 173–212.

Haas, E. B. (2001) 'Does constructivism subsume neofunctionalism?', in T. Christiansen, K. E. Jørgensen, and A. Wiener (eds), *The Social Construction of Europe* (London: Sage), pp. 22–31.

Haas, E. B. (2004) 'Introduction: institutionalism or constructivism?', in E. B. Haas, *The Uniting of Europe: Political, Social and Economic Forces, 1950–1957*, 3rd edn (Notre Dame, IN: University of Notre Dame Press), pp. xii–lvi.

Haas, E. B. and Schmitter, P. C. (1964) 'Economic and differential patterns of political integration: projections about unity in Latin America', *International Organization* 18/3: 705–38.

Haas, J. and Rubio, E. (2017) 'Brexit and the EU budget: Threat or opportunity', Jacques Delors Institute Policy Paper, 2017, vol. 183.

Haas, P. M. (1998) 'Compliance with EU directives: Insights from international relations and comparative politics', *Journal of European Public Policy* 5/1: 17–37.

Haas, P. M. and Haas, E. B. (2002) 'Pragmatic constructivism and the study of international institutions', *Millennium: Journal of International Studies* 31/3: 573–601.

Habermas, J. (2012) *The Crisis of the European Union: A Response* (Cambridge: Polity Press).

Hacker, B. and van Treeck, T. (2010) *What Influence for European Governance?* (Berlin: Friedrich Ebert Stiftung).

Haigh, N. (ed.) (1992) *Manual of Environmental Policy* (London: Longman).

Haigh, N. (2016) *EU Environmental Policy: Its Journey to Centre Stage* (London: Routledge).

Halikiopoulou, D. and Vlandas, T. (2017) 'Voting to leave: economic insecurity and the Brexit vote', in B. Leruth, N. Startin, and S. Usherwood (eds), *The Routledge Handbook of Euroscepticism* (London: Routledge), pp. 444–55.

Hall, P. (1986) *Governing the Economy: The Politics of State Intervention in Britain and France* (Cambridge: Polity Press).

Hall, P. and Soskice, D. (2001) *Varieties of Capitalism* (Oxford: Oxford University Press).

Hall, P. A. and Taylor, R. C. R. (1996) 'Political science and the three institutionalisms', *Political Studies* 44/5: 936–57.

Hallin, D. C. and Mancini, P. (2004) *Comparing Media Systems. Three Models of Media and Politics* (Cambridge: Cambridge University Press).

Hamilton, D. and Quinlan, J. (eds) (2005) *Deep Integration: How Transatlantic Markets are Leading to Globalization* (Brussels: Centre for Transatlantic Relations/Centre for European Policy Studies).

Harlow, C. (2002) *Accountability in the European Union* (Oxford: Oxford University Press).

Haroche, P. (2020) 'Supranationalism strikes back: a neofunctionalist account of the European Defence Fund', *Journal of European Public Policy* 27/6: 853–72.

Hart, K. (2015) 'The fate of green direct payments in the CAP reform negotiations' in J. Swinnen (ed.), *The Political Economy of the 2014–2020 Reforms of the Common Agricultural Policy: An Imperfect Storm* (Brussels and London: Centre for European Policy Studies/Rowman and Littlefield International), pp. 245–76.

Hart, K. and Baldock, D. (2019) 'The emerging agricultural policy frameworks in the four UK administrations A briefing for the UK Land Use Policy Group' December, IEEP, 1–10.

Hartlapp, M., Metz, J., and Rauh, C. (2014) *Which Policy for Europe? Power and Conflict inside the European Commission* (Oxford: Oxford University Press).

Hartley, T. C. (1996) 'The ECJ, judicial objectivity and the constitution of the EU', *Law Quarterly Review* 112: 95.

Hartley, T. C. (2007) *The Foundations of European Community Law*, 6th edn (Oxford: Oxford University Press).

Harvey, B. (1993) 'Lobbying in Europe: the experience of voluntary organizations', in S. Mazey and J. R. Richardson (eds), *Lobbying in the European Community* (Oxford: Oxford University Press), pp. 188–200.

Hayes-Renshaw, F. (2009) 'Least accessible but not inaccessible: lobbying the Council', in D. Coen and J. R. Richardson (eds), *Lobbying the European Union: Institutions, Actors, and Issues* (New York: Oxford University Press), pp. 70–88.

Hayes-Renshaw, F. and Wallace, H. (2006) *The Council of Ministers*, 2nd edn (New York: St Martin's Press).

Hayes-Renshaw, F., Van Aken, W., and Wallace, H. (2006) 'When and why the EU Council of Ministers votes explicitly', *Journal of Common Market Studies* 44/1: 161–94.

Heipertz, M. and Verdun, A. (2010) *Ruling Europe: The Politics of the Stability and Growth Pact* (Cambridge: Cambridge University Press).

Helferrich, B. and Kolb, F. (2001) 'Multilevel action coordination in European contentious politics: the case of the European Women's Lobby', in D. Imig and S. Tarrow (eds), *Contentious Europeans: Protest and Politics in an Emerging Polity* (Lanham, MD: Rowman & Littlefield), pp. 143–62.

Helleiner, E., Pagliari, S., and Zimmerman, H. (eds) (2010) *Global Finance in Crisis* (London: Routledge).

Henke, R., Benos, T. De Filippis, F., et al. (2017) 'The new Common Agricultural Policy: how do Member States respond to flexibility?', *Journal of Common Market Studies* 56/2: 403–19.

Henning, C. R. and Kessler, M. (2012) 'Fiscal federalism: US history for architects of Europe's fiscal union', Peterson Institute for International Economics Working Paper, No 2012–1 (Washington, DC: Peterson Institute).

Héritier, A. (1996) 'The accommodation of diversity in European policy-making and its outcomes: regulatory policy as patchwork', *Journal of European Public Policy* 3/2: 149–67.

Héritier, A. (2002) 'The accommodation of diversity in European policy-making and its outcomes', in A. Jordan (ed.), *Environmental Policy in the European Union* (London: Earthscan), pp. 180–97.

Héritier, A., Kerwer, D., Knill, C., Lehmkuhl, D., Teutsch, M., and Douillet, A.-C. (2001) *Differential Europe: The European Union Impact on National Policymaking* (Lanham, MD: Rowman & Littlefield).

Hertz, R. and Leuffen, D. (2011) 'Too big to run? Analysing the impact of enlargement on the speed of EU decision-making', *European Union Politics* 12/2: 193–215.

Hervey, T. and J. McHale. (2015) *European Union Health Law: Themes and Implications* (Cambridge: Cambridge University Press).

High Representative (2016) 'Shared Vision, Common Action: A Stronger Europe. A Global Strategy for the European Union's Foreign and Security Policy', Brussels, June, available online at https://europa.eu/globalstrategy/sites/globalstrategy/files/eugs_review_web.pdf.

Hildebrand, P. M. (2005) 'The European Community's environmental policy, 1957 to 1992', in A. Jordan (ed.), *Environmental Policy in the European Union*, 2nd edn (London: Earthscan), pp. 19–41.

Hill, B. and Davidova, S. (2011) *Understanding the Common Agricultural Policy* (London: Taylor and Francis, Earthscan).

Hill, C. and Smith, M. (eds) (2011) *International Relations and the European Union*, 2nd edn (Oxford: Oxford University Press).

Hillion, C. (2010) *The Creeping Nationalisation of the EU Enlargement Policy*, SIEPS Report 6 (Stockholm: Swedish Institute for European Policy Studies).

Hingel, A. J. (2001) 'Education policies and European governance: contribution to the interservice groups on European governance', *European Journal for Education Law and Policy* 5/1–2: 7–16.

Hirst, P. and Thompson, G. (1996) *Globalization in Question: The International Economy and the Possibilities of Governance* (Cambridge: Polity Press).

Hix, S. (1994) 'The study of the European Union: the challenge to comparative politics', *West European Politics* 17/1: 1–30.

Hix, S. (1998) 'The study of the European Union II: the "new governance" agenda and its rival', *Journal of European Integration* 5/1: 38–65.

Hix, S. (2005) *The Political System of the European Union* (Basingstoke: Palgrave).

Hix, S. (2007) 'The EU as a polity (I)', in K. E. Jørgensen, M. A. Pollack, and B. Rosamond (eds), *Handbook of European Union Politics* (London: Sage), pp. 141–58.

Hix. S. (2018) 'When optimism fails: Liberal intergovernmentalism and citizen representation', *Journal of Common Market Studies* 56/7: 1595–613.

Hix, S. and Høyland, B. (2011) *The Political System of the European Union*, 3rd edn (Basingstoke: Palgrave Macmillan).

Hix, S., Noury, A., and Roland, G. (2005) 'Power to the parties: cohesion and competition in the European Parliament, 1979–2001', *British Journal of Political Science* 35/2: 209–34.

Hix, S., Noury, A. G., and Roland, G. (2007) *Democratic Politics in the European Parliament* (Cambridge: Cambridge University Press).

Hobolt, S. B. (2014) 'A vote for the President? The role of *Spitzenkandidaten* in the 2014 European Parliament elections', *Journal of European Public Policy* 21/10: 1528–40.

Hobolt, S. and Spoon, J.-J. (2012) 'Motivating the European voter: parties, issues and campaigns in European Parliament elections', *European Journal of Political Research* 51: 701–27.

Hodson, D. (2009) 'Reforming EU economic governance: A view from (and on) the principal-agent approach', *Comparative European Politics* 7/4: 455–75.

Hodson, D. (2011a) *Governing the Euro Area in Good Times and Bad* (Oxford: Oxford University Press).

Hodson, D. (2011b) 'The EU economy: the eurozone in 2010', *Annual Review of the European Union, Journal of Common Market Studies* 49/1: 231–50.

Hodson, D. (2013) 'The little engine that wouldn't: supranational entrepreneurship and the Barroso Commission', *Journal of European Integration* 35/3: 301–14.

Hodson, D. (2015) 'The IMF as a de facto institution of the EU: A multiple supervisor approach', *Review of International Political Economy* 22/3: 570–98.

Hodson, D. and Puetter, U. (2019) 'The European Union in disequilibrium: new intergovernmentalism, postfunctionalism and integration theory in the post-Maastricht period', *Journal of European Public Policy* 26/8: 1153–71.

Hoffmann, S. (1966) 'Obstinate or obsolete? The fate of the nation-state and the case of Western Europe', *Daedalus* 95/3: 862–915.

Hoffmann, S. (1989) 'The European Community and 1992', *Foreign Affairs* 68/4: 27–47.

Hoffmann, S. (1995) 'Introduction', in S. Hoffmann (ed.), *The European Sisyphus: Essays on Europe 1964–94* (Oxford: Westview), pp. 1–5.

Hoffmann, S. (2000) 'Towards a Common European Foreign and Security Policy', *Journal of Common Market Studies* 38/2: 189–98.

Hogan, M. J. (1987) *The Marshall Plan, Britain and the Reconstruction of Western Europe, 1947–1952* (Cambridge: Cambridge University Press).

Holland, M. and Doidge, M. (2012) *Development Policy of the European Union* (Basingstoke: Palgrave Macmillan).

Hooghe, L. (2001) *The European Commission and the Integration of Europe: Images of Governance* (Cambridge: Cambridge University Press).

Hooghe, L. (2012) 'Images of Europe: how Commission officials conceive their institution's role', *Journal of Common Market Studies* 50/1: 87–111.

Hooghe, L. and Marks, G. (1996) '"Europe with the Regions": channels of regional representation in the European Union', *Publius: The Journal of Federalism* 26(1): 73–92.

Hooghe, L. and Marks, G. (1997) 'The making of a polity: the struggle over European integration', *European Integration online Papers (EIoP)*, 1/4.

Hooghe, L. and Marks, G. (2001a) *Multi-level Governance and European Integration* (Lanham, MD: Rowman & Littlefield).

Hooghe, L. and Marks, G. (2001b) 'Types of multi-level governance', *European Integration online Papers (EIoP)*, 5/11.

Hooghe, L. and Marks, G. (2004) 'Does identity or economic rationality drive public opinion on European integration?', *PS: Political Science and Politics*, 37/3: 415–20.

Hooghe, L. and Marks, G. (2007) 'Sources of Euroscepticism', *Acta Politica* 2–3: 117–27.

Hooghe, L. and Marks, G. (2009) 'A postfunctionalist theory of European integration: from permissive consensus to constraining dissensus', *British Journal of Political Science* 39/1: 1–23.

Hooghe, L. and Marks, G. (2020) 'Is liberal intergovernmentalism regressive? A comment on Moravcsik (2018)', *Journal of European Public Policy* 27/4: 501–8.

Horkheimer, M. (1982) [1937] *Critical Theory* (New York: Seabury Press).

Hout, W. (2010) 'Governance and development: changing EU policies', *Third World Quarterly* 31/1: 1–12.

Howarth, D. and Quaglia, L. (2014) 'The steep road to European banking union: constructing the Single Resolution Mechanism', *Journal of Common Market Studies* 52: 125–40.

Howarth, D. and Sadeh, T. (2010) 'The ever incomplete single market: differentiation and the evolving frontier of integration', *Journal of European Public Policy* 17/7: 922–35.

Howarth, J. (2000) 'Britain, NATO, CESDP: fixed strategies, changing tactics', *European Foreign Affairs Review* 16/3: 1–2.

Howorth, J. (2014) *Security and Defence Policy in the European Union* (Basingstoke: Palgrave Macmillan).

Hübner, D. C. (2018) 'The decentralized enforcement of European law: national court decisions on EU directives with and without preliminary reference submissions', *Journal of European Public Policy* 25/12: 1817–34.

Hudson, J. and Lowe, S. (2004) *Understanding the Policy Process* (Bristol: Policy Press).

Hurrell, A. and Menon, A. (1996) 'Politics like any other? Comparative politics, international relations and the study of the EC', *West European Politics* 19/2: 386–402.

Hurrelmann, A., Gora, A., and Wagner, A. (2015) 'The politicization of European integration: more than an elite affair?', *Political Studies* 63/1: 43–59.

Hyde-Price, A. (2008) 'A "tragic actor"? A realist perspective on "ethical power Europe"', *International Affairs* 84/1: 29–44.

Imig, D. and Tarrow, S. (eds) (2001) *Contentious Europeans: Protest and Politics in an Emerging Polity* (Lanham, MD: Rowan & Littlefield).

Inglehart, R. (1970) 'Public opinion and regional integration', *International Organization* 24/4: 764–95.

Institute for European Environmental Policy (2013) *Environment undermined in CAP deal*, June, Brussels.

IPES (2019) 'Towards a Common Food Policy for the European Union: the Policy Reform and Realignment that is required to build Sustainable Food Systems in Europe' http://www.ipes-food.org/pages/CommonFoodPolicy

Jabko, N. (2006) *Playing the Market: A Political Strategy for Uniting Europe, 1985–2005* (Ithaca, NY: Cornell University Press).

Jachtenfuchs, M. (1997) 'Conceptualizing European governance', in K. E. Jørgensen (ed.), *Reflective Approaches to European Governance* (Basingstoke: Macmillan), pp. 39–50.

Jachtenfuchs, M. (2001) 'The governance approach to European integration', *Journal of Common Market Studies* 39/2: 245–64.

Jachtenfuchs, M. (2007) 'The EU as a polity (II)', in K. E. Jørgensen, M. A. Pollack, and B. Rosamond (eds), *Handbook of European Union Politics* (London: Sage), pp. 159–73.

Jack, B. (2013) 'Article 260(2) TFEU: An Effective Judicial Procedure for the Enforcement of Judgements?' *European Law Journal* 19/3: 404–21.

Jackson, P. T. (2011) *The Conduct of Inquiry in International Relations* (London: Routledge).

Jacoby, W. (2004) *The Enlargement of the EU and NATO: Ordering from the Menu in Central Europe* (Cambridge: Cambridge University Press).

Jacqué, J. P. (2011) 'The accession of the European Union to the European Convention on Human Rights and Fundamental Freedoms', *Common Market Law Review* 48/4: 995–1023.

Jarman, H., Rozenblum, S., and Huang, T. (2021) 'Neither protective nor harmonized: The cross border regulation of medical devices in the EU', *Health Economics, Policy and Law* 16/1: 51–63.

Jeffery, C. (1996) 'Regional information offices in Brussels and multi-level governance in the EU: a UK–German comparison', *Regional & Federal Studies* 6/2: 183–203.

Jeffery, C. (1997) *The Regional Dimension of the European Union. Towards a Third Level in Europe?* (London: Frank Cass).

Jensen, C. S. (2000) 'Neofunctionalist theories and the development of European social and labour market policy', *Journal of Common Market Studies* 38/1: 71–92.

Jensen, C. S (2020) 'While we are waiting for the superbug: constitutional asymmetry and EU governmental policies to combat antimicrobial resistance', *Journal of Common Market Studies* 58: 1361–76.

Joerges, C. and Kreuder-Sonnen, C. (2017) 'European Studies and the European crisis: legal and political science between critique and complacency', *European Law Journal* 23/1–2: 118–39.

Joerges, C. and Neyer, J. (1997) 'From intergovernmental bargaining to deliberative political processes: the constitutionalisation of comitology', *European Law Journal* 3/3: 273–99.

Johnson, B. (2020) 'Statement made on 3 February 2020' available at https://questions-statements.parliament.uk/written-statements/detail/2020-02-03/HCWS86

Jones, E. (2010) 'Merkel's folly' *Survival* 52/3: 21–38.

Jones, E. (2018) 'Towards a theory of disintegration', *Journal of European Public Policy* 25/3: 440–51.

Jordan, A. (2002) *The Europeanization of British Environmental Policy* (Basingstoke: Palgrave).

Jordan, A. and Adelle, C. (eds) (2012) *Environmental Policy in the European Union*, 3rd edn (London: Routledge).

Jordan, A. and Fairbrass, J. (2005) 'European Union environmental policy after the Nice Summit', in A. Jordan (ed.), *Environmental Policy in the European Union*, 2nd edn (London: Earthscan), pp. 42–6.

Jordan, A. and Liefferink, D. (eds) (2004) *Environmental Policy on Europe: The Europeanization of National Environmental Policy* (London: Routledge).

Jordan, A. and Matt, E. (2014) 'Designing policies that intentionally stick: policy feedback in a changing climate', *Policy Sciences* 47/3: 222–47.

Jordan, A. and Moore, B. (2020) *Durable by design? Policy Feedback in a Changing Climate* (Cambridge: Cambridge University Press).

Jordan, A. and Schout, A. (2006) *The Coordination of the European Union* (Oxford: Oxford University Press).

Jordan, A. and Tosun, J. (2012) 'Policy implementation', in A. Jordan and C. Adelle (eds), *Environmental Policy in the European Union*, 3rd edn (London: Routledge).

Jordan, A., Wurzel, R., Zito, A., and Brückner, L. (2005) 'European governance and the transfer of "new" environmental policy instruments in the EU', in A. Jordan (ed.), *Environmental Policy in the European Union*, 2nd edn (London: Earthscan), pp. 317–35.

Jordan, A., Huitema, D., van Asselt, H., Rayner, T., and Berkhout, F. (eds) (2010) *Climate Change Policy in the European Union* (Cambridge: Cambridge University Press).

Jordan, A., Benson, D., and Rayner, T. (2013) 'The governance of sustainable development in the EU: synthesis and analysis', in R. Cörvers, P. Glasbergen, and I. Niestroy (eds), *European Union, Governance and Sustainability* (Heerlen: Open University in the Netherlands).

Jordan, G., Halpin, D., and Maloney, W. A. (2004) 'Defining interests: disambiguation and the need for new distinctions'. *British Journal of Politics and International Relations* 6(2): 1–18.

Jordana, J. and Trivino-Salazar, J. C. (2020) 'Where are the ECDC and the EU-wide responses in the Covid-19 pandemic?', *The Lancet* 385/10237: 1611–12.

Jørgensen, K. E., Pollack, M., and Rosamond, B. (eds) (2007) *Handbook of European Union Politics* (London: Sage).

Journal of European Public Policy (2005) 'Special issue: the disparity of European integration—revisiting neo-functionalism in honour of Ernst Haas', 12/2.

Judge, D. and Earnshaw, D. (2009) *The European Parliament*, 2nd edn (Basingstoke: Palgrave).

Judt, T. (2005) *Postwar: A History of Europe Since 1945* (New York: Penguin).

Juncker, J. C. (2014) 'A New Start for Europe: My Agenda for Jobs, Growth, Fairness and Democratic Change. Political Guidelines for the next European Commission'. Opening Statement in the European Parliament Plenary Session, available online at http://ec.europa.eu/priorities/docs/pg_en.pdf.

Juncker, J. C. (2017) 'State of the Union', address to the European Parliament, 13 September, available online at http://europa.eu/rapid/press-release_SPEECH-17-3165_en.htm.

Juncos, A. E. (2012) 'Member state-building versus peacebuilding: the contradictions of EU state-building in Bosnia and Herzegovina', *East European Politics* 28/1: 58–75.

Juncos, A. E. (2013) *EU Foreign and Security Policy in Bosnia. The Politics of Coherence and Effectiveness* (Manchester: Manchester University Press).

Juncos, A. E. (2020) 'Beyond civilian power? Civilian CSDP two decades on, in D. Fiott (ed.), *The CSDP in 2020. The EU's legacy and ambition in security and defence*', Paris: EU-ISS, available at https://www.iss.europa.eu/sites/default/files/EUISSFiles/CSDP%20in%202020_0.pdf

Juncos, A. E. (2021) 'Vaccine Geopolitics and the EU's Ailing Credibility in the Western Balkans: Carnegie Europe' available at https://carnegieeurope.eu/2021/07/08/vaccine-geopolitics-and-eu-s-ailing-credibility-in-western-balkans-pub-84900

Junk, W. M., Crepaz, M., Hanegraaff, M., Berkhout, J., and Aizenberg E. (2020) 'Interest Representation during the Corona Virus Crisis. Results from the European Union and Nine European Countries'. Summary Report, available at: https://sites.google.

com / view / michelecrepazcom / home / projects / intercov-project

Kaelble, H. (1994) 'L'Europe "vécue" et l'Europe "pensée" aux XXe siècle: les spécificités sociales de L'Europe', in R. Girault (ed.), *Identité et Conscience Européennes aux XXe Siècle* (Paris: Hachette), pp. 27–45.

Kaiser, R. and Prange, H. (2002) 'A new concept of deepening European integration? The European research area and the emerging role of policy coordination in a multi-level governance system', *European Integration online Papers (EIoP)*, 18.

Kallas, S. (2005) 'The need for a European transparency initiative', SPEECH / 05 / 130, 3 March, European Foundation for Management, Nottingham Business School, Nottingham.

Karp, J. A., Banducci, S. A., and Bowler, S. (2003) 'To know it is to love it?: satisfaction with democracy in the European Union', *Comparative Political Studies* 36 / 3: 271–92.

Karppi, I. (2005) 'Good governance and prospects for local institutional stability in the enlarged European Union', *Journal of East–West Business* 11 / 1–2: 93–117.

Kassim, H., Peterson, J., Bauer, M. W., Connolly, S. J., Dehousse, R., Hooghe, L., and Thompson, A. (2013) *The European Commission of the 21st Century: Administration of the Past or Future?* (Oxford: Oxford University Press).

Kassim, H., Connolly, S., Dehousse, R., Rozenberg, O., and Bendjaballah, S. (2017) 'Managing the house: the Presidency, agenda control and policy activism in the European Commission', *Journal of European Public Policy* 24 / 7: 653–74.

Katzenstein, P. J. (1996) *The Culture of National Security: Norms and Identity in World Politics* (Boulder, CO: Westview).

Katzenstein, P. J. (ed.) (1997) *Tamed Power: Germany in Europe* (Ithaca, NY: Cornell University Press).

Katzenstein, P. J., Keohane, R. O., and Krasner, S. (1998) 'International organization and the study of world politics', *International Organization* 52 / 4: 645–85.

Kaunert, C. (2011) *European Internal Security: Towards Supranational Governance in the Area of Freedom, Security, and Justice* (Manchester: Manchester University Press).

Kauppi, N. and Trenz, H. J. (2021) 'Dynamics of (De) politicization in an Emerging European Political Field and Public Sphere', in C. Wiesner (ed.), *Reconsidering EU politicization*, (Basingstoke: Palgrave), pp. 153–74.

Keane, R. (2004) 'The Solana process in Serbia and Montenegro: coherence in EU foreign policy', *International Peacekeeping* 11 / 3: 491–507.

Keohane, R. O. (1988) 'International institutions: two approaches', *International Studies Quarterly* 32 / 4: 379–96.

Keohane, R. O. (1989) *International Institutions and State Power: Essays in International Relations Theory* (Boulder, CO: Westview).

Keohane, R. O. and Hoffmann, S. (eds) (1991) *The New European Community: Decision Making and Institutional Change* (Boulder, CO: Westview).

Keohane, R. O. and Nye, J. (1975) 'International interdependence and integration', in F. Greenstein and N. Polsby (eds), *Handbook of Political Science* (Andover, MA: Addison-Wesley).

Keohane, R. O. and Nye, J. (1976) *Power and Interdependence: World Politics in Transition* (Boston, MA: Little, Brown).

Keohane, R. O. and Nye, J. S. (1997) 'Introduction: The End of the Cold War in Europe' in R. O. Keohane, J. S. Nye, and S. Hoffmann (eds), *After the Cold War International Institutions and State Strategies in Europe, 1989–1991* (Cambridge, MA: Harvard University Press), pp. 1–18.

Ketola, M. (2015) 'Sociological dimensions to Euroscepticism', in S. Usherwood, N. Startin, and S. Guerra (eds), *Euroscepticism in the EU: New Dimensions in Opposition to European Integration* (Cheltenham: Edward Elgar).

Keukeleire, S. and Delreux, T. (2014) *The Foreign Policy of the European Union* (Basingstoke: Palgrave Macmillan).

Keune, M. and Marginson, P. (2013) 'Transnational industrial relations as multi-level governance: interdependencies in European social dialogue', *British Journal of Industrial Relations* 51 / 3: 473–97.

Kitschelt, H. (1986) 'Political opportunity structures and political protest: anti-nuclear movements in four democracies,'. *British Journal of Political Science* 16 / 1: 57–85.

Kleine, M. (2013) *Informal Governance in the European Union: How Governments Make International Organizations Work* (London and New York: Routledge).

Kleine, M. and Pollack, M. (2018) 'Liberal Intergovernmentalism and its critics', *Journal of Common Market Studies* 56/7: 1493–509.

Klingemann, H. D., Fuchs, D., and Zielonka, J. (eds) (2006) *Democracy and Political Culture in Eastern Europe* (London: Routledge Research in Comparative Politics).

Klüver, H., Braun, C., and Beyers J. (2015) 'Legislative lobbying in context: towards a conceptual framework of interest group lobbying in the European Union', *Journal of European Public Policy* 22/4: 447–61.

Knill, C. and Lenschow, A. (1998) 'Coping with Europe: the impact of British and German administration on the implementation of EU environmental policy', *Journal of European Public Policy* 5:/4: 595–614.

Knill, C. and Liefferink, D. (2007) *Environmental Politics in the European Union* (Manchester: Manchester University Press).

Knill, C. and Tosun, J. (2009) 'Hierarchy, networks, or markets: how does the EU shape environmental policy adoptions within and beyond its borders?', *Journal of European Public Policy* 16/6: 873–94.

Knio, K. (2010) 'Investigating the two faces of governance: the case of the Euro-Mediterranean Development Bank', *Third World Quarterly* 31/1: 105–21.

Knodt, M., Greenwood, J., and Quittkat, C. (eds) (2011) *Journal of European Integration*, 33/4 (issue entitled 'Territorial and functional interest representation in EU governance').

Knodt M., Ringel, M. & Müller, R. (2020) 'Harder' soft governance in the European Energy Union, *Journal of Environmental Policy & Planning*, 22:6, 787–800.

Kohler-Koch, B. (1999) 'The evolution and transformation of European governance', in B. Kohler-Koch and R. Eising (eds), *The Transformation of Governance in the European Union* (London: Routledge), pp. 14–35.

Kohler-Koch, B. (2010) 'Civil society and EU democracy: "Astroturf" representation?', *Journal of European Public Policy* 17/1: 100–16.

Kohler-Koch, B. and Eising, R. (eds) (1999) *The Transformation of Governance in the European Union* (London: Routledge).

Kohler-Koch, B. and Quittkat, C. (2013) *De-Mystification of Participatory Democracy: EU-Governance and Civil Society* (Oxford: Oxford University Press).

Kohler-Koch, B. and Rittberger, B. (2006) 'Review article: the "governance turn" in EU studies', *Journal of Common Market Studies* 44/1: 27–49.

Kohler-Koch, B. and Rittberger, B. (eds) (2007) *Debating the Democratic Legitimacy of the European Union* (Lanham, MD: Rowman & Littlefield).

Kohler-Koch, B. and Rittberger, B. (2009) 'A futile quest for coherence: the many frames of EU governance', in B. Kohler-Koch and F. Larat (eds), *European Multi-Level Governance: Contrasting Images in National Research* (Cheltenham: Edward Elgar), pp. 3–18.

Koop, C., Reh, C., and Bressanelli, E. (2021) 'Agenda-setting under pressure: Does domestic politics influence the European Commission?' *European Journal of Political Research* doi: 10.1111/1475-6765. 12438.

Koopmans, R. and Statham, P. (eds) (2010) *The Making of a European Public Sphere. Media Discourse and Political Contention* (Cambridge: Cambridge University Press).

Kopecky, P. and Mudde, C. (2002) 'Two sides of Euroscepticism: party positions on European integration in East Central Europe', *European Union Politics* 3/3: 297–326.

Kornezov, A. (2017) 'Social rights, the Charter, and the ECHR: caveats, austerity, and other disasters', in F. Vandenbroucke, C. Barnard, and G. de Baere (eds), *A European Social Union after the Crisis* (Cambridge: Cambridge University Press), pp. 407–32.

Krahmann, E. (2003) 'Conceptualising security governance', *Cooperation and Conflict* 38/1: 5–26.

Krämer, L. (2012) 'The European Court of Justice', in A. Jordan and C. Adelle (eds), *Environmental Policy in the European Union*, 3rd edn (London: Earthscan), pp. 113–31.

Krastev, I. (2012) 'European disintegration? A fraying union', *Journal of Democracy*, 23/4: 23–30.

Kriesi, H., Grande, E., Dolezal, M., Helbling, M., Höglinger, D., Hutter, S., and Wüest, B. (2012) *Political Conflict in Western Europe* (Cambridge: Cambridge University Press).

Kröger, S. (2009) 'The open method of coordination: part of the problem or part of the solution?', Paper presented at the workshop 'Nouveaux' Modes de Gouvernance et Action Publique Européenne, 23 January, Section d'études européennes de l'AFSP, PACTE/IEP de Grenoble, Grenoble.

Kröger, S. and Friedrich, D. (eds) (2012) *The Challenge of Democratic Representation in the European Union* (Basingstoke: Palgrave).

Kronsell, A. (2005) 'Gender, power and European integration theory', *Journal of European Public Policy* 12/6: 1022–40.

Kuhn, T. (2019) 'Grand theories of European integration revisited: does identity politics shape the course of European integration?', *Journal of European Public Policy* 26: 1213–30.

Kuiper, P., Wouters, J., Hoffmeister, F., de Baere, G., and Ramopoulos, T. (2013) *The Law of EU External Relations: Cases, Materials, and Commentary on the EU as an International Legal Actor* (Oxford: Oxford University Press).

Kurpas, S., Grøn, C., and Kaczynski, P. M. (2008) *The European Commission after Enlargement: Does More Add up to Less?*, CEPS Special Report (Brussels: Centre for European Policy Studies).

Ladrech, R. (1994) 'Europeanization of domestic politics and institutions: the case of France', *Journal of Common Market Studies* 32/1: 69–88.

Laffan, B. (2014) 'Testing times: the growing primacy of responsibility in the euro area', *West European Politics* 37/2: 270–87.

Laffan, B. (2018) *Europe's Union in Crisis: Tested and Contested* (Routledge: London), pp. 1–208.

Laffan, B. (2019) 'How the EU27 Came to Be', *Journal of Common Market Studies* 57: 13–27.

Laffan, B. and Shaw, C. (2006) 'Classifying and Mapping OMC in Different Policy Areas', Report for NEWGOV, 02/D09.

Landmarks (2007) *The European Public Affairs Directory (EPAD)* (Brussels: Landmarks sa/nv).

Larsen, T. and Andersen, S. (2007) 'A new mode of European regulation', *European Journal of Industrial Relations* 13/2: 191–8.

Laurent, P. H. (1970) 'Paul-Henri Spaak and the diplomatic origins of the common market, 1955–56', *Political Science Quarterly* 85/3: 373–96.

Laursen, F. (ed.) (2006) *The Treaty of Nice: Actor Preferences, Bargaining and Institutional Choice* (Leiden: Martinus Nijhoff).

Laursen, F. (ed.) (2012) *The Making of the EU's Lisbon Treaty: The Role of Member States* (Bern: Peter Lang).

Lavallée, C. (2012) 'From the rapid reaction mechanism to the instrument for stability: the empowerment of the European Commission in crisis response and conflict prevention', *Journal of Contemporary European Research* 9/3, ISSN 1815-347X.

Lavenex, S. (2001) 'The Europeanization of refugee policy: normative challenges and institutional legacies', *Journal of Common Market Studies* 39/5: 825–50.

Lavenex, S. (2004) 'EU external governance in "wider Europe"', *Journal of European Public Policy* 11/4: 680–700.

Lavenex, S. (2011) 'Concentric circles of flexible "European" integration: A typology of EU external governance relations', *Comparative European Politics* 9: 372–93. https://doi.org/10.1057/cep.2011.7.

Lavenex, S. and Uçarer, E. M. (eds) (2002) *Migration and the Externalities of European Integration* (Lanham, MD: Lexington Books).

Leconte, C. (2010) *Understanding Euroscepticism* (Basingstoke: Palgrave Macmillan).

Leibfried, S. and Pierson, P. (eds) (1995) 'Semi-sovereign welfare states: social policy in a multi-tiered Europe', in S. Leibfried and P. Pierson (eds), *European Social Policy: Between Fragmentation and Integration* (Washington, DC: Brookings Institution), pp. 43–77.

Leibfried, S. and Pierson, P. (2000) 'Social policy: left to court and markets?', in H. Wallace and W. Wallace (eds), *Policy-making in the European Union*, 4th edn (Oxford: Oxford University Press), pp. 267–92.

Leinen, J. and Méndez de Vigo, I. (2001) *Report on the Laeken European Council and the Future of the Union*, A5–0368/2001, October, Brussels.

Lenaerts, K. and Gutierrez-Fons, J. A. (2014) 'To say what the law of the EU is: methods of interpretation and the European Court of Justice', *Columbia Journal of European Law* 20: 23–61.

Lenaerts, K. and Van Nuffel, P. (2011) *European Union Law*, 3rd edn (London: Sweet and Maxwell).

Lenaerts, K. and Verhoeven, A. (2002) 'Institutional balance as a guarantee for democracy in EU governance', in C. Joerges and R. Dehousse (eds), *Good Governance in Europe's Integrated Market* (Oxford: Oxford University Press), pp. 35–88.

Lenschow, A. (1999) 'Transformation in European environmental governance', in B. Kohler-Koch (ed.), *The Transformation of Governance in the European Union* (London: Routledge), pp. 39–60.

Lenschow, A. (2005) 'Environmental policy', in H. Wallace, W. Wallace, and M. Pollack (eds), *Policy-making in the European Union*, 5th edn (Oxford: Oxford University Press), pp. 305–72.

Lenschow, A. (2012) 'Studying EU environmental policy', in A. Jordan and C. Adelle (eds), *Environmental Policy in the European Union*, 3rd edn (London: Routledge), pp. 49–72.

Lenschow, A. (2021) 'Studying EU environmental policy', in A.J. Jordan. and V. Gravey, (eds), *Environmental Policy in the European Union*, 4th edn (London: Routledge).

Leruth, B. and Lord, C. (2015) 'Differentiated integration in the European Union: a concept, a process, a system or a theory?', *Journal of European Public Policy* 22/6: 754–63.

Leruth, B., Startin, N., and Usherwood, S. (eds) (2018) *Routledge Handbook of Euroscepticism* (Abingdon: Routledge).

Leuffen, D., Schuessler, J., and Gómez Díaz, J. (2020) 'Public support for differentiated integration: individual liberal values and concerns about member state discrimination', *Journal of European Public Policy* 1–20, https://doi.org/10.1080/13501763.2020.1829005

Lewis, J. (2003) 'Institutional environments and everyday EU decision making: rationalist or constructivist?', *Comparative Political Studies* 36/1: 97–124.

Lewis, J. (2005a) 'Is the Council becoming an upper house?', in C. Parsons and N. Jabko (eds), *With US or against US? The State of the European Union*, Vol. 7 (Oxford: Oxford University Press), pp. 143–71.

Lewis, J. (2005b) 'The Janus face of Brussels: socialization and everyday decision making in the European Union', *International Organization* 59/4: 937–71.

Lewis, J. (2017) 'The Council of Ministers of the European Union', in *Oxford Research Encyclopedia of Politics* (Oxford: Oxford University Press).

Liberatore, A. (1993) 'Problems of transnational policy making: environmental policy in the EC', *European Journal of Political Research* 19/2–3: 281–305.

Lieber, R. J. (1972) 'Interest groups and political integration: British entry into Europe', *The American Political Science Review* 66/1: 53–67.

Liefferink, D. and Andersen, M. S. (1998) 'Strategies of the "green" member states in EU environmental policy-making', *Journal of European Public Policy* 5/2: 254–70.

Lindberg, L. N. (1963) *The Political Dynamics of European Economic Integration* (Stanford, CA: Stanford University Press).

Lindberg, L. N. and Scheingold, S. A. (1970) *Europe's Would-be Polity: Patterns of Change in the European Community* (Princeton, NJ: Prentice-Hall).

Lindberg, L. N. and Scheingold, S. A. (eds) (1971) *Regional Integration: Theory and Research* (Cambridge, MA: Harvard University Press).

Lindblom, C. (1959) 'The science of muddling through', *Public Administration Review* 19/2: 79–88.

Locher, B. and Prügl, E. (2009) 'Gender and European integration', in A. Wiener and T. Diez (eds), *European Integration Theory*, 2nd edn (Oxford: Oxford University Press), pp. 181–97.

Loconto A. and Fouilleux E. (2019) 'Defining agroecology: Exploring the circulation of knowledge in FAO's Global Dialogue', *International Journal of Sociology of Agriculture and Food* 25/2, pp. 116–37.

Ludlow, N. P. (2006) *The European Community and the Crises of the 1960s: Negotiating the Gaullist Challenge* (London and New York: Routledge).

Lumbroso, S., Gravey, V. (2013) 'International negotiations and debates: to what extent do they hinder or foster biodiversity integration into the CAP?'

IDDRI—Study, 13/2: 1–46, available at https://www.iddri.org/en/publications-and-events/study/international-negotiations-and-debates-what-extent-do-they-hinder-or (accessed 4 March 2021)

Lynch, P. N., Neuwahl, N. W., and Rees, N. (eds) (2000) *Reforming the European Union from Maastricht to Amsterdam* (London: Longman).

McAuliffe, K. (2011) 'Hybrid texts and uniform law? The multilingual case law of the Court of Justice of the European Union', *International Journal for the Semiotics of Law* 24/1: 97–115.

McGowan, F. and Wallace, H. (1996) 'Towards a European regulatory state', *Journal of European Public Policy* 3/4: 560–76.

McGowan, L. (2007) 'Theorising European integration: revisiting neofunctionalism and testing its suitability explaining the development of EC competition policy', *European Integration online Papers (EIoP)*, 11/3: 1–17.

McLaren, L. N. (2006) *Identity, Interests and Attitudes to European Integration* (Basingstoke: Palgrave).

Macmillan, C. (2009) 'The application of neofunctionalism to the enlargement process: the case of Turkey', *Journal of Common Market Studies* 47/4: 789–809.

Macron, E. (2016) 'Initiative for Europe', speech, Paris, 26 September, available at https://www.diplomatie.gouv.fr/en/french-foreign-policy/european-union/events/article/president-macron-s-initiative-for-europe-a-sovereign-united-democratic-europe.

Macron, E. (2017) 'Initiative for Europe', address at the Sorbonne, Paris, 26 September, available online at http://international.blogs.ouest-france.fr/archive/2017/09/29/macron-sorbonne-verbatim-europe-18583.html.

Mahé, L.-P. (2012) 'Do the proposals for the CAP after 2013 herald a "major" reform?', Policy Paper No. 53, Notre Europe, March.

Maher, I., Billiet, S., and Hodson, D. (2009) 'The principal–agent approach to EU studies: apply liberally but handle with care', *Comparative European Politics* 7/4: 409–13.

Mahoney, C. and Beckstrand, M. (2011) 'Following the money: EU funding of civil society groups', *Journal of Common Market Studies* 49/6: 1339–61.

Majone, G. (1994) 'The rise of the regulatory state in Europe', *West European Politics* 17/3: 77–101.

Majone, G. (1995) 'The development of social regulation in the European Community: policy externalities, transaction costs, motivational factors', EUI Working Paper, Florence.

Majone, G. (ed.) (1996) *Regulating Europe* (London: Routledge).

Majone, G. (1999) 'The regulatory state and its legitimacy problems', *West European Politics* 22/1: 1–24.

Majone, G. (2009) *Europe as the Would-be World Power: The EU at 50* (Cambridge: Cambridge University Press).

Majone, G. (2014) *Rethinking the Union Post-crisis: Has Integration Gone too Far?* (Cambridge: Cambridge University Press).

Mandel, E. (1970) *Europe versus America: Contradictions of Imperialism* (London: New Left Books).

Mandelkern Group (2001) 'Mandelkern Group on Better Regulation Final Report', November, Brussels.

Manners, I. (2002) 'Normative power Europe: a contradiction in terms?', *Journal of Common Market Studies* 40/2: 235–58.

Manners, I. (2006) 'Normative power Europe reconsidered: beyond the crossroads', *Journal of European Public Policy* 13/2: 182–99.

Manners, I. (2007) 'Another Europe is possible: critical perspectives on European Union politics', in K. E. Jørgensen, M. A. Pollack, and B. Rosamond (eds), *Handbook of European Union Politics* (London: Sage), pp. 77–95.

Manners, I. (2008) 'The normative ethics of the European Union', *International Affairs* 84/1: 45–60.

Manners, I. and Whitman, R. (2003) 'The "Difference Engine": constructing and representing the international identity of the European Union', *Journal of European Public Policy* 10/3: 380–404.

Manners, I. and Whitman, R. (2016) 'Another theory is possible: Dissident voices in theorising Europe', *Journal of Common Market Studies* 54/1: 3–18.

March, J. G. and Olsen, J. P. (1989) *Rediscovering Institutions: The Organizational Basics of Politics* (New York: Free Press).

Marks, G. (1992) 'Structural policy in the European Community', in A. Sbragia (ed.), *Europolitics: Institutions and Policy-making in the 'New' European*

Community (Washington, DC: Brookings Institution), pp. 191–224.

Marks, G. (1993) 'Structural policy and multi-level governance in the EC', in A. Sbragia (ed.), *The Euro-Polity* (Boulder CO: Lynne Rienner), pp. 391–411.

Marks, G. and Hooghe, L. (2001) *Multi-level Governance and European Integration* (Lanham, MD: Rowman & Littlefield).

Marks, G., Hooghe, L., and Blank, K. (1996) 'European integration from the 1980s: state-centric v. multi-level governance', *Journal of Common Market Studies* 34/3: 341–78.

Marks, G., Neilsen, F., Ray, L., and Salk, J. E. (1996) 'Competencies, cracks, and conflicts: regional mobilization in the European Union', *Comparative Political Studies* 29/2: 164–92.

Marks, G., Scharpf, F. W., Schmitter, P. C., and Streeck, W. (1996) *Governance in the European Union* (London: Sage).

Marsh, D. (2009) *The Euro* (New Haven, CT: Yale University Press).

Marshall, T. H. (1975) *Social Policy* (London: Hutchinson).

Marshall, D. and Bernhagen, P. (2017) 'Government–business relations in multilevel systems: the effect of conflict perception on venue choice', *West European Politics* 40/5: 981–1003.

Martinsen, D. S. (2017) 'The European Social Union and EU legislative politics', in F. Vandenbroucke, C. Barnard, and G. de Baere (eds), *A European Social Union after the Crisis* (Cambridge: Cambridge University Press), pp. 459–76.

Mastenbroek, E. (2006) 'EU compliance: Still a "black hole"?', *Journal of European Public Policy* 12/6: 1103–20.

Mastenbroek, E. and Martinsen, D. S. (2018) 'Filling the gap in the European administrative space: the role of administrative networks in EU implementation and enforcement', *Journal of European Public Policy* 25: 422–35.

Mattila, M. (2008) 'Voting and coalitions in the Council after the enlargement', in D. Naurin and H. Wallace (eds), *Unveiling the Council of the European Union: Games Governments Play in Brussels* (Basingstoke: Palgrave Macmillan), pp. 23–36.

Mattli, W. and Stone Sweet, A. (2012) 'Regional integration and the evolution of the European polity: On the fiftieth anniversary of the Journal of Common Market Studies', *Journal of Common Market Studies* 50/s1: 1–17.

Mätzke, M. (2012) 'Institutional resources for communicable disease control in Europe: diversity across time and place', *Journal of Health Politics, Policy and Law* 37/6: 967–76.

Mazey, S. and Richardson, J. R. (2002) 'Pluralisme ouvert ou restreint? Les groupes d'interêt dans l'Union européenne', in R. Balme, D. Chabanet, and V. Wright (eds), *L'Action Collective en Europe* [Collective Action in Europe] (Paris: Presses de Science Po.), pp. 123–61.

Mearsheimer, J. J. (1990) 'Back to the future: instability in Europe after the Cold War', *International Security* 15/1: 5–56.

Mearsheimer, J. J. (2010) 'Why is Europe peaceful today', *European Political Science* 9/3: 387–97.

Menon, A. (2009) 'Empowering paradise? ESDP at Ten', *International Affairs* 85/2: 227–46.

Menon, A. (2011) 'European defence policy: from Lisbon to Libya', *Survival* 53/3: 75–90.

Menon, A. and Sedelmeier, U. (2010) 'Instruments and intentionality: civilian crisis management and enlargement conditionality in EU security policy', *West European Politics* 33/1: 75–92.

Mérand, F., Foucault, M., and Irondelle, B. (2012) *European Security since the Fall of the Berlin Wall* (Toronto: University of Toronto Press).

Merkel, A. (2010) 'Protecting the euro to preserve the European vision', 19 May.

Merlingen, M. (2012) *EU Security Policy: What it Is, How it Works, Why it Matters* (London: Lynne Rienner Publishers).

Messerlin, P. (2001) *Measuring the Costs of Protection in Europe* (Washington, DC: IIE).

Meyer, C. (2006) *The Quest for a European Strategic Culture: Changing Norms on Security and Defence in the European Union* (Basingstoke: Palgrave Macmillan).

Meyer, C. (2009) 'Does European Union politics become mediatized? The case of the European Commission', *Journal of European Public Policy* 16/7: 1047–64.

Michailidou, A. (2017) '"The Germans are back": Euroscepticism and anti-Germanism in crisis-stricken Greece', *National Identities* 19/1: 91–108.

Michailidou, A. and Trenz, H. J. (2015) 'The European crisis and the media: media autonomy, public perceptions and new forms of political engagement', in H. J. Trenz, C. Ruzza, and V. Guiraudon (eds), *Europe in Crisis: The Unmaking of Political Union?* (Basingstoke: Palgrave Macmillan), pp. 232–50.

Michailidou, A. and Trenz, H. J. (2020a) 'EU Differentiation, Dominance and the Control Function of Journalism', Arena Working Paper 1/2020, Arena: University of Oslo, https://www.sv.uio.no/arena/english/research/publications/arena-working-papers/2020/wp-01-20.html.

Michailidou, A. and Trenz, H. J. (2020b) 'Journalism and trust: the weaponization of fake news in trust-building', Arena Working Paper.

Milner, S. (2000) 'Introduction: a healthy scepticism?', *Journal of European Integration* 22/1: 1–14.

Milward, A. S. (1992) *The European Rescue of the Nation State* (London: Routledge).

Molitor, B. (1995) Report of the Group of Independent Experts on Legislation and Administrative Simplification, COM(95)288 final, May, Brussels.

Monar, J. and Wessels, W. (eds) (2001) *The European Union after the Treaty of Amsterdam* (London: Continuum).

Monciardini, D. and Benson, D. (2019) 'Plastic Regulation across Europe and the UK', 7th EELF Annual Conference, Environmental Law for Transitions to Sustainability, Utrecht, 28–30 August.

Monnet, J. (1976) *Mémoires* (Paris: Fayard).

Monti, M. (2010) 'A new strategy for the single market: at the service of Europe's economy and society.

Moran, M. (2002) 'Review article: understanding the regulatory state', *British Journal of Political Science* 32/2: 391–413.

Moravcsik, A. (1991) 'Negotiating the Single European Act: national interests and conventional statecraft in the European Community', *International Organization* 45/1: 19–56.

Moravcsik, A. (1993) 'Preferences and power in the European Community: a liberal intergovernmentalist approach', *Journal of Common Market Studies* 34/4: 473–524.

Moravcsik, A. (1994) 'Why the European Community Strengthens the State: Domestic Politics and International Cooperation', Harvard University Center for European Studies Working Paper Series No. 52.

Moravcsik, A. (1998) *The Choice for Europe: Social Purpose and State Power from Messina to Maastricht* (Ithaca, NY: Cornell University Press).

Moravcsik, A. (2001) 'A constructivist research programme for EU studies', *European Union Politics* 2/2: 219–49.

Moravcsik, A. (2002) 'Reassessing legitimacy in the European Union', *Journal of Common Market Studies* 40/4: 603–24.

Moravcsik, A. (2005) 'The European constitutional compromise and the neofunctionalist legacy', *Journal of European Public Policy* 12/2: 349–86.

Moravcsik, A. (2009) 'Europe: the quiet superpower', *French Politics* 7: 403–22.

Moravcsik, A. (2012) 'Europe after the crisis: how to sustain a common currency', *Foreign Affairs* May/June.

Moravcsik. A. (2018) 'Preferences, power and institutions in 21st-century Europe' *Journal of Common Market Studies* 56/7: 1648–74.

Moravcsik, A. and Vachudova, M. A. (2003) 'National interests, state power and EU enlargement', *East European Politics and Societies* 17/1: 42–57.

Morgenthau, H. (1985) *Politics among Nations: The Struggle for Power and Peace*, 6th edn (New York: Knopf).

Morillas, P. (2020) 'Autonomy in intergovernmentalism: the role of de novo bodies in external action during the making of the EU Global Strategy', *Journal of European Integration* 42/2: 231–46.

Mügge, D. (2011) 'From pragmatism to dogmatism: European Union governance, policy paradigms and financial meltdown', *New Political Economy* 16/2: 185–206.

Murdoch, Z. and Trondal, J. (2013) 'Contracted government: unveiling the European Commission's contracted staff', *West European Politics* 36: 458–69.

Naômé, C. (2008) 'EU enlargement and the European Court of Justice', in E. Best, T. Christiansen, and P. Settembri (eds), *The Institutions of the Enlarged European Union. Continuity and Change* (Cheltenham: Edward Elgar), pp. 100–19.

Naurin, D. (2007) 'Backstage behavior: lobbyists in public and private settings in Sweden and the European Union', *Comparative Politics* 29/2: 209–28.

Naurin, D. and Wallace, H. (eds) (2008) *Unveiling the Council of the European Union: Games Governments Play in Brussels* (London and New York: Palgrave Macmillan).

Neuwahl, N. and Kovacs, C. (2021) 'Hungary and the EU's rule of law protection', *Journal of European Integration* 43/1: 17–32.

Newman, A. L. (2008) 'Building transnational civil liberties: transgovernmental entrepreneurs and the European Data Privacy Directive', *International Organization* 62/1: 103–30.

Neyer, J. and Wiener, A. (2011) *Political Theory of the European Union* (Oxford: Oxford University Press).

Nicolaïdis, K. and Schmidt, S. (2007) 'Mutual recognition on trial: the long road to services liberalization', *Journal of European Public Policy* 14/5: 717–34.

Nicolson, F. and East, R. (1987) *From Six to Twelve: The Enlargement of the European Communities* (Harlow: Longman).

Niemann, A. (2006) *Explaining Decisions in the European Union* (Cambridge: Cambridge University Press).

Niemann, A. and Ioannou, D. (2015) 'European economic integration in times of crisis: a case of neofunctionalism?', *Journal of European Public Policy* 22/2: 196–218.

Niemann, A. and Schmitter, P. C. (2009) 'Neofunctionalism', in A. Wiener and T. Diez (eds), *European Integration Theory* (Oxford: Oxford University Press), pp. 45–66.

Niemann, A. and Speyer, J. (2018) 'A neofunctionalist perspective on the "European Refugee Crisis": the case of the European Border and Coast Guard', *Journal of Common Market Studies* 56/1: 23–43.

Norris, P. (2010) 'To Them That Hath' … News Media and Knowledge Gap', paper for Panel Session II. 1.: Political Knowledge and Information, PIREDEU User Community Conference, Brussels, 18–19 November.

Noutcheva, G. (2012) *European Foreign Policy and the Challenges of Balkan Accession: Conditionality, Legitimacy and Compliance* (London: Routledge).

Novak. S. (2013) 'The silence of ministers: consensus and blame avoidance in the Council of the European Union', *Journal of Common Market Studies* 51/6: 1091–107.

Nugent, N. (2010) *The Government and Politics of the European Union*, 4th edn (Basingstoke: Macmillan).

Nugent, N. and Rhinard, M. (2016) 'Is the European Commission really in decline?', *Journal of Common Market Studies* 54/5: 1199–215.

Nye, J. (2005) *Soft Power* (New York: PublicAffairs).

Nye, J. S. (1971) 'Comparing common markets: a revised neo-functionalist model', in L. N. Lindberg and S. A. Scheingold (eds), *Regional Integration: Theory and Research* (Cambridge, MA: Harvard University Press), pp. 192–231.

O'Neill, M. (1996) *The Politics of European Integration: A Reader* (London: Routledge).

O'Toole, F. (2018) *Heroic Failure: Brexit and the Politics of Pain* (London: Head of Zeus Ltd).

O'Toole, L. J. and Hanf, K. I. (2003) 'Multi-level governance networks and the use of policy instruments in the European Union', in T. Bressers and W. Rosenbaum (eds), *Achieving Sustainable Development: The Challenge of Governance across Social Scales* (Westport, CT: Praeger), pp. 257–79.

Obermaier, A. J. (2008) 'The national judiciary: sword of European Court of Justice rulings—the example of the *Kohll/Decker* jurisprudence', *European Law Journal* 14/6: 735–52.

Obstfeld, M. and Rogoff, K. (2009) 'Global imbalances and the financial crisis: products of common causes', Paper prepared for the Federal Reserve Bank of San Francisco Asia Economic Policy Conference, 18–20 October, Santa Barbara, CA, available online at http://elsa.berkeley.edu/~obstfeld/santabarbara.pdf.

Olson, M. (1965) *The Logic of Collective Action: Public Goods and the Theory of Groups* (Cambridge, MA: Harvard University Press).

Pacces A. and M. Weimer (2020) 'From diversity to coordination: a European approach to COVID-19', *European Journal of Risk Regulation* 1/2: 283–96.

Pachl, U. (2015) 'Repercussions of the European Commission's Better Regulation Agenda on Consumer Interest and Policy', *European Journal of Risk Regulation* 6/3: 375–7.

Padoa-Schioppa, T., Emerson, M., King, M., Milleron, J. C., Paelinck, J. H. P., Papademos, L. D., Pastor, A., and Scharpf, F. W. (1987) *Efficiency, Stability, Equity* (Oxford: Oxford University Press).

Panke, D. (2006) 'More arguing than bargaining? The institutional designs of the European convention and intergovernmental conferences compared', *Journal of European Integration* 28/4: 357–79.

Panke, D. (2010) *Small States in the European Union: Coping with Structural Disadvantages* (Aldershot: Ashgate).

Panke, D. (2011) 'Microstates in negotiations beyond the nation-state: Malta, Cyprus and Luxembourg as active and successful policy shapers?', *International Negotiation* 16/2: 297–317.

Panke, D. (2012a) 'Explaining differences in shaping effectiveness: why some states are more effective in making their voices heard in international negotiations', *Comparative European Politics* 10/1: 111–32.

Panke, D. (2012b) 'Being small in a big union: punching above their weights? How small states prevailed in the vodka and pesticides cases', *Cambridge Review of International Affairs* 25/3: 329–44.

Panke, D. and Haubrich Seco, M. (2016) 'EU and supranational governance' in J. Torfing and C. Ansell (eds), *Handbook on Theories of Governance* (Cheltenham: Edward Elgar), pp. 499–513.

Parker, O. (2012) 'The ethics of an ambiguous "cosmopolitics": citizens and entrepreneurs in the European project', *International Theory* 4/2: 198–232.

Parsons, C. (2010) 'Revising the Single European Act (and the common wisdom on globalization)', *Comparative Political Studies* 43/6: 706–34.

Partington, R. (2017) 'Are we happier after the Brexit vote? Only in England, official figures claim', *The Guardian* 8 November.

Patel, K. K. (2009) *Fertile Ground for Europe? The History of European Integration and the Common Agricultural Policy since 1945* (Baden-Baden: Nomos).

Paterson, W. E. (2011) 'The reluctant hegemon? Germany moves centre stage in the European Union', *Journal of Common Market Studies* 42/1: 57–75.

Pearce, J. and Sutton, J. (1983) *Protection and Industrial Policy in Europe* (London: Routledge).

Pe'er, G., Dicks, L., Visconti, P., et al. (2014) 'EU agricultural reform fails on biodiversity', *Science* 344/6188: 1090–2.

Pe'er, et al. (2020) 'Action needed for the EU Common Agricultural Policy to address sustainability challenges', *People and Nature* 2/2: 305–16.

Peers, S. (various) 'Legislative updates', *European Journal of Migration and Law*—various issues.

Peers, S., Hervey, T. Kenner, J., and Ward, A. (2014) *The EU Charter of Fundamental Rights: a Commentary* (Oxford: Hart Publishing).

Pelkmans, J. (1997) *European Integration, Methods and Economic Analysis* (London: Longman).

Pelkmans, J. (2010) 'Required: a bold follow-up to Monti', *CEPS Commentary 22*, July, Brussels.

Pelkmans, J. and de Brito, A. C. (2012) *Enforcement in the EU Single Market* (Brussels: Centre for European Policy Studies).

Pelkmans, J. and Winters, A. (1988) *Europe's Domestic Market* (London: Royal Institute of International Affairs).

Pelkmans, J., Hanf, D., and Chang, M. (2008) *The EU Internal Market in Comparative Perspective, Economic, Political and Legal Analyses, Vol. 8* (Berlin: Peter Lang Publishers).

Pérez-Solórzano Borragán, N. and Smismans, S. (2012) 'The EU and institutional change in industrial relations in the new member states', in S. Smismans (ed.), *The European Union and Industrial Relations* (Manchester, Manchester University Press), pp. 116–38.

Persson, T. and Tabellini, G. (1996) 'Federal fiscal constitutions: risk sharing and redistribution', *Journal of Political Economy* 104/5: 979–1009.

Peterson, J. (1995) 'Decision making in the European Union: towards a framework for analysis', *Journal of European Public Policy* 2/1: 69–93.

Peterson, J. (2008) 'Enlargement, reform and the European Commission: weathering a perfect storm?', *Journal of European Public Policy* 15/5: 761–80.

Peterson, J. and Bomberg, E. (2009) *Decision-making in the European Union* (Basingstoke: Palgrave Macmillan).

Phelan, W. (2011) 'Why do the EU member states accept the supremacy of European law? Explaining supremacy as an alternative to bilateral reciprocity', *Journal of European Public Policy* 18/5: 766–77.

Phinnemore, D. (2013) *The Treaty of Lisbon: Origins and Negotiation* (Basingstoke: Palgrave).

Piattoni, S. (2009) 'Multi-level governance: a historical and conceptual analysis', *Journal of European Integration* 31/2: 163–80.

Piattoni, S. (2015) *Civil Society and Legitimate European Governance* (Cheltenham: Edward Elgar).

Piattoni, S. (ed.) (2015) *The European Union: Democratic Principles and Institutional Architectures in Times of Crisis* (Oxford: Oxford University Press).

Pierson, P. (1998) 'The path to European integration: a historical institutionalist analysis', in W. Sandholtz and A. Stone Sweet (eds), *European Integration and Supranational Governance* (Oxford: Oxford University Press), pp. 27–59.

Pierson, P. (2004) *Politics in Time: History, Institutions, and Social Analysis* (Princeton, NJ: Princeton University Press).

Piris, J.-C. (2010) *The Lisbon Treaty: A Legal and Political Analysis* (Cambridge: Cambridge University Press).

Pisani-Ferry, J. and Posen, A. (eds) (2009) *The Euro at Ten: The Next Global Currency?* (Washington, DC: Peterson Institute for International Economics/ Bruegel).

Pohl, B. (2013) 'Neither bandwagoning, nor balancing: explaining Europe's security policy', *Contemporary Security Policy* 34/2: 353–73.

Poiares Maduro, M. (2007) 'Interpreting European law: judicial adjudication in the context of constitutional pluralism,' *European Journal of Legal Studies* 1/2: 137–52.

Polanyi, K. (2001) *The Great Transformation: The Political and Economic Origins of Our Time*, 2nd edn, Foreword by Joseph E. Stiglitz, Introduction by Fred Block (Boston, MA: Beacon Press).

Pollack, M. A. (1997) 'Representing diffuse interests in the European Union', *Journal of European Public Policy* 4/4: 572–90.

Pollack, M. A. (2002) *The Engines of Integration: Delegation, Agencies and Agenda-setting in the EU* (Oxford: Oxford University Press).

Pollack, M. A. (2005) 'Theorizing the European Union: international organization, domestic polity, or experiment in new governance?', *Annual Review of Political Science* 8/1: 357–98.

Pollack, M. A. (2007) 'Rational choice and EU politics', in K. E. Jørgensen, M. A. Pollack, and B. Rosamond (eds), *Handbook of European Union Politics* (London: Sage), pp. 31–55.

Pollack, M. A. (2009) 'The new institutionalisms and European integration', in A. Wiener and T. Diez (eds), *European Integration Theory*, 2nd edn (Oxford: Oxford University Press), pp. 125–43.

Pollack, M. A. (2012) 'Theorizing the European Union: realist, intergovernmentalist and institutionalist approaches', in E. Jones, A. Menon, and S. Weatherill (eds), *The Oxford Handbook of the European Union* (Oxford: Oxford University Press).

Pollex, J. and Lenschow, A. (2020) 'Many faces of dismantling: hiding policy change in non-legislative acts in EU environmental policy', *Journal of European Public Policy* 27/1: 20–40.

Poloni-Staudinger, L. (2008) 'The domestic opportunity structure and supranational activity: an explanation of environmental group activity at European Union level', *European Union Politics* 9/4: 531–58.

Pop, V. (2014) 'Juncker defends lobby-friendly restructuring of commission services', *EUObserver*, September, available online at https://euobserver. com/institutional/125802.

Poux, X. and Aubert, P.-M. (2018) 'An agroecological Europe in 2050: multifunctional agriculture for healthy eating', *IDDRI* https://www.iddri.org/en/ publications-and-events/study/agroecological-europe-2050-multifunctional-agriculture-healthy-eating

Presidency of the EU (2009) 'Declaration by the Presidency on the Western Balkans', Gymnich Meeting with the Western Balkans, Hluboká nad Vltavou, 28 March.

Puchala, D. J. (1971) *International Politics Today* (New York: Dodd Mead).

Puchala, D. J. (1999) 'Institutionalism, intergovernmentalism and European integration: a review article', *Journal of Common Market Studies* 37/2: 317–31.

Puetter, U. (2006) *The Eurogroup: How a Secretive Group of Finance Ministers Shape European Economic Governance* (Manchester: Manchester University Press).

Puetter, U. (2012) 'Europe's deliberative intergovernmentalism: the role of the Council and European Council in EU economic governance', *Journal of European Public Policy* 19/2: 161–78.

Puetter, U. (2014) *The European Council and the Council: New Intergovernmentalism and Institutional Change* (Oxford: Oxford University Press).

Purnhagen, K., de Ruijter, A., Flear, M., Hervey, T., and Herwig, A. (2020)', 'More competences than you knew? The web of health competence for European Union action in response to the Covid-19 outbreak', *European Journal of Risk Regulation* 11/2: 297–306.

Putnam, R. (1988) 'Diplomacy and domestic politics: the logic of two-level games', *International Organization* 42/3: 427–60.

Quittkat, C. and Kohler-Koch, B. (2011) 'Die Öffnung der europäischen Politik für die Zivilgesellschaft: das Konsultationsregime der Europäischen Kommission', in B. Kohler-Koch and C. Quittkat (eds), *Die Entzauberung partizipativer Demokratie: Zur Rolle der Zivilgesellschaft bei der Demokratisierung von EU-Governance* (Frankfurt aM: Campus), pp. 74–97.

Radaelli, C. M. (1998) 'Governing European Regulation: The Challenge Ahead', RSC Policy Paper No. 98/3, European University Institute, Florence.

Radaelli, C. M. (2003) 'The Open Method of Coordination: A New Governance Architecture for the European Union?', SIEPS Report 2003/1, Swedish Institute for European Policy Studies, Stockholm, available online at http://eucenter.wisc.edu/OMC/Papers/radaelli.pdf.

Rasmussen, A. (2020) 'How has Covid-19 changed lobbying activity across Europe?' Blog post LSE Blog: EUROPP European Politics and Policy, 17 June, available at https://blogs.lse.ac.uk/europp-blog/2020/06/17/how-has-covid-19-changed-lobbying-activity-across-europe/.

Rasmussen, M. K. (2016) '"Heavy fog in the Channel. Continent cut off"? British diplomatic relations in Brussels after 2010', *Journal of Common Market Studies* 54/3: 709–24.

Rauh, C. and Schneider. G. (2013) 'There is no such thing as a free open sky: Financial markets and the struggle over European competences in international air transport', *Journal of Common Market Studies* 51/6: 1124–40.

Ray, L. (2003a) 'Reconsidering the link between incumbent support and pro-EU opinion', *European Union Politics* 4/3: 259–79.

Ray, L. (2003b) 'When parties matter: the conditional influence of party positions on voter opinions about European integration', *Journal of Politics* 65/4: 978–94.

Ray, L. (2007) 'Mainstream Euroskepticism: trend or oxymoron?', *Acta Politica* 42: 153–72.

Rees, W. (2011) *The US–EU Security Relationship: Tensions between a European and a Global Agenda* (Basingstoke: Palgrave Macmillan).

Reif, K. and Schmitt, H. (1980) 'Nine second-order national elections: a conceptual framework for the analysis of European election results', *European Journal of Political Research* 8/1: 3–44.

Reilly, A. (2004) '"Governance": agreement and divergence in responses to the EU White Paper', *Regional and Federal Studies* 14/1: 136–56.

Reinalda, B. and Verbeek, B. (2004) 'Patterns of decision making within international organizations', in B. Reinalda and B. Verbeek (eds), *Decision Making within International Organizations* (London: Routledge), pp. 231–46.

Renda, A., and R. Castro (2020) 'Towards stronger EU governance of health threats after the COVID-19 pandemic', *European Journal of Risk Regulation* 11/2: 273–82.

Rhodes, M. (1995) 'A regulatory conundrum: industrial relations and the "social dimension"', in S. Leibfried and P. Pierson (eds), *Fragmented Social Policy: The European Union's Social Dimension in Comparative Perspective* (Washington, DC: Brookings Institution), pp. 78–122.

Rhodes, M. and van Apeldoorn, B. (1998) 'Capital unbound? The transformation of European corporate governance', *Journal of European Public Policy* 5/3: 407–28.

Rhodes, R. A. W. (1996) 'The new governance: governing without government', *Political Studies* 44/4: 652–67.

Riddervold, M. (2016) '(Not) in the hands of the member states: how the European Commission influences EU security and defence policies', *Journal of Common Market Studies* 54/2: 353–69.

Ripoll Servent, A. (2018) *The European Parliament* (Basingstoke: Palgrave Macmillan).

Ripoll Servent, A. and Roederer-Rynning, C. (2018) 'The European Parliament: A Normal Parliament in a Polity of a Different Kind', *Oxford Research Encyclopaedias*, Politics. (Oxford: Oxford University Press USA).

Risse, T. (2000) '"Let's argue!" Communicative action in international relations', *International Organization*, 54/1: 1–39.

Risse, T. (2002) 'Nationalism and collective identities: Europe versus the nation-state?', in P. Heywood, E. Jones, and M. Rhodes (eds), *Developments in Western European Politics* (Basingstoke: Palgrave), pp. 77–93.

Risse, T. (2005) 'Nationalism, European identity and the puzzles of European integration', *Journal of European Public Policy* 12/2: 291–309.

Risse, T. (2009) 'Social constructivism and European integration', in A. Wiener and T. Diez (eds), *European Integration Theory* (Oxford: Oxford University Press), pp. 144–60.

Risse, T. (2010) *A Community of Europeans? Transnational Identities and Public Spheres* (New York: Cornell University Press).

Risse-Kappen, T. (1996) 'Exploring the nature of the beast: international relations theory and comparative policy analysis meet the European Union', *Journal of Common Market Studies* 34/1: 54–81.

Rittberger, B. (2005) *Building Europe's Parliament: Democratic Representation beyond the Nation State* (Oxford: Oxford University Press).

Robinson, D. (2015) 'The multiplying of judges of the ECJ' Brussels blog, *Financial Times*.

Rodt, A. P. (2014) *The European Union and Military Conflict Management: Defining, Evaluating and Achieving Success* (London: Routledge).

Rosamond, B. (2000) *Theories of European Integration* (Basingstoke: Palgrave).

Rosamond, B. (2005) 'The uniting of Europe and the foundations of EU studies: revisiting the neofunctionalism of Ernst B. Haas', *Journal of European Public Policy* 12/2: 237–54.

Rosamond, B. (2007) 'European integration and the social science of EU studies: the disciplinary politics of a sub-field', *International Affairs* 83/2: 231–52.

Rosamond, B. (2016) 'Brexit and the Problem of European Disintegration', *Journal of Contemporary European Research* 12/4.

Rosenau, J. N. and Czempiel, E.-O. (1992) *Governance without Government: Order and Change in World Politics* (Cambridge: Cambridge University Press).

Rosenau, J. N. and Durfee, M. (1995) *Thinking Theory Thoroughly: Coherent Approaches in an Incoherent World* (Boulder, CO: Westview).

Ross, G. (1995) 'Assessing the Delors era and social policy', in S. Leibfried and P. Pierson (eds), *European Social Policy: Between Fragmentation and Integration* (Washington, DC: Brookings Institution), pp. 357–88.

Rozbicka, P. (2011) 'Myths and reality of EU policy processes and interest-group participation: why are interest groups not as successful as they would like to be?', PhD thesis, European University Institute, Florence.

Ruggie, J. G. (1982) 'International regimes, transactions and change: embedded liberalism in the post-war economic order', *International Organization* 36/2: 379–416.

Ruggie, J. G. (1998) *Constructing the World Polity: Essays on International Institutionalisation* (London: Routledge).

Ruggie, J. G., Katzenstein, P. J., Keohane, R. O., and Schmitter, P. C. (2005) 'Transformation in world politics: the intellectual contribution of Ernst B. Haas', *Annual Review of Political Science* 8/1: 271–96.

Rutten, M. (2002) *From Saint-Malo to Nice: European Defence—Core Documents* (Paris: Institute for Security Studies).

Rutz, C., Dwyer, J., and Schramek, J. (2014) 'More new wine in old bottles? The evolving nature of the CAP debate in Europe, and prospects for the future', *Sociologica Ruralis* 54/3: 266–84.

Ryner, M. (2012) 'Financial crises, orthodoxy and heterodoxy in the production of knowledge about the EU', *Millennium: Journal of International Studies* 40/3: 647–73.

Sánchez-Barrueco, M.-L. (2020) 'Litigation as a means to solve conflicts between the European Parliament and the Council: one size does not fit all', in Cardwell, P. J. and Granger, M.-P. (eds), *Research Handbook on the Politics of EU Law* (Cheltenham: Edward Elgar).

Sanders, D. and Bellucci, P. (eds) (2012) *The Europeanization of National Polities? Citizenship and*

Support in a Post-enlargement Union (Oxford: Oxford University Press).

Sanders, D., Magalhaes, P., and Toka, G. (eds) (2012) *Citizens and the European Polity: Mass Attitudes Towards the European and National Politics* (Oxford: Oxford University Press).

Sandholtz, W. (1998) 'The emergence of a supranational telecommunications regime', in W. Sandholtz and A. Stone Sweet (eds), *European Integration and Supranational Governance* (Oxford: Oxford University Press), pp. 134–63.

Sandholtz, W. and Stone Sweet, A. (1997) 'European integration and supranational governance', *Journal of European Public Policy* 4/3: 297–317.

Sandholtz, W. and Stone Sweet, A. (eds) (1998) *European Integration and Supranational Governance* (Oxford: Oxford University Press).

Sandholtz, W. and Stone Sweet, A. (1999) 'European integration and supranational governance revisited: rejoinder to Branch and Øhrgaard', *Journal of European Public Policy* 6/1: 37–41.

Sandholtz, W. and Stone Sweet, A. (2012) 'Neofunctionalism and supranational governance', in E. Jones, A. Menon, and S. Weatherill (eds), *Oxford Handbook of the European Union* (Oxford: Oxford University Press), pp. 18–33.

Sandholtz, W. and Zysman, J. (1989) '1992: recasting the European bargain', *World Politics* 42/1: 95–128.

Sarmiento, D. (2013) 'Who's afraid of the Charter; The Court of Justice, National Courts and the new framework of fundamental rights protection in Europe', *Common Market Law Review* 50: 1267–304.

Sbragia, A. M. (1993) 'EC environmental policy', in A. W. Cafruny and G. G. Rosenthal (eds), *The State of the European Community* (Boulder, CO: Lynne Rienner), pp. 337–52.

Sbragia, A. M. (1996) 'Environmental policy: the "push-pull" of policy-making', in H. Wallace and W. Wallace (eds), *Policy-making in the European Union*, 3rd edn (Oxford: Oxford University Press), pp. 235–55.

Sbragia, A. M. (2000) 'Environmental policy', in H. Wallace and W. Wallace (eds), *Policy-making in the European Union*, 4th edn (Oxford: Oxford University Press), pp. 293–316.

Sbragia, A. M. (2005) 'Institution building from below and above: the European Community in global environmental politics', in A. Jordan (ed.), *Environmental Policy in the European Union*, 2nd edn (London: Earthscan), pp. 201–24.

Sbragia, A. M. and Damro, C. (1999) 'The changing role of the European Union in international environmental politics', *Environment and Planning C* 17/1: 53–68.

Scharpf, F. W. (1988) 'The joint-decision trap: lessons from German federalism and European integration', *Public Administration* 66/3: 239–78.

Scharpf, F. W. (1997) *Games Real Actors Play: Actor-Centered Institutionalism in Policy Research* (Boulder, CO: Westview).

Scharpf, F. W. (1999) *Governing in Europe: Effective and Democratic?* (Oxford: Oxford University Press).

Scharpf, F. W. (2002) 'The European social model: coping with the challenges of diversity', *Journal of Common Market Studies* 40/4: 645–70.

Scharpf, F. W. (2006) 'The joint-decision trap revisited', *Journal of Common Market Studies* 44/4: 845–64.

Scharpf, F. W. (2010) 'The asymmetry of European integration, or why the EU cannot be a "socialmarket economy"', *Socio-Economic Review* 8/2: 211–50.

Scharpf, F. W. (2011) 'Monetary union, fiscal crisis and the preemption of democracy', LEQS Paper 36, London School of Economics and Political Science.

Scheutze, D. (2017) 'Parliamentary democracy and international treaties', *Global Policy* 8: Supplement 6: 7–13.

Schimmelfennig, F. (2001) 'The Community trap: liberal norms, rhetorical action, and the Eastern enlargement of the European Union', *International Organization* 55/1: 47–80.

Schimmelfennig, F. (2014) 'European integration in the euro crisis: the limits of postfunctionalism', *Journal of European Integration* 36/3: 321–37.

Schimmelfennig, F. (2015) 'What's the news in "new intergovernmentalism": a critique of Bickerton, Hodson and Puetter', *Journal of Common Market Studies* 53/4: 723–30.

Schimmelfennig, F. (2018a) 'Brexit: differentiated disintegration in the European Union', *Journal of European Public Policy* 25/8: 1154–73.

Schimmelfennig, F. (2018b) 'Liberal Intergovernmentalism and the Crises of the European Union', *Journal of Common Market Studies* 56/7: 1578–94.

Schimmelfennig, F. and Sedelmeier, U. (2002) 'Theorizing EU enlargement: research focus, hypotheses, and the state of research', *Journal of European Public Policy* 9/4: 500–28.

Schimmelfennig, F. and Sedelmeier, U. (2004) 'Governance by conditionality: EU rule transfer to the candidate countries of Central and Eastern Europe', *Journal of European Public Policy* 11/4: 661–79.

Schimmelfennig, F. and Sedelmeier, U. (eds) (2005) *The Politics of European Union Enlargement. Theoretical Approaches* (London: Routledge).

Schimmelfennig, F. and Sedelmeier, U. (2020) 'The Europeanization of Eastern Europe: The External Incentives Model Revisited', *Journal of European Public Policy* 27/6: 814–33.

Schimmelfennig, F. and Wagner, W. (2004) 'Preface: external governance in the European Union', *Journal of European Public Policy* 11/4: 657–60.

Schimmelfennig, F. and Winzen, T. (2017) 'Eastern enlargement and differentiated integration: towards normalization', *Journal of European Public Policy* 24:2, 239–58.

Schimmelfennig, F., Engert, S., and Knobel, H. (2006) *International Socialization in Europe: European Organizations, Political Conditionality and Democratic Change* (Basingstoke: Palgrave).

Schmidt, S. K. (2007) 'Mutual recognition as a new mode of governance', *Journal of European Public Policy* 14/5: 667–81.

Schmidt, S. K. (2018) *The European Court of Justice and the Policy Process* (Oxford University Press).

Schmidt, V. A. (2006) *Democracy in Europe: The EU and National Polities* (Oxford: Oxford University Press).

Schmidt, V. A. (2018) 'Rethinking EU governance: from "old" to "new" approaches to who steers integration', *Journal of Common Market Studies* 56: 1544–61.

Schmitter, P. (1969) 'Three neofunctional hypotheses about international integration', *International Organization* 23/1: 161–6.

Schmitter, P. C. (2004) 'Neo-neofunctionalism', in A. Wiener and T. Diez (eds), *European Integration Theory* (Oxford: Oxford University Press), pp. 45–74.

Schmitter, P. C. and Lefkofridi, Z. (2016) 'Neofunctionalism as a theory of disintegration', *Chinese Political Science Review* 1: 1–29.

Schneider, G., Steunenberg, B., and Widgren, M. (2006) 'Evidence with insight: what models contribute to EU research', in R. Thomson, F. N. Stokman, C. H. Achen, and T. Koenig (eds), *The European Union Decides* (Cambridge: Cambridge University Press), pp. 299–316.

Schoenefeld, J. and Knodt, M. (2020) 'Softening the surface but hardening the core? Governing renewable energy in the EU', *West European Politics* 44(1): 49–71.

Schonfield, A. (1973) *Europe: A Journey to an Unknown Destination*, Reith Lectures 1972 (London: BBC).

Schultze, C. J. (2003) 'Cities and EU governance: policy-takers or policy-makers?', *Regional and Federal Studies* 12/1: 121–47.

Schütze, R. (2016) *European Constitutional Law*, 2nd edn (Cambridge: Cambridge University Press).

Schütze, R. (2017) *From International to Federal Market: The Changing Structure of European Law* (Oxford: Oxford University Press).

Scott, J. and Trubek, D. M. (2002) 'Mind the gap: law and new approaches to governance in the European Union', *European Law Journal* 8/1: 1–18.

Scully, R. (2005) *Becoming Europeans? Attitudes, Behaviour and Socialisation in the European Parliament* (Oxford: Oxford University Press).

Scully R., Hix, S. and Farrell, D. M. (2012) 'National or European parliamentarians? Evidence from a new survey of the Members of the European Parliament', *Journal of Common Market Studies* 50: 670–83.

Sedelmeier U. (2008) 'After conditionality: post-accession compliance with EU law in East Central Europe', *Journal of European Public Policy* 15/6: 806–25.

Serricchio, F., Tsakatika, M., and Quaglia, L. (2013) 'Euroscepticism and the global financial crisis', *Journal of Common Market Studies* 51/1: 51–64.

Shackleton, M. (2012) 'The European Parliament', in J. Peterson and M. Shackleton (eds), *The Institutions of the European Union*, 3rd edn (Oxford: Oxford University Press), pp. 124–47.

Shapiro, M. (1992) 'The European Court of Justice', in A. M. Sbragia (ed.), *Europolitics* (Washington, DC: Brookings Institution), pp. 123–51.

Shaw, J. and Hunt, J. (2009) 'Fairy Tale of Luxembourg?: Reflections on Law and Legal Scholarship in European Integration' in Phinnemore, D. and Warleigh, A. (eds), *Reflections on European Integration* (Basingstoke: Palgrave Macmillan), pp. 93–108.

Shore, C. (2011) 'European governance or governmentality? The European Commission and the future of democratic government', *European Law Journal* 17/3: 287–303.

Siune, K. and Svensson, P. (1993) 'The Danes and the Maastricht treaty: the Danish EC referendum of June 1992', *Electoral Studies* 12/2: 99–111.

Sjursen, H. (2006) 'The EU as a "normative" power: how can this be?', *Journal of European Public Policy* 13/2: 235–51.

Skelcher, C. (2005) 'Jurisdictional integrity, polycentrism, and the design of democratic governance', *Governance* 18/1: 89–110.

Skogstad, G. (2003) 'Legitimacy and/or policy effectiveness? Network governance and GMO regulation in the European Union', *Journal of European Public Policy* 10/3: 321–38.

Skogstad, G. and Verdun, A. (eds) (2009) *The Common Agricultural Policy: Policy Dynamics in a Changing Context* (London: Routledge).

Slater, M. (1982) 'Political elites, popular indifference, and community building', *Journal of Common Market Studies* 21/1–2: 67–87.

Smeets, S. (2015) *Negotiations in the EU Council of Ministers: 'And All Must Have Prizes'* (Colchester: ECPR Press).

Smismans, S. (2004) *Law, Legitimacy, and European Governance: Functional Participation in Social Regulation* (Oxford: Oxford University Press).

Smismans, S. (2006a) 'New modes of governance and the participatory myth', *European Governance Papers* 6/1: 1–23.

Smismans, S. (ed.) (2006b) *Civil Society and Legitimate European Governance* (Cheltenham: Edward Elgar).

Smismans, S. (2008) 'New modes of governance and the participatory myth', *West European Politics* 31/5: 874–95.

Smismans, S. (2009) 'European civil society and citizenship: complementary or exclusionary concepts?', *Policy & Society* 27/4: 59–70.

Smismans, S. (2010) 'The European Union's fundamental rights myth', *Journal of Common Market Studies* 48/1: 45–66.

Smith, M. (2001) 'The Common Foreign and Security Policy', in S. Bromley (ed.), *Governing the European Union* (London: Sage), pp. 255–86.

Smith, M. (2004) 'Toward a theory of EU foreign policy-making: multi-level governance, domestic politics, and national adaptation to Europe's Common Foreign and Security Policy', *Journal of European Public Policy* 11/4: 740–58.

Smith, M. E. (2008) *Europe's Foreign and Security Policy: The Institutionalisation of Cooperation* (Cambridge: Cambridge University Press).

Smith, S. (2001) 'Reflectivist and constructivist approaches to international theory', in J. Baylis and S. Smith (eds), *The Globalization of World Politics: An Introduction to International Relations*, 2nd edn (Oxford: Oxford University Press), pp. 224–49.

Snell, J. (2019) 'Cassis at 40', *European Law Review* 4: 445–6.

Snowdon, C. (2013) 'Euro Puppets: The European Commission's remaking of civil society', IEA (Institute of Economic Affairs) Discussion Paper No. 45.

Spaak, P.-H. (1956) *The Brussels Report on the General Common Market*, June, Brussels.

Standard Eurobarometer (2015) Public opinion in the European Union, No. 83 Spring https://ec.europa.eu/commfrontoffice/publicopinion/index.cfm/Survey/getSurveyDetail/instruments/STANDARD/yearFrom/1974/yearTo/2015/surveyKy/2099.

Standard Eurobarometer (2019) Report: Media use in the European Union. No. 92, autumn https://europa.eu/eurobarometer/surveys/detail/2255.

Standard Eurobarometer (2020) Public opinion in the European Union, No. 93 Summer, https://ec.europa.eu/commfrontoffice/publicopinion/index.cfm/Survey/getSurveyDetail/instruments/STANDARD/surveyKy/2262.

Startin, N. (2018) 'How the referendum was lost. An analysis of the UK referendum campaign on EU membership', in B. Leruth, N. Startin, and S. Usherwood (eds), *Routledge Handbook of Euroscepticism* (Abingdon: Routledge), pp. 456–87.

Startin, N. and Krouwel, A. (2013) 'Euroscepticism re-galvanized: the consequences of the 2005 French and Dutch rejections of the EU constitution', *JCMS: Journal of Common Market Studies* 57/1: 65–84. https://doi.org/10.1111/j.1468-5965.2012.02301.x.

Stasavage, D. (2004) 'Open-door or closed door? Transparency in domestic and international bargaining', *International Organization* 58/2: 667–703.

Statewatch (2011) 'The Effects of Security Policies on Rights and Liberties in the European Union, and their Export beyond the EU's Borders', Statewatch Analysis No. 11/11, available online at http://www.statewatch.org/analyses/no-128-sec-lib-eu.pdf.

Statham, P. (2008) 'Political party contestation over Europe in public discourses: emergent Euro-scepticism?', ARENA Working Paper Series, 2008/08, ARENA, University of Oslo.

Statham, P. and Trenz, H. J. (2014) 'Understanding the mechanisms of EU politicization: lessons from the Eurozone crisis', *Comparative European Politics* 13/3: 287–306.

Stavrakakis, Y. and Katsambekis, G. (2014) 'Left-wing populism in the European periphery: the case of SYRIZA', *Journal of Political Ideologies* 19/2: 119–42.

Steenbergen, M. R., Edwards, E. E., and de Vries, C. E. (2007) 'Who's cueing whom? Mass-elite linkages and the future of European integration', *European Union Politics* 8/1: 13–35.

Steffek, J., Kissling, C., and Nanz, P. (eds) (2007) *Civil Society Participation in European and Global Governance: A Cure for the Democratic Deficit?* (Basingstoke: Palgrave Macmillan).

Stein, E. (1981) 'Lawyers, Judges, and the Making of a Transnational Constitution', *American Journal of International Law* 75: 1–27.

Stephenson, P. (2010) 'Let's get physical: the European Commission and cultivated spillover in completing the single market's transport infrastructure', *Journal of European Public Policy* 17/7: 1039–105.

Stoker, G. (1998) 'Governance as theory: five propositions', *International Social Science Journal* 50/155: 17–28.

Stone Sweet, A (2000) *Governing with judges: Constitutional Politics in Europe* (Oxford: Oxford University Press).

Stone Sweet, A. (2004) *The Judicial Construction of Europe* (Oxford: Oxford University Press).

Stone Sweet, A. (2010) 'The European Court of Justice and the judicialization of EU governance', *Living Reviews in European Governance* 5/2: 5–50.

Stone Sweet, A. and Brunell, T. L. (1998) 'Constructing a supranational constitution: dispute resolution and governance in the European Community', *American Political Science Review* 92/1: 63–81.

Stone Sweet, A. and Brunell, T. L. (2004) 'Constructing a supranational constitution', in A. Stone Sweet (ed.), *The Judicial Construction of Europe* (Oxford: Oxford University Press).

Stone Sweet, A. and Caporaso, J. (1998) 'From free trade to supranational polity: the European Court and integration', in W. Sandholtz and A. Stone Sweet (eds), *European Integration and Supranational Governance* (Oxford: Oxford University Press), pp. 92–134.

Stone Sweet, A. and Sandholtz, W. (1998) 'Integration, supranational governance, and the institutionalization of the European polity', in W. Sandholtz and A. Stone Sweet (eds), *European Integration and Supranational Governance* (Oxford: Oxford University Press), pp. 1–26.

Streeck, W. (1999) 'Competitive Solidarity: Rethinking the "European Social Model"': MPIfG Working Paper 99/8, September 1999 available at http://www.mpifg.de/pu/workpap/wp99-8/wp99-8.html.

Streeck, W. and Schmitter, P. C. (1991) 'From national corporatism to transnational pluralism: organized interests in the single European market', *Politics and Society* 19/2: 133–65.

Strumia, F. (2016) 'European Citizenship and EU Immigration: A Demoi-cratic Bridge between the Third Country Nationals' Right to Belong and the Member States' Power to Exclude', *European Law Journal* 22/4: 417–47.

Stubb, A. (1996) 'A categorisation of differentiated integration', *Journal of Common Market Studies* 34/2: 283–95.

Stuckler, D., Reeves, A., Loopstra, R., Karanikolos, M., and McKee, M. (2017) 'Austerity and health: the impact in the UK and Europe', *European Journal of Public Health* 27/suppl_4: 18–21.

Sultan, B. and A. Mehmood (2020) 'Pakistan and the BRICS Plus in the new era: a perspective of neo-functionalism', *Asian Journal of Middle East Islamic Studies* 14: 447–63.

Sun, J. M. and Pelkmans, J. (1995) 'Regulatory competition in the single market', *Journal of Common Market Studies* 33/1: 67–89.

Surridge, P., Wager, A., and Wincott, D. (2021) 'Comfortable Leavers: The Expectations and Hopes of the Overlooked Brexit Voters: UK in a Changing Europe', available at https://ukandeu.ac.uk/research-papers/comfortable-leavers-the-expectations-and-hopes-of-the-overlooked-brexit-voters/

Sutcliffe, J. B. (2000) 'The 1999 reform of the structural regulations: multi-level governance or renationalization?', *Journal of European Public Policy* 7/2: 290–309.

Suvarierol, S. (2008) 'Beyond the myth of nationality: analysing networks within the European Commission', *West European Politics* 31/4: 701–24.

Szapiro, M. (2013) *The European Commission. A Practical Guide* (London: John Harper).

Taggart, P. (1998) 'A touchstone of dissent: Euroscepticism in contemporary Western European party systems', *European Journal of Political Research* 33/3: 363–88.

Taggart, P. and Szczerbiak, A. (2002) 'The party politics of Euroscepticism in EU Member States and Candidate States', SEI Working Paper No. 51, Opposing Europe Research Network Working Paper No. 6. Falmer, Brighton: Sussex European Institute, University of Sussex.

Taggart, P. and Szczerbiak, A. (2005) 'Three patterns of party competition over Europe', Paper presented at the conference 'Euroscepticism: causes and consequences', 1–2 July, Amsterdam.

Taggart, P. and Szczerbiak, A. (eds) (2008) *Opposing Europe? The Comparative Party Politics of Euroscepticism, Vols I and II* (Oxford: Oxford University Press).

Tajfel, H. (1970) 'Experiments in intergroup discrimination' *Scientific American* 223/5: 96–102.

Tallberg, J. (2002) 'Paths to compliance: enforcement, management, and the European Union', *International Organization* 56(3): 609–43.

Tallberg, J. (2006) *Leadership and Negotiation in the European Union* (Cambridge: Cambridge University Press).

Tarta, A. (2017) 'A framework for evaluating European social media publics: The case of the European Parliament's Facebook page', in M. Barisione and A. Michailidou (eds), *Social Media and European Politics. Rethinking Power and Legitimacy in the Digital Era* (London: Palgrave), pp. 143–65.

Taylor, P. (1975) 'The politics of the European Communities: the confederal phase', *World Politics* 27/3: 335–60.

Taylor, P. (1993) *International Organization in the Modern World: The Regional and the Global Process* (New York: Pinter).

Taylor, P. (1996) *The European Union in the 1990s* (Oxford: Oxford University Press).

The Telegraph (2017) 'Italy commits to up to €17bn to rescue two stricken banks in "pragmatic" interpretation of EU bailout law', 26 June.

Terpan, F. (2015) 'Soft law in the European Union— The changing nature of EU law', *European Law Journal* 21/1: 68–96.

Terpan, F. and Saurugger, S. (2020) 'The politics of the Court of Justice of the European Union' in P. J. Cardwell and M.-P. Granger (eds) *Research Handbook on the Politics of EU Law* (Cheltenham: Edward Elgar), pp. 31–66.

Thielemann, E. (1998) 'Policy networks and European governance: the Europeanisation of regional policy-making in Germany', *Regional and Industrial Research Paper Series* 27: 1–39.

Thomson, R. (2009) 'Actor alignments in the European Union before and after enlargement', *European Journal of Political Research* 48/6: 756–81.

Thomson, R. (2011) *Resolving Controversy in the European Union: Legislative Decision-making before and after Enlargement* (Cambridge: Cambridge University Press).

Thomson, R. and Hosli, M. O. (2006) 'Explaining legislative decision-making in the European Union', in R. Thomson, F. N. Stokman, C. H. Achen, and T. Koenig (eds), *The European Union Decides* (Cambridge: Cambridge University Press), pp. 1–24.

Thomson, R., Stokman, F. N., Achen, C. H., and Koenig, T. (eds) (2006) *The European Union Decides* (Cambridge: Cambridge University Press).

Thym, D. (2015) 'When Union citizens turn into illegal migrants: The Dano case', *European Law Review* 40/2: 249–62.

Tilley, J. and Garry, J. (2007) 'Public support for integration in the newly enlarged EU: exploring differences between former communist countries and established member states', in M. Marsh, S. Mikhaylov, and H. Schmitt (eds), *European Elections after Eastern Enlargement*, CONNEX Report Series No. 1 (Mannheim: MZES Mannheim Centre for European Social Research, University of Mannheim), available online at http://www.mzes.uni-mannheim.de/

projekte/typo3/site/fileadmin/BookSeries/Volume_One/Ch06_chapter_final.pdf; http://www.mzes.uni-mannheim.de/projekte/typo3/site/index.php?id=596.

Toal, G. (2005) 'Being geopolitical', *Political Geography* 24/3: 365–72.

Tocqueville, A. de ([1835] 1961) *Democracy in America* (New York: Schocken).

Tömmel, I. and Verdun, A. (eds) (2008) *Innovative Governance in the European Union* (Boulder, CO: Lynne Rienner).

Trachtenberg, M. (2006) 'De Gaulle, Moravcsik and Europe', *Journal of Cold War Studies* 2/3: 101–16.

Trading economics (2021a) 'Spain Youth Unemployment Rate', https://tradingeconomics.com/spain/youth-unemployment-rate

Trading Economics (2021b) 'Greece Youth Unemployment Rate', https://tradingeconomics.com/greece/youth-unemployment-rate

Tranholm-Mikkelsen, J. (1991) 'Neo-functionalism: obstinate or obsolete? A reappraisal in the light of the new dynamism of the EC', *Millennium: Journal of International Studies* 20/1: 1–22.

Trauner, F. and Ripoll Servent, A. (eds) (2015) *Policy Change in the Area of Freedom, Security and Justice: How EU Institutions Matter* (New York: Routledge).

Treib, O. (2014) 'Implementing and complying with EU governance outputs', *Living Reviews in European Governance* 9/1.

Treib, O., Bähr, H., and Falkner, G. (2007) 'Modes of governance: towards a conceptual clarification', *Journal of European Public Policy* 14/1: 1–20.

Treib, O., Bähr, H., and Falkner, G. (2009) 'Social policy and environmental policy: comparing modes of governance', in U. Diedrichs and W. Wessels (eds), *The Dynamics of Change in EU Governance: Policy-making and System Evolution* (Cheltenham: Edward Elgar), pp. 103–31.

Trenz, H.J. (2004) 'Media coverage on European governance: Exploring the European public sphere in national quality newspapers', *European Journal of Communication* 19/3: 291–319.

Trenz, H. J. (2008) 'Understanding media impact on European integration: enhancing or restricting the

scope of legitimacy of the EU?', *Journal of European Integration* 30/2: 291–309.

Trenz, H. J. (2010) 'In search of the popular subject: identity formation, constitution-making and the democratic consolidation of the EU', *European Review* 18(1): 93–115.

Trenz, H. J. (2018) 'Euroscepticism as EU-polity contestation' in B. Leruth, N. Startin, and S. Usherwood (eds), *Routledge Handbook of Euroscepticism* (Abingdon: Routledge), pp. 293–305.

Trenz, H.J., Heft, A., Vaughan, M. and Pfetsch, B. (2020) 'Resilience of Public Spheres in a Global Health Crisis', Weizenbaum Series, 11. Berlin: Weizenbaum Institute for the Networked Society—The German Internet Institute. https://doi.org/10.34669/wi.ws/11.

Triandafyllidou, A. (2018) 'A "refugee crisis" unfolding: "real" events and their interpretation in media and political debates', *Journal of Immigrant & Refugee Studies* 16/1–2: 198–216.

Tridimas, T. (2018) *The European Court of Justice and the EU Constitutional Order, Essays in Judicial Protection* (London: Hart Publishing).

Trondal, J. (2010) *An Emergent European Executive Order* (Oxford: Oxford University Press).

Trondal, J. and Jeppesen, L. (2008) 'Images of agency governance in the European Union', *West European Politics* 31/3: 417–41.

Trondal, J., van der Berg, C., and Suvarierol, S. (2008) 'The compound machinery of government: the case of seconded officials in the European Commission', *Governance* 21/2: 253–74.

Truman, D. B. (1951) *The Governmental Process: Political Interests and Public Opinion* (New York: Alfred A. Knopf).

Tsebelis, G. (1990) *Nested Games: Rational Choice in Comparative Politics* (Berkeley, CA: University of California Press).

Tsebelis, G. (1994) 'The power of the European Parliament as conditional agenda-setter', *American Political Science Review* 88/1, 128–42.

Tsebelis, G. (2008) 'Thinking about the recent past and the future of the EU', *Journal of Common Market Studies* 46/2: 265–92.

Tsebelis, G. and Garrett, G. (1997) 'Agenda setting, vetoes and the European Union's co-decision procedure', *Journal of Legislative Studies* 3/3: 74–92.

Tsoukalis, L. (1997) *The New European Economy Revisited* (Oxford: Oxford University Press).

Tsoukalis, L. (2011) 'The JCMS annual review lecture: the shattering of illusions—and what next?', *Journal of Common Market Studies* 49/1: 19–44.

Turkina, E. and Postnikov, E. (2012) 'Cross-border inter-firm networks in the European Union's Eastern neighbourhood: Integration via organizational learning', *Journal of Common Market Studies* 50/4: 632–52.

Turner, J. C. (1985) 'Social categorization and the self-concept: a social cognitive theory of group behaviour', in E. J. Lawler (ed), *Advances in Group Processes* (Greenwich, CT: JAI Press), 77–122.

Uberoi, E. (2016) European Union Referendum 2016, Briefing Paper Number CBP 7639, House of Commons Library, 29 June.

Uçarer, E. M. (2001) 'Managing asylum and European integration: expanding spheres of exclusion?', *International Studies Perspectives* 2/3: 291–307.

Uçarer, E. M. (2013) 'The area of freedom security and justice', in M. Cini and N. Pérez-Solórzano Borragán (eds), *European Union Politics*, 4th edn (Oxford: Oxford University Press), pp. 281–95.

Uçarer, E. M. (2014) 'Tempering the EU? NGO advocacy in the area of freedom security and justice', *Cambridge Review of International Affairs* 7/1: 127–46.

UK Parliament (2014) 'The role of the European Scrutiny Committee: stages of scrutiny', available online at http://www.publications.parliament.uk/pa/cm201314/cmselect/cmeuleg/109/10906.htm.

USA (2021) Interim National Security Strategic Guidance, March, https://www.whitehouse.gov/wp-content/uploads/2021/03/NSC-1v2.pdf accessed 30 April 2021.

Vachudova, M. A. (2005) *Europe Undivided: Democracy, Leverage and Integration after Communism* (Oxford: Oxford University Press).

Van Acken, W. (2012) 'Voting in the Council of the European Union: Contested decision-making in the EU Council of Ministers, 1995–2010', Swedish Institute for European Policy Studies, No. 2, September.

van Apeldoorn, B. (1992) *Transnational Capitalism and the Struggle over European Integration* (London and New York: Routledge).

van Asselt, H. (2010) 'Emissions trading: the enthusiastic adoption of an alien instrument?', in A. Jordan, D. Huitema, H. van Asselt, T. Rayner, and F. Berkhout (eds), *Climate Change Policy in the European Union* (Cambridge: Cambridge University Press), pp. 125–44.

van der Eijk, C. and Franklin, M. N. (eds) (1996) *Choosing Europe? The European Electorate and National Politics in the Face of Union* (Ann Arbor, MI: University of Michigan Press).

van Keulen, M. (1999) *Going Europe or Going Dutch: How the Dutch Government Shapes European Policy* (Amsterdam: Amsterdam University Press).

Van Rompuy, H. (2011) 'The Economic and Political Challenges for Europe'. Official Opening of the EUI's Academic Year 2011–2012: 11 November, the European University Institute (EUI), Florence.

Van Rompuy, H. (2012) 'Towards a genuine economic and monetary union', Report, 5 December.

Vandenbroucke, F. (2017) 'The idea of a European social union: a normative introduction', in F. Vandenbroucke, C. Barnard, and G. de Baere (eds), *A European Social Union after the Crisis* (Cambridge: Cambridge University Press), pp. 3–46.

Vandenbroucke, F., Barnard, C., and de Baere, G. (eds) (2017) *A European Social Union after the Crisis* (Cambridge: Cambridge University Press).

Vanhercke, B., Sabato, S., and Bouget, D. (eds) (2017) *Social Policy in the European Union: State of Play*, Eighteenth annual report (Brussels: ETUI).

Vasilopoulou, D. (2013) 'Continuity and change in the study of Euroscepticism: plus ça change?', *Journal of Common Market Studies* 51/1: 153–68.

Verdun, A. (1996) 'An "asymmetrical" economic and monetary union in the EU: perceptions of monetary authorities and social partners', *Journal of European Integration* 20/1: 59–81.

Verdun, A. (2000) *European Responses to Globalization and Financial Market Integration: Perceptions of Economic and Monetary Union in Belgium, France and Germany* (Basingstoke: Palgrave Macmillan).

Verdun, A. and Zeitlin, J. (2018) 'Introduction: the European Semester as a new architecture of EU socioeconomic governance in theory and practice', *Journal of European Public Policy* 25/2: 137–48.

Versluis, E. and Tarr, E. (2013) 'Improving compliance with European Union law via agencies: The case of the European Railway Agency', *Journal of Common Market Studies* 51/2: 316–33.

Versluis, E., van Keulen, M., and Stephenson, P. (2011) *Analysing the European Union Policy Process* (Basingstoke: Palgrave).

Vestlund, N. M. (2015) 'Changing policy focus through organizational reform? The case of the pharmaceutical unit in the European Commission', *Public Policy and Administration* 30/1: 92–112.

Vollaard, H. (2014) 'Explaining European disintegration', *Journal of Common Market Studies* 52/5: 1142–1159.

Vollaard, H, van de Bovenkamp, H., and Martinsen, D. S. (2016) 'The making of a European healthcare union: a federalist perspective', *Journal of European Public Policy* 23/2: 157–76.

Von der Leyen, U. (2019) 'Political Guidelines for the Next European Commission', https://ec.europa.eu/info/sites/default/files/political-guidelines-next-commission_en_0.pdf accessed 30 April, 2021.

von Homeyer, I. (2004) 'Differential effects of enlargement on EU environmental governance', *Environmental Politics* 13/1: 52–76.

Votewatch (2011) 'Voting in the 2009–2014 European Parliament: How Do MEPs Vote after Lisbon?' Third Report, available online at http://www.votewatch.eu/blog/wp-content/uploads/2011/01/votewatch_report_voting_behavior_26_january_beta.pdf.

Votewatch (2014) 'Super Grand Coalitions EPP-SD-ALDE Approves the New European Commission', available online at http://www.votewatch.eu/blog/super-grand-coalition-epp-sd-alde-approves-the-new-european-commission.

Wæver, O. (2009) 'Discursive approaches', in T. Diez and A. Wiener (eds), *European Integration Theory* (Oxford: Oxford University Press), pp. 163–80.

Wallace, H. (2002) 'The Council: an institutional chameleon', *Governance* 15/3: 325–44.

Wallace, H. (2010) 'An institutional anatomy and five policy modes', in H. Wallace, M. A. Pollack, and A. R. Young (eds), *Policy-making in the European Union* (Oxford: Oxford University Press), pp. 69–104.

Wallace, H. (2017) 'The JCMS annual review lecture: In the name of Europe', *Journal of Common Market Studies* 55/8: 8–18.

Wallace, H. and Reh, C. (2020), 'An Institutional Anatomy and Five Policy Modes' in Wallace, H., Pollack, M.A., Roederer-Rynning, C., and Young, A.R. (eds) (2020) *Policy-Making in the European Union*, 8th edn (Oxford: Oxford University Press). 67–105.

Wallace, W. (1982) 'European as a confederation: the Community and the nation-state', *Journal of Common Market Studies* 21/1: 57–68.

Walters, W. (2004) 'The frontiers of the European Union: a geostrategic perspective', *Geopolitics* 9/2: 674–98.

Waltz, K. (1979) *Theory of International Politics* (New York: McGraw Hill).

Warleigh, A. (2000) 'The hustle: citizenship practice, NGOs and policy coalitions in the European Union—the cases of auto oil, drinking water and unit pricing', *Journal of European Public Policy* 7/2: 229–43.

Warleigh, A. (2001) '"Europeanizing" civil society: NGOs as agents of political socialization', *Journal of Common Market Studies* 39/4: 619–39.

Warleigh, A. (2003) *Democracy in the European Union: Theory, Practice and Reform* (London: Sage).

Warleigh-Lack, A. (2006) 'Towards a conceptual framework for regionalization: bridging "new regionalism" and "integration theory"', *Review of International Political Economy* 13/5: 750–71.

Warleigh-Lack, A. and Drachenberg, R. (2011) 'Spillover in a soft policy era? Evidence from the open method of co-ordination in education and training', *Journal of European Public Policy* 18/7: 999–1015.

Warleigh-Lack, A. and Rosamond, B. (2010) 'Across the EU studies-new regionalism frontier: an invitation to dialogue', *Journal of Common Market Studies* 48/4: 993–1013.

Weale, A. (2005) 'European environmental policy by stealth', in A. Jordan (ed.), *Environmental Policy in the European Union*, 2nd edn (London: Earthscan), pp. 336–54.

Weale, A., Pridham, G., Cini, M., Konstadakopulos, D., Porter, M., and Flynn, B. (2000) *Environmental Governance in Europe* (Oxford: Oxford University Press).

Weiler, J. H. H. (1997) 'Legitimacy and democracy of Union governance', in G. Edwards and A. Pijpers (eds), *The Politics of European Treaty Reform* (London: Pinter), pp. 249–87.

Weiss, F. and Kaupa, C. (2014) *European Internal Market Law* (Cambridge: Cambridge University Press).

Wendt, A. (1999) *Social Theory of International Politics* (Cambridge: Cambridge University Press).

Werts, J. (2017) 'The European Council as manager of crises', text of lecture provided at Summit Dissemination Conference, Europaïsche Akademie Berlin, 17 January.

Wessels, W. (1997) 'Ever closer fusion? A dynamic macro-political view on integration processes', *Journal of Common Market Studies* 35/2: 267–99.

Wessels, W. (1998) 'Comitology: fusion in action—politico-administrative trends in the EU system', *Journal of European Public Policy* 5/2: 209–34.

Wessler, H., Peters, B., Brüggemann, M., Kleinen-von Köningslöw, K., and Sifft, S. (2008) *Transnationalization of Public Spheres* (Basingstoke: Palgrave Macmillan).

Wettestad, J. and Jevnaker, T. (2016) *Rescuing Emission Trading: The Climate Policy Flagship* (London: Palgrave Macmillan).

Weyand, S. (2020) 'Presentation on EU Open Strategic Autonomy and the Transatlantic Trade Relationship', American Institute for Contemporary German Studies, 16 September https://www.aicgs.org/video/eu-open-strategic-autonomy-and-the-transatlantic-trade-relationship/.

Whitaker, R., Hix, S., and Zapryanova, G. (2017) 'Understanding Members of the European Parliament: Four waves of the European Parliament Research Group MEP survey', *European Union Politics* 18/3: 491–506. https://doi.org/10.1177/1465116516687399.

Widgren, M. (1994) 'Voting power in the EC decision making and consequences of the different enlargements', *European Economic Review* 38/4: 1153–70.

Wiener, A. (2006) 'Constructivism and sociological institutionalism', in M. Cini and A. K. Bourne (eds), *Palgrave Advances in European Union Studies* (Basingstoke: Palgrave), pp. 35–55.

Wiener, A. and Diez, T. (eds) (2009) *European Integration Theory*, 2nd edn (Oxford: Oxford University Press).

Wildgen, J. K. and Feld, W. J. (1976) 'Evaluative and cognitive factors in the prediction of European unification', *Comparative Political Studies* 9/3: 309–34.

Wille, A. (2013) *The Normalization of the European Commission: Politics and Bureaucracy in the EU Executive* (Oxford: Oxford University Press).

Wolfe, J. D. (2011) 'Who rules the EU? Pragmatism and power in European integration theory', *Journal of Political Power* 4/1: 127–44.

Wolkenstein, F. (2020) 'The revival of democratic intergovernmentalism, first principles and the case for a contest-based account of democracy in the European Union', *Political Studies* 68/2: 408–25.

Wong, R. and Hill, C. (eds) (2011) *National and European Foreign Policy: Towards Europeanization* (London: Routledge).

Wonka, A. (2008) 'Decision-making dynamics in the European Commission: partisan, national or sectoral?', *Journal of European Public Policy* 15/8: 1145–63.

Wonka, A. and Rittberger, B. (2011) 'Perspectives on EU governance: an empirical assessment of the political attitudes of EU agency professionals', *Journal of European Public Policy* 18/6: 888–908.

Woolcock, S. (2012) *European Union Economic Diplomacy: The Role of the EU in External Economic Relations* (Farnham: Ashgate).

Wright, T. (2012) 'What if Europe fails?', *The Washington Quarterly* 35/3: 23–41.

Wurzel, R. K. W. (2008) 'Environmental policy', in J. Hayward (ed.), *Leaderless Europe* (Oxford: Oxford University Press), pp. 66–88.

Wurzel, R. K. W. (2012) 'The Council of Ministers', in A. Jordan and C. Adelle (eds), *Environmental Policy in the European Union*, 3rd edn (London: Routledge), pp. 75–94.

Young, A. (2006) 'The politics of regulation and the single market', in K. E. Jørgensen, M. A. Pollack, and B. Rosamond (eds), *Handbook of European Union Politics* (London: Sage), pp. 373–94.

Young, A. (2014) 'Europe as a global regulator? The limits of EU influence in international food safety standards', *Journal of European Public Policy* 21/6: 904–22.

Young, A. (2015) 'Liberalizing trade, not exporting rules: the limits to regulatory co-ordination in the EU's "new generation" preferential trade agreements', *Journal of European Public Policy* 22/9: 1253–75.

Young, A. R. (1997) 'Consumption without representation? Consumers in the single market', in H. Wallace and A. R. Young (eds), *Participation and Policy-making in the European Union* (Oxford: Clarendon Press), pp. 206–34.

Youngs, R. (2019) 'Democracy after the European Parliament Elections', Brussels: CEPS https://www.ceps.eu/ceps-publications/democracy-after-the-european-parliament-elections accessed 30 April 2021.

Zahn, R. (2015) 'Common sense' or a threat to EU integration? The Court, economically inactive EU citizens and social benefits' *Industrial Law Journal* 44/4: 573–85.

Zaller, J. (1992) *The Nature and Origins of Mass Opinion* (Cambridge: Cambridge University Press).

Zaun, N. (2018) 'States as gatekeepers in EU asylum politics: explaining non-adoption of a refugee quota system', *Journal of Common Market Studies* 56/1: 44–62.

Zeitlin, J. and Vanhercke, B. (2018) 'Socializing the European Semester: EU social and economic policy co-ordination in crisis and beyond', *Journal of European Public Policy* 25/2: 149–74.

Zhelyazkova, A. and Thomann, E. (2021) 'Policy implementation', in A. J. Jordan., V. Gravey (eds), *Environmental Policy in the European Union*, 4th edn (London: Routledge).

Zito, A. R. (2001) 'Epistemic communities, collective entrepreneurship and European integration', *Journal of European Public Policy* 8/4: 585–603.

Zito, A. R. (2005) 'The European Union as an environmental leader in a global environment', *Globalizations* 2/3: 363–75.

Zürn, M. and de Wilde, P. (2016) 'Debating globalization: cosmopolitanism and communitarianism as political ideologies', *Journal of Political Ideologies* 21/3: 280–301.

Zysman, J. (1994) 'How institutions create historically rooted trajectories of growth', *Industrial and Corporate Change* 3/1: 243–83.

Index